The Letters of William Lloyd Garrison

EDITED BY

WALTER M. MERRILL AND LOUIS RUCHAMES

PUBLISHER'S NOTE

A word of explanation about the cooperation of the editors of this edition. Some time before 1960, each of the editors, unknown to the other, had embarked on the task of editing Garrison's letters. Each had secured a publisher: Professor Merrill, Harvard University Press; Professor Ruchames, University of Massachusetts Press. On learning accidentally of one another's efforts, the editors decided to cooperate in issuing one edition. The University of Massachusetts Press and Harvard University Press, after mutual discussions, concluded that the latter should assume the responsibility for publishing the work.

In arriving at their decision to cooperate, the editors agreed to combine the letters which each had gathered separately as well as to unite in a systematic search for letters that had thus far been overlooked. Repositories of manuscript letters, including libraries, state and local historical societies, and manuscript dealers, in the United States and abroad, were checked. In a number of instances, collections of uncatalogued letters were also searched and additional letters found. During the past two years, several hundred new letters have been discovered and incorporated in the collections. Thus, whereas the original plan called for an edition of four volumes, it appears that ultimately the number of volumes will reach six and perhaps eight.

In the allocation of responsibilities, the editors have divided the material by periods as follows:

1822–1835 — Walter M. Merrill   1850–1860 — Louis Ruchames
1836–1840 — Louis Ruchames   1861–1869 — Walter M. Merrill
1841–1849 — Walter M. Merrill   1870–1879 — Louis Ruchames

Each editor assumes complete responsibility for his volumes.

William Lloyd Garrison in 1846

The Letters of
William Lloyd Garrison,

Volume III

NO UNION WITH SLAVE- HOLDERS

1841-1849

EDITED BY WALTER M. MERRILL

The Belknap Press of Harvard University Press

Cambridge, Massachusetts 1973

© Copyright 1973 by the President and Fellows of Harvard College
All rights reserved
Distributed in Great Britain by Oxford University Press, London
Printed in the United States of America
Library of Congress Catalog Card Number 75-133210
SBN 674-52662-7
Book design by David Ford

With gratitude to the Garrison staff —
cooperative, efficient, indispensable

ACKNOWLEDGMENTS

In the cooperative effort of editing the letters of the current volume, I am grateful to many institutions and to many individuals. Let me mention, first of all, the generous support of two institutions: the National Endowment for the Humanities and Drexel University. The former granted substantial support to the project beginning in the spring of 1970; the latter, the editor's university, provided matching funds under the endowment grant, and overhead costs, and, during the interim period, funds for the payment of salaries. Also significant has been financial support from three members of the Garrison family: Marian K. Chubb (formerly Mrs. Philip McKim Garrison), Eleanor Garrison, and especially Robert H. Garrison. I continue to be grateful to Louis Ruchames, editor of alternate volumes of Garrison's letters.

I want to thank various libraries, historical societies, and individuals for furnishing photocopies and for permission to publish the Garrison letters in their collections. Since more than half of the letters printed in this volume are to be found at the Boston Public Library, special mention should be made of that collection. I am grateful also to the American Antiquarian Society, Bostonian Society, Columbia University Libraries, Essex Institute, Harvard College Library, Henry E. Huntington Library, Historical Library of the Religious Society of Friends (Dublin), Historical Society of Pennsylvania, McGill University Library, Marietta College Library, Massachusetts Historical Society, New-York Historical Society, Astor, Lenox and Tilden Foundations of the New York Public Library, Pierpont Morgan Library, Radcliffe College Library, Rhodes House Library (Oxford), Smith College Library, and Wichita State University Library.

I would especially like to thank Sarah Dunning Schear, Richard A. Ehrlich, and Sidney Kaplan for permission to publish letters from their private collections.

The research for this volume could never have been completed without an efficient and gifted staff, who have cooperated in transcrib-

Acknowledgments

ing and collating letters, in identifying persons and events, in corresponding with libraries and historical societies, and in reading and collating galley and page proofs. Especially to be commended for their work on volume III, although they have not worked simultaneously, are Marion E. Jarrett, Dr. Frank M. Laurence, Rebecca R. McBride, Dr. Alice J. Nearing, William B. Remington, Nancy A. Sahli, Patricia B. Wells, and Nancy Zurich. Also helpful were John S. Bartolomeo, Charlotte G. Harp, Helene E. Hoffman, Adeline G. Merrill, Margaret B. Merrill, Anita Sama, Dr. Frank Saul, and Lee Weinberg. Our primary researchers in the Boston-Cambridge area have been, first, Elizabeth L. Forsythe and currently Ruth D. Bell. Dr. C. Duncan Rice has worked on British research problems.

In addition to those mentioned above, the following persons have made special contributions to the research: John Alden, keeper of rare books, Boston Public Library; John B. Blake, chief, History of Medicine Division, National Library of Medicine, National Institute of Health; William H. Bond, librarian, Houghton Library, Harvard University; John D. Cushing, librarian, Massachusetts Historical Society; Harriet R. Cabot, curator, Bostonian Society; Diane M. Dorsey, curator of manuscripts, Schlesinger Library, Radcliffe College; Elizabeth Droppers, reference librarian, Harvard College Library; Elizabeth S. Duvall, Sophia Smith Collection, Smith College Library; Kimball C. Elkins, curator, Harvard University Archives; Olive C. Goodbody, curator, Historical Library of the Religious Society of Friends (Dublin); Thompson R. Harlow, director, Connecticut Historical Society; Michael D. Heaston, curator of special collections, Wichita State University Library; Carolyn E. Jakeman, Houghton Library, Harvard University; Elizabeth B. Knox, curator, New London County Historical Society; Richard C. Kugler, director, Old Dartmouth Historical Society Whaling Museum (New Bedford, Massachusetts); James Lawton, curator of manuscripts, Department of Rare Books and Manuscripts, Boston Public Library; Alzina C. Loveless, town historian, Skaneateles, New York; Marcus A. McCorison, director and librarian, American Antiquarian Society; David C. Mearns, chief, Manuscript Division, Library of Congress; Mary-Elizabeth Murdock, director, Sophia Smith Collection, Smith College Library; Ellen M. Oldham, curator of printed books, Boston Public Library; Dorothy M. Potter, librarian, Essex Institute (Salem, Massachusetts); Stephen T. Riley, director, Massachusetts Historical Society; Walter M. Whitehill, director, Boston Athenaeum; Richard N. Wright, president, Onondaga Historical Association (Syracuse, New York).

The following institutions have been extremely cooperative and helpful: Albany Public Library, Andover-Harvard Theological Library,

Acknowledgments

Carnegie Library of Pittsburgh, Chicago Historical Society, Cleveland Public Library, Connecticut Historical Commission, Douglas County Historical Museum (Lawrence, Kansas), Harrisburg Public Library, Haverford College Library, Historical Society of Old Newbury (Newburyport, Massachusetts), Historical Society of Western Pennsylvania, Kansas State Historical Society, Lexington (Kentucky) Public Library, Lynn Historical Society, Maine Historical Society, Mariners Museum (Newport News, Virginia), Minnesota Historical Society, Nantucket Historical Society, New Hampshire Historical Society, New Jersey Historical Society, New York State Historical Association, Oberlin College Archives, Ohio Historical Society, Pejepscot (Maine) Historical Society, Pennsylvania Historical Museum and Commission (Harrisburg), Plymouth Antiquarian Society, Rhode Island Historical Society, Salem Public Library, Springfield (Massachusetts) City Library, Trinity College Library, United States Military Academy Library, University of Kentucky Libraries, Western Reserve Historical Society, and Yale University Library. Generous research assistance was provided by many British institutions including Bristol Archives Office, British Museum, Central Library of Belfast, Dr. Williams's Library (London), Dublin Public Library, Exeter City Library, Library of the Religious Society of Friends (London), Liverpool City Library, Manchester Central Library, Mitchell Library (Glasgow), National Library of Scotland, National Maritime Museum (London), National Library of Ireland, Newcastle-on-Tyne City Library, John Rylands Library (Manchester), and University of London Library. There are, in addition, countless other persons and institutions to whom I am indebted for help.

All the efforts of libraries, researchers, and editors would be of little effect without the judgment, skill, and taste of the staff of the Harvard University Press. I want to express special gratitude to Mark Carroll, former director, to Eleanor D. Kewer, former chief editor for special projects, to Ann Louise McLaughlin, and to Elizabeth W. Pitha, who was copy editor not only for this project but earlier for my biography *Against Wind and Tide*.

Walter M. Merrill

Philadelphia
July 1973

CONTENTS

List of Illustrations   xix

Editorial Statement   xxi

I ORGANIZATION AND APPEAL: 1841–1842   1

1.   To James H. Garrison, January 4, 1841
2.   To Samuel J. May, January 5, 1841
3.   To George W. Benson, January 7, 1841
4.   To Edmund Quincy, January 12, 1841
5.   To John H. Tredgold, January 29, 1841
6.   To Elizabeth Pease, February 1, 1841
7.   To Parker Pillsbury, February 23, 1841
8.   To Elizabeth Pease, March 1, 1841
9.   To John A. Collins, April 1, 1841
10. To Elizabeth Pease, June 1, 1841
11. To Nathaniel P. Rogers, July 15, 1841
12. To Unknown Recipient, July 26, 1841
13. To Elizabeth Pease, September 16, 1841
14. To Gamaliel Bailey, Jr., September 27, 1841
15. To Sumner Lincoln, November 8, 1841
16. To Edmund Quincy, November 9, 1841
17. To Francis Jackson, November 26, 1841
18. To George W. Benson, December 17, 1841
19. To George W. Benson, January 9, 1842
20. To George W. Benson, January 28, 1842
21. To George W. Benson, January 29, 1842
22. To Henry G. and Maria W. Chapman, February 19, 1842
23. To Richard Allen, February 27, 1842
24. To Richard D. Webb, February 27, 1842
25. To Charles L. Corkran, February 27, 1842
26. To Abel Brown, March 18, 1842
27. To Sarah M. Douglass, March 18, 1842
28. To George W. Benson, March 22, 1842

Contents

29. To Edmund Quincy, April 4, 1842
30. To George W. Benson, April 11, 1842
31. To Henry C. Wright, April 12, 1842
32. To the Executive Committee of the American Anti-
    Slavery Society, May 9, 1842
33. To George W. Benson, May 13, 1842
34. To Elizabeth Pease, May 15, 1842
35. To Nathaniel P. Rogers, June 7, 1842
36. To George Bradburn, June 10, 1842
37. To Samuel J. May, June 10, 1842
38. To Elizabeth Pease, July 2, 1842
39. To Richard Allen, July 2, 1842
40. To George W. Benson, July 8, 1842
41. To the Editor of *Zion's Herald*, August 27, 1842
42. To George W. Benson, September 10, 1842
43. To Edmund Quincy, September 12, 1842
44. To Henry C. Wright, October 1, 1842
45. To George W. Benson, October 11, 1842
46. To George W. Benson, October 14, 1842
47. To Helen E. Garrison, November 21, 1842
48. To Helen E. Garrison, November 27, 1842
49. To John T. Norton, December 17, 1842

II DISUNION: 1843–1845   118

50. To George W. Benson, February 25, 1843
51. To Elizabeth Pease, February 28, 1843
52. To Richard D. Webb, February 28, 1843
53. To Hannah Webb, March 1, 1843
54. To Henry C. Wright, March 1, 1843
55. To George W. Benson, March 3, 1843
56. To Joshua T. Everett, March 4, 1843
57. To Louisa Gilman Loring, March 19, 1843
58. To James N. Buffum, March 24, 1843
59. To Henry C. Wright, April 1, 1843
60. To Elizabeth Pease, April 4, 1843
61. To George W. Benson, April 8, 1843
62. To George W. Benson, April 15, 1843
63. To Phoebe Jackson, May 1, 1843
64. To *The Liberator*, May 9, 1843
65. To David Lee Child, May 14, 1843
66. To George W. Benson, June 12, 1843
67. To George W. Benson, June 20, 1843
68. To Edmund Quincy, July 6, 1843
69. To Maria W. Chapman, July 7, 1843

Contents

70.   To *The Liberator,* July 14, 1843

71.   To Francis Jackson, July 15, 1843

72.   To Francis Jackson, August 2, 1843

73.   To Henry W. Williams, August 2, 1843

74.   To *The Liberator,* August 2, 1843

75.   To Francis Jackson, August 16, 1843

76.   To Henry W. Williams, August 23, 1843

77.   To Abby Kelley, September 8, 1843

78.   To Francis Jackson, September 9, 1843

79.   To *The Liberator,* September 17, 1843

80.   To George W. Benson, September 24, 1843

81.   To Sarah T. Benson, October 7, 1843

82.   To Laura Stebbins, October 7, 1843

83.   To *The Liberator,* October 13, 1843

84.   To Sarah T. Benson, October 14, 1843

85.   To George W. Benson, November 6, 1843

86.   To Elizabeth Pease, December 1, 1843

87.   To Daniel O'Connell, December 8, 1843

88.   To Louisa Humphrey, December 15, 1843

89.   To Henry C. Wright, December 16, 1843

90.   To Anne W. Weston, December 19, 1843

91.   To Edmund Quincy, January 5, 1844

92.   To Louisa Gilman Loring, January 5, 1844

93.   To *The Liberator,* January 8, 1844

94.   To Helen E. Garrison, January 12, 1844

95.   To *The Liberator,* January 15, 1844

96.   To George W. Benson, January 15, 1844

97.   To William Chalmers, April 27, 1844

98.   To James B. Yerrinton, May 7, 1844

99.   To George W. Benson, June 10, 1844

100.   To George W. Benson, June 25, 1844

101.   To George W. Benson, August 26, 1844

102.   To Samuel J. May, September 28, 1844

103.   To Henry C. Wright, October 1, 1844

104.   To Christopher Robinson, November 27, 1844

105.   To Edmund Quincy, December 14, 1844

106.   To Elizabeth Pease, December 14, 1844

107.   To John Bailey, January 10, 1845

108.   To Louisa Gilman Loring, January 11, 1845

109.   To the Editor of the *Daily Mail*, February 1, 1845

110.   To John Bailey, February 13, 1845

111.   To Richard D. Webb, March 1, 1845

112.   To Levi Woodbury, March 14, 1845

113.   To Lucretia Mott, May 8, 1845

114.   To George W. Benson, May 19, 1845

115.   To Francis Jackson, July 2, 1845

116.   To Elihu Burritt, July 16, 1845

Contents

117. To Samuel J. May, July 17, 1845
118. To Edmund Quincy, July 18, 1845
119. To James Miller McKim, July 19, 1845
120. To Unknown Recipient, July 25, 1845
121. To William Endicott, July 31, 1845
122. To James Miller McKim, August 6, 1845
123. To Charles Sumner, August 23, 1845
124. To Erasmus D. Hudson, September 12, 1845
125. To Henry C. Wright, November 1, 1845

III   BRITISH MISSION: 1846   326

126. To Louisa Gilman Loring, January 1, 1846
127. To Francis Jackson, January 12, 1846
128. To Samuel J. May, February 16, 1846
129. To Sydney Howard Gay, March 21, 1846
130. To Sydney Howard Gay, March 31, 1846
131. To James Miller McKim, May 3, 1846
132. To Sydney Howard Gay, May 7, 1846
133. To Samuel E. Sewall, May 15, 1846
134. To Henry C. Wright, June 1, 1846
135. To Unknown Recipient, June 1, 1846
136. To James Miller McKim, June 12, 1846
137. To Sydney Howard Gay, June 12, 1846
138. To Elizabeth Pease, June 16, 1846
139. To Francis Jackson, July 15, 1846
140. To Helen E. Garrison, July 18, 1846
141. To Edmund Quincy, July 19, 1846
142. To Charles K. Whipple, July 19, 1846
143. To Helen E. Garrison, July 26, 1846
144. To Edmund Quincy, August 1, 1846
145. To Helen E. Garrison, August 4, 1846
146. To Helen E. Garrison, August 4, 1846
147. To Helen E. Garrison, August 11, 1846
148. To Helen E. Garrison, August 13, 1846
149. To Edmund Quincy, August 14, 1846
150. To Elizabeth Pease, August 14, 1846
151. To Helen E. Garrison, August 18, 1846
152. To Edmund Quincy, August 18, 1846
153. To Thomas Clarkson, August 19, 1846
154. To John B. Estlin, August 19, 1846
155. To Richard D. Webb, August 19, 1846
156. To Thomas Clarkson, August 26, 1846
157. To Henry C. Wright, August 26, 1846

Contents

158. To Henry C. Wright, August 27, 1846
159. To Edmund Quincy, August 29, 1846
160. To Francis Jackson, September 2, 1846
161. To Helen E. Garrison, September 3, 1846
162. To Richard D. Webb, September 5, 1846
163. To Mary Howitt, September 7, 1846
164. To John B. Estlin, September 8, 1846
165. To Helen E. Garrison, September 10, 1846
166. To Richard D. Webb, September 12, 1846
167. To Helen E. Garrison, September 17, 1846
168. To Edmund Quincy, September 18, 1846
169. To Henry C. Wright, September 18, 1846
170. To Henry C. Wright, September 21, 1846
171. To Henry C. Wright, September 23, 1846
172. To Richard D. Webb, September 25, 1846
173. To Richard D. Webb, September 30, 1846
174. To *The Liberator*, October 3, 1846
175. To Elizabeth Pease, October 12, 1846
176. To *The Liberator*, October 20, 1846
177. To Richard D. Webb, October 24, 1846
178. To Elizabeth Pease, October 25, 1846
179. To Richard D. Webb, October 29, 1846
180. To Unknown Recipient, November 3, 1846
181. To Baring Brothers, November 3, 1846
182. To Sarah Hilditch, November 4, 1846
183. To Elizabeth Pease, November 15, 1846
184. To Marcus Morton, November 27, 1846
185. To James Freeman Clarke, November 28, 1846
186. To the Editor of the *Christian Witness*, December 4, 1846
187. To George W. Benson, December 11, 1846
188. To Samuel J. May, December 19, 1846

IV WESTERN MISSION: 1847   465

189. To Louisa Gilman Loring, January 7, 1847
190. To Anne W. Weston, February 23, 1847
191. To Richard D. Webb, March 1, 1847
192. To Henry C. Wright, March 1, 1847
193. To Elizabeth Pease, April 1, 1847
194. To *The Liberator*, May 11, 1847
195. To Sydney Howard Gay, May 15, 1847
196. To Heman Humphrey, June 15, 1847
197. To George W. Benson, June 26, 1847
198. To Richard D. Webb, July 1, 1847
199. To Heman Humphrey, July 9, 1847

Contents

200. To Joseph Merrill, July 12, 1847
201. To John B. Estlin, July 16, 1847
202. To Henry C. Wright, July 16, 1847
203. To George W. Benson, July 24, 1847
204. To John B. Vashon, July 27, 1847
205. To Louisa Gilman Loring, July 30, 1847
206. To Helen E. Garrison, August 3, 1847
207. To Helen E. Garrison, August 9, 1847
208. To Helen E. Garrison, August 12, 1847
209. To Helen E. Garrison, August 16, 1847
210. To Helen E. Garrison, August 20, 1847
211. To *The Liberator*, August 25, 1847
212. To Helen E. Garrison, August 28, 1847
213. To Helen E. Garrison, September 18, 1847
214. To Stephen S. Foster, October 12, 1847
215. To Helen E. Garrison, October 19, 1847
216. To Helen E. Garrison, October 20, 1847
217. To Helen E. Garrison, October 26, 1847
218. To Ellis Gray Loring and Francis Jackson, December 2, 1847
219. To Edmund Quincy, December 4, 1847
220. To Joseph Ricketson, December 4, 1847
221. To Edmund Quincy, December 8, 1847
222. To George W. Benson, December 17, 1847

V ANTI-SABBATH CONVENTION
AND FATHER MATHEW: 1848–1849

540

223. To Theodore Parker, January 3, 1848
224. To James and Lucretia Mott, January 10, 1848
225. To Edward M. Davis, January 10, 1848
226. To Samuel J. May, January 10, 1848
227. To Samuel J. May, April 7, 1848
228. To George W. Benson, April 20, 1848
229. To Maria W. Chapman *et al.*, April 20, 1848
230. To Theodore Parker, April 20, 1848
231. To Sydney Howard Gay, April 27, 1848
232. To Sydney Howard Gay, May 1, 1848
233. To George W. Benson, May 3, 1848
234. To Elizabeth Pease, May 3, 1848
235. To George W. Benson, May 17, 1848
236. To Francis Jackson, July 13, 1848
237. To Edmund Quincy, July 16, 1848

Contents

238.   To William Ballantyne Hodgson, July 17, 1848
239.   To William Rathbone, July 17, 1848
240.   To Helen E. Garrison, July 18, 1848
241.   To Maria W. Chapman, July 19, 1848
242.   To Helen E. Garrison, July 23, 1848
243.   To Helen E. Garrison, July 26, 1848
244.   To Francis Jackson, July 31, 1848
245.   To Eliza Jackson Merriam, August 9, 1848
246.   To Edmund Quincy, August 10, 1848
247.   To Robert F. Wallcut, August 28, 1848
248.   To Nathaniel Barney, September 8, 1848
249.   To Adeline Roberts, September 20, 1848
250.   To Eliza Jackson Eddy, October 3, 1848
251.   To Elizabeth Pease, October 3, 1848
252.   To Helen E. Garrison, October 10, 1848
253.   To Helen E. Garrison, October 18, 1848
254.   To George W. Benson, October 29, 1848
255.   To Francis Jackson, November 5, 1848
256.   To Abby G. Thayer, November 17, 1848
257.   To Samuel May, Jr., December 2, 1848
258.   To Joseph Congdon, December 15, 1848
259.   To Joseph Ricketson, January 2, 1849
260.   To Joseph Ricketson, January 22, 1849
261.   To Edmund Quincy, March 16, 1849
262.   To Henry Clay, March 16, 1849
263.   To Theodore Parker, April 9, 1849
264.   To *The Liberator*, May 8, 1849
265.   To Helen E. Garrison, May 9, 1849
266.   To Sydney Howard Gay, May 22, 1849
267.   To Sydney Howard Gay, May 25, 1849
268.   To Sydney Howard Gay, June 6, 1849
269.   To Elizabeth Pease, June 20, 1849
270.   To Elizabeth Pease, July 17, 1849
271.   To Ralph Waldo Emerson, July 20, 1849
272.   To Theobald Mathew, July 26, 1849
273.   To Charles Sumner, July 27, 1849
274.   To Samuel May, Jr., July 28, 1849
275.   To Elizabeth Pease, July 31, 1849
276.   To Theobald Mathew, September 7, 1849
277.   To Theobald Mathew, September 14, 1849
278.   To Theobald Mathew, September 28, 1849
279.   To the Financial Committee of *The Liberator*, September 28, 1849
280.   To Theobald Mathew, October 5, 1849
281.   To Theobald Mathew, October 12, 1849
282.   To Sydney Howard Gay, October 25, 1849
283.   To Francis Jackson, December 13, 1849

Contents

APPENDIX   679

284.   To William B. Earle, March 13, 1841
285.   To Isaac T. Hopper, May 7, 1846
286.   To the Secretaries of the Glasgow Emancipation
            Society, June 1, 1846
287.   To Elizabeth Buffum Chace, June 26, 1847

Index of Recipients   687

Index   689

LIST OF ILLUSTRATIONS

Frontispiece

William Lloyd Garrison in 1846, engraving from a daguerreotype made in Dublin in October 1846.
Courtesy of the Library of Congress.

Page 33

Antislavery meeting in Exeter Hall, London, 1841, engraved by H. Melville, after a drawing by Thomas Hosmer Shepherd.
Courtesy of the Library of Congress.

Page 34

The Liberator, January 1, 1841.
Chart showing the arrangement of exhibits at the Anti-Slavery Fair held at Marlboro Hall the preceding December.

Page 159

George Thompson in 1842, an engraving by Charles Turner, from an oil painting by George Evans.
Courtesy of the National Portrait Gallery, London.

Lucretia Mott in 1841, from an oil painting by Joseph Kyle.
Courtesy of Lucia Garrison Norton Valentine, Princeton, New Jersey.

Frederick Douglass in about 1847, from a daguerreotype.
Courtesy of the Historical Society of Pennsylvania.

Gerrit Smith in about 1849, from an engraving by John Chester Buttre.
Courtesy of the Library of Congress.

Page 160

Nathaniel Peabody Rogers in 1846, from the chalk and charcoal drawing by Henry B. Brown, which was engraved by Frederick Halpin as a frontispiece for *A Collection from the Newspaper Writings of Nathaniel Peabody Rogers* (Concord, New Hampshire, 1847). Rogers himself says in the collection (p. 354): "My individual objection to the picture . . . is its sad degree of likeness."
Courtesy of the Library of Congress.

List of Illustrations

Father Theobald Mathew in about 1849, from a daguerreotype by Mathew B. Brady.
Courtesy of the Library of Congress.

William Lloyd Garrison in 1846, painted in Boston by William Page. Members of the Garrison family have never considered this painting a good likeness, preferring the Dublin daguerreotype used as a frontispiece for this volume. (See Wendell Phillips Garrison and Francis Jackson Garrison, eds., *The Words of Garrison*, Boston, 1905, pp. 114–115.)
Courtesy of the Museum of Fine Arts, Boston.

William Lloyd Garrison in about 1846, from a lithograph by the Philadelphia firm of P. S. Duval, on stone by Albert Newsam. Although the date cannot be established with absolute certainty, the similarity to the Page portrait in face and costume suggests the same year. Francis Jackson Garrison dates the lithograph 1846–1847 on a card attached to the ambrotype copy in the possession of the editor.
Courtesy of the Sophia Smith Collection, Smith College Library.

Page 317

Cover of antislavery sheet music by Jesse Hutchinson, Jr., dedicated to Garrison's New Hampshire friend Nathaniel P. Rogers (Boston, 1844).
Courtesy of the Free Library of Philadelphia.

Page 318

William Lloyd Garrison to James Miller McKim, August 6, 1845. The stationery is engraved with a well-known antislavery seal, which changes to the feminine gender the original motto "Am I not a man and a brother." Designed in 1787 for the Committee for the Abolition of the Slave Trade, the earlier seal was widely used as an antislavery emblem by individuals and organizations like the Anti-Slavery Society, founded in London in 1823, and the British and Foreign Anti-Slavery Society, founded in 1839.
Courtesy of the Boston Public Library.

Page 501

Silver tea and coffee service presented to Garrison October 21, 1846, by John Wigham, Jr., on behalf of the antislavery ladies of Edinburgh. The set was valued at £40, and Garrison was subsequently shocked to find that customs officers in Boston charged him $60 duty, a fee for which he was ultimately reimbursed by female friends in Boston.
Courtesy of the Massachusetts Historical Society.

Page 502

William Lloyd Garrison to Henry C. Wright, July 16, 1847. Reproduced here is the second page of the letter, showing the way in which the letter sheet was folded to form a small envelope with stamp and address. In this letter Garrison announces his forthcoming trip to "the far West" with Frederick Douglass and expresses his confident enthusiasm for the rapid progress of the cause.
Courtesy of the Boston Public Library.

EDITORIAL STATEMENT

VOLUME III contains all of Garrison's letters known to the editor for the period 1841–1849, including fragments. The text of these letters has been established from autograph manuscripts or in their absence from the best available copy, whether written, typed, or printed; the exact source is given in the descriptive notes. An attempt has been made to arrange the letters in chronological order, though in some instances — especially when two or more letters were written on the same day — the chronology is uncertain.

The letters have been grouped in five periods, according to dominant themes, except when long trips (to England in 1846 and to the western United States in 1847) result in a sufficiently large annual accumulation to warrant their being grouped separately. Each of the five periods is introduced by a brief essay designed to assist the reader in fully understanding the letters to follow.

Format of the Text

1. Each letter is numbered and placed according to its chronological position in the entire sequence of letters, with the exception of such letters as have been printed in the appendix owing to their recent discovery.

2. Since all the letters are from Garrison, the editor has used a uniform heading, simply printing the name of the recipient in its usual spelling.

3. Each letter is also given a uniform date line using verbatim Garrison's original words, the editor having supplied when necessary additional information in square brackets. In those letters dated by Garrison at the bottom of the text, the date has been supplied twice: in square brackets at the beginning and as intended by Garrison at the end.

Editorial Statement

Text of the Letters

1. The salutation is uniformly placed but follows Garrison's original wording.

2. The editor has endeavored to supply with scrupulous accuracy the text of each letter as presented in its source. Garrison's misspellings have been followed, his cancellations omitted. Obvious slips, like the repetition of a word or phrase, have been silently corrected.

3. The complimentary close and signature are worded precisely as in the source, but uniformly placed. The punctuation of such signatures as are transcribed from printed sources follows the printed format.

4. Simple postscripts are uniformly placed following Garrison's signature. Marginal notations clearly intended as postscripts are transcribed as such, with notes explaining their position in the manuscript. Marginal notations intended by Garrison to be read at a particular position in the text are so placed.

5. Certain editorial situations are described by the following symbols:

[. . .] A lacuna in the manuscript or other source. If the lacuna consists of more than a word or two, its extent and nature are explained in the notes.

[   ] Editorial insertion.

[   ] Garrison's brackets.

☞ ☜ Garrison's method of emphasis.

Descriptive Notes

1. The source of the letter is supplied without number immediately following the text, the only abbreviations used being the conventional ALS for "autograph letter signed" and AL for "autograph letter" without signature. When the source is other than an autograph, its nature is described.

2. Known previous publications of the letter, whether in whole or in part, have been indicated.

3. Wherever the manuscript is in such poor condition as to interfere with transcription, that condition is described.

4. Efforts have been made to identify all recipients.

Notes

1. Consecutively numbered notes for each letter are placed immediately following the descriptive notes.

2. The editor has endeavored to identify persons referred to in the

text of the letters, as well as to explain references and allusions not immediately clear in context, the extent of the notes being determined by the importance of the person or the allusion. The editor has also tried to identify Garrison's quotations, but some of the authors quoted are so obscure as to make identification virtually impossible.

3. Quotations from the Bible have been verified or identified in the King James version, which seems to be the only one Garrison used. For quotations from Shakespeare, we have followed the standard concordance: John Bartlett, *A Complete Concordance . . . of Shakespeare* (New York, 1967). This book follows the Globe edition of 1891.

4. In order to avoid monotonous repetition the editor has not cited such commonly used secondary sources as the following. *Appleton's Cyclopaedia of American Biography, Dictionary of American Biography, Dictionary of National Biography, Encyclopaedia Britannica, Oxford Companion to American Literature, National Cyclopaedia of American Biography.*

The following sources have been abbreviated as indicated:

AWT. Walter M. Merrill, *Against Wind and Tide, a Biography of William Lloyd Garrison* (Cambridge, Mass., 1963)

Life. Wendell Phillips Garrison and Francis Jackson Garrison, *William Lloyd Garrison, 1805–1879: The Story of His Life, Told by His Children* (New York, 1885–1889)

OHAP. Samuel Eliot Morison, *The Oxford History of the American People* (New York, 1965)

PMHS. Proceedings of the Massachusetts Historical Society

Sheffeld. Charles A. Sheffeld, ed., *History of Florence, Mass., including a Complete Account of the Northampton Association of Education and Industry* (Florence, Mass., 1895)

ULN. Winifred Gregory, ed., *American Newspapers, 1821–1936: A Union List of Files Available in the United States and Canada* (New York, 1937)

ULS. Edna Brown Titus, ed., *Union List of Serials in Libraries of the United States and Canada* (New York, 1965)

Weld-Grimké Letters. Gilbert H. Barnes and Dwight L. Dumond, eds., *Letters of Theodore Dwight Weld, Angelina Grimké Weld and Sarah Grimké, 1822–1844* (Gloucester, Mass., 1965)

I ORGANIZATION AND APPEAL: 1841–1842

BY 1841 GARRISON had firmly established himself as an outstanding leader in the abolition movement.[1] His resolution of 1831, "I will be heard!" had been fulfilled: for he had completed a decade as editor of *The Liberator* in spite of almost insuperable financial difficulties and the persistent criticism of some friends and all enemies. In fact, he maintained through crisis after crisis personal editorial control of the paper, which was his in the sense that few influential organs of public opinion have ever belonged to one man. Although he controlled no antislavery society to the same extent, Garrison had risen to a position of considerable power in both the Massachusetts and the national societies. For in the schism of 1839–1840 he had been able to muster the majority vote on the crucial and divisive issues, so that the moderates were obliged to split away from the old organizations and form new ones, such as the short-lived Massachusetts Abolition Society and the more durable American and Foreign Anti-Slavery Society. Understandably, Garrison was convinced by this time that moderates in New York, like Arthur and Lewis Tappan, Elizur Wright, and Theodore D. Weld, with their burgeoning conviction that abolition should be effected through political means, had been repudiated by the majority of conscientious abolitionists; and he virtually banished their names from his letters of the 1840's, only occasionally mentioning them even in *The Liberator*. Not all twentieth-century historians would agree with Garrison's analysis. The Barnes-Dumond thesis, for instance, is predicated on the perhaps questionable assumption that after 1841 the main current of antislavery energy had shifted from New England to New York.[2]

1. The major source for material in the introductions to this volume is *AWT*; other sources will be separately cited. Quotations, even though they may appear in *AWT*, are cited to their original sources.
2. See, for example, Gilbert Hobbs Barnes, *The Antislavery Impulse, 1830–1844* (New York, 1933).

1

Since the dissidents had taken with them, by transfer to the New York State Anti-Slavery Society, the *Emancipator*, once the official organ of the national society, it was necessary for the Garrisonians to establish a new paper. The *National Anti-Slavery Standard* was the result. The new paper was kept alive during 1840 primarily by Mrs. Maria W. Chapman, and in 1841 Lydia Maria Child, assisted by her husband, became the editor, the position being taken by David Lee Child in 1843 and by Sydney Howard Gay, assisted by Mrs. Chapman and Edmund Quincy, in 1844.

Although Garrison certainly was in 1841 conscious of his increased power as a leader in the antislavery movement, his letters show him by no means arrogantly self-satisfied. They reveal, rather, a man resting after strenuous controversy, a man more often defensive than offensive, a man intent on readjustment and consolidation after the fervor, the excitement, the violence of the 1830's.

For the years 1841 and 1842 forty-four of Garrison's letters have been preserved, some of them short, some of them routine, many concerned exclusively with family matters: the death of Mary Benson, his wife's sister, the death of James Garrison, his only brother, who lived his last year as an invalid in Garrison's house. Outstanding are the long letters to his Scottish friend Elizabeth Pease, in which he summarizes what has happened in the world of American reform and defends his own actions. He seems to consider Miss Pease not only a close friend and associate in reform but also the one whose judgment will determine his British standing, and he was anxious that his reputation be untarnished in England, Scotland, and Ireland. He defends the old organization in Massachusetts and in the nation against attacks from the moderates. He defends himself against charges of infidelity and religious heterodoxy, he defends the British mission and the person of John A. Collins, he defends himself in the controversy with his former partner, Isaac Knapp, and with his friend Nathaniel P. Rogers. He gives Elizabeth Pease a view of family illness and death and other personal problems. He even discusses John Humphrey Noyes and the influence on himself of his philosophy of perfectionism.

Perhaps the most significant event discussed in the letters of 1841–1842 is the appearance on the American scene of what is called the Irish Address, a document initially signed by 60,000 Irishmen, including Daniel O'Connell and Father Theobald Mathew. The address was brought to this country in December 1841 by Charles L. Remond, distinguished black abolitionist and close associate of Garrison, when he returned from a British mission. The address appealed to Americans of Irish descent, urging that they treat Negroes as equals and that they support the abolitionists. At an expanded annual meeting of the

Massachusetts Anti-Slavery Society held in Faneuil Hall in January 1842, Garrison read the address aloud, and many of the assembled abolitionists attested to their Irish descent and enthusiastically supported the address. Following the meeting *The Liberator* furnished extended publicity, but many of the Irish-Americans remained indifferent. Irish prelates and the Irish press attacked both the abolitionists and the document itself, even impugning its authenticity.

At any rate, consideration of the Irish and their problems helped Garrison formulate an idea that had been flickering through his mind. The Irish wished repeal of their union with England; abolitionists should urge repeal of theirs with slavery.[3] In *The Liberator* of May 6, 1842, Garrison printed a long editorial, "Repeal of the Union," in which he argued that the Constitution was "a covenant with death" and should no longer be permitted to bind together the North and the South. Beginning with the issue of May 13 he printed the following as the superscription to the editorial column: "A REPEAL OF THE UNION BETWEEN NORTHERN LIBERTY AND SOUTHERN SLAVERY IS ESSENTIAL TO THE ABOLITION OF THE ONE, AND THE PRESERVATION OF THE OTHER."

1

TO JAMES H. GARRISON

Boston, Jan. 4, 1841.

My dear James:

I am sorry to hear that you feel discontented with your present situation — that your health is not good — and that you seriously think of leaving Brooklyn for Boston. You complain of having too much hard work to perform, and say that George expects as much from you as from a well man. I am sure that it is not the desire of George, or of any of the family, that you should labor so as to injure yourself in the least. Far otherwise. They wish you to do just what you please by way of bodily exertion, and no more. They have said so repeatedly, and they mean just what they say. The difficulty is, you try to perform too much; and your ambition is more than a match for your strength. You further say — "This way of working all the time, and receiving nothing for it, does not please my fancy."[1] You entirely mistake the feelings of bro. George, if you suppose he is not willing to make you a liberal compensation for your labor. He will get you any kind of clothing that you want; and if you are "almost in rags," it is certainly

3. See especially his letter to George W. Benson, March 22, 1842.

not his fault, but yours, in not making your wants known. Why, dear James, do you hesitate to make known your feelings to him, and also state your necessities? He feels a brotherly interest in your welfare, and will rejoice to improve every opportunity to make your condition comfortable and pleasant. As to what I have done for you, let it not be named. You are welcome to it all, and to as much more as I may, from time to time, be able to do for you; and the only remuneration that I want is, to see you leading a sober and virtuous life. And I can truly say, that I have been exceedingly rejoiced in spirit to hear such good things about you from George and the girls.[2] They praise you highly, and have supposed that you would like them well enough to remain in Brooklyn for some time to come. I hope you will do so. Let me entreat you not to come to any hasty conclusion about leaving, but to deliberate well and long before you make up your mind to change your situation. You think you can find a place in Boston where you can get an easy living; but this is by no means certain. One thing *is* certain, however: you cannot live in this city, and go among your old associates, without falling into temptation, and making yourself wretched and miserable. This is your misfortune. The petition which our Saviour has taught us to offer up is, "Lead us not into temptation." [3] If we are conscious of our own weakness before its terrible power — if we desire to escape from wrath and ruin — ought we not to avoid the society of those, as far as practicable, who care not how soon we go down to a grave of infamy, and who are themselves the victims of debauchery and intemperance? Dear James, I do not wonder that you feel, occasionally, somewhat lonesome and "down-hearted," in consequence of seeing so few with whom you are acquainted; but is it not better that you should be surrounded by a few choice friends, than by a host of those who will lead you astray, while they pretend to regard your welfare? Remember that you have now an excellent opportunity to recover yourself in every particular, and to begin the world anew. Do not lose it — do not despise it — do not deem it a hardship. So long as you have any appetite for ardent spirit — so long as you are not sure that you can resist its sorcery power — take the advice of a brother who loves you as he does himself, and remain where you will be the least exposed to be tempted and overcome. Liquor has been your worst foe. It has made you die a thousand deaths — robbed you of all your hard earnings — subjected you to a vast amount of suffering — and made shipwreck of your moral nature. You ought to hate, fear, avoid it, at all times and under all circumstances, as you would the bite of a rattlesnake, or the infection of the plague. Pray to God for strength to sustain you, and make up your mind, in the spirit of a moral hero, no more to touch, taste or handle the unclean thing. Then will you live in a new world, and be a new

4

creature. Then will you be able exultingly to exclaim — "Old things are passed away! Behold, all things are become new!" [4]

You wish me to send you a dollar, so as to enable you to come to Boston on foot. I have written to George to give you some money, and also to supply you with clothing. When you were here, I frankly but kindly told you why George and myself felt so reluctant to give you money: it was because of our fears that it would be spent in a manner not conducive to your welfare. Dear James, will you blame us for this? It is for your temporal and eternal good that we do it, though it may seem a hardship. Still, if you will take the responsibility, you shall have money, from time to time, as well as clothing; and I hope it will be wisely spent. ☞ Do not think of walking to Boston. At this inclement season of the year, it would be a rash act, and would in all probability put in peril your existence.

I shall send you in the next Liberator bundle, a Russian Lotion for Chilblains, which I hope will cure your feet.[5] How anxious I am that you should guard yourself from the cold as much as possible! Remember the old adage — "An ounce of prevention is worth a pound of cure" — especially in your present feeble state of health.[6]

If George cannot find suitable cloth in Brooklyn for your pantaloons, write me word immediately what kind you want, and I will forward it by the bundle. If I could be sure of fitting you, I would send on a pair already made up. Can I get you any thing else?

We are all well, and Helen and mother send their kind remembrances.[7]

Your loving brother,

Wm. Lloyd Garrison.

ALS: Garrison Papers, Boston Public Library.

James Holley Garrison (1801–1842) was Garrison's elder brother, who for twenty-two years served as a merchant seaman and a sailor in the British and then American navies. Suffering from alcoholism and a "fistulous abscess," he made his home after 1839 with the Garrisons, and then with Mrs. Garrison's family, the Bensons, at Brooklyn, Connecticut. In his final year of life he returned to his brother's home. (Walter M. Merrill, ed., *Behold Me Once More, The Confessions of James Holley Garrison*, Boston, 1954.)

1. The letter from which Garrison quotes has not been preserved.

2. George William Benson (1808–1879), who was currently operating the family farm in Brooklyn, Connecticut, was an active reformer and a consistent supporter of Garrison; he gave frequent public lectures and served as officer in various antislavery societies. In 1833–1834 he was one of Prudence Crandall's strongest supporters in the controversy over her school for Negro girls. In 1842, having sold the Benson farm, he moved to Northampton, Massachusetts, to become a founding member of the Northampton Association of Education and Industry, which functioned until 1846. During the following four years he was engaged in various textile enterprises. His last years were spent in Lawrence, Kansas. The "girls" were George W. Benson's spinster sisters, Mary (1797–1842), Sarah Thurber (1799–1850), and Anna Elizabeth (1801–1843). (*Life.*)

3. Matthew 6:13.

4. II Corinthians 5:17.

5. The Russian Lotion for Chilblains was a famous patent medicine which had been introduced in 1806 as "The Russian Salve Vegetable Ointment." It was alleged to cure, in addition to chilblains, sore eyes, piles, burns, frostbite, etc. (See an advertisement in *The Liberator*, April 11, 1851.)

6. Garrison quotes a maxim common in the nineteenth century; it was among those to be collected by T. C. Haliburton in 1843.

7. Helen Eliza Benson Garrison (1811–1876) married William Lloyd Garrison in 1834. A native of Providence, she had moved to Brooklyn, Connecticut, with her family. Although diffident by disposition and domestic by inclination, she was dedicated to her husband's cause. Helen's mother was Sarah Thurber Benson (1770–1844), a modest, self-denying, shy woman. She spent the winter of 1840–1841 with the Garrisons in Boston. (*AWT*.)

2

TO SAMUEL J. MAY

Boston, Jan. 5, 1841.

My dear Brother:

It is not too late to wish you a happy new year — the happiest you have ever yet known. O, that the whole earth were filled with happiness! O, that poor, diseased, miserable, depraved man, as a race, was redeemed from all iniquity, that henceforth he might lead a blissful existence! What can make us happy but the love of God shed abroad in our souls — that love which "worketh no ill to his neighbor, and is the fulfilling of the law"? [1] The soul that delights in God is happy, come what may — even in the midst of adversity, suffering, persecution, martyrdom. It is in this sense that we are conquerors, and more than conquerors, through Him who hath loved us, and given himself for us. [2]

On New Year's Day, how many unmeaning wishes are expressed by community for the happiness of each other! If those wishes were really sincere — if they were based upon disinterested benevolence — the whole state of human society would be almost immediately regenerated — all crime, all poverty, all misery, would disappear. It is, too, often, a mere form of words — a form which, while it seems to partake of kindness, is rather an exhibition of human selfishness. — But I did not take up my pen to moralise.

Our annual meeting, you know, is swiftly approaching. [3] We shall, of course, make application for the Hall of the House of Representatives [4] for one evening, on that occasion, and there is no reason to doubt that it will be granted to us, as usual. Loring and Quincy have signified their willingness to speak on the occasion; and I want you to be ready to do so also. [5] The several speeches ought not to occupy more than half an hour each, so that we may have as many speakers as practicable. You can prepare a resolution on any topic you choose, and speak to it. As the meeting is to be in the State House, before Senators and Representatives, it might be well to hold up the encroachments of slavery upon the rights, liberties and interests of the people of the north, and to show the necessity of a speedy and an absolute dissolution of co-partnership between Liberty and Slavery, as now existing in this country. But suit yourself as to this matter — only consent to be one of the speakers.

I give you this early invitation, in order that you may have some little time to prepare yourself, if any be needed. We shall have, I trust, a good anniversary. Let old Plymouth send a good strong delegation, with father Sprague at the head.[6] How far Mr. Bishop intends to give us trouble, I do not know; but he is very obstinate and wayward — and, having publicly committed himself, will no doubt do what he can to make trouble.[7] We shall try to be prepared for every emergency. Don't fail to be on hand.

Helen and the children are in good health, and also mother.[8] We desire to be cordially remembered to Mrs. May, and regret that we have not yet had the promised visit from her. Will she not come up to the annual meeting?

Yours, affectionately,

Wm. Lloyd Garrison.

ALS: Garrison Papers, Boston Public Library.

Samuel J. May (1797–1871) was a Unitarian minister and radical abolitionist (one of the founders of the New England Anti-Slavery Society in 1832). Formerly the minister in Brooklyn, Connecticut, where he married Garrison and Helen Benson in 1834, he was currently the minister in South Scituate, Massachusetts. His wife was Lucretia Flagge Coffin (c. 1802–1865). Shortly before his death he published *Some Recollections of Our Antislavery Conflict* (Boston, 1869), which is of special value for its biographical sketches of prominent reformers.

1. Garrison adapts Romans 13:10.

2. Garrison adapts Romans 8:37.

3. The annual meeting of the Massachusetts Anti-Slavery Society was to be held on January 27.

4. Of Massachusetts.

5. Ellis Gray Loring (1803–1858) was a distinguished Boston lawyer and philanthropist who had been an original member of the New England Anti-Slavery Society. Although his antislavery views were more conservative than Garrison's, he continued to be a major financial contributor to the cause and to *The Liberator*.

Edmund Quincy (1808–1877), son of Josiah Quincy, was an author and editor as well as abolitionist, who joined the cause in 1837. A consistent supporter of Garrison, he edited *The Liberator* during the editor's absence in 1843, 1846, and 1847 and was to be the editor of the *National Anti-Slavery Standard* in 1844.

6. Seth Sprague (1760–1846), father of Peleg Sprague, was a prominent Methodist layman and merchant of Duxbury, Massachusetts, who had for many years been a member of the state legislature. (*Life*.)

7. Joel Prentiss Bishop (1814 1001), formerly a clerk for the Massachusetts

Anti-Slavery Society, had called for a public explanation of certain adjustments in the treasurer's accounts. At the annual meeting, May presented a report assuring the society that the financial records were in proper order; Bishop filed a minority report (see *The Liberator*, December 25, 1840, January 1, and February 5, 1841). Bishop joined the abolitionists who opposed the Garrisonians but was active chiefly as a lawyer. (*Life.*)

8. By this time there were three Garrison children, George Thompson (1836–1904), William Lloyd, Jr. (1838–1909), and Wendell Phillips (1840–1907). George, the least successful of the Garrison children, was to move frequently from job to job. He came into some prominence during the Civil War as a lieutenant in a Negro unit, the 55th Massachusetts Regiment. William, as a wool broker, was to become the conservative businessman among the children. Wendell Phillips, the most intellectual of the children, was to become a distinguished editor. (*AWT.*)

3

TO GEORGE W. BENSON

Boston, Jan. 7, 1841.

My dear George:

So! you have sold yourself out of house and home! Then "the world is all before you where to choose" another abode, as it was to Adam when he was expelled from Paradise.[1] Now, your name is not Adam, but Benson — and Brooklyn is not Paradise, though it is certainly a very pleasant country town. You may shed "some natural tears," as our first parent did, (so Milton says,) at the thought of parting — but, never mind it — a thousand years hence, it will be a very trifling matter to us and to the world.[2] I hope the seller and buyer of your estate have both traded to good advantage, and are both equally satisfied with the transfer. — Where do you intend to locate yourself? I say, you must come somewhere in this vicinity. Do you hear? What say you to a little social community among ourselves? Bro. Chace is ready for it; and I think we must be pretty bad folks if we cannot live together amicably within gunshot of each other.[3] My Garrisonian battery shall not harm any of you, unless you new organize, go for a third party, or apologize for slavery.[4] In that case, look out!

I had written the accompanying letters to you and James, to send them by mail; but as I found they would reach you only one day earlier than by the bundle, I concluded to defer their transmission. You write that bro. James has got rid of his fit of the blues, and is now in good spirits. This is cheering intelligence. Doubtless, his bodily debility affects his mind, and at times makes life really burdensome. I wish he could be persuaded to take one or two Thompsonian courses; but, in case he should, he ought to be very careful not to take any cold afterward; otherwise, they would do him more harm than good.[5] If he can make up his mind to remain with you until you break up, I shall be glad: after that time, he may return to me, and some other plan must be devised for him. It does not seem probable that he will again be able to go to sea as an able-bodied sailor; and it is certain that he cannot reside in or near Boston, without being in the way of temptation, which he will not be able to resist. If he could only be effectually cured of the love of strong drink, all would go well with him, and he might be safely trusted any where. Strange that when he has suffered so much from that accursed poison, he will still use it as often as opportunity presents itself. "O that men should put an enemy into their mouths to steal away their brains," and degrade their manners and morals! [6] But James is now to be pitied, rather than blamed. He has been in a bad school, on board of a man-of-war, to learn sobriety, virtue, righteousness; and our surprise should be, that he is no worse than he is. He has many excellent and noble traits; and if he could summon manhood enough to overcome the sin that so easily besets him, he might yet be a blessing and an ornament to society.

In my other letter, I have urged you to be present at the annual meeting of our State Society toward the last of this month; and now that you have sold a portion of the estate, I hope you will not fail to come. Bro. Chace wants to see you very much; and you will have a good opportunity to see and consult with bro. [Samuel J.] May and other friends as to your future course. Do not fail, therefore, to come.

By the Liberator of this week, you will see that Gerrit Smith still feels a friendly interest in the welfare and continuance of the Liberator, sends ten dollars in aid of it, and says that the abolitionists of the country will never allow the pioneer paper to go down.[7] His letter will be a bitter pill to new organization and third par[t]yism, and arrives at a most seasonable period; for our subscription list is daily becoming smaller. We have lost, since last January, nearly 500 subscribers, over and above all additions; besides cutting off two or three hundred delinquent subscribers. Several of those who have hitherto stood firmly by the paper, have ordered their subscriptions to be stopped. The Sabbath Convention has been more than they could tolerate; and to save the formal observance of the first day of the week, they are willing that slavery should be perpetuated.[8] How we shall get along, I do not see; but "the Lord will provide."

Please settle with Theodore [9] for the butter, and I will pay you whatever balance may be due.

Your brother,

Wm. Lloyd Garrison.

ALS: Garrison Papers, Boston Public Library; printed partly in *Life*, III, 25.

1. John Milton, *Paradise Lost*, XII, line 646.
2. John Milton, *Paradise Lost*, XII, line 645.
3. William M. Chace or Chase (1814–1862), a bachelor, had been a Providence wool merchant and onetime partner of George W. Benson before joining a utopian farm community. Although he had been an active abolitionist for many years, having served as an agent of *The Liberator*, he became in the 1840's so dedicated to "no-government" principles that he opposed organization even within the antislavery movement. He was later to become an active member of the Republican party. (See his obituary, *The Liberator*, September 5, 1862.)
4. After 1839 the phrase "new organization" referred to the conservative faction within the antislavery movement which opposed the radical attitude of the Garrisonians toward many issues, including the church and clergy, woman's rights, the Constitution, and disunion. Unlike the Garrisonian old organization, the new organization was committed to abolition through political action and was, therefore, closely allied with the antislavery, third-party movement.
5. Garrison distrusted orthodox medical practitioners and had confidence in Dr. Samuel Thomson (1769–1845), whose name he frequently misspells. Thomsonian treatments, or "courses," were calculated to raise body temperature by the prescription of various herbs, vapor baths, and the like, on the theory that all disease was caused by cold.
6. Garrison adapts Shakespeare, *Othello*, II, iii, 292.
7. Gerrit Smith (1797–1874) was a wealthy man with extensive real estate holdings in New York state. He was one of the most generous philanthropists of his day, having contributed to numerous organizations and reforms, including abolition. The letter from Smith to which Garrison refers was printed in *The Liberator*, January 8, 1841. Garrison was especially pleased by Smith's assertion that if abolition failed, the blame would fall on religious sects which opposed it.
8. The convention to which Garrison refers was held in Boston, November 17–20, 1840, at the Chardon-Street Chapel (see *Life*, II, 421–438). It was attended by a great variety of people, including Emerson, who wrote the fullest account of it in his essay, "The Chardon-Street Convention." He said: "If the assembly was disorderly, it was picturesque. Madmen, madwomen, men with beards, Dunkers, Muggletonians, Come-outers, Groaners, Agrarians, Seventh-day-Baptists, Quakers, Abolitionists, Calvinists, Unitarians and Philosophers, — all came successively to the top, and seized their moment, if not their hour, wherein to chide, or pray, or preach, or protest." (*Lectures and Biographical Sketches, The Works of Ralph Waldo Emerson*, Boston, 1883, X, 374.)
9. Probably Theodore Scarborough (1814–1850) of Brooklyn, Connecticut, who married Caroline Simmons, became a member of the Northampton Association in April 1842, and was in charge of the agricultural department there. (Sheffeld, p. 104; Brooklyn town records.)

4

TO EDMUND QUINCY

Boston, Jan. 12, 1841.

My dear Quincy:

The Board meeting appointed to hear the annual report takes place to-morrow, but it must be deferred until Friday or Saturday, as I have not been able to get the report ready; so you need not come to the city until further intelligence on the subject be sent to you. In the mean time, you may scold, denounce, threaten, excommunicate me, and give me over to be buffetted; and I will promise to remain through it all, "calm as a summer's morning." [1] The fact is, the Board ought to have given me earlier notice, that they wished the report to be printed in season for the annual meeting. Whether it can now be done, I am not sure, even if I can complete the report this week. There arises a query in my mind, whether it is competent for the Board to print a report, independently of the action of the Society. This was proposed at the last annual meeting, but the proposition did not obtain.

I shall endeavor to hold myself in readiness to attend your county meeting next week; and if I can bring any body with me, it shall be done.[2] — You say that you shall rely upon my giving a lecture in the evening. I would much prefer that others should take part on the occasion; and I hope that you, at least, will hold yourself in readiness to do so. If, however, nobody else will talk, I will.

Friend Knapp tells an alarming tale about what is to be done at the annual meeting! [3] Andover, Methuen, Reading, (and perhaps some other towns,) are coming down in strong delegations to oust the present Board of Managers, put Baron Stow in the place of Francis Jackson, and establish an organ of the Society, in rivalry of the Liberator! [4] Friend K. says that the specimen number of the paper will be circulated at the annual meeting. How much of pretence and bluster there is in all this, and how much of reality, I do not know; but we ought to be prepared for every emergency. Our ranks are not yet purified, and we have yet to pass through many a severe trial. Whether we shall have as many as Gideon's army [5] left in the old organization, time must determine. What say you? Is your reliance upon God or man? Are you sorry that you have become such a fanatic? Or do you say with triumphant assurance, "I know in whom and in what I have believed"? [6]

Have you seen the atrocious attack upon bro. Collins, by Torrey, in the last Abolitionist? [7] Ought not our Board to take some action upon it, in justice to Collins?

Remember, you are to be one of the speakers at the State House. Be faithful and fearless.

My best regards to your excellent lady. Believe me,

Your loving friend,

Wm. Lloyd Garrison.

ALS: Garrison Papers, Sophia Smith Collection, Smith College Library.

1. Not identified.
2. The meeting of the Norfolk County Anti-Slavery Society was held at Dedham on the 20th and reported, over the signature of Edmund Quincy as

president, in *The Liberator* of the 29th. At that meeting Garrison was appointed to the business committee, which drew up a series of resolutions. In the evening he spoke for nearly two hours.

3. Isaac Knapp (1804–1843) was the old friend and partner of Garrison. When in 1835 the management of *The Liberator* became too much for him, the partnership was dissolved, although Knapp remained as printer. In 1839 he sold out his remaining interest in *The Liberator* to Garrison and friends. Despite their later differences, Garrison continued to profess concern about Knapp's well-being; see his letters to George W. Benson, December 17, 1841, and to Elizabeth Pease, May 15, 1842. (*Life.*)

4. Baron Stow (1801–1869) was a Baptist minister and former Garrisonian who had separated from Garrison's society over the issue of woman's rights. (*Life.*) The attempt to unseat Francis Jackson as president of the Massachusetts Anti-Slavery Society was unsuccessful. Apparently no new rival paper was circulated at the meeting.

Francis Jackson (1789–1861) was a wealthy Boston merchant who took an active part in municipal affairs. A vigorous abolitionist and reformer, he served many years as president of the Massachusetts Anti-Slavery Society and vice-president of the American Anti-Slavery Society. He supported Garrison's views on many issues, including woman's rights, and was one of his closest friends. On several occasions his support was not only moral but financial. Garrison's last child (born October 29, 1848) was to be named for him. (*Life.*)

5. An allusion to Judges 7:1–25.

6. Garrison adapts II Timothy 1:12.

7. Charles T. Torrey (1813–1846) was a Yale graduate and Congregational clergyman who left the ministry to devote himself full time to the antislavery cause. In 1839, disagreeing with Garrison's radical views, he became one of the founding members of the new organization, the Massachusetts Abolition Society. At the time of Garrison's letter he was temporarily editing that society's official publication, the *Massachusetts Abolitionist*. It was in this paper that he attacked John A. Collins (c. 1810–1879), the general agent of the Massachusetts Anti-Slavery Society, who was on an unsuccessful fund-raising mission to England. (*Life.*)

5

TO JOHN H. TREDGOLD

Boston, Jan. 29, 1841.

J. H. Tredgold:

In accordance with instructions given to me by the Board of Managers of the Massachusetts Anti-Slavery Society, I transmit to your Society the following preamble and resolution.

Yours, respectfully,

Wm. Lloyd Garrison.

———
———

At a meeting of the Board of Managers of the Massachusetts Anti-Slavery Society, held at the Society's Room, 25, Cornhill, on Monday, the 25th January, 1841, the following preamble and resolution were unanimously adopted:

Whereas this Board has recently seen in the official organ of the "Massachusetts *Abolition* Society,["] certain charges or insinuations intended to implicate the integrity of our respected brother John A. Collins; and whereas this Board has, through two of its members, investigated and ascertained the groundless character of the charges or insinuations aforesaid; and whereas similar charges have been made against him in other quarters for the same purpose, and obviously meant to destroy his influence among our anti-slavery brethren in Great Britain, with whom he is now residing on an important and responsible mission from the American Anti-Slavery Society, therefore,

Resolved, That this Board hereby expresses its full and unimpaired trust in the integrity and faithfulness of our brother, John A. Collins, and recommend him to the respect and confidence of the friends of emancipation universally.

Ordered, That a copy of the foregoing resolution be forwarded by the Corresponding Secretary of this Society to the Secretary of the London Committee of the British and Foreign Anti-Slavery Society.[1]

Wm. Lloyd Garrison,
Cor. Sec'y of the Mass. A.S. Society.

ALS: Anti-Slavery Society Papers, Rhodes House Library, Oxford University.

The preamble and resolution were printed as a part of the official report of the meeting of the Massachusetts society over the signature of the president, Francis Jackson, in *The Liberator*, January 29, 1841, the same day that Garrison wrote to John Harfield Tredgold (c. 1798–1842), secretary of the British and Foreign Anti-Slavery Society.

1. The London Committee is the name commonly used to designate the executive committee of the British and Foreign Anti-Slavery Society, the conservative organization founded in 1839.

6

TO ELIZABETH PEASE

Boston, Feb. 1, 1841.

My dear friend:

I am grieved, distressed, to think that I have only five minutes left to send you a hasty scrawl; for I owe you a whole quire of letters, and you shall yet have them, rely upon it. — I send you, however, something equivalent to many letters — to wit, a box, containing 200 copies of our Annual Report,[1] and some other things — all which you will distribute in the most judicious manner possible, from the London Committee down to, or rather *up* to any others who may have their minds filled with prejudice against our old anti-slavery organization. You will see that our Report grapples with all the charges against us, and that they are met by us in the most triumphant manner. As for Colver's attack upon bro. Collins and myself, it is most atrocious; but it will be seen in all its enormity in due time.[2]

I find that the duties cannot be paid on this side of the Atlantic on the pamphlets, &c. contained in the box; but our Society will pay all the expenses, as soon as you will let us know what they are. The box is directed to the care of Wm. Rathbone, Esq. Liverpool.[3] Pray get it as soon as you can. If bro. Collins has not left, give my love to him. I am very sorry I have not time to send him a line. — My best regards to your father, mother, dear Thompson, &c.[4] O, for three hours time!

Your admiring friend,

Wm. Lloyd Garrison.

E. Pease.

ALS: Villard Papers, Harvard College Library.

Elizabeth Pease (1807–1897), the daughter of wealthy English Quaker Joseph Pease (1772–1846), was an active and enthusiastic supporter of the antislavery cause and became Garrison's lifelong friend. In 1853 she was to marry Professor John Nichol of the Glasgow Observatory. (Joseph Foster, *Pedigrees of the County Families of Yorkshire*, London, 1874, II; *Life*.)

1. Of the Massachusetts Anti-Slavery Society.
2. Nathaniel Colver (1794–1870), a self-educated clergyman and reformer, had since 1839 been the pastor of the First Free Baptist Church in Boston (later to be called Tremont Temple). As an abolitionist Colver had followed not Garrison but the more moderate group of New York reformers. Recently, in letters to the London Committee and in a speech at a meeting of the Massachusetts Anti-Slavery Society, he had attacked both John A. Collins and Garrison. (*Life*.)
3. William Rathbone (1787–1868), son of a successful merchant family in Liverpool, was active in various areas of reform and philanthropy. He had also been the mayor of Liverpool in 1837.
4. George Thompson (1804–1878) was the English abolitionist and politician whom Garrison first met in 1833. Thompson had visited the United States as an antislavery lecturer in 1834–1835. During this tour his radical views delighted Garrison but enraged so many of his audiences that he was obliged for safety to return to England. He was to make subsequent trips to this country in 1850 and in 1864. Throughout the years Thompson continued to be Garrison's closest British associate and one of his best friends. (*Life*.)

7

TO PARKER PILLSBURY

BOSTON, Feb. 23, 1841.

Dear brother Pillsbury:

I had engaged, before receiving your kind letter, to be present at a meeting of the Essex County Anti-Slavery Society, which is to be holden on the very day of your meeting at Exeter.[1] If I could be in two places at once, I should certainly be with you on Thursday next, as well as with my anti-slavery friends in old Essex; but, as this is impracticable, and as I cannot properly get a release from my engagement, I can merely give you a few hasty lines, expressive of my regret that it so happens that I cannot comply with the invitation contained in your letter.

Let me say, do not despair of New-Hampshire! It is true she has sinned desperately in heart, in her hatred of a people meted out and trodden under foot, and is this moment prostrate in the dust before the Moloch of slavery. It is true her religion turns out to be devoid of humanity, and her republicanism is of a spurious quality. It is true, a very large majority of her inhabitants seem to be deaf to the cries of bleeding humanity, and to glory in their shameful opposition to the sacred cause of emancipation. Still, I renew the injunction, do not despair of New-Hampshire! She has still a conscience and a heart left, though both are awfully corrupted; and, proud and hardened as she may be, — yea, harder than her own granite rocks, — it is in the power of truth to melt and subdue her. The evil spirits that now possess her, and that now exclaim that they are tormented before their time, (though it is precisely the right time,) will doubtless rend her terribly in being cast out, but *they have not power to take her life*, and she shall yet be saved even as by fire. I am not sure that New-Hampshire is not destined to be foremost in the anti-slavery struggle, religiously and politically; and to be as conspicuous for her consecration to the cause of human liberty as she is now for her devotion to the cause of slavery.

You are in the midst of as glorious a conflict as the earth has witnessed — the contest of the few against the many, the weak against the strong, liberty against oppression, humanity against cruelty. O, do not falter — do not yield one inch — do not grow weary — and be assured of victory! Your cause is a sacred one — your principles are invincible — your measures rational and just. Let the enemies of freedom rave and howl as they may, and appear in what guise they may; let them brand you as infidels, disorganizers, and the offscouring of all things; let them say all manner of evil things against you falsely; what matters it?[2] *what matters it?* Glory in those proofs of your fidelity to God and humanity, and be strengthened by them mightily to the end of the conflict.

Give all the sympathies of my heart to dear Rogers, and to brothers Foster and Wright, and to all others who abhor slavery, and believe me to be, under all circumstances,[3]

Yours, in opposition to all evil,

WM. LLOYD GARRISON.

Printed: *Herald of Freedom*, March 5, 1841.

Parker Pillsbury (1809–1898), although born in Massachusetts, spent much of his life in New Hampshire. Trained as a Congregational minister, he had left the pulpit in 1840 to become a full-time reformer. Currently the general agent of the New Hampshire Anti-Slavery Society, he was later to hold a similar post with both the Massachusetts and the American societies. He succeeded Nathaniel P. Rogers as editor of the *Herald of Freedom*, a position he held between 1845 and 1846. (*Life.*)

1. Both the Essex County (Massachusetts) society and the New Hampshire Anti-Slavery Society were founded in 1834. According to *The Liberator*, February 19, 1841, the Essex County meeting was scheduled for Thursday, February 25, and the New Hampshire meeting for Wednesday, the 24th.

2. Garrison alludes to Matthew 5:11.

3. Nathaniel Peabody Rogers (1794–1846) was a practicing lawyer until 1838. At that time he established in Concord, New Hampshire, an antislavery paper, the *Herald of Freedom*, which he edited until 1845, when through a controversy with the state antislavery society he lost control. For many years Rogers was a close associate of Garrison's, though they became alienated during the dispute concerning the *Herald of Freedom*. (*Life.*)

Stephen Symonds Foster (1809–1881), a graduate of Dartmouth who abandoned a clerical career in favor of full-time reform, became an antislavery lecturer in 1840. Like Garrison, with whom he was closely associated, he was an active nonresistant. He was to marry abolitionist Abby Kelley in 1845. (*Life.*)

Henry Clarke Wright (1797–1870), originally a hat maker, became a minister in 1823 and a professional reformer in 1835. He remained during the years one of Garrison's closest associates in the cause of abolition and of nonresistance. From 1842 to 1847 he toured England on a mission sponsored by the New England Non-Resistance Society. The author of many moralistic and antislavery works for children, he was also one of the most frequent contributors to *The Liberator*. (*Life; AWT.*)

8

TO ELIZABETH PEASE

Boston, March 1, 1841.

Dear Friend:

As usual, I find myself driven into a corner at the very time, to use a nautical phrase, when I want the most "sea-room." Our mutual friend Joseph Adshead leaves immediately in the steamer for Liverpool, and I must communicate all I have to say in the course of five or ten minutes.[1] I have had no opportunity to converse with him since his unexpected arrival in this country, as he has been on the move continually; and I am yet ignorant whether he came in reference to the British India movement, or for some other object.[2]

I am very much obliged to you for your letter by the Britannia,[3] and do not regret, on the whole, that bro. [John A.] Collins has concluded to remain until the sailing of the steamer of the 4th inst.; though I trust he will not miss coming at that time, for his presence here now is indispensable. In whatever he has been called to encounter, on your side of the Atlantic, by the evil spirit that reigns there, as well as here, in the anti-slavery ranks, I deeply sympathize with him. The attempt of Nathaniel Colver to injure his character is exciting among all the true-hearted friends of our cause among us an intense feeling of indignation and abhorrence; and in the sequel it will be sure to recoil upon the head of that unhappy man. Equally abortive will be the effort of N. C. to affect my religious character by his absurd and monstrous statement to Joseph Sturge, that I have headed an infidel convention.[4] Even supposing the charge were true, I should like to know by what authority British *abolitionists*, as such, undertake to judge me, for this cause, *on the anti-slavery platform.* I need not say to you, that the charge is both groundless and malicious; that my religious views are of the most elevated, the most spiritual character; that I esteem the holy scriptures above all other books in the universe, and always appeal to "the law and the testimony"[5] to prove all my peculiar doctrines; that, in regard to my religious sentiments, they are almost identical with those of Barclay, Penn, and Fox;[6] that, respecting the Sabbath, the church, and the ministry, Joseph Sturge and I (if he be a genuine Friend) harmonize in opinion; that I believe in an indwelling Christ, and in his righteousness alone; that I glory in nothing here below, save in Christ and him crucified; that I believe all the works of the devil are to be destroyed, and our Lord is to reign from sea to sea, even to the ends of the earth;[7] and that I profess to have passed from death unto life,[8] and know by happy experience that there is no condemnation to them who are in Christ Jesus, who walk not after the flesh, but after the spirit.[9] The truth is, N. Colver has a mortal antipathy to all the distinctive views of Friends, and he regards them all as infidel: yet he writes to Joseph Sturge as though he fully agreed with him as to the nature of the Sabbath, and as though I held to purely infidel views on this subject!! Why does not Joseph Sturge, as an honest man and a sincere friend to the anti-slavery cause, (I will not refer to his former professions of personal friendship for me,) inform me by letter of what he has received from N. Colver and others, touching my religious character? Why does he not express a wish to hear what I can say in self-defence? I confess, I am grieved and astonished at his conduct, and am forced to regard him much less highly than I once did. By the next packet, I hope to be able to address a letter to him on this subject.

I am sorry, very sorry, (and very much surprised, too,) that bro. Collins should have applied to the London Committee for aid or approbation. It was an error of judgment, simply; but, after what we, who sent him out, have said of [that] Committee, it looks upon the face of it like an [impo]sition.[10] We supposed he would make his appeal to the abolitionists at large, and take his chance accordingly. I fear, also, that he may not have been so guarded at all times in his language as could have been desirable, respecting the transfer of the Emancipator — a transfer that was certainly very dishonorable, and wholly unworthy of the character of those who participated in it.[11] Yet I doubt not that the mission of J. A. C[ollins]. will do much for our persecuted enterprise.

For what you have done to aid him, we all feel under the deepest obligations. May Heaven reward you a hundred fold! Fear not that truth shall not triumph over falsehood, right over wrong, and freedom over *slavery*.

The box, containing the Annual Reports, &c., failed to be got ready for the steamer, and so it was forwarded in a packet-ship from New-York. Please let our friends in Scotland and Ireland have copies of the Report — also O'Connell, Bowring, Ashurst, Howitt, Buxton, Clarkson, Thompson, &c. &c.[12] See that all the members of the London Committee are supplied. The duties upon the box must have been heavy; and if J. A. C. did not pay them, let me know what they came to, and our Society will forward you the money. We do not expect or desire you to be at any charge for the same.

I send you a few extra Liberators for distribution, containing the action of our State Society upon N. Colver's charges, and also sundry speeches by Bradburn, Colver, and others.[13] The sheet can be cut in two. Send it where it may be most needed — one to Sturge in particular.

We hear pleasing intelligence from Mr. and Mrs. Chapman at Hayti.[14] His health is better, and they are both in fine spirits. Wendell Phillips and wife are now probably at Leghorn.[15] The fate of the Amistad captives will soon be determined. J. Q. Adams is now pleading their case in the most powerful manner.[16] It is impossible to predict the result. — My best regards to your father and mother. — There is no one in the world that I have a stronger desire to see again than yourself.

Yours, gratefully,

Wm. Lloyd Garrison.

ALS: Garrison Papers, Boston Public Library; printed partly in *Life*, III, 2–4.

1. Joseph Adshead (1800–1861) was a reformer from Manchester, England. A prolific pamphleteer, especially during the last ten years of his life, he became nationally known for his interest in the ragged school movement and for his work on prison reform. (Letter to the editor from C. Duncan Rice, Yale University, December 23, 1968.)

2. Garrison refers to the efforts of various British reformers to improve the conditions of subjects in India by educating the British public about their problems.

3. A steamship on the Cunard Line, which had made its first run from Liverpool to Boston in 1840.

4. Joseph Sturge (1793–1859), a member of the Society of Friends, was active in many reforms including, in addition to abolition, universal suffrage, peace, and temperance. He had been one of the founders of the British and Foreign Anti-Slavery Society and was the leading force on the so-called London Committee. Garrison could never convince him and the committee that the New York abolitionists and their new organization were unworthy of support. (*Life.*) The "infidel convention" was the Chardon-Street anti-Sabbath convention held in Boston, November 17–20, 1840.

5. Isaiah 8:20.

6. Robert Barclay (1648–1690), William Penn (1644–1718), and George Fox (1624–1691), early Quaker leaders who had suffered for their cause.

7. Zechariah 9:10.

8. I John 3:14.

9. Romans 8:1.

10. Garrison and the London Committee had clashed regarding the seating of women delegates from the United States at the World's Anti-Slavery Convention held in London in 1840.

11. The *Emancipator* had been the official organ of the American Anti-Slavery Society since its founding in 1833. In April of 1840, however, the executive committee of the American Anti-Slavery Society, then dominated by the New York abolitionists who were hostile to Garrison, had sold the paper, ostensibly because the paper's debts were becoming unmanageable. In the controversy which ensued, the Garrison group claimed that the committee had no authority to sell this essential property of the national society. The *Emancipator* continued to be published as the organ of the New York Anti-Slavery Society, while the *National Anti-Slavery Standard* subsequently became the publication of the American Anti-Slavery Society. (*Life.*)

12. Garrison lists a group of distinguished British reformers: Daniel O'Connell (1775–1847) was a lawyer, abolitionist, and advocate of repeal of the Irish union with England. John Bowring (1792–1872) was an English linguist, political economist, and member of Parliament as well as an advocate of many reforms. William H. Ashurst (1792–1855) was an enthusiastic believer in American democratic principles, who contributed frequently to *The Liberator* under the pseudonym "Edward Search." William Howitt (1795–1879) was a poet and prolific author on such diverse subjects as literature, nature, and spiritualism. Sir Thomas Fowell Buxton (1786–1845) vigorously advocated abolition during his career in Parliament. Thomas Clarkson (1760–1846), most scholarly of the group, spent his energies seeking information about the British slave trade and slavery in the West Indies and urging abolition. Author of many tracts and books, he supplied to parliamentary reformers the facts, the statistics, and often the argument essential to effect abolition.

13. George Bradburn (1806–1880) was a resident of Nantucket and, for several years prior to 1841, a Whig member of the Massachusetts House of Representatives. In 1844 he was to join the Liberty party and in 1848 to become editor of the Lynn *Pioneer*. (*Life.*)

14. Henry G. Chapman (1804–1842) was a prosperous Boston merchant and financial supporter of the antislavery movement, whose persistent ill health induced him to make trips to Haiti in search of a cure. (*Life.*) Maria Weston Chapman (1806–1885) was one of the most active members of the Boston Female Anti-Slavery Society; in 1840 she served as a delegate to the World's Anti-Slavery Convention. She was the author and the editor of numerous antislavery publications.

15. Wendell Phillips (1811–1884), of aristocratic Boston background and Harvard education, was, before the Civil War, a great champion of most of

Garrison's doctrines. His dynamic ability as a lecturer made him a major figure in the circle of Massachusetts reformers. In 1837 he married the wealthy Ann Terry Greene (1813–1886), who was an invalid much of their married life. (*Life.*)

16. Garrison refers to the internationally famous *Amistad* case. A group of about fifty African slaves had mutinied against their Cuban captors on the Spanish ship *Amistad* in June 1839, killing the captain and the cook. The *Amistad* was found drifting off Long Island by an American ship and was brought to New London, Connecticut, where the slaves were tried for mutiny and piracy. Judge Andrew T. Judson, who years earlier had been one of the prosecutors in the Prudence Crandall case, ordered the slaves remanded to the Spanish government. With John Quincy Adams as one of the defense attorneys, the decision was appealed to the Supreme Court in 1841. In a landmark decision in the antislavery movement, the *Amistad* captives were freed. (Louis Filler, *The Crusade Against Slavery,* New York, 1960, pp. 167 ff.)

9

TO JOHN A. COLLINS

Boston, April 1, 1841.

Dear Friend:

We had confidently anticipated your arrival in the Caledonia,[1] in consequence of the assurance held out in one of your letters, that you would leave for home in the steamer of the 4th ultimo; and our disappointment was very great in not seeing you. Doubtless, you have acted in the best possible manner for the GOOD CAUSE, according to your views of duty; and we trust that your mission will be crowned by Heaven with complete success.[2] But, though it may seem to you, and to our beloved co-workers on the other side of the Atlantic, that you can do more good by remaining yet longer abroad, than by returning home, yet we are extremely anxious that you should return with the least possible delay, and resume your General Agency in behalf of our Society. We have been compelled to suspend all our agency operations during your absence, and we rely upon you to put the machinery in motion again. The friends of the Massachusetts Anti-Slavery Society begin to complain somewhat loudly, because our Board has no agents in the field; and, consequently, they are not disposed to contribute so liberally to the funds of the Society as they would, if they could see us sending forth lectures to stir up the people. There is no other person, at present, to whom we can look, except yourself. We believe that, however much you may achieve for our cause in England, you can do more for it by being at your old post. In this opinion, all our friends agree: and it is our unanimous wish, therefore, to see and greet you, face to face, on the soil of the Puritans.

At a special meeting of the Board of Managers of the State Society, held on the 29th ultimo, the following preamble and resolution were adopted:

"Whereas, the interests of our Society require the early resumption, by our brother John A. Collins, of his agency in Massachusetts — therefore,

Resolved, That Mr. Collins be requested to return from his present mission in England, at the earliest possible moment consistent with his sense of duty; and that Messrs. Garrison and [Ellis Gray] Loring be a committee to write him on this subject."

It is in accordance with the above instructions, that we address this letter to you — deeming it unnecessary to urge your return by any additional importunity of our own. You have our deepest sympathies, in consequence of the ruthless assaults that have been made upon your character and mission by those who have seceded from the anti-slavery ranks, as originally organized, but we calmly wait for a triumphant acquittal in the progress of events. We would invoke the choicest blessings of the Almighty upon all those who have given you the right hand of fellowship abroad. We are confident that they will never have cause to regret their espousal of the interests of the American Anti-Slavery Society.

We remain, fraternally yours,

Wm. Lloyd Garrison,
Ellis Gray Loring.

ALS: Garrison Papers, Boston Public Library. Although this letter bears two signatures, it is written in Garrison's hand.

1. Launched in 1840 for the Cunard Line as a sister ship to the famous *Britannia.* (David B. Tyler, *Steam Conquers the Atlantic,* New York, 1939.)

2. Collins' mission was so unsuccessful that he was obliged to borrow the money for his return passage on a later voyage of the *Caledonia,* which reached Boston on July 17. Garrison and others were annoyed by the long delay in his return (see *Life,* III, 17, and *The Liberator,* July 23, 1841).

10

TO ELIZABETH PEASE

Boston, June 1, 1841.

Beloved Friend:

Your last epistle was refreshing to my spirit. I am happy to know that, notwithstanding all the wicked devices of the relentless spirit of sectarianism to blast my character in England, you are still my friend, faithful and true, and cannot be made to believe a lie. While the machinations of my enemies give me no uneasiness, and have never deprived me of one hour's sleep — and while I esteem it a very small thing to be judged of man's judgment [1] — it would argue on my part great insensibility of mind, if I did not feel truly and deeply grateful for all that you have done in my behalf, and to promote the welfare of our primitive anti-slavery organization. — Elizabeth, you have won for yourself the esteem and admiration of all those whose good opinion you could desire, at this crisis, on this side of the Atlantic. We know, from experience, what you have been called to suffer in espousing an unpopular cause; how friends have been converted into enemies; how your good has been evil spoken of; and how large an amount of moral courage you have needed, as well as faith in God, to sustain you in all your trials. Be of good cheer! If we suffer with Christ, shall we not also reign with him? [2] Let us rejoice that we are counted worthy to suffer for his sake.

It is a most extraordinary thing, that I am put on trial for my religious opinions among the abolitionists of England! Pray, what have they to do with those opinions, *as abolitionists?* Who are they, but persons belonging to every religious sect, every political party, every shade of religious belief? Standing with them on the anti-slavery platform, what right have I to rebuke, censure or denounce them for a difference of views on other subjects? Or what is their justification for making an attack upon me, in this behalf? I am willing to give them the right hand of fellowship, in an anti-slavery capacity. Why cannot they exhibit as catholic a spirit toward myself?

It is equally extraordinary, that my bitterest opponents in England are found in the Society of Friends — seeing that I am persecuted here for the crime of cherishing their peculiar sentiments, substantially, in regard to the sabbath, the church, and the ministry — and seeing, too, that those who have raised a hue-and-cry against me are "hireling priests"! [3] The head and front of my offending [4] consists in my being a Quaker indeed! How shall it be accounted for, that such men as Joseph Sturge and Josiah Forster are disposed to believe all that may emanate from the lips of those sturdy upholders of priestcraft, Nathaniel Colver and Amos A. Phelps? [5] I am an "infidel," forsooth, because I do *not* believe in the inherent holiness of the first day of the week; in a regular priesthood; in a mere flesh-and-blood corporation as constituting the true church of Christ; in temple worship as a part of the new dispensation; in being baptized with water, and observing the "ordinance" of the supper — &c. &c. &c. I am an "infidel," because I *do* believe in consecrating all time, and body and soul, unto God; in "a royal priesthood, a chosen generation"; in a spiritual church, built up of lively stones,[6] the head of which is Christ; in worshipping God in spirit and in truth, without regard to time or place; in being baptized with the Holy Spirit, and enjoying spiritual communion with the Father — &c. &c. If this be infidelity, then is Quakerism infidelity.

With regard to the "Church, Sabbath and Ministry" Convention, it should be understood that it was called not to determine what is or is not inspiration, or whether the bible is or is not the only rule of faith and practice, but simply to hear the opinions of "all sorts of folks," in relation to the Church, the Sabbath, and Ministry — leaving every one free to appeal to that standard, which, in his judgment, might seem to be infallible.[7] Hence, the Convention could not have properly entertained or decided upon any "extraneous" question. — It was a trick of priestcraft, to induce the Convention to cut off free discussion, that led to the introduction of the bible test by Colver, Phelps, [Charles T.] Torrey, St. Clair, &c.[8] These disorganizers and defamers resorted to this device merely to make capital for new organization, and to bring a false accusation against the leading friends of the old organization, some of whom happened to be in the Convention. All who were present saw at once the spirit that animated this band of priestly conspirators; so that they took the cunning in their own craftiness, and carried the counsels of the froward head-long.[9]

You state that Anna Braithwaite has made certain accusations against me, founded upon remarks alleged to have been made by me at her house.[10] Far be it from me to accuse her of wilful misrepresentation; but this I deliberately affirm, that she is mistaken, and that the language which she attributes to me, or any thing equivalent to it, never came from my lips. I shall write to her on this subject.[11] As to my remark at William Ball's, which has made me "an offender for a *word*," I did not suppose that it could be misapprehended by any one, especially a Friend; but, that it has been, only shows that "blindness has happened in part unto Israel." [12] By having Christ incarnated in each one of us, I meant no more than the apostle did when he said — "If any man have not the spirit of Christ, he is none of his"; — when he said — "If Christ be *in you*, the body is dead because of sin, but the spirit is life because of righteousness"; — when he said — "I am crucified with Christ; nevertheless, I live; yet not I, but *Christ liveth in me*"; — when he said — "Until Christ *be formed in you*"; — when he said — "That Christ may *dwell in your hearts* by faith"; — when he said — "Christ *in you* the hope of glory"; — when he said — "When Christ, who is *our life*, shall appear," &c.; — when he said — "Know ye not your own selves, how that *Jesus Christ is in you*, except ye be reprobates?" — when he said — "If any man be *in Christ*, he is a new creature." [13] I meant all this, precisely this, *and no more*.

I was endeavoring to rebut the Calvinistic dogma, that we cannot be perfect in this life, and must look to an outward Saviour to make amends for our own wickedness by his personal righteousness. I was inculcating the duty of personal holiness — of putting on Christ, and so, *by a figure*, INCARNATING him in our own bodies — of exercising that faith which overcomes the world — of believing the declaration, that "he that is born of God doth not commit sin." [14] And this is "infidelity," in the estimation of Anna Braithwaite! Is it so? You will remember that we had some religious conversation together — especially on our way to Windsor; and that I was strenuous in contending for "total abstinence" from sin, and "immediate, unconditional, everlasting emancipation" from the bondage of Satan, through our Lord Jesus Christ. I believe the reception of this doctrine is essential to salvation, and that it is because it is so seldom preached and believed, that our nominal christianity is so spurious. If Christ cannot cleanse me from all sin here, he cannot do it any where. If he cannot save me in this world, then it is because the devil is mightier than he. How much sin may I commit, and be delivered from the power of sin? How much may I serve Belial, and yet be loyal to Christ? How much impiety is compatible with holiness? How can that faith which overcomes the world, be overcome by any thing that is in the world?

Have you attentively read the little religious work I left with you, by J. H. Noyes? If you have done with the file of the Perfectionist which I left in your care, I will thank you to send it to me by a private conveyance whenever perfectly convenient. [15]

We are all waiting impatiently for the arrival of our bro. [John A.] Collins, who proposes to leave Liverpool on the 4th inst. He has made no small stir in Glasgow, and I trust given a powerful impulse to the cause of universal reform on your side of the waters. I long to see him, and hear from his own lips all his adventures. He has had to pass through a severe ordeal; but I hope it will appear, in the sequel, that the smell of fire is not to be found in his garments. [16] I am delighted to hear how well my dear friend Remond behaves. [17] He is a moral hero, and will be cordially received for his fidelity to our cause whenever he returns to the United States. Convey to him my warmest regards, and assure him that though I am a very neglectful correspondent, I am nevertheless his very faithful friend. I prize his letters to me very highly, and wish him to multiply the number.

Joseph Sturge is with us, and behaving in a very mean and cowardly manner. I have seen him, but he was not at all disposed to free conversation. He is acting wholly with the new organizers, and yet in a namby-pamby manner. He is not adapted to the present state of our country. What he is attempting to do, I cannot distinctly learn;

but I suppose his visit has some reference to the getting up of another pseudo "World's Convention."

The late meetings of the American A. S. Society surpassed all, in point of zeal and interest, I have ever attended in New-York.[18] The New-England Convention has just closed, and it has been a grand one.[19] Mrs. Child is now at the head of the Standard, and every thing looks well.[20]

Your admiring friend,

Wm. Lloyd Garrison.

☞ Prepare for a genuine World's Convention in Boston in 1843!! [21] — After meeting held in Chardon street Chapel last week, W. L. Garrison chairman, and N. P. Rogers secretary, it was unanimously voted, that a Committee be appointed to call a World's Convention to consider the subject of Human Rights in all its bearings, &c. &c. The following are the Committee: — W. L. Garrison, Lydia Maria Child, Nathaniel P. Rogers, Maria W. Chapman, Robert Purvis, Lucretia Mott, Wendell Phillips, Abby Kelley, Henry C. Wright, Samuel J. May, William Bassett, Edmund Quincy, Charles C. Burleigh, Francis Jackson, &c.[22] More anon. Remember me kindly to all at home. A brother's love to George Thompson and my best regards to Prof. Adam.[23]

ALS: Garrison Papers, Boston Public Library; a handwritten transcription is to be found in the Villard Papers, Harvard College Library; also printed partly in *Life*, III, 10.

1. I Corinthians 4:3.

2. Garrison alludes to II Timothy 2:12.

3. "Hireling priests" seems not to be a specific quotation, but rather a cant phrase used in anticlerical arguments.

4. Shakespeare, *Othello*, I, iii, 80.

5. Josiah Forster (1782–1870), an orthodox English Quaker teacher and author, was an early advocate of abolition. He had conducted boarding schools at Southgate and at Tottenham and was for many years a member of the Friends Educational Society. (*Annual Monitor*, 1871, pp. 26, 191.)

Amos A. Phelps (1804–1847) had been active in the antislavery movement during the 1830's and was among those who revolted against Garrison's leadership in 1839. At that time Phelps became recording secretary of the anti-Garrisonian Massachusetts Abolition Society. He spent his last years preaching in Boston churches. (*Weld-Grimké Letters*, I, 115.)

6. Two references, inverting the phrasing, to I Peter 2:9 and 2:5.

7. In this paragraph Garrison discusses the second session of the Church, Sabbath and Ministry Convention (the so-called Chardon-Street Convention). At the first session, November 17–20, 1840, the convention had debated the resolution that the Sabbath had no sanctity by divine authority; the third session, October 26–28, 1841, debated the sanctity and authority of the church as an institution. The purpose of the second session, March 30–April 1, 1841, was to debate the resolution: "That the order of the ministry, as at present existing, is anti-scriptural, and of human origin" (*The Liberator*, April 9, 1841). But before this resolution could be introduced, Alanson St. Clair, acting for the conservative,

proclerical group, introduced a different resolution to the effect that scripture represented "the paramount and the only authoritative rule of religious faith and duty." Though it had not been the intention of the convention to consider such a resolution, it was debated and finally defeated, the majority of the convention not wishing to limit the discussion of the ministry question to appeals to the authority of scripture. The defeat of St. Clair's resolution played into the hands of the conservatives. To the public it would seem that the radicals, including the Garrisonians, were "infidels," denying the authority of scripture.

8. Alanson St. Clair (1804–1877), a Congregational minister, had broken with the Massachusetts Anti-Slavery Society in the schism of 1839–1840 to join the Massachusetts Abolition Society. (*Life.*)

9. Garrison alludes to Job 5:13.

10. Anna Braithwaite (1788–1859), wife of Isaac Braithwaite of Kendal, Westmorland, England, was a prominent English Quaker minister deeply interested in the antislavery movement. (*Annual Monitor*, 1861, p. 15.) On June 20, 1840, during Garrison's most recent visit to England, the Braithwaites had entertained him and others at a dinner party (see Garrison's letter to Helen, June 29, 1840, *Letters*, II, 654; see also Anna Davis Hallowell, ed., *James and Lucretia Mott, Life and Letters*, Boston, 1884, p. 158). Presumably it was on this occasion that Garrison made the remarks in question.

11. The letter Garrison intended to write to Mrs. Braithwaite has not been preserved.

12. William Ball (1801–1878), an English Quaker, gave a tea for a large company at Tottenham, June 25, 1840, at which time Garrison seems to have spoken at length on the subject of perfectibility (see Hallowell, *James and Lucretia Mott, Life and Letters*, pp. 161–162).

Garrison quotes Isaiah 29:21 and, with an inversion of phrasing, Romans 11:25.

13. Garrison's series of biblical quotations is taken from Romans 8:9, 10; Galatians 2:20, 4:19; Ephesians 3:17; Colossians 1:27, 3:4; and II Corinthians 13:5, 5:17.

14. I John 3:9, adapted.

15. Garrison questions Elizabeth Pease about a tract by John Humphrey Noyes (1811–1886) — perhaps *A Treatise on the Second Coming of Christ* (Putney, Vermont, 1840). (Robert Allerton Parker, *A Yankee Saint*, New York, 1935.) He also refers to the official organ of Noyes and his associates, the *Perfectionist*, which had been briefly published in 1834 in New Haven and continuously after 1837 in Putney, Vermont (for a time under the title the *Witness*), ceasing publication in 1846.

Noyes, a graduate of Dartmouth who studied theology at Andover and Yale, was one of the most stimulating of nineteenth-century social theorists and utopian reformers. Having himself attained, as he thought, a state of perfect sinlessness, he developed a theology combining adventist and perfectionist beliefs. Translating his theory into practice, he established in 1836 in Putney, Vermont, a utopian community which later became notorious for its group marriages. Public outrage and legal action eventually forced the group to move to New York state, where, in 1848, they founded the Oneida community.

16. Garrison refers to Daniel 3:27.

17. Charles Lenox Remond (1810–1873), an outstanding Negro orator, was for many years an agent and lecturer for the Massachusetts Anti-Slavery Society. He went to England in 1840 as a representative of the American Anti-Slavery Society to the World's Anti-Slavery Convention. He stayed on to lecture in England and Ireland, returning to the United States in December 1841.

18. The annual meeting of the American Anti-Slavery Society had been held May 11–14 at the Broadway Tabernacle.

19. The annual New England Anti-Slavery Convention had been held May 25–27 at the Chardon-Street Chapel in Boston.

20. Lydia Maria Child (1802–1880), wife of lawyer David Lee Child, was

both author and abolitionist. From 1841 to 1843, with her husband's assistance, she edited in New York City the *National Anti-Slavery Standard*, organ of the American Anti-Slavery Society.

21. This proposed convention was never held.

22. Robert Purvis (1810–1898), son of a white South Carolina cotton broker and a mulatto mother, was a founder of the American Anti-Slavery Society in 1833 and a loyal Garrisonian abolitionist. Perhaps his most important contribution to the antislavery movement was his leadership in the Underground Railroad.

Lucretia Coffin Mott (1793–1880), wife of James Mott, was a minister in the liberal Hicksite branch of the Society of Friends and an active reformer. Her energies as reformer were directed towards woman's rights as well as abolition.

Abby Kelley (1811–1887), originally a teacher, was also an abolitionist and woman's rights advocate. In 1840, like Lucretia Mott and Lydia Maria Child, she had attended in London the World's Anti-Slavery Convention, which had refused to recognize women as delegates. In 1845 Abby Kelley married Stephen S. Foster.

William Bassett (1803–1871), originally a Quaker but by this time a Unitarian, had been an organizer of the Chardon-Street Convention. A staunch Garrisonian, he was active on *The Liberator*'s finance committee. In 1844 Bassett joined the Northampton community. (*Life*.)

Charles C. Burleigh (1810–1878), a lawyer by training, was a Garrisonian lecturer and editor. He became increasingly committed to the anti-Sabbath and woman's rights movements.

23. William Adam (c. 1797–1881) had a varied and interesting life, as scholar and reformer. Born in Scotland, he became a professor at Harvard (Oriental languages), an abolitionist, a missionary to India, a distinguished editor, and an author of several valuable reports on Indian life. In 1842, along with George W. Benson, he became one of the founders of the Northampton community. (Letters to the editor from Archie Motley, manuscripts librarian, Chicago Historical Society, June 1, 1970, and Sally R. Johnson, India Office Records, Foreign and Commonwealth Office, January 5 and 13, 1971.)

11

TO NATHANIEL P. ROGERS

Boston, July 15, 1841.

Dear Rogers:

It was out of my power to visit you on Saturday last, according to your invitation, in consequence of the absence of Helen and myself to Newburyport. Bro. Pillsbury and myself have just this moment returned from the County meeting at Plymouth yesterday — and an excellent meeting it was.[1] As I now purpose seeing you in Concord on Saturday next, and thus presenting you a living epistle nearly six feet long,[2] I shall add no more than that we are all well at home, and all desire to be most affectionately remembered to you and yours.

Yours, fraternally,

Wm. Lloyd Garrison.

ALS: Collection of Mrs. J. P. Learmont, McGill University Library.

1. The annual meeting of the Plymouth County Anti-Slavery Society was held Wednesday, July 14. (*The Liberator*, July 23, 1841.)

2. Only "five feet nine to ten," according to his sons (*Life*, IV, 319).

12

TO UNKNOWN RECIPIENT

Cambridgeport, July 26, 1841.

My Afflicted Friend:

We have just heard, by a letter from sister Ann,[1] of the death of your estimable mother. I hasten, in the midst of pressing engagements, to send you a few lines, in order to express the deep sympathy I feel in your case, at this juncture. You are now fatherless and motherless — in which bereaved condition I have been placed for the last eighteen years; and I know, therefore, how to condole with you at your loss. Happy is it for you that you have not been left an orphan in infancy, in childhood, or in early life. Unspeakably happy is the thought, too, that you have given yourself to God, in spirit and in truth, so that you can look up to him with more than filial resignation as unto a Heavenly Parent, and devoutly exclaim, "Not my will, but thine be done!"[2] As your day is — a day of trial and of visitation[3] — so may your strength and consolation be. It is cheering to my spirit to believe that you do not sorrow as those who are without hope

AL: Merrill Collection of Garrison Papers, Wichita State University Library.

The "Afflicted Friend" to whom this unfinished letter is addressed, though unidentified, is presumably someone known to the Bensons in Brooklyn, Connecticut, or its vicinity.

1. Anna Elizabeth Benson, Helen Garrison's spinster sister, a dedicated abolitionist and Garrison's best friend among his sisters-in-law. (*Life*.)

2. Luke 22:42.

3. A reference to Isaiah 10:3.

13

TO ELIZABETH PEASE

Boston, Sept. 16, 1841.

My very dear friend:

Perhaps, on looking at my signature, you will remember that I was in England last year, in company with a friend named [Nathaniel P.] Rogers, of New-Hampshire, and received many kindnesses at your hands; that I first met you in London, and afterward at Manchester and Liverpool; and that I have some acquaintance with George

Thompson. Under these circumstances, you will excuse the liberty I take in writing a hasty scrawl to you, (for the steamer is to leave almost immediately,) without a better acquaintance.

* * * * * *

Seriously, my esteemed friend, I have allowed so many steamers to return to England, without forwarding a single letter to you, that I feel as though I ought to have a fresh introduction to you, to recall myself to your remembrance. If you judge of my friendship, my gratitude, by the number of my epistles, you will be constrained to entertain a very poor opinion of me — and so will all my other dear friends, (whose worth and kindness are forever graven on my heart,) on the other side of the Atlantic. But I am neither ungrateful nor forgetful. In imagination, I am with you all, continually; for I hail you as kindred spirits, and shall ever feel specially grateful to Heaven for have [having] been permitted to commune with you, face to face! So much by way of apology and explanation.

Tell dear Thompson, that I fling the arms of my affection around his neck, and press him more closely than ever to my bosom, for his manly, fearless and eloquent defence of the American Anti-Slavery Society and its friends, at the last meeting of the Glasgow Emancipation Society.[1] He has "defined his position" in the most satisfactory manner; and though, in so doing, he may, and doubtless will, lose the friendship of some on both sides of the Atlantic — yet, let him be assured, he has done a good work for his own soul, strengthened and enlarged his reputation as a reformer for all time, and won for himself the confidence and love of those, "of whom the world is not worthy."[2] My prayer for him is, that he may be faithful in all things unto the end, that he may at last receive the crown of life.

Tell those faithful brethren, William Smeal and John Murray, that the course pursued by them, and the noble Society with which they are connected, and of which they are the soul, is mightily encouraging to the true-hearted abolitionists in America; that, though it is seldom they hear from us personally by letter, our eyes are continually upon them, and our ears ever open to hear their cheering words; and that they are *not* laboring in vain, nor spending their strength in vain.[3] O no! The same message may be conveyed to our dear Irish friends in Dublin, — the Webbs, the Allens, the Haughtons, — whose names I never mention but with deep emotion, often to the suffusion of my eyes with tears.[4] You have all stolen my heart — and what can I say more?

Our anti-slavery struggle is constantly increasing in vigor and potency; and never were our spirits better, or our blows more effective, or our prospects more encouraging, than at present. Our fall and winter campaign will be carried on with unwonted energy. The return of our friends Phillips, Chapman, and [John A.] Collins, infuses new life into the general mass. The people are every where eager to hear. I am covered all over with applications to lecture in all parts of the free States. The many base attempts that have been made to cripple my influence, and to render me odious in the eyes of the people, have only served to awaken sympathy, excite curiosity, and to open a wide door for usefulness. Thus has the Lord taken the cunning in their own craftiness, and carried the counsels of the froward headlong.[5]

The holy cause of non-resistance is also making sure progress, and conviction has seized upon many minds. It is destined to bless and save the world; for, in essence, it [is] the consummation of the gospel of Christ. Next week we are to hold, in this city, the annual meeting of the New-England Non-Resistance Society, at which we expect to see our beloved friend Lucretia Mott, as well as many other eminent friends of bleeding humanity.[6] If I were rich, what would I not give, if you could be present with us also? You must certainly make a trip to our shores, ere long. Will you not do so?

A most frightful riot has occurred in Cincinnati, Ohio, the particulars of which you will see in the Liberator.[7] The types and press of the Philanthropist have been for the third or fourth time destroyed — the dwellings of several abolitionists and colored persons sacked — several lives have been lost, and persons badly wounded — &c. &c. The cause of the riot was a quarrel between some white "rowdies" and two or three colored persons — the former having been the assailants. The course pursued by the city authorities of Cincinnati has been most criminal. They were virtually at the head of the mob! The result of all this, painful and humiliating as it is, will be, I am sure, the furtherance of the anti-slavery enterprise. "The Lord maketh the wrath of man to praise him, and the remainder he restrains." [8]

I have recently taken a jaunt, with dear N. P. Rogers, to the White Mountains in New-Hampshire, and must say that the scenery of the Granite State, is, in some respects, superior to that of Scotland.[9] But the mail closes in a few moments, and here I must abruptly terminate this almost illegible scrawl.

My family are all well. My wife admires and loves you, and desires to be remembered to you in the bonds of a pure friendship. Please give my choice remembrances to your father and mother, and to all inquiring friends. Let me hear from you soon — and believe me to be,

Ever your faithful friend,

Wm. Lloyd Garrison.

Elizabeth Pease.

ALS: Garrison Papers, Boston Public Library.

1. Thompson's address before the Glasgow Emancipation Society, as reprinted from the Glasgow *Argus*, appeared in *The Liberator*, September 10.

2. Garrison adapts Hebrews 11:38.

3. William Smeal (1793–1877), by religion a Friend, by trade a grocer, was for many years the co-secretary of the Glasgow Emancipation Society (founded in 1833). Along with John Murray (died 1849), the other co-secretary and the founder of the society, Smeal was influential in persuading the Glasgow society to favor the old organization American Anti-Slavery Society when it came under strong attack during Collins' controversial visit. (*Life.*)

4. Richard Davis Webb (1805–1872) was a charming and humorous Dublin printer and reformer (advocate of abolition, temperance, and nonresistance). He and his wife Hannah (1809–1862), also an active abolitionist, were among Garrison's best European friends and most frequent correspondents. (*Life.*)

Richard Allen (1803–1886), husband of Anne Webb, was an orthodox Friend, whose business was in linen and muslin. He was increasingly active in the anti-slavery and temperance causes, though he was somewhat more conservative than the Webbs and the Haughtons. He was secretary of the Hibernian Anti-Slavery Society. (Letter to the editor from C. Duncan Rice, Yale University, June 2, 1970.)

James Haughton (1795–1873), a corn and flour merchant in Dublin, was active in the causes of temperance, abolition, peace, education, and the abolition of capital punishment. Haughton had founded the Hibernian Anti-Slavery Society in 1837 and was currently its president. He was a staunch supporter of Garrison, although in the decades following this letter he tended to leave Hibernian abolition leadership to Webb. (Letter to the editor from C. Duncan Rice, Yale University, June 2, 1970.)

5. Garrison adapts Job 5:13.

6. A peace convention had been held in Boston September 18–20, 1838. As a result of this meeting the New England Non-Resistance Society was founded, and Garrison became the corresponding secretary. The annual meeting for 1841 occurred September 21–22; for a report of this meeting see *The Liberator*, October 1.

7. *The Liberator*, September 17, carried reprints from several Cincinnati papers concerning the riot, which appears to have begun with a quarrel between whites and blacks on August 31. On three successive nights the quarrel developed into an open battle with clubs and guns and even cannon. The *Philanthropist*, the first antislavery paper in the West, had been founded in 1836 by James G. Birney; since 1837 it had been edited by Gamaliel Bailey. Editorially it expressed the view that slavery should be abolished by political action. For a reprint of the *Philanthropist*'s analysis of the riot see *The Liberator*, September 24, 1841.

8. Psalms 76:10, adapted.

9. The week's tour with Rogers, begun at Concord, New Hampshire, on August 23, was a characteristic combination of business with pleasure: of anti-slavery meetings and speeches with scenic carriage drives and a horseback ascent of Mount Washington. Garrison wrote little about this excursion, but Rogers recorded it fully in columns of the *Herald of Freedom*; much of what he had to say was reprinted, after his death, in *A Collection from the Miscellaneous Writings of* . . . (Boston, 1849), pp. 160–192.

14

TO GAMALIEL BAILEY, JR.

BOSTON, Sept. 27, 1841.

DEAR SIR, —

In accordance with a unanimous vote of the Board of Managers of the Massachusetts Anti-Slavery Society, at a meeting held in Boston this day, at 25 Cornhill, it is our privilege to transmit to you the enclosed draft for one hundred dollars, as a donation from the treasury of the Society, to be applied to the purchase of another press for the Philanthropist, in the place of that which was recently destroyed by the mob in Cincinnati. This sum, though trifling in itself, is nevertheless large, in view of the pecuniary ability of the Massachusetts Society at the present time. It is presented to you, by the Board, in the name of the members and friends of that Society throughout the Commonwealth, as a token of the abhorrence with which they unitedly regard the late riotous proceedings in your city — of the esteem and admiration in which you are held by them, for the rare moral courage and noble fidelity to the cause of bleeding humanity, which you exhibit at this perilous crisis, as well as for what you have done and suffered on other trying occasions — and of their determination never to give up the conflict with slavery, until it be extirpated from the American soil. It is not doubted that the abolitionists of Ohio will promptly rally to your aid, and erect a new anti-slavery press for every old one that the minions of the slaveholding power may mutilate or destroy. This should be done without delay. The action of the friends of freedom, in such an emergency, should be as rapid as the motion of light, and as resistless as the tide of Niagara. Let there be no faltering — no delay — no cant about the duty of acting cautiously and prudently — no counselling to suspend operations until a more favorable period. NOW is the best, the only time; and to act boldly and uncompromisingly is the highest dictate of wisdom, the best caution, and the soundest policy. Whoever is for turning back, or beating a retreat, or discontinuing the publication of the Philanthropist even for an hour, betrays a weak and cowardly, if not a treacherous and wicked spirit. Give no heed to such counsellors; but 'trust in the Lord, and do good,' [1] and he will be 'a very present help in time of trouble.' [2] Cincinnati has been fully disgraced: it is anti-slavery alone that can redeem her character. Her children shall yet rise up, and call you and your persecuted coadjutors blessed.[3] Your country, deemed from her great iniquity, shall rank you among her truest friends, and her

Antislavery meeting in Exeter Hall, London, 1841

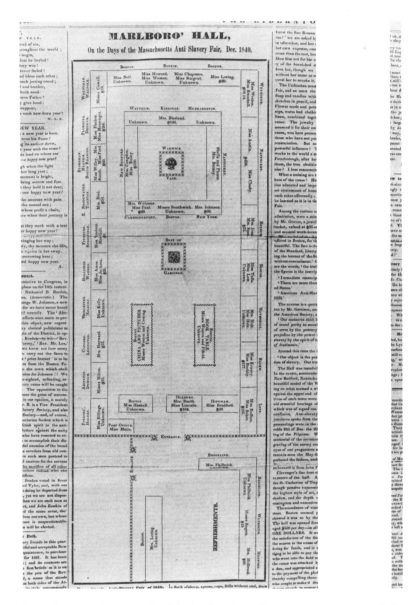

The Liberator, January 1, 1841, showing the arrangement of exhibits at the Anti-Slavery Fair held at Marlboro Hall the preceding December

noblest benefactors. Judging from the past, we are confident that you will remain firm and faithful to the end.

The sympathies of thousands, in this section of the country, are deeply excited in behalf of the colored population of Cincinnati, whose cries have entered into the ear of the Lord of Sabaoth.[4] May they have grace vouchsafed to them from on high, so as not to return evil for evil, but blessing for cursing — remembering that it is always better to suffer wrong than to do wrong.[5] Let them be assured that the wrath of their enemies shall be made instrumental to the deliverance of all who are in bonds.

The Board, in forwarding the enclosed mite, feel none the less gratified to be able to give this expression of their sympathy and esteem because they have very seriously differed in opinion with the Philanthropist, in regard to the unhappy division which has taken place in the anti-slavery ranks within the last two years. However much they may have lamented this disagreement, they have never doubted the purity of your motives, while they have ever highly appreciated your editorial candor and ability. They bid you God speed.

In behalf of the Board,

WM. LLOYD GARRISON, }
WENDELL PHILLIPS, } *Committee.*

Printed: *The Liberator*, October 1, 1841.

Gamaliel Bailey, Jr. (1807–1859) had edited the Cincinnati *Philanthropist* since 1837. Mob attacks on the paper had taken place before and would take place again, but the *Philanthropist* continued publication. In 1843 it became the daily *Herald and Philanthropist*. It ceased publication in 1846, when Bailey went to Washington to edit the *National Era*, the official weekly journal of the American and Foreign Anti-Slavery Society, which published many works by Whittier, Theodore Parker, Harriet Beecher Stowe, and others active in the cause.

1. Psalms 37:3.
2. Psalms 46:1.
3. Proverbs 31:28, adapted.
4. James 5:4.
5. Garrison paraphrases I Peter 3:9 and 3:17.

15

TO SUMNER LINCOLN

BOSTON, Nov. 8, 1841.

MY DEAR BROTHER:

My desire to be with you at your county meeting in Gardner, on the 17th inst., is very great; but with my present engagements, I must forego this pleasure.

The fidelity which you have so long exhibited as an abolitionist, in every emergency, has served greatly to exalt you in my estimation; and the noble spirit manifested by the people under your care, in conceding to you the right of free speech and action, is worthy of all commendation. When it will be my privilege to see them and you, I cannot tell; for I have a great dislike to travelling in the winter, especially in a stage-coach. Be assured, however, that I need no urging in this matter; and gladly will I avail myself of the first convenient opportunity to visit you.

The wickedness of this nation, in enslaving one sixth portion of the inhabitants, is so enormous, that it would be as easy to fill infinite space with solid matter as to cover it up; and whoever understandingly justifies it, or goes about hunting up apologies for those who are imbruting the image of God, clearly reveals himself to be an unprincipled man, and the enemy of Christ, whatever may be his religious pretensions. The case is a plain one. The test is sure. He who sees the Bible withheld, by the hand of tyranny, from millions who are living in a state of heathenism, and feels no anguish of spirit, does not believe in the Bible. He who sees the marriage institution trampled under foot, and men and women compelled to herd together like cattle, and does not glow with holy indignation, is impure in heart. He who sees his fellow-creatures chained, lacerated, maimed, murdered with impunity, and cries not out against the deed, is cruel in spirit. He who sees human beings sold in the shambles, with cattle and swine, under the hammer of the auctioneer, in lots to suit purchasers, and can excuse the transaction, is before God no better than a man stealer.

If it be truth that saves, then, if we would rescue our guilty country from destruction, we must speak the truth, whether it cost us our reputation or our life. It must be spoken in love, or else it will never be faithfully spoken, nor courageously applied to the conscience. Let us cheerfully make up our minds to be hated for Christ's sake; and when thus hated, let us not forget his injunction, 'Rejoice, and be *exceeding glad*; for great is your reward in heaven!' [1]

It is for the wicked, not for the righteous, to be cast down. He who says that God is on his side, yet cowers before the foe, makes his God a pigmy, instead of one mighty to save. The Christian fears nothing. By faith he has overcome the world, and there is nothing in the world to subdue him. He knows that Christ, the Captain of his salvation, is stronger than the Adversary; of what should he be afraid? When was it ever known that Truth slunk from the presence of Falsehood? When was ever Oppression at ease in the presence of Liberty? Who chases a thousand, or puts ten thousand to flight? They who worship God, or bow down to Mammon?

With a righteous cause, sustained by the mighty God of Jacob, what have we to fear? How can we be otherwise than courageous? Why should we not go forward, and possess the promised land?

This is no dream of enthusiasm — no flight of fanaticism. 'The battle is the Lord's,' [2] not ours. In the name of the Lord, let us do valiantly. He will give us the victory. Already the ranks of the enemy are broken, and despair is stamped upon every countenance. Already much territory has been won, many standards captured, and numerous fortresses reduced to heaps of ruin. Our cry, our watchword, must be — 'Onward! Onward!' [3] 'The Son of God goes forth to war,' and they who will not 'follow in his train' shall be destroyed.[4]

I trust a right spirit will pervade your meeting — a free, hearty, indomitable spirit. Look not to 'distinguished advocates from abroad,' and lean upon no arm of flesh.[5] If the Lord be with you, let that suffice. Tolerate nothing like formality in your meeting, but make it social, familiar, free. Then, whether you obtain help from abroad or not, your meeting will be profitable to yourselves, and advantageous to the perishing slaves.

Your admiring friend,

WM. LLOYD GARRISON.

Sumner Lincoln.

Printed: *The Liberator*, November 26, 1841.

Sumner Lincoln (1799–1890), a graduate of Yale College and Yale Theological Seminary, was a Unitarian minister at Gardner, Massachusetts (see Waldo Lincoln, *Lincolns of New England*, Worcester, Mass., 1926, p. 172). Lincoln had apparently invited Garrison to the meeting of the Worcester County North Division Anti-Slavery Society, which was held at Gardner, November 17.

1. Matthew 5:12.
2. I Samuel 17:47.
3. Garrison, Henry C. Wright, and others used "Onward! Onward!" as a kind of rallying cry; see Garrison's editorial in *The Liberator*, December 3, 1841, and Wright's letter, dated October 10, 1841, in the same issue.
4. Garrison refers to Reginald Heber's hymn "The Son of God Goes Forth to War"; see also last line thereof.
5. Garrison refers playfully to himself and to George Thompson's controversial visit of 1835; he also alludes to II Chronicles 32:8.

---

1 6

TO EDMUND QUINCY

Boston, Nov. 9, 1841.

Dear Quincy:

When I saw you at Hingham, on Thursday,[1] I forgot to remind you that the annual meeting of the Rhode-Island Society will be held in

Providence on Thursday and Friday of the present week.[2] I was glad to hear you say at Wrentham, that you intended to be at the meeting; and I sincerely hope that nothing will arise to prevent the carrying of that intention into effect. It is really a crisis with our anti-slavery friends in Rhode-Island, and they need all the aid and encouragement we can give them at the present time. Green, Chace, and others, in the plenitude of their *individuality*, (though acting by combination,) will probably make an attempt to take the life of the Society.[3] Besides, the infamous proscription of the colored citizens of that State, by the pseudo reformers in their proposed Constitution, should be met at the Providence meeting, and exposed in all its nakedness.[4] You are expected to be present without fail; and there will be the more need of your going, as there is little probability that Wendell [Phillips] will be able to go.[5]

Yours, lovingly,

Wm. Lloyd Garrison.

ALS: Garrison Papers, Sophia Smith Collection, Smith College Library.

1. At the meeting of the Plymouth County Anti-Slavery Society at Hingham, Massachusetts, on November 4.

2. The sixth annual meeting of the Rhode Island Anti-Slavery Society (founded in 1836) was to be held November 11–13. (See *The Liberator*, November 19, 1841; see also the issue for February 6, 1836.)

3. In this period the old organization Garrisonian societies were under attack not only by the proponents of conservative new organization but also by proponents of "no organization."

Christopher A. Greene (1816–1853) was a partner of William M. Chace in the utopian farm community already mentioned (letter to George W. Benson, January 7, 1841) and shared his views (see *Life*, III, 24). Both men opposed antislavery societies on the grounds that they were sectarian, and they believed that supreme efforts in the abolition movement had to be individual. The Rhode Island society survived their opposition.

4. Garrison refers to the efforts of the Suffrage party in Rhode Island, whose reform of the state constitution would not in fact extend the vote to Negroes.

5. Evidently Quincy was unable to attend the meeting.

17

TO FRANCIS JACKSON

Boston, Nov. 26, 1841.

My Dear Friend:

I hasten to inform you of the downfall of *Turkey*! Yesterday, at 2 o'clock, precisely, a very gallant attack was made by our forces in all quarters at once, our *Garrison* being in prime spirits and excellent condition. From the very first moment, the victory was evidently ours.

Grease, so long held in captivity, was immediately extricated, and its independence is, of course, settled beyond controversy. The *right wing* of the enemy's forces was carried by myself in person, without any loss, and the *left* by my eldest son, who displayed extraordinary zeal and valor. You may confidently announce that *Turkey* has not a leg left to stand upon! Acting on the popular maxim, that "to the victors belong the spoils," we made clean work even of the *bones,* and found some rare *pickings.* The women and children, inspirited by the prospect of a successful onslaught, could not be restrained from taking part in the engagement, and they exhibited, through out, the firmness of veterans; and, certainly, looking at the matter in a *patriotic* point of view, it would be hard to say that they acted "out of their appropriate sphere." One of the boys said he would go *"neck* or nothing." [1] Another was disposed to *breast* any danger, in order to gratify his warlike appetite. A third was inclined to occupy a *posterior* position, and "thereby hangs a *tail!*" [2] Our knives did great execution, cutting and carving the enemy fatally; and even our teeth were used to great effect. Rather *Turkish* this, to be sure, for civilized persons; but in war, you know, "the end sanctifies the means." [3] There was not a drop of blood shed on our side, and not a wound received, except a mere scratch which I accidentally inflicted on my finger by my own weapon, in the ardor of attack.

I hasten to communicate this intelligence to you, as it cannot fail to be gratifying; especially as you nobly incited us to the conflict, and avowed your readiness to "take the responsibility." We have unanimously come to the conclusion, that *Francis* Jackson is a better man and a better general than *Andrew,* and deserves incomparably more at the hands of his countrymen.[4]

Hoping and believing that nothing will ever occur to blight your laurels, I remain, with *Thanksgiving,*

Your faithful and much obliged friend,

Wm. Lloyd Garrison.

Francis Jackson.

P.S. My muse insists upon recording the event in rhyme — as follows:

SONNET.

Shout, all ye nations! *Turkey* is no more!
  Complete, perpetual, is its overthrow!
  Thanks-giving day was struck the fatal blow: —
Let bells be rung, let cannon loudly roar,
And nothing human *Turkey's* fate deplore!
  Its pride and pomp are in the dust laid low —

> *Grease* is delivered from a fiery foe,
> And all its tears and agonies are o'er!
> Let Tyranny with terror now turn pale,
>   (Fierce as a wolf, and sightless as an owl) —
> Its *end* is near, (and "thereby hangs a *tail*,")
>   And die it must, by fair means or by *fowl*!
> Thy cause, O Liberty! can never fail,
>   Though traitors curse, and demons rage and howl.

ALS: Villard Papers, Harvard College Library.

1. "Neck or nothing" was recorded in 1678 in John Ray, *English Proverbs* (p. 347), and has been used by many writers since.

2. Garrison refers to a common maxim found in Shakespeare and many other writers.

3. This proverb has been used by various authors as far back as the Romans.

4. For an expression of Garrison's hostility see especially his letter to Andrew Jackson, July 27, 1824, *Letters*, I, 23–29.

18

TO GEORGE W. BENSON

Cambridgeport, Dec. 17, 1841.

Dear George:

You will see, by the accompanying Circular, what mischief is brewing, and what a hostile position is assumed toward me, the Liberator Committee, and the Massachusetts A. S. Society, by my old, erring and misguided friend [Isaac] Knapp, and his more crafty and malignant abettors — to wit, Smith, Bates and [Joel Prentiss] Bishop.[1] I have every reason to believe that it was drawn up by Bishop, and that it has been sent to a great number of persons in all parts of the country. A copy was sent to our venerable friend Seth Sprague, at Duxbury, (the superscription being in Bishop's handwriting,) who, thinking I might not have seen it, promptly and kindly forwarded it to me, with the following characteristic lines:

"Respected Friend — I received the enclosed Circular a few days since, by mail; and, although I think it most likely that you are informed that it is in circulation, yet it is possible that you may not. I see that there is another storm brewing. If the devil was ever chained, certainly he has been let loose on the old Massachusetts A. S. Society.

Yours, with much respect,

Seth Sprague."

Thus far, we have not deemed it expedient to take any notice of the Circular, in the Liberator. The committee will probably wait until the first number of the "truc"(!!) Liberator shall have made its appearance, when it will, doubtless, be necessary for them to make a calm and plain statement of the facts in the case. This, of course, will suffice to satisfy all candid and honorable minds; for nothing can be more absurd, or more untrue, (as you well know,) than the charges brought against them and myself in the Circular. So artfully, however, is the Circular drawn up, and so widely has it been disseminated, that it will probably do a great deal of mischief, and penetrate where no reply will be allowed to follow. I presume it will be widely disseminated in England, and not unlikely through the agency of the London Committee. Well, I can truly say, "none of these things move me," Having a good conscience, and feeling willing to bear unrepiningly any cross that my Heavenly Father may see fit to put upon me, I will not fear what man can do to me, nor allow my mind to be disquieted by the machinations of men or devils. Happy is the man who makes innocence his companion, and who feels the assurance that he is crucified to the world.

You will doubtless be anxious to know what is Knapp's prospect of success in the publication of his new paper. I have no means of knowing; but take it for granted that, among the numerous enemies of the anti-slavery cause in general, of the Massachusetts A. S. Society in particular, of the Liberator, and of myself, (slavery, pro-slavery, new organization, and priestcraft, all combined,) he will not find it a very difficult matter to obtain an amount of funds sufficient to enable him to publish several numbers of the scandalous publication. The editing of the paper will be done, I presume, by Bishop, who will take the opportunity to disgorge all the venom he has been concocting for these two years against the old organization. — As soon as the paper is issued, I will send you a copy.

The receipts of the Liberator, for the present year, will fall short of its expenses to the amount of about $500. This sum will probably be made up by the kindness of friends. If you can obtain any new subscribers for the new year, in your region, or any one else, send their names along as a new year's present.

I wish you could be at our Fair next week.[2] — But you, and Prof. [William] Adam, and D. L. Child, must not fail to attend the annual meeting of our State Society in January next.[3]

Within the past fortnight, up to the present hour, our house has been turned into a hospital. The influenza has attacked almost every member of the family with great violence. Mother was first taken — then Mary — then Anna — then Sarah — then Helen — then the children — and then Eliza.[4] They were all brought down within a few days of each other, and have had a very serious time of it. Mary,

Sarah and Anna have been confined to their beds. Their coughs have been very bad, attended with fever and sore throat. I am happy to say they are all now convalescent, though it will be some time before they will fully recover. Anna has not yet left her room: the others are able to come below stairs. I have had a very light attack. The weather for some time past has been wet and spring-like, and the atmosphere humid and foggy; and no doubt the influenza will spread like a malignant epidemic far and wide. We are anxious to hear from you and yours, and trust you have not been afflicted as we have been. I do not know when I can visit Northampton; but if you will come to our State meeting, perhaps I will return with you. Give my best regards to Wm. Adam and D. L. Child. Say to friend Child that I received his letter, and will do as he desires me, with much pleasure; highly approving as I do of his article in the Standard. — So! we are once more gagged in Congress, and by a most villanous *ruse!* [5] Never mind — "once more to the breach!" [6] — Mother, all the sisters, wife, and James [H. Garrison], desire to be affectionately remembered to Catharine [7] and yourself.

Yours, truly,

Wm. Lloyd Garrison.

☞ *Write soon.*

ALS: Garrison Papers, Boston Public Library; partly printed in *Life*, III, 39–40. This letter is written on the same sheet as a note to Garrison signed by Isaac Knapp and dated December 8, 1841, in which Knapp refers to the same circular.

1. In this circular, dated December 6, Isaac Knapp claimed that he had been wrongfully deprived of his rights and interests in *The Liberator* by the "treacherous course" of Garrison, the *Liberator* committee, and the Massachusetts Anti-Slavery Society. Knapp announced his intention to start a new paper, the "true" *Liberator*, to be called *Knapp's Liberator*. The circular requested funds to cover the cost of printing the first issue. Apparently only one issue of *Knapp's Liberator*, dated January 8, 1842, was printed.

Two of the signers of Knapp's circular have not previously been identified. Little is known of John Cutts Smith (born John Smith Cutts) except that he had been one of the founders of the New England Anti-Slavery Society. (*Life.*) Hamlett Bates (1814–1880), a printer by trade, had worked as a bookkeeper in *The Liberator* office and was later to become a constable, a justice of the peace, and finally a judge. (Obituary, Boston *Advertiser*, October 25, 1880.) On the circular Smith and Bates testified to the validity of Knapp's claim, announcing that they would receive funds on behalf of *Knapp's Liberator*.

2. The annual antislavery fairs were a major source of funds for the Massachusetts Anti-Slavery Society. The eighth annual Massachusetts Anti-Slavery Fair was held December 22–25 at Amory Hall, Boston.

3. The annual meeting of the Massachusetts Anti-Slavery Society was held January 26–28 at the Melodeon, Boston.

David Lee Child (1798–1874), a Boston lawyer active in a variety of reforms, had for some years been one of Garrison's most capable supporters. Following a trip to Belgium in 1836, he constructed in Northampton, Massachusetts, the first American beet-sugar factory, which failed after approximately seven years of operation. In July 1843 he succeeded his wife as editor in New York of the

National Anti-Slavery Standard, a post he relinquished the following May. See Garrison's letter to *The Liberator,* July 14, 1843, and his editorial in *The Liberator,* May 17, 1844.

4. Eliza has not been positively identified, though she may have been a servant in the Garrison household.

5. Child's article in the *National Anti-Slavery Standard* was reprinted in *The Liberator,* December 24, 1841. In the previous session of Congress a gag rule had been passed which effectively prevented petitions on abolition from being presented. In a recent political maneuver, Congress had voted to retain the rule for the present session. For a review of the gag rule situation see *The Liberator,* December 17 and 24.

6. Garrison's adaptation of Shakespeare, *Henry V,* III, i, 1.

7. Catharine Knapp Stetson Benson (born 1808), wife of George and sister of Garrison's friend James A. Stetson.

19

TO GEORGE W. BENSON

Boston, Jan. 9, 1842.
Sabbath Evening.

My dear bro. George:

I can find it in my heart to wish you and yours, a happy new year — meaning by that term, a year without an end — that is, perpetual felicity. But we live in a perishing world, where every thing but hope in God is evanescent; the dearest ties of life are continually sundering; we know not what a day may bring forth; and we can be happy only on condition that our entire being is swallowed up in the will of God.

I write to you now for a special and somewhat urgent purpose. Dear sister Mary lies in a condition too critical to render it justifiable to keep you in ignorance of it. Three weeks ago, this evening, she was taken with violent spasms in the stomach, from which, after trying various remedies, she could obtain no relief, except by swallowing a mixture of spirits of hartshorn and laudanum. I felt very reluctant to her using this narcotic mixture; but, as she was in great agony — as she could get relief in no other way — and as she had before tried it with great success — we could not refuse it. It soon gave her temporary relief — after which, she had a violent attack of the cholera morbus, which reduced her very low, and which was with difficulty removed. Next, she was attacked with a very hard cough, attended with loss of appetite, and the return of her spasms. Mother and the rest of the household did all that could be done without medical aid, under such circumstances; but she grew no better. Mary did not appear to have strength or inclination to try the Thompsonian treatment, as she formerly made a pretty thorough trial of it, to no good effect. She had no desire to call in a "regular" calomel physician; and, of course, we had none. But she had, for some time, felt a growing interest in the homoepathic mode of treatment (in which interest I also shared, to some extent) — and we all concluded to send for a homoepathic physician, not daring any longer to assume the responsibility of the case ourselves. We therefore called in Dr. Wesselhoeft, the German doctor who is our near neighbor, — the friend and companion of Dr. Follen in Germany, — who is a most amiable and excellent man, and doubtless well understands his profession.[1] He has been assiduous in his attention for several days past, calling frequently by day and by night, and studying Mary's case with great vigilance and solicitude; but, up to the present hour, he has not been able to alter the aspect of her case. Some of her symptoms are better, some worse; but, on the whole, I am apprehensive that this is her last sickness, and that she is gradually wasting away. Certain it is, unless sudden and unexpected relief be obtained for her, she cannot survive much longer. Her cough, at times, is dreadful; and she has a permanent inflammation in the diaphragm which causes her great distress. Although her form is greatly emaciated, her face is swollen — probably from local nervous irritability. — She endures every thing as patiently as a lamb, although a great sufferer. I know not how this letter may find you at home; but, if it be in your power to come to Cambridgeport, let me urge you to do so without delay. It is impossible to foresee events, or accurately to calculate chances; but I am painfully impressed with the conviction, that Mary cannot continue many days, unless something remarkable takes place in her case. All the family enter into these apprehensions, and therefore wish to see you immediately, if practicable. Perhaps if you were here, some other treatment might be given, that would have a better effect. At any rate, it will be a great consolation to Mary to see you, especially if this shall prove her last sickness. You will need no more on this point.

Sarah and Anna are both in delicate health, and have been afflicted with severe colds. Mother is pretty well, considering how much she has had thrown upon her. I have just recovered from a most violent attack of influenza, which confined me to my room for days. I took two full Thompsonian courses. Helen is in as good health, as usual — and also the children. The health of poor James does not improve, and sometimes he is very low in spirits. He would undoubtedly be speedily better, if he had some kind of employment. How is it with you and your dear family? Sending to them the affectionate regards of all at home, and hoping to see you here in a few days, I remain, as ever,

Your loving brother,

Wm. Lloyd Garrison.

N.B. Wendell Phillips gave a lecture on slavery in this place, this evening, in the Town Hall, to a crowded auditory. It was eloquently delivered and well received. He has also just recovered from a severe attack of the prevailing influenza.

Do not fail to give my warmest regards to those talented and estimable friends, D. L. Child and William Adam.

The first number of "Knapp's Liberator" was issued yesterday. [Hamlett] Bates, [Joel Prentiss] Bishop, and J. Cutts Smith, are the principal writers. The articles are so low and scurrilous, and exhibit so much venom that I shall probably take no notice of the paper in the Liberator.[2]

ALS. Garrison Papers, Boston Public Library.

1. Garrison mentions two distinguished German immigrants, Robert Wesselhoeft (1797–1852) and Charles Follen (1796–1840). By training a lawyer, Wesselhoeft was suspected of being a revolutionary. He was so harassed by official government maneuverings that in 1840 he emigrated from Germany to the United States. Having observed Priessnitz's water cure at Graefenberg, he resolved to practice the treatment himself in America and accordingly obtained medical degrees first from the University of Pennsylvania and then from the University of Basel (Switzerland). From 1845 until his death he conducted a thriving water cure establishment and edited the *Green Mountain Spring Monthly Journal* in Brattleboro, Vermont. (Mary R. Cabot, *Annals of Brattleboro, 1681–1895*, Brattleboro, 1922, II, 563–584, and *The Liberator*, July 4, 1845.) Follen, who had died tragically in a steamboat fire, was a Unitarian minister and a professor at Harvard College until 1835, when his "Address to the People of the United States" (drafted for the first convention of the New England Anti-Slavery Society and printed in *The Liberator*, September 6, 1834) resulted in the termination of his contract. As Samuel J. May put it (*Some Recollections of Our Antislavery Conflict*, Boston, 1869, p. 254), "The funds for the support of his professorship at Cambridge were withheld. . . ."

2. It is true that *Knapp's Liberator* was never mentioned in the pages of *The Liberator*. The issue of January 28, 1842, did contain a letter signed by Francis Jackson, Ellis Gray Loring, Samuel Philbrick, William Bassett, and Edmund Quincy which defended Garrison and *The Liberator* against the charges made by Knapp, but even this letter did not specifically mention Knapp's circular or his paper.

---

2 0

TO GEORGE W. BENSON

Friday — noon — Jan. [28, 1842].[1]

Dear George —

In addition to what Helen has written, I will add, that Mary had a pretty comfortable night last night, and this forenoon has exhibited no special distress, although she is obviously altered for the worse, and is in as low and languishing a state as she can be, and live. I have consulted the Dr. [Robert Wesselhoeft] in regard to your coming down, and he thinks you had better come without delay, if you can arrange matters at home, so as to enable you to leave. Of course, you will not be able to reach here before Monday night. By that time, it is certain in the Dr.'s mind, that all doubt will cease respecting her fate. He says she may now be taken away at any moment — he can predict nothing certain. We must be prepared for a change from hour to hour. It seems to me that Mary cannot continue this terrible conflict with disease much longer; and the chance is, that she may not survive until your arrival. Still, she may linger for several days more. Perhaps you will think it best to wait until you hear again from us. I will write again to-morrow, hoping that you will be able to receive my letter before Monday morning.

I brought George home from Providence, having the quincy and lung fever upon him. The two courses that I have given him have worked remarkably well, but the child is still quite sick, and it will be some days, under the most favorable circumstances, before he will be himself again.

The meetings of our State Society, I am informed, have been interesting, but I have not been able to attend them, except a portion of yesterday afternoon and last evening. Our meeting in the State House, last evening, was a grand one, and crowded to excess.[2] It was addressed by Col. Miller of Vermont, J. C. Fuller of western New-York, [George] Bradburn, [Nathaniel P.] Rogers, Abby Kelley, [Charles L.] Remond, Douglas, W. Phillips, and myself.[3] Phillips made a splendid effort. All the speakers were cheered, and not a breath of opposition was manifested in any part of the immense assembly. Bradburn was tremendously severe and sarcastic, as usual.

[☞ Since the above was written, your letter has come to hand, and gratified we were indeed to hear that you found all well at home. Perhaps, before coming, you had better wait to receive another letter from me; but we should be glad, if convenient, for you to come immediately.]

Our meeting in Faneuil Hall, advertised in the Liberator to be held this morning, will not be held till this evening. Possibly we may have a row, for it is deemed lawful at all times in that Hall to make more or less disturbance.[4] The Irish Address may excite Yankee blood.[5] It is a great triumph, however, to have been granted the use of the Hall by the city authorities. — Philip Scarborough is here from Brooklyn.[6] He says it has been very sickly in that village. Joseph Stetson has lost one child, 3 years old, and has another very low.[7]

Yours, ever,

Wm. Lloyd Garrison.

ALS: Garrison Papers, Boston Public Library.

1. On the manuscript the date has been corrected from "Jan. 30" to "Jan. 28," which was a Friday, and the year 1842 supplied, perhaps by Wendell Phillips Garrison.

2. The Massachusetts State House on Beacon Street was designed by Charles Bulfinch (1763–1844) and built between 1795 and 1800. (Walter M. Whitehill, *Boston, A Topographical History,* Cambridge, 1959, p. 59.)

3. Jonathan Peckham Miller (1796–1847) fought so bravely in the Greek revolution in the 1820's that he was called "the American Dare Devil." Following his return to the United States he practiced law and gave much of his energy and his money to the antislavery cause. In 1840 he was the Vermont delegate to the World's Anti-Slavery Convention in London.

James Cannings Fuller (1793–1847) was an English Quaker who had settled in Skaneateles, New York, in 1834. A picturesque and somewhat eccentric person, he gave generously of his time and his financial resources to abolition and other reforms. (Joseph Crosfield, "North Carolina Yearly Meeting of 1845," *Bulletin of the Friends Historical Society of Philadelphia,* 3–120, February 1910.)

Frederick Douglass (c. 1817–1895), whose name Garrison often misspells, was the son of a Negro mother and white father. He had escaped from slavery in 1838 and become interested in the antislavery cause through reading *The Liberator.* In 1841 he came into prominence when he spoke so successfully at a convention of the Massachusetts Anti-Slavery Society at Nantucket that he was appointed an agent of that society. Almost at once he became one of the most powerful and effective speakers in the cause. In 1845 he published the sensational *Narrative of the Life of Frederick Douglass, an American Slave,* and thereafter he spent two years in England and Ireland.

4. Garrison refers to the meeting "For the Abolition of Slavery in the District of Columbia," which was perhaps postponed until the evening in order to avoid a conflict with the tenth annual meeting of the Massachusetts Anti-Slavery Society, which was held at the Melodeon between the 26th and 28th. In his report of the District of Columbia meeting Garrison asserted that the old "Cradle of Liberty" (Faneuil Hall, built in 1742, important as a political auditorium since the Revolution) had never witnessed a more enthusiastic meeting (see *The Liberator,* February 4, 1842).

5. When Charles L. Remond returned from England in December 1841, he brought with him an "Address of the Irish People to their Countrymen and Countrywomen in America," urging support of the abolitionists and signed eventually by 70,000 persons, including Daniel O'Connell, the mayor of Dublin, and Father Theobald Mathew (for an identification of Mathew see Garrison's letter to Richard Allen, February 27, 1842). The address, which was printed in *The Liberator,* March 25, 1842, had less effect on Irish Americans than the abolitionists anticipated.

6. Philip Scarborough (born 1788) of Brooklyn, Connecticut, was a farmer and an active abolitionist. (Typed transcription of Brooklyn Vital Records, Massachusetts Historic Genealogical Society, Boston, pp. 58–59.)

7. Joseph Stetson (born 1798), from Boston, was a brother of Catharine Knapp Stetson, George W. Benson's wife. He kept a temperance hotel, the Central House, in Nashua, New Hampshire. (John S. Barry, *A Genealogical and Biographical Sketch of the Name and Family of Stetson,* Boston, 1847, p. 33.)

2 1

TO GEORGE W. BENSON

Boston, Jan. 29, 1842.
Saturday noon.

Dear George:

I wrote to you yesterday, in relation to sister Mary's case; since which, she has grown worse, and this morning, early, was for some time supposed to be dying. The family hardly think that she will be able to outlive this day.[1] You will therefore hasten to us at the earliest practicable period.

We had a great and glorious meeting, last night, in Faneuil Hall. 3 or 4000 present — very many Irishmen, to hear the Irish Address — every thing went off in the most enthusiastic manner. No opposition from any quarter. I was called to preside. The meeting was addressed by [George] Bradburn, [Edmund] Quincy, Col. [Jonathan P.] Miller, J. C. Fuller, W. Phillips, [Charles L.] Remond, [Frederick] Douglas, &c.

In great haste,
Yours, in every trial,

Wm. Lloyd Garrison.

ALS: Garrison Papers, Boston Public Library.

1. Mary Benson died on January 29, 1842.

2 2

TO HENRY G. AND MARIA W. CHAPMAN

Boston, Feb. 19, 1842.

Esteemed Friends:

At a meeting of the Board of Managers of the Massachusetts Anti-Slavery Society, in this city, on the 16th instant, — the fact having been communicated of your intention to leave immediately for Haiti, in order to seek the restoration of Mr. Chapman's health, — it was, on motion, unanimously

Voted, That our respected friends and coadjutors, Henry G. and Maria W. Chapman, be requested and authorized to act as the official representatives of the Massachusetts Anti-Slavery Society during their sojourn in Haiti; and to obtain such information as may be in their power, especially from official sources, respecting the true condition of that republic, in order that the friends of liberty and equality in this country may be the better enabled to repel the calumnies of the enemies of Haitien independence, and of negro emancipation; and thus to hasten the day when that emancipation shall be gloriously realized in the United States, in the redemption of three millions of slaves now pining in bondage — and that independence fairly and honorably acknowledged by the Congress and Government of our own country.

Wm. Lloyd Garrison, Cor. Sec'y.

To Henry G. and Maria W. Chapman.

ALS: Merrill Collection of Garrison Papers, Wichita State University Library.

The same day that Garrison wrote this letter he wrote another, which has apparently not been preserved, to Joseph Balthazar Inginac, Secretary of the Haitian Republic, asking that the Chapmans be appropriately received by officials of the government. Inginac replied April 1, 1842 (see *The Liberator*, April 29, 1842) expressing agreement with Garrison's abolitionist views and regretting that he and President Jean Pierre Boyer were unable to receive the Chapmans because they were about to leave Haiti. A year later (see *The Liberator*, April 28, 1843), after the government of Boyer and Inginac had been overthrown, Garrison wrote an editorial supporting the revolution as "the triumph of the people over usurpation and misrule, consummated with scarcely the shedding of a drop of blood."

2 3

TO RICHARD ALLEN

Boston, Feb. 27, 1842.

My beloved friend Allen:

The face of any one from this country, who has not debased his manhood or corrupted his moral sense by his residence in a land of slavery, and who has from an early period most heartily espoused our persecuted anti-slavery enterprise, will, I am sure, at all times be a welcome sight to you; and none the less welcome when you learn that he, to whom that face belongs, is a native of your own dear Emerald Isle, who came to this country when he was quite a lad. I therefore make no apology for introducing to you my very amiable and worthy friend, Thomas Davis, now and for many years a resident of Providence, Rhode-Island.[1] He is in a somewhat precarious state of health, and he goes across the Atlantic expressly to try the beneficial effects of a sea voyage, and with a natural and strong desire once more to see his dear native land. Among my numerous friends, I prize him very highly for his many virtues and excellencies, and earnestly hope that he will gain even more than he anticipates from his transatlantic journey; for he finds it in his heart to live only that he may do good.

You will find in him a person of beautiful simplicity of character, and equally unassuming and intelligent. As he is personally acquainted with all the "old organized" abolitionists in whom you feel the deepest interest, you will be able to glean from him much unwritten unprinted information respecting our proceedings in this quarter. Ask him as many questions as you please, and he will be most happy to answer them all.

Richard Allen, I love you! But, I confess that, as a lover, I have shown myself to be a very indifferent correspondent; and on the bended knees of my overcharged heart, I sincerely crave your pardon. You may well demand, if the memory of Ireland be still dear to me — if the delightful scenes in which we participated in Dublin have not entirely faded from my recollection — if I regard you as a man who is more precious than the gold of Ophir [2] — if I feel any gratitude for your multitudinous kindnesses — why I have not more frequently proved all this by epistolary evidence. Attribute it not to any oblivion of mind — not to intentional neglect — not to any abatement of my friendship — but to my worst enemy, PROCRASTINATION, from whose chains I desire immediate, total, and unconditional emancipation. The truth is — as you may readily suppose — my *American* anti-slavery engagements keep me very busily employed; and that which I would do for my beloved Irish friends, that do I not. As soon as I find that one steamer leaves this port for Liverpool, without carrying a letter from me, I feel assured that, ere the time for the departure of another shall arrive, I shall be fully prepared to send one to this, and another to that friend abroad, perhaps a score in all! But the next opportunity catches me in the same predicament, and I am left to heave the unavailing sigh, and to hang my head for shame.

Richard Allen, (now, all jealousy aside!) I love your wife! I congratulate you both upon your union with each other. Give my most respectful and cordial remembrances to her, and all good wishes for your happiness here, and in that other and better world, "where the wicked cease from troubling, and the weary are at rest." [3]

Richard Allen, I love your Dublin friends, and am sure that I should love all who are out of Dublin if I only knew them; for is it not true that "birds of a feather flock together"? Tell that noble man, James Haughton, to scold me — tell all the Webbs to denounce me — tell that singularly delicate and loving spirit, Geo. Downes, to rebuke me sternly — tell all within your social and philanthropic circle to make black marks against me — because of my neglect to keep unbroken the chain of epistolary correspondence between us; — I will not grow angry, nor complain, but confess that you are merciful in not erasing my name from the tablets of your memories. [4] Thanks, thanks to you all!

As for the cause of emancipation on this side of the Atlantic, it is now in a palmy state, and our hearts are filled with hope and joy.

How mortified, how indignant, how astonished you will be to hear that the noble Address to your countrymen in America, signed by Daniel O'Connell and Father Mathew, and a mighty host, is spurned and denounced by the Irish papers in Boston! [See the Liberator.] [5]

Your affectionate friend,

Wm. Lloyd Garrison.

ALS: Allen Papers, Friends' Historical Library, Religious Society of Friends, Dublin.

1. Thomas Davis (1806–1895) had in 1817 settled in Providence, where he became a manufacturer of jewelry. His first wife was Helen Garrison's friend Eliza Chace (c. 1809–1840), his second, Pauline Kellogg Wright (1813–1876), both ardent abolitionists. Davis was to become active in politics, serving in the Rhode Island Senate (1845–1853), the United States House of Representatives (1853–1855), and the Rhode Island House of Representatives (1887–1890).

2. An adaptation of Isaiah 13:12.

3. Job 3:17.

4. George Downes (c. 1790–1846), who was educated at Trinity College, Dublin, and was a cataloguer there, worked with the Ordnance Survey, and was a verse and topographical writer. (Letter to the editor from P. Henchy, National Library of Ireland, January 6, 1971.)

5. Father Theobald Mathew (1790–1856) was a Franciscan priest of the Capuchin order. In 1838 he inaugurated the total abstinence movement in Ireland and carried on crusades in Irish, Scottish, and English cities. He visited the United States between 1849 and 1851.

The Irish papers to which Garrison refers are the Boston *Pilot* and the *Catholic Diary*. The *Pilot* began publication in Boston in 1835 as the *Literary and Catholic Sentinel*; in 1836 it became the Boston *Pilot* and continued publication until 1856. The *Diary* is probably the *New England Reporter and Catholic Diary*, an Irish Catholic weekly established at Lowell, Massachusetts, in 1841, and moved to Boston in February 1842. The paper, whose founder, editor, and publisher was James B. Clinton, appears to have stopped publication in 1845. (Eugene P. Willging and Herta Hatzfeld, *Catholic Serials of the Nineteenth Century in the United States*, Washington, D.C., 1963–1967, pp. 100–101.) Garrison refers in particular to an article printed in the *Pilot* which was reprinted in *The Liberator*, February 25, and to an article from the *Catholic Diary* which was reprinted in *The Liberator*, March 4. Garrison was also angry with the Boston *Morning Post* for reprinting the *Pilot* article with a laudatory introduction (see *The Liberator*, February 18).

---

2 4

TO RICHARD D. WEBB

Boston, Feb. 27, 1842.

Dear Richard D. Webb:

I cannot take my pen up to write merely a few lines to introduce a beloved friend to your acquaintance, without feeling my heart leap within me at the thought of you and yours. Am I not deserving of all praise for being so prompt and punctual in discharging my epistolary and other obligations to you and my other Dublin friends? Don't you and they feel ashamed at not having answered the "heap" of letters (which, *sub rosa*, I meant to have written, but have not,) to be forwarded to your beautiful city? Won't you all try to do better hereafter, if I will forgive you? O, but I am like the culprit, who, having been guilty of theft, in order to prevent being seized, lustily cried out, "Stop thief!" Well, seize me, shake me, and doing any thing except execute me. If you kill me off, I shall never be able to make any amends for my past misdoings: so, be merciful.

Seriously, dear friend, you have had just cause to complain of me, and I dare say have marvelled greatly at my inattention. I should feel unhappy indeed, if I thought even a suspicion had passed through your mind, that my regard for you had somewhat lost its intensity, or that, being absorbed in the anti-slavery conflict at home, I had nearly forgotten those hospitable, kind-hearted, devoted friends in Dublin, who made the brief sojourn of dear [Nathaniel P.] Rogers and myself in your city an Eden-like residence.[1] I have explained, in a hasty scrawl to our mutual friend, Richard Allen, the why and wherefore you have not oftener heard from me. I will therefore dismiss this topic, once for all, by assuring you that it will be easier for a camel to go through the eye of a needle,[2] than for Richard D. Webb to be forgotten or to go unappreciated by Wm. Lloyd Garrison.

The bearer of this is a dear and intimate friend of mine, (as well as a native of Ireland,) Thomas Davis, for many years a resident of Providence, in the State of Rhode-Island — about 40 miles from Boston. He came over to this country when quite young, and now visits his native land in quest of health. He will sail from New-York for Havre, from thence he will visit Paris, from thence to London, &c. &c. to Dublin — hoping to return in all the month of June. You will find him a modest, intelligent and amiable man, with the most liberal and catholic feelings, and with a heart as expansive as suffering humanity. He was among the earliest who rallied under the anti-slavery standard, and from that hour to the present has been more true and faithful than the needle to the pole — for that sometimes vibrates and wavers. He is personally acquainted with Rogers, [George] Bradburn, Abby Kelley, M. W. Chapman, and all who are of any note in the anti-slavery cause in this region. He will be most happy to sit down with you in social converse, and tell you all about our movements, the present position and prospects of our great enterprise, and answer all your inquiries.

Henry G. Chapman and his wife [Maria W.] have just sailed for

Hayti, on account of the feeble and very dangerous state of his health. We shall miss his wife until her return, as though a hundred of our best men were laid low. I fear that *he* may never come back.

This letter (even if I had time to extend it) will be received by you at too late a period to give you any anti-slavery intelligence, — provided you receive the Liberator regularly. We have had a tremendous excitement in Congress, arising from the presentation of a petition for the peaceable dissolution of the American Union, by John Q. Adams; but it has resulted in frightening the boastful South almost out of her wits, driving the slaveholding representatives to the wall, and in effecting a signal victory for the cause of liberty and its advocates.[3]

Our meeting in Faneuil Hall, to unrol the Irish Address, with its sixty thousand signatures, was indescribably enthusiastic, and has produced a great impression on the public mind. I am sorry to add, and you will be not less ashamed to hear, that the two Irish papers in Boston sneer at the Address, and denounce it and the abolitionists in true pro-slavery style. I fear they will keep the great mass of your countrymen here from uniting with us.

I desire to be specially remembered to your accomplished wife [Hannah], of whose genius, taste, talent and heart, I entertain an exalted opinion. Also to your worthy brothers, their families, and all the other friends.

I am with all my heart your friend,

Wm. Lloyd Garrison.

ALS: Garrison Papers, Boston Public Library; extract printed in *Life*, III, 44.

1. Garrison refers to their visit during the summer of 1840.
2. Garrison alludes to Matthew 19:24.
3. In December 1838 a resolution designed to eliminate discussion of slavery was put to the House of Representatives by Charles G. Atherton of New Hampshire. The resolution was adopted and became known as the gag rule. John Quincy Adams fought tirelessly against it. As part of his campaign for the right of petition, he presented to the House on January 24, 1842, a petition from citizens of Haverhill, Massachusetts, praying that for sectional reasons the Union of the States be peaceably dissolved, and moved its reference to a select committee with instructions to report against it. Although the document may be regarded as a satire on the proposed dissolution of the Union, it caused turmoil in the House. The members spent days in presenting and discussing resolutions prepared in a caucus of southern members stating that Adams should be severely censured. After eleven days of excitement, Adams offered to drop the subject if the resolution of censure were tabled, thus ending all attempts to suppress an "offender" by threats of censure. Moreover, Adams continued to oppose the gag rule and finally succeeded in having it lifted in December 1844. (For an account of Adams' presentation of this petition see *The Liberator*, February 4, 1842.)

2 5

TO CHARLES L. CORKRAN

Boston, Feb. 27, 1842.

My dear Corkran:

I am extremely happy to have an opportunity to introduce to you a beloved friend of mine, (Thomas Davis, of Providence, Rhode-Island,) who is to leave immediately for England and the Continent, in quest of health. You will be pleased with each other as the friends of bleeding humanity, and also as originating from an Irish stock. Mr. Davis left Ireland when he was a boy, and intends visiting the land of his nativity before he returns. For the last ten years, he has been a warm and faithful supporter of the anti-slavery enterprise, and through every ordeal has passed without having the smell of fire upon his garments. He will pass a few days in Paris; and as he will be a stranger in a strange land,[1] and ignorant of the French language, whatever kindnesses you may show to him, I shall appreciate as really done to myself. As he is perfectly familiar with all our anti-slavery proceedings, and personally acquainted with all our leading abolitionists, he will be able to answer any inquiries that you may wish to make, and to give you much valuable information. I will merely add, that the anti-slavery excitement is daily increasing in this country — that the powers of slavery are shaken — that the friends of justice, humanity and free[do]m are active, resolute, indomitable — that a crisis is [n]ear at hand, which, though it may possibly end in a dissolution of the American Union, will inevitably result in the downfall of our nefarious slave system.

The letter that I received from you, dated at Paris, in June last, was full of thrilling interest to me; and, being persuaded that it would be perused with more than ordinary pleasure by the numerous readers of the Liberator, I took the liberty to insert it in my paper.[2] I feel ashamed that so long a time has elapsed since its receipt, without sending my grateful acknowledgments to you at an earlier period. Most happy shall I be to hear from you, either verbally or by letter, (more especially by letter,) as often as you can find an opportunity to communicate with me. It is possible that you are no longer in Paris. As soon as I am informed of your location, I will try to be very prompt in sending you another letter.

It gave me great pleasure to learn that your mind had been seriously exercised on the subject of non-resistance, since we parted in Dublin — (O memorable visit, and painful separation!) The more you examine that subject, in the light of Christianity, the deeper will be your conviction, I am confident, that it is pregnant with the redemption of a war-making, sin-ruined world. No proposition commends itself more clearly to my understanding and heart than this: — Whatever form of religion justifies war, or the use of carnal weapons to redress wrongs and punish enemies, is antagonistical to the gospel of Christ, and based upon the sand of human selfishness and worldly policy. Christ came to save, not to destroy men's lives — to lay down his own • life for his enemies and murderers, rather than do them the slightest injury by way of retaliation or self-defence. He also came to set us an example that we should follow his steps; "who, when he was reviled, reviled not again; WHEN HE SUFFERED, he *threatened* not; but committed himself to Him that judgeth righteously." ³ It seems to me most plainly to follow, that no man has a right to claim to be a disciple of Christ, who is not prepared to lay down his life for his enemies, or who is disposed to support those kingdoms and governments which now fill the world, and which, being upheld solely by military power and brute force, crush and curse mankind. — I do not mean to say, that they who are not prepared either to adopt or to carry out these principles, are destitute of religious sentiment; for I believe that sentiment may be strong and active in them, restraining them from the commission of crime, and mightily influencing their every day walk and conversation, but I mean to say that they are not Christians — i.e. that they are not new creatures in Christ Jesus,⁴ the ransomed of the Lord,⁵ dead to the world, and alive to God. "Now, if any man have not the spirit of Christ, he is none of his." ⁶ That spirit cannot co-exist with a desire to destroy men's lives on any pretext, however plausible, nor with an unwillingness of mind to suffer the loss of all things, for Christ's sake. O for the consummation of all that Christianity is adapted to do for the world! O for the speedy approach of that time when nation shall no longer lift up sword against nation, but the whole human race shall, "like kindred drops, mingle into one"! ⁷ Wishing you the enjoyment of all good things, I remain,

Yours, against all forms of iniquity,

Wm. Lloyd Garrison.

ALS: Garrison Papers, Boston Public Library.

Charles L. Corkran is listed in Dublin directories for 1841–1843 as living at 88 Great Brunswick Street. According to *The Liberator*, July 30, 1841, at the time of Garrison's visit to Dublin in 1840 Corkran was the editor of the Dublin *Weekly Herald*. (An extensive search has failed to yield any information about the publication of this paper.)

1. Exodus 2:22.
2. Corkran's letter, which was printed in *The Liberator*, July 30, 1841, shows a familiarity with Garrison's circle and expresses interest in abolition, in temperance, in peace, and in problems concerned with British India.

3. I Peter 2:23.
4. A paraphrase of II Corinthians 5:17.
5. Isaiah 35:10.
6. Romans 8:9.
7. Garrison adapts Isaiah 2:4 and quotes William Cowper, *The Task*, Book II, line 19.

---

2 6

TO ABEL BROWN

BOSTON, March 18, 1842.

DEAR BRO. BROWN: —

I have not had time to consult with Mr. Remond, since the receipt of your letter; but I will venture to say, in his behalf, that, (*Deo volente*,) he will be present at your Anti-Slavery Convention in April, bringing with him the Irish Address, to which are appended the honored names of Daniel O'Connell and Father [Theobald] Mathew, and the authenticity of which some bastard Irishmen (for they cannot have a drop of genuine Irish blood running in their veins,) have had the folly and hardihood to deny.[1] Under the same provision, you may also expect to see me at the same time; and if I can persuade my eloquent friend, Wendell Phillips, to accompany us, I shall do so.

The Address is worthy of any people that ever lived. It is a noble gift of Ireland to America, strengthening her claim to be the

'First flower of the earth, and first gem of the sea.' [2]

It will prove an Ithuriel spear, causing every toad that it touches to start up in the shape of a devil; and unerringly determining who are the real friends of impartial liberty, and who are ready to 'bow the knee to the dark spirit of slavery.'[3] Until I am compelled to believe otherwise by evidence which it would be folly to dispute, I shall cling to the opinion that the great body of our Irish fellow-citizens mean to be found on the side of the oppressed (for is not Ireland oppressed?) the world over. But it must be remembered that they are liable to be led astray by unprincipled politicians, by time-serving leaders, and by designing priests. We must be more active to disseminate light and truth among them, and to let them have a copy of the Address, every man for himself. They have come to this fair land to escape from the chains of British tyranny; and now, will they, dare they, in their turn become the worst of oppressors, by helping to prop up the diabolical system of American slavery? Such apostacy is not to be tolerated as possible, even in imagination, for one moment. Let no Irishman claim to be the friend of O'Connell or of Ireland, who is not an abolitionist. If such there be, Ireland and O'Connell will indignantly disown him. The man who shouts for 'Repeal,' and yet is willing to shake hands with the southern slaveholders, is a loathsome hypocrite, and stands unmasked in his true character before an impartial universe. As an abolitionist — as a friend of justice — as a man and a christian — I am for the repeal of the union between England and Ireland, because it is not founded in equity, because it is not a blessing, but a visible curse to the Emerald Isle, and because eight millions of people are abundantly able to govern themselves, without the *ruinous aid* of 'foreign interference.' On the same ground, and for the same reason, I am for the repeal of the union between the North and the South — *alias,* between LIBERTY and SLAVERY — which is incomparably more unequal, more profligate, more intolerable, and more blighting, than that which ostensibly exists on the other side of the Atlantic. In both cases, IMMEDIATE AND UNCONDITIONAL EMANCIPATION will be the cry and the watchword of every consistent lover of Liberty.

Rely upon it, there is a stupendous conspiracy going on in the land. What means this sudden interest of the slave plunderers in the cause of Irish Repeal? They are shouting at the top of their lungs in favor of 'Repeal,' as though there was nothing in the world so abhorrent to their minds as oppression! When the wolf attempts to put on the aspect of the lamb, beware! Again, what means this sudden regard for the sacredness of 'southern institutions,' on the part of the leading Irish declaimers at the Repeal meetings at the South, and in other parts of the country? I will tell you. The game is this: 'You tickle me, and I will tickle you!' In other words, the bargain obviously is, (and you will shortly see it demonstrated in the Liberator,) that the South shall go for Repeal, and the Irish, as a body, shall go for southern slavery! — Here is a 'union,' most unnatural and horrible! [4] I most firmly believe that such an agreement has been entered into by the selfish Repeal demagogues at the North, and the mercenary slave-drivers at the South. And will our hard-working, liberty-loving, Irish fellow-countrymen allow themselves to be bought for such a purpose, and at such a price? Heaven forbid! What! they to be made the body guard of the infernal slave system! Do they not know that O'Connell refuses to shake hands with an American slaveholder, and ranks no man as true to liberty who is not an abolitionist?

Let your 'Tocsin' ring out its loudest notes of alarm, and summon a mighty gathering of free spirits in April.

Yours for the repeal of the union between freedom and despotism, the world over.

WM. LLOYD GARRISON.

Printed: *The Liberator*, April 8, 1842.

Abel Brown (1810–1844), a clergyman, was one of the founders of the Eastern New York Anti-Slavery Society and the publisher of the *Tocsin of Liberty*. (C[atherine]. S. Brown, *Memoir of Rev. Abel Brown, by His Companion*, Worcester, Mass., 1849).

1. The convention to which Charles L. Remond was to bring the Irish Address was for the purpose of founding the Eastern New York Anti-Slavery Society (see *The Liberator*, April 15, 1842). Among the most famous "bastard Irishmen" to doubt the authenticity of the Irish Address was Bishop John J. Hughes of New York (1797–1864); he urged the Irish to repudiate the address even if it did prove to be genuine (see his letter to the New York *Courier and Enquirer* as reprinted in *The Liberator*, March 25, 1842). A so-called Irish organization which also challenged the authenticity of the document was the Baltimore Repeal Association (see *The Liberator*, April 22, 1842).

2. Thomas Moore, "Remember Thee," stanza 2, line 2.

3. Although the passage in quotation marks has not been specifically identified, it follows a series of allusions to Milton's *Paradise Lost*, IV, 788–814.

4. Articles relevant to the South's attitude toward Irish Repeal appeared in *The Liberator*, March 25 and April 1, 1842.

27

TO SARAH M. DOUGLASS

Boston, March 18, 1842.

My dear Friend,

I hear that your beloved Mother is now an angel in heaven! [1] Are you in tears? Then it is on account of *your* loss, and not because *she* has not gained immensely by the transition from this to "another and a better world." [2] My tears shall mingle with yours; but we will not sorrow as do those who are without hope. Our hope is in God, and therefore it is sure and steadfast. Death is not a calamity to the righteous, it is not even a trial. Jesus, the Conqueror, has plucked its sting, and robbed the Grave of its victory.[3] What is mortal, must necessarily obey the laws of mortality. If from the dust the body was taken, why should we marvel, or grow morbid in our minds, when the dust receives its own? [4] The sun rises and sets — day and night succeed each other — spring and summer, autumn and winter, are regular in their season. These are common events; but are they more common, or more natural, than the decay of our mortal bodies? Yet somehow or other, the occurrence of death seems almost always untimely — strange — unnatural. And yet, who would desire to live in the flesh time without end? It is the will of God that we should die, and it is of very little importance whether we be called away early or late, if we can at all times heartily say, "Thy will, O God, be done." [5] It is enough that decay can never blight the spiritual flower; that the soul is stamped with immortality; that Christ is the Resurrection and the life; [6] and that the rest prepared for the righteous is eternal.

I should be glad to hear more of the particulars of your Mother's death. What was the nature of her illness? did she retain her senses to the last? I will not inquire as to her readiness to depart, for I feel assured that it was only for her to know the will of her Creator, cheerfully to submit to it. How vividly are her features impressed upon my memory! How pleasant was the smile that she habitually wore! how musical her voice! how gentle and Christ like her spirit! how keen and exquisite her susceptibilities of mind! It always refreshed my spirit to visit your house, and enter into conversation with her; and never shall I forget how cordial was the greeting on her part, on every such occasion. Should I be permitted to visit Philadelphia again, I shall undoubtedly realize her loss much more sensibly than I can do at present. I hope that your dear Father sustains his great bereavement with christian resignation and fortitude.[7] I entertain a high respect for him, and desire you to give him my warmest sympathies and my best regards. Whether we meet again on earth, or not, let us all be, "Dressed for the flight, and ready to be gone." [8] How is your own health? Are you still residing under the family roof? Is teaching still your vocation? What has been Robert's success, since his return from Europe? [9] Does he contemplate pursuing his profession in Philadelphia? Do you perceive any change for the better, in your city, on the score of prejudice? Has the union of the Freeman with the Standard increased the anti-slavery spirit among you? [10] Our venerable friend James Forten has also paid the debt of nature.[11] When I was in Philadelphia the last time, he was complaining of ill health; but I did not then suppose that I should behold him no more on earth. But who can tell what a day or an hour may bring forth? He was a man of rare qualities, and worthy to be held in veneration to the end of time. He was remarkable for his virtues, his self respect, his catholic temper, his christian urbanity. An example like his is of inestimable value, especially in the mighty struggle now taking place between liberty and slavery — reason and prejudice. It is pleasing to know that he met death calmly and happily. I hear that, almost in the hour of dissolution, he desired to be cordially remembered to me, and other abolition friends. This fact deeply affects me and animates my heart.

You have now in Philadelphia, our mutually beloved friend Henry C. Wright. The world hates him, because he is not of the world. He is one of the most indefatigable and enlightened reformers that have ever suffered in the cause of righteousness. Yet how much is he slandered, how widely contemed, how basely misrepresented! May his health, strength, and life long be precious in the sight of the Lord!

If you should [chance] [12] to see Dr. Moore and wife, James Mott and wife [Lucretia], Mrs. Forten and family, and other dear and well known friends of mine, please remember me to them individually with great affection.[13]

I remain yours in the bonds of christian sympathy,

Wm. Lloyd Garrison.

Handwritten transcription: Garrison Papers, Boston Public Library.

Sarah Mapps (sometimes spelled Mappes) Douglass (1806–1882), from a prosperous Philadelphia Negro Quaker family, taught for many years and eventually took charge of the Preparatory Department of the Institute for Colored Youth, where she lectured on physiology and hygiene. (Anna Bustill Smith, "The Bustill Family," *Journal of Negro History*, 10:638–644, October 1925.)

1. Grace Bustill Douglass (died 1842), the daughter of Cyrus Bustill, kept a millinery store on Arch Street in Philadelphia. (Smith, "The Bustill Family.")

2. August F. F. von Kotzebue, *The Stranger*, I, i.

3. Garrison alludes to I Corinthians 15:55.

4. Garrison alludes to Genesis 3:19.

5. Possibly Garrison adapts Matthew 6:10.

6. John 11:25.

7. Robert M. J. Douglass, hairdresser, is described in the Anna Bustill Smith article cited above (p. 643) as "a highly respected, scholarly, Christian man."

8. Not identified.

9. Robert M. J. Douglass, Jr. (1809–1887), was a portrait painter who had studied in various art academies at home and abroad, as well as with Thomas Sully. He was to acquire a studio on Seventh Street in Philadelphia, where, in addition to painting he made daguerreotypes, taught shorthand, and even gave lessons in French and Spanish. (Smith, "The Bustill Family.")

10. In fact, Garrison refers not to the merger of two papers but to the suspension of the *Pennsylvania Freeman* (official organ of the Eastern Pennsylvania Anti-Slavery Society) and the transfer of a thousand subscriptions from that paper to the *National Anti-Slavery Standard*.

The *Standard* had been founded in 1840 at the time the Garrisonians gained control of the American Anti-Slavery Society as the official organ of that society. Sustained at first largely through the efforts of Mrs. Chapman and then through funds raised at the antislavery fairs, it had a succession of editors and co-editors from Oliver Johnson to Lydia Maria Child, to David Lee Child, and ultimately to Sydney Howard Gay, assisted by Mrs. Chapman and Edmund Quincy. Although the *Standard* never had the stability of *The Liberator* and many members of the national society preferred the latter, the *Standard* did in fact survive Garrison's paper, since it was still being published separately in 1870 when it was merged into the *National Temperance Advocate*, later the *National Advocate*. (*ULN*; *Life*, II, 359–360.)

11. James Forten (1766–1842), father-in-law of Robert Purvis, was a wealthy and highly respected Negro leader in Philadelphia. Garrison held him in high esteem, and Forten's opinions of the American Colonization Society had influenced his own. Notice of Forten's death was printed in *The Liberator*, March 11, 1842. It was said that thousands of people attended his funeral.

12. An emendation inserted in brackets above the line, apparently by Wendell Phillips Garrison.

13. Robert Moore (c. 1763–1844) was a Philadelphia Quaker physician and close friend of the Motts. His wife, Esther (c. 1774–1854), was especially active in the antislavery and woman's rights movements. (Philadelphia city directories; *Life*; and obituary, *Pennsylvania Freeman*, January 2, 1845.)

James Mott (1788–1868), husband of Lucretia Coffin Mott, was a birthright Quaker and, since 1827, a member of the liberal Hicksite branch. Although moderately successful in the wool business, he was dedicated primarily to reform. He was a founder of the American Anti-Slavery Society in Philadelphia in 1833, a delegate to the World's Anti-Slavery Convention in London in 1840, and, throughout the 1840's, an advocate of woman's rights.

28

TO GEORGE W. BENSON

Boston, March 22, 1842.

Dear George:

As Sarah and Helen have written letters to dear Anne, (whose health we are glad to hear is improving,) I presume they have written somewhat minutely, in regard to all domestic affairs; and I will not, therefore, travel over the same ground. As for young Thurber, I have failed to see him personally, but left your letter, to-day, in the hands of his wife.[1] I shall probably either see or hear from him to-morrow. His wife says she is much attached to Boston; and though willing to go to Northampton, if they can thus better their condition, yet I think it rather doubtful about their going, especially if his prospects here shall brighten as the spring opens. But you shall be informed of his decision, as soon as it is made up.

If all be well, (and, so mutable are all things here below, we can promise nothing as to the future without prefixing an *if*,) I shall go to Albany about the 21st of April, in company with C. L. Remond, to attend an anti-slavery convention which our friends intend to get up in that city, with special reference to the Irish Address. We shall carry that Address along with us. There is a pretty large Irish population in Albany, and an Irish Repeal Association;[2] but the Argus has had the effrontery and folly to deny the authenticity of the Address, and, of course, a meeting called with especial reference to it will be pretty sure to be well attended, and to create a wholesome excitement.[3] In going or returning, I shall endeavor to visit Northampton, (most probably on returning,) and, if practicable, make Remond accompany me. I intend, if I can, to add Wendell Phillips to our company. So, you may make your arrangements, at your leisure, for at least one "incendiary" meeting in your place.

Do not forget to suggest to my friend [David L.] Child, the importance of preparing, without delay, a stirring Address to the friends of the American Anti-Slavery Society, urging them to take prompt and effectual measures to insure a full attendance at the approaching anniversary, from all parts of the free States; and setting forth, in strong terms, the necessity of a large representation, on the occasion.[4] For my own part, I avow myself to be both an Irish Repealer and an American Repealer. I go for the repeal of the union between England and Ireland, and for the repeal of the union between the North and the South. We must dissolve all connexion with those murderers of fathers, and murderers of mothers, and murderers of liberty, and traffickers in human flesh, and blasphemers against the Almighty, at the South. What have we in common with them? What have we gained, what have we not lost, by our alliance with them? Are not their principles, their pursuits, their policies, their interests, their designs, their feelings, utterly diverse from ours? Why, then, be subject to their dominion? Why not have the Union dissolved in form, as it is in fact — especially, if the form gives ample protection to the slave system, by securing for it all the physical force of the North? It is not treason against the cause of liberty to cry, "Down with every slaveholding Union!" Therefore, I raise that cry! And, O, that I had a voice louder than a thousand thunders, that it might shake the land, and electrify the dead — the dead in sin, I mean — those slain by the hand of slavery.

How marvellously Providence works! The Irish Address, I trust, is to be the means of breaking up a stupendous conspiracy, which I believe is going on between the leading Irish demagogues, the leading pseudo democrats, and the southern slaveholders. Mark three things. First — The Irish population among us is nearly all "democratic." Second — The democratic party is openly and avowedly the defender and upholder of the "peculiar institution" of slavery. Third — The cry in favor of Irish Repeal is now raised extensively throughout the South, and sustained by the leading democratic journals, — and why? To secure the aid of the Irish voters on the side of slavery, and to bring their united strength to bear against the anti-slavery enterprise! Also, if possible, by sending over donations to Ireland, to stop [Daniel] O'Connell's mouth on the subject of slavery, and to prevent any more "interference," on that point, from that side of the Atlantic! Hence, I observe, at the Repeal meetings, in various parts of the country, resolutions and declarations which amount to sacred pledges, that those "repealers" will stand by southern institutions, at all hazards! Now, by the Address, which will cause every toad to start up into a devil as soon as he is touched, we shall be able to probe this matter to the bottom. If O'Connell and our friends in Ireland remain true to us, and renew their spirited attacks upon American slavery, and cry out against this unholy and frightful league between southern slave-drivers and his countrymen in America, then it will put down at the South this pretended sympathy for Ireland, and be the means of advancing our movement still more rapidly.

In this week's Liberator, I shall publish copious extracts from O'Connell's speeches, for the last ten years, against American slavery.[5] They will scathe like lightning, and smite like thunderbolts. No man, in the wide world, has spoken so strongly against the soul-drivers of this land as O'Connell.

Is it not heart-cheering to know that the British government will not give up the slaves of the Creole?[6]

I trust all your hopes will be realized, in regard to your undertaking. Look well to the present, and the future will take care of itself.

For a few days past, I have been somewhat feverish, and do not feel in a very good condition now.

Remember me with a brother's affection to Anne and Catherine, and give my friendly remembrances to Wm. Adam, D. L. Child, &c.

Yours, faithfully,

Wm. Lloyd Garrison.

ALS: Garrison Papers, Boston Public Library; extract printed in *Life*, III, 49–51.

1. George Thurber (1821–1890), a cousin of George W. Benson, was a well known botanist, who was forced to resign his post in the New York Assay Office in 1856 because of his abolitionist views. He served as editor of the *American Agriculturist* from 1863 to 1885.

2. A reference to the associations organized in the United States during the 1840's to send money and moral support to the parent organization in Dublin headed by Daniel O'Connell.

3. Garrison did not reprint the Albany *Argus* article but alluded to it briefly in *The Liberator*, March 25, 1842. The *Argus* was founded in 1826 and survived, with various changes of title, until 1920. (*ULN.*)

4. A call for the anniversary meeting, reprinted from the *National Anti-Slavery Standard*, appeared in *The Liberator*, April 29, 1842.

5. Extracts from O'Connell's speeches were printed in *The Liberator*, March 25, 1842.

6. On November 7, 1841, the slaves on board the brig *Creole*, bound from Norfolk to New Orleans, revolted. The ship sailed for Nassau, where the leaders of the uprising were held for mutiny and murder. Eventually they were released, the British government having refused to extradite them or to indemnify their owners. Articles pertaining to the *Creole* case were printed in *The Liberator*, December 24 and 31, 1841, and March 4, 11, and 18, 1842. There was agitation, especially in the South, suggesting that the United States declare war on England over the case.

2 9

TO EDMUND QUINCY

Boston, April 4, 1842.⎫
Monday Evening. ⎭

My dear Quincy:

I have seen George Bradburn, and received your note, with regard to my lecturing in Dedham, on Fast (alias *Farce*) Day evening.[1] You seem to be anxious that I should come, and I am as anxious at all times to oblige you; but such is the present condition of my head, (and what can I do without a clear head on that occasion?) that I think it would really be hazardous to call a meeting on the strength of my coming. Within the past fortnight, I have been severely afflicted and tormented with an inflammation in my head, (I am generally regarded as *hot-headed*, you know, but this is something superadded to my burning "fanaticism,") arising from the gathering of ulcers in my ears, of a malignant type. My distress has been, at times, very great; and the nature and *location* of the disease have been such as almost wholly to incapacitate me from attending to any business. At the present hour, the inflammation has very much subsided, but the radical cause of the difficulty remains apparently untouched. I have almost wholly lost the power of hearing on one side of my head, and am somewhat apprehensive that it may be a permanent loss. I take no pleasure in conversation, in consequence of this infirmity, and should feel very oddly to address an audience. Under these circumstances, I confess, it would be more agreeable to my feelings not to be necessitated to visit Dedham on Thursday next.

Besides, in reflecting upon the matter, I am led to think that, even were I in good mental and bodily condition, it would be better to have a meeting on some other occasion.

In the first place, "the game is not worth the candle." [2] For me to go to Dedham to hear Dr. Burgess preach on the subject of slavery, and then to go into a public examination of his sentiments, (or for any other prominent anti-slavery lecturer to do so,) would seem to argue that the Dr. is a formidable opponent.[3] This is what I mean about "the game," &c.

Secondly, it has been whispered about, probably, that I intend to review Dr. B's sermon; and although this fact might and probably would induce people to attend, yet it would excite local prejudices, and perhaps be regarded as a personal attack, with personal motives,

&c. &c. I do not think it would present the best opportunity to be *impartially* heard in behalf of the slave.

Thirdly, it will be difficult to conceal the fact from Dr. Burgess, as to the object of my visiting Dedham at such a time, to hear him preach on the subject of slavery; and he may thus be induced, by a clerical *ruse*, to shape his discourse so as to present as few objectionable points as possible, and yet not commit him to the abolition side of the question. I would rather let him speak out his mind freely, with no "foreign influence" to bias his mind; at the same time, let there be "a chill" among the congregation — Edmund Quincy, for instance — taking notes, to be used as may seem expedient hereafter.

Lastly, you have just had two lectures from Bradburn, which might suffice *pro tempore.*

This is my present condition, and these are my present feelings. Bro. [John A.] Collins says he entertained the same views when the plan was first proposed, though he afterwards consented to waive them. It would be all-sufficient to state, that, in consequence of my ill-health, the lecture would be postponed until a future occasion.

If, notwithstanding all this, you find that you must hold your meeting, then, I can only say, I will come, and do the best that I can, with an utterly unprepared mind, and a body, or rather head, ill at ease. But spare me this task, if possible. I submit the whole to your friendship and judgment. Let me hear from you by Wednesday evening.

Bro. Collins has been confined to his house for a few days past, (most of the time to his bed,) by an attack of pleurisy. He is better to-day, though not able to go out. Unless he is careful, he will make himself a sick man for some time to come.

We are to have two public meetings, this week, in the Marlboro' Chapel, (on Wednesday and Thursday evenings,) to be adressed by Bradburn and [Wendell] Phillips.[4] Should my lecture at Dedham be given up, I think you had better come to the city on Thursday evening, and participate in the proceedings.

Great events are succeeding each other with such rapidity, that the mind is almost overpowered. It seems, after all, that the invasion of Texas by the Mexicans turns out to be a small affair; but it will prove large enough in the sequel, and greatly to the detriment of Mexico, I fear.[5]

Your faithful friend,

Wm. Lloyd Garrison.

P.S. I was sorry not to be able to attend the "Bible Convention."[6] "The spirit was willing, but the flesh was weak."[7] It appears to have been a failure.

ALS: Special Collections, University of Arizona Library.

1. The fast and thanksgiving days of early New England had their roots in religious practices brought from England. By the beginning of the nineteenth century, all the New England states except Rhode Island were keeping annual spring fasts during the month of April. The date in Massachusetts, officially recognized and proclaimed by the governor, was usually the first Thursday.

2. Montaigne, *Essays*, Book II, chapter xvii.

3. George Burgess (1809–1866), at this time rector of Christ Church (Episcopal), Hartford, was to become bishop of Maine in 1847.

4. Marlboro Chapel (seating 1,800 people) was erected in 1836 for a group known as the "First Free Congregational Church"; it was located at the rear of the Marlboro Hotel, 229 Washington Street. (Boston city directory, 1837; *Bowen's Picture of Boston*, Boston, 1838.)

5. In *The Liberator*, April 1, a report was printed that Texas had been invaded and San Antonio captured. Such exaggerated accounts of the fighting in Mexico were commonplace. An article in *The Liberator*, May 6, dismissed the earlier report as "veriest humbug," the invading army being only a few hundred marauders on the frontiers.

6. The "Bible Convention," organized by Ralph Waldo Emerson, Bronson Alcott, Maria Weston Chapman, and Edmund Quincy to debate whether the Bible had divine authority, was held on March 29 at the Masonic Temple in Boston. (*The Liberator*, January 21, 1842.)

7. Garrison adapts Matthew 26:41.

---

3 0

TO GEORGE W. BENSON

Cambridgeport, April 11, 1842.

My dear George:

I avail myself of the opportunity, by Mr. Silloway,[1] who intends leaving in the morning for Northampton, to send you a few hasty lines; hoping that you will allow us to hear from you at your earliest convenience.

Your cousin [George] Thurber has called repeatedly to inquire, whether I had received any intelligence from you, relative to his going to N.;[2] and great has been his perplexity of mind, in consequence of your silence. After you wrote to have him come up, he was willing to do so, without any delay, provided he could obtain a loan to settle various petty debts, and to enable him to get to N. with his family, and such furniture as would be both convenient and necessary for them to have on their arrival. This would require about thirty dollars. Unless such an arrangement could be made, he did not feel as if he could consent to leave Boston, in debt. I gave him encouragement to believe, (from what passed between us in regard to his pecuniary situation when you were here,) that you would be able to make the necessary arrangement, though I told him how sorely you and your associates were tried, at the present time, for funds. I wrote to you immediately by mail, respecting the predicament in which he was placed, but have received no tidings from you; which has led me to suppose that you have been absent from home, or too unwell to write. Since he made up his mind to be with you, he has had, and *refused*, two good offers of employment during the spring and summer; and it will, therefore, be a severe disappointment to him, in case he fails of going to N. What makes it more perplexing to him is, he has been compelled to break up house-keeping, as the house that he occupied has been let to another person; and, of course, he does not wish to hire another dwelling, while this negociation is pending. His wife is at present with her sister in East Boston, and as he dare not seek permanent employment, he is now doing little or nothing from day to day. The owner of the house which he formerly occupied, he says, has offered to loan him the thirty dollars, if he will let him have his furniture as security; the said furniture to be forfeited, if the money be not returned within two months. But Thurber is apprehensive that the man is not trustworthy, and that, if he should take the loan, he shall be put to much trouble and difficulty in getting back his furniture, which, of course, is worth a great deal more than that amount, and which he does not wish to sacrifice at auction. He therefore still waits to hear from you, with much anxiety. If I had the money, I would loan it to him at once; but it happens that I am peculiarly straitened at this moment, especially in consequence of having accommodated two friends (before I knew how it would be with Thurber,) to the amount of fifty-five dollars, who will not be able to repay me for at least a month to come. The loan that he needs is not large in itself; and yet it is large in a case where funds are so important in the commencement of an enterprise like yours at N. If you cannot let him have it now, it will greatly relieve his mind to hear from you.

I have been thinking of attending a meeting at Albany, on the 20th and 21st inst.; but, in the last Liberator, (as you probably saw,) I intimated that I should not go, as I presumed from the call it was to be a Liberty Party Convention.[3] Within a day or two, however, I have received a letter from the Editor of the Albany Tocsin, in which he says I have misapprehended the grand object of the meeting, which is, to organize an "Eastern N.Y. Anti-Slavery Society," on the old organization basis, so far at least as the equal rights of men and women are concerned. With this explanation and assurance, I have concluded to change my mind, and to go to Albany next week. Whether Remond will be able to accompany me, or not, I do not yet know.[4] I shall calculate to visit you on my return, so as to be with you a week from next Saturday, and remain until Monday. Should any thing occur to break this arrangement, you shall be apprised of it without delay. Should I visit N., I should not object to having a meeting on Saturday, and also on Sunday evening, if it should be deemed best. But you had better wait until you hear from me again.

I have not been well for a fortnight past. My old scrofulous complaint in the head has returned, and raged with great violence, causing me much suffering, and making mental effort extremely irksome. Willie is quite sick with a fever — probably the scarlet fever, though of this I am not yet certain. I have given him three moderate courses,[5] — not without benefit, — but he is still a sick child. Should he continue to linger, I think of consulting Dr. Wright.[6] Bro. James is about as usual — sometimes quite feeble, and anon cheerful and active.

The mission of bro. H. C. Wright, I fear, will fail for the want of funds.[7]

Love to your wife, and a kiss for each of the children.

Your loving brother,

Wm. Lloyd Garrison.

ALS: Garrison Papers, Boston Public Library.

1. Probably a misspelling of the name Jason H. Sulloway from Canton, Connecticut, who was after April 17, 1842, a member of the Northampton Association of Education and Industry. (Sheffeld, p. 104.)

2. Northampton, that is, the Northampton Association.

3. Garrison refers to the issue of April 8. He opposed the Liberty party (founded in New York state in 1840) on the grounds that abolition was a moral issue and that abolitionists could not conscientiously seek their goal by voting for third-party candidates within a system organized under a pro-slavery Constitution.

4. In *The Liberator*, April 15, Garrison corrected his impression that the Albany meeting would be a Liberty party convention and announced his intention, health permitting, to attend. An account of that meeting, however, does not mention Garrison as being present, though Charles L. Remond did attend (see C[atherine] S. Brown, *Memoir of Rev. Abel Brown, by His Companion*, Worcester, Mass., 1849, p. 115).

5. Thomsonian courses.

6. John Harvey Wright (1815–1879) received an A.B. degree from Amherst College in 1834 and his M.D. from Harvard in 1838. He was admitted to the Massachusetts Medical Society in 1837. (Letter to the editor from Jonathan Prude, researcher, September 1970.)

7. In *The Liberator*, March 25, Garrison had announced the intention of the New England Non-Resistance Society to send Henry C. Wright on a mission to England and Ireland in the cause of nonresistance, abolition, and other reforms. An urgent appeal was made for funds so that Wright could leave in two or three weeks. Contributions were slow in coming, however, and Wright did not leave until September. He remained abroad until 1847.

3 1

TO HENRY C. WRIGHT

Boston, April 12, 1842.

Dear bro. Wright:

Our application for funds to meet the expenses of your visit to England does not, as yet, meet with that success which is desirable. Only about fifty or sixty dollars have been subscribed: of this sum, $20 by John C. Gore, of Roxbury, and $5 by Alfred Wells, of Western New-York, who has also transmitted a lock of his hair as a token of his brotherly regard for you.[1] I wrote to our bro. Couoe, at Portsmouth, for such assistance as he might find it within his ability to afford; but he writes, in reply, that the numerous claims upon him, and the various responsibilities which at this time rest upon him, and the utter prostration of business, (so far as *profits* are concerned,) render it impracticable for him to give any essential aid.[2] He informs me that he intends visiting this city in the course of a few days, when he will call upon me, and talk more about the mission. Some of our friends, I think, are a little selfish. They do not wish to lose you, and argue that you cannot now be spared for a purpose. For my own part, I cannot allow any one of them to surpass me in strong personal attachment to you, and in estimating at a high rate the value of your labors at home; but I think, in this case, my vision is more comprehensive than theirs, and am sure they do not understand how matters and things are, on the other side of the Atlantic, so well as myself. Though there will be some delay in procuring all the funds necessary for your mission, the mission itself must not be given up. You will not be able to arrive in season to attend the London anniversaries,[3] as I at first hoped; but I think you will be aided so as to start immediately after our New-York anniversary,[4] which is rapidly approaching. Great will be the disappointment abroad, if you should fail to cross the Atlantic this spring or summer. Do not, I pray you, give up the hope or intention of going. It will require some little time, of necessity, to hear from our friends in various parts of the country; and as money at the present time is very scarce, the contributions will come in more slowly than they would under more favorable circumstances.

You have probably seen Rogers's characteristic flourish about your mission.[5] He evidently thinks you had better remain here, and then he also thinks it would be well for you to go. You see in what a dilemma your friends are placed; but I think it must be gratifying to you to perceive how highly your labors are appreciated by those whose esteem is worth having.

Has not our excellent friend, Mrs. [David L.] Child, been somewhat over scrupulous, in refusing to publish [6] the resolutions adopted by the Ex. Com. of the Non-Resistance Society, relative to your mission? I confess, I was not a little surprised at her refusal; but, of course, it does not originate in any hostility to your mission, or any want of personal regard for yourself. But I think that, in this instance, she stands up so straight as to lean a little backward.

I can scarcely use my pen, I am so ill. For the last fortnight, I have had a slow fever hanging upon me, which now more distinctly assumes the aspect of scarlet fever, with which George and Willie are now quite ill. Probably other members of the family will yet be brought down by it.

Isaac Knapp has just lost his wife.[7] Poor creature! she has had to encounter many sorrows and trials since she married him, and her future prospects were such as not to render life very desirable.

Bro. Bacon will tell you all the local intelligence that is afloat here.[8] We have heard of the safe arrival of Mr. and Mrs. Chapman at Hayti; but no letters have been received from them.

Wishing to be affectionately remembered to all the members of your family, and to all the other dear friends in P[hiladelphia]. I remain,

Your sick but faithful friend,

Wm. Lloyd Garrison.

ALS: Garrison Papers, Boston Public Library.

1. John C. Gore (1806–1867) contributed money and land to the Massachusetts Anti-Slavery Society for the purpose of building a meeting house. He was a life member of the society and served as vice-president from 1843 to 1852. (*The Liberator*, September 9, 1842, February 2, 1844, February 6, 1852.)

Alfred Wells (1814–1867) was a lawyer who owned the Ithaca *Journal and Advertiser*. He served as a congressman from 1859 to 1861 and held several local offices in western New York. (*Who Was Who in America*.)

2. Samuel Elliott Coues (1797–1867), father of ornithologist Elliott Coues, had many literary and humanitarian interests, including the cause of nonresistance. He became president of the American Peace Society around 1842. In 1853 he moved from Portsmouth, New Hampshire, to Washington, D.C., where he worked in the Patent Office.

3. In May.

4. The ninth annual meeting of the American Anti-Slavery Society in New York, May 10–13, 1842.

5. Garrison refers to Nathaniel P. Rogers' article on Henry C. Wright's mission which appeared in the *Herald of Freedom*, April 1, 1842. Rogers was not so much in favor of Wright's remaining in the United States as Garrison would imply. He wishes the mission well and urges its financial backing. Much of his article excoriates the clergy and churches of England, as well as America, for hypocrisy concerning slavery and peace. Wright's mission, according to Rogers, will reveal unconquerable "moral truth" to the common people and expose "how true the clerical slander is." Garrison did not reprint this article in *The Liberator*.

6. In the *National Anti-Slavery Standard*.

7. Adeline B. Knapp, wife of the former publisher of *The Liberator*, died April 11, 1842. (For her obituary see *The Liberator*, April 15, 1842.)

8. Benjamin C. Bacon (1803–1874) was a founding member of the New England Anti-Slavery Society and was in charge of the books sold at the anti-slavery office in Boston. (*Life.*)

3 2

TO THE EXECUTIVE COMMITTEE OF THE AMERICAN ANTI-SLAVERY SOCIETY

Boston, May 9, 1842.

DEAR FRIENDS: —

After much reflection, I have come to the conclusion not to be present at the annual meeting of the Parent Society, in New-York. The motives which induced me to forego the pleasure of being with you, on that interesting and important occasion, I trust will be accurately understood, and duly appreciated. In a recent number of the Liberator, I ventured to state, (not with the intention of committing the society to any definite course of action, but merely on my own responsibility,) that among the topics that would undoubtedly be presented for discussion at the meeting in New-York, would be the subject of a repeal of the Union between the North and the South — or, in other words, between liberty and slavery — in order that the people of the North might be induced to reflect upon their debasement, guilt, and danger, in continuing in partnership with heaven-daring oppressors, and thus be led to repentance.[1] In behalf of the Society, you have deemed it both necessary and proper, publicly to disclaim any such purpose; and have left the country to infer, not only that no such topic will be introduced, but that its discussion would be foreign to the object of anti-slavery enterprise — that it does not legitimately come within the constitutional sphere of the society. Under these circumstances, I am most anxious that a free and unbiassed opinion should be expressed by the society on this point, and that every appearance of personal anxiety on my part, as to its decision, should be avoided. I am determined not to allow it to be said, that the society was influenced by my presence and activity, to reverse the position of its Executive Committee — to disclaim the disclaimer — and to occupy new and untenable ground, in relation to this great question of repeal. It is for this reason that I remain at home.[2] I think the Executive Committee have seriously erred in judgment, but I do not esteem them any the less, and am as ready to give them my hearty co-operation for the overthrow of slavery, as at any previous period of my life.

A difference of opinion and an abandonment of principle are heaven-wide from each other. Of the latter, I do not believe the committee will ever be guilty. I hope nothing will be done hastily, unkindly, or rashly; and that the blessings of the Almighty will be with you all.

With unabated regard, I remain, yours, to the end of the conflict,

WM. LLOYD GARRISON.

Printed: *The Liberator*, May 27, 1842; reprinted in *Life*, III, 55–56.

The members of the executive committee of the American Anti-Slavery Society were James S. Gibbons, David Lee Child, William P. Powell, Abby H. Gibbons, James Hudson, Roswell Goss, Thomas Van Renselaer, Charles Marriott, Isaac T. Hopper, Lucretia Mott, Lydia Maria Child, and Oliver Johnson. (Of this group only Lucretia Mott, Lydia Maria Child, and David Lee Child have been previously identified.)

James Sloan Gibbons (1810–1892) was a Philadelphia merchant and banker who wrote many articles on banking and finance; he also wrote the memorable Civil War song, "We are coming, Father Abraham, three hundred thousand strong." He was a prominent member of the American Anti-Slavery Society and a strong supporter of the *National Anti-Slavery Standard*, once having mortgaged his furniture to keep the paper from going bankrupt.

William P. Powell was a Negro member of the American Seaman's Friend Society, under whose auspices he kept a temperance "Sailor's Home" at 330 Pearl Street, New York City, where Garrison was to stay in October 1849. An advertisement for the boarding house appeared in *The Liberator*, May 3, 1850. Powell was to visit Great Britain in 1851. (For his letter about that trip see *The Liberator*, February 7, 1851.)

Abigail Hopper Gibbons (1801–1893), wife of James Gibbons, was an abolitionist, philanthropist, and educator, with a special interest in prison reform.

James Hudson has not been identified.

Roswell Goss (c. 1809–1847) had operated the Graham House at 63 Barclay Street, New York, for many years. According to his obituary in *The Liberator*, September 24, 1847, he had been a member of the board of the Massachusetts Anti-Slavery Society when he had lived in Boston, prior to moving to New York.

Thomas Van Renselaer (also spelled Rensalaer and Rennselear) was the proprietor of a restaurant in New York City. By 1839 he was sufficiently prominent in abolition circles to be considered by Gerrit Smith for a mission to Liberia to investigate the conditions of the Negro colony, but supposedly his Garrisonian views on nonresistance and no-government prevented his selection. (See his letter to Garrison, March 24, 1839, in Anti-Slavery Letters to Garrison and Others, Boston Public Library.) For several years (apparently between 1847 and 1850) he edited in New York the *Ram's Horn*, on which at one time it is reported that Frederick Douglass was assistant editor. (*The Liberator*, September 13, 1844, August 20, 1847.)

Charles Marriott (died 1843) was a New York Hicksite Quaker. An advocate of the free produce idea, he also served as a director of the American Anti-Slavery Society. In 1841 Marriott was censured by the Society of Friends, along with Isaac T. Hopper and James S. Gibbons, because of an article in the *National Anti-Slavery Standard*. (Thomas E. Drake, *Quakers and Slavery in America*, New Haven, 1950, pp. 160–162.)

Isaac T. Hopper (1771–1852) was a Quaker abolitionist who was especially active in the Underground Railroad in Philadelphia and in New York. He was also deeply involved in prison reform.

Oliver Johnson (1809–1889), antislavery leader and editor, was an old friend and associate of Garrison's. During his trips to Britain in 1833 and 1840, Garrison had entrusted the editing of *The Liberator* to Johnson. In 1849 Johnson was to become editor of the *Anti-Slavery Bugle* (Salem, Massachusetts) and from 1853 to 1865 he was associate editor of the *National Anti-Slavery Standard*.

1. The article to which Garrison refers appeared in *The Liberator*, April 22, and subsequently in various New York City papers. The resulting publicity caused such a considerable public reaction against the forthcoming anniversary meeting of the American Anti-Slavery Society that the executive committee released to the New York press a circular (reprinted in *The Liberator*, May 6), asserting that disunion was not one of the society's causes and that the agenda for the meeting had not been determined.

2. Although Garrison then decided, in the interest of inviting an appearance of public harmony, not to attend the anniversary meeting, he did not change his own views on disunion.

---

3 3

TO GEORGE W. BENSON

Cambridgeport, May 13, 1842.

Dear George:

You need no assurance from me, that I deeply sympathize with you and Catharine, in the recent bereavement which you have both sustained.[1] The beautiful child upon which your affections were so strongly placed, and which was so full of promise, has been suddenly taken from you, as the flower perishes when plucked from the stem that gave it nourishment. It lies not, however, in the bosom of the earth, but has been transplanted to a heavenly soil, and to a brighter clime. No strange thing has happened unto you; and yet it is an event which greatly tries the soul, and calls for the exercise of faith and resignation in an extraordinary degree. I have no reason to doubt that you have gone through this trial in an exemplary manner, and that in the will of God, your own is swallowed up.

Having had our share of sickness, under our own roof, we know how to feel for you, in having had a similar experience in your own family. While we mingle our sympathies in view of the loss of your babe, we are proportionably glad to hear that the other children are convalescent. May this letter find your entire household in the perfect enjoyment of health.

As Sarah and Helen have written to you and Catharine, I take it for granted that they have stated all the particulars in regard to Anne's illness, and shall not add any thing on this point. Cambridgeport is evidently a place which does not agree with her health, and therefore she will do wisely to spend the summer either at Providence or Northampton.

You will see, by the Liberator of to-day, that I did not go to New-

York, and the reasons why I remained at home. I regretted to be absent from the meeting on account of the stormy aspect of things, created by the diabolism of the New-York daily press; but, in consequence of the peculiar position in which I stood to the Executive Committee, by their unfortunate disclaimer, I deemed it very important that the action of the American Society, at its present anniversary, should be entirely unbiassed by any thing that I might say or do; so that it might appear, beyond all cavil, that the Society marked out its own course, and came to its own conclusions, without any aid from me. I hear that the meetings are proceeding in a very quiet manner, and that none of the sons of Belial have rallied either to molest or make afraid.[2] The great question of a repeal of the Union has been boldly and earnestly discussed; but I do not know how the debate terminated. To-morrow morning, all our Eastern delegates will return — about 250 of whom went on in the Mohegan, via Stonington — and then all the particulars will be made known.[3] I have not at any time supposed that a majority even of old organizationists are prepared openly to go for repeal; for the question is one of recent agitation, and should be carefully examined before a verdict is made up, either *pro* or *con*. Yet I have no doubt whatever, that, in the progress of the discussion, all who mean to be consistent, uncompromising abolitionists will ere long be found on the side of repeal.[4]

As for the disclaimer of our New-York friends, I am sorry it was made; not only as it took a false position, but as it was extended under circumstances that seemed to indicate a lack of self-possession, and an improper dread of mobocratic violence. It was certainly an error of judgment; but how different is this from a dereliction of principle! It need not, and will not, I trust, create any breach of friendship, or lead to personal alienation, in any quarter.

Dr. [Robert] Wesselhoeft fully intended to go to Northampton, in the morning, with Mr. Mack; but the illness of the girl who lives in his family has interposed to baffle his intention.[5] He still hopes to visit you in the course of a fortnight. He will cease to be our neighbor after the next week.

Mr. Mack was enabled to sell only a small portion of his furniture. The company at the auction was v[ery] small, and few seem disposed to buy on any terms.

As you were prevented from going to New-York, I shall cherish the hope of seeing you in Boston at the New-England Convention.[6] By your regard for the cause, you must make an effort to give your attendance on that occasion. Bring with you, if practicable, our able, enlightened and beloved friends D. L. Child, Wm. Adam, and Dr. Hudson — and as many more as you can muster.[7]

It is my intention, should nothing occur to prevent, to visit Northampton toward the last of June, with Helen, and one or two of the children. I wish to be with you when Nature is in her best attire, and exhibits her brightest charms. We will endeavor not to incommode you.

The times are portentous, and what lies before us, who can tell? In storm or sunshine, I remain,

Yours, in brotherly ties,

Wm. Lloyd Garrison.

☞ I got up at early dawn this (Saturday) morning and walked in to Boston to the depot, expecting to find Mr. Mack as Dr. W. said he was in the city, but he did not go from the depot, though he may have taken the cars at Brighton. I had letters to send by him from Sarah, Anne, Helen, and Eliza; but must wait for another opportunity. The throat distemper with which Anne has been attacked, has been very painful and protracted. After a fortnight's dosing, in vain, we called in Dr. [John Harvey] Wright, and he very soon administered relief.

James continues in a feeble state. The fistulous abscess near his lungs will, in all probability, terminate his existence; though he may yet linger for months. How much more cheerfully could I regard his exit from this evil world, if I could see in him a spirit reconciled to God!

I do not see any prospect of our raising money enough to defray bro. [Henry C.] Wright's expenses that must necessarily be incurred by a mission to England. Perhaps it is all for the best; but I relinquish the hope of his going with great reluctance.

ALS: Garrison Papers, Boston Public Library; partly printed in *Life*, III, 54–55.

1. Eliza Davis Benson (born February 1841) had died of scarlet fever.

2. So inflammatory was the subject of repeal of the Union that it was feared rioters might try to break up the meetings.

3. The *Mohegan* of the James Hand line, a brig of 161 tons launched in 1838, sailed along the coast north of Philadelphia. (Carl C. Cutler, *Queens of the Western Ocean*, Annapolis, 1961, p. 540.)

4. The question of repeal of the Union was vigorously debated at the convention for three days. In the end, however, it was decided that no vote should be taken regarding disunion. Thus, the society delayed committing itself on the repeal issue for the current year (see *The Liberator*, May 20, 1842).

5. David Mack (1804–1878) was a Yale graduate and lawyer who had conducted a private school at Cambridge before helping to found the Northampton Association of Education and Industry in 1842. In 1845, after the resignation of William Adam, Mack became head of the association's education department. (Alice Eaton McBee, *From Utopia to Florence*, Northampton, Mass., 1947; see also letter to George W. Benson, July 8, 1842.) Dr. Wesselhoeft's servant has not been identified.

6. The ninth annual New England Anti-Slavery Convention was held May 24–27 at the Chardon-Street Chapel, Boston.

7. Erasmus D. Hudson (1805–1880) supplemented his practice of medicine

by serving the American Anti-Slavery Society as a general agent, 1837–1849. A member of the Northampton community in the 1840's, he moved to New York City in 1850, where he practiced orthopedic surgery.

---

3 4

TO ELIZABETH PEASE

Boston, May 15, 1842.

My very dear friend:

If I am the most neglectful of all your correspondents, I shall ever aim to be the most faithful of all your friends. This may seem paradoxical, though the asserter is full of sincerity and truth.

Two years ago, I was preparing to embark for England, in company with my increasingly beloved friend, N. P. Rogers. Though crowded with delightful incidents and remarkable events, in the aggregate they appear only like two moments — two flashes of thought — two glances of the eye. Thus does the soul assert its immortality, and bid defiance to the lapse of time. It can more easily sustain the weight of an eternity, than the body the wear and tear of a century. But when I closely scan those two years in detail, they seem to embrace a large portion of my existence. Scene after scene rises before my mental vision, with such distinctness and freshness, that I seem to be living in the past, and to have no connection with the present, no interest in the future. I have taken an affectionate farewell of all my American friends — I have given the last look to my native land — I am all afloat on the vast Atlantic, now impeded by protracted calms, now hurrying onward by favoring gales, and anon tempest-shaken — I hail the Irish coast in the distance — I am walking in the streets of commercial Liverpool — I am flying on the wings of steam toward "the capital city of mankind" — I am in the midst of the roar and commotion of London! — But I must pause, or Memory will occupy the remainder of this sheet, large as it is, in recapitulating events which, however deeply interesting to me as reminiscences of the past, are too well known by you to be chronicled in this epistle.

Some time has elapsed since I received a letter from you. You were somewhat ill at that time, and under medical treatment. Although I am deeply your debtor, on the score of epistolary exchanges, yet as you ever esteem it to be more blessed to give than to receive, your silence has led me to fear that you have not yet fully recovered from your sickness. If this be so, I can sympathize with you from experience. Since the new year came in, all the members of my family have been more or less ill. At one time, we were all on the sick list — mother, three sisters, wife, children, our "help," my brother, and myself! The children have had the measles, scarlet fever, coughs, and the usual ills which childhood is "heir to." [1] My wife's eldest sister, Mary Benson, died about the first of February, after a most distressing illness; but happy in her mind as an angel — and all

"Dressed for the flight, and ready to be gone." [2]

She was a member of the orthodox Society of Friends, and greatly beloved by a very large circle of acquaintance. When I first knew her, she was strongly influenced by sectarian prejudices, though her spirit was always lovely; but she gradually rose above the dominion of sect, till she rejoiced in the complete enfranchisement of her soul. Her dying testimonies were precious. My own brother has been an invalid in my house for more than two years past, and is gradually habitancing towards the grave, his disease being incurable. My brother-in-law [George W. Benson] has just lost a beautiful babe [Eliza Davis Benson], fourteen months old, and been otherwise afflicted. These, indeed, are ordinary events; for in what climate is disease not found — in what nation, or among what people, has death ceased to destroy? Our bodies are of the earth, earthy: why should we marvel that the dust returns to dust? [3] It is strange, it is wonderful, that while there is no event more common, none more certain, than death; yet there is none which jars the chords of the soul so rudely, or which takes mankind so completely by surprise. Why is this? Is it because

"All men think all men mortal but themselves"? [4]

This solves the enigma, in part; but it is also owing, doubtless, to the uncertainty of the period when "the inevitable hour" [5] shall transpire. In her apostrophe to Death, Mrs. Hemans thrillingly says —

"We know when moons shall wane;
When summer birds from far shall cross the sea;
When Autumn's hue shall tinge the golden grain; —
But who shall teach us when to look for thee?

Is it when Spring's first gale
Comes forth to whisper where the violets lie?
Is it when roses in our path grow pale?
They have *one* season, *all* are *ours* to die!" [6]

Is this any cause for lamentation? Is it not the merciful arrangement of our Heavenly Father? Do we not look upon the dissolution of our mortal bodies with too much apprehension, as though it were a frightful or an unnatural event? Is not Christianity dishonored by the manner in which death is regarded by many of its professors? Are they not too apt to speak of it as a mysterious dispensation — to hoist black signals of distress for public observation, as though a dreadful calamity had happened — to disfigure their faces, that they may appear unto men to *mourn?* In what sense can a natural event be said to be mysterious, or a dispensation of Divine Providence? Away with all this! "Now is Christ risen from the dead!" Let that be our exultation — our song — our triumph. "O Grave! where is thy victory? O Death! where is thy sting?"⁷ Let us rejoice that we are mortal — that we are not always to be pilgrims and strangers in this sin-blighted world. If the gospel does not make those who truly embrace it stoical, neither does it make them misanthropic. It is the will of God that our bodies should moulder in the dust, and that our souls should live forever. The will of God be done! From the *heart* let us say it.

I have not written to you, nor to any of my friends across the ocean, any thing respecting a petty conspiracy which was made, a short time since, to injure my character, and that of some of the most prominent friends of the anti-slavery cause in this city and vicinity, in connexion with the Liberator; nor would I now go into any explanation of the matter, were it not for the information which has reached me, that Charles Stuart ⁸ (once among my most ardent friends, but now bitterly hostile in spirit, because I cannot see eye to eye with him on the subject of woman's rights, non-resistance, &c. &c.) is industriously engaged in circulating, in various parts of England, copies of a paper issued in this city, (only one number having made its appearance,) entitled "Knapp's Liberator," in order to prove that I am no better than a swindler or a knave! *"Et tu, Brute!"* ⁹ Is it possible that my old friend Stuart can be guilty of this mean and wicked conduct? Have I indeed fallen so low in his estimation, that he regards me as a villain in practice, as well as a heretic in speculation? So it would seem, if what I hear of him be true. For this and for other acts of injustice and unkindness, on his part, toward myself, I make all possible allowance on account of his peculiar temperament, and most cheerfully forgive him, even as I pray to be forgiven by my Father who is in heaven, for all the offences which I have committed against him or my fellow-man, in thought, word or deed.

It is proper, under these circumstances, that you should have at least a brief statement of the facts in the case; especially as my silence in the Liberator, respecting the charges thus brought against me and the Liberator Committee, may have seemed unaccountable to you and others, being ignorant of the reasons for that silence.

I am charged with having defrauded my former partner in business, Isaac Knapp, of his share in the ownership of the Liberator; and Francis Jackson, Ellis Gray Loring, Samuel Philbrick,¹⁰ Edmund Quincy, and William Bassett, (men of the best reputation, and of perfect integrity of character,) with being accomplices in this swindling plot!!

To those who are personally acquainted with the parties implicated, (putting myself out of the question,) this charge is not only monstrous, but ludicrous. Sooner than intentionally to commit a dishonest act, I believe every one of them would rather perish at the stake. In this instance, they have allowed themselves to be libelled with impunity — some, because they are non-resistants, and therefore cannot go to law; others, because they know that no defence is needed from them against such accusers; and all, because they are too elevated in mind to descend to gratify personal selfishness and petty spite by a public conflict. I have been induced to preserve unbroken silence in the Liberator, for two reasons: first, and mainly, out of pity and long-suffering toward my unfortunate and erring friend Knapp; and, secondly, because I knew that he was only a tool in the hands of three obscure, designing individuals, who had their personal ends to gratify, and who were eager to obtain even an infamous notoriety through the columns of the Liberator.

Let me give you the facts in a nut-shell. Mr. Knapp and myself commenced the Liberator in January, 1831, without a single subscriber. For a time, we were partners in business. Our subscription list gradually increased, but the expenses of the paper much exceeded its income; and had it not been for the assistance which was generously afforded us by a few individuals out of their own pockets, we could not have sustained the Liberator a single year. In 1835, the partnership between Mr. Knapp and myself was dissolved; he continuing to be the printer, and I the editor of the paper. Every year, donations to a considerable amount were required to keep the paper in existence; but this pecuniary burden was borne with great cheerfulness by a few personal friends, because they believed that they could not devote their money to a better purpose, and that the downfall of the Liberator would prove a serious injury to the anti-slavery enterprise. Here it is necessary to state, that Mr. Knapp is constitutionally a feeble man, with little or no energy, with no business adaptation, and without any kind of order or method in conducting the affairs of this life. Still, he fancied that he could do business to great advantage, and had a passion to engage in it on a large scale. Besides being very imprudent in printing various anti-slavery works, (which at that early period could be much more easily given away than sold,) on his own responsibility, he subsequently opened an anti-slavery depository in this city, from which he might have obtained a handsome income, if he had been a truly business man; for the sales rapidly increased up to the hour of the unfortunate division in the anti-slavery ranks, and amounted annually to a pretty large sum. Instead of keeping his accounts in regular order, he allowed them to remain in confusion — being, in numerous instances, unable to tell how much he owed others, or how much others were indebted to him. At length, his affairs became desperate; he could not meet his payments; the sight of his creditors, and their continual duns, vexed his spirit, and drove him to despondency; he neglected his business, and in an evil hour secretly resorted to the intoxicating bowl; his temper became soured, his vision obscured, his moral sense injured, and he made himself a burden to our cause, and a prey to self-inflicted misery. Most unfortunately, too, he had the infatuation to marry a young girl — a mere doll, feeble in mind and fond of dress — who was in every respect unfitted to his situation and wants. He seemed to doat upon her very weaknesses, and she was unquestionably very strongly attached to him. Poor afflicted one! Within a short time, she has been called to find a refuge from grief and suffering in the silent tomb.[11] It was a happy release for her. I hope it will not prove detrimental to her bereaved partner. They ought never to have been united together. But "love is blind," it is said — and the adage was exactly verified in this instance.

Many and loud were the complaints of the friends of the Liberator, respecting the indolence of Mr. Knapp, and his inattention to business. At last, those who had generously kept the paper alive by their timely donations, unanimously came to the determination, that they would no longer to contribute of their substance to sustain it, unless an arrangement could be made to relieve it of the needless pecuniary burden which was imposed upon it, in consequence of Mr. K's idleness and dissipation. In the autumn of 1839, meetings were held by those who were most deeply interested in this matter, in Boston, (among whom were Mr. and Mrs. [David Lee] Child, Mr. and Mrs. [Henry G.] Chapman, F. Jackson, E. G. Loring, E. Quincy, W. Bassett, &c.) at which the feelings of the friends of the Liberator were fully and frankly made known, in regard to the connection of Mr. Knapp with the paper. It was ascertained that, by another arrangement, from one thousand to fifteen hundred dollars per annum, which they had long been paying Mr. Knapp to support him in doing nothing, and worse than nothing, could be owed to the anti-slavery cause and to the paper. They were still willing to meet all needful expenses, but not to be defrauded in this manner, from year to year, especially when their kindness was so deplorably perverted. The facts in the case could not be denied. A committee was appointed to confer with Mr. Knapp, in order to effect the desired arrangement in an amicable and equitable manner. This he entered into with much reluctance, of course. As a matter of experiment, it was agreed that he should waive all right and title to any part of the Liberator for the term of two years, — he being paid such remuneration as impartial referees might feel disposed to award. It was further agreed that, during this period, the pecuniary concerns of the paper should be managed by a responsible committee, in whom its friends could feel the utmost confidence; and, consequently, the present committee kindly consented to act in this [c]apacity, to the universal gratification of the frien[ds] of the Liberator. When the question of remuneration was submitted to the referees, (who were all quite friendly to Mr. Knapp,) they summoned a number of practical printers as witnesses to determine the amount that ought to be awarded to Mr. Knapp. On being asked, of what pecuniary value a newspaper could be, which sunk one or two thousand dollars per annum over and above its receipts, they, of course, said, none whatever. Two things were essential to the continuance of the Liberator; first, that I should be connected with it as its editor; and, secondly, that its pecuniary affairs should be so managed as to inspire confidence among its benefactors and friends; and neither of these could be done on the old plan. As a matter of kindness and good will, rather than of equity, the referees decided that I should pay Mr. Knapp $150 — half of it to be paid yearly. This decision was cheerfully met on my part.

To say that I separated from my friend Knapp with great reluctance and pain of mind — that I exerted myself to the utmost to retain him as printer of the Liberator — that I greatly compassionated his forlorn condition, and did every thing in his behalf that friendship and sympathy could suggest — is simply to assert the truth, which all my friends in this quarter know full well. But *the existence of the Liberator depended upon this new arrangement*; and justice to those who had to sustain it required that it should be made.

This arrangement was to expire in two years by its own limitation — that is, on the first day of January, 1842. So economical and excellent has it proved, that, with a much less number of subscribers than the paper had at the time of the transfer, it last year amply defrayed all its expenses from its receipts, instead of taking from the pockets of its friends some $1500 or more in private donations, as it formerly did while in the hands of Mr. Knapp. Can those friends be blamed for being unwilling to squander so large a sum upon idleness and improvidence? And what right had Mr. Knapp to insist upon this exaction, seeing that he was of no benefit to the cause or the paper?

After we separated, I endeavored to stimulate Mr. Knapp to active exertions to retrieve his character, and promised to exert all my influence to aid him, if he would lead a sober and industrious life. I pointed out to him a mode in which I felt certain that he could do well for himself; and I assured him that all my friends were his friends, who would cheerfully contribute to his relief, provided he would only respect himself, and evince a disposition to work for a livelihood. Instead of listening to this advice, or to the friendly suggestions of others, he gave himself up to idleness, the use of strong drink, and even to gambling — often wandering about, not knowing where to find a place of rest at night — leaving his poor wife a prey to grief and shame and making a complete wreck of himself. For a number of weeks, I sheltered him and his wife under my roof — assisted him in other respects — and collected for him between thirty and forty dollars, from a few friends in a distant place; for, kindly disposed as were the anti-slavery friends in this region toward him, it was in vain to solicit aid from them, so long as he gave himself to the intoxicating bowl and the gambling table. You perceive what returns he has made for my kindness; but my heart yearns over him, and I cannot reproach him.

Before the time of the transfer had expired, (some eighteen months,) Mr. Knapp failed in business, and conveyed all the property in his hands to his creditors. He was indebted to them to the amount of several thousand dollars, a very small portion of which was realized by them. Among other things which legally and equitably fell into their hands was his interest in the Liberator, namely, half of the subscription list, as the other half had never been alienated by myself. From that time he had no more claim as a proprietor in the establishment than yourself. No negotiation could be had with him any more than with Prince Albert.[12] The property belonged to his creditors, and it was for them to decide how they would dispose of it.

As the last year was drawing to its close, it was deemed desirable and important by the Liberator Committee, that the former interest of Mr. Knapp in the paper should be purchased of his creditors, or else that some other arrangement should be made which should leave me untrammelled in the management of the Liberator. Accordingly, they deputed Mr. Loring to see the assignee, and to state him the facts in the case, with a view to causing a legal transfer to be made. Mr. Loring discharged this duty most fairly and honorably. He informed the assignee that the property in the paper was only nominal; that it had always been a losing concern; and, therefore, that he could offer for Mr. Knapp's interest in it only a small amount, ($25,) in order to a legal adjustment of the matter.[13] It was further stated to him, that, in case this offer should be refused, I should issue a new paper on the 1st of January, 1842, to be entitled "Garrison's Liberator," which would effectively settle the matter without cost; for it was important, since Mr. Knapp had no longer any direct interest in it, that the control of the paper should be exclusively in my hands. The assignee said he would confer with the creditors. He did so, and they very readily accepted Mr. Loring's offer. The transfer was then made to me in a legal manner; and thus, both legally and morally, all right and title to any part of the subscription list ceased for ever on the part of Mr. Knapp and his creditors. And this is the fraudulent conduct of which the Liberator Committee and myself have been guilty!

Since the fall of 1839, Mr. Knapp has not manifested the slightest interest in the anti-slavery cause, but has done all that he could, in connexion with certain selfish and unprincipled individuals, to injure my character, to destroy confidence in the Massachusetts Anti-Slavery Board, and to alienate the friends of our sacred enterprise from each other. This shows that he has never been an abolitionist from *principle*. This discovery makes my heart ache.

Backed up by three individuals, whom he knew to be deadly hostile to myself, to the Massachusetts A. S. Society, and to the most prominent advocates in our ranks, — upon whose word or bond no reliance could be placed, — and who were selfishly as well as maliciously animated in seeking to restore him to his former situation, — Mr. Knapp endeavored to purchase back his half of the Liberator, and once more to have the exclusive control of the financial concerns of the paper. But the Committee could not consent to make any contract with him; for the reasons which, two years before, had imperatively required that his connexion with the paper should cease, not only remained in full force, but had been strengthened by his subsequent conduct.

☞ If he had been permitted to resume his former position, the Liberator would inevitably have gone down. No confidence was placed in the promises that he made, or in his ability or willingness to labor. As for his backers, they were known to be of a hateful spirit, and personally the determined enemies of the old organization and myself. All of them, like poor Knapp, ("Birds of a feather flock together,") were *out of employment*, and hoped to feather their nest in case he could obtain the control of the paper — one by acting as a travelling agent, another by being the book-keeper, and the third by acting as editor, if they should succeed in inducing me to retire; for, even while he was negotiating with the Committee, Mr. Knapp repeatedly said that the Liberator would do much better without than with me. Thus, "coming events cast their shadows before," [14] and we profited by the warnings thus given. — Now these are the persons who have got out "Knapp's Liberator," (you will observe that Knapp says nothing on his own responsibility, but is a mere tool in their hands,) and filled its columns with the vilest insinuations and the most venomous slanders, in order to prove — first, how shamefully Mr. Knapp has been *swindled* out of his property! — secondly, with what perfect disinterestedness they have acted in this matter!! — and thirdly, how selfish and sordid have been the Liberator Committee and its editor!!! You will not marvel, my dear friend, that we have refused to notice their scurrility, and to dignify them by a personal controversy. No reply was needed in Massachusetts — nor, indeed, in any part of this country. The whole affair has proved an abortion — the vile conspiracy has resulted in nothing but infamy to those who formed it. Now, only to think of the eagerness of Capt. Stuart to blast my moral character by circulating "Knapp's Liberator" abroad! Verily, he knows not what he does.[15]

Your grateful friend,

Wm. Lloyd Garrison.

N.B. You will pardon me for going so fully into these particulars; but I felt it due to you that you should be put in possession of them, in order that you may be enabled to counteract the evil course pursued by Capt. Stuart. If you can, you may let him read this letter, and perhaps he will be induced to atone for his conduct. You may let any other persons read it, who feel any interest in the matter. It is, in itself, a very small affair; but it has been magnified by the malice of enemies, and on that account deserves some notice. One strong reason why I have allowed my still dear but misguided friend Knapp to stab my character with impunity is, an unwillingness to expose his criminal behavior for the last three years before the world, as it is known only to a comparatively small number even of the abolitionists in New-England. I have covered his shame and guilt from the public eye, with the mantle of brotherly kindness and christian charity, and for a time to the injury of my own character. My reward is sure. ☞ The annual meeting of the American A. S. Society has just been held in New-York [16] — and though attempts were made to stir up a mob, every thing went off peaceably and triumphantly. We are all in excellent spirits.

ALS: Garrison Papers, Boston Public Library; partly printed in *Life*, III, 41–42.

　　1. Garrison alludes to Shakespeare, *Hamlet*, III, i, 63.
　　2. Not identified.
　　3. Garrison alludes to I Corinthians 15:47 and to Genesis 3:19.
　　4. Edward Young, *Night Thoughts*, "Night I," line 424.
　　5. Thomas Gray, "Elegy Written in a Country Churchyard," line 35.
　　6. Felicia Dorothea Hemans (1793–1835) was among Garrison's favorite poets. He quotes from her "The Hour of Death," stanzas 6 and 7.
　　7. Garrison quotes I Corinthians 15:20 and adapts I Corinthians 15:55.
　　8. Charles Stuart (1783–1865), a captain retired from the East India Service and a conservative abolitionist. (*Life.*)

9. Shakespeare, *Julius Caesar*, III, i, 77.

10. Samuel Philbrick (1789–1859), formerly a leather merchant and for many years treasurer of the Massachusetts Anti-Slavery Society as well as a generous contributor to that society and to *The Liberator*. (*Weld-Grimké Letters*, I, 400–401, and *Life*.)

11. Adeline B. Knapp had died April 11.

12. Prince-consort of England (1819–1861).

13. Wording thus in manuscript.

14. Thomas Campbell, "Lochiel's Warning," line 56.

15. Garrison alludes to Luke 23:34.

16. May 10–13.

---

3 5

TO NATHANIEL P. ROGERS

Boston, June 7, 1842.

Dear Rogers:

At the time of our late N[ew]. E[ngland]. Convention, a young colored lad [1] came to one of our meetings, in the capacity of a runaway chattel; and as he was anxious to follow the North star even into Canada, (the sun of republican liberty being too brilliant for his weak vision to gaze at,) a collection was taken up for him, amounting to about fourteen dollars, to aid him on his way. In addition to this sum, our colored friends here gave him some six or seven dollars. He was also furnished with a trunk, and a good supply of clothes. He then took his flight for Canada, via Concord, but, to our surprise, found his way back to this city yesterday.

His statement is as follows. On arriving at Concord in the stage, he saw you, from whom he received a note, (which I have now in my possession,) to Denison R. Burnham, of Plymouth, and to Edmund Carleton, of Littleton, soliciting their friendly offices, &c.[2] At dusk, (the first day,) the stage stopped at a tavern, where he tarried over night. The next morning, he resumed his journey in the stage, and continued travelling until dusk; when, on stopping at the tavern, who should open the door of the stage, but his southern master! He was seized by the collar, and hurled by his master violently to the ground, who swore that he would make an example of him on his return to the South. He immediately regained his feet, and ran at the top of his speed near a river, pursued by his master and two or three others, but succeeded in making his escape by plunging into a pine thicket, leaving behind him his trunk, in which he had put his money (some $10 or $12) for safe-keeping, at your suggestion, as well as his clothes. After wandering about for some time, greatly afflicted and dismayed, he got on the right road to Nashua, to which place he travelled, where he got into the cars, and came to this city.

The boy tells his story very artlessly, and appears to be honest and sincere. I do not see what motive he can have to make up such a story, if it be not true. The only part of it that seems to be remarkable is the coincidence of meeting with his master, so far up in New-Hampshire. But, according to the statement of the lad, he is an opulent and very extensive slaveholder, and accustomed every summer to visit the North. Probably he was wending his way to the White Mountains; and he might have been in this city, when the lad made his appearance at our Convention, and so have learnt some thing about his intended flight to Canada. How humiliating it is to think of an innocent fellow-being thus hunted, and worried, and despoiled, on the soil of New-England! — Of what value is the religion or the democracy of the people?

This unfortunate lad will remain with us, until we can ascertain whether he can recover his trunk. — He does not remember the name of the place where he met his master; but it was where the stage was to stop for the night, the second day after he left Concord; and he thinks that the town next beyond it was called Lancaster. You will probably be able to determine this matter without much difficulty. He says that the stage-driver seemed to be the only one who was disposed to befriend him, at the time that he came in contact with his master. Perhaps he had arrived at Littleton, and a line from you to friend Carleton may be the means of our obtaining his trunk and money. The trunk was, I believe, a brown hair one, of an oblong square, with a strap around it. Should it be recovered, it may be forwarded by the first safe conveyance, to the care of Henry W. Williams, 25, Cornhill, Boston.[3]

[George] Bradburn brings a good account of your Concord meetings. He was much pleased with his visit. He says that bro. [Stephen S.] Foster spoke like one of the old prophets, under full inspiration; and the more he becomes acquainted with him, the more he is constrained to esteem and respect him. May Heaven bless and guide the noble abolition band of New-Hampshire, to the end of the conflict!

I am sorry that I saw so little of you and yours, during your late visit to Boston; but I did not think it right to claim a monopoly of your company, when there were so many friends who were so desirous of enjoying it. I did not mean that you should leave the city, without my seeing you again — but so it happened. May we meet again soon, and finally never to part! My affectionate regard to your wife and family.

Ever yours,

Wm. Lloyd Garrison.

ALS: McKim-Garrison Collection, New York Public Library.

1. Not identified.
2. Denison R. Burnham (1799–1876) was the owner of the Pemigewasset Inn in Plymouth, New Hampshire. He served in several sessions of the state legislature and was noted for his kindness to the poor and needy. (Ezra S. Stearns, *History of Plymouth, New Hampshire,* Cambridge, Mass., 1906, I, 434–435.)
    Edmund Carleton (1797–1882), a lawyer, was one of the organizers of the Littleton, New Hampshire, chapter of the American Anti-Slavery Society. His home was a station on the Underground Railroad. (Charles Bell, *The Bench and Bar of New Hampshire,* Boston and New York, 1894.)
3. Henry Willard Williams (1821–1895) was at this time a general agent of *The Liberator.* Later he studied medicine at Harvard (graduating in 1849) and abroad. Settling in Boston, he became a distinguished ophthalmologist.

---

3 6

TO GEORGE BRADBURN

Boston, June 10, 1842.

My dear friend:

At our Board meeting this morning, it was voted that your term of service be extended a fortnight longer from the time of its regular expiration, in order to enable you to attend the meetings on the Cape, if you can make it convenient to do so.[1] If you will come to this city on Wednesday next, you will find a free conveyance to Barnstable in one of the packets on the evening of that day. It is my intention to accompany you. I trust our trip will be a pleasant and a useful one.

With much regard,
    Your faithful coadjutor,

Wm. Lloyd Garrison.

Geo. Bradburn.

ALS: Villard Papers, Harvard College Library.

1. Bradburn had been traveling as a lecturer for the Massachusetts Anti-Slavery Society. His term as lecturer having been extended, he accompanied Garrison to a series of antislavery and nonresistance meetings beginning in Barnstable, Massachusetts, June 16. For lists of the lectures planned see *The Liberator,* April 8, 22, 29, 1842.

---

3 7

TO SAMUEL J. MAY

Boston, June 10, 1842.

Dear bro. May:

Our friend Jairus Lincoln calling at our office this morning, I showed him your letter in regard to the time of holding the annual meeting of the Plymouth Society, at East Abington; when he said it would not answer; but he would see you on the subject, and let me know the result.[1]

We have had a Board meeting this morning, and by their request I would state to you that, early in the fall, we shall be glad to employ you as one of the agents of the Mass. A. S. Society, provided you can make your arrangements at Scituate [2] in a manner satisfactory to yourself, and feel disposed to consecrate yourself to the preaching of anti-slavery doctrines, that the prison-doors may be opened, and the captives set free.[3]

We are all pretty well at home. Our best regards to Mrs. May.

In haste,

Your loving friend,

Wm. Lloyd Garrison.

N.B. You will see, by the Liberator of this day, that a series of meetings on anti-slavery and non-resistance is to commence next week on the Cape. Can you not exchange with bro. Wolcott, and attend some of them? [4]

ALS: Garrison Papers, Boston Public Library.

1. Jairus Lincoln (1794–1882), a Harvard graduate in the class of 1814, was conducting a boarding school for young ladies at his home in Hingham, Massachusetts, during the 1840's. In 1843 he was to publish a book of antislavery melodies. (Letter to the editor from Julian C. Loring, Hingham Historical Society, August 30, 1970.) The annual meeting of the Plymouth County Anti-Slavery Society, of which May was president, was to be held in East Abington, Massachusetts, on June 30.

2. South Scituate, Massachusetts, where May lived.

3. Perhaps a reference to Isaiah 61:1.

4. Perhaps Wolcott is a variant spelling for the name of Robert F. Wallcut; see the letter to Unknown Recipient, June 1, 1846.

---

3 8

TO ELIZABETH PEASE

Boston, July 2, 1842.

Beloved Friend:

Your prompt reply to my last letter was peculiarly gratifying, as it brought me the welcome information of your restoration to health, at least so far as to enable you once more to resume your pen. I had begun to feel quite anxious in regard to your illness, but am now greatly relieved in my mind.

The health of my own family, at the present time, is good, and my own is excellent. My dear Helen fully reciprocates your friendly remembrances, and longs to see and become personally accquainted with you. Your arrival in the United States would be hailed with gladness by thousands of as warm and excellent friends of bleeding humanity, as the world has ever known. When may we hope for that joyous event to transpire? Do not say with O'Connell, that you will not visit us, so long as our soil is polluted by the footprints of a slave; for, by your coming, you will be able to do much to erase those footprints forever.[1] Remember, that a trip in the steamer from Liverpool to Boston is now but a very slight excursion. We shall insist upon your making us a social visit, (Deo volente,) at some future period not very far distant, in company with our mutually beloved friend George Thompson, whose reception would be enthusiastic in the extreme. Dear Thompson can scarcely realize how great is my admiration, how fervent is my love, for him. It is seldom I write to him, but he has an abiding place in my heart; and I trust nothing will ever occur to alienate us from each other. May his strength be equal to his day!

You will perceive what a hornet's nest I have stirred up, by calling for a dissolution of the union between the free and the slave States of this republic. The disclaimer of the Executive Committee of the Parent Society, on this subject, just before the last anniversary in New-York, was a very weak and precipitate affair, and has been condemned by the abolitionists, *nem. con.*[2] It expressed far more than they really intended to convey, and I believe they all heartily regret its publication. It was an error of judgment, committed under circumstances of great peril, and not a compromise of principle. You may be assured, that an issue is fast making up to this effect — Slavery must be abolished, or the Union dissolved. A more atrocious compact was never made since the fall of Adam. Its dissolution is required by every principle of morality, justice, and religion. The agitation of this question is destined to rock the country to its centre, but they who have received a kingdom which cannot be moved have no reason to be afraid. It is only those things which are made, that can be shaken down.[3]

> "His hand the good man fastens on the skies,
> Nor feels earth move, nor heeds its idle whirl." [4]

Happy are they who feel that they stand on the eternal rock, and that their faith has overcome the world.[5] Instead of crying "peace, peace, when there is no peace," [6] they are continually praying that God would "overturn, overturn, and overturn," [7] every portion of Satan's empire. How can the righteous tremble? Is he not as bold as a lion? Is it not the wicked who flee when no man pursueth? [8]

I have not yet thanked you for a little work which you forwarded to me last fall, on the subject of christian perfection, written by a member of the Society of Friends.[9] I have read it with much pleasure. To me, the doctrine is unspeakably precious. -- This world can never be redeemed, until it be received into the hearts, and acted out in the lives, of the professed followers of Christ. But, oh! how it is hated, scoffed at, and rejected as a damnable heresy, by the religious teachers of the day, and by those who are led by these blind guides! [10] There is no practice, however vile — no sin, however impious — which is not now compatible with a christian profession. Slaveholders, warriors, worshippers of mammon, enemies of holiness, are all embraced in the christian fold. No marvel, therefore, that all Christendom is full of selfishness, pollution, oppression, and violence, and ripening for destruction. All this proves that the religion of the day is spurious, and that few are found to believe in Christ. Now the axe must be laid to the root of the tree,[11] and total abstinence from sin and immediate emancipation from the chains of Satan be insisted on as the reasonable duty of every human soul, and as essential to christian character, or in vain will [be] every isolated effort in favor of temperance, abolition, moral reform, political equality, &c. &c. to raise mankind from their fallen condition. If it be true, that he who has not the spirit of Christ is none of his [12] — that there is no condemnation to those who are in Christ Jesus — that they who are born of God cannot do wickedly — that they only are christian, who are dead to sin, and alive to God [13] — then it is certain, that of the millions who profess to have passed from death unto life,[14] scarcely a fraction may be regarded as having a just claim to the title which they assume. While professing to be free, they at the same [time] acknowledge that they are in bondage. They make provision for sin in the flesh, by declaring that none can live without sin. What but unbelief hinders them from exclaiming, "Thanks be to God, who giveth us the victory, through our Lord Jesus Christ"? [15]

Our dear brother, Henry C. Wright, expects to leave for England soon after the 1st of August. We know not how to spare him; but, remembering that the field is the world, and desiring to disseminate the heavenly doctrine of non-resistance abroad as well as at home, we are reconciled to his leaving us for a time. I know you, as well as others, will give him a cordial reception, and gladly use your influence to get him a hearing before the people. I am sure you will admire the simplicity of his manners, the serenity and benevolence of his spirit, the uprightness of his walk and conversation, and the devotion which he manifests to the cause of Christ, in all its branches. His style of preaching is blunt and severe, but calm and affectionate; and in the social circle, he is a delightful companion. His great forte lies in addressing little children, over whom he exerts complete mastery. Place him in the midst of a crowded assembly of children, and he never fails to produce a deep impression upon their minds. Heaven bless his mission.

We are making vigorous efforts to carry on our anti-slavery campaign, and our prospects are daily brightening. But my sheet is full — and so is my heart. Believe me that I am

Your much attached friend,

Wm. Lloyd Garrison.

ALS: Garrison Papers, Boston Public Library; a handwritten transcription of an extract is to be found in the Villard Papers, Harvard College Library.

1. Garrison was present at the meeting in London's Exeter Hall, July 13, 1833, when Daniel O'Connell made the remark referred to here, and O'Connell's speech is reprinted in *The Liberator*, November 23, 1833. O'Connell's precise words were: "I have often longed to go [to America] . . . ; but so long as it is tarnished by slavery, I will never pollute my foot by treading on its shores."

2. *Nemine contradicente*: no one contradicting.

3. Hebrews 12:27–28.

4. Not identified.

5. Garrison alludes to Exodus 33:21 and John 16:33.

6. Jeremiah 6:14.

7. An adaptation of Ezekiel 21:27.

8. Garrison adapts Proverbs 28:1.

9. Not identified.

10. Matthew 23:24.

11. An adaptation of Luke 3:9.

12. Romans 8:9.

13. An adaptation of Romans 6:11.

14. I John 3:14.

15. I Corinthians 15:57.

---

3 9

TO RICHARD ALLEN

Boston, July 2, 1842.

My dear friend Allen:

I am getting into your debt immensely, and what is more, you are so generous that you seem to be determined that I shall not get out of it. You do not hear from me, by way of epistolary interchange, very often; but I hope you take it for granted that I am (what is really the case) very thankful for your numerous favors, and always ready to acknowledge how great a debtor I am to you. Pray, (mark my boldness!) do not be weary in well-doing,[1] but let me hear from you as often as convenient. Your letters are read with interest here, by the friends of all good enterprises, and will prove very serviceable to us in our great struggle against the powers of darkness. It is so difficult, however, to read your handwriting, that I presume you observe many blunders in the printing of your epistles. When you write the names of *persons* and *places*, please be a little more particular in forming your *letters*; for blunders here are very easily made.

I do not wonder that you blush, and hang your head, to see the unkind and insolent reception which the Irish Address has met with, on this side of the Atlantic, at the hands of your exiled countrymen. It is now quite apparent that they will go *en masse* with southern men-stealers, and in opposition to the anti-slavery movement. This will not be done intelligently by them, but they will be effectually controlled by a crafty priesthood and unprincipled political demagogues. When we had our great meeting in Faneuil Hall, we took all parties by surprise. Our Irish fellow-citizens, who were then present, acted out their natural love of liberty, to the life; for, at that time, they had not been instructed how to act by their leaders, and the Pilot and Diary, and other Irish papers here, had not opened their batteries. Since that time, however, they have wholly kept aloof from us, and it is impracticable to get them to listen to us. So much more potent is the influence of American slavery over their minds, than that of Father [Theobald] Mathew and Daniel O'Connell combined!

Let me state one fact, as a sample of many others that might be given. Some time after the Faneuil Hall meeting, we held two public meetings in the Marlboro' Chapel, (a central, popular and spacious building,) which were extensively advertised in our daily papers, and in large placards that were posted around the city.[2] It was announced, that the Irish Address would be presented on those occasions, for the inspection of all persons, and especially that of our Irish fellow-citizens, in order that all doubts in regard to its genuineness might be put at an end. It was also stated that the speakers would be Wendell Phillips and George Bradburn. Where were our Irish friends? They did not show themselves even in the form of a meagre representation, but avoided our meetings as though the pestilence (instead of the Irish Address) were to be uncovered for the destruction of the city! Even to this hour, not a single Irishman has come forward, either publicly or privately, to express his approval of the Address, or to avow his determination to abide by its sentiments. It is horrible to think that so large a mass of your countrymen, who have known what it is to suffer from oppression, and who have torn themselves away from their native shores, in order to find freedom in this land of boasted liberty, should be enlisted in support of the most horrible system of slavery that the earth has ever known.

We are all grieved and astonished to see in what manner these frightful developments are received by Daniel O'Connell.[3] O, how altered are his tone and aspect! But I cannot yet give him up.

I must close abruptly; for the steamer is to start immediately, and I send this hasty scrawl by a private conveyance. Tell dear Richard D. Webb that I have a long letter for him on the stock, and mean to launch it, and send it to Dublin, without delay. My best regards to him, his estimable wife, yours do., James Haughton, all the dear Webbs, my beloved friend [George] Downes, &c. &c.

☞ Our anti-slavery campaign, for the ensuing year, we mean to prosecute with great vigor. The prospect before us is promising. All hearts are full of hope, all hands are strong.

Heaven bless you, dear one, in all your labors of love!

Yours, faithfully,

Wm. Lloyd Garrison.

ALS: Anti-Slavery Society Papers, Rhodes House Library, Oxford University.

1. An allusion either to Galatians 6:9 or II Thessalonians 3:13.
2. The meetings Garrison refers to were held in Marlboro Chapel, April 6 and 7, 1842, and were addressed by George Bradburn and Wendell Phillips. See *The Liberator*, April 15, 1842, for Garrison's immediate reaction to the low attendance. It should be noted, however, that *The Liberator* did not advertise the meetings, except in a small insertion, April 8, the day after the second meeting was held.
3. Garrison's condemnation of O'Connell may be due in part to the latter's accepting aid for the Irish Repeal Association from repeal associations in America which condoned slavery. The controversy over this issue, which arose in the spring of 1842, caused O'Connell to declare that he thought the best policy was to try to convince those Americans who were assisting repeal that slavery was evil, but to do so in a conciliatory manner.

40

TO GEORGE W. BENSON

Boston, July 8, 1842.

Dear bro. George:

The bearer of this, Mr. Wolcott, has been introduced to me, by an esteemed friend, as an individual of amiable disposition and high moral worth — a true abolitionist — and a friend of reform. He has become interested in your social and fraternal community at Northampton, and now visits the place for the purpose of seeing with his own eyes, and hearing with his own ears, and coming to some definite conclusions as to his future course. He is a mechanic, and the more to be respected and appreciated than if he were "a gentleman." I believe it is his wish to connect himself with your association, provided that step[s] can be taken to mutual satisfaction.[1]

It is now uncertain, whether I shall be able to visit your place this summer, as the state of Helen's health will not allow her to accompany me. Our dear mother would be gratified to see you all in N., and would gladly seize the first opportunity to do so, were it not for her reluctance to leave Helen, under present circumstances. Still, it is possible that we may conclude to take a hasty trip to N. in all this month.

Anne has been in Providence, as you are doubtless aware, for some time past. Yesterday, Sarah left us, to spend the remainder of the summer in P. I have no doubt that their health and spirits will be improved by the change, though we are sorry to lose their company. There is no society for them in Cambridgeport.

I saw Dr. [Erasmus] Hudson yesterday morning, on his return from Maine, where he has had some interesting adventures, and made some stir with his anti-slavery "fanaticism," in company with George Foster.[2] He went as far as Bangor. — He left here in the afternoon train of cars for Millbury, in which place he was to have lectured last evening. He showed me a letter from you, in which you requested him to procure a suction breast-pipe. I told him that I would attend to the matter, and will do so without delay. I happened to see, fortunately, a new breast-pipe, which has been recently invented, combining all the good properties of the old, and adding others to them, so as to make it far superior to any thing now in the market. It has the recommendation of Warren, Channing, and other of our eminent physicians.[3] Its cost is $3: — the old one cost $3,50. I have not yet ascertained where it is for sale, or I would forward you one by Mr. Wolcott. I intend to purchase one for my own family use.

How did you spend the 4th? Not in noisy revelry or "patriotic" display, I know. I went to Lowell, and addressed a large, respectable, and most attentive assembly, for the space of two hours, in a beautiful grove: —

"The groves were God's first temples" — [4]

and they are far better places in which to plead for suffering humanity, than any of the "steeple-houses" in the land — provided the weather be favorable. I used the largest liberty of speech, on the occasion, and spoke, I trust, in the spirit and with the earnestness of one who felt that he was bound to "remember them that are in bonds as bound with them." [5] My speech was very favorably received.

You must try to get up a celebration on the first of August.[6] [David L.] Child, [William] Adam, [Erasmus] Hudson, Hill,[7] [Theodore] Scarborough, &c. &c. shame on you, if you fail to remember that day in a manner that will "tell" upon the anti-slavery enterprise! You have got an abundance of materials to work with, and see to it that you astonish and overwhelm the quiet, rest-loving people of Northampton with your glorious rant and revolutionary fanaticism on the birth-day of West-India emancipation.

[John A.] Collins is now acting as General Agent, pro tempore, of the National Society. He will do for it all that zeal, energy, tact, and indomitable perseverance, can accomplish. We are laying our plans to bring on a general engagement with the enemies of liberty, with the least possible delay. Look out for a spirited fall campaign!

What a horrible state of things exists in Rhode-Island! What calamity can be more unendurable to a free people, than to be placed under the absolute despotism of martial law? For that is a law which tramples all civil government into the dust, and repeals all the laws of God. With the Suffrage party, I have very little sympathy, because, while they protest against a land holding aristocracy, they insolently and basely exclude, by their Constitution, all colored citizens from voting at the polls; but I have still less sympathy with the Charter party. They are behaving in a way that will assuredly bring a fearful retribution, ere long.[8]

Mother, Helen, and James, (whose health, I am happy to say, is no worse,) unite with me in wishing to be cordially remembered to Catharine, M. E. Sulloway and husband, &c.[9]

Affectionately yours,

Wm. Lloyd Garrison.

ALS: Garrison Papers, Boston Public Library.

1. Garrison refers to a utopian, joint-stock company, the Northampton Association of Education and Industry, which was established in April 1842, with George W. Benson as a founding member. During the four years of its existence, the community, which owned 470 acres of land near Northampton, including houses, timberland, a saw mill, and a silk factory, had a total membership of approximately 210, from eight states. (Sheffeld.) Although Garrison tended to be indifferent to utopian reform, he was concerned for the welfare of this particular community.

Mr. Wolcott has not been identified.

2. George J. Foster (1810–1876), an attorney, had for a number of years been actively associated with and even employed by the Massachusetts Anti-Slavery Society. (Letter to the editor from Jonathan Prude, researcher, September 1970.)

3. John Collins Warren (1778–1856) was a professor of anatomy and surgery at Harvard Medical School. In 1846 he was to give the first demonstration of surgery on a patient anesthetized with ether. Walter Channing (1786–1876), brother of William Ellery Channing, had been professor of obstetrics at Harvard since 1815 and its dean since 1819. Like Warren, Channing was a pioneer in the use of anesthetics.

4. William Cullen Bryant, "A Forest Hymn," line 1.

5. Hebrews 13:3.

6. The British West Indian slave trade had been abolished in August 1833, the measure passing the House of Commons August 7 and receiving the Royal Assent August 28. It was customary to celebrate the anniversary of the emancipation on August 1.

7. Samuel L. Hill (1806–1882), a native of Rhode Island, had been in the textile business in Willimantic, Connecticut, before becoming one of the organizers of the Northampton Association. After the dissolution of the community, Hill remained in the area, engaging in the manufacture of silk and eventually founding a school named the Hill Institute which is still in operation. He also helped to organize the Free Congregational Society. (Sheffeld.)

8. Garrison refers to the violence in Rhode Island over the framing of a state constitution and the extension of suffrage. At this time the state did not have a constitution, the governor and assembly tracing their authority to the charter granted by Charles II. The charter government, or party as Garrison calls it, limited voting rights to a small percentage of citizens with substantial land holdings.

In 1840 the Rhode Island Suffrage Association was established to press for the extension of franchise (Garrison objected because Negroes were not included). When the assembly refused the association's demands a People's or Suffrage party, as Garrison calls it, was formed, which late in 1841 held its own constitutional convention and organized a statewide election to approve the new constitution.

Although the assembly did not recognize this new constitutional document, it did declare a convention to draft a constitution of its own. But so much sympathy had been engendered for the People's party that the assembly's constitution was defeated. In April 1842 the People's party elected Thomas W. Dorr (1805–1854) governor even though a recent law had declared "illegally" elected officials guilty of treason. Meanwhile, the Whigs had reelected Samuel W. King (1786–1851) governor, and so two separate governments claimed responsibility to rule the state.

In the days following King's inauguration Dorr was in effect the leader of an insurrection, but his forces were so small and badly organized that Governor King easily prevailed by calling out the official militia, declaring martial law, and issuing an order for Dorr's arrest. Dorr fled the state but returned the next year to stand trial, serving one year of a life term before public sympathy forced the legislature to annul his sentence.

9. The marriage of Mary Eliza Pierce to Jason H. Sulloway is recorded in *The Liberator* for June 10, 1842.

41

TO THE EDITOR OF *ZION'S HERALD*

[August 27, 1842.]

SIR —

I am perfectly aware how extremely difficult it is for a priest to be an honest man, in things pertaining to the kingdom of God; for the position which he occupies, being obtained by usurpation, requires the use of cunning and falsehood to sustain it. I am not surprised, therefore, to perceive in the Herald of the 24th ultimo, an editorial article, in which you say, referring to some remarks which I made in the Liberator, respecting the recent Sabbath Convention in Western New-York —

'If this is not infidelity in *spirit* as well as *sentiment*, WE KNOW NOT WHAT IT IS — *infidelity rabid with audacity*. It is precisely in the strain of Tom

Paine and of most kindred minds, who have acquired any note by their spleen against the labors of good men.['] ¹

No man in this country receives more of priestly vituperation, or cares less for it, than myself. It is seldom that I take the trouble to correct any misrepresentation of my views or motives; and I do so in the present instance only because it enables me to present a striking illustration of the absurdity and hollowness of that 'infidel' outcry which is raised against me, as a reformer, by a time-serving and hireling priesthood.

In the first place, I charge you with being most unjust to me, and dishonest toward your readers, in mutilating my article on the New-York Convention, so as to suppress the most important portion of it, on the SCRIPTURAL soundness of which, I felt authorized to make those strong introductory animadversions, which you have copied into the Herald, accompanied with your pious denunciations of me as an infidel of the 'Tom Paine' * school. If I shall say that you did not dare to lay it all before the public, because you were conscious that it could not be refuted, and that it would render ridiculous your accusations against me, I might possibly be mistaken. In order, therefore, to test your courage and fairness on this point, I annex the following extracts, as the remainder of the article which you are pleased to term 'infidelity in spirit as well as sentiment — infidelity rabid with audacity' — and request you to insert it in your columns:

[It is unnecessary to republish the extract here alluded to. It contained my offer of a handsome reward to any person who would prove, from the Bible, the first day of the week to be 'the holy Sabbath' — and also my views of the spiritual nature of the new dispensation.]

Now I call upon your readers to observe, that my rabid and audacious infidelity consists solely in appealing to the SCRIPTURES OF THE OLD AND NEW TESTAMENTS, for the orthodoxy of my sabbatical views, and offering a liberal reward to any person who will show when or where Jehovah, or Christ, or the apostles, enjoined the observance of the first day of the week as 'the holy Sabbath.' Instead of allowing them to become acquainted with this fact, you carefully suppressed it; and instead of paying any attention to my SCRIPTURAL CHALLENGE, you heaped upon me the coarsest anathemas! I am constrained to believe that he who will act thus unfairly and dishonestly, cannot have any true reverence, either for the first day, or any other day of the

* Though Mr. Paine was an infidel, it does not seem to me that christian courtesy will call him by any other than his proper name, though priestly contempt may, for the lack of argument.²

week; or, at least, that he is conscious of his inability to refute my positions by scriptural or rational evidence. If 'the sabbatical observance of the first day of the week is without any foundation in scripture,' then it follows that they are guilty of playing off 'a religious imposture,' who attempt to enforce it upon the people, in the name of the Lord; and that they are 'either groping in legal blindness,' i.e. are under the law, 'or aiming to substitute the form of godliness for the power thereof.' Perhaps you can show, from scripture, that we are under obligation to keep that day as 'the holy Sabbath.' By so doing, you will not only be able to obtain a handsome reward, but also to convict me of setting at nought a sacred command. Will you try? Or will you refuse to publish this communication in the Herald, and again brand me as a rabid and audacious infidel?

In the second place, I charge you with unfairness in hiding from your readers the fact, that my views of the Sabbath are essentially the same as were entertained and avowed by Luther, Melancthon, Tyndale, Calvin, Paley, Foster, Whitby, Roger Williams, Belsham, Priestly, Fox, Penn, Barclay, and other eminent men of various religious denominations.[3] Were those men 'infidels in spirit as well as in sentiment'? Did they write on this subject, 'precisely in the strain of Tom Paine and of most kindred minds'?

In the third place, I charge you with superlative folly and gross slander, in making 'infidelity,' (ay, of the worst kind!) to consist in rejecting YOUR views of the sanctity of the first day of the week! I call such an assumption priestly insolence, and feel authorized, in the spirit of Christian fidelity, to do so. Are the Seventh-day Baptists 'infidels' for observing, as the Sabbath, the day set apart in the fourth commandment? [4] The Society of Friends has always openly repudiated the dogma, that, in the gospel dispensation, one day is more holy than another. Is that a Society of Infidels?

In the fourth place, I charge you with injustice in causing your readers to remain wholly ignorant of the grounds on which I brought my censures against the sabbatical movement in the Western New-York. *You* knew, but *they* did not, that I advocated the consecration not merely of one day in seven, but of all time, to the service and glory of God — a serving in newness of spirit, and not in the oldness of the letter — justification by faith — the liberty wherewith Christ hath made us free. Strange infidelity this! You knew, moreover, that in the very number of the Liberator, in which the sabbatical remarks appeared which have filled you with holy horror, there was an article from my pen in vindication of the doctrine of Christian perfection, — a doctrine which Methodists claim to regard as unspeakably precious.

'The head and front' of my infidelity 'hath this extent — no more.' [5]

I believe that, in Christ Jesus, the believer is dead unto sin, and alive unto God [6] — that whosoever is born of God overcometh the world [7] — that Christ is the end of the law for righteousness, to every one that believeth,[8] and the true Sabbath, of which the Jewish was only typical. I believe that priestcraft, and sectarism, and slavery, and war, and every thing that defileth or maketh a lie,[9] are of the devil, and destined to an eternal overthrow. I remain,

Yours, in perpetual 'infidelity' to the cause of unrighteousness,

WM. LLOYD GARRISON.

Boston, Aug. 27, 1842.

Printed: *The Liberator*, September 9, 1842.

The editor of *Zion's Herald and Wesleyan Journal*, a Methodist paper published in Boston since 1823, was Abel Stevens (1815–1897). Although he called himself an abolitionist, Stevens supported the right of the slaveholders to church membership.

1. The remarks by Garrison to which *Zion's Herald* of August 24 objected consisted of an article, almost one column long, in *The Liberator*, August 19, under the title "Sabbatical Movement." Stevens quotes only a short part of the article, and fails to mention the lengthy section in which Garrison offers a reward of $1,000 to anyone who can prove that there is biblical or apostolic support for Sabbath observance.

Garrison's quotation of the *Herald*'s comments is accurate except for punctuation, especially the addition of italics and small capitals. On September 21 Stevens published a short paragraph acknowledging receipt of Garrison's "furious tirade" and suggested that the rest of the article in *The Liberator* was "but a contrivance to get into our columns futile arguments against the Christian Sabbath." The paragraph indicates that Garrison's letter was never printed and never would be.

2. In 1845, when Garrison read Thomas Paine's religious works, apparently for the first time, he was virtually to reverse this earlier condemnation, impressed as he was by Paine's honesty and insistence on reason as the prime weapon against error.

3. Garrison cites a group of English and Continental religious leaders, reformers, and theological scholars: from Germany, Martin Luther (1483–1546) and Melanchthon (1497–1560); from Switzerland, John Calvin (1509–1564); and from England, Robert Barclay (1648–1690), Thomas Belsham (1750–1829), John Foster (1770–1843), George Fox (1624–1691), William Paley (1743–1805), William Penn (1644–1718), founder of the state of Pennsylvania, Joseph Priestly (1733–1804), William Tyndale (c. 1492–1536), Daniel Whitby (1638–1726), and Roger Williams (1604–1684), founder of the settlement at Providence.

4. The Seventh Day Baptists differ from other Baptists in their adherence to Saturday as their Sabbath. Their reasoning is that Christ and his apostles observed the Old Testament (Saturday) Sabbath. Led by Stephen Mumford, they first organized as a separate church body in the United States in 1672, at Newport, Rhode Island. (Frank S. Mead, *Handbook of Denominations in the United States*, 5th ed., Nashville and New York, 1950, pp. 49–50.)

5. Shakespeare, *Othello*, I, iii, 80–81.

6. Romans 6:11.

7. I John 5:4.

8. Romans 10:4.

9. Revelation 21:27.

4 2

TO GEORGE W. BENSON

Boston, Sept. 10, 1842.

Dear George:

Most heartily do I congratulate you on the gift of a fine boy [Thomas Davis Benson], to supply the vacant place of your departed little one, Eliza Davis; and happy am I to hear that Catherine has succeeded so well on the cold water, tee-total, Washingtonian plan.[1] And now, in return, let me say, yesterday forenoon dear Helen presented me, for the fourth time, with a noble boy [Charles Follen Garrison], "a little superior to any thing before him," possibly. He weighed about 10 lbs., and, of course, in that particular, must take the precedence of yours. It is a happy coincidence of births, united as we are by the most tender and endearing ties of life. Helen has never before had so comfortable a time. At 7 o'clock, she was well at the breakfast table; at 8 o'clock, her pains began to come on slightly; at 9, bro. [Oliver] Johnson (who, with his wife, and James Boyle, happened to be with us) got into the omnibus, and went to Boston for Mrs. Alexander; at 10 Mrs. A. arrived at the house; and at 11, A.M. the babe was born![2] This was quick work, and seemed almost like a dream. Helen remains in a very comfortable state, and she has a most excellent nurse, who came very promptly as soon as she was sent for.

We are somewhat disappointed that the babe proves to be a boy, and yet, I trust, none the less thankful. We have not yet given him a name, but shall probably call him either Charles Follen or Francis Jackson. Which shall it be?

I am much obliged to you for sending me the account of the slave case, and will make use of it in the next Liberator.[3]

Will not my Quaker friends think I have given them a severe dose in yesterday's paper?[4]

Elias Smith has started on his mission to Maine.[5] I hope he will succeed; but it is doubtful. His wife is not yet confined.

Bro. James continues very feeble, and looks very much emaciated. His cough does not seem to trouble him a great deal, but his lungs are probably incurable.

I write in great haste. All the family, of course, are delighted to hear the good news from Northampton, and desire me to send their congratulations to you and Catherine.

Yours, affectionately,

Wm. Lloyd Garrison.

N.B. Henry Williams says Babb, of Bath, has paid $3.00 on your acct.[6] The money waits your order.

ALS: Garrison Papers, Boston Public Library.

1. The Washingtonian Movement was a crusade dedicated to total abstinence, which flourished between 1840 and 1845. The movement included both women and men, for there were Martha Washingtonian Societies as well as those for the Sons of Temperance. All these groups encouraged abstinence by moral suasion, shunning political action.

2. James Boyle, born in Lower Canada of a Catholic family, became a revivalist preacher in Vermont and in Connecticut and subsequently, under the influence of John Humphrey Noyes, a perfectionist. After serving for a time as lecturer and financial agent of the Ohio Anti-Slavery Society, he joined the Northampton Association, where he remained until 1845. (*Life.*)

Janet Alexander (c. 1784–1845), a native of Scotland, was instructed in midwifery by Dr. James Hamilton, professor of midwifery at the University of Edinburgh. She arrived in Boston in 1819 and until her death was actively engaged in the practice of her profession, being able to boast that she had never lost a patient. (See *The Liberator*, February 6, 1846.)

3. Garrison refers to the *Creole* case (see his letter to George W. Benson, March 22, 1842). The account, printed in *The Liberator*, September 9, consisted of correspondence between Daniel Webster and Lord Ashburton. Webster was at this time secretary of state. Alexander Baring, First Baron Ashburton (1774–1848), English politician and financier, had been sent to America in 1842 to settle some disputes over boundaries and over the extradition of criminals and to discuss methods the United States and Great Britain might take to suppress the slave trade. The result of the negotiations was the Webster-Ashburton Treaty. In the three letters Garrison prints, Webster decries British policy in violating the security of American vessels in British ports, citing the case of the *Creole*. Ashburton evades the issue and suggests it should be settled not in Washington but in London. Webster concludes the correpondence by conceding this point. He is insistent, however, in the name of President Tyler, that Great Britain must prevent such incidents in the future.

4. In describing what Garrison calls "the outrageous scenes" which took place in the Friends meeting house at Lynn, when Thomas P. Beach and Stephen S. Foster attempted to address the meeting on the subject of slavery, Nathaniel P. Rogers made some uncomplimentary remarks about the Quaker form of worship. These comments were deeply resented by the Quakers, especially by Rebecca Weeks (spelled Weekes in *The Liberator*) of Farmington, New York, who wrote a long poem rebuking Rogers. Although Garrison printed the verses in the issue of September 9, he took Rogers' side in the dispute. In a long editorial he censured the modern Society of Friends as being "as much under the dominion of priestcraft, as much led by outward observances, and as much swayed by public opinion, as any other sect." (See Garrison's letter to Helen E. Garrison, November 21, 1842.)

5. Elias Smith (c. 1815–1887), a former Methodist minister, was at this time an antislavery leader and an intimate associate of Garrison's. (*Life.*)

6. Robert Babb, a blacksmith, was secretary of the Bath Anti-Slavery Society (letter to the editor from Doris M. Rowland, curator, Pejepscot Historical Society, Brunswick, Maine, June 26, 1970).

4 3

TO EDMUND QUINCY

Boston, Sept. 12, 1842.

My dear Quincy:

We want you to come in from Dedham on Thursday,[1] if practicable, to attend a special meeting of the Executive Committee of our Non-Resistance Society, at Mrs. Southwick's, at 3 o'clock.[2] This meeting will be in relation to our annual meeting, and to the Non-Resistant. It is a long time (altogether too long a time) since we had a Committee meeting; and if we do not mean to have our paper go down, once for all, the wheels of our Society blocked up beyond the power of moving, and the non-resistance enterprise a mere "flash in the pan," we must bestir ourselves accordingly. I wish you would write a good rousing article for the Liberator, in regard to the annual meeting, (which we now contemplate holding on the 18th, 19th and 20th of Oct.) urging a large attendance, &c.[3] I will say something editorially besides. [Un]less[4] some extra exertions are made, I fear our meeting will prove a meagre affair. So it ought not to be. I confess, I am somewhat mortified and surprised to see how little regret seems to have been felt by non-resistants, in regard to the suspension of the Non-Resistant. But let us prepare ourselves to have a redeeming meeting in October.

Yours, lovingly,

Wm. Lloyd Garrison.

N.B. On Friday last, my wife presented me, for the fourth time, with a fine boy, weighing 10 lbs. The mother and babe are both doing remarkably well. It cannot be denied that "Garrisonism" is on the increase.

ALS: Garrison Papers, Sophia Smith Collection, Smith College Library.

1. September 15.

2. The semimonthly organ of the New England Non-Resistance Society, the *Non-Resistant*, was first published in January 1839. The editorial committee consisted of Garrison, Mrs. Chapman, and Quincy, though Garrison wrote little for the paper. The *Non-Resistant* had so many financial difficulties that publication was suspended in June 1842. (*Life.*)

Thankful Hussey Southwick (1792–1867), wife of Joseph Southwick, was an active abolitionist and nonresistant. (*Life.*)

3. Although as president, Quincy signed the call in *The Liberator* for the meeting of the nonresistance society (see the issues for September 16, 1842, and subsequent weeks), the "good rousing article" did not appear before the meeting. He did write a series of editorials for the paper during Garrison's absence in western New York state (see the issues for November 18, December 2, 9, 16, 23, 30, 1842, and January 6, 1843; some of these editorials appeared after Garrison's return).

4. "Our less" on manuscript.

4 4

TO HENRY C. WRIGHT

Boston, Oct. 1, 1842.

Dear bro. Wright:

Unless the Sheridan shall have an uncommonly quick passage, or the Acadia an unusually long one, across the Atlantic, this hasty epistle will probably anticipate your arrival in Dublin, and so take you agreeably by surprise.[1] Fully was it my intention to send by you a bundle of letters, to my English, Scotch and Irish friends; but my anti-slavery engagements in New-Hampshire interfered, and occupied precisely the time that I had intended to devote to letter-writing. I can imagine how you felt, under these circumstances; and can share equally in your regret. [Nathaniel P.] Rogers and [Charles L.] Remond told me at Somersworth, and [George] Bradburn at Nantucket, that they had equipped you with letters to our beloved friends abroad; and I suppose others have seized the opportunity to write by you. You will not stand in need, therefore, of any special introduction from me to our transatlantic coadjutors. Indeed, you are already too well known among them to require an introduction. I am as sure that you will be hospitably and cordially received by them, as I am that the sun is shining gloriously this first day of October. How my heart leaps to think of your visit! O that I could be with you, to sympathize, to rejoice, to labor with you! But what do I say? How can loving, kindred spirits ever be separated? Are they not one by affection, choice, affinity? Matter separates but matter. To the soul, there is "no more sea," [2] no geographical boundaries, no mountain barriers. Then, remember that I am separated from you only in bodily form; but as for my heart, with all its aspirations, hopes, good wishes, and love without measure, it is with you. I know what is the heart of a stranger, in a strange land; [3] how lacerating it is to the feelings to be exiled from home, wife, children and friends — to have a mighty ocean heaving its billows between one's own native land and the foreign soil on which it is his lot to stand — to think of what may transpire in one's absence, by the vicissitudes of time, and the ravages of death; but I know, too, by delightful experience, that he who trusts in God, and whose meat and drink it is to do the will of his Heavenly Father, will be sustained under every trial — will be richly compensated for whatever sacrifices he may make in the cause of bleeding humanity — and will not lack any good thing.

You well know, dear brother, that I have felt the deepest interest in your mission to England, and have done what I could (I am sorry it has been so little) to forward it. My own convictions still remain strong, as they were at the beginning, that the mission will do good to yourself, and to the various great moral and philanthropic enterprises of the age. No one can be more sorry to part with you, for a time, than myself; but my belief is unfaltering that, by kindling a fire abroad, you will communicate warmth to us here at home. What an ample field is before you! How many eyes, both of affectionate friends and bitter enemies, are fastened on you! My prayer is, that you may be endowed with grace and wisdom from on high, and persevere in well-doing to the end.

> "A cloud of witnesses around,
> Hold thee in full survey: —
> Forget the steps already trod,
> And onward urge thy way!" [4]

To my dear Dublin friends — the [Richard D.] Webbs, [Richard] Allens, [James] Haughtons, &c. &c. — convey the choicest expressions of my personal regard and love. Seldom do they hear from me by letter, but they are never absent from my remembrance. I cherish toward them peculiar feelings of friendship and admiration, and yearn in spirit for the time when I may again behold them face to face.

To John Murray and William Smeal, in Scotland, (in particular,) give my affectionate regards, and assure them of my increasing esteem for them. Their kindness to me was very great, and I long for the opportunity and ability to repay it.

To George Thompson and Elizabeth Pease say, that, should I love them any more than I do, I should be guilty of the sin of idolatry. They are, indeed, very dear to me.

Three weeks ago,[5] my dear Helen presented me with a fourth son, whose name we shall call Charles Follen. The mother and child are both doing remarkably well. Thus, it is undeniable that, in spite of all opposition, "Garrisonism" is on the increase!

I intended to write much more, but have been greatly hindered by company this morning — & the mail is to close in a few moments. Adieu! Write soon — Heaven bless and prosper you!

Yours, ever,

Wm. Lloyd Garrison.

ALS: Garrison Papers, Boston Public Library; extract printed in Glasgow Female Anti-Slavery Society, *Second Annual Report*, 1843, p. 16.

1. The *Sheridan* was a sailing ship of the Dramatic Line which had been on the New York-Liverpool run since 1837. (Carl C. Cutler, *Queens of the Western Ocean*, Annapolis, 1961.) The *Acadia*, a wooden paddle steamer with auxiliary sail and sister ship to the *Britannia*, served on the Cunard Line between 1840 and 1849. (Frank E. Dodman, *Ships of the Cunard Line*, New York and London, 1955.)

2. Revelation 21:1.
3. Exodus 2:22.
4. Garrison quotes the second stanza of the hymn (words by Philip Doddridge and music by Handel) "Awake, my soul, stretch every nerve."
5. September 9.

---

4 5

TO GEORGE W. BENSON

Boston, Oct. 11, 1842.

Dear George:

If this should find you in Providence, I hope you will be induced to return home to Northampton by the way of this city and Cambridgeport. We all want to see you, especially at this crisis in regard to the sickness of poor dear James. He certainly cannot continue much longer. Indeed, for a week past, we have been looking daily for his demise. He is emaciated to a mere skeleton, and is scarcely able to sit up long enough, once in twenty-four hours, to have his bed made. Last night he passed very comfortably, and still remains so. Probably he will die suddenly. He has exhibited a great deal of patience and fortitude during his illness. How far he is really conscious of his situation, and what are his real feelings, if he considers his case hopeless, I am not yet sure.

I want to see you, also, in regard to some pecuniary matters. My expenses, this year, in consequence of James's illness, and in other ways, have been very considerable; so that I now stand in debt, over my salary, $150; and should James be taken away, the funeral expenses would probably amount to $50 more. What is worse, the receipts of the Liberator up to the 1st inst. have fallen short of the expenses nearly $200 — so that I have not been able to get the $100 due me for my last month's services. October 1st being regular quarter day, and of course the time for settlement with creditors, found me unable to pay either my rent, or my grocer's bill, and my credit is, of course, suffering. What to do, I know not. [Ellis Gray] Loring is unable to loan me any thing; so is Southwick; [1] [Samuel] Philbrick has advanced $50 to pay the paper-maker; [Francis] Jackson has lost ten thousand dollars within a year, and is, of course, very much pinched. He has, nevertheless, loaned me $50. This gives me no special relief. In regard to yourself, I know that you are crushed under the weight of pecuniary responsibilities, in connexion with your great movement at Northampton; and I have no idea of giving you any trouble. But I should like to see you, and perhaps we may devise something together as "a committee of ways and means." I have little doubt that the Liberator affairs will be made square at the end of the year, by the receipts, and by donations; but it is the *present*, rather than the *future*, that now troubles me.

Helen is badly troubled with gatherings in her ears, which are extremely painful. The babe is thriving finely. We still keep our nurse, partly on James's account.[2] She will remain only a few days longer.

Yours, affectionately,

Wm. Lloyd Garrison.

P.S. Since the above was written, I have received your letter of yesterday, containing a check for $40, in relation to dear Mary's board. I have no doubt it is all right, after the most rigid business agreement; but I kept no account. This will aid me to that amount, and it arrives very opportunely.

ALS: Garrison Papers, Boston Public Library.

1. Joseph Southwick (1791–1866), husband of Thankful Hussey Southwick, was a Quaker abolitionist who was later to disagree with Garrison over the issue of disunion. (*Life*; see also Sarah Hussey Southwick, *Reminiscences of Early Anti Slavery Days*, Cambridge, Mass., 1893.)

2. The nurse, Mrs. French (she is named in the following letter to George W. Benson, October 14, 1842), has not been positively identified, although she may be the same Mrs. French listed in an index in the Department of Rare Books and Manuscripts of the Boston Public Library as a spiritualist faith healer in the 1860's.

46

TO GEORGE W. BENSON

Cambridgeport, Oct. 14, 1842.

Dear bro. George:

The sufferer is at rest from his bodily pains. My poor afflicted brother James threw off his mortal habiliments this morning, at 3 o'clock, but death had no power over his spirit. Till within half an hour of his departure, his sufferings were very great; but he finally died so quietly, that I supposed he had fallen asleep, and did not discover my error until at least half an hour after the event had transpired. As his case had long been hopeless, his release from the flesh is cause of consolation, rather than of sorrow. He retained his senses to the last, and died with all possible fortitude and resignation, being perfectly aware that his end was approaching. We shall consign his mortal remains to the tomb on Sunday afternoon, toward evening;

and I need not say that we shall be extremely gratified if you can arrange your business, so as to be with us on the occasion. But I do not wish you to feel under any special obligations to be here, if you have important concerns to attend to elsewhere. Come, if you can without too much inconvenience; if you cannot, it is well. I would say the same to dear Anna and Sarah. If they wish to stay longer in Providence, it would not be best for them to come merely to attend the funeral. If otherwise, we are all ready to welcome them back immediately. Remember that you must all consult your own convenience and wishes.

Dear mother arrived safely yesterday, at 11 o'clock, A.M. We were very much disappointed in not seeing you at the same time, as we were expecting you both in company together, and were thinking it a fortunate circumstance that you would arrive here in such an emergency. I have also been hoping that you would not fail to attend our Non-Resistance anniversary next week; for that cause needs the personal presence of every true friend on that occasion.[1]

Fortunately, Mrs. French, our excellent nurse, remains with us to this hour, and has been of very great service to poor James, in his illness. She expects to be called to another place every moment.

I intend that the funeral arrangements and ceremonies shall be as plain, simple, and *free*, as possible. Liberty of speech shall be given to all who may attend. I shall probably have a testimony to bear again[st] the war system, the navy, intemperance, &c. in connection with J's history, and also against that religion which sustains war and its murderous enginery.[2]

A letter was sent to Anna, yesterday, by mail, from Helen. I forgot the bundle, until it was too late.

I shall direct this letter to Anna, lest you shall not be in Providence, and the letter remain unopened.

Our best regards to bro. Anthony and Charlotte and to the sisters.[3]

Yours, by every tie of love,

Wm. Lloyd Garrison.

ALS: Garrison Papers, Boston Public Library; extract printed in *Life*, III, 72.

1. The meeting was held at Marlboro Chapel on October 30.
2. Garrison carried out his intention, and the speech caused some stir among the guests (see Garrison's letter to Henry C. Wright, March 1, 1843).
3. Charlotte Benson Anthony (1803–1886), a sister of Helen Benson Garrison, had married in 1826 Henry Anthony (1802–1879). Although Anthony lived in Providence, a city Garrison often visited, he is seldom mentioned in the letters since he was too conservative to be a congenial Garrisonian. It is probably the Benson sisters to whom Garrison refers.

4 7

TO HELEN E. GARRISON

Waterloo, Nov. 21, 1842.

My dear Helen:

Up to the present time, "all's well" with me; but, as I anticipated before I left home, I have been so busily occupied in attending meetings and seeing friends, letter-writing has been out of the question. I am now at the dear hospitable home of Thomas M'Clintock, and at this moment am writing in a room crowded with rampant abolitionists, whose tongues are all in motion, and their hearts in joyous commotion.[1] Whether, under these circumstances, I shall be able to write an intelligible scrawl, is at least quite problematical. "To begin with the beginning."[2] I arrived at the Brighton depot half an hour before the cars came along; from thence I took the train for Albany, where I arrived at 7 o'clock, in the midst of a cold rain-storm. I might have immediately taken another train onward, and arrived at Rochester (450 miles from Boston) on Sunday afternoon. Wishing to keep my rest unbroken, I concluded to tarry over night, and went to a Temperance hotel near the depot,[3] and in the morning left for Utica, arriving in that beautiful city at 2 o'clock, P.M. Here I concluded to remain until the next morning. On going up Genesee-street, in quest of a temperance house, I met Alvan Stewart going to church.[4] We shook hands with each other, and he *politely* asked me to go and stop with him over night. I declined, not wishing to incur any special obligations at that time, or in that quarter; but, on his invitation, I spent the evening with him and James C. Jackson, (whose head-quarters are now in Utica,) and we had a talk on a great variety of topics, not excepting third partyism.[5] I spoke very plainly on the last topic, and made them both rather uneasy; for poor James evidently felt that he stood on a sandy foundation. Early on Monday morning, I left in the cars for Rochester, and arrived at that place in the afternoon, where I met with a most cordial reception from friends Post, Burtis, and others.[6] Dear bro. Collins, to our astonishment, arrived from Buffalo the same evening, in feeble, but improved health. Abby Kelley did not get along till the next day at noon. She came from Waterloo, in company with friend M'Clintock, wife, and daughter Mary.[7] Our meetings continued in Rochester, three times a day, from Tuesday morning until Friday, 1 o'clock, P.M. In consequence of the bad weather, and the very bad state of the travelling, and the uncertainty of my arrival, &c. &c., there were not so many delegates from abroad as were expected; though some came a distance of 30 or 40 miles. In the day time, our meetings were respectably attended in point of numbers, and by some of the choicest spirits in the land. In the evening, they were crowded to overflowing. They were held in the Second Presbyterian Church. The deepest interest was manifested in them from the opening to the close. W. L. Chaplin was present, and endeavored to act the champion for the third party; but he made miserable work of it.[8] On taking the vote on a resolution, condemnatory of that party, it was carried by a very large majority, though all persons were allowed to express their views. The result was most unexpected to myself, in as much as nearly all the abolitionists in this section of the country have been carried away by this unwise measure. Neither [Charles L.] Remond nor [Frederick] Douglass was present, but there was no lack of speech-making. I have had to talk a great deal, of course, — for there has been a special curiosity to see and hear me; and it is a satisfaction to me to know, that my remarks have been received with much favor generally. On Friday afternoon, I started from Rochester for Farmington, in company with J. A. Collins, J. C. Hathaway, and Abby Kelley, in Joseph [Hathaway]'s team.[9] It was a very blustering and severe day, and we suffered considerably from the cold, but had a warm reception on our arrival at Farmington. The next day, we had two meetings in the Orthodox Quaker meeting-house, which were addressed by Abby and myself — principally by W. L. G. The day was raw and gusty, and the audience in the forenoon not very large; but in the afternoon, the house and gallery were well-filled, though very few Quakers were present, owing to a strong prejudice against us, as well as to the weather. In the evening, a large company (chiefly Quakers) assembled at Hathaway's house, — among them R. Weeks, the one who wrote the verses in regard to Rogers's description of the "Scene in the Quaker meeting-house in Lynn" — (nothing, however, passed between us directly on that point.) [10] We talked on phrenology, mesmerism, anti-slavery, non-resistance, &c. In the morning, Joseph took his team, and brought us to Waterloo, where we arrived yesterday (Sunday) at 1 o'clock. At 2, P.M. the Court House was crowded by a dense assembly, which was addressed by Collins and myself. Last evening, another crowded auditory convened at the same place, and were addressed by Abby, Jacob Ferris, (a splendid young orator,) and myself — I occupying the greater part of the time, in blowing up the priesthood, church, worship, Sabbath, &c. as they now exist.[11] A very deep impression was evidently made. This evening, I am to deliver a lecture on slavery in the same place; and at 12 o'clock at night shall leave in the cars for Syracuse, to attend the conventions to be held in that place, commencing to-morrow forenoon. This is pretty close work, and draws upon all my mental and physical powers; but, thus far, my health remains good, and my lungs do not seem to suffer from so much speaking. Collins's pleuritic complaint hangs on to him, and his whole constitution seems to be greatly impaired. He will probably not return until after the Utica conventions. Abby Kelley is tasking her lungs too severely, and ought to be more careful for the future. She will continue in this part of the country during the winter.

My dear one, how are you and the little ones, and all the household? Do send me a letter to Utica, and give me all the little domestic particulars that you can think of. I shall hasten back to you, on the wings of love, as soon as possible. To-day we are all thrilled with emotion to think that poor Latimer's case is to be decided now.[12] Great interest is felt in it here and elsewhere, and thousands are waiting with much anxiety to learn the result of the trial. All hope that Latimer will be rescued. The Liberator has just come, and is extremely interesting. A thousand kisses for you and the babe and boys, and love to all.

Your loving husband,

Wm. Lloyd Garrison.

ALS: Garrison Papers, Boston Public Library; partly printed in *Life*, III, 63–67.

Garrison had gone to central and western New York state (leaving Boston November 12 and returning December 3) to attend conventions of the American Anti-Slavery Society in Rochester, Syracuse, and Utica. His mission was to counteract William Goodell's attack on the American Anti-Slavery Society, expressed in an address read at the Liberty party convention, in Syracuse early in October. Goodell claimed that the society indirectly encouraged proslavery political parties by not supporting the Liberty party. Although *The Liberator* pronounced Garrison's tour a great success, he became so seriously ill with scarlet fever upon his return that he was unable to resume editorial duties until the issue of January 20. (*The Liberator*, November 4, 18 and December 16, 23, 1842.)

1. Thomas McClintock (c. 1792–1876) was a druggist in Waterloo, New York, having moved there in 1836 from Philadelphia. A Quaker, he was the author of the *Basis of Religious Association*, which marked the beginning of the Congregational or Progressive Friends movement. As part of this movement McClintock organized a new yearly meeting at Waterloo. (*Friends Intelligencer*, 33:89, 1877.)

2. Lord Byron, *Don Juan*, Canto I, stanza 7, line 2.

3. The Temperance House, located at 77–79 Broadway.

4. Alvan Stewart (1790–1849) of Utica, New York, was a lawyer and abolitionist. In 1835 he had called the convention at Utica which established the New York State Anti-Slavery Society and became its first president. Unlike Garrison, he saw slavery as a political issue and wished to work for its overthrow by political means. In 1840 he was one of the organizers of the Liberty party and ran on its ticket for governor of New York. He received only a few hundred votes.

5. James Caleb Jackson (1811–1895) was a physician and abolitionist. With Nathaniel P. Rogers he edited the *National Anti-Slavery Standard* for a year beginning in June 1840. He was editor of the *Liberty Press* in Utica, 1842–1844, and editor of the Albany *Patriot*, 1845–1846. In 1847 he was to be a sponsor of the Liberty League, a fourth party growing out of the Liberty party.

6. Garrison mentions two abolitionists from Rochester, New York, who were also interested in spiritualism, Isaac Post (1798–1872) and Lewis B. Burtis (c. 1793–1868). In 1845 Post and his wife resigned from the Society of Friends, on the grounds that their membership interfered with antislavery activity. Burtis was by occupation a stove manufacturer. (Rochester *Union & Advertiser,* June 16, 1868.)

7. Mary Ann McClintock (Mrs. Thomas) was one of the women who was to help draft the call for the Seneca Falls woman's rights convention in 1848.

8. William Lawrence Chaplin (1796–1871) was an abolitionist who was active in forming the Liberty party. (*Life.*)

9. Joseph Comstock Hathaway (1810–1873) was a Quaker farmer and abolitionist of Waterloo. In 1832 he married Esther Aldrich. (Elizabeth Starr Versailles, *Hathaways of America*, Northampton, Mass., 1965, p. 250.)

10. Garrison refers to Rebecca Weeks (born c. 1795), who, according to the 1850 census, lived in Farmington, New York. He printed her poem concerned with the form of Quaker worship (spelling the name Weekes) in *The Liberator,* September 9, 1842. (See Garrison's letter to George W. Benson, September 10, 1842.)

11. Jacob Ferris is mentioned in *The Liberator,* May 19, 1843, as a resident of New York City; he may be the Jacob Ferris listed as a chairmaker in *Longworth's American Almanac, New York Register, and City Directory.*

12. George Latimer, a Negro slave, had escaped from Norfolk, Virginia, to Boston with his wife and child. Arrested without warrant on a charge of theft, he was brought before Judge Lemuel Shaw. When he was denied the right to trial by jury, his case became a cause célèbre. As a result of the public clamor and the many petitions circulated on Latimer's behalf, he was released; and in 1843 the Massachusetts legislature passed a personal liberty act forbidding justices to participate in the capture of fugitive slaves and law-enforcement officers to hold them. (*Life.*)

48

TO HELEN E. GARRISON

Syracuse, Nov. 27, 1842.

Dear Wife:

I wrote to you a hasty letter from Waterloo, giving you some of the outlines of my visit to Rochester. Although many interesting events have occurred since that time, I shall wait till I see you before I go into the particulars. Up to this hour, I have enjoyed myself far beyond my expectations. The spirit of hospitality, in this section, exceeds any thing to be found in New-England, with comparatively rare exceptions. Money is about "as scarce as gold dust," but there is no lack of food and the other necessaries of life, and to these you are heartily welcome. All the towns that I have visited are uncommonly agreeable in their appearance, and exhibit a neatness, taste and regularity, that have taken me by surprise. If the aspect of things is so pleasant now, in bleak winter, what must it be in the prime of summer? I wish you could be with me, and so do many others, who would delight to extend to you the warm hand of friendship. If all things shall go well with us, and our means will allow of it, what say for a trip with me, next summer, to Niagara Falls?

The friends at Waterloo were the kindest of the kind. I delivered three addresses in that place, to crowded houses, — the last on Monday evening, — the effect of which was visibly beneficial to our cause. At 12 o'clock that night, I left in the cars for Syracuse, accompanied by friends [John A.] Collins (who was far from being well) and J. C. Hathaway, where we arrived at 5 o'clock, A.M. G. W. Pryor, Jacob Ferris, W. O. Duvall, and Abby Kelley arrived during the forenoon, in a private conveyance.[1] We all came to the splendid mansion, occupied jointly by Stephen Smith and Wing Russell, (formerly of New-Bedford,) where we, and many others, have all been entertained with a hospitality and kindness never exceeded in my experience.[2] Poor Collins had to go to bed at once, and has scarcely been able to sit up even to this hour. To-day he is somewhat better, and may possibly leave to-morrow afternoon for Utica, under my care. He has had all possible attention paid to him, and as good nursing as he could have obtained in this wide world. He is nearly disabled from the service, at least for some time to come. This morning, (Sunday,) G. W. Pryor, S. S. Foster, Abby Kelley, and Mrs. Russell, left for Vernon, on their way to Utica, in a carryall. The day is cold and blustering, and a snow-storm beginning to set in.

On Tuesday forenoon, our Convention opened in this place, under circumstances by no means auspicious.[3] Not a meeting-house could be obtained for us, and we were forced to meet in a hall three stories high, called "Library Hall." Handbills had been placarded about the town, announcing that Abby Kelley, C. L. Remond, Frederick Douglas, and W. L. Garrison would be at the Convention; but, notorious as we are, and great as is the curiosity usually manifested to see and hear either of us singly, our meeting in the forenoon consisted only of eleven persons, all told! These were nearly all of our own company. We appointed J. C. Hathaway President, and J. N. T. Tucker Secretary, and then adjourned.[4] In the afternoon, we had a small audience; but, such was the feeling we excited in the meeting, by our scorching remarks and "ultra" resolutions, the hall was crowded in the evening, when I opened my budget of heresies on the subject of temple worship, the church, the priesthood, the Sabbath, &c. which created no small stir. The next day, S. S. Foster arrived, and we soon had the town in commotion. During the day, a considerable number of persons were in attendance, and the discussions assumed so exciting an aspect, that, at the close of the afternoon meeting, it became apparent that we should have a riot in the evening — all in defence of the clergy and the church! When the evening came, the hall was densely filled, partly by a highly respectable assemblage, and partly by a troop of mobocrats, having their pockets filled with rotten eggs and other missiles. Jacob Ferris opened the meeting in a short but eloquent speech, which, as it contained nothing specially offensive, was listened to without disturbance. Our friend S. S. Foster then took the platform, and was allowed to proceed without much interruption until he made his favorite declaration, in his most excited manner, that the Methodist Episcopal Church is worse than any brothel in the city of New-York. Then came such an outbreak of hisses, cries, curses! All order was at an end. Several ruffians rushed toward the platform to seize Foster, but were not allowed to reach him. The tumult became tremendous. Several citizens, who were well known, attempted to calm the storm, but in vain. Rotten eggs were now thrown, one of which was sent as a special present to me, and struck the wall over my head, scattering its contents on me and others. Next, a number of benches were broken, and other damage done; and, finally, the meeting was adjourned, in much disorder, to meet at the same place the next day, at 10, A.M. We all got through the mob safely, though they kept a sharp look-out for Foster and myself, having prepared, as it was said, tar and feathers to give us a coat without any cost to ourselves.

In the morning, (Thursday,) we met agreeably to adjournment; but, on the opening it was announced that we could not have the use of the hall during the day, unless we would become responsible for all damages that might be done to the building; and that we could not be allowed to occupy the hall in the evening, on any conditions, such was the excited state of the public mind. This announcement led to a most animated discussion. We refused, of course, to give any such guaranty, as that would be a strong inducement to the mob to do all the injury they could to the hall. Syracuse was held up to the infamy of the world, in terms of merited severity, as a town under mobocratic sway, worthy to be associated with Boston, New-York, and Utica, in 1835. Finally, the requisition was withdrawn, and we were allowed to continue our meetings through the day, but not in the evening. In the afternoon, Foster obtained a very respectful hearing in defence of his terrible charge against the Methodist Church, and produced an impression decidedly in his favor. He was followed by a pettifogging lawyer and editor, named Cummings, in reply, who kept the audience in a roar of laughter by his ridiculous nonsense and silly buffoonery.[5] He was put forward by the mobocrats, (as well as another lawyer, named Hillas,) as the champion of Church and State; but all he said worked mightily in our favor.[6] At dark, a motion was made that we adjourn *sine die*; but our opponents outnumbered us, and voted to adjourn the meeting until the next morning. The hall, however, was not opened to them, and we, of course, did not go to the place. The whole town is in a ferment. Every tongue is in motion. If an earthquake had occurred, it would not have excited more consternation, or made more talk. But we have no doubt that the result will be good for our cause. We sent the resolutions we intended to discuss in the Convention, relating to the church and the clergy, to the clergymen in this place, by a committee; but the corrupt and cowardly creatures did not dare to come and discuss them with us before the people. To-day, however, (Sunday,) in "coward's castle," [7] they are denouncing us as "infidels," &c. and warning the people against us. This, too, will do good. Already the tide is turning in our favor, and, in a short time, genuine anti-slavery will obtain a strong foothold here.

Our next Convention is to be held at Utica, on Tuesday next, and will continue in session at least three days.[8] As bro. Foster will be there, I presume we shall have a repetition of the scenes in Syracuse, as he is remarkably successful in raising the spirit of mobocracy wherever he goes. Possibly, we may have quiet meetings; but, come what may, may we all be faithful to the cause. I could wish that bro. Foster would exercise more judgment and discretion in the presentation of his views; but it is useless to reason with him, with any hope of altering his course, as he is firmly persuaded that he is pursuing the very best course.

On Friday evening next, I expect to lecture in Albany, and on Saturday night hope to embrace you and the dear children again, in health and safety. I yearn to see and kiss my sweet babe in particular; and yet it will not do for me to begin to make any exceptions, for one after another comes up, and they are all so dear to me that I cannot be invidious. Tell my dear George, and Willie, and Wendell, to be good boys, and help you all they can, until my return; and father will bring them some playthings when he gets home.

I am pretty well worn down with exertion. During the ride from Waterloo to this place, in the night, I took cold, and have been troubled with influenza ever since; so that I have spoken at our meetings here with great difficulty, in consequence of hoarseness. I am now better. Fear not about my taking care of myself. On my return, I have many marvellous things to relate to you about animal magnetism, having seen many experiments, and in which I am a full believer.[9] What can I send but a loving heart to you, and affectionate remembrances to all the household?

Yours, in holy bonds,

Wm. Lloyd Garrison.

☞ I think nothing had better be copied from this for the Liberator, till my return.

ALS: Garrison Papers, Boston Public Library; printed in *Life*, III, 67–71.

1. George W. Pryor was a member of the executive committee of the Skaneateles Anti-Slavery Society and until 1838 head of the Quaker-influenced Skaneateles Female Seminary. (Dwight Bruce, *Onondaga's Centennial*, 1896, I, 987, 994.) W. O. Duvall, who appears not to have been a resident of Syracuse, has not been identified.

2. Stephen Smith (1776–1854), a Quaker of New Bedford, became prominent in the shipping business in New York City before establishing in Syracuse the Onondaga Solar Salt Company. His house was to become a noted station on the Underground Railroad.

Wing Russell (1803–1844), Stephen Smith's brother-in-law, was also a native of New Bedford, where he kept an apothecary shop. In 1835 he and his wife Elizabeth moved to Syracuse to join the colony that had grown up around Smith's salt manufactory. When his health failed, Russell returned to New Bedford, where he died. (For both Smith and Russell see Rebecca Williams Hawes, "Abraham and Zerviah [Ricketson] Smith and their Nineteen Children," *Old Dartmouth Historical Sketch*, No. 30, New Bedford, Mass., 1910.)

3. An antislavery convention was held at Library Hall in Syracuse, November 22–24, 1842. Brief accounts of the meeting appeared in the local paper, the *Onondaga Standard*, November 23, 30, 1842.

4. J. N. T. Tucker (c. 1802–c. 1865) was a Baptist minister and printer. He edited the Syracuse *Democratic Freeman* until 1846. Moving to Brooklyn, he edited the Brooklyn *Freeman*, better known as the *Advertiser*. In 1854 he was tried for the murder of his four-year-old son but was acquitted on grounds of insanity and committed to a mental institution from which he later escaped. (Letter to the editor from Richard N. Wright, president, Onondaga Historical Association, December 12, 1970.)

5. Hiram Cummings was founder and editor of the *Empire State Democrat and United States Review* from 1840 to 1843. (Bruce, *Onondaga's Centennial*, I, 573.)

6. Garrison misspells the name of David Duncan Hillis (c. 1808–1859), who had moved to Syracuse in 1837. In 1844 he was to be made surrogate of the county. From 1850 until his death his law firm, Hillis and Morgan, figured in many important trials. (Letters to the editor from Richard N. Wright, November 7 and December 12, 1970.)

7. A pulpit, often described as "six feet above argument," referring to the elevation of the pulpit and the inability of the congregation to argue with the clergyman.

8. The Utica antislavery convention was held in the Congregational church between November 29 and December 1, 1842, for the purpose of discussing abolition and of organizing a New York state antislavery society. A disapproving review in the Utica *Daily Gazette*, December 13, 1842, implied that Garrison had attempted to incite disorder of the "neophytes" in the audience, possibly because he expected "mobocratic" scenes similar to those encountered in Syracuse.

9. Animal magnetism was the name given to the influence supposed to operate in hypnotism, or mesmerism as it was known in Garrison's day (after Friedrich Mesmer, the Austrian physician, 1734–1815).

4 9

TO JOHN T. NORTON

Cambridgeport, Dec. 17, 1842.

My Dear Sir:

Your letter of the 12th instant has just been received, and I hasten to answer it, although I am compelled by severe illness to employ for that purpose the hand of a friend. I am just recovering from an attack of Scarlet fever, which has reduced me to the brink of the grave, and which must be my excuse if I do not enter into all the topics suggested by your letter as fully as you may think their importance deserves.

I do not think such a Conference as you suggest would be of any service to the A. S. Cause; because I think it must be based upon admissions to which I cannot give my assent. My presence there would imply 1st. that it is "minor differences", that keep the individuals you mention, from acting in concert with myself & the other members of the Amercian A. S. Society; 2d. that any "unhappy divisions" exist among the true Abolitionists of the country; 3d. that "the great *vital* and *essential* principles of Abolition are held *in common* by all Abolitionists" — supposing you intend to include the individuals you mention in that number; 4th., that "matters of opinion & modes of action, not necessarily connected with, & belonging to, the subject of Slavery" have ever been brought upon the A. S. Platform by them who now occupy it; 5th. that such an union as you propose "*is* practicable" between such men as myself and such men as those you mention, their state of mind being what their actions indicate; — to all which propositions I must enter my distinct, peremptory & unqualified dissent.

The Abolitionists of the Country, embodied in the American & Massts. A. S. Societies, with whom I am identified, stand in the same position, & present the same front to Slavery, that they have ever done since the commencement of the campaign. Their Platform is the same it has ever been. If "minor differences" have caused any persons to leave it — they who remain upon it are not to blame. In my opinion, the true Abolitionists of the country were never more united among themselves, as to all the essentials of doctrines & measures, than at the present time. The individuals you mention I cannot consent to meet in the way you propose, because by so doing I should recognize them as *Abolitionists*, to which character I think they have forfeited all claim by their conduct in times past & present, — by what they have done, & what they have left undone. I refer, in part, to the circumstances attending the transfer of the Emancipator, & the mismanagement of the other property of the Am. A. S. Society; to the false issues which were made up before the world as to the causes of the Secessions of 1839 & 1840; to the slanders & libels which were circulated in this country & in Europe respecting myself & other Abolitionists, for the purpose of destroying the confidence of the A. S. Public in our integrity & moral character. Of these things the persons in question were guilty, either as principals or as accessories, either by their direct agency, or by the silence of an affected neutrality.

The Abolitionists of the Country, I repeat, stand where they have always done. They cannot move from their position to secure the coöperation of any persons whatever, without compromising their principles. They are ready to welcome to their ranks all manner of persons who wish to enlist in the warfare against Slavery. If the gentlemen whom you wish me to meet have repented of their wrong-doings towards the A. S. Cause & its supporters and wish to make confession & reparation, they will be received with open arms, & all that is past will be forgiven. But no concessions can be made to secure their coöperation that may imply that their action has been otherwise than blameworthy in the highest degree.

This imperfect sketch of my views on this subject will satisfy you that, in my opinion, such a conference would be of no advantage as long as the persons you wish me to meet remain unrepentant, & continue to justify their course in the particulars to which I have alluded, & in others to which I have not had time to refer; — and when they do see the error of their ways and wish to amend them, it will be clearly unnecessary. All they will have to do, in such case, will be to express the state of their minds & to return to active duty upon the Platform, & by the side of the friends, they have deserted.

I have gone into my reasons for declining your proposition at some length — though by no means in as full & satisfactory a manner as I could have wished — because I supposed from the circumstance of your making this application to me that the facts in the case are not fresh in your mind. Pray excuse the length of this letter & all its imperfections in consideration of the circumstances under which it was written.

I am truly yours

Transcription in the hand of Edmund Quincy: Garrison Papers, Boston Public Library.

John Treadwell Norton (1795–1869), a prominent businessman in Farmington, Connecticut, had written on December 12, 1842, a circular letter to Garrison, Joshua Leavitt, Gerrit Smith, Lewis Tappan, Theodore D. Weld, and John Greenleaf Whittier, proposing the conference to which Garrison refers in this letter. Garrison's quotations from Norton's letter are accurate. (For a fuller identification of Norton see letter to Elizabeth Pease, September 1, 1840, n. 7, *Letters*, II, 687; Norton's letter is preserved in the Garrison Papers, Boston Public Library.)

II DISUNION: 1843–1845

GARRISON'S CONCEPT of disunion, which he had been evolving during 1842, was translated into official action in 1843–1844. At the eleventh annual meeting of the Massachusetts Anti-Slavery Society in January 1843 the discussion centered on the Constitution and the Union. On the third day of the meeting Garrison introduced a resolution, which was officially adopted: "That the compact which exists between the North and the South is 'a covenant with death, and an agreement with hell' — involving both parties in atrocious criminality; and should be immediately annulled." [1] Beginning with *The Liberator* for March 17, Garrison substituted this resolution for the superscription to the editorial column he had used during the preceding year.

The same crucial constitutional question was introduced for a three-day discussion at the annual meeting of the American Anti-Slavery Society, May 7–9, 1844. A series of radical resolutions resulted, condemning the Constitution and urging dissolution of the Union. Loyal abolitionists were enjoined to support no political party dedicated to preserving the Union and ideally to refrain from all voting. Climactic was the following: "Henceforth, therefore, until slavery be abolished, the watchword, the rallying cry, the motto on the banner of the American Anti-Slavery Society shall be, 'NO UNION WITH SLAVE-HOLDERS!' " [2] The final vote on these resolutions stood at fifty-nine in favor, twenty-one opposed. Protests signed by eight men, including lawyers David Lee Child and Ellis Gray Loring, were read into the minutes. Garrison was happy with the results; bold and revolutionary steps, he thought, could not be taken without opposition. He was especially pleased to report in *The Liberator*, September 22, that the cry NO UNION WITH SLAVEHOLDERS had been heard across the Atlantic, where at the tenth annual meeting of the Glasgow

1. *The Liberator*, February 3, 1843.
2. *The Liberator*, May 24, 1844.

Emancipation Society the American Anti-Slavery Society had been congratulated for its bold policy of disunion.

In the meantime, another issue drew Garrison's attention. In the spring of that year the Free Church of Scotland, determined that individual congregations should be able to appoint their own ministers, broke away from the established Scottish church, forfeiting in the process state support. It was decided that contributions should be sought from Presbyterian churches everywhere — in America as well as in Britain. Surprisingly, the drive for funds met with a warm reception in Charleston, South Carolina, where impassioned sermons filled collection trays with what the abolitionists considered blood-stained money. Under the leadership of Garrison's group abolitionists insisted that the tainted money should be returned at once to South Carolina.

By this time Henry C. Wright, Garrisonian to the core, was in Britain, journeying from town to town, rising early, lecturing late, and in between writing his autobiography and letters for *The Liberator* (an average of two a week). As usual he testified for peace, against slavery, and also against the Free Church of Scotland. But the Scots were impervious even to such an indefatigable man as Henry Wright, for the Free Church returned not a shilling of their southern collection.

Social reorganization, another contemporary issue which aroused the imagination of many nineteenth-century Americans, interested Garrison little, even though his brother-in-law, George W. Benson, was one of the founders and leading spirits of the Northampton Association of Education and Industry. It is true that for some three months in the summer of 1843 Garrison lived with his family in Northampton, where he was closely associated with the Bensons and other residents of the community, but his sojourn there was owing more to his need for an extended rest than to curiosity about the community's experiment. The dozen letters he wrote from Northampton contain few references to the community and no real speculations about reforming society. Rather he describes the beauty of the scenery and the dearth of reading materials, especially newspapers, confessing that he is "famishing for intelligence." [3] The monotony was relieved only by occasional antislavery and temperance meetings in Northampton and vicinity and by writing letters to family and associates. His physical health improved as his boredom deepened. Garrison's visit to Northampton demonstrated clearly that he was a man of action, not a social philosopher.

While he was at Northampton Anna E. Benson, Helen's sister who was living with the family, died. A calamity more disruptive of family

3. Garrison's letter to Francis Jackson, July 15, 1843.

life was his wife's dislocation of her right arm in a carriage accident, probably caused by Garrison's inept driving. The fact that Helen was pregnant with Fanny, to be born the following December, added to Garrison's feeling of guilt about the accident. He took her to doctor after doctor and literally spent weeks catering to her wishes and seeking the recovery of her health.

During this period Garrison had a conflict between personal and professional loyalties that was to cause him considerable anguish. Nathaniel Peabody Rogers had been a radical abolitionist at least as early as 1832 when he read Garrison's *Thoughts on African Colonization.* From a distinguished New England family of ancient lineage and himself a man of real charm who put Garrison at ease despite the difference in their backgrounds, Rogers was the kind of person with whom Garrison was proud to associate. He was a successful New Hampshire lawyer and editor of the Concord *Herald of Freedom.* Garrison and Rogers had become good friends in the summer of 1840, following the abortive World's Anti-Slavery Convention in London, when they toured Scotland and Ireland together. In the spring of 1841, after a series of antislavery lectures in Massachusetts, in Connecticut, and in New Hampshire and after attending the national antislavery meeting in New York City, Garrison joined Rogers on a visit to Philadelphia. In August they took an excursion together through the White Mountains in New Hampshire. In the summer of 1843 Rogers was prevailed upon to visit Northampton during Garrison's residence there. In short, by the time the trouble started in the summer of 1844 the two men were close friends.

In July 1844 Garrison heard that Rogers' paper, the *Herald of Freedom,* had ceased publication, and he responded as a good friend and associate would. He praised Rogers and insisted that the paper must be sustained. Publication was soon resumed but under the auspices of the state society. When at the next annual meeting of the New Hampshire society Rogers made a public disturbance by objecting to the election of officers on the grounds that officers were of little value to a society, Garrison was astonished. Such action logically extended might abolish both the Massachusetts and the American societies, he thought. But in public he was gentle with Rogers: "It is not for true-hearted friends to apologize to each other for a difference of opinion on questions of this character. A difference in the choice of instrumentalities, or modes of action, is not a difference in spirit." [4]

Then the case of the *Herald of Freedom* was complicated by the serious illness of Rogers, which left the paper under the de facto control of its printer, John R. French, who also happened to be the

4. *The Liberator,* July 26, 1844.

fiancé of Rogers' favorite daughter. At this juncture the board of the New Hampshire society appointed, with the approval of French, a special fact-finding committee consisting of Wendell Phillips and Edmund Quincy, with Garrison as chairman. Although the committee exonerated the board, it recommended that Rogers remain as editor of the paper. When the *Herald of Freedom* refused to print the report of the committee, Garrison "was almost disposed to doubt the evidence of my own senses." [5] By the summer of 1845 Garrison had to admit that Rogers was ungrateful, unprincipled, and unbalanced on the subject of no-organization.

Another issue of national significance was also occupying Garrison's thoughts in the early 1840's. He was concerned about the strong likelihood that slavery would be extended by the addition to the Union of another southern state. As early as the spring of 1842 he warned against the imminence of the annexation of Texas and a war with Mexico. Toward the end of 1843, even more convinced that annexation would be morally wrong and politically imprudent, he urged readers of *The Liberator* to petition Congress for disunion, reproducing sample petitions for their use. By the spring of 1844 he had decided that with the addition of a new slave state New England had no alternative but secession. When in May of the same year Calhoun and others signed a treaty of annexation, he predicted the ruin of agriculture, of commerce, and of manufacturing, and then war with England, and ultimately civil war. As annexation became a reality in the following year the pages of *The Liberator* thundered with unrestrained epithets. It was a "deed of perfidy, black as . . . Egyptian darkness," "a crime unsurpassed in the annals of human depravity!" Garrison urged citizens of Massachusetts "to recall their Senators and Representatives from the hall of Congress — to treat the General Government as a nullity. . . 'NO UNION WITH SLAVE-HOLDERS.'" [6]

5. *The Liberator*, December 13, 1844.
6. *The Liberator*, March 7, 1845.

---

5 0

TO GEORGE W. BENSON

Boston, Feb. 25, 1843.

Dear bro. George:

I have been intending, ever since my recovery from my severe illness, to write a long letter to you; but, while I never lack in good intentions, in reference to epistolary correspondence with my friends, it is seldom that I carry any of them out.

Instead of a long letter, I must now write very briefly, as I am limited for time. This is chiefly to inform you that dear mother is now quite ill with an intermittent, slow fever. She was taken on Saturday last, with cold shiverings and vomiting. We gave her a lobelia emetic, which operated kindly, and the next day she appeared to be better. We found it necessary, however, soon afterward, to give her another; but as she could not take a regular course, it did not make much alteration in her case. On Wednesday, it was deemed advisable to call in Dr. [Robert] Wesselhoeft, who has since regularly prescribed for her. He does not consider her immediately dangerous, but is somewhat apprehensive that she may fail in strength. If he can keep that up, there will be no difficulty in effecting her restoration. She has considerable appetite, and, on the whole, is not so weak to-day as she was yesterday. Should her symptoms grow worse, we shall apprise you of the fact by the earliest mail. It might be well for you not to be absent from home on a long journey, at this time, until the crisis is past. As yet, I do not feel alarmed in regard to her case, and trust she will yet be spared to us many years.

The health of sister Ann is about the same as usual — and that is miserable indeed. She is almost compelled literally to starve herself, though having all the while an excellent appetite, on account of the difficulty of digestion. She is taking the Dr's powders, but as yet they have produced no beneficial effect. Her spirits are low, and she feels very much discouraged.

Sarah has a good deal on her hands just at this time, but holds out better than could be expected with her frail constitution.

Helen is pretty well worn down with care and anxiety. Our babe [Charles Follen Garrison] is now cutting his teeth, and suffers severely, so that he has little rest, day or night. Wendell continues feeble, with scarcely any appetite, and a bad cough.

I am not yet fully recovered from the consequences of my fever, and at times walk with much difficulty. So you see we still have a sick house.

Hoping that all your household are well, and promising you to write again in a few days, I remain, in haste,

Lovingly yours,

Wm. Lloyd Garrison.

ALS: Garrison Papers, Sophia Smith Collection, Smith College Library.

5 1

TO ELIZABETH PEASE

Boston, Feb. 28, 1843.

My dear friend Elizabeth:

Before receiving yours of the 31st Dec. (enclosing an excellent letter from Joseph Barker, which shall be given to the readers of the Liberator next week, and which would have had a much more prompt insertion if it had not been for the pressure of other matters,) I had almost begun to feel apprehensive that, for some cause or other, I had unwittingly given you offence — so long a time had transpired since I had received a letter from you.[1] It is true that I have no special claim on your time or attention; it is true that, of all correspondents, I am the most procrastinating, (my epistles being "few and far between" — O that it were in my power to make them "like angels' visits"!)[2] and therefore have no right to complain of any body, on that score; but, knowing how generous is your spirit, and with what facility and despatch you use the pen, I scarcely knew how to interpret your silence. It seems your state of health has been so delicate as to require abstinence from continued mental effort and epistolary correspondence. — It is cheering news to hear that you are better. Be careful lest a relapse come upon you; and consult your own necessities, even at the risk of being misapprehended, for a time, by your numerous friends. I, too, have been ill, severely so, and know experimentally how to sympathize with those who are prostrated on beds of sickness. During my confinement of more than six weeks to my chamber, I felt with the poet Thomson to exclaim —

"O, who can speak the vigorous joys of health!
Unclogged the body, unobscured the mind!
The morning rises gay with pleasing stealth —
The temperate evening falls serene and kind!"[3]

My dear Helen was called to summon all her fortitude and devotedness as a wife and a mother, and faithfully did she perform her part. With a babe at her breast, a husband sick almost unto death, and three children lying ill at the same time of that dreadful disorder scarlatina, she nobly passed through the ordeal; and it was not until we were all convalescent, that her exhausted frame gave out, when she was brought down by a slow, intermittent fever, from which she has since happily recovered. Truly, we have been afflicted as a household, but the wings of divine love and mercy have overshadowed us all the while.

I join with you in the regret, that it was not my good fortune to become acquainted with your excellent friend, Joseph Barker, during my last visit to England. His writings evince a most amiable and christian spirit, and a mind resolutely bent in knowing and obeying the truth, at whatever sacrifice. The correspondence which has thus been opened between us, I trust will long be continued. He cannot shower his epistles upon me too copiously. O, such spirits are too rare in our world, and it is for this reason that the world is "upside down," yea, in ruins. But the work of redemption is assuredly going on, and Christ shall yet have the heathen for a possession, and reign "from sea to sea, and from the rivers to the ends of the earth." [4]

Dear Henry C. Wright, it appears, you have not yet seen. I commend him to your friendship and confidence as a tried spirit, a loving friend of the human family, a humble follower of the Son of God.[5] You will find him to be a man of child-like simplicity, absorbed in his one desire to go about doing good, of unpretending manners, frank and bold in the declaration of his sentiments, and of a remarkably social and affectionate spirit. He is not calculated to captivate an audience by his eloquence, but he finds no difficulty in securing their attention by the sincerity of his manner, the startling novelty of his doctrines, and the vigor with which he lays the axe at the root of the tree.[6] We miss him from our ranks, more and more, and shall hardly be able to reconcile ourselves to a prolonged absence on his part abroad. Still, it is for him, and not for us, to mark out his course, and to determine in what part of the vineyard of the Lord he shall labor. When you see him, I dare say your mind will be greatly refreshed by the communications it will be in his power to make to you, respecting our reformatory operations in this country. He knows "every rope in the [ship] [7]" — is familiar with all the transactions of the last ten years — and is personally acquainted with nearly all the leading abolitionists and non-resistants on this side of the waters. Just take a peep into his diary, or get him to read from its pages, and you will find many things of a curious and an instructive nature. I am much pleased to hear that you so highly appreciate his little volume, "A Kiss for a Blow," and trust it will find a ready sale in England.[8] Your advice and counsel will be of great service to him as to his best method of getting before the people. May the God of peace crown his labors with abundant success, and return him in safety to his native land!

The intelligence which you communicate respecting Dwarkananth Tagore excites painful anxiety for the welfare of our beloved friend George Thompson.[9] I thought, from the first, that the mission of G. T. was one of doubtful utility and great personal hazard; but now, "clouds and shadows" do indeed rest upon it. Let us, however, hope for the best.

The present condition of England strikes me not only as extremely melancholy, but as absolutely frightful. What a spectacle, in a country famous for its industry and its fertility, to see vast multitudes of the people famishing for bread! What is to be the end of all this? Of all your reform parties, not one goes far enough — not one is based on the broad, immovable foundation of human rights — not one raises the standard of christian revolt against the powers of darkness. The repeal of the Corn Laws may do something for the relief of the people — the extension of the right of suffrage may ultimately do more; but these measures are not radical, but only palliative.[10] Palliation, it may be said, is better than unmitigated suffering; and so it is, *pro tempore*; but there is nothing so good as a blow aimed at the right source. The people are crushed beneath an overgrown monarchy and a bloated aristocracy, and are made the victims of an atrocious alliance between Church and State. Why not then boldly aim for the destruction of these? I confess it excites my derision, and awakens indignant feelings in my bosom, when I read the proceedings of your Anti-Corn Law men, your Free Suffrage declaimers, your roaring Chartists, at their soirees and on other social or convivial occasions, and see that Queen Victoria, and Prince Albert, and the rest of the royal brood, are complimented in "sentiments," and cheered as if they were the benefactors of old England! [11] The watchword should be, — at the risk of martyrdom, or execution for high treason, — Down with the throne! Down with the aristocracy! Down with the accursed union between Church and State! The rights of God and man should be defended at all hazards. Of course, I desire the shedding of no blood, but only the utterance of great and terrible truths, and the use of those weapons which are mighty, through God, to the pulling down of strong holds. None but non-resistants, in deed and in truth, in spirit and in life, are qualified to carry on such a warfare. Some of them would probably die as martyrs; but this is far better than that a whole people should perish. Without a miracle, if things continue long in their present state, it seems to me England cannot escape a bloody revolution.

Say to your venerable father [Joseph Pease], that I have forgotten neither his personal kindness to myself, nor his philanthropic zeal in the cause of universal emancipation. May his useful life long be spared to the world. I will thank you to convey to your mother-in-law [12] my respectful remembrances. The death of so benevolent a man as Jonathan Backhouse must be severely felt among you.[13] Whose turn it may be next to put off this mortality, it is impossible to foresee, nor is it material. "That life is long which answers life's great end." [14]

So! there is to be another General Anti-Slavery Convention held in London, in June next — and the whole world of women have been duly notified that none but "gentlemen" will be admitted as members! [15] Of course, the American Anti-Slavery Society and its auxiliaries will not consent to be represented on the occasion, even by "gentlemen." I hope bro. Wright will go into the gallery to take notes, and that he will also make his arrangements so as to attend the London anniversaries in May.[16] Farewell, beloved friend!

Wm. Lloyd Garrison.

ALS: Garrison Papers, Boston Public Library.

1. Garrison refers to Joseph Barker (1806–1875), an English printer and former Methodist minister, whose letter he printed March 10, 1843. The letter is an expression of Barker's rather conservative religious views.

Garrison had apparently not heard from Elizabeth Pease since her letter of October 31, 1842 (printed in *The Liberator*, January 20, 1843).

2. Thomas Campbell, *The Pleasures of Hope*, Part II, line 377.

3. James Thomson, *The Castle of Indolence*, II, stanza 58, lines 1–4.

4. Psalms 72:8.

5. It is ironic that Garrison with his highly developed sense of social propriety should have been the one to introduce Henry C. Wright and Elizabeth Pease, for there developed between them a rather unconventional relationship. Sometime in 1843 Wright became very ill, and Miss Pease took it upon herself to nurse him back to health. In the process they fell deeply in love, and later in the year were often seen together. Eventually, Wright, who despite a wife and family in America, knew that he was unusually susceptible to the charms of girls and young ladies, resolved that he must see her no more. (Louis Billington, "Some Connections between British and American Reform Movements, 1830–1860, with Special Reference to the Anti-Slavery Movement," unpublished master's thesis, University of Bristol, 1966, pp. 175–176.)

6. Garrison adapts Luke 3:9.

7. Garrison mistakenly writes "shape" instead of "ship," the word indicated for the common nineteenth-century maxim to which he undoubtedly refers.

8. Henry C. Wright's book of moralistic stories for children, dedicated to the principle that evil should be countered with good, was published in Boston in 1842. For Garrison's laudatory review of the book see *The Liberator*, September 9, 1842.

9. Dwarkananth Tagore (1794–1846), grandfather of the poet, was a wealthy Indian merchant, whose firm of Carr, Tagore, & Company had been founded in 1834. (Krishna Kripalani, *Rabindranath Tagore*, New York, 1961.) Since the pertinent passage of Miss Pease's letter of December 31, 1842, has apparently not been preserved either in manuscript at the Boston Public Library or in published form in *The Liberator*, one can only speculate concerning the nature of her "intelligence . . . respecting Dwarkananth Tagore," though her letter of October 31, 1842, indicates that she considers him somewhat less than reliable. (An excerpt from the letter of December 31 did appear in Garrison's editorial comment concerning Barker's letter in *The Liberator*, March 10, 1842. See letter to Elizabeth Pease, December 1, 1843.)

10. The Corn Laws prohibited or discouraged the importation of foreign grain. Richard Cobden and the Anti-Corn-Law League were largely responsible for the repeal of the laws in 1846.

11. The Free Suffrage Declaimers advocated the abolition of the property qualification for voting then current in England. The Chartists, mostly from the working classes, were political reformers active in England between 1837 and 1848. They had formulated a "People's Charter," consisting of six demands concerned directly or indirectly with suffrage.

12. An old usage meaning "stepmother." Mrs. Pease has not been identified.

13. Jonathan Backhouse (1779–1842) was an English banker and railway promoter. Both he and his wife were ministers of the Society of Friends in Great Britain and had traveled extensively in the United States during the 1830's trying to heal the schism among the Quakers. (Elbert Russell, *The History of Quakerism,* New York, 1943.)

14. Edward Young, *Night Thoughts,* "Night V," line 773.

15. This meeting convened June 13, 1843, at Freemasons' Hall. At an earlier convention sponsored by the British and Foreign Anti-Slavery Society (June 1840) the British majority had refused to seat Lucretia Mott and other American women delegates, and Garrison protested such denial of woman's rights by refusing to participate at the convention, merely observing the proceedings from the balcony. (*AWT,* pp. 165–168.)

16. Garrison refers to the annual meeting of the British and Foreign Anti-Slavery Society.

---

5 2

TO RICHARD D. WEBB

Boston, Feb. 28, 1843.

My dear Webb:

I knew that you was a modest man, before I received your last favor, written on a part of the sheet occupied by our friend H. C. Wright. He speaks in eulogistic terms of "the Dublin friends — the Webbs, the [Richard] Allens, the [James] Haughtons," &c. — which, having seen, you are apprehensive will appear in the Liberator. "It would only make any one (who may read the Liberator in Ireland) laugh at its inaccuracy and exaggeration." Have you yet to learn, that among the penalties inflicted on true reformers, during their life-time, is that of being praised, (rarely does praise come, however,) by those who are intimately acquainted with them, far more highly than they themselves can endure, or the generation in which they live are willing to endorse? Think not to be appreciated by the public, while duty compels you to act the part of moral Ishmaelites. Doubtless, there are thousands in Ireland, who are at all times ready to laugh when they hear the philanthropic labors of such "fanatics" and "incendiaries" as yourselves represented as exerting a powerful influence on the public mind, and as worthy of the highest commendation. Let them laugh! The laugh of such scorners is a stronger panegyric than that which excites it. I sincerely believe you are doing a great and good work, in the spirit of christian zeal and charity; that you are sowing imperishable seed for a bountiful harvest; that you are kindling a beacon-light that shall yet be plainly visible on both sides of the Atlantic; that it is not given to you to know what will be the extent of your influence, or the result of your labors in the great field of christian philanthropy. I believe Henry C. Wright simply does you justice in his letter, and speaks of you "without partiality and without hypocrisy." I believe it is not wrong to say, "Well done, good and faithful servants!" though it is not for mortals to add — "enter ye into the joy of your Lord."[1] Hence, (in spite of your protestation, and at the risk of making you ridiculous in the eyes of many,) I shall certainly not mutilate H.C.W's letter, my dear Dublin friends. If I thought you were capable of being inflated by any such notice, I would suppress it; but your feet, I trust, are so firmly planted on an eternal foundation, that they never can be shaken, either by the breath of flattery, or the wave of persecution. Go on in your noble work, "in the patience of hope and the labor of love," remembering that it only requires faith, "like a grain of mustard seed," to cast mountains of prejudice and corruption into the sea.[2] In your weakness, you are strong. "Thrice is he armed who hath his quarrel just."[3]

It is so seldom I write to you, my dear Webb, (to my shame it is here recorded — but, do I not love and admire you, nevertheless?) and so many events of surpassing interest are constantly transpiring, here and abroad, worthy of notice and criticism, that when I attempt to endite an epistle for your eye, I am deeply perplexed to know where to begin, or what to omit. I feel as if I must take passage at once in the steamer, for Dublin via Liverpool, and hold a "palaver" with you and others, in your great, beautiful and wretched city, for at least a month — and so be "a living epistle," known and read of you all. This being confined to pen, ink and paper, where time is limited, and the heart has a world of freight on board of it to discharge, is terrible bondage. It is better than total non-intercourse, but scarcely better than throwing crumbs to those who are famishing for lack of regular meals. Reading and writing do not come by nature, but conversation does; and, hence, I love to talk a great deal better than I love to write.

It appears that you have heard of my recent severe illness. Now that I have recovered from it, it seems to me like awaking from a frightful dream. On the score of loathsomeness, the scarlatina (as I had it) is next to the small-pox. My family have all been quite ill, but are now happily convalescent. I have now four children, (all boys,) the youngest of whom is about six months old, and bears the name of a great and good man, who was lost in the steamer Lexington, two years ago — and who was endeared to me by many considerations — Charles Follen, formerly of Germany.[4]

We are driving our anti-slavery operations with rail-road speed, and success every where crowns our efforts. The result, I doubt not, will be the dissolution of the Union. I have no expectation that the bloody-minded South will be brought to repentance, but only to a terrible retribution. You may expect to hear of more exciting scenes and stormier times among us than have yet been witnessed; for, though we have passed through various important crises, the great crisis of all is yet to come!

I am very much obliged to you, and others of your loving circle, for occasional numbers of the Dublin papers; and in them I am glad to see the reports of your meetings in the Royal Exchange.[5] It is a fortunate circumstance that you are thus able to get your sentiments before the reading public; but the time is coming (mark that!) when you will not be permitted to do this. — But here I close abruptly to say a word to your beloved Hannah, begging to be affectionately remembered to those whose names it is here needless to specify.

Your faithful friend,

Wm. Lloyd Garrison.

ALS: Garrison Papers, Boston Public Library.

1. Garrison telescopes Matthew 25:23.
2. Garrison adapts I Thessalonians 1:3 and Matthew 17:20.
3. Shakespeare, *2 Henry VI*, III, ii, 233.
4. The *Lexington* was a wooden paddle steamer built in 1836 by Bishop and Simmson in New York City. A fire broke out on January 13, 1840, while she was en route from New York to Stonington, Connecticut, and of the 110 passengers on board only four survived. The disaster was the subject of a well-known Currier and Ives print.
5. The Royal Exchange is now City Hall, at Cork Hill, Dublin. It was designed by Thomas Cooley and built between 1769 and 1779. (Letter to the editor from C. Duncan Rice, Yale University, December 26, 1970.)

53

TO HANNAH WEBB

Boston, March 1, 1843.

Esteemed Friend Hannah Webb:

Chivalry, while it practically crushes and degrades woman, theoretically concedes that the wife is "the better half" of the husband. Of one thing I feel quite sure, that you twain, Richard and Hannah, are one, and where there is only one, there is no division into greater or less. Long may you live together on earth, one in spirit and purpose, and for ever be united beyond the grave in one glorious destiny! Such is my prayer.

I thank you for the Sybilline leaf which you and Richard conjointly sent to me by the last steamer.[1] It is an awakener of the most delightful reminiscences. That visit to Dublin! To be so cordially entertained by strangers, being a "foreigner" — to be welcomed to their fire-sides and their hearts — to obtain their confidence and esteem so literally on so short an acquaintance — when I forget it all, may my tongue cleave to the roof of my mouth! I know not that I have ever thanked you, formally, on paper, for your kindness to me during my brief sojourn in Dublin. I only know that "the thankless oft are noisiest in their thanks," [2] and that my heart has ever since, like a fountain, been welling over with the chrystal waters of gratitude. But, no more on this point — you will say.

I feel rejoiced to hear that you have all been pleased with the s[oci]ety of that simple-hearted, strong limbed, indomitable laborer in the vin[eyard] of the Lord, Henry C. Wright. He is indeed "a man and a brother." [3] His [. . .] goes out, like the universe of God, embracing all things in its circumference. On its altar, the fire of divine love seems to be continually burning. There are none so low in the abyss of human degradation and mystery, none so remote by geographical position, whom the arms of his philanthropy do not embrace. If he is "a man of one idea," the idea is this — that "love is the fulfilling of the law," [4] and that to dwell in it is to dwell in God. You say that some who have listened to him have been edified, "and some shocked." For a long time to come, it will be his mission, I apprehend, to shock, rather than to edify. Your land, as well as ours, is in an awful condition — totally incapacitated to listen to the truth with calmness. It needs to be shocked and shaken as by an earthquake. The truths that he will utter will make the ears of the people to tingle; [5] but all those who are seeking for light, and who rejoice to walk in it, will hear him gladly. I trust he will declare the whole truth, whether men will hear or forbear.

Referring to my boys, you ask — "How dost thou contrive about school? Does Helen teach them herself?" We are necessitated to do pretty much as our neighbors. George and William attend a private school, kept by an excellent young woman, who, though not specially interested in this subject of non-resistance, has an excellent "faculty" of managing children, without a frequent resort to pains and penalties. [6] Our boys (as far as they are developed) have a large share of independence and firmness, and require a steady guidance. Between schools, it is difficult to keep them at all times shut up in the house; and if they play out of doors, they are liable to hear improper language from vicious boys. It is a perilous career, in this world of ours as society is now constituted, from childhood to old age; and every parent has just cause to feel anxious for the future course and welfare of his children.

At last, in the Commonwealth of Massachusetts, human beings who love each other may be united together in "holy wedlock," even though the hue of their skin may not perfectly harmonize! Doubtless you have seen something in the Liberator about an "intermarriage law" here, by which the marriage of white and colored persons is declared null and void.[7] It was an old law, made more than a hundred years ago, in the days of slavery on the soil of the Pilgrims. As it was a war upon human rights, and a disgrace to our statute books, the abolitionists have endeavored, for the last six years, to procure its repeal by petitioning the Legislature; but they have sustained an annual defeat until the present session, when success has perched upon their standard. The law has been repealed — and thus another staggering blow has been given to the monster prejudice. Our object has been not to promote "amalgamation," but to establish justice, and vindicate the equality of the human race. Regretting that I have neither time nor space to write more, and wishing you and yours the choicest blessings of heaven, I remain,

Your grateful friend,

Wm. Lloyd Garrison.

ALS: Garrison Papers, Boston Public Library.

Little is known of Hannah Webb except that she was the wife of Richard Davis Webb.

1. By "Sybilline leaf" Garrison simply means a letter. The expression derives from the legend of the Cumaean sibyl, who wrote her prophecies on palm leaves.

2. Not identified.

3. "Am I not a man and a brother?" is the motto on the seal of the British and Foreign Anti-Slavery Society.

4. Romans 13:10.

5. A reference to either I Samuel 3:11, II Kings 21:12, or Jeremiah 19:3.

6. Although the school Garrison refers to has not been positively identified, an advertisement in *The Liberator*, March 12, 1847, refers to a Miss Whitney, who kept a school on Chauncy Place in Boston, a neighborhood where several of Garrison's associates, including the Chapman family, lived.

7. In *The Liberator*, February 10, 1843, the repeal of the intermarriage law is reported, along with the names of all who voted. Garrison suggests that his readers treat those who voted against repeal "as unprincipled men 'who glory in their shame.'" For further comments on the marriage law see *The Liberator*, February 24, 1843.

---

5 4

TO HENRY C. WRIGHT

Boston, March 1, 1843.

Dear bro. Wright:

Your letter from Dublin of Jan. 30th was duly received by the last steamer, and perused with intense interest and pleasure. For the deep sympathy which you express in regard to my late illness, and your congratulations on my being convalescent, accept the gratitude of my heart. It has been the severest ordeal through which my mortal frame has ever been called to pass. All the dear children had the scarlatina in a dangerous form, but my own case was far the most perilous. I can conceive of nothing more loathsome than this disorder, except the small-pox. Not being able to administer Thompsonian courses to myself, or to remove to an infirmary, I put myself under the medical care of Dr. [Robert] Wesselhoeft, (a German, and the intimate friend and companion of the lamented [Charles] Follen,) who is a homœopathist, and have no cause to regret the step. For three months, my house was a hospital. First, the children all had the chicken-pox; then, all but the babe had the scarlatina; then, I was next prostrated with the same disorder; then, dear Helen was seized with a nervous fever; and, finally, sister Ann (whose chronic complaints seem to be incurable) was reduced quite low. The health of sister Sarah was also very much shattered by fatigue and anxiety. At present, we are all convalescent, but none of us, as yet, perfectly restored. Mrs. Benson now lies confined to her bed by a slow, intermittent fever, but we trust her sickness will not be unto death. My poor, afflicted brother James was happily released from suffering a few weeks after your departure; I say happily, because as his disorder was incurable, and subjected him to intolerable pain, we could not desire his prolonged existence on earth.[1] He died in a calm and quiet state of mind; and at last so slight was his struggle with the "last enemy," [2] he had probably been dead half an hour before I was aware of it, though I was watching (alone) by his couch. I thought he was in a serene slumber, and was rejoicing that he was able to obtain some repose. At his funeral, (we had a crowded house,) after a prayer, &c. from our beloved Samuel J. May, I addressed the assembly at some length, especially in reference to the navy in particular, and the war-system in general, and held up the religion of the United States in its true character. My remarks were very pointed, and produced some sensation among the warring sectarians who were present.

Another son has been added to my family since you left, and a fine, noble boy he is — of course! He bears the honored name of Charles Follen.

Happy am I to find that your appreciation of my dear friends in Ireland is as exalted as my own; that your intercourse with them has been mutually instructive and pleasant; that they know nothing of weariness or apathy in carrying on the great work of human redemption; and that they shrink from nothing that is right, and fear nothing but what is wrong. Heaven bless them in their basket and in their store,[3] and may they be filled with all the fulness of God, which is love without measure, pure, disinterested, inexhaustible! How much I think of them — admire them — love them; how eagerly I catch at every scrap of intelligence from them; how watchfully I observe all their movements in the various philanthropic enterprises, to the promotion of which they have dedicated their lives; with what gladness I receive and read their epistles; and how I yearn for that happy day (will it ever come on earth?) when we shall be permitted again to see each other, face to face; they little know, because their humility leads them to form a slight estimate of themselves, and of their philanthropic labors. Besides, judging me by an epistolary standard, as a test of friendship, they have no reason to suppose that I am very enthusiastic in my attachment to them; for they have been shamefully neglected by me, on that score. You know something of my aversion to the pen, and of my procrastinating habits, and therefore can make some allowance for me. In *intention*, I have written to them whole reams of letters; but, in reality, they scarcely receive one from me during a twelvemonth. To be sure, my time is very much occupied in our various reformatory enterprises at home; but I will [no]t try to shelter myself behind this fact, in order to screen myself from merited reprehension. All I can now say is, tell them that I am truly growing penitent, and hope to "bring forth fruits meet for repentance" [4] very speedily. Convey to them, individually, my best wishes and most grateful remembrances.

It seems, by the date of your letter, that you have not yet had a personal interview with that peerless woman, Elizabeth Pease. She writes to me that she is strongly desirous of seeing you, and feels confident that your mission was undertaken at the right time, and will be productive of great good. Her contribution of £20 in aid of your invaluable little work [5] is characteristic of her generous spirit. You will find her as complete a specimen of womanhood as can be found on the earth. She is endowed with more than Roman (because it is Christian) firmness, with great conscientiousness, with true courage, with sterling independence, and with a strong and comprehensive intellect. She is not merely "an honor to her sex," but a blessing to the world. May her light shine brighter and brighter to the perfect day!

You will regret to learn that there is, at present, no probability that the "Non-Resistant" will be renewed in its publication — at least, for some time to come. This is, I think, to be attributed partly to the want of energy on the part of our Executive Committee, and partly to your absence. We miss you exceedingly in the cause of non-resistance, and can scarcely be reconciled to the thought of your remaining abroad any length of time. Do not infer from all this, however, that I am led to view our sublime and holy movement as on the retrograde; for I am satisfied that converts to it are daily multiplying, and that it has received an impetus which no opposition will be able to frustrate. But our time, our means, our labors are so absorbed in seeking the emancipation of our enslaved countrymen, that we cannot do as much specifically and directly for non-resistance as it would otherwise be in our power to perform. We shall try to do more for the future.

The subject of capital punishment, within a few months past, has been widely discussed in the land, and is fast increasing in public interest. As usual, at the outset of every reform, the clergy (as a body) are contending stoutly in favor of the gallows. It is a divine institution, and the very corner-stone of christian security. A public debate has lately been held in the Broadway Tabernacle, New-York, between Mr. T. O'Sullivan, the editor of the Democratic Review, and the *Reverend* George B. Cheever — the latter for strangling, and the former against it. The Rev. Dr. Cox also pitted himself, on the same occasion, against Mr. Greely, the editor of the Tribune.[6] The Evangelist, in the successive numbers, has published Cheever's argument, which occupies more than [...] columns of that paper. It raises (as well as the Obse[rver] Baptist Advocate) a shout of triumph, and declares that O'Sullivan [...] completely vanquished.[7] From other and more impartial sources it is conceded that O'Sullivan was "used up," being no match (especially in biblical exegesis) for the parson. Cheever's fancied Gibraltar position is, "Whoso sheddeth man's blood," &c.[8] This, he affirms, was a law given through Noah to all mankind, which is not superseded, repealed, or in any degree impaired by the christian dispensation, but is in perfect harmony with it! I wish I could send you the numbers of the Evangelist containing his argument; but, having no spare copies, and intending to review it in the Liberator, (and possibly in a pamphlet,) I am unable to do so at present. Cheever exhausts panegyric upon the benevolence and moral efficacy of the gallows, and likens it to one of the planets in the firmament, to a beacon-light, to "a sun shot into chaos"![9] His argument is both ingenious and vigorous, and will do considerable mischief. Discussions have been held in this city on the same subject, at which I was not able to be present. Petitions are now before our Legislature, praying for the abolition of capital punishment.

After a warm conflict, the intermarriage law has passed through both houses of our Legislature, and only needs the Governor's signature (which will undoubtedly be affixed to it) to be complete.[10] Thus has another tremendous blow been given to the monster prejudice. We have not been equally successful in regard to the rail-road question, and shall therefore "try again."[11] Never were the aspects of the anti-slavery cause so auspicious as at the present time. In this Commonwealth abolitionism is now scarcely able to find one public opponent. The Latimer affair has produced a mighty sensation, not only "from Berkshire to Cape Cod," but from one extremity of the country to the other. The Latimer petition to our Legislature contained more than sixty-five thousand names; and that to Congress, more than fifty-one thousand[.] The latter was entrusted to John Quincy Adams, and has caused intense excitement among the slaveholding banditti in the House of Representatives. The former was presented to our House by a son of Mr. Adams, and he has made a favorable report on the same in behalf of the committee to whom it was referred, but no action has yet been taken on it [12]

Our Anti-Slavery Fair, in December, was the most splendid and successful of the series.[13] The contributions of our transatlantic coadjutors excited great curiosity and admiration on the part of the visitors, and were gratefully appreciated by all the friends of genuine abolitionism in this region. It is by such co-operation that the great idea of human brotherhood becomes a living reality, and national animosities are doomed to an ignominious death. "One good turn" begets as well as "deserves another."

The Miller excitement increases as the time draws near for the fulfilment of the prediction.[14] A considerable number of worthy abolitionists have been carried away by it, and, for the time being, are rendered completely useless to our cause. But the delusion has not long to run, and let us rejoice.

Among the public men, who have recently died, are Commodore Hull, Bishop Griswold, Peter A. Jay, and Judge Thacher of this city.[15]

I hope to hear from you by every steamer that leaves Liverpool for Boston. Your letters will be read by thousands with deep interest in the Liberator. — Be extremely careful of your health. Let me know in what way I can be of any service to you. I hope to be more punctual hereafter in my correspondence with you. All our Boston friends, together with the members of my household, desire special remembranc[e] and wish you every blessing; but none more heartily than

Your loving friend,

Wm. Lloyd Garrison.

ALS: Garrison Papers, Boston Public Library.

1. James Holley Garrison died on October 14, 1842.
2. I Corinthians 15:26.
3. Deuteronomy 28:5.
4. Matthew 3:8.
5. Probably *A Kiss for a Blow* (Boston, 1842).
6. Garrison refers to a meeting at one of the city's most active assembly halls (340–344 Broadway, between Worth Street and Catherine Lane), listing among

the disputants on this occasion four prominent New Yorkers: John Louis O'Sullivan (1813–1895), whose initial Garrison mistakes, George B. Cheever (1807–1890), Abraham Liddon Cox (1799–1864), and Horace Greeley (1811–1872), whose name Garrison mispells.

O'Sullivan, who opposed capital punishment, was both journalist and diplomat; he had established in 1837 (along with S. D. Langtree) the *United States Magazine and Democratic Review*, noted for publicizing nationalistic and expansionist views. O'Sullivan himself probably originated the phrase "manifest destiny." From 1844 to 1846 O'Sullivan was to be editor of the New York *Morning News*.

George B. Cheever, at this time pastor of the Allen Street Presbyterian Church in New York, defended capital punishment on biblical grounds and favored the continuation of compulsory Bible reading in the public schools, but he was also an active abolitionist.

Abraham Liddon Cox, physician as well as minister and the brother of Samuel Hanson Cox, had been active in the American Anti-Slavery Society since its inception. (*Life.*)

Horace Greeley was the editor of the New York *Tribune*, which he had founded in 1841. The paper was rapidly becoming outstanding in the city. Greeley's views about slavery were as inflexible as Garrison's own, and the *Tribune* frequently expressed opinion favorable to the abolitionists. Greeley was active in many other reforms also, including the abolition of capital punishment. In the 1850's Greeley became active in the Free-soil movement, and following the Civil War he became the presidential candidate for the Liberal Republican and the Democratic parties.

7. Garrison mentions two New York City papers. The *Evangelist* was published between 1830 and 1902 (with various subtitles) when it merged into the *Christian Work and the Evangelist*, later becoming simply the *Christian Work*. The other paper is probably the *Baptist Advocate* (1839–1845), which was superseded by the *Recorder*. (*ULS*.)

8. Genesis 9:6; the rest of the sentence is as follows: "by man shall his blood be shed: for in the image of God made he man."

9. The Cheever-O'Sullivan debate was reported in the *Evangelist*, February 9, 16, and 23, 1843. The issue of February 9 contains Cheever's phrase "a sun shot into chaos."

10. The governor was Marcus Morton (1784–1864), a Democrat, who had served in that office since 1839. Morton had in fact approved the repeal of the intermarriage law February 25. (Letter to the editor from Anna E. Lima, assistant state librarian, the Commonwealth of Massachusetts State Library, February 17, 1971.)

11. The "rail-road question" refers to the use of "Jim Crow cars"; see Garrison's letter to Helen E. Garrison, September 17, 1846, n. 2.

For Wendell Phillips' speech on the subject of prejudice against Negroes on railroad trains see *The Liberator*, February 18, 1842.

12. Garrison refers to Charles Francis Adams (1807–1886), who had studied law under Daniel Webster and was first elected to the Massachusetts House of Representatives in 1840. Originally opposed to abolition, he gradually came to a better understanding of the issues at stake, becoming an advocate of the antislavery cause, but, unlike Garrison, he was disposed to compromise.

13. The first antislavery fair had been held in 1834, when it raised $300 for the New England Anti-Slavery Society. It became an annual event, raising for the Massachusetts Anti-Slavery Society as much as $5,250 in 1856. Following that year the bazaar was replaced by the National Anti-Slavery Subscription, which raised $6,117.02 in 1859. During the Civil War this type of fund-raising venture became less successful.

14. William Miller (1782–1849) of Low Hampton, New York, led the Second Advent movement in the United States. The movement was based on the conviction that the world is evil and will be destroyed by divine intervention, allowing only the righteous to be saved. Miller predicted that the second advent would

occur between March 1843 and March 1844. In *The Liberator*, November 8, 1844, Garrison described Miller and his followers as led "by a deplorable fantasy of the brain."

15. The four men who share the same year of death had little else in common. Isaac Hull (1773–1843), a ship captain by the age of twenty-one, was in charge of the Boston Navy Yard between 1815 and 1823 and of the navy yard in Washington between 1829 and 1835. Alexander Viets Griswold (1766–1843), an Episcopal clergyman since 1794, in 1810 elected bishop of the Eastern Diocese (Massachusetts, Maine, Rhode Island, Vermont, and New Hampshire), of which he became in 1838 presiding bishop. Peter Augustus Jay (1776–1843), a lawyer by profession, was the son of Chief Justice John Jay and brother of judge and moral reformer William Jay. He served in various public and charitable offices in New York state and was an active abolitionist as early as 1816 when he was a member of the New York state assembly. Peter Oxenbridge Thacher (1776–1843) had been judge of the municipal court in Boston. Garrison had focused attention on him sporadically during the spring and summer of 1832. At the opening of the court session Judge Thacher had given a long charge to the jury describing indictable offenses, citing the example of a paper that preached such hostility and hatred as might lead to revolt or insurrection in other states. (*Life.*) Other papers identified the paper as *The Liberator*, and Garrison reprinted a number of their articles attacking Thacher and defending freedom of the press, limiting himself to brief and restrained comments (see *The Liberator*, April 7, May 5, July 28, August 18, 1832).

55

TO GEORGE W. BENSON

Boston, March 3, 1843.

Dear bro. George:

I am happy to send you the intelligence, that, since my last letter, mother has continued steadily to improve in health, and may now be regarded as decidedly convalescent, and therefore out of danger. She is, of course, yet weak, but her appetite is good, and by care it will not be long before she will be about the house again.

I do not know who was the author of the communication from Dorchester, that was published in the Liberator, giving a thrust at your Association about equal rights, &c. I published it [1] without note or comment, feeling quite certain that I should be furnished with such a reply as was sent to me by Wm. Adam, a man who would be constantly rising in my estimation, if that were possible; for I have long regarded him as one of the noblest specimens of manhood to be found among our race.[2]

We (that is, myself and household) are highly gratified at the fiscal success of your operations, thus far, and trust you will have no occasion, on any ground, to regret the experiment you are making.

The bearer of this, (a son of Peleg Clarke, of Coventry,) is probably well known to you.[3] He informs me that he visits Northampton to take a peep at your little community, with some intention of becoming an individual part of it.

I talk of leaving Cambridgeport, by and by, and removing to the city. Ellis Gray Loring is desirous that we should occupy his house, and we shall probably do so, but not till the fall. Our friends in Lynn are anxious to have me locate myself in that place. James N. Buffum has an excellent house to let, in a very pleasant situation.[4] On some accounts, I should like to reside in Lynn; but the distance is rather too great from the city.

Give our united loving remembrances to Catherine, and our friendly regards to all who are with you.

Yours, ever,

Wm. Lloyd Garrison.

ALS: Garrison Papers, Boston Public Library.

1. In *The Liberator*, February 10, 1843.
2. Professor Adam's reply was published February 24. It denied the allegation that women had been excluded from voting at a recent antislavery convention in Northampton and defended the integrity of the Northampton Association.
3. Garrison may refer to John L. Clarke, whose father, Peleg Clarke (1784–1875) was a homeopathic physician and late in life became president of the Rhode Island Homoeopathic Society (George A. Morrison, Jr., *The 'Clarke' Families of Rhode Island*, New York, 1902, p. 125).
4. James N. Buffum (1807–1887), an active abolitionist from Lynn, Massachusetts, was vice-president of the Friends of Social Reform, a Fourier organization in which George W. Benson was also active. In 1845–1846 he went on tour through Britain and Europe with Frederick Douglass. (*Life.*)

---

5 6

TO JOSHUA T. EVERETT

Boston, March 4, 1843.*

Esteemed Friend:

I am compelled, through bodily weakness, (the lingering consequence of my recent severe illness,) to decline the kind and urgent invitation of my friends in Leominster, to be present at the meeting of the Worcester County Anti-Slavery Society, in your town on Wednesday next. You need no assurance from me, that it would give me much pleasure to be able to participate in the proceedings of the meeting, for various reasons: — first, to gratify those dear friends, and to show my appreciation of their kindness; secondly, to remove some of those

* This letter was not written for the public eye; but it is published at the request of the Convention. — Ed. Lib.

monstrous misapprehensions which exist in many minds, in regard to my principles and sentiments; and, lastly, to aid in the further advancement of our heaven-sanctioned enterprise, which has for its object the glory of God and the welfare of our race.

You pleasantly remark, in your letter, that I am regarded, by some persons in your region, as 'a monster in human shape.' What it is that makes me so frightful in their eyes, I do not know; but I am prepared to say with Paul, 'If I be an offender, or have committed any thing worthy of death, I refuse not to die.' [1] In what consists my criminality? In refusing to go with a multitude to do evil — to seek human applause and popularity — to abandon principle for expediency — to walk by sight instead of by faith? [2] In toiling, for many a weary year, to undo the heavy burdens and let the oppressed go free? [3] In proclaiming the equal rights of the whole human race, without regard to color, clime or sex? In striving to cause swords to be beaten into ploughshares, and spears into pruning-hooks, that the nations of the earth may learn the art of war no more? [4] Is it in preaching salvation from sin in this life, through the righteousness of Christ wrought out in the soul of him who is born of God? Is it in striving to bring a spurious religion and a false worship into disrepute, and to vindicate Christianity from the dreadful aspersions which have been cast upon it by its nominal professors? To these charges, I plead guilty. They constitute 'the head and front of my offending.' [5] For which of these will any *Christian* take up stones to stone me?

You allude to some others in your vicinity, who wish to 'have it distinctly understood that they are old organizationists, *but not of the Garrison class.*' If they simply mean by this, that they fully coincide with my views of the awful enormity of slavery, and of the duty of all slaveholders *immediately* to let their slaves go free, but do not agree with me in some of my religious views, then I have only to say, that this disclaimer is absurd, gratuitous and unreasonable. For is it not a fact that, on the anti-slavery platform, we have persons of every variety of doctrine and sentiment, both religious and political; but who, on the subject of slavery, are 'mingled into one, like kindred drops?' [6] Because I am an abolitionist, am I to be shunned, or held up to odium, if I do not agree with others on points foreign to the anti-slavery enterprise? In being an abolitionist, have I no right to think, speak and write on any other subject of a controverted nature? Have I not as much liberty as my accusers? Do I differ any more widely from them than they do from me? When have I refused to join hand in hand with *them* for the extermination of slavery on our soil, because of a difference of views in religion or politics? Who can justly accuse me of indulging in religious, sectarian or political partyism, as an abolitionist? I have a right to demand of others, the charity and good-will which I exhibit toward them. Rely upon it, my dear friend, that they who claim to be abolitionists, 'but not of the Garrison stamp,' will generally, if not invariably, be found to be inimical not only to some of my peculiar religious sentiments, but to my *abolitionism*, which is too uncompromising in principle, too decisive in action, too impartial in application, to suit their bigoted, time-serving spirit. They hate me for my fidelity to bleeding humanity. They need another baptism. They do not 'remember them that are in bonds as bound with them.' [7] Their religion is one that comes by observation, and has a human priesthood, a worldly sanctuary, and ordinances of divine service. They are not abolitionists from *principle*. They love a right eye or a right hand much better than they love the cause of Christ.[8] I leave such cavillers and persecutors in the hands of God, who will assuredly render to every one according to his works.[9] From the inmost recesses of my soul, I pity them, and pray for the purging of their moral vision, and the enlarging of their minds. I have no fear that time and posterity will not do me ample justice. I labor not for this age, or to obtain the verdict of this generation. No man, of any nation, shall be able justly to accuse me, either in time or eternity, of refusing to acknowledge him as 'a man and a brother,' or advocating doctrines of a sectional or hostile character. 'My country is the world — my countrymen are all mankind.' [10]

Feeling assured in spirit that your meeting will be owned and blessed by the God of the oppressed, and confiding in you, that you will be faithful to the end, in nothing wavering, and confident of a final victory, I remain, with much esteem,

Your unfaltering coadjutor,

WM. LLOYD GARRISON.

Printed: *The Liberator*, March 31, 1843.

Joshua Titus Everett (1806–1897) spent most of his life in Princeton, Massachusetts. He was widely known in Worcester County and elsewhere as a reformer. An early convert to the antislavery cause, his house was always open to the fugitive slave. For many years he held the office of president of the Worcester County North Division Anti-Slavery Society and was an occasional contributor to *The Liberator*. He was a member of the Massachusetts legislature from 1833 to 1835 and at the time of his death was the oldest ex-member of the General Court. (Letter to the editor from Edith M. Maynard, librarian, Worcester Historical Society, October 27, 1970.)

1. Acts 25:11.
2. Garrison reverses II Corinthians 5:7.
3. Isaiah 58:6.
4. Garrison adapts Isaiah 2:4.
5. Shakespeare, *Othello*, I, iii, 80.
6. Garrison adapts William Cowper, *The Task*, Book II, line 19.
7. Hebrews 13:3.

8. Garrison refers to Matthew 5:29–30.

9. Garrison adapts Proverbs 24:29.

10. The original form of Garrison's motto for the head of *The Liberator* read, "Our country is the world — our countrymen are mankind," and appeared with the first issue, January 1, 1831.

---

5 7

TO LOUISA GILMAN LORING

Cambridgeport, March 19, 1843.

Esteemed Friend:

I obtained, a few days since, at Mrs. [Maria W.] Chapman's, a most beautiful and acceptable present, which you had the kindness to leave in her care for me. In the inkstand, I found a *golden* token of your friendship, the value of which I prize at a far higher rate than its market worth — though, in these "hard times," that is not inconsiderable. I am very much pleased with the inkstand. Something like it I have for a long time very much needed; for my writing-materials (for an editor) are of a most shabby character. The workmanship of it is exceedingly ingenious and elaborate; and if I knew who made it, I should like to compliment him for his skill and patience. I suppose, however, it is of foreign manufacture.

I need not tell *you* that this is not the first, second or third time that I have been indebted to you for a kindness done to me and mine; nor need I multiply words to assure you that my bosom is swelling with grateful emotions, in view of your friendship and benevolence. I am also a debtor to your estimable husband, to a large extent, and shall always hold in grateful remembrance his manifold kindnesses since we struck hands together for the emancipation of our enslaved fellow-countrymen, and the salvation of our native land.

Hoping ever to deserve and retain your confidence, esteem and friendship, by my fidelity to truth, mercy and love, I remain,

Your grateful friend,

Wm. Lloyd Garrison.

Mrs. E. G. Loring.

ALS: Ellis Gray Loring Family Papers, Radcliffe College Library.

Louisa Gilman Loring (1797–1868), the wife of Ellis Gray Loring, was also a zealous abolitionist and generous contributor to the cause. The Lorings' home was a center for abolitionists and later for the care of fugitive slaves. (*Life.*)

5 8

TO JAMES N. BUFFUM

Cambridgeport, March 24, 1843.

My dear Buffum:

After carefully estimating the advantages and disadvantages of a residence in Lynn, as compared with one in the city, — and after listening to the opinions of several friends on this point, — we (i.e. all the family) have come to the conclusion that, all things considered, it will be more convenient and satisfactory for us to remove to the city, than to make Lynn our dwelling-place. On many accounts, we should prefer to live in your "free and equal" town, but there are other considerations which lead us to believe that, as a whole, we should find ourselves better situated in Boston than in any other place in its vicinity. Nevertheless, we are highly obliged to you for having given us the opportunity to examine, and (if we chose) to occupy the convenient and pleasantly located house that you hold in trust. Our regard for the dear friends in Lynn is very strong, in some cases rising to admiration; and greatly should we rejoice to be allowed to have daily intercourse with them; but of this pleasure we must be deprived, at least for the present. Under existing circumstances, if the choice of removal had been left to us between Lynn and any other place except Boston, we should undoubtedly have decided in favor of Lynn. It is not yet certain to what part of the city we shall go, but probably the "South End" — perhaps to the house now occupied by our esteemed friend Ellis Gray Loring, who is desirous to let it to us.

When you next call at our respected friend Daniel Johnson's, please inform the family that, since her return home, sister Anne has been nearly all of the time confined to her bed, and it will probably be some time (if ever) before she becomes convalescent.[1] She is daily attended by Dr. [Robert] Wesselhoeft, our German homœopathic physician, who thinks her case somewhat critical, and describes her disorder as being exceedingly difficult to manage. Thus far, his prescriptions do not seem to have produced any beneficial effects; nor is Anne's faith in this mode of treatment very strong. We must leave the result in the hands of Him "who does not willingly afflict the children of men,"[2] being prepared for every event in his providence.

Say to those hospitable friends, that we shall ever gratefully remember their christian kindness during our abode under their roof, in such afflicting circumstances. Anne frequently expatiates on the motherly and sisterly attention that was unceasingly shown to her by

Miriam and Abby, and desires me to convey her love and heart-felt thanks to them as one deeply their debtor.[3] Helen and Sarah also unite in sending their affectionate remembrances.

I trust you found your beloved wife and child well on your return from your anti-slavery tour, and that you all continue in the enjoyment of good health. Surely, to him who has a loving and faithful wife, and who is equally loving and faithful toward her, "there is no place like home." [4]

Your much obliged friend,

Wm. Lloyd Garrison.

ALS: Garrison Papers, Boston Public Library.

1. Daniel Johnson (born 1768) was a shoemaker of Lynn. (Lynn city directories.)

2. An adaptation of Lamentations 3:33.

3. Miriam Johnson, a Quaker, who had married Daniel Johnson in 1828, was treasurer of the Women's Anti-Slavery Society of Lynn and represented Massachusetts at the 1838 Anti-Slavery Convention of American Women. The Johnsons' house was a station on the Underground Railroad. Abby was the Johnsons' daughter. (Letters to the editor from Jonathan Prude, researcher, September 1970, and from Diane Liesinger, curator, Lynn Historical Society, June 3, 1970.)

4. John Howard Payne, "Home Sweet Home," *Clari, the Maid of Milan,* Act I.

59

TO HENRY C. WRIGHT

Boston, April 1, 1843.

Dear bro. Wright:

Can you tell me when the time will come that "there shall be no more sea"? [1] Probably, in a literal sense, never. Yet I would that the Atlantic, "that great and wide sea, wherein are things creeping innumerable, both small and great beasts," [2] were not rolling its billowy barriers between us! Not that I do not want you to be in England, but that I want you to be in America. A separation so wide, though not incompatible with the unity of the spirit, is a severe trial. But I will not complain so long as I know that you are laboring in the vineyard of the Lord, and endeavoring to promulgate the great, vital, all-embracing truth, that all mankind belong to one brotherhood, and constitute one family. Your mission is one of love and peace, marred by no selfish considerations, restricted by no geographical boundaries, governed by no sectarian motives. Its object is to reconcile all people, that they may be "no more strangers and foreigners, but fellow-citizens with the saints, and of the household of God; built upon the foundation of the apostles and prophets, Jesus Christ himself being the corner-stone." [3] Nevertheless, benevolent as it is, and much as it is needed in every part of the earth, it will subject you to the contempt of some, to the hatred of others, to the opposition of the great multitude. But you know the conditions — "no cross, no crown." [4] May your zeal be unquenchable, your faith strong as the pillars of the universe, your courage equal to every emergency.

It is difficult to determine, whether England or America demand the liveliest sympathy. Both are laden with iniquity; both are perverse and desperate in heart; both are full of the elements of self-destruction. England has more suffering and poverty universally diffused among her population — more ignorance and degradation — more governmental oppression and religious bondage. But England is not cursed by slavery. That dreadful system, which embodies more crimes, calamities, woes and horrors than any other devised by Satanic subtlety, belongs to America. It is her curse, her opprobrium, her destroyer. Is it in the course of destiny, that both England and America shall perish? As nations, with rival governments based on murderous violence, unquestionably it is. They both take the sword, and in process of time they will both perish by the sword; and great and terrible will be their fall.[5] But, as in other cases of national retribution, a remnant shall be saved, who shall stand forth as witnesses for God, to testify against all dependance on an arm of flesh, and in favor of recognizing the Prince of Peace as the honored one whose right it is to reign "from sea to sea, and from the rivers to the ends of the earth." [6] Surely, the sword shall not devour for ever, but love shall finally subdue all things.

Since you left us, but little has been said or done on the subject of non-resistance, as a distinct enterprise; yet it is certain that the good seed which has been scattered so liberally, especially by yourself, is destined to bring forth an abundant harvest. The question of capital punishment is attracting special attention at this time, and during the present year will be more thoroughly discussed than it has been hitherto. The debate in New-York between Cheever and O'Sullivan, — the former in favor of the gallows, the latter for its abolition, — will lead to extensive inquiry and conversation on this subject.[7] I wish I could send you Cheever's argument, by the steamer of to-day; but I have not been able to procure a copy of it in pamphlet form, in which it has made its appearance in New-York. The committee in our State Legislature, to whom our petitions against capital punishment were referred, have reported unfavorably, and their report has been adopted. The N. E. Puritan, N. Y. Evangelist and Observer, and other papers of this stamp, are rampant in their zeal to uphold the gallows.[8] But that relic of barbarism, I trust, is soon destined to be swept away from the soil of Massachusetts. Imprisonment for life is the substitute proposed; but this is equally at war with the spirit of Christianity, though, for the time being, it would be an indication of progress. In the order of human advancement, the abolition of the gallows must precede that of imprisonment.

A new question has been started, and is urged with some zeal on the consideration of the people, in relation to the right of individual property. Bro. [John A.] Collins is the most active in this movement, and will probably resign his anti-slavery agency in the course of a few weeks, in order to devote himself exclusively to its promotion. Of his benevolent desire to aid and bless our suffering race, I have no doubt; but I do not think his judgment is sufficiently solid, or his moral perceptions sufficiently clear, or his system of moral philosophy sufficiently christian, to render him a safe and successful leader. He seems to be an earnest convert to Robert Owen's absurd and dangerous dogma, that men are "the creatures of circumstances" — not sinful, but unfortunate — not inwardly corrupt, but outwardly trammelled — and that it is by association alone, in a distinctive community formed on the basis of equal rights and equal property, that the regeneration of the world is to be effected.[9] His theory is, that it is as wrong, for principle, for one man to claim absolute ownership to his hat or his coat, as it is for another to claim a human being as his property. For human beings to buy and sell to and of each other, even on terms of exact reciprocity, he regards as a wrong, and contends that every body should help himself, according to his necessities, (he being the sole judge,) wherever the means of subsistence and comfort exist. This, he thinks, should be universally agreed to all. Of course, he does not advocate the taking away from another of any thing against his consent. I only give you his theory. Time and room forbid my saying any thing more.

I have not heard from your family since you left, but presume they are well. They, doubtless, keep you apprised of their situation.

Our friend Joshua Coffin is at present in this region, lecturing to good acceptance respecting the tour that he made to the South, two or three years [ago].[10]

Wendell Phillips, Edmund Quincy, the Chapmans, the Westons, the [Joseph] Southwicks, &c. are all well as usual, and nothing special has transpired in our social circle to communicate to you.[11] You are remembered with much affection by all, and all as one desire to have an abiding-place in your memory. Some of them will write to you very shortly — probably by the next steamer.

As to my home concerns, we are still at Cam[bridgeport] but think soon of removing to Boston, and occupying our friend E. G. Loring's house at the south end. Ever since we have resided at the port, in the house which we now occupy, (though you know it is very pleasantly situated,) we have had some one or more of the members of our family sick. All have been sick, in turn — two (bro. James and sister Mary) have died. Mrs. Benson has just recovered from a severe illness, and sister Ann is now confined to her bed, and is in a precarious situation. She may not survive many weeks. You will not wonder, therefore, that we deem our situation an unhealthy one, and think it prudent to change our place of residence.

Georgie, Willie and Wendy all keep you in lively remembrance, and long for an opportunity to hug and kiss you.

Give my kind remembrances to dear Elizabeth Pease, and all the other dear friends.

Yours, affectionately,

Wm. Lloyd Garrison.

P.S. Write to me as often as possible. The postage I will most cheerfully pay.

☞ I hope you will be a looker-on, *in the gallery*, at the London Anti-Slavery Convention, in June.[12] [Rev. Nathaniel] Colver, [Amos A.] Phelps and Leavitt have been appointed, by the "new organization" *clique*, to attend as delegates, and will accept the appointment, provided they can raise the funds.[13] I have no doubt that Phelps and Colver feel specially desirous to visit England, in order to injure our influence, and stir up sectarian enmity against us, as much as in them lies. I hope you will carefully note their proceedings. The former has been very sick, and for a time it was doubtful whether he would recover, but he is now better, and would like a sea-voyage for the benefit of his health. Not a single delegate will be sent to the London Convention, either by the American A. S. Society or any of its auxiliaries. It is too *"gentlemanly"* a body for the "common people" and — *women!*

Our worthy friend James Cannings Fuller has gone to England, and will join the Convention; but he will do so on his own responsibility. I wish he would make a protest against the exclusive character of that assembly, and then *mount to the gallery*. Henry Colman will sail next week, from New-York, for Liverpool.[14] He also will probably join the Convention, "on his own hook." I wrote to you by J. C. F., and shall try to send you another letter by H.C. I hope you will see them both. I trust none of *our* English, Scotch or Irish friends will be members of the Convention. Pray, make your arrangements to attend the London anniversaries in May. It will be a good opportunity for you to become acquainted with many excellent individuals.

☞ So! you have not seen Elizabeth Pease! Then you have not seen the paragon of her sex. Give my regards to all our true-hearted friends in Ireland. Dear Helen, mother, and the sisters, unite with me in love to you. We invoke Heaven's choicest blessings on your head.

ALS: Garrison Papers, Boston Public Library; extract printed in Glasgow Female Anti-Slavery Society, *Second Annual Report*, 1843, pp. 16–17.

1. Garrison adapts Revelation 21:1.
2. Psalms 104:25.
3. Ephesians 2:19–20.
4. William Penn, *No Cross, No Crown* (1668).
5. Garrison refers to Matthew 26:52.
6. Psalms 72:8.
7 See Garrison's letter to Henry C. Wright, March 1, 1843.
8. The *New England Puritan* began publication in Boston in 1840; during its first year it was known as the *Puritan*. In 1849 it merged into the *Boston Recorder*. (*ULS.*) The New York *Observer* was founded in 1823 and continued publication until 1912, when it merged into *Christian Work*. (*ULS.*) The *Evangelist* has been previously identified.
9. Robert Owen (1771–1858), English social reformer, wrote down the principles Garrison quotes in *A New View of Society, or Essays on the Principle of the Formation of the Human Character* (London, 1813). In his New Lanark mills in Scotland he pioneered in industrial reforms and later founded a new firm with Jeremy Bentham and Quaker William Allen. His interest in educational philanthropy led him to establish infant schools in England. In 1817 he became interested in the possibility of establishing socialist communities, and in 1825 a disciple of his experimented with one near Glasgow. In 1826 Owen himself set up a colony at New Harmony, Indiana. After both communities had failed, Owen returned to Great Britain, where he became increasingly interested in socialism.
10. Joshua Coffin (1792–1864), teacher and historian, was one of the founders of the New England Anti-Slavery Society and served as its recording secretary. He was a fat, good-natured man of whom Garrison thought highly. (*Life.*)
11. Garrison probably refers to two of the five Weston sisters, Caroline (1808–1882) and Anne Warren (1812–1890). Although not so well-known or so influential as their older sister Maria Weston Chapman, they were ardent abolitionists who expressed their sentiments in many poems and articles in the antislavery journal *The Liberty Bell*. The Weston sisters kept a school in a house on Boylston Street, site of the present Boston Public Library. (*Life.*)
12. The second World's Anti-Slavery Convention met in London during the week of June 13. See *The Liberator*, July 7, 1843, and July 28, 1843. The latter issue contains correspondence from Henry C. Wright, who attended the convention.
13. Joshua Leavitt (1794–1873), clergyman, abolitionist, and editor, had earlier differed with Garrison concerning the policies of the American Colonization Society, of which Leavitt was a member. A vigorous and sometimes abusive writer, he edited the *Evangelist* beginning in 1831, the *Emancipator* in 1837, the *Ballot Box*, supporting J. G. Birney, before the election of 1840, and from 1848 to his death, the *Independent*.
14. Henry Colman (1785–1849) was a Unitarian minister and agricultural expert. From 1837 to 1841 he was engaged in making an agricultural survey of Massachusetts, and from 1843 to 1848 he studied agriculture in Europe.

6 0

TO ELIZABETH PEASE

Boston, April 4, 1843.

Beloved Friend:

It seems, by his last letter, that Henry C. Wright had not yet visited Darlington. Doubtless, ere this, he has had the pleasure of seeing you, face to face. During his absence, our non-resistance enterprise languishes, for lack of an efficient public lecturer. Do not regard us as selfish, if we express the hope that he will return to us at an earlier period than he had decided upon at the time he took his departure. A man, with his principles and feelings, is "more precious than the gold of Ophir." ¹ England and America both need his labors; but, bad as we are, there is more freedom of speech and better materials to carry on the work of reform here, than with you in "the old world." Still, it is for him, rather than for us, to determine what part of the immense field of christian philanthropy he can occupy to the greatest advantage.

Do you mean to attend the London Anti-Slavery Convention, in June next? It is needless to ask, whether you mean to be a member of it; because as you are nothing better than a woman, and no "gentleman," and as none but *gentlemen* are to be admitted to a seat in the same, of course this is out of the question. But the *gallery*, you know, is reserved for the inferior species of our race; and a capital point of observation it is.² Can any thing be more contemptible than this exclusive spirit toward women? In what respect is it less wicked than that which of old led the Jews to have no dealings with the Samaritans? If, in Christ Jesus, there is neither male nor female, but all are one, why not in the work which Christ Jesus came to perform? — namely, to bind up the broken-hearted, to proclaim liberty to the captives and the opening of the prison to them that are bound.³ It is no answer to say, that the sphere of woman differs widely from that of man; for though this is true, in regard to certain responsibilities and duties which arise from the peculiarity of her sex, it does not touch the question of her intellectual and moral equality. Where moral, and not physical power is to be wielded, for the emancipation of the human race, what hinders woman from participating in its exercise on equal terms with man? In such employment, her sex, instead of being adverse to her usefulness, is admirably calculated to facilitate her labors.

A woman now sits on the throne of England. I am not aware that such a position is deemed incompatible with her sex, either by Churchmen or Dissenters. Nay, I have never heard that even the London Committee have objected to it. What more have the advocates of woman's rights claimed than this? Yet women are not to be allowed a seat in an Anti-Slavery Convention, simply because they are — women! Have you ever heard of those who strain at a gnat, and swallow a camel? [4]

It seems that the London Peace Society has called a General Peace Convention, to meet in London on the 22d of June next.[5] It is to consist of "all *persons* nominated by Peace Societies and Associations, at home or abroad; by Religious Bodies or Societies, and Philanthropic, Literary, or Scientific Institutions; by vote of the London Committee; and appointed at public meetings of towns or districts, specially convened for the purpose." I hope this body will be put to the test, whether it regards women as persons. Why are the members limited to those who shall be deputed to act as the representatives of others? Why not throw the doors wide open, and invite all to assemble who are for beating swords into ploughshares, and spears into pruning-hooks, that no more blood may be shed on the earth? [6] Nay, why not let even the advocates of war come, and present their side of the question? I see, by the Programme, that "no discussion of the fundamental principle is to be allowed." This limitation may be useful for the despatch of business, but I do not think it will be found advantageous for the cause of Peace. Precious as the time of the Convention may be, should any person arise to speak, avowing opinions in opposition to its proceedings, I hope he will be permitted to express his mind fully, and be listened to with patience and candor. I wish it were in my power to attend this Convention; but I trust H. C. Wright will not fail to be present on so important an occasion. Among the topics to be discussed is "the essential sinfulness of war, and its direct opposition to the spirit and precepts of Christianity, the prosperity of nations, and the true interests of mankind." This opens a wide field of inquiry, from the investigation of which, I hope the Convention will not shrink, lead where it may. I do not see how we can show "the essential sinfulness of war," without showing "the essential sinfulness" of the army and navy, rival national boundaries, conflicting national interests, governments based on physical force, &c. &c. If the axe be not laid at the root of the tree,[7] little can be done by lopping off the branches.

Petitions have recently been presented to the Legislature of Massachusetts, praying for the abolition of capital punishment; and, in case this prayer should not be granted, requesting that such clergymen as advocate judicial homicide should be appointed hangmen! [8] This has caused much fluttering among the clergy and their friends, who affect to regard these petitions as most insulting to their cloth, and as an outrage on their *holy* profession. It certainly places them in a ludicrous dilemma; for it cannot be degrading to do what God requires — and if he requires capital punishment in certain cases, why should they who claim to be the expounders of his will, and the teachers of his law, object to inflicting the penalty by their own hands — especially since they are to be well paid for the sanguinary job? Something curious and instructive will come out of all this.

At present, our land is somewhat extensively agitated by those who are sounding "the midnight cry," [9] and inculcating the dogma that the Second Advent of the Messiah, and the destruction of this world, are to be witnessed during the present year.[10] These events, many believe, are to transpire in all this month. Thousands have been converted to this strange faith; and the effect of the excitement has been, in many instances, to produce insanity. Multitudes, who were formerly engaged in the various moral enterprises of the age, have lost all interest in works of practical righteousness, and think and talk of nothing else but the burning up of the world. — Deluded people! to be expecting that which took place 1800 years ago! To dream of a literal destruction of this glorious creation! To imagine that Christ is to make his appearance literally on a cloud, &c.! They are yet in their sins, because they deny that Christ has appeared the second time without sin unto salvation.[11]

With us, at this time, the earth is covered with snow and ice; but it is all summer in my heart, and my esteem for you and other dear friends abroad is in full bloom. Farewell!

Yours, truly,

Wm. Lloyd Garrison.

P.S. I was much pleased with the excellent letter which you forwarded to me from Joseph Barker. I have not yet found time to write to him; but in your next note to him, please to inform him that I intend doing so shortly, and that other favors from him are strongly solicited by me. I regret, with you, that I had no opportunity to become acquainted with him in England; for I feel certain that we agree with each other in all the essential points of Christianity, and in believing that love is the fulfilling of the law.

I shall send this letter by Henry Colman, a highly respected and intelligent friend, who is to sail from New-York, this week, to Liverpool, for the purpose of making an agricultural survey of Europe. He intends to be in London at the sitting of the Anti-Slavery Convention; and I hope you will have an opportunity to become personally acquainted with him. You will be delighted with his frankness, urbanity, and benevolent disposition. My choicest regards to your parents, H. C. Wright, and other well-known friends.

ALS: *Battles and Leaders of the Civil War*, I, Henry E. Huntington Library.

1. Garrison could refer to any of a number of biblical passages, such as Job 28:16.
2. Garrison makes reference to his having withdrawn to the gallery when in 1840 the first World's Anti-Slavery Convention had excluded women delegates.
3. Isaiah 61:1.
4. Matthew 23:24.
5. The peace convention was held the week following the abolition convention. On June 30 letters were written to Garrison by Richard D. Webb, Henry C. Wright, and Elizabeth Pease, who agreed that the peace convention accomplished little, since the time was occupied not by discussion of crucial issues but by the reading of papers and the passing of resolutions. (*The Liberator*, July 28 and September 1, 1843.)
6. Garrison alludes to Isaiah 2:4.
7. A reference to Luke 3:9.
8. In *The Liberator*, April 28, 1843, Garrison writes an editorial urging the abolition of capital punishment and attacking the Reverend George B. Cheever for favoring the death penalty.
9. An allusion to Matthew 25:6.
10. Garrison refers to the Adventist movement, which had evolved under the leadership of William Miller during the 1830's. Garrison's description of the nation's response is not exaggerated. The movement had been extensively publicized through the founding of Adventist papers in leading cities and the circulation of many pages of propaganda. In 1845, despite the failure of his prophecies, Miller founded the Adventist church.
11. Garrison alludes to Hebrews 9:28.

61

TO GEORGE W. BENSON

Cambridgeport, April 8, 1843.

Dear George:

We have been waiting anxiously to receive a letter from you, in regard to the unfortunate and afflicting case of your dear boy — supposing that you went immediately from Providence to *Northampton*, on hearing of the disaster.[1] Sister Charlotte has relieved our minds of the suspense we were in, by sending us your letter to her, which you wrote at Brooklyn, and which contained the cheering information that the child was out of danger. It seems you had not then returned home. We wish, however, to receive further particulars from you, directly.

We all remain about as well as when you were with us, except Anne, whose case is exceedingly critical, if not altogether hopeless. Dr. [Robert] Wesselhoeft is evidently much disturbed in mind on her account, as her complaints are so complicated as to baffle all his medical skill. He shakes his head ominously when asked as to the probability of her recovery, and appears to be floating on a sea of uncertainty in the application of his medicines. Thus far, what he has given her has had no other effect than greatly to distress her system, though I am sure he is doing all that lies in his power to relieve her. What is quite unfortunate, Anne has no confidence in the homœopathic mode of cure, and this makes her to despond; though she does not feel as if she could muster courage enough to say to him, that she would prefer to try something else. She would like to try a few Thompsonian courses, and I should like to have her, as well as the rest of the family; but we all want your advice, before we take any new steps. Anne is now confined to her bed, all the time, excepting the few moments that are occupied in making her bed. She is very feeble, and considerably emaciated. For a fortnight past, the swellings in her legs have disappeared, till within a few days. The right leg is now badly swollen, up to her thigh. The left is, as yet, unaffected in this manner. Her cough continues somewhat troublesome. The Dr. is perplexed, he says, to decide whether her disease is a consumption of the bowels, or dropsy of the bowels. In a case of "life and death," like this, I think we should not, from motives of delicacy, persist in a mode of treatment, repugnant to the wishes of our dear suffering sister, and apparently inefficacious. More than three weeks have elapsed since the Dr. took her case in hand, and she has gradually been growing worse ever since. It is not certain, of course, that any other mode of treatment would have been attended with any better results. Still, I know that mother, Sarah and Helen, (as well as Anne and myself,) would prefer to have something else tried; but they do not like to say much about it. A large bill of expense is now running up, to no purpose. — This is not to find fault with our excellent friend, the Dr., but simply to state to you the facts as they exist up to this hour. We do not know how pressing are your engagements at the present time; but we think Anne's case is so extremely critical, that it is of some importance that you should visit us again at your earliest conveyance. In the mean time, it might be well for you to write to Dr. W. stating that you had heard that Anne, in his opinion, was in a very dangerous situation; and if he felt satisfied that he could not do her any special good, that he would inform the members of the family to this effect; and if, by the desire of Anne, they should proceed to try something else, begging him not to consider such a change as made out of disrespect to him or his practice. From these hints, you will know how to fashion your letter, if you cannot conveniently come to us, and determine what is to be done on the spot.

Give our special regards to Catherine, and assure her that we all deeply sympathize with her in the dreadful calamity which happened during your absence.

In great haste, but with much love,

Yours, ever,

Wm. Lloyd Garrison.

ALS: Garrison Papers, Sophia Smith Collection, Smith College Library.

1. A search of relevant newspapers and correspondence has failed to disclose what the "disaster" was and whether it occurred to Henry E., George, Jr., or Thomas Benson.

---

6 2

TO GEORGE W. BENSON

Boston, April 15, 1843.

My dear George:

Your letter was received by due course of mail. Since that time, sister Anne has remained about the same — perhaps is somewhat worse. She is not, as yet, we think, aware how sick she is; for she talks of getting better, but Dr. [Robert] W[esselhoeft]. thinks she had better not yet be informed as to the critical nature of her disease. He now says that she is tending towards a consumption, and I presume in reality has no hope of her recovery. Anna has no intention of trying any other medicine, until (as she says) he restores her to as comfortable a state as he found her, which may not be in his power. Sarah is deeply affected by the prospect of Anna's possible dissolution; and the crisis is deemed so alarming, that she and mother (as well as Helen and myself) earnestly desire your presence with as little delay as possible. We know how extremely inconvenient it will be for you to leave home at this period, but we also feel that the case is such as demands a brother's attention, especially when so much reliance is placed by us all on your judgment. Without a consultation with you, we know not what to do — and, in fact, we can do nothing, for Anna would probably be influenced, at this time, only by yourself.

I sympathize most deeply with Sarah. The care of tending and watching Anne has almost entirely devolved on herself for several weeks past, and her nervous system is, consequently, very much affected. Mother is still comparatively an invalid, and Helen, by the multiplicity of her cares, is unable to render much assistance.

Dr. W. has not said any thing about receiving a letter from you, and we thought it not best to break the matter to him. I trust you wrote to him as guardedly and delicately on the subject as possible; for he is a man of very tender feelings, and is certainly exerting himself to the utmost in prescribing for Anne.

My own health is precarious. The swelling in my left side is growing worse, and I am in continual pain. The disorder which afflicts me I *feel* to be very serious. In a few days, I am to undergo a strict surgical examination, that I may know the worst. The will of the Lord be done.[1]

We shall not remove to this city [Northampton] till the 1st of June — nor at that time, unless a decided change for the better shall take place in Anna's case. She is at present wholly confined to her bed.

I wish you would make a formal application to our excellent friend William Adam, for the admission of George Thompson this spring to your community as a scholar, &c. If we can make any arrangement of this kind, it will relieve us of a great deal of care and anxiety. Mrs. Boyle[2] says that she would most cheerfully take the superintendence of him. I wish to know, first, whether you can receive him soon — and, secondly, on what terms. He seems to be delighted with the idea of going to N[orthampton]., and I have no doubt would be well contented.

Little Charlie is troubled somewhat with a scrofulous humor on the head and near the mouth.

Hoping you will be able so as to arrange your affairs as to be with us shortly, I remain, with much love to Catherine,

Yours, affectionately,

Wm. Lloyd Garrison.

ALS: William Lloyd Garrison Papers, Massachusetts Historical Society.

1. Acts 21:14.
2. Laura Boyle (c. 1804–1852), the wife of James Boyle (see her obituary, *The Liberator*, July 30, 1852).

63

TO PHOEBE JACKSON

Cambridgeport, May 1 — June 10, 1843.

A word as to my health. For a fortnight past I have been quite unwell, & do not yet feel much better. I have had a severe cold, and (what is quite rare with me) a troublesome cough. During the late sessions of the N. E. A. S. Convention,[1] I was compelled to be almost entirely dumb, on account of hoarseness; & the trifling effort that

I then made to be heard, especially in reading the 'Address to the Slaves' at the great meeting in Faneuil Hall, has since been very injurious to my lungs.[2]

On Tuesday last, I was examined by Dr. [John C.] Warren, of Boston, in regard to the swelling in my left side, wh. has caused me so much bodily pain & uneasiness for some time past. I had previously been examined by three other physicians. Truly, 'who shall decide where doctors disagree?'[3] No one of these agrees with another. Dr. [Robert] Wesselhoeft feels certain that it is a tumor beneath the skin, under the ribs, having blood-vessels attached to it, and partaking somewhat of the nature of a polypus. Dr. Green thinks it is an enlargement of the spleen![4] Dr. Bowditch is confident that it is neither the one nor the other, but hesitates to say positively what it is.[5] Dr. Warren says it is a great enlargement of the 'colon,' and of other intestinal parts connected with the stomach.

Two persons have examined me in a clairvoyant state, and they disagree with all the doctors, and with each other! Miss Gleason, (one of the two, formerly of Providence, I believe,) could not see that any thing affected my left side, but said that I had been considerably troubled with my right side — a piece of intelligence which was entirely new to me! — Miss Wilkins (the other clairvoyant, who has had perfect success in her examination of numerous other persons) has examined me three times, & on each occasion has been evidently much distressed, entering fully into my pains from sympathy.[6] She says that there is a collection of brownish matter near the heart, with small blood vessels attached to it, & that there is great danger of sudden death, either from the matter ultimately overflowing the heart, or the bursting of blood vessels. She also says that my liver is covered with small white blisters, in a state of suppuration, & that the lower parts of my lungs are withered from exhaustion, &c. This is truly a formidable description, but I am not yet able to credit the whole of it. In the course of a few days I expect to be examined by another clairvoyant, who is very remarkable in her way, and also by another physician.

Transcription of an extract of a letter written in the hand of Wendell Phillips Garrison: Garrison Papers, Boston Public Library; shorter extract printed in *Life*, III, 83.

Phoebe Jackson (1807–1887) of Providence, Rhode Island, whose name Garrison sometimes spells Phebe, was a sympathetic friend of the Garrisons throughout the years. She helped take care of Henry E. Benson when he was ill in Providence in 1836. (See Garrison's letter to Henry E. Benson, August 4, 1836, n. 3, *Letters*, II, 151–152.)

1. The tenth annual New England Anti-Slavery Convention, held in Boston from May 30 to June 1, 1843 (reported in *The Liberator* for June 9, 1843).

2. Garrison's "Address to the Slaves of the United States" was initially delivered

in Faneuil Hall, May 31, 1843. The speech referred to the principles of the Declaration of Independence and stressed that the goal of the antislavery cause was the achieving of "liberty, equal rights, equal privileges" for all American Negroes. Garrison also came out against colonization and emphasized the non-violent character of abolitionism. The speech was printed in *The Liberator*, June 2, 1843.

3. Alexander Pope, *Moral Essays*, Epistle III, line 1.

4. Henry Bowen Clarke Greene (1800–1848) received his M.D. degree from Harvard in 1819 and an A.M. from Bowdoin in 1828. He practiced medicine first in Saco, Maine, and then in Boston. (Letter to the editor from Jonathan Prude, researcher, July 10, 1970.) Dr. Greene's diagnosis of Garrison's disorder was confirmed by the post-mortem examination in 1879. (*Life.*)

5. Henry Ingersoll Bowditch (1808–1892), physician and abolitionist, was a follower of Garrison and a member of the "Latimer Committee," which was formed in 1842 to defend George Latimer, a runaway slave. He was associated with the Massachusetts General Hospital from 1838 until his death; many public health measures were instituted through his efforts.

6. In the Boston city directories, a Fanny Wilkins and an Elizabeth Gleason appear in 1849 and 1855. Nothing further is known about them.

---

6 4

TO *THE LIBERATOR*

NEW-YORK, May 9, 1843.

MY DEAR FRIEND:

It is now 2 o'clock, P.M. We have just concluded our anniversary meeting, and a very spirited and effective one it has been, in the judgment and feeling of all who were present.[1] It was not held in the Broadway Tabernacle, as usual; for though that could have been obtained for the purpose, such were the ungracious, yet perfectly characteristic airs assumed by that small-hearted, mean-spirited man, David Hale,[2] (one of the editors of the Journal of Commerce,) in relation to our having it, the Executive Committee would not gratify him, but hired Apollo Hall, a beautiful and spacious room, which was crowded to overflowing by as cheering an array of human countenances as was ever presented in a great and glorious cause. Whether by accident or design, in some of the papers our meeting was notified to be held (without authority, of course) in the Tabernacle, and in others in Apollo Hall, 110, instead of 410, Broadway.[3] This latter mistake was made even on some of the printed cards which are usually prepared by the booksellers for gratuitous distribution; so that amid this confusion of notices, it is highly probable that many persons were unable to find our real place of meeting. Yet we had no room for more — the hall being densely occupied by a most attentive and evidently delighted assembly.

The chair was occupied (in the absence of our worthy President, Lindley Coates,[4]) by Francis Jackson, of our city, of whose spirit and character I need say nothing, for they are widely known in the republic. The Annual Report, as a whole, was an admirable document, and was read in the best manner by our giant-hearted coadjutor Joseph C. Hathaway, of Farmington, N. Y. Its adoption was moved by Jacob Ferris, in a brief but pertinent and eloquent speech. As I took no memorandum of the Treasurer's Report, my attention at the moment of reading it being diverted elsewhere, I cannot give you an accurate account of the receipts and expenditures of the Society during the past year. James Munroe, of Plainfield, Ct. was the first regular speaker; and he acquitted himself with the ability of a veteran in the cause of reform.[5] — He demonstrated, in the most logical, eloquent and conclusive manner, that slaveholding must necessarily be hostile to national prosperity, safety, morality and religion, and called on all the friends of God and our country to rally for its extirpation. He was succeeded by Frederick Douglass, who supported a resolution, affirming that the anti-slavery movement was the only earthly hope of the slave population. He spoke in a very feeling and impressive manner, as the representative of his enslaved brethren and sisters. Abby Kelley then made a brief address, in behalf of the manacled women of the South, and deepened the impression made by the remarks of Douglass. I did not intend to speak on the occasion, and left home with an implied pledge that I would endeavor to keep still, in consequence of my recent ill state of health; but I could not remain dumb, especially in view of the progress of our cause in the Old Bay State, which constituted the theme of my remarks, in connexion with the 'Latimer case,' and the passage of the law by our Legislature, making it a penal offence for any of our State officers to assist a slaveholder in seizing his fugitive slave.[6] I was followed by Wendell Phillips, in a speech of surpassing eloquence and boldness, which elicited great applause, and which called upon all the friends of God and man to place the Church and State under their feet, and to make the present reform worthy of the Genius of Christianity and the Spirit of Liberty. A hiss being heard on the statement of his revolutionary proposition, it kindled afresh the fire of his eloquence, and drew from him a torrent of lofty and soul-stirring declamation, worthy of the best efforts of our revolutionary struggle. All the resolutions were adopted with perfect unanimity, and with strong emphasis. Our Hutchinson friends came on with us from Boston, but for some reason, (I know not what,) they were not present in the assembly — much to the disappointment of us all.[7] Nothing was wanting but the melody of their sweet voices to perfect the tone of the meeting. We have delegates from the far West — even as far as Indiana; and the prospect is, that all our meetings will be of the right character and of the deepest interest. But the mail will close speedily, and I must drop my pen.

Yours, faithfully,

WM. LLOYD GARRISON.

Printed: *The Liberator*, May 12, 1843.

This letter is addressed to *The Liberator* by way of James Brown Yerrinton (1800–1866), its printer since 1841, who not infrequently during Garrison's brief absences assumed editorial duties. (*Life.*)

1. The tenth annual meeting of the American Anti-Slavery Society was held in New York, May 9–11. See reports of the meeting in *The Liberator*, May 19, 26, and June 2, 1843.

2. David Hale (1791–1849) became business manager of the New York *Journal of Commerce* in 1827, the year it was founded by Arthur Tappan. In 1831, along with Gerard Hallock, he assumed complete control of the paper, introducing new methods of gathering news that brought great prosperity. Since 1840 Hale had owned the Broadway Tabernacle, which he rented for public meetings and for religious services. Garrison could never forgive the *Journal of Commerce* for its opposition to *The Liberator* and his radical abolitionism.

3. According to the New York city directories, Apollo Hall or "Apollo Gallery" was located at 412 Broadway.

4. Lindley Coates (1794–1856) was a resident of Lancaster County, Pennsylvania. A Quaker, he had been named a manager by the American Anti-Slavery Society at the time of its founding in 1833 and served as president from 1840 to 1843. His home was a station on the Underground Railroad. (See obituary, *The Liberator*, June 27, 1856, and R. C. Smedley, *History of the Underground Railroad in Chester and Neighboring Counties of Pennsylvania*, Lancaster, 1883, pp. 84–89.)

5. James Munroe (1821–1898), a native of Connecticut, was persuaded by Garrison to become an antislavery lecturer. In 1846 he was graduated from Oberlin College, where he taught for many years. He held several political offices in Ohio and served in the United States House of Representatives from 1871 to 1881. (R. S. Fletcher, *A History of Oberlin College*, Oberlin, Ohio, 1943, p. 390.)

6. The law is printed in *The Liberator*, March 3, 1843.

7. The Hutchinsons were one of the most famous musical families of nineteenth-century America. Garrison probably refers to the quartet comprised of Adoniram Judson Joseph (1817–1859), Abigail Jemima (1829–1892), John Wallace (1821–1908), and Asa (1823–1884). Organized in 1841, the quartet went on many tours of the United States and in 1845, one to Europe. Although the original quartet disbanded in 1849 when Abby married, members of the family remained active in music throughout the century, introducing such songs as "Tenting on the Old Camp Ground" and "Rally Round the Flag." In 1855 several of the brothers founded the town of Hutchinson, Minnesota. The story of the Hutchinson family can be found in Carol Brink, *Harps in the Wind: the Story of the Singing Hutchinsons* (New York, 1947).

George Thompson in 1842

Lucretia Mott in 1841

Frederick Douglass in about 1847

Gerrit Smith in about 1849

Nathaniel Peabody Rogers in 1846

Father Theobald Mathew in about 1849

Garrison in 1846, painted by William Page

Garrison in about 1846, from a lithograph
by P. S. Duval, on stone by Albert Newsam

6 5

TO DAVID LEE CHILD

BOSTON 14 May, 1843.

DEAR FRIEND, —

By the recent choice of the American anti-slavery society, Francis
Jackson, William Lloyd Garrison, Ellis Gray Loring, Anne Warren
Weston, Edmund Quincy, Wendell Phillips & Maria Weston Chapman,
were constituted members of the executive Committee of that society.
Among the most important of the duties involved in our acceptance
of that trust, is the appointment of an editor for the Standard.

It is not easy to find in combination all the various and opposite
qualities required for the perfect fulfilment of the duties of this office;
and if our application to yourself prove unsuccessful, we hardly know
where to look for one capable of filling it. Suffer us to appeal, therefore, at the outset, to your disinterested and devoted love of the cause,
entreating you, as you value its prosperity, not to withhold your abilities from its support at this important moment, how-little agreeable
or however painful their exercise in the capacity of editor of the
Standard may be.

We know how difficult as well as uncomfortable it necessarily is,
to act as the organ of a society. We know that it requires iron strength
and almost superhuman magnanimity to be at once the official leader
& the servant, — the champion & the ambassador, — as well as the
brother of the abolitionists. We see and feel all that is implied in
being the editor of the Official organ of such a body as the American
Anti-Slavery Society, arrayed in behalf of such a cause, in the midst
of enmity so deadly, and opposition at once so violent, so subtle and
so unscrupulous. We take into consideration the fact, that the Standard, being the organ of the whole society, cannot be a free paper
in the same sense that the Liberator, the organ of an individual, is
so; but must, in the nature of things, be to the American society, what
the Whig & Democratic organs are to those parties; the difference
being in the nature of our object, — the promulgation of righteous
principles by righteous means; while theirs is the advancement of
men by any means. We see, therefore, that the only way to provide
for the freedom of an editor of the Standard is to select one who
is in agreement with the society, and who can yet bear to be misrepresented & misunderstood on account of that agreement. He will
be called an ignorant fanatic, to make him draw a line of distinction [1]
between himself and some members of the society: an infidel and
a radical, to make him shrink from the side of others: perchance a

161

quietist to make him deny anti-slavery fellowship to yet others. He will be made to bear, in his own body, the individual sins of the whole anti-slavery fraternity. But if he knows and feels the benefits & the satisfaction of associated action and of the friendship that springs from it, he will be unmoved by the efforts to destroy it, and heedless of the disparaging observations of those who disguise their indifference under the name of philosophy, and their hatred under the name of love. He will easily bear to be called a small-minded man, labouring for a small object; the slave of an association, sacrificing his individuality by submitting to work in its trammels. But, notwithstanding all that is trying and irksome, our confidence in your devotedness, strength of mind, courage, fortitude, penetration & brotherly feeling makes us turn to you in the earnest hope of securing your great ability and high quallifications for the service of the cause at this difficult & painful post.

We greatly regret your necessary absence from the annual meeting; and therefore subjoin a statement of its tone and temper; hoping nothing therein will be discordant with your own: for greatly as we desire to secure your services for the society, we should be as much above requiring the slightest sacrifice of your righteous Freedom, as you would be above making it.

The meeting was a most satisfactory one, being more than commonly well attended & unanimous. All the debates, resolutions & selections of Officers, showed how strong was the determination to transcend, morally, both church & state in the prosecution of our enterprise; yet to confine it within the strictest limitations of anti-slavery proper. The society declared its conviction that all sects & parties in the United States are corrupted by slavery; and pronounced the conduct of those who remain in connection with them, inconsistent with the requisitions of anti-slavery principle, though not incompatible with membership in the anti-slavery society. As all sects & parties were alike condemned, it consequently followed that no portion of the society's means was to be used in controversy respecting the comparative merits of any. We ought, in the plainness of Friendship to state here, that your letters from Washington [2] were, on this account disapproved, even by those members of the Am. Soc. who are Whigs in principle; and that the most inflexible determination was universally expressed never to permit the Standard to be managed or modified in the slightest degree in such a way as to give pleasure either to Whig, Democratic or Liberty party leaders; to seceders from the American Society, or to half-way abolitionists. Especially from our official paper must all effort be banished to make out a good case for either political party. Justice to the slave requires the condemnation of both; & the columns of the Standard are too precious to be given to the trifling task of demonstrating a grain of wheat in two bushels of chaff. The society opposes the third political party as decidedly as either of the others, though for different reasons; believing it under any circumstances a blunder; and, while it retains James G. Birney as its presidential candidate, the Emancipator as its organ, & continues to be governed by the motives in which it originated, a crime.[3] At the same time the society gives credit for purity of purpose, to vast numbers who ignorantly espouse it.

The broad & deep distinction in character between the original anti-slavery movement & that spurious embodying of the secession from it popularly called New organization, was noticed & branded anew. It was the pervading spirit of the society more than ever to rely upon the strong enunciation of Truth as to the character of slavery & slaveholders, & to the solemn energy of united action against the system, for the awakening of the publick conscience to the work of its abolition and for security from the embarrassment of hypocritical professions & the incumbrance of selfish help.

If in these points you agree with the society's plan of operations for the year, to which we as its Executive Committee stand pledged, we most earnestly entreat you to act with us as editor of the Standard in carrying them out; assuring you of our warmest sympathy, our most hearty co-operation & our most strenuous support.

Hoping to receive your reply as soon as possible,

We are your affectionate friends and co-labourers in the cause.

> WM. LLOYD GARRISON,
> President of the A.A.S.S.
> MARIA WESTON CHAPMAN, Cor. Sec.

Written in the hand of Maria W. Chapman, signed by her and by Garrison: Miscellaneous Manuscripts, New-York Historical Society.

Although this letter seems to have been composed by Mrs. Chapman to represent the consensus of discussion at a meeting of the executive committee, it has been retained as a part of the Garrison canon because it is signed, addressed, and slightly revised in his hand. Moreover, it seems likely that the meeting in question was dominated by him.

Edmund Quincy in a letter to Richard D. Webb, June 27–July 26, 1843 (*Life*, III, 92), emphasized the importance of selecting the right editor for the *Standard*. "Great opposition," he said, "was made to David Lee Child on account of his bias towards Whiggery, but the matter was referred to the Executive Committee to do the best they could in the premises. The meeting went off with the greatest harmony possible." At any rate, Child accepted the post, though he relinquished it the following May, when a committee of three succeeded him: Maria W. Chapman and Edmund Quincy, with Sydney Howard Gay as resident editor (see *The Liberator*, May 17, 1844).

1. The word "distinction" is in Garrison's hand.
2. It is not certain what "letters from Washington" are referred to, though

they must have expressed some of the Whig views thought inappropriate for the official organ of the society. During later months in the year Garrison defended Child's right to state his Whig preferences (*The Liberator*, December 8 and 22, 1843). Beginning in February 1844 Child began to publish both in *The Liberator* and in the *Standard* a long series of letters from Washington, which contained far too much political party talk to please a radical Garrisonian (see *The Liberator*, February 23). By summer Garrison was thoroughly disillusioned, and he expressed shock that Child was supporting Henry Clay for President (see *The Liberator*, July 5 and November 8, 1844).

3. James Gillespie Birney (1792–1857) was a lawyer whose interest in colonization and the restriction of the domestic slave trade dated from the middle twenties. In 1832 he had been commissioned as an agent of the American Colonization Society. He was nominated for President at a state convention in New York in 1839 and by the Liberty party in 1840 and in 1843. Although Birney had many qualities Garrison admired, the two men were in sharp disagreement regarding reliance on political action to effect abolition. (*Life.*)

---

6 6

TO GEORGE W. BENSON

Boston, June 12, 1843.

Dear George:

You are waiting, doubtless, to receive some definite information respecting our removal to Northampton. I have also been waiting to know what word to send you, and have therefore hesitated to write in a state of uncertainty. Ann is considerably better than she has been, and we all think she will be able to be removed to Northampton by the 1st of July, at which time my lease will expire. In case she cannot be removed at that time so far, an arrangement will be made to take some rooms for her, and mother and Sarah, in Elias Smith's house; but you shall have another letter on the subject, more definite, in a few days.

My calculations now are to leave for Northampton, with my family, on Friday or Saturday of next week — the 23d or 24th inst. Angelette will not go with us; and we shall determine about hiring a girl, when we get to our farm-house.[1] Please inform the friend with whom we are to board, of our coming. Phebe Jackson is exceedingly desirous of spending several weeks with us, if she can obtain board under the same roof. Let me know whether it will be practicable to have the necessary arrangements made. We shall be very glad to have her company.

Mother thinks you had better remove all the furniture belonging to her and the sisters, to Northampton, in case they are able to go; but she desires to know your mind on that point.

Olive Gilbert, of Brooklyn, has been residing with us for a fortnight past, and will remain a few days longer.[2] She intends making a visit to Vermont, before she returns home.

We are expecting a visit from sister Charlotte every day.

Our New-England Convention was a truly inspiring occasion.[3] But how did it happen that not a single abolitionist made his appearance from Northampton?

Has our friend D. L. Child left your place for New-York. We have been earnestly hoping to see him in Boston, before he takes charge of the Standard, and trust we shall not be disappointed.

I am still troubled with various complaints. What with my side — bleeding piles — a sore throat, and a cough — you may suppose I need nothing more to place me on the sick list.

Last Tuesday, Dr. [John C.] Warren made a careful examination of my side, in the presence of Dr. [Henry I.] Bowditch. He says it is neither a tumor, nor an enlargement of the spleen, but a great distension of the intestinal parts connected with the stomach, and more troublesome than dangerous. Dr. [Robert] Wesselhoeft laughs at his opinion, and is confident that his own is the correct one. "Who shall decide when doctors disagree?"[4] The examination, though tenderly managed, gave me great pain for several days afterward. I think Dr. Wesselhoeft is near[er] right than Dr. Warren; but Dr. Bowditch fully agrees with the latter.

I see, in the New-York Tribune of Saturday, a very favorable notice of the Northampton Association, from Benjamin C. Bacon, in which he repels certain aspersions cast on its religious character. I will copy it into the Liberator, either this week or the next.[5]

We have had most dismal weather for a fortnight past — cold, wet and dreary. — Have you had any better in N[orthampton].?

Give my brotherly regards to James Boyle and his wife [Laura] — to Emily Farwell, (all remain well at her father's house) — and to Catharine.[6] You shall receive another letter from me before I set out for N.

Yours, with overflowing affection,

                         Wm. Lloyd Garrison.

ALS: Garrison Papers, Boston Public Library.

1. Although she has not been identified, Angelette was apparently a young woman hired by the Garrisons to help in the care of the children; Garrison occasionally spells her name "Angenette" or "Angy."

2. Olive Gilbert (born 1801) was a native of Brooklyn, Connecticut, where she lived until 1872. She then moved to Franklin, Massachusetts, and finally, in 1881, to Vineland, New Jersey. She is chiefly known for having written the biography of Sojourner Truth, an ex-slave whom she befriended. (Letter to the editor from Ruth D. Bell, researcher, April 30, 1971.) Published in 1850, the *Narrative of Sojourner Truth* included an introduction by Garrison.

3. Garrison refers to the meeting held May 30–June 1, 1843. Three daytime sessions met in the Miller Tabernacle on Howard Street and two evening ones in Faneuil Hall. On the evening of May 31 Garrison delivered an "Address to the Slaves of the United States," which was printed in *The Liberator*, June 2.

4. Alexander Pope, *Moral Essays*, Epistle III, line 1.

5. The letter to which Garrison refers appears not to have been published in *The Liberator*.

6. Emily Farwell (1808–1887), a native of Waltham, Massachusetts, was the daughter of William and Rebecca Farwell. A search through the files of the city clerk in Waltham has failed to yield any more information about the family.

6 7

TO GEORGE W. BENSON

Boston, June 20, 1843.

Dear George:

Your letters by Mr. Clark and by mail have been duly received.[1] We are now beginning to pack our things, and to turn our household furniture and wares upside down. On Thursday, we shall endeavor to complete the removal of all that belongs to us; leaving what belongs to mother and the sisters subject to your disposal, at the time of your coming. Should we succeed according to our expectations, we shall take the cars for Wilbraham on Friday morning, and hope to see you on the arrival of the stage in Northampton in the afternoon. Possibly, in case of stormy weather, we may not arrive till Saturday, but we shall try to get through on Friday.

As yet, we have not succeeded in finding a suitable girl to go with us, and do not expect to, at this late period. Angelette would be glad to go with us, we have no doubt, but she is a poor washer and ironer, and very slovenly in the performance of her work. You may therefore say to the man, who thinks his wife will answer our purpose, that he had better send for her, and we shall have no difficulty about the wages, provided she fulfils her part of the engagement satisfactorily. We think that nine shillings a week is as high as ought to be allowed, and cannot give more. It is higher wages by 25 cents than is usually given where all the work of a family is to be done, in this quarter. The sooner she comes, the better.

We do not yet know, whether Phebe [Jackson] will go to N[orthampton]., or, if she should, at what time she will be with us, as we have not yet heard definitely from her on the subject. I shall write to her this afternoon. She has intimated that she should probably wish to stay about a month, but perhaps will be glad to stay longer.

Helen intends bringing with her sheets, pillow-cases, towels, &c. &c.

I do not know how we shall be able to manage with our children, on the score of sleeping. Perhaps George, William and Wendell can all sleep, side wise, in one bed. We shall then want a crib, or something equivalent to it, for Charles. I suppose it can be easily obtained in N.

Mother and Helen wish you to ascertain from the man already alluded to, all that you can respecting his wife's capability, disposition, &c.; and to have the bargain so run as to be no longer binding than shall be agreeable to the parties.

Yesterday, Ann had a slight relapse, but feels better to-day. The weather is now really summerish and charming, and already it is reviving to my feelings. I hope my sojourn in N. will not be in vain, in regard to bodily health.

The Bunker Hill pageant is over, and the President [Tyler] has left us for Springfield.[2] There was an immense concourse of people, of course, and the military display was very great, and to my mind very painful. The Masons and Odd Fellows turned out somewhat numerously, as well as audaciously — and so did "the reverend clergymen," and all the embryo priests belonging to Andover Theological Institution.[3] I did not hear Webster, but merely got a glance at him as he stood on the platform.[4] His address is published, but I have not yet had time to read it. I saw Tyler many times, and heard him speak in reply to an address that was made to him in the town-hall, in Charlestown, yesterday. He is a Virginian — a slaveholder — and no Roman, except his nose, which is wholly and hugely so. He brought with him a slave young man to wait on him — not one of his own slaves, but owned by a relative of his, who, I understand, has been promised his freedom on his return — undoubtedly, to keep him from running away here. Tyler has taken no notice of the letter we sent to him, asking for an interview, to present the Address of the New-England A. S. Convention.[5] He has, in fact, had no time to see us, but it is rather shabby in him not to send us a word in reply. We have got just what we expected from him — nothing; but he has got our Address, and so has the country, and our great purpose is accomplished. His reception here was civil, respectful, decent — nothing more. Last night, Mr. Legare, of his Cabinet, died in the city; so the report is this morning.[6] Judge Simmons, of the Police Court, is also dead.[7] So is Hon. Barker Burnell, of Nantucket.[8] He died in Washington. So perish high and low.

Olive Gilbert leaves us this afternoon, to visit Vermont with a cousin of hers, Mr. Cleveland.[9] She is an excellent woman, and combines in her person many fine qualities. In the fall she expects to visit Northampton.

Hoping to see you on Friday, when we shall be able to discourse about many things, and to find you all well and happy, I remain,

Your affectionate brother in love, as well as in law,

Wm. Lloyd Garrison.

ALS: Garrison Papers, Boston Public Library.

1. Garrison undoubtedly refers to the same person who delivered an earlier letter to George W. Benson (March 3, 1843); his name was apparently John L. Clarke.

2. A great celebration on June 17, 1843, heralded the completion of the Bunker Hill Monument. Following a parade, including military and fraternal organizations and thirty bands, a ceremony was held at the monument, where Daniel Webster gave the principal address. Later in the day a dinner was given in Faneuil Hall. Webster's speech was published in pamphlet form by Tappan and Dennet of Boston.

3. Garrison disliked both the Free and Accepted Masons and the Independent Order of Odd Fellows. In a *Liberator* editorial, May 26, 1843, he attacked the Odd Fellows, chiefly because, like the Masons, they were a secret order. He called the society "a species of Freemasonry, and probably the same thing in substance," and added that he thought the name "disgustingly silly."

Garrison's reference to Andover Theological Seminary reflects an animosity dating back to 1835, when some clerical supporters of the Colonization Society tried to check the advance of abolitionism by dividing Garrison's forces. Although they were ultimately unsuccessful, they were able to persuade the Andover students not to have any connection with the American Anti-Slavery Society. For an account of the affair see *Life*, I, 468–475.

4. Daniel Webster (1782–1852), orator, diplomat, and statesman, was secretary of state under President Tyler until Whig pressure forced him to resign in May 1843. In the 1840's and 1850's he became the eloquent champion of preservation of the Union. Although he was a strong critic of slavery, he believed that disunion was a worse evil and that the antislavery forces were becoming too militant.

5. Garrison refers to the "Address to the Slaves of the United States," which he had delivered at the New England Anti-Slavery Convention, May 31, 1843.

6. Hugh S. Legaré (1797–1843) of Charleston, was a man of many careers, all of which he pursued with distinction. He was in turn lawyer, scholar, journalist, diplomat, and politician. A close friend of John Tyler, he was appointed attorney-general in 1841, and when Webster resigned as secretary of state, Tyler made Legaré *ad interim* secretary.

7. William Simmons (1782–1843), a Harvard graduate, was senior justice of the police court of Boston. (*The Liberator*, June 23, 1843.)

8. Barker Burnell (1798–1843) was a Whig politician who served in the Massachusetts legislature and, from 1841 to 1843, in the United States House of Representatives. (*Who Was Who in America.*)

9. Impossible to identify, since there were many Cleveland cousins.

6 8

TO EDMUND QUINCY

Northampton, July 6, 1843.

All hail to thee, my rural friend! Art thou surrounded with trees and shrubbery, — enjoying the quietude and retirement of a country life, — breathing the pure, fragrant, elastic atmosphere of summer, — so am I. In these things, then, we are equal. But, for the matter of natural scenery — hill and dale, mountain and meadow, the sublime and beautiful, ranging continually "from grave to gay, from lively to severe" [1] — I defy Dedham, or any other place that I have yet seen, to compare with Northampton. It fully satisfies my somewhat extravagant expectations; for reality here is extravagance elsewhere. As for the village itself, — meaning thereby the houses, shops, fences, &c. &c., — though it has some beautiful "country seats," as a whole it wears the aspect of dilapidation, and lacks that trim, careful, nice appearance, which characterises some of the villages in the immediate vicinage of our great brick-and-mortar metropolis. "As the mountains are round about Jerusalem," [2] so are the hills round Northampton. In all other features, these two notable places widely differ. For am I not a competent judge, having seen the Panorama of Jerusalem, by Catherwood? [3] Two of the hills here are so bulky and elevated as to wear a mountainous aspect, and are called Mount Holyoke and Mount Tom. The former is not quite so high as the latter, and the curious generally throng to the top of it; but our friend David Lee Child (a good judge in such matters, having travelled in England and Europe) says the best view is obtained from the top of Mount Tom, and that it surpasses any that he has seen elsewhere. I have not yet summoned energy enough to seek so lofty an altitude; for, "ah! who can think how hard it is to climb!" [4] And having no wings, not even a small balloon, but a lame side, I look, and pause, and wait, until "a more convenient season." [5] Besides, having seen the sky-supporting mountains of New-Hampshire and Vermont, — "whose name is legion," [6] — and having stood with my feet on the head of Mount Washington, I am not so deeply impressed by these imitations, as other travellers are who have never seen the original copies.

As for the people of Northampton, be not too inquisitive, for I can give you no real information on this point. As a proof of the personal esteem in which I am held, and of my ripening popularity, (this is the growing season, you know,) I have not yet received a single invitation to break bread with any one in the town, or to enter into any one's house, though I have been here nearly a fortnight, and my coming was heralded in the Gazette.[7] Now, don't you grow sick from envy. I admit that you are as good a man as I am, and deserve to have all possible honors heaped on your head.

"Now are *our* brows bound with victorious wreaths!" [8]

In what else does the hospitality of this world appear but in the erection of hospitals? Not, however, for fanatics and incendiaries; and therefore you and I must look elsewhere for civility and bread. We have committed crimes not easily to be forgiven, having opposed the sacred order of the clergy, and pleaded for good-for-nothing niggers!

Some of us resolved that no better day could be found, on which to speak in defence of our enslaved countrymen, than the fourth of July; and we therefore determined to hold a meeting in the town, for that purpose. We engaged the Town Hall, (a meeting-house being out of the question for such "infidels,["]) and got some handbills printed and circulated at a late hour; but when the time of meeting came, lo! the doors of the Hall were closed against us, and we were unceremoniously turned into the street. We organized our meeting directly opposite the Hall, under the protecting shadows of two umbrageous trees, Prof. [William] Adam presiding, and David Lee Child acting as Secretary. Baring my head, (not to the pitiless storm, but to the clear blue sky,) [9] and mounting literally a stu[mp,] I addressed a respectable, decorous and attentive audience, for more than an hour, on the hypocrisy and cruelty of this brazen republic, in scathing language, and was followed in a caustic speech by James Boyle, who came nearer home, and spoke of the clergy of the place, and the religionists of the day, in the most withering terms. Dr. [Erasmus] Hudson and Mr. Child intended to address the meeting, but they were so well satisfied with what had been said, and with the deep impression that had evidently been made, that they thought it best to hold their peace. So much for our first reception in Northampton.

I am residing at a farm-house about three miles from the centre of the town, and about one mile from the Industrial Community. Our accommodations are simple and rude, but those with whom we board are kind and friendly, and we contrive to pass our time very pleasantly. Till within the last three days, we have had such melting weather as to make any intellectual or physical effort a weariness to the flesh. I have not been sufficiently long in the place to know whether my health will probably be benefitted by my residence here; but no better place can be found, and the experiment will be fairly made. My side is no better, but rather worse, at present, from an imprudent act which I committed a day or two since; but I trust the severe strain I then received will produce no permanent mischief, though it has caused me great pain.

Health and happiness to thee and thine, Edmund of Dedham! Assist me, to thy utmost extent, in serving up a weekly repast for the readers of the Liberator, and receive, in return, as compensation, my poor thanks, and the admiration and thanks of thy delighted readers, on both sides of the Atlantic ocean.

As the poet Gray said to his friend Walton, "Next to the pleasure of hearing you, is the pleasure of hearing from you. Next to the pleasure of seeing you, is the pleasure of seeing your hand-writing." [10] Pray, take the hint, and send me an epistle as soon as convenient.

Your faithful friend,

Wm. Lloyd Garrison.

ALS: Garrison Papers, Sophia Smith Collection, Smith College Library.

1. Alexander Pope, *An Essay on Man*, Epistle IV, line 380.
2. Psalms 125:2.
3. Frederick Catherwood (1799–1854), British panoramic painter and world traveler, executed the drawings for the *Panorama of Jerusalem* and possibly the painting itself. Garrison probably saw the work in New York, where it was on exhibition from 1836 to 1842, when it was destroyed by fire (see Victor W. Von Hagen, *Frederick Catherwood, Architect*, New York, 1950).
4. James Beattie, *The Minstrel*, I, stanza 1, line 1.
5. Garrison adapts Acts 24:25.
6. Adaptation of Mark 5:9.
7. Garrison refers to a weekly Northampton publication, called at this time the *Hampshire Gazette*. The newspaper appeared from 1786 until 1918 under several different names. (*ULS*.)
8. Shakespeare, *Richard III*, I, i, 5.
9. Allusion to Shakespeare, *King Lear*, III, vii, 59 and III, iv, 29.
10. Garrison reproduces the passage fairly accurately, although he incorrectly identifies the source and one of the persons concerned. The letter in question, dated November 14, 1735, was written *to* the English poet Thomas Gray (1716–1771) by his friend Richard West, whom Garrison mistakenly calls Walton. For the text of the letter, see Paget Toynbee and Leonard Whibley, eds., *Correspondence of Thomas Gray* (Oxford, 1935), I, 33.

69

TO MARIA W. CHAPMAN

Northampton, July 7, 1843.

My dear Mrs. Chapman:

From a sequestered spot in one of the prettiest towns in our great and wide country, I salute you. Hither I have come in quest of that, which, when possessed, is too frequently regarded as of little consequence; but which, when lost, is regarded above all things else on earth — to wit, health. If it is to be obtained for me any where, why not here, where all is fragrance and purity in the atmosphere, sublime and beautiful in the scenery, and peace and quietude among a rural population? Nothing troubles me, at present, except the swelling in my left side, which is still painful, and for which I scarcely expect to obtain permanent relief. I have just been reading a new mode of curing all diseases, in [John Humphrey] Noyes's "Perfectionist," published in Putney, Vt.[1] It is for the sick person to have faith that God will heal him instantly, and according to his faith it will be! This, you will perceive, is a panacea not to be purchased at the store of any druggist; and as I have *no faith* in it, there is no chance of its doing me any good. It is not almighty power and goodness, but human folly and marvellousness, that I distrust in this instance. Sure I am, that I most earnestly desire that the will of the Lord may be done in my case; [2] but I do not think there is any perceptible difference in the size of the swelling, on that account. My "wonder" is too small to induce me to place any reliance on the prescriptions of fanaticism. For the present, I must seek relief in homœopathy, diet, and exercise.

I suppose you are now located at Weymouth. Do you find Nature any less gay, beautiful and young, than when in childhood you gazed on her charming face? Is the sun less effulgent — is the moon less fair — are the stars less brilliant, than of old? Yet have they all advanced in years, and are much older than antiquity. They do what we perishable mortals cannot — fling defiance to Time, and support the weight of centuries as easily as though it were lighter than gossamer. Flesh and blood cannot compete with them, yet I defy them to outlive us. Let not matter vaunt itself against spirit. On the brow of the latter is stamped IMMORTALITY; and though its external drapery must fade, nothing shall be able to mar or mutilate ITSELF. A pleasant, joyous summer to you, in the beautiful place of your nativity! May your heart be as light as the song of birds is sweet; your intellect clear as as a cloudless sky; your path thickly strewed with the flowers of love and friendship as the concave of night with stars.

You have visited Northampton, and therefore need no description of it. I understand that there are no visiters, this season, at the hotels, from abroad. Such as "pass by on the other side" [3] must be ignorant of the attractions it holds out to tourists. Ride in whatever direction you choose, the mind is filled with admiration and delight at the opulence and beauty of the scene. Newburyport must yield the palm to Northampton, though in some of its features it is decidedly superior. I have not yet become acquainted with any of the people, and can say nothing intelligently on that point. We were not allowed to occupy the town hall, on the 4th inst., for an anti-slavery meeting, after having engaged it, but were forced to organize in the open air. It was a spirited affair.

I see nothing, as yet, from your pen in the Liberator. I am sure that the omission has arisen from your other numerous engagements, for your good will is boundless, and your readiness to serve the cause almost beyond comparison or competition. There is scarcely a person in the wide world to whom I am so deeply indebted, in a variety of modes, as to yourself; and though I have given you in return few words expressive of my gratitude, be assured that my heart is none the less full of thankfulness.

I write in haste, as the bearer of this is to leave town immediately. How I yearn to see the countenances of my beloved Boston friends! It seems as if a month had elapsed since my departure.

My general health is improving, though the complaint affecting my left side remains in about the same state. Helen and the tribe of boys are all very well and happy. She sends you her best remembrances.

Please convey to my esteemed friends in Chauncey Place, the warmest expressions of my personal esteem and gratitude.[4] I trust they are well, and enjoying the peace of Heaven in their minds. My best regards also to your estimable parents and sisters.[5]

I intend to be at the Springfield Convention [6] on Tuesday, as do also Dr. [Erasmus] Hudson and James Boyle. We intend to have a due observance of the first of August in this place.

☞ Mr. [David L.] Child expects to be in Boston in all this week.

AL: Garrison Papers, Boston Public Library. The complimentary close and signature have apparently been cut off the bottom of the manuscript sheet.

1. Garrison refers to a three-part article, "The Natural Laws Subordinate to Spiritual Power," two parts of which had been printed in the *Perfectionist*, June 15 and July 1, 1843; the third would appear July 15.
2. A reference to Acts 21:14.
3. A reference to Luke 10:31–32.
4. Mrs. Chapman, by this time widowed, lived in Boston at 39 Summer Street, one of the defining boundaries of Chauncy Place.
5. Warren Weston (c. 1780–1855), of Pilgrim descent and living in Weymouth, Massachusetts, was the father of Mrs. Chapman and her sisters Anne, Caroline, Deborah, Emma, and Lucia. He was married at this time to his second wife Ann or Anne (died 1878); the sisters' mother was Nancy Bates Weston (1785–1839). (For Captain Weston's obituary see *The Liberator*, November 9, 1855; see also *Life* and Garrison's letter to Francis Jackson, November 3, 1855.)
6. The Massachusetts Anti-Slavery Society Convention to be held in Springfield, July 10–11.

7 0

TO *THE LIBERATOR*

NORTHAMPTON, July 14, 1843.

MY DEAR FRIEND —

Before coming to this place, I had heard such encomiums bestowed on the beauty of its position and appearance, as to excite high-wrought expectations and a lively curiosity in my breast, in regard to it. These have been abundantly realized; so that I, too, am prepared to join the throng of admirers, and to concede to Northampton the palm for romantic loveliness and the most charming scenery over every other place that I have yet visited in our flourishing Commonwealth. I have long claimed for Newburyport, my own beloved native place, an unrivalled location, and attractions of the most bewitching character; but, on the whole, Nature has showered her gifts with a more prodigal hand on Northampton. Each of these places has features peculiar to itself, which place it beyond comparison. Here I miss the Merrimack river, rolling majestically in its broadest dimensions towards the Atlantic, and also the sight of that great ocean in the distance; but ample compensation is made in the proximity of the Connecticut river, and in view of the sublime range of hills which surrounds this place on every side. Ride in whatever direction you choose, if you have any taste for the sublime or beautiful, you will be filled with delight, and constantly induced to exclaim, in the devout spirit of the royal singer of Israel, — 'O Lord, how manifold are thy works! in wisdom hast thou made them all: the earth is full of thy riches . . . Thou greatly enrichest it with the river of God, which is full of water; thou waterest the ridges thereof abundantly; thou settlest the furrows thereof; thou makest it soft with showers; thou blessest the springing thereof. Thou crownest the year with thy goodness; and thy paths drop fatness.' [1] At first, the atmosphere seemed to be so laden with perfume as to be almost oppressive, so great was the contrast with the rank smells of our crowded city. The pride of this place, as furnishing the finest sites for dwellings, is Round Hill, which is indeed a gem of exceeding beauty, and which reminds me of English scenery in connexion with princely opulence. The highest elevations are Mount Tom and Mount Holyoke; of which the latter is the popular resort, though the altitude of the former is somewhat greater, and the view from which, (in the opinion of a friend [David Lee Child] who has been something of a traveller on both sides of the Atlantic,) is surpassingly magnificent. I intend visiting them before my return; for though 'the eye is never satisfied with seeing,' [2] it is the medium through which an immense amount of satisfaction is conveyed to the mind. I will then give you my 'impressions.' Having seen the Welch and Scottish mountains, and stood on the summits of the Green mountains of Vermont and the White mountains of New-Hampshire, these do not strongly affect my imagination, as their height, I believe, does not exceed one hundred feet. Yet in appearance they approach to the sublime, and form a striking contrast with the intervales and meadows in their vicinage.

This is the residence of Sylvester Graham,[3] who has encountered his share of the world's obloquy for attempting to reform it from some of its beastly habits, but who has displayed a martyr's spirit and front in giving utterance to his convictions of truth, as it relates to the bodily as well as spiritual redemption of mankind. Though not a convert to all his views, I admire his firmness, his courage, and his manifest desire to bless mankind by showing them how, in his opinion, they best can 'glorify God in their bodies and spirits, which are his.'[4] Comparatively few have been found disposed to adopt his dietetic theory, in all its minutiæ; but tens of thousands of persons have been happily affected by his lectures and writings, and saved from the direful effects of a vitiated appetite; though, of this great multitude, few, I am apprehensive, are disposed to acknowledge their indebtedness to him. Shame on them for their lack of gratitude and magnanimity! But this is the fate of every reformer, in his day and generation. Time and posterity will take care of his memory.

Our able and vigorous anti-slavery coadjutor, D. L. Child, is still here, but expects to leave for New York (via Boston) in all next week, to assume the editorial management of the Standard. Success has not crowned his efforts in the sugar-beet cultivation,[5] but he has probably done all that any one could have done, in his circumstances, and deserved something more than success. He has toiled early and late, in season and out of season, not 'like a slave,' but like a freeman and 'with a will,' and far more severely than a human being ought to toil. He has exhibited immense energy and resolution, and, especially for one 'bred to the law,' and fond of literary pursuits, astonishing industry. The location of the land which he has tilled is very pleasant, and he has made some substantial improvements on it. I regret, for the sake of humanity, as well as for his own sake, that his experiment has failed; for an additional blow would be given to slavery, if free sugar could supplant that which is raised by slave labor — as it will, unquestionably, at a day not far distant. The Standard, under his care, cannot fail to be an ably conducted journal. He has great qualities of mind, and has been identified with the anti-slavery cause from an early period. Standing aloof, as he does, from every religious sect and political party, (though of religion and politics he has his own views,) I confide in him to pursue an impartial course, as editor of the Standard, — to give credit to whom credit may be due, — to regard the success of our cause as paramount to all questions of national policy, — and to give no quarter either to spiritual or political wickedness in high places. It is to be hoped that Mrs. CHILD will be a liberal contributor to the Standard, especially to its literary department, and that the distinguishing elements of their character will be blended together in the management of the paper.

The town of Northampton (by which term I now mean the houses, stores, &c.) wears an air of dilapidation, and will not compare in architectural taste and beauty with many other places in the State, though it has a few handsome buildings. Aside from its delightful location, it presents no features either of an impressive or interesting character. The spirit of enterprise appears to be exiled from it, and it has the misfortune to be under the control of a few wealthy men, who, having more than a sufficiency of this world's goods, have long since retired from business, and seemingly wish not to be disturbed in their repose even by the hum of prosperity. A rail-road is talked of between this place and Springfield, and some steps have been taken towards its commencement; but how soon it will be completed, is extremely uncertain.

Inviting as is Northampton to all tourists and sojourners from our great cities during the summer season, I am told that the hotels are yet vacant, and that the prospect is, that they will continue to remain so. Let it be made accessible by rail-road, and no doubt multitudes would be induced to visit the place, who now 'pass by on the other side.' [6]

My present location is about three miles from the centre of the town, in a spot quite rural and picturesque. My acquaintance with the inhabitants is so limited, that I can report nothing of their civility or hospitality. Besides my unpopularity as an abolitionist in this region, religious bigotry reigns with despotic sway over the minds of the people, and inflames their prejudices against me on account of my contending for that liberty wherewith Christ makes his followers free. It is melancholy to see those, whom God has made to serve him, so priest-ridden, and bewitched by carnal observances, and misled by sectarian creeds. Though I find 'none so poor' [7] (with scarcely an exception,) as to give me a friendly welcome to the town, yet I have no complaint to make, but feel happy in the assurance that I am not slighted for any evil that I have done, but for my fidelity in exposing the religious and political impostures of the times. With the amiable Cowper, I can rejoicingly say —

['] 'Tis my happiness below,
    Not to live without the cross,
But a Saviour's power to know,
    Sanctifying every loss.' [8]

There are a few choice anti-slavery spirits here, but these reside chiefly in the 'Community.' Some days prior to the fourth of July, we resolved to celebrate that day by an anti-slavery meeting in the town; and accordingly deputed a committee (Dr. [Erasmus] Hudson and James Boyle) to apply for the town hall, for that purpose. The person who has charge of the hall was seen by them, and agreed to let us have it. Notices of the meeting were sent to the different clergymen, to bo road from their pulpits, but none complied with the request, excepting the Baptist and Unitarian.[9] Some fifty handbills were printed, and posted in various parts of the town, informing the people of our intentions, and inviting them to attend; but these were torn down by the lawless spirit of pro-slavery almost immediately, so that comparatively few persons were notified of the meeting. The morning of the 'glorious fourth' came, and a small band of us assembled at the town hall, but found the doors closed against us, and no one to tell us for what cause! The friends of impartial liberty were thus turned into the street, rudely and dishonorably, with this alternative — either to hold their meeting in the open air, or to shake off the dust from their feet on the town, and go elsewhere. Nothing daunted, they immediately organized in front of the hall, under two finely over-shadowing elm trees, by calling that unblenching friend of human rights, Prof. WILLIAM ADAM, to the chair, and appointing DAVID LEE CHILD secretary. I then addressed the assembly at some length, after reading a portion of the first chapter of Isaiah, making my remarks as applicable to the day and the occasion as it was in my power, and exposing the awful guilt and hypocrisy of the American people in pretending to be worshippers at the shrine of Freedom, and to be praising God for their deliverance from a foreign yoke, while they were keeping in abject bondage a population larger than that of all New-England! The words that I uttered were those of 'truth and soberness' [10] — and though they were calculated to make the ears of the wicked to tingle, and the hearts of the hypocritical to writhe in agony, yet they were such as the oppressed in all ages and in all climes have loved to hear, such as became a freeman, such as ex-hibited slavery in its true colors, and such as left the whole country without excuse for its abominable deeds. It was the first time that I ever mounted literally a stump as a rostrum from which to address the people, and I found much more freedom of spirit on it than I had ever found in a pulpit. James Boyle followed me in a speech of great cogency and power, in which he went into an examination of the religious aspects of our cause, and demonstrated that, for the continuance of slavery in our land, the American church and clergy are pre-eminently guilty, and deserve to be abandoned by all who fear God or regard man. He made some very pointed allusions to the pro-slavery position of the clergy in Northampton, and their subserviency to public opinion. 'You will find them all ready enough,' he said, 'to countenance the temperance picknick, to be held this afternoon, because the popular gale sets strongly in that quarter; but not to attend a meeting like this, or to advocate a cause so unpopular as ours.' It was the intention of Dr. Hudson and D. L. Child to be among the speakers on the occasion, but they both felt unwilling to offer any remarks, lest (as they said) they should weaken, rather than deepen the impressions that had been made on the minds of the audience. The broadest invitation was repeatedly given to all who were present, to participate in the proceedings, and especially to deny (if they could) the soundness of any of the positions that had been assumed, or the arguments that had been offered, or the allegations that had been made; but no one ventured to appear in defence either of Church or State. An elderly gentleman, named Taylor,[11] (not a resident of the town, I believe,) stepped forward, and said that he was as much of an abolitionist as any body, and hated slavery as much as Mr. Garrison did; that I had spoken in 'unmeasured terms' of slavery, but he had no fault to find on that score; but that I had not told the people what they could do to abolish the system. He thought we had nothing to do with it; it was a part of the compact, and incorporated into the Constitution; and it was our duty to support it until that Constitution should be amended, though he was decidedly opposed to all political action on the subject! After premising that I knew not how to speak in *measured* terms of a system so unclean and impious as is slavery, and that they who have an object to effect are seldom found lamenting that they know not what to do, and that the grief of abolitionists is, that so much is to be and can be done, and that there are so few to do the work, I proceeded to show in what manner and on what grounds the people of the North were justly chargeable with upholding slavery, and, consequently, how they might extricate themselves from their present guilty relations. But, if I satisfied others on that point, I did not convince Mr. Taylor, who shook his head, and reiterated his declaration, that, slavery being sanctioned by the Constitution, we were bound to sustain it as law-abiding citizens. He argued that, so long as it was in the statute book, the law of the land was of paramount authority to the law of God. I admired his honesty in avowing this monstrous doctrine — a doctrine which is practically enforced as orthodox by the great body of our religious and political leaders, though in the abstract conceded to be heretical. He was quite certain, moreover, that the abolitionists had retarded the abolition of slavery many years — an assertion which Messrs. McDuffie, Calhoun, Clay & Co. would rejoice to see demonstrated as a fact, and which indicates either profound ignorance or consummate effrontery, by whom soever made.[12] This was easily disposed of, and the meeting was then dissolved.

Our audience was probably twice as numerous as it would have been in the hall, from the novelty of the gathering in the open air. Among the listeners, I am told, was the Rev. William Allen, D. D. formerly President of Bowdoin College.[13] I wish he had taken the stump, and defined his position on this momentous question. The weather was delightful, and the proceedings throughout were perfectly orderly; not the slightest disrespect being shown, in a single instance.

There are three newspapers published here — two whig, and one democratic. The Courier[14] and Gazette (both whig) took no notice of the meeting, — whether from motives of policy, or in the spirit of contempt, I do not know; but in giving, as they did, an account of the manner in which the day was observed in the town, their silence in regard to a meeting held under such peculiar circumstances, in so public a manner, and with such a noble object in view, is certainly not creditable to their humanity or courtesy.

In the Democrat, — which has for its motto, as if purposely to illustrate its rottenness, 'Uncompromising hostility against every form of tyranny over the mind of man,' — appeared an editorial sketch of the meeting, which was chiefly confined to a personal attack upon myself, and to a broad caricature of what was said and done on the occasion, expressed in the language and spirit of the lowest blackguardism.[15] I send you a copy of the paper, containing the article, which I wish you to place in the receptacle provided for such ebullitions in the columns of the Liberator. It furnishes additional evidence of the fact which has long since been demonstrated to the world, that there is nothing under heaven so devoid of principle, so callous to shame, so reprobate in spirit, so profligate in practice, so impudent in pretension, so hypocritical in conduct, so heartless in feeling, or so villanous in design, as the existing DEMOCRACY of the United States, falsely so called.

> ['‚]Who can with patience for a moment see
> The medley mass of pride and misery,
> Of whips and charters, manacles and rights,
> Of slaving blacks and democratic whites,

And all the piebald policy that reigns,
In free confusion, o'er Columbia's plains?
To think that man, thou just and gentle God,
Should stand before thee with a tyrant's rod,
O'er creatures like himself, with souls from thee,
Yet dare to boast of perfect liberty!!' [16]

Alluding to me, the editor of the Democrat politely says — 'He began with a lie in his mouth, by saying that he was refused admittance into the town hall.' [17] The facts respecting our being excluded from the hall are precisely such as I have already mentioned. The plea now made, in order to get rid of the odium which must ever attach to such unworthy conduct, is, that the hall had been previously engaged to the ladies engaged in the Temperance celebration on that day. But it avails nothing — for, first, the hall was not occupied during the forenoon, if at any other period in the day, either by the ladies or by others, but remained empty and locked throughout our meeting; secondly, it was a piece of deception to give us the assurance that we should occupy the hall, if it had been already promised to others; and, thirdly, whether such an agreement had been made in behalf of the ladies, or not, no one presented himself to enlighten us on this point, or to prevent any misapprehension that might arise under the anomalous circumstances of the case, or to correct any of our statements. 'Finding that no one contradicted him in his falsehood,' continues the editor — I give you his name, 'Rinaldo R. Taylor' — 'he made the most of it by a long harangue against the town, [a false assertion,] and thanked heaven that he was allowed to speak in the open air' — [that is true.] 'He said that $5000 had been offered for his poor head by some lynching characters at the South.' [18] Those lynching characters were the Senate and House of Representatives of Georgia, backed up in legal form by the Executive of that State. This atrocious attempt, by the offer of a large bribe, on the part of a sovereign State, to secure the abduction and subsequent murder of a citizen of Massachusetts, guiltless of any and every crime, and simply for advocating universal liberty and equality, is treated by this 'democratic' traducer as a capital joke, but which, in the matter of dollars and cents, he thinks was carried a *little* too far — for, 'judging from the effect of his preaching here, we should say that it was a very extravagant offer.' Ha! ha! ha! What can be more droll or witty? Now, it may be safely affirmed that the man who can thus treat an offer so murderous, needs nothing but the opportunity and the courage to perpetuate any crime within the scope of human transgression. With his own hands he tears off the mask of his profession, and reveals himself in his true character. But the editor adds — 'Indeed it is our firm belief, that if these lynchers were to pay Wm. L. Garrison, editor of the Boston Liberator, and David L. Child, editor of the New-York Standard, the $5000 to keep their heads on their shoulders, and employ them in delivering lectures about the country, it would be a better speculation [for slavery, of course,] than to chop off their heads.' Slang like this is the popular 'democratic' currency. But, mark the argument! D. L. Child and W. L. Garrison will do more to perpetuate slavery, by 'delivering lectures about the country,' than the chopping off of their heads would do to secure the same end; therefore, let them live! But, should the 'lynchers' be, after all, the more sagacious in this matter, why then the heads of these fanatical abolitionists ought to be chopped off, by a just regard for our 'constitutions and laws,' and as a good 'speculation'!

I am next charged with having used 'disgusting language, not only against departed patriots, both clerical and laymen, but against the constitutions and laws framed by them,' &c. Why did not this patriotic democrat expose the injustice of my remarks on the spot? Why did he skulk from manly discussion, and by silence give his consent to the accuracy of all that was advanced by the speakers? Doubtless, on that occasion, he felt that discretion was the better part of valor,[19] as did a certain redoubtable hero of old, whose lies, like his own, were 'gross as a mountain, open, palpable.'[20] Why, in giving an account of the meeting, does he suppress the fact, that all persons who were present, whether friendly or hostile to the anti-slavery movement, were invited to give utterance to their sentiments; and that, though charges of a grave character were urged against both Church and State, and repeated solicitations made to have them corrected if they were not true, no one came forward — no, not even to screen the clergy of the place from condemnation, or to convict me of 'lying,' in regard to the town hall? He knows that when our opponents were called on to say in what manner we had disturbed the truth —

> 'There was silence, deep as death,
> And the boldest held his breath
> For a time' — [21]

until he could utter his ribaldry through the medium of the 'Northampton Democrat.'

Again — 'The clergy came in for the greatest share of abuse, and were told to extend the solemnization of the marriage vow to the horses in the stables, the cattle in the yards, and the pigs in the pens.' This the critic calls 'disgusting balderdash,' but, in the true spirit of knavery, he does not state in what connexion this language was used; that it was simply an illustration — the *argumentum ad hominem* — to show the folly of those who, while they maintain that slaves are justly the chattels personal of their masters, affect to regard the suppression of the marriage institution among them as a great evil! As if property stood in virtuous need of the marriage vow!

But I must close. Let the article in the Democrat appear in the next number of the Liberator, without abridgment, and send a copy to its courteous and veracious editor.[22]

Yours, for free discussion,

WILLIAM LLOYD GARRISON.

Printed: *The Liberator*, July 28, 1843. This letter was sent to *The Liberator* by way of its printer, James B. Yerrinton.

1. Garrison quotes freely from Psalms 104:24 and 65:9–11.
2. Ecclesiastes 1:8, with a substitution of "never" for "not."
3. Sylvester Graham (1794–1851), a minister and reformer, active in the temperance movement, was known principally for his writings and lectures on the relationship of diet and regimen to health. He advocated the use of pure and natural foods, exercise, and Spartan living arrangements.
4. Garrison adapts I Corinthians 6:20.
5. At Northampton, where he erected the first (but short-lived) sugar-beet factory in the United States.
6. Garrison refers to Luke 10:31–32.
7. Shakespeare, *Julius Caesar*, III, ii, 126.
8. Garrison quotes almost exactly from William Cowper, *Olney Hymns*, "Welcome Cross," lines 1–4.
9. Horace D. Doolittle (1807–1880), the Baptist clergyman, and Rufus Ellis (1819–1885), the Unitarian clergyman, were both supporters of the antislavery cause. (See Eve O. Cochran, *A Centenary History of the First Baptist Church of Northampton, Massachusetts, 1826–1926*, Northampton, 1926, pp. 15–16 and Nathaniel Lauriat, *The History of Unitarianism in Northampton, 1824–1954*, Northampton, Mass., n. d., p. 5.)
10. Acts 26:25.
11. Not identified.
12. These three men, all southerners by birth and lawyers by training, possibly constituted more of a triumvirate in Garrison's eyes than in their own. All opposed the abolitionist movement, but with different reasons and with different emphases. George McDuffie (1790–1851) served as governor of South Carolina and as member of the House and Senate. He used his apparently outstanding abilities as orator and debater in support of nullification. John C. Calhoun (1782–1850) of Charleston, South Carolina, had a long record of service in the government — in Congress, as Vice-President, and at the cabinet level. He was consistently proslavery and fought for the exclusion of antislavery petitions from Congress. Henry Clay (1777–1852) of Kentucky, "The Great Compromiser," served as congressman, senator, and secretary of state. His famous talent for compromise characterized the tone and tactics with which he supported emancipation.
13. William Allen (1784–1868), a clergyman, was well known in New England at this time as scholar, preacher, and poet; he was the compiler, in 1809, of the *American Biographical and Historical Dictionary*, one of the earliest volumes of this type. He served as president of Bowdoin College from 1819 to 1838, at which time he moved to Northampton, Massachusetts, where he pursued literary activities for the rest of his life.
14. A daily Northampton newspaper founded in 1829. (*ULN.*)
15. The Northampton *Democrat*, a weekly newspaper, was founded in 1840 and was known for a short time in 1841 as the Northampton *Democrat and*

Hampshire County Advertiser. It appears to have ceased publication in 1854. (*ULN*.)

16. Thomas Moore, "To the Lord Viscount Forbes from the City of Washington," lines 139–148. Garrison quotes exactly except for punctuation and the substitution of "policy" for "polity."

17. Rinaldo R. Taylor took over the editorship of the Northampton *Democrat* in June 1843. In the issue of December 19, 1843, he announced that he was leaving his editorship and had no future plans. Taylor appears not to have been a native of Northampton; the town records show neither his birth nor death date. (*The Liberator*, July 14, 1843.)

18. In 1831 the Georgia legislature, believing that *The Liberator* was inciting slave revolts, passed a bill offering a reward of $5,000 to anyone who arrested Garrison and brought him to trial in that state.

19. Adaptation of Shakespeare, *1 Henry IV*, V, iv, 122.

20. Shakespeare, *1 Henry IV*, II, iv, 250.

21. Thomas Campbell, "Battle of the Baltic," stanza 2.

22. The article from the *Democrat* appeared in *The Liberator*, July 28, 1843.

71

TO FRANCIS JACKSON

Northampton, July 15, 1843.

My Dear Friend:

I see you as freshly with the eyes of my memory, as though you stood before me; yet a distance of nearly one hundred miles separates us from each other. This is done by mental clairvoyance, without the aid of animal magnetism. Believe me, I am neither asleep nor dreaming, though I have just had a comfortable *siesta*, in a natural way. I hear you, also, in the same manner that I see you; but both seeing and hearing belong to the past, in this instance, and though delightful in the shape of reminiscences, they give no knowledge of the present, and are far from being actualities. In plain English, (for I am getting to be too mystical,) how you look *now*, whether you are well or ill, whether you are at home or abroad, on what topic you are conversing, or what you are doing, I really cannot tell. On these points I need information, and therefore should be highly gratified to receive a letter from you, giving me all the particulars. But much should I prefer to see you — "in the flesh," as we say, or in the form of "a living epistle," to use an apostolic phrase — in this romantic village, that we might ascend heavenward together, at least as high as the top of Mount Holyoke, and, I was about to say, never part company with each other! But, without an instantaneous translation, such a continual juxtaposition would hardly be convenient for either of us, in a business way. Yet I hope that the time will arrive, (but that time pertains to eternity,) when, our mortal having put on immortality, we shall "meet to part no more," [1] where we shall enjoy the contemplation of scenes infinitely more beautiful and glorious than are to be found in the enchanting valley of the Connecticut. Do you not intend to escape from the heat, dust, languor and confinement of a city life, in mid-summer, for a few days at least? Or have you done so already? If you have not, pray let Northampton stand first on your list of preferences, and give to the spurious humanity of the place, by your presence, "the assurance of a man." [2] But I will not be selfish. It is my friendship for you that is thus suggestive and urgent.

I am fresh from a jaunt to Springfield, in company with James Boyle and Dr. [Erasmus] Hudson, to attend the anti-slavery convention in that place. The ride was transcendantly fine, and afforded an amount of enjoyment not to be derived from the possession of one hundred millions of dollars, in hard cash. If my organs of ideality, eventuality, locality and memory, be not larger now than they were a week since, they are certainly more active. Yet I cannot describe what I have seen and felt. If, with the curse that still rests upon it, (not an arbitrary curse, however — not an irreversible, almighty fiat, but the original curse growing out of, and perpetuated by, man's disobedience, which has prevented the desert wilderness from blossoming like the rose, and produced briers and thorns in afflicting luxuriance,) Nature presents so ravishing an aspect, what will be her appearance when that curse shall have been removed, and there shall be nothing to hurt, molest, or make afraid? when love shall cover the earth, "as the waters cover the sea"? [3] when peace and plenty shall be as abundant as the light of heaven?

Our convention at S. was not numerously attended, — for, though these are emphatically "the times that try men's souls," [4] the farmer does not leave his plough, nor the mechanic his work-shop, nor the merchant his counter, as was done in our *first* revolutionary war, — but we had a choice selection of people, and a very spirited time. Not less than six or eight clergymen were present, with a fair sprinkling of the leading politicians in the place; but though we brought the most tremendous charges against Church and State, and challenged all who were present to refute our positions, not one of our opponents ventured to take the floor. I am persuaded that a deep and salutary impression was made on the occasion. For further particulars, see the next Liberator.

The "Northampton Association" is struggling bravely and hopefully for success, against the embarrassments of the times, against the prejudices of the community, against the formidable difficulties necessarily attendant on every such enterprise at the outset, against the cry of infidelity, raised by priestcraft and bigotry. As it is yet in its infancy, it is too early to predict the result of this experiment; but I trust it will be cheering to the friends of universal reform. If the members of the Association prove true to themselves, and allow no root of bitterness to spring up among them, I see no serious obstacle in the way of their success.

Our esteemed friend D. L. Child will probably be the bearer of this letter, as he told me, a few days since, that he should endeavor to leave for Boston, without fail, to-morrow. I regret that the Standard has been so long without an editor, and that our friend has been unable to settle his affairs in this quarter at an earlier period. He has been a hard worker on his land, and has not failed in his beet sugar experiment for any lack of industry or energy on his part. I am sorry that he has received no other compensation for his severe toil and philanthropic intentions, than the consciousness of having tried to do good. Of course, you and the other dear friends in the city will have an interview with him, and freely interchange thoughts with each other, respecting the points on which we feel so deep a solicitude.

What has transpired in the world, or even in Boston, since I left, I do not know, as I get little or no intelligence here. Cut off from my weekly examination of papers from all parts of the country, and scarcely seeing one for many days in succession, I am famishing for intelligence. A remedy for this will soon be applied in the shape of a bundle of papers, which is hereafter to be forwarded to me by Harnden's express, once a week, from 25, Cornhill.[5]

We have had intensely warm weather (a few days excepted) since our arrival. Though only three weeks have transpired, it seems as though we had been absent nearly as many months. Our location is a pleasant one, but very retired, about three miles from the centre of the town. My health is better, in some respects, than it was before I came, but my left side continues troublesome. Helen and the children are all very well, the latter being thoroughly browned in their complexion by their unwonted exposure to the sun. Pleasant as is the country, we shall all be happy to return to the city by the first of October. My wife desires to be specially remembered to you and Harriet, and to Mr. and Mrs. Merriam — and we twain, you know, are one.[6]

Your grateful friend,

Wm. Lloyd Garrison.

ALS: Garrison Papers, Boston Public Library.

1. I Corinthians 15:53 and the hymn by Bourne Hall Draper and Heinrich C. Zeuner, "Ye Christian Heralds, Go, Proclaim," stanza 3, line 2.
2. Shakespeare, *Hamlet*, III, iv, 62.
3. Isaiah 11:9.

4. Thomas Paine, *The American Crisis*, No. 1 (December 23, 1776).

5. The William F. Harnden Company, of Boston, provided express package-carrying service. (Boston city directory.)

6. Garrison refers to Francis Jackson's wife, Harriet, and to his daughter, Eliza Jackson Merriam (1816–1881), and her husband, Charles D. Merriam (c. 1814–1845). Eliza Merriam was active in abolitionist circles at this time, and had served as treasurer of the Boston Female Anti-Slavery Society in 1841. Her husband was equally active in the abolition movement, and was a life member of the Massachusetts Anti-Slavery Society. (Letter to the editor from Jonathan Prude, researcher, September 1970.)

72

TO FRANCIS JACKSON

Northampton, August 2, 1843 ⎱
Wednesday night, 10 o'clock ⎰

Beloved Friend:

Your sprightly and most animating letter of the 26th ult. has just been put into my hands, and read with a thrill of delight. The *"living epistle"* is yet to come, which will be still better; but this, now before me, is pleasure enough for one night, at least. Though I have never learnt to dance, I feel as if I could now do so, even without the aid of music, or, rather, with the aid of the music of your epistolary voice. I will try — so, here goes! * * * There! "I've done the deed: didst thou not hear a noise?" [1] I will ask no one's opinion as to the beauty or propriety of the execution. What is done by a glad and grateful heart is always done in proper and beautiful style.

You rightly judge in presuming that, eager as I am for intelligence, I do not care to learn "the prices of stock or merchandize," excepting in the single article of cotton, as pertaining to the overthrow of slavery; but I am delighted to hear what you are doing to enlarge the South Cove, for the benefit of a great city, a noble commonwealth, and a long line of posterity.[2] No one knows better how to lay a broad and solid foundation than yourself. I would rather be the conqueror of those four acres of "flats," than of Napoleon Bonaparte; and I certainly regard you as a much greater hero than the Duke of Wellington; though the compliment is a poor one.

Most happy am I to be informed, that William F. White has gone on the great Western anti-slavery tour.[3] Considering his age, his education, and his family connexions, his case is a remarkable one, and full of promise. The Conventions which he will attend, will doubtless serve to augment his intellectual and moral power, and make him yet more useful in the mighty cause of freedom. I admire all I have seen of him, except his mustaches, which I heartily abominate.

All your items of anti-slavery intelligence are interesting. The donation of Thomas Sturge is not only liberal, but far beyond any thing that I had expected from that quarter; and it is not less timely than liberal.[4] See what it is to walk by faith! How or where the money was to be obtained, to meet the expenses growing out of our numerous Western Conventions, we could not certainly tell; but we had faith to believe it would be forthcoming, and according to our faith, so already it has been to us. I only regret that our worthy friend [Samuel] Philbrick, through doubt, had to record his vote against this magnificent movement in behalf of down troddon humanity. But no one will rejoice more heartily than himself at its success.

The gift of land, by J. C. Gore, is another pleasing indication, that his religion is of a practical nature, and not sectarian. Your sabbatical survey of the land, to ascertain its dimensions and qualities, was worthy of the Christian dispensation. It was a good deed, though not a better day than any other of the week. The taking possession of the land, "in the name of the Massachusetts Anti-Slavery Society," was an impressive and novel act, well calculated to make a sensation in any pro-slavery region. Abolition is surely "dying away."

Not the least delightful part of your letter was the intelligence, that you and my dear [Nathaniel P.] Rogers intend visiting Northampton on Saturday next. Whether the priestcraft and pro-slavery of this place will sanction the deed, or not, we will make our arrangements for visiting Mount Holyoke on Sunday next, and climbing heavenward as high as practicable. James Boyle, and other kindred spirits, will accompany us. Pray, tarry with us a few days, if you can. This is a glorious region for scenic beauty and grandeur; but perhaps it is familiar to you. We shall have a pleasant time together, I am sure.

I will be at the American hotel,[5] in this place, on your arrival on Saturday afternoon, with a vehicle to convey you both to the "Community," where you will receive a plain but hearty welcome from the members thereof. I do exceedingly regret that I am so circumstanced as to be unable to offer you and Rogers a bed and room; but I am only a boarder, having very poor accommodations for myself, and there is not an inch of spare room in the house. But you shall be welcome to our table, and partake of such fare as we have set before us from day to day. I shall be with you in the Community nearly all the time, and endeavor to "gipsey" with you in all the region round.

My wife heartily reciprocates your kind remembrances, and is delighted at the thought of so soon seeing you and N.P.R. She is quite unwell, at present, with a sudden attack of the cholera morbus, but her case is not, as yet, a severe one. All the children are in excellent bodily condition; and little Charles Follen is a bouncer indeed. He would certainly take the premium at any public exhibition of babes in the old Bay State, not on the score of beauty, but of specific gravity. He is just learning to stand on his own legs.

We must have one anti-slavery meeting in the town before you leave — perhaps on Sunday evening. I want Rogers to give priestcraft and sectarism in this bigoted region, "a touch of his quality" [6] before he leaves. Tell him that my heart leaps to embrace him, and that my affection for him cannot be described in words. Heaven send you a fair day on Saturday, and grant us all a pleasurable meeting. I write in haste. Much that I want to say, I must leave unwritten.

Your admiring friend,

Wm. Lloyd Garrison.

ALS: Garrison Papers, Boston Public Library.

1. Shakespeare, *Macbeth*, II, ii, 15.
2. The South Cove, that area directly across the channel from South Boston, was after 1833 the site of a major urban redevelopment project under the direction of the South Cove Company of which Francis Jackson was an agent. Land had been reclaimed; streets, a railroad station, and the United States Hotel (then the largest in the country) were to be constructed. (Walter Muir Whitehill, *Boston: A Topographical History*, Cambridge, Mass., 1968.)
3. William A. White (1818–1856), whose initial Garrison mistakes, was a native of Watertown, Massachusetts, and a graduate of Harvard. A lecturer and journalist, he was an ardent abolitionist as well as a temperance advocate. (*Life.*)
4. Thomas Sturge (c. 1787–1866) was a successful Quaker businessman who was also a generous philanthropist and reformer. (*Annual Monitor*, 1867, p. 135.)
5. The American House, located on Pleasant Street at Pearl, a stopping place for the stage heading south. (*Hampshire Gazette*, September 24, 1844.)
6. Shakespeare, *Hamlet*, II, ii, 460.

73

TO HENRY W. WILLIAMS

Northampton, August 2, 1843.

Dear Henry:

I have but a moment to write a few lines to you, as the party by whom this is to be sent will leave immediately. In answer to your inquiries respecting my health, I would state, that it is decidedly better than it was at Cambridgeport; but as for the complaint in my side, it remains in about the same state. Probably it has a life of its own, and is governed by its own laws, and will long continue to be more or less troublesome. Helen and the children are all remarkably well.

Well, the glorious anniversary of W[est]. I[ndian]. emancipation is over. In this town, we succeeded in getting the largest meeting-house opened for us, in which we held meetings all day, and though our audiences were not large, they were of the right stamp. A very admirable address was delivered by Prof. [William] Adam, and speeches were made by James Boyle, myself, and other individuals. Every thing went off in a highly satisfactory manner. I long to hear how the meetings at Lowell and Dedham were attended, and shall eagerly look to the Liberator for information.

By the way, I wrote to you or friend [Oliver] Johnson, requesting that *two* copies of the Liberator might be sent to me regularly. Last week *none* was received, either by the mail or the bundle. Please see that the mistake is corrected. If you can spare three or four copies of the last number, you may send them along for distribution in this quarter.

Mr. Stetson informs me that he paid $60 to you, on my account.[1] You may retain this sum in your hands, until my late landlord shall present his bill for the quarter's rent.

Should there be any money, that is due me for the last month, you may send it to me by the first safe conveyance, as I wish to settle my bill for board as promptly as possible.

I shall send a packet of letters, editorial matter, &c. in the course of all this week.

Desiring to be affectionately remembered to all the friends, I remain,
Your much obliged friend,

Wm. Lloyd Garrison.

ALS: Villard Papers, Harvard College Library.

1. James A. Stetson (1801–1893) was the brother of Catharine, George W. Benson's wife. A resident of Brooklyn, Connecticut, after 1825, he made carriages, worked for a while as a salesman for a Northampton, Massachusetts, factory, and finally returned to Brooklyn, where he became a farmer. He was an active Mason, temperance advocate, Unitarian, and Republican. (*Commemorative Biographical Record of Tolland and Windham Counties, Connecticut,* Chicago, 1903, pp. 961–962.)

7 4

TO *THE LIBERATOR*

NORTHAMPTON, August 2, 1843.

MY DEAR FRIEND —

In addition to the anti-slavery observance of the 11th ultimo, in this town, there was a public temperance celebration on the part of the Cold Water Army, Martha Washingtonians, &c.[1] In the procession, there were not less than seven or eight hundred children, with badges and banners — a very pleasing spectacle. It was gratifying to perceive, that, strong as is the aristocratic spirit in this quarter, no distinction was made among them on account of *complexion.* Colored children were not only allowed to walk in the procession, but in some instances were coupled with white ones; and I saw no token of contempt or disapprobation among the numerous spectators. 'This is progress,' I said to myself, abolition progress. True, to cease from a cowardly and wicked persecution of the weak and innocent is not a very meritorious act; but it is an indication, in a case like this, that the spirit of humanity has not labored in vain for the last ten years, and that justice and equality shall yet be established in our borders. The pic nic was held in a beautiful orchard, and was bountifully supplied with choice refreshments. The Courier states that there were about four hundred loaves, or, as estimated by one gentleman, a ton of cake, upon the tables! Plain food would have been better, on such an occasion; but there are comparatively few who have yet learnt to be 'temperate in all things.' [2] The temperance cause has had its days of persecution and reproach, (I remember them well,) when the influential, the wise, and the pious, stood aloof from it in the spirit of contempt or anger; but it is now riding on the topmost wave of popularity, and all classes are doing homage to it. Public opinion has signed the teetotal pledge, and hence, priests and politicians, and all who seek honor one of another, are now graciously disposed to *patronize* it, and to manage the whole movement. This fact was strikingly illustrated in the celebration alluded to. To show you how much THE PEOPLE had to do with it, I send you the following order of services, which I presume was followed without variation:

1st, Music by the Band. 2d, Prayer by *Rev.* William Allen, D. D. 3d, Song by the Cold Water Army. 4th, Address by the *Rev.* Rufus Ellis. 5th, Song by the Glee Club. 6th, Address by the *Rev.* E. P. Rogers.[3] 7th, Music by the Band. 8th, Address by *Rev.* H. D. Doolittle. 9th, Song by the Cold Water Army. 10th, Address by the *Rev.* Orange Clark.[4] 11th, Song by the Glee Club. 12th, Address by *Rev.* Charles Wiley.[5] 13th, Music by the Band. 14th, Refreshments. 15th, Songs by the Cold Water Army.

Six speakers, and not a layman among them all — none but clergymen! What will become of the temperance enterprise, if it be entrusted to such hands? Look at that order of services again! You see in it the contrivance of *Sect,* as well as of *Craft.* Every religious denomination in the town furnishes its priestly representative, excepting the Methodist, the omission not being intentional. It was not a meeting at which THE PEOPLE could have any chance to be heard, or free speech could be uttered with *lay* simplicity and plainness. No provision was made for any but ORDAINED AND DIVINE SPEAKERS. How these spoke I do not know; but, doubtless, to the gratification of Sect, and the furtherance of Craft. As an old teetotaller, I protest against every such arrangement. If the clergy will have *one day in seven,* in which to harangue the people, without 'let or hindrance,' I think it is rather a hard case if the people cannot be allowed at least *one day in the year* especially on the fourth of July, on which to talk with each other, in public assembly, on matters pertaining to their dearest interests. That seventh day monopoly is one of terrible power and injustice, that ought not to be tolerated one hour longer; nor would it be, if it had not made its vassals afraid of their own shadows. I groan in spirit to behold the time when it will be universally seen in its true character, and repudiated in the name of Christianity; and when they who are determined to uphold it shall become

> 'Vile before all the people, in the light
> Of a world's liberty!' [6]

The 'Washingtonian movement' is, as yet, to a very considerable extent, under clerical management, which will be the death of it, unless the laity take full possession of it; and just so far as they are daring to do so, are the clergy withdrawing their countenance from it. L. M. Sargent [7] complains that the Washingtonians are beginning to discard religious formalities and the aid (?) of the priesthood, at their meetings, and even to hold their meetings in the open field on Sunday, before the sun goes down; but the complaint arises from a superstitious attachment to a religion that 'comes by observation,' and instead of being just cause of alarm or grief, is one of the most encouraging signs of the times, in regard to the certainty of human progress. But let the true Washingtonians understand, that a persistance in this course, on their part, will bring down upon their heads the anathemas of these holy usurpers, and they will be branded as 'infidels' of a dangerous character — the more dangerous, because they, in imitation of one Jesus of Nazareth, are going about, doing good. Many will be induced to leave their ranks, but their cause will only make better progress.

By the term 'clergy' or 'priesthood,' I wish to be understood not preachers of truth, but the leaders of sects; such as claim to be divinely appointed in a sense that places them above, and the people below; such as practically array themselves against human equality, and claim, by virtue of their office or position, the confidence and respect of the community.

Yesterday was the anniversary of a day that has given birth to the most extraordinary and glorious event of the present century, the celebration of which will doubtless be observed until not a slave be left to clank his chain in any part of the world. I wanted to be at the great gathering of anti-slavery spirits at Dedham — at the convention in Lowell — and wherever jubilee meetings were held on that day; but I could only be in one place, and at one meeting and found it more convenient to be here than any where else. We made application, through a large committee, for the First Congregational meeting-house — one of the most commodious in the Commonwealth — with very little hope of success; but our request was granted, (not without hesitancy and fear on the part of the parish committee,) and we accordingly occupied it all day. Our meetings were not thronged, as they ought to have been, and as they would have been, if the clergymen of the place had exerted themselves to induce the people to attend; but, though few of the village residents were present, a respectable number convened from the neighboring towns, the members of the Industrial Community turned out *en masse*, in true abolition style. Our widely and worthily known colored friend, DAVID RUGGLES, was called to the chair, and presided in a very satisfactory manner.[8] Until he was afflicted with ophthalmy, he devoted himself to the task of breaking the fetters of his oppressed countrymen with indomitable courage and unconquerable zeal. His sight is somewhat better, but far from being restored, the loss of which affects not only himself, but very seriously the cause of the hunted fugitive. Dr. E. D. Hudson and Frances Judd acted as Secretaries.[9] As usual, at the opening of the meeting, an opportunity was given for vocal prayer; but no one was moved to improve it. And this is now a customary occurrence in all our reformation meetings, in which such a course is pursued, whether in the city, or in the country. This omission of a religious formality, which has so long enslaved the human mind, and which is the product of any thing but the true spirit of prayer, is another hopeful sign, though it will cause formalists and pharisees to groan in spirit, and to lift up their hands in holy horror. It also shows how purely mechanical and ceremonial this mode of extorting vocal prayer has been, and is, as generally adopted; for when reliance on the priest ceases, and no one is urged to go through with the performance, the result is usually silence, though many devout souls are present. The public praying in our land is far from being in accordance with the teachings and example of Christ, and is manifestly done to be seen of men.

In the forenoon, an elaborate and instructive address was delivered by Prof. WILLIAM ADAM, in which the leading features of the anti-slavery movement in England, and the glorious results of West India emancipation, were delineated in a manner that gave high satisfaction to the audience. I hope to procure this address for publication in the Liberator, and am sure it will be read with pleasure and deep interest.[10]

In the afternoon, addresses were made by James Boyle, our truly noble-minded friend Sumner Lincoln, (formerly of Gardiner,) Thomas Hill,[11] (a promising young man, belonging to the 'Community,') Wm. F. Parker,[12] Stephen Rush,[13] and myself. The address by young Hill was well conceived and well spoken, and evinced a growing intellectual and moral capacity. Parker and Rush are also members of the 'Community.' The latter is a fugitive from the land of chains, whips and bowie knives, and six months ago stood under the lash of the driver as a beast of burden. He has made great proficiency in reading and writing since he came here, and has conducted in a very exemplary manner. His heart was full of gratitude to God, and he found it difficult to give utterance to his feelings on the occasion; but he spoke sensibly and earnestly, in the spirit of one who had worn the galling shackles of bondage, and who was rejoicing in the blessings of liberty. He said that he was induced to run away by hearing of Latimer's case; and that as Massachusetts had given succor and protection to George Latimer, he thought he would try his luck in the same manner. He was also induced the more readily to escape, by hearing his master and other slaveholders cursing the abolitionists, of whom he formed a high opinion from that circumstance.

Several choice anti-slavery hymns were sung between the addresses, with the spirit and understanding also. I trust a salutary impression was made on all present. Thus ended our observance of the first of August in Northampton.

Yours, in haste,

WM. LLOYD GARRISON.

Printed: *The Liberator*, August 18, 1843.

1. The Cold Water Army was founded about 1835 by the Reverend Thomas P. Hunt. The army, composed of children and youths, took pledges of total abstinence and wore badges with slogans such as "Here we pledge perpetual hate to all that can intoxicate." (*Standard Encyclopaedia of Alcohol Problems.*)
The Martha Washington Societies were an outgrowth of the Washingtonian Movement, a temperance crusade founded in 1840 (letter to George W. Benson, September 10, 1842).

2. I Corinthians 9:25.

3. Ebenezer P. Rogers (1817–1881) was a Yale graduate, who after studying at Princeton Theological Seminary entered the Congregational ministry in 1840. He served numerous congregations throughout the United States, being at Edwards Church in Northampton from 1843 to 1846. His final call was at South Reformed Church in New York City. (Obituary, New York *Times*, October 25, 1881.)

4. Orange Clark (c. 1797–1869) served St. John's Parish in Northampton from April 27, 1842 to April 7, 1843. In 1850 he moved to San Francisco, where

he was chaplain of the United States Marine Hospital and was active in other religious activities. (Letter to the editor from Ruth D. Bell, researcher, March 24, 1971, citing records of the Diocese of Massachusetts.)

5. Charles Wiley (1810–1878), Congregational minister, attended Columbia and Princeton and was a graduate of Auburn Theological Seminary. He was pastor of the First Church in Northampton from 1837 until he moved to Utica in 1845. For a time he was president of Milwaukee University, and finally settled in East Orange, New Jersey. (Isaac S. Hartley, *Historical Discourse Delivered on the Occasion of the Semi-Centennial Year of the Reformed Church*, Utica, New York, 1880.)

6. John Greenleaf Whittier, "Clerical Oppressors," stanza 12, lines 3–4.

7. Lucius Manlius Sargent (1786–1867), antiquary and author, who wrote many tracts on temperance. (Edward J. Lowell, "Memoir of Lucius Manlius Sargent, A.M.," *PMHS*, 3:309–312, 1886–1887.)

8. David Ruggles (c. 1811–1849) was a Negro abolitionist who had been an agent of *The Liberator* in New York City as early as 1835 (*The Liberator*, February 28 and September 26, 1835). He had been active in the Underground Railroad in New York, having helped 600 fugitives (including Frederick Douglass) escape in three years (see report of the soirée in his honor, *The Liberator*, August 20, 1841). About the time the Northampton community was organized he was in generally ill health and had lost his sight. Members of the community nursed him back to health, and he subsequently organized in Northampton his own water-cure establishment, giving Garrison extensive treatment in the summer of 1848. (Obituary, *The Liberator*, December 21, 1849.)

9. Frances P. Birge Judd (c. 1820–1894) was the wife of Hall Judd, the first citizen of Northampton to join the community. After her husband's death in 1850 Mrs. Judd remained active in the antislavery movement. (Northampton town records.)

10. The address was not printed in *The Liberator*.

11. Although Thomas Hill (1818–1891) was not on the official list of members of the Northampton community, he may have been related to the three families of Hills (Samuel L., Sally, and Matilda) who were. Thomas Hill had already demonstrated that he was an extraordinary young man. After having served as apprentice first to a printer and then to an apothecary, he entered Harvard College, distinguishing himself in mathematics and science, even winning the Scott Medal from the Franklin Institute, and graduating in 1843. He was to graduate from the divinity school in 1845 and then to be a minister for fourteen years at Waltham, Massachusetts. Later in life he became president first of Antioch (1859–1862) and then of Harvard College (1862–1868). He published innumerable works, both theological and scientific.

12. William F. Parker (born 1811), resident of Nantucket, had entered the Northampton Association in October 1842. Director of the Mechanical Department, he apparently moved after 1851 to Cleveland, for he is listed in the Cleveland city directories as a carpenter working at Wasson's railroad car factory. After the edition of 1869–1870 he is no longer listed; it may be assumed that he died about that time, although no cemetery record has been found for him in Cleveland. (Letter to the editor from Edouard A. Stackpole, president, Nantucket Historical Association, March 29, 1971; Sheffeld.)

13. Little is known of Stephen Rush except that he was originally from New York City, that he was a member of the committee of arrangements for the celebration of British West India emancipation, August 1, 1843 (Northampton *Democrat*, July 25, 1843), and that he entered the Northampton Association November 4, 1843, and withdrew April 23, 1846. (Sheffeld.)

7 5

TO FRANCIS JACKSON

Northampton, August 16, 1843.

My Dear Friend:

If the pleasure I received, in consequence of your visit to this place, was not equal in amount to your kindness in making it, I can only give as a reason, that your kindness is not easily matched. You do not need the assurance, that we were all sorry that you could stay no longer with us; and our importunity would have been far more strenuous than it was, to have your sojourn with us prolonged, if we had not known that you needed nothing of the kind on our part. Mightily have we been comforted and strengthened by the presence of our beloved [Nathaniel P.] Rogers, (for which we are primarily, nay wholly, indebted to you,) who has gained the friendship and admiration of the entire "Community," and whose absence now is felt as a severe bereavement. I will tell you nothing of my jaunt with him to Greenfield, to Mount Holyoke, (we made it "a Sabbath day's journey,") [1] or to Springfield — the last the most pleasant and the most painful, as it separated us from each other, to meet we know not when; of our meetings under the majestic pine tree, with those who can not only endure, but enjoy, free speech and free investigation; of our social interviews with the "Community" members, and our rambles together in the region round about; because as you have seen him, and as he is now probably with you, you have had, doubtless, all the particulars on these points. His visit has been a visible blessing to us all. He has spoken to us words of encouragement, of peace, of good will, of "faith, hope, charity"; [2] and these have been listened to profitably and gratefully.

For a whole week after you left us, we had rainy weather, and so were deprived of many an excursion which I had planned to take with Rogers; but within ourselves we had plenty of sunshine, with the spirit of song, and our journeys were made heavenward, in the regions of intellect and soul, and wondrous and beautiful things we found by the way. But we neither made nor visited any "castles in the air," nor attempted to gather up any moonshine. We were perfectly agreed in the opinion, that the world is turned upside down, and that it ought to be turned downside up, and we thought it a practicable affair. We were not appalled at its bulk or weight, for we regarded it as of small dimensions in the arms of Spirit. We plotted treason against Church and State, and all that characterises them, and so were full of loyalty to Truth and Right. What else we said and achieved, will it not be recorded in the columns of the Herald of Freedom, or the Liberator?[3] *Nous verrons.*

I have now lying before me the Utica Whig, of Aug. 1st, in which is the letter of Judge Bacon, of that place, giving an account of his visit to John Quincy Adams, at Quincy, to which reference was made while you were here.[4] Alluding to Mr. A's remarks on slavery, Judge B. says — "He [Mr. A.] saw little prospect or hope of such a result [the abolition of slavery by compensating the slaveholders] being brought about by the consent or aid of the slave-holding States, with their present cherished views and principles; and when it was intimated to him that a considerable portion of those inhabiting the free States would not consent to this mode of settling the question, because it would be making a compromise with sin, he replied, that he considered them too, [the abolitionists, technically so called,] to be "as crack-brained a set," as the southern fanatics were on the other side of the question." I have copied the language accurately, in case you think it best to make any use of it in a letter to Mr. Adams on the subject. Whether it is worth while to make a serious matter of it, I am somewhat in doubt; but you will observe that the words, "as crack-brained a set," are given in quotation marks as the identical words used by Mr. Adams, to describe his opinion of the abolitionists. I have very little doubt that he uttered the language attributed to him; for I am constrained to think that he cares no farther for the abolitionists than they can be made to subserve his own purposes on the great question of the right of petition. Consult with our friends, and see whether it is best to put "the old man"[5] ungrateful and abusive to the torture. If so, let him be placed on an epistolary rack without delay, and let us see what we can get out of him by way of confession — whether he will be able to "save his *Bacon*," and how he will do it.

I shall send this hasty effusion to you by a worthy son of the Emerald Isle, who has long been in the employ of Mr [David Lee] Child, but who, failing to get employment here, is wending his way to Boston, to find something to do. Mr. and Mrs. Child were very much attached to him, and he was to them. I believe Mr. [Ellis Gray] Loring knows him personally; and between you both, perhaps he will be able to obtain labor, so that he may get bread. Possibly, you can contrive to give him a chance on the "South Cove."

If dear Rogers be with you, tell him that G[eorge]. T[hurber]. and myself arrived home from Springfield at 7 o'clock, P.M. On our way, we saw four dove hawks, and a bald eagle of a startling size, in very close proximity to us. His flight was a majestic one. If I had, like him, the power to fly, you would soon see, at your door in Hollis-street,

Your affectionate friend,

Wm. Lloyd Garrison.

Francis Jackson,
Hollis-Street,
Boston, Mass.

ALS: William Lloyd Garrison Papers, Massachusetts Historical Society; a typed transcription is preserved in the Merrill Collection of Garrison Papers, Wichita State University Library.

1. Acts 1:12.
2. I Corinthians 13:13.
3. The *Herald of Freedom*, founded in Concord, New Hampshire, in 1836, was the organ of the New Hampshire Anti-Slavery Society. Nathaniel P. Rogers assumed the editorship in 1838, after the death of the original editor, Joseph H. Kimball. In 1844 Rogers and the New Hampshire society became involved in an irreconcilable controversy which is the subject of subsequent letters from Garrison. By 1846 the paper was to merge with the *Pioneer* of Lynn, Massachusetts, to become the *Pioneer and Herald of Freedom*, owned by Christopher Robinson. (*Life*.)
4. The Utica *Whig* is not listed in Gregory's *Union List of Newspapers* or anywhere else searched. Possibly Garrison is referring to the *Oneida Whig*, which is listed under "Utica" as a weekly published from May 20, 1834, to October 15, 1853.
Ezekiel Bacon (1776–1870) was a native of Massachusetts, where he had served in the state legislature between 1805 and 1806. Later he was a member of Congress (1807–1813) and first comptroller of the United States Treasury (1813–1815). Following his service in the federal government he moved to Utica, New York.
5. A common nickname for John Quincy Adams, also called "the old man eloquent."

---

7 6

TO HENRY W. WILLIAMS

Northampton, August 23, 1843.

Dear Henry:

With the exception of a letter, giving the particulars of the calamity which befell my dear wife and her mother, by the upsetting of a wagon, (addressed to Oliver [Johnson],) I have not put pen to paper for a week past, having had my time incessantly occupied in looking after the sick ones — watching, &c. It is a week to-night since I have been divested of my clothing on retiring to rest, and you may easily imagine that, by this time, I am pretty well tired out. Helen's arm is steadily improving, but the broken bone has not yet begun to unite, but will probably do so in a day or two. She has suffered a good deal of pain, and finds it extremely embarrassing to nurse her child. Mrs. Benson is getting slowly along, but it is uncertain whether she will be ever able to walk again, except as a cripple. Her sufferings, at times, have been very great. Sister Ann is quite low, and evidently failing fast. Altogether, we are in afflicted circumstances.

I have received no bundle from Boston since Francis Jackson came here — a fortnight last Saturday — an interim too long. If any has miscarried, please give me information to this effect, and state when and how the bundle was sent. If none has been sent, please forward one by the Express line without delay.

I sent a line to you, some days since, saying that if you could forward me $50, either by mail or in the bundle, I should be extremely glad to receive it, in order to liquidate my board bill, &c. The late accident will involve me in considerable additional expense for medical attendance, &c. Forward me what you can soon, be it much or little. Our Northampton sojourn will be a dear one, after all.

The bearer of this is Mr. Gaylord,[1] of Utica, N.Y. who is interested in the various industrial association schemes, and who has made the "Community" at this place a hasty visit, for the purposes of information, &c. He will visit Ripley's Community at Roxbury.[2] He appears to be an excellent man — is acquainted with Collins and his scheme, and can give you information about them, if you should desire it.[3]

I have neither spirit nor time to add any thing more than that I am,

Faithfully yours,

Wm. Lloyd Garrison.

ALS: Merrill Collection of Garrison Papers, Wichita State University Library.

1. Possibly Frederick G. Gaylord of 218 Genesee Street, listed in the 1842–1843 Utica directory as having no occupation.

2. Garrison refers to Brook Farm, West Roxbury, Massachusetts, the most famous of the nineteenth-century American experiments in communal living. George Ripley (1802–1880), Unitarian minister turned Trancendentalist, was the community's moving spirit and president from its founding in 1841 to its dissolution in 1847. In subsequent years he had a distinguished career as editor and literary critic.

3. John A. Collins and others had founded a communal farm near Skaneateles, New York. The community was dedicated to the rejection of conventional religious beliefs. Although traditional marriage customs were retained, the community permitted divorce and reared children communally. Like Brook Farm and other communities, this one continued only briefly, being disbanded after excessive dissension among the members, in 1846.

7 7

TO ABBY KELLEY

Northampton, Sept. 8, 1843.

My Dear Friend:

Your letter, sent from Waterloo [New York], came to hand too late to enable me, or any one else in the "Community," to go to Springfield, in season to meet you on your arrival at that place; and as you did not come yesterday afternoon in the stage from Springfield, I presume you wended your way directly to Boston. I am extremely sorry that the notice of your intentions was not received seasonably, for there is no one whom I am more anxious to see, face to face, at the present time, respecting the attitude and prospects of our anti-slavery enterprise, than yourself.

I have only a very few moments allowed me, in which to write these hasty lines, and therefore am unable to make a reply to your letter, to the extent that I could wish.

Respecting the article in the Standard, to which you allude, I certainly think it is quite defective, in certain particulars, and calls for a reply from those whose vision is clearer than that of our friend D.L.C[hild].[1] That reply I intended to make in the Standard, as soon as I read the article; but, since the late unfortunate accident to my dear Helen and her mother, (in addition to the fact that our beloved sister Anne has, for a fortnight past, been extremely low, and will not probably survive twenty-four hours longer,) I have had so much anxiety, so much care thrown upon me, and so little rest at night, that I have not been in a condition to prepare an article even for the Liberator, or scarcely to look at a book or newspaper. This is the sole cause of my silence; but I shall try to get something into the next Standard, if possible. I do not feel any special trepidation respecting this matter, though I regret that D.L.C. does not more keenly apprehend the philosophy of the anti-slavery reform. Let us not be hurried into any act that may gratify our enemies, rather than benefit our own side. Fidelity on our part will yet make all things straight, I hope, at head quarters.

I have not time to say a word respecting the Buffalo Convention.[2] James and Lau[r]a Boyle send their loving regards to you, and long to see you here. Will you not return from Boston via Northampton?

Yours, faithfully,

Wm. Lloyd Garrison.

☞ I shall probably remain here two or three weeks longer.[3]

ALS: Kelley-Foster Collection, Worcester Historical Society.

1. Since the reply to Child's article was apparently not printed, it is difficult to know which "defective" article Garrison means, though it was undoubtedly one stressing his Whig views (see the notes to Garrison's letter to Child, May 14, 1843, for a discussion of Child's political deficiencies).

2. The National Convention of Colored Citizens, with Amos Beman as president, was held in Buffalo, August 15–19, 1843. During the proceedings a controversy arose between the Reverend H. H. Garnet and Frederick Douglass over the efficacy of militant action, Garnet advocating a relatively violent approach to the problem of Negro rights. The convention resolved to support the Liberty party, but Douglass and Charles L. Remond dissented from this view, casting the only two opposing votes. (For discussions of the convention see *The Liberator*, September 22, 1843, and Charles Wesley, "The Participation of Negroes in Anti-Slavery Political Parties," *Journal of Negro History*, 29:43–45, 1944.)

3. Garrison left Northampton Tuesday, September 22; see his letter to George W. Benson, September 24, 1843.

7 8

TO FRANCIS JACKSON

Northampton, Sept. 9, 1843.

My very dear Friend:

The time for my return to Boston is rapidly drawing to a close; but where I am to be located, or to find a shelter for my family, I do not know. Have you yet seen or heard of any tenement, that answers to the description that I gave you when you were here? If so, will you write me the particulars about it as to the rent and the location? If you have not, I should also like to hear from you at your earliest convenience. I understand that my friend Oliver Johnson has been for some time absent on a visit to Vermont, and therefore suppose he has had no opportunity to find a house for me, as he promised to do, if he could. Should he now be at home, I wish you would converse with him in relation to this matter, as we had some idea of taking a house in company, provided we could find a suitable one. As a matter of choice, on account of my children, (that they may not disturb any one under the same roof,) I should prefer being in a tenement alone with my family, if exactly the right one can be procured. The rent must not be over $300,[1] and as much less as practicable. If our friend [Ellis Gray] Loring's house is still to let, and nothing better offers, and he will put the rent down to $250, I may conclude to occupy it; though I should much prefer a modern built house. I do not wish you positively to engage any house for me; but as soon as you hear of a good chance, I will make a trip to Boston, and come to some conclusion without delay. Is the house in Carver-street still empty? and if so, what is the lowest rent that will be taken?

My wife's broken arm is slowly mending, but is still useless, and very painful; and I fear it will be a long time before she will again obtain the use of it. Her mother is not yet able to walk, but her case is probably not so bad as was at first apprehended. Our sister Anne has almost finished her earthly career, and cannot survive long. For the past week, we have been expecting her dissolution hourly. Thus, you perceive, we are involved in affliction.

If I had time, I should like to occupy the remainder of this sheet with other topics. But I write in haste, and can only add that I am

Your faithful friend,

Wm. Lloyd Garrison.

ALS: Garrison Papers, Boston Public Library.

1. Per year.

---

7 9

TO *THE LIBERATOR*

Northampton, Sept. 17, 1843.

My Dear Friend:

Since the unfortunate accident which happened to my wife and my aged mother-in-law, by the upsetting of the vehicle in which they were riding, (partly through my own unskilfulness,) I have been too much distressed in mind, and too busily employed in discharging the peculiar responsibilities growing out of the case, to send you any thing in an editorial shape for the Liberator. In the case of Mrs. Garrison, it happens that a bad matter has been rendered worse, in consequence of the physician whom we employed having mistaken a dislocation of the elbow for a fracture of the coronoid process; so that, after nearly five weeks of suffering, her arm is in a more critical state than it was at the time of the accident.[1] Surgical as well as medical blunders are too common on the part of those who have been taught in the schools, to confer much credit on those 'nurseries of learning and science.' It was the right arm that was injured, the temporary (if, happily, it shall prove only temporary) loss of the use of which, where four young boys (one of them a nursing babe) are hourly needing a mother's special care and labor, is quite a serious affair, as you may easily conceive.

On discovering the real condition of the arm, I at first concluded to go directly to Boston, and obtain the surgical aid of Dr. [John C.] Warren or Dr. Hayward, especially as I felt anxious to be at my editorial post at the earliest opportunity; but, on learning that Dr. Sweet, the celebrated bone-setter, (the son of a still more celebrated father now deceased,) resides in Franklin, about ten miles from Norwich, Ct., and being made acquainted with several extraordinary cures performed by him, I have concluded to leave this place to-morrow for his residence, believing that he will restore the use of the arm in less time, with far less pain, and with greater certainty, than any surgeon to be found in the city.[2] He is, it is true, an unscientific man, in the technical use of the term, and has never been to college, and knows very little of books; but he has, in an eminent degree, what is sometimes called a peculiar 'gift' or 'ruling passion' for his profession, and has had constant practice for more than thirty years, having been put to the business by his father at the early age of eleven years. Perhaps some of my friends will be surprised to learn that, in this emergency, I have resorted to 'a quack' for aid; for the inquiry is as often and as incredulously made now, as it was eighteen hundred years ago — 'Can any good thing come out of Nazareth?'[3] 'Is not this the carpenter's son?'[4] But I have long been convinced that there is incomparably more of quackery, and less of truth, *in* the schools of law, physic and divinity, than *out* of them. Certainly, I dare to employ the man, who, in my opinion, can do better service to me or mine than any other person, whether he be or be not popular with the age in which he lives. Possibly, I may have cause to regret that I did not prefer some Boston surgeon to Dr. Sweet; but I have not the slightest apprehension on that score, and you shall in due season be made acquainted with the result.

On Friday afternoon last, we consigned to the grave the mortal remains of one long tenderly beloved by us, ANNE E. BENSON, a daughter of the late venerable GEORGE BENSON, of Brooklyn, Ct. (formerly of Providence,) in the 42d year of her age, and a sister of my wife.[5] She was among the gentlest, purest spirits that ever dwelt on earth, and lived and died in the christian faith. Her heart was in all the various reforms of the age; and though, in consequence of her long protracted bodily infirmities, and of her great natural diffidence, she was unable to make herself conspicuous or active in carrying them forward, she nevertheless took a lively and an abiding interest in every effort to promote the happiness of the human race, especially in the beneficent cause of anti-slavery. In her religious sentiments, she closely approximated to those which are held by the Society of Friends, though she was too free to be attached to any particular sect. The religious services at her funeral were of a very simple character, such as she desired, and with no one to enact the part of a priest on the occasion. Her body was buried in a beautiful pine grove near the house in which she yielded up her mortal existence, and there it will gradually return to the dust from which it was taken. She was so remarkably childlike and innocent, so completely separate in her spirit and affections from an evil world, that the beautiful lines of Mrs. Hemans, addressed to a deceased infant, may be almost as strictly applied to her:

> 'Thou wast so like a thing of light,
>   That Heaven benignly called thee hence,
> Ere yet the world could breathe one blight
>   O'er thy sweet innocence;
> And thou, that brighter world to bless,
> Art passed, with all thy loveliness.' [6]

How grand, consolatory, inspiring, glorious, is the thought of immortality! What though this 'earthly house of our tabernacle' [7] be dissolved?

> 'Life is real, life is earnest,
>   And the grave is not its goal;
> 'Dust thou art, to dust returnest,'
>   Was not spoken of the soul.' [8]

I have just received the painful intelligence of the death of one who was formerly a partner with me in business, who commenced the publication of the Liberator with me, who for several years exhibited much interest in the cause of the slave, and with whom, from boyhood, I had been in terms of the closest intimacy. I allude, of course, to Isaac Knapp. In an evil hour he was led, by adversity and business mismanagement, to put the cup of intoxication to his lips; and for the last three or four years sustained a wretched existence, though he made several attempts (alas! how ineffectual!) to return to the path of rectitude. You are perfectly familiar with the causes, necessities and motives which led to his disconnexion with the Liberator, and which rendered that disconnexion absolutely essential to the existence of the paper. You know (as well as all the true and enlightened friends in Boston and its vicinity) that that step was taken with the kindest feelings towards himself, and with a sacred and paramount regard to the welfare of the anti-slavery enterprise. But, unhappily, such was his diseased state of mind and of body at that time, and subsequently, and so recklessly did he throw himself into the hands of a few ignorant and malevolent individuals, who made him their dupe and tool, that he became excessively hostile in spirit toward his best friends, and even widely estranged from me personally — regarding us all as his enemies, and bringing against us the most absurd and unjust accusations. But let the veil of oblivion be drawn over this short period of an otherwise useful life; for even in this particular, he deserves pity rather than censure, and never can I find it in my breast to say a bitter word of him. He was naturally amiable, kind, and obliging even to excess; and had a benevolence that was ever gratified in relieving the necessities of others, though not always regulated by sound discrimination and a strict regard to his pecuniary ability. He never hesitated to share his last morsel of bread with those who were in distress, and he cherished the strongest abhorrence of a covetous or mean disposition. He was altogether too generous to chaffer in trade; and having no business adaptation, he consequently involved himself deeply in debt while attempting to carry on business. It was thus he became depressed in spirit, and, instead of calmly submitting to the stroke of adversity, vainly sought to find relief from his sorrows (as millions have done before) in the intoxicating bowl. For the first six or seven years after the Liberator was started, he was a faithful coadjutor in the anti-slavery cause, and greatly is that cause indebted to him for what he did and suffered in its behalf, during that stormy and perilous period of its history. I am not sure that I could have commenced the printing of the Liberator, had it not been for his uniting with me in partnership, and partic-ipating in the labors and necessities of my lone situation. And a most loving, faithful, devoted friend and brother was he to me! Gratefully and exultingly do I proclaim it, that at no time did I perceive in him either a thought or wish to dilute or soften the truth on the subject of slavery, or to lower, even to the slightest conceivable extent, the anti-slavery standard; no, not even in the gloomiest hour of our cause, when we were in daily expectation of falling victims for our advocacy of the rights of our enslaved countrymen, and when a different kind of policy might have given us bread and safety, but at the expense of humanity. Dropping a tear of pity over his sad fate, let us ever associate his name with those who never turned their backs upon a great and good cause, because it was unpopular.

I have also received tidings of the demise of the amiable, unassum-ing, tender-hearted, unfaltering CHARLES MARRIOTT, formerly of Hud-son, N. Y., but for several years past a resident in the city of New-York. He was a native of England, but came over to this country, I believe, in early youth, at which period he began to be deeply interested in the labors of Wilberforce and Clarkson for the abolition of the African slave trade.[9] From the first appearance of the Liberator, he became a subscriber to it, and contributed many excellent articles to its col-ums, from time to time — among others, an 'Address to Members of Congress,' which I subsequently put in a tract form, and sent to every member of Congress.[10] His spirit was truly dove-like, and no one could 'know him but to love him,'[11] on account of his signal moral worth and tender sympathy for the oppressed. I shall ever revere the memory of that good man.

I may not be able to occupy my editorial chair until the expiration of some three or four weeks; but the paper gains by my absence in point of interest and ability, and the readers of the Liberator will therefore have nothing to regret in consequence of my absence.[12] My health has considerably improved by my sojourn in Northampton; and, grateful for the opportunity which has been granted me to repair my wasted bodily energies, I hope to be more useful to the cause of universal liberty and righteousness, on my return home, than I have been for some time past.

Your affectionate friend,

WM. LLOYD GARRISON.

Printed: *The Liberator*, September 29, 1843.

1. Garrison refers to Chauncey Austin Hall (1811–1856), a graduate of the University of Pennsylvania Medical School who practiced in Northampton from 1837 to 1850, where he was the medical superintendent of the Round Hill Water Cure. After 1850 he lived in Hartford, Connecticut, and Madison, Wisconsin. (*Amherst College Biographical Record*, 1963, p. 21.)

2. Dr. Warren has been identified; the other two doctors were practitioners of entirely different training and experience. George Hayward (1791–1863), a Harvard graduate with a medical degree from the University of Pennsylvania, was a professor of the Harvard Medical School and one of the surgeons-in-chief at the Massachusetts General Hospital. He was later to be the first to use ether as an anesthetic during a major operation.

Stephen Sweet (1798–1874) came to bonesetting as a family craft, for he was the son, grandson, great-grandson, and great-great-grandson of "natural bone-setters." He himself passed his skill on to several of the children of his three marriages, the most famous being John Byron Sweet. On two occasions Dr. Sweet was elected to the state legislature, though both times he refused to serve. (Letter to the editor from Elizabeth B. Knox, secretary and curator, New London County Historical Society, January 14, 1970.)

3. Garrison adapts John 1:46.

4. Matthew 13:55.

5. George Benson (1752–1836), the father of Helen Benson Garrison, had been a successful Providence businessman, though he had retired to Brooklyn, Connecticut, dedicating his last years to abolition, temperance, and pacifist activities. (*Life.*)

6. Garrison slightly misquotes Felicia Hemans, "Dirge of a Child," stanza 3.

7. An adaptation of II Corinthians 5:1.

8. Henry Wadsworth Longfellow, "A Psalm of Life," stanza 2.

9. William Wilberforce (1759–1833) was the English philanthropist and anti-slavery crusader who was largely responsible for the success of the West Indies Emancipation Bill, although he did not live to see its passage. Throughout his adult life he agitated against slavery, not only in the House of Commons, to which he was first elected in 1780, but in association with Thomas Clarkson (previously identified), Joseph Sturge, Garrison himself, and others. A leader of the evangelical "Clapham Sect," he established its organ, the *Christian Observer*.

10. Marriott's address was printed in *The Liberator*, November 26, 1831.

11. An adaptation of Fitz-Greene Halleck, "On the Death of Joseph Rodman Drake," lines 3–4.

12. Although no one other than Garrison was officially editing *The Liberator* during his absence in Northampton, Edmund Quincy did write some editorials and Henry W. Williams, the general agent of the paper, was apparently in charge of the office. (See editorial comment in *The Liberator*, June 23, 1843.)

---

8 0

TO GEORGE W. BENSON

Boston, Sept. 24, 1843.

Dear bro. George:

On taking leave of you, on Tuesday morning, we continued our *stage-coaching* to Wilbraham, which place we reached one hour and a quarter before the arrival of the cars; so that we had ample time to rest, with our little ones. We were very fortunate in not being crowded, having had only one inside passenger in addition to our own company, and the distance was travelled in a very pleasant manner, without any of us experiencing any special fatigue. On taking the cars, I left my surtout at the Wilbraham depot, (having so many other things to look after,) but was fortunate enough to recover it on Thursday, at Worcester, on my return from Connecticut. Helen and I parted with Anne,[1] and Angelette, and the boys, at Worcester, with no little anxiety of mind on account of the last named, especially Charlie, who from that hour was doomed to cease obtaining his living by tugging away at his mother's breast, and henceforth to eat as do children of a larger growth.

We arrived at Greenville on Tuesday evening, and received a very sisterly welcome from Augusta Reed and Louis[a] Humphrey — (I am not sure that the latter name is correct.) [2] After giving them such information as they desired respecting the "Community," and talking over sundry matters pertaining to our anti-slavery enterprise, we retired to rest, not having been able to ascertain whether Dr. [Stephen] Sweet was at home, or absent. Soon after breakfast, the next morning, I took Helen and Augusta into a carry-all, and drove to Franklin, about 10 miles from Norwich. On arriving at the summit of an elevated piece of ground, on which stoo[d a] meeting-house, a parsonage house, and one or two others, I accosted a man who was mowing near his house, and asked him whether he could tell me where Dr. Sweet lived. "I am the man," was his reply. "Then you are the man for me." So, after first taking a survey of the mighty prospect to be seen from such a glorious location, we drove up to the Doctor's door; and, putting aside his scythe, he proceeded to look into our case without delay. As soon as he saw Helen's arm, he pronounced it (without touching it) to be a *dislocation* of the elbow, and said that Dr. [Erasmus D.] Hudson was entirely correct in his judgment of it, and that Dr. [Chauncey A.] Hall had utterly misapprehended the case, for there had been no *fracture*. He also said that if he could have had the management of it at the time of the accident, he would not have asked for more than one minute to set the arm; but now it would prove a difficult matter, in consequence of the length of time that had elapsed, and the mal-treatment of the case. The dislocated bone was surrounded with a bony substance that had been formed by an effort of nature to accommodate itself to the injury, the removal of which would require some time, by absorption. He should not think of attempting to set the bone under ten days or a fortnight, during which time the arm must be bathed three times a day in as hot water as could be borne, and covered with a liniment of his own preparation, in order to soften the parts, and relax the tendons, ligaments, &c. Even then, a good deal of pain would be unavoidable in setting the bone, which, after being put in its proper place, would probably require his care a fortnight longer, before she could use her arm. He stated that he had had three or four similar cases within a few months, and there was then a young lad at his house, who had arrived the day before, and whose case was almost precisely similar to Helen's. On being asked if he thought he could effect a permanent cure in her case, he replied that he had never yet failed doing so in any instance. On hearing him say that it would require a month to mend the arm, Helen began to shed tears, at the thought of being so long separated from her children and myself; and I also felt somewhat cast down, not that I thought the time unreasonably long, but because I deeply sympathized with Helen, and knew not how, at such a crisis, I could either remain with or be absent from her. As the Dr's inspection would not be necessary for the first fortnight, and it would be quite as expensive to board in that vicinity as the railroad fare from Norwich to Boston, and back again, would amount to, we concluded to come directly to Boston, and accept of the hospitality of our kind friends, the [Joseph] Southwicks; and we accordingly took the afternoon train of cars for Worcester, at which place we stopped over night, (at the Temperance Hotel,) and on Thursday morning took the cars for this city. Our friends have given us a warm and sympathetic reception, though some of them probably think that we are very foolish to think of going so far again to have H's arm set, especially by a "quack," when the great Dr. [John C.] Warren is so near at hand; but, from what I saw and heard of Dr. Sweet, I have more confidence in his judgment, knowledge and skill, in mending dislocations and fractures, than in all the surgeons of Boston put together. Should our dear mother not speedily recover from her injury, I would earnestly propose her going to see Dr. Sweet. It is sad to think that Dr. Hall so long grossly misapprehended H's case, to the infliction of so much needless suffering on her, and well nigh to the permanent loss of her right arm. On ascertaining the facts in the case, and how great has been his blunder, I should not think he would feel as if he could keep the money I paid over to him. These I shall communicate to him as soon as the arm is mended, and he may then follow his own sense of justice. Here our friends think he should rather pay damages than exact fees. We shall probably leave for Norwich and Franklin a week from to-morrow — (Monday.)

On leaving us at Worcester, the remainder of our company arrived in Boston, without having experienced any trouble on their way, in reference to the children, neither of whom cried or whimpered during the whole journey. Charlie was "as merry as a grig"[3] all the way, and never was happier since the day of his birth. He has been weaned without any difficulty, and has a good appetite, and looks as hearty as ever. Wendell also enjoys himself very much, and is in excellent health. Angelette will probably remain with us until our return from Norwich, though she is not well qualified to take the responsibility of the children during our absence. Perhaps we may conclude to take the children with us, and discharge her from further service.

Since my arrival, I have been almost constantly occupied in "hunting up" a house in which to live — and, truly, as there are at present four or five hundred to let, (and a large portion of these entirely new ones,) it is a somewhat difficult matter to make a selection among so many. I think, however, that we shall take a house in Pine-street, near Washington-st., at the South end, (about a quarter of a mile this side of Mr. [Ellis Gray] Loring's,) which is wholly new, and has never been occupied, and is very neat, beautiful, and commodious, having eleven sleeping rooms, two parlors, and two kitchens — being made to accommodate two families. The rent is $350, and a lease must be taken for three years. The house is one of a long and beautiful block, and is quietly as well as centrally located. Tell mother and Sarah, that we have already selected the room for them to occupy, if they will take up their abode with us during the winter. We calculate that Oliver Johnson and his wife will take some rooms with us so that our rent will be only about $250. They are still absent in Vermont, in consequence of the sickness of Oliver's father, who was in a dying state at the last accounts.[4]

Yours, affectionately,

Wm. Lloyd Garrison.

☞ In the course of this week, we shall transmit to you a bundle, in which you will find letters, newspapers, &c. We shall want Willie to return home as soon as we get to housekeeping. We hope to hear of the health and good behaviour of the boys, and desire to be affectionately remembered to all the members of the community.

ALS: Garrison Papers, Boston Public Library.

1. Anna Elizabeth Benson (1834–1870), the eldest daughter of George W. Benson, who was to marry Dr. Edward Percy in 1852.

2. Augusta Reed (c. 1799–1848) was a long-time subscriber to *The Liberator* and a supporter of abolitionism. (Obituary in *The Liberator*, September 1, 1848.)

Louisa Humphrey (1800–1869) was among the early advocates of the anti-slavery cause and a friend and co-worker of Abby Kelley Foster. According to her obituary, "only her constitutional modesty, and a retiring disposition which shrank from public notice, prevented her from being ranked among the foremost agitators for human rights in this country." (*National Anti-Slavery Standard*, July 3, 1869.)

3. Probably a corruption of "a merry Greek," an expression appearing in England as early as the sixteenth century and used frequently in the eighteenth.

4. Ziba Johnson (died 1843) had settled in Peacham, Vermont, in 1795; no other information is available about him.

---

8 1

TO SARAH T. BENSON

Franklin, Ct. Oct. 7, 1843.

Dear Mother:

I wrote to bro. George soon after we arrived in Boston, but have not received a word of intelligence from him since we left Northampton. Helen and myself feel extremely anxious to hear how you are getting along, — whether you and Sarah intend visiting Boston or Providence this fall, — and what is the state of her health, and Catherine's. In the new house we have taken on lease in the city, (in Pine-street, at the South end,) [1] we have already selected a good room for Sarah and yourself, or for either of you, in case you cannot come together — though we desire to have you both under our roof. But we will not be too urgent in this matter. You both know our mind, and, "being of age," can decide for yourselves; in which decision we shall cheerfully acquiesce, whatever it may be.

After having applied hot water and Dr. [Stephen] Sweet's liniment to Helen's arm, three times a day, for the space of ten or twelve days, on Monday afternoon we took our departure from Boston in the cars for Norwich — or, rather, for Greenville, where we passed the night with our hospitable anti-slavery friends, Augusta Reed and Louisa Humphrey. On Tuesday forenoon, we took a carriage, and drove up to this place, and fortunately found Dr. Sweet at home. We found he had procured for us a comfortable boarding-place at the house of Col. Hazen, (about half a mile from his own residence,) to which we at once directed our steps.[2] The Colonel had left that morning with his daughter for South Hadley, the latter intending to enter the Holyoke Seminary at that place; and it was not till last evening that he reached home.[3] In despite of his military title, he looks any thing but warlike, and appears to be nothing more than a plain farmer. We shall probably have some talk on the subject of peace and war before we separate. He is a member of the orthodox church, but how badly priest-ridden, I cannot yet tell. His wife is a pleasant, quiet woman, who, with a young daughter, (in addition to ourselves,) constitutes his entire household. His house is a very ancient one, into which he has recently removed, having given up the handsome and commodious one which he occupied to his son, who has recently married. We have a good parlor, well furnished, with a bed-room adjoining, and they are all very attentive to us. They spread a most bountiful table, so that we have an excess of good things to eat, and are constantly in danger of eating too much. — [How unlike, in every particular, our situation at Mrs. W's! [4] A greater contrast, in the way of providing, it would be difficult to present.] We are feasting on nice peaches and apples, even to repletion. But how lonely we feel! Not a child in the house, and our four dear little boys a long distance from us, and they separated from each other. Truly, this is suffering complete bereavement. But we have this consolation — they are in good hands, and will lack for no care or attention; and we hope soon to see at least three of them gathered around the domestic hearth. When we left Boston, Wendell and Charles were in good health. We left them in the care of Angenette [Angelette], at Mrs. [Joseph] Southwick's — though Wendell will probably remain with Anne Mann's, during our absence.[5] On parting with us, he was [so] offended that he could not go too, that he struck Helen a blow on the bonnet, as she attempted to kiss him, and attacked me with the zeal of a small steam-engine. But, notwithstanding his freaks of this kind occasionally, he is a most affectionate child, and is never so happy as when he can be with us.

Mr. and Mrs. Johnson have returned from Vermont, in good health, and will occupy a part of the house with us. They admire its arrangement, as I think you will when you see it. There are eleven sleeping rooms above the parlor, and two good kitchens. They are to have three of the chambers, which will leave us seven, one of which (in the attic) I intend to make my editorial sanctum sanctorum. Oliver buried his father during his absence, who died of congestion of the brain, and was delirious for a long time.

"But what of Helen's arm?" you will ask. On Tuesday afternoon, Dr. Sweet examined it, but concluded not to operate on it till the following day. On Wednesday forenoon, he came with his son,[6] (a young man who is already something of a bone-setter, "a chip of the old block,") and they both made great efforts to restore the dislocated bone to its proper place; but they could only start it a very little, so callous has it grown, and so great was the anguish it caused Helen. In consequence of the shock given to her nervous system, the Dr. will postpone another trial until to-morrow. The case is a difficult one, and cannot be remedied suddenly, without giving Helen more pain than she can well bear; and even by a gradual process, she will have to suffer a great deal. O, what a lamentable accident it has proved! But the most afflicting thing is, the sad blunder of Dr. [Chauncey A.] Hall in mistaking, for five long weeks, a dislocation for a fracture. Any time within the first week, the bone might have been set easily. We may have to remain here a month, possibly; but Dr. Sweet is a perfect master of his profession — and this is our consolation.

Hoping to hear from you all soon, through a letter from George, and wishing to be affectionately remembered by all the household, I remain,

Yours, filially,

Wm. Lloyd Garrison.

P.S. Helen wishes to know whether she did not leave her black silk cape at the factory, as she cannot find it among her things. It may be sent (if found) by Willie, when he comes down, if no earlier opportunity is presented. We have received an excellent letter from Laura Stebbins, giving a good account of George and Willie.[7] Helen left a bundle in Boston, to be forwarded by Mr. [James A.] Stetson, containing some cloth to be made into a jacket for George, &c. Has it been received?

Helen has had no difficulty with her breasts since she weaned Charles.

I have written letters to Dr. Thurber and Olive Gilbert.[8]

Saturday forenoon. — Dr. Sweet has called in, and thinks he had better defer operating on Helen's arm until Monday. It is evident that he is doubtful whether he shall succeed, in consequence of the ossification which has taken place. Dear Helen is in much distress of mind, and thinks she cannot be helped; and my own mind is greatly afflicted at the thought of her having a stiff arm for life. But you shall hear again from us soon.

ALS: Garrison Papers, Sophia Smith Collection, Smith College Library. In the left margin of page 3 of this letter, the following sentence appears in Helen Garrison's hand: "Our furniture was removed from Cambridgeport before we left Boston."

1. 13 Pine Street, where the Garrisons remained until June 1849.

2. Henry Hazen (c. 1790–1845) was probably a colonel in the state militia. He and his wife, Sarah Gifford Hazen, apparently operated a boarding house for travelers like the Garrisons. (Letter to the editor from Elizabeth B. Knox, secretary and curator, New London County Historical Society, January 14, 1970.)

3. Hazen's daughter has not been identified, the only Miss Hazen on record at Mount Holyoke College apparently not belonging to this family.

Mount Holyoke Seminary, at South Hadley, Massachusetts, had been founded in 1837 by Mary Lyon. The curriculum was patterned after that of Amherst College; it was the first institution of higher learning for women in the United States.

4. Mrs. W. has not been identified.

5. Possibly Garrison refers to Anne E. Mann (1774–1849), who was born in England and died in Lynn. In *The Liberator* at this time are advertisements for a millinery store in Summer Street being kept by A. E. Mann — probably the same person. (Letter to the editor from Jonathan Prude, researcher, September, 1970.)

6. Not identified, owing to the fact that Dr. Sweet had several sons who were bonesetters.

7. Laura Stebbins (c. 1794–1865) was a native of the Northampton area and a member of the Northampton Association of Education and Industry in 1843–1844. Although the town records indicate that she had married Armanda Wood in 1827, she was still being referred to by her maiden name at the time of this letter.

8. Dr. Thurber has not been identified.

---

8 2

TO LAURA STEBBINS

Franklin, Ct. Oct. 7, 1843.

Esteemed Friend:

On Monday last, we (i.e. Helen and I) took the cars in Boston for Norwich, and arrived in this village the next day — our object, to have Dr. [Stephen] Sweet set the dislocated elbow. Just before starting, your welcome letter was put into my hand, for which we proffer as many thanks in return, as there are words contained in it, and a thousand more. It gave us the only intelligence yet received from Northampton, since our departure; and great was the parental relief we experienced on perusing it. Having never before been separated from our dear children, we naturally feel a peculiar solicitude to hear of their welfare; and I trust the love we cherish for them makes us feel yet more keenly for the terrible situation of those, whose offspring are liable at any moment to be torn from their arms, and sold into interminable slavery. To hear that George and William are well, gives us pleasure; to hear that they are pretty good boys, and that you are encouraged to believe that they will be kind and obedient, is still more comforting. I trust you will continue to inform us, from time to time, respecting their behaviour, and that you will have no occasion to write that they are growing disobedient and unruly. We are sure that they will find in you a watchful and true friend, and we desire them to listen to your advice as they would to our own. Our anxiety is solely on your account, not on theirs — that is, we are afraid that you will give yourself too much trouble on their account. William will have to remain somewhat longer than we anticipated on leaving N., for the prospect now is, that we shall have to remain here two or three weeks from this date; It being pretty evident, from the experiment already made by Dr. Sweet, that the dislocated elbow can be mended only by a slow process, in consequence of mal-treatment, and the length of time that has elapsed since the disaster. Happy indeed shall we be when that right arm (and what is more needed in a family than a mother's right arm?) shall be restored to active use. O, it was a sad day when the wagon was upset, containing my unfortunate mother-in-law, and my dear wife and child [Wendell Phillips Garrison]; and more unfortunate was it when we called in the aid of a physician, who, however amiable and well-meaning, has proved that he utterly misapprended the case. But vain are all regrets for the past. Nor is it for us not to borrow trouble of the future, but to live in THE PRESENT, and to meet exigencies as they may arise.

As Dr. [Chauncey A.] Hall was obtained by our beloved friend David Mack, we are apprehensive that he will feel troubled in mind about it. But he has no cause for self-reproach. Like the good Samaritan, he flew to our relief as soon as he saw our distress, and endeavored to procure for us what he deemed the best surgical aid. He has a lasting claim on our gratitude for his kindness.

Dr. Hall will be sorry to hear, I am sure, that he made so great a mistake. He may be skilful, notwithstanding he has erred so widely in this case; for mistakes of this kind are by no means rare on the part of country physicians, who have very little practical knowledge of surgery. It is a remarkable coincidence that, at this moment, there is a colored woman [1] at Dr. Sweet's, from Willimantic, whose elbow was dislocated the last week in June, precisely in the same place as Helen's; and the physician she employed declared that her arm was broken, put splints around it, and treated it like a broken limb! — Such ignorance is scarcely pardonable. If a physician be conscious that his knowledge of surgery, especially of bone-setting, is imperfect, he ought to warn his patients of this fact, and direct them to some more intelligent and certain authority. Within a few months, Dr. Sweet has had several cases like Helen's, all of which have been misapprehended by the "regular faculty." Yet *he* is regarded as a quack!

Give our friendly regards to Roxcy Brown, and tell her that her letter to Augusta Reed and Louisa Humphrey, at Greenville, procured for us a most hospitable reception on the part of those kind-hearted and excellent women, who deserve to occupy a place in the esteem of all true-hearted reformers.[2] They are looking towards the Northampton "Community" with deep interest, and may yet offer themselves for membership. Should they apply, I hope there will be room for them.

Say to our esteemed friend Emily Farwell, that we have both visited her parents' home, and were happy to find them all well. My visit was unavoidably a short one, and I was not able, therefore, to say much to them about matters and things in the "Community." They were glad to hear of Emily's health, and were expecting her home soon; and they expressed the hope that she would remain with them through the winter.

To Laura Boyle we desire to be remembered in terms of strong affection and heart-felt gratitude. I shall try to write to her from this place. I wish I could ascertain where James [Boyle] and Dr. [Erasmus] Hudson are lecturing in this State. They are very much needed in Norwich and Greenville, and I should be glad to have them visit those places during my residence in this region.

And to what one of all the "Community" household do we not desire to be kindly remembered? To our pleasant and intelligent friend [Fortune R.] Porter — our rough spoken but warm-hearted friend [Charles] Wiley — our promising friend Thomas Hill — our unfortunate but worthy friend [David] Ruggles — our fortunate but long oppressed friend [Stephen] Rush — our kind friend [Samuel J.] May — our blunt but true-hearted friend [William F.] Parker — our sterling friend Hiram Wells — our pleasant and amiable friend Paine — &c. &c. — and to all of the gentler and better sex, (better in practice, taking mankind at large, not by nature,) for whose names there is no room on this sheet — we send friendly salutations.[3] Hoping to hear from you again soon, I remain,

Yours, with much esteem,

                        Wm. Lloyd Garrison.

☞ Do you still continue your "infidel" meetings? If so, with what success? Let not our friends "forsake the assembling of themselves together,"[4] because they have no particular one to rely on to make a speech. Speech-makers and speech-making they do not need, and the less they have of them, the better — provided they will themselves become talkers, not, however, for the sake of talking, but in order to promote free inquiry and advancement in knowledge. Tell them I want to publish some fresh testimonies from them in the Liberator, in relation to the anti-slavery enterprise, non-resistance, woman's rights, religious liberty, &c. &c.

☞ Mr. Mack has kindly stipulated to take George Thompson under his supervision, on the return of his wife. This will relieve you of considerable anxiety and care. Should either of the boys need any thing they have not got to make them comfortable, their uncle George or aunt Sarah is authorised to procure it for them on my account.

☞ Special remembrances to our beloved friends Hall Judd and wife Sophia Ford the Haywards, [Theodore] Scarboroughs, &c.⁵ We gratefully remember the kindness of Mrs. Adam.

ALS: Merrill Collection of Garrison Papers, Wichita State University Library.

1. Not identified.

2. Abigail Roxanne Brown (1816–1906) was a native of Connecticut who moved to the Northampton community in 1842, where she met Lorenzo D. Nickerson (1811–1893); she married him in 1844. The Nickersons moved to New York state and later to Appleton, Wisconsin, where Lorenzo became a prominent businessman. (*Commemorative Biographical Record of the Fox River Valley, Counties of Brown, Outagamie and Winnebago*, Chicago, 1895, pp. 554, 557; and Sheffeld, p. 103.)

3. Fortune R. Porter has not been further identified.

Hiram Wells (1813–1859), European by birth, was active in New England social and political movements. A charter member of the Northampton Association, he had in 1842, with Horace D. Doolittle, submitted to Congress a list of grievances, including complaints of unequal taxation and of government support for slavery. (Letter to the editor from Carol Hagglund, researcher, March 3, 1971.)

Oliver Dwight Paine (born 1819) was a native of Chesterfield, Massachusetts. He joined the Northampton community in April 1842 and left it in June 1845. (Chesterfield Town Records, microfilm, Forbes Library, 3:64, 1796–1842, and Sheffeld, p. 104.)

4. An adaptation of Hebrews 10:25.

5. Hall Judd (1817–1850) was a native of Northampton and a clerk by profession. He entered the community in 1842. (Letter to the editor from Elizabeth Duvall, bibliographer, Smith College Library, June 1, 1970.)

Sophia Ford (1802–1885), a native of Dedham, was a member of the Northampton Association, 1843–1845, and later became tutor to the children of such men as Bronson Alcott, Ralph Waldo Emerson, and William Ellery Channing. (Walter Harding, "Thoreau's Feminine Foe," *PMLA*, 69:110–116, March 1954.)

Josiah Hayward (died 1874) was a mason from Salem, Massachusetts, who entered the Northampton community in 1843, leaving the following year. He married Sarah Lord in 1825. (Salem Vital Records and an obituary in the Salem *Register*, April 20, 1874.)

8 3

TO *THE LIBERATOR*

FRANKLIN, Ct., Oct. 13, 1843.

MY DEAR FRIEND:

Having stated, in my last letter, that I was about proceeding with Mrs. Garrison to Franklin, Connecticut, from Northampton, for the purpose of obtaining the opinion of Dr. STEPHEN SWEET, the great 'natural bone-setter,' (using this term as significant of something not to be obtained in the school of surgery,) respecting the nature of the injury done to her right arm by being thrown out of a vehicle two months since, I will now give you the result of our visit to this place.

After driving our carriage to the top of a high hill in Franklin, (from which is seen one of the finest prospects in all New-England,) and not knowing where the object of our search resided, I hailed a man who was industriously at work with his scythe in a field near the road-side, and asked him whether he could tell me where Dr. Sweet was to be found. 'I am the man,' said he. 'Then you are the man I want to see,' I replied. We were quite fortunate in finding him at home, — for we had come at a venture, — as he is constantly sent for in all directions, by those who are acquainted with his extraordinary skill in all dislocations and fractures of the bones. We drove up to the door of his house, (a large, misshapen, antiquated dwelling,) and soon introduced ourselves to him, and were in turn introduced to his family, consisting of his wife and a troop of children, some of whom are already beginning to prove that, in the work of bone-setting, as well as in other particulars, they are (to use a homely but familiar illustration,) 'chips of the old block.'

You will recollect that our physician at Northampton decided, that the injury done to Mrs. G's arm was a fracture of the coronoid process of the ulna, at the elbow; and that, for about five weeks, the arm continued to grow worse, instead of better, without his discovering his error. Fortunately, our anti-slavery friend, Dr. E. D. Hudson, who was absent from the 'Community' at the time of the accident, was induced to look at the case. After a careful examination, he stated that, in his opinion, there was a dislocation, but no evidence of any fracture, and advised us to procure forthwith the best surgical aid, as it was then a difficult affair. This led us to consult Dr. Sweet, as our first choice. As soon as the bandage was removed, on taking a single glance at the arm, without touching it, he said it was a plain case of dislocation. The humerus, or fore-arm bone, was driven out of its place, and lay over the radius and ulna more than an inch.

There was no fracture. This was the third or fourth case he had been called to remedy, of precisely the same character, within a short time, every one of which had been ignorantly treated by the attending physician as a case of fracture! What a satire on the boasted 'science' of the schools! He declined attempting to reduce the dislocation at that time, on account of the great suffering that must unavoidably be inflicted by such a harsh operation, but prescribed the frequent application of his liniment to the arm, for some ten or twelve days, in order to soften and elongate the contracted cords and tendons; at the end of which period, we again visited him. Seven weeks had now elaped since the accident happened; during all which time, ossification had been going on around the lower part of the humerus, thus tending to bind it firmly to the radius and ulna, and also in the socket, from which the humerus was driven. This is always a formidable obstacle in replacing dislocated bones, as every surgeon knows. Dr. Sweet is not a man to make any flourishes, or to boast of his skill. On asking him, at our first visit, whether he thought he could effect a cure, he simply replied, 'I have never yet failed to do so, in a similar case; but I can tell better after I have made a trial. Every thing depends on the ossification that has taken place, as nothing else lies in the way.' I have now the unspeakable satisfaction to inform you that, to-day, the Rubicon has been passed, and the humerus adjusted to its natural position, without any kind of machinery, and simply by the skilful pressure of his all-powerful hands. Mrs. G. sustained the painful operation with much courage and fortitude, and mingled the smiles of joy with the tears of suffering when it was finished — such smiles as none but a wife and a mother can give, under such circumstances. Of course, the arm is still considerably swollen, and must remain so until the inflammation (a favorable symptom) subside, and the ossified matter, now broken up, be removed by absorption. Several weeks must elapse before it can be used freely, and without pain; but the work has been effectually done.

Since we have been here, Dr. Sweet has been called to reduce another dislocated elbow, which was also mistaken for a fracture, and treated as such for some time, by a 'regular' physician. Was I very far from the truth, do you think, when I said in my last letter, that 'there is incomparably more of quackery in the schools of law, physic and divinity, than out of them'?

I make no other complaint of the physician we first employed than is conveyed in the simple facts of the case. He erred through misconception, not wilfully — an error which, from his gentlemanly demeanor and sympathetic feelings, I am sure he will as deeply regret as we do ourselves, as it had well nigh resulted in the loss of the use of a right arm for life. Mistaking a dislocation for a fracture, he did probably all that needed to be done in the latter case, but to no good result.

The truth probably is, that not one physician in a hundred knows how to manage such cases; and of the body of those who make surgery their study, in a 'scientific' form, very few are competent to discharge the duties of their profession. They are continually blundering — mistaking one thing for another — mutilating, or leaving to perish, or cutting off limbs unnecessarily — and inflicting much needless pain on those whose sufferings they are employed to alleviate. — What is the testimony of Dr. Sweet, on this subject — of one who has never even once advertised that he is ready to attend to all cases of bone-setting, who has never published any of the numerous certificates in his possession in regard to his skill, so averse is he to making a display of himself, or to imitate the impudent example of many a genuine quack? It is this — that, during a constant practice of more than thirty years, he has scarcely found one 'regular' surgeon who understood his business; and his most frequent and worst cases have been those which have been managed, or rather mismanaged by the 'faculty,' who often do more mischief than good. On asking him how many times, during his long practice, (as the most sagacious are sometimes liable to err,) he had mistaken the cases of those who had come to him — as, for instance, a fracture for a dislocation, or *vice versa* — he replied, 'In not a single instance; and I have set more bones than could be piled in my house.' This was said emphatically, but without vanity, and beyond all doubt truthfully. This region is crowded with witnesses of his remarkable success. Unquestionably, he has not his equal as a bone-setter — for with the other branches of surgery I believe he does not meddle — in the United States.

I am constantly hearing, from various individuals with whom I happen to come in contact, accounts of the successful efforts of Dr. Sweet, in cases of extreme difficulty. Among these are the following:

A teamster had a load weighing 6900 lbs. run over his legs, (half way below the knee,) which were ground into ruts about four inches deep, and shockingly crushed. He is now well and active, without any apparent injury having been sustained.

Another man had a load of heavy green oak wood run over his right foot, across the instep, crushing it to pieces, and over his left limb, a little above the ankle joint, which was ground into a rut six inches deep so tightly as to require an axe (it being winter) to cut out the frozen earth around it. He was entirely cured, and at work as usual, the next season.

A lady, now living in Chaplin, was thrown from a wagon, and sustained a compound fracture above the ankle joint, so that the points of the bone protruded into the ground, two or three inches. Two surgeons were employed, who attempted to reduce it, and put on a paste dressing, which was not removed till the expiration of six weeks; at which time, the wound having sloughed, and the bandage rotted, Dr. Sweet was employed by the patient to examine the case. He did so, in the presence of the two surgeons, who declined removing the bandage, and insisted that the wound was doing well. On taking off the dressing, it was found to be thronged with maggots! The lady complained of experiencing a burning, crawling sensation in the wound. The attending surgeons said this was caused by the knitting of the bones together! Dr. Sweet told them that it was owing to the maggots having taken possession of the wound internally, and told them they must extract them immediately; but this they could not do. He then opened the wound, and took from the limb nearly a pint of corrupt matter and living maggots. Under his care, the lady recovered the use of her limb.

A lawyer of Macon, Georgia, had a son born with a club foot. A surgeon was employed, at an early period, for a whole year, to straighten the foot, but without success. The best surgical skill that Philadelphia could afford was next sought, and tried in vain. The child was then placed, for a short time, under the care of the celebrated Dr. Mott, of New-York, but he could give no relief.[1] Subsequently, the afflicted father made a visit to his brother at Norwich, who was a physician, and who recommended the employment of Dr. Sweet in the case. In the course of a few weeks, the boy (then six years old) was perfectly cured. This is only one among scores of similar instances that might be enumerated.

A person employed in a factory in Greenville, (Norwich,) was caught by one of his arms by the belt of the picker, and carried over the drum upwards of one hundred times, through a space of about fourteen inches. His clothes were nearly all torn off, and the plastering was widely stained with his blood, mingled with pieces of flesh. He was supposed to be dead when extricated, but soon became sensible. The physicians, who were summoned, said he could not live an hour, and declined attempting to relieve him. Dr. Sweet was summoned in haste, by the friends of the unfortunate sufferer. He examined the man, and found that his shoulders, ribs, and breast were all badly lacerated — his left arm broken near the shoulder — his right arm broken in three places between the shoulder and elbow, much hemorrhage having taken place — his right knee broken in pieces, and partially dislocated — two of the bones of the toes of his right foot loose in his stocking — a compound fracture of the left leg — one of the condyles of the pelvis, near the back, knocked off — his skull fractured above his left eye — his scalp cut to the skull, and rolled up some distance — and his whole body covered with bruises and lacerations. For twenty-four hours, Dr. Sweet bent himself without cessation, to the task of mending the fractures, dislocations, &c. &c. The man is now in good health, and again actively employed in the factory.

I might give the particulars of another case, almost precisely similar, excepting somewhat more formidable, attended with an equally astonishing result; but it is not necessary.

Dr. Sweet is about forty-seven years old — of the average height — strongly and compactly, though not very stoutly built — has a well cast head, filled with a good stock of sound common sense — is remarkable for his mechanical ingenuity and accurate observation — and is singularly endowed with those natural gifts, which admirably qualify him for his profession; the absence of which, no amount of scholastic knowledge (though excellent in its place) can ever supply. Long may he live to relieve, bless and save suffering humanity! I warmly commend him to universal patronage; for what is distance, or time, or money, where a limb is to be saved from deformity or from perishing? All who come will find that his charges are very reasonable; and the poor will always find him compassionate and generous. Some surgeons, with but a tithe of the immense number of cases he has had, have made independent fortunes by the fees they have taken; but Dr. Sweet is a man of very moderate means, owning an ordinary farm of about two hundred acres, and living in a very simple manner. His education has been extremely limited, he being emphatically a self-taught, self-made man, and his knowledge of books is scanty, excepting the great book of Nature. If he had the literary ability, and the disposition vigorously to take up the question of surgical reform, he has facts enough in his possession to electrify the whole country, and to cover with confusion the faces of the so-called [']learned faculty.' His father,[2] who died a few years since, was also a famous bone-setter; but neither father nor son has placed on record any of his remarkable cures, nor even kept a private list of the most difficult ones. What a pity, and what a loss!

I see it stated, in a Norwich paper, that Dr. SAMUEL THOMPSON, of Boston, the founder of the Thompsonian system, is dead. No candid person, it seems to me, can become acquainted with the history of that 'unscientific,' though genuine medical reformer, without being filled with indignation and disgust at the shameful persecution he encountered for having dared to convict the learned medical world of ignorance and folly — and with admiration of the courage, fortitude and perseverance which he manifested at all times, and under all circumstances. I hesitate not to say, that he is to be reckoned among

the world's benefactors, ay, and the world's martyrs. It was in my
own native place, (Newburyport,) that he was first cast into a loathsome dungeon, on the idle charge of having hastened the death of
a patient, by mal-practice — a charge maliciously stirred up against
him by some of the medical faculty, who can fill whole grave-yards
with their victims, in accordance with 'the will of God,' and *secundem
artem*, without suffering in their reputation, or being put on trial for
man-killing. Furious was the war waged against him, and against all
who dared to uphold him. It was as much as any man's character was
worth to avow himself a Thompsonian. But how has truth triumphed
over falsehood — innocence over calumny — right over wrong — nature
over 'scientific' imposture! Formerly, by legal enactment, it was lawful
to swindle any Thompsonian practitioner out of his fees, and he could
bring no action against any of the swindlers! Now, Thompsonianism
is every where fast becoming reputable — has spread throughout the
entire country — has its thousands of infirmaries, and its hundreds of
thousands of disciples — and is continually multiplying its triumphs.
All this mighty change Dr. Thompson lived to see, and died at a good
old age,[3] having done not only the State, but the world, some service
— great service. Though I do not say or believe, that he has exhausted
the field of medical discovery or improvement, (for it will not be
given to any single mind to do this, for we are progressive beings,
and something better still undoubtedly lies beyond, in due season to
be revealed,) yet I am satisfied, both from experience and observation
of its excellent results, that his system of medical treatment is incomparably superior to that of any which the schools deign to approve.
I am glad that it is not too late for me to encounter some odium for
making this public avowal, for I do not care to make my voice heard
in a popular shout.

Franklin is a small village, lying about eight miles northwest of
Norwich, having a scattered population of about one thousand. As
far as I can learn, the inhabitants are profoundly ignorant of all the
reforms of the age, except that of temperance, which has made some
progress here, though the taverns continue to deal out their 'distilled
death and liquid damnation,' and much remains to be done.[4] Notorious
as I am elsewhere — at a greater distance — here nobody appears to
have heard of me — no, not even of my being an 'infidel'! Here, therefore, I can move about, without terrifying any body, and just as
respectably as any one else! I intend, however, to make a public
revelation of myself to such of them as may choose to hear me lecture,
on Tuesday evening next, when I shall endeavor to contrast the religion
of the United States with Christianity, the religion of Jesus Christ.
The Rev. Dr. Nott is the venerable rabbi who is settled over the

orthodox church in this place.[5] He preaches regularly without a colleague, though he is about ninety years old, and has been here over this one parish over sixty years! Two entire generations, therefore, have been subjected to the weekly penalty of listening to his barren, sectarian, priestly theology, which is of the most rigid sort. The condition of the people under him (as well as that of many other congregations which are somewhat · similarly situated,) strongly reminds me of the deplorable, yet ludicrous case of Sinbad the sailor, on whose shoulders the old man of the sea rode so long and so unmercifully.[6]

We are pleasantly situated in the family of Col. Henry Hazen, and shall probably return to Boston in the course of ten days.

Yours, for deliverance to all who are bowed down,

WM. LLOYD GARRISON.

Printed: *The Liberator*, October 27, 1843.

1. Valentine Mott (1785–1865), known at the time as a brilliant and daring surgeon, received his training at the Medical Department of Columbia College and in Great Britain. Although he devoted his efforts principally to the teaching and practice of surgery, and wrote little of major medical interest, he did amass an outstanding collection of medical books to be known subsequently as the Mott Memorial Library.

2. Benoni Sweet (1760–1840), a native of Rhode Island and a bonesetter by profession, as were his progenitors for four generations. (Letter to the editor from Elizabeth B. Knox, secretary and curator, New London County Historical Society, January 14, 1970.)

3. An allusion to Genesis 15:15.

4. Garrison perhaps adapts a passage from Robert Hall, *Works, with a Brief Memoir of His Life by Olinthus Gregory and Observations on His Character as a Preacher* (New York, 1842), III, 34.

5. Samuel Nott (1754–1852), a graduate of Yale, served for seventy years as the pastor of the Congregational church in Franklin, Connecticut.

6. Garrison refers to one of the adventures in "Fifth Voyage of Sindbad the Seaman," *The Book of a Thousand Nights and a Night* . . . translated and annotated by Richard F. Burton (the Burton Club, c. 1910), VI, 50–53.

---

8 4

TO SARAH T. BENSON

Franklin, Ct., Oct. 14, 1843.

Dear Sarah:

I have endeavored to keep our Northampton friends informed of the progress that has been made in reducing Helen's dislocated elbow, and now take up my pen to give you the latest intelligence on that point, knowing how great must be the anxiety felt by you and mother, and all the other members of the household.

The first effort of Dr. [Stephen] Sweet, to reduce the dislocation, met with very slight success; the second started the bone a little; the third pushed it back about an inch. Yesterday he made his fourth attempt, and you will all rejoice to hear that "the Rubicon was passed" — in other words, the bone was restored to its true position, as far as the ossified state of the parts would allow. The arm is yet badly swollen, and very painful; but this is a good symptom. Probably a week will be necessary to allay the swelling, and two or three before Helen can begin to use her arm with any freedom. But how fortunate it is that we came here! Had we not done so, there is no probability that the arm would have been saved from perishing, even though our Boston surgeons had had the management of the case. I am satisfied that there is no bone-setter in all the United States equal to Dr. Sweet, and assiduously shall I improve every convenient opportunity to make his merits known, and to persuade those who have broken or fractured bones to put themselves under his care. How is our dear mother? Can she walk without a cane? If not, I think we should lose no time in having her come to Franklin, in order that Dr. Sweet may apply his skill to her case.

Up to this hour, we get no intelligence from any of you, and you can therefore imagine how great is our desire to receive a letter. But as we shall return to Boston on Friday or Saturday next, no letter had better be directed to me at this place. — Perhaps bro. George has already written to me at Boston.

We shall want William to be sent down to the city by the first favorable opportunity. His board is to be settled for from the 1st of October, (up to which time I believe it was paid,) and his tuition from the time of its commencement. If bro. George will see to it, I will see that he is made good. Our house is No. 13, Pine-street, at the south end, where William may be left. The sooner he can come, (provided he does not reach Boston before Friday or Saturday,) the more easy we shall be in our minds. Georgie will probably be very reluctant to part with him, but I hope he will soon be reconciled to the separation. We long to see them both, and regret that we must be separated even from one of them, for any length of time. May we hear a good account of them.

The last that we heard from the little ones at Boston, they were merry and in good health, and did not appear to miss us at all.

Oliver [Johnson] and his wife have removed their furniture into our house, and arranged their rooms, as well as a good deal of our furniture, which we were forced to leave in a state of utter confusion. Should William be sent down before we get home, they will be glad to attend to him; so that no good opportunity should be lost to send him to Boston, on account of our absence, which is so soon to end.

I have written letters from this place to Dr. Thurber, Olive Gilbert, sister Charlotte, Phebe Jackson, Elizabeth A. Pierce [1] at Brooklyn, and several others.

I perceive, by a Norwich paper, that the celebrated Dr. Samuel Thompson recently died in Boston. There is a point at which it is not in the power of steam, lobelia and cayenne to save from the grasp of death. "The inevitable hour" [2] comes to all.

We are hoping that you and mother will spend the winter with us, and shall have a room set apart expressly for that purpose. But we will not urge either of you beyond your inclinations. I hope you will not fail to make Charlotte a visit this fall.

Helen one day happening to refer to the spot that you have on your breast, Dr. Sweet said he had a salve which he felt confident would readily cure it, whether the sore should prove to be scrofulous or cancerous. I shall procure some of the salve, and, from what he has told me of its healing effects in similar cases, I have little doubt that it will save you from much pain and danger. You shall receive it by the first convenient opportunity, with directions how to apply it. You need not fear of its doing you any injury.

Dr. Sweet has examined my side, and says it is a sheathing (of a coagulated substance) partly under and partly over the ribs. He thinks wearing his plasters will give me great relief, and effect possibly a cure. I shall try them without delay.

Tell bro. George that I forgot to pay Mr. Ashley for reducing the heels of my new boots. [3] Will he discharge the debt?

Elder Coe saw sister Charlotte a few days since in Providence. [4] She and her household were well.

Yours, lovingly,

Wm. Lloyd Garrison.

N.B. Please say to bro. George, that I shall be glad if he can make it convenient to get somewhere about one hundred pounds of good butter put down for me at the earliest practicable period. If he cannot, he will let me know soon.

Whatever clothing, or other articles, that Georgie may need, from time to time, let them be procured without consulting me, and charged to my account.

Should it so happen that it will be inconvenient to board and educate Georgie this winter in the Community, let him be sent home, whenever that time may come. He must be constantly cautioned against pulling beyond his strength, as he has a narrow chest, and has already injured himself in that way.

How consolatory it is to think that our dear Anne, though taken away from us, is in the full enjoyment of heavenly felicity!

ALS: William Lloyd Garrison Papers, Massachusetts Historical Society.

1. Elizabeth A. Pierce, not identified.
2. Thomas Gray, "Elegy Written in a Country Churchyard," stanza 9, line 3.
3. George Ashley (1819–1875), a shoemaker by trade, had interests ranging from church music to politics. He was to serve in 1844–1845 as a member of the Northampton Association. (Francis Bacon Trowbridge, *The Ashley Genealogy, a History of the Descendants of Robert Ashley of Springfield, Massachusetts*, New Haven, 1896, p. 316.)
4. William Coe (1804–1872), a minister, was an ardent abolitionist who named three of his sons after leaders in the movement. (Henry F. Coe, *Descendants of Matthew Coe*, Boston, 1894, pp. 21–23.)

85

TO GEORGE W. BENSON

Boston, Nov. 6, 1843.

Dear George:

According to the request contained in your letter, received on Thursday, I was prompt in my attendance at the depot on Friday evening, when I had the satisfaction to take our dear mother and sister Sarah by the hand, and to clasp in my arms my dear little Willie. The journey did not seem to fatigue them much, though they were all glad, of course, to get to No. 13, Pine-Street. They all continue well; and next week we shall be looking to see you in our family circle. We have concluded to have Georgie spend the winter with us, and wish you to bring him with you, "bag and baggage." Next spring and summer, should things turn out favorably, he may reside in the Community; but during the winter, we wish him to be in the city. Whatever is due for his boarding, tuition, clothing, &c., please settle, and also Willie's account, and I will pay you.

Sarah forgot to bring with her the salve for Willie's forehead, and hopes you will remember to take it with you.

We are sorry to hear of poor little Tommy's ill health, and hope that the perilous crisis has passed with him.[1] We are equally glad to hear of Catherine's safe delivery, and that the new comer is not less beautiful than weighty.[2]

All the sympathies of my heart are proffered to Hiram Wells, whose terribly afflicting case is one deserving of the strongest commiseration.[3]

We deeply sympathize with our friend Stetson and his wife, in the loss of their eldest boy.[4] How frail are the ties of life!

It seems you have had a narrow escape of your life, by being thrown from a wagon. For an *unfortunate* man, you are the most *lucky* of any within the scope of my acquaintance. "May you live a thousand years!"

Helen's arm is slowly, though steadily improving. It still remains somewhat stiff, but she can use it considerably.

Sophia Foord was with us during the non-resistance meetings. Our anniversary was a quiet and pleasant one. She will not return to N[orthampton]. under two or three weeks.

In great haste, and with a horrible pen in my hand, I remain,

Yours, affectionately,

Wm. Lloyd Garrison.

N.B. I think of attending the anniversary of the R. I. State Society, of Providence, on Wednesday and Thursday.

ALS: William Lloyd Garrison Papers, Massachusetts Historical Society.

1. Garrison refers to Thomas Davis Benson (born 1842). No other information is available about him.

2. Garrison alludes to Mary Benson (born 1843), George Benson's sixth child. In 1863 she married William L. Soule in Kansas. (Letter to the editor from Jonathan Prude, researcher, September 1970.)

3. At the time of this letter, Wells had lost part of his right hand in an industrial accident. He was ultimately to die in a boiler explosion in his machine works in Florence, Massachusetts. (Sheffeld, p. 240.)

4. Garrison refers to Ebenezer Witter Stetson (1833–1843), the eldest son of James A. and Dolly W. Stetson.

---

8 6

TO ELIZABETH PEASE

Boston, Dec. 1, 1843.

My Beloved Friend:

If, instead of this meagre and hasty epistle, I could send you a ream of letter-paper, closely written over, I should hardly then begin to discharge the epistolary debt (as well as the debt of gratitude for your numerous kindnesses) which I owe you. Month after month has glided away, without bearing from me any token of that devoted friendly attachment which I have felt for you from the first hour of our acquaintance. But my silence has not been owing to any diminution of personal esteem, for that is increasing continually. After the sad accident which befell my dear wife and her aged mother, through my unskilfulness, my mind was so distressed, and I sympathized so deeply in their sufferings, that for several weeks I could neither put pen to paper nor scarcely read a page. My health, which was then beginning to improve, became again seriously impaired, and a total relaxation of mind seemed to be absolutely necessary to expedite its recovery. It is now, I am happy to say, incomparably better than it was in the spring. Be assured that I shall endeavor to guard it with all due care; for, phrenologically speaking, my caution is pretty well developed, — rash and fanatical as my enemies affect to consider me.

Helen's arm, since it was put right by Dr. Sweet, has improved surprisingly, and she can now use it with a good deal of freedom, though it will require more time for its entire recovery. Her mother was not so badly injured as we at first apprehended, and she is now wholly recovered from the effects of the fall. My four little boys are all in blooming health, and quite as full of activity as it is desirable to see. The youngest (Charles Follen) is just beginning to go alone. I wish you could behold the little troop, as they swarm round me to bestow on me the kisses of their affection, and to tell me all that they know, in order that they may have their stock of information augmented. Dear children! may they be spared to do much toward rescuing this ruined world of ours from sin and misery!

What *will* my dear brother Henry C. Wright think or say of me, in consequence of my long silence? He knows that I love him too well to lose sight of him in my memory for a moment. How tenderly have I sympathized with him in his sickness! He is copious in his expressions of gratitude to you for your more than sisterly regard for his welfare and recovery, and tells me that you have been his angel-preserver and benefactor. We all feel in Boston that the continuance of his precious life, up to this time, is mainly owing to you as an instrument in the Divine hands. I need not supplicate Heaven to bless and reward you; for no one can do good, in the right spirit, without being blessed.

You will be pleased to hear of the safe arrival of Prof. Walker [1] and Samuel May. It is refreshing to my spirit to hear them expatiate on the noble spirits with whom they came in contact abroad. By the former, I received your truly generous donation of money to assist me at the present time in my pecuniary embarrassment, and it filled my heart too full for utterance. You will beg me to spare a profusion of words, and I will therefore only add, that never was a donation received at a more seasonable period. It came like manna from heaven. The Liberator is yet painfully struggling against wind and tide, and the hatred toward it for its fidelity to the cause of christian reform is rather increasing than diminishing. The "powers that be" in Church and State, especially a powerful and an ungodly priesthood, are straining every nerve to crush it; and, at times, it seems as if they would triumph. Our list of subscribers is very much reduced, and for the last three or four months I have received nothing by way of salary.

I state this to you, because I know it will give you great satisfaction to hear that your donation was made under circumstances that render the receipt of it peculiarly acceptable. Your previous donations were equally serviceable. Yet, knowing as I do how many objects of charity and philanthropy at home you are constantly aiding, and how heavy must be your expenditures, it makes me almost shrink from accepting your generous gifts.

A thousand thanks to you, my dear friend, for the beautiful bag which, at the kind suggestion of H. C. W., you have forwarded to me. I will preserve it as a choice keep-sake, for your memory will ever be very dear. Helen admires it, and unites with all her soul with me in expressions of gratitude for all your manifold kindnesses.

Has our beloved George Thompson yet returned from India?[2] I am suffering in spirit for want of an epistolary communion of soul with him.

I am afraid that Henry C. Wright will suffer seriously in his health by remaining in England during the present winter. Ought he not to return home?

The Chapmans, Westons, Phillipses, Quincys, &c. are all well as usual, and actively engaged in carrying on the anti-slavery conflict. The time for holding the annual Fair is at hand, and all hands (especially the female ones) are "busy as bees" in preparing for it.[3]

Next Monday, Congress convenes at Washington. We are anticipating a more stormy session than the country has ever yet seen. Every effort is now making on the part of the South to annex Texas to the Union, and we are apprehensive it will succeed. Heaven knows what is to become of this guilty nation.

But I must close in haste, and most abruptly. You shall hear from me again by the next steamer.

With great admiration and affection, I remain,
Your faithful friend,

Wm. Lloyd Garrison.

ALS: Villard Papers, Harvard College Library.

1. James Walker (1794–1874), a Unitarian minister and professor of theology at Harvard, who was subsequently president of that institution (1853–1860).

2. The exact dates of Thompson's visit to India as the agent of the British India Society are not known, although a number of reports concerning the visit were published in the *British Friend*, May 31, 1843–January 31, 1844. Thompson was to investigate land reform and Indian labor, but there is some evidence that he was diverted from making objectionable criticisms by Indian landowners who wanted to preserve the status quo. He returned to Britain under a retainer from the Rajah of Sattara (see Garrison's letter to Helen E. Garrison, September 3, 1846.)

3. The tenth annual Massachusetts Anti-Slavery Fair opened on December 19, 1843, in Amory Hall, Boston.

8 7

TO DANIEL O'CONNELL

[December 8, 1843.]

SIR:

The great heart of bleeding humanity in the United States is swelling with gratitude and expanding with hope, in consequence of your eloquent and masterly reply to the pro-slavery Letter of the Cincinnati Repeal Association.[1] That reply is a staggering blow to the American slave system, and will mightily strengthen the hands of the friends of immediate and unconditional emancipation on this side of the Atlantic.

As soon as the necessary arrangements could be made, after the receipt of your Reply by the Liverpool steamer, a public meeting of the citizens of Boston and vicinity was held in Faneuil Hall, (world-famous as the 'Old Cradle of Liberty,' and historically identified with the revolutionary struggle of 1776,) to hear it read, and to take such action upon it as its merits might seem to require. You will be glad to hear that a large number of Irish residents in this city were present, and listened with respectful attention to the reading of the Reply. As a copy of the proceedings, in an official shape, (transcribed by a colored lad, whose penmanship it will gratify you to see,) will accompany this letter, and also a copy of 'The Liberator,' containing a sketch of the speeches on that occasion, I need not here attempt to describe them.[2] I deem it both a privilege and an honor to have been selected to read your Reply to so large a number of Bostonians and Irishmen. The same privilege and honor were conferred on me, a few days previous, by the abolitionists of Rhode-Island, at the annual meeting of their State Society, held in Providence, where your reply was heard with thrilling emotions, and responded to in the most enthusiastic manner.

Among the atrocious calumnies against the American abolitionists, which have been sent over to you by some of your recreant countrymen, and one which you seem to think is not entirely without foundation, is the following: that they are bitterly hostile to Irishmen, both as foreigners and as Catholics! Coming from such a source, I am surprised that your sagacious mind should have given it the slightest credence, for I hold that those who justify reducing God's rational creatures to the condition of goods and chattels, or who attempt to palliate the guilt of slaveholders, are incompetent to testify, in the court of truth and equity, against the persecuted and fearless friends of negro emancipation — as I also hold that the malignant foes of the righteous cause of repeal are disqualified to be regarded as good witnesses against DANIEL O'CONNELL *as a Repealer*. Let me assure you that the accusation is utterly untrue, and no evidence can be produced to sustain it. The genuine abolitionists of the country, as a body, are of the number, 'of whom the world is not worthy,'[3] though despised and rejected, as was JESUS, the Prince of emancipators, by the chief priests, scribes and pharisees. I hesitate not to affirm, that, of all associated people on the face of the globe, they are the least wedded to sect and party, and the most catholic in their feelings towards the whole human race. Instead of being hostile to such of your oppressed countrymen as have come hither, they are the only persons who really respect or sympathize with them; and so far from being bigoted against Catholicism, they have surprisingly emancipated themselves from sectarian bondage, and find occasion to make a thousand charges against Protestant, to one against Catholic pro-slavery. The Protestant clergy and church, as such, have been desperately arrayed against this movement, from the first hour that the flag of immediate emancipation was unfurled to the breeze.

When I visited England in 1833, to put an end to the impostures of ELLIOTT CRESSON, respecting the American Colonization Society, you treated me with great kindness and cordiality, as did my lamented friend, the late JAMES CROPPER, and also THOMAS FOWELL BUXTON, ZACHARY MACAULY, WILLIAM ALLEN, JOSEPH STURGE, GEORGE THOMPSON, and other eminent philanthropists.[4] You then signed with alacrity the famous Protest against the American Colonization Society, which bore at its head the potent name of WILLIAM WILBERFORCE; and it was by *your* advice that I called a public meeting in Exeter Hall, in opposition to that nefarious combination, at which you made one of your most powerful speeches.[5]

When I saw you at the general Anti-Slavery Convention, and at your lodgings in London, in 1840, your manner was very gracious toward me, and your commendation of myself most emphatic.

When I visited Dublin, you did me the honor to call on me at the house of my respected friend, RICHARD D. WEBB, as soon as you heard of my arrival in the city, and again received me in the most cordial manner. I have spoken on the same platform, in the same public meetings, in Exeter Hall, Freemasons' Hall,[6] &c. with yourself, in favor of the cause of Temperance, and against American slavery and East India servitude.[7]

Fourteen years ago, I stood up almost single-handed against this guilty nation, and in the sacred name of God demanded the immediate liberation of every slave on the American soil; nor have I ceased, day or night since, to enforce that demand. I have thus served two full apprenticeships in the cause of negro emancipation. My life has been in continual peril, as 'the head and front' of anti-slavery offending.[8] During that period, I have been as much hated, as much calumniated, as much feared, as yourself.

Why do I allude to these facts? In the spirit of vanity? No. I have never yet courted the notice of any man, and even my enemies will bear witness that I have never feared the frown of any, knowing, as did a despised apostle of old, that it is a very small thing to be judged of man's judgment, and that every human being must give account of himself to God, not to man.[9] But I have regretted to perceive in you, within a few months past, for reasons which, to me, are perfectly inexplicable, a disposition to travel widely and frequently out of your path, to attack me personally in the most contemptuous manner, and (if you are reported correctly in the Dublin journals) *an affected ignorance of my character and labors as an abolitionist.* You have seized the most extraordinary occasions to hold me up to derision and odium in Ireland — to wit, in the meetings of the Repeal Association, where accusations could be made, but not answered, by reason of the broad Atlantic rolling between us — by stigmatizing me, *while denouncing American slavery*, as 'a maniac in religion,' and referring to me as 'a man *called* Lloyd Garrison,' whose company *as an abolitionist* you rejected, and also that of all his anti-slavery associates! Now, I will venture to say, you cannot accurately tell what are my religious opinions; but if you are familiar with them, I appeal to your magnanimity, good sense, and 'sober second thought,' to say, whether it is legitimate business for you, or any other man, *at a Repeal meeting*, to attack the theology of one who is *a decided friend of Repeal*, and an uncompromising abolitionist, and one who, notwithstanding *your* peculiar religious sentiments, has always spoken of you in terms of eulogy, and has never written a line to your disparagement. What if we are not agreed in abstract religious speculations, or respecting religious rites and ceremonies — as *abolitionists*, as *Repealers*, may we not walk harmoniously together? Must a man be a *Catholic*, in order to belong to the Repeal Association? Are Repeal meetings the right places in which to settle points of theological controversy? Why, then, I ask, in the spirit of candor, charity and fair dealing, have you attempted to stain my religious character, *and to cripple my labors in the abolition of slavery*, by pointing the finger of reproach at me as a *heretic*? Is such conduct worthy of Daniel O'Connell? What toad or serpent has been pouring his 'leprous distillment' [10] into your ear, in order to make us enemies of each other? Surely, I do not err when I hazard the assertion, that you have not been self-moved in this matter.

You avow the greatest respect for JOSEPH STURGE, and have eulogized his character on various occasions. Yet, on matters of religious faith and duty, how wide is the difference between a Catholic and a Quaker! Why is he not 'a maniac in religion' as well as myself, seeing that I more cordially endorse the grand distinctive principles of Quakerism, than I do those of any other sect?

If I had arrayed myself against the cause of *Irish Repeal*, then, indeed, it would have been not only justifiable, but commendable in you, to have censured me, *on that ground*. Or, if I had abandoned the *anti-slavery cause*, then, when speaking on the subject of American slavery, — whether at a Repeal meeting or elsewhere, — your rejection of my company, *for that cause*, would have been to the point. But as I am *a Repealer* — as I am *an abolitionist*, for whose seizure the sovereign State of Georgia offers a reward of five thousand dollars — I think you have erred in attacking me as you have done in so gratuitous and offensive a manner. Am I not right in this view of the case? And if I am, I have no need to suggest to your generous mind what ought to be done by you at the next meeting of the Repeal Association at the Corn Exchange, or in Conciliation Hall.[11]

Hoping you will mightily foil all the machinations of your wily enemies, and be triumphant in your peaceful efforts for Repeal, and wishing a long life for yourself, and freedom and prosperity for oppressed and suffering Ireland, I remain,

Yours, in every conflict for the right,

WILLIAM LLOYD GARRISON,
Chairman of the Meeting in Faneuil Hall.

Printed: *The Liberator*, December 8, 1843; reprinted in the *Herald of Freedom*, December 15, 1843.

1. The Cincinnati Repeal Association had sent a contribution to the Irish Repeal Association accompanied by a letter in support of slavery in the United States. O'Connell was so shocked that Irishmen in America could be proslavery that he wrote an address, approved by the Committee of the Irish Association, urging all Irishmen to work for the abolition of slavery and prejudice. On November 18, 1843, Garrison read O'Connell's address at Faneuil Hall, where it received a generally, though not unanimously, favorable response. (*The Liberator*, November 10, 17, 24, 1843.)

2. Garrison refers to the issue dated November 24, 1843. The "colored lad" has not been identified.

3. Hebrews 11:38, with a substitution of "is" for "was."

4. Garrison refers to several reformers not yet identified in this volume. Elliott Cresson (1796–1854), a Philadelphia Quaker merchant and philanthropist, was an ardent supporter of the American Colonization Society and traveled widely in the United States and Great Britain to enlist funds for its support.

Founded in 1817 under the sponsorship of Henry Clay, Daniel Webster, James Madison, and John Marshall, by 1827 the American Colonization Society had settled 15,000 Negroes in Africa, and was generally looked on in both the North and the South as a noble Christian enterprise. Garrison's initial opposition to the object of resettlement of American Negroes stems from around 1830 and is documented in his *Thoughts on African Colonization* (1832). The opposition of Garrison and the anticolonizationists to Cresson reached its height during the summer of 1833.

James Cropper (1773–1840), a wealthy English Quaker merchant, was committed to the abolition of slavery in the West Indies. He was also one of the first English abolitionists to oppose the American Colonization Society.

Zachary Macaulay (1768–1838), whose name Garrison misspells, was an unstinting English abolitionist, who experienced the evils of slavery firsthand by working on a plantation in Jamaica and by serving as governor of Sierra Leone. He was one of the founders in 1823 of the Anti-Slavery Society.

William Allen (1770–1843), an English Quaker, was a scientist by training. An energetic abolitionist, he was unique in the scope of his friendships, which ranged from Wilberforce and Clarkson to Czar Alexander I.

5. Garrison refers to a protest, dated July 1833 and signed by twelve leading British abolitionists (not including Clarkson), which was presented to him during his visit to England. This protest represented to Garrison the ultimate victory in his campaign against colonization.

Exeter Hall (seating capacity, 3,000), built on the Strand in London in 1831 and used for concerts and various reformist meetings, was the site of the anticolonization meeting mentioned by Garrison. (Henry Benjamin Wheatley, *London Past and Present*, London, 1891, II, 26.)

6. In Great Queen Street, London.

7. By "East India" Garrison probably means India.

8. Garrison adapts Shakespeare, *Othello*, I, iii, 80.

9. Garrison refers to St. Paul and paraphrases I Corinthians 4:3–4.

10. Shakespeare, *Hamlet*, I, v, 64.

11. The Corn Exchange and Conciliation Hall were adjacent structures located on Burgh Quay in Dublin. The former was the usual meeting place of the Irish Repeal Association and the latter, the scene of some of O'Connell's greatest triumphs. (Adam and Charles Black, *Black's Guide to Dublin*, Edinburgh, 1866.)

---

8 8

TO LOUISA HUMPHREY

Boston, Dec. 15, 1843.

Dear Friend:

I owe you a long string of apologies for having been so dilatory in sending you a letter, informing you of our situation in Boston; but as the payment of the debt, in that shape, would be good for nothing, I will merely say that I have purposed a hundred times, since our arrival home, to write you a long epistle, expressive of the high esteem dear Helen and myself cherish for you and Augusta [Reed], and of the deep gratitude we feel toward you both for your acts of disinterested kindness to us during our visits to Greenville; but some hindrance or engagement has interposed to prevent the carrying out of those many good intentions.

I write now in haste; and as you will be desirous to learn, first of all things, what is the present condition of Helen's arm, I will state that, for some time after we came back, we continued very faithfully to apply warm baths and Dr. [Stephen] Sweet's liniment to the arm, and seemed to make some progress in bending it upward; but for the last three or four weeks, we have done little toward a restoration, for there is evidently something wrong in the matter — at least a partial dislocation of one of the bones — an obstruction which prevents us from bending the arm to any extent — so that the arm, though very much improved since we saw you, still continues to look out of shape, to be at times quite painful, and comparatively of little service. How much my poor wife has suffered since the accident took place, by which she was so severely injured! How great a misfortune has been the loss of the use of that right arm! It is probable that she has slipped one of the bones out of its place by lifting so much with it, and by attempting to do so much about her household affairs. Knowing that if I called in any of our Boston surgeons to put the arm right, after the panegyric I had published in the Liberator upon Dr. Sweet's skill, and not feeling any more confidence in them than I had done before, and deeming it an act of justice and duty that he should be apprised of the difficulty, I wrote to Dr. Sweet, some time ago, telling him the state of the case, and proposing to meet him with Helen at your residence without delay, if he would send me word what day he would be in Greenville. After waiting most anxiously for a fortnight for his reply, a letter came from him, apologizing for his delay in writing, saying that he had been absent, &c.; and appointing Saturday of that week for us to be at your house. But ever since that time, our house has been like a hospital on a small scale; for every member of the family has been ill with a severe attack of the influenza, excepting myself, and none of them are yet fully restored to health. First, Mrs. [Oliver] Johnson, a friend residing with us, was taken down with it; then Helen's sister Sarah; then Helen herself, and very violently; then all the children, the little babe somewhat dangerously; and then Mrs. Benson. I have therefore written to Dr. Sweet, requesting him to make us a flying visit, telling him we shall not be able to go to him, for some time to come, if at all; and we hope to see him the present week. I feel reluctant to consult any one else; yet, if he cannot come, it will be necessary for us to do so.

You see what liberties I took with your letter, and perhaps you will blame me for doing so; but I felt confident the publication of it would be deeply interesting to the readers of the Liberator, and usefully serve to illustrate religious hypocrisy and pro-slavery rottenness.[1] I endeavored to be as careful as possible, so as not to expose any thing that might be deemed strictly private. I am curious to hear what has been said about it in your region. Does Coit recognise his portrait? [2] Knapp's *praying* allusions to me exhibit priestly assurance and cant in a strong light.[3] They amused me a good deal; but I could not help pitying the dupes of such a man.

There is shortly to be a convention in this city, in regard to social reorganization, at which I expect to meet James Boyle, bro. George Benson, David Mack, and perhaps other members of the Northampton Community.[4] I will say to James all that was omitted in the printing of your letter, respecting his visiting Greenville again. It is evident that the subject of "Communities" or "Associations" is exciting more and more interest among the people, and especially among those who are actively engaged in works of benevolence and philanthropy. I have had no time to examine the subject, and am therefore a mere learner — not, I trust, as respects the spirit which should actuate every human being, but as to the details of social cooperation and the basis of community arrangement. Nothing can be made plainer to my mind than that mankind may and should dwell together in unity, as one great family; that their interests are all one and the same, and not diverse and antagonistical; that there should be no monopoly, no favouritism, no rich, no poor, no high, no low, among them. But all this can be brought about by no mere external organization or local colonization, (though either of these may be a powerful means to a glorious end,) but by a discernment and hearty embrace of the truth, and by a readiness to walk in the footsteps of the Son of God. It is only they who walk by faith, and not by sight,[5] who can overcome, and be delivered from the evil that is in the world — not faith in sectarian creeds and observances, but in the promises of the one living and true God, which shall never fail.

I hope this will find you and Augusta comfortable in body and happy in mind. Helen and I think and talk of you frequently — always with pleasure, always gratefully. She sends her sisterly regards and her best wishes to you both. A letter from either of you will always be welcome, and should either or both of you at any time come to Boston, do not fail to make our habitation your home — (No. 13, Pine-Street.)

Yours, faithfully,

Wm. Lloyd Garrison.

P.S. On Sunday evening before last, I addressed an immense assembly in Lynn, for more than two hours, in defence of "Come-out-erism," and against the popular views of the Clergy, the Church, the Sabbath, Worship, &c.[6] The discourse obtained a hearty response from many minds, and has produced no little sensation in that place. Let us not be discouraged by the number or power of our spiritual foes, remembering that "the battle is the Lord's," [7] and that error and imposture must certainly pass away. Great revolutions are sometimes effected in a very summary manner, and apparently from very small causes. The fall of spiritual Babylon will probably be not less sudden than great, "for strong is the Lord God who judgeth her." [8] Let our confidence in the triumph of justice and love be like a rock, against which the billows of opposition beat in vain. It is for the unbelieving and wicked to be afraid, but the righteous to be bold as a lion.[9]

☞ Please give our kind regards to Mr. and Mrs. Kennedy.[10]

ALS: Manuscript Collection, The Bostonian Society.

1. Garrison refers to a letter printed in *The Liberator* December 1, 1843, signed "An Abolitionist." According to the writer, Garrison's recent lecture in Greenville had set the town in an uproar, chiefly because Garrison said that northern churches and clergy were anti-Christian.

2. William Henry Coit (1792–1872) was a Greenville manufacturer and merchant who took an active part in educational, benevolent, and religious enterprises. (Letter to the editor from Elizabeth B. Knox, secretary and curator, New London County Historical Society, January 14, 1970.)

3. Jacob Knapp (1799–1874) was a Baptist minister and revivalist who claimed to have converted more than 100,000 people during his lifetime. Garrison's reference to Knapp's "*praying* allusions" is explained in Louisa Humphrey's letter. In a public prayer in his church, although he was himself an antislavery advocate, Knapp called Garrison an infidel and agent of the devil. (*Autobiography of Elder Jacob Knapp*, Boston, 1868.)

4. A "Convention of Friends of Social Reform" was held in Boston December 26–29, 1843. Organized to spread information about Fourierism and associationism as a cure for social problems, the gathering was sponsored by members of communities like Brook Farm and the Northampton Association, as well as by private citizens. Similar conventions were also held at Worcester (December 12–13) and Leominster (December 15–16). For an account of the Boston meeting see *The Liberator*, January 5, 1844.

5. An adaptation of II Corinthians 5:7.

6. "Come-outer" was the name originally applied to certain religious dissenters or reformers who separated themselves from an established organization. Such a group flourished in New England about 1840, including that group of nonresistance abolitionists who advocated "coming-out" from church and state because of the attitude of both toward slavery. The term was also applied to radical political reformers. (Mitford Mathews, *Dictionary of Americanisms*, Chicago, 1951.)

7. I Samuel 17:47.

8. Revelation 18:8.

9. Garrison adapts Proverbs 28:1.

10. There were several people with the name Kennedy living in the Greenville area. It is impossible to determine which ones Garrison means.

8 9

TO HENRY C. WRIGHT

Boston, Dec. 16, 1843.

My dearly beloved friend —

As I hastily seize my pen, at the last hour prior to the sailing of the steamer, my cheeks crimson with shame and regret to think that I have allowed days, weeks, months to transpire, without sending you a single epistle. During all that time, I have been in affliction with my family, in consequence of sickness — the unfortunate accident which happened to my dear Helen and her mother — and the long protracted sufferings and death of our lamented sister Anne. I will not, however, occupy any portion of this sheet with apologies; for to inflict these upon you, would be most unsatisfactory, and quite needless. Surely, you know me too well to imagine that my affection for you has diminished — that I do not feel any special interest in your sublime christian mission abroad — that I am not with you, in spirit, in all your anxieties, cares, labors, sacrifices and triumphs. You are as dear to me as one human being ought to be to another, and I feel that we are united by the indissoluble bonds of faith and love. Judge me not by the number or quality of my letters. I am a dilatory correspondent, as you well know; and whoever has any epistolary correspondence with me must "let patience have her perfect work." [1]

A brief letter which I have lately received from my dear friend Richard Allen informs me that you were then sitting by his side, and in tolerable health. I have been dismayed at the accounts of your illness, previously received; especially to hear that you have a strong tendency to consumption, and that your lungs are seriously affected. But the last intelligence cheers my heart, and I trust you will do nothing rashly to jeopard your valuable life. It is painfully evident that the climate of England is not friendly to your constitution; and I have been alarmingly apprehensive that you would fall a victim to it, ere long, in connexion with your arduous labors. In my opinion, you ought to risk your life no longer by remaining abroad, but to return home as soon as practicable — perhaps not during the present winter, but early next summer; and when you do return, as a sea-voyage is so injurious to your system, you ought to come in a Cunard steamer from Liverpool, so as to be as few days on the passage as possible. [2] If you are really in no special danger by remaining in England, why then I will not so earnestly urge your return; and yet I want to see and embrace you, and to have you laboring once more with and among us. We miss you prodigiously. Little has been done, directly, to promote the heaven-born cause of non-resistance since you left. No agent has been found to take the field, and the Executive Committee of our little Non-Resistance Society are so occupied with their anti-slavery labors and responsibilities, that they have neither the time nor the means to put any efficient machinery into motion. Yet do not suppose that any reaction has taken place. The cause is certainly advancing, and thousands are beginning to feel an interest in its principles, who were formerly disposed to regard it as wild and chimerical.

We had an interesting annual meeting of the Society in October last;[3] and though the number in attendance was not large, except at the evening sessions, those who were present were the best friends of reform in all its branches. Our resolves were of a radical nature, and calculated, one would suppose, to awaken opposition on the part of those who are hostile to non-resistance; but, though there was free utterance allowed to all, not an opponent appeared, except during the last evening; and then none other than our indescribable friend G. W. F. Mellen, who tried to defend Liberty party and government — with what success you can readily imagine.[4] Edmund Quincy declining to act any longer as President, Adin Ballou was chosen in his place, and Edmund was transferred to the Executive Committee.[5] We intend to imitate the admirable plan adopted in England to scatter light and information, by publishing a series of tracts on various topics, occupying from two to eight pages. We hope that Adin Ballou will be induced to act as a lecturing agent for a considerable portion of the year, and also our bro. John M. Spear of Weymouth.[6]

Great fears are entertained that Texas will be annexed to the Union at the present session of Congress. It was supposed that President Tyler would strongly recommend the annexation in his message, but he has had the cunning not to do so, knowing that, if he did, a tremendous excitement would ensue throughout the entire North.[7] His language toward Mexico is insulting and belligerent; he intimates that the United States will declare war against her, unless she recognize the independence of Texas, or cease molesting her! There is no telling what a day will bring forth. Congress is corrupt enough to do any thing. The right of petition has again been cloven down, and no excitement has followed. This would not be borne in England, but Slavery is a more corrupting, more terrible power than Monarchy. Anti-slavery is indubitably lengthening its cords and strengthening its stakes; but it has a mighty work yet to perform. If the abolitionists would only be more uncompromising and more courageous in their dealings with the foe, they would achieve a hundred victories where they now obtain only ten. Multitudes of them yet need to be emancipated from their sectarian and party shackles, and to stand fast in the liberty of Christ.

The annual Massachusetts Fair will open in a few days, and we think under favorable circumstances. The articles received from Ireland excite our admiration and gratitude. Heaven bless the generous spirits there, who, with but a small portion of this world's goods in their possession, and surrounded by distress and poverty in every form, have contrived to show that their hearts are as expansive as suffering humanity, and that their benevolence is not confined to the Emerald Isle on which they reside. Would that I could see them all individually, take them by the hand, and, as the mouth-piece of three millions of the most wretched creatures to be found on the face of the earth, express the feelings of my heart in view of their kindness! Truly, I want to see Ireland again, more than words can express; and especially do I desire to see Dublin. The [James] Haughtons, [Richard D.] Webbs, [Richard] Allens, &c. &c. do not know how much they are beloved by me, because I cannot tell them, and have no means to make it strikingly manifest. Extraordinary people they are — abounding in all good traits of mind, heart and intellect. I *must* see them again — but how or when? Alas! I cannot tell. Will none of them make us a visit? Is it really impracticable for such an arrangement to be made? Next summer, certainly, some one or more of them (the more the better) must come over and reciprocate the visit we made them in 1840. Every thing shall be done to make their visit delightful, and without any pecuniary expense to them during their sojourn among us.

Please say to Richard Allen, that his present of four valuable and neatly wrought linen shirts has come safely to hand, for which I beg to proffer him my most grateful thanks. If I knew who made them, I would also send my compliments to her, for her skill with the needle. These tokens of friendship are more valued by me than all worldly honors and emoluments.

I have received presents, also, in money, from dear Webb and others in Dublin, to sustain the Liberator. Elizabeth Pease has also made a most generous donation for the same object. These gifts have helped to preserve the existence of the paper during the present year; and without them, though entirely unexpected, I know not what could have been done to get along. Our subscription list is very much reduced, and the hatred of the enemies of God and man towards the Liberator is increasing continually. It often seems to me that there is no alternative left but to let the paper go down; but the good providence of God has thus far sustained it, and brought signal relief in the hour of extreme distress. Tell dear Webb that, with his large family, and limited means, and many calls for charity, I cannot feel as if I ought to retain what he has sent over; and yet I know it would hurt his feelings for me to send it back to him.

My health is very much improved, but my family continues to be afflicted with sickness. Within the last three weeks, every member of it, except myself, has had a most violent attack of the influenza, attended with a fever and a bad cough, but they are now all convalescent. Helen has again partially dislocated her elbow, by over-exertion, and will probably have to go to Connecticut again to see Dr. [Stephen] Sweet. We are now living in the city, in Pine-street, at the south end. Oliver Johnson and his wife are living under the same roof with us. George Thompson is now a very tall boy, active in work or play, but dull as a scholar. He can scarcely spell the simplest words, though he has been to school some four or five years! He abhors a book, and would much prefer that reading and writing should come by nature, than be obtained in any other method. He is far from being a dunce, but he is too restless to give any attention to his books. However, I feel no anxiety on that score. Hereafter he may take a sudden start, and be an inveterate book-worm. William is a much better scholar than George, and is getting along fast enough. Wendell has mastered the alphabet, and is the brightest and most beautiful boy of the lot. — They all remember you with great vividness, and frequently ask when they shall see and frolic with you again. Charles is now beginning to walk alone, and bids fair to be a fine boy. These constitute my earthly jewels. My affection for them is strong and pure, but not idolatrous. It shall be my aim to bring them up to be a blessing to the world.

Bro. George W. Benson is still located in the "Northampton Community," which promises to be a very successful experiment. James Boyle and his wife are also members of the same community. The subject of social reorganization is attracting general attention, and exciting a growing interest. Many schemes are in embryo, and others have had a birth, and are now struggling for an existence. As experiments, to bless our race, I feel an interest in them all, though I am not very sanguine as to the result of this new species of colonization.

John A. Collins is almost entirely absorbed in his "Community" project at Skaneateles, and is therefore unable to do much directly for the anti-slavery cause. He goes for a community of interest, and against all individual possessions, whether of land or its fruits — of labor or its products; but he does not act very consistently with his principles, though he says he does the best he can in the present state of society. He holds, with Robert Owen, that man is the creature of circumstances, and therefore not deserving of praise or blame for what he does — a most absurd and demoralizing doctrine, in my opinion, which will make shipwreck of any man or any scheme under its guidance, in due season. Still, it cannot be denied that circumstances are often very unfavorable to the development of man's faculties and moral nature; and if, by a reorganization of society, these can be rendered more favorable, — as doubtless they can, — let it take place. But it is an internal rather than an outward reorganization that is needed to put away the evil that is in the world.

But the last five minutes have come, before the closing of the mail, and I must bring this hasty scrawl to a close, by begging you to let me hear from you as often as convenient, even if you get little or nothing from me in return; and by sending kind remembrances to you, without number, from all the family, and thousands of warm-hearted friends, to whom you are unspeakably dear. To all the Dublin friends give the latest assurances of my unquenchable love for them.

Yours, affectionately,

Wm. Lloyd Garrison.

ALS: Garrison Papers, Boston Public Library.

1. James 1:4.
2. The Cunard Line, founded in 1839, was unchallenged by competition until the 1850's.
3. The fifth annual meeting of the New-England Non-Resistance Society, held in Boston, October 30, 1843.
4. George W. F. Mellen (c. 1804–1875) was a chemist at 49 Chatham Street, Boston, who published in 1841 a book entitled *An Argument on the Unconstitutionality of Slavery.* (See Garrison's letter to John A. Collins, December 1, 1840, n. 9, *Letters*, II, 727.)
5. Adin Ballou (1803–1890), a Universalist clergyman and reformer, was the founder of the Hopedale Community, the first of the Utopian enterprises. He persistently maintained his nonresistance position even during the Civil War. Ballou spent his later years engaged in literary activities.
6. John Murray Spear (1804–1887), a Universalist minister and reformer, was interested in the plight of prisoners and was active in helping former convicts adjust to freedom. In 1845, with his brother, Charles, he began publishing *The Hangman,* later known as *The Prisoner's Friend.*
7. On the final day of his term as President, John Tyler implemented the joint congressional resolution of February 1845, offering Texas annexation and statehood.

---

9 0

TO ANNE W. WESTON

Tuesday Evening.
[December 19, 1843.] [1]

My Dear Friend:

Having taken it for granted, that the extraordinary violence of the storm would prevent the gathering of any number of friends at the

Bazaar this evening, and having, therefore, made no preparation to speak to edification, I beg to throw myself upon the indulgence of such as may be present, and to be excused for non-attendance, especially in view of the lateness of the hour, and of a night's editorial labor before me. It is scarcely possible that any thing could fall from my lips, calculated either to enlighten or encourage those who are so well-read and so thoroughly posted up in regard to our sacred cause.

Yours, in great haste,

Wm. Lloyd Garrison.

Miss A. W. Weston.

ALS: Garrison Papers, Boston Public Library.

1. This letter was undoubtedly written on the day the antislavery fair opened, or Tuesday, December 19. In his report of the fair in *The Liberator*, January 12, 1844, Garrison expresses his surprise that in spite of the violent storm and the bad condition of the streets the bazaar had raised $2,800 for the cause.

---

9 1

TO EDMUND QUINCY

Boston, Jan. 5, 1844.

My dear Quincy:

At our Board meeting on Tuesday, you were unanimously chosen to write the Annual Report this year.[1] They all specially desire that you should do so — and I am most anxious that you should, as well as Mrs. [Maria W.] Chapman. I promise to stand by your Report as far as my conscience and judgment will allow; and more you will not exact of me. Accompanying this is a hasty synopsis of topics I have made, from which you can make a selection. Friend [Oliver] Johnson will examine a file of the Standard, and send you the result by Monday. To-morrow, I leave for New-Hampshire, to be gone ten days. In haste,

Yours, faithfully,

W. L. Garrison.

ALS: Garrison Papers, Sophia Smith Collection, Smith College Library.

1. Quincy both wrote the report for the Board of Managers and delivered it at the twelfth annual meeting of the Massachusetts Anti-Slavery Society in Faneuil Hall, January 24–27.

9 2

TO LOUISA GILMAN LORING

Boston,
Jan. 5, 1844.

Esteemed Friend:

On returning home from my office, this evening, Helen put into my hands your kind note; enclosing the generous sum of twenty dollars as a token of your good will and friendship for me and mine. Most heartily do I thank you in my own behalf — in hers — in that of my four little ones. As the receipts of the Liberator (from every source) fell short of its expenses about two hundred dollars, during the past year, your donation is peculiarly acceptable.

Your friendship I prize beyond the value of rubies; and when I say yours, I mean, also, that of Mr. [Ellis Gray] Loring; — for you twain are indeed one — one in affection, one in philanthropy, one in virtuous excellence, one in modest worth, and one in your long continued kindness toward myself.

May 1 never justly forfeit your confidence in my integrity and uprightness! My admiration of the magnanimity and catholic spirit of you both, is stronger than words can express. If you cannot agree with me in all my opinions, you are not for suppressing the honest utterance of them, but feel disposed to sustain the freedom and independence of the Liberator. I am quite as fallible as other men — quite as liable to err — but I am sure of one thing, that I love the truth, that I desire to save and bless the human race, that I am against whatever detracts from the glory of God or the welfare of the world, as far as I can discern aright.

Helen feels deeply indebted to you for your many kindnesses, and gratefully unites with me in wishing you and Mr. Loring many a happy new year

Hastily, but heartily,

Your much obliged friend,

Wm. Lloyd Garrison.

Mrs. Louisa Loring.

Handwritten transcription: Garrison Papers, Boston Public Library.

9 3

TO *THE LIBERATOR*

MILFORD, N. H. Jan. 8, 1844.

DEAR FRIEND:

I am now on a flying visit to the Granite State, and shall probably be absent from my editorial post some ten or twelve days. Who can eulogize too extravagantly the rapidity and comfort of a rail-road conveyance at this inclement season of the year? My ride from Boston to Nashua was as pleasant as though it had been on a June morning, with flowers in bloom, and Nature clad in her most gorgeous habiliments. The car had summer weather inside, so that it was a matter of perfect indifference to the passengers how Boreas raged around it. Absorbed in reading, I found myself at Nashua almost unconsciously. Success to all rail-road enterprises, the world over! Humanity can contemplate them with delight, even though old Mammon may, for a time, endeavor to make them subservient to his own base purposes. They will bring the human race together in a manner and under circumstances that will mightily hasten the time when 'nation shall no longer lift up sword against nation, neither shall they learn war any more.' [1] O for the day when peace, plenty, joy and righteousness shall pervade our wo-begone, sin-stricken earth universally!

I was somewhat disappointed in not meeting my beloved friend N. P. ROGERS at Nashua, though I hope to see him before my return home. Seeing a temperance hotel near the depot, I went into it, forgetting that it was kept by an esteemed acquaintance of mine, JOSEPH STETSON. I believe his is the only hotel in the place, that is conducted on strictly temperance principles; and I need not urge on the teetotal travelling community the duty of sustaining it by their patronage. Mr. STETSON is a worthy, industrious man, who has long been manfully struggling against adverse fortune, and who deserves all possible encouragement in his present position; for a great deal yet remains to be done for the cause of temperance in Nashua.

I found a strong hearted abolition friend of this place at N. waiting to convey me in his sleigh to Milford.[2] It was my first sleigh-ride for the season; and as the road was in a most excellent condition, and our horse a good traveller, we came almost with the fleetness and ease of steam conveyance.

In this town the anti-slavery forces are nominally strong — probably more so than those of any other place in New-Hampshire. At the last election, the Liberty party cast one hundred and one votes; and there were from thirty to fifty abolition voters who did not vote, from consciencious scruples and other causes. There is a wide division, an impassable gulph, here, between the friends of old and new organization — the former being considerably in the minority, but as active, courageous, uncompromising, generous, out-and-out abolitionists as can be found on any portion of the globe. They are nearly all 'come-outers,' of the truest mould and the best stamp; and by their words of truth and deeds of power, they cause priestcraft and sectarism, in all this region, to gnaw their tongues for pain. The new organizationists go *en masse* with the Liberty party, with the priesthood, and with sect, and are as hollow and spurious as religious imposture could desire. Morally speaking, they say nothing and do nothing, except to slander and assail those faithful champions of our cause, who are directing their energies for the overthrow of 'the bulwarks of American slavery.' They have no controversy with religious pro-slavery, but are noisy and voluble when election day comes, and active in their endeavors to secure for themselves the loaves and fishes of office. Voting the Liberty party ticket is with them 'the end of the law for righteousness to every one that believeth'[3] that James G. Birney ought to be President of the United States. Morally speaking, I am more and more convinced, by inquiry and observation, that the Liberty party, as such, *in New-England*, is utterly unprincipled, and the most insidious, and therefore the most dangerous foe with which genuine anti-slavery has to contend. I am pained, I am surprised to learn, from various quarters, that there are many who call themselves 'old organized abolitionists,' who cast their votes with the Liberty party, though they know, in this part of the country at least, it was 'conceived in sin, and brought forth in iniquity,'[4] that its leaders are not trust-worthy, and that a large majority of its supporters are making use of it as a substitute for moral action, and as a foil to ward off the blows which are aimed at a pro-slavery church and priesthood. Let them not say that they are reduced to the alternative of voting with that party, in consequence of the pro-slavery character of the whig and democratic parties. It is not true. If they must vote, they can testify against all these parties by scattering their votes on those in whom they can confide. But I think duty requires of them, as abolitionists, not to vote at all, but to 'let the dead bury their dead,'[5] to refuse to sustain the present Constitution of the United States, and to demand, in the name of God and humanity, a dissolution of our blood-cemented, atheistical Union.

On Saturday evening, I lectured to the people on slavery, and yesterday, in the forenoon and afternoon, addressed them at considerable length on Non-Resistance, the Ministry, Church, Worship, the Sabbath, &c. There were many more present than I expected to see.

In the evening, I listened to a temperance lecture from a young Irishman, of considerable talent and address,[6] but was sorry to hear him advocate 'legal suasion' for the rum-sellers — in other words, the use of club law, the sword and bayonet, in order to manifest the *love* of *Washingtonians*, and the *spirit* of the *Lamb of God!*

But I write in haste, and must add some further particulars in my next letter. I start immediately for New Ipswich.

Yours, faithfully,

WM. LLOYD GARRISON.

N.B. Just remind the genuine friends of anti-slavery in and out of Massachusetts, that they are expected to rally in great strength at the annual meeting of the State Society on the 23d instant in Boston, in order that the State House and Faneuil Hall may rock beneath their tread, and resound with their voices.[7]

Printed: *The Liberator*, January 12, 1844.

1. With one minor substitution, a quotation from Isaiah 2:4.
2. Leonard Chase (1811–1869), a manufacturer and merchant, came originally from Millbury, Massachusetts. (Letter to the editor from Margaret S. McCormack, Milford Historical Society, New Hampshire, September 15, 1970.)
3. Romans 10:4.
4. An adaptation of Isaiah 59:4.
5. Matthew 8:22.
6. Not identified.
7. According to the account in *The Liberator*, February 2, 1844, the meetings began on January 24.

94

TO HELEN E. GARRISON

New Ipswich, Jan. 12, 1844.

Dear Helen:

I wrote a few lines from Milford for the Liberator of this week, giving a sketch of my lecturing in that place on Saturday evening and all day Sunday. On Monday, I came to this place (which is about 14 miles from M.) in an open sleigh, and with a spirited horse, in company with my esteemed friend Leonard Chase. The mercury was almost down to zero, and the wind blew the snow somewhat violently, and "cut like a razor"; but we were well protected by good buffalo skins, and felt the cold very slightly. I had my ears tied up snugly; and if I can contrive to keep them warm, I care very little either for the blasts of old Boreas, or for the stealthy ruffian Cold. We arrived about 2 o'clock at friend Hammond's, and were received by him and his warm-hearted wife (who is a gem of a woman) in the most affectionate and hearty manner.[1] They have one of the snuggest, best contrived, prettiest little cottages that you have ever seen. It reminds me of the time when we made our romantic sojourn in the Roxbury cottage — a remembrance which always excites a thrill of pleasure in my bosom.[2] I do not wonder that Mrs. Hammond feels reluctant to be separated from this dear spot, and from this her native place; but they will probably go to the Northampton Association in the spring, and most valuable acquisitions they will be. Heaven prosper that Association in all good things! Its failure would cause the enemies of equal rights and radical reform to shout aloud for joy. Mr. Hammond intends leaving for Northampton next week, on a flying visit to confer with bro. George, at his request.

The first thing you will be anxious to hear about is my health. I am quite as well as usual, and have taken no cold since I left home. The weather has been cold, but pleasant — the mercury having once fallen as low as 4 degrees below zero. Our cottage is warmed by a furnace, so that it is kept in a very comfortable state. You know my habitual *cautiousness*, and so need give yourself no uneasiness on my account.

The next thing you will be anxious to hear about is my portrait, and what is the probability of its being an accurate one. I arrived so late on Monday, that nothing could be done on that day. I have sat three times, and already such progress has been made as to warrant the belief that success will crown friend Hammond's efforts. He feels a great deal of anxiety — perhaps too much — in regard to it, and will try to do his best. Phrenologically, he has form and imitation large, but he is somewhat deficient in the organs of constructiveness, color and ideality. He is evidently possessed of genius and talent, but has had very poor opportunities to perfect himself in the art. His wife has excellent critical powers, and will aid him very much by her suggestions in regard to my features. I hope, for your sake, dear Helen, that the portrait will be a true one; for I know it will give you great delight to possess a copy of it.[3]

The next thing you will wish to know is, when I shall be at home. At the earliest hour possible — for when did I ever choose to remain needlessly away from you and the dear little ones? But this is not to answer your inquiry. Well, then, you may expect to see me on Wednesday night. The painting at this season cannot be hurried, as it is somewhat difficult to dry it; hence, a little more time will be required on that account. I wish to give friend Hammond all the time I can conveniently spare, in justice to himself, and for the sake of obtaining a good portrait. You need no assurance from me, that I wish to be with you, even this very hour if it were possible; especially on account of your lame arm and household affairs.

My presence in this place creates a good deal of sensation, and in the region round about. I have already given three public lectures — two on slavery, and one on non-resistance. One evening, I occupied the Methodist meeting-house; the other evenings, the schoolhouse, where I am to lecture all day next Sunday, on Worship, the Church, the Ministry, the Sabbath, &c. My audiences have been large, and highly respectable, notwithstanding the mad-dog cry of "infidel," raised against me by the Irreverend Mr. Lee and his sattellites.[4] He refused to read the notice for my lectures, but it was read by the Baptist and Methodist clergymen [5] — though none of these have attended my meetings. A considerable number of Mr. Lee's church members and congregation, however, have been present. As far as I can learn, my lectures have produced a deep and salutary impression, and I trust will serve to aid the cause of God and down-trodden humanity, universally. On each occasion, I begged the people to consider the meeting as free to them as to myself — to interrupt me, if they should wish to, at any stage of my remarks — to propound any objections — to raise any inquiries — to start any difficulties, &c. &c.; but not a single individual had any thing to say, on any point — though I attacked the church, the clergy, the whig, democratic and liberty parties, in the most unsparing manner! At the close of my non-resistance lecture last evening, (I spoke for two hours, and though the house was crowded, the audience seemed to be spell-bound to the end,) a good Second Advent woman rose, and made a few excellent remarks — saying that she felt free to speak in a meeting where William Lloyd Garrison was, and endorsing every word that had fallen from my lips. She did not say that the world was about to be destroyed, but her language implied as much. There are a number here, who embrace the views of Mr. [William] Miller, and continue steadfast in his doctrine. They are "come-outers" from the churches and hold a separate meeting of their own. Such persons must have veneration and marvellousness to a great degree, and while they are under such excitement, reason and argument are of very little avail in convincing them of their delusion.

The Liberty party here is made up of very worthless materials. It rules the town, politically.

Persons have come from a long distance to hear me. Among these have been Dr. Bachelder and his wife from Marlboro', (22 miles off.) [6] They arrived yesterday, and heard me last evening. He will return home to-day, but she will probably remain over the Sunday. He is the one who wrote to Oliver [Johnson], about my eulogy on Dr. [Stephen]

Sweet and Dr. [Samuel] Thompson; [7] but he said nothing to me about it, and treated me with great cordiality, earnestly inviting me to visit his place. His wife, he says, is a thorough-going "Garrison *man*." But I must stop. Mr. and Mrs. Hammond send friendly greetings to you and Mr. and Mrs. Johnson. Love to all.

Ever yours,

W. L. Garrison.

ALS: Garrison Papers, Boston Public Library.

1. Elisha Livermore Hammond (1799–1882), married to Eliza Preston of New Ipswich, New Hampshire, was a committed abolitionist and temperance reformer. By trade a farmer and an artist, he was shortly to join the Northampton Association, in which he was active until 1846. During the last thirty five years of his life he continued to live in the vicinity. (Sheffeld, pp. 221–224.)

2. Garrison refers to the cottage in which he and Helen lived during the first months of their marriage.

3. The portrait has apparently not survived.

4. Samuel Lee (1803–1881), a graduate of Yale College and Theological Seminary, served as pastor of the First Congregational Church in New Ipswich from 1836 until his retirement in 1860. (Charles H. Chandler, *The History of New Ipswich, N.H.*, Fitchburg, Mass., 1914, pp. 127, 129, 514.)

5. Not identified.

6. James Batcheller (1791–1866), a physician living in Marlborough, New Hampshire, was married to Persis Sweetser (died 1851). A graduate of Dartmouth, Dr. Batcheller served in both houses of the state legislature and was a strong advocate of temperance and abolition. (Charles A. Bemis, *History of the Town of Marlborough*, Boston, 1881, pp. 201–203.)

7. See Garrison's letter to *The Liberator*, October 13, 1843.

---

9 5

TO *THE LIBERATOR*

New Ipswich, (N.H.) Jan. 15, 1844.

Dear Friend:

On Monday last, I was brought to this village by my worthy friend Leonard Chase, of Milford, who, for several years past, has been among the foremost and most devoted advocates of the anti-slavery cause — having nobly laid on its altar his means, time, talents, reputation, health, every thing, and suffered persecution in proportion to his fidelity. At the present time, he is in deep affliction at the recent death of his estimable wife and two children, all torn from his embrace within the space of a month or six weeks.[1] Thus, thrice has his peace been slain by the darts of the 'insatiate archer,'[2] in the most affecting manner; but his is the sorrow of tender affection, not of gloomy misanthropy — for lofty and immoveable is his faith in God. His wife was indeed a partner, and a 'help meet for him.'[3] She was endowed with

unusual moral courage, a clear perception of truth and right, great
patience and forbearance under strong provocation, affections of the
most generous and expansive nature, and a capacious heart. Her manners were unobtrusive and quiet, but with her natural modesty she
combined rare independence and firmness of character. While her
sympathies were specially drawn toward our wretched slave population, hers was not a local philanthropy, nor a mind of 'one idea.' She
was not afraid freely and fairly to investigate any subject; and wherein
she discovered herself to be in error, or truth to lead, she was prompt
to walk in the light [4] that was vouchsafed to her. In every one of the
reforms, now struggling for the mastery over an evil world, and which
shall in future times make the present age famous, she took a peculiar
interest; and the certainty of losing caste by espousing them was one
of the strong inducements that led her to be a humble witness in their
behalf. She and her husband had long been members of an orthodox
church; but having had their vision purged so as clearly to perceive
the inherent rottenness of every such sectarian organization, and the
entire falsity of that religion which 'comes by observation,' [5] and which
consists mainly of temple worship, sabbatical observances, and carnal
ordinances, they refused any longer to be connected with it. Up to
that time, they were in 'good standing' and excellent repute; but, as
soon as they sundered the fetters of spiritual usurpation, their names
were cast out as evil, and a most malignant spirit was exhibited toward
them by those who professed to be — *par excellence* — the meek and
lowly disciples of Christ. When their little daughter died, they dispensed with the mummery of a priestly performance at the funeral;
and when she and her babe soon followed that little one to her
heavenly abode, again no forms were observed at the funeral, but
every mind was left free to give utterance to its thoughts and feelings.
On each occasion, the coffin was not stained with the ordinary hue:
the first was made of white pine, and allowed to retain its natural
color — the second was painted of a bluish aspect. These *alarming*
departures from customary usages excited great sensation in the godly
(?) town of Milford, and every pious formalist and sanctimonious
hypocrite rolled up their eyes and lifted up their hands in holy horror.
Enslaving human beings, and war with all its atrocities, were not to
be compared in enormity with such conduct. All tongues became busy
respecting this 'infidel' innovation, nor to this hour have they found
rest. What scandal they have uttered, what fictions fabricated, what
caricatures put in circulation, I will not stop to relate. Miserable revilers! in vain do ye strain at a gnat, while ye without difficulty swallow
a camel! [6] O, the hateful character of the popular religion of the day!
It is a frightful imposture — dishonoring to God, degrading to man,

a curse to the world. But it shall fall — for the winds and rains of truth and freedom are descending upon it — and 'great shall be the fall thereof.' [7]

Our ride from Milford to New Ipswich was rather uncomfortable to the body, the mercury ranging nearly to zero, and a strong wind prevailing, blowing the loose snow and 'cutting like a razor'; but our hearts were warm, and full of enjoyment.

My present visit to this place is for a special object, you know — an object which I think will be successfully attained, though it is something that will interest my friends more than it does myself — and it is for their sake alone it is undertaken.[8] I find it will be necessary for me to remain here a few days longer than I at first contemplated; so that you may not expect to see me before Saturday evening.

Though I did not come here with a view to lecturing, I have given five public addresses on Slavery, Non-Resistance, and Christianity, at the request of friends — the two last yesterday (Sunday) in the fore-noon and afternoon. My audiences have been uniformly larger than I anticipated; for here, as elsewhere, priestly malice, *in an anti-slavery garb*, has long been busy in holding me up to the people as an 'infidel,' and the enemy of all righteousness, because I do not shun to 'declare the whole counsel of God,' [9] whether men will hear or forbear. Some of my auditors have come five, ten, and even twenty miles, to hear me; so much am I indebted to my calumniators for the prevailing curiosity to see and hear what I may have to say. Thus are the cunning caught in their own craftiness; and they who have made a pit for the innocent have themselves justly fallen into it.[10] One thing is certain — if they who have listened to me have not been convinced that all my views are sound on the various topics on which I have discoursed, their minds have been disabused, to a very great extent, in regard to my principles and purposes. I will add, that all my meetings have been as free to others as to myself. I have invited interrogation, objection and reply, in regard to any of the doctrines I have advanced; but no one seemed disposed to say a single word in opposition, notwithstanding they were of a most startling and radical character. Rely upon it, the SECOND REFORMATION has begun, and in ten years a mighty moral and religious revolution will have been witnessed on both sides of the Atlantic. Tyranny may rage, and priestcraft writhe and howl; but 'strong is the Lord God who judgeth them,' [11] and he shall dash them in pieces as a potter's vessel.[12]

The orthodox clergyman here is SAMUEL LEE, who pretends to be an abolitionist, but whose *support* of our cause is a thousand times more detrimental to it than the most violent *opposition* of an avowed enemy. He refused to read a notice of my lectures on slavery to 'his people,' and was careful to abstain from giving any countenance to them. He is a conceited spiritual rabbi, on a Lilliputian scale, who combines in his character — as priests generally do — the tyrant ruler and the vassal time-server. Verily, he has his reward — or, if not, it shall be given to him in due season.

Yours in haste,

WM. LLOYD GARRISON.

Printed: *The Liberator*, January 19, 1844.

1. Garrison refers to Chase's wife, Mary Isabelle Dickey (1814–1843), who apparently had died in childbirth, along with her infant, in mid-December; and to his daughter, Frances Elvira Chase (1841–1843), who had died in mid-November.

2. Edward Young, *Night Thoughts*, Night I, line 212.

3. Genesis 2:18.

4. Possibly a reference to I John 1:7.

5. Garrison's adaptation of Luke 17:20.

6. Garrison paraphrases Matthew 23:24.

7. Garrison adapts Matthew 7:27.

8. As early as 1841 the abolitionists had been concerned about the recalcitrance of the people of New Hampshire to reform (see Garrison's letter to Parker Pillsbury, February 23, 1841). Even dedicated abolitionist Nathaniel P. Rogers had been so resistant to systematic organizations that he was about to begin an unfortunate controversy with the New Hampshire Anti-Slavery Society over the control of the *Herald of Freedom*, supposedly the official organ of the society. Garrison was starting, to use Abby Kelley's description (*Life*, III, 120), "to upturn some of the hard soil of New Hampshire." He was to be followed in subsequent months by Frederick Douglass, Parker Pillsbury, Stephen S. Foster, and others.

9. A reference to Acts 20:27.

10. Garrison adapts I Corinthians 3:19 and Psalms 57:6.

11. With one substitution, a quotation from Revelation 18:8.

12. Garrison adapts Psalms 2:9.

---

9 6

TO GEORGE W. BENSON

New Ipswich, N. H., Jan. 15, 1844.

Dear George:

Our friend [Elisha L.] Hammond (whom you are expecting to see at Northampton this week, and under whose hospitable roof I am now abiding, that he may make on canvass another face like unto mine,) is extremely sorry that it will not be in his power to visit you, according to your appointment and his desire, at the present time; but he thinks it is highly probable that he shall attend our annual meeting next week in Boston, where he presumes you will be, and he is calculating that you and James Boyle will make a visit to New Ipswich, immediately after that meeting.

The obstacle that interposes to prevent his going to Northampton, now, is — MYSELF. So, excuse him, and blame me, if you please. You know I have come hither to get, if possible, (what no artist has yet been able to make,) an accurate portrait of the arch incendiary Garrison, in order that an engraving may accompany the volume of my writings, which has been projected by my friend [Oliver] Johnson, but which, I apprehend, will not be very soon completed.[1] Bro. Hammond has artistic genius, but he has lacked the necessary opportunities, means, time and practice, which are necessary to perfect one in so divine an art. He has undertaken the task, in my case, "with fear and trembling," but there is no doubt that he will "work out" a good portrait, that will be deemed worthy of "salvation," rather than destruction.[2] His anxiety to succeed well, however, has served more to embarrass than to aid him; for, after spending three days on his first sketch, he threw it aside, and began another, which, at the close of the third sitting this day, looks so much like me, that I think none of my friends would need a formal introduction to it. We shall need the remainder of this week to complete it. I have not known how to spare the time; but the great gratification which will be given to my friends, on both sides of the Atlantic, should he succeed, induces me to be absent awhile from my post. I shall probably be in the city on Friday, but, at farthest, on Saturday evening, if no unforeseen obstacle prevent.

I am very much pleased with Mr. Hammond. He is a most amiable man, modest, quick to discern the truth, prompt to walk in the path of duty, heartily interested in every reform, and anxious to promote the welfare of mankind. He has genius accompanied with perseverance, and will yet shine as an artist, should scope be given to his efforts. He seems to be strongly inclined to join your Association, and will certainly be a valuable member, should he do so.

Mrs. Hammond is a very interesting woman, of excellent good sense and pleasing manners, a thorough-going reformer without fanaticism, as cheerful as a canary-bird, and a first-rate wife. This is her native place — here she has always lived — here she was married — here she is comfortably situated — and here are her relations, friends and acquaintance. Hence, it is not surprising that she rather hesitates in regard to removing to Northampton, especially as she has no personal knowledge of your operations. If he shall decide to go, however, she will readily go with him. They are now living in a sweet little cottage, which he erected several years ago, and on which he will have to make a considerable sacrifice, in case he sells it.

Friend Hammond has drawn the plan of a Community House, which he will show and explain to you, either at Boston or here.[3] As a great deal depends on that structure, I hope no pains will be spared to make it in a high degree attractive and convenient. Deliberate well before you decide, and consult the best models to be found either in theory, or in actual existence.

I hope you will not fail to be at our annual meeting. We have engaged the State House for two evenings, and shall hold our other meetings either in Faneuil Hall or the "Miller Tabernacle." [4]

A letter which I have just received from Oliver Johnson informs me that all at home are as well as usual. Little Charlie has been somewhat ill with teething, and Angy [Angelette] has had an attack of fever, but they were both on the recovery.

Remember me with brotherly love to Catharine, and affectionately to the children. I wish the friends connected with the Association to be assured, that I feel a special interest in their welfare, and shall gladly avail myself of every convenient opportunity to say a good word in behalf of your reformatory enterprise. May love and peace abound among you all. Please give my regards to Mr. and Mrs. [David] Mack, Mr. and Mrs. [William] Adams [Adam], Mrs. [James] Boyle and sister, &c.

Yours, lovingly,

Wm. Lloyd Garrison.

ALS: Garrison Papers, Boston Public Library.

1. Although Johnson did not finish this projected volume, *Selections from the Writings and Speeches of William Lloyd Garrison,* collected by Robert F. Wallcut, was published in Boston in 1852.
2. Garrison adapts Philippians 2:12.
3. There is no firm evidence that the new community house was ever built.
4. The Miller Tabernacle, the center for the Second Advent movement in Boston, was located on Howard Street and was dedicated May 4, 1843. Accommodating several thousand persons, it was frequently used for public meetings. (Ira V. Brown, "The Millerites and the Boston Press," *New England Quarterly,* 16:592–614, December 1963.)

97

TO WILLIAM CHALMERS

Boston, April 27, 1844.

Dear Sir —

The anniversary of the American Anti-Slavery Society will be holden in the Apollo Hall, 410, Broadway, in the city of New-York, on Tuesday, May 7th. In behalf of that Society, I cordially invite you to be present at the meeting, and to be one of the speakers on that occasion, to testify against that 'sum of all villanies,' American slavery.[1] The great distinctive doctrine of the Society is, that immediate emancipation is the duty of the master and the right of the slave.

Respectfully yours,

WM. LLOYD GARRISON,
President of the American A. S. Society.

Printed: *The Liberator*, May 8, 1846. This letter, along with related correspondence, was first printed in the Edinburgh *Witness*, May 21, 1845.

William Chalmers (1812–1894), a Scots clergyman, was the son of Thomas Chalmers, the theologian and moderator of the Free Church of Scotland. He left the Presbyterian church in 1843 and became a well-known polemicist for the new Free Church. (Letter to the editor from C. Duncan Rice, Yale University, December 26, 1970.)

1. Chalmers declined the invitation because of Garrison's stand on the Sabbath question (see *The Liberator*, May 8, 1846). The quotation is from John Wesley, *Journal*, February 12, 1772. (See *Journal*, New York, 1906, III, 461.)

---

9 8

TO JAMES B. YERRINTON

NEW-YORK, May 7, 1844.

MY DEAR FRIEND YERRINTON:

It is now two o'clock, P.M. Our anniversary meeting in the Apollo Hall has just closed; and as the mail will close soon, I can send you only a very brief sketch of the proceedings.

The meeting was opened with some introductory remarks by myself, in which I congratulated the Society that, on this its tenth anniversary, it still maintained its original impregnable and sublime position, as the uncompromising foe of slavery — as the untiring friend of universal emancipation; that its principles remained unshaken, its doctrines uncorrupted, its measures rational, energetic and effective, its purposes humane, glorious and godlike; and that its victories over prejudice and pro-slavery continued to be frequent, heart-inspiring and magnificent. I congratulated it, moreover, that it is still feared, detested and assailed by all that is corrupt, oppressive and demoniacal in the land — still the terror of oppressors — still the hope of the oppressed — still the sheet anchor of American honor, justice and freedom; that while its members and friends are reviled and rejected in their native land, they are admired and applauded by the friends of freedom and philanthropy throughout the world, who are bidding them God speed, and continually eulogizing their noble deeds. Finally,

I congratulated them on having enlisted in a great and glorious cause — the sacred cause of liberty; that on their side they had their country's Declaration of Independence — the Bible — the Gospel of Jesus Christ — The Lion of the tribe of Judah and the Lamb of God — the Eternal Spirit of Truth — the Lord Almighty — and with all these, the certainty of final victory over all opposition.

I alluded to the circumstances under which we met, as of thrilling interest and deep importance, in view of the strong efforts that were making to annex Texas to this country for the express purpose avowedly to perpetuate and extend slavery and the slave trade; and gave it as my deliberate conviction and emphatic testimony that, with or without Texas, the time had come for the American Anti-Slavery Society to hoist the banner of 'Repeal,' and to declare the American Union at an end. I urged upon the friends of liberty to be united in this great revolutionary measure, and to allow nothing to alienate them from each other.

> 'At last conspire!
> In one immortal cause as brothers blend
> To one immortal end!
> Be knit with one desire —
> Think as one mind, and move
> As one gigantic body, strong
> To cope with injury and wrong:
> By calm resolve — which rage
> Shall but make firmer still —
> Bid down another, better, golden age
> Of constancy and will!' [1]

After the reading of the 4th chapter of Hosea, prayer was offered by Dr. Brisbane of Ohio, who has so nobly emancipated all his slaves.[2] Adin Ballou, of Hopedale, Mass. then made a very clear, cogent and eloquent speech on the superiority of moral over political power in every great moral and christian reform, and as necessary to induce that change in public sentiment, by which alone any effective political action could be consummated. The speech was worthy of the man and the occasion — and that is praise enough. After he had finished, up sprang the *Reverend* Charles W. Denison, and declared in a tumid, ridiculous and atheistical speech, that the doctrine advanced was destructive of the moral government of God!!! [3] He then went on ranting about the ballot-box as being the power and wisdom of God — the weapon sanctioned by Jesus Christ — and the only effectual mode to overturn slavery and regenerate the world!! He made an attack on non-resistants, and argued the divinity of human government. He said he had a right to speak and be heard in the meeting, and that he was carrying out his anti-slavery every where. All this was sufficiently impudent and shameless, in one who, in 1840, attempted to destroy the American A.S. Society, by secession with others from its platform, because Abby Kelley was placed on a business committee! I felt it my duty to unmask this base apostate, and to tear off the hide from this wolf in sheep's clothing. Charles C. Burleigh followed in a speech that ground the trumpery speech of Denison to powder; and the meeting closed by an impressive speech from Abby Kelley, who gave a narrative of the rise and progress of the anti-slavery cause in the United States, and of the division that took place in 1840. Her speech was very powerful.

We have a strong company of true-hearted men and women, from various parts of the Union, and shall no doubt have a spirited time at our subsequent meetings.

Yours, in great haste,

WM. LLOYD GARRISON.

Printed: *The Liberator*, May 10, 1844.

1. Not identified.
2. William Henry Brisbane (1803–1878) was a native of South Carolina who, at great financial sacrifice, had freed his slaves and moved to the North. He was a prolific author, his works including *The Fanatic or the Perils of Peter Pliant* (1846), *Slaveholding Examined in the Light of the Holy Bible* (1847), and *Amanda: A Tale for the Times* (1848). For a summary of his antislavery position and Garrison's opinion of him see *The Liberator*, March 1, 1844. (*Who Was Who in America.*)
3. Charles Wheeler Denison (1812–1881) was editor of the Philadelphia *World*. One of the founders of the American Anti-Slavery Society, he left the old organization in 1840 over the issue of woman's rights. During the Civil War he was to propagandize the northern cause in England, where he later edited a paper for Americans. (See *Weld-Grimké Letters*, I, 123.)

99

TO GEORGE W. BENSON

Boston, June 10, 1844.

Dear bro. George:

Catharine arrived at our house from Nashua and Lowell, on Friday, where she has had a very pleasant visit. Her mother came with her, but is stopping elsewhere in the city, and will go with her to Northampton.[1] They will leave for N. on Friday morning next, and Helen and myself will accompany them. Mother and Sarah will go to Providence immediately on our return home. Mother continues quite feeble, and is troubled occasionally with a slow fever, with loss of appetite. She is evidently not long for this evil world, but is ready for her departure at any moment. Her life has been a long and useful one. Sarah has just taken the cars for Lynn, to spend the night with the [Oliver] Johnsons, who were so kind to Anne when she was taken ill under their roof. I do not know when James Boyle [will] be in the city, but I hear that he was at the Concord (N. H.) meeting last week, and that it was a grand one.[2] Your wife and babe are well. Tell George Thompson [Garrison] we are coming, and shall rejoice to see his dear young face again. Love to all the friends.

　　　Yours, ever,

　　　　　　　　　　　　　　　　　　　Wm. Lloyd Garrison.

ALS: Garrison Papers, Boston Public Library.

　　1. Mary Alexander Stetson, who had married Benjamin Stetson in 1793, was the mother of Catharine Knapp Stetson Benson, the wife of George W. Benson. (John S. Barry, *A Genealogical and Biographical Sketch of the Name and Family of Stetson*, Boston, 1847, p. 33.)

　　2. The annual meeting of the New Hampshire Anti-Slavery Society was held in Concord on June 5, 1844; a brief account appears in *The Liberator*, June 21, 1844.

100

TO GEORGE W. BENSON

　　　　　　　　　　　　　　　　　Boston, June 25, 1844.

Dear George:

　　As I expected, the information that I was forced to convey to Mrs. Paul, respecting the difficulty of her being received at the Community at the present time, filled her with much distress of mind, and blotted out the last star of hope that was left beaming for her.[1] Our friends, the [Joseph] Southwicks, were also greatly disappointed; for though they are hospitable and generous to a fault, they are naturally desirous (after having entertained her for so long a time) that she should find some retreat that she can call or regard as her home. My heart aches for this unfortunate, but amiable and excellent woman. Her case is one that strongly appeals to us as the friends of humanity, and especially as abolitionists. She is indeed a stranger in a strange land,[2] without friends or relatives, without any certain abiding place, and without knowing where to direct her footsteps; and all this, solely because, being destitute of the vulgar prejudice against a colored complexion, she married in England the Rev. Nathaniel Paul, a man of fine personal appearance and talents, but one of those who are regarded by the pseudo democrats and christians of this country as belonging to an inferior race. Her sufferings on the score of this prejudice, since she came over, have been those of a martyr, which she has borne with christian resignation and fortitude.

I wish to make one more effort in her behalf. You will pardon me for my importunity, for I feel a degree of personal responsibility in regard to her, in consequence of my becoming acquainted with her at the time of her marriage in England. I know exactly how you are situated at the Community, both as to room and as to pecuniary matters. I know it was only the additional weight of an ounce that broke the camel's back, and that the load which you all have to carry is a very heavy one indeed. Yet I trust the proposition which I am about to make will be accepted by you, as it will involve no expense to yourselves, but will rather prove a service. It is this. If you will take Mrs. Paul under your sheltering care for a year, (after which time, other arrangements can be made,) you shall be guaranteed a dollar a week for her board, (which I suppose will cover the cost of it,) or if that be not sufficient, one dollar and a half; you at the same time receiving all that she can earn during the year; and Mrs. Southwick says she will be able to do much, either with her needle, in the silk department, or in some other kinds of labor — and she will not be backward in trying to do whatever lies in her power. The Southwicks will pay half of her board, and I can beg the other half from other friends, if necessary. She will need little or no clothing during the year, as she has a sufficient quantity to carry her through. She has also a mattrass and bed clothes, which she can carry with her. Under these circumstances, I am sanguine that you will contrive to let her be with you. As to accommodations, she will cheerfully put up with any that you can give her, however humble.

My dear George, do not let "nay" be said to this proposition, if possible. Words and entreaties I would multiply, if it were necessary. Lay this matter before your committee at once, and let me hear from you without delay. A state of suspense is one of extreme pain, frequently, and none can be more so than the present. I have encouraged Mrs. Paul to hope that this new arrangement will be successful.

Mother and sister Sarah went to Providence on Friday afternoon, and a letter from Charlotte informs us that they are doing well.

Yours, in great haste,

Wm. Lloyd Garrison.

☞ Write soon.

ALS: Garrison Papers, Boston Public Library.

1. Little is known about Mrs. Nathaniel Paul except that she was English and was feeling the prejudice meted out to those who had crossed the racial line in marriage. Garrison's attempt to have her admitted to the community was apparently unsuccessful; the list of members does not contain her name. (Sheffeld, pp. 103–105.)

Nathaniel Paul (died 1839) was a Baptist minister sent in 1832 to England to raise funds for the Wilberforce Settlement, the Canadian refuge offered by the British Colonial Government to fugitive slaves and free Negroes. During Garrison's trip to England in 1833, Paul was his constant companion; indeed, Garrison borrowed money from him for his return passage. The two men did not meet again after 1833. (Obituary in *The Liberator*, July 26, 1839.)

2. Exodus 2:22.

---

1 0 1

TO GEORGE W. BENSON

Boston, Aug. 26, 1844.

Dear bro. George:

Your letter of last night, announcing the death of our beloved mother, has just come to hand. It is an event for which we have been endeavoring to prepare our minds; and now that it has taken place, we trust to be able to meet it in the spirit of christian faith and resignation. She was truly "one of the excellent of the earth," worthy of all praise and admiration. Advanced as she was in years, she did not outlive her usefulness. It is painful to part with one so beloved, yet it is all right. We shall, I trust, join her, and all the other members of the endeared family who have been removed, in that other and better world. Helen is in tears, and will miss mother exceedingly. Poor dear Sarah! my heart is full of sympathy for her, for this fresh blow must strike her very heavily. But let us all say from the heart, "The will of the Lord be done," [1] and it will go well with us.

We shall leave in the morning train for Providence. Mr. [Samuel J.] May happens to be in the city, though I have not yet seen him; but I have no doubt he will accompany us to P., if no insuperable obstacle prevent.

Yours, in brotherly sympathy,

Wm. Lloyd Garrison.

ALS: Garrison Papers, Boston Public Library.

1. Acts 12:14.

102

TO SAMUEL J. MAY

[Boston, September 28, 1844.]

P. S. My esteemed friend Spooner wishes me to add a postscript.[1] I know where your heart is so well, and how ready you are to do what in you lies to hasten that day of jubilee for which you have so long prayed and labored, that I am sure you will not need any of my entreaties to be added to those of Mr. Spooner, to induce you to attend the meeting at Plymouth,[2] if you can conveniently make your arrangements to do so. Plymouth county is specially dear to your heart, and the people generally have a very high regard for you. Do go, if possible, and see them, and let them once more see and hear you. You are aware, perhaps, that poor Mr. Briggs has sadly faltered, and is no longer go[ing] onward to perfection.[3] Your visit might be the means of doing him great good, for it is a pity that he should utterly apostatize.

We are all well at home. Bro. George left us on Thursday for Bath, Me., and will return to the city in a day or two. He wants to have an interview with you, and has left a note for you at 25, Cornhill.

My best regards to Mrs. May.

Yours, lovingly, as ever,

Wm. Lloyd Garrison.

Holograph postscript signed: Garrison Papers, Boston Public Library. These paragraphs appear in a letter to Samuel J. May from Bourne Spooner.

1. Bourne Spooner (1790–1870) was an abolitionist from Plymouth, Massachusetts, who extended hospitality to George Thompson during his visit in 1851. (*Life.*)

2. Of the Plymouth County Anti-Slavery Society on October 2, 1844.

3. Probably George W. Briggs (1810–1895), pastor of the First Church in Salem in later years, who was in Plymouth in 1844. (Letter to the editor from Dorothy M. Potter, librarian, Essex Institute, Salem, December 23, 1970.)

103

TO HENRY C. WRIGHT

Boston, Oct. 1, 1844.

My Beloved Friend:

It is sometimes said of a person, that "he ought to be hanged," without meaning any thing very sanguinary by such an expression.

In view of my epistolary delinquencies, and of the long, long period that has elapsed since I wrote to you, I feel, not exactly that I deserve to be strangled, but mortified to a most humiliating extent. How it is that you have let me off so easily — without giving me a single reproachful look — without sending me one word of complaint — I am at a loss to imagine; but your forbearance and magnanimity are worthy of eternal renown, and I would certainly celebrate them in immortal verse, if I only knew how. It is utterly idle for me to attempt to palliate my silence, on the plea of occasional ill health — domestic affairs — editorial duties — the responsibilities of the anti-slavery cause — or any thing of the kind. Alas! too long a period of time has elapsed for me to escape under cover of such a plea. It would be useless, too, for me to tell you how many long and affectionate epistles I have projected in my mind, for your perusal, within the present year; but as these were never completed, and have only been mere abstractions, any intelligence of that kind would only serve to aggravate rather than mitigate my criminality. As one steamer after another has left this port, without carrying one word of brotherly love and cheer from me to you, I have blushed, sighed, and resolved that "the next steamer" should certainly not depart, until I had prepared an epistle of astounding length, and filled to repletion with things fresh, novel and interesting. But, alas! when the day of her departure came, it found no such document begun, and me too busy to think of even subscribing my name to any thing. As it is, I am driven into a corner, and must write in full gallop, if I would not lose the mail which is to close at noon, this day.

You must indulge me in expressions of regret. I am pained to think that, during your long residence in Graeffenberg, not a line was received from me to comfort you while passing through your terrible "water cure," and living among a people "of a strange speech." [1] You have been desperately ill — have taken long journeys — have resided for months in Austria — have been restored to health, and almost literally have "passed from death unto life" [2] — and at length have returned back to England — and yet, all this period, I have sent you nothing in the shape of an epistle, to tell you of the mingled emotions of anxiety, alarm, hope and joy, which have filled my breast. O, this is too bad — it is abominable! And yet you have been as dear to me as the apple of my eye. There is no one, on the wide earth, among the great circle of my friends, for whom I entertain greater love and respect. Your views of the nature, spirit and design of Christianity, — of the brotherhood of the human race — of the corruption of existing political, religious and governmental institutions — are more nearly identical with my own, than those of almost any other individual. In your welfare — in all your labors and trials — in all that you are endeavoring to accomplish in behalf of the human family — I take a deep, abiding, thrilling interest. God be with you to the end of the conflict here below, and bless you eternally!

Your recovery as it were from the jaws of death, by a process as extraordinary as it has proved efficacious, is a matter of astonishment and delight to your numerous friends on this side of the Atlantic. Have you not heard the shout of joy that has gone up from us? Yet we rejoice with fear and trembling, lest, after all, there may be a relapse, either in consequence of the cure not being radical, or from your want of caution in speaking and lecturing on your favorite themes. We are apprehensive, too, that the climate of England is not adapted to your constitution; for it seems to have exerted a deleterious influence upon you ever since you landed in that country. Do be careful of yourself — see that you are not consumed by the fire of your philanthropy — curb your disposition to labor beyond measure — believe in "the limitations of human responsibility," though not as laid down by that selfish and cowardly teacher of morality, President Wayland.[3]

You must return home! — and with as little delay as possible! This is the unanimous opinion of your friends in this country. We admit that "the field is the world"; [4] we are sure that you are sowing precious seed abroad, that will ultimately produce a rich harvest; we know that the genuine friends of Christian peace, in Europe, are "few and far between"; [5] we perceive many good reasons for your remaining among a people who are so frightfully victimized by the war spirit; yet, notwithstanding all this, we are satisfied that the best position for you to occupy is to be found in the United States. If the peace of this country can be maintained, the peace of the world will follow almost as a necessary consequence. In regard to the cause of negro emancipation, have we not always said that we can assail slavery more successfully by remaining at the North, than by going to the South? So, in regard to the blessed cause of non-resistance, we can attack the war spirit to more advantage by occupying a position the least embarrassed by the presence of military power, than we can by going into its presence, and attempting to take the citadel before we have gained a single outpost.

I do not know but the season has too far advanced for you to think of returning home until next spring; and yet to spend the winter in Scotland may be more perilous to your health, than for you to take your chance in our cold, clear, wintry climate. But you must not tarry longer than next spring, unless the voice and the providence of God clearly determine otherwise. In an unselfish spirit, we long to see you again, and to embrace you in the flesh. Give due heed to these suggestions, and decide according to your own convictions of duty; and when you write to me again, let me know your mind on these points.

The annual meeting of our Non-Resistance Society occurs on the 29th instant. At that meeting, I presume a resolution will be passed, urging your speedy return home to your former field of labor. The Society, I regret to say, has had only a nominal existence during the past year — and, indeed, ever since your departure. It is without an organ, without funds, without agents, without publications. Yet, I rejoice to add, on the other hand, that the cause of non-resistance is gaining new adherents continually, through the radical character of the anti-slavery movement. At present, that movement is first in the order of progress and reform on this soil, in which every non-resistant is most deeply interested, and which absorbs nearly all our time and means; and this is the reason why our Non-Resistance Society, as such, gets so little of our attention. But should you return, our Board would be inspirited to put forth vigorous efforts, and I feel confident that you would be sustained in a pecuniary point of view.

Your letters from Graeffenberg, as published in the Liberator,[6] giving an account of the "Water Cure" and its peasant founder, have excited a wide and lively interest among all classes, and been extensively copied by the journals of this country. This will be gratifying intelligence to your benevolent mind. Who can tell how many invalids will be saved from an untimely grave by your sickness — or, rather, by the knowledge of the simple mode of your restoration to health? Thus it is ever with our Divine Benefactor: —

> "Behind a frowning providence,
> He hides a smiling face."

And how true it is that

> "Blind unbelief is sure to err,
>   And scan his works in vain:
> God is his own interpreter,
>   And he will make it plain." [7]

Certainly, it has been made very plain in your case; and thus it is that through individual suffering and self-sacrifice, the world is to be redeemed, both morally and physically.

I regard your sojourn in Graeffenberg as of vast importance, prospectively, on other grounds than the remedy made known for "the ills which flesh is heir to." [8] Your social intercourse with so many persons from the various nations of the earth — the declaration to them of your peculiar views — the greatness of your spirit as exhibited to them in transcending all geographical boundaries, and pouring contempt on all national pride and glory — the inculcation of the great doctrine of human brotherhood — the presentation of Christianity in a new, glorious, sublime form — what may not follow from all this?

By the last steamer, I received from you a voluminous mass of manuscript, containing several letters, and also the sketches of men and things you made at Graeffenberg, and on your return to England. For this and all similar favors, I return you my warmest thanks; for they give additional interest to the Liberator, and contain the noblest sentiments, expressed in plain and simple language. You will perceive that I have commenced their publication, in order. The remainder will appear in subsequent numbers. Unfaithful as I am on the score of epistolary reciprocity, I trust — knowing that it does not arise from any lack of personal interest or remembrance — you will still continue your favors, and let me hear from you as often as convenient. Through the Liberator, you will be able to address and to influence many minds. Speak out your whole mind on all subjects which concern the redemption of our race, let who will take offence at truth and honesty.

Politically, the American Anti-Slavery Society has "passed the Rubicon," in regard to this blood-cemented Union; and on its banner is inscribed the motto, "No Union with Slaveholders." No step has yet been taken in our cause, so trying to those who profess to be abolitionists, or that is destined to make such a commotion in Church and State. It will alienate many from our ranks, but their defection will be our gain. "The battle is the Lord's," [9] not man's, and victory shall be achieved not by numerical superiority — not by physical might or power — but by the Spirit of Truth, and the omnipotence of Love.

The adherents of Liberty party, in order to justify voting, are impudently claiming the U. S. Constitution is and was intended to be, by those who originally framed and adopted it! Even Gerrit Smith has stultified himself so far as to have written a long letter to John G. Whittier, maintaining the same absurd doctrine.[10] Nay, he has gone so far as to eulogize those diabolical provisions respecting the prosecution of the slave trade for twenty years — the putting down of slave insurrections by the government — the three-fifth representation of the slaves through their masters — as decidedly anti-slavery in their character and tendency! He is now completely absorbed in electioneering in behalf of James G. Birney and the Liberty party, and has consequently gone backward since you left for England. He is a very unstable man, and his course is full of contradictions. He puzzles me to decipher his character more than any other man of my acquaintance. Still, I mean to let charity and patience have their perfect work in regard to him; for, after all, he seems to be a noble-hearted and benevolent man, but his head is often sadly at fault. I wish, if you get time, you would address a letter to him, on his new political career, and his strange interpretation of the Constitution, reminding him of the awful responsibility he is thus taking upon himself, and of the concessions he has made to you, on various occasions, respecting the divinity of non-resistance. In his letter to Whittier, he perseveres in calling the American A. S. Society a Non-Resistance Society, because it will not support a pro-slavery Constitution!

Among those who have left us, on account of our "no union" doctrines, is George Bradburn. Poor man! there is more of the politician than of the Christian in his composition, and therefore he clings to political action, even if it must be at the expense of principle. To think of his now being a partisan of the pseudo "Liberty party," and in full fellowship with such men as [Joshua] Leavitt, Birney, Stanton, and the like! [11] "To such base uses do men come at last," [12] who are not prepared to sell all that they have, that they may follow Christ! [13] But I hope our friend Bradburn will get his eyes open, and speedily change his course.

The anti-slavery cause is moving on majestically, "against the wind, against the tide," notwithstanding the incumbrance of Liberty party.[14] We are in the midst of another Presidential campaign, and the rival parties are holding immense mass meetings in all parts of the country, to ensure a triumph. The democratic party is committed, body and soul, to the slavocracy; and the whig party, having Henry Clay at its head, is scarcely less committed on the same side — though, so far as the annexation of Texas is concerned, its tone is very different from the other. It is extremely uncertain how the election will turn, though the chances rather incline to the side of Clay. You must not be surprised, however, if Polk [15] should be elected by a decided majority. Just at this moment, we are reserving our anti-slavery strength, and preparing ourselves to make an onslaught on public sentiment, as to the disunion question, as soon as the Presidential campaign shall have terminated. The Liberty party is increasing numerically, made up of the selfish and superficial, with some exceptions, and will probably cast in this State twelve thousand votes, and in the whole country one hundred thousand.[16] A more unscrupulous man than Joshua Leavitt is not at the head of the press in this country. Whittier is editing a Liberty party journal at Lowell,[17] but it is a tame affair politically; for he has too much decency, self-respect and conscience to make a prime politician.

The Anti-Slavery Standard, in the hands of Quincy, Chapman and Gay, is radical and spirited, of course, and will do good service.[18]

Dear [Nathaniel P.] Rogers is still driving his inimitable pen with railway speed, though I think he occasionally runs off the track, and sometimes mistakes a mole-hill for a mountain. He now avows unmitigated hostility to every organized society, and regards a president or chairman as an embryo Caligula or Nero. Just at this moment, there is a most unpleasant controversy going on between him and young French,[19] the printer of the Herald of Freedom, on the one side, and S. S. Foster and the Executive Committee of the N. H. State A. S. Society on the other. It relates to the ownership and management of the Herald. I hope it will be amicably settled, and without any impeachment of character.[20]

Wendell Phillips and his wife are yet protracting their summer residence at Nahant, but will soon return to the city. She is still a poor debilitated invalid, requiring almost his constant presence, so that his anti-slavery sphere of labor is necessarily quite restricted. They both have my tenderest sympathy and warmest love.

John A. Collins is at the Skaneateles Community, except when he is travelling and lecturing in its behalf. He no longer takes any apparent interest in the anti-slavery enterprise, but rather regards it as a very small affair. Theoretically, he is afloat on the dark ocean of atheism, without compass, chart, or rudder, or solitary star at night for guidance. He subscribes to [Robert] Owen's philosophy, that man is the creature of circumstances, and therefore not accountable — not worthy of any praise or blame for any of his actions. Yet, like Owen, he has much to say about the regeneration of the world, and claims to have found in his theory, coupled with his "no property" doctrines, a panacea for all the ills of life. Alas! for his delusion.

In August, I had the pleasure of seeing your wife and May and Dr. Stickney, in Philadelphia.[21] They were then in good health, but longing for your return; and their eyes brightened when I told them that I meant to throw a lassoo across the Atlantic, by which I was in hopes soon to bring you back, a captive to my loving skill and prowess.

We have had another bereavement in our family. Our venerable and estimable mother, Mrs. Benson, paid the debt of nature a short time since, and was buried at Providence. Sister Ann died a year ago at Northampton — sister Mary and my brother James the year before. Sister Sarah's health is very frail; she has a bad cancer on her breast, and is probably to tarry but a short time here below. But these, though afflicting, are natural events; and to us, as well as to others, must come at last "the inevitable hour." [22] Let it come, in God's good time, and a good life shall make it any thing but a gloomy event.

My own health is tolerably good, but will not admit of any laborious effort. The disease in my left side is gaining ground, and greatly distending it, causing me much pain, and threatening serious consequences. I must give up public lecturing, and hold my peace for some time to come, if I would not cut short the thread of my earthly existence. I am about to put myself under medical treatment — a mixture of homœopathy and hydropathy — for as we have no hydropathic establishment in the country, the latter process can only be imperfectly carried out.

Dear Helen is in very good health; so are the children. George Thompson is at the Northampton Community, getting his education. But my sheet is filled, and I have no room for domestic particulars. All send their love.

I have served R. D. Webb and wife, (O, admirable couple!) R. Allen, James Haughton, Elizabeth Pease, John Murray, William Smeal, &c. as badly as I have you, in regard to my correspondence. Say to them all I pine in spirit to see them, and love and esteem them highly. God bless you all.

Yours, lovingly, faithfully, to the end,

Wm. Lloyd Garrison.

Should you be in want of funds, at any time, either for your necessities abroad, or to enable you to return home, do not hesitate to apprise me of the fact.

ALS: Garrison Papers, Boston Public Library.

1. Henry C. Wright stayed at the health resort in Graeffenberg in Austrian Silesia (now northeast Czechoslovakia) for about six and one-half months to take the water cure. The resort was located on the family homestead of Vincenz Priessnitz (c. 1800–1851), who originated the system of hydropathy around 1829. At Graeffenberg patients were subjected to an inexorable series of treatments, all involving pure cold water, whether in the form of beverages, of wet compresses, or of baths. Graeffenberg became so famous that it drew people from around the world and became the model for many similar centers.

Garrison's biblical reference is to Ezekiel 3:5.

2. John 5:24.

3. Francis Wayland (1796–1865) was president of Brown University from 1827 to 1855. He made liberal changes in the curriculum, enlarged the university facilities, and was famous as a teacher. Garrison refers here to Wayland's comment in his *Limitations of Human Responsibility* (1838) that abolition was being used as a tool by third-rate politicians, and to his belief that it was possible to be both a Christian and a slaveholder.

4. An adaptation of the motto of both the New England Non-Resistance Society and *The Liberator* ("Our Country is the World — Our Countrymen are All Mankind").

5. Thomas Campbell, *Pleasures of Hope*, Part II, line 378.

6. Intermittently, May-August, 1844.

7. William Cowper, *Olney Hymns*, "Light Shining Out of Darkness," stanza 4, lines 3–4, and stanza 6, with the word "work" changed to "works."

8. Garrison slightly misquotes Shakespeare, *Hamlet*, III, i, 62–63.

9. I Samuel 17:47.

10. John Greenleaf Whittier (1807–1892) was the distinguished New England poet whose verse Garrison had first published in *The Free Press* in 1826. Garrison launched Whittier not only as poet and abolitionist but also as editor, and Whittier edited over the years several papers: the *American Manufacturer* (1829), the

Essex Gazette (1830 and 1836), the *New England Weekly Review* (1830–1832), and the *Pennsylvania Freeman* (1838–1840). One of the founders of the American Anti-Slavery Society, Whittier was active also in the Massachusetts society. After 1840 Whittier and Garrison diverged as abolitionists, since Whittier, being more politically oriented, transferred from the American to the American and Foreign Anti-Slavery Society.

The letter from Gerrit Smith to John Greenleaf Whittier, dated July 18, 1844, and printed in *The Liberator*, August 31, 1844, maintains that the federal Constitution is an antislavery document which, if strictly followed, would result in abolition. Smith says, however, that the moral climate of the country, in the North as well as the South, is such that the provisions of the Constitution have been and will continue to be interpreted in a way to favor the continuation of slavery.

11. Henry B. Stanton (1805–1887) was one of the students who left Lane Theological Seminary in 1835 because of its opposition to their antislavery work. He joined James G. Birney in his abolitionist activities and soon became an agent of the American Anti-Slavery Society. After his marriage to Elizabeth Cady, the woman's rights leader, he practiced law in Boston, later moving to New York state and running successfully for state senator. After the Civil War he was to devote most of his time to journalism, being connected with the New York *Tribune* and *Sun*.

12. An adaptation of Shakespeare, *Hamlet*, V, i, 3.

13. Matthew 19:21, Mark 10:21, and Luke 18:22.

14. Although there seems to be no specific literary source for Garrison's phrase, it was a common maxim that the conjunction of wind and tide was an irresistible force. Perhaps the literary statement of the idea closest to Garrison's is Shakespeare, *3 Henry VI*, IV, iii, 58–59.

15. James K. Polk (1795–1849), eleventh President of the United States.

16. The Liberty party received 10,860 votes in Massachusetts, 65,608 nationally, and no electoral votes.

17. The *Middlesex Standard*, which Whittier edited from July 1844 to March 1845.

18. Sydney Howard Gay (1814–1888) was a journalist and author. After an early career in finance and law, he became in 1842 a lecturer for the American Anti-Slavery Society. In 1844 he became resident editor of the society's official organ, the *National Anti-Slavery Standard*, with the assistance of Maria W. Chapman and Edmund Quincy; he continued as chief editor for thirteen years. Deciding in 1857 that the antislavery cause no longer required his full attention, he joined the staffs of the New York *Tribune* and the New York *Evening Post*. At the time of his death he was writing a life of Edmund Quincy.

19. John Robert French (1819–1890), who edited various New England and Ohio papers and later served in the United States Treasury and Congress. (*The Liberator*, December 13, 1844, February 14, 1845, and *Life*.)

20. The complicated controversy over the control of the *Herald of Freedom* had been in progress since the summer. Although the paper was the organ of the New Hampshire Anti-Slavery Society, its editor, Nathaniel P. Rogers, and its printer, John R. French, his prospective son-in-law, had been shifting the paper away from the control of the society's board of managers. In June, without consulting the board, Rogers and French briefly suspended publication of the *Herald* in order to pay outstanding debts. After the money had been raised, publication resumed, but the controversy continued. (See *The Liberator*, November 8, 29, December 6, 13, 27, 1844, January 3, 10, May 16, 30, June 6, 13, 20, 1845. Rogers' death is mentioned, without comment, by substitute editor Edmund Quincy, October 23, 1846.)

21. Pierre LeBreton Stickney (c. 1814–1887) received his M.D. from Jefferson Medical College of Philadelphia in 1842, becoming a member of the Massachusetts Medical Society in 1847. He practiced first in Philadelphia (see the city directories

of 1844 and 1845) and later for many years in or near Springfield, Massachusetts. (See *The Massachusetts Medical Society: a Catalogue of its Officers, Fellows, and Licentiates, 1781–1893*, Boston, 1894, p. 174. Information also supplied in letter to the editor from John B. Blake, chief, History of Medicine Division, National Library of Medicine, June 29, 1971.)

May is unidentified.

22. Thomas Gray, "Elegy Written in a Country Churchyard," stanza 1, line 3.

104

TO CHRISTOPHER ROBINSON

Boston, Nov. 27, 1844.

My dear friend Robinson:

I do not know how you are situated as to family affairs, business engagements, &c., at this juncture; but I have seized my pen to say, that, knowing as I do your deep interest in the welfare of the Herald of Freedom, in dear bro. [Nathaniel P.] Rogers, in all that appertains to the integrity and success of the anti-slavery cause, it is my earnest hope and desire that you will be able to be at the meeting of the N. H. Anti-Slavery Society on Friday and Saturday of this week, in order to effect, if possible, (and is it not possible?) an amicable arrangement of the unhappy difficulty which has sprung up between the Board and the Publisher of the Herald, respecting the proprietorship of that paper — a difficulty which has now a very threatening aspect, and will do great mischief, if it be not settled in a brotherly spirit.[1] I am anxious that as many of the Lynn friends should go to Concord as possible, especially yourself, friend Clapp, and J. N. Buffum.[2]

You will excuse the suggestion, and believe me.

Ever, your loving friend,

Wm. Lloyd Garrison.

ALS: Miscellaneous American Autographs, Pierpont Morgan Library.

Christopher Robinson (1799–1876), a prominent shoe manufacturer in Lynn, Massachusetts, was the owner of two Lynn papers, the *Essex County Washingtonian* and the *Pioneer*. In 1846 the *Pioneer* merged with what had been Nathaniel P. Rogers' paper to become the *Pioneer and Herald of Freedom*. (Letter to the editor from Diane Liesinger, curator, Lynn Historical Society, June 3, 1970.)

1. The committee (chaired by Garrison) appointed to settle the controversy could not persuade Rogers and French either to change their stand or to remain with the *Herald*. In the issue of December 6, 1844, they announced that the paper was being discontinued.

2. Henry Clapp (1814–1875) was a lecturer on temperance and abolition and one of Rogers' strongest supporters. For a time he edited the Lynn *Pioneer*.

1 0 5

TO EDMUND QUINCY

Boston, Dec. 14, 1844.

My dear Quincy:

By the advice of our friends Jackson and Philbrick, I have written a letter to Andrew Robeson, of New-Bedford, respecting the new typographical dress so much needed for the Liberator, and submitting to his benevolence the situation of the pecuniary affairs of the paper, in this particular.[1] I understood you to say that you intend visiting New-Bedford next week, and that you would endeavor to see him on the subject. I hope you will do so, whether he transmits any thing or not before your arrival, particularly because you are a member of the financial committee; and it might be satisfactory to him to converse with you. The whole amount required is about $300, in addition to the sale of the present fonts of type in use, as old type metal, to be recast at the foundry. The original cost of the printing-office was $600; of which sum Francis Jackson advanced $200, E. G. Loring $200, and Samuel Philbrick $200 — they being joint owners of the same. They are willing to sink their interest in the original purchase, so far as the types are concerned, toward procuring the new dress. Having done so much, I am very anxious that the $300 should all be collected from other sources; but the Liberator has very few wealthy friends, though it has a great many poor ones, in a pecuniary sense. If Nathaniel Barney were at home, I have no doubt that he would cheerfully contribute a liberal sum; but he is absent from the country.[2] Samuel Philbrick thought that friend Robeson might take the whole load on his shoulders, "without feeling it." Perhaps so — but it is easy to be free with other people's money, and to determine what they can do "as well as not." If friend R. should give $100, or even $50, I should esteem it a generous deed. Could not Samuel Rodman be prevailed on to contribute something, and one or two others in New-Bedford?[3] I feel the more unembarrassed in making the present appeal, as it is literally in behalf of the cause — and as it [is] not my wish or intention to have any exclusive *personal* interest in the contemplated purchase, beyond that of a fellow-soldier in the anti-slavery conflict. Each contributor is to be an absolute proprietor in the materials, to the amount of his contribution — the property to be purchased in the name of the financial committee of the Liberator, and held in trust by them. True, it will in all probability be an outright gift to the cause; but it ceases to be a *personal* affair, and, in case of personal dereliction, can at any time be claimed by the proprietors. Under these circumstances, perhaps you will feel no hesitancy in asking some of the rich New-Bedford friends, whether they will do something toward the object. The sum is comparatively trifling; and it is for this reason, as well as for not unnecessarily exposing the pecuniary condition of the Liberator to the world, that our friends Jackson and Philbrick deem it best that no public appeal should be made through the Liberator, and that the sum required should (for various reasons) be made up by two or three individuals at most.

Knowing your readiness to aid in this matter, to the extent of your ability, and hoping that your visit to New-Bedford will be pleasant to yourself, and serviceable to our cause, I remain,

Yours, faithfully, to the end,

Wm. Lloyd Garrison.

Edmund Quincy.

ALS: Garrison Papers, Sophia Smith Collection, Smith College Library.

1. Andrew Robeson (1787–1862) was a New Bedford businessman, philanthropist, and reformer, who served as an officer in both the Massachusetts and the American Anti-Slavery Societies. He was especially generous in his financial contributions to Garrison. (See Garrison's letter to Edmund Quincy, June 19, 1838, n. 1, *Letters*, II, 373.)

2. Nathaniel Barney (1792–1869) was a native of Nantucket, where he was an importer and manufacturer of whale-oil products and owned an interest in whaling ships. An indication of his generosity is that he gave the accumulated dividends from his stock in the New Bedford Railroad to Garrison for use in the cause as a reparation for the common railroad policy of discriminating against Negro passengers. (Letter to the editor from Edouard A. Stackpole, president, Nantucket Historical Association, May 29, 1970.)

3. Samuel William Rodman (1814–1906), after graduating from Harvard in 1834, spent a few years reading law and touring Europe before returning to New Bedford to engage in the whaling business. (Harvard Class of 1834, *50th Year Memorial.*)

106

TO ELIZABETH PEASE

[Boston, December 14, 1844]

My Esteemed Friend —

I eagerly improve this opportunity to unite with my dear Helen in returning heart-felt thanks for your generous remembrances, and to acknowledge the receipt of your note, with "The Peace Reader," "The Peace Almanac," and the circulars, intended for myself.[1] The Almanac is truly *multum in parvo*, and a capital pacific instrumentality. The

Reading-Book deserves to find a place in every school and in every family. I intend to make copious selections from it for the Liberator, and will give it an editorial notice.[2] I have read your letter in the Christian Witness with much pleasure, and shall give all who read the L. a chance to peruse it.[3] Wide as the Atlantic is, the philanthropic mind holds a mastery over it, and by giving utterance to its thoughts and feelings, can exert a powerful influence on multitudes beyond the great deep.

Helen has briefly alluded to an unpleasant difficulty between the Managers of the New-Hampshire Anti-Slavery Society and the Herald of Freedom, the particulars of which you will see in the Standard and Liberator. It is greatly to be deplored, but I cannot believe it is to sunder the ties of friendship between bro. [Nathaniel P.] Rogers and his Boston friends. His articles on the subjected have been written in a highly irritated state of mind, and in bad taste; but much allowance is to be made for him on the score of sickness, and also of his sanguine nervous temperament. Still, he and [John R.] French are entirely in the wrong, and I regret that dear R. should have become a party to the rashness, self-conceit and usurpation of that young man. But French is his prospective son-in-law, and this has warped his judgment, and obscured his vision. He has retired from his editorial post, and the Herald is discontinued *pro tempore*; but it will be speedily started again, and probably under the editorial care of Parker Pillsbury, who is a noble soldier in the cause, and has a great deal of tact and talent. Rogers is to make us a visit next week; and as we have not had a personal interview with him since the trouble commenced, we fondly hope it will be productive of good to us all. His health is very slender, but he is slowly on the recovery. We shall endeavor to keep his pen employed, to the extent of his physical ability, if the present breach can be healed.

You will see that George Bradburn has left us in an ill-tempered and violent manner, and gone over to the "Liberty party," alias the "New Organization." Alas for political ambition! In view of so many cases of personal alienation and anti-slavery defection as have taken place in our ranks, from time to time, I feel more and more how important is the declaration of the prophet — "Cursed is he that trusteth in man, or maketh flesh his arm." [4] — I wish you could have seen our little anti-slavery group at Mrs. Chapman's, a few evenings since, opening the boxes from England, and exam[in]ing their beautiful and choice contents for the Fair. It was a scene for a painter. Be assured, we feel far more than we can express of gratitude, and in due season shall make a formal and public acknowledgment. — You will rejoice to hear that the Congressional Gag Law has been repealed by a decided majority, but the annexation of Texas is probably certain.⁵ You see why I can add no more.

Affectionately yours,

Wm. Lloyd Garrison.

N. B. Monday noon, Dec. 16.

My dear wife has just presented me with a fine babe — *a girl*.⁶ Both mother and child are doing remarkably well.

ALS: Villard Papers, Harvard College Library. Garrison's letter is written on the same large sheet that begins with Helen's appreciative thanks for Christmas presents.

1. The correct title of "The Peace Reader" was *The Peace Reading-Book* (edited by H. G. Adams, London, 1844). It contained selections from the Bible, history, philosophy, and poetry, all of them about the evils of war. The preface blamed the continuance of war on the tendency of educators to emphasize worldly glory and to extol military success and suggested that children should rather be taught the importance of meekness, charity, and the return of good for evil. "The Peace Almanac" has not been identified.

In addition to the books mentioned above, Miss Pease sent a dress for Helen and books for the children.

2. No selections from *The Peace Reading-Book* or references to it appear in *The Liberator*. Throughout the year 1845, however, Garrison prints many "peace pledges" and often mentions the peace movement.

3. The *Christian Witness and Church Member's Magazine* was published in London by the Congregational Union of England and Wales from 1844 until 1864; a new series was begun in 1865 and lasted six years. (*ULS*.)

Garrison did not reprint Elizabeth Pease's letter in *The Liberator*.

4. Garrison refers to Jeremiah 17:5.

5. For a detailed discussion of the gag law, its history and eventual repeal, largely through the efforts of John Quincy Adams, see Garrison's letter to Richard D. Webb, February 27, 1842.

6. Helen Frances (Fanny) Garrison (1844–1928) was born December 16. She was to marry Henry Villard, and upon his death in 1900 she began a career of philanthropy and social reform. She served as a member of the advisory committee of the National Association for the Advancement of Colored People, labored for the woman's suffrage movement, and in her last years devoted her energy to the cause of peace and nonresistance. From 1897 to 1922 she headed the Diet Kitchen Association, which established public milk stations for children in New York City.

107

TO JOHN BAILEY

Boston, Jan. 10, 1845.

My dear friend Bailey:

When I seconded your motion, in the Liberator, for a public meeting in New-Bedford, respecting poor Boyer's case, and the villanous conduct of Capt. Ricketson, I was careful not to say that any one from this quarter would be present, because I could not then tell, as I had not then seen Wendell Phillips; but I felt, and still feel, whether speakers could be obtained from abroad or not, our anti-slavery and colored friends in your town ought to meet, and adopt suitable resolutions on the subject.[1] I am sorry to say that Wendell says it will not be possible for him to visit New-Bedford at present, though he is anxious a meeting should be held. As for myself, I am also unable to attend. Two of my children are quite unwell with cough and fever; and my wife is still confined to her chamber. I am very sorry it so happens. [Stephen S.] Foster and [Frederick] Douglass are in New-Hampshire, and [Charles L.] Remond is on the Cape. There is no other person to whom we can apply. Still, hold your meeting, even if it be a small one, and let your own souls speak out.

Yours, in haste,

W. L. Garrison.

ALS: Simon Gratz Autograph Collection, Historical Society of Pennsylvania.

John Bailey (1788–1883), watchmaker and jeweler, lived in New Bedford most of his life. In 1855 he was to serve as vice-president of the Massachusetts Anti-Slavery Society and later as managing editor of several antislavery papers, including the *Path Finder* and the *Peoples Press*, both begun in 1854. (Letter to the editor from Jonathan Prude, researcher, September 1970.)

1. Gilbert Ricketson (died c. 1854–1855) of Fall River, Massachusetts, was master of the schooner *Cornelia* out of New Bedford. Sailing north from Norfolk, Virginia, he discovered a runaway slave named Rudder and returned him to Norfolk. Ricketson's steward, a free Negro from New Bedford named Henry Boyer, was implicated in the case and was sentenced to four years in the Virginia Penitentiary. Although there is no record that the public meeting Garrison suggests was ever held, the Massachusetts Anti-Slavery Society, during its annual meeting on January 25, 1845, did pass a resolution expressing indignation at Ricketson's action. See Garrison's letter to John Bailey, February 13, 1845. (*The Liberator*, January 3, and February 21, 1845.)

108

TO LOUISA GILMAN LORING

Boston, Jan. 11, 1845.

Dear Mrs. Loring:

To say that the note, enclosing $20 as a fresh token of your friendly regard and good wishes on the commencement of the new year, is received by us with thankful hearts, is simply to declare that we are not unfeeling; for, surely, the least that can be done by the receivers of benefits, is to acknowledge the kindness of the benefactor. But this gift is prized by us far above its pecuniary value, as it is a substantial assurance of the continuance of your personal esteem and confidence, which we should lament to forfeit under any circumstances, and hope ever to retain. How much we are indebted to you and your estimable husband, through the strange vicissitudes and fiery trials of many years, we need not declare, and you will not be desirous to remember; but it is all recorded on the tablets of our hearts, and will be immortal in our memories. We will not express the hope that you *may* be amply rewarded for your friendly countenance and pecuniary aid, lest it should imply that you have not derived, from the deeds themselves, *as soon as performed*, an amount of pleasure constituting a rich recompense; but we are happy to believe that you can experimentally testify to the truth of the declaration, — "It is more blessed to give than to receive." [1] And yet it is a very blessed thing "to receive," when the gift is bestowed by the hand of friendship, and serves to relieve actual necessities, as we can testify.

It is not too late to wish that this may prove to you and yours, the brightest and happiest year you have yet experienced in this "vale of tears" [2] — (thanks to kind Heaven for the promise, that the time is coming when "all tears shall be wiped away," [3] and this discordant world shall be "filled with the abundance of peace"!) [4] What lies before us — "through what new scenes and changes we must pass" [5] — whether our remaining days on earth are to be few or many — is not yet a matter of revelation; but, that we can be happy, in the purest and highest sense of the term, be the mutations of our life what they may, is most certain, provided we be always animated by love and good will to our fellow-creatures. "To be good is to be happy," [6] is a trite adage, which no one seems to reject or discredit as an abstract truth, (like the boasted declaration, that "all men are created equal,") but which few practically regard. "Evil! be thou my good!" [7] is often the exclamation of many an erring soul in search of happiness; but it is not possible to gather grapes from thorns, nor figs from thistles.[8] We must *be* right to *feel* right, and then it is *all* right.

The congratulations of our friends on the recent birth of a daughter to us, add greatly to the pleasure we feel on that score. The little one did not arrive in season to be called a new year's gift from a beneficent Creator, but we are quite willing to receive her as such, ay, and to cherish her as a perennial favor. We think she is a bud of promise — a tolerably pretty babe — and deserving of all the kisses we bestow on her — of course! You shall judge for yourself whenever you can make it convenient to take a peep at her. We shall demand for her the rights of a human being, though she be a female. We value her at a high rate; but she is worth precisely as much as any other child, and no more. How valuable, then, are they all!

Wishing you to give to Mr. [Ellis Gray] Loring our warmest regards, and to accept for yourself the assurances of our love and respect, we remain,

Your grateful friends,

Wm. Lloyd Garrison,
Helen E. Garrison.

ALS: Ellis Gray Loring Family Papers, Radcliffe College Library; a handwritten transcription of this letter is to be found in the Garrison Papers, Boston Public Library.

1. Acts 20:35.
2. William Cowper, *Conversation*, line 881.
3. Adaptation of Revelation 7:17.
4. Garrison adapts Psalms 72:7.
5. Inaccurately quoted from Joseph Addison, *Cato*, V, 1, 12.
6. Nicholas Rowe, *The Fair Penitent*, III, i, 101.
7. John Milton, *Paradise Lost*, IV, 110.
8. Garrison adapts Matthew 7:16.

109

TO THE EDITOR OF THE *DAILY MAIL*

[Boston, February 1, 1845.]

Sir —

I observe in the Mail of yesterday morning, an editorial paragraph respecting the recent Faneuil Hall Convention, in which the proposition submitted by me to that body is denounced as 'treasonable.'[1] — That proposition was purely hypothetical, and simply provided for an emergency which appears to be inevitable, and which we must be prepared to meet in the spirit of freedmen. Assuming what the Address, subsequently adopted by the Convention, explicitly set forth, that the annexation of Texas to the United States, in the form and for the purpose contemplated, would be not only an infraction of the Constitution, but 'the overthrow of it' — an utter prostration of all State rights, and a dissolution of the Union — it suggested the expediency of summoning another Convention of the People of Massachusetts, after the consummation of this frightful act of tyranny, to form a new government for themselves, the Union of 1789 having then ceased to exist. 'If this be treason,' as Patrick Henry once exclaimed,[2] 'make the most of it.' For a similar 'treasonable' doctrine, I refer to a somewhat 'blurred and tattered parchment,' called the Declaration of Independence: — 'We hold these truths to be self-evident . . . . That all governments derive their just powers from the consent of the governed . . . . That whenever *any form* of government becomes destructive of

these ends, [the preservation of liberty and equality,] it is the right
of the people to alter or to abolish it, and institute a new government,
laying its foundation on such principles, and organizing its powers in
such form, as to them shall seem most likely to effect their safety and
happiness.' [3]

You venture to say, what I will venture to question, that 'Massachusetts will remain true to the Union, however other States may
violate the clearest provisions of the national compact.' [4] If you deem
such a declaration either patriotic or christian, you are ignorant of
the quality of the Puritan spirit, dead to the inspiration of liberty,
and blind to the signs of the times. Our revolutionary fathers did not
say — 'The colonies will remain true to the mother country, however
the Parliament may violate the clearest provisions of the British Constitution.' — No! They promptly repelled the slightest encroachments
of their rights, and, unfurling the banner of revolution, inscribed on
it — 'Resistance to tyrants is obedience to God.' [5] There are those, alas!
who, claiming to be their descendants, and professing to glory in their
indomitable spirit, have so basely degenerated as to cringe under the
lash of the slave-driver, and to bow their necks to the yoke of tyranny,
lest they be guilty of 'treasonable' conduct! Their slavish servility they
dare to call patriotism. When 'the clearest provisions of the national
compact' are trampled upon by other States, expressly to extend and
perpetuate slavery, 'Massachusetts will remain true to the Union,' by
declaring it to be no longer in existence, and by providing new safeguards for her rights and liberties — and false to it by clinging to the
form when the substance has vanished.

You say — 'It is indeed unfortunate, that one hair-brained man
should be thus permitted to defeat a truly wise and patriotic purpose.'
And yet you add — 'True, not half a dozen persons in the Convention
would probably support this project; but still it goes out to attaint
the proceedings'!! [6] If this be reason, what is folly? Whatever may be
the character of the project alluded to, I alone am responsible for it;
and, most assuredly, I am proud to take that responsibility. The Convention is to be tried by its own declarations and acts; and he who
shall attempt to hold it accountable for the opinions or propositions of
any of its members, will deserve to have the brand of FOOL or KNAVE
stamped on his forehead. All that it is *guilty* of, is the Address which
it adopted, and the appointment of a committee of correspondence. [7]

In your opinion, 'it ought to have thrown out Garrison's treasonable
resolution at once.' [8] The whole body of Southern slave-mongers will
add, that the author of the resolution ought to have been thrown out
along with it. This shows that while, in this matter, you are in their
company, they excel you in 'patriotism.'

My object, however, is not to defend myself against your absurd charge of treason, but to repel an insinuation which severely reflects on my honor and honesty as a man. You say — 'Mr. Garrison was not, we understand, a delegate to the Convention, and he professes to believe in the principle of no-human government. He had, therefore, no right to intrude himself, for good or evil, upon the deliberations of that body.'[9] I care not for your opinion that I am a 'hair-brained man,'[10] but when you attempt to stain the integrity of my character, it is too grave a matter to be suffered to pass unnoticed. My right to sit as a member of that Convention was as valid as that of any other member. I was chosen as one of the delegates from Ward 10, (in which I reside,) with seven others, without a dissenting vote; and my certificate of membership, signed by the chairman and secretaries of the meeting, was duly presented to the Convention.[11] It was, I have reason to believe, the most numerously attended Ward meeting held in the city. I submit to your sense of propriety, whether you were justified in giving this libellous accusation to the public, without further inquiry.

In conclusion, allow me to say that, whatever may be my views of government, they do not disqualify me from joining an assembly of the people to protest against the annexation of Texas as a most wicked and unlawful act.

Requesting that you will insert this letter in your paper of Monday,[12] as an act of personal justice and editorial fairness, I remain,

Yours, for universal liberty, and no union with slaveholders,

WM. LLOYD GARRISON.

Boston, Feb. 1, 1845.

Printed: *The Liberator*, February 7, 1845.

Edward C. Purdy was in 1845 the editor of the rather insignificant Boston *Daily Mail* (1840–c. 1856). He and John N. Bradley were also the publishers of the paper, and their office was at 14–16 State Street. (Letters to the editor from Ruth D. Bell, researcher, January 19, June 6, 1971.)

1. The Convention of the People of Massachusetts was held in Faneuil Hall on January 29–30, 1845, to take action against the proposed annexation of Texas. The chief accomplishment of the meeting was the adoption of the "Address to the People of the United States," which opposed annexation not only because it was unconstitutional but because it would further spread slavery. Although predominantly Whig, the meeting reflected all shades of political opinion. Among the other delegates were Francis Jackson, Ellis Gray Loring, and Samuel J. May. For an account of the meeting and the text of the address see *The Liberator*, January 31 and February 7, 1845.

2. In his speech on the Stamp Act, May 29, 1765, before the Virginia House of Burgesses.

3. Garrison quotes accurately from the Declaration, altering, for emphasis, some of the punctuation.

4. This quotation does not appear in the *Daily Mail* editorial.

5. Garrison misquotes the seal of Thomas Jefferson (c. 1776), substituting "Resistance" for "Rebellion."

6. Here Garrison quotes correctly.

7. The original committee of correspondence consisted of Stephen C. Phillips of Salem, Charles Allen of Worcester, John C. Gray of Boston, Charles F. Adams of Boston, and William B. Calhoun of Springfield; it was then enlarged by the appointment of James Fowler of Westfield and James G. Carter of Lancaster.

Stephen Clarendon Phillips (1801–1857) was a merchant and Whig who had also served as a member of Congress. In 1848 he was to be the leader of the Free-soil convention in Worcester. A strong supporter of the antislavery cause, he advocated the abolition of segregated schools in Salem. He died in the burning of the ship *Montreal* on the St. Lawrence River. (*The Liberator*, July 3, 1857.)

Charles Allen (1797–1869) was a Harvard graduate and jurist. Active in the Free-soil movement, he was to be elected to Congress in 1848 and in 1850. After many years of service in the lower courts and other branches of government, he was to become chief justice of the Superior Court of Massachusetts in 1859.

John C. Gray (1793–1881) was a lawyer from Boston. Besides being active in the Texas convention, he was a resident member of the Massachusetts Historical Society. (Letter to the editor from Ruth D. Bell, researcher, March 24, 1971.)

William Barron Calhoun (1795–1865) was a lawyer, politician, and educator. He began to practice law in Springfield in 1822, later becoming a member of the state legislature, a member of Congress (1834–1843), and a holder of several other public offices. He wrote many articles on social and educational issues.

James Fowler was a lawyer about whom little is now known, except that he was active in the Massachusetts Historical Society, that he was in 1842 involved in some undesignated but questionable legal proceedings, and that some people thought him a broken if not an insane man. (For oblique references to him see the letters from Ira Pettibone to Amos A. Phelps during 1842, the Phelps Papers, Boston Public Library.)

James Gordon Carter (1795–1849) was an educational reformer whose theories were far ahead of his time. For example, he favored the inductive method of learning as opposed to memorization and recommended the establishment of normal schools. He served in both the House and the Senate, where, as chairman of the committee on education, he was able to effect the passage of many progressive measures.

Charles Francis Adams, the son of John Quincy Adams, has been previously identified.

8. This quotation does not appear in the *Daily Mail* editorial.

9. Here Garrison quotes correctly.

10. Also correctly quoted.

11. The chairman of the convention was John Mason Williams (1780–1868), one of the justices of the Court of Common Pleas of Massachusetts. His writings include *Nullification and Compromise, a Retrospective View*, published in New York in 1863. (Library of Congress Catalog.)

The secretaries were George T. Curtis, James B. Congdon, John M. Earle, and John Greenleaf Whittier.

George Ticknor Curtis (1812–1894) was a lawyer of national distinction, who practiced in Boston, in New York, and often in Washington. He also had a political career, serving in the Massachusetts legislature (1840–1843) and in the next decade as United States commissioner. Although in the famous Dred Scott case he defended the freedom of Scott, as United States commissioner he angered abolitionists by supporting the Fugitive Slave Act of 1850.

James B. Congdon (1802–1880) was one of New Bedford's most prominent citizens, serving as cashier of the Merchants' Bank for more than thirty years, as chairman of the town's board of selectmen, as city treasurer, and as tax collector. He was prominent in both the abolition and temperance movements and was influential in establishing the first free public library in the United States. (Letter to the editor from Richard C. Kugler, director, Old Dartmouth Historical Society, December 22, 1970.)

John Milton Earle (1794–1874) was a journalist and legislator. Manager and editor of the Worcester *Spy* from 1823 to 1858, he served twice (1844–1846 and 1850–1852) in the General Court of Massachusetts and was to become a member of the upper house in 1858. An early supporter of the antislavery cause, he also had an interest in science. (See Garrison's letter to Helen E. Garrison, April 22, 1839, n. 6, *Letters*, II, 454.)

12. As Purdy did, in the issue of February 3, 1845.

110

TO JOHN BAILEY

Boston, Feb. 13, 1845.

Dear Friend Bailey:

You and our other friends in New-Bedford will be greatly disappointed in not seeing, in this week's Liberator, the call for a Convention in your place next week. But, under all the circumstances, I did not dare publish such a call, lest there should be a great failure in the end. Wendell [Phillips] assured me positively that he could not attend, either next week, or for some time to come. I had no time to hear from Samuel J. May or Edmund Quincy — [Charles L.] Remond and [Frederick] Douglass were absent, laboring in the Granite State — it did not seem to me probable that the Hutchinsons could be obtained — and as for myself, I of course could not risk my health and strength to any great extent. These, therefore, are the reasons why no call appears in the Liberator. I am sorry it so turns out, and you will be sorry too. I see the opportunity is a good one, arising out of Capt. [Gilbert] Ricketson's infamous conduct, (rendered still worse by his impudent and profligate defence,) to make a grand anti-slavery stir in New-Bedford, and regret the arrangements cannot be made according to the desire of the friends. If Wendell had answered in the affirmative, I should have said "ditto to Mr. Burke," at all hazards.[1]

I am sorry that friend Ray is disposed to give any countenance to the unjust and unwarrantable attempt of [Nathaniel P.] Rogers and [John R.] French to get up another Herald of Freedom.[2] You will see, by this week's Liberator, what I think and have felt compelled to say of that attempt.

Please give my best regards to friend Emerson,[3] to the Westons,[4] to Mrs. Bailey, and all the members of your family.

Yours, for the truth and the right,

Wm. Lloyd Garrison.

ALS: Autograph Collection, Harvard College Library.

1. The "Mr. Burke" referred to is the infamous William Burke (1792–1829) of Edinburgh, who progressed from robbing graves in order to sell the bodies to doctors for dissection to throttling the victims himself. The slang term "to burke" meaning "to stifle" arose about 1829, the year Burke was executed, and by 1840 had come to mean "to hush up." (*A Concise Dictionary of English Slang*, New York, 1956.) Garrison uses the term in connection with his suppression in *The Liberator* of a call for an antislavery convention in New Bedford.

2. Although not positively identified, "friend Ray" could be Isaiah C. Ray (1804–1882), a native of Nantucket, who was a boot and shoe merchant in New Bedford in the 1840's but shifted his calling to law in the 1850's. In 1844 at the American Anti-Slavery Society convention in New York he had been appointed to the committee on finance. (See *The Liberator*, May 24, 1844; also letter to the editor from Richard C. Kugler, director, Old Dartmouth Historical Society, May 25, 1971.)

French had announced that since their paper had been suppressed, he and Rogers were going to reestablish it under the title *The Herald of Freedom*. Garrison disparaged the plan in an editorial in *The Liberator*, February 14, 1845. When the first issue of *The Herald of Freedom* was printed in March, Garrison said that it ought to be called *The Usurper* (see *The Liberator*, March 21, 1845). In 1845, with the dissolution of the New Hampshire Anti-Slavery Society, both *Heralds* ceased publication. (*Life.*)

3. Ralph Waldo Emerson (1803–1882), the distinguished essayist and poet, by temperament wished to remain aloof from active reform, believing, as he said in *Self-Reliance*, that the individual, even the slave, must elevate himself. Despite his inclination, he did commit himself to abolition and on occasion spoke to groups of abolitionists.

4. Several Weston households are known to have existed in New Bedford during the 1840's. Only one family member, however, Deborah Weston (born 1814), a daughter of Warren Weston and sister of Maria Weston Chapman, is known to have been active in abolition in 1845. She participated in a protest against the New Bedford Lyceum for its refusal to admit a Negro to membership (Zephaniah W. Pease, ed., *The Diary of Samuel Rodman, 1821–1859*, New Bedford, 1927, p. 269).

111

TO RICHARD D. WEBB

Boston, March 1, 1845.

My beloved friend Webb:

"Out of sight, out of mind." So runs the proverb. But every proverb is not true; at least, not always. Your case, for instance, is a notable exception. Believe me, you have an abiding place *in* my mind and heart; and it is not necessary to see you, face to face, to quicken my remembrance of your worth and genius. Still, like a true lover, I frequently "sigh like a furnace" [1] to get another glimpse of your countenance, and to see your dear household once more "in the flesh." We are told of a time when "there shall be no more sea." [2] Do you think the Atlantic will cease to roll between us in our day? If so, how soon, and by what process? Will its "kindred drops" so "mingle into one," [3] as to cause the absorption or evaporation of that one great drop? Is this the way in which Ireland will be "annexed" to the United States? On this point, I am somewhat skeptical. Besides, I am in a hurry, and cannot wait to see the solution of a problem like this. I am growing old daily, (to say nothing about an hourly progress,) and I suspect you are in the same predicament. When, in 1840, we for the first time mingled our affections together, and looked each other kindly in the face, we were somewhat fresh and young, you know, and also agile and sportive. Alas! already, almost five long years have since been added to our uncertain term of earthly existence. Now, I cannot endure the thought of our being two "venerable old gentlemen" before we embrace each other again. You must come over and pay me a friendly visit, by the next steamer — if practicable! Remember, I have been over to Dublin to see you and yours. Remember, too, the old adage — "One good turn deserves another." To be sure, the ocean which separates us is about as broad as it ever was; but then the time of crossing it has been astonishingly abridged, requiring on the average only a fortnight. It will yet be reduced to a week, before either of us shall have reached the age of three score years and ten, if either survive so long. That is my prophecy. But only think of it! In fourteen days, it is in your power to be here in our midst in Boston! Would not your arrival make a commotion among us? Try, and see. A Yankee welcome can never compare with an Irish one; but we will do our best. Seriously — can you not make it in the way of business, as well as of friendship, to come over and see us? Of course, Hannah must come too, if she can. In the name of the Commonwealth of Massachusetts, I enjoin it upon Henry C. Wright to return home without delay, and to bring you two with him, and also James Haughton, and Richard Allen, and as many of your noble brothers, as he can entice or compel, without too flagrantly violating his non-resistance principles.

Procrastinating man that I am! Here it is the 1st of March, and within a few hours of the departure of the Liverpool steamer. I have a volume of things to write about, but scarcely a page of it shall I be able to complete. But I am relieved in mind to know that Edmund Quincy is your faithful and attentive correspondent; so that you are kept pretty well advised of matters and things as they pertain to our little friendly circle in Boston and its vicinage. As to the anti-slavery enterprise, as you see the Standard, Liberator and Herald of Freedom, you are kept pretty well instructed as to the most prominent events connected with it. Apparently, the slaveholding power has never been so strong — has never seemed to be so invincible — has never held such complete mastery over the whole country — has never so successfully hurled defiance at the Eternal and Just One — as at the present time; and yet never has it in reality been so weak, never has it had so many uncompromising assailants, never has it been so filled with doubt and consternation, never has it been so near its downfall, as at this moment. Upon the face of it, this statement looks absurdly paradoxical; but it is true, nevertheless. We are groping in thick darkness; but it is that darkest hour which is said to precede the dawn of day. As a nation, slavery has horribly corrupted us, so that we "make haste to shed innocent blood," [4] and neither fear God nor regard man; but there are hundreds of thousands of our population who will not bow the knee to Baal,[5] and we may yet obtain a glorious victory.

I have little doubt that Texas is now a member of the American confederacy. The next mail from Washington will unquestionably bring the last decisive action of the Senate on the subject, and that will be in favor of annexation.[6] There is a bare possibility that the nefarious project may again be defeated; for the vote will be a very close one. But the prize is too great to be put in peril by the sturdiness of one or two opponents, and they will be bribed to any extent that may be necessary. The history of this Texan movement, from its commencement to the present time, I verily believe has no parallel for villany and inhumanity, connected with the most despotic purposes. We have been betrayed by a party, making the highest pretensions to democracy. It is the shameless defection of the Northern portion of the Democratic party, that has given this bloody and atrocious triumph to the South. But the greediness of the Slave Power will not be satisfied with the annexation of Texas. Its settled purpose is to conquer all Mexico, and on its fertile plains to establish slavery and the slave trade.

Perhaps nothing has operated so powerfully on the public mind, in favor of annexation, as the hue-and-cry which has been so artfully raised against the alleged design of England to subjugate Texas to her own will and purpose, in order to cripple the commerce and manufactures of the United States, and put in jeopardy our glorious "democratic institutions" — the most cherished of which is the institution of slavery! There is among us a great deal of fear and hatred of England; and it is only necessary for the leading political demagogues to make their appeals to this infernal disposition, and they can achieve whatever feat of scoundrelism they wish to perform. Unhappily, at this juncture, in connexion with slavery, the hatred of the Irish population among us toward England is of a bitter and most implacable type, and it all goes in favor of the annexation of Texas, through motives of terror or revenge. It is a most deplorable circumstance that, religiously and politically, almost the entire body of Irishmen in this country are disposed to go with the accursed South for any and every purpose, and to any extent. The patriotic and Christian appeals which have been made to them by Daniel O'Connell and Father [Theobald] Mathew, and others of their countrymen at home, on this subject, have not had the slightest perceptible effect on their minds. They are a mighty obstacle, therefore, in the way of negro emancipation on our soil. Truly, they know not what they do.[7]

I must say a few words, respecting the deplorable alienation which has taken place in the mind of our once beloved friend [Nathaniel P.] Rogers towards some of his old and warmest friends. He has needlessly and criminally involved himself in a matter, in which neither his character nor his editorial independence was in the slightest degree implicated. John R. French, the late printer of the Herald, is a young man of a very irascible temper, wilful and obstinate to a proverb, and stocked with self-conceit; though he possesses some good qualities. He is, moreover, prospectively, the son-in-law of friend Rogers. His management of the Herald, and his treatment of the Board of Managers of the New-Hampshire Society, have been disgraceful and arrogant in the highest degree. It is quite needless for me, in this letter, to go into the details of his case, as you have doubtless read all that has been published, on both sides of the question. It was strictly a *business* affair, and we all supposed could be amicably settled; and I have no doubt would have been, had not friend Rogers given French such bad counsel, and come to his rescue in so gratuitous and violent a manner. The special meeting of the New-Hampshire Society, which was called expressly to have the affair fully and impartially investigated, was a meeting held in accordance with the expressed wishes of French, and before it he declared it to be his determination to go, and openly meet the issue. Rogers advised him to treat the meeting with contempt, and not to make any defence; being conscious, as it is now apparent, that, if F. should put himself on trial, all the facts were against him, and a verdict must be rendered accordingly. French, however, in the absence of friend Rogers from Concord at that time, had the *imprudence* to attempt to defend himself at the meeting; and the committee of arbitration, (on which were Wendell Phillips, Edmund Quincy, Anne Warren Weston, and myself,) after a long and searching examination, were compelled to pronounce him in the wrong; though they treated him, in their report, with quite as much delicacy and charity as the facts warranted. I wish you would reperuse that report, and mark how careful is its phraseology, and what it was that the committee undertook to decide. That report was basely refused a place in the Herald, together with the proceedings of the meeting — and this was done with the sanction of friend Rogers!

It was never dreamed by any of us, that the affair would become so serious, or that any tie of friendship would be ruptured by it. For my own part, I resorted to every expedient, consistent with good faith and honor, to effect a reconciliation. I had, in private, long and earnest interviews with Rogers and French, and affectionately besought them to weigh the consequences that must inevitably grow out of a persistance in their course. Various propositions were made to them to take the Herald, on as long a lease as they could desire, or under the supervision of the Board as to the *financial* department, leaving friend Rogers in the possession of that unlimited editorial freedom which he has always enjoyed, and which nobody among us has desired to see abridged; — but all in vain. They behaved precisely like the dog in the manger.[8] They had grown so "free" as to be disregardful of right and justice, and to claim exemption from all accountability. They would brook nothing in the shape of friendly counsel or admonition. We were viewed as impertinent intermeddlers, treated with contempt, and finally branded as enemies. For a long time, we clung to the hope that the illness of Rogers was mainly the cause of his extraordinary behaviour; but even this is gone — for now that he is recovered, he is more unkind and imperious than ever, and cannot speak peaceably to us. This is a development of character most afflicting and astounding to us. We see, or think we see, in him, (unless we ourselves are the victims of a wild delusion,) an entire destitution of magnanimity, a wanton disregard of the rights of others, a disposition to play the autocrat, a criminal shuffling with respect to his own declarations and admissions, and a pitiable inflation of mind, as though he had distanced all others engaged in the work of Reform. In attacking others from whom he dissents, no one is habitually more severe and unsparing than himself; yet I have never known one more sensitive when he is criticised by others, or so restive under the gentle reproof of affectionate and faithful friends. I think he has never forgiven James Haughton for venturing to express his regret at the manner in which he (Rogers) satirized [Daniel] O'Connell's table devotions. Now, this is a great infirmity, to say the least. Certainly, we ought to remember that, in every strife, there are blows to take, as well as blows to give; and we ought to receive them in good temper and with manly endurance. Especially should we receive with patience and kindness the admonitions of our *friends*, and love them all the more cordially for their rare fidelity; for, alas! how prone are friends to wink at each other's failings, under circumstances that require a prompt and frank rebuke!

For the last [eig]hteen months, friend Rogers has had a strong tendency of mind toward speculative atheism. He does not care to recognize the existence of God; he does not seem to think it is of any consequence to determine whether there be any such being; he does not have any faith in immortality beyond the grave; he is captivated by Owen's theory of no property as a personal right; and he has run into folly on the subject of freedom, and joined those whom Milton so aptly describes:

"License they mean, when they cry liberty." [9]

Having thus made shipwreck of his religious faith, it does not greatly surprise me that he has lost sight of the claims of justice, in the matter of the Herald of Freedom, and that he is in an irritable and most unhappy state of mind. As to mere speculative opinions, I care nothing about them, except when I plainly see that they are injurious to the temper and conduct of those who embrace them.

Friend Rogers has a growing horror of all *organized* societies, and fancies that to seek their extinction is the first duty of man, and "the end of the law for righteousness" [10] to every one who will join in this Quixotic crusade. To have a chairman or secretary at a meeting is an enormity not to be tolerated; committees are tyrannical usurpers; boards of managers are soul-killing "corporations." Order and system, however simple, are viewed by him with uneasiness, and even alarm. On this subject, he has really lost his wits, and become a raving monomaniac. But the most ludicrous part of it is, that he fancies a cruel conspiracy has been formed by his old friends to crush him, on account of these harmless absurdities! Hence, he persists in declaring that, though an issue has been made with J. R. French, respecting the printing of the Herald, it is a mere trick, a hypocritical manœuvre; because the real design is to drive him from his editorial chair, and thus prevent him from propagating his opinions in regard to organizations and free meetings!! The fact, that we had never even noticed his peculiar views on that subject, so trifling did we consider them, goes for nothing. The fact, that he and French have had a transfer or lease of the Herald repeatedly proffered to them, even since the outbreak, goes for nothing. The fact, that all his Boston friends, from whom he has now cut loose, have remonstrated with him against leaving the Herald, goes for nothing. The fact, that while he was editor of the Herald, from no quarter did any voice come, objecting to his "no organization" notions, goes for nothing. The fact, that the committee of investigation earnestly expressed the hope that satisfactory arrangements would be made with himself and French for editing and printing the Herald, goes for nothing. The fact, that the Board have never ceased to offer him the editorial chair *unconditionally*, goes for nothing. The fact, that the State Society, at its last meeting, unanimously instructed the Board to procure his services, without any restraint upon his mind or pen on any subject, goes for nothing. He is, alas! the victim of "the genius of corporation"!!! He is a martyr to his devotion to "free meetings" and a "spontaneous press"! If this be not monomania, what is? He persists, moreover, in saying that the Herald of Freedom is dead; and he and French have issued proposals for raising it up from the grave! This last act is capping the climax of folly and injustice, and it excites universal surprise and regret. Of course, he has a party with him, but it is a very small one indeed, and composed of those on whom no permanent reliance can be placed, as they are generally of an impulsive and eccentric character, and led by a blind sympathy rather than by reason and justice. They are generally those who have either lost their balance religiously or else some old grudges to gratify against the Liberator, the Standard, the Massachusetts or American Society, or the Boston abolitionists. I cannot believe the new paper will succeed, whether its title be "*the Herald of Freedom,*" or any other; but it may obtain a short, spasmodic existence. At present, Rogers makes use of Henry Clapp's paper, "The Pioneer," as his organ.[11] A word as to Clapp. He has considerable talent, and the zeal of a new convert; but lacks judgment and good sense — is impulsive and vain — tries to imitate Rogers in his style of writing and speaking — fancies that, next to R., *he* is the greatest *reformer* extant, "the pioneer" of the new world — is not to be relied on, I fear — and will prove a dangerous *friend* to Rogers. He fails to perceive the difference between the step *ridiculous*, and the step *sublime*, and is full of inflation.

Our old friend George Bradburn has left us in a towering passion, and joined the pseudo "Liberty party." These are *trying* times, certainly.

The number of those who are raising the cry, "No Union with Slaveholders," is steadily increasing.[12] The position of disunion is palpably the only one we can consistently or innocently occupy as the advocates of the slaves, as the friends of freedom, and as the obedient children of God. It must prevail, at last.

The shirts which were kindly forwarded to me by your brother James were safely received, and prized most highly.[13] I desire you to communicate to him my warmest thanks for this fresh memorial of his friendship, and assure him that it is estimated by me infinitely above the mere market value of the articles sent.

Tell your beloved wife that her wishes, expressed some time ago in a note, are now realized, as well as my own. Ten weeks ago, my dear Helen presented me with a fine little daughter; so that the account now stands — four boys and one girl. I have named her after my wife and mother — "Helen Frances." We are all in the enjoyment of health: my own is very much improved.

As many affectionate remembrances as there are stars in the sky to Henry C. Wright, Richard Allen, James Haughton, all the Webbs, Maria Waring, &c. &c.[14]

Yours, with intense affection,

Wm. Lloyd Garrison.

☞ Did bro. H. C. Wright ever get a letter from me, addressed to your care? He has never acknowledged its receipt. I presume his family are all well, or I should have heard from Philadelphia. I meant to have written to him by this steamer, but it is now too late.

ALS: Garrison Papers, Boston Public Library; extract printed in *Life*, III, 143.

1. An adaptation of Shakespeare, *As You Like It*, II, vii, 148.
2. An adaptation of Revelation 21:1.
3. William Cowper, *The Task*, Book II, line 17.
4. Isaiah 59:7.
5. An adaptation of Romans 11:4.
6. The joint resolution of Congress admitting Texas was in fact passed on the very day Garrison wrote this letter.
7. Luke 23:34.
8. Garrison refers to the famous fable of Aesop.
9. John Milton, "On the Detraction which Followed upon my Writing Certain Treatises," II, line 11.
10. Romans 10:4.
11. Beginning November 5, 1846, the Lynn *Pioneer* was to merge with the *Herald*, to become the *Pioneer and Herald of Freedom*. (Letter to the editor from Diane Liesinger, curator, Lynn Historical Society, June 10, 1970.)
12. The phrase "No Union with Slaveholders" originated in an address "To the Friends of Freedom in the United States" on the tenth anniversary of the American Anti-Slavery Society (see *The Liberator*, May 24, 1844). Garrison's phrase became, in effect, the motto of the society.
13. James Henry Webb (c. 1796–1878) lived in Kingstown, Dublin. (*Annual Monitor*, 1880, p. 173.)
14. Maria Waring (1818–1874) of Dublin was Webb's sister-in-law and a loyal Garrisonian abolitionist. She later married Dr. James George Palmer. (Letter to the editor from Olive C. Goodbody, curator, Friends' Historical Library, Religious Society of Friends, Dublin, July 16, 1970.)

112

TO LEVI WOODBURY

[March 14, 1845.]

SIR: —

I acknowledge the receipt, under your frank, of a copy of the speech on the annexation of Texas, delivered by you in the Senate of the United States, February 17, 1845.

I should be sorry to be thought lacking in courtesy toward any human being; but where there is no foundation for personal respect, neither honesty nor justice will tolerate even the semblance of it. I shall tell you what I think of your political character, in plain language and with great brevity.

You are one of those political demagogues, who are more injurious to a nation than pestilence or famine; whose selfishness is the only god whom they recognize or adore; whose ambition must be gratified, at whatever sacrifice of moral principle, and though hecatombs of innocent victims perish to effect its object.

You profess to be a democrat — a stanch, unflinching, genuine democrat — a devout worshipper at the shrine of Liberty, and an uncompromising foe to Tyranny.

This is to your shame and condemnation. It greatly mitigates the criminality of those who, engaged in acts of villany, wear no mask and put on no cloak, but exhibit themselves in their true character. Your profession, instead of extenuating, only serves to deepen your guilt.

You a democrat! Then is Satan, when disguised as an angel of light, no devil! *You* the enemy of oppression! Then was Benedict Arnold a patriot to the hour of his death! *You* a supporter of the Declaration of Independence! Then was Judas a faithful adherent of his Lord!

Sir, you are a political hypocrite. This you know. The plainness of my charge may astound you, but its correctness your conscience will endorse to the letter. If democracy be the assertion of human liberty and equality, — the vindication of the rights of all men, irrespective of caste or clime, — then you are no democrat. You are the friend, the companion, the eulogist of men-stealers. The blood which is dripping from their hands stains your own in the warm grasp of social and political fellowship. You have done much, and are eager to do more, to multiply the victims of their tyrannous rule and murderous rapacity. — John Tyler, John C. Calhoun, George McDuffie, and Levi Woodbury, are equally the *friends of the people*; or, to substitute fact for irony, 'the best of them is as a brier — the most upright is sharper than a thorn-hedge.' [1] As were the princes and judges of Jerusalem, in the days of Ezekiel, so are they: 'like wolves ravening the prey, to shed blood, and to destroy souls, to get dishonest gain.' [2]

Of course, you was one of the 'democratic' conspirators in the Senate, who recorded their votes unanimously in favor of the annexation of Texas to the United States. The object of that measure you knew, beyond the possibility of a doubt, was to extend and perpetuate the horrible system of American slavery — to multiply new slave States — to establish a precedent for the seizure of the whole Mexican empire, in due season, and its annexation to this country, in order that an illimitable scope might be given to that spirit of rapine, conquest and oppression, which now holds entire mastery over us. Yet you had the barbarity to support it. It was a deed of violence to the Constitution, which stains your soul with the crime of perjury; it was an act of perfidy toward Mexico, which, to the latest posterity, will consecrate to infamy the names of those who perpetuated it; it was a conspiracy against the liberties of the world, yet formed and consummated in the sacred name of freedom, to extend its area, and multiply republican institutions!

Here is your speech — smooth, plausible, adroit, yet all the more detestable that it is so. You are one who puts darkness for light, and light for darkness; who calls evil good, and good evil; [3] and against whom Heaven pronounces a woe. You commence with a bold misstatement, as though you were repelling a slander. 'We are all wronged,' you say, 'when charged with supporting the resolution as a high-handed measure of party supremacy.' How do you make the wrong appear? Has not Texas been annexed by a party vote, and for a party purpose? What says the Globe, on this matter of 'party supremacy'?

'With Texas and its train of new States — with Florida and Iowa and Oregon — the whole northwest — bringing the giant force of their incorruptible democracies to sustain the already dominant popular party in the Union, all the Machiavelian policy, the intrigue and corruption, the cunning combinations and political machinery, plied by federalism heretofore with partial success, will for the future be plied in vain.' [4]

What says the Boston Post?

'The vote in Congress decides one thing — that this is a great party measure, and the *Democracy of the Union must stand upon it, or not at all.* They will stand upon it, as they did upon the Louisiana question, firmer than ever. It is destined to give an *unchanging ascendancy to the Democratic policy of our national government.*' [5]

Yes! the democratic party relies for its supremacy on its alliance with the Slave Power, and has obtained that supremacy by means the most profligate, and for purposes the most atrocious.

Desirous to cloak the villany of your party, you say — 'Let it not be understood that this was an attempt to appropriate to ourselves the lands of a weak and unoffending neighbor, without his consent, by a sort of piratical seizure.' Sir, your virtuous indignation burns in vain, at the thought of this imputation being thrown upon the country. The dismemberment and annexation of Texas have been nothing less than 'a sort of piratical seizure,' as all Christendom knows, and no man living better than yourself. On this point, you do not need a single additional ray of light. You know when Texas was invaded, how she was revolutionized, and why she has been annexed to the United States. We have 'appropriated to ourselves' this vast territory, for the purposes of slavery, because 'our neighbor,' Mexico, is 'a weak and unoffending neighbor,' and crime and cowardice are generally found in close companionship. If Mexico had been strong like England or France, we should not have dared to do as we have done, even with all our land-stealing rapacity and pro-slavery desperation.

When you say that, 'under this Constitution, which has been in existence fifty years, *without stain or reproach* (!) we have never seized upon a foot of land belonging to any neighbor,' do you mean to quibble with the term *neighbor?* Have the Cherokees, have the Seminoles and the other Indian tribes, lost not 'a foot of land' by our plundering disposition? Are not their cries continually going up to Heaven, that a righteous retribution may fall upon us for our horrid cruelties toward them — for driving them from their fertile lands, extinguishing their council fires, spilling their blood, and conspiring for their extermination? * But what if, for fifty years, we had committed no trespass: would that fact render venial an act of perfidy and robbery, committed by us at the close of that period? For half a century, we stole from none of our neighbors, whether powerful or weak; therefore, we are incapable of committing a theft! Such is your logic.

Sir, robbery is, and always has been, the grand business of this nation — its prominent characteristic and ruling passion. As a people,

* I had scarcely written these sentences, before the following paragraph met my eye, in the Vicksburg Sentinel of the 18th ultimo.[6] It refers to the Choctaw Indians:

'The last remnants of this once powerful tribe are now crossing our ferry on their way to their new home in the Far West . . . They are going away! With a visible reluctance which nothing has overcome but the stern necessity which they feel impelling them, they have looked their last on the graves of their sires — the scenes of their youth — and have taken up their slow toilsome march, with their household gods among them, to their new home in a strange land. They leave names to many of our rivers, towns, and counties; and so long as our State remains, the Choctaws, who once owned most of her soil, will be remembered.'

we 'have used oppression, and exercised robbery, and have vexed the poor and needy: yea, we have oppressed the stranger wrongfully.' [7] If we have not been distinguished for land-stealing, the fact is to be accounted for simply on the ground that our domains were already sufficiently extensive for our purposes. We have signalized ourselves by atrocities of a deeper dye, and which 'overpass the deeds of the wicked'; [8] — for in our skirts is found the blood of innocence; and our traffic is in 'slaves and the souls of men.' [9]

Has wounded and bleeding Africa no charges to prefer against us at the bar of God, for invading her territory, giving her beautiful villages to the consuming fire, slaughtering countless numbers of her inoffensive children, and dooming to the chains and stripes of a fright-ful servitude, such of them as survived the horrors of 'the middle passage'? [10] You have the cool assurance to declare, that the Constitu-tion is 'without stain or reproach' — in the face of the damning fact, that, under that Constitution, — for twenty long years after its adop-tion, — the piratical slave trade was prosecuted by us as a lawful commerce; and even to this day, is protected by our national flag. 'Shall I not visit, for these things? saith the Lord. Shall not my soul be avenged on such a nation as this?' [11]

The inhabitants of Texas have long been proverbial for their in-famous character. By common consent she has been denominated 'the great valley of rascals' — a chosen refuge for all swindlers, counter-feiters, burglars and cut-throats, escaping from the United States.[12] Doubtless, she has a few, a very few worthy citizens; but, as a whole, her population is nothing better than a vast banditti, surrounded by the forms of law. Yet, so corrupt are you in sentiment, so debased in spirit, so abject in servility, you hail them as 'our brethren, our kith and kin, men who have worshipped at the same altars (!) with us, who have been educated at the same schools, and *trained up to the same republican principles'!!* Again, you eulogize them as 'our own brethren — our own children — our fellow-soldiers, who have fought with us side by side; our fellow-patriots, who, like ourselves, have contended for their liberties and independence, and, *like ourselves*, have established A FREE CONSTITUTION'!! Nay, a third time you are impelled to utter the language of panegyric, in contemplating their virtuous and *democratic* character! They are 'a people more than leavened by Americanism — a people possessing unity of birth and religion — unity of education — unity of social habits — unity of prin-ciples, throughout, with *ourselves and our immortal fathers* — trained to REPUBLICAN forms and self-government long enough and strong enough'!!! [13]

Are you not ashamed of yourself, Senator Woodbury? What do you mean by that cabalistical word 'democracy'? Liberty to buy, sell, steal and flog negroes, and to lynch abolitionists, *ad libitum?* Do you not know that no man's life is safe in Texas, who proclaims himself hostile to slavery? Do you not know that, by the 'free Constitution' of Texas, no free colored person is allowed to remain on her soil? Do you not know that, by the same instrument, slavery is made perpetual? Do you not know that these Texians, 'trained up to the same republican principles with ourselves,' are systematic slave traders, slave speculators, and slave plunderers, who neither fear God nor regard man? And yet you glory in their character and deeds! Away, to Texas! or hide yourself from the presence of the virtuous and good! Your democracy is a sham.

Lamenting the prostitution of your talents, reprobating the dishonesty of your course, and loathing the very name of a pro-slavery democrat, I remain,

Your plain-spoken friend,

WM. LLOYD GARRISON.

Printed: *The Liberator*, March 14, 1845.

Levi Woodbury (1789–1851) was a United States senator, cabinet officer, and associate justice of the Supreme Court. A Dartmouth graduate and lawyer by profession, his first elective office was that of governor of New Hampshire (1823–1825). While opposed to slavery, Woodbury thought that the laws upholding it must be obeyed until repealed. He advocated free public schools, prison reform, and poor relief.

1. Micah 7:4.
2. Ezekiel 22:27.
3. Isaiah 5:20.
4. The Washington *Daily Globe* and the *Semi-Weekly Globe*, February 27, 1845.
5. Boston *Post*, January 30, 1845.
6. The quotation Garrison refers to appeared in the Vicksburg *Daily Sentinel*, February 18, 1845, and he quotes with reasonable accuracy.
7. Garrison quotes Ezekiel 22:29, changing the word "they" to "we."
8. Jeremiah 5:28.
9. Revelation 18:13.
10. "The middle passage" refers to the Atlantic Ocean.
11. Jeremiah 5:9.
12. Statements about Texas like Garrison's were common, even in the South. For example, Charles Hooton, an Englishman who visited Texas in 1845, wrote in his book, *St. Louis' Isle, or Texiana* (London, 1847, p. 15): "Texas generally may with safety be regarded as a place of refuge for rascality and criminality of all kinds." In the Savannah *Republican*, May 11, 1844, Texas is alluded to as a refuge for convicts: "To all intents and purposes, Texas has been the Botany Bay of the United States for the last eight years."
13. Throughout this letter Garrison quotes Woodbury's speech accurately, adding his own italics.

1 1 3

TO LUCRETIA MOTT

[May 8, 1845.]

Be assured I will do every thing in my power, to give the Biography of the devoted Lundy a wide circulation, and a favorable reception.[1] My admiration of the fearless determination, the untiring perseverance, the unconquerable spirit, the far-reaching philanthropy of this remarkable man, is not abated by the lapse of time; but increased the more I contemplate the state of the country at the time he labored, to extirpate from our land the direful curse of slavery. I shall ever remember him with gratitude, as well as admiration, and I ratify your declaration, that "there is certainly much due to his memory."

What tho' he labored under some mistakes — what tho' he did not perceive all the steps necessary to be taken, before the slave system could be destroyed, have we not all of us erred in some particulars and been continually learning something in regard to our duties and responsibilities, that we did not know or perceive at the beginning of our work? Lundy in his day was a prodigy — and he deserves a high place among the benefactors of mankind

Handwritten transcription of extract: Villard Papers, Harvard College Library; also printed, with a few editorial changes, in the *Pennsylvania Freeman*, May 22, 1845, and in *The Liberator*, August 1, 1845.

1. Benjamin Lundy (1789–1839), a Quaker, was an active abolitionist as early as 1816 when he urged the formation of antislavery societies. From 1821 to 1835 he published the *Genius of Universal Emancipation*. During these years Lundy was interested in the question of colonizing freed Negroes and made many trips to explore possible locations. In 1829 Garrison joined Lundy, upon his request, as associate editor of the *Genius*, but Garrison's vitriolic writing led to legal action and his quick departure from the editorship. From 1836 to 1838 Lundy published the *National Enquirer and Constitutional Advocate of Universal Liberty*, which was devoted to exposing what Lundy considered the slaveholders' plot to annex Texas. In 1838 this paper was taken over by John G. Whittier, who changed its name to the *Pennsylvania Freeman*. The forthcoming biography to which Garrison refers is by Thomas Earle, *The Life, Travels and Opinions of Benjamin Lundy, Including His Journeys to Texas and Mexico; with a Sketch of Contemporary Events, and a Notice of the Revolution in Hayti* (Philadelphia, 1847).

1 1 4

TO GEORGE W. BENSON

Boston, May 19, 1845.

Dear bro. George:

We did not send George on Saturday, on account of the severe storm. This morning looks bright and pleasant, and he must take his chance alone; for we have been waiting in vain, for some time, for some one going to Northampton, in whose care to send him. I trust he will reach the Community safely.

In the last Albany Patriot [1] is a letter from its editor, James C. Jackson, written from New-York city, in which is given to the public the following extraordinary declaration: —

"On my way back to this city, I called and saw James Boyle and wife at Newark, N.J. He is a clerk in a hosiery store. James has learned the character of the Garrison clique to perfection. To use his own language, they are "devils incarnate." He gave me a full history of his battles with Garrison, Phillips, Mrs. Chapman, &c., about their attempts to cover up the rascality and meanness of J. A. Collins; said that they admitted many charges against Collins, but declared it would not do to say it *aloud* — it would be giving New Organization advantage. Said Garrison is as thoroughly enslaved as man can be; that he says only what Mrs. Chapman allows, on controverted points; and told me some things about the controversy in New-Hampshire between [Nathaniel P.] Rogers and [Stephen S.] Foster and Abby Kelley worth preserving, inasmuch as the tribe contemplate a descent upon our State this season. Coming as they do from Boyle, they are entitled to consideration, these things are. *He was very glad to see me*; inquired after all *the Liberty men* whom he had known in our State, and *bade us all success* as the TRUE and EFFECTIVE representatives of the principles of liberty."

Now, dear George, is it within the scope of *possibility* that our friend Boyle used such language as the above to that base apostate from our cause, James C. Jackson? I will not believe it, until I hear it confirmed substantially by Boyle himself. Yet its appearance in the Patriot looks as if there must be some foundation for it; for would Jackson be so great a fool to put it forth publicly, as "a lie made out of whole cloth," when he would thus certainly expose himself to refutation and shame? James has never had any "battles" with me, or with Phillips or Mrs. Chapman, about Collins; and if we have become "devils incarnate" in his eyes, we must have fallen with the rapidity of the apostate angels. What is to come next?

Do you read Rogers's Herald of Freedom? It grows more and more conceited, and more and more venomous. His malignity will surpass his former friendship.

With much love to Catharine, I remain,

Yours, unswervingly,

Wm. Lloyd Garrison.

ALS: Garrison Papers, Boston Public Library.

1. A weekly paper (c. 1841–1848), originally called the *Tocsin of Liberty* and purchased by Jackson in 1844. (*ULN.*)

115

TO FRANCIS JACKSON

Wednesday Morning.
July 2, 1845.

My Dear Friend:

It is settlement day with me for another quarter of the year, and I find myself in the same predicament (owing to the non-payment of a debt of $50 due me from another) that I was at the previous quarter. As I am anxious to keep my credit good with my landlord, &c., if you can loan me $50 (fifty) till the expiration of the present month, when I shall receive my monthly stipend, you will greatly oblige me.

It may happen to be quite inconvenient for you to do so. In that case, I will apply elsewhere.

Yours, truly,

Wm. Lloyd Garrison.

☞ Should it be convenient to make the loan, I will hand you a receipt for the same when I see you. I am very busy to-day at my office; have not been well for several days past.

ALS: Garrison Papers, Boston Public Library.

The recipient of this letter, although not specified on the manuscript, is undoubtedly Francis Jackson, whom Garrison regularly addresses as "My Dear Friend," and from whom he often borrows money; moreover, the letter is so attributed in the collection at the Boston Public Library.

116

TO ELIHU BURRITT

[Boston, July 16, 1845.]

DEAR SIR —

It is not with any wish or intention to wound your feelings, or to do you the slightest injustice, that I have placed in a department of the Liberator, long since consecrated as the 'Refuge of Oppression,' an extract of a letter addressed by you to SAMUEL LEWIS, Esq., of Cincinnati, and read in the great Liberty party Convention, held in that city on the 11th ultimo; [1] but solely to indicate my estimate of the actual position to which you stand committed by that extract, adverse to the cause of God and the rights of man. I am unwilling to believe, however, that you mean to do an evil deed, or to connive at wickedness on the part of others; and therefore I wish to call your attention to what may have been written in great haste, and without due consideration of the language used by you in regard to the AMERICAN UNION.

You are a scholar; and none the less for being a self-taught one. As a linguist, your proficiency has been so great as to secure for you the title of 'the learned blacksmith.' Hence, no one knows better than yourself the force and meaning of words; how important it is, especially in all grave discussions, that they should be used with care and precision; what they generally signify, and how are popularly understood. With the diplomatist, language may be 'the art of concealing thought'; but with him who is upright in heart, it is the symbol of truth and honesty, both in purpose and action.

You strongly reprobate a dissolution of the Union, and represent those who are in favor of such a measure as exhibiting a 'pusillanimous distrust in God.' In your opinion, it is a 'suicidal arm' that would strike the blow; for the Union is 'the concentrating nucleus of the hopes and interests of the future ages of humanity' — 'the child of all that the progressive ages of humanity have produced of freedom and virtue' — 'the ISAAC of the race, in which all the nations of the earth should be blessed' — 'the whole moral power we have and need to abolish slavery' — 'worth the world to the destiny of human nature for the abolition of slavery.' The idea of its dissolution is a 'treacherous' one, that should be 'banished from every American heart' — for its lineaments are 'Satanic,' though it may assume 'the guise of an angel of light.' [2] In short, you seem to regard the American Union with as much reverence as if it were the stone, 'cut out without hands,' which Nebuchadnezzar saw in his troublous dream, and which became a great mountain, and filled the whole earth; or as if it were 'the New Jerusalem, coming down from God out of heaven,' which John describes with so much pious enthusiasm.[3]

On this subject, your language astonishes, shocks, appals me! If it be not used deceitfully — if it be not a mere flourish of rhetoric — if it mean what the people in this land, what the people in other lands, will understand it to mean, without some new and extraordinary interpretation — then I am constrained to pronounce it in a high degree impious, and worthy of all condemnation. But if you really mean nothing by it, or something existing only in the imagination, then are you trifling with common sense and the human understanding, and worshipping at an unknown shrine.

The American Union — what is it? Is it of heaven, or of men? Is it a fanciful abstraction, or a living reality? Is its scope local or universal? Has it geographical boundaries, or does it embrace the globe? What are its height and depth, its length and breadth? On what basis does it rest? For what was it designed, and what is its irresistible tendency? Is it imbued with the spirit of peace and good will to the human race, or is it at war with all the prerogatives of God, with the gospel of his dear Son, with the sacred and inalienable rights of man?

These questions are pregnant with meaning. How will you answer them? Or will you refuse to give a reason for the faith that is in you, in regard to this matter? Believe me, dear sir, I have no desire to be hypercritical, but feel deeply serious on this subject.

The words, 'American Union,' have but one meaning in the popular mind; and whatever you may have intended to express by them, in your letter to the Cincinnati Convention, you cannot doubt that they convey essentially the same idea to the great body of the American people. This Union is nothing more, nothing less, than what those who framed it intended it to be. It is the work of men's hands, and therefore may be imperfect, oppressive, or monstrous. In your eyes, it seems to be without spot or blemish — 'the end of the law for righteousness'[4] to every one that lives under it — so sacred that 'Nature itself would repel the profane disruption of a system, to whose integrity every stream, from the Sabine to the St. Johns, is as necessary as any vein in the human body'!! And it is your object to make all others regard it in the same heavenly light! Those who call for its dissolution you would have branded as traitors, and treated as under Satanic influences!

Such, also, is the estimate placed upon it by James K. Polk, the President of the United States, in his inaugural address. He says — 'The *inestimable* value of our federal Union is felt and acknowledged by all . . . New communities and States are seeking protection under its aegis, and multitudes from the Old World are flocking to our shores to participate in its blessings. Beneath its benign sway, peace and prosperity prevail . . . These are some of the blessings secured to our happy land by our federal Union. To perpetuate them, it is our sacred duty to preserve it. Who shall assign limits to the achievements of free minds and free hands, (!) under the protection of this glorious Union? *No treason to mankind, since the organization of society, would be equal in atrocity to that of him who would lift his hand to destroy it* (!) He would overthrow the noblest structure of human wisdom, which protects himself and his fellow-man (!) He would stop the progress of free government, (!) and involve his country either in anarchy or despotism. He would extinguish the fire of liberty, (!) which warms and animates the hearts of happy millions, and invites all the nations of the earth to imitate our example' (!!) [5]

I need not tell you who is James K. Polk, nor under what circumstances he was elected to the presidential office. Professing to be a democrat of the purest stamp, he does not scruple to enslave men, women and children, and to stand forth as the representative and advocate of a most bloody and heathenish system, which degrades to a level with four-footed beasts as large a population as swarms in all New-England. Almost unknown to the country — possessing talents of an ordinary character — he was nominated for the Presidency solely because he was ascertained to be in favor of committing the greatest crime of the age, namely, the annexation of Texas, in order to give ample scope and security to southern slavery. The party by which he was chosen as its truest representative also claims to be democratic, and makes the loudest professions of regard for liberty and equal rights; but among all the languages of the globe, words cannot be found adequately to describe its unparalleled hypocrisy and heaven-daring profligacy. It has a cannibal appetite for human flesh and blood, which seems to grow rapacious in proportion to the number of its victims. Dead to shame, its conscience seared as with a hot iron, and possessed of a legion of devils, it is desperately bent on perpetrating every crime that can inflame heaven, or curse the earth. I need not dwell on these facts, because they are as familiar to you as to myself; but I cannot refrain from asking you, how it happens that you and James K. Polk regard with so much attachment the same federal Union, if it be (as you say it is) 'the concentrating nucleus of the hopes and interests of the future ages of humanity,' — 'the ISAAC of the race, in which all nations should be blessed'? You profess to be an anti-slavery man, — an unflinching abolitionist. I am wholly at a loss, therefore, to know how you and Mr. Polk harmonise so perfectly in your views of the Union. Is he deceived, or are you, in regard to its true character? Or do you mean one thing by it, and he quite another? What is your meaning?

The American Union is but another name for the American Constitution. There was no such Union until the adoption of that Constitution; and the repeal or abrogation of the latter will be the dissolution of the former. How, dear Sir, with the Madison Papers in your hands — with the history of the country before your eyes — with full knowledge of the fact, that the people have always been in favor of slavery, and have never been willing to leave one square foot of State or national territory, on which a fugitive slave might claim protection and redress — you can eulogize that Constitution as 'the Isaac of the race,' or give it any countenance, either as an abolitionist or the friend of universal peace, is to me quite incomprehensible.[6] I am constrained to regard it with unutterable abhorrence, and to labor for its subversion by all just and righteous means. Truly, as did those of old, against whom the prophet testified, — 'We have made a covenant with death, and with hell are we at agreement'; and like them we have the impious assurance to say, 'When the overflowing scourge shall pass through, it shall not come unto us; for we have made lies our refuge, and under falsehood have we hid ourselves.' But I hear the voice of God saying, 'Your covenant with death shall be annulled, and your agreement with hell shall not stand: when the overflowing scourge shall pass through, then shall ye be trodden down by it. Judgment also will I lay to the line, and righteousness to the plummet; and the hail shall sweep away the refuge of lies, and the water shall overflow the hiding place.'[7] My soul exclaims — 'THE WILL OF GOD BE DONE.['][8]

You are against a dissolution of the Union! So is John Tyler, so is John C. Calhoun, so is James K. Polk, so *was* Andrew Jackson! Is not this to strike hands with thieves, and to consent with adulterers? For how can two walk together, except they are agreed? and what fellowship hath light with darkness?[9]

I have some other thoughts on this subject, which I must reserve for another letter. In the mean time, assuring you of my desire to be a co-worker with you in every righteous enterprise, I remain,

Yours for a dissolution of every pro-slavery alliance, and the reign of Christ throughout the earth,

WM. LLOYD GARRISON.

Boston, July 16, 1845.

Printed: *The Liberator*, July 18, 1845.
    Elihu Burritt (1810–1879), the so-called "learned blacksmith," was both linguist and reformer. He was especially dedicated to the cause of world peace. In 1846 he was to organize in England the League of Universal Brotherhood; two

years later he helped arrange the Brussels Peace Congress. Late in life he retired to New Britain, Connecticut, devoting himself to farming, writing, and teaching languages.

1. Burritt's letter was printed in *The Liberator*, July 18, 1845.

Samuel Lewis (1799–1854), the first superintendent of common schools in Ohio, was one of the most influential founders of the public school system in that state. In 1841, with Salmon P. Chase and others, he organized the Liberty party, which nominated him for Congress in 1843 and 1848, and for governor in 1846, 1851, and 1853.

2. Garrison quotes Burritt's letter correctly.

3. Garrison quotes from and alludes to Daniel 2:31–35 and Revelation 21:2.

4. Romans 10:4.

5. Garrison's quotations from Polk's inaugural address are accurate except for variations in the punctuation (see Renzo D. Bowers, *Inaugural Addresses of the Presidents*, St. Louis, 1929, pp. 191–192).

6. A three-volume edition of the papers of James Madison, edited by H. D. Gilpin, had appeared in 1840. Garrison had himself made those parts of the papers concerned with the Constitution readily available by printing excerpts in *The Liberator* (September 13, 1844) and by publishing a fuller pamphlet (January 1845).

7. Isaiah 28:15, 18, and 17.

8. Garrison refers to Matthew 6:10.

9. Garrison adapts Amos 3:3 and II Corinthians 6:14.

117

TO SAMUEL J. MAY

Boston, July 17, 1845.

Beloved Friend:

I am determined not to measure your friendship by the number of letters I receive from you; and I protest against your forming any estimate of my love for you by any such standard. Each of us is busy in his sphere, and much leisure is not a thing known to either of us. Though, in a bodily sense, you are further removed from me than ever, yet you are as near and dear to me in spirit as though you were constantly by my side. I deny the verity of the proverb, in your case — "Out of sight, out of mind." It may apply in some cases, to some persons; but not to me or to you.

How do you find yourself situated in Syracuse? As to the place itself, though I visited it in the winter season, it impressed me favorably.[1] Of the inhabitants, I could form no just opinion, because I had no time to become acquainted with them. Some of them mobbed our anti-slavery convention; but such things have been done in Boston, you know — and I think pretty well of Boston, nevertheless. The few friends I met with in Syracuse were among the kindest of the kind, the truest of the true; and never shall I cease to remember them with gratitude and love. Especially shall I ever feel under heavy obligations to the lamented Wing Russell and his estimable wife, and to Stephen Smith and his wife. Their hospitality was really munificent, and their countenance and co-operation, at that trying period, of great service to the persecuted but godlike cause of anti-slavery. Do not fail to proffer them my warmest regards and my most grateful recollections. I wish it were in my power to make a visit to you all, before the summer vanishes; but I can only commune with you in spirit — for here my body must be imprisoned.

The abolitionism which surrounds you, I presume is generally of the Liberty party stamp. How much does it differ from the new organization of *the* East? It has, no doubt, some excellent supporters, in intention, among the mass; but, as a political affair, there cannot be much real vitality in it. I trust your anti-slavery and Christian testimony is against any political action under the present pro-slavery, war-sanctioning Constitution of the United States. You have seen the Disunion and Anti-Slavery Peace Pledges in the Liberator.[2] How many are there in Syracuse, who are prepared to affix their signatures to them? Whatever doubt or hesitancy there may be, on the part of some, respecting the Disunion Pledge, I should like to look in the face the professed abolitionist or peace man, who is unwilling to sign the Peace Pledge. We intend to canvass the free States on this subject; and that it is a vital movement is demonstrated by the outcries of the enemies of the brotherhood of the human race. Let us be found wholly on the side of God and his dear Son, and have no part nor lot in the kingdom of darkness.

A short time since, I received a Syracuse paper, (probably sent by you,) in which is a communication, complaining of a peace discourse delivered by you, as though it were a very treasonable affair. I read it with a smile, and the gladness to know that you were determined to be faithful to the Master whom you profess to serve; whose kingdom is one of peace and righteousness, whose mission it is to beat all murderous weapons into useful instruments, and who came to save men's lives, not to destroy them. May you be strengthened from on high to declare the whole counsel of God, not fearing what men may say of you, or do to you.[3] There must be no compromise of principle, even to save father or mother, wife or sister, children or friends. All is lost where the truth is surrendered.

My attention has recently been drawn to the subject of Phonography and Phonotypy, and I want you, as a friend of universal reform, to look into it; for I am persuaded you will be delighted with it, as I have been. It is a new system of writing and printing, invented by Mr. Isaac Pitman, a teacher in Bath, England, by which the ignorant masses may be taught to read and write in an almost incredibly short space of time — compressing the labor of months into weeks, and of years into months.[4] As a teacher, and a scholar, you know how monstrous and endless are the absurdities and perplexities of English orthography, and how laborious is the ordinary mode of writing. But here is a system devised, which brings order out of chaos, makes every thing plain, simple, consistent, and infallibly sure, surpasses stenography in the rapidity of writing, and is perhaps next in importance to the discovery of printing in the fifteenth century. It is making great progress in England, and is receiving in this quarter a strong impetus. Several hundred persons in this city, (a large number of school teachers included,) have already taken lessons in it, among whom I am one. Our teacher is Mr. Augustus F. Boyle, an English young gentleman, who has been teaching the French language for the last three years, and who enters into this new reform with zeal and spirit.[5] He will probably hand this letter to you, as he leaves immediately to attend a convention of teachers, which is to be held in a few days in Syracuse. As he will be able to give you all the information you may desire in regard to this matter, I need not add any more. I understand Mr. Peirce, of the Normal School, is much interested in it.[6] This evening we meet to form an American Phonographic Society.[7]

With much love to your wife and Susan,[8] in which Helen warmly joins, I remain, faithfully,

Yours for the cross and the crown,[9]

Wm. Lloyd Garrison.

ALS: Garrison Papers, Boston Public Library; partly printed in *Life*, III, 148.

1. Garrison is looking back to his visit to Syracuse in the winter of 1842.
2. The pledges to which Garrison refers were printed in *The Liberator*, July 18, 1845. Signers of the disunion pledge were expected to make all possible efforts to foster "peaceable dissolution of the Union." In particular they were committed not to countenance the election of any candidate whose office required the taking of an oath to support the Constitution. Signers of the peace pledge were obliged not to support any war that might result from the annexation of Texas or from any other war "designed to strengthen or perpetuate slavery."
3. Garrison alludes to Isaiah 2:4, Luke 9:56, and Acts 20:27.
4. Isaac Pitman (1813–1897) had developed a system of shorthand based not upon orthographic but upon phonetic principles. The system was introduced to Boston in 1845 by Samuel P. Andrews. Garrison was so interested in phonography that he gave it much publicity in *The Liberator* (see the issues for July 11, 18, October 17, 1845; January 16, March 20, April 10, 1846; and January 1, 1847).
5. Augustus French Boyle (1818–1894) was the English assistant to Samuel P. Andrews. Not only did he teach the new system in Boston and, beginning in 1847, in New York, but he also collaborated in preparing *The Complete Phonographic Class Book* (1845). (Letter to the editor from Joan Gibbs, archivist, University of London Library, December 31, 1970.)
6. Cyrus Peirce (1790–1860), a graduate of Harvard College and Divinity School, became a minister, then a teacher, and later the principal of various high

schools. He is chiefly known, however, for his reform and reorganization of the public school system of Massachusetts.

7. It is seldom realized that Garrison was instrumental in founding the American Phonographic Society, becoming a member of its executive council.

8. Susan Coffin, Mrs. May's sister.

9. An allusion to William Penn's *No Cross, No Crown* (1669).

118

TO EDMUND QUINCY

Boston, July 18, 1845.

My dear Quincy:

Thanks for your letter. If I am able to be any where on the first of August, I intend being at the Dedham gathering; but I hope no great amount of *speaking* responsibility will be imposed upon me, as my bodily health is poor, and as I shall be severely tasked during my attendance upon the Pennsylvania meeting, which is to be held in a few days afterward. — I hope our Pic Nic will be worthy of the day, in spirit, action, and numbers.[1]

I have not seen the number of "*The* Herald," to which you allude, and therefore know nothing more of its contents than what you communicate. You may rest assured that I have done with R. and his paper.[2] My last review of his course was declared to be final; and I shall keep my word, unless something so monstrous turns up, on his part, as to make some allusion to him absolutely necessary. It must be monstrous indeed, to change my determination. I have lost all curiosity to see his paper, and therefore do not think of borrowing it for perusal. Sadly do I feel in view of R's downward course; for I fear he will never rise again, though he vauntingly take for his motto, "Excelsior." Among those who have discontinued the Liberator, on account of their sympathy with Rogers, are William Bolles of New London, and Peleg Clarke of Coventry.[3]

Yesterday we had an informal meeting of our Executive Committee, to examine the present condition of the Standard, as presented by Mr. [Sydney Howard] Gay at the request of our Treasurer. The subscription list has received a severe shock, and is much more reduced than I had supposed; and, according to Mr. Gay, the prospect of its still further reduction is quite certain, unless some vigorous efforts are made to increase its dimensions. That the list is so small is not owing to the lack of editorial ability, but mainly, if not solely, to the position which it occupies in regard to the Church and State. The expense of keeping the Standard afloat is so great, that friend Gay thinks it a question deserving of serious consideration, whether it is best to continue the paper. For my part, I am prepared to say, the Standard must not be struck, so long as we have a single shot left in the locker. Its bare existence is worth a very large sum to our cause, which cannot be so well expended in any other manner.

This is a trying period to us all. The enemy has never dreaded or hated us more than at the present time — the highest proof we can have of our fidelity and efficiency! The subscription list of the Liberator, like that of the Standard, is becoming reduced, and a new subscriber is rarely obtained. Well, the paper has seen many a dark hour, but deliverance has again and again been vouchsafed to it in a most remarkable manner. When the time shall come that it can be sustained no longer, it shall disappear with its flag nailed to the mast-head.

Please give my warm congratulations to Mrs. Quincy on the happy birth of another child; [4] and trusting that she and the babe are doing well, I remain, my dear Q.,

Your faithful friend,

Wm. Lloyd Garrison.

ALS: Garrison Papers, Sophia Smith Collection, Smith College Library.

1. The Norfolk County meeting of the Massachusetts Anti-Slavery Society was to be held on the morning of August 1, 1845, in the town hall of Dedham. Following the formal meeting the group adjourned to "the Grove" for discussions and a picnic. Garrison was elected "President of the Day" and made a lengthy speech (reprinted in *The Liberator*, August 15, 1845).

The "Pennsylvania meeting" refers to that of the Eastern Pennsylvania Anti-Slavery Society to be held in the Old Kennett Meeting-house, Chester County, August 11, 1845.

2. Nathaniel P. Rogers and the *Herald of Freedom*.

3. William Bolles (1800–1867), the successful proprietor of the publishing and bookselling firm of W. & J. Bolles in New London, Connecticut, was a Swedenborgian and a radical abolitionist. He was the author of the popular *Bolles' Spelling Book*, the editor of a *Phonographic Pronouncing Dictionary of the English Language*, and the compiler of *The Complete Evangelist*, a gospel history of the life of Christ. (New London *Daily Star*, July 22, 1867.)

4. Morton Quincy (1845–1849).

119

TO JAMES MILLER McKIM

Boston, July 19, 1845.

My dear McKim:

Your letter contains several items of interest and encouragement, respecting the aspect of our cause in your vicinity, which I have read with great pleasure. Though the position which fidelity to our anti-slavery professions requires us to occupy, — a total separation from Church and State, and a warfare upon both as the existing bulwarks of the slave system, — is a trying one, in a worldly sense, yet I am sure that it is impregnable, and will give us more power over the nation, and do more to hasten the overthrow of slavery, than any other that we could possibly occupy. It will cause a still further reduction of our numbers, (though, thank Heaven! we have not many more to lose,) but it will also serve to demonstrate to the fearful and unbelieving, that, in a righteous enterprise, "one shall chase a thousand, and two put ten thousand to flight" — and that "the wicked flee when no man pursueth, but the righteous are as bold as a lion."[1] O, to be exactly in the right — to stand on an immovable foundation — to have reason and truth with us — to have the strong arm of God to sustain us — what strength, what confidence, what joy, what assurance of victory, it imparts! It destroys all fear of man — it keeps the moral vision clear — it makes absurd and worthless, as well as criminal, any substitution of expediency for principle, of policy for honesty. Come what may, it enables the soul to be always confident and erect — to perceive the end from the beginning — to be exceeding glad when a scoffing world is expecting to see it filled with despair.

Be assured that I have a yearning desire to be with you as early next month as practicable, and that I stand in need of no entreaties to convince me that our cause in Eastern Pennsylvania.[2] But my bodily condition is such that I must use great caution in regard to what I may promise, or undertake to perform. I ought to be at the Water Cure infirmary at Brattleboro', Vt., under the care of my physician, Dr. Wesselhoeft, rather than attending anti-slavery meetings, or attempting to lecture before the public.[3] I have scarcely recovered from the shock my system received at the last New-England Convention.[4] My lungs are now very easily affected — my left side is permanently diseased — and I suffer a great deal in my spine. Hence, while the spirit is willing, the body is weak.[5]

I do not, now, see how I can be with you before Saturday noon, August 9th. If I can make my arrangements to come a day or two earlier, I will try to let you know in season. You may, if you please, make two appointments for me to "sermonise" in your city on Sunday, the 10th; and in the evening, I will give an anti-slavery lecture, if Wendell Phillips be not there to act as my substitute.[6] He is now residing out of the city,[7] and I have neither seen nor heard from him for several weeks. I am mightily apprehensive that he will fail of being at your State meeting; but I do not know to what extent he has pledged himself to you that he will be present. You will, of course, see that he has a letter, enforcing upon him the importance of his attendance; and he shall have one from me, if I fail to see him personally, as persuasively as I can write it. We must resolve "not to take NO for an answer," on his part. I think you had better advertise, that the lecture on Sunday evening will be delivered by him, or, in case of a failure, by myself as his substitute. I must make my arrangements, so as to return home by Saturday evening, August 16th. I regret that I cannot remain longer; but I feel sure that my health, as well as my home duties, will prevent me.

Please say to my beloved friend, Edward M. Davis, that "the progress of our cause" is too huge a theme for me to grapple with at present, and I cannot, therefore, comply with his kind request.

When you see Thomas S. Cavender, please inform him that I would gladly comply with his request, to send him a copy of the Liberator of November 3d, 1843, if it were in my power; but all the back numbers of the paper, up to January 1, 1845, have been disposed of.[8]

It will not be convenient for my wife to visit Philadelphia the present season. Her babe is but seven months old, and she shrinks from the idea of taking the little one on so long a journey, anxious as she is to see Philadelphia and the beloved friends in it. She reciprocates your friendly remembrances.

The thought of soon seeing my endeared friend, Lucretia Mott, gives me a thrill of pleasure. I hope to find her strength equal to her day. Pray give my loving regards to her and her husband [James], and to all the members of their family. My best regards to all the other friends, whose names it is unnecessary to recapitulate.

I have not seen [Nathaniel P.] Rogers's "*The* Herald of Freedom," for several weeks, and cease to feel the least curiosity as to its contents. His fall has been like that of Lucifer, and I fear he is never to rise again. All his flourishes about a free press, free speech, and free meetings, I regard as nothing better than the ostentation of cant.

Hoping nothing will arise to prevent my shaking hands with you in a few days, I remain, to the end,

Yours for the cross and the crown,

Wm. Lloyd Garrison.

ALS: Garrison Papers, Boston Public Library; printed partly in the *Pennsylvania Freeman*, July 31, 1845.

James Miller McKim (1810–1874) was a Presbyterian minister who relinquished his pastorate to devote his energies to the antislavery cause. His son Charles Follen McKim became a well-known architect; his daughter Lucy married Wendell Phillips Garrison.

1. Garrison quotes part of Deuteronomy 32:30 and Proverbs 28:1.
2. The incomplete predication in this sentence is Garrison's. McKim had invited Garrison to address a public meeting in Philadelphia, scheduled at Temperance

Hall for August 10, and Garrison had selected the Sabbath question as his topic. Two hostile reviews of his two-hour speech are reprinted in *The Liberator*, September 12, 1845. Henry Grew defended the speech in the *Pennsylvania Freeman*, September 11, 1845.

3. Dr. Robert Wesselhoeft had opened his water cure infirmary May 29, 1845.

4. Garrison appears to be suffering from some ailment caught at the annual convention at the Marlboro Chapel, May 27–29, 1845.

5. Garrison adapts Matthew 26:41.

6. Although the *Pennsylvania Freeman* for July 3, 1845, announces that Wendell Phillips will speak at the annual meeting of the Eastern Pennsylvania Anti-Slavery Society in Kennett Square on August 11, he appears not to have attended either this meeting or the earlier one in Philadelphia.

7. In Natick, Massachusetts, apparently.

8. Thomas S. Cavender, listed in the Philadelphia city directory as a conveyancer at 348 North 5th Street, was on the staff of the *Pennsylvania Freeman*

120

TO UNKNOWN RECIPIENT

BOSTON, JULY 25, 1845.

DEAR FRIEND: — The Executive Committee of the American Anti-Slavery Society have just met for the purpose of consulting as to the best mode of promoting the cause, during the ensuing six months. After a careful examination and comparison of the whole subject, they have resolved to address, personally, every devoted friend of the Society, in order to obtain his or her personal exertions at the point where they are at this moment most needed, to increase the circulation of the Standard.

We are, at the present moment, free from embarrassing debt. This freedom has been won by exhausting labors, imposed on a few individuals, and not by the liberality of the Society at large. We say not this by way of reproach; for in no benevolent society does the responsibility of the pecuniary burden, or of the laboring oar, ever fall impartially. We simply state the fact, that the knowledge of it may bring us help. We should not dream of sending such a communication as this to every one who *calls* himself a brother in the cause. It comes to you, dear friend, and a few others who have devoted themselves, with us, to make the sacrifices of life and labor in its behalf, which we pray God to bless, as a notification of the imperative need of immediate aid.

Of course, unless energetic effort be made now, we shall be as deeply in debt as ever at the end of the year. Not until we have done our utmost, do we call upon you for that co-operation which we never have sought, and feel sure that we never shall seek in vain.

Our duty to lend all present strength to the support of the Standard, appears clear from its indispensable necessity to the cause, and to the Society as the servant of the cause. It is our common organ and means of communication with the world, and with each other; — the repository of all facts and documents of the times, which can help us to a better understanding of our obstacles and fulfilment of our duty: and it is ever where the STANDARD should be — in the van of the march, or the thick of the battle.

But, above all, is it of consequence that it should be sustained, as the advocate of absolute morality and right on the subject of human freedom, in a land where the moral nature of men has been so nearly quenched by sixty years of compromise and guilty prosperity. The Standard is the representative of the AMERICAN ANTI-SLAVERY SOCIETY; and the AMERICAN ANTI-SLAVERY SOCIETY represents and leads, and wisely directs the Anti-Slavery movements it has originated. We witness, daily, the salutary and conservative effects of our high principled and deep rooted enterprise. Church and State, — party and sect, — society and individuals, — are all continually moved in a strong and altogether unexampled manner. The effect of a vigorous application of our principle of immediate repentance and renunciation, to the sin of sustaining, by participation, the pro-slavery government of the United States, — to the sin of swearing to support, as they are, the bloody compromises of the Constitution, — has been of unparalleled efficacy in sending through the community the idea of the horrible nature of slavery, and the thought of emancipation. That principle of immediate individual reform; of withdrawal of moral influence from the wrong scale, to place it in the right; of choosing, unhesitatingly and openly, whom we will serve, — the mammon of unrighteousness, or the LIVING GOD; of "taking, (in the emphatic language of Scripture,) the LORD's side;"[1] — that true and noble principle, that impregnable and holy position, have been the salvation of the cause, at the critical moment when the irksomeness of labor, the loss of novelty, and the delusion of hoping some other road to our object than through men's hearts, had well-nigh prevailed to scatter a movement, that outward assault had been tried upon for years in vain. It is as the occupant of this noble and only true position, that the Standard should be sustained with all our power, even were it not ably conducted in less important respects.

In our cause, as in the great Christian movement of which it is a portion and an emblem, "one thing is needful;" — and the Standard and the American Anti-Slavery Society have chosen the good part.[2] This makes it our *duty* to serve and to sustain both to the uttermost. We are thereby secured from "the incumbrance of selfish help;" —

shown who is false and dangerous to our cause in the world of profession; — freed from the pernicious and shameful attempts of such as are knowing enough to see the growing importance of the cause, while they are at the same time base enough to try to absorb it into their several partisan and sectarian schemes, for the promotion of their own selfish ends.

This is the distinctive characteristic which we have been most desirous to secure for the Standard as your organ, and to exhibit, ourselves, as your chosen servants for the cause, — the characteristic of entire disinterestedness. Dear and valued as our Society and our official organ are, it is only in a secondary sense. We rather choose that both should perish, doing right, than exist in temporising, and apparently flourishing connection with wrong. Extinction for such a reason would more promote our object, than existence prolonged by compromise. While a few of us remain faithful, the selfish efforts of others will be used instrumentally, by Divine Providence, for the furtherance of the cause. How blameable, then, not to make the exertion that will secure the continuance of agitation, and all its consequences of partisan and sectarian effort; partial and selfish labor; sincere, but mistaken devotedness. Let the American Society die, because of the dying out of the zeal and devotedness of its members, and see how speedily all the movements, which are the fruits of its living energy, in the churches, the legislatures, the parties, would die out. If we wish to excite and continue such movements as that of Cassius M. Clay in Kentucky, we must urge forward the American Anti-Slavery Society, with its visible representative — the Standard; for all such approximations to right principle, feeling and action, in the various movements of the times, have been from the beginning the fruit of our own adherence to the exact right.[3]

We desire the friends who may have been, at times, under the delusion of the early Christian disciples, looking to see the triumph of our association as "a temporal kingdom," (so to speak) — as a powerful partisan institution, which should be a source of honor and emolument to its supporters, while accomplishing the work of abolition — to remember that such is not, in human affairs, the outward and visible sign of fidelity to the right, — of success in its advocacy. We are able, as a Society, to show the world the true signs; — on one side, a little band, everywhere spoken against, without temporal means or advantage of any kind which the world can either give or take away; and on the other, an awakened nation, resisting unsuccessfully the progress of the truth which that little band exists to promulgate.

No one can help seeing, at a glance, that the more faithful we are, the greater must be the difficulty and the harder the dint of effort, by which our operations are to be sustained. The more explicit, uncompromising and effectual upon the nation is our common organ, the Standard, the less support can it derive from its subscription list. Men do not willingly pay, beforehand, for their own conviction of sin; though, when converted, they bring forth for the conversion of others, a hundred fold.[4] Here, then, is the present and most urgent need of help — the circulation of the STANDARD.

We have entirely neglected, during the past year, the duty of obtaining subscribers, in our anxiety to pay off debts and furnish lecturers. We must now, therefore, while out of debt, and before the lecturing season arrives, atone for this long neglect. By a simultaneous effort to extend the circulation of the Standard, we should not only disseminate so much more anti-slavery truth, but we should be doing it in such a way as to prepare the ground before the lecturing agent, against the beginning of next winter, and we should thereby have saved the funds which usually come into our hands at that season, and which, in past years, have been devoted to payment of the debts of the Standard, and should be able to sustain lecturing agents to take advantage of the long evenings and the leisure of the people.

Independent of the indispensable necessity of sustaining the Standard to sustain the cause, we have other inducements to offer to the general reader. A series of articles is in preparation, embodying all that was worthy of note in the sojourn of H. G. and M. W. Chapman in the Island of Haiti — a spot most interesting to the lovers of freedom, and the friends of the human race. These will appear weekly, until a good degree of information shall have been given on the manners, laws, institutions, history, character, resources and prospects of the Haitians.[5]

It will be recollected that the French Government sent hither, some years since, a commission to examine our prison discipline, consisting of M. Alexis de Toqueville and M. Gustave de Beaumont.[6] They took the opportunity to examine, also, our government and manners; and while M. de Toqueville, in his "Democracy in America," gave the world his observations on the former, M. de Beaumont conveyed his impressions of the latter in a very interesting novel, entitled "Marie, or Slavery in the United States;" which has passed through many editions in France, but which has never appeared in this country, owing to the subserviency of northern publishers to southern slaveholders. This work is to be translated for the Standard, and to appear in weekly numbers in the miscellaneous department. It is admirably adapted to dissipate the degrading prejudice against race, which is at once the cause and the effect of slavery, and which forms the basis of all the obstacles we have to encounter.

Our extensive exchange list, and the increasing attention we gain from the South, are both strong motives for exertion to sustain our organ. We wish your instant help, at this, the critical moment, to ensure the continuance of this important influence upon the corps-editorial of the country, and upon the best hearts at the South. We learn that the Standard is regularly filed in the Southern reading rooms, even at New Orleans, and eagerly read.

Our main reliance for the continuance of so efficacious an instrumentality is the exertions of such devoted friends as yourself, for doubling our subscription list, that our present economical system of cash payments may not be broken in upon, and that the five hundred delinquent subscribers whom we have just struck off the list, may be replaced with such as may both profit by the paper, and help to sustain it.

The expenses of the paper are reduced to the lowest practicable point, and amount to far *less than those of any other paper of equal size*, on account of the great amount of gratuitous labor the committee bestow upon it. We only ask the friends of the cause not to forget that the time we thus expend in their service, takes from our ability to earn and economise, so that it precludes as large an appropriation of funds from our small personal means as we could otherwise make.

We look to you, at this moment, for instant, needed, indispensable aid. We entreat you, for your own sake, as the best anti-slavery economy — for the slave's sake, as the best anti-slavery agitation, "doctrine, reproof, correction and instruction in righteousness" [7] — *to go yourself,* from door to door, in your neighborhood, and obtain subscribers. Is it not practicable to obtain five additional subscribers in your parish? Do it, we entreat you. That number added from every parish in your State only, would give an immense subscription list. But we hope and trust that a specific effort, made by you, will be far more successful in your vicinity. If, for any reason, you think it in your case a surer mode, (as there is sometimes a delicacy about asking one's own neighbors a question which we would yet gladly have them asked,) to hire a true-hearted, faithful, competent person, on the usual terms of periodical agencies — i.e. 50 cents for each copy paid for in advance — *we hereby authorize you to do so on our behalf.* [This should be resorted to with caution, not only as a less economical method, but as presenting a temptation to one not faithful, to betray the cause or the truth, for the sake of obtaining a subscriber.]

In view of the malignant and indefatigable calumnies by which we are opposed, it will be well to assure all who are asked to subscribe, of the falsity of the frequent charge, that the Standard and the American Society have more than a single object — the abolition of Slavery.

☞ *No other end is advocated. We defy the strictest scrutiny*. Our religious views are as various as the degrees between high Calvinism and low Unitarianism; but we should despise ourselves, did we use the means and instrumentalities intrusted to us for the slave, for any other purpose, however good.

The first of August might be advantageously devoted to this work of obtaining subscribers. Not only on those few occasions, where a crowd affords an opportunity, but *everywhere* that the day dawns upon an abolitionist, who is asking himself how a day's work can be best made serviceable to the cause. But ☞ it is not a *day's* work alone, that is needed. *Let this be a six months' work with you*, and a broad foundation of future usefulness and success will have been laid. ✍

You may safely promise a paper as entertaining and interesting as the single subject of Slavery and its collateral bearings will admit; for we have made the requisite arrangements to insure such a paper.

But it will be open, faithful, and uncompromising, in a degree second to none, and to a degree which will make it incumbent upon us all to effect an extensive circulation, in the exact proportion that it renders that duty more difficult to fulfil.

Praying God to speed you in this, the most pressing service of this juncture, we are,

Your faithful and diligent servants for the cause,

WM. LLOYD GARRISON, *Pres. Am. A. S. Soc.*

WENDELL PHILLIPS, ⎫
M. W. CHAPMAN,   ⎬ *Secretaries.*
         ⎭

Printed form letter: Garrison Papers, Boston Public Library; Villard Papers, Harvard College Library.

1. An adaptation of Exodus 32:26.
2. Garrison adapts Luke 10:42.
3. Cassius Marcellus Clay (1810–1903), a colorful and sometimes violent man, was a politician and ardent abolitionist. In 1845 he founded at Lexington, Kentucky, the *True American*, an antislavery journal which hostile citizens tried to suppress by shipping its equipment to Cincinnati; Clay then published it from that city. He later took the paper, renamed the *Examiner*, to Louisville. Clay fought with distinction in the Mexican and Civil Wars and was a close friend of Abraham Lincoln. During the 1860's he served as United States minister to Russia.
4. Garrison echoes Matthew 13:23.
5. Ten "Haitian Sketches" were printed in the *National Anti-Slavery Standard*. The first, signed "C.," appeared June 12, 1845; the others appeared irregularly thereafter until November 13, 1845.
6. Garrison mentions two distinguished French writers and politicians, Alexis, Comte de Tocqueville (1805–1859), and Gustave de Beaumont (1802–1866). Tocqueville and Beaumont had been sent to the United States in 1831 to study the American prison system. The most important product of this joint tour was Tocqueville's *De la Démocratie en Amérique* (originally published in 1835, an

English translation appearing in New York in 1838). Garrison also refers in this paragraph to Beaumont's book *Marie, ou l'Esclavage aux États-Unis* (Paris, 1835), for which the author received a prize from the Académie Française and which was serialized in the *National Anti-Slavery Standard* between July 17 and December 18, 1845.

7. II Timothy 3:16.

121

TO WILLIAM ENDICOTT

Boston, July 31, 1845.

Friend Endicott:

We have supposed that there would be a pic nic held to-morrow by our true-hearted friends in Lowell, and, accordingly, entered into an agreement with our Scottish friend John Campbell Cluer [1] to attend it as one of the speakers who could be relied upon on the occasion; but we find, at this late hour, that our Lowell friends have failed to make the necessary arrangements, and that there is to be a Liberty party gathering in that city. Mr. Cluer is here, ready to fulfil his engagement. We should be very glad to have him go to Dedham or to Waltham; but as there will be no lack of speakers at either of those places, and as there is considerable uncertainty whether Rev. Mr. Stetson or Dr. Channing [2] will be present at your meeting, (indeed, I understand Dr. C. will not be able to attend,) we have requested friend Cluer to give you a lift, in genuine Scottish style, at Danvers. I think he will be quite an acquisition for the occasion; and as it is *British* West India emancipation (would it were *American* also!) that is to be celebrated to-morrow, it will not be "foreign interference" for him to have a hand in the affair. [3]

Our good friends at the gathering will see that his expenses from New Bedford, and something in addition, are given to him, as this is expected in his particular case, or at least was, if he went to Lowell. He is very poor, and needs sympathy and assistance as a stranger and an exile, both for himself and wife and child. He is disengaged, so that he can lecture on any of the reforms of the day in any of the towns in Essex County, if the friends wish to engage his services.

I send by him a letter which has just been received by Mr. Whipple,[4] our General Agent, from the Hon. Stephen C. Phillips, of Salem, which should be read, *emphatically*, at your gathering. It is quite brief, but contains *multum in parvo*, and gallantly commits him to the advocacy of the anti-slavery cause as paramount to all other political considerations.

Hoping that you will all have "a first rate time," and that a staggering blow will be given to our slave system, I remain, in haste,

Yours, come what may,

William Lloyd Garrison.

William Endicott.

ALS: Miscellaneous American Autographs, Pierpont Morgan Library.

William Endicott (1809–1881) of Danvers, Massachusetts, a lineal descendant of Governor John Endecott of Massachusetts, pursued the craft of morocco dressing, but because of his independent means retired early to follow humanitarian pursuits. He withdrew from the Baptist communion to attend the Unitarian church. Active in the antislavery movement, he wrote often for abolition papers. (Alfred P. Putnam, "History of the Anti-Slavery Movement in Danvers," *Danvers Historical Collections*, 30:22–23, 1942.)

1. Listed in the New Bedford city directory for 1845 as a temperance lecturer residing at 11 Sears Court.

2. Caleb Stetson (1795–1870), a graduate of Harvard College and of the divinity school, was a clergyman, a hypnotist, and an abolitionist. (*PMHS*, 9:128, 1895.)

William Henry Channing (1810–1884), nephew of William Ellery Channing, was a Unitarian clergyman who was for a time connected with Brook Farm and the Religious Union of Associationists. He was a strong advocate of abolition, temperance, and woman's rights.

3. In Massachusetts, West Indies Emancipation Day celebrations were held in Danvers, Lowell, Waltham, Dedham, Duxbury, Fall River, and Leicester (*The Liberator*, July 25, 1845).

4. Charles King Whipple (1808–1900) was treasurer of the New England Non-Resistance Society and assistant editor of the *Non-Resistant*. He also helped edit *The Liberator* during Garrison's third English mission in 1846. (*Life*.)

1 2 2

TO JAMES MILLER McKIM

Boston, Aug. 6, 1845.

My dear McKim:

The letter written jointly by dear Lucretia Mott and yourself was duly received, and was read with great pleasure. Say to her that I shall be delighted once more to see her in the flesh, and to be a sojourner in her family. I have not seen or heard any thing directly from Wendell Phillips, but have written to him on the subject, and presume he will faithfully redeem his pledge, and be with us. Caroline Weston will accompany us, and one or two female friends from Plymouth rock. [Frederick] Douglass intended going with us, but cannot, as he is to sail in the Liverpool steamer, from this port, on the 16th inst., with James N. Buffum. As to my Sunday lectures, I will give you one on "The Sabbath, as a Christian institution," and another on "The Duty

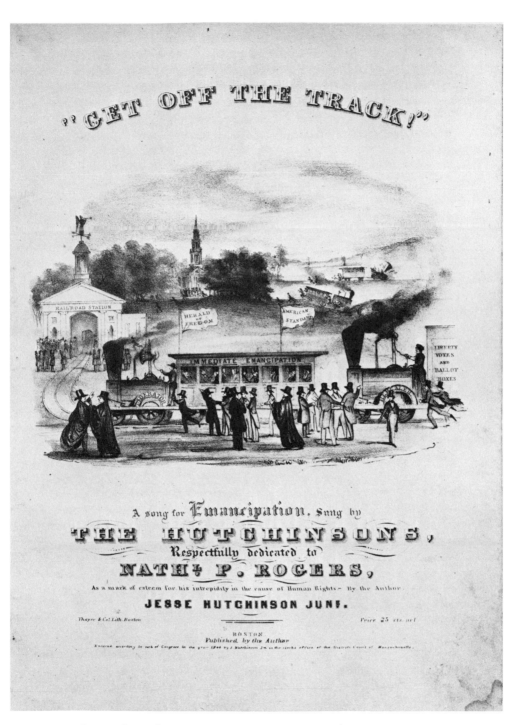

Cover of antislavery sheet music by Jesse Hutchinson, Jr., 1844

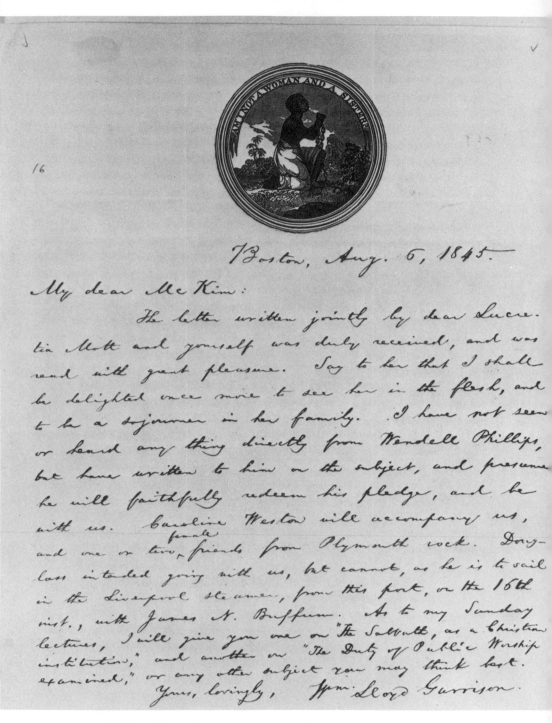

16

Boston, Aug. 6, 1845.

My dear McKim:

The letter written jointly by dear Lucretia Mott and yourself was duly received, and was read with great pleasure. Say to her that I shall be delighted once more to see her in the flesh, and to be a sojourner in her family. I have not seen or heard any thing directly from Wendell Phillips, but have written to him on the subject, and presume he will faithfully redeem his pledge, and be with us. Caroline Weston will accompany us, and one or two female friends from Plymouth rock. Douglass intended going with us, but cannot, as he is to sail in the Liverpool steamer, from this port, on the 16th inst., with James N. Buffum. As to my Sunday lectures, I will give you one on "The Sabbath, as a Christian institution," and another on "The Duty of Public Worship examined," or any other subject you may think best.

Yours, lovingly, Wm. Lloyd Garrison.

William Lloyd Garrison to James Miller McKim, August 6, 1845

of Public Worship examined," or any other subject you may think best.[1]
Yours, lovingly,

Wm. Lloyd Garrison.

ALS: Garrison Papers, Boston Public Library.

1. Garrison refers again to his public lecture scheduled for Sunday, August 10, in Temperance Hall, Philadelphia.

123

TO CHARLES SUMNER

Boston, August 23, 1845.

Dear Sir:

It is with great pleasure I comply with your request, to send your friend, Mrs. Rathbone of Liverpool, a copy of my prison sonnet, in my handwriting.[1] That sonnet was pencilled by me upon the wall of the prison, almost as soon as I was put into my cell — a cell which had just been vacated by a murderer, who was executed for his crime. I remained in prison forty-nine days. It is needless to add, that my imprisonment did not change my views of slavery or the slave trade!

I avail myself of this opportunity to thank you for your Fourth of July oration, on "The True Grandeur of Nations." I deeply regret that I was not present at its delivery; for I should like to have seen its effect on the countenances of those who delight in military parade, and whose God is the God of battles, not of peace. The manner in which they writhed at the dinner table demonstrated how mighty and invincible is the truth, and how much more potent are spiritual than carnal weapons. Their denunciations and reproaches are your best commendations; but you will also receive the fervent benedictions of all the true friends of the human race. In view of the war-clouds which now hang over our guilty country, your oration is singularly timely. That it may greatly aid in stopping the effusion of human blood, and hastening the epoch when men shall learn war no more,[2] is the fervent desire of

Your admiring friend,

Wm. Lloyd Garrison.

Charles Sumner, Esq.

ALS: Merrill Collection of Garrison Papers, Wichita State University Library.
Charles Sumner (1811–1874), to be known after 1851 as the leader among the abolitionists in the Senate, was before the Fourth of July speech Garrison lauds a little-known Boston lawyer. For the text of the speech see Sumner, *The Works of* . . . (Boston, 1875–1883), I, 5–132.

1. Garrison sends to Elizabeth Grey Rathbone (c. 1790–1882), wife of Liverpool philanthropist William Rathbone, a copy of his "Freedom of the Mind," the most famous of his poems, which he had written on the wall of his cell during his imprisonment in Baltimore in the spring of 1830. The sonnet was first printed in *A Brief Sketch of the Trial of William Lloyd Garrison, for an Alleged Libel on Francis Todd, of Massachusetts* (Baltimore, 1830), p. 8.

2. Garrison adapts Isaiah 2:4.

124

TO ERASMUS D. HUDSON

Boston, Sept. 12, 1845.

My Dear Brother:

So it seems, you are in prison, for daring to call for the interposition of the Habeas Corpus in behalf of a female slave in the Old Bay State! [1] And arrested, too, on complaint of the very person, for whom you kindly intended to secure the boon of freedom! Well, we have had many strange and extraordinary cases take place, both in the Commonwealth and out of it, since the anti-slavery enterprise was started; but this rather surpasses any of them — at least, in some of its features. Of course, it is not the "chattel personal," but the knavish "owner" of the girl, who has brought this malicious, yet ludicrous suit against you. Depend upon it, he will never bring this suit to trial; but let him, if he dare. His object, no doubt, is, simply to give you annoyance and trouble, and to put you to some expense; impudently supposing that he will thus deter abolitionists from ever again attempting to interfere with "slave property" on our "free soil," even in a legal and constitutional manner. I really hope that the trial will take place — it will be a great anti-slavery occasion, "rich" beyond all legal precedent.

Wendell Phillips is at present residing at Natick, but the Liberator of to-day will inform him of your situation. He will rejoice to plead your case. Ellis Gray Loring says he will gladly assist him as counsel to any extent in his power; and so will Samuel E. Sewall. But, I repeat, Hodgson will never come to trial.

It was best, *pro tempore*, for you to allow yourself to be locked up in jail, to illustrate slaveholding audacity, and to make the case a startling one to the Commonwealth; but this having been done, the friends in Boston think you had now better let bail be given for your appearance at court, that you may be restored to your family; and if any is wanted, you can call upon Francis Jackson and Ellis G. Loring, who will be happy to respond to your call. Perhaps, however, you may choose to remain in jail, for reasons that do not occur to us; but we do not like the idea of your being locked up for a month, unless there be something special to be gained by it to our good cause.

Please let us hear from you again, in regard to this matter. In the mean time, I bid you be of good cheer, and remember that

"Stone walls do not a prison make,
Nor iron bars a cage." [2]

My liveliest sympathies are with your wife and family, who, I trust, will be liberally remembered by the friends in Springfield during your incarceration.[3]

The letter I have published in the Liberator, respecting your case, is from Dr. Church.[4] Yours was not received in season for this week's paper, but shall be printed next week.[5]

I write in haste, as I am just leaving for Gloucester. Whether in prison or out of it, I remain

Faithfully yours,

Wm. Lloyd Garrison.

ALS: Collection of Sidney Kaplan, Amherst, Massachusetts.

1. Hudson's good nature and conscientious principles caused him to become entangled in the case of the slave Catharine Linda. The property of W. B. Hodgson of Savannah, Georgia, she told a fugitive slave who was friendly with Hudson that she would like to be free. The fugitive slave took immediate action, arranging that a complaint be drawn up against Hodgson, and Hudson signed the document. After the complaint was filed, Catharine Linda, remembering her parents and children in Georgia, told the court in Northampton that she had decided to remain with the Hodgsons. For a few weeks Hudson thought the case closed, but then he was approached by the sheriff who advised him to apologize to Hodgson in order to avoid legal action. Refusing to cooperate, Hudson was served with a warrant under a complaint in the name of Catharine Linda. He was confined in the Springfield jail for almost three weeks before he was persuaded to accept money for bail offered not by Loring and Jackson as suggested in Garrison's letter, but by two local residents, John Payson Williston and Dr. Jefferson Church. For reasons the editor has been unable to determine, verdict in the case was delayed until the November term of 1848 when Hudson was found guilty and fined $30.67. (*The Liberator*, September 12 and 19, October 3, 1845; Springfield *Daily Republican*, September 9 and 19, 1845; Records of the Massachusetts Supreme Judicial Court, case number 254, Catherine [*sic*] Linda v. Erasmus D. Hudson; letter to the editor from John E. Powers, Clerk, Supreme Judicial Court, County of Suffolk, Commonwealth of Massachusetts, January 28, 1972.)

2. Richard Lovelace, "To Althea from Prison," stanza 4, lines 1–2.

3. Hudson and his wife, Martha Turner of New Marlboro, Massachusetts, ultimately had three sons, two of whom survived their father. (*Medical Register of New York, New Jersey, and Connecticut,* 1881–1882.)

4. The letter from Dr. Jefferson Church (1802–1885) was printed in the issue for September 12, 1845. After graduating from the Pittsfield Medical College in 1825, Dr. Church practiced briefly in Peru, Massachusetts, before settling in Springfield, Massachusetts. He was well known in the area both as a doctor and as a nonresistant abolitionist, and, much as he disagreed with his militancy, he was to become a close friend of John Brown. Dr. Church's house was one of the principal stations on the Underground Railroad. (Letter to the editor from

Dorothy Mozley, genealogy and local history librarian, Springfield City Library, January 14, 1972.)

5. The letter did appear in *The Liberator*, September 19, 1845.

125

TO HENRY C. WRIGHT

Boston, Nov. 1, 1845.

My dearly beloved bro. Wright:

I begin with a very sincere and humble confession. If there ever was a man, (and there has been many a one,) who deserved to receive the "cut direct" at the hands of his friends, for his epistolary remissness, I am that man. If I were a man of property, and the bargain were possible, I would give a large portion of it if I could possess your executive perseverance with the pen. I feel ashamed to think how few letters you have received from me since your long absence from this country; and especially in view of the many communications I have received from you, both for my private perusal and for the columns of the Liberator. How you find time to perform so vast an amount of epistolary labor, and at the same time to deliver so many public lectures, is to me a matter of astonishment. For the journal of your travels to and from Graeffenberg, and also respecting the water cure process at G., I wish to return you my very warmest thanks; and not for myself alone, but also in behalf of all the readers of the Liberator.[1] If ever a tourist used his eyes, and improved every moment of his time, to see all that was to be seen, and know all that was to be known, you seem to have done so. The manner in which you blend with your descriptions of natural scenery, and of the habits and manners of the people among whom you sojourned, moral and religious reflections, and reformatory sentiments, is as edifying as it is original and unique. In printing your journal, I presume we have committed many typographical blunders, especially in giving the names of places and persons; but we have done the best we could. You are aware that your manuscript is at times somewhat difficult to decipher. The paper on which you have written has been very thin, and the matter very closely run together; so that it has required much perseverance and a practised eye to avoid making errors in the sense, at once serious and ludicrous. But we have been a thousand times compensated for all the trouble we have been at, and all the perplexity we have experienced; and are apprehensive that we shall be always your debtor. Be assured that you are affording much gratification, and conveying much instruction, to those who are in the habit of reading the Liberator; that you cannot write too often; that your health, welfare, location and movements, are matters of deep interest to thousands; and that you are sowing broadcast the seeds of a world-wide reformation.

In all the trials through which you have been called to pass, in advocating the great doctrine of human brotherhood, (which is but another designation of the gospel of peace which Jesus came to proclaim and exemplify,) you have had our liveliest sympathy. Scribes and Pharisees have assailed you, after the ancient manner, as a disturber of the peace, as not of God because you do not keep the Sabbath day, as seeking to turn the world upside down; but your faith has remained steadfast, and your sufficiency has been of God. I rejoice at your boldness and fidelity — a stranger, as you are, in a strange land.[2] The times require great plainness of speech, and the most radical measures of reform. Alas! how few are found willing to endure any sufferings, to make any sacrifices, to encounter any perils, in the service of God! How many stand ready to run any hazard, to grapple with any danger, in the service of Satan! Let but a war be proclaimed, no matter for what purpose, and they will enlist by thousands at the rate of a few shillings a day, to kill or be killed. The standard of Philanthropy has few to rally around it, whilst that of Revenge is thronged.

Last week, the annual meeting of the Non-Resistance Society took place in Boston, and it was by far the most profitable of any we have ever held.[3] As to the Society itself, it has had only a nominal existence since you left us; as we have not been able to find a suitable person to go forth into the lecturing field — all our non-resistant lecturers, such as C. C. Burleigh, Abby Kelley, S. S. Foster, and Parker Pillsbury, being almost wholly engaged in the anti-slavery movement. On your return, we shall endeavor to give a new impulse to the cause of non-resistance. Its converts are steadily multiplying, and it has ceased to be assailed so wantonly and abusively as formerly.

At the meeting alluded to, a resolution respecting your absence abroad and your return to this country, was adopted by acclamation. You will see it in the Liberator of this week.[4] We are fully aware, we think, of the importance of your presence and labors in England; and we therefore feel delicate about urging your return home; but you will understand that all are desirous to see you at the earliest practicable period. I hope you will make your arrangements to return in the spring, in company with our beloved friends James N. Buffum and Frederick Douglass, in season to be present at the annual meeting of the American Anti-Slavery Society in May; or, at the latest, at the grand meeting of the New England A.S. Society, in Boston, the last of that month.[5]

The kind reception which James and Frederick have already met with abroad, is exceedingly gratifying to the faithful friends of emancipation here. They are worthy of all possible confidence and encouragement, as you well know. How refreshing it must be to your spirit to see them, and to get from them all the intelligence that you can, as from "living epistles," respecting a thousand things about us, which can never be obtained from our anti-slavery papers, or from private letters! And they will leap for joy to see you. Pray get out of them every thing that you can; for they have crowded budgets of information, which it will be worth your while to search to the bottom. I am afraid they will find so much work to be done, that they will not return home so soon as they contemplated when they left us; but they must remember how [mig]hty is the conflict going on here, and how few [. . .] there [are] to engage in it on the side of God and human right.

I fully intended (did you ever know a man of better intentions than myself?) to write letters by this steamer to R. D. Webb, James Haughton, Elizabeth Pease, and Douglass and Buffum; but constant interruptions of company, as well as business matters, have again foiled me. Say to Richard D. Webb, that I cherish for him the warmest affection and the highest esteem; and the catholic spirit in which he treats my silence proves him to be an uncommon man. I bless the day when I became acquainted with the dear Dublin friends. It will ever constitute a joyous and most important era in my existence. As for Elizabeth Pease, I do not deserve ever to have another letter from her; but she *must* do me the justice to believe that my omission to write has not been intentional. There is not a woman living, whose friendship I more highly esteem than hers.

My health is better than usual. Helen and the dear children are all very well, and often are you the subject of our thoughts and conversation. With best love to all the friends, and great personal regard for yourself, I remain,

Yours, ever,

Wm. Lloyd Garrison.

ALS: Garrison Papers, Boston Public Library.

1. By the time of Garrison's letter Henry C. Wright had become the most faithful and the most voluminous of *The Liberator's* correspondents. The first installment of the journal to which Garrison refers (dated July 10, 1845) appeared in *The Liberator*, October 10, 1845. Subsequent installments as well as letters addressed to Wright's wife and to his daughter were printed at regular weekly intervals thereafter until February 13, 1846; for Garrison's description of the journal as a whole see the issue for February 13. Wright's contributions to the columns of *The Liberator* continued at frequent intervals throughout the remaining twenty years of the paper's publication.

2. Garrison adapts Exodus 2:22.

3. The annual meeting of the New England Non-Resistance Society, held in the Chapel under the Museum, Tremont Street, October 16–17, raised a total of $47.58 (see *The Liberator*, October 31, 1845).

4. The resolution to which Garrison refers, which eulogizes Wright and his mission abroad as well as urging his return, was inadvertently omitted from the report of the meeting printed on the last page of the issue for October 31 but was inserted apologetically by Garrison on the second page of the same issue.

5. Garrison must mean the Massachusetts Anti-Slavery Society, since that society had replaced the New England Anti-Slavery Society in 1835.

III BRITISH MISSION: 1846

BY THE SPRING of 1846 the United States was at war with Mexico. Although Garrison branded the war "the most atheistical and impious . . . ever recorded in the gory pages of History,"[1] he himself became more personally involved with another war, that against the Free Church of Scotland, and that war had reached a stalemate. On April 21 the Glasgow Emancipation Society held a large public meeting at which Douglass, Thompson, and Wright all demanded that the money collected from American slaveholders be returned. In his speech Thompson eulogized Garrison, introducing a resolution "that we extend to Mr. Garrison an invitation to visit this kingdom, to cheer us by his presence, and encourage us by his counsels."[2] When the Massachusetts Anti-Slavery Society agreed to raise funds for his visit, Garrison could hardly refuse doing what indeed he wanted most to do in the world: make another trip to Britain.

Preparations for the trip were extensive. In addition to routine planning and packing there was the elaborate ceremonial of saying farewell — a process which always fascinated Garrison more than he realized. Most spectacular was the meeting in Boston of free colored friends on the eve of his departure. It was an extended testimonial meeting with shouts and cheers and applause. Of the various oratorical gestures the fullest was Garrison's own (three columns in *The Liberator*, July 24, 1846), in which he recounted the activities of his sixteen years as an abolitionist, concentrating on the accomplishments of his two earlier British missions. "I now go," he said, "at the suggestion of British abolitionists, to aid in exposing the iniquity of the Free Church. Her representatives are blameworthy, not because they got money in the Southern States, but because they got it most foully by keeping silence on the subject of Slavery." He explained that he was also going to see George Thompson, Frederick Douglass, and

1. *The Liberator*, December 25, 1846.
2. *The Liberator*, May 29, 1846.

Henry C. Wright. Finally, "I leave you at a critical hour. War is raging over our land, but it only indicates the enormous growth of our previous wickedness." The meeting ended with the passing of a series of resolutions commending Garrison for past service and expressing confidence in the new mission. "We offer him the grateful homage of our hearts, and promise that while he remains the 'William Lloyd Garrison of the past,' the bond of union between us can never be severed."

Perhaps no one was so conscious of the void left at Garrison's departure on July 16 as Edmund Quincy, who had been prevailed upon to edit *The Liberator* in his absence. In an editorial stressing the importance of the mission (printed in the same issue as Garrison's speech), he paid tribute to Garrison: "In view of the greatness of the harvest and the fewness of the Laborers, it is hard to miss, even for a season, the giant arm and gleaming sickle of the foremost of the reapers." He wished that Garrison could "multiply himself among mankind" so that he could serve in several places at the same time. At least he counted on the regular help of Charles K. Whipple, and he hoped for the frequent assistance of Mrs. Maria W. Chapman and Wendell Phillips.

The first events after Garrison's tedious and often fog-bound voyage did not prove so much to his liking as the farewell of friends in Boston. In fact, he must have sensed the parallel between what happened at the World's Temperance Convention in London on August 4 and what had occurred at the international antislavery convention in 1840. When Garrison rose in the meeting to reprimand the Reverend Edward Norris Kirk, Boston's distinguished Congregational minister, for what he considered a proslavery speech, the audience's initial applause turned into angry objections. Garrison retired from the meeting and avoided further participation.

Other meetings were more harmonious and more successful. At the Crown and Anchor Tavern on August 10, there was founded the Anti-Slavery League, a society dedicated to the abolition of slavery in all nations, especially the United States, where it was suggested that the league work not with the new American and Foreign Anti-Slavery Society but with the old American Anti-Slavery Society. Speechmaking at the meeting by Douglass, Garrison, Thompson, and Wright consumed some six hours, but only the Reverend Edward Kirk left the room early.

As a matter of policy and to save precious time Garrison soon decided that during the current mission he would avoid as many public meetings as possible and concentrate on making personal contacts with editors, writers, and those most directly involved with

British public opinion. He became acquainted with Douglas Jerrold, editor of *Punch*, who was glad to reprint a number of articles from *The Liberator*. He also made arrangements with the editor of the *Daily News* (founded by Charles Dickens) to give coverage to news about the abolition movement in the United States. He renewed acquaintance with William and Mary Howitt, closely associated with the *People's Journal*, in which a biographical sketch of Garrison's life was to appear in September. He had breakfast with John Bowring, reformer and influential member of Parliament. He spent one Sunday with moral-suasion Chartists William Lovett and Henry Vincent and another Sunday with William H. Ashurst, who under the pseudonym Edward Search was already a frequent contributor to *The Liberator*. He also cultivated Joseph Barker, a wealthy printer whose new press, Garrison thought, was destined to revolutionize man's cultural life by making books available at unbelievably low prices.

In short, Garrison did his best to expand the journalistic outlets for his radical abolitionism throughout Britain. But, despite his resolution to the contrary, he continued to attend public meetings in many cities in England, Scotland, and Ireland. In Scotland he not only lectured on abolition but preached against the Free Church at every turn of the road. In Edinburgh he had a special honor, for 250 ladies presented him with a handsome tea and coffee service (later an embarrassment owing to the $60.00 duty imposed at the Boston Custom House). In Glasgow there was a special public breakfast in his honor. In Ireland he took time to visit friends, and he made a sensational speech in Belfast.

Although it was so hectic a trip that there was insufficient time for relaxation and sleep and Garrison resolved to avoid such a strenuous trip in the future, his health seemed to improve as his activities became more frenzied. In fact, he was probably relieved to substitute excitement and adulation for the routine life in Boston, with its regular editorial duties and the chores and inevitable illness at home.

Garrison sailed from Liverpool on November 4, landing in Boston on the seventeenth. The next month, almost on his own birthday, Helen presented him with a second daughter, Elizabeth Pease Garrison — it was a fitting birthday present, and the name honoring as it did his Scottish friend and supporter seemed a fitting conclusion to his mission abroad.

A few days after the birth of Lizzy Pease, Garrison was deeply involved with the National Anti-Slavery Bazaar, an annual fund-raising event in Boston since 1834. The fair this year was especially exciting since the tables in Faneuil Hall were brimming with articles Garrison had collected abroad. It was this bazaar that James Russell Lowell celebrated in "Letter from Boston," (reprinted in *The Liberator,* January 8, 1847), which read in part:

> There's GARRISON, his features very
> Benign for an incendiary,
> Beaming forth sunshine through his glasses
> On the surrounding lads and lasses
> (No bee could blither be, or brisker), —
> A picwick somehow turned John Ziska,
> His bump of firmness swelling up
> Like a rye cupcake from its cup.
> And there, too, was his English tea-set,
> Which in his ear a kind of flea set,
> His Uncle Samuel for its beauty
> Demanding sixty dollars duty
> ('T was natural Sam should serve his trunk ill,
> For G., you know, has cut his uncle)
> Whereas, had he but once made tea in 't,
> His uncle's ear had had the flea in 't,
> There being not a cent of duty,
> On any pot that ever drew tea.

126

TO LOUISA GILMAN LORING

Boston, Jan. 1, 1846.

My dear Mrs. Loring:

Your kind note, with the generous donation contained in it, was carefully put into my hand this afternoon by the young man who brought it.[1] It is a double assurance of your unaltered friendship — a good word and a liberal deed. I am sure you will be gratified to know that your gift will serve to relieve me from some pecuniary embarrassments under which I have been laboring, in consequence of the paucity of the receipts of the Liberator for the last six months. If I were "making money," I should hardly feel free to accept of it; nor, in that case, would you deem it desirable to proffer it. Thus far, a kind Providence has sustained me, and in many a dark hour suddenly cast its cheering light upon my pathway. My experience has been a singular and deeply interesting one, for the last fifteen years. At no time have I been delivered from the bondage of pecuniary embarrassment; and yet, in each extremity, a way has been opened for my relief, wholly unexpected to me.

To-day is the commencement of another new year. Dear Helen unites with me in proffering to you and your husband [Ellis Gray

Loring] the warmest desires for your happiness, not only for the present year, but for many years to come.

Yours, with much thankfulness and esteem,

Wm. Lloyd Garrison.

ALS: Ellis Gray Loring Family Papers, Radcliffe College Library; a handwritten transcription of this letter is to be found in the Garrison Papers, Boston Public Library.

1. Not identified.

127

TO FRANCIS JACKSON

Boston, Jan. 12, 1846.

My Dear Friend:

The presentation of your likeness, together with the note of $50 due you since last July, affords me an opportunity to express, on paper, the strong sense which I cherish of the many obligations under which I labor toward yourself. I improve it for the relief of my own mind, and not because I suppose you need or wish any such acknowledgments, to convince you of my gratitude.

First, as to your daguerreotype likeness. I have made my choice of the two specimens which you sent to me, in accordance with your request.[1] Either of them I should prize highly; each in some respects is better than the other; and both are so good, that I have found it difficult to determine which to prefer.

When I ventured to ask such a favor of you, I did so from an earnest desire to possess the features of one, whose friendship I deem it true and substantial honor to enjoy, for whose character I cherish the warmest sentiments of admiration, and whose life is consecrated to the furtherance of the cause of truth, justice, liberty, philanthropy. Your ready compliance with my request is another proof of your kindness, to be added to the many instances which had previously transpired. I will take care to preserve the gift, if possible, so that my children, who are now all too young to understand any thing of my history, in their maturer years may be enabled to gaze upon the countenance of one who was their father's friend, coadjutor and benefactor, and also a friend to the whole human family.

As to the gift of the note of hand, I feel deeply embarrassed, and, as a matter of business, would much prefer to liquidate it as soon as possible. I certainly owe you an apology. When I obtained the loan, I confidently expected to be able to return it in the course of thirty days, on the receipt of my monthly stipend; but the receipts of the Liberator began to diminish at least two or three months earlier than usual in the year — (the *pinching* time generally falling between September and January) — so that it was not until the first of the present month that I received much of my dues, and then barely enough to pay for my groceries, rent, &c. My usual salary has fallen short the past year about $160. To that amount, and something more, I am still honestly in debt to various individuals. I owe my friend Samuel Philbrick $100, and you $50, on the note which you so generously wish me to accept. I want to pay you both, in good faith, according to promise. But I have felt that I could rely on your friendly indulgence, better than on that of my landlord and other creditors. Of course, there being a deficiency in the receipts of the Liberator the past year, it cripples me to the full extent that I have mentioned; but I have no claim on the receipts of the present year to make good my salary for 1845, and must do the best I can under the circumstances.

It would hurt your feelings if I should return you the note until it be paid, and it hurts my feelings to think that I have not had the means to cancel it. If it were not a business transaction originally, I should feel somewhat differently about it, though the act of kindness would be the same on your part.

I will not extend this explanatory and apologetical part of my letter; for I know how strongly averse you are to any thing like a pointed allusion to your good deeds.

Hoping ever to be one with you in spirit and purpose, and wishing for you and yours the choicest of Heaven's blessings, I remain,

Your faithful and much obliged friend,

Wm. Lloyd Garrison.

Francis Jackson.

ALS: Garrison Papers, Boston Public Library.

1. The daguerreotypes of Francis Jackson have not been identified.

128

TO SAMUEL J. MAY

Boston, Feb. 16, 1846.

Dear brother May:

I perceive, by the Utica Liberty Press, which has just come to hand, that Hiram Wilson announces that he is to be in Syracuse on the 18th instant, to attend a meeting called in aid of Anti-Slavery Missions.[1]

Enclosed are twenty-two dollars. Ten dollars are from the "Lynn Women's Anti-Slavery Sewing Circle," sent to my care by Miriam B. Johnson, Treasurer, to whom I wish friend Wilson would please send a line, acknowledging the receipt of the money.[2] This donation is "to aid the Canada Mission." The other twelve dollars were collected by Spencer Hodges, of Foxboro', Mass. from friends in that town, to be exclusively appropriated to the distribution of the Bible among the refugees in Upper Canada, in accordance with an appeal put forth some time since in the Oberlin Evangelist by Mr. Rice, an associate (I believe) of our friend Wilson.[3] There is a balance of 50 cents, which I cannot send, (the whole sum collected at Foxboro', being $12.50,) and a portion of which I shall take to pay the postage on this letter. The remainder shall at any time be handed over to H. W's order, to any person in this city. I wish he would immediately send a line to Spencer Hodges, acknowledging the receipt of the money — as I told him and Miriam B. Johnson, that I would endeavor to get acknowledgments from Mr. Wilson to them. We cannot be too exact in such matters.

It is possible that Mr. Wilson may have left Syracuse before you receive this. If so, please send the money to him, if you know where he is. If not, keep it until further notice.

You see what use I have made of your kind letter, in the last number of the Liberator.[4] It was very refreshing to my spirit. Hope you will pardon me for what I have done. I regret that I have not a moment, now, to occupy in sending you a long and loving reply. We are all pretty well at home. Helen unites with me in proffering much love to you all.

Ever yours,

Wm. Lloyd Garrison.

ALS: Garrison Papers, Boston Public Library.

1. The Utica *Liberty Press* was a weekly newspaper published from 1843 to 1849. (*ULN.*)

Hiram Wilson (1803–1864), a graduate of Oneida Institute, was one of the student rebels at Lane Seminary in 1835. He graduated from the Oberlin Theological Department in 1836. After serving as an antislavery agent in Ohio, he spent most of his career in Canada helping Negro fugitives. In 1842 he was one of the founders of a manual-labor school, the British-American Institute of Science (referred to by Garrison as "the Canada Mission"), located near London, Ontario. (Robert S. Fletcher, *A History of Oberlin College*, Oberlin, Ohio, 1943, I, 246–247, and Robin W. Winks, "'A Sacred Animosity': Abolitionism in Canada," *The Antislavery Vanguard*, ed. Martin Duberman, Princeton, 1965, pp. 309, 335–336.)

2. Little is known of the Lynn Women's Anti-Slavery Sewing Circle, except that Abby Kelley was its secretary in 1837.

3. Spencer Hodges may be either the father (1783–1865) or the son (1812–1892); little is known of either. (Letter to the editor from Florence C. Bleumer, special librarian, Boyden Library, Foxborough, Massachusetts, July 8, 1970.)

The Oberlin *Evangelist* was a semimonthly religious periodical, published 1838–1862. (*ULS.*)

Isaac J. Rice was a Presbyterian minister who had attended Hamilton College and Auburn Theological Seminary. Since 1838 he had operated a mission school for Negroes near Amherstburg, Ontario, which also served as a terminus for the Underground Railroad. (Wilbur H. Siebert, *The Underground Railroad from Slavery to Freedom*, New York, 1899, pp. 194, 200, 214; *General Biographical Catalogue of Auburn Theological Seminary, 1818–1918*, Auburn, N.Y., 1918, p. 64.)

4. May's letter was printed in *The Liberator*, February 13, 1846.

---

1 2 9

TO SYDNEY HOWARD GAY

Boston, March 21, 1846.

My dear Gay:

Our Executive Committee are anxious that an official notice of the approaching annual meeting of the American Anti-Slavery Society should appear, *without fail*, in the next Standard.[1] Will you write such notice, stating that the meeting will continue in session three or four days, and append to it my name as President, and Wendell Phillips and Maria Weston Chapman as Secretaries? It would be well, if you can, to write at least a short editorial article, respecting the importance of this meeting, &c. If you have not yet secured the Broadway Tabernacle for the anniversary meeting, I would do so immediately, as we are anxious to keep our old position before the public.

I am just starting for the New Bedford Convention, and write in great haste.[2]

With my best regards to Mrs. Gay,[3] I remain,

Yours, with high esteem,

Wm. Lloyd Garrison.

S. H. Gay.

ALS: Sydney Howard Gay Papers, Columbia University Libraries.

1. At this time the executive committee of the American Anti-Slavery Society consisted of Garrison, Francis Jackson, Wendell Phillips, Mrs. Maria W. Chapman, Edmund Quincy, Charles L. Remond, Anne Warren Weston, William H. Channing, Joseph C. Hathaway, Sydney Howard Gay, Sarah Pugh, and Daniel Carmichael. Only the last two have not been previously identified.

Sarah Pugh (1800–1884) had been a delegate to the World's Anti-Slavery Convention in London in 1840 and was described by Lucretia Mott in her letter to Richard D. Webb of February 21, 1847, as "a lady of leisure." A resident of Philadelphia, she was particularly active in the antislavery and woman's rights movements. (*Life.*)

Daniel Carmichael is known to be from the New York City area, probably Brooklyn, though he does not appear in city directories for the appropriate years. He was married to Eliza Otis, and they were the parents of the better-known

Henry Carmichael, who was born in 1846. (Daniel is mentioned in the *National Anti-Slavery Standard*, May 21, 1846, and in the *Biographical Dictionary of America*, under "Henry Carmichael.")

An announcement of the annual meeting of the American Anti-Slavery Society appeared in the *National Anti-Slavery Standard*, March 26, 1846, and subsequent issues. The names of Garrison, Phillips, and Mrs. Chapman were mentioned, as requested. An editorial signed "G." appeared April 9, 1846, speaking in general terms of the progress of the antislavery movement since the society was formed but warning that much remains to be done. The Broadway Tabernacle was secured for the meeting, which was held May 12, as announced.

2. The New Bedford convention met March 20–22. Garrison was present at the meeting, serving on the business committee and addressing the gathering (*The Liberator*, March 27, 1846).

3. Elizabeth J. Neall Gay (1819–1907), a Philadelphia Friend who had attended the World's Anti-Slavery Convention in London in 1840 and married Sydney Howard Gay in 1845. (*Friends' Intelligencer*, 64:816, 1907.)

130

TO SYDNEY HOWARD GAY

Boston, March 31, 1846.

My dear Gay:

Lewis Hayden has just informed me that he intends leaving for Detroit this afternoon, via New-York; and I avail myself of the opportunity (though in a prodigious hurry at this moment) to answer the inquiries contained in yours of the 23d.[1]

Benjamin Lundy first established his paper in Greenville, Tennessee, in the "seventh month" of 1820.[2] The Liberator was commenced January 1, 1831. I believe the next anti-slavery paper that was started was the Emancipator, in the city of New-York, under the editorial care of Charles W. Dennison; but I am not positive as to the time it commenced. I believe, however, it was in 1834 — it may have been the year previous, before the organization of the American Anti-Slavery Society.

Lewis Hayden has won the esteem and friendship of all with whom he has become acquainted, and is a rare young man. Should he conclude to return, and take up his abide in New Bedford, I think he can be made very serviceable to our cause. He needs to be more with us, fully to understand the position that we occupy, in regard to Church and State; but he is an apt scholar, and has made very good progress in a very short time. I have not had a good opportunity to hear him speak in public; but I believe he has generally acquitted himself to good acceptance. His chief embarrassment seems to be, to find language to express the facts of his history, and the thoughts and emotions of his mind.

It is none too early to be making strong appeals, in the Standard and Liberator, respecting the importance of a large attendance of delegates at the annual meeting in May; for, without such appeals, I am afraid that but comparatively few will be present. The time is rapidly approaching, and will soon be consummated.

My best regards to your wife, and all possible felicity to you both, now and ever.

Your faithful coadjutor,

Wm. Lloyd Garrison.

P.S. If you see my beloved friend, H. W. Williams, before he sails to-morrow for Havre, give him my most cordial adieu and grateful remembrances [3] I feel under great obligation to him, for many kind services that he has rendered to me, year after year, and wish him great success and prosperity in his future career. Our paper goes to press one day earlier this week than usual; so that I am suddenly baffled in my intention to write my friend Williams a farewell letter.

ALS: Sydney Howard Gay Papers, Columbia University Libraries.

1. Lewis Hayden (1816–1889) was a fugitive slave from Kentucky who became a close friend of Garrison. A leading Negro citizen of Boston, he opened a clothing store there in 1849. (*Life*; *The Liberator*, June 29, 1849.)

2. Garrison's recollection is slightly inaccurate. According to Lundy's *Autobiography*, the *Genius of Universal Emancipation* was first established in Mount Pleasant, Ohio, in January 1821. After a few issues it was moved to Greenville, Tennessee, where it was published until the summer of 1824, when Lundy removed it to Baltimore. It was there in 1829 that Garrison became an associate editor of the paper until he founded *The Liberator* in 1831. The *Genius* ceased publication with Lundy's death in 1839.

3. Williams was leaving for France to study medicine.

131

TO JAMES MILLER McKIM

Boston, May 3, 1846.

My dear McKim:

As you are republishing my essays on "The Constitution and Political Action," I hasten to inform you of a blunder in the last (3rd) number, which occurred during my absence from the city, in the "making up." [1]

At the close of the third paragraph, ending thus — "fear not to walk in the path of obedience" [2] — *dele* the next paragraph, commencing, "In proof of the soundness of these views," and ending, "Supreme Court of the United States," and put it *between* the paragraph, ending "if need be, by the national arm," and the next paragraph, commencing, "Such, then, being the nature of the American Union," &c.[3]

I regret that this blunder should have occurred in the Liberator, and am somewhat apprehensive this letter will arrive too late to have the article printed correctly in the Freeman. If this should be the case, please make the correction in your *inside* form.

Do try to induce as many of our Philadelphia friends to be at the annual meeting as possible, at New-York. I am afraid our meeting will be smaller than usual, and I feel very anxious that our *best* heads and hearts should be present. I hope it will be possible for James and Lucretia Mott to be present. My best regards to them, your wife, and all the beloved circle.

Yours, truly,

W. L. Garrison.

ALS: Collection of Richard A. Ehrlich, Boston, Massachusetts.

1. Garrison's articles were published in *The Liberator*, April 17, April 24, May 1, 1846; in the *Pennsylvania Freeman*, April 23, April 30, May 7, 1846.
2. An instance in which Garrison seems to invent his own biblical-sounding entreaty by combining familiar phrases like "Fear not: for I am with thee" (Isaiah 43:5) and "Enter not into the path of the wicked" (Proverbs 4:14).
3. McKim made the suggested corrections.

132

TO SYDNEY HOWARD GAY

Boston, May 7, 1846.

My dear Gay:

It was thought by the Executive Committee, that it would save you some trouble to get the placards for our anniversary in New-York printed in this city. We accordingly send you 300 copies, and trust you will employ a faithful "bill-sticker" to put them up in the best places in New-York. Especially, let Broadway have the benefit of a considerable number. Two or three should be put up at the Tabernacle, and half a dozen should be reserved for the Lecture Room,[1] to be put up at the door on Wednesday and Thursday. Is it best to have the lot posted on Monday afternoon, or early on Tuesday morning? I should think on Tuesday, provided they can be posted in *good season* for the Tabernacle meeting, which meeting I am apprehensive will be a comparatively small one, unless special pains are taken to notify the great public. I feel the more anxious about it, as the American & Foreign Anti-Slavery Society are to hold their anniversary in the Tabernacle, in the afternoon of the same day. The judicious distribution of the accompanying placards is important mainly in regard to our Tabernacle meeting, as it is not to be supposed that the attendance on our subsequent meetings will be large. But enough respecting *them*.

You will, of course, see that our meetings are duly advertised in some of the daily papers. I would put into the advertisements, the names of the speakers as given in the placards. It is yet somewhat doubtful whether Wendell Phillips will be able to speak, in consequence of the feeble state of his health; but I think he will not fail us, as I have just seen him, and he is improving. We hope Abby K. Foster [2] will not decline speaking in the Tabernacle, as she is an object of special interest, and I have no doubt will acquit herself ably.

We thought it prudent, for the safety of our *placard*, not to put on to it our motto, "No Union with Slaveholders," lest it should be torn down, and our money thus thrown away.

I am inclined to think that we shall want the Lecture Room till Friday, 2 o'clock, P. M. If so, can we have it?

[Edmund] Quincy, Phillips, [Parker] Pillsbury, myself, &c. intend taking the Long Island rout on Monday morning, so as to be in N. Y. in the evening. Can you make it convenient to greet us at the landing-place?

I shall accept the kind invitation of Isaac T. Hopper to stop at his house.

Can any thing be done to direct delegates to cheap boarding-houses? How many can the Graham House accommodate? [3]

I deeply sympathize with your beloved wife, in the severe loss which she has experienced by the death of her venerated father.[4] My best regards to her.

Yours, faithfully,

Wm. Lloyd Garrison.

ALS: Sydney Howard Gay Papers, Columbia University Libraries.

1. Of the American Anti-Slavery Society library.

2. The former Abby Kelley, who had married Stephen S. Foster, December 31, 1845.

3. The Graham Boarding House, established by Roswell Goss, was located at 63 Barclay Street, New York City. (New York city directory.)

4. Daniel Neall (c. 1783–1846) of Philadelphia, father of Elizabeth Neall Gay, was a loyal Garrisonian abolitionist. It was he who, in May 1838, presided over the ill-fated antislavery meeting in Philadelphia's Pennsylvania Hall which ended with the hall's being burned by a mob. (Obituary in *The Liberator*, May 8, 1846.)

133

TO SAMUEL E. SEWALL

Boston, May 15, 1846.

Dear Sir:

For various reasons, I must decline being one of "The General Committee of Arrangements for the funeral of the Rev. C. T. Torrey" — but I scarcely need add, that I shall not suffer his cruel imprisonment and melancholy death to pass by, without making them as efficacious as possible in hastening the downfal of the nefarious slave system.[1]

Yours, faithfully,

Wm. Lloyd Garrison.

Samuel E. Sewall.

ALS: Merrill Collection of Garrison Papers, Wichita State University Library.

Samuel E. Sewall (1799–1888), attorney, was a descendant of the first American abolitionist, Judge Samuel Sewall. He was also a cousin of Samuel J. May. (*Life.*)

1. Garrison refers to the arrest of Charles T. Torrey (1813–1846) in Baltimore in 1844 for helping escaping slaves across the borders of Virginia and Maryland. After a notorious trial, Torrey was convicted and sentenced to six years' hard labor in the state penitentiary. In prison his mind and body deteriorated, and after serving slightly more than a year, he died of tuberculosis. His body was carried to Boston where he was honored, at a public funeral, as a martyr to the cause of abolition.

134

TO HENRY C. WRIGHT

Boston, June 1, 1846.

My dear brother H. C. W.:

Our New-England Anti-Slavery Convention has just closed its sessions in "the old Cradle of Liberty"; and it has been the most numerously attended, the most spirited, the most earnest, the most radical, and the most auspicious and effective, of any of the series — and that is bestowing upon it a spendid eulogy.[1] The present iniquitous war in which this country is now engaged with plundered, stricken, inoffensive Mexico, was a prominent subject of discussion, and the boldest words were uttered against the American government, and loyalty to it was denounced as rebellion against God. The excitement produced was so great, that Faneuil Hall was closed against us the last evening, lest there should be (as there would unquestionably have been) a mob! Of course, we shall turn this occurrence to good account. William Henry Channing and Theodore Parker distinguished themselves for the bravery of their language, and the revolutionary and "treasonable" doctrines which they enunciated.[2] Never before have such meetings been held in this Commonwealth, or in this country. The pillars of the government are falling — the foundations of existing institutions are shaking — Church and State are tottering to their over-throw. Multitudes are lifting up their voices for a new union and a new government, in which nothing oppressive or unchristian shall enter. The times are stirring and eventful indeed. We are living years in days. Every moment is big with a sublime event. Let us remember that they only can be saved — they only be entitled to the crown — who endure unto the end. I feel as full of hope, faith and strength, as my soul can hold. In the midst of all the commotions around me, my peace is as a river.[3] My song continually is — "The Lord reigneth, let the earth rejoice." [4]

Your recent grand meeting in Glasgow filled our Convention with joy and exultation, and its proceedings will deeply affect public sentiment throughout this country. Such blows never fall without a stunning effect. If "that blood-stained money" should be sent back to the South, it would produce an immense sensation here, and fall like an avalanche upon the slave system. The aid that it would give to our glorious anti-slavery movement cannot be estimated — certainly, not overrated. I sincerely hope the Free Church will return the money, make an unequivocal confession of wrong, and declare slaveholders to be totally unfit to belong to "the household of faith," [5] or recognized as the children of God.[6]

My time is so limited, (to a few moments, for the mail closes directly,) my heart is so full, that I shall fail in saying any thing worth communicating in this sheet. As to the kind and brotherly invitation that has been given to me to visit Scotland this summer, I dare not say, now, that I will or can comply with it; but nothing would give me so much joy as to be able to do so. You shall know more definitely about it by the next steamer. It was cordially resolved, by the N. E. Convention, that I ought to go, in case my health will allow, and I can make the necessary arrangements. How to leave my family, how to leave the Liberator, how to leave the country, at the present great crisis, I do not know; but I know that I will consider the matter carefully, and that nothing but insuperable obstacles will induce me to say "nay" to the invitation. Still, your expectations must not be too highly raised.

You must say to Elizabeth Pease, George Thompson, Frederick

Douglass and James N. Buffum, &c. &c. that I am utterly unable to write to them by the present conveyance; but I fondly hope to present to them "a living epistle," ere long. If not, they shall have written messages, which shall tell them anew, how I love and cherish them all, in my inmost soul.

Dear brother, your labors abroad are appreciated at home, as of immense value to the cause of liberty and righteousness. Heaven preserve your health, and grant us the privilege of soon embracing each other.

Ever yours,

Wm. Lloyd Garrison.

ALS: Garrison Papers, Boston Public Library.

1. The annual New England Anti-Slavery Convention was held in Faneuil Hall May 26–28, 1846.
2. Theodore Parker (1810–1860) was a Unitarian clergyman, a scholar, and a linguist. His theological views, especially those put forth in *A Discourse of Matters Pertaining to Religion* (1842), provoked much controversy. He was an active abolitionist and became one of John Brown's enthusiastic supporters.
3. Garrison adapts Isaiah 48:18.
4. Psalms 97:1.
5. From Galatians 6:10.
6. For a fuller discussion of this controversy see two introductions to this volume: "II Disunion: 1843–1845" and "III British Mission: 1846."

135

TO UNKNOWN RECIPIENT

BOSTON, JUNE 1, 1846.

DEAR FRIEND:

We take the liberty, in behalf of the Executive Committee of the AMERICAN ANTI-SLAVERY SOCIETY, to submit to you the following statement with regard to the NATIONAL ANTI-SLAVERY STANDARD, the organ of the Society.

The Standard is the vehicle through which the principles and measures of the American Anti-Slavery Society are explained and enforced. It is unnecessary, therefore, to say that it maintains the most advanced position that the American Abolitionists have as yet taken up. Its business is to keep an incessant watch upon Slavery, and upon everything that countenances or sustains it, and to be ever vigilant to expose and counteract their devices. Its pages reflect, as in a mirror, the ever-changing aspects of Slavery, of Pro-Slavery, and of Anti-Slavery. It is, therefore, interesting and valuable, as we apprehend, to the philosophical or the philanthropic observer of these portentous elements of our passing history, who may not in all respects agree with the philosophy or the method of reform which it inculcates, as well as to those who cordially accept them both.

The Standard is exclusively devoted to the *Anti-Slavery* reform. Being the organ and the property of a Society made up of persons of every shade of opinion on other subjects, propriety and good faith require that it should confine itself to the agitation of the one subject on which they are of one mind. The *facts* of other reforms will be recorded, as part of the "general intelligence" of the paper; but the discussion of their merits will form no part of its business.

While the Standard will continue to be exclusively an Anti-Slavery paper, yet, with regard to Slavery, and to the measures and principles of the Society for which it speaks, it will invite the freest and fullest discussion. It will be, so to speak, not more an *Anti-Slavery* than a *Pro-Slavery* paper; inasmuch as its columns will be open to the Slave-holder and his friends as freely as to their adversaries. We only desire the triumph of the Right and the Truth, and have established our paper as a fair field in which their just supremacy may be vindicated.

In addition to its Anti-Slavery intelligence and discussions, the Standard will contain a well-digested summary of foreign and domestic news, and a large amount of literary and miscellaneous reading. Its excellence in these respects we believe to be generally acknowledged by its present readers. No pains will be spared to make it not only a sound Anti-Slavery, but an excellent Family, newspaper.

The immediate management of the paper will remain in the hands of its present resident editor, SYDNEY HOWARD GAY, whose editorial tact and eminent talent have been sufficiently proved by the experience of two years, to need any eulogy of ours. In addition to the invaluable services of Mr. GAY, the Executive Committee have been fortunate enough to secure the promise of regular contributions to the editorial department from a number of persons, all of them well known as thorough Abolitionists, and some of them equally celebrated in the republic of letters. When we mention MARIA WESTON CHAPMAN, WENDELL PHILLIPS, ELIZA LEE FOLLEN, WILLIAM HENRY CHANNING, JAMES RUSSELL LOWELL, DAVID LEE CHILD, EDMUND QUINCY, and THOMAS T. STONE, as some of those upon whose regular assistance Mr. GAY can depend, in his editorial labors, we think that we shall not be thought extravagant in our confidence that the Standard will be surpassed by no paper in the country in the amount or variety of the talent which it will command.[1] The names which we have enumerated are those of only a portion of the contributors on whom we rely in America, and we are confident that we shall also be favored with the contributions and correspondence of some of the first talent in Great Britain and Ireland.

Having thus endeavored to make the Standard one of the *best* papers in the land, the Executive Committee have determined to endeavor to give it the widest possible circulation by making it one of the *cheapest*. They intend, therefore, from the commencement of the seventh volume (June 4th) to furnish it to subscribers at ONE DOLLAR per annum, being one half its present price, without reducing its size or diminishing its amount of matter. This they are enabled to do from the circumstance that all the labors of the non-resident contributors are *strictly and entirely gratuitous*, and the expenses of the paper at New York are reduced to the lowest possible point by a rigid and self-denying economy on the part of the resident editor. Having no wish to make the paper a profitable concern, and only desiring that it should pay its actual expenses and be read as extensively as possible, the Committee have made this change, in the belief that both objects would thus be most readily accomplished.

Our object in addressing you, at this time, is to ask your cooperation in this matter. To invite you, if not already a subscriber, to subscribe; or, at any rate, to lay these facts before such of your friends and neighbors as you judge best, and to procure their names, if they are willing to give them. The experience of such of the Committee as have made the attempt, has satisfied them that it is no difficult matter to procure subscribers, on the present terms. Scarcely any one to whom the paper has been shown, the names of the contributors recounted, and the price stated, has refused to subscribe. We believe that a great addition to the present number of subscribers and readers can be obtained, at the expense of a very little personal effort on the part of the friends of the paper and the cause. That effort we invite you to make, as your reasonable service to the Slave, to whom we all acknowledge so heavy a debt of duty.

We shall send you herewith a copy of the paper, (if you are not a subscriber,) as a specimen of its size, &c. You will remember, should you be disposed to assist us, that the terms are, *strictly and invariably*, "IN ADVANCE." It is important that what you do should be done quickly; and we would ask the favor of you ☞ TO RETURN THIS CIRCULAR, WITHIN ONE FORTNIGHT FROM THE TIME YOU RECEIVE IT, WITH THE NAMES AND MONEY YOU HAVE OBTAINED, IF ANY; BUT AT ANY RATE TO RETURN IT, THAT WE MAY KNOW WHAT TO DEPEND UPON, ☜ directed either to SYDNEY H. GAY, 142 Nassau Street, New York, or to ROBERT F. WALLCUT, 25 Cornhill, Boston.[2]

In confident hope of your cordial cooperation with us in this attempt to disseminate Anti-Slavery truth, we are, very truly and respectfully, your friends.

             WILLIAM LLOYD GARRISON, PRESIDENT.
WENDELL PHILLIPS, Secretary.

Printed form letter: Garrison Papers, Boston Public Library.

1. Eliza Lee Cabot Follen (1787–1860), the widow of Professor Charles Follen, was a prominent abolitionist. She was also the author of children's books, the editor of teachers' manuals, and active in the Sunday school and other educational movements.

James Russell Lowell (1819–1891) was distinguished as poet, essayist, editor, and abolitionist. He had early editorial connections with the *Pioneer: A Literary and Critical Magazine,* the *Pennsylvania Freeman,* and the *National Anti-Slavery Standard.* Later in life, after he had established himself as a man of letters, he became the editor of the *Atlantic Monthly,* and subsequently he was associated with the *North American Review.* In addition to his extensive literary and editorial functions, Lowell was an active abolitionist, whose *Anti-Slavery Papers* were published in two volumes in 1902.

Thomas T. Stone (1801–c.1875) was a Unitarian minister who had during the past year been a lecture agent for the Massachusetts Anti Slavery Society. On July 12 he was to be installed as the minister of the First Unitarian Church of Salem, Massachusetts. (*Who Was Who in America.*) For further information about Stone see *The Liberator,* July 24, 1846, in which are printed an article about his installation at Salem and an editorial tribute by Edmund Quincy.

2. Robert Folger Wallcut (1797–1884), a graduate of Harvard's famous "abolition class" of 1817, was the Unitarian minister at North Dennis on Cape Cod. (*Life.*)

136

TO JAMES MILLER McKIM

Boston, June 12, 1846.

My dear McKim:

You are requested to give the accompanying proceedings an insertion in the next Freeman.[1] Perhaps something may be done to forward the mission, in your section of the country. I do not wish to go to England at the expense of two or three individuals, but shall feel much more gratified if the sum that will be needed should be made up by a general co-operation of the friends, so as to burden nobody. I trust that the mission will not only pay for itself, in a pecuniary sense, but in the end be the means of securing valuable and permanent pecuniary aid to the cause, through the Fair, &c.

The time has been when a mission of this kind would have excited a lively sensation among our colored friends in New-York and Philadelphia, and elicited from them some assistance; but our cause seems to have transcended them as a body, both as it respects the Church and State — religion and politics. How would my old friend Joseph Cassey feel about the mission?[2]

Yours, on both sides of the Atlantic,

Wm. Lloyd Garrison.

ALS: Garrison Papers, Boston Public Library.

1. Garrison refers to the resolutions passed by the executive committee of the

American Anti-Slavery Society, June 11, 1846, concerning his proposed English trip, which he had been invited to make by the Glasgow Emancipation Society. The resolutions accredited him as a representative of the American society and proposed that the treasurer, Francis Jackson, open a special subscription for the furtherance of the mission. It was also resolved by the state (Pennsylvania) executive committee that J. M. McKim cooperate with Jackson by receiving and forwarding special subscriptions from eastern Pennsylvania. The proceedings were printed in the *Pennsylvania Freeman,* June 18, 1846.

    2. Joseph Cassey (c. 1790–1848) was a prominent Philadelphia Negro and longtime Garrison supporter. (*Life*; *The Liberator,* January 28, 1848.)

137

TO SYDNEY HOWARD GAY

Boston, June 12, 1846.

Dear Gay:

It is the request of the Executive Committee, that you will give the accompany[ing] proceedings an insertion in the next Standard.[1] If you please, you can write an additional paragraph about the mission, in your editorial capacity. What remains to be done, pecuniarily, must be done quickly. I do not wish to go to England at the expense of some three or four individuals. It will be far more gratifying to my feelings, to have the friends generally contribute a little to the mission — the expense of which, and a good deal more, I trust, will be returned to the American Society, by the additional aid that I hope to procure for it abroad.

With my best regards to your wife, I remain,

Yours, on both sides of the Atlantic,

Wm. Lloyd Garrison.

ALS: Sydney Howard Gay Papers, Columbia University Libraries.

1. The proceedings were published in the *National Anti-Slavery Standard,* June 18, 1846.

138

TO ELIZABETH PEASE

Boston, June 16, 1846.

Beloved Friend:

A few moments before the mail closes for Liverpool, I seize my pen to say, that, while I feel ashamed, in view of the time that has elapsed since I last forwarded a line to you, I hope ere long to be able to assure you, in *propria persona*, face to face, in Darlington itself, that you have never at any moment been divorced from my remembrance, and that there is no one among my friends for more whom I cherish higher respect or stronger esteem than for yourself. In an epistolary way, I must give it up — I am incorrigible — my good intentions are rarely carried into execution. All the Irish and Scottish friends have been neglected, as though I had no gratitude, no endurance of friendship, no memory of their existence! Yet I respect, love, remember them all, more than ten thousand letters can express. If I did not feel assured that you and they are long-suffering and forgiving in spirit, I should feel greatly disheartened, and almost afraid to write again. Frederick Douglass, James N. Buffum, and Henry C. Wright, have special cause to reproach me for my silence; and yet they never will distrust my love.

My dear friend, you have had a heavy bereavement in the death of your loved and loving father [Joseph Pease], and deeply have I shared it with you. Fondly did I cherish the hope, when I bade him farewell in 1840, that I should see him again in the flesh. But it has pleased the Almighty to transfer him to a better world, to a higher sphere of usefulness, and to more exalted society; and though it is natural that our tears should fall, at an event which takes the loved one from our side, yet it is not for us to be filled with gloom, but with Christian resignation.

It is not *positively* certain that I shall go to England this season; but it is, now, more than probable that I shall leave here for Liverpool in the steamer of 16th July. Please inform William Smeal, George Thompson, R. D. Webb, and Henry C. Wright, to this effect. My heart bounds within me at the thought of seeing you all once more. I have not time to add another line, except that I remain, as hitherto, and hope to till time with us shall be no longer — nay, for ever —

Your faithful friend,

Wm. Lloyd Garrison.

Elizabeth Pease.

ALS: Villard Papers, Harvard College Library.

139

TO FRANCIS JACKSON

(July 15 '46)

Friend Jackson —

A day or two since, I received a letter from a gentleman in New-York city, (which I have mislaid in my hurry,) enclosing fifty dollars, to pay for his pledge to that amount, made either at the annual meeting of the Mass. A. S. Society in January, or at the meeting of the American Society in New-York. There can be but one person, in such a case, and therefore you or friend Philbrick will set it right, & duly acknowledge it.[1]

Yours, truly,

W. L. G.

ALS: Sydney Howard Gay Papers, Columbia University Libraries.

1. At the foot of the page following Garrison's paragraph are two notes in the hand of Francis Jackson, suggesting that the donor is probably James Eddy (for an identification of him see Garrison's letter to Eliza Jackson Eddy, October 3, 1848) and asking that Sydney Howard Gay see James Eddy to "ascertain from him if he was the donor & for what object he made it."

140

TO HELEN E. GARRISON

SATURDAY, July 18 [1846] —
11 o'clock A.M.

MY DEAR WIFE:

We are now within two hours' sail of Halifax, but advancing cautiously, being surrounded by a dense fog, which is pretty sure to be met with on this coast at all seasons of the year, and which is always the source of embarrassment, and sometimes of peril, to navigation. It defies all nautical skill and calculation, and is therefore more unmanageable than a 'young hurricane.' We started with the wind 'dead ahead,' and it continues so to this hour. I have not, as yet, been positively seasick, (though I am always sick of the sea,) but my stomach has been in a state of semi-rebellion nearly all the way. Twice I have been unable to go to the table; and for at least one half of the passage I have been in my berth. In a day or two, however, I shall hope to be myself again, and a little more beside, as I usually grow more robust, in proportion to the length of the voyage.

Thus far, nothing has occurred worth relating. We have on board 107 passengers, Englishmen, Frenchmen, Spaniards, Americans, &c.; yet brother men all. Several clergymen, I understand, are with us, on their way to the Evangelical Alliance Convention, or the World's Temperance Convention.[1] We have at least one southern man, a General Flournoy of Kentucky, a delegate to the Temperance Convention, and I hope not a slaveholder.[2]

❋ ❋ ❋ ❋ ❋ ❋ ❋ ❋ ❋

3 o'clock, P.M.

The fog still continues, only growing more dense. It is impossible to say precisely where we are, though we cannot be very far from the land. The 'leads' are constantly going, to ascertain how deep is the water. Now we have more than 100 fathoms; now it is 90; now it is less than 70; now it is 27! This is 'shoaling' very fast. We are going at the rate of only four or five miles an hour. Capt. Hewitt, the commander, is said to be a very experienced officer, and evidently feels how great is the responsibility resting upon him.[3] I have just said to him that we had better be ten days too cautious, than one hour too precipitate. We have a regular pilot on board, who left Boston with us. We are now in 24 fathoms of water. Scarcely five minutes have elapsed, and the Britannia strikes hard with her bows on a reef! Some say, we have run against a rock; others, that we are on a sandy bottom. One thing is certain — the steamer is hard and fast, with only 2½ fathoms at her bows, and four or five fathoms at her stern and side. This is a moment of intense seriousness, not unattended with feelings of alarm; but there is no outcry, and no very perceptible agitation among the passengers. Some are resorting to their life-preservers, in case we are compelled to leave in the boats. The false keel of the vessel, at the bows, has broken off, and floated away; but, happily, there is no leak. We can see the bottom, which is sandy, and covered with grass. Our wheels are reversed, and every effort is making to 'back out.' Our first attempts are abortive; but, in the course of five or ten minutes, to the joy of all, we are once more afloat. In a few minutes, we strike again, nearly midship, and anxiety is again on every countenance. Our boat is out, with the second mate and four or five seamen, sounding with the lead in various directions, so as to find deep water, and a way of escape. We are evidently on a reef. Some think it is 'Cow Bay' — others, that we are near the 'Devil's island' — but it is all guess-work.[4] The night is approaching, which adds to our perplexity; but once more we are afloat! A small coasting vessel is dimly seen through the fog; our boat goes to it for information, but the captain can give none, as he says he is not acquainted with the coast, and does not know where he is. He declines coming any nearer to us, and we lose sight of him entirely. We have two cannon on board, which have been fired repeatedly; and though they must be heard at a great distance, we get no response. The sun is now nearly at its setting, and the curtain of fog is lifted for a short time, so as to enable us to get a tolerable observation. We are again in deep water, and for safety stand off from the coast, and retrace our steps. Fog, fog, fog — nothing but fog; and this continues all night. When shall we have clear weather?

Sunday morning — 6 o'clock.

I have just left my berth, and come on deck. The fog still continues, but we are now in plain sight of the land, not far from Camperdown, — say 15 or 20 miles from Halifax. At eight o'clock, we are along side of the wharf — all safe, and in good spirits. How long we shall remain here is uncertain. There is to be an examination of the bottom of the steamer, and probably her false keel is to be repaired. Of course, all will be made right and fast before we leave. Give yourself no anxiety, as to the remainder of the voyage. All the more vigilance will be exercised, in consequence of the escape we have made.

We saw the steamer Cambria, some distance from us, early on Friday morning, having on board (I suppose) our beloved friend James N. Buffum and the Hutchinson family.[5] They probably arrived in Boston, on Friday evening. I would have given several guineas, if I could have seen J. N. B. for one hour. My loving regards to him.

Yours, till death,

WM. LLOYD GARRISON.

Printed: *The Liberator*, August 7, 1846.

1. The Evangelical Alliance Convention was an international conference of some twelve hundred evangelical churchmen representing several Protestant denominations, including the Free Church of Scotland. Its purpose was to foster a new spirit of unity on the major moral issues of the age, to continue the fight against Roman Catholicism, which was making substantial gains at this time, and to establish a permanent ecumenical alliance. The convention met in London, August 19, 1846, but disunity over the slavery question made the formation of a permanent alliance impossible. Garrison followed the proceedings with great interest, mentioning the Evangelical Alliance in many of his letters and editorials during August and September. (Letter to the editor from C. Duncan Rice, Yale University, June 1970.)

The World's Temperance Convention, the first of its kind, was held under the auspices of the National Temperance Society of England in the Literary Institute, Aldersgate Street, London, during the week of August 4, 1846. Although more than 300 delegates attended, all but thirty-three were from Great Britain. (*Life.*)

2. Extensive search has not discovered a General Flournoy from Kentucky, though there was a Georgia politician, John Jacobus Flournoy (1808–1879), who was active in temperance and other reforms. (Ellis Merton Coulter, *John Jacobus Flournoy, Champion of the Common Man in the Antebellum South*, Savannah, 1942.)

3. John Hewitt has not been further identified, although Charles Dickens describes him as follows: "A well-made, tight-built, dapper little fellow; with a ruddy face, which is a letter of invitation to shake him by both hands at once: and with a clear, blue, honest eye, that it does one good to see one's sparkling image in" (*American Notes*, London, 1842, p. 10).

4. Cow Bay is both a bay and a town in the eastern passage from Halifax to the Atlantic Ocean. Devil's Island is an island in the same passage.

5. The *Cambria* was a Cunard wooden sidewheeler, built in 1845, weighing 1,422 tons gross. She was employed on the Boston-Halifax-Liverpool and the New York-Liverpool runs. (Frank E. Dodman, *Ships of the Cunard Line*, London and New York, 1955, pp. 31, 131.)

1 4 1

TO EDMUND QUINCY

HALIFAX, Sunday morning, 10 o'clock, ⎫
July 19, 1846. ⎭

MY DEAR QUINCY:

The average trip of the steam-ships from Boston to Halifax is, I believe, about forty hours. Ours has occupied sixty-six. With a head-wind all the way, and a dense fog half of the way, we made comparatively slow progress. Yesterday afternoon, we struck on a reef, and had a very narrow escape, the particulars of which, I have communicated in a letter to my wife. At this moment, the carpenters are at work, repairing the damage which was done to the Britannia, (entirely at the bows,) and it is expected that we shall be ready to start this afternoon. I believe no one of our numerous passengers thinks of remaining behind, in consequence of this accident. They all behaved with remarkable firmness and composure — none more so than the ladies. There was no screaming, no weeping; though tears have fallen, and screams been uttered, in cases of far less peril. Capt. [John] Hewitt showed by his countenance, that he felt it to be a very serious occasion; but he exhibited the best qualities of a commander, and succeeded in extricating us from our perilous situation with the least possible excitement.

This will be my fifth voyage, and third mission, across the Atlantic. I could wish, as a matter of personal accommodation, that there was 'no more sea' [1] — for I very much prefer land to water, as a basis for travelling; but what would please me, would not please others, and far be it from any one to think that either the land or the ocean can be safely dispensed with! He may do what he can to abridge distances, by additional speed, and thus to 'annihilate time and space' [2] — but to more than this he may not aspire.

Hitherto, I have not found the society of those with whom I have crossed the Atlantic, at all calculated to relieve the tediousness of the voyage. Though dressed as gentlemen, and claiming to be such, they have generally shown themselves to be vulgar in taste, and perverse in appetite; giving themselves up to wine, brandy, gin, whisky and porter drinking, smoking and chewing that nauseous weed tobacco, playing cards for gain as well as amusement, and carousing more or less boisterously to a late hour. Of course, it was useless to expect to find in them, sympathy for any of the reforms of the day. Anti-slavery they could not tolerate; tee-totalism excited their contempt; 'the way of peace, they knew not;' [3] non-resistance to enemies, they scoffed at. In the present instance, there seems to be considerable improvement. A fair proportion of the passengers goes for total abstinence; there is less smoking than usual; less also of profanity; and those who call for the intoxicating drink, are evidently restrained in the use of it by the abstemiousness of those who sit around them. Perhaps we shall have more of excess, after we are fairly launched on the broad Atlantic; but I hope not.

We are all 'foreigners' on board — that is, we hail from the various quarters of the globe; the larger proportion, of course, being Englishmen and Americans. Persons are talking around me in 'an unknown tongue,' [4] not as a matter of privacy, not to conceal from me or others what they have to say, but in the language which they understand, and in social intercourse. I am not apt to be over-curious; but I wish I could understand them — I wish I knew what they were talking about! It is very painful to me to hear human speech, and yet as nothing better than jargon. This 'confusion of tongues' [5] on earth is no irrevocable ordination of God, rely upon it. It is a shame and a curse to mankind. We must get rid of it, for 'order is Heaven's first law'; [6] and the way to get rid of it is to see and feel that it is unnatural and monstrous, and to conspire for the discovery of a universal language. A man has really no more need to use two dialects, than he has to eat with two mouths, or to walk with four legs! What if he sojourn in the East or West, the North or South? What if he be a European, American, African or Asiatic? Has he not the same vocal powers of utterance? Why not speak, then, so as to be understood by every body? As for your learned men — your linguists — they can be dispensed with as readily as any other class of supernumeraries, when every body talks as every body ought to talk. You see what a hobby this is with me, and how confidently I dogmatize about it; but, remember, I am in the midst of a Babel confusion, without an interpreter, and endurance has passed its bounds. All hail to Phonography and Phonotypy, as the first steps in the grand march toward the universal redemption of human speech from the yokes and fetters now fastened upon it!

It is an effort for me to hold my pen. I am weak and dizzy from the effect of the voyage to this place, and ought to go ashore to derive new strength from the embrace of mother earth.[7] But, it being uncertain at what hour we start, I feel in duty bound to send you this poor epistle, rather than to occupy my time in rambling about the town. On the water, it is almost impossible for me to think with precision, or to write in an intelligible manner; and it is almost as difficult a task for me to read any volume, however interesting. I feel more like becoming oblivious to every thing around me, — to pen, ink, paper, and books, — until my feet are once more planted upon the dry land.

On Friday, I succeeded in giving Theodore Parker's 'Sermon of War' a careful perusal; and though on listening to its delivery, I derived great satisfaction, the reading of it has much enhanced its value, in my estimation.[8] It ought to be put into the hands of the PEOPLE — I use this word in an emphatic sense. Let every farmer, mechanic, working-man, operative, have a copy of it. Ten thousand dollars could not be better expended than in giving it a gratuitous circulation throughout the country. Its arguments and appeals go home to the understanding and conscience; its facts and figures are as irresistible as demonstration itself. I like the vigor of its rebuke, the strength of its denunciation, the boldness of its implication, the freshness of its style. I saw, in a late number of the Christian Watchman, a carping, sneering, bigoted review of this sermon, by its anti-reform, anti-human, anti-christian editor, Crowell, whose name you will find on the list of the Executive Committee of the American Peace Society, together with that of Hubbard Winslow! [9] It is an outrage on decency for such men to pretend to be the friends of peace.

I wish I could be with you all, in bodily presence, at your celebration of the approaching First of August. In spirit, I shall see and commune with each one of you. Whether in the body, or out of it, I am for universal liberty — and ever

Yours, affectionately,

Wm. Lloyd Garrison.

ALS: Merrill Collection of Garrison Papers, Wichita State University Library; also printed in *The Liberator*, August 7, 1846.

1. Revelation 21:1.
2. An adaptation of Alexander Pope, *Martinus Scriblerus, or, the Art of Sinking in Poetry*, chapter XI, lines 20–21.
3. Isaiah 59:8.
4. I Corinthians 14:2.
5. A reference to the Tower of Babel, Genesis 11.
6. Alexander Pope, *An Essay on Man*, Epistle IV, line 49.
7. Garrison refers to the mythological giant Antaeus.
8. Parker's sermon on war was preached at the Melodeon in Boston on Sunday, June 7, 1846, and published "by request," three editions being printed in 1846.
9. The *Christian Watchman* was a national Baptist paper founded in Boston in 1819 and surviving today in Somerset, New Jersey, after many name changes, as the *Watchman-Examiner*. (*ULS.*) William Crowell (1806–1871), a Baptist clergyman and journalist, edited the *Watchman* from 1840 to 1850. Migrating to St. Louis, Missouri, he edited there from 1851 to 1861 a similar publication, the *Western Watchman*. The author of several religious works, he preached extensively throughout the United States. (John Howard Brown, ed., *The Biographical Dictionary of America*, Boston, 1904.)
Crowell's review of Parker's sermon, published in the *Christian Watchman*, July 3, 1846, describes it as "a discourse, erroneously called a sermon," and says that "so far as it is a peace discourse we like it." Crowell objects, however, to Parker's emphasis on how much was spent on the war, alleging that such matters are not proper subjects for Sabbath discussion. He further calls the sermon intel-

gious in spirit and intent because of its "thrusts and sneers at the belief of evangelical Christians."

The American Peace Society was organized May 8, 1828, in New York by William Ladd, for the purpose of abolishing war. Although this was the first national organization of its type, local groups, such as Samuel J. May's Windham County Peace Society, had been formed during the early 1820's, some of which affiliated with the new society. The movement centered in the northeastern states, and its growth was such that in 1841, the year of Ladd's death, 1,500,000 tract pages were distributed. During the 1850's, as a result of disillusionment over wars in Europe and the impending crisis in America, the movement declined. (Merle E. Curti, *The American Peace Crusade, 1815–1860*, Durham, N.C., 1929.)

Hubbard Winslow (1799–1864) was a Congregational clergyman who succeeded Lyman Beecher in his Boston pastorate. He was a colonizationist, an active member of the American Peace Society, and the author of several religious and moral works.

1 4 2

TO CHARLES K. WHIPPLE

HALIFAX, [July] 19, 1846.

MY DEAR WHIPPLE:

We were less than three days on the trip from Boston to Halifax, (an unusually long one for a steamer,) yet it seemed to me that each day was equal in duration to a week at home. I have just been refreshing my spirit by walking through the principal parts of the town, and especially in taking a bird's eye view of the magnificent prospect that is afforded from the huge fortification that is in progress of completion, on a very elevated summit.[1] Nothing can be more pleasing than the land or water view. Every thing delighted me but that devil-invented fortification, and these tiger-chained soldiers who met me wherever I wandered. I wanted to disarm the latter and demolish the former, but not by brute force, or the aid of gunpowder. The moral abhorrence which war excites in my soul, causes me instinctively to recoil whenever I see a soldier, as I should to see a rattlesnake running at large. Why are these soldiers here? why is this costly fortification erected? It is because it is apprehended that we, Americans, will one day attempt to conquer the Canadas, *vi et armis*. Shame on us that we should put any body in fear of his life! Are we assassins, are we murderers? I fear we are not to be trusted as a people. And yet, if the people of the provinces were non-resistants — if they would send their soldiers away, and dismantle their fortifications, and spike their cannon, and declare that, for our evil they will invariably return us good — they would be entirely safe from our rapacity and violence; and I fear nothing else will protect them.

This matter of war and conquest reminds me of the horrible designs of our government upon Mexico. I am anxious that, to the final termination of hostilities, the Liberator should bear a steady, oft-repeated and faithful testimony against the Executive that provoked the Mexican war — against the Congress that sanctioned it — against the parties that encourage it — against every individual that does not protest against it. No matter what may be the success of the American arms, it cannot alter the criminality of the war. The more success, the more crime, and the more guilt. The more Mexicans slain, the more murders committed. It is a distinct, all-crushing pro-slavery movement. The enemies of slavery, therefore, should consider it to be the chief anti-slavery work which they are now specially called upon to do, to endeavor to paralyze the power of the government, that Mexico may be saved, and the overthrow of the Slave Power hastened. It is appalling to think of the guilt which Massachusetts incurs, in volunteering to engage in this war. Is not this land, are not the people, ready for destruction — is it not to be feared that they are beyond repentance, whose shameless motto is, 'Our country, right or wrong'? [2] Where are the ministers of the gospel of peace — where are the churches which claim for their leader the Prince of Peace — where are the virtuous, the humane, the just, in a crisis like this? Do they imagine that they can remain dumb, and not be chargeable with all the blood that may be shed in this unholy conflict? In view of this profession, they should hear the voice of heaven, — 'Ye are my witnesses, saith the Lord.' [3] Let them testify, long and loud — in season and out of season — in clear and explicit language. They who ask, 'What good will it do?' are such as hold the truth in unrighteousness, and have no abiding faith in God.[4] No righteous testimony, even from the humblest soul, was ever yet borne in vain.

Your faithful friend,

WM. LLOYD GARRISON.

Printed extract: *The Liberator*, August 21, 1846.

This extract is mistakenly dated in *The Liberator* "June 19." Garrison was not in Halifax in June, but is known to have been there July 19; see his letter of that date to Edmund Quincy.

1. Garrison refers to the Halifax Citadel, specifically the fourth fort to be constructed on the summit of Citadel Hill. Although construction had begun in 1828, it was still going on at the time of Garrison's visit. By 1870 the Citadel was virtually obsolete, although it served various military functions until the end of World War II. In 1956 it became a National Historic Park. (Pamphlet, *The Halifax Citadel*, sent to the editor by J. A. Sanford, Fort Anne National Historic Park, Annapolis Royal, Nova Scotia.)

2. Stephen Decatur, "Toast Given at Norfolk," April 1816.

3. Isaiah 43:1.

4. Garrison adapts Romans 1:18.

143

TO HELEN E. GARRISON

At Sea — [July] 26, 1846.

My Dear Wife:

The world is wide, and it has many places of attraction, and there are many good people in it; but, to me, there is no place so dear as my own cherished home, no one who has so large a share of my love as yourself, no objects so attractive as our beloved children. That I have consented to cross the Atlantic, and to be separated from you for the space of three or four months, is a proof, not that my love has abated in intensity — not that it is no cross for me to sojourn abroad — not that I am forgetful of the sacred claims which are binding upon me as a husband and a father — but that, to some extent, at least, and in a positive sense, I remember those who are in bonds as bound with them,[1] and am willing to make in their behalf, real and large sacrifices. Situated as you are, with no mother or sister or friend with you — with five young children, needing continual guidance and watchfulness — and in other respects requiring my special solicitude, and making my presence particularly desirable — I feel that you are signally manifesting the spirit of self-sacrifice in being willing to have me undertake my present mission, in accordance with my own convictions of duty, and the strong desires of the friends of emancipation, on both sides of the Atlantic. May Heaven preserve you and all our dear children, and enable me to return home in safety within the time allotted for my mission. It is not till I go far from you, that I begin to realize how essential is your presence to my happiness, and that I [am] aware of the measure of my love. I need no assurance from you, that you fully reciprocate all my feelings, and that your affection for me is strong and enduring.

Here we are on the wide ocean, the tenth day of our departure from Boston, and something like two thousand miles on our journey. During all this time, we have been surrounded with fog, so that we have not been able to take a single lunar observation — fog from Boston to Halifax — fog from Halifax to the Grand Banks — fog from the Grand Banks to Cape Race — fog for breakfast, fog for lunch, fog for dinner, fog for tea, and fog all night and all day. Of course, my brain is in a fog, my thoughts are foggy, and my letter will be very foggy. By the time you will receive this, I hope we shall have fair weather, and a clear sky.

Fortunately, we have had no rough weather, and [2] the wind has been entirely in our favor, and quite gentle. We left Halifax on Monday morning last, with additional passengers, — not, however, without some slight apprehension as to our safety, in consequence of the damage done to the Britannia, by striking on a reef near Halifax. Two who came with us from Boston, — delegates to the World's Temperance Convention, — left us at Halifax, being afraid to proceed. With my usual caution, — for you know that I am a cautious man, — I hesitated, and hardly knew whether to proceed, or to return home. I felt that, while the danger was not imminent, there was some risk — and so did all the other passengers. On Tuesday, some alarm was created, by the discovery that the steamer was leaking considerably, and that the channel to the pumps was so obstructed, that the water could not be pumped out. To open this channel, it was necessary to remove a large quantity of coal; after which, by the aid of our engine, there was no difficulty in keeping the steamer free. Still, the fact that she is constantly leaking, and requiring the pump to be kept in continual operation, creates more or less uneasiness on board; and very thankful shall we be, when our voyage is ended, and we are once more safely on the land. Having been so long detained at Halifax, it is not probable that we shall be in Liverpool before the 31st instant, or the first of August — though some are sanguine enough to think we shall arrive by the 30th inst. You know my great aversion to the sea, and it is greatly increased by the present trip. I dislike the confinement — the company is not such as I should prefer — to write, costs me many painful efforts — I take no pleasure in reading, for my brain is in a whirl; and though I have been sea-sick for only two or three days, I have felt disposed to keep to my berth a large portion of my time, rather than to be on deck; consequently, the hours have passed away as with wings of led, and each day has seemed almost interminable. On retiring to rest at night, I have merely divested myself of my boots, coat, vest and collar, and, putting on my gown, laid down on the outside of the bed-clothes — with but two exceptions. Almost every night, I have been wholly indisposed to sleep; and, O! how long the night has been! In the solitude and darkness, dear Helen, your image has been constantly before me; and all the eventful scenes through which we have passed, since we pledged to each other eternal love and fidelity, have successively and vividly presented themselves to my mind. The remembrances of the past are both sad and joyous. I have been carried back to the time when I first visited Brooklyn, and was welcomed in the dear family circle, and saw you in the freshness and simplicity of girlhood, and received the pure tokens of love at your hands. Alas! what changes have taken place in that sweet domestic circle, where the very peace of paradise seemed to prevail, as though it were never to have an end. Every thing was so tranquil, every thing so happy, there was nothing to suggest thoughts of mortality and decay. Frances died a few months before my acquaintance with you began; then how soon was our beloved Henry snatched from us in the bloom and spring-time of life! [3] Almost immediately, your venerable sire was next called away. Next followed our beloved Mary, and the[n] our never-to-be forgotten Anne, and then dear and excellent mother. The old homestead has passed into other hands, and Brooklyn has ceased to be a place of resort, almost a place of interest. I do not bring up these reminiscences to sadden your mind; but they have passed like images before the mirror of my memory, as I have been lying in my berth, unable to sleep, though it was time for profound repose. Almost twelve years have rolled away, since in marriage we two became one; and if beloved ones have been taken from us, kind Heaven has been pleased to crown our union with five dear children, who are still preserved to us. I have thought much of them, as well as of you. What do you think I discovered in the pocket of my gown, a day or two since? A pair of stockings belonging to our own and only pet daughter, Fanny! You should have seen me when I made the discovery — how I smiled, how I exulted, how I kissed and pressed to my heart the tiny little things! It was next to having her in my arms, and seeing her sweet face, and hearing her pleasant voice. I feel much concerned to hear what is the state of her health, and whether her complaint has been removed. If it has not, you should not suffer another moment to pass, without procuring the advice and aid of Dr. Guise.[4]

Liverpool, July 31, 1846.

Your heart will leap to see, by this, that we have come safely to port. We arrived this afternoon at 3 o'clock, it being just 15 days since we left Boston. Had we not been detained by the accident at Halifax, we should have completed the voyage in 13 days. Nothing has occurred on our way, worthy of special notice. Since the 26th, we had tolerably clear weather, and a fair wind. All Liverpool is in a state of enthusiastic excitement, in consequence of the visit of Prince Albert, and so crowded that it is said that every hotel is full to repletion, and several guineas, in some instances, were proffered for a night's lodging, with a slight entertainment. All the vessels in the port (an immense number) have colors flying at their mast-head, which present the gayest appearance I have ever seen. The attachment to royalty in this country borders closely on idolatry.

Who should I find at the dock, waiting for me, but those two beloved friends, Henry C. Wright and Richard D. Webb of Dublin? They have been in the city since Tuesday, every moment anxiously awaiting my arrival. I will not attempt to describe our interview. It was loving and affectionate, on both sides, of course. Great was their joy to see me. We went immediately to the Temperance Hotel in Clayton Square, where we shall remain till Monday morning, when we shall leave for London.[5]

Monday evening, Aug. 3.

It is now about 11 o'clock. I am in London, at the residence of dear George Thompson, who was at the depot on my arrival, and took bro. Wright and myself home. His wife and four of the children are now absent from the city — two are at home. His own mother is residing with George, and though in the 76th year of her age, is uncommonly sprightly and entertaining. He and H. C. W. send their cordial regards to you. To morrow, the World's Temperance Convention begins. [Henry] Clapp is in the city. But my sheet is full. Farewell, dearest!

Wm. Lloyd Garrison.

☞ Give my special remembrances to Mr. and Mrs. Prideaux.[6] How comes on the little boy? I will have some fun with him when I return. Tell Ellen that I have been delighted to see Ireland even at a distance.[7] Give her my warm regards.

ALS: Garrison Papers, Boston Public Library; a press copy of the first two pages appears in the Garrison Papers, Sophia Smith Collection, Smith College Library.

Garrison misdates this letter August 26, at which time he was already in England, since he had landed at Liverpool on July 31. Moreover, the last two pages of the letter have the dates July 31 and August 3. The correct month July has been supplied on the manuscript in the hand probably of Wendell Phillips Garrison; the editor follows this emendation.

1. An adaptation of Hebrews 13:3.

2. Since the corner is torn off the manuscript page, the words "weather, and" are supplied from the press copy at Smith.

3. Frances Benson (1794–1832) was a spinster sister of Helen E. Garrison. (*Life.*)

Henry Egbert Benson (1814–1837), Helen's brother and Garrison's close friend, lived in Providence from 1831 to 1834. He was an agent for *The Liberator* and for Samuel J. May's Unitarian paper, the *Christian Monitor and Common People's Adviser*. He also traveled with George Thompson in 1834–1835, as assistant and companion. (*Life.*)

4. Christian F. Geist (1806–1872), whom Garrison often calls Dr. Guise, was born in Germany and began practice in Boston in 1842. (Letter to the editor from Jonathan Prude, researcher, September 1970.)

5. The hotel, of which William Brown was the proprietor, was located at 20 Clayton Square. (*Gore's Directory of Liverpool and Its Environs*, London, 1847.)

6. James Prideaux (1809–1846), of 13 Pine Street, was a professor of music whose advertisements for "pianoforte, playing and singing" appeared in *The Liberator* almost weekly until August 14, 1846. (Letter to the editor from Jonathan Prude, researcher, September 1970.)

7. Ellen, the Garrisons' Irish servant, has not been further identified.

144

TO EDMUND QUINCY

Liverpool, August 1, 1846.

My Dear Quincy:

The Britannia arrived at this port yesterday afternoon, much to the satisfaction of all the passengers, and to the relief of many minds here, as our detention at Halifax gave rise to considerable uneasiness. The damage she sustained by running upon a reef not far from the entrance of the harbor, caused her to leak considerably during the passage; but as the pump was worked by the engine which propelled her, there was no difficulty in keeping her free. Fortunately, we encountered no gale, and the wind was generally favorable, so that we could make use of our canvass; but, for the first ten days, we were completely enveloped in the fog, of which I have had *quantum suff.* to satisfy me for a long time to come. We had fog from Boston to Halifax — fog from Halifax to the Grand Banks — fog from the Grand Banks to Cape Race, and a long distance beyond; — fog at breakfast, fog at lunch, fog at dinner, fog at tea, and fog all night and all day. Nothing occurred on the voyage worth putting on record, excepting when the first glimpse of the sun was caught. Surely, "it is a pleasant thing to behold the light of the sun," [1] especially after such a fog.

For two days past, Liverpool has been in a state of loyal delirium, in consequence of the visit of Prince Albert by special invitation, for the three-fold purpose of laying the corner-stone of a large and costly building for the benefit of seamen — being present at the formal opening of a new dock called by his name — and gratifying public curiosity.[2] The newspapers give the particulars of the movements, appearance, sayings and doings of the Prince, in a manner that not merely "borders on the ridiculous," but is childish in the extreme. The best thing that can be said of him is, that he is a harmless, well-behaved, good-looking young man, has no distinctive character, and is a mere appendage to the throne. But he is the husband of Victoria; and, whether from gallantry or a fondness for display, the people almost idolize Victoria. This visit of Prince Albert has been a costly affair to individuals, and to the city. The number of people drawn by it into Liverpool from the surrounding country was immense. Human ingenuity was exhausted to give brilliancy and effect to the spectacle. Never did I behold so gorgeous a sight as was presented by the shipping in the harbor, ten thousand flags of all colors, shapes and nations floating in the breeze, and meeting the eye in every direction. Not arriving till the afternoon of the day of the grand celebration, we were a little too late to see the ceremonies performed, for the particulars of which, see any of the Liverpool papers.

Before the Britannia got along side of the dock, my heart leaped with delight to recognize in the crowd of speakers, waiting impatiently to give me a loving greeting, Henry C. Wright and Richard D. Webb, of Dublin. I felt at once repaid for the peril we encountered near Halifax, for all the loss of comfort by the prevalence of fog across the Atlantic, and for the separation from the beloved friends in Boston. Happy, indescribably happy was our meeting. Henry is in good health, and time and toil excessive seem to have made no impression upon him. His cure at Graefenberg appears to have been an effectual one. Richard, when I left Liverpool for Boston in 1840, came expressly from Dublin to give me the parting hand; and now he has come expressly to be the first to welcome me once more to the shores of England. I will not attempt to describe the pleasure I have already derived from his company. He is a man of genius, full of Irish wit and pleasantry, but, better than all this, true to the claims of suffering humanity, a clear-sighted abolitionist, and a world-embracing spirit. Of Henry C. Wright, I need say nothing. My appreciation of his character and labors is too well known to require any declarations from me at this time, on that point.

Being teetotallers all, we have made Brown's temperance hotel, in Clayton-square, our head-quarters; and I would recommend this hotel, and its worthy and attentive keeper, to the special patronage of the friends of temperance from the United States, visiting Liverpool. On Monday, we shall leave for London.

London, August 4, 1846.

We arrived from Liverpool last evening, having James H. Webb, (a brother of Richard,) his wife, and Maria Waring, in company with us. It was a delightful journey. O, the beauty of England! Our long-beloved, faithful and ever-devoted friend George Thompson met us at the depot, and took Henry and myself home with [him], — though Mrs. Thompson is at present absent for the benefit of her health, at Gravesend. Notwithstanding the immense popularity which has attended his brilliant career of philanthropy in this country — notwithstanding the honors which have been so prodigally heaped upon him — he still appears the same simple, unaffected man that he did during his memorable sojourn with us in New-England, in 1835 — a year never to be forgotten in the annals of American history.[3] This indicates a noble mind and a truly great man. I shall spare no pains to persuade him to return with me to the United States. He thinks it will not be possible for him to do so, such are his engagements; but he fully intends being with us, *Deo volente,* at no distant day.

To-day, the World's Temperance Convention will commence its deliberations. Of course, I shall not fail to be present, and to send you some account of its proceedings. I must conclude abruptly, desiring to be affectionately remembered to all the true-hearted.

Yours, faithfully, to the end,

Wm. Lloyd Garrison.

ALS: Mellen Chamberlain Autograph Collection, Boston Public Library; also printed in *The Liberator*, September 11, 1846.

1. A reference to Ecclesiastes 11:7.
2. Garrison refers to the Sailors' Home, designed in the Elizabethan style, which was to be completed in 1850 at a cost of £50,000. It became one of Liverpool's best-known charities, providing seamen with room, board, and medical care at moderate expense. He also refers to Albert Dock, which had just been completed at a cost of £782,265. (*The Adelphi Hotel Guide to Liverpool*, Liverpool, 1872, pp. 71–79.)
3. According to Garrison's view, 1835 was memorable as the year of violent opposition to abolitionists: there were riots in Philadelphia; George Thompson was mobbed in Concord, New Hampshire; in Boston both Thompson and Garrison had been symbolically attacked by the erection of gallows in front of the Garrison house; and in the same city Garrison's life had been endangered when a mob seized him as a surrogate for Thompson.

145

TO HELEN E. GARRISON

London, August [4], 1846.

My Dear Helen:

I am filled with consternation — with sorrow — with anguish. The steamer has returned from Liverpool, carrying no letter from me to you, or to any one else! What will you think of me? How great will be your disappointment! I anticipate you in the shedding of tears. The way in which this calamity happened was this. I had completed the letter to you, which you will receive with this, dated Liverpool, excepting some half a dozen lines, and just before leaving for London, when my good friend Richard D. Webb, wishing me to go with him to a particular place, assured me that I could finish the letter in London, and send it by the morning train to Liverpool, in season for the steamer, as he had ascertained that such was the arrangement made between the two places. It seems he was misled by false information. I finished the letter to you, and wrote another to Edmund Quincy, and sent it to the London Post Office at an early hour in the morning; but the letters came back with the tidings on the part of the bearer, that no mail goes to-day for the steamer. This seems to me almost incredible, because there is ample time for the mail to reach Liverpool, in season. But here are the letters! That to Edmund Quincy is not specially important; but this one to you, — you to whom hours must seem like days, and days like weeks, and weeks like months, — you, who, in consequence of the serious accident the Britannia encountered near Halifax, must feel intense anxiety to hear of my safe arrival in England, — is of as much value as the evidence of a loving and devoted heart, the fidelity and attachment of a fond husband and father. It is too much for me to imagine your feelings, on failing to get this epistle. I can realize, (because I know the strength of your love for me,) how your heart must leap to hear of the arrival of the steamer — with what impatience you must wait to have the mail assorted — with what loving confidence you must expect to get an epistle from me — and, hence, the joyous emotions that must possess your breast; but I dare not think of the shock, the grief, the astonishment, resulting from the announcement — "There is no letter from your husband!"

There is one thing that mitigates my grief, and will, to some extent, your own. R. D. Webb and H. C. Wright both fortunately mailed letters for Boston at Liverpool, announcing my safe arrival, and the fact that they were on the dock to embrace me as soon as I landed; so that you will be at ease, in regard to two most important points to you — to wit, my arrival and health. Be assured, there shall be no failure by the steamer on the 19th.

I am stopping at the house of my dear friend George Thompson, and shall make it my head quarters as long as I remain in London. His house is handsomely furnished, and very pleasantly located, having a yard in front, and also a spacious piece of ground in the rear of the house, with gravelled walks, &c. It is about three miles from the heart of the city, though, to an American eye, it is as much in the city as Pine-street is in Boston. Every thing is furnished for my accommodation, so that I lack nothing. To be once more with George, is a revival of days gone by. He is still the same loving, faithful friend — the same playful, mirthful, entertaining companion — the same modest, unpretending man — the same zealous and eloquent advocate — the same warm and sympathizing friend of suffering humanity — that he was eleven years ago, when he was in our country. I do not perceive that either time, or his immense labors, have made any striking change in his personal appearance. He looks about as young as he did in the U.S. He has fallen into one injurious habit, and that is, the inordinate use of snuff. Like all snuff-takers, he uses it almost unconsciously. Of course, I have borne my testimony against his box and its contents. He has too much good sense to take offence, and too much honesty to attempt to extenuate his conduct; so he simply smiles, and hears me with all kindness. If I can induce him to give up this habit, and sign or take the tee-total pledge in regard to snuff, I shall feel as if it were worth the trouble and expense of coming to London; for, should this habit continue to grow upon him, it will seriously impair his voice, and thus greatly injure him as a public speaker.

Dear wife, it now seems to me as if I could never again be induced to be separated from you for so long a time, or by so wide an obstacle to our union as the ocean. Whatever of yearning desire you may feel to see and embrace me, be assured it is *fully* reciprocated by

Your loving husband,

Wm. Lloyd Garrison.

ALS: Garrison Papers, Boston Public Library; extract printed in *Life*, III, 156.

Garrison misdates this letter August 1; in fact he did not reach London until late in the evening of the third, on which date he was still writing the letter begun July 26 which missed the Liverpool steamer. Since a later letter to Helen is also dated the fourth, it is certain that this one was written earlier that same day. These inferences are supported by the fact that someone has on the manuscript questioned whether the date were not August 4 rather than August 1.

146

TO HELEN E. GARRISON

London, August 4, 1846.

This day the World's Convention began its sessions.[1] The cause which it seeks to promote being the first that I ever publicly espoused, I went to the meeting, for the purpose of observing its proceedings. It was held in a comparatively small room, and the public were not allowed to listen to the discussions. Though not a delegate from any temperance society at home, I was politely furnished (with others) with a ticket, which admitted me as a member of the convention; but I soon perceived that the same spirit which controlled the anti-slavery convention in 1840, had entire mastery over this. In the course of the afternoon session, the Rev. Mr. Kirk, of Boston, incidentally defended the American slaveholders, and eulogized the Sabbath as worthy of being maintained by pains and penalties, 'not in the name of the Lord, but on the ground of expediency.'[2] As soon as I could, I rose to reply, and was at first received with very great applause; but the moment I began to rebuke Kirk for his conduct, sundry individuals raised the cry of personality, and protested against the discussion of extraneous topics! Great excitement followed, and the result was, that Kirk took back his pro-slavery sentiment, not to repudiate it, but to avoid the issue, and escape censure. Every thing in the convention is under the most stringent regulations. As for free discussion, its toleration is out of the question. I do not think, after the treatment that I have received, that I shall attend another session. Not that the convention at all sympathized with Kirk, for they did not; but they were afraid of giving offence, or of getting into a controversy on another topic, aside from the object which had specially brought them together. Still, they behaved quite unfairly, and are under too much 'management' to suit me — though Henry Clapp, notwithstanding his horror of an organized meeting on our side of the Atlantic, can act as Secretary, and discover nothing to dislike or censure!

The temperance cause, in this kingdom, has made very little progress, especially among the 'respectable' and 'good society' folks. Almost wherever I go to partake of the hospitalities proffered to me, decanters of wine are on the table, and not to take a glass of this poison is an act of singularity which immediately excites notice and observation.

Printed extract: *The Liberator*, September 11, 1846; reprinted in *Life*, III, 157–158. This fragment is printed with the explanatory note: "We give, by permission, the following extracts of a letter from Mr. Garrison to his wife."

1. The World's Temperance Convention began on Tuesday, the fourth, and ran through the rest of the week (*The Liberator*, September 18, 1846).

2. Edward Norris Kirk (1802–1874) was a graduate of Princeton Theological Seminary who became a prominent evangelist and lecturer in behalf of temperance, missions, and abolition. From 1842 to 1871 he served as pastor of the Mount Vernon Congregational Church in Boston and was known as one of the outstanding preachers of his time. The quotation from Kirk's speech cannot be verified, since it was not printed in *The Liberator*; in consideration of Kirk's honorable record of antislavery activity, both past and to come, it is possible that Garrison quotes him out of context or misreads his intent.

147

TO HELEN E. GARRISON

London, Aug. 11, 1846.

My dear Helen:

This, you know, is my third visit to London. If, at first, its vastness and splendor overwhelmed me, my astonishment is rather increased than diminished, the more I attempt to take its dimensions, and look into its wonders. There are two positions in which I feel myself "less than nothing, and vanity" [1] — a mere mote in the sun-beam — on the Atlantic ocean, and in London, the central point of human existence. Not an hour passes over my head, but I deplore your absence and long to have you by my side. The throng of people is immense, without end, go where you will — and yet this is the season of the year when tens of thousands of the inhabitants are out of the city, rusticating in the country, or enjoying themselves by the sea-shore. The Thames river presents a curious spectacle, at all hours. In addition to the multitude of vessels from various parts of the globe, the river is crowded with steamers of all sizes and descriptions, gliding up and down with great velocity, and carrying multitudes of people, who are enabled to travel a long distance for a mere trifle. Nothing can be more animating or picturesque than to stand on any one of the fine bridges which span the Thames, and look up and down the river, to see the innumerable conveyances which are flying in every direction. As for the streets in London, their name is legion, and in length many of them seem interminable. Yet, huge as is the city, and complicated as are its arrangements and mysterious as are its modes of existence, every thing goes on with a regularity and precision truly marvellous. There is no violent collision — scarcely any jostle — the mechanism is perfect, "like clock-work" — and no one is allowed or expected to interfere with another.

Gravesend is now a place of resort, though it was once notorious for the resort of sailors and lewd women. It is 20 miles down the Thames. Mrs. Thompson has been residing there for a few weeks, with her children, for the benefit of their health. I have just been down with George Thompson, where I spent the night, and had a very pleasant entertainment. The place was full of visitors, and the scene was a very lively one. In the evening, we went to a beautiful garden, of immense extent, called Rosherville, some two or three miles from Gravesend, which has been reclaimed from a worthless soil, and beautified and adorned in a truly wonderful manner. The next morning, we all came up together — Mrs. Thompson and the children will remain at home for the season. The latter are six in number — two boys and four girls.[2] The two eldest girls are quite tall, and on the whole interesting. They all lack animation, and bear a much stronger resemblance to their mother than to their father.

It is still doubtful whether I shall be able to see Elizabeth Pease before my return. She is now living in a retired place in the country, and sees nobody. Her health is very critical. She has probably an enlargement of the heart, and in her early days was subject to epileptic fits. The sickness and death of her almost idolized father [Joseph Pease] have caused a great prostration of her physical system.

There is another thing, prevalent in this city, which is calculated to shock and overwhelm a good man from the United States. It is the immense number of prostitutes, who swarm the streets every night for the vilest purposes. You must remember that London is almost as light in the night as it is in the day-time; hence, every person is readily seen and identified. But these poor creatures know no shame, and are driven to this disgusting course by the most terrible necessities. They are of all grades in appearance, from the most fashionably dressed to the most ragged. They are very importunate to all passers-by, often taking them by the arm, and frequently accosting them in a familiar manner. Hence, there is a perpetual temptation, and a very formidable one, held out, especially to young, unmarried men, to be licentious. In fact, personal purity on the part of married men, I am told, is scarcely regarded at all, taking them in a mass. Last evening, I was waiting for an omnibus, in company with a venerable friend, in front of the Lord Mayor's [3] mansion, when a very handsomely dressed young lady passed me, with a parasol in her hand, and gave me the most earnest glances, in a manner revealing her desire, yet not boldly or impudently. She had a sweet countenance, almost pensive, and a beautiful form. After advancing a few steps, she stopped, turned round, and in the most insinuating manner acted as though she expected me to go with her. There she stood, in expectancy, until the omnibus came along, and I was whirled out of her sight. My heart sunk within me to think of the horrid fate of that unfortunate creature. She seemed to me like one just entering on her frightful career. I thought of her as a sister — as *my* sister — seduced, it may be, by some villain, who had pledged to her eternal fidelity. I thought of her as a daughter, — as *my* daughter — once the hope, the pride, the ornament of the family circle — now a castaway, and forever shut out from virtuous society. To think of such a one selling her body nightly, for a few shillings to furnish her with bread — no matter to whom, provided she can obtain the price! What unutterable loathing must possess her soul — and yet, so inexorable is society, this she must do, or die of starvation in the streets. O, horrible doom! As I rode home to George Thompson's, a long distance through the city, I observed multitudes of others, (for they are easily detected,) some standing at the corners of the streets, others in front of public buildings which are much frequented, and others sauntering along, looking every one boldly in face whom they hoped to victimize. It is an awful state of society, requiring the most sturdy virtue and the deepest religious principle to save one from contamination.

Lovingly yours, and yours only,

Wm. Lloyd Garrison.

ALS: Garrison Papers, Boston Public Library; extract printed in *The Liberator*, September 25, 1846.

1. An example of Garrison's use of biblical language without reference to a specific text.

2. The six Thompson children were Elizabeth, Edith, Amelia, Louisa, Garrison, and Herbert. Elizabeth died in 1847 and Garrison in 1851. Amelia was to marry F. W. Chesson; Herbert (c. 1835–1867) had been born in the United States. Since the Thompson family records are scant, information about the children is meager. (Letter to the editor from C. Duncan Rice, Yale University, December 26, 1970.)

3. John Johnson (died 1848), politician and would-be member of Parliament, Lord Mayor of London, 1845–1846. (Letter to the editor from Betty R. Maste, deputy keeper of records, Corporation of London, April 21, 1971.)

148

TO HELEN E. GARRISON

London, Aug. 13, 1846.

Dear Wife:

The steamer which left Boston on the 1st inst. arrived in Liverpool in the unprecedented short passage of 10 days and 18 hours, as if animated by a desire to bring me that intelligence from home, which I so much wanted to receive. George Thompson has just put into my hands, two Standards, two Liberators, a letter from dear Wendell Phillips, another from Edmund Quincy, and two from yourself. I have devoured the contents of the whole of them, with an appetite which, though it would be difficult to satiate, is to some extent appeased. Edmund has taken up the editorial pen in earnest, and by his industry and vigor makes a full and racy editorial department. He will throw me into the shade entirely, both as to quantity and quality. Wendell, alluding to our accident off Halifax, humorously remarks — "Had it been an *American* steamer, with our "neck or nothing" principles aboard, I should have wished to come back; but careful Mr. Bull may be trusted — and wherever he'll put his little finger, a Yankee may trust his life." This is literally true. The characteristics of the two parties are seen in their watch-words — that of "Mr. Bull" being, "*All right!*" — that of "Brother Jonathan",[1] "GO AHEAD!"

The sudden and severe illness of Mr. [James] Prideaux has made me feel very sad, and deeply do I sympathize with his devoted wife in this heavy affliction. What a resolute, heroic woman she is! To think of her leaving a sick-bed, after so short a confinement, at so much hazard to herself and her little one! But such is the love of woman. By your last letter, there seems to be a chance for his recovery, though his case is extremely critical. I shall feel great anxiety to hear again from you, in regard to his fate. Do every thing that you can to relieve them in this hour of trial, and express to Mrs. P. my warmest sympathies.

The conduct of Lovejoy, about the carriage, was certainly very arbitrary; but he was probably actuated by good motives.[2]

It afflicts me to think that dear little Fanny is still troubled with her complaint. Something ought to be done to relieve her speedily, or it may become chronic. I hope you will not delay sending for Dr. [Christian] Guise [Geist]. I think he will be able to prescribe successfully for her. At least, it is desirable that he should know precisely her case. Henry C. Wright thinks (and his judgment is of much value) that if she could take, two or three times a day, a "sitz bath," — i.e. sit in a bowl or pan, somewhat shallow, with three or four inches of water, as long as you could amuse her, — it would be highly beneficial. I would try it — the experiment can do no harm. I am glad the dear little sufferer is such a comfort to you at night, and in some measure supplies my absence. Tell her that "papa" longs to hug and kiss her, to carry her on his shoulder, to sing to her, to dance with her, to walk out into the streets with her, that she may see all the pretty things. You may *almost* smother her with kisses for my sake. All that you give, I will repay with interest on my return.

You cannot be too careful, at this season of the year, either in regard to yourself or the children, as to the bowel complaint. I do not think that ripe fruit is at all dangerous, but far otherwise. The only danger lies in eating it in an unripe or decayed state.

I do not wonder that you were greatly alarmed for my safety, on hearing of our disaster near Halifax, through the Boston papers, and on the return of some of the passengers to Boston; especially, as you had received from me, at the time you wrote, no assurance on that score. I wrote a long letter to you at Halifax, describing the accident — another to Quincy, and another to [Charles K.] Whipple, designed for the Liberator — but none of them appear to have been received. I paid the postage on them, and cannot doubt that they were all safely received the next day after the steamer left.

I hope, by this time, George and William are located in Northampton, where I would let them remain until my return — certainly, allow George to stay, without fail. His absence will be a great relief to you all, and he will be far happier in the country than in the city. As to his learning, a few weeks will make no difference worthy of a moment's consideration. Without having G. or W. at home, you will have care and trouble enough with the other children. Rest assured, dear wife, I feel heartily in spirit to share your burdens and trials, and long to be with you at this moment, that I may relieve you of much of that heavy anxiety which I know continually presses upon you. Endeavor to preserve as much serenity of mind as possible. Remember your delicate situation — and how intimate is the unborn child with a mother's feelings and pulsations. Do not give way to despondency or excitement: your child will through life be affected by your present condition. As for Wendy, Charley, and Fanny, remember that they are little children, and allow them to caper as freely as they will, without chiding them too often, provided they do nothing *very* bad. Provide amusement for them in some shape or other, and give them the assurance that if they will be good children, I will bring them some pretty presents from London on my return. O for an hour's frolic with them!

Give my best regards to Ellen. Tell her that I have had the warmest manifestations of Irish friendship and kindness, in the persons of the [Richard D.] Webbs, [James] Haughtons and [Richard] Allens of Dublin; and when I get to the Emerald Isle itself, I am certain of receiving a hearty welcome in all quarters. I shall probably visit Dublin, Belfast and Cork. If Ellen will send me word where her relatives reside, I will either go and see them, or write to them respecting her situation. So seldom have we called her by her full name, that I have forgotten it; so, be particular in sending it to me. It would give me great pleasure in informing her friends as to her connexion with our family, and the value we place upon her as a faithful associate.

I write nothing to you for insertion in the Liberator, except I expressly so direct. As to the progress I am making, with regard to the object of my mission, you will learn the particulars in the letters I shall write to Quincy, or the other editors *pro tem.*, for the public eye. On Monday, we are to hold our first public meeting in this city, at the Crown and Anchor tavern, which will be addressed by myself, Douglass, Wright, Thompson, Henry Vincent, and others.[3] On Wednesday, the Evangelical Alliance will be held, and there will probably be some excitement in it. growing out of the question, whether slaveholders shall be admitted to it.[4] There will be a considerable number of pro-slavery American priests present, whose sojourn here will be any thing but comfortable.

Hereafter, till further notice, letters must be addressed to me at Glasgow, Scotland, to the care of William Smeal. I shall take a final leave of London probably in ten or twelve days, for Bath, Bristol and Exeter.

Mrs. Thompson has returned from Gravesend, with all the children. She is in good health, and looks quite as young as she did when in Boston. The children are not handsome, but remarkably quiet — far too much so, for me — and very studious. She has a dear little baby girl, about 16 months old, and even more delicate than *sis*. I play with her a good deal, and almost fancy she is mine. Give my special regards to all the [Francis] Jacksons and [Charles D.] Merriams, as well as to other friends. Farewell!

Lovingly yours,

Wm. Lloyd Garrison.

ALS: Villard Papers, Harvard College Library.

1. The sobriquet for the United States later supplanted by the term "Uncle Sam."

2. Joseph C. Lovejoy (1805–1871) was a brother of Owen and Elijah P. He had been principal of Hallowell Academy, then pastor of the Universalist church, Oldtown, Maine, and was currently minister of the church at Cambridgeport, Massachusetts. It is uncertain what Garrison means by his "conduct . . . about the carriage." (Dwight L. Dumond, ed., *Letters of James Gillespie Birney, 1831–1857*, New York, 1938, p. 716.)

3. Garrison refers to the first public meeting of the recently organized Anti-Slavery League, to be held August 17, 1846. The Crown and Anchor Tavern, located in the Strand at the corner of Arundel Street, was famous for its earlier associations with Johnson, Boswell, and Reynolds; in 1847 it was to become the Whittington Club. (Letter to the editor from C. Duncan Rice, Yale University, July 25, 1969.)

Henry Vincent (1813–1878), who had married Lucy Chappell Cleave in 1841, was a lecturer and political agitator. He was one of the leaders in the Chartist movement, dedicated to extending and reforming suffrage.

4. This world convention of Protestant sects did produce plenty of excitement. The dilemma was how to meet in a spirit of unity to discuss moral issues when there were so many irreconcilable attitudes on the great moral question of slavery. Crisis followed crisis until the American proslavery delegates were able to pass a resolution that all references to slavery be deleted from the proceedings. For Garrison's contemptuous reaction to this measure as well as his account of the convention as a whole see *The Liberator*, October 2, December 11, 1846, and *Life*, III, 164 ff.

---

1 4 9

TO EDMUND QUINCY

LONDON, August 14, 1846.

MY DEAR QUINCY:

It gives me unalloyed satisfaction to believe, that my mission to this country will be productive of the best results to the cause of emancipation in our own country; and I hope it will be of some service to the cause of liberty and equal rights in this. Thus far, I have received a cordial welcome on the part of those whose co-operation is specially desirable, and who are the most to be relied on in every emergency. The spirit of reform is busily at work here, in a thousand different ways; and, truly, the number of abuses to be removed, and grievances to be redressed, is multitudinous. Happily, such labor we are spared, because the particular abuses and grievances, to which I allude, are not found among us; and, were it not for our great, overshadowing, execrable slave system, our land would be incomparably the glory of all lands, and our people the admiration of the world. All those who are truly engaged in any of these reformatory movements, as a matter of uncompromising principle, will assuredly give the faithful men and women, who rally around the American Anti-Slavery Society, their warmest sympathies, and, as far as practicable, their aid. If we are in advance of them, they will not raise the senseless cry of "ultra-ism," but will march steadily onward, as light shall be shed upon their pathway, and new moral discoveries be made by them. We want none to co-operate with us, who are not prepared to stand by us in every emergency — that is, of course, so long as we are faithful to the principle which now binds us together — a world-wide principle, vindicating all human rights, and consulting all human interests.

I told you and my other cherished associates, before embarking for the old world, that it would not be my object to multiply superficial friends to our movement, by keeping out of sight its radical tendencies, or its unpopular features; but rather to seek the personal acquaintance of those who are able to appreciate fidelity to a great and good enterprise, who are animated by a spirit of disinterested benevolence, who cherish the world-reconciling doctrine of the brotherhood of the human race, who are participating in unpopular movements at home, and who are determined never to be driven from their convictions of duty.

I intend to hold as few public meetings as possible, consistently with the full and most effective discharge of my mission; for these are attended with very considerable expense, and necessarily consume more time in their arrangement than I can well spare, in view of the limited period of my absence from Boston. If, therefore, you should not see me reported frequently in the newspapers as having addressed public assemblies, you must not infer from this silence that I am not devoting myself in the best manner, and with assiduity and sound judgment, to the discharge of the delightful task which I have voluntarily assumed.

It will be my object, as far as practicable, to become personally acquainted with those who have the control of the press in this country, or who, by their literary efforts, are moulding the public sentiment, in order to secure their co-operation with us, as occasion may offer, by recording their testimony against American slavery, its patrons, abettors and apologists; and by thus helping to swell that tide of moral indignation, which, rising like a deluge, shall ultimately sweep the foul system of slavery from the earth.

Soon after my arrival in this city, I called to see Douglas Jerrold, (having a letter of introduction to him from an esteemed friend in

Liverpool,) and was highly gratified with the interview.[1] Jerrold, you know, is a writer who has sprung somewhat suddenly into notoriety, especially as the principal editor of the inimitable *"Punch"* — a journal which has an immense circulation here, and which has consecrated the somewhat dangerous weapons of wit and satire, and the perilous art of caricature, to the cause of humanity, and in behalf of popular liberty. In addition to his contributions to 'Punch,' he publishes a weekly magazine, which exhibits much tact and industry, and, though of a graver character than 'Punch,' is equally on the side of the people. The facts which I was enabled to lay before him during our brief interview, (for I purposely made it brief, being an editor myself, and knowing that long visits are often a great annoyance, however interesting the visitant,) respecting American slavery, and the influence it exerts for evil upon this country and throughout the world, seemed to be new to him, and to excite his special attention. He promised to give us a helping hand for its overthrow, and has since manifested his sincerity in copying various articles from the Liberator into his magazine. Jerrold appears to be about 35 years of age, and has an intellectual countenance, though his personal appearance is not peculiarly striking. May he continue to consecrate his fine talents to the advancement of the human race, and he will thus embalm his literary reputation, so that it shall go down to posterity undecayed, and in full proportion.

I have had a pleasant interview with the editor of the Daily News, the paper which Charles Dickens started — (Dickens is now absent, on the continent.) [2] It will be in his power, and from what fell from his lips it will be his wish, to inform the public mind, from time to time, through his columns, of the workings of slavery in America, and the successes of the anti-slavery movement. Richard D. Webb has kindly promised to cull from the Standard and Liberator, such items as may do good service here, and forward them occasionally for publication in the News, as far as the editor may find room and inclination for their insertion.

I have also a letter of introduction to John Saunders, Esq., connected with the People's Journal, but he is now absent from the city.[3] William Howitt, the poet, the author, the friend of universal liberty, is also connected with that journal. I became acquainted with him, and Mary Howitt, his gifted wife, during my visit to London in 1840, and was then much interested in them.[4] On Sunday, the 9th, in company with R. D. Webb and Fredcrick Douglass, (after hearing a discourse from the celebrated Unitarian preacher, W. J. Fox,) I spent the day with them much to my delight and edification.[5] William Howitt is uncommonly 'good looking,' for an author — has a fine intellectual and moral development of the brain — thinks quickly, writes vigorously, and converses with great fluency. I should take him to be a man of keen sensibility, and thus capable of enjoying or suffering far beyond the mass of men. But suffering is an affliction, of which there is no trace on his bright and animated countenance. You may rely upon his remembering us in our struggle, and giving us a seasonable word of encouragement. His wife is not less hearty in her good will, or less radical in her views. She shows herself to be a superior woman, in the simplicity of her manners and the naturalness of her deportment. Her literary reputation creates no self-inflation of mind, and it seems to be her aim to write in a way that shall equally instruct and amuse, and especially to promote the welfare of our race.

I have not yet seen Mr. Miall, the editor of the Nonconformist, who wields a vigorous pen, and exercises considerable influence over the dissenting party whom he represents.[6] I shall try to do so, however, before I leave London.

This morning, I took breakfast with our friend Dr. John Bowring, M. P., accompanied by George Thompson and Frederick Douglass. He is very entertaining and affluent in the social circle, and deeply imbued with the spirit of humanity. He has long been interested in our cause, and is still disposed to render us all the service in his power.

Among those whom I was desirous to see on coming to England, (having known something of their labors in behalf of the working classes, and for the promotion of peace and temperance,) were Henry Vincent and William Lovett.[7] My acquaintance with them has even heightened my esteem and added to my list of cherished friends. Vincent is a young man, ardent, untiring, and remarkably gifted as a public speaker; and has met with great success in his philanthropic labors throughout the united kingdom. It is his purpose, at some future day, to make us a visit, and help the cause of humanity along during his sojourn. You may be sure that he will be true as steel to us, and not add another to the catalogue of recreants from England, (mostly of the clerical order,) who have bowed the knee to the Baal of slavery [8] on landing on our shores. We will give him a warm reception whenever he comes. He has the happiness to be united in wedlock with one of the most intelligent and reformatory women in England or America. I have rarely met with one, so comprehensive in her views, so vigorous in her understanding, or so remarkable in her conversational powers. I spent the day with them, last Sunday, at their residence at Stoke Newington. Their house adjoins the one in which that world-honored philanthropist, John Howard, used to reside.[9] Douglass, Wright, James Haughton and his two daughters, with other friends, were also present; and it was a day long to be remembered.

William Lovett is at the head of the moral suasion Chartists, as opposed to the violent course of Feargus O'Connor and his associates.[10] He has great perseverance and good sense, and is exerting a most salutary influence over the minds of the laboring classes of England. *Of course*, he is with us, 'heart and soul,' and will be a valuable auxiliary.

I have very many things to communicate, but I have allowed my visits so to occupy my time as to leave little opportunity for recording events as they transpire. I have requested dear Henry C. Wright and George Thompson to write by the next steamer, so as to supply my omissions, giving such particulars of our doings as they think will be cheering to the readers of the Liberator.

Unfortunately, the letter which will accompany this, dated the 3d instant, was detained by the erroneous impression that it could be mailed in London, in season for the Liverpool steamer of the 4th. I felt sadly about it, because the letter which I had written to my wife was also detained for the same reason.

The World's Temperance Convention, it is generally agreed, was as great a failure, in point of freedom and spirit, as the psuedo World's Anti-Slavery Convention in 1840. There were between two and three hundred delegates present — among those from the United States, Rev. Drs. Beecher, Patton and Marsh, and Rev. Mr. [Edward N.] Kirk.[11] You shall receive the particulars of it in another letter.

Ever faithfully yours,

Wm. Lloyd Garrison.

ALS: Merrill Collection of Garrison Papers, Wichita State University Library; also printed in *The Liberator*, September 11, 1846. Since the manuscript is incomplete, four paragraphs have been transcribed from the printed version (beginning with "of the workings of slavery" in the sixth paragraph and ending with "Vincent is" at the beginning of the second sentence of the tenth paragraph). Two brief emendations written above the lines of the manuscript in a hand other than Garrison's or Quincy's ("great" for "good" in the middle of the second paragraph and "in this" added near the beginning of the fifth paragraph) have been preserved in our text as they were in that printed in *The Liberator*.

1. Douglas William Jerrold (1803–1857), originally in the printing business, had become a successful playwright and man of letters. He contributed regularly to most of the leading magazines of his day, in particular, *Punch*, the distinguished illustrated weekly comic periodical, founded in 1841. At the time Garrison wrote this letter Jerrold had founded and was editing two weekly magazines: *Douglas Jerrold's Shilling Magazine* (January 1845–June 1848), to which Garrison probably refers; and *Jerrold's Weekly News* (July 1846–December 1849), known from 1846 until 1848 as *Douglas Jerrold's Weekly Newspaper*.

2. Garrison refers to John Forster (1812–1876), the English biographer and critic, who edited the *Daily News* for some months during 1846. A close friend of Dickens, Forster's *Life of Charles Dickens* (London, 1872–1874) is the work by which he is best remembered.

Charles Dickens (1812–1870) had founded the *Daily News* in 1846 and edited the paper during the first three months of its existence (January–March). The trip to Europe to which Garrison refers led him to Switzerland, where he wrote *Dombey and Son,* never returning to his editorial post. Dickens was an outspoken opponent of slavery and had expressed himself strongly on the subject during his visit to the United States in 1842.

3. John Saunders (1810–1895) was an English novelist and dramatist. In January 1846 he founded the *People's Journal,* which he edited for about two years. The paper continued publication under the original name until June 1849; in July of that year a new series was issued under the title *People's and Howitt's Journal,* which was published until June 1851.

4. Mary Howitt (1799–1888) was, like her husband, a Quaker and a poet. The Howitts collaborated on many works. Mrs. Howitt was also a noted translator, devoting herself to Scandinavian literature; between 1842 and 1863 she translated into English many of the stories of Hans Christian Andersen.

5. William Johnson Fox (1786–1864) was a Unitarian preacher, politician, and man of letters. He was an editor of the *Monthly Repository* and the intimate of many prominent men, including John Stuart Mill. A leading figure in the Anti-Corn-Law League, he served as a member of Parliament after 1847; his most notable achievement was to be the introduction of a compulsory education bill in 1850.

6. Edward Miall (1809–1881) was an English Congregational minister and journalist. Besides editing the *Nonconformist,* he helped to found the British Anti-State Church Association in 1844, and later served as a member of Parliament. Garrison admired his newspaper because it strongly advocated the antislavery cause.

7. William Lovett (1799–1877) was a champion of the working classes and the cause of universal brotherhood. In his autobiographical *Life and Struggles* (London, 1876) he mentions a delightful evening spent with Garrison, Frederick Douglass, and Henry C. Wright at the home of J. H. Parry. (*Life and Struggles,* New York, 1920, II, 328.)

8. An adaptation of Romans 11:4.

9. John Howard (1726–1790) was an English philanthropist and prison reformer. He reported his findings in 1777 in *The State of the Prisons in England and Wales, with Preliminary Observations, and an Account of some Foreign Prisons.* During the last years of his life he devoted himself to research on the means for prevention of plague and for guarding against the spread of contagious diseases.

10. Feargus Edward O'Connor (1794–1855), a zealous reformer, favored the use of physical force in the cause of radical doctrines. In 1837 he established at Leeds the newspaper *Northern Star* and became an intense advocate of the Chartist movement.

11. Lyman Beecher (1775–1863), father of Henry Ward Beecher and Harriet Beecher Stowe, was from 1832 to 1850 president and professor of theology at Lane Theological Seminary, Cincinnati, Ohio. Although Beecher was an abolitionist, he was a colonizationist and too conservative for Garrison.

William Patton (1798–1879), a Presbyterian minister and author, was one of the founders of Union Theological Seminary in 1836. He resigned his pastorate in 1852 and devoted the rest of his life to writing and missionary work.

John Marsh (1788–1868) was a Congregational clergyman and temperance reformer. In 1836 he became editor of the press established by the American Temperance Union and supervised the publication of the *Journal of the American Temperance Union* and the *Youth's Temperance Advocate.*

150

TO ELIZABETH PEASE

London, Aug. 14, 1846.

Beloved Friend:

I did not believe it possible that I should allow so many days to elapse, after my arrival in London from Liverpool, before sending you at least a few hasty lines; but the bustle and excitement of this immense city, — this focal point of human existence, — have been over-powering to me — and with the many things I have had to do, and the persons I have had to see, time has passed away very rapidly. There are so many things that I wish to communicate to you, that I know not how or where to begin. The first thing is in regard to your health. I feel great solicitude on that account. The loss of your dear father [Joseph Pease] was a bereavement of no ordinary character to yourself, as well as a public loss to the cause of bleeding humanity. I am aware how near and dear you were to him — how near and dear he was to you; and therefore I do not wonder that his loss has inflicted a severe blow upon you, from which you have not yet recovered. But I hope, dear friend, that nothing of gloom is cherished by you, as though "some strange thing" had happened to you[1] — as though life were no longer a desirable thing. The mind has a wonderful sympathy with the body, and the body with the mind. As to the death of this mortal frame, the loss of relatives and friends, we should be prepared for them as events which may at any moment transpire. Among all the operations of nature, I know of nothing more beautiful and benef-icent than the enfranchisement of the spirit from its bodily tenement. Death is never an enemy, though he is represented in a hideous form, and we are taught to regard him with terror. God, our loving Creator, makes no enemies to do us harm. The transitions through which we are called to pass, are but steps in the march of an eternal progress. Nobody really dies — no one is really buried. Why should not that which is mortal change and perish? But the spirit is not made of dust, and hence it is not subject to the laws of mortality. We must either believe in God, or become atheists. If God is immortal, then, being made in his image, we too shall live for ever. If there be no God, still we repine in vain at the operations of nature or chance. Let us, then, bow to what is inevitable, in the spirit of resignation; and if we believe in immortality, show by our walk and conversation that we are of the number who exultingly ask — "Where is thy sting, O Death? Where is thy victory, O Grave?"[2] I forbear holding out to you induce-ments to bear your great loss in a serene, though chastened spirit; for I feel sure that you do so.

It is still doubtful, whether the state of your health will allow me to see you before my return to the United States. You shall run no risk on my account. Much as I long to see and converse with you, I will do neither at the peril of your health. But I will cherish the hope that you will steadily continue to improve, and that we shall have more than one interview before the ocean shall intervene between us — perhaps never again to be permitted to see each other on earth. I do not know that I should have been induced to have undertaken my present mission, if I had not been animated by the desire to see you once more in the flesh, and by the expectation of having your good counsel and active co-operation. Ignorant of your true situation, I had fondly hoped that we should be much together, — knowing as I did how deep was your interest in the early triumph of that good cause, to which I have dedicated my life, as well as in other reformatory enterprises. But, "not our will, but thine, O Lord, be done." [3]

My happiness in being with dear Henry C. Wright, once more, is a cup full to overflowing. A braver or better spirit — one more true to principle, or more self-denying in action, or more sublime in purpose — where is it to be found? Under the most trying circumstances, he has stood erect, where millions would have fallen. If he is "a plain, blunt man," [4] he is also a good one. If he lacks in worldly prudence, he is not deficient in heavenly wisdom. It is not for such a man to be widely honored in his day and generation, but posterity will shout his praises, loud and long. Heaven reward you for all that you have done for him! He speaks of your kindness frequently, and with deep emotions of gratitude. The pecuniary assistance he has received from you has been extremely generous, as well as indispensable to the furtherance of his mission of peace and good will to the people of this land. Without your aid, he must have returned home, long ere this, frustrated in all his great purposes. Under God, he is indebted to you for the preservation of his valuable life. This he feels and acknowledges — and for this, millions have cause to bless you.

Dear Elizabeth, having many letters to write home by the next steamer, I can add no more at present. Do not attempt to answer this, for I shall not look for a reply — not, at least, till you can write without injury to yourself. What we have already done in this city, shall be communicated hereafter. On Monday evening, we are to have a public meeting [5] at the Crown and Anchor, the proceedings of which will be fully reported, and a copy forwarded to you. The prospect is encouraging.

Farewell! Affectionately yours,

Wm. Lloyd Garrison.

ALS: Villard Papers, Harvard College Library.

1. I Peter 4:12.
2. Garrison slightly misquotes I Corinthians 15:55.
3. Garrison uses one of the many variants of "thy will be done" (Matthew 6:10).
4. Shakespeare, *Julius Caesar*, III, ii, 223.
5. Of the new British society, the Anti-Slavery League.

151

TO HELEN E. GARRISON

LONDON, Aug. 18, 1846.

DEAR HELEN:

This is a beautiful morning, and I lack nothing to complete my enjoyment but your own dear presence, and that of the children. O that I could embrace you all, and bestow upon you as many kisses as my affection would prompt! But here I am, — the wide ocean rolling between us, and my work but just begun. It was my hope to be able to leave for home in the steamer of Oct. 4th; but it seems, now, impracticable for me to get away before the 19th. Henry C. Wright is also so circumstanced, that he will not be able to leave till that time. This will make the delay of a fortnight, which will be very long to you, and also to me; but yet it is only a fortnight, and it is better that we should consent to this temporary separation, than that my mission should be left in an imperfect state. It bids fair to be serviceable to an extent surpassing my most sanguine expectations. We have formed an Anti-Slavery League for all England, and last evening held a public meeting, which was fully attended by a most intelligent, respectable and enthusiastic assembly.[1] I would have readily given several guineas, if you and the Boston friends could have been spectators. It was a real old organized anti-slavery meeting, such as was never before held in this metropolis. George Thompson was in the chair, and made a brief but earnest speech, in which he referred to me in a very kind and complimentary manner. Henry C. Wright made the opening speech, and it was "a scorcher," and received great applause. I followed him — and on rising, was received by the assembly with a tempest of applause, they rising from their seats, swinging their hearts, and cheering loudly. I made a long speech which elicited the strongest marks of approbation. Douglass was received in a similar manner, and made one of his very best efforts. I never saw an audience more delighted. Henry Vincent made the closing speech, which was eloquently uttered, and warmly cheered. James Haughton, at the commencement, presented a resolution, welcoming us all to England,

&c. &c. Rev. Mr. [Edward N.] Kirk, of Boston, was in the meeting, but he found the atmosphere too warm for him at last, and left the room. We began at half past 6, P. M., and did not adjourn till 12 o'clock, very few having left at that late hour. Every thing was encouraging in the highest degree.

Dearest, you have my heart. I shall think of you in the din of public excitement and the silence of privacy. My health is excellent, as I trust yours is. Love to all the dear friends without specification. Write by every steamer.

Yours ever,

W. L. G.

ALS: Garrison Papers, Boston Public Library; printed partly in *Life*, III, 160.

1. As the introduction "III British Mission: 1846" indicates, the Anti-Slavery League was formed to promote Garrisonian abolitionism in England, unlike the already existing British and Foreign Anti-Slavery Society, which worked with the new organization, the American and Foreign Anti-Slavery Society. (*Life*, III, 159–164.)

152

TO EDMUND QUINCY

LONDON, Aug. 18, 1846.

DEAR QUINCY:

The announcement of the formation of an "ANTI-SLAVERY LEAGUE" in this city, to act in co-operation with the American Anti-Slavery Society, will be glad tidings to you all. This deed was done at a meeting of choice friends of liberty, held at the Crown and Anchor tavern, (famous as the head quarters of agitation,) on Monday, the 10th inst. Last evening, we held a public meeting at the same place, in behalf of the League, and in furtherance of my mission. Tickets, 6d. each. The large hall was filled by a most intelligent and respectable assembly; and if you and the American friends could have witnessed the scene, I am sure you would have rejoiced abundantly in spirit. Our invaluable coadjutor, GEORGE THOMPSON, was called to the chair, with expressions of strong enthusiasm. He made a brief, but, of course, an eloquent speech, in which he stated the object of the meeting, and the purposes of the League; and concluded by commending Henry C. Wright, Frederick Douglass and myself, to the esteem and co-operation of the friends of freedom throughout the land. He sat down, warmly applauded.

A resolution was then offered by our sterling friend — "the truest of the true" -- JAMES HAUGHTON, of Dublin, welcoming us to the old world, and giving us the assurance of a cordial reception wherever we might travel, as the friends of the slave, and the representatives of the American Anti-Slavery Society. He accompanied it with a few pertinent remarks — for, like our efficient coadjutor, FRANCIS JACKSON, he is a man of deeds, rather than of words — when, on sitting down, up sprung the Rev. John Howard Hinton, and attempted to make an issue, hostile to the purposes of the meeting, by saying that he was not prepared to vote for the resolution, because he was in favor of the American and *Foreign* Anti-Slavery Society![1] He had no one to respond to him, and it was not deemed worth while to make any reply to him, to the disarrangement of the order of proceedings. On taking the vote, all hands were lifted in favor of it, except those of five individuals — one of whom was a Mr. Collier of New-York, (the once notorious Dr. Collier of Boston, it is said,)[2] who, in the course of the meeting, attempted to apologize for the American men-thieves, and to cast a slur upon the speakers. He was listened to as well as could be expected, under the circumstances; but when he alluded to our friend Douglass as *"that colored man,"* in the true spirit of American color-phobia, the whole audience burst out in such a thunder-tone of disgust and indignation, that he sunk upon his seat as if a thunderbolt had smitten him.

Henry C. Wright made the opening speech, and it *"told"* with immense effect upon the assembly. He exhibited the naked horrors of slavery, and in the language of Christian rebuke, bore a faithful testimony against all the abettors and apologists of that foul system. His speech was continually interrupted by electric bursts of applause.

I followed him in a speech of considerable length, and was received with a degree of enthusiasm which I found it incomparably more difficult to support, than all the opposition to be met with in America.

Frederick Douglass was even more rapturously received, and made one of his very best efforts.

Henry Vincent concluded the meeting with a short, but highly eloquent speech, and the meeting broke up at 12 o'clock!

For further particulars, I must refer you to the letters of H. C. Wright & George Thompson.[3]

Hastily, yours,

Wm. Lloyd Garrison.

ALS: Merrill Collection of Garrison Papers, Wichita State University Library; also printed in *The Liberator*, September 11, 1846.

1. John Howard Hinton (1791–1873) was an English Baptist minister, the author of the *History and Topography of the United States* (London, 1830–1832).
2. Not identified.

3. Perhaps Garrison refers to letters of Wright and Thompson in general. Several appropriate letters by Wright were printed in *The Liberator*, September 25. The Thompson letters to which Garrison refers were apparently not printed in the paper.

153

TO THOMAS CLARKSON

London, Aug. 19, 1846.

Venerable Friend:

It was my privilege to see you in 1833, though, alas! at that period, your sight was gone. I shall never forget your words to me — "I believe I have lost it in a good cause." No one in the wide world could entertain a doubt on that point. Happily, you have since measurably recovered from your blindness, to the joy of your friends, and much to your own comfort. In 1840, I endeavored to see you before you left London, but failed doing so, much to my regret, as I was unable afterward to visit you at Ipswich. I am once more, and for the third time, on English soil, in behalf of three millions of my enslaved fellow-men in the United States, and for the promotion of the cause of emancipation universally. I have completed forty years of my life; and it gives me great and unalloyed satisfaction to think that I have given a very considerable portion of that period, (more than sixteen years — a brief term indeed, in comparison with your own protracted labors,) to the cause of God, the promotion of impartial liberty, the rescue of down-trodden humanity. Be the remainder of my life long or short, I consecrate it to the same good work, with an unfaltering trust in an almighty arm, not being willing to accept deliverance from calumny, persecution and outrage, if it must be obtained through a compromise of principle, or by ceasing to remember those who are in bonds as being bound with them.[1] It gives me unspeakable consolation to know, that there are two classes, at least, in the United States, who are convinced of my fidelity to the heaven-originated cause, which I have so long publicly espoused — namely, the slaveholders and the slaves. The testimony of such witnesses cannot be strengthened by that of any other class.

It is impossible for you, beloved friend of God and man! — ay, for any one on this side of the Atlantic — fully to understand the workings of Slavery in America; how entirely it has subjugated both Church and State to its evil purposes; how absolute is its sway through the length and breadth of the land; how it controls every interest, and directs every movement, in any way affecting its own existence; to what perils it has exposed those who have dared to confront it; what sacrifices it has imposed on the faithful and unshrinking band of abolitionists, who have been willing to count nothing dear to them, so that they might deliver those who are oppressed, out of the hands of the spoiler.[2] I am happy to add, that, in spite of the mountainous obstacles which have been thrown into the pathway of emancipation, our cause has advanced far beyond our most sanguine expectations, and is hourly increasing in strength and numbers. We want to secure for it the blessing and co-operation of the friends of freedom in every land, especially in England.

In order that you may be minutely apprised of the present position of the anti-slavery cause in the United States, and that I may see you, if allowable, once more in the flesh, it is my intention to leave in the morning train of cars for Ipswich, to-morrow, (Thursday,) to seek a brief interview with you, accompanied by my esteemed friend, Mr. George Thompson, whose name and labors are familiar to you, and Mr. Frederick Douglass, the gifted and eloquent fugitive slave from America, who has lectured with so much acceptance, in various parts of the united kingdom, during the past year. We trust the state of your health will be such as to permit you to see us, at least for a few moments; but, great as would be our disappointment not to have an interview with you, we would not subject you to any discomfort or inconvenience, in order to secure it. We are perfectly aware how essential it is, at your advanced age, that you should see as few visiters as possible, and that your mind should be kept from any undue excitement. Whatever may be your decision, we shall most cheerfully acquiesce in it.[3] We intend returning to London in the evening train.

Assuring you that no name is more highly venerated by the truly good and philanthropic in America, than your own — and trusting that a gracious Providence will permit you to see the entire overthrow of American slavery, before you are called to your heavenly home — I remain, with profound esteem,

> Your humble coadjutor,
>
> Wm. Lloyd Garrison.

Thomas Clarkson.

ALS: Thomas Clarkson Collection, Henry E. Huntington Library.

1. Hebrews 13:3. Garrison often uses this quotation or a slight variant of it.
2. Garrison inverts the meaning of II Kings 17:20.
3. This visit of August 20 was the last meeting Garrison had with Clarkson. For more details about the visit see his letter to Thomas Clarkson, August 26, 1846.

154

TO JOHN B. ESTLIN

London, Aug. 19, 1846.

Esteemed Friend:

Your very kind note was duly put into my hands; and it is with great pleasure I inform you, that, *Deo volente,* I intend leaving London for Bristol on Monday next, (24th inst.) in company with my eloquent coadjutors, George Thompson and Frederick Douglass. We propose being with you till Wednesday, when we shall leave for Exeter, to remain there till Friday — which day we shall endeavor to pass at Bath, and so return to London on Saturday. This will be far too hurried a visit to suit *me,* but I am afraid to promise any thing more. During our brief sojourn in Bristol, we shall submit ourselves entirely to your disposal. Should it be deemed best, by you and other friends, for us to hold a public meeting, you are authorised to announce one for Tuesday evening.

I wish you could have been with us, at our public meeting on Monday evening last, at the Crown and Anchor; because I am sure it would have given you great pleasure to see how cordially the several speakers were received, and with what bursts of enthusiasm the sentiments uttered by them were endorsed. Never have I seen a more animated assembly. It was highly intelligent, and quite numerous. George Thompson was called to the chair, who made some eloquent introductory remarks. He was followed by James Haughton of Dublin, H. C. Wright, W. L. G., F. Douglass, and Henry Vincent. The meeting began before 7 o'clock, and did not close till midnight — scarcely any having retired, even at that late hour. A pretty full report of the proceedings will appear in the London Universe of Friday.[1] I will endeavor to send you a copy. Nearly all the other city journals have noticed the meeting in respectful terms, and thus have given that publicity to our movement which is so essential to its success.

The Anti-Slavery League which has been formed, if energetically conducted, cannot fail to make a deep impression on the public mind, on both sides of the Atlantic. Whatever it may do toward overthrowing American slavery by righteous instrumentalities, (and it is to be taken for granted that none others will be used,) I feel assured will return in rich blessings on England, and essentially aid, in the most direct manner, the cause of freedom throughout the world. I am happy to know that you are disposed to give it your countenance.

Anticipating much pleasure in my contemplated visit, I remain,

Yours, with much esteem,

Wm. Lloyd Garrison.

N.B. After further consultation, we have concluded to remain in Bristol until Thursday or Friday. George Thompson thinks he can be with us only one day, just to attend the public meeting, should it be deemed best by you to have one. He will come, in that case, on Tuesday or Wednesday, as you shall decide. Please let us hear from you before we leave for Bristol on Monday.

Your kind offer of hospitality, I shall gratefully and gladly accept.

Should you see my worthy friend H. C. Howells, (perhaps you are not acquainted with him,) please tender him my thanks for his letter, and inform him of my intention in regard to Bristol.[2]

ALS: Garrison Papers, Boston Public Library.

John Bishop Estlin (1786–1855), a resident of Bristol, was a noted ophthalmic surgeon. He was an active advocate of the causes of temperance, abolition, instruction of the poor, religious tolerance, and the suppression of medical frauds.

1. The London *Universe* was published from January 1846 to August 1848. (Letter to the editor from C. Duncan Rice, Yale University, June 2, 1970.)

2. The reference is possibly to the H. C. Howells listed in the Bristol directories from 1812 to 1849 as a writing master and, subsequently, boarding school keeper at a number of different locations. His name does not appear in the directories after 1849. (Letter to the editor from Mary E. Williams, assistant archivist, Bristol Archives Office, June 24, 1971.)

155

TO RICHARD D. WEBB

London, Aug. 19, 1846.

My dear Webb:

That plodding, faithful, indefatigable, unparalleled pen-driver, — the fanatical, disorganizing, infidel Henry C. Wright, — is writing to you, at this moment, a sketch of our sayings and doings since you left us, (and your absence is felt by me like a heavy bereavement,) especially in regard to our meeting at the Crown and Anchor, on Monday evening last; so that it will be wholly unnecessary for me to go into the particulars. When I tell you, that it was a real, old-fashioned, old-organized, American anti-slavery meeting, (such, I am quite certain, as was never before held in *England*,) you will understand me to imply all that was bold, uncompromising, undissembling, hearty, enthusiastic. At an early stage of the proceedings, an attempt was made to distract and divide the assembly, by the Rev. John Howard Hinton, who, on the presentation of a resolution by James Haughton, welcoming us to England, &c., rose and declared that he could not vote for it, because he went with the American and *Foreign* Anti-Slavery Society![1] This annunciation elicited not a single note of approbation, and the resolution was adopted by acclamation. Under these circumstances, it was not deemed necessary, by any of us, to say one word in reply; though, if it had not been for interrupting the order of our proceedings, as previously marked out, I should have given such an exposure of that Society as would have caused the reverend intruder to deplore his folly for a long period. Dear H. C. W. made the opening speech, in his characteristic plain, faithful, direct manner, which excited an intense feeling, and elicited much applause. I followed him at considerable length, and was received with the most gratifying evidences of cordiality. Frederick [Douglass], on rising, drew forth a perfect storm of applause. His speech was exceedingly happy, both in regard to manner and matter. Both he and H. C. W. excoriated [Edward N.] Kirk, [William] Patton, [John] Marsh, et cet., for the deceitful course which they are pursuing in this country, in regard to the anti-slavery movement in the United States. Thus far, "the work goes bravely on." [2]

I received, by the last steamer from Boston, two long letters from dear wife, one from Wendell Phillips, and another from Edmund Quincy — together with copies of the Standard and Liberator. Also, a short letter from James N. Buffum. Nothing special has transpired since I left, but all eyes are turned to this country, to see what will be the results of my mission. My beloved Helen sighs over my absence, and longs for my speedy return — (I should blush if she did not!) — but she desires the mission to be first, and herself secondary, at this juncture. I have written to her, that I shall not be able to leave till the 19th of October, instead of the 4th, as I had resolved to do before leaving home. Happily, all are well at home, so that I have no special anxiety on that score.

Dear Richard, I am yearning to see you under your own roof, in the midst of your own beloved family. I will not attempt to tell you how much I love and admire you, or with what gratitude I regard your manifold kindnesses to me; because I know you shrink from all such declarations, and because I think they are quite superfluous at any time between those whose friendship is based upon principle, and whose hearts are one. Peace, joy, eternal bliss, be with you and yours! As for your cherished Hannah, you know what I think of her, in part. Ten thousand kind remembrances to her.

Faithfully yours,

Wm. Lloyd Garrison.

P.S. I trust my much esteemed friend Maria Waring arrived safely in Dublin. There are few, very few, on my list of friends, for whom I cherish a more sincere regard.

ALS: Garrison Papers, Boston Public Library.

1. Haughton's resolution welcoming Garrison, Frederick Douglass, and Henry C. Wright and pledging aid in the cause was printed in the London *Universe*, August 21, 1846, and reprinted in *The Liberator*, October 2, 1846.

2. Colley Cibber, *Richard III* (*Reviv'd with Alterations*), III, i, 156.

156

TO THOMAS CLARKSON

Bristol, Aug. 26, 1846.

Dear & venerated Friend:

By the kindness of George Thompson, to whose care it was addressed, I have just received your note, which brings me the afflicting intelligence that you have been quite ill since I had the unspeakable happiness to see you, & that you feel as if it might be the last epistolary effort of your life. My spirit is overwhelmed. I have earnestly desired, if not inconsistent with the will of Heaven, that you might be spared to see the day when the millions of wretched slaves, who are yet clanking their chains & smarting under the lash in the United States, would go forth from their dark prison house singing jubilee songs, and sending up praise & thanksgiving to God.[1] It appears however, that your labours on earth are nearly ended, and that you are, "Dressed for the flight, and ready to be gone,"[2] to another, & happier state of existence. From that sublime position, you shall ultimately see the fulfilment of your desires, and the consummation of your wonderful efforts, in abolition of slavery throughout the world. For is not the God whom we serve, true & faithful to his promises? Does he not frown on the oppressor? Is not his sympathy with the oppressed? Is it only a question of time when the arm of tyranny shall be broken, and the prey delivered out of the hand of the spoiler[?] Stimulated by your great and good example, I hereby solemnly renew my pledge never to abandon the cause of the perishing slave, relying upon God to sustain me by his grace, (as he has hitherto done) in the darkest hour, & remembering the solemn admonition, that "he that endureth *to the end*, the same shall be saved."[3]

Be the blessings of those who are ready to perish, upon your head! The cheering light of heaven fall upon you, as you pass through the dark ["]valley of the shadow of death!"[4] Extreme felicity be yours, in that Kingdom into which nothing that is false or oppressive can enter, and which is full of peace & holiness! Having never shrunk from the cross, may you now wear the crown![5]

My recent visit to Playford Hall will never be forgotten. It is one of the many thrilling incidents of my life, to which I shall frequently recur, with mingled emotions of joy and sadness. In the prostration of your physical powers, I deeply sympathized; but I was equally surprised and delighted to find how active was your mind, and how lively was the interest you continue to feel in the cause of universal emancipation. On bidding you farewell, I saw that you were very strongly affected; & most fully were your feelings reciprocated by me, and by those dear friends & coadjutors who accompanied me, George Thompson and Frederick Douglass. On such an occasion, words become powerless.

The very friendly & hospitable reception given to us by Mrs. Clarkson [6] will ever constitute a claim upon our gratitude. May she live to see the utter & universal overthrow of that terrible system, which you have so long & so untiringly laboured to destroy. I desire to be kindly remembered to her, and your estimable daughter in law.

Your wishes and instructions, in regard to the unfinished manuscript, shall be scrupulously followed.[7] It will be of great service to the Anti-Slavery Cause in the United States, where your name is venerated by all those, "of whom the world is not worthy." [8]

With commendable solicitude, you wish me, "not to mix up any extraneous matters with our sacred cause!" On this point I know that you and Mrs. Clarkson have been grossly deceived. I solemnly declare, that he who affirms that I have attempted to make any such mixture, is either ignorant, or a calumniator. It is not on this rock (as you intimate) that we have split in the United States. Be assured that this is a weak devise of the Enemy, to destroy our influence and cripple our movement as faithful, uncompromising abolitionists. The American Anti-Slavery Society is not, as is wickedly alleged, an ["]Anti-church, anti-ministry, anti-sabbath, no-government society," but unswerving in its course, and single in its object — to wit, the abolition of Slavery.

Farewell! In another world all things shall be clearly revealed.

Lovingly yours,

W. L. Garrison.

Thomas Clarkson

Handwritten transcription: Thomas Clarkson Collection, Henry E. Huntington Library.

1. Garrison loosely adapts Isaiah 42:7 and 42:12.
2. Not identified.
3. Garrison quotes Matthew 10:22, adding the words "the same."
4. Psalms 23:4.
5. Garrison refers to William Penn, *No Cross, No Crown* (1669).
6. Identified in the notes to Garrison's letter to Unknown Recipient, November 3, 1846.
7. Garrison refers to Clarkson's "Hints for the American People in the Event of a Dissolution of the Union." At this time, since the paper was incomplete,

Clarkson reserved the right to revise it. On August 25 he wrote to Garrison to say that because of his ill health the paper must be considered concluded. Among other comments in the paper Clarkson had said, "I consider, then, the dissolution of the Union, by affording the opportunity of making such a change, among the greatest blessings; and, in all probability, nothing but a dissolution of the Union could produce such a glorious opportunity." (See *Life*, III, 168–169.)

8. Hebrews 11:38.

157

TO HENRY C. WRIGHT

Bristol, Aug. 26, 1846.

My Dear Henry:

We arrived in this place on Monday afternoon, at half past 5 o'clock, and found our attentive friend Mr. [John B.] Estlin at the station, with his phaeton,[1] ready to convey us to his elegant residence. In the evening, a choice circle of friends, men and women, assembled at his house to greet us, and we had a very pleasant time. Yesterday afternoon, we had a public meeting at the Victoria Rooms, (a splendid building,) which was attended by a most select assemblage, the Mayor of the city presiding on the occasion, who introduced us in a very handsome manner.[2] The hall was filled — a considerable part of the assembly being members of the Society of Friends, of the affluent class. Very marked attention was paid to our remarks, and all seemed to be highly gratified; but, to me, it was any thing but an animated time. So much formality and *selectness* takes all the warmth out of me; and I felt as dull and flat as though I had neither perception nor instinct. Frederick [Douglass] seemed to labor under embarrassment, but he did much better than myself. I thought he would greatly disturb the Mayor, and our cautious and considerate friend Mr. Estlin — the former, by his severe remarks upon slaveholders as "vagabonds" and "villains," (for you will recollect that Bristol is the head quarters of the West India planters in this kingdom, and it was bringing up old reminiscences not the most pleasant to them and their friends) — and the latter by his "indiscriminate" assault on the American church and clergy. How the mayor really felt at such plain talk, I cannot say; but he concluded the meeting with some commendatory remarks; — and, to my surprise, Mr. Estlin took exception at nothing that was said, but seemed to be very much pleased, and declared that he believed a very salutary impression had been made. The more I see of him, the more I am satisfied that he means to be a true friend of the cause, and that he is the main spoke in the anti-slavery wheel, in all this region.

Last evening, we had a large circle of persons, of various religious denominations, convened at friend Estlin's, and a most animating conversation followed, on a variety of topics, but chiefly on *non-resistance* — when I gave them all my heresies on that point. I wish you could have seen us, — yes, and been one of the group. I had half a dozen opponents, ministers, lawyers, merchants, &c.; but they were so effectually answered, that they knew not which way to turn. The discussion, however, was very amicably conducted. Some would say, that it was very poor policy to be talking about such subjects, if I wished to secure aid to the anti-slavery cause, and to make my mission a successful one. Thank God! it is not policy, but principle, by which I mean to be governed in my intercourse with my fellowmen; and while I desire at all times to be governed by a sound judgment, and not to be guilty of rashness, I will not desist from declaring "the whole counsel of God," as opportunity may offer, whether men will hear or forbear.[3] As Wendell Phillips on[c]e finely remarked — "God has not sent me into the world to abolish slavery, but to do my duty." It seems to me that our intercourse with our fellowmen will be to little benefit, if we confine ourselves to the consideration of topics about which we are already agreed, or which are of a trivial character. Phrenologically speaking, my caution is large, and my combativeness not very active; and as I pay no regard whatever to the question of numbers, but every thing to the question of right, I am not very forward in the work of proselytism.

I have received a very kind note from Francis Bishop of Exeter, in which he says, in relation to the coming of Douglass and myself to that place — "I have spoken to several friends on the subject, and they all agree that a public meeting is most desirable.[4] We have accordingly decided on having such a meeting on Friday evening, in the largest and best public room in Exeter. The people only want to know the facts of American slavery, to be heart and soul with you. I trust we shall form an auxiliary to the League in Exeter." We are to meet with a select number of friends at Bishop's residence, to-morrow (Thursday) evening. Thus, you see, our way is fully prepared before us.

Mr. Estlin thinks there ought to be an auxiliary to the League in Bristol. This will probably be agreed upon at the close of our meeting this evening. Thus far, every thing here looks auspiciously.

Frederick is stopping with a very wealthy and estimable member of the Society of Friends, who a few weeks since was gulled out of £50 by the Broad-street Committee.[5] What will Sturge and Scoble say to his giving us the right hand of fellowship?[6]

Your note has just been received, for which many thanks. I am thankful James Haughton has given the *argumentum ad hominem* to Dr. [John] Marsh.[7]

What tidings in regard to the Evangelical Alliance? Did you see Nelson after I left? [8]

George Thompson writes that he thinks it extremely doubtful whether he can be with us this evening. This is depressing to us.

With assurances of my high regards to William Smeal, John Murray, and the dear friends at Glasgow; I remain, hastily,

Yours, ever,

W. L. Garrison.

ALS: Garrison Papers, Boston Public Library; partly printed in *Life*, III, 169–171.

1. A light, open, four-wheeled carriage.

2. The Victoria Rooms had been built in 1842 next to the Queen's Hotel and the Fine Arts Academy at a cost of some £20,000; the main hall held 2,000 persons standing and 1,300 seated. (W. F. Mack, *New Illustrated Guide to Bristol and Clifton*, Bristol, 1856.)

John Kerle Haberfield (1785–1857), a solicitor by profession, served in various city offices and six times as mayor; he was to be knighted in 1851. (Letter to the editor from Elizabeth Ralph, city archivist, Bristol Archives Office, December 29, 1970.)

3. An adaptation of Acts 20:27 and Ezekiel 3:11.

4. Francis Bishop (1813–1869), a Unitarian minister in Exeter, had tried during the year before Garrison's visit to organize a Garrisonian society. In London in 1854 he was to reduce the General Anti-Slavery Conference to chaos by supporting Parker Pillsbury's demands for an endorsement of Garrison. After 1856 he worked in Liverpool as a Unitarian slum missionary. (Letter to the editor from the Reverend F. Kenworthy, Unitarian College, Manchester, England, December 23, 1970.)

5. Douglass' Quaker friend has not been identified. The Broad Street Committee is the executive committee of the British and Foreign Anti-Slavery Society, so called from its address at 27 New Broad Street. Garrison seems to imply that Douglass is at odds with the British and Foreign Anti-Slavery Society, which was associated with the anti-Garrisonian "new organization." In fact, Douglass had at this time extensive contacts with members of that society, especially with John Scoble.

6. John Scoble (c. 1810–c. 1868), an independent clergyman who was active in the British and Foreign Anti-Slavery Society, was after 1840 the chief British rival to George Thompson. In 1853 he was to emigrate to Canada, where he worked in the British-American Institute of Science and played a minor role in politics as a supporter of the Toronto Clear Grit movement. (Letter to the editor from C. Duncan Rice, Yale University, May 13, 1968.)

7. Since the letter from Wright to which Garrison refers has apparently not been preserved, the precise meaning of Garrison's allusion remains obscure. It is known, however, that Haughton was criticizing Marsh for concentrating on the temperance cause rather than linking it to the all-inclusive antislavery movement. In his letter to John Marsh of August 25, 1846, Haughton says: "You denounce those who make, sell, or consume them (spirits), in justly indignant terms, as men who are 'verily guilty against their brother.' Is not the Anti-Slavery question a kindred question? . . . Why not tell the slaveholder, and his no less guilty apologist, as you did last night, in burning language, in Exeter Hall, tell the dealers in strong drinks, that they are unworthy to receive the hand of Christian fellowship?" (*National Anti-Slavery Standard*, October 1, 1846.)

8. Isaac Nelson (1812–1888) was a leading figure in the Presbyterian church

in Ireland and probably the only nationally known abolitionist in Ulster. Although he was the persistent opponent of the Evangelical Alliance, he was also an active member of the British and Foreign Anti-Slavery Society and was not at this time sympathetic to Garrison. (Letter to the editor from C. Duncan Rice, Yale University, April 16, 1969.)

158

TO HENRY C. WRIGHT

Bristol, Aug. 27, 1846.

Dear Henry:

We held our public meeting, last evening, in the large hall, formerly occupied by the [Anti-Slavery] League; and though the tickets were put at 6d. and 3d., the hall was filled in every part, and many had to stand up in the aisles. We were much disappointed (i.e. Frederick and myself) that George Thompson was not able to be with us, though his absence was not complained of by any of the Bristol friends. As it happened, there was no room for an additional speaker, unless Frederick and I had made shorter speeches; for our meeting did not close till half past 10 o'clock. George Thomas, a wealthy and influential Friend, presided, and made some very excellent introductory remarks.[1] Frederick made one of his very best speeches, which produced a powerful effect. We were both warmly responded to by the audience. It was agreed that another public meeting should be held at the same place, next Wednesday evening — Frederick to give the lecture. Every thing in this quarter looks highly encouraging.

Yours, in haste,

W. L. G.

ALS: Garrison Papers, Boston Public Library.

1. George Thomas (1791–1869) was a distinguished philanthropist and reformer who lived in Bristol, where he was one of the founders of the Bristol General Hospital and chairman of the city's charity trustees. (*Annual Monitor*, 1871, p. 125.)

159

TO EDMUND QUINCY

London, Aug. 29, 1846.

My Dear Quincy:

I need not tell you any thing in regard to the writer of the following generous and encouraging letter.[1] He is, you know, a distinguished solicitor of this great city, with whom it was my good fortune and delightful privilege to become acquainted during my visit to this country in 1840. His place of residence is at Muswell Hill, a few miles out of London; and a more charming spot it is difficult to find on the wide surface of the earth. Since he wrote this letter, he-has returned home, and I have had the happiness to pass a day with him, in company with George Thompson, Frederick Douglass, and other friends — the celebrated Unitarian preacher, W. J. Fox, being of the party. Mr. Ashurst is a man of true republican simplicity of manners, — a gentleman in the highest sense of the term, — an admirer of republican principles, but not of the sham democracy of America, — of great sagacity and extensive information,   deeply interested in all the reforms of the age, — the special friend of the laboring classes, — and one of the earliest and most efficient advocates of the penny post system, the benefits of which to England cannot be easily exaggerated.[2] Although his letter to me was not written for publication, yet I venture to send it to you for that purpose, because I am sure it will be read with delight and profit by all who take any interest in the cause of Universal Reform.

Yours, faithfully,

WM. LLOYD GARRISON.

Printed: *The Liberator*, September 25, 1846.

1. Garrison refers to William Henry Ashurst, whose letter was published in *The Liberator*, September 25, 1846, immediately following Garrison's to Quincy. Ashurst encourages Garrison in his work, applauds the efforts of George Thompson, and discusses, among other subjects, British India.

2. Around 1837 Sir Rowland Hill proposed that postage on all letters received and delivered anywhere in Britain should be at the uniform rate of one penny per half-ounce. He further proposed the sale of stamped covers, which would enable postage to be collected in advance. Despite opposition by the post office, public pressure led to adoption of a bill establishing uniform penny postage on August 17, 1839; by January 10, 1840, the new rate was in effect throughout the United Kingdom.

160

TO FRANCIS JACKSON

London, Sept. 2, 1846.

My Dear Friend Jackson:

I meant to have written you a long letter, ere this, on matters & things here, but time is so rapid in his movements, and I am so busy, that I have not been able to do so. I have only a moment to say, that

I am well, and that the mission is prospering gloriously. I hope all is well with you. My best love to all your household.

I must throw myself on your kindness to see that my quarterly bills are met on the 1st of October, holding me responsible for what may be advanced. I would not trouble you, were I on the other side of the "big pond." My dear friend Wendell Phillips, I am sure, will be glad to co-operate with you. I can add no more, now, except that I am,

Affectionately yours,

Wm. Lloyd Garrison.

Francis Jackson.

ALS: Garrison Papers, Boston Public Library.

161

TO HELEN E. GARRISON

London, Sept. 3, 1846.

My doubly dear Helen:

Procrastinating as usual, here I am at the desk of dear George Thompson, at the last moment before the closing of the mail for Boston, with pen in hand to send you a few words of greeting, a thousand kisses for the dear children, and unfeigned assurances of my health, which never fails to be excellent in this climate. My cheeks are quite ruddy, and I have little doubt that, on my return home, you will find me in a much better bodily condition than when I left you. That word *home* excites a yearning sensation within me; but I must not think too much about it, or I shall be quite unfitted to discharge the duties of my mission. Happily, the 19th of October is fast approaching, when (Deo volente) I shall embark in the Liverpool steamer direct for No. 13, Pine-street; for though my visit here is delightful in a high degree, nothing can supply your place, or make good the absence of the children.

You see I am still in London. But you must not infer that I have been stationary here since my arrival in this city. I have been to Bristol, and held two public meetings, — one of them composed of the selectest sort, the mayor presiding — the other of a more popular cast, largely attended, and enthusiastically supported. Douglass was with me, and, of course, wherever he goes, the lion of the occasion. We had a number of private parties, and no pains were spared to make our visit an agreeable one. From Bristol, we went to Exeter, where we met with a cheering reception, and had a large and glorious meeting. I left Frederick there, to give another lecture, and am to go down to Birmingham to-morrow, with Geo. Thompson, to hold a public meeting in the evening, where Douglass has promised to meet us. I shall then return to London, and spend two or three days in correspondence, and then go to Sheffield and Leeds, to hold public meetings, and perhaps continue on to Darlington, should Elizabeth Pease have returned from her sojourn in the country. Her health is still precarious, but somewhat improving. Thence I shall return to London, to attend a great and final anti-slavery meeting in Exeter Hall,[1] with special reference to the Evangelical Alliance, and its troubled and indefinite action on the subject of slavery. It will make a deep sensation here, beyond all doubt. Thompson has promised to make one of his strongest efforts, and Douglass will do his part on the occasion. Henry C. Wright will not be able to be with us, as he is now in Dublin, superintending the publication of his little work on Non-Resistance.[2]

In addition to addressing a large meeting at the Crown and Anchor, I have spoken at a public meeting, gotten up by Thompson in regard to the atrocious case of the afflicted Rajah of Sattara, (of which comparatively little is known in America, excepting by Phillips, Quincy, and Mrs. [Maria W.] Chapman.)[3] I was cheered to the echo, not so much in consequence of what I said, though that was warmly responded to, but because Thompson told them a few particulars of my labors in the anti-slavery cause in America. Last evening, I addressed a large meeting of the moral suasion Chartists, for the space of two hours, in the National Hall, George Thompson in the chair, and, of course, warmly commending me to the affection and co-operation of the workingmen of England.[4] I wish you could have been present, to see the enthusiasm that was excited. When I rose to address them, the applause was long protracted and overpowering. Peal after peal, like a thunder-storm, made the building quake; and at the conclusion of my remarks, they gave me nine hearty cheers, and adopted by acclamation a highly flattering resolution. I did not appear before them in my official capacity, or as an abolitionist, technically speaking, but on my own responsibility, uttering such *heresies* in regard to Church and State as occurred to me, and fully identifying myself with all the unpopular reformatory movements in this country. This will probably alienate some "good society folks" from me, but no matter. I know that the cause of my enslaved countrymen cannot possibly be injured by my advocacy of the rights of all men, or by my opposition to all tyranny.

I have done a good deal in private, as well as in public, to advance the great object I have in view; and though with me day is turned into night, and night into day, I contrive to keep in good health, which fact will give you as much comfort as any that I could possibly send you.

I have spent a very delightful Sunday at my old friend, William H. Ashurst's, at Muswell Hill, as charming a spot as the earth presents, — *almost*. Thompson and Douglass were with me, and a large social gathering — among whom was the celebrated and eloquent Unitarian preacher, William J. Fox, who, after preaching his forenoon sermon, (it was Sunday,) came and spent the remainder of the day with us, engaging in sport after dinner in rolling balls on the green sward, and for healthful exercise. It was a day long to be remembered.

I have twice visited William and Mary Howitt, at their residence in Clapton. They are a remarkable couple, and widely known in the world of literature. I am to spend to-night with them. Mary is kindly preparing for the "People's Journal," an auto-biography of my life, which will, no doubt, aid me in no small degree in the prosecution of my mission.[5] It will be published in a few days, and you shall have a copy by the next conveyance.

I shall derive great assistance from the co-operation of William Lovett and Henry Vincent, the leaders of the moral suasion Chartists — the friends of temperance, peace, universal brotherhood. They are true men, who will stand by us to the last — men who have been cast into prisons in this country, and confined therein, (the former one year, the latter twenty months,) for pleading the cause of the starving operatives in this country, and contending for universal suffrage. Such men I honor and revere.

I hardly know what I should do without the assistance of George Thompson. A more generous, disinterested, faithful champion of the Right, cannot be found. He has every thing to do — a world of business upon his hands — and yet, he contrives to lend me a helping hand at any moment, and to any extent. The indebtedness of our cause to him is immense. Whenever he goes over to the United States, he shall have a reception that shall form a striking contrast to the treatment he experienced in 1835. Mrs. Thompson and the children are well, and all desire to be kindly remembered.

I was very much disappointed not to receive a line from any one, especially from you, by the last Liverpool steamer; but, remembering how I allowed a steamer to go off without sending a scrap of intelligence to you, or to any one else, I, of course, have no right to complain. But, dear Helen, do not imitate my bad example. Try to send me a few lines by every steamer, directing your le[tt]ers to the care of William Smeal, Glasgow.

I shall write, by this conveyance, to our friend Francis Jackson, to see that you are provided with the amount necessary to meet my quarterly bills on the 1st of October, so that you will have no anxiety on that score.

Say to all the friends, that I am getting along swimmingly; and I am now a thousand times satisfied, that I could not have arrived at a more auspicious period. Great results are to be the fruits of this well-timed mission.

Our Anti-Slavery League will soon enrol a multitude of noble men and women on its list of members; and *all* our anti-slavery coadjutors in the U. S. must become members of it also. The price of a ticket is only 25 cts.

As I have delayed too long, (how shamefully characteristic!) to write any thing specially for the Liberator by this opportunity, you may show this hasty scrawl to Mrs. Chapman, and let her make out of it such an editorial article as she shall think proper, in her own language.[6]

I am delighted with the manner in which the Liberator has been conducted.

W. L. G.

AL: Garrison Papers, Boston Public Library; the manuscript was edited by Edmund Quincy, the substitute editor, and partly published in *The Liberator*, September 25, 1846. The letter was also partly printed in *Life*, III, 172–173. We have here transcribed the letter from the manuscript, except for the closing paragraph and the signature, which appear only in the version printed in *The Liberator*.

1. On September 14.

2. Wright's *Defensive War Proved to be a Denial of Christianity and of the Government of God*, although published in London, was printed in Dublin by Webb and Chapman.

3. Pratap Singh, Rajah of Satara (died 1847), had retained Thompson to plead in London that he had been unjustly removed from authority in his state by the British. Garrison obviously reflects Thompson's point of view; in fact it is questionable whether the rajah had any just claims for redress. (See C. U. Aitchison, *A Collection of Treaties, Engagements, and Sanads Relating to India and Neighboring Countries,* Calcutta, 1931, VIII, 361–363.)

4. Extensive search in libraries in this country and England has failed to identify the National Hall to which Garrison refers. It has been suggested that either Garrison is mistaken in the name of the hall or that "the Chartists renamed a public hall for the occasion." (Letter to the editor from Donovan Dawe, principal keeper, Guildhall Library, London, October 18, 1972.)

5. Mary Howitt wrote a "Memoir of William Lloyd Garrison," which appeared in the *People's Journal*, September 12, 1846; it was autobiographical in the sense that Garrison supplied her with all the material. The memoir was also reprinted in the *Pennsylvania Freeman*, March 25, 1847, and partly in the *National Anti-Slavery Standard*, November 12, 1846.

6. No Chapman editorial based on material in this letter appears in *The Liberator*. Apparently Quincy's edited excerpt of Garrison's letter took its place.

162

TO RICHARD D. WEBB

Birmingham, Sept. 5, 1846.

My dear Webb:

I am now at the house of our friend Arthur Naish, and seize my pen to give you a few hasty lines, in compliance with the request contained in your note to him.[1]

George Thompson came down from London with me yesterday afternoon. Frederick Douglass arrived from Worcester at about the same time. Since I parted from him at Exeter, he has had an enthusiastic public meeting at that place, and another at Bristol, — in both of which places, we held meetings together; and in both, an anti-slavery league has been formed, auxiliary to the London League, under very cheering auspices. Our friend [Francis] Bishop, at Exeter, is an admirable co-worker, and spared no pains to make our visit an eminently successful one. I had an interview with John Dymond, the Quaker banker, (the brother of Jonathan Dymond,) and, finding that his mind had been tainted by the Broad-street Committee, gave him a full statement of the partial and injurious course pursued by that Committee, in relation to myself and the American Anti-Slavery Society.[2] I inferred that a favourable impression was left upon his mind, inasmuch as he seconded one of the resolutions that were adopted at the public meeting.

Our meeting here, last evening, was more fully attended than we had anticipated, and the sentiments that were uttered met with a very hearty response. Thompson went into the subject with his accustomed fidelity and eloquence. It was nearly 11 o'clock before we adjourned. We had no chairman; for the very good reason that no one was willing to occupy the chair, at such short notice. We got along, however, without any difficulty. I regret that I must return to London to-day, and Frederick must leave for Carlisle, as we ought to hold another public meeting here.

On Wednesday last, I addressed an enthusiastic meeting of the "moral suasion" Chartists, at the National Hall in London, Thompson in the chair. I did not appear in behalf of the American Anti-Slavery Society, or as an abolitionist in the technical sense, but on my own individual responsibility, and gave utterance to some of the "heresies" which I cherish, in regard to the cause of Reform universally. The text which I took was — the effect of American slavery on the progress of liberty throughout the world. I fully identified myself with the struggling reformers against Church and State, in this kingdom; and I was equally delighted and surprised to see how warmly my sentiments, however ultra, were responded to. At the conclusion, the large assembly gave me nine cheers, and three more for the American abolitionists. You will see a full report of the proceedings, in the London Inquirer, the editor of which has called upon me, and promised to do all that he can to promote the League, both in his private capacity, and as an editor.[3]

The Evangelical Alliance has died, "making no sign"[4] on the question of slavery, though for a whole week it suffered and agonized over it.[5] Its proceedings will excite disgust and indignation in every true breast. It has been unanimously decided by the friends in London, that we must hold a great public meeting in Exeter Hall, for both sides of the Atlantic, with express reference to the doings of the Alliance; and I have no doubt we shall have an immense meeting. Thompson, Douglass and myself are to be the principal speakers. We all deeply regret that dear H. C. Wright cannot be with us. The meeting is to be held on Monday, Sept. 14, and we intend to make it as effective as possible.

As many thanks as there are words in the note you sent to me at London. I will act upon your suggestions, as far as practicable. At the present time, one public meeting in London will do more for this kingdom, and especially for America, than two or three elsewhere. I cannot now determine how soon I shall be in Scotland; but, be assured, I am anxious to visit it without a moment's unnecessary delay, and then to get to the Emerald Isle. Letters may be forwarded to me till the 13th inst. to the care of George Thompson, Waterloo Place, London.

I will not fail to see Joseph Barker. When I leave London "for good," (which I hope will be not later than the 14th or 15th inst.) I shall probably go to Leeds, Sheffield, Newcastle, (on my way to Darlington,) and so continue on rapidly to Edinburgh.

Your two pamphlets, respecting the Bazaar and the farewell proceedings in Boston, have been received, and will give essential aid to my mission. Blessings on you and your co-workers!

I suppose dear Wright is with you. To him, James Haughton and family, to your father and brothers, and especially to your estimable wife, give my affectionate remembrances.[6] All the Naish family desire to be kindly remembered to you and Henry.

This morning, Thompson, Douglass and myself are to take breakfast with Joseph Sturge, by special invitation. [He was not at our meeting last evening.] I shall try to do justice to our cause. The result of the interview you shall soon learn.

Farewell! — Ever yours, lovingly,

Wm. Lloyd Garrison.

R. D. Webb.

☞ Mary Howitt will soon have her sketch of my life completed.

ALS: Garrison Papers, Boston Public Library.

1. Arthur John Naish (1816–1889), of a conscientious Birmingham Quaker family, was himself a dedicated reformer, being especially interested in abolition, peace, and temperance. Naish's collection of Quaker books, pamphlets, and tracts became the basis of the Bevan-Naish Library, now the property of the Society of Friends.

2. John Dymond (c. 1791–1861), the son of John and Olive Dymond of Exeter, was active in the temperance, antislavery, and peace movements. He held the office of Guardian of the Poor in Exeter and was an elder in the Society of Friends. (*Annual Monitor*, 1863, p. 33.)

Jonathan Dymond (1796–1828), by profession a linen draper, was a moral and theological writer. In 1825 he founded a peace society in Exeter and served with it until his death. His most famous work, posthumously published in 1829, was *Essays on the Principles of Morality and on the Private and Political Rights and Obligations of Mankind*.

3. The London *Inquirer* (founded in 1842 and still being published today) was edited between 1842 and 1847 by William Hincks (1794–1871), minister of Stamford Street Chapel, London. He later emigrated to Toronto, where he taught natural history. (Letter to the editor from the Reverend Roger Thomas, Wolding-ham, Surrey, England, May 5, 1971.

4. An adaptation of Shakespeare, *2 Henry VI*, III, iii, 29.

5. The Evangelical Alliance was moribund rather than dead, for the convention in question had merely been adjourned. Garrison correctly predicted that the delegates' confusion over the slavery question would mean the demise of the kind of stable and unified ecumenical alliance the convention had planned.

6. Richard D. Webb's father was James Webb (1776–1854), a resident of Grange near Lurgan in northern Ireland. (Letter to the editor from Olive C. Goodbody, curator, Friends' Historical Library, Religious Society of Friends, Dublin, February 4, 1971.) Richard D. Webb's brother Thomas (1806–1884) of Dublin was active in many reform organizations, including the Dublin Temperance Society (founded in 1829), of which he was one of the first members. He also worked on a translation of the New Testament. (*Annual Monitor*, 1885, p. 196.) Webb's brother James Henry has been previously identified.

163

TO MARY HOWITT

5 Waterloo Place,
Sept. 7, 1846.

Esteemed Friend:

I send herewith a copy of the "People's Journal," with a few corrections in the Memoir, which can probably be made without any difficulty. Adopt such only as you think proper.

The personal interest that you have taken in my case lays me under heavy obligations to you, which I shall not easily be able to discharge. The effect of the Memoir will, I trust, be serviceable to the anti-slavery cause, by removing many absurd prejudices against myself, and securing in its behalf a more general interest on both sides of the Atlantic. Its publication will impress me with the importance of seeking an onward and upward course, till the close of life, — not to obtain fame or panegyric, but that I may be more and more true to those obligations and duties which God has imposed upon me, and in the faithful discharge of which, it will be impossible for me to have lived in vain. And not to have lived in vain is to have done something toward rebuilding this dilapitated world, lessening the misery and augmenting the happiness of mankind, and hastening that enrapturing period when

"The noise of war shall cease from sea to sea,
And married nations join in harmony." [1]

It gives me unspeakable pleasure to have secured the friendship and approbation of one, who is so widely and justly esteemed as yourself, whose labours are so unceasingly and powerfully directed to the intellectual, moral and physical improvement of the human race, and whose spirit is world-wide in its scope and catholicity. May you long live to scatter blessings far and wide, and to be hailed by millions as an angel-spirit, sent to cheer the good, reclaim the wandering, and make the earth a dwelling-place of love and peace.

I am also highly gratified in having secured the esteem and co-operation of your gifted husband [William], whose genius, talents and philanthropy are all consecrated to the noble task of overturning old abuses and hoary usurpations, and securing liberty and justice for those who are the victims of oppression, in all climes.

My pencil was promptly received, as forwarded through the post; but I was sorry thus to trouble you, through my forgetfulness.

I expect to leave London for Sheffield and Leeds, on Wednesday morning, to return again on Saturday.

Your much obliged friend,

Wm. Lloyd Garrison.

Mary Howitt.

ALS: Merrill Collection of Garrison Papers, Wichita State University Library.

1. William Cullen Bryant, "After a Tempest," stanza 5, lines 4–5. Garrison changes "dwell" to "join."

164

TO JOHN B. ESTLIN

London, Sept. 8, 1846.

My Esteemed Friend:

I am compelled to send you this very hasty note, this evening, instead of a long letter, as I fully contemplated this morning; but, what with various other letters I have had to write, and continual interruptions on the part of visiters, my time is so far consumed that I shall barely be able to finish this, in season for the mail.

All thanks to the ladies for their *resolutions*.[1] They shall be duly considered, and the result declared to them in an official epistle.

Your letters lay me under fresh obligations. I do not like to use many words, to express my indebtedness — for a poet has truly said, that

"The thankless oft are noisiest in their thanks" —[2]

but I wish you to be assured, that I fully appreciate your distinterested kindness; and I trust you will never have cause to regret the confidence you have reposed in me.

I will endeavour to see James Martineau, without fail — and also the other Unitarian friends, whose names you have forwarded to me.[3] The interview may be of some service to our good cause.

I have just finished a letter to Mrs. Armstrong, in reply to one from her, inquiring why aid cannot properly be given to the Philadelphia Liberty Party Bazaar, as well as to the Boston Bazaar.[4] My answer perhaps you will see, although it is necessarily brief, as I wrote it in haste. I hope none who desire to be friendly to the American Anti-Slavery Society will aid the Philadelphia Bazaar, which is hostile to the very existence of that Society, and would rejoice at its extinction this hour.

It gave me great satisfaction to hear of the successful meeting you held, after I returned to London; and though Frederick [Douglass] was unguarded in one of his expressions, in regard to the Unitarian communion table, I am certain it was far from his intention to make an invidious fling. — I wish you had had a better acquaintance with him, which the brevity of his visit prevented. He has very amiable qualities, and thus far at least has run well in the race of humanity. As to his means of support, he is chiefly dependant upon the sale of his Narrative;[5] but I believe he is at this time receiving a small stipend from the Edinburgh friends, though they do not defray his travelling expenses.

To-morrow morning, I shall go to Leeds, to see Joseph Barker, who has written to me a most urgent and cordial letter. I shall not attempt to hold a public meeting in that place, for lack of time; but on Friday evening, George Thompson, Frederick and myself will hold a meeting in Sheffield, in the Friends' meeting-house. On Saturday, we shall return to London, to prepare for our great Exeter Hall meeting, respecting the Evangelical Alliance, on the ensuing Monday. On the succeeding Wednesday, I expect to bid a final farewell to London, and go directly to Glasgow. I will try to apprise you of my course, from time to time.

I will see that a copy of the Liberator is duly forwarded to your address.

Your kind attentions to my esteemed and afflicted friend Abdy, I feel with as lively emotions as though they had been shown to myself.[6]

Your account of the interview with certain visiters in Bristol, from Boston, amuses me, — it is so characteristic of the great portion of the American people. And yet, such a state of mind is most lamentable — is it not? O, what an evil work slavery has done upon otherwise excellent people! How it blinds their vision, and blunts their moral sense!

I will readily take charge of the drawing which you cannot pack in your box for the Bazaar. Where will you send it — to London or to Liverpool? I would suggest the latter place, if it can be safely entrusted with any one until I leave for Boston.

Your Bazaar notices are timely and shall be judiciously distributed.

My National Hall speech will do no harm, but good, I trust.

Gratefully yours,

W. L. Garrison.

J. B. Estlin

☞ To your daughter, Miss Park, Mrs. Carpenter and family, Mr. James, &c. &c. please convey my warm regards.[7]

ALS: Garrison Papers, Boston Public Library.

1. The ladies to whom Garrison refers were probably the members of the Bristol and Clifton Auxiliary Ladies' Anti-Slavery Society. A search through the minute book of this group (at the Dr. Williams's Library in London), however, has failed to yield any reference to a group of resolutions passed around this time. It is possible that they were the work of a private group of ladies rather than the official action of an organization. The "official epistle" to which Garrison refers appears not to have survived. (Letter to the editor from Kenneth Twinn, Dr. Williams's Library, London, October 29, 1970.)

2. Not identified.

3. James Martineau (1805–1900), brother of Harriet, was an English philosopher and clergyman. Ordained in 1828, he was in 1840 appointed professor of mental and moral philosophy and political economy at Manchester New College, a position he held for forty-five years.

4. Garrison refers to the wife of George Armstrong (died 1857), prominent Unitarian minister in Bristol, who was one of the most enthusiastic Bristol workers

for the Boston Bazaar. She was a member of the Bristol and Clifton Auxiliary Ladies' Anti-Slavery Society. (Ralph Henderson, *A Memoir of the Late Rev. George Armstrong* . . . , London, 1859.)

The second annual antislavery fair sponsored by the Liberty party was held December 21–24, 1846, in the lecture room of Franklin Hall (Sixth Street below Arch).

5. Garrison refers to *The Narrative of the Life of Frederick Douglass, an American Slave* (Boston, 1845), a 125-page book with a preface by Garrison and an introductory letter by Wendell Phillips, which was one of the major documents in the antislavery movement.

6. Edward Strutt Abdy (1791–1846), educated at Jesus College, Cambridge, was best known for his writings on America, the most famous being *Journal of a Residence in the United States* (London, 1835).

7. Mary Estlin (born c. 1820), John B. Estlin's only daughter, was the most important British female Garrisonian except Elizabeth Pease and Jane and Eliza Wigham. Active in the Bristol and Clifton Ladies' Anti-Slavery Society, she was to lead it in 1851 to declare its independence from the British and Foreign Anti-Slavery Society and its devotion to Garrisonian principles. She corresponded with many abolitionists at home and abroad and visited the United States in 1868. (Letter to the editor from Elizabeth Ralph, city archivist, Bristol Archives Office, February 11, 1971.)

Although a thorough search has been made, little is known of Miss Park except that she was a friend of Mary Estlin, active in the Bristol and Clifton Ladies' Anti-Slavery Society, and probably a Unitarian.

Mrs. Carpenter is probably Mrs. Lant Carpenter (Anna Penn, died 1856), mother of Mary Carpenter (letter to John B. Estlin, July 16, 1847) and Philip Carpenter (letter to Samuel J. May, December 19, 1846).

William James (1808–1876) was a Unitarian minister who served a congregation at Lewin's Mead, Bristol, from 1842 until his death. He published a number of funeral discourses and other pamphlets. (Letter to the editor from F. Kenworthy, principal, Unitarian College, Manchester, England, December 10, 1970.)

165

TO HELEN E. GARRISON

Leavy Greave,
Sheffield, Sept. 10, 1846.

My Dear Helen:

I have just ascertained that the steamer Great Western [1] will sail from Liverpool on Saturday, for New-York; and though I have just arrived at this place from London, (via Leeds,) and have many friends to see, and a public meeting to attend, I must not fail to improve this opportunity, in advance of the steamer which sails for Boston on the 19th inst.

I am here at the house of some dear Quaker friends, Mary Brady and her sister, whose residence is a most delightful one, and whose interest in the anti-slavery cause in America is lively and hearty. [2] Sheffield, you know, is famous for its cutlery, and is nearly as populous as Boston. The scenery round it is beautiful and romantic in the extreme. I visited it in 1840, in company with poor [Nathaniel P.] Rogers and George Thompson, and passed a night at Winco Bank, at the picturesque residence of Mrs. Rawson, a lady who is still here, and on whom I mean to call before I leave the place, if practicable.[3] It was at her house that I met the celebrated poet, James Montgomery.[4] He was invited to meet me at Mary Brady's, last evening, in company with others, but had to decline doing so, on account of his ill health. He has promised to be at our public meeting this evening. Frederick Douglass is to be with me, and is expected from Shields this afternoon. George Thompson has promised to come down from London, and take part in our proceedings, if he can. We are to have the Friends' meeting-house — the first one that has yet been offered to us in this country, and I presume will be the last; for the opposition to us, in this country, runs almost exclusively in the channels of Quakerism, in consequence of the poisonous influence exerted by the Broad-street Committee in London, of which Joseph Sturge is a member. By the way — a few days since, George Thompson, Douglass and myself went to Birmingham, (the residence of Sturge,) and there held a large public meeting, and were invited by Joseph to take breakfast with him. We did so — and, in the presence of a considerable number of his relatives, for more than an hour, I had a very plain and faithful conversation with him, in regard to his treatment of me personally as an abolitionist, and to the unfair and dishonorable course of the London Committee toward the American Anti-Slavery Society. I have not time to give you the particulars of the interview; but it was one of confusion to himself, and it deepened my conviction that he is any thing but a candid, straight-forward man. My *facts* he did not attempt to invalidate, but he shuffled in a manner truly pitiable.

Your letter, by the Great Western, was as unexpected as it was precious. I was, indeed, greatly disappointed that I received none from you by the last Boston steamer, (none from any of the friends — I did not deserve any, and very properly got my deserts!) but I did not chide you even in spirit, — for I have no need of any thing, dearest, to satisfy me that you cherish a strong and deathless affection for me — an affection which I wish you ever to believe is fully reciprocated by me. You say, in your letter, that my disappointment will teach me to sympathize with you, in your grievous disappointment at not receiving a letter from me. How sadly I felt, at missing the steamer, I will not repeat — I have told you all about it, in the letters that were transmitted by the last steamer. You were not intentionally forgotten — no! no! that would be *impossible*. You are in my thoughts by day and by night; and, O that it were possible for you to be with me! The dear children, too — am I not sighing to embrace them, and to be with you all again at the earliest practicable period? Heaven graciously preserve you all, till we are permitted to see each other under our dear family roof!

It will be impossible for me to leave Liverpool till the 19th of October. You can, therefore, write to me by the steamer of the 1st of October, and I beseech you to do so. Letters and papers must be addressed to me, to the care of "William Rathbone, Esq., Liverpool." Inform my good friend [Robert F.] Wallcutt of this direction.

The tidings which you communicate of the death of my esteemed and my much attached friend [James] Prideaux really shock me. Though, in a previous letter, you gave me an account of his severe illness, I was not willing to believe that his recovery was ever a matter of uncertainty. How transitory is life! His noble wife, — alas! now widow, — has all the sympathies of my heart, and I desire you to proffer them to her as from one who will ever be her steadfast friend. To think of the dear babe, so early left without a father! But such is mortality, and we must not murmur at what is ordered from above.

Convey to those dear and attentive friends, Edmund Jackson and wife, my gratitude for all their kindnesses displayed to you and the children, during my absence.[5] Words are cheap, and therefore I will not multiply them, especially as I am sure that a profusion of thanks would be more painful than gratifying to them. The same thing is true of my dear and obliging friend Francis Jackson, and his peerless daughter, Mrs. [Eliza Jackson] Merriam. When I get home, I will say to them something of what I feel on this subject.

My grateful regards and acknowledgments to dear Wendell Phillips, R. F. Wallcutt, and the other friends, for their remembrance of you and yours.

Poor dear little sis! I am greatly distressed on account of her complaint. Don't fail to consult Dr. [Christian] Guise [Geist].

I trust you will have no trouble in discharging our quarterly bills on the 1st of Oct. Do not fail to put the note into friend Jackson's hand, that I enclosed for him in my last letter. Wendell will gladly co-operate with him to advance any money that you may require — and you need not hesitate to receive their assistance, as I will see it is all duly repaid.

I am in excellent health and spirits, and have not had a sick day since I landed at Liverpool.

H. C. Wright is now in Dublin. I shall leave, with Douglass, for Scotland, next week, almost immediately at the close of our great Exeter Hall meeting, which we are to hold on Monday next, in

London, for the purpose of thoroughly dissecting the Evangelical Alliance, for its tortuous and cowardly course on the subject of American slavery.

I have only to repeat, that my mission promises to be of great service to our cause, and that I am more and more satisfied that it could not have been undertaken at a more auspicious period. I am constantly busy, and every day making warm personal friends, and friends to our movement. Between now and the 19th of next month, I have a great deal of travelling to perform, many public meetings to hold, and many social circles to instruct. I will leave no stone unturned, and will put into operation all the machinery possible.

H. C. Wright will return with me. It is doubtful, whether Frederick will return till the next steamer afterward, as he is desirous of crossing in the Cambria, with Capt. Judkins — the same vessel which brought him over.[6] He is in sound health, and every where creates a deep sensation, and makes a powerful impression.

If you should happen to see my true-hearted friend, James N. Buffum, give him my heart's love, and my warmest thanks for his letter, to which I will reply by the next steamer. Tell him the place and spot from which I am writing, and that the Bradys desire to be cordially remembered to him. They speak of him with great affection, and trust he will one day again visit England, and be a guest under their roof.

Write me all the particulars about home, by the steamer of the 1st. Tell the boys to be kind, loving, and obedient, till my return, and I will bring them a variety of presents — some tools, &c. &c.

The friends in various quarters are busily working for our Faneuil Hall Bazaar, and the prospect is favorable to a larger quantity of useful and valuable articles being sent over, this season, than at any former period. Many inquiries are made after Mrs. [Maria W.] Chapman, whom I never fail to represent as "number one" in our great enterprise.

Remember your peculiar situation, dearest, and be careful not to expose yourself to any mishap. I am sorry little sis gives you so much trouble, and requires so much attention. Beware how you allow her to do you a serious injury.

I have much, every thing to say but no time, no space, is left. Dear wife! dear boys! dear girl! kisses and blessings without end for each and all. On the 5th of November, you may hope to embrace

Your loving and ever attached husband,

Wm. Lloyd Garrison.

Helen E. Garrison.

P.S. I have been to see Joseph Barker, at Leeds. He is one of the most remarkable men on this side of the Atlantic, having sprung up from a beggar boy to the position of a great, active and glorious-minded reformer. He has recently had a steam power press presented to him by his friends, and will work a revolution in cheap printing in England, to an extent unparalleled in the world. It is worth coming over here to commune with such a spirit, and to secure his co-operation with us. We think of starting a monthly periodical, to be the organ of the League we have formed, and to be called "The Anti-Slavery League," and we shall probably employ Joseph Barker to print it.[7] Joseph has lost many of his old friends for having embraced the Unitarian faith, (though he does not call himself by any sectarian name,) but he is not the man to confer with flesh and blood, in adopting and carrying out what he conceives to be the truth. Unitarianism is as odious in this country as "infidelity" is in ours — but, thus far, those who have most zealously espoused my mission have been the Unitarians.

If my dear Mrs. Chapman would write a letter to Mr. J. B. Estlin, 47 Park-street, Bristol, thanking him and his daughter in particular, and the Bristol friends in general, for their kind and generous reception of me, and their noble efforts to give us all the assistance in their power in behalf of the Bazaar, I am sure it would be extremely gratifying to them, and arrive at an opportune moment. Mr. Estlin is one of the most distinguished surgeons and oculists in England, and though exceedingly cautious and circumspect in all that he does, is a true and estimable man, who is doing more for us than almost any other person in England.

I will copy, verbatim, the letter of James Montgomery to Miss Brady:—

"The Mount, Sept. 9, 1846.

Dear Friend:

I thank you for the note of invitation to meet Mr. Garrison at Leavy Greave, on Thursday evening. The time with me is past, I fear, to take any active part in such labors as formerly were my duty and delight to attempt, however feebly. I have been much indisposed, during the last four weeks, from two attacks of the prevailing malady, and am too weak and low in spirit for *speaking* exertions; but I am a *good* hearer, and, unless otherwise prevented, shall be glad to attend Mr. G's lecture on American slavery. You will excuse my absence on Thursday evening.

I am, truly,

Your friend and servt.

J. Montgomery."

The original letter I shall bring with me as an autograph for the Fair.

I shall not be able to see Elizabeth Pease till two or three days before my departure for Boston. She is very slowly improving in health, and is under strict medical control — as well as watched and guarded, in a painful manner, by some of her relatives, who exceedingly dislike Henry C. Wright and myself, and who are hand-in-glove with the Broad-street Committee.

I have not yet seen Harriet Martineau, and hardly expect that pleasure, as she is now absent from her mountain residence at Ambleside; but I shall try not to miss an interview.[8] I understand that she is in good health.

Mary Howitt has completed her auto-biography of me for the People's Journal. You shall have a copy of it, by the Boston steamer.

Among the dear friends, to whom I desire special remembrances, you must not forget my faithful friend [James B.] Yerrinton. If it be possible, amid the multiplicity of my engagements, to send him a letter by next steamer, I will do so. I have very many letters to answer on this side of the Atlantic.

I wish a purse could be made up for Henry C. Wright, on his return, as a testimonial of regard for his disinterested, indefatigable and invaluable services here. He will return moneyless, I presume, and really ought to be remembered. If this were suggested to James N. Buffum, I have no doubt he would see the project "carried through by daylight" — for there are multitudes who would gladly contribute their mites for this object. Adieu.

☞ In writing to dear Sarah, George and Charlotte, do not fail to give my special and most brotherly regards. Love to Ellen.

ALS: Garrison Papers, Boston Public Library; extract printed in *Life*, III, 174.

1. A paddle steamer built in 1837, the speed and profits of which helped to establish the superiority of steam over sail for transatlantic passenger service. (Frank E. Dodman, *Ships of the Cunard Line*, London and New York, 1955, pp. 8, 126.)

2. Mary Brady (c. 1789–1851) and her sister Rebecca (c. 1795–1860) kept a ladies' boarding and day school for many years at Leavy Greave. Mary Brady was known as a strong-minded Quaker whose drastic methods of discipline were long remembered in Sheffield families. (Letter to the editor from John Bebbington, city librarian and information officer, Sheffield City Libraries, August 18, 1970.)

3. Mary A. Rawson (c. 1802–1887) was one of Garrison's faithful British supporters. Garrison visited her in 1840, 1846, and 1877. (*Life.*)

4. James Montgomery (1771–1854) was an English poet and journalist who edited the Sheffield *Iris* for more than thirty years. He held strong views on reform and was imprisoned for them in 1795 and 1796. He was especially eloquent in his denunciation of the slave trade.

5. Edmund Jackson (1795–1875), the brother of Francis Jackson, was a pros-

perous businessman and generous contributor to the cause of abolition. (Garrison's letter to *The Liberator*, September 7, 1832, n. 5, *Letters*, I, 165).

6. Commodore Charles Judkins was a famous master of the Cunard line. He had a reputation for seamanship which made him almost a legendary figure. When he made a thirty-day round trip between Boston and Liverpool in the winter of 1839–1840 he approached a record. It was also said of him that his manner was such a striking blend of geniality and sternness that he was both admired and feared by crew and passengers alike. (F. Lawrence Babcock, *Spanning the Atlantic*, New York, 1931.)

7. It seems certain that no copy of *The Anti-Slavery League* was ever issued.

8. Harriet Martineau (1802–1876), the sister of the English philosopher and divine, James Martineau, successively advocated in her writings Unitarianism, the abolition of slavery, mesmerism, and positivism. Her views were always controversial.

166

TO RICHARD D. WEBB

Leavy Greave,
Sheffield, Sept. 12, 1846.

My dear Webb:

On Thursday,[1] I left London for Leeds and Wortley, expressly to see Joseph Barker. It was a long distance to ride, but I would cheerfully have gone five times as far, rather than to have missed the opportunity of becoming personally acquainted with such a man. I found him in his quiet home, for he had written to me that he was at leisure, and longed to embrace me. Of course, we had much to say *to* each other, and something *of* each other; and each of us being ready and rapid in conversation, a great deal of information was mutually given and received. In the evening, a considerable number of choice spirits, of both sexes, came together at his house, and we had a highly interesting interview, which lasted till a late hour. The next morning, I took a survey of his premises, went into his printing-office, set some types just to see how natural it seemed, examined his steam power-press which he has recently had presented to him, &c. &c. It is, you know, his desire and aim to effect a revolution in this country, in regard to cheap literature; and I trust the friends of *the people*, especially of the labouring classes, who have few or no books of any kind, will assist him in every way in their power. I got Joseph to collect such books and tracts as had been written by him, and put them into a bundle; and when he had done so, I was really astonished at the multitude of his productions. It is almost a miracle of talent and perseverance for one to have performed, one who has had no advantages of education, and who at one time was literally a street beggar. He is really a great thinker — has a far reaching and comprehensive mind — is possessed of a gloriously free spirit — and writes with astonishing ease and copiousness, as well as remarkable good sense. I venerate such a man. All the popular great men of the day are pigmies, in contrast with him. He will be an anti-slavery auxiliary, of no small value. I almost felt sad in bidding him farewell.

We dined with Joseph Lupton, of Leeds, where we had a cordial reception, and had a few more friends to be added to my list.[2] On Thursday afternoon, at 4 o'clock, I took the cars for Sheffield, and in the evening arrived at the beautiful and quiet retreat, occupied by those noble women, Mary and Rebecca Brady, (who, *en passant*, desire me to solicit you to make them a visit, and to give you their kind remembrances — for they entertain a high opinion of you, as who does not?) I found a circle already assembled to welcome me, (chiefly young Friends,) and I need not add, our time went off both rapidly and pleasantly.

Yesterday forenoon, I went to various places with James Wall, a very worthy and respectable Friend, and dined at his pleasant residence, in company with a few individuals.[3] Our public meeting was to be in the evening, at the Friends' meeting-house; but the hour for holding it had nearly expired, without the appearance of Frederick Douglass, who was to have been with us from Carlisle and Shields (where he had been lecturing) at a much earlier period in the day. The name of George Thompson, too, had been put upon our placards, and he also "came up among the missing" — but he made no positive pledge that he would come. At last, Frederick made his appearance. I did not anticipate either a large or spirited meeting — for I was quite weary in body, and Frederick was still more so. Besides, I was told that Sheffield was a place that at no time had manifested an anti-slavery spirit, during the struggle for West India emancipation; — and, moreover, there happened to be, last evening, a concert given by Grisi, Lablache, &c., which put a formidable rival into the field against us, at least as affecting certain classes.[4] But, to the result. The Friends' spacious meeting-house was crowded to overflowing — the aisles deeply filled by persons standing from seven to nearly eleven o'clock — and hundreds unable [to] gain admittance. It was a most animating spectacl[e,] and a more delightful meeting I have not yet seen in England. Every thing went off very happily. Edward Smith [5] was in the chair, and spoke very kindly in regard to Frederick and myself. F. D. sold, on the spot, a considerable number of his Narrative. James Montgomery, the poet, was present, and was evidently most deeply affected. I made a direct appeal to him, in my speech, to write a poetical effusion, expressly with reference to American slavery —

and the audience applauded "to the echo." [6] He is, at present, in poor health; but I trust he will act upon the hint I gave him. This (Saturday) morning, we are to have a large party to breakfast, and in the afternoon, F. D. and myself will return to London. Love to your dear wife [Hannah], H. C. Wright, Thomas [Webb] and his wife — *et al.*

Faithfully yours,

Wm. Lloyd Garrison.

☞ Joseph Barker is with me this morning. — He came over to our meeting, last evening, from Leeds.

☞ A great meeting at Exeter Hall is to be on Monday evening next.

ALS: Garrison Papers, Boston Public Library.

1. "Thursday" corrected to "Wednesday" in another hand.

2. Joseph Lupton, a successful wholesale cloth merchant of Leeds, was an active Unitarian and a loyal Garrisonian, who worked closely with Mary Estlin and Sarah Pugh. In 1853, with Wilson Armistead, he was to form the radical Leeds Anti-Slavery Association, the only British organization to include both men and women on its executive committee. (Letter to the editor from C. Duncan Rice, Yale University, December 23, 1968.)

3. Garrison probably refers to the James Wall (c. 1800–1883) who is described in the *Annual Monitor* (1884, p. 119) as "of Kew, late of Sheffield"; he may be the same person designated as a farmer in the Sheffield city directory of 1852.

4. Garrison mentions two of the most distinguished Italian opera singers of the period, Giulia Grisi (1811–1869), soprano, and Luigi Lablache (1794–1858), bass. (E. Blom, *Grove's Dictionary of Music and Musicians*, 5th edition, London, 1954.)

5. Edward Smith (1800–1868), an iron manufacturer and leading member of the Society of Friends at Sheffield. (Letter to the editor from C. Duncan Rice, December 23, 1968.)

6. Shakespeare, *Macbeth*, V, iii, 53, adapted.

167

TO HELEN E. GARRISON

Muswell Hill,
near London, Sept. 17, 1846.

My Dear Wife:

I wrote you a few hurried lines from Sheffield, on Friday last, and sent them by the steamer Great Western, which sailed the next day for New-York, from Liverpool. I trust they will reach you in season for you to send me a reply by the Boston steamer of the 1st of Oct.; for I should be sadly disappointed not to hear from you again, before leaving for the United States.

The meeting held by [Frederick] Douglass and myself, on Friday evening, in Sheffield, in the Friends' meeting-house, (a spacious one,) was attended by a dense throng of persons, and presented a brilliant appearance. Hundreds were unable to gain admission. Edward Smith, a leading member of the Society of Friends, presided. Among others who were present, was James Montgomery, the celebrated poet. He seemed to be deeply affected — his countenance continually changing "from grave to gay, from lively to severe," [1] as the horrors of slavery were revealed, and the absurdities of its apologists exposed. In the course of my speech, I alluded to him by name, and invoked him to let his muse record her execration against the slave system and all its abettors. He is now quite advanced in years, and in poor health; but I hope he will do what I suggested.

I remained at Sheffield until Sunday morning, receiving visits and making others in return. The dear friends with whom I stopped, Mary and Rebecca Brady, did every thing in their power to aid me; and I shall ever remember their kind attentions with gratitude. They are admirable women — true reformers — whose acquaintance repays one for crossing the wide Atlantic.

On Saturday, I visited Mrs. [Mary] Rawson, at her Eden-like abode at Wincobank, and was most cordially received, though I could stop only a few hours. It was at the house of this estimable lady, that I first met Montgomery, in 1840, George Thompson and [Nathaniel P.] Rogers then being with me. Although six years had elapsed since my former visit, every thing looked so natural that it seemed to me as if not an hour had intervened. Those years have made a slight impression upon the countenance of Mrs. Rawson, but the natural scenery (which is around her dwelling) remains unchanged; and its beauty is truly ravishing. I am constantly sighing, dear Helen, that you are not here by my side, for more than a thousand reasons — and among others, that you cannot see the enchanting landscape views which crowd upon my sight in all directions, as I travel through this wonderful land. I desire, moreover, to have you with me, that you may become personally acquainted with some of the dearest persons in the world.

On Sunday, I returned to London, a long distance by rail-road, and very much fatigued by the ride. I do not feel able, for economy's sake, to ride in what are called the "first class" cars, which are exceedingly comfortable, though nothing remarkable, except for their high price. The second and third class are perfectly execrable, and look as if they were made for the transportation of convicts, [rather] than for the accommodation of the traveling public. They are like our "Jim Crow" cars, but a large portion of what are considered "respectable" people travel in them.[2] As to the beauty and comfort of our steam-boats and rail-way cars, we in America far transcend those in England; but, in many other things, we come short.

On Monday, Thompson and myself busied ourselves in some little preparation for the Exeter Hall meeting, which we were to hold that evening, with special reference to the course pursued by the Evangelical Alliance, on the subject of American slavery. Frederick joined us in the afternoon, having left Sheffield in the morning. Our meeting was a very triumphant one. The vast hall was densely crowded, and presented a brilliant spectacle. The interest and feeling manifested by the vast audience were of no ordinary character. Many of the friends, and some of the members of the Alliance were present, some of them in no very amicable state of mind toward us. None of the American delegation showed their heads. I spoke first, after some excellent prefatory remarks from the chairman, the Rev. John Burnett, a very able and independent man.[3] My speech was frequently interrupted by a certain portion of the audience, in a rowdyish manner, something after the pattern we occasionally exhibit in Boston and elsewhere. My remarks frequently stung to the quick, and the snakes hissed and twisted as though they felt that the hour of doom had come. Still, the applause overpowered all the opposition — but the interruption was very considerable, and made my speech less consecutive than it otherwise would have been. Knowing that Thompson and Douglass were to follow me, I had more to say about the sectarian character of the Alliance, than about its pro-slavery action; and this it was that called down upon my head the special "blessings" of the priests and their tools in the vast assembly. Thompson, though quite poorly all day, acquitted himself with more than ordinary ability, and made so powerful an impression that he swept away all symptoms of opposition; so that, when the resolutions were presented for adoption, only three or four hands were raised in opposition to them! Douglass followed in a very effective speech, and was warmly applauded. We regard the result of the meeting as a great triumph, and as giving a staggering blow to the Alliance at the very moment most opportune.

My manner of expressing my thoughts and feelings is somewhat novel, and not always palatable, in this country, on account of its plainness and directness; but it will do more good, in the end, than a smoother mode. At least, I think so, and will "bide my time." I am led to be more plain-spoken, because almost every one here deals in circumlocution, and to offend nobody seems to be the aim of the speaker. *If I chose*, I could be as smooth and politic as any one; but I do not so choose, and much prefer nature to art.

On Tuesday evening, I went with Mrs. Thompson, Douglass, and J. B. Daily [4] of Philadelphia, to the Vauxhall gardens, where I saw the most brilliant exhibition of lamps and fireworks, as well as extraordinary feats in horsemanship and manual dexterity. I shall have a variety of marvels to tell to the dear boys, on my return; for I have not time now to go into particulars. There is no end to sight-seeing in London, but I am too busy to go round much for that purpose.

Yesterday, till 4 o'clock, I busied myself about sundry matters, when I came out here to this delightful spot, (of which you have frequently heard me speak in terms of admiration,) accompanied by Thompson and his wife, and J. R. Daily.[5] Our friends, the [William H.] Ashursts, received us with open arms; and a cheering time of it we had till after midnight — Thompson being in his pleasantest humor, and I feeling in a very happy mood. I have risen early this morning, (though I did not retire to rest till morning,) to write you this hasty scrawl, as it is the only proof of my love that I can show you on this side of the Atlantic. The morning is beautiful indeed. All nature looks as if no curse had ever been inflicted upon it. It is not God, but man, who has brought woe into the world. For the past six weeks, the weather has been uncommonly fine — indeed, for England, quite extraordinary. At neither of my former visits has it ever been so warm and so settled. There has scarcely been a shower. When I was here in 1840, not a day elapsed for two months, that we had not at least a sprinkling of rain. My health continues very good, notwithstanding the great fatigue of visiting, holding public meetings, being at social circles, answering correspondence, through which I have to pass. I have done with very little sleep since I left home, and must continue to do without it until my return.

I was slightly disappointed that I got no letter from you by the last Boston steamer, though as you wrote but a few days previous by the Great Western, I will not complain. The only epistle I received was from Edmund Quincy, who gives me, in his humorous way, a good scolding for not writing more for the Liberator. I assure you, and him, and all the other friends, that I have had my hands full here, both day and night. The penny post system, in this country, induces almost every body to write, and every day there are many notes to be answered, which is no small task. If I have not sent much original matter for the Liberator, I certainly have not failed to send more printed matter, respecting my proceedings, than the Liberator will be able to publish for some time. It is not of much consequence as to my writing letters for the Liberator; but the manner in which I am doing up my work here is of no small importance; and, that I have not been idle a moment, but have been sorely pressed by a multiplicity of engagements, George Thompson will testify. The truth is, I ought to have come over at least two or three months earlier than I did, though I shall do a great deal for our cause, even in the limited time which my visit must occupy. But this is crowding things together too hastily for comfort.

My excellent and devoted friend Quincy is really putting his soul into the Liberator, and by his industry and ability is making it a very racy sheet. It will appear very dull after my return.

Quincy sends me a letter from Henry Clapp, which appeared in the Lynn Pioneer of the 27th ultimo, written from this city.[6] It exhibits folly and knavery, affected magnanimity and viperous malice, in about equal proportions. It was written from this city. He seems to be comforted with the belief, that nobody knows there is such a person as William Lloyd Garrison in England! "So far," he says, "in this country, I haven't met a dozen persons who knew Mr. Garrison by name." Well, a man's notoriety *is* limited, to be sure — much more than he is apt to imagine — but this declaration of Clapp only shows that the company which he has kept has been of a very equivocal character, to say the least, both as to intelligence and virtue. If I am so little known here, how ludicrous is the outcry that he and Rogers have made, about my blasting C's character in a foreign land!! But even Clapp must now confess that as many as *two* dozen persons have heard of me here; for, to say nothing of two former visits to England, of the vast multitudes who have heard my name, and cheered loudly, (through George Thompson's public labors,) and of the numerous meetings I have already held in various parts of the kingdom, it must be very galling to the spirit and painful to the eyes of Mr. Clapp to see my portrait in the People's Journal staring him in the face in every corner in London, and handbills daily distributed to the passing multitude, reading thus — "A Portrait, by H. Anelay,[7] and a Memoir, by Mary Howitt, of William Lloyd Garrison, is contained in No. 37 of the People's Journal." I saw placards posted about the streets in Leeds, when I was there a few days ago, making the same announcement, but in a more conspicuous manner. So much for not being known!

Clapp was at our Exeter Hall meeting on Monday evening last, and sat directly in front of the platform, looking in a sinister and troubled manner. What he is doing here, or with whom he is associating, I cannot find out. Once or twice, he has been accidentally encountered by some one of my friends, when he has taken the opportunity to whine about my unjust treatment of him, and to express the admiration which he still entertains for me! There is in him such a mixture of folly and knavery, that it gives rise to feelings equally ludicrous and disgusting. Of course, it will be his business, while he remains in this country, to do me all the injury in his power, as secretly as possible; but his mischief will react upon himself.

Henry C. Wright will probably return with me, though it is not certain, as many here are extremely anxious, in view of the peculiar state of our cause, to have him remain awhile longer; but, though I am sure his labors here would be of immense service, we need him so much on our side of the water, I shall not tolerate his remaining behind. Frederick Douglass will not return till next May, in season for our New-England Convention. This I have strongly advised, for many important reasons. If he and H. C. W. were both to return home now, in the present embryo state of the "Anti-Slavery League," we should lose a great deal of what otherwise will be permanently secured to us. He is really doing a great work, and the people are every where desiring his presence. The poor fellow is — naturally enough — sighing to see his wife and children, but he is satisfied that it will enhance his personal safety, and be the better for them in the end, to remain here until spring. In a pecuniary point of view, he is doing very well, as he sells his Narrative very readily, and receives aid in donations and presents, to some extent. He has done with the Joseph Sturge party entirely, and will be careful how he is caught again with chaff.[8]

I have not asked for any pecuniary assistance here, and have received nothing, even incidentally, to the amount of a farthing. The truth is, those who feel a special movement in our cause are generally far from being wealthy, and they are more or less taxed to carry on the various reformatory movements in England. It costs a good deal to get up public meetings, and report the proceedings, and buy copies of the papers containing those proceedings, for gratuitous distribution, at home and abroad. Our Exeter Hall meeting cost nearly two hundred and fifty dollars, merely for the building, advertisements, placards, &c.; to say nothing about the expense of reporting, as we were anxious to have a full report; and this you will find in the London Patriot of this week.[9] You and the dear friends in Boston will read that report with great satisfaction, I am sure. I wish you all could have heard George Thompson *deliver* his speech. We have bought three hundred copies of the Patriot for circulation in America and England.

I endeavor to husband my pecuniary means as carefully as possible — with more parsimony than as if the money were my own; but the living in this country, in connexion with so much travelling, is very expensive, and money melts away very easily. To the end, I mean to save to the cause every farthing in my power; even often to my discomfort. In London, I have been residing with dear Thompson; and though he lovingly delights to entertain me, yet I shall not feel as if it were right to tax his hospitality for so many weeks, without making some remuneration; for his family is a large and expensive one, and it costs him a large sum to meet his necessary expenses. Of course, he will not be willing to receive a *quid pro quo*, in form — but I shall make presents to all the children and to Mrs. Thompson, enough to satisfy my conscience, that I have not too seriously burdened this dearly beloved and generous friend.

I will now give the particulars of my future route until the 19th of Oct., when I hope to embark for home. To-morrow, I go direct to Glasgow, expecting to arrive on Saturday evening, where I shall remain until the 23d inst.; thence to Edinburgh, and remaining till the 28th; thence to Dundee; thence to Belfast, Oct. 1st; thence to Dublin, 3d; thence to Cork, 6th; thence to Liverpool, (via Dublin,) 8th; thence to Wrexham, Manchester and Rochester, (to hold public meetings in all these places,) 9th to 14th; thence to Darlington, to see Elizabeth Pease, until the 17th; thence to Liverpool, to leave on Monday, the 19th. There — talk of a man's writing letters for the public eye, or to particular friends, under such circumstances! It is too much for body and mind — but I must try to accomplish it all. George Thompson will not be able to go with me to Scotland, but his company is not important, as he has so recently been there.

I can write no more. Dearest one, I love you better than I do my life. Be careful of your health, and say a thousand things to the dear children in advance for me. I hope they will try to be good, that they may deserve the presents which I intend to bring to them. With special remembrances to Mrs. [James] Pride[a]ux, Ellen, and all the beloved friends as one,

Yours, most lovingly,

W. L. Garrison.

☞ I shall return in the same steamer in which I came over, the Britannia. I should have preferred another, but she is a good sea boat.

ALS: Garrison Papers, Boston Public Library; extract printed in *Life*, III, 166–167.

1. Alexander Pope, *An Essay on Man*, Epistle IV, line 380.

2. A "Jim Crow car" was a railroad car for the exclusive use of Negroes, and the phrase was first used in 1841 to refer to a railroad car in Massachusetts. ("Jim Crow" as a generic term for Negro is said to derive from the minstrel show song of that name introduced by Thomas D. Rice in 1828.) Although attempts to pass legislation against such segregation were defeated, only a few cases were reported in the North after 1842. Wendell Phillips spoke eloquently on the subject of segregation on railroad cars; see *The Liberator*, February 18, 1842. (A full discussion of the problem is to be found in C. Vann Woodward, *The Strange Career of Jim Crow*, 2d edition, New York, 1966.)

3. John Burnet (1789–1862), Congregational minister, was a leading English dissenter, who opposed the principle of state-supported churches. He had in 1840 represented the Congregational Union of England and Wales at the World's Anti-Slavery Convention. (Letter to the editor from C. Duncan Rice, Yale University, December 26, 1970.)

4. Not identified.

5. Presumably Garrison refers to the J. B. Daily mentioned in the preceding paragraph.

6. The Lynn *Pioneer*, at this time edited by Henry Clapp, was apparently published under several different names between 1842 and 1849, the last three years as the *Pioneer and Herald of Freedom*. (Letter to the editor from Diane Liesinger, curator, Lynn Historical Society, June 10, 1970.)

7. Henry Anelay (died 1883), a landscape and historical painter who exhibited at the Royal Academy and elsewhere. (Letter to the editor from Joan Gibbs, archivist, University of London Library, August 18, 1970.)

8. Presumably, Garrison refers to Douglass' association with the British and Foreign Anti-Slavery Society and its London Committee, of which Sturge was the most powerful member. There was concern among Garrisonians, unnecessarily as it turned out, that Douglass might be too much influenced by the British group. (Letter of Maria W. Chapman to Richard D. Webb, in Philip Foner, *The Life and Writings of Frederick Douglass*, New York, 1950, I, 65.)

0. The London *Patriot*, a biweekly paper founded in 1832 and edited by Josiah Conder (1789–1855), bookseller and popular poet, was strongly nonconformist and abolitionist. It had closer ties, however, with the British and Foreign Anti-Slavery Society than with the Garrisonians. In 1867 the *Patriot* became the *English Independent*. The story Garrison refers to was reprinted in *The Liberator*, October 16, 1846.

168

TO EDMUND QUINCY

LONDON, Sept. 18, 1846.

MY DEAR QUINCY:

In your last epistle, you exclaim, "Write! write! write!" I am quite sure of one thing — you need nothing from my pen to give interest to the columns of the Liberator during my absence. I see, and am delighted to see, that you are resolved to occupy the editorial chair to some purpose. "You are extremely fortunate," said my friend George Thompson, after perusing the last two numbers of the Liberator, "in the person you have selected to fill your place." He is not alone in this opinion. Now this I say, not to flatter you, but to prove what I have just affirmed, that you are not in special need of editorial assistance. Moreover, if you receive but few and hastily written letters from me, you must confess that I keep you bountifully supplied with printed matter, giving you the proceedings of the various important public meetings that we have held, in different parts of the Kingdom, for the furtherance of my mission; by which you will see, ay, and be convinced too, that I have not been idle, but occupied in the most profitable manner. Be assured, it is expecting too much of one, situated as I am, that he will be a constant and voluminous contributor to a newspaper, three thousand miles across the Atlantic; and at the same time, accomplish in eight or ten weeks here, what ought to be the deliberate and systematic work of several months. I suppose I shall never visit this country again; but, if an opportunity should ever present itself, I shall be slow to embrace it, unless I can have time allowed me to take some degree of rest, to have some respite from mental excitement, to prosecute my labors without the loss of that natural repose which is so essential to the health of the body and the vigor of the mind. Recollect that I did not touch British soil until the 1st of August, and that the time allotted for my visit was only a few weeks; and that, consequently, a multiplicity of duties, engagements and services have had to be met, at once overwhelming and unescapable. See what is before me, until the 19th of October, when I hope to embark in the steamer Britannia for Boston. This evening, I shall take a final leave of London, and, getting such rest in the cars as I can, ride all night on my way to Glasgow, via Newcastle and Berwick-upon-Tweed, arriving at the former place to-morrow night. On Monday or Tuesday evening, we shall probably hold a public meeting, with special reference to the Free Church; and during the three days I can remain in that city, every moment must be occupied in visiting, or receiving visits. Frederick Douglass will be with me. On the 23d, we shall proceed to Edinburgh, where we shall remain till the 28th, improving our time to the best possible advantage. From thence, we expect to go to Dundee; from Dundee back to Glasgow; from Glasgow to Belfast; from Belfast to Dublin; from Dublin to Cork; from Cork to Liverpool, via Dublin; from Liverpool to Wrexham; from Wrexham to Manchester; from Manchester to Rochdale; from Rochdale to Darlington; from Darlington to Liverpool. All this to be completed within four weeks! Now talk of writing, to a man who has as yet found no time to sleep! "It be vary easy to cry, *blow louder!*" said an indignant French trumpeter, who had expended his last breath, "but vere is de vind?" [1] So it is easy to cry, "Write! write! write!" — but, where is the time and place? Under the most favorable circumstances, I am a bad correspondent; under the worst, what can you expect?

Yet it is reasonable that you should desire something from my pen, and right that the readers of the Liberator should expect it. But, seeing in what haste I am compelled to write, you must pardon every thing on the score of brevity and style.

By the last steamer, you were apprised of the fact, that the Evangelical Alliance was in trouble on the slavery question, not knowing how to get rid of it, puzzled to know what to do with it. To reconcile anti-slavery and pro-slavery, and to satisfy the friends of emancipation and the defenders of tyranny by the same act, and at the same time, is a difficult matter, even for the most learned rabbies, the most sagacious doctors of divinity. Nevertheless, they tried hard to do it, and spent day after day in anxious deliberation, fruitful in suggesting new combinations, but all to no purpose. The abolitionism of the British delegates was of that substance, out of which we in America so readily manufacture our "dough-faces"; [2] but the pro-slavery of the American delegates was as unbending as steel, and harder than adamant. Come what might — confusion, chaos, and wild uproar — they were dogged in their determination not to allow any thing to appear on the records of the Alliance, to any extent hostile to the nefarious slave system. They presented a solid, almost an unbroken phalanx, and triumphantly carried their point! But victory was obtained at a ruinous price. It shielded American slavery from condemnation, but it also defeated the grand object for which the Alliance was called — the formation of a universal, evangelical organization. In fact, the whole movement has ended in a manner, justly calculated to excite the ridicule and contempt of all Christendom. There is not even a fragment left of it. It has not even an isolated existence. What a fact to chronicle in the nineteenth century, that a body claiming to have been divinely suggested, and composed of the holiest men on earth, crumbled at the touch of the Slave Power, and vanished into thin air, so that it is no longer visible to the eye, or palpable to the touch! Heavenly harmony reigned, until a proposition was made to stigmatize theft as a crime, and to declare that a man-stealer was one who gave no satisfactory evidence that he had been "born again" — and, therefore, ought not to receive the hand of Christian fellowship. This was going too far! It was secular as well as personal in its bearings! It had something to do with this world, whereas the next is the all-important subject of consideration! Our American delegates — Beecher, Cox, Patton, Kirk, Emory, Morse, Olin, &c. &c. — could not restrain their indignation! [3] They felt wounded, defrauded, insulted — and declared that they would never submit to such dangerous interference! In their judgment, indiscriminately to put slaveholders beyond the pale of the Christian church was to cut off the members of Christ's body, and to crucify him afresh! In some cases, (what cases were not specified,) slaveholding was a damnable act — in others, it was a religious duty! Some slaveholders deserved to be sent to everlasting burnings — others were worthy of the highest seats in the regions of heavenly bliss! It was the Garrisonian abolitionists, who deserved to be treated as infidels, and any amount of condemnation bestowed upon them was just! It was impossible that they could be actuated by good motives, and it was certain that they had put back the cause of emancipation at least two centuries!

Well, they sat in secret conclave, not daring to let a single spectator be present, and forbidding any one to report their proceedings. They sighed, and groaned, and complained, and threatened, and waxed warm, and hinted at an explosion; the heavens were as brass over their heads; thick darkness was around them; they prayed, and prayed, and prayed, but either *their* god was asleep, or had gone on a long journey, for he heard them not.[4] Finally, they broke up in confusion, and all their professions of brotherly regard and christian principle were thus demonstrated to be hypocritical and impious in the extreme. In view of the circumstances of the case, their devotional exercises must have been intolerable to the ear of Him whose solemn command it is, to "remember them that are in bonds as bound with them," to "break every yoke, and let the oppressed go free," to "deliver him that is spoiled out of the hand of the oppressor." [5]

Such being the character and termination of this Alliance, we deemed it highly expedient to hold a grand public meeting in Exeter Hall, to review the proceedings of that body, and to make it the occasion of giving another powerful impetus to the anti-slavery movement, on both sides of the Atlantic. That meeting was held on Monday last; and though it was a free and open meeting, and thousands assembled on the occasion, not one of the American delegates ventured to make his appearance, and only one of all the English delegates took the platform in extenuation of the conduct of the Alliance — and he only added to the contempt for that body which had previously been felt by the audience. His name was Preston, a Baptist preacher — a man, I am assured on good authority, who has broken his temperance pledge, and has recently been seen in a state of intoxication.[6] Yet he had the priestly assurance to accuse me of seeking to subvert Christianity!

You will see the proceedings of the meeting reported at great length in the London Patriot, copies of which will be transmitted to you. I am sure they will be read with a thrill of pleasure by all the friends of bleeding humanity. George Thompson acquitted himself in a manner that electrified the vast assembly, and was frequently cheered from the beginning to the end of his powerful speech. Publish that speech without abridgment. If you can find room for all that was said, the importance of the occasion will amply justify you in doing so. We have the popular sentiment of England with us, and the religious press, even of the evangelical stamp, condemns the Alliance in no measured terms. At the close of our meeting, a gentleman, well known for his philanthropy, Luke J. Hansard,[7] but not hitherto specially interested in the anti-slavery movement, presented to the Secretary of the League [8] the following *bona fide*, but quaintly expressed order:—

"LONDON, 15th Sept. 1846.

Messrs. Hoare: [9]

Pay the Christian Emancipation Society for the total abolition of all slavery from man to man, which destroys the accountability of mankind to their God, — FIFTY POUNDS

(Private account.)

LUKE J. HANSARD."

The gift was equally liberal and seasonable.

Douglass and myself have recently held a meeting at Sheffield, in the spacious Friends' meeting-house, which was crowded to over-flowing, and the proceedings of which you will find in the accompanying Sheffield papers. Give such extracts as you may think proper.

Adieu! In haste,

Wm. Lloyd Garrison.

ALS: Garrison Papers, Sophia Smith Collection, Smith College Library; also printed in *The Liberator*, October 9, 1846.

1. Not identified.

2. In American slang of the period, northern men with southern principles.

3. Lyman Beecher, William Patton, and Edward Kirk have been previously identified. Samuel Hanson Cox (1793–1880), a Presbyterian clergyman and educator, was a founder of New York University and was director of Union Theological Seminary for thirty-six years. He was an early advocate of abolition and temperance.

Robert Emory (1814–1848), born in Philadelphia and graduated from Columbia University, was associated with Dickinson College for most of his life, as professor of ancient languages and as president of the college. He was also a Methodist Episcopal minister and author of *The History of the Discipline of the Methodist Episcopal Church* (New York, 1844).

Sidney Edwards Morse (1794–1871), who was graduated from Yale in 1811 and also studied at Andover Theological Seminary, was a minister, editor, and geographer. In 1823 he founded the New York *Observer*, an evangelical religious paper, and remained senior editor and proprietor until 1858. He was the inventor of cerography, a method of printing maps, and in 1866 was granted a patent for a "bathometer," a diving device.

Stephen Olin (1797–1851), a Methodist Episcopal clergyman, was president of Randolph-Macon College (1834–1837) and of Wesleyan University (1842–1851). As a delegate to the General Church Conference of 1844, he became a member of the committee which attempted unsuccessfully to reconcile the pro-slavery and antislavery factions. He was instrumental in organizing the Evangelical Alliance, and at the meeting to which Garrison refers he represented the New York and New England conferences of the Methodist Episcopal Church.

4. The phrase "the heavens were as brass" is an allusion to Deuteronomy 28:23; the "thick darkness" appears in so many places in the Bible that Garrison's reference is probably not specific. He also alludes to I Kings 18:27.

5. Garrison alludes to Hebrews 13:3, Isaiah 58:6, and Jeremiah 21:12.

6. Garrison probably refers to John Preston (c. 1786–1847), the General Baptist clergyman (ministries in London, in Melbourne, and in Macclesfield). At twenty-two he had become a student of Dan Taylor, the founder of the New Connexion of General Baptists; he also married one of Taylor's daughters. (Letter to the editor from E. F. Clipsham, librarian, The Baptist Union of Great Britain and Ireland, July 10, 1970.)

7. Luke James Hansard (born c. 1805), reformer, pamphleteer, and head of

the printing firm, L. and G. Hansard & Sons of London, a company best known for its printing of parliamentary papers. (Letter to the editor from C. Duncan Rice, Yale University, June 2, 1970.)

8. The secretary of the league, R. Smith, is not identified.

9. Referring to Hoare's, the only remaining private bank in London, founded in 1690 by Sir Richard Hoare (1648–1718) and presently located at 37 Fleet Street in a building constructed in 1829 on the site of the old Mitre Tavern. (*Blue Guide to London*, ed. Stuart Rossiter, London, 1965.)

169

TO HENRY C. WRIGHT

London, Sept. 18, 1846.

Dear Henry:

I leave almost immediately to-day, direct for Glasgow, via Newcastle, Berwick and Edinburgh, where I hope to arrive to-morrow night. As I am busy in writing home to dear Helen, and also for the Liberator, and have also a multitude of things to do, I can only send you this hasty scrawl to say, that, a few days since, I authorised George Thompson to write Messrs. Rickarby and Harding,[1] at Liverpool, to engage our passages in the steamer of the 19th Oct., supposing that there was no doubt of your determination to return with me, and knowing that it was highly necessary to secure our berths in season. A letter just received from the firm states that they have chosen an excellent room, containing two berths, for us — the price of the passage is £40"19s. each. It is large, but there is no getting comfortably over any cheaper.

Now, dear Henry, have I been too hasty in this matter? Do you mean to back out, and leave me to go home alone? I hope not. If I have, you must immediately write to me at Glasgow, because I am responsible for your berth, and must pay half forfeit, unless you go with me, or unless I can get some one to take your place. Frederick [Douglass] has concluded to remain during the winter, to lecture in various parts of England for the benefit of the [Anti-Slavery] League — and, therefore, there is the less necessity for your remaining, and the more for your going to America.

I wish you could be with me in Scotland, but will not urge you on that point. Frederick will join me on Monday at Glasgow. Dear Thompson will not be able to go to Scotland, but intends being at Manchester and Rochdale with us.

It is quite uncertain whether I shall visit Belfast. I am informed, by a letter just received from there, that [Isaac] Nelson and Stanfield are quite inimical in their feelings, and doing what they can to prejudice the minds of the people against me.[2] No one is prepared to go forward to get up a public meeting — and hence, I think of going the more speedily to Dublin, where I had much rather be, in the family of dear Webb.

You will see in the Patriot, a very full report of the speeches made at our Exeter Hall meeting on Monday evening last, in regard to the Evangelical Alliance. It was a tremendous and most triumphant meeting.

Many thanks to R. D. W[ebb]. for his letter. I regret I have not time to answer it. With best regards to him, his wife, all the Webbs, the [Richard] Allens, and the [James] Haughtons, I remain,

Yours, lovingly,

Wm. Lloyd Garrison.

H. C. Wright.

ALS: Garrison Papers, Boston Public Library.

1. James Rickarby and George Harding, partners in a commission merchant firm. (*Gore's Directory of Liverpool and Its Environs*, London, 1853).

2. Garrison probably refers to James Standfield (active 1809–1861) who is listed in the Belfast directories as a wholesale grocer. Standfield was an active abolitionist, serving for many years as secretary of the Belfast Anti Slavery Society, he was also closely associated with the Belfast Charitable Society. (Letter to the editor from C. Duncan Rice, Yale University, April 16, 1969.)

170

TO HENRY C. WRIGHT

Glasgow, Sept. 21, 1846.

Dear Henry:

I am now just where you have so long desired to see me, under the roof of Andrew Paton and sister, and sitting by their side.[1] I arrived here at 10 o'clock, on Saturday night, from London, in the midst of a drenching rain — our dear friend Paton being on hand at the station to give me his heartiest welcome. My ride from London was extremely fatiguing, and has caused me a great deal of bodily suffering. I left in the night train, and though travelling in a first class car, could get no sleep, the change in the weather had been so sudden, and the cold was so great. We arrived at Newcastle between 9 and 10 o'clock, A. M., and from thence drove by the coach to Berwick. I had to take an outside seat, and got thoroughly chilled through. Sixteen miles from Berwick, it began to rain steadily, and, having left my umbrella in London, I got considerably wet. On arriving in the cars at Edinburgh, we had to get out in the dark, and go through mud and water some distance, (no shelter being overhead,) with our luggage in our hands, to find the train for Glasgow. We finally got into a car, (pretty well drenched by this time,) and as we went along, supposed that we should have no more annoyance until we got to Glasgow; but the train almost immediately stopped, and we were ordered to leave it, and go to another. Such vexatious arrangements (or, rather, such want of arrangements,) I have never before seen. In fact, with all the boasted order and regularity which are said to prevail on this side of the Atlantic, in every department of life, I do maintain that nothing can be worse than the management on the rail-ways. — It is "confusion worse confounded." [2]

The consequence of this exposure has been a severe attack of rheumatism in all my limbs — and, what is quite unfortunate, (especially where so much private talking and public speaking is to be done in so short a time,) I am quite hoarse, and have considerable inflammation on the lungs. I do not easily recover my voice when it is affected in this manner; hence I shrink from the thought of addressing a public assembly at this time.

In consequence of the occupancy of the City Hall, we shall hold no meeting in Glasgow, until Wednesday evening of next week.[3] It is asking too much to solicit your company on that occasion; yet all the friends, as well as myself, are strongly desirous of seeing you. I wish you could also be with us at Edinburgh. Our arrangements are as follow — To-morrow evening, Frederick [Douglass] and myself will address a public meeting at Paisley, (spending the day with John Murray) — on Wednesday evening, we shall hold a meeting at Greenock — on Thursday evening, and also Friday evening, meetings at Edinburgh — on Monday evening, (probably,) a meeting in Dundee — on Tuesday, return to Glasgow — on Thursday, perhaps go to Belfast — and on Saturday be in Dublin.

It is really afflicting and most unsatisfactory to be hurried along in this manner. It gives me no time for deliberate preparation, and therefore my public efforts must necessarily be very crude; nor can I have any time to enjoy the society of friends. But what more can I do? I cannot protract my sojourn in this country longer than the 19th of October. My passage is engaged; and if it were not, I could not remain. I wrote to you from London, stating that I had ventured to engage your passage also; and I reiterate the expression of my hope, that you will not fail to go with me. I am aware how much remains to be done here — and, for that matter, there is enough to occupy your entire life, should it extend to the age of Methusaleh — but, remember home — your wife and family — the length of your absence — the amount of labour to be done in the United States —

the fewness of the labourers.⁴ Remember, too, that I am under a public pledge to bring you back with me! Be ready, therefore, for a start. Do not allow any entreaties to keep you in England over the ensuing winter.

Friend Paton received a note from you this morning, enclosing the printed sheets of your forth-coming work on Peace. I have taken a rapid glance at them, and think the arrangement is excellent, and, of course, that the argument is invincible. May the work be widely circulated on both sides of the Atlantic, and be mightily instrumental towards bringing the horrid war systems of this world to a perpetual end!

I am very much pleased with the freedom of mind which characterises friend Paton and Catharine. They are deserving of all that you have said of them.

William Smeal has been to see me two or three times, and spent the last evening here. He is in fine spirits, and "true as the needle to the pole." ⁵ We shall probably have a very crowded meeting here next week.

I long to be in Dublin. My warmest regards to dear [Richard D.] Webb and family, and all the other friends, "of whom the world is not worthy." ⁶

Ever yours,

W. L. Garrison.

H. C. Wright.

ALS: Garrison Papers, Boston Public Library.

1. Andrew Paton (1805–1884), a Glasgow abolitionist and associate of William Smeal, was an active supporter of the North during the Civil War. Paton's sister Catherine was a member of the Glasgow Female Anti-Slavery Society, which she served for several years as treasurer. (*Life.*)

2. John Milton, *Paradise Lost*, II, 996.

3. The city hall in Glasgow, being the only building suitable for large public assemblies at this time, was commonly used for Glasgow Emancipation Society meetings. It was built in the old street called the Candleriggs and was replaced around 1901. (Letter to the editor from C. Duncan Rice, Yale University, December 26, 1970.)

4. Garrison refers to either Matthew 9:37 or Luke 10:2.

5. Barton Booth, "Song," stanza 2, lines 1–2, first published in *The Hive* in 1726. (See *The Hive*, London, 1732, I, 111.)

6. Garrison adapts Hebrews 11:38.

171

TO HENRY C. WRIGHT

Glasgow, Sept. 23, 1846.

Dear Henry:

On Monday evening, I met a number of gentlemen, belonging to the Emancipation Committee, at one of the hotels; and we had a very pleasant interview, which lasted till midnight — Dr. Watson in the chair.[1] Our faithful friend John Murray was up from Bowling Bay; and I went down with him, yesterday morning, to his romantic and quiet residence, where I got a very kind reception from his wife and family, and spent a portion of the day with him in climbing the neighboring hills, and talking about you and the other anti-slavery friends who had visited Bowling Bay, at various periods — &c. &c. In the evening, we went to Greenock, where a meeting had been hastily, and, of course, imperfectly called, to be addressed by Frederick [Douglass], (who had preceded us thither,) and myself. It was held in a very large church, and a somewhat numerous and very respectable audience was present. Frederick opened the meeting, and, in the course of his speech, dealt very faithfully with the Free Church, which caused some hissing among the snakes belonging to that brood; but this was trifling, in comparison with the amount of applause bestowed. In following him, I adverted to the hissing, and invited to the platform, any one in the assembly, who was prepared to deny the charges which had been brought against the Free Church, Drs. Candlish, Cunningham, Chalmers, &c.[2] But,

> "There was silence, deep as death,
> And the boldest held his breath" — [3]

and we thus "finished off" the hissers for the remainder of the evening. Our meeting broke up at 10½ o'clock, with much enthusiasm, and it was voted that there should be an auxiliary anti-slavery league formed in Greenock. More will need to be done in that place, as I am told that it is sadly lacking in intellectual activity and moral life.

Murray, Douglass and myself staid over night at the Temperance hotel, and this morning I came up to Glasgow, via Bowling Bay.

I am laboring under a severe attack of influenza — have a constant headache, and am quite hoarse — and, what is quite unfortunate, must go immediately to Paisley, on writing this, to address a public meeting with Frederick. To-morrow, I must hurry to Edinburgh, to be present at a meeting in the evening; but I feel more like being on the sick list. Alas! "necessity knows no law."

Another note from you — and one that makes it difficult to be satisfactorily answered. I see how it is — you are not satisfied that duty requires your return home this fall, in consequence of the peculiar state of our cause in this country, arising out of the course pursued by the Evangelical Alliance. — I confess, I see many weighty reasons for your remaining till spring — and I shall leave the matter entirely to your own unbiassed convictions of duty. How to return without you, I do not know — I am under a sort of pledge to see that you and Douglass return with me — and I have waited a fortnight longer than I first intended, to be sure that you would not give me the slip. Besides, your passage is engaged, and I know not whether it can be recalled, or not — though I will write to Liverpool, and see if it can be done. I am bound to add, that Murray, [William] Smeal and [Andrew] Paton are decidedly of the opinion, that you ought not to leave till spring. A letter from Geo. Thompson just received, states that he is overwhelmed with correspondence about the League and the Alliance, and needs two amanuenses and a private secretary to keep pace with it. I see how much there is to be done, and the great importance of its being done. All I desire is, that you may be where you can be the most usefully employed. I will, therefore, not urge you to return with me. Wait till I see you in Dublin, before a decision be absolutely determined on.

I cannot delay my visit. There are imperative reasons for my return home in the steamer of the 19th.

With loving regards to all the dear friends in Dublin, I remain,

Ever yours,

W. L. Garrison.

H. C. Wright.

ALS: Garrison Papers, Boston Public Library.

1. George Watson (c. 1792–1849) was president of the Faculty of Physicians and Surgeons of Glasgow (1845–1846). In his obituary of February 23, 1849, the Glasgow *Herald* describes him as taking an interest in "everything relating to the spread of liberal opinion, freedom of conscience, and the promotion of the happiness of men of all climes and colours."

2. Robert Smith Candlish (1806–1873) was minister of the important parish of St. George's in Edinburgh and was one of the founders of the Free Church of Scotland.

William Cunningham (1805–1861) was also active in the Free Church movement. Since he was an experienced public speaker, he visited the United States in 1843 to explain the movement but was criticized because of his association with slaveholders.

Thomas Chalmers (1780–1847) was responsible for many innovations in the church, including reorganization of the Glasgow parish system and the administration of poor relief. In 1823 he became professor of moral philosophy at St. Andrews. He helped to found the Free Church of Scotland and was its first moderator.

3. Thomas Campbell, "Battle of the Baltic," stanza 2, lines 7–8.

172

TO RICHARD D. WEBB

Edinburgh, Sept. 25, 1846.

My Beloved Friend:

Your note was received last evening, just as I was leaving the house to attend (with [Frederick] Douglass) our first public meeting in this city. The audience was considerably numerous, but not crowded, but will probably be much larger this evening. I gave a brief history of the American Anti-Slavery Society, and vindicated it and myself from the slanders which had been brought against it; and then proceeded to criminate and rebuke the Free Church, with special allusions to [Thomas] Chalmers, [Robert S.] Candlish, and [William] Cunningham. Frederick took up the Evangelical Alliance, and, as we say in America, "handled it without mittens." The applause was frequent and hearty, though there were a few serpents in the assembly who hissed. An invitation was given to any one to come forward, and defend either the Free Church or the Alliance; but no one ventured to enter the lists.

On Tuesday evening, we had a very good meeting in Greenock; but a much larger and incomparably more spirited one at Paisley, on the next evening. On the whole, it surpassed every meeting I have witnessed on this side of the Atlantic. Cheers for the Paisley weavers!

This forenoon, we are to address our anti-slavery female coadjutors in this place. On Monday evening, we expect to address a public meeting in Dundee. We are talking about having another public meeting in Edinburgh, on Tuesday evening, but I shall try to evade it, and get to Glasgow, preparatory to our great meeting in that city on Wednesday evening. There will probably be another meeting held on Thursday evening. On Friday morning, we shall go to Belfast, and address a public meeting that evening, if our friends are disposed to appoint one. I have just written to our friend John R. Neill, to this effect.[1] I hope to be in Dublin some time during Sunday. It grieves me, beyond all expression, to think that I can remain with you and yours, only a day or two, unless I give up my visit to Cork, which place I am quite anxious to see, even as a matter of curiosity. Of course, I shall expect to address no public meeting, either in Dublin or Cork, but to enjoy the social circle of friends that may wish to see me. Still, make whatever arrangements you please. If I had better go to Cork, (and I think you will say so,) pray write to our friends there, and say I will be with them on Tuesday evening, Oct. 6th, and remain till Thursday morning, when I must return to Dublin, and leave in the evening packet of that day for Liverpool, *without fail,* to meet Geo. Thompson the next morning at Brown's hotel, and proceed to Wrexham, Manchester and Rochdale, as a public meeting is arranged in each of these places. This plan is beyond alteration, and I must govern myself accordingly.

Do not incur the trouble or expense of coming to Belfast, as I shall remain in that place less than 24 hours; but it will gladden my heart to see you in Liverpool, just prior to my embarkation. ☞ We are to have a grand meeting in Liverpool on Monday evening, Oct. 19th, (as the steamer, fortunately, is not to sail till the 20th,) when we must have Thompson, (he has promised to be there,) [Henry C.] Wright and Douglass, and finish off "superbly."

Say to dear Henry, that I have seen his letter to William Smeal, and trust he has received the note I sent to him, a day or two since. I should be very glad to see him in Glasgow, next week, of course; but would prefer to see him in Dublin, and to have him go with me to Cork. Let him remain, then, till I come to Great Brunswick-street, where certain great men reside.[2] It will be a great relief to his mind, to assure him that, on mature consideration and a careful survey of the whole ground, I am entirely satisfied that he can do more by remaining on this side of the Atlantic, this winter, *by far,* than by returning to the United States.

Love to your dear wife — &c. &c.

Faithfully yours,

W. L. Garrison.

R. D. Webb.

☞ Frederick will not go with me.

ALS: Garrison Papers, Boston Public Library.

1. John R. Neill may have been the watchmaker and jeweler listed in the Belfast street directories for the period 1843–1884.

2. The Webbs lived at 176 Great Brunswick (now Pearse) Street. (*Almanac, Register, Directory 1846,* Pettigrew and Oulton, Dublin.)

173

TO RICHARD D. WEBB

Glasgow, Sept. 30, 1846.

My Dear Webb:

I have this moment arrived from a visit to Edinburgh and Dundee, and lose no time in replying to your note, which has just been put into my hands. It is "as clear as preaching" — and a great deal more so — that I cannot go to Cork, much as I desire to see the place, and especially the dear friends who reside there. I had no idea that the distance was so great, but supposed it would be a short and easy jaunt. If you have sent word to any one in Cork, that I intend to visit it, pray write immediately, and explain how I am situated, and express my deep regret that I cannot come.

I do not think I shall remain over Sunday, in Belfast, but shall endeavour on that day to get to Great Brunswick-street, Dublin; but, if otherwise, I will take the mail train on Monday, according to your suggestion.

I hope to see your cousins, the Webbs, in Belfast, and will do what I can to set them right, especially the "better half." [1]

We (Frederick [Douglass] and myself) have held two public meetings in Edinburgh, which were well attended, though not crowded, as many people were absent from the city. — I have no time to give you the particulars — you shall have them when we meet. We had also a social ladies' meeting, which was highly interesting, and they seemed to be greatly delighted. Last evening, at one of the hotels, we had a tea party, Councillor Stott in the chair, nor did we separate (and then most reluctantly) till near midnight. [2]

Our meeting at Dundee, on Monday evening, though very suddenly called, was a capital one. The evening was very dark and stormy, but the hall was crowded, and the enthusiasm great. An anti-slavery society was organized on the spot.

My regret in not being able to visit Cork is greatly diminished by the delightful thought that I shall have more time to spend in Dublin than I had allotted to myself.

Distribute the love in my heart, in any quantity, among all the Dublin "fanatics and infidels."

Yours, to the end,

Wm. Lloyd Garrison.

N.B. Another note from you! Well — as to Wrexham. I am aware it is a small place, but it was Geo. T[hompson]'s desire that I should visit it with him — and if he will alter our arrangement, I shall be happy to stay longer in Dublin. But *you* must influence him by letter.

ALS: Garrison Papers, Boston Public Library.

1. It is known that Richard D. Webb had several first cousins once removed in Belfast, but they have not been identified by name.

2. Joseph Hood Stott (died c. 1857), leather merchant, was currently serving on the town council of Edinburgh. In subsequent years he was to hold several local offices. (Letter to the editor from W. H. Makey, city archivist, Edinburgh Corporation, April 22, 1971.)

1 7 4

TO *THE LIBERATOR*

Belfast, Oct. 3, 1846.

It is now early in the morning. I am on the soil of the Emerald Isle, having just arrived at this place from Glasgow. ❋ ❋ ❋ ❋ ❋ ❋ ❋ ❋ ❋ ❋ ❋ I leave on Monday morning for Dublin, the friends are beginning to pour into the house, — at noon there is to be a public meeting, this evening there is to be a social gathering, &c. &c. What, then, can I give you, except the merest outlines of my movements since I wrote to you last?

I wish, through you, to say to all my friends, once for all, that epistolary correspondence with them, or even for the Liberator, has been impracticable on my part; and I will abide by the verdict of all, with whom I have been associated on this side of the Atlantic, in regard to this inability. I can give you no adequate conception of the constant and overpowering engagements and duties which are pressing upon me. These are accumulating as fast as the time for my return home is drawing to a close. The amount of labor, through which I have passed, especially within the last fortnight, has been far greater than I supposed it possible my physical frame could endure. I have been hurried from place to place, and held meeting after meeting, and turned day into night and night into day, and spoken in public, and talked almost incessantly in private, and come into contact with all sorts of minds, so that it is a marvel to me that, mentally, I am not in a fever, and, physically, entirely prostrated. Besides all this, I am receiving letters from all parts of the kingdom, earnestly desiring my presence, and expressive of the most kindly feelings; and it is no small task to send replies to these.

Nothing but facts like these could have prevented me from sending letters to my particular associates and friends in America; and I am sure that a knowledge of them will fully exonerate me, in their minds, from the suspicion, that I have forgotten them.

Just see how I have been employed since the 18th ultimo. Up to the evening of that day, I was excessively busy, in the office of our dear and indefatigable friend, George Thompson, writing letters to you and others, and mailing various newspapers and documents, giving an account of the public meetings which I had addressed in behalf of my mission; for, although I came over here with an almost settled purpose not to address many meetings of this character, yet, through the irrepressible zeal and earnest entreaty of the friends in various quarters, I have had to address many thousands of the people in a public manner; and I will just add, that, in every instance, I received the most enthusiastic demonstrations of regard, and a 'God speed you!' uttered ten thousand times over in the most hearty and fervent manner. In fact, both in public and in private, I have been received with a cordiality quite overpowering; for my poor services are abundantly overrated.

On the evening of the 18th, I bade farewell to London — the city of cities — and took the cars for Glasgow, via Newcastle-on-Tyne. Up to that time, the weather had been remarkably bland, and I had not received any detriment to my health; but a cold wet storm came on, and a severe change of the weather — severe from its suddenness — ensued. I rode all night, and arrived in the morning at Newcastle, comple[te]ly chilled, and physically exhausted, having been unable to sleep any on my journey. From thence I proceeded, by coach, to Berwick, a distance of sixty or seventy miles; and as I was obliged to take an outside seat, and the day was cold and stormy, I was still more prostrated on arriving at Berwick. From thence I took the cars for Glasgow via Edinburgh, arriving at the former place in the evening, about 11 o'clock, in the midst of a heavy rain. At the station, I was met by a very dear and excellent friend of the anti-slavery cause, Andrew Paton, who took me to his residence, where I received a hearty welcome from his sister Catherine, one of a small but devoted band of true-hearted women in Glasgow, whose labors in the cause are beyond all praise.

This was Saturday evening. On Sunday, I found myself laboring under a violent attack of influenza, (which has since become somewhat prevalent,) and my voice seriously impaired through hoarseness. I had desired to be in special good condition, especially as to lungs, on visiting Scotland; for I was aware that I was expected to do a good deal of work in a very few days. Hence, I was myself depressed in view of my situation. My lungs were in a state of irritation, but they were to have no opportunity to rest — for public meetings I must address, and talk I must in the social circle, which I am very fond of doing, you know.

On Monday, our untiring and very popular friend, Frederick Douglass, came to Glasgow — thenceforth to continue laboring with me, from place to place, until my return to the United States. We had anticipated holding a public meeting, on that evening; but, as the City Hall, (a truly immense one,) was to be occupied during the week with an exhibition of statuary, and as our friends were desirous that we should have our meetings in it, we concluded to alter our arrangements. In the evening, we met the members of the Glasgow

Emancipation Committee at the Eagle Hotel,[1] — Dr. [George] Watson
in the chair, — where we had a social chit-chat, over a cup of tea, and
formed a personal acquaintance which will ever be to me a source of
grateful recollection.

On Tuesday morning, we went to Bowling Bay, about ten miles
down the river Clyde, to the residence of John Murray, — a man too
well known on your side of the Atlantic to need any eulogy from me,
— accompanied by that veteran in the cause of Christian reform, who
came up the day previous to give us his benediction. His place of
abode combines the picturesque, with the beautiful and sublime, in
an eminent degree; but I have no time to indulge in drawing pictures,
or to recapitulate the many pleasant objects that I saw. During the
day, we climbed the lofty hills which rise somewhat precipitously
behind his dwelling, and had a magnificent prospect opened to us.
James N. Buffum, (of whose illness I regret to hear,) will remember
the spot, and his memorable collision with one of Lord Blantyre's
servants, as well as his correspondence with his lordship, in regard
to it.[2] The latter of Lord B., I am told, was not only very civil, but
quite creditable to his character.

In the evening, we went down to Greenock, and held a very
spirited meeting with special reference to the guilty position of the
Free Church of Scotland — no one venturing to say one word in its
defence. The next day we went to Paisley, and in the evening had
the most crowded and enthusiastic meeting I have yet seen on this
side of the Atlantic. I shall never forget it. Commend me to the
weavers and other operatives in Paisley, for intelligence, sagacity, and
appreciation of right sentiments!

On Thursday, we went to Edinburgh, and in the evening addressed
a large assembly, and were greatly applauded. On Friday, at noon,
we addressed a meeting of ladies; and in the evening held another
public meeting, with great success. On Monday, we went to Dundee,
and spoke to a large assembly, convened almost at an hour's notice,
and in the midst of a rain-storm, — and though it is one of the strong-
holds of the Free Church, — our severest accusations against it were
continually responded to by loud cheers. On Tuesday, we returned to
Edinburgh, and in the evening attended a tea-party that was given
to us, as a farewell expression of confidence and friendship on the
part of our Edinburgh friends — of whom, as well as of others, I shall
speak more fully on my return home — for I shall not be able to get a
moment's time here to do justice to my feelings, in regard to their
numerous acts of kindness. I am under very heavy obligations to the
unwearied cooperation and warm hospitality of the Rev. James
Robertson, of Edinburgh, the intelligent, faithful, and uncompromising

Secretary of the Scottish Emancipation Society.[3] We have formed for each other a friendship, which I trust will never be broken. He is truly a most valuable acquisition to our cause.

On Wednesday, we returned to Glasgow, and in the evening held a meeting in the City Hall, of the right stamp, and under cheering circumstances. On Thursday, at noon, we addressed a full meeting of ladies, which seemed to give great satisfaction. In the evening, we held another meeting in the City Hall, which was equally cheering with the others, and terminated near midnight. Yesterday morning, about seventy ladies and gentlemen gave us a public breakfast at the Eagle Hotel, and I only regret that I have not time to tell you all about it. As a testimonial of affectionate regard to myself, it was overpowering to my feelings. At half past 11 o'clock, we bade farewell to Glasgow, (to the [Andrew] Patons, the [William] Smeals and numerous other liberal friends,) and went to Kilmarnock, where we addressed several hundred persons, hastily summoned together, and received their benediction — and, after taking tea with a number of choice lovers of our good cause, we took the cars for Ardrossan, and at that place went on board a steamer for Belfast, making the passage in seven hours, and arrived here this morning.

Thus I have given you the meagre outlines of a most eventful and successful series of meetings, held during the last fortnight in places more or less remote from each other, and every one of them presenting peculiar features of interest. The labor devolving upon me has been excessive, but I am happy to say that my influenza has entirely left me, and I am really in good health and spirits, — good even to a marvel. A public meeting is appointed for us this day, at one o'clock. Two of the Belfast papers are singularly violent at my coming, and raising the mad-dog cry of 'infidel! infidel!' against me, and publishing the most atrocious falsehoods, so as to deter the people from attending the meeting.[4]

5 o'clock.

We have just returned from the meeting. The hall was well filled, and with a highly respectable audience. I had to speak at great length, and, in spite of the efforts of the press to make me odious, succeeded in obtaining the candid support and strong applause of an overwhelming majority of those who were present. In fact, I have never had any difficulty, either in America or this country, in commending the cause which I plead, and the doctrines which I enunciate, to any audience that will give me a candid hearing. My speech will probably create no small stir in this place, and I am beset on all sides to remain, and hold another public meeting in Belfast, with Douglass. This I cannot do, but must go to Dublin on Monday, to remain there till Thursday, and from thence go to Liverpool, to hold public meetings in Wrexham, Manchester, Rochdale, Newcastle, Darlington, and finally Liverpool. Is not this driving business with steam power?

    ❖   ❖   ❖   ❖   ❖   ❖   ❖   ❖

Though I have engaged my passage in the steamer of the 19th, yet it is possible I may remain till the 4th of November. There are a thousand weighty reasons why I should remain another fortnight — but I will not do so, unless I should I feel it to be imperative. ❖ ❖ ❖ ❖

Yours, &c. &c.

WM. LLOYD GARRISON.

Printed: *The Liberator*, October 30, 1846.

   1. Mentioned in Andrew Aird, *Glimpses of Old Glasgow* (Glasgow, 1894), as part of a district later swept away by the railways.

   2. Charles Walter Stewart, twelfth Lord Blantyre (1818–1900), who at one time was an officer in the Grenadier Guards, served in the House of Lords from 1850 to 1892. He married the sister-in-law of Garrison's friend the second Duchess of Sutherland. The barony of Blantyre became extinct in 1900. What Lord Blantyre's servant did to offend James Buffum is unknown. (Sir James Balfour Paul, ed., *The Scots Peerage*, Edinburgh, 1905, II, 91–92.)

   3. James Robertson (1803–1860) was a theological scholar, ordained in 1832 and appointed to the church of Ellon. In 1843 he became professor of divinity and church history at the University of Edinburgh. He was associated with the "Endowment Scheme" of the Church of Scotland.

   4. One of the articles referred to appeared in the Belfast *News-Letter*, October 2, 1846. The other article has not been identified.

175

TO ELIZABETH PEASE

Liverpool, Oct. 12, 1846.

My Beloved Friend:

Since I wrote to you, at London, I have made my excursion to Scotland, Ireland and Wales, (as far as Wrexham,) and am now just preparing to leave for Manchester, where we are to have a great meeting this evening, in regard to the Evangelical Alliance, in the Free Trade Hall.[1] Frederick Douglass and dear [George] Thompson went with me to Wrexham, where we had an excellent public meeting on Friday evening. Frederick is now in Manchester. George is with me, and will proceed in company to M., to take an important part in our public meeting. He has given his time, and influence, and means, and labours, to aid me in my mission, with a generosity and assiduity which greatly increase my already weighty obligations to him. The manner in which he has arraigned the Free Church of Scotland and the Evangelical Alliance, for their recreancy to the cause of the down-trodden slaves, is another striking proof of his moral courage, and his unswerving fidelity to the "Garrisonian" abolitionists of the United States.

Henry C. Wright arrived early this morning from Dublin, but went directly to Manchester without my seeing him, (George saw him for a moment,) but will participate in our proceedings this evening.

To-morrow (Tuesday) evening, we shall hold a public meeting in Rochdale — and on Wednesday evening, I hope to have the exquisite pleasure of seeing you, face to face, in Darlington. Whether Henry will accompany me, I do not know, but I shall try to induce him to do so.

I have promised to address a public meeting in Newcastle, on Friday evening — and on Saturday forenoon, a public breakfast is to be given to me at one of the hotels. Dear G. Thompson will probably be with me at N.

Never have I been called to endure so much mental excitement and bodily fatigue as during the last four weeks. I have had no respite, and as for sleep, it has been almost entirely banished from my eyes. Yet my health, to my amazement, continues firm, though for a time I was greatly prostrated in Scotland by a severe attack of influenza.

I heard that you passed through Edinburgh, while I was in that city! — How poignant was my regret, that it was not in our power to see and commune with each other, at that time!

Wherever I have been, I have met with a most cheering reception; and, at every public meeting, the people have responded in thunder-tones to my views on the subject of slavery and its abettors. I have ten thousand things to communicate, but must forbear until we meet.

Dear George sends his loving remembrances. I hope your health is steadily improving.

Admiringly, your faithful friend,

Wm. Lloyd Garrison.

N.B. Frederick Douglass and Henry C. Wright will not return to the United States until next spring. It is possible that I may remain a fortnight longer, (though my passage is engaged for the 20th inst.) — this will be determined in a day or two. I shall not be able to remain in Darlington longer than till Sunday morning — or Monday, at the latest — as we are to hold in Liverpool a public meeting, on the evening of Monday next, to be addressed by G. T., H. C. W., F. D., and myself. Should I decide to remain in this country till the 4th of November, my arrangements will be such as to prevent me being with you again, after our approaching interview; so that we must improve the hours as much as possible in conversing about the state of our great cause on both sides of the Atlantic, though you must not incur the slightest risk to your health, in seeing me. On this condition, alone, ought you to be willing to grant me an interview. Adieu!

ALS: Garrison Papers, Boston Public Library.

1. Garrison refers to the second Manchester building of this name, constructed in 1843 primarily for political meetings with a seating capacity of seven to eight thousand people. In 1855–1856 this building was replaced by a third Free Trade Hall. (Letter to the editor from C. E. Makepeace, local history librarian, Central Library, Manchester, June 14, 1971.)

176

TO *THE LIBERATOR*

LIVERPOOL, Oct. 20, 1846.

I send a hastily written letter to you, (I am always compelled to write in haste,) by the last steamer, in which I intimated that there was some probability of my remaining here till the 4th of November, although my passage was then engaged for the steamer which sails to-day. I am sure that, if you knew precisely how I am situated, and how immensely important it is that I should remain here a fortnight longer, (when I mean to let nothing detain me any longer from returning,) you would willingly give your consent to have me remain — nay, you would urge me to remain. If my health be continued, (and it is now excellent,) during the next two weeks, by the aid of dear [George] Thompson, I expect to do a great work for abolition, in addition to what has already been achieved. To-morrow, — or, rather, this afternoon, (for it is now past one o'clock in the morning, and I am to have no sleep, because it is my only chance to send you a line,) Thompson, [Frederick] Douglass and myself will leave here for Edinburgh, thence to Dundee, Perth, Inverness and Aberdeen, thence to Glasgow, Belfast and Dublin, and thence to Liverpool and Rochdale, and back again to Liverpool, at which place we are to hold public meetings, and make a fresh assault upon the Evangelical Alliance and the Free Church of Scotland. These meetings will not fail to make a great excitement, and will constitute the keystone to the arch of my mission to this country. It is every thing to be able to have the company of George Thompson with me in Scotland. During my recent tour, he was not able to go with me; and though Douglass and I got along exceedingly well, and were every where received with great enthusiasm by the people, yet G. T. is the one to inspire the people in a manner which throws all others into the shade. He is greatly beloved and honored in Scotland, though his faithful rebuke of the Free Church has lost him many friends. Mr. Thompson will go with us to Edinburgh.

I have so many things to say to you, that I know not how to commence. At Belfast, after our public meeting, we had a large tea-party in the evening, at one of the hotels, which was attended by a very respectable company, and a pleasant and profitable time it was.

From Belfast I rode on a coach from Portadown to Drogheda, a distance of more than 60 miles — and, oh! the amount of human suffering, filth and destruction, which met my eye during every step of the journey. I was frequently melted to tears, and for the first time in my life saw human beings, especially women and children, in a situation that made me almost lament their existence. Yet I was assured that I saw the best portion of the laboring poor in Ireland! Alas! for them, with the famine which is sorely pressing them, in consequence of the entire failure of the potato crop — the food on which they have subsisted from time immemorial.[1] Multitudes, beyond a doubt, — in spite of all that the government can do to give relief, — will miserably perish for the want of the absolute necessaries of life. O, the poor women! O, the poor children! O, the poor babies! Heaven send them speedy succor!

On my way from Drogheda to Dublin, in the cars, an accident happened to the train coming in the opposite direction, by which several cars ran off the track, but no injury was sustained by the passengers, fortunately, though it detained us some time. I expected to have arrived at early tea-time at Richard D. Webb's, where a large company of friends, (the [James] Haughtons, [Richard] Allens, &c.) with some who had come from Cork, Limerick and Waterford, — a distance, in some instances, of more than 100 miles, — had assembled at an early hour to give me a warm greeting; but I did not arrive till about midnight. A few had then left, but we had a joyous time, I assure you. Frederick was not with us, but dear Henry C. Wright *was*. I have not time to give the particulars of all that I saw, heard and did, during my three days' abode under the roof of R. D. W. This I must omit till we meet. It was a delightful sojourn, as you may readily imagine, and nothing was left undone to make me both comfortable and happy. James H. Webb and Thomas Webb, (the brothers of Richard,) and James Haughton and Richard Allen, were all as kind and attentive as brothers could be. H. C. W. and myself held one public meeting in Dublin, which was not very fully attended, but it was one of great interest, and has caused more excitement in the city than all other anti-slavery meetings ever held there before, in consequence of our review of the action of the Evangelical Alliance.

I left Dublin with much regret, on Thursday eve — the 9th inst., and arrived in the steamer at Liverpool the next morning, where I found Geo. Thompson and Frederick waiting for me at Brown's hotel, Clayton square. From thence, we went immediately to Wrexham, in Wales, to our warm-hearted friends, Sarah and Blanche Hilditch, (the latter deaf and dumb,) who gave us a sisterly welcome.[2] In the evening, we held a public meeting in the town hall, which was densely packed until near midnight — and the expression of enthusiasm, on the part of those present, was overwhelming. On Sunday we left Wrexham for Liverpool, and in the evening met a number of select and highly respectable people at the house of Dr. Hodgson, (a very talented man, who is at the head of the Mechanic's Institution in this town,) among whom was Mrs. Ames, an intimate friend of Mrs. [Eliza Lee] Follen, and Mrs. Balfour of London, a lady who is delivering public lectures in regard to the condition and rights of women with great success.[3] On Monday morning, we went to Manchester, and in the evening addressed a meeting of four thousand persons in the immense Free Trade Hall, (H. C. Wright having joined us,) who gave us a most enthusiastic welcome and a unanimous verdict of approval in our condemnation of the Alliance. It was a glorious meeting. On Tuesday evening, we spent a few very pleasant hours at the house of H. B. Peacock, a most accomplished gentleman; and Henry and I passed the night at Mrs. R. R. More's.[4]

We all parted at Manchester on Wednesday morning — Thompson for London — Douglass for Rochdale — Wright for Dublin — and I for Darlington, where I arrived in the evening, and was doubly welcomed by dear Elizabeth Pease, whom I found in a better state of health than I had anticipated, though still delicate. She is a noble woman, and her mind is throwing off many of the shackles of sect, which bind so closely nearly all who are attached to any sect. Our interview was far too short, as I had to go to Newcastle on Friday evening, where Thompson and myself held the most densely crowded and enthusiastic meeting I have yet seen on this side of the Atlantic. The next morning, we had a public breakfast given to us, and a fine time we had of it — the Rev. George Harris, a noble hearted Unitarian minister, in the chair.[5] The mayor of Newcastle, who is allied to the aristocracy, though a warm friend of every beneficent reform, and greatly esteemed, presided at our public meeting.[6] I saw, in Newcastle, Harriet Martineau's mother and her sister, Mrs. Greenhow.[7] On Saturday, we returned to Darlington. I got letters from my beloved friend — *ours*, I mean — Francis Jackson, and another from Quincy.

None of them, however, get letters from me! Nor is this owing to procrastination — and, of course, not to a lack of love and gratitude on my part — but really and truly to an entire absorption of my time in a manner which leaves me not a moment to myself. *Impossibilities* no man can perform. None of you can conceive of the series of employments into which I am constantly plunged. It is difficult for me to find time to eat — regular and necessary sleep is wholly out of the question. Letters from various parts of this kingdom — from known and unknown friends — are daily pouring in upon me like a deluge. I cannot begin to answer a tithe of them. I am hurried from place to place, from meeting to meeting, with great velocity, and the labor of months is compressed into weeks. The Liberator has very little from my pen, but the anti-slavery cause never before received such aid from me as at the present time.

Yesterday, [Monday] we left Darlington for Liverpool — a long distance — and held a public meeting here in Concert Hall, Lord street. We had no Liverpool 'philanthropists' to occupy our platform — for some reason, they chose to stand aloof — but our meeting was gloriously successful, and attended by a most brilliant assembly, whose verdict in our favor, and against the Alliance, was all that we could desire, all that could be given. We go immediately to Scotland.

Alas! the steamer leaves in a few moments, and I can add no more. Tell Mrs. [Maria W.] Chapman, that our worthy friend, Edward S. Abdy, is no more. He died a few days since at Bath.

Printed: *The Liberator*, November 20, 1846.

1. Potatoes had become the national food of Ireland as early as the reign of Charles II. This dependence on one crop was accompanied by periods of scarcity and want throughout the eighteenth and early nineteenth centuries, and the ultimate danger of complete crop failure was augmented by a rapid growth in population to over 8,000,000 by 1845. When the crop failed in 1846, a dreadful famine ensued. Despite public and private efforts at relief, between 200,000 and 300,000 persons died of starvation or disease during the next two years.

2. Garrison supplies the only information as yet known about the Hilditch sisters.

3. Although Mrs. Ames is too obscure to be identified, William Ballantyne Hodgson (1815–1880) and the Balfours were well known in British reform and political circles. Hodgson, educational reformer and political economist, was born in Edinburgh and educated at the university there. He became principal and lecturer in various schools and universities in Scotland and in London.

Clara Lucas Balfour (1808–1878), wife of James Balfour of the Ways and Means Office in the House of Commons, was a temperance lecturer and the author of various publications.

4. H. B. Peacock (1801–1876) was a journalist prominent in musical and dramatic circles in Manchester. (Letter to the editor from Frank Taylor, keeper of manuscripts, The John Rylands Library, Manchester, August 17, 1970.)

Garrison misspells the name of Rebecca Fisher Moore, wife of Irish barrister Robert Ross Rowan Moore, who had attended the 1840 World's Anti-Slavery Convention as a supporter of the British India Society. (Letter to the editor from C. Duncan Rice, Yale University, February 14, 1969.)

5. George Harris (1794–1859) had been since 1845 minister of Hanover Square Chapel in Newcastle. He was also active as editor of the *Christian Pilot and Pioneer* and as political and educational reformer.

6. Thomas Emerson Headlam (1777–1864), originally a physician and for many years president of the University of Durham Medical School, was a prominent public figure in Newcastle, serving as a popular mayor of that city during the 1830's and 1840's. (Letter to the editor from A. Wallace, city librarian, Newcastle upon Tyne City Libraries, August 20, 1970.)

7. Harriet Martineau's mother, Elizabeth Rankin Martineau (died 1848), was the daughter of a Newcastle wholesaler grocer and sugar refiner. Harriet's eldest sister Elizabeth (1794–1850) had married in 1820 Newcastle surgeon Michael Thomas Greenhow. (R. K. Webb, *Harriet Martineau*, New York, 1960.)

177

TO RICHARD D. WEBB

Dundee, Oct. 24, 1846.

My dear Richard:

You have already been apprised, by a note from George Thompson, that it will be impracticable for us to visit Dublin, as we originally designed. I can readily imagine how you and the other very dear friends in your city will feel at the intelligence; but I am sure that neither you nor they will regard this alteration in our plans as arising from any lack of desire, on our part, to see and embrace you all. Our fortnight's work is laid out, I believe, to the best advantage, and every moment of the time is to be assiduously employed. Our last meeting will probably be held in Rochdale, on Monday evening, Nov. 2d, though it is possible that we may have a farewell meeting in Liverpool, on the evening of the 3rd. We shall not be able to go to Belfast — and this will be another disappointment to our Irish friends. But it is a great distance to go, merely to hold a single meeting, and we must abandon our purpose, in that particular.

Our meeting in Newcastle surpassed in spirit, and in numerical pressure, every other that I have attended in Britain. This was all the more gratifying, as the anti-slavery committee in that place, (under the influence of the London Committee,) took no part in getting it up; but did what they could, probably, to prejudice the minds of people against me. The next day, we had a public breakfast given to us, at one of the hotels.

I spent two days at dear Elizabeth Pease's quiet residence, and found her in a more comfortable state of health than I had anticipated. She fully expected H[enry]. C. W[right]. would accompany me, and had his chamber all prepared for him, and was, of course, somewhat disappointed at his absence. We had interesting conversations on a great variety of subjects, and I was happy to find that she is not to be moved by any mad dog cry of "infidelity" that may be raised against me, or dear Henry. I bade adieu to that noble woman with feelings of regret too strong for utterance, and with increased admiration of her character. She seemed to be impressed with the idea, that she should never see me again in the flesh; but I trust we shall meet many, many times here below, on this or the other side of the Atlantic.

We had an excellent meeting in Liverpool on Monday evening last, (the 19th,) though not a single Liverpool man appeared on our platform! We did the best we could with our own forces, and put George Thompson into the chair as President of the League. The audience was large, and rendered a hearty and unanimous verdict in our favor.

On Tuesday, we took the cars for Fleetwood, (G. T., F. D[ouglass]., Mrs. Thompson, Mr. Farmer our reporter,[1] and myself,) arriving in the evening — and from thence took the steamer for Ardrosson, having had a troublous night on the water, and so passed on to Edinburgh, through Glasgow, arriving at the former place a short time before the public meeting in the evening. The meeting was numerously attended, and went off with great interest — not a single Free Church man venturing even to hiss at any thing that was said or done. An elegant tea service, from the anti-slavery ladies in Edinburgh, was presented to me, by the chairman, before the audience, and also a silk purse containing ten sovereigns.[2] Such tokens, while they are cheering to me at the present crisis, when such malignant efforts are making to cover me with popular odium, make me feel as though I had yet to perform much, fully to deserve them.

On Thursday evening, Douglass and I held a meeting in Kirkcaldy, which was got up in the course of a few hours. Notwithstanding the haste, and that every one present had to pay for admission, we had six or eight hundred present; and a "royal time" we had of it.

Yesterday, we came to this place, George Thompson being with us. All the meeting-houses but one were closed against us, on account of my "infidelity"! We had a good attendance, and a spirited meeting, nevertheless. This evening, we are to speak in Perth; on Monday evening, in Aberdeen; on Wednesday evening, in Glasgow; in Edinburgh, on Thursday evening.

Will it be in your power to take the steamer on the evening of Nov. 2d for Liverpool, with H. C. W.? Let none of you come, if it will put you to serious inconvenience. Remind dear J. H. W[ebb]., and R. Allen, of their promise to let me have their Daguerreotype likenesses.

With boundless love to Hannah [Webb], Henry [C. Wright],

Thomas and James [Webb], and their families, J. Haughton, the Allens, &c. &c. I remain

Lovingly yours,

W. L. Garrison.

ALS: Garrison Papers, Boston Public Library.

1. William Farmer was a journalist who was closely associated with W. W. Brown and other British abolitionists. (Letter to the editor from W. Edward Farrison, professor emeritus of English, North Carolina Central University, Durham, July 15, 1971.)

2. The tea service, which was to cost Garrison duty he could ill afford, is now deposited at the Massachusetts Historical Society (see illustration, p. 501). The chairman who presented the tea service on behalf of the ladies of Edinburgh was John Wigham, Jr. (1782–1862), a prominent Quaker philanthropist of the city who had been active in innumerable local and national reforms, including abolition and peace. (Obituary, *Scotsman*, April 30, 1862; *Annual Monitor*, 1863, p. 180.)

178

TO ELIZABETH PEASE

Perth, Oct. 25, 1846.

Dear Elizabeth:

It is not a dream that I have been at Feethams, and taken you by the hand, and sat by your fireside, and partaken of your hospitality, and conversed with you about the great interests of humanity, and the glorious reforms of the age; but, our time was so limited, and our intercourse was unavoidably so brief, that the visit seems almost to have been like a vision of the night. How deeply have I lamented your illness, since I came over to this country; and how often I have wished that you could have been present in the social circle, or in the public meeting, as I have journeyed from place to place! When we parted, you intimated that it was probably the last time we should see each other again in the flesh. Such a thought I will not cherish for a moment. True, we "know not what a day may bring forth," [1] and human life is at all times most uncertain; but I will fondly cherish the hope, that we may meet many, many times, both on this and on the other side of the Atlantic — *especially on the other side.* Should your health be fully restored again, (and you must take it for granted that it will be, that thus a cure may be hastened, for the mind has a wonderful effect upon the body,) I trust a good Providence will permit you to visit the shores of New-England, to receive the cordial welcome of a thousand hearts, and the warm grasp of a thousand hands. The thought of seeing you, one day or other, under my roof, in the presence of my family, gives me exquisite pleasure. My dear Helen would rejoice to greet you, and to have an opportunity to express to you her grateful feelings for all the kindnesses you have showered upon us. I believe you would love her like a sister; and, exalted as is her opinion of you, she would esteem you yet more highly on a personal acquaintance, if this were possible. Never did a husband have a more affectionate or more faithful wife; never were children blessed with a more watchful and assiduous mother. The prospect of being once more with them, in the short space of four weeks, causes my heart to leap within me for joy; but I shall have some drawback upon this joy, in leaving many dear friends on this side of the Atlantic, whose daily society I shall yearn for in spirit, and whose presence is inspiring to my heart.

I will not, my dear friend, press this matter of a transatlantic visit any further, at the present time. I suppose it now looks chimerical to you — and, of course, it is not to be seriously entertained, under present circumstances. You will pardon me for suggesting it to you — and let it be left to the disposal of kind Heaven, in the yet undeveloped future. Even should my life be spared, it does not seem probable that I shall ever again cross the Atlantic; but, among the powerful inducements I should feel to renew my visit, the pleasure of again taking you by the hand would certainly be paramount.

At Liverpool, I first broke the seal of the parcel you put into my hands, and found the beautiful purse, with its contents and the note. Valuable as was the gift, in a pecuniary sense, the friendship which dictated it I prize as beyond all estimate; because I believe you to be one of the best women of the age. This I should not venture to say, if I did not feel assured that you regard me as incapable of offering adulation to any human being; nor would you tolerate it, for a moment, if you had not entire confidence in my sincerity. My esteem for you is based upon the solid conviction, that you love truth, and justice, and righteousness, for their own sake; that you are a fearless seeker after what is right and good; that you have a heart which deeply sympathizes with suffering humanity; that you cherish a deep abhorrence of dissimulation and cant; and that you are determined to be true to your convictions of duty, be the consequences what they may.

The only hesitancy I feel in retaining what you generously put into the purse, as a token of regard for dear Helen and myself, (20 sovereigns,) is the knowledge of the fact, that the calls upon your benevolence are incessant, and that the recipients of your bounty are increasingly numerous. But I will not disguise the fact, that, struggling as is the Liberator continually against wind and tide, and pecuniarily embarrassed as it is at present, your gift is most acceptable, and shall be sacredly appropriated.

And now, dear Elizabeth, I bid you farewell, promising to be a more attentive correspondent for the future than I have been hitherto, and praying that your valuable life may be greatly prolonged. That I may ever be worthy of your esteem and friendship, is the desire of
Your grateful and admiring friend,

Wm. Lloyd Garrison.

Elizabeth Pease.

P.S. Our meeting at Liverpool, last Monday evening,[2] was fully attended, and went off with great spirit — [Frederick] Douglass and [George] Thompson principally occupying the time; but not a single Liverpool man appeared on our platform! The American influence, through commercial interchange, is very considerable; and the Evangelical Alliance is too "respectable" a body for the very "respectable" in society to join in assailing it for the present. They must first ascertain how the popular current is likely to run. Well, we can get along without them, perhaps much better than with them. The heart of THE PEOPLE is sound, and they give us, in every instance, their hearty approbation.

On Tuesday, we left Liverpool, via Fleetwood, Ardrossan and Glasgow, for Edinburgh. The voyage from Fleetwood to Ardrossan was very irksome, the sea being much excited, and many of the passengers quite sick. We arrived in Edinburgh on Wednesday afternoon, only a few hours before the evening meeting, very much exhausted, (especially dear Thompson,) and quite unfit, both in mind and body, to address a public assembly. The meeting was a very good one, nevertheless — for when did G. T. ever make a poor speech? On that occasion, an elegant silver tea-service was presented to me by the chairman, John Wigham, Jr., in behalf of the anti-slavery ladies of Edinburgh — a gift which I shall prize to the close of life, as a token of respect and confidence extended to me at a time when the most malignant attempts were made in England and Scotland, by the unprincipled partisans of the Free Church and the Evangelical Alliance, to cripple my efforts, and destroy my religious character.

On Thursday evening, Frederick and I addressed a large assembly at Kirkcaldy, (summoned at a few hours' notice,) and were very warmly received. On Friday evening, George Thompson united with us in addressing a meeting in Dundee. Only one church (and that not a large one) in the place could be obtained for us. "Garrison is an infidel," was the cry — "he does not believe in our holy Sabbath" — therefore, give him no countenance as the advocate of the perishing millions in America, who are clanking their chains in hopeless despair!

Rely upon it, dear Elizabeth, you are to have the same exhibitions of priestly rancor and hatred toward myself, on this side of the Atlantic, that have been for so many years witnessed in the United States. No matter — it will all turn out well, in the end. This hue-and-cry will only serve to excite inquiry among the people as to my real sentiments, and they will see, in due season, how grossly they have been deceived. The cunning shall be caught in their craftiness, and the counsels of the froward carried headlong.[3]

Yesterday, we came to this city, from Dundee, in a steamer borne on the noble river Tay; but the weather was dismal and stormy, so that we lost (what I much desired to see) a good prospect, and saw very little of the river scenery. It was a bad evening for our meeting — for, in addition to the inclement state of the weather, it was Saturday night, preparatory to the administration of "the Sacrament," and the people were religiously at their several places of worship. We had, nevertheless, about 400 persons present, and a very satisfactory meeting.

It was our intention to hold a meeting in Aberdeen on Monday evening, and the friends in that place are expecting us, without fail; but we find that we shall be compelled to ride on the outside of the coach all night to-night, and we dare not run this risk to our health. So, we shall send word to this effect to our Aberdeen friends, and hold another public meeting in this place to-morrow evening. On Wednesday evening, we are to have a meeting in Glasgow; on Thursday, another in Edinburgh; on Friday evening, G. T. will deliver a lecture in regard to British India, and the case of the Rajah of Sattara; on Saturday evening, we shall be in Carlisle; on Monday evening in Rochdale; and on Tuesday, in Liverpool. — On Wednesday, the 4th, I shall leave for "home, sweet home." Shall I hear from you before my departure?

W. L. G.

ALS: Garrison Papers, Boston Public Library.

1. An adaptation of Proverbs 27:1.
2. October 19.
3. Garrison adapts Job 5:13.

179

TO RICHARD D. WEBB

Glasgow, Oct. 29, 1846.

My dear Webb:

Last evening, we had one of the largest and most enthusiastic meetings, in regard to the Free Church, thc Evangelical Alliance, and the Letter of Dr. Wardlaw, that I have seen on this side of the Atlantic.[1] Notwithstanding there was another very popular meeting of the citizens, last evening, the immense City Hall was crowded to its utmost, hundreds of men and women being compelled to stand *five hours* — i. e. from 7 till 12 o'clock!! You will see, by the Argus, what we did — although the report, of course, gives but a faint idea of the meeting.[2] Has not [George] Thompson put Dr. Wardlaw "in a fix," as we say in America?

We leave, in a few minutes, for Edinburgh, where we are to hold forth this evening.

What I desire particularly to say to you, in this note, is, do not go to the risk, trouble and expense of coming all the way to Liverpool, merely to give me the parting hand — especially, if the weather be stormy. This is a disagreeable season of the year to be on the water, and every voyage is attended with more or less danger. Of course, I want to see you, of all men; but, I will not allow myself to be gratified, to the discomfort of one of the dearest and most cherished friends I have in the world.

Tell dear H. C. W[right]. not to come to Liverpool, (he suffers so much on the water,) unless he does not intend to return to Dublin. I do not need either his or your presence, or that of any other Dublin friend, to assure me of your love.

With the best regards to Hannah, and the entire circle, I remain, in haste,

Ever yours,

W. L. Garrison.

R. D. Webb.

ALS: Garrison Papers, Boston Public Library.

1. Ralph Wardlaw (1779–1853) was a Congregational minister and a professor of systematic theology at the Glasgow Theological Academy; and he was widely known in the United States for his theological writings. It was at his invitation that Harriet Beecher Stowe visited Scotland in 1853.

In this paragraph Garrison refers to the controversy that had arisen in the Evangelical Alliance between Wardlaw and Thompson. Although the precise letter to which Garrison refers has not been found, the situation was as follows: Wardlaw had originally come out against any blanket statement that slaveholders should be admitted to the alliance, but later he accepted a compromise resolution that each branch of the alliance should decide grounds for membership. This was too conservative a view for Thompson, who insisted that the British should cooperate with the American branch only if it excluded all slaveholders.

2. The Glasgow *Argus*, which was published from 1833 to 1847, was a liberal Glasgow biweekly, the organ of local abolitionists, corn-law leaders, and other reformers. It was run by "The Clique," a reform junta who had James Oswald of Shieldhall elected as reform member of Parliament for the city in 1832 and maintained him in office until 1847; it was later edited by Charles Mackay. (Letter to the editor from C. Duncan Rice, Yale University, June 2, 1970.)

180

TO UNKNOWN RECIPIENT

Liverpool, Nov. 3, 1846.

My Dear Madam:

Your letter of the 29th ult. has just been put into my hands; and though I am in the midst of pressing engagements & duties, in consequence of preparing to leave in the steamer Acadia for Boston, I lose no time in sending you a reply.

You desire me to return you the manuscript which Mr. [Thomas] Clarkson put into my hands, containing his views on the Dissolution of the American Union, in connexion with the subject of slavery.[1] Why you wish me to return it, you do not state, excepting that you "would not like to lose it." I intend to preserve it, with all care & fidelity, both for its intrinsic value, and as a token of his regard for my anti-slavery services in the U. S. I must, therefore, respectfully decline complying with your request, trusting that you will readily see that I must necessarily prize the Mss. very highly, and that no other person in the world, inasmuch as it was entrusted to my care by Mr. Clarkson, has so valid a claim to its possession as myself.

When I visited Mr. Clarkson, I did not know or imagine that he had any such manuscript. He gave it to me, not only without solicitation, but as much to my surprise as pleasure. Moreover, he gave me full liberty to do with it whatever I might deem best; but, before its publication in any form, he desired me to revise it carefully with my esteemed friend Geo. Thompson, and to make such alterations as the sense or grammar might require. The copy of it, which appeared in the London Patriot, was given *verbatim*, with a very few trifling corrections, in no wise affecting the sentiments of the writer.

Why do you object to my retaining the Ms.? Or on what ground do you claim a right to it, transcending my own? Or why do you reproach Mr. Thompson, as though as he had committed a serious wrong? You express "deep sorrow for what has taken place." Why are you thus sorrowful? Is it because the Ms. was given to me, in preference to some other person? or because you disapprove of the sentiments expressed by Mr. Clarkson? If on the former ground, I shall be sorry to be deemed by you unworthy of this mark of confidence and respect; if on the latter, I can only say, that I believe those sentiments are worthy of the name and fame of Clarkson, and thus believing, I am persuaded their publication will greatly promote the abolition of American slavery, — however startling to some, in their application to that "covenant with death," [2] the Am. Constitution.

AL: Garrison Papers, Boston Public Library.

Although this letter is clearly in Garrison's hand, it is not signed and it is corrected to an extent unusual for Garrison; conceivably it is not the copy sent to the recipient — in fact the letter may not have been sent at all. Moreover, the identity of the intended recipient is uncertain. She could be Catherine Buck Clarkson (c. 1773–1856), daughter of William Buck, a prosperous yarn maker of Bury St. Edmunds, who married Thomas Clarkson in 1796. It seems unlikely, however, that Garrison would have written in this tone to a recently bereaved lady. Another possibility is that it may have been written to Mary Clarkson Dickinson, niece and former daughter-in-law of Thomas Clarkson, who had in 1843, six years after the death of her first husband (Clarkson's son Thomas), married the Reverend W. W. Dickinson. (Earl Leslie Griggs, *Thomas Clarkson, the Friend of Slaves*, London, 1936, p. 168.)

1. Garrison refers to Clarkson's "Hints for the American People in the Event of a Dissolution of the Union," which had appeared in the London *Patriot*, October 1, 1846.

2. Isaiah 28:15.

181

TO BARING BROTHERS

Liverpool
November 3 1846

Gentlemen,

The letter of Credit from Messrs. Saml. May & Co Boston [1] which I have lodged in your hands, authorizes me to draw for the sum of £50, in addition to the sums I have already received. This I hereby authorize you to pay to Mr. George Thompson whose receipt will be your discharge   I annex his signature.

I remain   Gentlemen
Your obcdt. Servt.

Wm. Lloyd Garrison

Thompsons Signature
Geo. Thompson

Transcription in the hand of George Thompson: Garrison Papers, Boston Public Library

Baring Brothers, one of the most prosperous of English financial houses, had been in operation since 1770. In 1846 control of the firm lay in the hands of Alexander Baring, Lord Ashburton, who had been highly successful in extending the business to the United States.

1. A hardware and metals store at Broad and State Streets, founded by Samuel May (1776–1870) and currently owned by his sons John Joseph May and Frederick W. G. May. (Letter to the editor from Ruth D. Bell, researcher, April 30, 1971.)

182

TO SARAH HILDITCH

[November 4, 1846] [1]

On board of the Acadia, ⎱
waiting for the mail.   ⎰

My much esteemed friend:

With a full heart and suffused eyes, I have watched the little steamer, conveying you and the other dear friends again to the shore, till it was lost in the distance. I know not how to express my feelings, in view of such a demonstration of personal friendship, and sympathy and regard for the cause which I humbly advocate. On an occasion like this, words are powerless. Yet I want to tell you how much I feel indebted to you for your sisterly reception, your ardent co-opera-tion, your self-sacrificing spirit, your words of encouragement and love, your unremitted devotion to the cause of poor bleeding, fettered, crushed humanity. I shall ever feel grateful to Heaven, for having been permitted to become acquainted with you and dear Blanche [Hilditch], whose case excites my utmost sympathy, my warmest admiration, my brotherly regard. Tell her, that though I was com-pelled to be mute in her presence, not knowing what signs to make to hold intelligent converse with her, I felt that our spirits needed no vocal ut[terance.]

Farewell to my dear and attentive friend, Mr. Clare! [2] May he be a faithful witness for God, and ever have his head covered in the day of battle.[3] I shall give him a choice place in my heart.

Farewell to you, to Blanche! I say the word with a sorrowful spirit. I desire to remain behind awhile, for a thousand reasons; but ten thousand demand my return home to the United States. My dear wife is waiting to embrace me with open arms — my children are shouting joyously in anticipation of my return — a thousand friends are waiting impatiently to greet me. Adieu! adieu! More I would add, but the mail has arrived, and I must hastily close.

Ever faithfully and gratefully yours,

Wm. Lloyd Garrison.

ALS: Merrill Collection of Garrison Papers, Wichita State University Library.

1. Garrison is known to have sailed from Liverpool on this date.
2. Garrison may refer to Joseph Clare (c. 1817–1860), who was between 1846 and 1853 minister of the Baptist Chapel on Chester Street in Wrexham. (Letter to the editor from A. G. Veysey, county archivist, Flintshire County Council, December 23, 1970.)
3. Garrison adapts Psalms 140:7.

183

TO ELIZABETH PEASE

Halifax, Nov. 15, 1846.

Dearly beloved Friend:

With a head full of confusion, but with a heart overflowing with kind and grateful emotions, I seize my *pencil* to announce to you our safe arrival at this place, in the remarkably quick passage of eleven days from Liverpool; and as we are only 400 miles from Boston, we shall probably reach that city on Tuesday, (to-day is Sunday,) thus making our entire voyage in thirteen days — the shortest passage ever made, I believe, by any steamer, at this season of the year. The weather has been unexpectedly bland, and we have very fortunately escaped without encountering a single gale of wind — though we have had a few squalls, with some rough sea. Short as the voyage has been, in reality, it has seemed almost interminable to me. I have been sick and wretched nearly all the passage, beyond every thing that I have ever before experienced. Till within the last two days, I have scarcely sat up an hour a day, but have kept to my berth, unable to relish any food, unable to digest such as I took, unable to sleep during the long and almost seemingly endless nights, and wholly disinclined to make any acquaintance among the passengers, or enter into conversation with any one. O, I *do* dislike the ocean, as a highway of transportation! Commend me to dry land, and railway carriages! My wretched hours were happily solaced by thinking of my visit to Feethams, (too short, alas! too short,) and of the numerous and dearly beloved friends I had left behind me, and of the interesting scenes through which I had so rapidly passed during my sojourn in Britain. They were relieved, too, by the transporting thought that I was rapidly approaching my cherished home, and, Providence permitting, soon to be permitted to embrace my dear wife and children. If any man was ever blessed with an affectionate and loving wife, I am that man; and if ever children had a watchful, assiduous, devoted mother, mine have. I tell Helen that the only fear I have is, that her attachment for me is carried to an undue extent. She always feels my absence so keenly, that I never leave home without great reluctance; though she never wishes me to forego the discharge of any duty to please her. May I ever prove worthy of one so confiding, faithful, and loving!

How many things I shall have to communicate on my return home! It will be a busy time with me, both with the tongue and pen, for some weeks to come. Our Bazaar week will doubtless be one of great animation, and I shall have to be a sort of fixture to it, until its termination. I hope we shall not be deprived of the use of Faneuil Hall; for, in that case, we shall really be put into a serious predicament, as we have no other hall in the city large enough for our purpose. There are several boxes of articles for the Bazaar in the Acadia.

I pray you, dear E., to let me hear from you, as often as convenient. I feel much solicitude on the score of your health, and long to hear of your complete restoration. I am determined not to abandon the hope, (smile as you will,) of one day seeing you in Boston, and under my roof! "Hope on, hope ever," says Miss Leslie, and it shall be my motto.[1]

In writing at any time to Mary Martin, please convey to her my warmest remembrances, and assure her that she stands high on my list of friends.[2]

I desire to be cordially remembered to your amiable brother John and his excellent wife.[3]

My head whirls — it is a painful effort to write even a sentence — and I must hastily bid you adieu!

Faithfully yours,

Wm. Lloyd Garrison.

E. P.

ALS: Garrison Papers, Boston Public Library.

1. Probably Garrison refers to Eliza Leslie (1787–1858) of Philadelphia, who became well known for cookbooks and later for stories published in *Godey's Lady's Book*; in 1848 she published a novel, *Amelia, or a Young Lady's Vicissitudes*. The specific quotation has not been found in her works.

2. Mary Martin (1806–1848) of Waterford (near Cork), wife of temperance reformer Edward Martin, was a staunch Garrisonian who worked closely with Richard D. Webb. (Letter to the editor from C. Duncan Rice, Yale University, June 2, 1970.)

3. John Beaumont Pease (1803–1873), one of Darlington's leading citizens, was active especially in Christian and temperance reforms. (Letters to the editor from M. Y. Ashcroft, county archivist, North Riding of Yorkshire County Council, August 18, 1970, and W. A. L. Seaman, county archivist, Durham County Council, August 27, 1970.)

1 8 4

TO MARCUS MORTON

BOSTON, Nov. 27, 1846.

SIR —

I am sure you will not deem it any impeachment of your intelligence or impartiality, if I respectfully ask you to review a decision, which, as Collector of this port, you gave a few days since, and by which I was unexpectedly taxed nearly sixty dollars; because the wisest and best men sometimes err in judgment, and see and correct their error, on more mature deliberation.

The case, you will remember, is simply and exactly this:— On making a visit recently to Edinburgh, in Scotland, a number of the ladies and gentlemen of that city, desirous of evincing their personal regard for me, presented to me a silver tea service, with an inscription, which has been appraised in value at £40, and taxed 30 per cent. The facts were stated to you, and you kindly consented to examine the law, and see whether this token of friendship might not properly be allowed to pass, duty free. I did not see you afterward, but was told by your clerk, that you had decided in favor of exacting the duty. It was accordingly paid; for, though it was a tax that I was not able to meet, without some pecuniary embarrassment, I could not think of allowing such a token to remain in the hands of the Government, to be disposed of at public vendue.

Unquestionably, your decision is sustained by the *letter* of the tariff law, but I cannot think it is by its *spirit*; and it is for this reason, I desire you to re-examine the grounds of your decision. With legal matters, as a lawyer and a judge, you are much better conversant than myself; but I believe I do not err in supposing, that it is the spirit of a law, and the unquestionable design of those who enacted it, which are to be consulted, rather than its letter.

The duty imposed on foreign silver plate, by the law of Congress, I conceive to affect only the case of importation, for sale and profit, or where the plate has been purchased as a matter of personal taste, convenience or luxury; but it seems to me that it was never intended to be applied, and that by no just or liberal construction can it apply, to *a token of personal and public regard*, such as is rarely bestowed, and such as was proffered to me in Edinburgh. It was not a purchase, on my part, nor was it imported as a matter of profit or speculation; but it is, I am persuaded, a fair and just exception to a general rule. The inscription upon it shows the origin and design of the gift, (of which I presume you have no doubt,) and renders it unsuitable for sale or transfer, at least while I am living.

You are to be commended for your determination to discharge the onerous duties devolving upon you as an officer of the customs, in a faithful and impartial manner; but, in every case which presents a doubtful aspect, whether it fairly comes within the spirit of the law, I think it will be generally conceded, that the verdict should be rendered in favor of the citizen, rather than that of the government; because an error of judgment in the particular instance may prove a very serious pecuniary injury to the citizen, but cannot possibly thus affect the government. Such a case, I respectfully submit, is mine, as already explained to you.[1]

Yours, for strict equity,

WM. LLOYD GARRISON.

Printed: *The Liberator*, December 25, 1846.
   In *The Liberator* immediately following the text of this letter is a note explaining that the tea service in question is on display at the Faneuil Hall Bazaar.

   1. Morton remained adamant to Garrison's appeal, but a group of women friendly to the cause were later to reimburse him for the amount of the duty. For Garrison's acknowledgment of their contributions see his letter to Louisa Gilman Loring, July 30, 1847, and *The Liberator* of the same date.

185

TO JAMES FREEMAN CLARKE

Boston, Nov. 28, 1846.

Dear Sir —

If you have no objection, will you be so kind as to read the following notice to your congregation to-morrow? — and oblige

Yours, truly,

Wm. Lloyd Garrison.

☞ The annual meeting of the New-England Non-Resistance Society will be held in the Marlboro' Chapel, Hall No. 1, on Thursday and Friday next, (day and evening,) commencing at 10 o'clock, A.M. The friends of universal peace and good will are cordially invited to attend.

Adin Ballou, President.

ALS: Villard Papers, Harvard College Library. An identical note of the same date addressed to Theodore Parker, with part of the postscript torn from the bottom of the sheet, is to be found in the William Lloyd Garrison Papers, Massachusetts Historical Society.
   James Freeman Clarke (1810–1888) was a graduate of both the college and the divinity school at Harvard. After spending seven years as minister of a Uni-

tarian church in Louisville, Kentucky, he became in 1841 the minister of Boston's Church of the Disciples. A Transcendentalist in philosophy, he was the author of innumerable sermons and books, including *Anti-Slavery Days* (Boston, 1884). He was an active member of various educational boards and was involved in virtually all the reforms of the day.

---

1 8 6

TO THE EDITOR OF THE *CHRISTIAN WITNESS*

[December 4, 1846.]

Sir —

By an editorial article in your last number, it appears to be my misfortune, — possibly my crime, — not to advocate the anti-slavery cause in a manner agreeably to your taste. You 'are not exactly at ease' respecting me. Neither are the American slaveholders, nor their apologists — nor do I intend to allow them any repose, until they break every yoke, and let the oppressed go free.[1] I have come to the country as the accredited representative of the free colored and slave population of the United States — a population, (to use the descriptive and affecting language of scripture,) peeled, scattered, meted out, and trodden under foot of men.[2] For seventeen years they have recognized me as their faithful friend and uncompromising advocate, offered up in my behalf their prayers, and bestowed upon me their benedictions. If, sir, *you* are not, *they* are 'exactly at ease' respecting my course. I prefer their judgment and testimony, in this particular, even to yours.

You declare 'that there are great difficulties in the way of our comfortable co-operation with Mr. Garrison.' The American slaveholders and their apologists are placed in a similar dilemma. What those difficulties are, you do not distinctly specify. As an abolitionist, I maintain that slaveholding, under all circumstances, is a heinous sin against God, and ought to be immediately abandoned; and that slaveholders are men-stealers, and not the followers of Christ. On this foundation is based the anti-slavery movement in the United States, as was the movement in this country for the overthrow of West-India slavery. Are you willing to stand upon it, and maintain it, at whatever cost? If so, then I do not know why, as an *abolitionist*, we cannot comfortably co-operate with each other.

It seems that my speech in Exeter Hall, in review of the proceedings of the Evangelical Alliance, gave you serious offence, though you 'attended the meeting in the spirit of candor.' Are you sure this spirit guided your pen in writing the article on 'SLAVERY,' which appeared in the last Christian Witness? I do not wish to be personal; but I must be explicit. Upon the face of it, I am constrained to say, that a more unjust and calumnious article was never sent forth to excite popular prejudice, or to decry the character of the friends of the American Anti-Slavery Society.

You 'unhesitatingly affirm that, in England, Mr. Garrison will command small sympathy, and few friends, among either the wise or the good.' Then, certainly, it must be either on account of the badness of my cause, or the badness of my character. That cause is the cause of impartial liberty, and needs no vindication. Whether I have done aught to promote it — whether I have suffered or perilled any thing in its behalf — let tyrants and persecutors bear witness. If, then, I have not been false to it, at any time, nor been disposed to shrink from a pitiless storm of popular fury in attempting to carry it forward, why should not *many* of the 'wise and good,' in England, give me their sympathy and co-operation? Thus far, at least, I have had no cause to complain of the reception which has been given to me in England, Scotland, Ireland and Wales. I have addressed many public meetings, and in every instance the thronging multitudes have given me their enthusiastic approbation. Possibly, they were not the 'wise and good' — possibly, they were the foolish and wicked. Personally, they were strangers to me; but this I know — they showed themselves to be the uncompromising friends of the slave, and pronounced a righteous verdict of condemnation against the pseudo 'Free Church' of Scotland, and its guilty ally, the Evangelical Alliance. I make my appeal to the people of this country — not to any professional class of men — and cheerfully leave my cause and character in their hands.

You say that I 'seem to have made the science of offence a special study,' and opprobriously remark, that I have, as you think, 'attained to a high proficiency.' If you mean to say that I seek to give offence, in an evil spirit, or for malicious purposes, your charge is as unfounded as it is serious. My aim is to reconcile the human race, not to foment jealousies and divisions — to throw down, not to build up or support those partition walls, which prevent the people of all nations from 'mingling into one, like kindred drops.'[3] But there can be no peace without purity — no union without righteousness — no love without liberty. Though Jesus declared that, by the promulgation of his gospel, the father should be arrayed against the son, the son against the father, and all the family relations be violently sundered, yet, without a paradox, he was the Prince of Peace, and came to reconcile us all to God.[4]

The prophets, under the old dispensation — the Savior and his apostles — 'the noble army of martyrs and confessors' — were all accused of 'making the science of offence a special study,' and 'attaining to a high proficiency.' Now, they are venerated and honored; but, in their day, they were regarded as 'pestilent and seditious fellows,' 'the off-scouring of all things,' blasphemers and infidels, and unworthy to live.[5] Read the first and fifty-ninth chapters of Isaiah, and see the mode adopted by that ancient disturber of the peace to avoid giving offence to those whom he sought to reclaim! How very 'prudent,' 'judicious[']' and 'guarded' he was in the use of language, and in the accusations he preferred against the house of Israel!

To your charge against me, I beg leave to borrow, in extenuation of my conduct, the words of Luther — 'Almost all men condemn the tartness of my expressions; but I am of opinion, that God will have the deceits of men thus powerfully exposed; for I plainly perceive, that those things which are softly dealt with in our corrupt age, give people but light concern, and are presently forgotten. If I have exceeded the bounds of moderation, the monstrous turpitude of the times has transported me. Nor do I transcend the example of Christ, who, having to do with people of like manners, called them sharply by their proper names — such as, an adulterous and perverse generation, hypocrites, a brood of vipers, children of the devil, who could not escape the damnation of hell.' [6]

You represent me as 'breathing a spirit of fierce hostility to Evangelical religion, cherishing a feeling of bitter contempt for its institutions, its ministers and professors.' You are very careful to suppress all evidence on this point; for the all-sufficient reason, that you can find none. In vindicating the cause of the suffering and the dumb in the United States, what religious sect or political party have I spared? What one of them all have I ever censured for its peculiar religious faith or political creed? If I have assailed 'institutions,' 'ministers,' or 'professors,' it is because they are enlisted on the side of the oppressor, and not because they are 'Evangelical.' For a similar reason, and in a similar manner, I have assailed other denominations, popularly regarded as heretical. My course towards them all has been 'without partiality and without hypocrisy.' I have not allowed myself to be a respecter of persons or parties. Why, then, do you 'go out of the way' to promulgate such an accusation against me, through your widely circulated magazine?

But, you are not content with grossly misrepresenting me — you must also asperse the characters of others, equally innocent. 'Such,' you add, 'we have the fullest reason to believe, are all the characteristics of his party in America'; and as an 'illustration' of this, you quote a resolution, adopted at the last annual meeting of the American Anti-Slavery Society, — 'W. L. Garrison in the chair,' — as follows:—

'Resolved, That this Society rejoices in the present declining state of American religion, inasmuch as it voluntarily comes forth to baptize and to sanctify slavery, which Mahommedanism abolishes, and Catholicism condemns; and that it will endeavor to warn the world, particularly the so-called heathen portion of it, against its influence.'

This is only a portion of the resolution as it was adopted by the Society.[7] I do not object to it as it is quoted, but endorse it to the letter, with all my understanding and heart. But why mutilate it? Why put a period where you only find a comma?

To this simple, clear, common-sense, and Christian resolution, you are pleased to append the following extraordinary commentary: 'Decline is the precursor of dissolution. If, then, the decline of religion gives joy to this Society, surely its extinction would excite rapture. The principle, then, of this Society is INFIDELITY! Its meet motto, we infer, is, *Let Christianity perish, that the slave may go free!* * * * Is, then, the hope of the slave founded on the extinction of Christianity? Is it come at last to this? Such, at least, is not yet the doctrine for the people of England.' (!!!)

Sir, I am told that you are an intelligent and honest man. I trust the good opinion of your friends is well founded. But your head is evidently confused, if your heart is all right. It requires a large amount of that charity 'which thinketh no evil, and beareth all things,'[8] to exonerate you from the suspicion of wilfully placing a false and monstrous construction upon the language of the resolution. What! the principle of the American Anti-Slavery Society is 'infidelity'! Why, sir, ever since it was organized, this Society has been the vindicator and champion of Christianity, against the foul and impious aspersions cast upon it by the great body of the American clergy, who maintain that it sanctions the enslavement of the rational creatures of God! What! an 'infidel' Society employing lecturers to defend the Bible as an anti-slavery volume, and denouncing its suppression among the slave population as a crime against 'the life of the soul'! — asserting that the true ministers of Christ are ever found on the side of the oppressed, and that the true church of Christ gives no shelter to those who hold their fellow-men in slavery. What! the 'meet motto' of the American Anti-Slavery Society is, '*Let Christianity perish, that the slave may go free!*' Sir, is this *your* motto — 'Let the slave be kept in his chains, that Christianity may live'? Point me to a religion which connives at human degradation and bondage, and I will show you a religion which is from beneath, and not from above. At the very moment you are assuming to vindicate Christianity, you are making it identical with a man-enslaving, soul-destroying religion — the religion of America; and thus are you found among its worst enemies and defamers!

Commenting on the resolution, you say — 'If the decline of religion gives joy to this Society, surely its extinction would excite rapture.'

The decline of what religion? The *Christian* religion? No. *American* religion! Yes. And why? The reason is concisely and strongly given in the resolution: — 'Inasmuch as it voluntarily comes forth to baptize and to sanctify SLAVERY'! It is a religion of whips and chains, of branding-irons and bloodhounds, of pollution and blood, of tyranny and heathenism! Reason enough why the American Anti-Slavery Society, and why all who love God and their fellow-creatures, should rejoice at its decline; for its gradual dissolution is a sure sign that Christianity is abroad in America, demanding liberty for all who are in bonds, and asserting her rightful supremacy over the land! The anti-slavery movement is the great Christian movement of the age, and whatever is hostile to it is 'Infidelity' in the worst sense of that term. You admit that 'the American churches, in this matter, are steeped in guilt' — not sullied, not tainted but *steeped in guilt!* Then, according to your own showing, their religion is vain — they are 'cages of unclean birds.' [9] The Anti-Slavery Society rejoices that they are in a declining state; and for this you call it an 'infidel' body!! I am unable to comprehend either your logic or your morality; but it seems to me that you are clearly condemned out of your own mouth.[10]

As to warning the heathen world against the influence of 'American religion,' this seems to be quite unnecessary. Our missionaries to the Karens [11] have written home, that their vocation is gone; for the Karens, having ascertained that the Americans are a slaveholding and slave trading people, refuse to listen to the teachings of the missionaries, on the ground that if they become Christians, they will be liable to be reduced to slavery! So that, even now, the 'so called heathen' are rising in judgment against the so called Christianity in America!

You inform your readers, that the 'American Anti-Slavery Society is a wise, a noble, a powerful, laborious and efficient confederacy, enjoying the confidence of the mass of the slave's true friends, and meriting that of this country.' This is strictly true. It is my privilege to represent this Society, and to be its presiding officer. Doubtless, you meant to praise the American *and Foreign* Anti-Slavery Society, which was organized by a seceding faction in 1840 to destroy the Parent Society, which has not a single agent in the field, which has no treasury, which exists only in name, a[n]d which is embodied in the person of Mr. Lewis Tappan! [12]

Appealing to you to give this a prompt insertion in the Christian Witness, as an act of simple justice, I remain,[13]

Yours, for truth, liberty and Christianity,

WM. LLOYD GARRISON.

Printed: *The Liberator*, December 4, 1846.

John Campbell (1794–1867), Congregational minister, author of many ecclesiastical works, especially on the subject of missions, and newspaper editor, founded the *Christian Witness* in 1844. Together with the *Christian Penny Magazine* and the *British Banner* (founded in 1846 and 1849 respectively), the paper reflected Campbell's strong opposition to Roman Catholicism, ritual, and rational theology.

In *The Liberator*, December 4, 1846, are printed Campbell's editorial from the October *Christian Witness* to which Garrison refers, Garrison's own letter, Campbell's reply, and a commentary by Edward Search (William Henry Ashurst).

1. Garrison adapts Isaiah 58:6.
2. Garrison adapts Isaiah 18:2.
3. Garrison quotes loosely from William Cowper, *The Task*, Book II, line 17.
4. Garrison paraphrases Mark 13:10, 12, 13.
5. In this paragraph Garrison mingles quotations from the *Book of Common Prayer* (*Te Deum laudamus*), Campbell's editorial, and I Corinthians 4:13.
6. The quotation from Luther has not been identified.
7. The rest of the resolution reads, ". . . especially as being extended by American Board of Commissioners for Foreign Missions, whose definitions and defence of Slavery have proved the depravity of that body to be unparalleled in the history of the nations they are laboring to convert." The resolution was introduced by Parker Pillsbury of New Hampshire; comment by Pillsbury is also included in *The Liberator*, May 22, 1846, in which the resolution is printed.
8. Garrison compresses I Corinthians 13:4, 7.
9. Garrison refers to Revelation 18:2.
10. Garrison refers either to Job 15:6 or Luke 19:22.
11. A race of hill people in Burma, one branch of which, the White Karens, was readily converted to Christianity.
12. Lewis Tappan (1788–1873) was one of the founders of the New York Anti-Slavery Society and the American Anti-Slavery Society. He and his brother Arthur worked with Garrison until they broke with him on the issue of combining other reforms with abolition. Lewis took a leading role in forming the American and Foreign Anti-Slavery Society and became its first treasurer. Especially aware of the international scope of the American cause, he maintained a close relationship with the British and Foreign Anti-Slavery Society and attended the international antislavery convention in London in 1843. Unlike Garrison, he felt that slavery could be abolished within the Union through the cooperation of churches. In 1846, Tappan became treasurer of the new American Missionary Association, which was explicitly committed to the cause of the Negro.
13. Garrison's letter was not printed in the *Christian Witness*.

187

TO GEORGE W. BENSON

Boston, Friday morning, 10, A.M.
Dec. 11th, 1846.

Dear George:

The Garrisonian ranks are filling up. This morning, dear Helen presented me with a new comer into this breathing world, — a daughter, — and the finest babe ever yet born in Boston! [1] Both mother and child are doing well — as I trust you all are at home.

In haste, with loving remembrances,

Wm. Lloyd Garrison.

G. W. Benson.

ALS: Garrison Papers, Boston Public Library.

1. Elizabeth Pease Garrison (1846–1848).

188

TO SAMUEL J. MAY

Boston, Dec. 19, 1846.

My Beloved Friend:

The receipt of your kind letter, welcoming me home again from my foreign mission, was next to the pleasure of taking you by the hand. You see what liberty I ventured to take with a portion of it, in the Liberator, which I thought would be gratifying to many of our friends on both sides of the Atlantic.[1] I hope I committed no breach of confidence.

The first intelligence I have to communicate is, that, on the 10th instant, I completed my 41st year — (shades of the patriarchs, Abraham, Isaac and Jacob! I am getting to be venerable) — and on the next morning, (as a pleasing coincidence, it ought to have been, i.e. might have been, on the same day,) Helen presented me with a darling babe — (the sixth! patriarchal again!) — as fine a one as was ever yet born into this breathing world — yours excepted, of course, "as a matter of politeness" *before folks* — a daughter, too, but not, like Byron's Ada,[2] "*sole* daughter of my *house* and heart,"[3] for two good reasons: — the first is, I have one other daughter — and the second is, though Byron owned a house, I don't, but am a tenant at will. We have given the name of Elizabeth Pease to the new comer, and shall be entirely satisfied if she prove to be as good as her namesake. Helen is very comfortable, except when she attempts to nurse the babe, being somewhat troubled with her breasts. I am always glad to hear of any new accession to the Garrisonian ranks, though there are many in the land who will take no pleasure in the news.

I felt very glad, as did Helen, that Susan [Coffin] was enabled to remain under our roof, and to cheer dear wife with the pleasure of her company, during a considerable portion of my absence abroad. We shall always feel under special obligations to her. She has not yet returned to Scituate, but thinks of doing so in a few days. During the past week, she has been visiting at Dr. Moriarty's, at the North end.[4]

The very day on which I returned home, anticipating my arrival an hour or two, sister Sarah came from New-York and Providence, and conveyed to us the good news that Dr. Doolittle had succeeded in curing the cancerous tumor on her breast, though it was not entirely healed up.[5] Within a few days, it has given her considerable pain, and it is possible she may have to go to New-York again, to consult the Dr. She has exhibited, through all her sufferings, great patience and fortitude, as well as all the other graces which adorn her excellent character. Deeply have we sympathized with her; but, though we are not wholly divested of anxiety on her account, we trust she is out of danger.

All my children are at home, and at present enjoy good health, excepting little Fanny, who is somewhat weak and feeble in constitution. I find such a family to be a considerable drawback on my public usefulness, especially in regard to lecturing and travelling in further-ance of the anti-slavery cause; and it is also a heavy burden on Helen, who has no additional help to that of Ellen. We must do as well as we can, under the circumstances. I would not have the number of our children less; but it is difficult to look after so many, and at the same [time] to discharge the duties of my position as a "leading" abolitionist.

I long to see you, face to face, to talk about the incidents attending my British mission. Now that it is over, it seems to me very much like a pleasant vision of the night — pleasant and dream-like, all except the passage to and from England, which was a reality, beyond all doubt. I shall never get reconciled to the ocean. Though I am fond of agitation, it does not run in that line. Commend me to dry land, to keep an erect attitude and a bold front. I always get thrown, when-ever I attempt to wrestle with the Atlantic: —

"Calm or convulsed, in breeze, or gale, or storm." [6]

You will be pleased to hear, that among the foremost to give me their hearty approval, and to aid me in my mission, were Unitarian friends. I am under great obligations to Francis Bishop, William James, H. Solly, Philip Carpenter, George Harris, and other Unitarian clergymen, and have formed for them a strong personal friendship, which they appear heartily to reciprocate.[7] By a letter just received from my dear friend [Francis] Bishop, he informs me that, since I left, his wife has given birth to a daughter, whom they have named Caroline *Garrison* Bishop.[8] This is an indication of their personal regard for me. James Martineau was absent from Liverpool when I was there, and I did not see him. I was told that he is considerably prejudiced against the true anti-slavery band in this country, and sympathizes with such men as Drs. Dewey and Parkman.[9] I meant to have visited Harriet [Martineau], at Ambleside, before my return; but she left for Egypt, a few days before I sailed, and I missed the coveted opportunity. I saw her mother [Elizabeth] and sister [Elizabeth Greenhow] at Newcastle. Religiously, the Unitarians in England are regarded as little better than infidels; but I found them to be much better than their revilers and persecutors.

Nothing could have been more timely than my mission. No three months of my life were ever spent more profitably to the cause of religious and personal freedom. The blow that was given to the Evangelical Alliance, by our bold, prompt and scathing condemnation of it, was like a thunder-bolt from heaven. If I had not gone to England at that time, there is little doubt that the pro-slavery action of the Alliance would have been winked at by the religious public in Britain, and thus slavery would have secured in its defense the religious sanction of the evangelical portion of Christendom. You have seen, no doubt, the result of the proceedings of British Alliance at Manchester.[10] Slaveholders are declared to be ineligible to a seat in that body. Very much is due to the indefatigable exertions of Henry C. Wright, Frederick Douglass, and George Thompson. I trust we shall have all three of them with us next summer.

Dear Helen and Sarah charge me to give you, and Mrs. May, and Charlotte, their warmest regards and lively remembrances.[11] Their feelings are those of

Your affectionate friend,

Wm. Lloyd Garrison.

Saml. J. May.

☞ I send you, by this mail, your pencil case, enclosed in a newspaper, hoping it will reach you safely. It was left here by Dr. Winship.[12] I also send you, Mary Howitt's sketch of my life, in the People's Journal. The portrait is a bad one.

ALS: Garrison Papers, Boston Public Library; partly printed in *Life*, III, 171–172.

1. May's letter, dated November 26, appears in *The Liberator*, December 4, 1846.
2. Augusta Ada Byron (1815–1852), who married William, first Earl of Lovelace, in 1835.
3. Lord Byron, *Childe Harold's Pilgrimage*, Canto III, stanza 1, line 2.
4. Joseph Moriarity (1812–1847) received his M.D. from Harvard in 1834 and for a time served as hospital physician at Deer Island. He lived at 31 Salem Street, Boston. (*Quinquennial Catalogue of Harvard University, 1636–1915*, Cambridge, 1915, p. 604; obituary in *The Liberator*, December 10, 1847.)
5. According to various New York City directories, this is probably Dr. Adrastus Doolittle, who is listed as a botanic physician with offices at 245 Centre Street.
6. Not identified.
7. Garrison mentions, in addition to the already identified Francis Bishop and William James, two Unitarian ministers, Henry Solly (1813–1903), and Philip Pearsall Carpenter (1819–1877). Solly was a prolific pamphleteer who was greatly interested in establishing working men's colleges. Carpenter, originally a Presbyterian and later an Anglican minister, was a philanthropist and reformer who in his later years became dedicated to the science of conchology. (Letter to the

editor from F. Kenworthy, principal, Unitarian College, Manchester, England, December 10, 1970.)

8. Caroline Garrison Bishop has not been further identified.

9. Orville Dewey (1794–1882) was a Unitarian clergyman and author who held pastorates in many states and was the fourth president of the American Unitarian Association (1845–1847). Since he was a critic of abolitionists and slaveholders alike, he was censured in both North and South.

Francis Parkman (1788–1852) was a graduate of Harvard and Edinburgh. A Unitarian clergyman, he served as pastor of the New North Church in Boston from 1813 to 1849. He taught theology at Harvard and was the author of several religious works.

10. This meeting was of great significance to Garrison, for it proved that victory over the Evangelical Alliance had been won. After the convention adjourned, delegates from each country were to meet to establish branches of the permanent alliance. The British delegates, meeting in Manchester on November 4, resolved almost unanimously to exclude slaveholders, thus returning to the position originally taken by the Birmingham committee. Garrison was slightly dissatisfied with the resolution, since he believed it had been passed less from true antislavery spirit than as the result of the pressure of public opinion. The effect, however, was a victory for his efforts to rouse public sentiment in England against the alliance. That the resolution was passed on the very day Garrison sailed for America, November 4, was a sign that he had closed his English tour in triumph. (*The Liberator*, December 11, 1846.)

11. Garrison refers to Charlotte G. Coffin (1809–1889), the sister of Mrs. Samuel J. May, Lucretia Flagge Coffin. (Letter to the editor from Jonathan Prude, researcher, September 1970.)

12. Garrison misspells the name of Charles William Windship (1773–1852), a graduate of Harvard with an M.D. from Glasgow, who lived in Roxbury and practiced medicine in Boston for many years. (Boston City directories; *Quinquennial Catalogue of Harvard University, 1636–1895*, Cambridge, 1895.)

IV WESTERN MISSION: 1847

URING THE FIRST HALF OF 1847 Garrison's life returned to normal. He resumed his regular editorial work, gave occasional public lectures on abolition, on peace, on various political topics, especially the Mexican War and disunion. He spoke at the annual meetings of both the Massachusetts and the national antislavery societies. The events of 1847 crucial to him came later in the year.

Up to 1847 Garrison's influence as an abolitionist extended along the eastern coast and farther east to Great Britain. The western United States had been left to moderate abolitionists, like Theodore D. Weld, though Garrison had been involved in the spring of 1843 with plans to abolitionize that area. At the New England antislavery convention that year one hundred conventions were planned for the country west of the Hudson. Garrisonians, under the leadership of John A. Collins and Frederick Douglass, proceeded to hold meetings in towns throughout central and western New York, Ohio, Indiana, and western Pennsylvania, but Garrison himself stayed in the East.

In 1847, however, Garrison became more directly involved with the western antislavery movement. He explained in a brief editorial in *The Liberator*, March 19, 1847, that he had long planned to lecture in the West, though his tour had been postponed by the recent mission to England. August, he said, would be the time for him to go west. By the middle of July plans were complete: first, he would attend the meeting of the Eastern Pennsylvania Anti-Slavery Society in Philadelphia; then, accompanied by Frederick Douglass, he would go to Harrisburg, to Pittsburgh, and on to Ohio.

Douglass, former slave turned eloquent abolitionist, had returned in April 1847 from a strikingly successful British tour, where he and Garrison had often appeared on the same platform. He was without doubt one of the most effective orators in the cause. Garrison thought him an ideal choice for colleague on this new tour.

The trip west can be followed in detail by readers of Garrison's letters. It started on schedule and proceeded with relatively few untoward incidents through western Pennsylvania and into Ohio, where Douglass and Garrison were joined by Stephen S. Foster. But the pace was fast and the opportunities for rest infrequent, and both Douglass and Garrison grew tired. By the time they reached Cleveland, Garrison was so exhausted that he became seriously ill with a high fever. For five weeks he lay in bed, too sick even to write letters to his wife. In the middle of October Henry C. Wright, just returned from England, appeared in Cleveland like a ministering angel, determined to take his good friend home to Boston. On the twenty-first they started the long journey; on the twenty-seventh Garrison was reunited with his family at 13 Pine Street.

Still weak from his long and serious illness in Ohio, Garrison recuperated during the last two months of 1847, while Quincy generously continued to edit *The Liberator*. Since the abolition movement generated at that time no crisis that demanded Garrison's attention, he spent his days at home with his family and talked with friends and associates. He did venture to speak briefly at a nonresistance meeting December 28, and he and Wright planned exciting events for the early months of 1848.

189

TO LOUISA GILMAN LORING

13, Pine Street,
Jan. 7, 1847.

My dear Mrs. Loring:

All that I can offer you, in return for your generous new year's token of friendship, are my poor thanks, and my heart-felt desires for your continual happiness and prosperity. I do not doubt the declaration of the Great Philanthropist, that "it is more blessed to give than to receive"; [1] and as I experience much pleasure in being the recipient of your kindness, yours must be greater, of course, in the bestowment of it — which thought greatly increases my own satisfaction.

You and your beloved husband [Ellis Gray Loring] have done much, for a long series of years, to strengthen my hands and encourage my heart in the prosecution of that sacred cause, which, though entitled to universal homage, has had to struggle against the most formidable opposition, and is still far from being popular. However, it must be as consoling to you, as it is to me, to know that a mighty change has been wrought in public sentiment, in favor of our imbruted countrymen, since we first became acquainted with each other. This revolution cannot go backward; for it is animated by the spirit of universal humanity, and sustained by the power of God. Great events are now in embryo, to which the present year will doubtless give birth, all tending to the overthrow of slavery, and the deliverance of those who are spoiled, out of the hands of the oppressor.[2] We have only to continue in the faithful discharge of the duties that may devolve upon us, serene in the midst of popular commotion, strong in the righteousness of our cause, and confident in the ultimate triumph of Right over Wrong.

I would improve this opportunity to return my grateful acknowledgements to Mr. Loring, for his donation in aid of my late mission to Great Britain — a mission already crowned with remarkable success, and which will constitute an important era in our anti-slavery history. I could not have crossed the Atlantic at a period more opportune; and never did I labor with so much success, in the same space of time.

Please give my warmest regards to Mr. Loring, in whose confinement I have deeply sympathized, though I have failed to see him since my return home. I will call in a day or two, hoping to find him much improved in health, and to have the pleasure of an interview with you both.

Mrs. Garrison desires to be gratefully and affectionately remembered to you and Mr. Loring. She and the babe are getting along very comfortably.

Your much obliged friend,

Wm. Lloyd Garrison.

ALS: Ellis Gray Loring Family Papers, Radcliffe College Library; a handwritten transcription of this letter is to be found in the Garrison Papers, Boston Public Library.

1. Acts 20:35.
2. An adaptation of Jeremiah 21:12 or 22:3.

190

TO ANNE W. WESTON

Boston, Feb. 23, 1847.

My Dear Friend:

It has suddenly occurred to me, this morning, that I am under an engagement to be in Weymouth, somewhere about the 1st of March

— on a Sunday. I sincerely hope it is not next Sunday. If it is, and if you have not made any positive engagement for me, I hope you will make none; or, if you have made any, pray get it deferred, if you can, for one week. My reason for making this request is, the steamer is to sail for Liverpool on Monday, and I want all day Saturday and Sunday to be scribbling letters to friends in England, Scotland and Ireland. On Thursday and Friday, I have got to sit for my portrait, as well as to attend to other matters.[1] Of course, if you have so committed me that I *must* come, why, then I will come. But I put myself in your hands, to dispose of me as you think proper, under these circumstances. I hope I shall be excused for one week.

I know not whether you are at home, or at New Bedford; nor is Mrs. [Maria W.] Chapman able to inform me. If you are absent, I will thank any of the family to send me a line by return of mail.

Ever yours, faithfully,

Wm. Lloyd Garrison.

Anne W. Weston.

ALS: Garrison Papers, Boston Public Library.

1. It is uncertain to what portrait Garrison refers. Among the known likenesses the closest in date is the daguerreotype taken in Dublin in October 1846.

191

TO RICHARD D. WEBB

Boston, March 1, 1847.

My dear Richard:

This is the first day of Spring, according to the calendar, but we have plenty of snow in the city, and the sleigh-bells are merrily jingling in all directions. I wish you were here, with Hannah and the children, and all the other Webbs, (the [James] Haughtons and [Richard] Allens inclusive, of course,) just at this time, to take a sleigh-ride with me, my wife, and six children, in one of our magnificent sleighs, drawn by some dozen horses, more or less. Wouldn't we create a sensation in the city? Wouldn't we "astonish the natyves" [1] in the suburbs? Wouldn't we mount to the top of Bunker Hill, (no great elevation, by the way,) and scour the revolutionary plains of Concord and Lexington, and see how much ice Wenham lake [2] can contain without bursting, and drive to Dorchester heights, where Washington marshalled his forces, and finally go whirling down to Lynn, where James N. Buffum resides, and, having taken him with his "facts" [3] on board, finish off by a jaunt along Lynn beach to famous

Nahant, — the resort of all who can get to it, and who have any taste for the sublime and beautiful. Or, we might go a few miles further, to my dear native place, Newburyport, where you should all be shown "the house where I was born," [4] the bones of Whitefield, the celebrated preacher, within a few steps of that house, and whatever else the place affords.[5] But the snow will soon be gone, and you are not here, and we shall lose that ride, and I am sorry. Your Daguerreotype likeness is before me, and it gives me great comfort. It is amazingly like you, only it does not talk audibly, and it is idle to ask it to take any thing to eat or drink at my table. I have the ability to talk to *it*, but what is the use of talking where one gets no response? I would much rather that the original were under my roof, but I place a high value on this imitation. If you were not a truly diffident man, I would tell you that the picture is very much liked by your unseen and personally unknown friends, who visit me from time to time; and all the others in my possession excite a great deal of interest and pleasure.

Only think of it! More than a third of a year has vanished since I was by your fireside, and pacing up and down the streets of Dublin with you! Pray, don't grow old, if you can help it. I defy your Daguerreotype to do so. "Time writes no wrinkles" on that.[6] The inanimate part, which I have of you, and that is but half of you, is at least secure. Luckily, that monster Time cannot take either of us by the fore-lock, because we are so bald; and therein we have the advantage of him, as he is said to have one, which let us seize as opportunity shall offer. Speaking of portraits, let me tell you that I have spoken to Mrs. [Maria W.] Chapman, to have hers taken for you; and she is willing to do so. You shall have it, ere long; and I mean to procure for you, also, one of Wendell Phillips, another of Edmund Quincy, another of Francis Jackson, another of Abby Kelley Foster, &c. There — what do you say to that? This is not to make faces at you, but for you. I do not mean to be denied — that is, outfaced — by any of those whom I have named. It is no light affair — and yet the light has every thing to do with it. James N. Buffum showed me a capital Daguerreotype of himself, intended for you, which I believe he has forwarded. "Hold! enough!" [7] you will exclaim; but where there are so many suggestive *heads*, it is difficult to bring the discourse to a close.

To more serious matters. As you regularly receive the Standard and Liberator, I deem it unnecessary to say much here, in regard to our anti-slavery doings. We realized from the Bazaar about a thousand dollars more than we did last year. This, on the whole, was an increase greater than we had any good reason to expect. Remember that we are the "forlorn hope" of the anti-slavery movement, and that we are in constant collision with all the religious sects and political parties. Our "Disunion" ground terrifies many, and offends more. There is no transcending it for the overthrow of slavery, and to occupy it requires a good deal of nerve. But it is invulnerable, and must ultimately be occupied by all the non-slaveholding States. A very considerable number of petitions, praying for the secession of Massachusetts from the Union, has already been presented to our Legislature, numerously signed by legal voters. This is encouraging; but a revolution so great, and involving such momentous consequences, is not hastily to be wrought out. We must "bide our time," and labour on diligently for the result. There is no other question so universally discussed as that of slavery, and within the last six months a most surprising change in public sentiment has undeniably taken place. The cowardly pro-slavery war which our national administration is waging with Mexico is producing a mighty reaction against the Slave Power, and, out of the slave States, is generally regarded with abhorrence. Mr. [John C.] Calhoun, who is the Napoleon of slavery, is evidently anticipating a "Waterloo defeat," in due season. You will see his speech in the last number of the Liberator.[8] He does not attempt to hide his fears as to the future. Unless slave States can be added to the Union as fast as free States, his cherished system of diabolism must ultimately be overturned. Mark his language. He is a man who means what he says, and who never blusters. He is no demagogue, but proud, incorrigible, merciless tyrant, though he expresses the hope that he is a kind master! Nicholas of Russia [9] would as complacently express the same hope.

The horrid particulars of the famine in Ireland have made a wide and profound sensation in this country. Contributions are pouring in from every quarter, and the amount of food, money and clothing, that will be contributed, will be very considerable; yet not a fiftieth part that ought to be done. But we must recollect that the idea of human brotherhood is as yet but very imperfectly developed in the world, and that, hitherto, each nation has left other nations to take care of themselves, without being specially concerned for their welfare. Still, enough will be given to save many thousands from starving, and to strengthen the ties of humanity, to the disregard of the selfish feelings of nationality. Boston, I trust, will not be outdone by any other place in the country.

Nantucket, which, eight months ago, was almost wholly destroyed by fire, (property to the amount of £200,000 having been consumed,) [10] in what the apostle calls "the abundance of its poverty," [11] has generously contributed $2200, or nearly £500 to the relief of your famished countrymen. Francis Jackson will transmit to you

£250, contributed by our anti-slavery friends, chiefly if not exclusively of the "old organization" stamp; but this is only a very small portion of what will be contributed by others, of the same stamp, whose gifts will be conveyed in various channels, indiscriminately, along with those of other citizens.

And now I have just begun, I must stop. With the most endearing remembrances to Hannah, and the whole circle of beloved ones in Dublin, I remain, with an overflowing heart,

Yours, faithfully,

Wm. Lloyd Garrison.

☞ Edmund Quincy desires me to give you his friendly salutations, and to make confession of epistolary delinquency on his part. He will send you a good long letter by the next steamer. He has been very busy with his Annual Report.[12]

☞ I am sorry to learn, by a letter from Mary Brady of Sheffield, that dear H. C. Wright was quite ill at her house. I trust his health is again fully restored. Should he happen to be with you, give him my loving regards.

☞ On the 11th of December, my dear Helen presented me with a charming babe, a girl, whom we have named Elizabeth Pease.

ALS: Garrison Papers, Boston Public Library; extract printed in *Life*, III, 217.

1. Not identified.
2. In Wenham, Massachusetts, a town about twenty miles northeast of Boston, the lake being an important source of ice for the Boston area.
3. Presumably a reference to Buffum's predeliction for facts and statistics.
4. Thomas Hood, "I Remember, I Remember," stanza 1, line 2.
5. George Whitefield (1715–1770) was an English evangelist, author, and pamphleteer, who first came to America in 1739. Preaching throughout New England, he was largely responsible for the "Great Awakening" in religious activity which occurred at that time. In all he made six journeys to the United States and is buried in Newburyport, Massachusetts, near the house in which Garrison was born. (*Who Was Who in America*.)
6. Garrison quotes Lord Byron, *Childe Harold's Pilgrimage*, Canto IV, stanza 182, line 8, adding an "s" to "wrinkle."
7. Shakespeare, *Macbeth*, V, viii, 34.
8. Calhoun's speech, printed in *The Liberator*, February 26, 1847, proposes that new states, at the time of their admission to the Union, should not have to declare themselves either slave or free.
9. The autocratic Nicholas I (1796–1855).
10. The fire in Nantucket was reported in *The Liberator*, July 24, 1846. A large portion of the business district, nearly four hundred buildings in all, was destroyed, and total losses were estimated at from $900,000 to $1,000,000. Although no lives were lost, several persons were injured and many lost their homes.
11. A reference to Luke 21:3–4.
12. Garrison probably refers to a report Quincy was preparing for the Norfolk County Anti-Slavery Society, of which he was president.

192

TO HENRY C. WRIGHT

Boston, March 1, 1847.

My dear Henry:

A letter from that excellent woman, Mary Brady, brings us the distressing intelligence of your illness at her house; though we are comforted by her assurance, that you seemed to be improving. You labor too abundantly, and are attempting to do too much; and, unless you restrain yourself far more than you have hitherto done, I am afraid you will suddenly break down beyond recovery. By the next steamer, I hope to receive a line from you, announce[ing] your complete restoration.

On returning home, I found I had gained six pounds of flesh — six pounds beyond what I had ever weighed before — notwithstanding all the fatigues and labours of my transatlantic tour. The climate of Old England is much more congenial to me than that of New England. It affects my voice and lungs much more to give one lecture here, than it did to deliver half a dozen abroad. At present, we are all in the enjoyment of health at home. The little babe, which was born unto us on the 11th of Dec. last, and to whom we have given the cherished name of Elizabeth Pease, is a fine little girl, and in a thriving condition. The father of four boys and two girls! think of that! Verily, Garrisonians are multiplying in this pro-slavery land.

I had hoped to write to dear E. Pease by this conveyance, but I have had to scribble so many letters to others, that my time is consumed. I write to you, crowded up to a few moments, and so shall not be able to say the hundredth part of what it is in my heart to utter. When you write to Elizabeth, assure her of my continual remembrance of her. She knows what a sadly delinquent correspondent I am at all times. I hope to hear that she is steadily gaining in health and strength.

I see it announced in the London Non-conformist, that you, and Frederick [Douglass], and dear George Thompson, contemplate coming to this country in May next. Is it so? The intelligence seems too good to be true. But a hearty reception awaits each and all of you, whenever you shall come — the sooner, the better, unless the exigencies of our cause abroad require still further delay. The Board of Managers of the Massachusetts Anti-Slavery Society, and the Executive Committee of the American Society, have unanimously voted to pay all the expenses that our friend Thompson may occur, in case he shall visit us, which it is earnestly hoped he will not fail to do at no distant day. Bring him with you on your return; and, if E. P. be well enough, try to induce her to come over at the same time. She ought to see the new world, and to give the friends of humanity here a chance to express their regard for her personally.

Let me know by the next steamer, if you can, *definitely*, as to the time you and Frederick think of returning. We ought to be apprised beforehand, in order to be prepared to give you an official reception. If you could arrive here in season to attend our New-England Convention, (and in order to do this, you would have to embark in the steamer of the 4th of May,) it would be highly gratifying, and most timely. But when we parted, you spoke of August as being the month in which you expected to return.

I presume all your family are well, as I hear nothing to the contrary. The same may be said of Frederick's family. I am sorry that I have no time to send him a letter by the Cambria. Heaven bless and sustain him in all his labours.

My dear Thompson must also be cheated out of a long epistle that is due to him. I wrote to him a letter of sympathy, as soon as you communicated to me the painful tidings of the death of his charming little girl; but I have received no reply, as yet, and am not sure that he got my letter.

I see that Henry Clapp is endeavouring to make use of our old organization friends abroad, that he spoke at the meeting of the Glasgow Emancipation Society, and that he was to address the people of that city again on the subject of slavery.[1] He is a wily creature, with considerable talent, but not to be trusted or encouraged. No one is more bitterly opposed to us than he is, in design and spirit.

We are making decided progress in our Disunion movement. Our Legislature, now in session, has before it many petitions, numerously signed by legal voters, asking that body to take measures for the peaceable secession of Massachusetts from the Union. We are surprised to find how many are prepared for this measure.

In Congress, at its present session, the subject of slavery, in connexion with our nefarious war with Mexico, has been the chief topic of discussion; and in the House of Representatives, the Slave Power has been defeated by a majority of ten votes, on a measure vital to its existence. By the Wilmot proviso, no slavery is to be allowed in any new territory that may be annexed to the Union.[2] In the Senate, that proviso will be voted down, of course, because there is a majority of slaveholding Senators in that body; but the triumph in the House is most unexpected, and demonstrates that anti-slavery is marching forward with irresistible power. "Read, mark, learn, and inwardly digest"[3] the speech of John C. Calhoun, in the Senate on this subject, as contained in the last Liberator. The Napoleon of slavery is anticipating a Waterloo in the future, and at no distant day.

Helen sends much sympathy and love to you, as well as many of your other friends. Accompanying this, is a letter for you from our indefatigable coadjutor Stephen S. Foster. Love to every body.

Ever yours,

Wm. Lloyd Garrison.

ALS: Garrison Papers, Boston Public Library.

1. *The Liberator* makes no mention of Clapp's appearance at the Glasgow Emancipation Society meeting. There is, however, a reference to another of his speeches which perhaps relates to his making "use of our old organization friends abroad." In *The Liberator*, February 26, 1847, a letter from Francis Bishop to Garrison appears, dated December 1846, Exeter (Devonshire), stating, "Henry Clapp lectured on American slavery at our Athenaeum in Exeter, on Saturday last."

2. Representative David Wilmot of Pennsylvania and some of his associates feared that the Mexican War would result in the annexation of territory in the southwest and an increase in the number of slaveholding states. Therefore, when President Polk requested $2,000,000 with which to make peace, Wilmot, with the support of Jacob Brinkerhoff of Ohio, decided to offer a proviso which would prohibit the establishment of slavery in any territory thus acquired. After a conference of northern Democrats, Wilmot rephrased his proviso and introduced it in Congress. The House passed the measure, but, as Garrison prophesied, the Senate did not. However, the proviso was finally enacted, on June 19, 1862, and slavery in the territories was forbidden.

3. From the *Book of Common Prayer*, the Collect for the Second Sunday in Advent.

193

TO ELIZABETH PEASE

Boston, April 1, 1847.

Beloved Friend:

Knowing how delicate and fluctuating is the state of your health, and therefore what a task it must be to you to attempt to carry on any epistolary correspondence, I feel under the most grateful obligations to you for your long and interesting letter, received by the last Liverpool steamer. It will be a poor return I shall make by the steamer which is to leave this port this forenoon, though I had hoped to send you an epistle as long as your own; but, in consequence of some exposure and too much public lecturing, I have been quite sick for the last three or four days, — the very time I purposed to give to my friends on the other side of the Atlantic, who are perhaps more constantly in my memory, than if they were only thirty miles, instead of being three thousand, from me. So vivid are my recollections of my late visit, — so much do I live in the spirit-world, — that at times I find it difficult to persuade myself that I am not still with you all, even in body as well as in mind. As for your own dear domicil at Feethams, it seems as if at any moment I could knock at your door, walk into the parlor, take you by the hand, and enter into social conversation with you.

On the 11th of December last, an addition was made to our group of children, (making half a dozen complete,) of a dear little girl, to whom we felt it to be both an honour and a privilege to give the name of Elizabeth Pease. I immediately sent the intelligence to George Thompson, (not having time to write to you by that conveyance,) supposing he would communicate it to you; but you appear to have first obtained it from Wendell and Ann Phillips. We have felt the more gratified in giving your cherished name to our dear babe, since we have received the afflicting tidings of the death of dear Thompson's charming little girl, whose loss I felt like a personal bereavement; for I became exceedingly attached to her during my visit to Chelsea. Our babe is really a beautiful one, and thrives finely. The boys are extravagantly fond of her, as well as little Fanny. I told them that I would put her name into rhyme to the extent of the English language, or as far [as] I could make a tolerably good jingle; and to show you how well I succeeded in this childish effort, I send you (at their request) the following: —

LIZZY PEASE

There sits mother at her ease,
With her baby, Lizzy Pease,
Lying softly on her knees. —
Kiss the darling, if you please —
Her lips are "like wine on the lees" — [1]
But be careful not to tease,
Though she'll bear a gentle squeeze. —
Hark! she is humming like the bees —
Like the lullaby of seas —
Like a music-laden breeze,
Making all the forest trees
Join in chorusses and glees! —
Milk from the breast with her agrees,
But not either bread or cheese.
Keep her warm, else she may freeze,
Or take a sudden cold, and sneeze,
And day and night shall cough and wheeze,
Till her little spirit flees,
(By the tyrant Death's decrees,
Who is never cheated of his fees,)
To where St. Peter turns the keys!

With your letter came one from H. C. Wright, announcing that he was on the recovery. Occasionally, I feel apprehensive lest he may never be permitted to return home. His case seems to be a peculiar one, and it is evident that he will have need of all the caution he and his friends can summon to save him from a premature grave. A life so valuable should be preserved to the latest period, consistent with the discharge of duties absolutely imperative.

[Frederick] Douglass, I see, is to return home in the Cambria on the 4th inst. This is somewhat earlier than he anticipated when I left him. Knowing how much still remains to be done for our cause abroad, I am sorry to have him leave; and then, seeing how mighty is the struggle going on at home, and how very few faithful and able lecturers we have in the field, I am rejoiced (as are his numerous friends) at the prospect of soon taking him by the hand. He will be warmly welcomed by the abolitionists, and, doubtless, more kindly regarded by people generally, in consequence of the generous and honorable reception given him in Great Britain. You will see, by the Liberator, that a few individuals here are loudly protesting against his ransom by the English friends, as though it were a violation of principle.[2] I can conceive of a wide difference of opinion honestly existing as to the expediency or necessity of the ransom; but when any attempt to affix a moral stigma to the deed, I am very much surprised at their conduct. Never have I entertained the opinion, for a moment, that it is wrong to ransom one held in cruel captivity; though I have always maintained, in the case of the slave, that the demand of the slaveholder for compensation was an unjust one. But I see no discrepancy in saying that a certain demand is unjust, and yet being willing to submit to it, in order to save a brother man, if this is clearly made to be the only alternative left to me.

This country is still prosecuting its murderous warfare against Mexico; but though the American forces have generally been victorious, recently the tide of events appears to be setting in favour of the Mexicans, and confirming the scriptural declaration, that "the race is not to the swift, nor the battle to the strong."[3] We have rumors, to-day, of a bloody engagement having taken place, with great loss on both sides, — General Taylor having been compelled to fall back on Monterey, with the loss of many of his officers.[4] I desire to see human life at all times held sacred; but, in a struggle like this, — so horribly unjust and offensive on our part, so purely one of self-defence against lawless invaders on the part of the Mexicans, — I feel, as a matter of justice, to desire the overwhelming defeat of the American troops, and the success of the injured Mexicans.

The distress in Ireland continues to excite much sympathy here, and contributions in money and food are daily made in all parts of the country. These will arrive too late to save thousands, now beyond all human aid; but they will prevent other thousands from dying of hunger. It is a singular spectacle we are now presenting to the world — with one hand, we are carrying desolation and death into a neighboring republic, and with the other supplying food and clothing to save from suffering and death, those who reside across the wide Atlantic.

Our Boston "clique," as poor [Nathaniel P.] Rogers used to bitterly call us, are all as well and as busy as usual. You are much in our remembrance; and we are cherishing the hope, however faintly, that we may yet see you in Boston. As I have not time to finish, so I have not tried to commence a letter to you; but I hope to send you a full answer to yours by the next steamer. Please give my affectionate remembrances to Mary Martin, and my regards to your brother [John Pease] and his wife. Helen cordially sends her love, and wishes you could a glance at her babe, with its sweet face and mild blue eyes.

Hastily, but truly, yours,

Wm. Lloyd Garrison.

ALS: Garrison Papers, Boston Public Library; a handwritten transcription of an extract is to be found in the Villard Papers, Harvard College Library.

1. Isaiah 25:6.
2. Garrison refers to the effort initiated by a Mrs. Richardson of Newcastle, England, to raise sufficient funds (about $750) to buy Douglass' freedom from his former master. The action excited great controversy in the United States. (See *The Liberator*, January 15, 29, March 5, 19, 1847.)
3. Ecclesiastes 9:11.
4. Zachary Taylor (1784–1850), twelfth president of the United States, pursued a military career for forty years. As commander of the Army of the Rio Grande, he was a leading force in the Mexican War. Garrison refers here to Taylor's attack on Monterey, when, after three days of fighting, the Mexican army capitulated and a lenient eight weeks' armistice was drawn up. This treaty was unacceptable to President Polk, who ordered hostilities with the Mexicans resumed.

194

TO *THE LIBERATOR*

NEW-YORK, [May] 11, 1847.[1]

MY DEAR FRIEND:

Our anniversary meeting has just closed. It was attended by a large throng of highly intelligent and reflecting persons, and the proceedings were of the most satisfactory and inspiring character. I am satisfied that an unusually powerful impression was made on the minds of those present. The attention they gave to the various speakers was deep and earnest, and they frequently responded in bursts of enthusiastic approval to the bold and stirring sentiments that were uttered. Occasionally, a few hisses could be heard from some evil spirits who were tormented just at the right time, but their opposition was very feeble, and only served to bring out all the better feelings of the audience in loud and protracted applause. The result has clearly demonstrated a wonderful change in public sentiment, especially in this city, within a comparatively short period. To-day, on our platform, doctrines were maintained, and sentiments advanced, in regard to Church and State, the Union and the Constitution, not only without uproar, but with strong approval, that would have subjected us to great peril, if they had been uttered a few years since. As sure as the sun shines, or water rolls, or the grass is growing, our anti-slavery leaven is fermenting the whole lump of society. God is with us, and never working more diligently for us, than when the clouds are the thickest, and the prospect most dubious. At the commencement of the meeting, I read portions of the 2d and 18th chapters of Jeremiah, which seemed to me singularly applicable to the history and career of this country — its deliverance from colonial vassalage, its subsequent forgetfulness of God, its grievous wandering from the path of justice, its worship of the Moloch of slavery, its liability to divine retribution. Our beloved and unswerving friend SAMUEL MAY, Jr., formerly of Leicester, but now of Brooklyn, Ct., followed in a devout and earnest prayer for guidance, strength, and victory over the dark spirit of oppression.[2] Mr. [Sydney H.] Gay, the editor of the Standard, then read a brief but gratifying report of the state of our cause and the action of the Society during the year. Francis Jackson, Treasurer, then read his report, by which it appears that the income and expenditures of the Society, since the last anniversary, have been nearly NINE THOUSAND DOLLARS, leaving a balance in the treasury of two hundred dollars. Wendell Phillips then offered the following resolution:

Resolved, That the duty of every American is to give his sympathy and aid to the anti-slavery movement; and the first duty of every citizen is to devote himself to the destruction of the Union and the Constitution, which have already shipwrecked the experiment of civil liberty, and bid fair to swallow up the hopes of every honest man in a worse than military despotism; assured that out of the wreck, we may confidently expect a State which will unfold, in noble proportions, the principles of the Declaration of Independence, whose promises made us once the admiration of the world.

This resolution was advocated by Mr. Phillips with that earnestness, boldness and eloquence, which mark him as the JAMES OTIS of the new revolution for liberty.[3] It had many passages of great power, which went through the vast assembly with electric effect.

The platform was next taken by Frederick Douglass, after I had made some introductory statements respecting his mission to England, his treatment on board of the Cambria, and the indignation of the British press universally, in relation to his exclusion from the cabin of that vessel.[4] I read the withering comments of the London Times on that disgraceful transaction, as a sample of English feeling respecting the American prejudice against a dark complexion. There were some in the audience, who plainly indicated that it caused their democratic ears to tingle. But when I announced the cheering sequel of this affair, that henceforth there is to be no proscription on account of color on board of the Cunard line, the pleasure that was exhibited by the audience, and the applause that followed, were worthy of a strictly British assembly.

The following is the resolution which was sustained by Douglass:

Resolved, That slavery is a system so demoralizing and inhuman, so impious and atheistical, so hostile to the cause of liberty and Christianity throughout the world, that to seek its immediate extinction in this and every other country where it is tolerated, is the right and the duty of the people of all nations, by all proper instrumentalities: — That this Society, as the representative of three millions of American slaves, proffers its grateful acknowledgments to the Christians and philanthropists of England, Scotland, Ireland and Wales, for the powerful testimonies that they have borne against the sin of slaveholding, under all circumstances, and especially in a land boasting of its civil and religious liberty — for their warm approval of the anti-slavery movement in the United States, and those who are its unflinching advocates — and for the charitable aid they have extended to us, in various ways, from time to time; assuring them that they have neither labored nor spoken in vain, and invoking them to continue their co-operative efforts, until the last slave on the American soil is set free.

Douglass was eminently successful in his speech, and was warmly applauded from beginning to end.

The meeting began at 10, and terminated at 1 o'clock, on the topmost wave of popular gratification. I regret that our stanch friend from the West, James W. Walker, had no opportunity, for lack of time, to address the assembly, but he will speak this evening at the Apollo Saloon.[5] We have quite a number of our truest friends brought together from various parts of the country, and I have no doubt our subsequent meetings will be highly interesting and edifying.

To-morrow evening, our colored friends in this city will give Douglass a grand reception meeting.

In haste, but with renovated spirit,

    Faithfully yours,

                                          WM. LLOYD GARRISON.

Printed: *The Liberator*, May 14, 1847.

1. In the printed version this letter is misdated "April 11"; in fact the annual meeting of the American Anti-Slavery Society is known to have occurred on May 11 (see the proceedings of the meeting, *The Liberator*, May 21, 1847).

2. Samuel May, Jr. (1810–1899), the cousin of Samuel J. May, was Garrison's lifelong friend and supporter. A Harvard graduate and Unitarian clergyman, he later became disillusioned with organized religion. In 1847 he became general agent of the Massachusetts Anti-Slavery Society and in 1848 was to join in signing the call for an anti-Sabbath convention. (*Life.*)

3. James Otis (1725–1783), the vehement Massachusetts publicist, politician, and Revolutionary leader, was one of Garrison's idols.

4. Douglass, owing to the prejudice of American passengers, had been excluded from the first-class berth he had paid for in advance, though he was finally allowed passage provided he remain in his cabin for the duration of the voyage. (See *The Liberator*, April 30, 1847, for Douglass' letter on the subject.) Garrison reprinted editorials from the *Times* and some eighteen other British papers in *The Liberator*, May 14, 1847. The *Times* said: "We, therefore, do not refrain from expressing our most intense disgust at the conduct of the agents of the *Cambria*, in having succumbed to a miserable and unmeaning assumption of skin-deep superiority by the American portion of their passengers." The whole controversy culminated in a letter from Mr. Cunard, proprietor of the steamship line, guaranteeing that in the future there would be no prejudice against the color of passengers on his ships.

5. James W. Walker of Leesburg, Ohio, was a lecturing agent for the Western Anti-Slavery Society. He was to speak at the meeting of the American Anti-Slavery Society, which convened at the Apollo Saloon (sometimes called the Apollo Rooms) on May 11. (*Life.*)

195

TO SYDNEY HOWARD GAY

[May] 15, 1847.

My Dear Gay:

Before leaving, I intended to request you to send me, in slips, as soon as printed, the official proceedings of the Am. A. S. Society, at its late meetings, so that I can insert them in the next Liberator. Please do so by the mail that leaves on Monday afternoon, if practicable, and I will reciprocate the favor in sending you the proceedings of the New-England Convention, in season for the Standard to publish them simultaneously with the Liberator.[1] Please, also, to request my friend Oliver Johnson to send me a copy of the Tribune, containing the

Tabernacle speech of Douglass, immediately; for if he has already done so, it has not come to hand.[2]

Yours, faithfully,

Wm. Lloyd Garrison.

S. H. Gay

ALS: Sydney Howard Gay Papers, Columbia University Libraries. The correct month is written on the manuscript in a hand other than Garrison's.

1. The annual New England Anti-Slavery Convention was held at Marlboro Chapel in Boston, May 25–27, 1847. The proceedings are reported in *The Liberator*, June 4, and in the *National Anti-Slavery Standard*, June 3, 1847.

2. Frederick Douglass spoke at the anniversary meeting of the American Anti-Slavery Society on May 11, 1847, describing and defending his conduct during his recent trip to England. His speech was printed in the New York (daily) *Tribune*, May 13.

196

TO HEMAN HUMPHREY

[Boston, June 15, 1847.]

Sir —

I give you all your clerical, divine, and official titles, though I have no respect for them whatever; and, what I regret to be compelled to add, none for yourself personally. I do not mean to be disrespectful, but I must be frank, explicit, truthful.

I have been aware that, for several weeks past, you have been in Boston and its vicinity, lecturing in various pulpits in behalf of a scheme of expatriation, which, in view of its origin, design, principles, measures, and tendencies, stands without a rival on the score of hypocrisy, villany, and impiety. Circumstances, however, prevented my hearing your discourse until Sunday evening last, at the old South church. That discourse has supplied me with several texts, from which I intend to preach as many sermons; and I feel fully qualified and commissioned to do so, though no priestly hands have ever been laid upon my head, and I have yet to receive the forms of ordination.

Do not suppose, for one moment, that I regard your agency as likely to result in making the nefarious scheme which it is designed to promote, successful and popular in this Commonwealth, in New-England, in any portion of the free States. You are too late in the field to be formidable. Within the last fifteen years, one of those revolutions which never go backward has taken place — a revolution in public sentiment at the North, which has almost obliterated from the memory of the people, even the existence of the American Colonization Society.

Whatever may be your talents and attainments, your zeal or perseverance, you can do nothing more than to give to the dead carcass spasmodic action, just so long as you apply to it your galvanic battery; but it is not within human ability to create life, or raise the dead. Years have elapsed since the Society which you so faithfully represent was sent reeling to an infamous grave. The thunderbolt which smote it with deadly effect was forged out of its own materials, and the indignant protestations of the free colored population of the country. In 1832, I gave to the world my 'THOUGHTS ON AFRICAN COLONIZATION,' — a work which almost immediately arrested the popularity of the scheme, and ere long alienated from it thousands of its most disinterested and efficient supporters, who had grossly misapprehended its real character and design; and which has ever since rested upon it like a fallen avalanche.[1] All this I affirm without vanity. It was neither strength of intellect nor skill in controversy, on my part, that accomplished the deed. My work was potent and irresistible, solely because every charge in it was DEMONSTRATED to be true, by an overwhelming mass of evidence extracted, not from what the opponents of the Colonization Society had written against it, not from any anti-slavery documents, but from the official organs and reports of the Society itself, and its auxiliaries. *That work no man has been able to invalidate or answer.* He who can disprove its statements must first be able to disprove the existence of slavery, the formation of any such body as the American Colonization Society, the publication of such a work as the African Repository, the authenticity of every Report purporting to have emanated from the Colonization Board of Managers at Washington.[2] He must do more than this. He must show that all the declarations and remonstrances of the free people of color against the doctrines and operations of the Society, which are recorded in my work, are bold forgeries, and diametrically opposite to the well known views of that persecuted class. My charges were the following, each one of which is vital, and all of which were proved, beyond refutation or doubt: —

I. The American Colonization Society is pledged not to oppose the system of slavery.

II. It apologizes for slavery, and justifies slave-holders.

III. It recognizes slaves as legitimate property — as sacred as any other.

IV. It increases the value of slaves.

V. It is the enemy of immediate abolition.

VI. It is nourished by fear and selfishness.

VII. It aims at the total expulsion of the colored population.

VIII. It vilifies and persecutes the free people of color, and prevents as far as possible their moral and social elevation in the United States.

IX. It deceives and misleads the nation.

The attempt to uphold the Colonization Society, at this late day, is serviceable to this extent: — it shows who are the real friends of the colored population, and consequently the uncompromising opponents of slavery, by their withdrawal from the Society; and who are the persecutors and despisers of that population, by their wilful adherence to it. Once, there were many truly benevolent and philanthropic persons at the North, who were zealous in their efforts and liberal in their gifts to crown it with success, because they sincerely believed it to be a sublimely beneficent movement; but their vision has since been purged — they have found that they were the victims of a stupendous imposture — and they have repudiated, with indignation and abhorrence, what they formerly regarded with pleasure and exultation. For those who still adhere to it, there is no excuse. They have eyes, but they see not; ears, but they hear not; hearts, but they feel not.[3] They willingly and eagerly seek the banishment of the free colored people to Africa, because they hate their presence, and are determined to trample upon them while they remain in the United States. They are not abolitionists, but the avowed and bitter enemies of the anti-slavery movement. They have no conscientious scruples that forbid their striking hands with the thieves, and consenting with the adulterers of the South. But their wickedness they attempt to hide under the cloak of philanthropy; the murderous prejudice which they cherish and defend, they declare to be natural, unconquerable, and a proof of their own Christian disinterestedness in seeking the expulsion of those with whom they affect to sympathize, and in whose temporal and eternal welfare they claim to take the deepest interest.

It is for this reason that I honestly said, at the commencement of this letter, that I feel no personal respect for you. It is but recently that you have become an agent of the Colonization Society. You cannot be ignorant as to its principles, doctrines and purposes. You support it, not as good men did formerly, through lack of correct information, but from an affinity of spirit with all that makes it what it is — mean, despicable, time-serving, unchristian. After listening to your discourse, I felt as a Christian to regard you with amazement, as an American to blush for you, as a man to rebuke you openly. I confess, knowing that the scheme which you represent is 'full of all deceivableness of unrighteousness,'[4] I went to hear from your lips, something so novel, so ingenious, so well calculated to allay suspicion, so guarded in its allusions and references, as to be totally unlike the mode of advocating the colonization conspiracy, that was adopted many years ago; but

I was mistaken. You dealt honestly with your hearers. The most revolting features of your scheme you presented without a mask, and as worthy of admiration. It was not a missionary enterprise that you advocated, except incidentally, but ☞ the AMERICAN COLONIZATION SOCIETY — its origin and design; and eulogized its founders and managers — such men-stealers as Henry Clay, John Randolph, Bushrod Washington — as worthy of undying renown.[5] Of nothing which it or they had said or done did you complain; to none of the views advanced by them did you take any exceptions. Be assured that I will measure you faithfully by your own standard; and if I fail to prove by it that you are a man whose religion is vain, and a shameless panderer to prejudice and slavery, then let me be covered with shame and confusion of face.

But let me not anticipate what I intend to prove. I will begin with the opening exercises on Sunday evening.

The first hymn that was sung was in reference to the 'enlargement and glory of the Church.' This enlargement is to be effected, it seems, by diminishing the population on one side of the globe, through the operation of oppressive laws, and the prevalence of a relentless spirit of caste — and by increasing it on the other, by the process of transportation. The 'glory of the Church' is to be augmented by her sanction and support of a scheme, which in a word and deed flatly denies that God has made of one blood all nations of men,[6] which was concocted to give security to slavery and the domestic slave-trade, and which derives a large portion of its revenue from the sale of fathers and mothers, husbands and wives, children and relatives, as chattels personal.

Prayer was offered by the Rev. Mr. Blagden, who has yet to exhibit the slightest interest in the anti-slavery cause.[7] The atrocious crimes of this nation were not remembered by him, but he 'thanked God that we live in a land of gospel light and liberty' — (from which, you attempted to show, it was absolutely necessary to colonize three millions and a half of the American people in a land of thick darkness and gross idolatry, in order that they might cease to be meted out and trampled under foot,[8] and rise to freedom and independence!) He warmly eulogized the Colonization Society and its founders, and represented its object as being in the highest degree benevolent and Christian. He expressed the hope that the colony at Liberia would result as gloriously as had that of the pilgrim fathers at Plymouth, in building up a mighty empire, and bringing millions into the glorious liberty of the sons of God! — (the liberty to traffic in human flesh, and to exterminate the aborigines of the country as wild beasts and dangerous reptiles!) [9] He prayed that God would cause the slaves to have the Bible put into their hands, and the marriage institution restored to them; — just as though God stood in the way, or needed to be supplicated to allow so reasonable a request as this! But he did not pray that the slaves might have complete justice meted out to them — that they might immediately be set free, and permitted to enjoy liberty and equality in this their native land. He 'remembered to forget' the cruelty and impiety of the southern slaveholders, and the aggravated guilt of their northern abettors. Next followed the hymn —

'From Greenland's icy mountains.' [10]

How could such a hymn be read or sung, on such an occasion, in the old South Church, without a deep blush of shame mantling every cheek? What, too, could be more horribly ludicrous, as well as superlatively impudent? You, and all who heard you, knew that three millions of the population of this country are not only unable to read the Bible — are not only destitute of the Bible — but are prohibited from possessing and reading it, by terrible penalties; and yet, sir, you read, and the choir sung, with all possible complacency, as though this whole country were a mountain of holiness —

> 'Shall WE, *whose souls are lighted*
> *By wisdom from on high —*
> Shall WE, to men benighted,
> *The lamp of life deny?*'

Then came the text — and such a text for such a discourse! It was the very same once chosen by Bishop Hedding, from which to deduce the rightfulness of slaveholding.[11] It was — THE GOLDEN RULE! 'Therefore, whatsoever ye would that men should do to you, do ye even so to them; for this is the law and the prophets.' (Matt. xii. 12.) [12] Your explanation and application of that rule must be reserved for comment till another number.[13] Such, you 'solemnly' declared, was your construction of it, that, before God, if you and your children were black, you would deem it both a duty and a privilege to be colonized from your native land, and sent to a heathen country, by those who would deny you the full enjoyment of your freedom at home. — How you would feel and reason, under such circumstances, I will try to imagine hereafter.

Abhorring the scheme which you are endeavoring to promote, and trusting that you will speedily find some decent and honest employment, from which to derive a livelihood, I remain, with all fidelity,

Yours, for liberty and equality on the American soil, now and forever,

WM. LLOYD GARRISON.

Boston, June 15, 1847.

Printed: *The Liberator*, June 18, 1847.

Heman Humphrey (1779–1861) was a Yale graduate and a minister who took a strong interest in the cause of temperance. He was president of Amherst College from 1823 to 1845.

1. Garrison's *Thoughts on African Colonization*, published in June 1832, was a 238-page pamphlet systematically condemning the American Colonization Society.

2. The *African Repository*, the organ of the American Colonization Society, was founded in 1825. In 1892 it was superseded by *Liberia*, which continued publication until 1909. (*ULS.*)

3. Garrison adapts Psalms 115:5–6.

4. II Thessalonians 2:10.

5. John Randolph (1773–1833), a brilliant but unstable man, served the United States government for many years as member of Congress and briefly as minister to Russia. Although he disapproved of slavery, he defended its constitutional safeguards and states' rights — hence Garrison's dislike for him. After 1818 his eccentricities in speech and action indicated mental abnormality, and his later years were passed in actual insanity.

Bushrod Washington (1762–1829) was a nephew of George Washington and served as justice of the United States Supreme Court from 1798 until his death. Although Washington favored abolition and served as the first president of the American Colonization Society, in 1821 he was bitterly criticized for selling fifty-four Mount Vernon slaves to a Louisiana purchaser. Washington retorted that since slaves were property he had a right to sell them and that he had sold the Negroes because they were disobedient and continually trying to escape.

6. Acts 17:26.

7. George Washington Blagden (1802–1884) was a graduate of Yale University and Andover Theological Seminary. After serving in several churches in the Boston area he became in 1836 pastor of the Old South Church, a post he held until 1872. (Hamilton Andrews Hill, *History of the Old South Church*, Boston and New York, 1890.)

8. An adaptation of Isaiah 18:7.

9. In 1821 the American Colonization Society selected Cape Mesurado as a home for the first group of freed Negroes to emigrate to Africa. The colony of Liberia was actually founded, however, by a white American, Jehudi Ashmun, between 1822 and 1828, and the name "Liberia" was invented in 1824 by the Reverend Ralph Randolph Gurley. Most of the immigrant population of Liberia were free Negroes who migrated from choice, but a few were freed for the purpose. Even with missionary aid their condition was not prosperous; moreover, they kept slaves. In 1847 the American colonists declared Liberia to be an independent republic, and it was so recognized by most of the great powers, with the exception of the United States, which delayed recognition until 1862. Commercial and financial ties between the United States and Liberia have always been strong.

10. Garrison quotes the title of the hymn by Reginald Heber written in 1819 and published in 1823. Farther down the page he quotes stanza 3, substituting "shall" for "can" in lines 1 and 3 and "by" for "with" in line 2.

11. Elijah Hedding (1780–1852), a bishop in the Methodist Episcopal Church, spent much of his ministerial career in New England and was instrumental in establishing the magazine *Zion's Herald*. He was a strong opponent of abolition.

12. Garrison gives the wrong citation and slightly alters Matthew 7:12.

13. See Garrison's letter to Heman Humphrey, July 9, 1847. In addition to his direct correspondence with Humphrey, Garrison wrote an introduction to an article entitled "The Colonization Conspiracy," which appeared in *The Liberator*, June 25, 1847. The article presented a series of resolutions passed at a meeting of the colored citizens of Boston on June 22. Among other things they cited the deviation from the Golden Rule by the American Colonization Society and called the society "practically an enemy to those whom it promises to aid."

197

TO GEORGE W. BENSON

Boston, June 26, 1847.

My dear George:

I do not know whether it will be in your power to procure the accommodation for me, that I very much need at the present time; but I do know that your own concerns are sufficiently onerous, without needing any addition to them, and that I am extremely reluctant to make even the suggestion to you.

On the 1st of July, (Thursday next,) my quarterly payments fall due, for groceries, rent, fuel, &c. &c. The past quarter, my expenses have been unusually great, in getting all the children their summer clothing, &c.; so that I shall need at least $100, to pay what I owe, in addition to what will be due me on my salary. — I have been so often befriended by Francis Jackson and Wendell Phillips, that I dislike to ask them again so soon; although I presume they would both assist me cheerfully to this extent. Still, if I can procure this sum elsewhere, I should be very glad. Helen has suggested that she has no doubt our good friend Thomas Davis, at Providence, would readily make the desired loan — (I should want it only for 30 days, till my next monthly payment was due) — but I would prefer that you should correspond with him, on the subject, if you think best, stating to him that I had applied to you for the loan, and you had ventured to ask the accommodation of him — &c. — *for thirty days.*

The time is so short, that whatever is done, should be done immediately. I am anxious to keep my credit untarnished, and have hitherto been able to do so, to an hour. There is nothing like it in securing confidence.

For the last three days, I have been sorely tormented with a severe attack of my old scrofula swelling and inflammation in the ear, but trust to get over it in a few days.

Fanny, during the same time, has been quite feverish, although she appears to have no positive complaint. Helen, the babe, and all the rest of the children, are well.

I hope dear Sister Sarah is steadily improving in health. She is in my thoughts continually. If the mail were not just closing, I should like to occupy the remainder of this sheet, in regard to her case. Give my warmest sympathies and tenderest love to her, and remember me affectionately to Catharine.

Please let me hear from you as soon as practicable, but do not let me put you to any great trouble.

Yours, faithfully,

Wm. Lloyd Garrison.

ALS: Garrison Papers, Boston Public Library.

198

TO RICHARD D. WEBB

Boston, July 1, 1847.

My dear Webb:

Many thanks for your interesting letter to Francis Jackson, detailing your observations during your late philanthropic mission among your famishing countrymen. You will find it in the Liberator this week.[1] I hope there are not many blunders in it; but, if there are, the fault will not be owing to the manuscript, which was very legibly written — by dear Hannah, I suppose — for *you* cannot write plain! I have not a good compositor in my office.

You see that we fanatics, here, have been constrained to differ with you, dear Richard Allen, and H. C. Wright, in regard to receiving the donations from the South for the relief of the starving among you; though we all agree with you in pronouncing judgment against the course of the Dublin Committee, in rejecting the aid proffered from London, because it was the proceeds of a theatrical entertainment, and accepting without a scruple whatever may have been given by the slaveholders.[2] I really think there is a broad line of demarcation to be drawn between a case in which money is obtained from the slaveholders solely because they are first recognized as "members of the household of faith,"[3] and that in which it is given voluntarily (as in the Irish case) without any sanction of slaveholding being either required, volunteered, or understood. But perhaps I am wrong.

You must refer to the numbers of the Liberator, for information in regard to the state of the anti-slavery question. We are in good spirits, and serene as heaven itself, though the opposition is still formidable, and the present crisis one of no ordinary trial, especially in regard to the atrocious war with Mexico. It is certainly not a popular war; it was begun and is carried on against the deep moral convictions of the sober portion of the people; its real object, the extension and preservation of slavery, no intelligent man honestly doubts; still, the diabolical motto, "Our country, right or wrong,"[4] gratifies national pride, appears in a patriotic garb, and obtains a sanction practically that is almost universal. Besides, the American arms have been crowned with extraordinary success; and there is little doubt that Generals Scott and [Zachary] Taylor will be "revelling in the halls of the Montezumas," in the city of Mexico, on the 4th of July, our "glorious day of freedom and national independence." [5] Again — the religious sectarists, who hate Catholicism, but *do not* love Christianity, exhibit much resignation, and no slight share of satisfaction, in view of the war. "It is the Lord's doings, and marvellous in *their* eyes." [6] It will help put down the "Man of Sin" — it will riddle with bomb-shells "the Mother of Harlots" [7] — it will open the way for the circu-lation of the Bible; the preaching of the gospel, the saving of souls from perdition — &c. &c.

Now, boldly and continually to denounce the war, under such cir-cumstances, as bloody and iniquitous — to impeach the government and the administration — to deplore instead of rejoicing over the vic-tories won by our troops — to wish success to the Mexicans, as the injured party, who are contending for their firesides and their country against enslaving and remorseless invaders — as you can easily imag-ine, subjects us to great odium, and brings down upon our heads the heavy charge of "treason" and "traitors to the country." But our testi-mony is not in vain. It burns like fire upon the national conscience.

Well, O'Connell has left his wide field of popular agitation, and removed to a new and mysterious sphere of existence.[8] Though he had many faults and failings, (Heaven be merciful to us all!) I honor his memory, and regard him with feelings of gratitude and respect. His death, at such a time, in the awful state into which his suffering coun-try is plunged, is truly affecting. Of course, the Repeal movement may be regarded as virtually at an end, I suppose.

How are you and the dear ones at home? How is it with James Haughton and family, and Richard Allen and wife? How is my well-remembered, much admired Maria Waring? How are *all* the Webbs, a noble race! If I could only leap across the Atlantic, and run no risk of coming short in making it, would I not be with you instanter, to hand you this letter, and to embrace you all? And, sure, *I would!*

Frederick Douglass and James N. Buffum are by my side, both in fine spirits, and both begging me to proffer to you, and all the Dublin friends, their loving regards.

Lovingly yours,

Wm. Lloyd Garrison.

ALS: Garrison Papers, Boston Public Library.

1. Webb's long letter (more than three columns) was printed in *The Liberator*, July 2, 1847.
2. The Dublin Committee, appointed under the central relief authority for

Ireland, had been charged with the responsibility of aiding those suffering from the famine.

3. An adaptation of Galatians 6:10.

4. A quotation from the famous toast given by Stephen Decatur in Norfolk, Virginia, in April 1816.

5. Winfield Scott (1786–1866) of Virginia had become a general during the War of 1812 and had been since 1841 the commanding general of the United States Army. He led the Mexican campaign of 1847 and was to capture Mexico City on September 14. The quotation applied to Scott may refer to "Marine Hymn," line 1, since the lyrics were composed in 1847.

6. Psalms 118:23, with the substitution of "their" for "our."

7. II Thessalonians 2:3 and Revelation 17:5.

8. Daniel O'Connell had died May 15, 1847.

199

TO HEMAN HUMPHREY

[July 9, 1847.]

SIR —

If there be any employment more despicable, or more reprehensible than that in which you are now engaged, I have yet to learn what it is. It seems to me if you had any true self-respect or manliness of character — if you were imbued with the spirit of Christianity, how-ever slightly — you would be ashamed of it, and instantly be induced to abandon it. Taking the text from which you preached at the Old South Church in this city — viz. the Golden Rule — as the standard by which to form a sound judgment in this case, you are convicted out of your own mouth of being engaged in a crusade equal[ly] irrational and oppressive — equally at variance with every principle of republicanism, and every precept of Christianity.

What are you trying to do? To persuade the white people of this country, that it would be a benevolent and Christian deed for them to transport to Africa, just as they are, in all their ignorance and wretchedness, the entire colored population, simply on account of their complexion! As a professed minister of Him, in whom 'there is neither Jew nor Greek, neither Barbarian nor Scythian, neither bond nor free,'[1] but all are one, you[2] are going about from city to city, from village to village, from one section of the country to another, declaring that the prejudice which is grinding the black man to the dust is invincible, and must in the nature of things continue in full operation, so long as he remains in this republic. Instead of rebuking it as vulgar, unnatural, malevolent and unchristian, you are stimulating it to increased activity, and doing what you can to confirm your detestable doctrine, that the proscribed can never be allowed to enjoy liberty and equality on the American soil. Instead of calling to repentance, those who are cherishing this sinful disposition, and flaming with righteous indignation in view of their cruel behaviour, you are finding a natural cause for it all in the fact, that the victims are of a sable hue, that God never intended they should dwell among us, and that their home is in benighted Africa. Are you not ashamed of yourself? The fact, that you readily find admission into the pulpits of the land, to inculcate sentiments so inhuman, so insulting to the beneficent Creator of the human family, so hostile to the world-reconciling doctrine of human brotherhood, is an awful commentary on the religion of the church. The fact that you can stand up in the presence of a public assembly, and enforce those sentiments without blushing, and without exciting against you a popular storm of moral indignation is a melancholy proof, not less of the obduracy of your spirit than it is of the brutal state of the community. Go, hide yourself, until a heart of flesh be given to you. Colonize yourself to some uninhabited island, and there remain, until you can learn to respect every human being as one created in the image of God. Blush to behold the light of day — blush to look into any mirror — until you are prepared to endorse the glorious sentiment, that, whatever may be his origin, complexion or estate, 'A MAN'S A MAN FOR ALL THAT.' [3]

I admit that you are faithfully representing the American Colonization Society, in declaring complexional caste to be both inevitable and invincible, so long as the white and colored population of this country remain together. It was the discovery of this nefarious doctrine, as the vital and animating sentiment of that Society, that first opened my eyes to the hypocrisy of its benevolent professions, and the villany of its character. In its official organ, and in all its publications, the Society has basely done — what you are doing — eagerly sought for every manifestation of *colorphobia*, and then argued that, being founded in nature, over which neither reason nor religion could have any control, it demonstrated the necessity of colonizing the victims of it on the coast of Africa! It is impossible for me to express the abhorrence I feel of an association organized on such a basis, and for such a purpose. It combines everything of meanness, duplicity, malignity, brutality, and impiety.

You will doubtless recollect, that, some fifteen years ago, through the crafty misrepresentations of ELLIOTT CRESSON, (at that time an agent of the American Colonization Society in England,) WILLIAM WILBERFORCE, with many other distinguished philanthropists in that country, was induced to recommend that Society as deserving of the cordial support of the friends of a down-trodden race. Perhaps you will also remember, that, in the year 1833, I went over to England, to expose the dishonesty of the course pursued by said Cresson, and to prevent the friends of negro emancipation from being swindled out of their money, by exposing to them the real design of this scheme of African colonization — to wit, the gratification of a ferocious prejudice, and the security of the slave system. If your memory fails you, in this particular, Mr. Cresson's is unquestionably fresh and lively, and he will be able to confirm my statements. In a comparatively short time, he was compelled to leave England in disgrace, having been convicted of cowardice and imposture before all the people. Wilberforce was at that time residing in Bath, at which place I visited him, for the purpose of disabusing his mind, and showing him that, in avowing himself to be the friend of the Colonization Society, he was practically causing the weight of his great influence to rest like an avalanche on the entire colored population of the United States. Though he had thus committed himself before the world, he had done so honestly, and under a gross misapprehension of the facts in the case; and therefore I found him to be in an ingenuous state of mind, with no pride of opinion to be wounded or humbled by any discovery of error. His mind was clear, his faculties vigorous; and never shall I forget the searching ordeal through which I passed on that occasion. On taking my leave of that great and good man, I told him that I should leave with him no documents written against the Colonization Society by its opponents, but simply the Fifteenth and Sixteenth Annual Reports of its Board of Managers, in one of which he would find an elaborate defence of the Society from the charges which had been brought against it; but expressing my deep conviction, that a careful perusal of those two Reports would excite his astonishment and disgust, and cause him indignantly to repudiate that Society, as an evil conspiracy. Smiling at the confidence I manifested in his speedy conversion, he thanked me for the documents, and promised to give them a candid and critical examination. The result may be told in a few words. In the course of a few weeks, I received a 'PROTEST AGAINST THE AMERICAN COLONIZATION SOCIETY,' the first name appended to which was that of WILLIAM WILBERFORCE, followed by those of Zachary Macaulay, Samuel Gurney, Lord Suffield, Dr. Lushington, Thomas Fowell Buxton, James Cropper, William Allen, Daniel O'Connell, and others.[4] In that Protest, the signers declare —

'To the destruction of slavery throughout the world, [mark that!] we are compelled to say that we believe the Colonization Society to be an obstruction . . . While we believe its pretexts to be delusive, we are convinced that its real effects are of the most dangerous nature. It takes its root from a cruel prejudice and alienation in the whites of America against the colored people, slave or free — This being its source, its effects are what might be expected; that it fosters and increases the spirit of caste already so unhappily predominant; that it widens the breach between the two races — exposes the colored people to great practical persecution, in order to force them to emigrate; and, finally, is calculated to swallow up and divert that feeling which America, as a Christian and a free country, cannot but entertain, that slavery is alike incompatible with the law of God, and with the well-being of man, whether the enslaver or the enslaved.

On these grounds, therefore, we must be understood utterly to repudiate the principles of the American Colonization Society. That Society is, in our estimation, not deserving of the countenance of the British public.'

No verdict was ever more just, no testimony more emphatic, than this. The lamented THOMAS CLARKSON pronounced the same judgment against the Society in 1840.

Do you wish to know, what Wilberforce found in the two Reports alluded to, to excite his Christian indignation, and to purge his vision? Among other things, the following impious language, as uttered officially in the 15th Report of the Managers:

'The race in question were known, as a class, to be destitute, depraved — the victims of all forms of social misery. The peculiarity of their fate was, that this was not their condition by accident, or transiently, but *inevitably* and *immutably*, whilst they remained in their present place, by a law as infallible in its operation, as any of physical nature.' * * 'Their residence amongst us is attended with evil consequences to society — *causes beyond the control of the human will* must prevent their *ever* rising to equality with the whites.' * * 'The Managers consider it clear that causes exist, and are operating to prevent their improvement and elevation to any considerable extent as a class, in this country, which are fixed, not only beyond the control of the friends of humanity, BUT OF ANY HUMAN POWER. *Christianity cannot do for them here, what it will do for them in Africa.* This is not the fault of the colored man, *nor of the white man, nor of Christianity; but an ordination of Providence, and no more to be changed than the laws of nature.* Yet, were it otherwise, did no cause exist but prejudice, to prevent the elevation, in this country, of our free colored population; still, were this prejudice so strong (which is indeed the fact) as to forbid the hope of any great favorable change in their condition, what folly for them to reject blessings in another land, because it is prejudice which debars them from such blessings in this! But, in truth, no legislation, no humanity, no benevolence can make them insensible to their past condition, can unfetter their minds, can relieve them from the disadvantages resulting from inferior means and attainments, can abridge the right of freemen to regulate their social intercourse and relations, which will leave them *for ever a separate and depressed class* in the community; in fine, nothing can in any way do much here to raise them from their miseries to respectability, honor and usefulness.' 5

The same monstrous, disgraceful, ferocious sentiments, you, Sir, are busy in promulgating even at this late day, under the mask of philanthropy. Was ever a greater affront offered to a just and righteous God than this? 'Have we not all one Father,' and has he not 'made of one blood, all nations of men'? [6] Three millions and a half of the people, in this country, are 'peeled, meted out, and trodden under foot' — but then, 'not by any fault of their own,' (that is true,) nor by the fault of others! [7] 'It is an ordination of Providence, and no more to be changed than the laws of nature'!!

WM. LLOYD GARRISON.

Printed: *The Liberator*, July 9, 1847.

1. An adaptation of Galatians 3:28.
2. *The Liberator* has a single quote, omitted here, before the word "you."
3. Robert Burns, "For A' That and A' That," stanza 3, line 4.
4. Samuel Gurney (1786–1856) was a wealthy Quaker banker of Norwich, England, who controlled the London bill-broking business of Overend, Gurney and Company, for forty years the greatest discounting-house in the world. He devoted the latter years of his life to charitable and philanthropic activities including abolition.

Edward Harbord, Baron Suffield (1781–1835), after a long and successful political career, became a radical reformer, dedicated chiefly to the abolition of the slave trade.

Stephen Lushington (1782–1873) was a distinguished lawyer and judge whose clients included Lady Byron and Queen Charlotte. He worked for the abolition of capital punishment, of the church rates, and of slavery, and was a steady supporter and adviser of Sir Thomas Fowell Buxton.

Garrison here quotes, with minor deletions, approximately the last half of the British philanthropists' renunciation of the American Colonization Society. The full text, under the heading PROTEST, was printed in *The Liberator*, October 12, 1833.

5. Garrison quotes accurately, extracting phrases from several parts of the report.
6. Malachi 2:10, Acts 17:26.
7. Garrison freely adapts Isaiah 18:7 and perhaps echoes Luke 23:4, 23:14, or John 18:38, 19:4, 19:6.

---

2 0 0

TO JOSEPH MERRILL

Boston, July 12, 1847.

Dear Friend:

I have just received the above letter from New-York, from John Hart of Cork, who, it seems, has arrived at that port, but is unable to get to Danvers for the lack of means.[1]

By the accompanying letter from the venerable and excellent William Martin, of Cork, you will see that he is necessitated to say some things respecting the conduct of John Hart, that are very discreditable to the latter.[2] His conduct to his poor mother, in her dire distress, appears to have been exceedingly base. The only palliation for it (if such a thing be possible) is, the horrid selfishness which famine is so apt [to] engender in the human heart.

I received your letter, inquiring after the case of Hart, and intended to answer it more promptly. The unintentional delay, however, enables me to send you the letter from John Hart, which was received by to-day's mail. Will you see that an answer is sent to him from some of his friends in Danvers? Though he has grievously sinned, he is still a suffering man; and if he can find bread and employment, may once more be restored.

In haste, I remain,

Yours, truly,

Wm. Lloyd Garrison.

Joseph Merrill, Danvers.

ALS: Autograph Collection, Essex Institute. Garrison's letter begins on the same sheet on which Hart wrote describing his financial predicament.

Joseph Merrill (c. 1814–1882), a currier, was active among the Danvers abolitionists. He eventually identified himself fully with Garrisonians and in 1863 was elected secretary pro tem of the Essex County Anti-Slavery Society. (The Reverend Alfred P. Putnam, "History of the Anti-Slavery Movement in Danvers," *Danvers Historical Collections*, 30:20–21, 1942.)

1. John Hart cannot be identified with certainty. He may have been the John Hart who in 1863 boarded with Michael Conley in Andover, Massachusetts, where he was apparently working in a file shop. (Alfred Poore, "Andover, Massachusetts, in the Year 1863," *Essex Institute Historical Collections*, 50:42, 1914.)

2. William Martin (1772–1853), a Quaker, was governor of the House of Industry in Cork. He is commonly known as the father of the temperance movement, the one who converted Father Mathew to the cause. (Letter to the editor from C. Duncan Rice, Yale University, June 2, 1970.)

201

TO JOHN B. ESTLIN

Boston, July 16, 1847.

My Dear Sir:

If you have utterly erased my name from the tablet of your memory, I can scarcely wonder at the act — so delinquent, on the score of epistolary attention, have I been to you, and the other dear friends at Bristol. I am mortified beyond measure to think that so much time has elapsed since my return home, without your receiving a single epistle from me. The truth is, I have purposed to do so much, from time to time, that I have done nothing. It has been in my heart to send you, the Misses Carpenter,[1] &c., epistles formidable in length; and hurried and perplexed on the eve of the sailing of each steamer,

I have shrunk from the task, and said — "Well, I must not, cannot send a few hasty lines, and therefore will wait till the next opportunity, when I will endeavour without fail, to send something worthy of perusal." Alas! that I am now only able to make this explanation — to assure you, and, through you, the other beloved friends of your circle, that my gratitude and regard are strong and overflowing, and that I am,

Faithfully and admiringly yours,

Wm. Lloyd Garrison.

ALS: Garrison Papers, Boston Public Library.
Although the manuscript does not designate the recipient, it was undoubtedly written to Estlin, who was Garrison's best friend at Bristol.

1. Probably Mary Carpenter and her sister or sisters. Mary Carpenter (1807–1877) was one of Mary Estlin's most important followers in the Bristol and Clifton Ladies' Anti-Slavery Society. She is better known, however, as a polemicist on education, her most important work being *Reformatory Schools for the Children of the Perishing and Dangerous Classes*, London, 1851. (J. E. Carpenter, *The Life and Work of Mary Carpenter*, London, 1879.)

202

TO HENRY C. WRIGHT

Boston, July 16, 1847.

My dear Henry:

It is just one year ago, to-day, since I bade adieu to my family and friends, and embarked for the shores of old England. How swiftly has the time sped! What mighty and numerous events have been crowded into it! Much of it seems to me like a dream; and yet I have been any thing but dreaming. That I have visited England, Scotland, Ireland, Wales, in *propria persona*, is a historical fact. On this point, I am sure I cannot be mistaken. I have met and given you a warm embrace; and taken by the hand, and communed, face to face, with the Thompsons, the Smeals, the Patons, the Murrays, the Wighams, the Webbs, the Haughtons, the Allens, the Peases, the Bradys, the Carpenters, the Estlins, and a host of other beloved friends and coadjutors, the recollection of whose unwearied kindness and zealous co-operation sets my heart to overflowing with emotion like a fountain deeply stirred. Absence from their immediate presence seems to me like a daily bereavement, and it makes me sad to think that I may never see them again in the flesh. Will none of them come over to America, to make us at least a flying visit? Try to induce as many of them as you can to accompany you to these shores. Assure them of such a reception as the grateful and the admiring know how to give. Be sure to come, first of all, to Boston, and from thence journey *ad libitum*. Ours is "a great country," as well as a very inconsistent and oppressive one. Here human society, institutions, customs, may be surveyed under new phases. Here the spirit of reform is more active and vital, and here human progress has taken greater strides, than in any other part of the world. Here are the most abundant means, the noblest opportunities, the greatest facilities, to promote the cause of humanity – of universal brotherhood.

So, it seems, you are to embark for home in the Caledonia of the 19th of August. I trust nothing will occur to baffle your purpose, for you are greatly needed here; and yet, I hardly feel reconciled to your leaving, so great is the field of reformatory usefulness abroad, and so few are the laborers to occupy it. After your return, there will be left behind no American representative of the anti-slavery cause. I have endeavored to imagine, but in vain, who shall next visit England, in due season, from our ranks. We have no one who can be spared, or who, if he could be for a few months, would be just *the* one to go, excepting Wendell Phillips; and he cannot, so long as his wife lives, and remains in her usual precarious state of health.[1]

I am sure it will be almost like breaking your heart-strings to leave the vast circle of beloved friends, with whom you have become so intimately acquainted, and to whom you are so much endeared – to leave them, not for a brief period, but with the strong probability of never seeing them again on earth. Your personal attachments are unusually strong, and therefore the more keen is your susceptibility. The separation will cause many a tear to flow, many a breast to heave, many a heart to grow liquid as water. But let not the sadness of the occasion overwhelm your soul. To sustain and comfort you, remember the pleasures of "home, sweet home" – that here are thousands who are yearning to greet you, and whose presence will fill your heart with gladness. Thus, dear Henry, may you find your strength equal to your day.[2] Thus doth God temper the wind to the shorn lamb.[3]

Toilsome and incessant have been your labors in the vast field of suffering humanity, and great shall be – may I not say, has been? – your reward. The seed that you have sown has been good seed, and a glorious harvest must be the consequence, to be reaped by each succeeding generation. Ever shall the true reformer find, that "scattered truth is never, never wasted."[4]

Should you leave Boston[5] at the time specified in your letter, you will probably arrive here about the 1st of September. At that time, I am sorry to add, I am to be in Ohio, – leaving here on the 1st of August, and not returning home till the 1st of October. But you will find my dear Helen and some of the children at home, and a chamber at your service, and a plate for you at the table. She will expect you without fail. Francis Jackson and other friends will also be desirous to entertain you. Doubtless, you will be anxious to reach Philadelphia as soon as convenient; but on my return, I shall hope to see you in Boston, and to devise plans for a fall and winter campaign against "the powers of darkness." [6]

I trust the voyage will prove to you far less detrimental than it did in going to England — (it can scarcely prove worse.) Be sure to take the steamer, and a berth in the first cabin. May every thing be propitious on the passage!

Assure all the dear friends at Glasgow, Edinburgh, Sheffield, Wrexham, Bristol, London, Darlington, Dublin, Cork, &c. &c., as you may have opportunity, that though they have few epistolary proofs of my remembrance of them, and my exalted appreciation of their character, yet I am neither forgetful nor ungrateful; but my spirit dwells much of the time with them, and they are continually in my thoughts to live and to die with them. It will at all times give me exquisite pleasure to hear from them, either by letter, or through the medium of others. I am mortified to think that I have been able to write to so few of them since my return; but the omission has not been owing even to a momentary forgetfulness of them.

Frederick Douglass will accompany me to "the far West" — and perhaps James N. Buffum. We shall go via Pennsylvania, and return by the way of Niagara falls.

I have neither time nor room to give you any particulars of the progress of our cause. From day to day, from hour to hour, indications are bursting out, both in the political and religious arena, of the onward march of anti-slavery. We are greatly strengthened and encouraged by what we see and hear.

I shall write to you by the steamer of the 1st of August, and address the letter to Mr. [William] Brown at the Temperance Hotel in Clayton Square, Liverpool, to whom I desire to be specially remembered when you see him — also to Dr. [William B.] Hodgson.

You must take it for granted that all your friends here wish to be cordially remembered to you, and that I am not less solicitous to send my warm regards to all the friends across the Atlantic.

Ever faithfully yours,

Wm. Lloyd Garrison.

H. C. Wright.

ALS: Garrison Papers, Boston Public Library.

1. By the time of Garrison's letter, Ann Phillips, who had been married to Wendell since 1837, was a chronic invalid. Although her illness may have been

psychosomatic, Phillips remained considerate and uncomplaining, often nursing her himself — on one occasion for sixty consecutive days without once leaving the house. (Ralph Korngold, *Two Friends of Man, the Story of William Lloyd Garrison and Wendell Phillips and Their Relationship with Abraham Lincoln*, Boston, 1950, pp. 170–172.)

2. Garrison adapts Deuteronomy 33:25.

3. Garrison uses the maxim found in the works of many French and English writers, most significantly in Laurence Sterne, *A Sentimental Journey*.

4. Not identified.

5. Apparently Garrison means Liverpool rather than Boston.

6. Garrison perhaps alludes to John Milton, *Paradise Lost*, III, 256.

203

TO GEORGE W. BENSON

Boston, July 24, 1847.

Dear George:

We have been greatly distressed at home to hear of the sad calamity that has befallen your dear wife and children, by being thrown out of a carryall.[1] Under all the circumstances, it is, perhaps, remarkable that no life was lost, and no limbs broken. But the contusions received, especially by Catherine, appear to have been severe and dangerous. The fortitude which she displayed, through all her sufferings, according to dear Sarah's letter, was entirely characteristic, and shows her to be one of ten thousand. Do let us hear from you, in regard to her present situation — how she is getting along, how the children are doing, and whether there will be left any permanent marks of the catastrophe.

Helen can feel a most lively sympathy for Catherine, having also been a sufferer in a similar manner. She joins with me in tendering to her the warmest sympathies.

Enclosed is a letter just received from our excellent friend Olive Gilbert. Please put it into Sarah's hands, who will be glad to peruse it, and who will answer it, if it be in her power. Our affectionate regards to her, with our yearning desires for her complete restoration to health. Tell her that Samuel J. May left Boston for Syracuse yesterday afternoon, having had a very gratifying visit among his friends.

Ever yours,

Wm. Lloyd Garrison.

ALS: Garrison Papers, Boston Public Library.

1. An account of the accident appears in *The Liberator*, July 30, 1847.

2 0 4

TO JOHN B. VASHON

Boston, July 27, 1847.

Friend Vashon:

For many years, your old friend has had a strong desire to visit Pittsburgh, but circumstances have conspired to prevent its gratification up to the present hour. Ere the lapse of another fortnight, however, I hope to be in your busy city, in company with my eloquent friend Frederick Douglass, on our way to Ohio. We shall not be able to remain in P. longer than two or three days; but, during that time, we shall be happy to address the white and colored citizens, in public, in relation to slavery, if suitable arrangements can be made for that purpose.

Nearly twelve years have rolled away since you were at my house. It was the memorable day of the eventful riot in this city, in October, 1835, when, after partaking of a dinner with you, I hurried to the anti-slavery meeting, from which I was taken by the mobocrats, dragged through the streets, almost denuded of my clothing, and finally incarcerated in prison to save my life. My hat was cut to pieces, but its place was supplied by another, which you had the kindness to buy for me at a venture as to the precise size required. How many important events have transpired since that time, all deeply affecting our glorious anti-slavery cause! What battles have been fought, what victories won, by the uncompromising and undaunted friends of emancipation! How wonderful and auspicious has been the change wrought in the public sentiment at the North! But I write in haste, and can only add that, I am still

Faithfully yours,

Wm. Lloyd Garrison.

N.B. We expect to be in Pittsburgh about the 10th of August.

Typed transcription: Villard Papers, Harvard College Library.

John B. Vashon (c. 1789–1854), a prosperous Negro barber and later the owner of the City Baths in Pittsburgh, was an active abolitionist. As early as 1831, as chairman of a group of black citizens, he wrote a series of resolutions opposing the American Colonization Society (see *The Liberator*, September 17, 1831). In this letter Garrison refers to the Boston riot of October 21, 1835, at which time Vashon was visiting the Garrisons. (See the letter to Vashon, December 8, 1832, *Letters*, I, 194, descriptive note.)

Silver tea and coffee service presented to Garrison October 21, 1846

Frederick Douglass will accompany me to 'the far West'—and perhaps James N. Buffum. We shall go via Pennsylvania, and return by the way of Niagara falls.

I have neither time nor room to give you any particulars of the progress of our cause. From day to day, from hour to hour, indications are bursting out, both in the political and religious arena, of the onward march of anti-slavery. We are greatly strengthened and encouraged by what we see and hear

I shall write to you by the steamer of the 1st of August, and address the letter to Mr. Brown at the Temperance Hotel, in Clayton Square, Liverpool, to whom I desire to be specially remembered when you see him—also to Dr. Hodgson.

You must take it for granted that all your friends here wish to be cordially remembered to you, and that I am not less solicitous to send my warm regards to all the friends across the Atlantic. Ever faithfully yours,

H. C. Wright.   Wm Lloyd Garrison.

William Lloyd Garrison to Henry C. Wright, July 16, 1847, second page

2 0 5

TO LOUISA GILMAN LORING

Boston, July 30, 1847.

My Dear Friend:

I had hoped to be able to comply with your invitation to make you and your beloved husband [Ellis Gray Loring] a visit at Brookline, accompanied by my beloved Helen; but the only thing I can do, in the hurry of preparing to leave home for the far West on Monday afternoon next, is to send you this brief and hastily written note, — a special object of which is to thank you very heartily for your kind donation of $10, towards remunerating me for the sum so unrighteously exacted of me at the Custom House, on account of the tea-service presented to me by my friends in Edinburgh, Scotland. Through the activity of that philanthropic and lovely woman, Mrs. E. F. Meriam, the whole amount has been raised, and put into my hands — and I will add, at a time when it proves specially acceptable, in consequence of a pressure of circumstances. To each of the donors, in this case, I desire to make my grateful acknowledgments.

Next to a fort, arsenal, naval vessel, and military array, I hate a Custom House — not because of the tax it imposed on the friendly Scottish gift, but as a matter of principle. I go for free trade and free inter-communication the world over, and deny the right of any body of men to erect geographical or national barriers in opposition to these natural, essential and sacred rights. Every government must be regarded as a tyranny, and unworthy of approbation, that erects or maintains such barriers. It also is controlled by a very short-sighted policy. — But this is not the place for a treatise on political economy.

During the next eight or nine weeks, I expect to travel many hundreds of miles, attend numerous public meetings, and address many thousands of the people in relation to the wrongs and sufferings of the three million captives in our land. The excursion will be attended with novelty all the way through, as I have hitherto seen very little of Pennsylvania and nothing of Ohio. I trust the mission will not be wholly in vain, brief as it must be on the score of time.

How great has been the progress of the anti-slavery cause since we became acquainted with each other! Yes, since the memorable year 1835! Through what trials, difficulties, misrepresentations, outrages, apostacies, mutations, has that cause passed; and with what a divine energy it has thus far overcome all opposition! "The best of all," as the dying John Wesley said, "God is with us." [1] That the cause of suffering humanity is his — that, in being faithful to it, we are continually and abundantly rewarded — that those who resist its march are sure to be vanquished — who can doubt? "Blessed are the merciful, for they shall obtain mercy." [2] All chains shall yet be broken, and freedom become universal.

Though it is very seldom I have the pleasure of seeing you and Mr. Loring, be assured that your friendship is very highly prized, and your kindnesses remembered with a grateful heart. My warmest regards to E. G. L.

Your much obliged friend,

Wm. Lloyd Garrison.

Mrs. L. Loring.

ALS: Ellis Gray Loring Family Papers, Radcliffe College Library; a handwritten transcription of this letter is to be found in the Garrison Papers, Boston Public Library.

1. Garrison quotes accurately from an anonymous work, *The Beauties of the Reverend J. Wesley, M.A.* (Philadelphia, 1817), p. 21.
2. Matthew 5:7.

206

TO HELEN E. GARRISON

Philadelphia, Aug. 3, 1847.

Dear Wife:

A year ago, this day, I arrived in London, and was, therefore, at a distance of three thousand miles from you. Now I am in Philadelphia, some three hundred miles away. So far as *separation* is concerned, it is the same whether we are hundreds or thousands of miles apart; but then, as a matter of speedy return, it is a matter of very great consequence as to what the relative distance may be. I could be with you in less than twenty-four hours, if necessary — that is comforting. But then, you will say, "you are but commencing your journey away from home, and are to be gone till the 1st of October." True, but no frowning Atlantic ocean is between us, and the time, after all, in reality, whatever it may be in feeling, is very short.

Nothing occurred on the way worthy of special remark. Our trip from Norwich to New-York was as serene and quiet as possible, where we arrived at 5 o'clock. At 9 o'clock, I crossed the ferry, and took the cars for Philadelphia — arriving at 2 o'clock, J. M. M'Kim being at the wharf to escort me to the dear home of our beloved friends, James and Lucretia Mott, who gave me a warm reception of course.

Aug. 7.

Our three days' meeting at Norristown closed last evening, and a famous time we have had of it.[1] Every day, two or three hundred of our friends from Philadelphia came up in the cars, and the meetings were uniformly crowded by an array of men and women, who, for thorough-going anti-slavery spirit, and solidity of character, are not surpassed by any in the world. [Frederick] Douglass arrived on the second day, and was justly the "lion" of the occasion; though a considerable number participated in the discussions, our friend Lucretia Mott speaking with excellent propriety and effect. Thomas Earle was present to annoy us, as usual.[2] Our meetings were not molested in any manner, excepting one evening, when Douglass and I held a meeting after dark, when a few panes of glass were broken by some rowdy boys while D. was speaking. It was a grand meeting, nevertheless, and the house crowded with a noble auditory to the end. The meetings will have a powerful effect in the prosecution of our cause for the coming year. It was worth a trip from Boston to Norristown, merely to *look* at those who assembled on the occasion. I regret that I have as yet found no time to write a sketch of this anniversary for the Liberator. As Sidney H. Gay was present, both the Standard and Penn. Freeman must be referred to for an account of it, prior to any that I shall be able to make of it.[3]

This morning, we leave in the cars for Harrisburg, which, though the capital of the State, is very much under the influence of Slavery. I do not anticipate a quiet meeting, but we shall bear our testimony boldly, nevertheless.

Nearly a week has elapsed of the eight allotted for my tour. No one will be more rejoiced when they are completed than

Yours, lovingly,

Wm. Lloyd Garrison.

ALS: Garrison Papers, Boston Public Library; partly printed in *The Liberator*, August 20, 1847, and in *Life*, III, 189–190.

1. Garrison refers to the meeting of the Eastern Pennsylvania Anti-Slavery Society, a brief account of which appears in *The Liberator*, August 27, 1847.

2. Thomas Earle (1796–1849) was a Philadelphia lawyer and editor and in 1840 the Liberty party candidate for Vice-President of the United States. He was strongly sympathetic to the abolitionists and in 1847 wrote a biography of Benjamin Lundy. But he disagreed with Garrison on some issues, particularly disunion; and it is likely that he came to the Norristown meeting as a heckler.

3. *The Liberator's* account of the meeting was reprinted from the article in the *Pennsylvania Freeman*, August 12, 1847; another article appeared in the *National Anti-Slavery Standard* on the same date.

2 0 7

TO HELEN E. GARRISON

Harrisburg, Aug. 9, 1847.

Dear Wife:

On Saturday morning, [Frederick] Douglass and I bade farewell to our kind friends in Philadelphia, and took the cars for this place, the capital of the State, a distance of 106 miles. Before we started, an incident occurred, which evinced something of that venomous pro-slavery spirit which pervades the public sentiment in proportion as you approach the borders of the slave States. There is no distinction made at Philadelphia in the cars, on account of complexion; though colored persons usually sit near the doors. Douglass took a seat in one of the back cars before I arrived; and while quietly looking out at the window, was suddenly accosted in a slave-driving tone, and ordered to "get out of that seat," by a man who had a lady with him, and who might have claimed the right to eject any other passenger for his accommodation with as much propriety. Douglass quietly replied, that if he would make his demand in the form of a gentlemanly request, he would readily vacate his seat. His lordly commander at once laid violent hands upon him, and dragged him out. Douglass submitted to this outrage unresistingly, but told his assailant that he behaved like a bully, and therefore precluded him (D.) from meeting him with his own weapons. The only response of the other was that he would knock D's teeth down his throat, if he repeated the charge. The name of this man was soon ascertained to be John A. Fisher, of Harrisburg, a lawyer; and the only palliation (if it be one) that I hear offered for his conduct is, that he was undoubtedly under the influence of intoxicating liquor.[1] This was a foretaste of the violence to be experienced on our attempting to lecture here, and which I anticipated even before I left Boston.

Though the cars (compared with our Eastern ones) look as if they were made a century ago, and are quite uncomfortable, yet the ride was far from being irksome, on account of the all-pervading beauty and opulence of the country through which we passed, so far as a fine soil and natural scenery are concerned. We passed through the counties of Philadelphia, Chester, Lancaster, and a portion of Dauphin; and through the whole distance, saw but a single spot that reminded us of our rocky New-England. Arriving at 3 o'clock, we found at the depot, awaiting our coming, Dr. Rutherford, an old subscriber to the Liberator, and his sister-in-law, Agnes Crane, both of them true and faithful to the anti-slavery cause in the midst of a perverse and prejudiced people; and also several of our colored friends, with one of whom, (Mr. Wolf, an intelligent and worthy man,) Douglass went home, having previously engaged to do so; while I went with Dr. Rutherford, and received a cordial welcome from his estimable lady.[2]

The Court House had been obtained for us for Saturday and Sunday evenings. Hitherto, nearly all the anti-slavery lecturers have failed to gather any considerable number together; but, on this occasion, we had the room filled, some of the most respectable citizens being present. At any early period of the evening, before the services commenced, it was evident that mischief was brewing, and an explosion would ultimately follow. I first addressed the meeting, and was listened to, not only without molestation, but with marked attention and respect, though my remarks were stringent, and my accusations severe. As soon, however, as Douglass rose to speak, the spirit of rowdyism began to show itself outside of the building, around the door and windows. It was the first time that a "nigger" had attempted to address the people of Harrisburg in public, and it was regarded by the mob as an act of unparalleled audacity. They knew nothing at all of Douglass, except that he was a nigger. They came equipped with rotten eggs and brickbats, fire-crackers and other missiles, and made use of them somewhat freely — breaking panes of glass, and soiling the clothes of some who were struck by the eggs. One of these bespattered my head and back somewhat freely. Of course, there was a great deal of yelling and shouting, and of violent exclamation — such as "Out with the damned nigger," &c. &c. The audience at first manifested considerable alarm, but I was enabled to obtain a silent hearing for a few moments, when I told the meeting that if this was a specimen of Harrisburg decorum and love of liberty, instead of wasting our breath upon the place, we should turn our back upon it, shaking off the dust of our feet — &c. &c.

Your Husband —

Wm. L. Garrison

P.S. I am about leaving in the cars for Pittsburg and I had to get a friend to close this Letter.[3]

W G

We were well pleased with the visit of Your Husband to this place

AL: Garrison Papers, Boston Public Library; printed in *The Liberator*, August 20, 1847; reprinted in *Life*, III, 190–192.

1. Garrison probably refers to John Adams Fisher (1799–1864), prominent Harrisburg attorney who specialized in ejectment and real property cases. In March 1860 he was to draft the act to incorporate Harrisburg. (*Twentieth Century Bench and Bar of Pennsylvania*, Chicago, 1903, II, 758.)
2. William Wilson Rutherford (1805–1873), a graduate of Jefferson Medical College in Philadelphia, was to practice medicine in Harrisburg for forty years.

He was surgeon to the Pennsylvania Railroad Company, president of the Harrisburg Gas Company, and withal one of the community's most public-spirited citizens. (William H. Egle, *History of the Counties of Dauphin and Lebanon in the Commonwealth of Pennsylvania* . . . , Philadelphia, 1883, p. 557.)

Dr. Rutherford was married to Eleanor Crain, sister of Agnes and daughter of Colonel Richard M. Crain.

Mr. Wolf has not been identified.

3. The complimentary close, the signature, the postscript, and the final sentence were written in the hand of the friend, who is described in Garrison's letter to Helen of August 12, 1847, as "a colored friend," a "Mr. Brown"; Brown has not been further identified. A second signature, "Wm. Lloyd Garrison," has been written in another hand above the almost illegible signature supplied by Brown.

2 0 8

TO HELEN E. GARRISON

Pittsburgh, [Friday] morning, Aug. [13], 1847.

Dear Wife:

I endeavored to complete a letter for you at Harrisburg, before leaving for this place on Monday morning, but was able to write only a portion of one, before it was time to be at the depot. In my perplexity, not knowing what else to do, I requested a colored friend to finish my letter, explaining to you the reason why he did so, and put it into the Post Office. He promised to do so, and I hope was faithful to his promise. As I left off, just as I was giving you the particulars of the rowdyish outbreak at our meeting at H., I requested Mr. Brown to mention that no attempt was made to molest me, and that [Frederick] Douglass escaped without any serious injury, although he was struck in the back by a stone, and a brickbat just grazed his head. All the venom of the rowdies seemed to be directed against him, as they were profoundly ignorant of his character, and it was the first time a colored man (or, to use their slang term, "a nigger") had attempted to address a public assembly in that place.

On Sunday, forenoon and afternoon, we addressed our colored friends in their meeting-house at H., at which a number of white ones were also present. The meetings were crowded, and a most happy time we had indeed. Not the slightest molestation was offered.

On Monday, we left Harrisburg in the cars for Chambersburg, a distance of fifty-four miles. On arriving, to our serious regret we found that the ticket which Douglass obtained at H. for Pittsburgh enabled him to go directly through in the 2 o'clock stage, while I should be compelled to wait until 8 o'clock, (it proved to be 11 o'clock,) in the evening. This was annoying and unpleasant in the extreme. Douglass had a hard time of it, after we parted. The route over the Alleghany mountains, although a very beautiful and sublime one, is a very slow and difficult one; and with a crowded stage, in a melting hot day, is quite overpowering. It seemed to me almost interminable — almost equal to a trip across the Atlantic. Douglass was not allowed to sit at the eating table, on the way, and for two days and nights scarcely tasted a morsel of food. O, what brutality! Only think of it, and then of the splendid reception given to him in all parts of Great Britain! On his arriving at Pittsburgh, however, a different reception awaited him, which was also intended for me. A committee of twenty white and colored friends, with a colored band of music, who had sat up all night till 3 o'clock in the morning, met him to welcome him to the place, and to discourse eloquent music to him.[1] Of course, they were greatly disappointed at my not coming at that time. I arrived toward evening, entirely exhausted, but soon recovered myself by a good warm bath. A meeting had been held in the afternoon in the Temperance Hall, which was ably addressed by Douglass.[2] In the evening, we held one together in the same place, crowded to overflowing. Yesterday, Friday, we held *three* large meetings, two of them in the open air, and concluded last night with the greatest enthusiasm. I have seen nothing like to it on this side of the Atlantic. The place seems to be electrified, and the hearts of many are leaping for joy.

This morning, Saturday, we are off for New Brighton, where we are to have a meeting this afternoon, and others to-morrow. I have not a moment of time, scarcely, left to myself. Company without end — meetings continuously from day to day — little or no sleep — it is the greatest difficulty I can find time to send you a single line in regard to my tour. As for the Liberator, I cannot give any sketch for the public eye, but hope to be able to do so in a few days.

When I get to Salem, Ohio, I shall hope to receive a good long letter from you, assuring me that you and the dear children are well, and giving me some information in regard to the absent ones at Princeton and Lynn. — How I want to hug the babe, and kiss dear little Fanny! — But they must wait until I get home. I have only time to add, that I am in good health, enjoying myself exceedingly. If my esteemed friend Miss [Charlotte] Coffin is with you, give her my warmest regards. Remember me affectionately to all inquiring friends.

Ever faithfully yours,

Wm. Lloyd Garrison.

ALS: Garrison Papers, Boston Public Library; extracts printed in *The Liberator*, August 20, 1847, where the letter is dated August 14, and in *Life*, III, 192–193, where it is dated August 12, the date supplied by Garrison on the manuscript. In fact, neither of these dates is correct; it was written on Friday, August 13, as can be established by reference to internal and external evidence. The "three large meetings" to which Garrison refers were held not on Friday the 13th but on

Thursday the 12th, as is reported in a letter from Frederick Douglass in the *National Anti-Slavery Standard*, September 2, 1847. Also, Garrison left Pittsburgh for New Brighton on August 13, the same day that he wrote the letter. The Pittsburgh *Daily Chronicle*, August 14, reports his departure with Douglass as of that date, and he himself in a letter to Helen, August 16, says that he left Pittsburgh on "Friday" (the 13th).

1. An allusion to Shakespeare, *Hamlet*, III, ii, 375.
2. Temperance Hall was located on the southeast corner of Smithfield Street and Diamond Alley in the downtown area of Pittsburgh. (Letter to the editor from Ruth K. Salisbury, librarian, Historical Society of Western Pennsylvania, February 23, 1971.)

209

TO HELEN E. GARRISON

Youngstown, (Ohio,) Aug. 16, 1847.

Dear Helen:

I scribbled a few hasty lines for you at Pittsburgh, just before leaving that busy, though dingy and homely city — a city which so closely resembles the manufacturing towns in England, that I almost fancied I was once more on the other side of the Atlantic. So, too, the enthusiasm manifested at our meetings was altogether in the English style. For example, at the close of our last meeting, three tremendous cheers were given for [Frederick] Douglass, three for [Stephen S.] Foster, and three for myself. Every thing passed off in the most spirited and agreeable manner.

On Friday, we took the steamer for Beaver, on the Ohio river, (which commences at Pittsburgh, the Monongahela and Allegheny rivers forming a confluence, and falling into it, just below the city,) and from thence rode to New Brighton, in an omnibus, some three or four miles, accompanied by several of our colored Pittsburgh friends, — J. B. Vashon and son, (George B.) Dr. Peck, Dr. Delaney, (editor of the Mystery, black as jet, and a fine fellow of great energy and spirit,) and others, where we had a most cordial welcome from Milo A. Townsend, and his wife and parents, Dr. Weaver, Timothy White, &c. &c.[1] Milo is one of the truest reformers in the land, and wields a potent reformatory pen, but his organ of hope is not quite large enough. There seems to be no branch of reform, to which he has not given some attention. New Brighton is a small village of eight hundred inhabitants, but there are several other villages in its immediate neighborhood. There have been a good many lectures on slavery given in it by our leading anti-slavery lecturers, such as Stephen and A. K. Foster, [Charles C.] Burleigh, [Parker] Pillsbury, Douglass, &c.; but the people generally remain incorrigible. The secret is, they are much priest-ridden — thus confirming afresh the assertion of the prophet, "like people, like priest." [2] The Hicksite Quakers have a meeting-house here, but they are generally pro-slavery in spirit.[3] No place could be obtained for our meeting, excepting the upper room of a large store, which was crowded to excess, afternoon and evening, several hundred persons being present, and many other persons not being able to obtain admittance. In the evening, there were some symptoms of pro-slavery rowdyism outside the building, but nothing beyond the yelling of young men and boys. Over our heads in the room, were piled up across the beams many barrels of flour; and while we were speaking, the mice were busy in nibbling at them, causing their contents to whiten some of our dresses, and thinking, perchance, that our speeches needed to be a little more *floury* — (flowery.) The meetings were addressed at considerable length by Douglass and myself, and also by Dr. Delaney, who spoke on the subject of prejudice against color in a very witty and energetic manner. Douglass was well nigh run down, and spoke with much physical debility. Among others at the meeting was Sarah Jane Clarke, the poetess, who has long been interested in the anti-slavery cause, — a handsome and interesting young woman.[4] I spent an hour at her father's house, in company with Douglass and Milo. Dr. Clarke is in a very feeble state of health, and terribly afflicted with the *tic doloreaux*.[5] Mrs. Clarke is a fine looking woman, and says she knew you in your childish days, as well as your father's family at Brooklyn. She is related to Daniel Tyler, who now occupies the old homestead.[6] It was very pleasant to meet with one who was acquainted with the Brooklyn people, and especially with those whose memories are so dear to us. Sarah [Benson] visited the spot last autumn.

Saturday forenoon, Milo, Dr. Peck, Dr. Weaver, Charles Schirras, and myself, ascended a very steep eminence across the river, three hundred feet high, where we had a beautiful prospect, reminding me somewhat of the view from the top of Mount Holyoke at Northampton, though it was not so fine or extensive, of course.[7] In descending, we went under the "Allum Rocks," which presented a very wild and picturesque appearance.[8] On reaching Milo's house, I was thoroughly tired out, and wet through and through by the perspiration. Indeed, throughout our journey, the weather has been uniformly and exceedingly warm, and I have been "wet to the skin" nearly all the time. To make frequent and long harangues, under such circumstances, is quite overpowering. I have never perspired so much in my life. The quantity of water thus exuded through the pores of the skin has astonished me, and I marvel that any thing is left of me in the shape of solid matter.

Saturday afternoon, at 4 o'clock, Dr. Peck, (he is a fine, [very] promising colored young man, son of my old friend John Peck, now of Pittsburgh, and formerly of Carlisle,) who has lately graduated at the Rush Medical College at Chicago, Douglass and I, took passage for this place (a distance of forty miles) in a canal-boat, it being the first trip of the kind I had ever made on a canal.[9] The day was excessively hot, and on the way, one of the horses was almost melted, and came within a hair's-breadth of losing his life. Colored persons are not allowed, usually, to sit at the table at regular meals, even on board of these paltry canal boats; and we expected to have some difficulty. When the hour for supper arrived, the captain came to us, and said he had no objection to our sitting down together, but he did not know but some of the passengers would object. "We will go and see," said I, with my feelings somewhat roused. Happily, no objection was made. Berths were also given to us all, but it was impossible for me to sleep in so confined an atmosphere, as the cabin was small, and thronged. The scenery on the route was very pretty. At 4 o'clock, yesterday morning, (Sunday,) we arrived here, and immediately came up to the "Mansion House," kept by N. Andrews.[10] It is a "rum tavern," but the landlord (strange to say) is friendly to our cause, and generally entertains the abolition lecturers without charge. This world presents some queer paradoxes, and this is one of them. Yesterday, we held three meetings in a beautiful grove, which were well attended. During the day, the burden fell chiefly upon me, as Douglass was entirely exhausted and voiceless. I am afraid his old throat complaint, the swelling of the tonsils, is upon him. He left for Salem after dinner, accompanied by Samuel Brooke, a distance of forty miles.[11] J. W. Walker, S. S. Foster, and Dr. Peck, helped to fill up the gap at the meetings. To-day, I leave for New Lyme, (40 miles off,) where the annual meeting commences on Wednesday, and will continue for three days.[12] Thus far, I have stood the fatigues of the tour better than I anticipated. As yet, I have not had a word of intelligence from home. I trust you have written to me at Salem. With many kisses for you and the children, and loving remembrances to all the friends, I remain

Ever yours,

Wm. Lloyd Garrison.

ALS: Garrison Papers, Boston Public Library; extract printed in *Life*, III, 193–195.

1. George B. Vashon (c. 1824–1878), son of the well-to-do barber John Vashon, was the first Negro to be graduated from Oberlin College (1844), from which he also received a master's degree (1849). A lawyer and educator, he was to become president of Avery College in Pittsburgh and, after the Civil War, a solicitor with the Freedmen's Bureau in Washington, D.C. (Letters to the editor from Ruth K.

Salisbury, librarian, Historical Society of Western Pennsylvania, February 23, 1971, and W. E. Bigglestone, Oberlin College Archives, March 1971.)

David Jones Peck, son of the John Peck mentioned later in this letter, was the first Negro graduate of an American medical school (see Leonard W. Johnson, Jr., "History of the Education of Negro Physicians," *Journal of Medical Education*, 42:440, 1967). There is a difference of opinion concerning the date of Dr. Peck's graduation: *Rush Medical College Catalogue* (Chicago, 1849), lists him as in the fifth commencement, 1848, whereas Johnson and *The Address Book of the Alumni of Rush Medical College* (Chicago, 1913–1914), give the same date as Garrison, 1847. Possibly, although he was a member of the class of 1847, the commencement exercise did not occur until 1848.

Martin R. Delaney (1812–1885) founded a Negro antislavery paper, the Pittsburgh *Mystery*, in 1843 but in 1847 withdrew to become co-editor of the *North Star* with Frederick Douglass. In 1849 Delaney was to begin the study of medicine at Harvard. He practiced in Pittsburgh and later in Chatham, Canada. In 1859 he headed the first Negro expedition to explore the Niger Valley in Africa. During the Civil War he was commissioned as the first Negro major in the United States Army and later filled various federal and commercial posts. (See William J. Simmons, *Men of Mark* . . . , Cleveland, 1887, pp. 1007–1015.)

Milo A. Townsend (1816–1877) was a Quaker abolitionist, schoolmaster, and editor of New Brighton, Pennsylvania. His paper, which Garrison calls the "organ of hope," was the New Brighton *Times*. (Letters to the editor from Charles W. Townsend, January 3 and March 8, 1971.)

Little is known about Charles Weaver (died 1851) except that he was a physician practicing in New Brighton. (The Reverend Joseph H. Bausman, *The History of Beaver County, Pennsylvania*, New York, 1904.)

Timothy White (1807–1885) was a Quaker carpenter whose home served as a station on the Underground Railroad. (John W. Jordan, *Genealogical and Personal History of Beaver County Pennsylvania*, New York, 1914, I, 531–533.)

2. Hosea 4:9.

3. In 1827 the Hicksite Quakers separated from the Orthodox to form their own division of the American Society of Friends. Named for the leader of the movement, Elias Hicks (1748–1830), the Hicksites minimized the importance of the historic Christ, emphasizing instead an abstract concept of the spirit of Christ within each man.

4. Sarah Jane Clarke (1823–1904), a native of New York state, moved to New Brighton in 1842 and in 1844 began writing poems and children's stories under the pseudonym "Grace Greenwood." In 1853 she married Leander K. Lippincott of Philadelphia. She was one of the first women in the United States to become a regular newspaper correspondent.

5. Thaddeus Clarke (1770–1854) was a physician and native of Connecticut. He was an uncle of Theodore D. Weld, Clarke's sister Elizabeth being Weld's mother. His wife was Deborah Clarke (c. 1791–1881).

6. Daniel Tyler (1799–1882), soldier and industrialist, was born in Brooklyn, Connecticut. He studied in artillery schools both in the United States and in France. In the 1840's he became president of several railroad companies. During the Civil War he was a brigadier general.

7. Charles Perry Schiras, or Schirras (c. 1824–1854), was a resident of Allegheny, now a part of Pittsburgh, and a good friend of the composer Stephen Collins Foster. The Schiras family also owned a farm near New Brighton. An ardent abolitionist, Schiras edited his own antislavery weekly, the *Albatross*. (Letter to the editor from Ruth K. Salisbury, librarian, Historical Society of Western Pennsylvania, December 2, 1970.)

8. Alum Rocks is a steep hillside on the west bank of the Beaver River. A trail winding about the cliff led to what was believed to be an Indian cave. (Letter to the editor from Nell Stafford, librarian, New Brighton Public Library, November 19, 1970.)

9. John Peck, wigmaker by trade, took an active part in trying to improve conditions for Negroes, using every effort to secure them equal educational opportunities as well as the right to vote and to hold office. He had served as president of the state convention of the Negro freemen of Pennsylvania held in Pittsburgh, August 23–25, 1841. (Letter to the editor from Ruth K. Salisbury, librarian, Historical Society of Western Pennsylvania, May 27, 1970.)

Dr. Peck and Garrison traveled on the Pennsylvania-Ohio Canal.

10. Norman Andrews (1799–c. 1882) was a native of Connecticut who came to Ohio at an early age, engaged in farming, and later established a general store at Paines Corners. About 1842 he moved to Youngstown and operated the Mansion House until about 1850, when he retired, although he retained ownership of the hotel until 1865. (H. Z. Williams, *History of Trumbull and Mahoning Counties*, Cleveland, 1882.)

11. Samuel Brooke (1808–1889), civil engineer and railroad route-explorer, was born in Maryland of a strongly antislavery family. Moving to Alliance, Ohio, in 1842, Brooke became general agent for the Ohio American Anti-Slavery Society and later for the Western Anti-Slavery Society. (Letter to the editor from Conrad F. Weitzel, reference librarian, Ohio Historical Society, September 18, 1970, citing W. H. Perrin, *History of Stark County, Ohio*, 1881, pp. 718–719.)

12. Garrison refers to the annual meeting of the Western Anti-Slavery Society, to be held August 18–20. This society had gone through a succession of name changes. Originally the Ohio Anti-Slavery Society, it became, following the schism of 1840, the Ohio American Anti-Slavery Society and in 1846 the Western Anti-Slavery Society.

210

TO HELEN E. GARRISON

New Lyme, (Ohio,) Aug. 20, 1847.

Dear Helen:

On Sunday last, I wrote a letter to you, dated at Youngstown, and another to friend [Robert F.] Wallcut, but left them on the table at the hotel, unsealed, without giving directions to any one to put them into the post-office, in my hurry to leave for this place. Whether they were sent to you, I do not know, but trust the landlord did for me what *I* meant to have done.

On our way to this place, we stopped on Monday night at a tavern in Hartford, a place settled originally by emigrants from Hartford, Ct. In the evening, a lecture was advertised to be given on Phonography by a Mr. Alexander,[1] (an abolitionist,) in the meeting-house. Before the meeting, the lecturer and a deputation of persons waited upon me, and urged me to go over and address the assembly at least for a few minutes, as there was a great curiosity to see me. I complied with their request, and spoke about fifteen minutes in favor of Phonography, and thus enabled the good folks to take a peep at the "elephant," but without his "trunk."

On Tuesday afternoon, we arrived at this little village, the place selected for holding our grand convocation in this State — the anniversary of the Western Anti-Slavery Society. Just after our arrival, a very severe rain-storm ensued, accompanied with heavy thunder and vivid lightning. It was well for our clothes, if not for our skins, that we escaped it. A great change in the weather at once took place, and the next day it was so cold that I wanted to be sitting by a rousing fire to feel comfortable. The clouds were dark and lowering, and it rained more or less frequently during the day. Our great tent, capable of holding four thousand persons, which was put up the day before, was blown down by the wind during the night, and, as it was thoroughly saturated with the rain, it required considerable effort to erect it again. Notwithstanding the unpropitious state of the weather, at an early hour vehicles of various descriptions began to pour into the place in great numbers. A small meeting-house or academy, close to the tent, was occupied by the Ladies' Fair, which I have, as yet, not found time to visit; but, for want of good management, I am told it is not likely to realize any considerable amount of funds for the cause, though I believe they have a good variety of articles.[2] We held two meetings in the tent on the first day, which were attended by a large concourse, among them some of the choicest friends of our cause in the land, — ay, and choicest women, too. Messrs. Giddings and Tilden, members of Congress, who have nobly battled for freedom in that body, were also present.[3] After the organization of the meeting, a poetical welcome to Douglass, [Stephen S.] Foster and myself, written by Benjamin S. Jones, was sung with exquisite taste and feeling by a choir, causing many eyes to be moistened with tears.[4] I then addressed the great multitude at considerable length, and was followed by Douglass in a capital speech. In the afternoon, we again occupied the [tent] most of the time. The interest manifested, from beginning to end, was of the most gratifying character, and all seemed refreshed and greatly pleased. As the night approached, there appeared to be some symptoms of rowdyism, and it became necessary for some of our friends to watch all night, lest the tent should be damaged. Yesterday, all day, our meetings were still more thronged — four thousand persons being on the ground. The Disunion question was the principal topic of discussion, the speakers being Douglass, Foster, and myself, in favor of Disunion, and Mr. Giddings against it. Mr. G. exhibited the utmost kindness and generosity towards us, and alluded to me in very handsome terms, as also to Douglass; but his arguments were very specious, and I think we had with us the understanding and conscience of an overwhelming majority of those who listened to the debate. As a large proportion of the abolitionists in this section of the country belong to the Liberty party, we have had to bring them to the same test of judgment as the Whigs and the Democrats, for supporting a pro-slavery Constitution; but they are generally very candid, and incomparably more kind and friendly to us than those of their party at the East.

To-day, (Friday,) we shall close this cheering anniversary; after which, Douglass and I must ride forty miles to attend another convention at Painesville, which commences to-morrow morning at 10 o'clock; at the conclusion of which, we must take another long jaunt, to hold meetings on Sunday at Munson. Our friends here have so multiplied the meetings, that not an hour is left us for rest. They are unmerciful to us, and how we are to fulfil all the engagements made, without utterly breaking down, I do not know. Douglass is not able to speak at any length, without becoming very hoarse, and, [in] some cases, losing the ability to make himself heard. This makes my [own] task the more arduous. On the whole, I am enabled to sustain it pretty well, and shall endeavor to act as prudently as I can.

Our reception has been very kind. The manners of the people are primitive and simple. The country, of course, looks like a newly settled one, as compared with our New-England States, but it is comparatively thickly settled on this Western Reserve.[5] In regard to contributing money towards carrying forward our cause, they are not so liberal as we are at the East; indeed, money here is not usually plenty, although they have every thing else in abundance.

No quotations must be made from my hasty scrawls to you for the Liberator. I have not a moment's time to prepare any thing fit for the public eye, and must refer our friends at home to the Bugle for information.

My best regards to the [Francis] Jacksons, Mrs. [Eliza Jackson] Meriam, the Wallcuts, and the other dear friends. Glad shall I be when my mission is ended.

With great love, yours, ever,

Wm. Lloyd Garrison.

P.S. Since my arrival here, I have had the pleasure of receiving a letter from you, dated August 8th, which was directed to Pittsburgh, and forwarded to me from that place. I devoured its contents with great eagerness, and felt a great burden of anxiety removed from my mind in consequence of it. I am hoping to receive another letter from you at Salem. You will see by the Liberator, at what time and place I am to be in western New-York, on my homeward route, and can calculate how to get a letter to me at any place seasonably. Pray let me have a letter, directed to the care of Samuel J. May, at Syracuse.

I do not wonder that you feel lonely, in my absence, and that of four of the children.[6] My anxiety to return is equal to yours to have me once more at home. Happily, should all go well with me as it has done thus far, the time will soon be completed, and the family circle will be again unbroken. I am sorry you were unable to communicate any information respecting George and William, though I presume they are well and happy. It was pleasant to hear from Wendell and Charles, that they were enjoying themselves finely at Lynn. Tell Fanny father wants you to kiss her many times for him, every day, until he returns home — and dear little Lizzy too. Your account of the funeral of the late Mrs. Chapman was very interesting. My warmest sympathy and regards to Mary.[7]

ALS: Garrison Papers, Boston Public Library; extract printed in *Life*, III, 196–198.

1. Not identified.

2. The Ladies' Fair at the Western Anti-Slavery Society meeting was similar to the annual bazaars in Boston, where miscellaneous items were sold for the benefit of the antislavery cause. Advertisements for this particular fair are to be found in *The Liberator*, July 16, 1847.

3. Garrison refers to two distinguished congressmen from Ohio, Joshua Reed Giddings (1795–1864) and Daniel R. Tilden (1804–1890). Elected as a Whig in 1838, Giddings crusaded for free debate on all matters relating to slavery and urged that the power of the federal government to tax free states for the support of slavery be rescinded. In 1848 he broke with the Whigs, becoming a member of the Free-soil party, and in 1854, following the repeal of the Missouri Compromise, he became a Republican. Tilden moved from Connecticut to practice law in Ohio. In 1843 he was elected as a Whig representative to the House, where he served until 1847. Late in life he became a probate judge of Cuyahoga County. (*Biographical Directory of the American Congress, 1774–1961*, pp. 1716–1717.)

4. Benjamin Smith Jones (1812–1862) of Salem, Ohio, was editor, with his wife Jane Elizabeth Jones (born 1813), of the *Anti-Slavery Bugle* from approximately 1847 until 1849, when he was succeeded by Oliver Johnson. The *Bugle*, which was the organ of the Ohio American Anti-Slavery Society, was published between July 1845 and May 1861. Its founding and its suspension were both announced in *The Liberator*, July 11, 1845, and May 10, 1861. (*Life*.)

5. The Western Reserve was a district in northeastern Ohio bordering on Lake Erie for about one hundred and twenty miles and comprising more than three million acres, with Cleveland as its population center. Although in the eighteenth century title to this land had been claimed by Connecticut, it was ceded in 1800 to the United States government.

6. As this letter indicates, Wendell and Charles were visiting at Lynn, possibly with the James N. Buffums; George and William were at Princeton, Massachusetts, perhaps visiting the Joshua T. Everetts. (See the letter to Helen E. Garrison, August 12, 1847.)

7. Sarah Greene Chapman (c. 1774–1847) was the wife of Henry Chapman of Boston and the mother of Henry G. Chapman and Mary Gray Chapman. Through the Boston Female Anti-Slavery Society, she paid the counsel fee in the Med case, which in 1836 (the first time in the history of the United States), applied English common law to slaves taken to a free state voluntarily by their masters, declaring them free. (*Life*.)

Little is known of Mary Gray Chapman (c. 1798–1874) except that like the rest of her family she was active in the antislavery cause.

2 1 1

TO *THE LIBERATOR*

RICHFIELD, Ohio, Aug. 25, 1847.

Our great anniversary meeting closed at New Lyme on Friday, the 20th inst. The discussions of the last day were of a spirited character, and up to the last hour the audience was immense. We adjourned at half-past 2 o'clock, P. M., and were then busily engaged for some time in shaking hands and bidding farewell to a host of friends. When the dense mass moved off in their long array of vehicles, dispersing in every direction to their several homes, some a distance of ten, others of twenty, others of forty, others of eighty, and others of a hundred miles, it was a wonderful spectacle. One man (colored) rode three hundred miles on horseback to be at the meeting! After taking some refreshment, we left New Lyme, about 4 o'clock, for Painesville, passing through Austinburg, and taking supper at the house of Cornelia and Betsy Cowles's brother, where we had a hearty welcome.[1] The girls arrived with [Frederick] Douglass soon after we did, who remained under their roof until the next morning, when he rode over to Painesville. The girls are very fine singers, especially Cornelia, and we sung together a number of songs before we left. Dr. [David J.] Peck, a highly intelligent and amiable young colored man, a graduate of Rush College, was my companion — Mr. Jackson, a colored citizen of P., carrying us in his two horse vehicle to the house of deacon Horace Ensign at Madison, where we arrived between 10 and 11 o'clock at night.[2] The deacon had invited us at New Lyme to spend the night at his house, but had retired with his family to rest, supposing we had concluded to stop in Austinburg. He, and his son, and daughter, soon made their appearance, and about midnight all was quiet again. The deacon is a Liberty party man, but very kind and hearty in his feelings towards us, and his house is always open to anti-slavery lecturers and runaway slaves. After breakfast, the next morning, we rode to Painesville, Lake county, (within three miles of Lake Erie,) arriving at 10 o'clock. It is a very pleasant and well-built village, the prettiest and most populous of any that we have yet seen — containing about 1500 inhabitants. The Telegraph, a Whig paper, is the only paper printed in it.[3] The politics of the place are strongly Whig. The same remark applies to nearly every town and village on the Western Reserve. Not having been invited to stop with any one at P., we went to Higley's tavern, to brush off the dust, wash ourselves, and prepare for the meeting.[4] The landlord came out, and took off our baggage, supposing that Dr. Peck was Mr. Douglass. I requested him to show us a chamber, and he did so, without saying a word. As soon as he left us, I said to my friend Peck, 'Dr., I am inclined to think, from the looks of the landlord, that our company is not desirable here.' In a few minutes, a person came into our room, saying that his name was Briggs — that he was the brother of the present Governor of Massachusetts — that he had taken the liberty of introducing himself to us in consequence of a conversation he had just had with the landlord, who declared to him, that no nigger could be allowed to sit at his table, and that if any such attempt were made, there would be a *muss* — not that he had any objection himself, but his boarders would not allow it.[5] A genuine specimen of American democratic, Christian colorphobia. Mr. Briggs invited us to his house, and we accordingly left the tavern. Our meeting was convened in a grove in the immediate vicinity, and several hundred persons were present.[6] Gen. Paine, a lawyer, (Liberty party,) presided.[7] The day was fine, and the attention given was all that we could desire. Most of the day's talking devolved on me. Frederick's voice was much impaired, and he had to have a bad tooth extracted during the meeting. I took dinner at Gen. Paine's with a company of friends, and at the close of the afternoon meeting, I went home to spend the night with J. Gillet, a true friend of our cause, and was very hospitably treated.[8]

On Sunday morning, Mr. Gillet carried me to Munson, (14 miles,) with his wife and another lady, in his carryall. The ride was a charming one, during which, I discussed all sorts of theological questions with Mrs. Gillet, a lady of considerable quickness of intellect. On arriving at Munson, we saw the great Oberlin tent in a distant field; but no village was to be seen, and only here and there a solitary log cabin. 'Strange,' said I to myself, 'that our friends should pitch their tent in such a place. From whence are we to get our audience?' But, on going to the spot, I found a large company already assembled, and in a short time the vast tent was densely filled, even to overflowing; so that the multitude was greater than we had even at New Lyme! It was a grand and imposing spectacle. Poor Frederick was still unwell, and could only say a few words in the forenoon; and in the afternoon, he absented himself altogether from the meeting, and put a wet bandage round his throat. This threw the labor mainly upon me, though our sterling friends S. S. Foster and J. W. Walker made long and able speeches, which aided me considerably. The enthusiasm was general and very great. We continued our meeting through the next day, with a large and most intelligent audience, and made a powerful impression. Douglass was much improved, and spoke with inimitable humor, showing up the religion of the South in particular, and of the country in general. At the close, Dr. Richmond, (one of our most intelligent and active comeouters, last from the Liberty party,) offered a series of resolutions, strongly commendatory to Douglass and myself, which were *unanimously* adopted by a tremendous 'Ay!' — after which, six cheers were given in the heartiest manner.[9] Altogether, it was the most interesting meeting I have ever attended in this country. (The preceding night, I stopped with Douglass, Dr. Peck, and Saml. Brooke, with an anti-slavery friend, Mr. Randall.) [10] Monday afternoon, we all started for Twinsburg, Brooke and I coming by the way of Chagrin Falls village, (where we stopped over night with Mr. Richardson, 'true blue,') and Douglass, Foster, &c. going by the way of Bainbridge.[11] In the morning, we rode over to Twinsburg, where we found collected in a beautiful grove about a thousand persons, whom Douglass and I addressed, at great length, both forenoon and afternoon. Douglass almost surpassed himself. It was a most gratifying occasion to all, and a good work was done. We were all hospitably entertained by a stanch abolitionist, Ezra Clark, a subscriber to the Liberator.[12] As at New Lyme, Painesville, Munson, and other places, multitudes crowded around us to give us their blessing and God speed, and to express the strong gratification they felt to see us in the flesh. A great many anti-slavery publications were sold, subscribers obtained for newspapers, &c. &c. Before dark we left for this place, at which to tarry over night, at the house of deacon Ellsworth, on our way to Oberlin.[13] To-day is commencement day at O., and we shall leave here soon after breakfast, hoping to arrive at O. in season for the afternoon exercises. I have long desired to see Oberlin, but do not expect to accomplish much in that place, as we are to have only one day's meeting, (to-morrow,) and a good deal of prejudice is cherished against me on account of my 'infidelity' and 'comeouterism.' We are prepared, however, to give our testimony, both in regard to the Church and State, whatever may be thought or said of us.

WM. LLOYD GARRISON.

Printed: *The Liberator*, September 10, 1847; extract printed in *Life*, III, 199–202.

1. Possibly Garrison refers to Edwin Weed Cowles, oldest brother of Betsey and Cornelia Cowles. A physician, he practiced in Mantua, Cleveland, and Detroit, and was the father of Edwin Cowles (the founder of the Cleveland *Leader*) and of Alfred Cowles (the business manager of the Chicago *Tribune*). Betsey Cowles (1810–1876), daughter of pioneer preacher Giles Hooker Cowles, was graduated from Oberlin in 1840 and became an important figure in educational reform as well as in the cause of woman's rights and abolition. At the second convention for woman's rights at Salem, Ohio, in 1850, she was elected president. Cornelia Cowles (c. 1807–1869), her sister's life companion, was a professional singer. (Harriett Taylor Upton, *History of the Western Reserve*, Chicago, 1910.)

2. Mr. Jackson has not been identified. Of Horace Ensign nothing is known except that his wife, Celestia Raymond, came in 1824 to Madison, Ohio, from Sherburne, New York. (Letter to the editor from Virginia R. Hawley, general reference supervisor, Western Reserve Historical Society, December 5, 1970.)

3. The Painesville (Ohio) *Telegraph*, a weekly newspaper, was founded in 1822 and continued publication under various titles until approximately 1918. (*ULN*.)

4. Homer Higley (1796–1857), a native of Connecticut who had served in the War of 1812, had moved to Painesville and become the proprietor of the American House. In 1835 he had been one of the organizers of the Painesville and Fairport Railroad. (Letter to the editor from Frances Slack, administrative secretary, Lake County Historical Society, September 10, 1970.)

5. Simon B. Briggs (1793–1863) was a brother of George N. Briggs, then governor of Massachusetts. Simon Briggs had lived in Painesville since 1843 and was probably a colonel in the state militia. (Painesville *Telegraph*, October 15, 1000.)

6. The Painesville *Telegraph* of August 25 confirms that the meeting was addressed by Garrison and Douglass and reports that perfect order was maintained throughout.

7. James Harvey Paine (1791–1879) was a general in the state militia and a leader in the antislavery movement in northern Ohio. In 1839 he organized a county branch of the Liberty party and in 1844 was chairman of the Ohio party convention. In 1848 he was to move to Milwaukee, where he and his son Byron argued successfully the unconstitutionality of the fugitive slave law before the state supreme court. (Painesville *Telegraph*, February 20, 1879.)

8. Garrison apparently refers to Isaac Gillet (1789–1850), Painesville farmer and general merchandiser. Besides being interested in abolition he was a supporter of the peace movement and a member of the national Liberty party committee. (Letter to the editor from Josephine C. Sheffer, Morley Library, Painesville, June 10, 1970.)

9. Probably Garrison refers to John Lambert Richmond (1785–1855), a Baptist minister and physician. In 1827 he had performed in Newton, Ohio, a Caesarean section, the first officially recorded in the American medical press. He had subsequently moved to Pendleton and then to Indianapolis, Indiana.

10. Garrison may refer to David Austin Randall (1813–1884), a Baptist clergyman and editor of the *Washingtonian*, the first temperance paper in Ohio.

11. Mr. Richardson has not been identified. One of the first instances of the term "true blue" meaning "faithful" occurs in Samuel Butler, *Hudibras*, Part I, Canto 1, line 189.

12. Ezra Clark (1807–1890) was a farmer and land clearer. A Methodist and native of Connecticut, he operated a station on the Underground Railroad. (Gertrude Van Rensselaer Wickham, ed., *Memorial to the Pioneer Women of the Western Reserve*, Cleveland, 1896–1897.)

13. Elijah Ellsworth (1785–1859), born in Connecticut, moved with his family to Ohio, where he became the minister of Richfield. (Letters to the editor from Warren Skidmore, head history librarian, Akron Public Library, December 1 and 8, 1970.)

2 1 2

TO HELEN E. GARRISON

Oberlin, Aug. 28, 1847.

My Dear Wife:

Though I have received no intelligence from you since your letter of the 8th inst., I withdraw for a few moments from the pressure of company, before leaving this place, in order to give you a very brief sketch (which I should be glad to make a very full one, if time would permit) of the meetings we have held, in furtherance of the anti-slavery cause.

You know that from the commencement of the Institution in Oberlin, I took a lively interest in its welfare, particularly on account of its springing up in a wilderness, only thirteen years since, through the indomitable and sublime spirit of freedom, by which the seceding students of Lane Seminary were actuated.[1] When Messrs. Keep and Dawes went over to England, a few years since, to obtain pecuniary aid in its behalf, from the friends of a freedom-giving Christianity, I commended them to the confidence and liberality of all British abolitionists; and while in that country with them in 1840, I did what I could to facilitate their mission.[2] Oberlin has done much for the relief of the flying fugitives from the southern prison-house, multitudes of whom have found it a refuge from their pursuers, and been fed, clad, sheltered, comforted, and kindly assisted on their way out of this horrible land to Canada. It has also promoted the cause of emancipation in various ways, and its church refuses to be connected with any slaveholding or pro-slavery church by religious fellowship, though it is said to be involved in ecclesiastical and political relations, which impair the strength of its testimony, and diminish the power of its example. From these, if they exist, it is to be hoped it will be wholly extricated, ere long, as light increases, and duty is made manifest. So thoroughly has the poison of slavery circulated through every vein and artery of this nation, that it infects every part of the body politic, whether religiously or politically considered.

The desire that I had long cherished to visit Oberlin was gratified on Thursday last. In company with [Frederick] Douglass, [Stephen S.] Foster, [James W.] Walker, and the indefatigable General Agent of the Western Anti-Slavery Society, Samuel Brooke, I arrived in season to attend the exercises of the graduating class in theology. The number of persons present was immense — not less than four thousand. The meeting-house is as spacious as the Broadway Tabernacle in New-York, but much better arranged. Two of the graduates took occasion, in their addresses, to denounce "the fanaticism of Come-outerism and Disunionism," and to make a thrust at those, who, in the guise of anti-slavery, temperance, &c. are endeavoring to promote "infidelity"! Prof. Finney, in his address to the graduates, gave them some very good advice — telling them that denouncing Come-outerism, on the one hand, or talking about the importance of preserving harmony and union in the church, on the other, would avail them nothing.[3] They must go heartily into all the reforms of the age, and be "anti-devil all over" — and if they were not ready to do this, he advised them to go to the workshop, the farm, or any where else, rather than into the ministry. This was talking very plainly — but if those young men should attempt to carry his advice into practice, where could they hope to find congregations and salaries?

Yesterday, at 10 o'clock, we began our meetings in the church — nearly three thousand persons in attendance. Another was held in the afternoon, another in the evening, — and this forenoon we have had another long session. Douglass and myself have done nearly all the talking, on our side, friend Foster saying but little. The principal topics of discussion have been come-outerism from the Church and the State. Pres. Mahan entered into the debate in favor of the U. S. Constitution as an anti-slavery instrument, and, consequently, of the Liberty party.[4] He was perfectly respectful, and submitted to our interrogations with good temper and courtesy. As a disputant, he is adroit and plausible, but neither vigorous nor profound. I shall say nothing about my visit here, for the public eye, until my return. What impression we made at Oberlin, I cannot say; but I was abundantly satisfied as to the apparent effect. I think our visit was an important one, and very timely withal. Douglass and I have been hospitably entertained by Hamilton Hill, the Treasurer of the Institution, an English gentleman, who formerly resided in London, and is well acquainted with George Thompson and other anti-slavery friends.[5] He is a very worthy man, and his lady is an amiable woman. They have a family of nine children. James Munroe and his wife are boarding in their family. I did not know before that James was married. His wife is a delicate looking young woman. He looks very slender, and I think will fall, ere long, a victim to pulmonary consumption. He inquired very particularly after you and all our household, and desired to be warmly remembered. He is now connected with the Faculty. We dined yesterday with Prof. Hudson, and were invited to dine with Pres. Mahan to-day, but could not afford the time.[6] Prof. Morgan called to see us, but my old friend James A. Thome has given us "the go-by" — why, I do not know.[7] Among others with whom I have become acquainted is Miss Lucy Stone, who has just graduated, and yesterday left for her home in Brookfield, Mass.[8] She is a very superior young woman, and has a soul as free as the air, and is preparing to go forth as a lecturer, particularly in vindication of the rights of woman. Her course here has been very firm and independent, and she has caused no small uneasiness to the spirit of sectarism in the Institution. — But I must throw down my pen, as the carriage is at the door, to take us to Richfield, where we are to have a large meeting to-day under the Oberlin tent, which is capable of holding four thousand persons.

Salem, Sunday night, Sept. 5, 1847.

Here I am, under the roof of Benj. S. and E. Jones, with a company below stairs singing a variety of songs and hymns — the Cowles, from Austinburg — while I am trying to do, what I have in vain sought to do, since I was at Oberlin — and that is, to finish this letter.

Our meetings at Richfield were eminently successful — five thousand present, and the weather superb. We held six meetings in all. Stopped with Dea. [Elijah] Ellsworth, a come-outer. From thence we went to Medina, and held two meetings in the court-house, which was filled with an intelligent audience. The effect produced good. — We next went to Massillon, and held three meetings in the Tremont Hall, to a respectable and deeply interested assembly. Stopped with R. H. Folger, a talented lawyer, and good abolitionist, and a relation of Lucretia Mott.[9] Next, we went to Leesburg, the residence of J. W. Walker — a long and tedious ride.[10] Stopped on the way over night at a tavern in Zoar, a place owned by an association of German communitists, and highly improved.[11] We held several meetings at Leesburg — attendance small, but much interest manifested on the part of those present. A Methodist priest [12] wished to know whether I believed in the inspiration of the Bible. This led to a rich scene. Stopped with Mr. Millisack,[13] an old subscriber to the Liberator, who has a beautiful situation. On the way from Leesburg to this place, stopped for the night at a miserable tavern in Augusta, and arrived here yesterday morning, and had the happiness to obtain a letter from you, giving me the assurance of all being well at home. Of course, I devoured every word of it greedily. We have held four immense meetings here — two yesterday, and two to-day — five thousand persons on the ground. Our friends are in the best possible spirits. The tide of anti-slavery is rising daily. Every thing looks encouraging. This afternoon, while a vast concourse was assembled in the tent, just as I had concluded my speech, a thunder storm broke upon us, and the rain poured down in torrents, giving us all a pretty thorough baptism — but the people would not disperse, and we looked the storm out of countenance, & wound up gloriously. Our dear friends,

James and Lucretia Mott, are here — Lucretia has spoken twice from our platform, and will go with us to other places. To-morrow, we leave for New Lisbon — on Tuesday and Wednesday, we must be at Warren — on Thursday and Friday, at Ravenna — on Saturday and Sunday, at Cleveland and then farewell to Ohio! My health is good, but I am excessively jaded out. Write to me at Syracuse.

Love to every body,

W. L. G.

ALS: Garrison Papers, Boston Public Library; extracts printed in *The Liberator*, September 17, 1847, and in *Life*, III, 202–205.

1. Oberlin Collegiate Institute, which in 1850 became Oberlin College, was chartered in 1834. In 1835 its newly established theological seminary (Congregational) admitted forty students from Lane Theological Seminary of Cincinnati. The students had left Lane because its board of trustees had forbidden discussion of the slavery question.

2. John Keep (1781–1870) was a Yale graduate and Congregational minister. In 1835 he became president of the board of trustees of Oberlin in which capacity he cast the deciding vote for the admission of Negro students to the school. Although intermittently resuming his pastoral duties, he spent most of his remaining years in service to Oberlin. (*Weld-Grimké Letters.*)

In 1839 William Dawes (1799–1888) was sent to England with John Keep on a fund-raising mission for the college. During this trip they collected $30,000, and Dawes served also as a delegate to the World's Anti-Slavery Convention of 1840. A trustee of Oberlin from 1839 to 1851, he was also active in the peace movement, and in 1847 was elected president of the Lorain County (Ohio) Peace Society. (Robert Samuel Fletcher, *A History of Oberlin College*, Oberlin, 1943.)

3. Charles Grandison Finney (1792–1875) was a revivalist and educator. In 1835, after the Lane Seminary affair, he was invited to establish a theological department at Oberlin, and was connected with the college for the rest of his life, acting as president from 1851 to 1866.

4. Asa Mahan (1799–1889) was a Congregational clergyman who in 1835 became first president of Oberlin, a position he held until 1850. Like Finney he had been connected with Lane Seminary and had assisted in the founding of the theological department at Oberlin.

5. Hamilton Hill (1794–1870) had acted as host to Keep and Dawes during their fund-raising tour in England. They persuaded him to come to Oberlin as treasurer, a post he held until 1864. Active in the peace movement, he attended the peace congress in Paris in 1849. He also helped establish a school for Negroes in the town of Oberlin. After his retirement from the college he returned to England. (Fletcher, *A History of Oberlin College.*)

6. Timothy B. Hudson (1814–1858) did not receive his bachelor's degree from Oberlin until 1847, but he taught Greek and Latin there during 1838–1841 and 1847–1858. He favored coeducation, was active in the peace movement, and took part in antislavery activities as an agent of the Ohio Anti-Slavery Society and a lecturer on abolition. (Fletcher, *A History of Oberlin College.*)

7. John Morgan (1803–1884) was a native of Ireland and a graduate of Williams College. While teaching at Lane Seminary he supported the students in the antislavery debate and was discharged. He then went to Oberlin, where he taught until his retirement in 1880. (*Weld-Grimké Letters.*)

James A. Thome (1809–1873), the son of a Kentucky slaveholding planter, went in 1833 to Lane Seminary under the influence of Theodore D. Weld. Having taken part in the debate there, he joined the exodus to Oberlin to become an antislavery lecturer and minister. In 1836 he went to the West Indies for the American Anti-Slavery Society. In 1838 he became professor of rhetoric and belles lettres at Oberlin and in 1849 pastor of a church in Cleveland, where he served until 1871. (*Weld-Grimké Letters.*)

8. Lucy Stone (1818–1893), formerly a self-educated teacher, had worked her way through Oberlin, where she became a radical advocate of abolition and woman's rights. An eloquent free-lance lecturer, as early as 1850 she was instrumental in organizing various woman's rights conventions. She founded the American Woman Suffrage Association, and in 1870 she raised funds to establish the *Woman's Journal*, which she and her husband, Henry Brown Blackwell, were to edit from 1872 until her death.

9. Robert H. Folger (1812–1899), from Chester County, Pennsylvania, was a cousin of Lucretia Mott's. He practiced law in Massillon, Ohio, and was to be a justice of the peace for fifteen years and a United States commissioner for fifty. He also took an active part in politics, at first working with the Liberty party and later with the Republican. (Letter to the editor from Margaret Hudson, assistant librarian, Massillon Public Library, May 26, 1970, citing *History of Stark County, Ohio*, edited by John H. Lehman.)

10. Leesburg (now called Leesville) is in Carroll County, Ohio.

11. Zoar, named for the town where Lot settled after fleeing from Sodom and Gomorrah, was a separatist religious community founded in 1819 by Joseph Michael Bimeler (c. 1778–1853), who led a group of refugees from Germany to Philadelphia and ultimately to Ohio. Thanks to Bimeler's leadership Zoar had developed a series of flourishing industries, but it was destined to be dissolved in 1898 because of internal dissension.

12. Not identified.

13. Not identified.

213

TO HELEN E. GARRISON

Cleveland, Ohio, Sept. 18, 1847.

My Dear Wife:

The bitter with the sweet — the thorn with the rose. Here I am — on my back; of course, "looking up," literally. I came to this place just a week ago, (with Douglass,) to complete my mission to Ohio, expecting to leave for Buffalo on Monday. Our first meeting was held in the large Advent Chapel, and was densely crowded, hundreds not being able to gain admittance.[1] Sunday forenoon, we held another crowded meeting in the same place; in the afternoon, to accommodate the throng, we went into a pleasant grove, where we addressed a large auditory. The effect produced at all these meetings seemed to be excellent. Unfortunately for me, the atmosphere in the grove was damp, and it sprinkled occasionally during the meeting — the clouds being very dark and lowering. But this, in itself, was a very trifling circumstance. My labors, for the last four weeks, had been excessive — in severity, far exceeding any thing in my experience. Too much work was laid out for both Douglass and myself, to be completed in so short a time; yet it was natural that our Ohio friends should wish to "make the most of us," whilst we were in their hands. Sunday night was a very restless one to me, and on Monday morning I arose, feeling as if my labors in Western New-York must be dispensed with. My brain was terribly oppressed, and highly inflamed — my system full of pain — my tongue began to give symptoms of a fever, that might be more or less protracted — and I felt indescribably wretched. In an hour, as it were, I was a crushed man — helpless as an infant. During the day, I went to the bed to which I am still confined. Thinking a Lobelia emetic would relieve my stomach, and possibly my head, I took one. It operated very gently, but nothing particularly offensive was ejected. In the evening, feeling it would be imprudent longer to tamper with so determined a foe, I sent for Dr. Williams, a skilful homœopathic physician, and gave myself unreservedly to his care.[2] My case he soon ascertained to be that of a bilious, intermittent type, with a tendency to typhoid. Tuesday, Wednesday and Thursday, were days of great restlessness, distress and anxiety; the fever was upon me in its strength; not a moment's sleep could I realize, day or night. It reminded me of my scarlatina sickness, though it was not quite so dreadful as that. Yesterday, I began to feel better, and have since been improving up to the present hour. I am now decidedly convalescent, though still exceedingly weak, as a matter of course. In the course of another week, I expect to be so far recovered as to leave for home. Eight hundred miles is the distance which separates us — 200 by steam across Lake Erie, and 600 miles by rail-road from Buffalo to Boston. This would be formidable indeed, without the power of steam. Now, my dear, I have given you the worst of the case, that you may have no scope left for the imagination. Possibly, you may see the following paragraph, which appeared (very imprudently indeed) yesterday in the True Democrat: —

"Mr. Garrison was so unwell as to be unable to proceed to Buffalo with his friends on Monday last. He is now at Mr. Jones's, quite low with the bilious fever. Visiters are prohibited by his physician from calling upon him." [3]

It is true, that, for a day or two, (so numerous were the calls upon me,) Dr. Williams forbade visiters coming to my room, but this was only a wise injunction. As my case is b[ecom]ing [4] known, it naturally brings in many persons, both from the city and neighboring villages, to make inquiries after my health. Benjamin and J. Elizabeth Jones, of Salem, have been to see me; so has a sister of S. S. Foster, who is residing here.[5] George Bradburn is a daily visiter at my bedside. Every body is kindly offering me all needed assistance. Fortunately, I am in one of the best families in the world, and have every thing done for me, by day and by night, that you could desire. I miss nothing, need nothing, but your dear presence, and that of the darling children. God preserve you all from harm. A thousand kisses for them — as many for you — on my return. Should you have written to me at Syracuse, I shall get the letter, as I intend to spend a day with dear S. J. May. Douglass left here on Tuesday noon.

Your *improving* husband,

Wm. Lloyd Garrison.

ALS: Garrison Papers, Boston Public Library; extract printed in *Life*, III, 205–207.

1. The Advent Chapel was located on Wood (now East Third) Street, between Rockwell and St. Clair Streets. It was a round brick building about sixty feet in diameter. (Cleveland city directory, 1845–1846, p. 122.)

2. Charles D. Williams (1812–1882), who came to Cleveland in 1846, had offices in the "Empire Block" (numbers 78–84 Superior Street). He was to help organize the Western College of Homœopathic Medicine in 1850, where he became professor of principles and practice of homœopathy. In the early 1860's he went from Cleveland to St. Paul, Minnesota, where he continued his medical practice and invented, with E. B. Berge, a new type of fire-alarm box. (Letter to the editor from Donald Empson, assistant reference librarian, Minnesota Historical Society, March 31, 1971.)

3. The Cleveland paper referred to could be either a daily or a weekly — that is, the *Daily True Democrat*, founded in 1847 and published under this title until December 1851 or the weekly *True Democrat*, founded in 1846 and published under this name until 1853. (*ULN*.)

Mr. Jones was probably Thomas Jones, father of the future Senator John Percival Jones of Nevada. With his wife Mary Ann, Thomas Jones emigrated from Herefordshire, England, to settle in Cleveland as a marble cutter. In 1844 he was elected treasurer of the Liberty Club of Cleveland, an antislavery organization. (Letter to the editor from Laszlo L. Kovacs, head history librarian, Cleveland Public Library, November 23, 1970.)

4. Probably "becoming," although the word cannot be supplied with certainty, since a piece of the page has been torn out.

5. Garrison refers to Sarah Foster (1805–1890), who was at this time a teacher in Cleveland. (James O. Lyford, *History of the Town of Canterbury, N.H., 1727–1912*, Concord, N.H., 1912, II, 136.)

214

TO STEPHEN S. FOSTER [1]
(Private.)

Cleveland, Oct. 12, 1847.

My dear Foster:

My head is so weak, and my hand so unsteady, that I fear you will scarcely be able to read this scrawl.

I had a very comfortable night last night, without taking any medicine, and have thus far passed a very comfortable day in bed, notwithstanding the exceeding gloominess of the weather.

I have been examining afresh the probable expenses of my illness;

and I am satisfied that they will not be one farthing less than one hundred dollars. Do not let the friends subject me to the mortification of being necessitated to say to any to whom I am indebted, "I have no money to pay you now, but my friends will settle with you hereafter." Spare me that necessity. I want every thing settled, cash down, before I leave Cleveland. After you have made an appeal in your effective manner at Randolph, let Samuel Brooke and J. W. Walker go among the audience, and take up such contributions as the friends may be disposed to make.[2] I suppose Samuel will take in trust what may thus be collected. Just ascertain, then, what the whole amount is, and ask Samuel what other money he has in his hands for the same purpose; then ascertain the sum total, and you will know precisely what is the balance needed to make up $100. If my expenses be less than I suppose they will be, what is left shall be remitted to the treasury [3] at Salem.

Do not forget to remind the Executive Committee, that at least $45 will be saved to the treasury, by your going home with me, instead of Samuel Brooke. This is a very fortunate circumstance.

I earnestly desire that you will abandon your contemplated discussion with Mr. Preston, and write to him why you do so.[4] I expect, now, to get up somewhat rapidly; and you had better gradually wind your way along from Salem to Cleveland. You can spend a day or two here, if necessary, very pleasantly.

My head is utterly confused, and I am exhausted. I must now take the penalty.

Give my warmest remembrances to all the friends of Peace and Liberty at Randolph. My benediction is upon them all.

    Yours, lovingly,

                    Wm. Lloyd Garrison.

    P. S. By the word "private" inside, I do not mean that such friends as S. Brooke, J. W. Walker, and other choice ones, should not peruse the letter, but only that no public use must be made of it. I have no doubt that every thing will be done that I require. My only apprehension has been, as to the promptness with which the settlement might be made. You must all pardon my sensibility on this point. I am weak and nervous.

ALS: Stephen and Abigail Kelley Foster Papers, American Antiquarian Society.

    1. According to an announcement in *The Liberator*, July 30, 1847, Stephen S. Foster had been selected as a last-minute replacement for James N. Buffum to accompany Garrison on his western tour.

    2. Randolph and all the towns referred to in this letter are in Ohio.

    3. Probably that of the Western Anti-Slavery Society.

    4. Possibly Garrison refers to James A. Preston (1815–1848), an 1841 graduate of Oberlin Theological Seminary, who subsequently became a missionary in

Jamaica. (Letter to the editor from Virginia R. Hawley, general reference supervisor, Western Reserve Historical Society, June 6, 1971.) The nature of Foster's "contemplated discussion with Mr. Preston" is unknown.

215

TO HELEN E. GARRISON

Cleveland, Oct. 19, 1847.

My Dear Wife:

I am going to try to write you a few lines, "with my own hand," [1] as Paul says; but whether I shall succeed, or not, is at least problematical. My hand is unsteady, and I am too weak, as yet, to make an effort of any kind without considerable difficulty.

The arrival in Cleveland of dear H. C. Wright took me almost as much by surprise, as if he had descended from the clouds. Of course, I was very deeply affected by his presence; but though my heart leaped to see him, I almost felt to regret that a few dear friends had taxed themselves to defray the expenses of his long journey from Boston to this city. But it is another instance of their unbounded kindness to me, and it presses upon my heart somewhat heavily. I am *so* glad that you did not come with him, much as I yearn to see you; for, under all the circumstances, it would have been not only a useless and expensive, but a very imprudent act. Indeed, at no stage of my illness did I deem it all advisable to send for you. I am specially glad, therefore, that you deemed it not best to come at this late period, during my convalescence. — But my heart's overflowing gratitude to those generous friends, who offered to defray all the expenses of your journey!

On another account, nothing could have been more opportune than the journey of H. C. W. at this time. The great National Liberty Party Convention will meet at Buffalo to-morrow and next day, and the occasion will doubtless be one of tremendous interest and excitement. There will, I think, be a complete blow-up of the party. In order that we may have a correct report of its proceedings, and "gather up the fragments that nothing may be lost," [2] I have urged Henry, (as there is really nothing for him to do here,) to go to Buffalo, and there watch the Convention as a cat does a mouse, allowing nothing to escape, and putting down in his note-book, every thing worth recording. Disliking to part from me, he at first hesitated; but, seeing the importance of having that body looked after, he consented to go, and accordingly took the steamer this forenoon for Buffalo, (accompanied by Saml. Brooke, who is also going on to Boston,) where he will remain until my arrival at B., which I trust will be in all this week.[3]

You will be glad to hear that I rode out yesterday, and enjoyed the ride, and also to-day with benefit. I am now only waiting for the arrival of S. S. Foster, who expects to be here on Thursday, when, if the weather be fair, we shall leave on Friday for Buffalo. In the course of a fortnight from this date, I hope to embrace you and the children in my arms.

I have lost twenty pounds of flesh by my illness, and am quite thin and weak. This effort has been most exhausting to me. I *must* stop. Best regards to all.

Your weary but loving husband,

Wm. Lloyd Garrison.

P. S. I have received a long, sympathetic and loving letter from brother George at Northampton, in which he gave me the glad intelligence that dear sister Sarah's health is very much better, and that in a few days she would go with him to Boston, and remain with us during the winter! How I long to see her!

☞ Let no more letters be addressed to me at this place. I shall be gone before their arrival.

ALS: Garrison Papers, Boston Public Library; partly printed in *Life*, III, 207–208.

1. An adaptation of Galatians 6:11.
2. An adaptation of John 6:12.
3. Letters from Henry C. Wright describing the convention and relevant events immediately preceding it can be found in *The Liberator*, November 5 and 19, 1847.

216

TO HELEN E. GARRISON

Cleveland, Oct. 20, 1847.

My Dear Wife:

As on a previous occasion, I received a letter from you last evening, only an hour or two after I had mailed one for you. It came quite unexpectedly, and its contents were of a comforting character. To be assured that all is well at home, and that you lack for nothing, is a very great relief to my mind. O, the blessing of health! it is seldom appreciated until it is taken from us. I hope to prize it, hereafter, more highly than I have hitherto done.

The kind and unceasing attentions of our esteemed friends, Mr. and Mrs. [Robert F.] Wallcut, to which you gratefully allude, certainly demand of me the liveliest expressions of thankfulness. These you will proffer to them. Our indebtedness to them is very great, and ever increasing.

You also refer to the kind and efficient assistance rendered by Mrs. Garneaux.[1] She is one of the ministering spirits of Love and Goodness in this world — too rare, alas! — and but for whom, the world would present a dreary aspect indeed. Give her my warmest remembrances.

I rather regret that you have weaned dear Lizzy at so early a period, but perhaps you have decided wisely. I was thinking that about the middle of December would be the most suitable time.

Tell dear little Fanny, that father is coming home soon, in accordance with her wishes.

I am glad to hear, beyond measure, that all the boys are behaving so well, and going to school so regularly. Especially am I glad to hear that George has been promoted in school, and is attending to his studies with so much interest. May they all try to improve every day, to be always kind to each other and to all around them, and to make you happy.

The trip of dear H. C. Wright from this place to Buffalo, yesterday, must have been as short and pleasant, as the trip from Buffalo to Cleveland was long and disagreeable. May I be as fortunate!

This is the last letter you may expect to receive from me at this place. My next I hope will be a living epistle, in *propria persona*.

I am expecting S. S. Foster daily. As soon as he arrives, I shall be for leaving without any delay, unless the weather should be stormy. That may detain us here several days, but I hope not.

You represent the state of sister Sarah's health to be far more feeble than did bro. George in his letter. Give her my sympathy and love.

I cannot specify the friends to whom I desire to be affectionately remembered. None of them are forgotten.

It is a most painful effort for me to write. This short letter has cost me the labor of hours.

Ever yours, lovingly,

Wm. Lloyd Garrison.

P. S. H. C. Wright will accompany me as far as Albany, and from thence go to Philadelphia. S. S. Foster will go with me as far as Worcester; and Saml. Brooke will go with me all the way through to Boston. You must have a bed ready for him.

Is it not strange that [Frederick] Douglass has not written a single line to me, or to any one, in this place, inquiring after my health, since he left me on a bed of illness? It will also greatly surprise our friends in Boston to hear, that, in regard to his project for establishing a paper here, to be called "The North Star," he never opened to me his lips on the subject, nor asked my advice in any particular whatever. Such conduct grieves me to the heart. His conduct [. . .] [2] paper has been impulsive, inconsiderate, and highly inconsistent with his decision in Boston.[3] What will his English friends say of such a strange somerset? I am sorry that friend [Edmund] Quincy did not express himself more strongly against this project in the Liberator.[4] It is a delicate matter, I know, but it must be met with firmness. I am sorry to add, that our friend Saml. Brooke is at the bottom of all this, and has influenced Douglass to take this extraordinary step, as he thinks the Bugle might as well be discontinued, or merged in Douglass's paper! Strange want of forecast and judgment! — But, no more now.

ALS: Garrison Papers, Boston Public Library; extract printed in *Life*, III, 209–210.

1. Eliza Jones Garnaut (1810–1849) was a native of Wales and matron of the Temporary Home for Destitute Females and Orphan Children in Boston. She belonged to the Moral Reform Society and supported antislavery, temperance, and peace. (*The Liberator*, September 7 and October 12, 1849.)

2. The letter is torn.

3. Garrison's attitude towards Douglass' founding of an antislavery paper invites extended explanation, not only because the story is complicated but because it reflects the growing rift between the two men. When Douglass returned from abroad in April 1847 he brought with him £ 500 from English friends, who had suggested that he use it either for his personal needs or to start his own newspaper. Garrison and others advised against such a publication on the grounds that there were many antislavery papers already (even several edited by Negroes), that it was doubtful whether enough subscribers could be found to sustain it, and that Douglass' greatest talent lay in speech-making, not editing. In *The Liberator*, July 9, 1847, it was announced that Douglass had abandoned the idea.

While lecturing with Garrison in Cleveland in September, Douglass seems to have reconsidered his decision, although his plans for the paper were certainly not concrete, for he eventually decided to publish it in Rochester rather than Cleveland. The first issue of the *North Star* appeared December 3, 1847. With Martin R. Delaney as co-editor for the first two years, publication continued for seventeen years, and soon Garrison seems to have lost his resentment. In *The Liberator*, January 28, 1848, for instance, he praised the first issues of the *North Star* and wished it success.

4. In announcing the founding of the *North Star* in *The Liberator*, October 1, 1847, Quincy remarked that there would doubtless be a difference of opinion among abolitionists as to the advisability of publishing the new paper and said that there would be disappointment at losing Douglass as a lecturer. Quincy did, however, wish the paper success.

217

TO HELEN E. GARRISON

Syracuse, Oct. 26, 1847.

My dear Helen:

I will confess to you, that I meant to have taken you by surprise, by arriving in Boston on Saturday evening next,[1] (Deo volente,) when I left Cleveland a week ago yesterday, without letting you know of my purpose. But brothers [Samuel J.] May and [Henry C.] Wright have "let the secret out" in their joint letter; and perhaps it is better that you should know exactly my design. It is true, "there's many a slip between the cup and the lip," and it is by no means certain that my strength will enable me to get along as fast as I hope to do.[2] But, thus far, I have endured the fatigues of the journey better than I anticipated. I hope all will be well to the end. Instead of Saml. Brooke, dear bro. Wright will go with me to Boston, so have a bed-room nicely prepared for him — hair-mattress, &c. We shall not probably arrive before 8 o'clock, in the evening. If we do not come then, look for us on Monday evening. Please let only a very few friends know of this arrangement — such as the [Francis] Jacksons, Mrs. [Eliza Jackson] Meriam, Mr. and Mrs. [Robert F.] Wallcut, W. Phillips, &c. — as I must see the friends generally by degrees, and I wish to have a very quiet Sunday at home. I shall not go to Northampton, unless the weather is fair — and only for the night.

Farewell, till we meet!

W. L. G.

ALS: Garrison Papers, Boston Public Library.

1. October 30.
2. Garrison quotes the ancient proverb which can be traced back to the Greeks, possibly to Homer.

218

TO ELLIS GRAY LORING AND FRANCIS JACKSON

Thursday Morning. [December 2, 1847.][1]

Dear friends Loring and Jackson:

The bearer of this — Henry Williams [2] — who appears to be a very worthy and industrious colored man, is in trouble in regard to certain articles of his, which are at present at the Worcester depot, and which he needs, but has not quite money enough to redeem them. He will tell you his simple story, in a few words. He does not ask for any gratuity, but only wants a little time to earn the money ($3) required to pay for the transportation of his things from New Haven. If my pockets were not entirely bare and empty, I would aid him to the extent of his wishes; for he has excellent recommendations of character from gentlemen residing in New Haven. I submit his case to your judgment and kindness.

Yours, truly,

Wm. Lloyd Garrison.

ALS: Garrison Papers, Boston Public Library.

1. The date is supplied in another hand, probably Wendell Phillips Garrison's.
2. Perhaps the "Henry Williams, col'd.," located on Christopher Street near Columbus, to be found in New Haven directories between 1844 and 1846.

219

TO EDMUND QUINCY

Boston, Dec. 4, 1847.

My dear Quincy:

If you can find time, I wish that, in the next Liberator, you would stick the nib of your pen into the vitals of the delinquent subscribers to the Liberator, and make them "shell out" what they owe, before the close of the year. You can exercise more freedom on that "delicate subject" than I can; and our pecuniary deficiency is so great, that we shall be warranted in calling pretty loudly upon delinquents.

After this next paper, I shall endeavor to relieve you of further editorial labor and responsibility. Most grateful do I feel to you, for your many kindnesses. But words are cheap, and I will not use them profusely.

Do you intend to notice Pierpont next week?[1] It seems to me he has had his "three days of grace" allowed him, and judgment should now be executed upon him.

Ever your much obliged friend,

Wm. Lloyd Garrison.

Edmund Quincy.

ALS: Garrison Papers, Sophia Smith Collection, Smith College Library.

1. John Pierpont (1785–1866), the grandfather of J. P. Morgan, was a Unitarian minister whose dedication to various reforms so offended his conservative parishioners at Hollis Street Church, Boston, that in 1845 he voluntarily resigned. Garrison refers to a controversy that had arisen between Pierpont and

Quincy. Pierpont had written an introduction to a collection of newspaper articles by Nathaniel P. Rogers in which Pierpont implied that Garrison, Quincy, Wendell Phillips, and Francis Jackson had sided against Rogers in the *Herald of Freedom* controversy because he did not share their views on nonresistance. Quincy wrote Pierpont a letter on November 9 refuting this charge and received a reply on November 14. Quincy wrote again on December 13, 1847 (see *The Liberator*, December 17, 1847), reiterating his denial. A final explanation from Pierpont in which he appeared to capitulate was printed in *The Liberator*, December 31, 1847.

220

TO JOSEPH RICKETSON

Boston, Dec. 4, 1847.

My Esteemed Friend:

I was highly gratified by the receipt of your kind letter, inviting me to be one of the lecturers before the New Bedford Lyceum.[1] Most happy shall I be to improve the opportunity, if my health will permit; and I am daily improving in that particular. You may, therefore, consider me engaged. Allow me as late a period for the delivery of the lecture as you can conveniently with your other arrangements. I am greatly obliged to you for the friendly interest you manifest in my case. Would that I could be an attendant at your anti-slavery meetings, to be held to-day and to-morrow in your place![2] My dear friend H. C. Wright, the bearer of this, is to be present, and a faithful witness to the truth he will be. God's blessings rest upon you all!

In great haste, I remain,

Your much obliged friend,

Wm. Lloyd Garrison.

Joseph Ricketson.

ALS: Charles G. Slack Collection, Marietta College Library, Ohio; a typed transcription has been preserved in the Garrison Papers, Boston Public Library.

Joseph Ricketson, Jr. (1815–1876), the son of a merchant and cashier of the Bedford Commercial Bank, was himself a merchant who in 1841 became a member of the committee of arrangements of the New Bedford Lyceum. His house was always open to Garrison and other abolitionists and reformers. (Daniel Ricketson, *New Bedford of the Past*, ed. Anna and Walton Ricketson, Boston, 1903, p. 18.)

1. The New Bedford Lyceum, founded in 1828, was probably the most prominent cultural institution in the city until 1907, when it was dissolved and its assets turned over to the Old Dartmouth Historical Society Whaling Museum. Garrison spoke at this lyceum regularly, but whether he was able to accept Ricketson's invitation this time is not known. (Letter to the editor from Richard C. Kugler, director, Old Dartmouth Historical Society, June 16, 1970.)

2. There is no mention of these meetings in *The Liberator*.

2 2 1

TO EDMUND QUINCY

Boston, Dec. 8, 1847.

Dear Quincy:

As I think of going to Northampton to spend a few days with bro. George, please consider yourself editor of the Liberator for another week at least; and if you can cook up a dish for [John] Pierpont and Lewis Tappan in the next number, do so.[1] They might as well be executed at the same time for their offences.

I have received a letter from David Ruggles, at Northampton, in which he says — "From what I can learn of your symptoms, you need to restore an equilibrium of circulation, and brace the nervous and muscular systems. Why can't you spend five or six weeks at a Water Cure, and accomplish it by a very moderate course of treatment? Come out here; and it will afford me the highest gratification to put you through, free of charge. I have, at present, but few patients, and can give you the very best attention."[2] This is certainly a generous offer, but I must decline it; though I have no doubt that such a course of treatment would do me immense service, as my nervous system is still very much impaired. My sleep at night is "next to nothing," mainly on account of the swelling and pain in my left side.

Yours, gratefully,

Wm. Lloyd Garrison.

ALS: Garrison Papers, Sophia Smith Collection, Smith College Library.

1. Quincy's controversy with Pierpont has already been described in Garrison's letter to Edmund Quincy, December 4, 1847. It is not clear why Garrison wanted Quincy to deal with Lewis Tappan. At any rate, the suggested article did not appear.

2. For information about David Ruggles and details of the water cure see Garrison's letters to Francis Jackson, August 2, 1843, and to Henry C. Wright, October 1, 1844. Garrison did not accept Ruggles' invitation on this occasion, but he did the following summer, as will be seen in subsequent letters. The water cure was frequently advertised in *The Liberator*, after May 21, 1847.

2 2 2

TO GEORGE W. BENSON

Boston, Dec. 17, 1847.

Dear George:

Was it not aggravating, after so long a separation, that we should be able merely to glance at each other, and to make but a single salutation, as we passed each other, "rail-road speed," between Boston and Providence? Great was my regret on being absent from home when you were here, for I had special desires to see you. For the last ten days, I have been thinking every day that I would jump into the cars for Springfield and Northampton, and spend a fortnight with you; but various domestic matters have prevented my doing so, and I now reluctantly "give it up." Helen has been more troubled, in regard to her "help," within the last four months, than during all the previous time for more than twelve years. Girl after girl has come, and proved inexperienced or worthless — how many, I will not begin to enumerate. To-day, we are to try again with a new hand — with what success remains to be seen. With our large family, to be without some one to do the cooking and washing, even for twenty-four hours, is a serious inconvenience. I am to have a fortnight longer to perfect my health, (which is very much improved,) before I resume the cares and responsibilities of the Liberator. My friend [Edmund] Quincy has been exceedingly kind and accommodating; and if my health required it, he would cheerfully remain at the editorial post almost any length of time, without charge. It will take me some time to wear the editorial harness easily, and I shall need to be cautious, for a while, how I indulge in long protracted mental effort.

A few days since, I received a very kind letter from my worthy friend Dr. [David] Ruggles, generously inviting me to spend some time at his water cure establishment, gratuitously, and try the effect of that process upon my system. Most grateful am I to him for his kind offer, and most readily would I embrace it, if I had not been so long absent from my post, and the cares of the family were not so onerous. — The swelling in my left side, near the diaphragm, is quite troublesome, since my fever, and Dr. [Christian F.] Geist, the homœopathic physician, is prescribing for it. He thinks it is of the nature of a polypus. You know there are conflicting opinions as to what it is, among the doctors.

My special object in writing is, to tell you how I am situated, pecuniarily, at the present time, and to ascertain whether you will be able to obtain for me the pecuniary relief desired, temporarily. The reduction of the price of the Liberator one half dollar, at the commencement of the last volume, lost us at least eight hundred dollars; but we were in hopes that the number of new subscribers that might thus be obtained would make up for this loss. In this, we have been wofully disappointed, our list of subscribers having increased scarcely any at all — perhaps not more than one hundred. The consequence is, that the Liberator is swamped, — i. e. considerably in debt to the paper maker, the printer, and the general agent.

According to my usual salary, three months' salary ($300) will be due to me on the 1st of January — every cent of which will be due to my creditors on that day. This large deficit in the receipts of the Liberator, I have little doubt, the financial committee will shoulder, with the aid of others, but not in season to save my credit, which, fortunately, I have been able to keep in the most punctual manner hitherto, and which I would not lose, if it can possibly be avoided, for a good deal. Hence, I am shivering and shaking, and at my "wit's end," in view of the near approach of the 1st of January. I owe you something, already, and am therefore loath to apply to you in this emergency; and yet, I want your counsel, if nothing more. Judging from the past, I have no doubt that my salary will be fully paid, probably in all January; but of this, of course, there is no absolute certainty, as the committee are not responsible to me for a farthing. As yet, however, they have never failed to make all good. Now, dear George, overwhelmed as you are with business, can you procure for me the desired loan of $300, in season for the 1st of January, to save my credit — taking for security the amount that is due me, my integrity as a man, and whatever belongs to me in the shape of personal property? If so, I shall feel relieved of a mountain weight, and will endeavor to repay the loan as soon as my accounts shall be squared with the committee. Should you desire an interview with me, on sending me word by return of mail, I will in the course of a few hours be at Bensonville in the course of a few hours; but, much as I desire to see you and Catherine, and the other friends, I should like to avoid the expense of the journey at this time, if practicable. Still, it may be necessary to see you, face to face; if so, I will cheerfully come. Helen is hoping, with me, that you will come down and be with us during Christmas week, to visit the Bazaar, &c. Can you not do so?

The late Mrs. [Sarah] Chapman generously bequeathed to me $100, which was paid to me on the day before Thanksgiving, and at a most timely period too. It enabled me to discharge sundry debts, which I otherwise could not have easily liquidated. Do the best we can, our family expenses are large, and increasing unavoidably with the growth of the children. Much do I wish to see and consult with you as to the future. We are all well. Love to your wife and children.

Yours, "in tribulation,"

W. L. Garrison.

☞ Of course, if the whole loan desired cannot be obtained, any portion of it will be acceptable.

ALS: Garrison Papers, Boston Public Library.

V ANTI-SABBATH CONVENTION
AND FATHER MATHEW: 1848–1849

THE LAST TWO YEARS of the decade of the 1840's were memorable to Garrison himself not for the continuation of his agitation for disunion, not for the end of the war with Mexico, not for the first woman's rights convention in Seneca Falls, New York, not for the election of Zachary Taylor, but for the Anti-Sabbath Convention in Boston, March 23–24, 1848, and for what Garrison considered the misconduct of Father Theobald Mathew, the Irish prelate who arrived in Boston in July 1849.

The Anti-Sabbath Convention was instigated primarily by Henry C. Wright and by Garrison. In many ways Wright had become Garrison's closest friend and colleague. With him Garrison did not feel the social barrier that separated him from Phillips and from Quincy, for both men were of lower middle-class stock and both Calvinistic in background, though not in current practice. It was true that Wright had had formal education Garrison lacked (he was a graduate of Andover Theological Seminary), but Garrison had leadership in the antislavery movement which Wright, who was slow in becoming an abolitionist, greatly respected. Wright had not joined the Massachusetts Anti-Slavery Society until 1835, but now he embraced Garrison's ultra views on abolition and followed all his extraneous reforms as well, supplying energy and ideas of his own, especially on nonresistance and the Sabbath question. Garrison was aware that during Wright's absence in Great Britain secondary reforms had been neglected; and he used the serendipitous leisure available during the recuperation from his serious illness to exchange ideas and to plan action.

Garrison involved many besides Wright in the discussions in what Quincy called "Helen's parlor." [1] From time to time during the last weeks of 1848 and the first of 1849 all the so-called Boston clique met

1. Henry C. Wright, "Diary to Maria," December 2, 1847, Boston Public Library.

there. Garrison's and Wright's plans for a public convention were approved, a carefully worded call was written, and signatures were sought — Garrison anticipating a thousand or more. Even before the public meeting, however, the response among Garrisonians was not uniformly favorable. Several of the most dependable abolitionists signed the call reluctantly, if at all. Quincy signed with the explicit understanding that he was not expected to promote the convention. "I was content," he said, "to ring the bell, but not to do any part of the preaching or evangelizing." [2] Both Wendell Phillips and Samuel J. May refused to sign. The call for the convention was published in *The Liberator*, January 21 and again February 18 and March 3.

In the meantime, Garrison kept his readers abreast of the reaction to the call from individuals and from the press. *The Liberator* became a forum of private and public opinion both on the advisability of having a convention and on the validity of the Sabbath as a religious institution. Between the first publication of the call (January 21) and the meeting itself (March 23–24) Garrison printed innumerable letters, articles, editorials, some of them supporting his point of view, others attacking it. Wright, of course, filled many columns as did Garrison himself, who published elitorials February 11, March 10, and March 17.

As Wright's unpublished diary makes abundantly clear, the two-day convention itself was in no sense an anticlimax to the previous publicity. Officers were elected. Garrison's alter ego, George W. Benson, became president and Quincy, no doubt reluctantly, one of the vice-presidents, and Garrison, modestly, became a member of the business committee. Speeches and resolutions were numerous: everyone from Theodore Parker to Lucretia Mott to Wright to Garrison spoke. In fact, Garrison could not restrain himself from speaking five times. Almost every speaker introduced resolutions, some as many as twenty. Lucretia Mott, it was generally agreed, made the most eloquent contribution. A mentally disturbed individual, Abby Folsom, who had acquired the reputation of being the ubiquitous pest of conventions, provided the comic relief.

As Garrison's letters show, the aftermath of the convention was not so much to his liking. When publicity about the meeting spread abroad, Elizabeth Pease, Garrison's British arbiter, was disturbed. She wrote to Phillips and Wright as well as to Garrison, complaining about *The Liberator*, which she feared might corrupt innocent persons. Garrison responded with page after page of defense.

More serious than criticism from Miss Pease were the illnesses

2. Edmund Quincy to Richard D. Webb, letterbook, March 9, 1848, Massachusetts Historical Society.

suffered by the Garrisons during the spring and summer of 1848. Influenza attacked one after another in the family. Garrison had a bad fever and cough; Helen and her sister Sarah were sick; and the baby, Lizzy Pease, always frail, died on April 20. Helen and Garrison mourned their first loss of a child, and Garrison rationalized that death was a part of life; daguerreotypes were recorded of the infant corpse.

Garrison's illness lingered into the summer, nourished, Quincy thought, by his proclivity for irregular diet and the "hell-broths of Thompsonianism." [3] Dr. David Ruggles offered Garrison without charge the facilities of his water cure establishment at Northampton; and, beginning in the middle of July, Garrison spent three miserable months with myriad applications of cold and hot water, the monotony in the eccentric sanitarium relieved only by the visit of his family in August.

Garrison returned to Boston in time for the birth of Francis Jackson Garrison on October 29. The Garrisons lived for the winter in their house at 13 Pine Street and then moved in March to 65 Suffolk (later Shawmut Avenue). On April 8 occurred an event that was to test Garrison's powers of rationalization and his fortitude more even than did the death of Lizzy Pease. Charlie Follen Garrison, six years old and handsome and robust, was suffering from what may have been a minor fever and digestive complaint. At Garrison's insistence he was given a homeopathic vapor bath so hot that it ultimately resulted in his death.

In July 1849 Garrison was aroused from the lethargy of illness and death by the appearance on the American scene of Father Theobald Mathew, the same Irish priest and reformer who had signed the Irish Address in 1841 urging his compatriots in the United States to shun prejudice against the Negro and to support the noble efforts of abolitionists. Although his present American mission was dedicated primarily to temperance, Garrison felt certain that Father Mathew would be eager to help further the cause of abolition. Father Mathew's was a triumphant procession from New York to Washington where the people and their leaders (some no doubt thinking of the Irish vote at forthcoming elections) thronged to pay him attention.

Garrison decided to invite Father Mathew to join the Massachusetts Anti-Slavery Society's celebration of the British West Indies emancipation at Worcester on August 3. As chairman of a reception committee he drew up a formal letter of invitation, which he and Dr. Henry I. Bowditch personally presented to the distinguished

3. For Quincy's discussions of Garrison's ill health see the copies of his letters to Richard D. Webb, letterbook, June 27, July 26, 1843; January 31, 1844; December 13, 1845; and January 13, 1853 (Massachusetts Historical Society).

cleric at the Adams House in Boston. Father Mathew indicated at once that he was sufficiently occupied during his current trip with the "slavery of intemperance," but Garrison urged that he study the letter and reply to it. When no written answer came from Father Mathew, Garrison fastened onto a new cause célèbre. He printed in *The Liberator*, August 10, the letter of invitation, a report of the interview, and various other editorial comments; in the nine weeks to follow he unleashed a veritable barrage of propaganda against Father Mathew, including five more letters of his own addressed to him. Father Mathew had the dignity to remain silent.

During 1849, despite illness and death in the family and his preoccupation with the Father Mathew case, Garrison engaged in many other activities, such as appearing with Wendell Phillips before the judiciary committee of the state legislature to argue for disunion, presiding at the British West Indies celebration in Worcester, and at the annual meeting of the American Anti-Slavery Society in New York City, attending the autumn meeting of the Pennsylvania Anti-Slavery Society, and writing extensively for *The Liberator* and for the *National Anti-Slavery Standard*. He also publicized and circulated in his state the earliest petition for woman's suffrage.

223

TO THEODORE PARKER

Boston, Jan. 3, 1848.

Esteemed Friend:

The names of a number of well known friends of universal reform are to be appended to this printed Call for a Convention. Should you feel so disposed, it would gratify them to see yours added to the number.[1] Please read the Call critically, and if you are willing to sign it, a line to that effect from you would be very acceptable.

Truly yours,

Wm. Lloyd Garrison.

Theodore Parker.

ALS: Garrison Papers, Boston Public Library.

1. Parker signed the call. The final version is printed in *The Liberator*, January 21, 1848. The convention was held in the Melodeon in Boston on March 23–24. George W. Benson was elected president, and among the vice-presidents were Francis Jackson and Edmund Quincy. The convention adopted resolutions opposing state designation of a single day of the week as the day of worship and rest, maintaining that not only was there no basis in scripture for such an act but that it violated basic principles of religious freedom. A complete account of the proceedings appears in *The Liberator*, March 31, 1848.

2 2 4

TO JAMES AND LUCRETIA MOTT

Boston, Jan. 10, 1848

Dear Friends —

In allowing your names to be appended to the Call for an Anti-Sabbath Convention, you have gratified many of your friends here, and given fresh evidence of possessing true moral courage. In the course of a few days, our list of signers will be completed, and then the Call will be printed in a circular form, and also in the *Liberator*. We have not yet heard from our valued friends, J. M. McKim & Charles C. Burleigh. They will, doubtless, readily allow the use of their names. We hope Charles will write the tract assigned to him by the Committee, on the history and nature of the Seventh-day Sabbath.[1] If he should prefer to treat upon some other branch of this subject, he can do so; but we hope he will *write*.

Please hand the accompanying leaves to dear Edward M. Davis.[2] I am glad that you have so worthy a son-in-law, who, I dare say, seems more like *a son indeed*. Long may he be spared to aid and bless suffering humanity.

I have nothing to offer you but my poor, though heartfelt, thanks for the token of your unabated friendship which was enclosed in your letter. I sometimes wish I were in a situation absolutely to decline the acceptance of every such gift — not from feelings of pride, or a desire to be cynically independent — but because "it is more blessed to give than to receive." [3]

I shall long remember our pleasant interviews in Ohio, with unalloyed satisfaction.[4] I marvel that Lucretia did not utterly break down under the pressure of her public labors. Aside from my severe illness at Cleveland, I rejoice that I was permitted to visit Ohio, & hope that my labors were not wholly in vain. Yours, Lucretia, I am sure were not.

How I wish you lived no further off than the next street — or, better yet, the next door! I long to commune with you both, face to face, from day to day. How will it be with us in the Spirit-land? Will time & space be annihilated?

Helen sends her loving remembrances. No one esteems you more highly than

Your attached friend,

Wm Lloyd Garrison

Transcription in the hand of Wendell Phillips Garrison: Garrison Papers, Boston Public Library.

1. The phrase "Seventh-day Sabbath" refers to the practice of celebrating the Sabbath on Saturday rather than Sunday, the Millerites or Second Adventists being the most prominent group advocating such a practice. Whether Burleigh wrote the tract Garrison requested is not known. *The Liberator* did print some "Remarks" Burleigh had made on the subject at the convention (see the issues for May 5 and 19, 1848).

2. Garrison refers to his letter to Edward M. Davis, January 10, 1848.

3. Acts 20:35.

4. On his western tour the previous summer Garrison had met the Motts in Salem, Ohio (see Garrison's letter to Helen E. Garrison, August 28, 1847).

225

TO EDWARD M. DAVIS

Boston, Jan. 10, 1848.

My Dear Friend:

Thanks to you for your prompt and generous response to the Call for a Convention to protest against penal legislation in favor of a Sabbatical observance, and to explode a mischievous delusion everywhere prevailing, that one day in the week is more holy than another — that we are to give one-seventh portion of our time to God, and the rest we may devote to "secular" matters! I regard this as one of the great reformatory movements of the age — and, assuredly, it will shake all Christendom — certainly all Priestdom. I am more and more convinced, that the prevalence of just views in regard to the Sabbath is essential to the deliverance of the people from the power of priestcraft and the bondage of false worship.

It was gratifying to receive the names of dear James and Lucretia Mott, to be appended to the Call. Theodore Parker has heartily signed it, and I presume William Henry Channing will also add his signature.[1] We shall have a select but potent array of names, of good men and women, worthy of primitive times, worthy of any age, and equal to any crisis. The Call will appear in next week's *Liberator* — then look out for an "orthodox" sensation in all parts of the land!

One great object of the Convention is, not merely for discussion, but for action — to place on record sentiments and doctrines, calculated to enlighten all inquiring minds. To this end, we have divided the Sabbatical question into various parts — each part to constitute a distinct essay for a tract, and the whole to form a volume, which shall cover the entire ground — as follows: —

I The Nature and History of the Seventh-day Sabbath — showing it to have been purely Jewish in its origin and design. By C. C. Burleigh.[2]

II History of the First-day Sabbath. By Theodore Parker.[3]

III The Worship of God — what is it? Henry C. Wright.[4]

IV The Physiological Argument — "Man and beast need rest." Wm. L. Garrison.

V The assumed judgments upon Sabbath-breakers. Edmund Quincy.

VI A compilation of the views of Luther, Calvin, Tyndale, Penn, Barclay, Fox, &c. &c. on the Sabbath question — with a running commentary. Wendell Phillips.

VII How Sabbatizing stands directly in the way of all the reforms of the age. Parker Pillsbury.

VIII How shall a day of rest be best observed by the people? Charles K. Whipple.

IX Tyranny of penal legislation in favor of the Sabbath. John W. Browne.[5]

If all these essays can be elaborately prepared, and presented to the Convention for their adoption, they will be of great value in carrying on the controversy throughout Christendom; for rely upon it, my dear friend, both sides of the Atlantic are to be shaken by this great question. Already, great agitation prevails in Scotland respecting the observance of the Sabbath. The blood-stained, pseudo "Free Church" is in the field, and Dr. [Robert S.] Candlish, I understand, has proposed that *ten thousand pounds* be raised to carry on their Sabbatical operations! A "Sabbath League" has been formed, intended to unite the various sects in one powerful combination, and to co-operate with the "American and Foreign Sabbath Union" in this country.[6] Hence the enemy is already in the field — the conflict has already commenced — and "God defend the right!"[7] Under these circumstances, our contemplated Convention may be regarded as specially opportune.

Your voluntary proposal, to give $50 towards carrying out the object of the Convention is equally generous and seasonable. In publishing the tracts alluded to, means will be needed to print them for distribution.[8] Other kind friends will doubtless contribute something to scatter light and knowledge on this subject. I hope you will be able to attend the Convention.

Please remember me kindly to your dear wife, and accept for yourself the assurances of my increasing regard.

Wm. Lloyd Garrison.

Edward M. Davis.

Handwritten transcription, signed by Garrison: Garrison Papers, Boston Public Library.

1. Channing did not sign the call.

2. A note has been added to this line, in Garrison's hand, reading: "(In fact, speaks first on tyranny of penal enactment then on other topic."

3. Another note in Garrison's hand reads: "(Sunday — a human institution)."

4. Another note in Garrison's hand reads: "(Christianity not a religion of time & place)."

5. John W. Browne (1810–1860) was a Boston lawyer who, as a Harvard student, had been an intimate friend of Charles Sumner. (*Life.*) The volume in which his essay appeared was entitled *Tyranny of Penal Legislation in Favor of the Sabbath.*

6. The Sabbath League, or Sabbath Alliance, was founded at Edinburgh, November 1, 1847, for the purpose of honoring the fourth Commandment and persuading everyone to obey it. An appeal to the electors of Scotland from the committee of the alliance, published in the *North British Advertiser*, May 8, 1852, was to express the sentiments of the society as follows: that the Sabbath was to them the symbol of their reverence for God and the secret of their superiority over other lands "in point of freedom with order, and of progress with tranquillity." The league was in existence as late as 1869. (Robert Cox, *The Literature of the Sabbath Question*, Edinburgh, 1865.)

The American and Foreign Sabbath Union was organized in Boston, April 1843. At the first annual meeting Thomas S. Williams, chief justice of the state of Connecticut, was chosen president. A resolution stressing the essential nature of Sabbath observance and requesting all persons to refrain from engaging in travel, amusement, or any secular business on Sunday was passed and incorporated into the constitution. The union also published a series of tracts called *Permanent Sabbath Documents*, which were attached to the annual report, and union lecturers traveled about the country speaking on Sabbath observance. (*First Annual Report of the American and Foreign Sabbath Union, presented April, 1844*, Boston, 1844.)

7. Shakespeare, *2 Henry VI*, II, iii, 55.

8. *The Liberator* does not mention the tracts alluded to, although Garrison informs his readers (March 31, 1848) that a full report of the convention, including the principal speeches, will be published in pamphlet form. Also, he acknowledges Davis' $50 contribution in the issue for April 21, 1848. Throughout May and June *The Liberator* prints lengthy reports of the speeches made by Parker (May 12), Burleigh (May 19), John W. Browne, Burleigh, and Garrison (June 2), Lucretia Mott (June 9), Garrison (June 16), Henry C. Wright (June 23), and Pillsbury and Stephen S. Foster (June 30). Burleigh, Parker, Wright, and Browne follow fairly closely the topics Garrison mentions in his letter. Lucretia Mott and Garrison emphasize that no day is holier than any other, and Garrison comments on the absurdity of a belief that God will punish with material calamity if Sunday is not observed; he blames the priests for keeping the people in fear.

226

TO SAMUEL J. MAY

Boston, Jan. 10, 1848.

My Dear Friend:

I send you the accompanying Call for a Convention to oppose penal legislation in regard to the observance of a Sabbath day, and to explode the mischievous delusion, that one day in the week is more holy than another. This Call has been drawn up with great care and deliberation, and sanctioned by a large committee of our best reformatory spirits. We wish to append to it a select number of names — such as are widely known, and will have a strong moral influence wherever known. If you approve of it, please write to me by return of mail, authorising the use of your name.[1] Among those who have already signed it are Wendell Phillips, Maria W. Chapman, Francis Jackson, Edmund Jackson, Edmund Quincy, Theodore Parker, Henry C. Wright, James and Lucretia Mott, Edward M. Davis, Charles K. Whipple, Stephen and Abby K. Foster, Parker Pillsbury, John W. Browne, C. F. Hovey, &c. &c.[2] I trust you will be pleased with this protest against legislative tyranny over conscience — this vindication of the real nature and spirit of Christianity. "Ye are my witnesses, saith the Lord."[3] Let us register our testimony against injustice and delusion while we may, that those who live in our day, and those who shall succeed us, may be all the better for our example.

I am considerably improved in health, but neither mentally nor physically as well as I was before my illness.

Susan [Coffin] is giving us the light of her pleasant countenance and kindly aiding Helen with her needle. She seems to be in excellent health. During the Fair, she passed her time at Edmund Jackson's, "on the Neck."[4]

Sister Sarah's health continues quite frail, but her hope of ultimate recovery is inextinguishable.

Helen and the children are as well as usual. All desire me to send their most affectionate remembrances to you, and your dear wife and family.

Bro. George has not been to Boston for some time, though we are expecting him daily. He has authorised me to put his name to the Call. Andrew Robeson, Nathl. Barney, C. C. Burleigh, Wm. H. Channing, will also probably sign.[5]

Yours, affectionately,

Wm. Lloyd Garrison.

ALS: Garrison Papers, Boston Public Library.

1. Either May did not sign the call or his reply reached Garrison too late to be included in the printed version appearing in *The Liberator*, January 28, 1848.

2. Charles Fox Hovey (1807–1859) was a rich Boston merchant and a member of the board of managers of both the Massachusetts and the American Anti-Slavery Societies. (*Life.*)

3. Isaiah 43:10.

4. "The Neck," or "Roxbury Neck," was the mile-and-a-half strip of land joining Boston and Roxbury, which kept Boston from being cut off as an island from the marshes of Back Bay. (Walter Muir Whitehill, *Boston: A Topographical History*, Cambridge, Mass., 1959.) "The Neck" has become many streets, including Washington Street, on which Jackson lived at number 773. (Boston directory.)

5. Of these, only Robeson and Burleigh signed the call.

2 2 7

TO SAMUEL J. MAY

Boston, April 7th, 1848.

My Dear Friend:

Last evening, a colored man called at my house, for the purpose of enlisting my sympathy and influence in his behalf, calling himself William Halyard, and seeking pecuniary aid to buy his mother, who is now (as represented) a slave in Maryland.[1] He is a mulatto, about 25 or 30 years of age, middle height, and very good looking and well-dressed. He brought with him, as credentials, a *printed* letter, purporting to be from your pen, which your good cousin[2] has copied verbatim on the third page of this sheet, and which Halyard coolly and repeatedly declared that you put into his hands, in the printed form. What I wish you would send me, by return of mail, (I will pay the postage — don't you,) [is] a letter, which I can publish, denying the authenticity of the document, and giving such information as you can in regard to this imposter.

All our family have been quite unwell for some time, Helen and myself in particular; and our babe is now lying quite sick with a lung fever. How it may turn with her is problematical. I write in haste, or I would add more. Our best love to your dear wife, Charlotte, and all the family.

Faithfully yours,

Wm. Lloyd Garrison.

ALS: Garrison Papers, Boston Public Library.

1. William Halyard has not been identified. May's reply to Garrison, together with Halyard's letters, which he presented to Garrison, are printed in *The Liberator*, April 21, 1848.

2. Probably Samuel May, Jr.

2 2 8

TO GEORGE W. BENSON

Boston, April 20, 1848.
3 o'clock, morning.

Dear George:

I do not know that you have been apprised of the illness of our dear babe, Elizabeth Pease, since she was taken down with the lung fever a fortnight last Monday, preceded by an attack of the influenza. For a time, we thought her somewhat dangerously sick, and soon called in the medical aid of our homœopathic friend, Dr. [Christian F.] Geist. For a few days past, though much emaciated, she has appeared to be slowly improving; so that we have had no serious apprehensions in regard to her case. Yesterday afternoon, however, her symptoms changed decidedly for the worse, and after considerable restlessness, she expired without a groan or struggle, quite imperceptibly indeed, in the arms of Mrs. [Eliza Jackson] Meriam, a little before 1 o'clock this (Thursday) morning. From her birth she has been a feeble child, and seldom in apparent good health. Her breathing apparatus always seemed defective, which indicated something of organic disease; but after her weaning, she gradually grew weak, and though rallying occasionally, was at last overcome by inflammation of the lungs. "Dust to dust, and the spirit to God who gave it." [1] We shall commit her dear remains to the earth tomorrow (Friday) afternoon, making the funeral as private and simple as practicable. You and Catherine have suffered a similar bereavement, and therefore know experimentally how to sympathise with us in our loss.[2]

For a month past, our house has been little better than a hospital. We have all been down with the influenza, and the attack has been of a violent character. I have been severely affected, with considerable fever and great pressure upon the brain, as well as a hard cough upon the lungs; and also with an erysipelas swelling and eruption in the face, besides being daily tormented with the St. Anthony's fire in my hands and feet, causing them to itch and swell very much. Of course, it is better that the humor should be out than be in. I am now slowly mending, with a "good for nothing" feeling hanging about me. Dear Helen has had a severe time of it. Her cold has been exceedingly troublesome, and constantly renewing; and having had so much anxiety of mind in regard to our suffering babe, and been deprived so long of her regular sleep, she is quite worn down. Sarah has also largely shared in the general epidemic, and is at present very weak, though cheerful and uncomplaining as usual. By and by, we shall all throw off this robe of mortality, and thus be delivered from "the ills that flesh is heir to." [3] To exist in a spiritual body, subject to no sickness or decay, is an animating thought, and may well reconcile us to a temporary sojourn here, while it makes the act of earthly dissolution far from being an event to be deplored.

Hoping that you and your dear family are all well, and that you will take special care of your own health, and transmitting the most affectionate remembrances from Helen and Sarah, I remain, dear George,

Yours, with immortal aspirations,

Wm. Lloyd Garrison.

P.S. Our beloved friend Henry C. Wright, after an absence of several weeks, lecturing in Worcester county on the things pertaining to the true kingdom of peace and humanity, returned to our house last evening. The babe has died since he retired to rest, and he is not yet apprised of the event. It is good to have so good a man here to sympathise with us in such an hour.

ALS: Garrison Papers, Boston Public Library.

1. Garrison adapts Ecclesiastes 12:7.
2. Garrison refers to the death of the Benson's one-year-old daughter Eliza Davis Benson on May 3, 1842.
3. Garrison slightly misquotes Shakespeare, *Hamlet*, III, i, 62.

229

TO MARIA W. CHAPMAN *ET AL.*

13 Pine Street,
Thursday afternoon.
(April 20, 1848.)

Dear Friends:

Early this morning, our dear babe, Elizabeth Pease, — who has been ill of a lung fever for a fortnight past, — winged her flight from this to "another and a better world." [1] No strange thing has happened unto us, more than unto others. "The inevitable hour" [2] comes at last to all. But if we did not feel our bereavement deeply and tenderly, it would indicate a want of parental affection such as is not seen even in those who are called savages.

We have designated 3 o'clock to-morrow (Friday) afternoon, as the time for the funeral services. If you are not otherwise engaged, we should be gratified to have you present on the occasion.

Yours, with much esteem,

W. L. and Helen E. Garrison.

Mrs. M. W. Chapman, daughter,
and sisters —
Miss Mary G. Chapman.

Handwritten transcription: Garrison Papers, Boston Public Library.

1. August F. F. von Kotzebue, *The Stranger*, I, i.
2. Thomas Gray, "Elegy Written in a Country Churchyard," stanza 9, line 3.

230

TO THEODORE PARKER

13 Pine Street,
Thursday afternoon.
April 20, 1848.[1]

Dear Friend:

Early ˙this morning, our dear babe, Elizabeth Pease, — who has benn ill of a lung fever for a fortnight past, — winged her flight from this to "another and a better world." No strange thing has happened unto us, in view of human mortality — nothing dark or mysterious; yet we feel our bereavement deeply and tenderly. We have designated 3 o'clock to-morrow (Friday) afternoon as the time for the funeral services. If you are not otherwise engaged, we should be gratified to have you present, and to express whatever sentiments the occasion may suggest, in such manner as may be to you most agreeable.

With great respect and esteem,

Your bereaved friends,

Wm. Lloyd and Helen E. Garrison.

Theodore Parker.

ALS: Garrison Papers, Boston Public Library.

1. Garrison supplied the date on the manuscript with a different pen and apparently at a later date, the year being given at the top of the page.

231

TO SYDNEY HOWARD GAY

Boston, April 27, 1848.

My dear Gay:

In reply to your note of inquiry, I am happy to say, that Theodore Parker authorises the use of his name as among the speakers at our anniversary in New York.[1] Lucretia Mott, when here, also intimated that she would be willing to speak on that occasion; and it would give additional interest to the meeting, to many, if her name were announced in the placards and advertisements. Can this be done in a way not to interfere with the Quaker doctrine of being "moved by the Spirit"? Try. Of course, we must have a speech from Wendell [Phillips], on the occasion; and one either from [Frederick] Douglass, or W. W. Brown, or [Charles L.] Remond.[2] The first would make the most impression — which shall it be? I am to write, to-day, to Philadelphia, at the request of our Executive Committee, asking Wm. H. Furness to be one of our speakers; and I shall request him to send you word, in season for your next Standard.[3]

What a discussion we have had in both houses of Congress on the slavery question! But how softly, cautiously, almost weakly, does Hale behave! [4]

Yours, faithfully,

Wm. Lloyd Garrison.

☞ Print a good lot of placards for the meeting — omitting whatever might needlessly cause them to be torn down.

ALS: Sydney Howard Gay Papers, Columbia University Libraries.

1. Garrison refers to the annual meeting of the American Anti-Slavery Society, which was to be held in New York City at the Broadway Tabernacle, May 9–11. A report of the proceedings can be found in *The Liberator*, May 19, 1848.

2. William Wells Brown (c. 1816–1884) escaped from slavery in 1834 and devoted the rest of his life to the antislavery cause. A member of the Massachusetts Anti-Slavery Society, he went to England in 1849 to lecture and was appointed a delegate to the peace congress held in Paris that year. Although his writings cover many fields, he is best remembered for the autobiographical *Narrative of William Wells Brown, a Fugitive Slave* (1847).

3. At this time the executive committee consisted of the following persons: William Lloyd Garrison, Francis Jackson, Wendell Phillips, Maria Weston Chapman, Edmund Quincy, Charles Lenox Remond, Anne Warren Weston, William Henry Channing, Eliza Lee Follen, Sarah Pugh, Sydney Howard Gay, and James Russell Lowell.

William H. Furness (1802–1896) was a Unitarian minister who spent his pastoral career at the Unitarian Church in Philadelphia. His two major interests were the antislavery cause and the study of the life of Jesus. He was also one of the first American scholars to study and translate German literature. Although Furness did not speak at the convention, he did send a sermon to Gay which was published in the *National Anti-Slavery Standard*, May 11, 1848.

4. John Parker Hale (1806–1873) began his political career in 1832 with his election to the New Hampshire state legislature. He subsequently served as United States district attorney, congressman, and senator. In 1847 he was nominated for the presidency by the Liberty party, but when the Free-soil party absorbed the Liberty party in 1848, he withdrew in favor of Van Buren. In 1852 he was to accept the nomination of the Free soilers and to poll 150,000 votes.

232

TO SYDNEY HOWARD GAY

Boston, May 1, 1848.

Dear Gay: —

It is about an even chance, whether I shall be well enough to be present at the anniversary meeting in New York, though I feel somewhat better to-day than I have done for some days past. Nothing shall keep me away, if I can help it; but I can make no speeches. You must advertise Wendell [Phillips] among the speakers at the Tabernacle. I am glad [Frederick] Douglass has promised to speak. It is not probable there will be time for [William W.] Brown to participate on that occasion, but at our other meetings, he will find frequent opportunities to speak. I am hoping [William H.] Furness will write to you, authorising you to make use of his name. As for Lucretia [Mott], I supposed she would object to being positively committed to make a speech; but there is no doubt that she will bear her testimony, if her mind should be stirred up. Perhaps it will be best to omit her name in the placards. I hope our meeting will be well attended, but am apprehensive the number of delegates will be small. Do you propose to hold evening meetings, publicly? It seems to me we had better omit these, and let us devote the evenings to business consultations, &c.

Faithfully yours,

Wm. Lloyd Garrison.

Please enclose to me in our package this week James B. Richards's note due the Amer. Soc.[1] — He sails for Europe on Friday & wants to pay it. — The note was given to Isaac T. Hopper — when he was Treas?

ALS: Sydney Howard Gay Papers, Columbia University Libraries.

1. James Bardwell Richards (1817–1886) was born in Ceylon and spent his childhood there and in India. He devoted his life to the study of mental retardation and in 1848 went to Europe to examine schools in London and Paris. In October of that year he started the first state school for the mentally retarded in Boston. Similar institutions were later established in New York and Pennsylvania. (*New England Historical and Genealogical Register*, 1887.)

233

TO GEORGE W. BENSON

[Boston, May 3, 1848.]

Dear George —

I have time to add only a word. I think it is quite likely I shall make you a visit on my return to New York, and be with you on Friday or Saturday, to spend a few hours; but do not stay at home, for a moment, on that account, especially as it is uncertain whether I shall visit you at all, on my way home. Something will depend upon the time I shall be able to leave New York. I wish you could make it in the way of business to be at our anniversary. Love to Catherine, &c.

Truly yours, sick or well,

Wm. Lloyd Garrison.

ALS: Garrison Papers, Sophia Smith Collection, Smith College Library. Garrison writes this note at the end of a letter from Helen E. Garrison to George W. Benson, dated May 3, 1848.

---

2 3 4

TO ELIZABETH PEASE

Boston, May 3, 1848.

My Dear Friend:

Our darling babe, who bore your beloved and cherished name, after a sojourn of sixteen months in the flesh, left us a few days since to reside where sickness and death are unknown, where all tears are wiped away, and where bright and beautiful spirits are rejoicing in the bliss of immortality. It is the first breach that has been made in our family circle — the first link that has been broken in the chain of our parental relationship. As a child, it seemed to us (perhaps we were partial) that she was uncommonly beautiful, and in a rare degree promising. The vacancy created in our household by her departure is a large one, and we miss her as though she had been many, instead of one. In consequence of my severe illness in Ohio last fall, she was weaned prematurely, and from that time to the hour of her flight, made very little progress in health, strength or size. She suffered unusually in getting her teeth; and at last had a severe attack of the influenza, which ended fatally in a lung fever. Up to the day of her decease, however, we apprehended no real danger respecting her case — nor did her physician, who supposed, with us, that she was in a convalescent state. Indeed, the previous night she reposed so well, that I went to my office in the morning, with an elastic step and a joyous spirit. I did not return till late in the evening, (our dear Henry C. Wright being with me, he having just arrived in the city, after a fortnight's absence,) when Helen informed me that a marked change had come over the babe during the afternoon, and that the doctor had just gone, having expressed his fears that the case might terminate fatally. Soon after midnight, she drew her last breath so gently, that no one perceived it: —

"Night dews fall not more gently to the ground,
Nor weary, worn-out winds expire so soft."[1]

It is all right; and though we weep, we do not complain. "Dust to dust, and the spirit to God who gave it,"[2] is the law of our creation, obedience to which will be exacted of us all. The event which has happened to us is a very common one indeed, in this mutable world; yet though millions of parents have anticipated us in a similar bereavement, it comes to us as though we were first in the painful experience. At the funeral, we invited a select number of highly valued friends, several of whom made remarks exceedingly appropriate to the occasion — Wendell Phillips and Theodore Parker in particular. We had two or three Daguerreotype likenesses of the dear little one taken, as she lay in that placid sleep of death; and though they are far from being what life would have expressed, or what we could have desired, still we prize them very highly. If we can find an opportunity to do so, we may send one of them to you.

No one misses, no one *can* miss, the vanished one so much as my dear Helen, whose watchfulness and care, by day and by night, for more than six months, were excessive. To see the cradle vacant — to be unable to clasp her babe to her bosom — to wake up in the night, and find no little one nestling by her side — all this seems to leave her almost solitary, although there are still five others left, each of whom she loves just as tenderly, and the loss of either of whom she would feel just as keenly. She is sure of your special sympathy, and desires to be affectionately and gratefully remembered to you, for whom she entertains the warmest esteem.

In the last two months, I have had a succession of catarrhal attacks, attended with a cough and symptoms of erysipelas, which have been so violent as to render it impracticable for me to give that attention to my editorial duties which is so requisite to one in my situation. Dear Henry is urging me very strongly to go to Dr. [David] Ruggles's Water Cure Establishment at Northampton, during the summer; and perhaps I shall do so, if I can make suitable arrangements in regard to the management of the Liberator during my absence from the city.

The influenza has been very prevalent in this region during the past season, and many have fallen victims to it. Every one of my family has been severely affected by it, Helen in particular; but, happily, we are all now on the mending hand. The loss of health is the loss of many blessings in one.

It is a source of lively joy to us, that the water cure has proved so efficacious in the restoration of your own health. Long may your valuable life be preserved; for this wretched, suffering world is sadly in need of benefactors. Please give to Dr. McLeod my special regards, and my best wishes for his entire success in the beneficent medical reform in which he is so zealously engaged.[3] I equally admire and appreciate those qualities of the head and heart which distinguish him, — his patience and perseverance, his indomitable courage and unconquerable will, his love of truth for its own's sake, his benevolence and sympathy of spirit, his readiness to discard what he discovers to be wrong, his determination to adhere to what he believes to be right. Many thanks to you for a copy of his invaluable work on

"The Treatment of Small Pox, Measles," &c. which I mean warmly to commend in the Liberator, as worthy of extensive circulation in this country.

H. C. W. has probably written to you, respecting his contemplated visit to Ohio, where he expects to labor during the summer.[4] I shall be sorry to lose his cheering companionship and invigorating personal presence all that time, but I know that the field he has chosen is a most interesting and useful one.

We shall soon be called to say farewell to our indefatigable co-adjutor Maria W. Chapman, who expects to leave Boston about the 1st of June, with her family, to reside two or three years on the continent of Europe. How "the cause" can get along without her immediate presence, here, I cannot tell.

How many things, dear friends, remain unwritten! Yet I have time and room merely to add that I am

Your faithful friend,

Wm. Lloyd Garrison.

ALS: Garrison Papers, Boston Public Library.

1. Robert Blair, "The Grave," lines 714 715.
2. An adaptation of Ecclesiastes 12:7.
3. William Macleod (1819–1875) was a physician at Ben Rhydding, Yorkshire. A graduate of the Royal College of Physicians at Edinburgh and the University of St. Andrews, Macleod was the author of *The Treatment of Small Pox, Measles, Scarlet Fever, Hooping Cough, &c., by the Water Cure and Homoeopathy* (Manchester, 1848). A more complete account of Dr. Macleod and his work can be found in Richard Metcalfe, *The Rise and Progress of Hydropathy in England and Scotland* (London, 1912).
4. Henry C. Wright's trip to Ohio is first reported in *The Liberator*, July 7, 1848, in a letter of his from Pittsburgh, dated June 17. Letters from Wright on his western tour appear almost weekly thereafter until the issue of December 15, where, in a letter dated November 19, 1848, he announced the conclusion of his mission. During the trip Wright lectured extensively, usually on antislavery topics.

235

TO GEORGE W. BENSON

Boston, May 17, 1848.

Dear George:

I have just received your kind epistle, informing me of your great disappointment at my not making you a visit, last week, as I fully purposed to do; and urging me to come up to Northampton the latter part of this week. My reason for giving you the slip was simply the unpropitious state of the weather in New York, which detained me so long as to defeat my intention — for it was absolutely necessary that

I should be at home on Saturday evening, and I did not leave until Saturday morning. My health is considerably better, just now; and for the present, I must forego the pleasure of visiting Northampton, as I cannot afford the expense of the journey, (in addition to that to New York,) — being more deeply in debt than I have been at any time for several years past, with no immediate prospect of getting out of it — as, with the utmost economy, I find that I am going behind-hand at least a dollar a day beyond my stipend. What to do, in order to reduce my expenses, and yet live in Boston, I know not; and on this account, I am extremely anxious to see you, that I may obtain your counsel and advice. But I hope you will be able to attend the New England A. S. Convention the last days of May, when we will talk over all needful matters.[1]

If I can avoid going into the water cure, I wish to do so, on many accounts; but should I conclude to try it, I would prefer to delay it till about the first of August, when my boys are to have a vacation of five weeks, and they can be sent into the country. In the mean time, as I am particularly troubled with the erysipelas and St. Anthony's fire, I think of making a full trial of Dr. Townsend's Sarsaparilla, if I can obtain the desired quantity by advertising in the Liberator.[2] You will say, "Better come to Northampton" — but I do not see how I can arrange my family affairs, &c.

Helen, for a fortnight past, has been severely afflicted with a boil under her left arm, so that I have had to call in the Dr. She is now somewhat better.

We had cheering meetings in New York — never better. We resolved, among other things, that God never made slaveholders, and therefore they do not belong to the human race, but are of monstrous and diabolical origin. Excelsior![3]

This week, I hope to be able to complete arrangements in regard to our poor afflicted Mrs. [Nathaniel] Paul, and will write to you again on Friday or Saturday. Love to all at home.

Ever lovingly yours,

Wm. Lloyd Garrison.

ALS: Garrison Papers, Boston Public Library.

1. The annual New England Anti-Slavery Convention was held at the Melodeon in Boston, May 30–June 1. The proceedings were reported in *The Liberator*, June 9, 1848.

2. During the nineteenth century sarsaparilla was used, like sulphur and molasses, as a spring tonic and cure-all. Although Ayer's and Hood's sarsaparillas, manufactured at Lowell, Massachusetts, were the two leading brands, they had close competition from the product of Dr. Samuel P. Townsend of New York. Dr. Townsend's product, advertised as "A Wonder and a Blessing," made him enough money to buy the home of A. T. Stewart, described at the time as the costliest mansion ever built in New York City. Townsend's sarsaparilla depot was

located at 126 Fulton Street, next to the office of the *Sun.* (Stewart H. Holbrook, *The Golden Age of Quackery*, New York, 1959, p. 46; New York city directory.)

3. Garrison refers to Henry Wadsworth Longfellow, "Excelsior."

236

TO FRANCIS JACKSON

Boston, July 13, 1848.

My Dear Friend:

I cannot find words to express my sense of the kindness of yourself and Wendell [Phillips], in enabling me to maintain a good credit with my landlord, grocer, &c. by advancing the amount which I owed to them on the 1st instant, and thus extricating me from a very painful pecuniary embarrassment — at a time, too, when it is so difficult even for good business men to obtain a loan at a high per centage. In spite of the utmost care and economy, my family expenses have gradually and unavoidably increased in my present situation, so as to require, as soon as practicable, an avoidance of some of those liabilities to company, &c. which now subject me to a considerable tax. I dread at any time to be in debt, both as a matter of honor and justice, and therefore constantly feel how necessary it is to be exceedingly careful how I get into it, even to procure bread for my children. Though neither you nor Wendell expressed any desire to have the money returned, and though I do not know how soon I shall be able to return it, yet I wish to recognize it as a *bona fide* debt, and therefore enclose an acknowledgment of your portion of the sum advanced — not as a matter of form, but of just obligation. It shall, at least, be a legible proof of your friendship, manifested at a time of universal pressure.

Hoping that you will all be safely returned from your Canadian tour, and that it will prove one of unalloyed enjoyment, I subscribe myself,

Your very grateful friend,

Wm. Lloyd Garrison.

Francis Jackson.

ALS: Garrison Papers, Boston Public Library.

2 3 7

TO EDMUND QUINCY

Sunday night.
[Boston, July 16, 1848.]

Dear Quincy:

Accompanying this, you will find a few selections, from which to make extracts, if you think best — and others on which to comment, such as Winthrop's oration at Washington; [1] the President's Peace Message; Seth Sprague's Taylor Speech at Bridgewater, (the degenerate son of a sainted sire,) — the scurrilous notice of our N. Y. anniversary in the article from the Scottish Guardian; the significant and honorable fact, that while the *Olive Branch* was the most sought after by the last Legislature, [2] the Liberator stood lowest on the list — and it should be stated that the $19.50 credited to the Libr. includes *two* years' pay, instead of one, as friend [Robert F.] Wallcut informs me. The Emancipator ranks next in popularity with the Puritan and the Recorder, as you will see. [3] How significant are such facts! — The article on "The Anti-Slavery Fairs" is worthy of insertion and comment. [4] Give M. M. Noah a lashing for his toad-eating letter. [5] Also, that blockhead and bigot, the Rev. A. K. Moulton, whose malignant article you will find in the "Refuge" this week, respecting our "Old Organized Meeting," alias the last N[ew]. E[ngland]. A. S. Convention. [6] — Also, Ben Hallett, for his pious address to the Sabbath School children. [7] What a scamp! — Copy the extract I have marked in William Goodell's almost interminable Liberty League Address in the Albany Patriot, and riddle it as you know how to do such things. [8] It would sting Goodell awfully to put it in the "Refuge," but it would not be inappropriate to that department — determine as you like.

The speeches of dear Wendell, at Philadelphia, or extracts from them, may be published as you find room, but not till he has revised them. Enough, you will say, to begin with.

I have thought it best to publish [John C.] Calhoun's speech this week, entire, [th]ough it will occupy a large portion of the inside. [9] Farewell!

W. L. G.

ALS: Garrison Papers, Sophia Smith Collection, Smith College Library.
The content of this letter makes it clear that "Sunday night" must be July 16, 1848, since Garrison is known to have left Boston for Northampton on Monday, July 17. As can be seen in the notes below, Quincy did use in the paper some of the materials left him by Garrison.

1. Garrison refers to Robert Charles Winthrop (1809–1894), a graduate of Harvard and law student in the office of Daniel Webster, who served in Congress

from 1840 to 1850 and was speaker from 1847 to 1849. Appointed to the United States Senate in 1850 upon the resignation of Daniel Webster, he was defeated for election in 1851 by Charles Sumner — owing at least in part to his own lenient attitude toward slavery. He served for thirty years as president of the Massachusetts Historical Society.

2. The *Scottish Guardian* was published in Glasgow from 1832 to 1861; the article in question did not appear in *The Liberator*. (Letter to the editor from C. Duncan Rice, Yale University, December 26, 1970.)

The Boston *Olive Branch* was printed between 1836 and approximately 1860. (*ULS.*)

3. Garrison probably refers to the *New England Puritan*, which was published in Boston from 1840 to 1849, when it was merged into the Boston *Recorder*.

4. "The Anti-Slavery Fairs" was printed in the column of *The Liberator* called "Refuge of Oppression," August 11, but without editorial comment.

5. Mordecai Manuel Noah (1785–1851) was a lawyer, playwright, and journalist of Sephardic Jewish ancestry. From 1817 to 1826 he edited the *National Advocate*. In 1841 he was appointed associate judge of the New York Court of Sessions, resigning the next year. Late in his life he edited *Noah's Times and Weekly Messenger*. Noah's "toad-eating letter" was a column which had appeared in his *Sunday Times*, attacking the abolitionists for treason against the Constitution and the church and for their "incendiary effort" to encourage "Sambo" to resist his oppressors rather than to improve his condition by "safe and gradual" means. Quincy reprinted the column in the "Refuge of Oppression" but without comment in *The Liberator*, July 28, 1848.

6. Albanus K. Moulton (1810–1873) was a Baptist clergyman who served congregations in Dover, New Hampshire, Portland, Maine, and Roxbury, Massachusetts. After suffering a nervous breakdown he retired to Iowa but was to return to active service in the 1860's. (G. A. Burgess and J. T. Ward, *Free Baptist Cyclopedia; Historical and Biographical*, Free Baptist Cyclopedia Co., 1889.) Moulton's article was in the "Refuge," July 21.

7. Benjamin Franklin Hallett (1797–1862) was a lawyer, politician, and editor who allied himself with reform causes. After 1838 he became less concerned with these than with allegiance to the Democratic party. By the 1860's he was to be quite willing to make concessions to the party's southern faction. Hallett's article was not used by Quincy.

8. William Goodell (1792–1878), a minister, lecturer, author, and editor, was an ardent reformer and abolitionist. In 1833 he was one of the organizers of the American Anti-Slavery Society. Unlike Garrison he believed that abolition could be accomplished under the Constitution and without dissolving the Union. In 1840 Goodell helped to organize the abolitionist Liberty party; in 1847, in order to broaden the party's platform to include other reforms, he established the Liberty League. The extract in question was apparently not printed.

9. Calhoun's speech on the bill to establish a territorial government in Oregon, delivered in the Senate, June 27, 1848, was reprinted in *The Liberator*, July 21, 1848. The point of contention over this bill was in the section prohibiting the extension of slavery into the territory. Calhoun argued that the federal government did not have the right to establish a territorial government which would preclude slaveholding citizens from immigrating there.

2 3 8

TO WILLIAM BALLANTYNE HODGSON

Boston, July 17, 1848.

My Dear Sir:

When I was in England in 1846, my cup of pleasure was largely filled by the personal introduction to yourself, which I had the good fortune to enjoy. Since my return home, I have not for one moment forgotten you, your dear family, or your kindness and hospitality, as unitedly shown on that occasion.

I wish you to become personally acquainted (you know her already by reputation) with Mrs. Maria Weston Chapman, the bearer of this, who leaves this city, with three of her children, for a temporary residence on the Continent via England, and whose philanthropic spirit and intellectual ability place her in the front rank of the noblest women of this or any other age. Her devotion to the anti-slavery cause, for the last fourteen years, has been unsurpassed; and no one has been more calm in the hour of peril, none more hopeful in the hour of darkness, none more active in the hour of general despondency, than herself. Our mutual friend, George Thompson, could give you, and would delight to do so, any amount of eulogy upon her character and merits. She has been the soul of our National Anti-Slavery Bazaar for many years, and the chief financier of the whole movement.

Mrs. Chapman will be accompanied by her sister, Miss Caroline Weston, one of the rare women of the world for moral heroism and intellectual acumen. Her labours in behalf of the slave have been unceasing, and most effective. How to spare her, for an hour, we scarcely know.

As I write in great haste, and as these beloved friends will be able to give you whatever information you may desire respecting matters and things in the United States, I will only add that I hold you in great esteem, and remain

Your admiring friend,

Wm. Lloyd Garrison.

Dr. Hodgson.

ALS: Garrison Papers, Boston Public Library.

2 3 9

TO WILLIAM RATHBONE

Boston, July 17, 1848.

Esteemed Friend:

Remembering the interest you feel in the cause of negro emancipation in the United States, and of suffering humanity universally, — and also your courtesy and hospitality, as shown to me during my last visit in Liverpool in 1846, — I take the liberty of introducing to you Mrs. Maria Weston Chapman, of this city, one of the most distinguished women of the age on this side of the Atlantic, and one of the most devoted and efficient laborers for the abolition of slavery in the wide world. Ever since the visit of George Thompson, Esq. to this country, in 1834, she has been conspicuously identified with the anti-slavery movement; and I do injustice to no one when I say, that she has surpassed us all in the influence and aid which she has brought to that movement. Her sister, who accompanies her, Miss Caroline Weston, is also remarkable for her devotion in the same good cause, for her strength of mind and clearness of moral vision, for her untiring energy and uncompromising adherence to principle. I am sure you will be pleased to know them, and they to know you, personally. They will remain but a few days in Liverpool, when they will sojourn awhile in London, and then proceed to the Continent, for the education of the children of Mrs. Chapman — probably in Paris. We know not how to spare them from our shores, but trust they will at last be returned to us in safety. The husband of Mrs. C., now deceased, was (as well as his father) a much respected merchant in Boston, and a faithful abolitionist.[1] He acted for many years as the Treasurer of the Massachusetts Anti-Slavery Society.

As these highly intelligent ladies are familiar with every thing relating to the past history and present condition of the anti-slavery cause, I need add nothing on this subject, except that the Slave Power is reeling under the blows that the friends of freedom are giving it, and we are all greatly encouraged by the signs of the times.

Wishing to be kindly remembered to your family, and to your brother Richard,[2] I remain,

Yours, with great esteem,

Wm. Lloyd Garrison.

William Rathbone, Esq.

ALS: Merrill Collection of Garrison Papers, Wichita State University Library.

1. Mrs. Chapman's husband was Henry G. Chapman, who had died in 1842; her father-in-law was Henry Chapman (1771–1846), an advocate of temperance

as well as abolition, whose principles prevented him from doing any business with the South. (Obituary, *The Liberator,* December 4, 1846.)

2. Richard Rathbone (1788–1860), husband of author Hannah Mary Reynolds and Clarkson's ally in the exposure of the Liverpool slave trade. (Letter to the editor from C. Duncan Rice, Yale University, December 26, 1970.)

---

2 4 0

TO HELEN E. GARRISON

Northampton, July 18, 1848.

Dear Helen:

The trip in the cars to this place, yesterday, was much more pleasant than the one I took with Fanny, as the heat was much less intense; but the dust and smoke were quite as disagreeable — so that I was not sorry when I arrived at the depot. There I met with our old friend David Lee Child, whom I had not seen for a long time, and the pleasure at meeting was mutual. There is to be a "Free Soil" Convention in this town next week; and to-morrow Mr. Child begins a short tour through the county, for the purpose of addressing the people, and urging upon them the importance of sending delegates to the meeting.[1] Bro. George drove down to the depot a few minutes after my arrival, and carried me and my baggage, with Mr. Child and Mrs. [Elisha] Hammond, (whom we took up by the way,) to Benson-ville. On the way, we discussed the affairs of the nation as vigorously and actively as possible. Speaking of Mrs. Chapman's visit to Europe, for educational purposes in regard to her children, Mr. Child expressed much surprise and wonder at her choice, and said that he had supposed there was not steam power enough to drag her away from the anti-slavery cause to the extent that her absence must necessarily require. With us, and many others, he regretted the step, and thought it an ill-advised one.

I found George's family all well, excepting little Sarah, who is afflicted with a bloody diarrhœa, but appears to be a little better this morning.[2]

Charlie had almost despaired of my coming, so that he gravely told Catherine, in the forenoon, that if I did not come when the cars got in, he must go right down to Boston; for he could not stay any longer. He was truly glad to see me, and kissed and hugged me with his usual fervor. He has behaved with great propriety, Catherine says, and is much less boisterous in his manner than when at home. But he says that he likes Boston better than he does Northampton, because he "cannot get used" to the latter place. He simply means

that he wants to be with us and the children; and now that he will
be able to see me every day, I have no doubt he will feel much more
contented. He goes to school regularly, and I have just met him on
the way, accompanied by Mary Benson and another little girl, who
were all singing the song, "O come, come away." [3] He asked me to
let him stay at home, but when I told him that I should not be able
to see him until toward night, he trudged along with the girls quite
resignedly. I gave him, yesterday, some nine or ten sticks of candy,
which he immediately distributed among Tommy, Mary, and the rest,
scarcely reserving a taste for himself. He is a generous little fellow,
as I hope all my boys will be.

Catherine was much obliged to you for your note, and the little
present accompanying it. I took tea with the family, as a farewell to
"tea" for some time.

Of course, I spent the night at the Infirmary. Dr. Ruggles was
rather desirous of giving me a "half bath" before I went to bed, but
I preferred to begin in the morning, and start, if not go through, "by
daylight." My bed is a single one, and being composed of straw, did
not feel quite natural; but I shall soon get used to it, though I should
prefer a good solid mattrass. I awoke as early as 3 o'clock, and heard
the packers stirring about, preparatory to packing their patients; and
though I knew I was not to be packed, yet I lay expecting every
moment to be summoned to my "half bath." It was not till 6 o'clock,
however, that my turn came, and the interim I spent in dreaming
that I had already gone through the process, and also of many other
things. The bath was refreshing, and after taking it, I had a fine
ramble, from which I have returned to write this hasty epistle to you.
In half an hour, I am to be rubbed down with a wet sheet. There will
be very little time allowed either for reading or writing. Indeed, the
Dr. enjoins abstinence from both, as much as possible. Our breakfast
was made up of wheat and rye bread, cracked wheat boiled like
hominy, stewed prunes, milk, and cold water. The Dr. does not wish
me to use much milk, as he says it is not good for my humor. He has
now eighteen patients in all.

Bro. George and Catherine expects you and the children here, at
vacation, without fail, and say they will be able to accommodate
you all, or to find accommodations. I hope you will come, of course,
but wish you to do as you may feel the most strongly inclined. George
intends visiting Boston either next week or the week after, and would
like to have you come with him at that time, if convenient.

You must write to me as you find leisure, for I shall feel anxious
to hear from you often. Tell Fanny, that dear little funny Sarah,
though so unwell, wants to know how Fanny is, and if she will not

come up and see her. Tell all the boys they must try to assist you as much as possible, and be just as good as they know how. George thinks we shall do wisely to remain where we are till Spring. Love to all.

Ever yours,

Wm. Lloyd Garrison.

ALS: Garrison Papers, Boston Public Library; partly printed in *Life*, III, 228–229.

1. The Free-soil party, formed in 1847 by a coalition of liberal Democrats and Whigs, was founded on the principle of opposition to the extension of slavery into the territory acquired by the Mexican War. In 1848 the party's candidates for President and Vice-President were Martin Van Buren and Charles Francis Adams.

2. Sarah Benson (1846–1925) was George W. Benson's seventh child. In 1864 she was to marry Horace E. Stone in Kansas. (Letters to the editor from Mrs. George T. Hawley, librarian, Kansas State Historical Society, June 1971, and Gail French Peterson, research director, Douglas County Historical Museum, Lawrence, Kansas, June 19, 1971.)

3. This is a song by W. E. Hickson, which is to be found in several collections, including John Piersol McCaskey, ed., *Favorite Songs and Hymns for School and Home* (New York, c. 1899).

241

TO MARIA W. CHAPMAN

Northampton, July 19, 1848.

My Dear Friend:

Sorely was I disappointed in not seeing you and Caroline [Weston], before I left Boston, as I fully intended to do, by going down to Weymouth; but I found so many things "to see to," preparatory to my departure for this place, as to employ every moment of my time. And here I am at the Water Cure establishment, fairly committed to this liquid mode of treatment, having taken the initiatory step yesterday morning. The experience of the first day runs thus: — a half bath (which I should consider a whole one and a quarter) at 5 o'clock, A. M.; rubbed down with a wet sheet thrown over the body at 11 o'clock; a sitz bath at 4, P. M.; a foot-bath at half past 8, P. M.; and at 5 this morning, a shallow bath, which is to be followed at 11 by a spray baptism. And so on to the end. Thus far I have not winced, nor uttered a sigh or groan. But this is only child's play at present, and therefore I may not boast. The weather is warm and beautiful, and it will require some time to bring on a "crisis." At every such period, great faith and resolution are necessary — just as at every pro-slavery outbreak. I have told Dr [David] Ruggles, that if he will rid me of my *humor*, he shall have all my *wit* as a perquisite, though I expect to be in any but a witty state of mind when the former is fully developed.

How to feel resigned to your separation from our little anti-Slavery band by a foreign residence of years, I scarcely know; but I know that the step has not been hastily taken on your part, and that there is not water enough in the Atlantic ocean to quench the flame of your philanthropy. At home or abroad, you will be equally untiring to promote that sacred cause in which you have so long and so effectively labored. Still, we shall miss you more than words can express. We have few suggestive, creative, executive minds; and such is your's, in an eminent degree. Your absence, therefore, will not be the absence of one individual, but of many in one. How joyfully I testify to the clearness of your vision in the darkest hours! to the serenity and bravery of your spirit in the most perilous times! to the steadfastness of your faith when almost all others were faltering! to your un-compromising adherence to principle, under the most powerful temptations! How immensely indebted am I to you for counsel, encouragement, commendation, and support! How could the Liberator have been sustained through such a conflict without your powerful co-operation? Where would have been the Boston Female Anti-Slavery Society but for yourself? How could the Massachusetts and American Anti Slavery Societies have put forth such exertions, in-dependently of your own? The National Bazaar — what does it not owe to you? I know what others have done — what sacrifices they have made, what labors bestowed, what impulses they have given — (I speak with special reference to the women in our cause) — and I remember them all with gratitude and admiration; but your position and influence have been pre-eminently valuable. — But I must quit this strain — it seems too much as if I were writing a biographical notice. Accept my thanks, fervent but poor, for all that you have done. Thus far, in battling for the right, and in contending with "principalities and powers, and spiritual wickedness in high places," [1] and in detecting what is spurious under the guise of abolitionism, and in rebuking treachery and profligacy of conduct on the part of those who, for a time, run well, we have seen eye to eye, and stood side by side. May we continue to do so while we have breath!

I did not write so many introductory letters as I wished to do — (but I hope you have received those which I left with Mr. [Robert F.] Wallcut) — but, on your arrival in London, our beloved friend George Thompson will enable you to see every one with whom you may desire to have an interview, either for your personal gratification, or the advancement of the cause of the slave. Proffer my heart's best affections to G. T., and assure him that he is a part of my existence, and that I watch all his movements with the deepest interest. I have never congratulated him on his election to a seat in the House of Commons, because I do not know by what oath or affirmation he may be bound, so far as fealty to the government is concerned; and because I have been somewhat apprehensive lest it should contract, rather than enlarge, his sphere of usefulness as a popular reformer, and a world-embracing philanthropist. It is a long time since I received a letter from him, and two or three of mine remain unanswered, if he ever received them; but I know that no mortal is more busily occupied than himself, and that his home correspondence is immense, to say nothing of his multifarious public duties and private engagements. Why I chiefly desire a letter from him, as soon as convenient, is, that I may know, for the artist's sake, what disposal has been made of Page's paintings, that were committed to his care a year ago last spring.[2] I feel some degree of responsibility in regard to those paintings; and never having been able to give Mr Page any information respecting them, since they were sent, it has been a source of much embarrassment to me. Pray give my most friendly and cordial remembrances to Mrs Thompson and all the dear children. On gazing, the other day, in Boston, at Bayne's panoramic view of London and the Thames, it seemed as if I was really there again in bodily form, and could call on G. T. and his family at any moment.[3]

I hope you and Caroline will not fail to see our much attached friend William H. Ashurst and his charming family at Muswell Hill, a perfect gem of a place, quite equal to Paradise before the fall. You will be delighted with them all, and they will be immensely gratified to see you. I cherish for Mr. Ashurst a profound regard, as a rare man on earth. His ability is unquestionable and great, his philanthropy expansive, his spirit catholic, his practical knowledge of men and things uncommon, his philosophy serene and comprehensive, and his perception of truth quick and steady. A most attentive and valuable correspondent of the Liberator has he proved for a long time past; and may it be a long time to come before his favors in that line will cease.

Should you happen to see dear Elizabeth Pease, (and I trust you will not fail doing so,) say every thing to her, for me, in the shape of good wishes, grateful remembrances, admiring reminiscences, &c. &c. Her sympathetic letter respecting the death of our dear little Lizzie was a cordial to the heart of Helen, and very strengthening to my own. What would the world be without such friendship? I know that she will be highly gratified on hearing that I am at last trying the "Water Cure."

Pray visit Bristol, if you can, to see that perfect gentleman, kind friend, and active friend of our cause, Mr [John B.] Estlin, and also his accomplished daughter [Mary Estlin] and others in that place, who have an abiding and a choice place in my memory.

Then as to the friends in Sheffield, Edinburgh, Glasgow, Belfast, and Dublin, &c. &c. to which of them do I not desire to be warmly remembered, should you see any of them?

How delighted will our cherished friend Mary G. Chapman be to embrace both you and Caroline, and the children, on the other side of the Atlantic! Alas! that I cannot be there too! Farewell!

Yours, with undying regard,

Wm. Lloyd Garrison.

M. W. Chapman.

Handwritten transcription: Garrison Papers, Boston Public Library; extract printed in *Life*, III, 229.

1. An adaptation of Ephesians 6:12.

2. It is known that Thompson had been sent the Page portrait of Garrison (painted 1846) that it might be exhibited in Great Britain. What other paintings were in Thompson's possession is uncertain, though William Page (1811–1885) is known to have painted during his Boston period (1844–1847) in addition to Garrison the following: John Quincy Adams, Charles W. Eliot, James Russell Lowell, Wendell Phillips, Josiah Quincy, Colonel R. G. Shaw, Charles Sumner. In 1849 Page moved to Italy, where for eleven years he enjoyed the reputation of being the leading American painter of his time. He produced not only portraits but also historical paintings. In his later years he settled in New York, and between 1871 and 1873 he was president of the National Academy. (Wendell Phillips Garrison and Francis Jackson Garrison, eds., *The Words of Garrison*, Boston, 1905.)

3. Walter McPherson Bayne (1795–1859) was a landscape and panorama painter. Born in England, he exhibited in London from 1833 to 1858. He lived in Boston during the 1830's and 1840's, and his work was shown at the Boston Athenaeum. His most famous painting was a panorama of a voyage to Europe, which was exhibited in several American cities between 1847 and 1856. (George C. Groce and David H. Wallace, *The New-York Historical Society's Dictionary of Artists in America, 1564–1860*, New Haven, 1957.)

242

TO HELEN E. GARRISON

Boston,[1] July 23, 1848.
Sunday Afternoon.

Dear Wife:

I have an opportunity to send you a few lines, and therefore improve it, though I have nothing special to communicate. Aside from the daily incidents which occur under the Water Cure roof, (and these are very slightly varied, and of no interest to any but the patients,) there is nothing in all this region to stimulate the mind, excepting a contemplation of the beautiful and grand in Nature — nothing occurring worth putting on record. Perhaps a continued residence in the country would operate upon me differently; but I have been so long accustomed to the bustle and excitement of a city life, that it is quite essential to the activity of my brain. My ideality is a large organ — so the phrenologists say, and so I believe; and if I were sufficiently transcendental to live in an ideal state, I could well enjoy the solitude of a country residence, where one is cut off from intercourse with society. But I see too many things on terra firma, that need to be corrected or destroyed — the earth is too much stained with human blood — there are too many of my race suffering for lack of food, trampled beneath the hoofs of tyranny, plundered of sacred and inalienable rights, groping in mental darkness, victimized by those twin monsters bigotry and superstition, wallowing in the mire of sensuality, and sighing to be brought into the glorious "liberty of the sons of God," [2] — to allow me to dwell in an ideal state, or to gaze upon imaginary rainbows in the clouds, pleasant as it might be under other circumstances: therefore my benevolence overtops my ideality, and makes me greatly prefer the practical to the fanciful. — I want, first of all, to see the horrid system of slavery abolished in this country; and then every thing else that is evil.

See what one can do, who has a tolerable share of firmness, when he has made up his mind to do it! I detest shams, deplore weaknesses, and have no opinion of cowardice, except "on instinct." You know how I used to revolt at the idea of a baptism of cold water at home — how flesh and blood recoiled at the thought of taking a bath fresh from the aqueduct. Well, here I have been almost a week; and every day, some four or five times, I have been packed in a wet sheet, or drenched from head to foot, or immersed all over, or subjected to a sitz bath, foot bath, &c. &c.; and in no instance have I uttered a groan, or heaved a sigh, or shed a tear, or faltered for a moment. Bravo! Allow me to praise myself; that privilege is fairly mine by conquest; and you may add a "well done, husband," if you please. How I shall deport myself in a "crisis," I will not predict. At such a time, it is lawful for every patient to have "the blues," but I believe in no case does anyone lose his appetite. Every one is hungry here, and eager to hear the bell rung for breakfast, dinner or supper, though the fare is extremely simple — no coffee, no tea, no butter, no milk, (a spoonful or two of cream,) no meat, (except a lean slice by special permission,) no hot bread, no warm dish of any kind. No one gets the gout by surfeit; but if he has it, when he comes, he is infallibly cured of it; for, as Solomon sagely says, "where there is no fuel, the fire goeth out." [3] You may think that I sigh for "the leeks and onions of Egypt," and murmur for meat as did the manna-surfeited Israelites; but I don't.[4] But enough of boasting.

As yet, I perceive no effect of the water upon my system; but to-morrow I am to commence wearing "fomentations," or wet compresses around the body. These will hasten a developement. What this may be, it is not easy to predict; but every thing in good time. "Sufficient unto the day," &c.[5]

Of the nineteen patients who are here, a majority are men. They are all well behaved, and very pleasant. I believe I am the gayest of the lot — perhaps it is because I am the least advanced in the "cure." My organ of mirthfulness is constantly excited, especially when I see a dozen men gravely sitting in what is called the "sitz bath," being one of the number (excepting the gravity) myself. This "exceeds all power of face," [6] it looks so comical — like a desperate, as well as unnatural, effort at incubation. Most of the females are young ladies, all of them remarkably silent, (for their sex, of course,) and none of them very interesting, (though I dare say they are all very worthy,) excepting a Miss Thayer from Rochester, N.Y.,[7] who, being a "Garrisonian" abolitionist, and a thoroughgoing reformer, must, of course, be very agreeable. She reminds me a little of Elizabeth Pease, of Darlington, though younger by one half. She is a rigid Grahamite, and deems it wrong to take the life of any animal for food — even to destroy a spider or snake. She was surprised, she said, to see me, yesterday, take up a stone to kill a snake which lay across my pathway, a few yards from the house, with his forked tongue thrust out in self-defence; though he got away unharmed. She is well acquainted with the anti-slavery friends in Rochester; and her sister is governess to the children of Frederick Douglass. Her disease is scrofula.

Yesterday, my esteemed friend, and worthy abolition coadjutor, Mr. Stephens, of Plymouth, brought his sister-in-law, Mrs. Bartlett, to try the effect of the water cure in her case, which is one of incipient pulmonary consumption.[8] He thinks he may himself come up next month, and go through a course, as his liver is badly affected. There does not seem to be any pro-slavery among the patients; if there really is, it has not been manifested by any word or sign, and I hope it will be washed out of them.

Bro. George is yet undetermined in regard to business. He is evidently at a loss to know what to do, and I wish I could relieve his mind on that score. He thinks, however, of visiting Andover and Boston in the course of a few days, and I hope you will be ready to come up to this place with him; though I will not urge you to do so, if for any reason you prefer to remain in Pine street. I long to see you and the children, especially my darling Fanny, whose likeness, as well as the best one of my own, you will please get at Mr. North's — telling him that I will settle with him for the same.[9]

I shall want, when you come, another pair of thin pantaloons, cheap, to wear here, no matter of what stuff. Please send or call at Mr. Curtis's, in Ann street, who knows and keeps my measures, and he will doubtless be able to find a pair already made that will answer the purpose.[10] If not, I can get a pair made in Northampton. Mr. Curtis, if he has a suitable pair, will charge the same to my account.

Bring with you, also, my best rubber overshoes; and if you have room, also my broad-toed pair of boots. I also need two more sheets.

Perhaps you had better buy *two* trunks, of a pretty good size. Friend [Robert F.] Wallcut will readily buy them for you, and probably cheaper than you can. I hope he will be in funds, so that he can advance you the month's salary. You will need considerable here for incidentals, as well as some for board. I have had to buy towels, linen for drawers, jean [11] and linen for compresses and body jackets, &c. &c.; so that I have but a trifle left. Our weekly washing will be something of an item.

Charles is well, and anxious to see you all. He is far more quiet than at home, and goes to school every day, but is to have a vacation in a day or two. Little Sarah [Benson] continues somewhat unwell, though she is a little better. Mrs. Rogers [12] is still at George's. Mrs. [Nathaniel] Paul is slowly improving, but a burden. I enclose a note for our landlord, which you can read, seal, and *direct*, as I have forgotten his christian name, and you will find it on his bill.

Yours, lovingly,

Wm. Lloyd Garrison.

ALS: Garrison Papers, Boston Public Library; extract printed in *Life*, III, 230–231.

1. Garrison mistakenly heads this letter "Boston"; on the manuscript "Northampton" is added above, probably by Garrison himself.
2. An adaptation of Romans 8:21.
3. Garrison adapts Proverbs 26.20.
4. Garrison adapts Numbers 11:5 and alludes to Exodus 16:35.
5. Matthew 6:34.
6. Alexander Pope, "Epistle to Dr. Arbuthnot," line 36.
7. Abby G. Thayer (born c. 1827), who married Isaac T. Chase in 1853. (Rochester *Daily Democrat*, September 22, 1853.)
8. Lemuel Stephens (born 1786), who was married to Sally Morton, was active in the antislavery movement. Mrs. Bartlett was probably Mary Morton, wife of Elkanah Bartlett. The Morton family were also Plymouth abolitionists. (Letters to the editor from Rose Briggs, curator, Plymouth Antiquarian Society, June 10 and 29, 1970, and Katharine F. Freeland, director, Plymouth Public Library, June 23, 1970.)
9. Garrison refers to the William C. North listed in the 1848–1849 Boston

directory as a "daguerrean" having his studio at 142 Washington Street and living at the Marlboro Hotel.

10. Garrison refers to John Curtis, Jr., whose clothing store was located at 6 Ann Street, Boston. (Boston city directory.)

11. The durable twilled cotton cloth often used for work clothes — hence our modern "jeans."

12. Mrs. Rogers has not been identified.

243

TO HELEN E. GARRISON

Bensonville, July 26, 1848.

Dear Helen:

A few minutes after I had forwarded my letters to you by Mr. Stephens, I received yours of Sunday last. I am induced to write thus early again, because from the description you give of the colored girl, who wishes to do your work, I am convinced that she will not answer your purpose. She is manifestly too young, too slender, and too inexperienced. You need some one at least as strong as Hannah; [1] and though this young girl may be very smart, and may think she can perform all that you must necessarily require of her, yet it is evident to me that she would become discouraged, or break down, in a short time. Besides, if she has been used principally to the taking care of children, I do not see how she can well understand the art of cooking. Of course, Mr. Taylor's testimony cannot avail aught, as he knows nothing about her.[2] Perhaps, however, you have made a positive engagement with her; and, if so, then I suppose you must take her, "for better, for worse," as she may happen to turn out.

As for Hannah, I pity her, and do not wonder that she is troubled at the thought of losing her place. You must make all due allowance for one in her situation, on the score of temper, and be careful to say or do nothing that shall excite her ill feelings. It is evident that she is attached to us, and would much rather live with us than with any other family. There is at least an equal chance that, if you lose her, you will get worse help. It is true, she lacks neatness, (and this is a serious deficit,) and is a very poor washer and ironer, (and this, too, is a great drawback,) but she is industrious, though not swift, kind, and ready to do any kind of work. She is also honest. If, during your absence from the city, she can obtain a situation to her mind, let her do so; but, if not, perhaps you had better retain her — at least till after your accouchement — letting her understand, however, that, whenever you can find one who can better fill her place, you will be induced to make the change, after giving her due notice. For Ellen's sake, I feel anxious that Hannah should be satisfied that we take an interest in her welfare. As a stranger in a strange land,[3] she is all the more to be tenderly regarded. I am sorry she is not all that we want, and all that is really desirable; but it will, doubtless, be extremely difficult to find a girl who, as a whole, will do better than herself at nine shillings a week.

I believe I requested you, in my last letter, to buy me a pair of thin pantaloons at Mr. [John] Curtiss's; but I wish to withdraw that request, as I shall be able to make my erminett ones answer my purpose; therefore, give yourself no trouble on that score. But I shall need the pantaloons I left in the closet — not the black ones, but of another color, and somewhat stout.

To-day, there is to be a free soil convention in Northampton, and several of us will go down this afternoon to judge of its character and spirit, — dispensing with our usual bath. The defection from the Taylor and Cass ranks, in this section of the State, appears to be considerable, and is every day increasing.[4] It seems probable, now, that there will be no choice of electors in Massachusetts, by the people, at the November election. I long to see the day when the great issue with the Slave Power, of the immediate dissolution of the Union, will be made by all the free States; for then the conflict will be a short and decisive one, and liberty will triumph. The free soil movement inevitably leads to it, and hence I hail it as the beginning of the end.

Wednesday Evening.

George and William safely arrived this afternoon at 3 o'clock; though they took the train for *Cabot*, at Springfield, and had to wait some time at that place until the Northampton train came along. I got my friend Mr. Bradbury to go to the depot for them, as I did not like to leave the meeting.[5] They immediately went on their way to Bensonville. They brought a letter from you, enclosing some money, and also one from my kind friend [Samuel J.] May, as well as a large bundle of newspapers, which I was very glad to receive. Mr. May thinks I had better relinquish my intention of receiving a bundle weekly to examine, lest it shall be a drawback upon my progress in the water cure; and he very considerately offers to make all necessary selections for the Liberator. But absence of newspapers will cause me more uneasiness of mind, than their examination will prove detrimental. Should I have a "crisis," however, I shall undoubtedly feel too unwell, for the time being, to read much without injury; and in that case, I will duly notify friend [Robert F.] Wallcut of the fact and not attempt the task.

[. . .]

As to the sheets, perhaps you had better wait till you come here before you purchase the cloth, or make any, as you will then know precisely the kind that are wanted. I suppose two more will answer. Fine ones are not required.

I hear from New York, that Mrs. [Sydney H.] Gay has presented her husband with a fine boy.

The daguerreotype likeness of dear little, charming, lovely, darling Fanny is greatly admired by all the ladies and gentlemen here, both for its execution and the beauty of the face. Mine is thought to be pretty good, but not entirely satisfactory. It is strange that neither nature nor art can succeed in getting a good likeness of me. Do not fail to bring our saluted Lizzy's with you.

Our kind friend Blanchard, I think, must have been disappointed that we did not take his house; and nothing but our peculiar situation at this time would have prevented our doing so.[6] If he should call on you again, assure him that we should have been much pleased to have had him for a landlord, and are greatly obliged to him for his kindness and attention. I esteem him highly [. . .]

AL: Garrison Papers, Boston Public Library; extract printed in *Life*, III, 231. Owing to a badly torn page of the manuscript, this letter is incomplete; one third of two pages, including the signature, is missing.

1. An unidentified servant.
2. Mr. Taylor has not been identified.
3. A reference to Exodus 2:22.
4. Lewis Cass (1782–1866), soldier, diplomat, and statesman, entered the War Department during the Jackson administration. He became minister to France in 1836 and was elected United States senator from Michigan in 1845. In 1848 he was nominated for President on the Democratic ticket.
5. Nothing is known of Cyrus Bradbury other than that he came from Boston to enter the Northampton community with two sisters, Elizabeth Ely and Sarah Elizabeth Bradbury, April 4, 1844, and that he withdrew December 2, 1844. (Sheffeld, p. 103.)
6. Joshua P. Blanchard (1782–1868) lived at this time at 13 Purchase Street, Boston. Most of the remaining years of his life, however, were spent at 4 Waverly Place. He served as secretary to the American Anti-Slavery Society from 1841 to 1848. (Letter to the editor from Jonathan Prude, researcher, September 1970.)

---

2 4 4

TO FRANCIS JACKSON

Boston,[1] July 31, 1848.

My Dear Friend:

Here's to your health, happiness and prosperity, in a mug of cold water, pure from the spring, the original "ale" of Adam in Paradise! There is nothing like water, now, you know — especially at a hydropathic establishment. The Welshman's rabbit was good boiled, baked, roasted, fried, or stewed; and with us who are here for the much desired "cure," water is good running, sprinkling, dripping, pouring, dashing — and whether you are standing, sitting or lying. What do you think of forty different applications of it to one's body, in one week — and from week to week from three to twelve months, according to the severity of the case? What do you think of as many large mugs of the same liquid taken internally during the same period? If this is not using the water power to some purpose in driving this bodily machinery, then there are no such things as cause and effect in the universe. One must have in him, or about him, a good deal of "the filth of the flesh" [2] not to be able to get rid of it by such a process. But as to the flesh itself, it is sure to be a gainer in the end, though one may lose a few pounds of it, along with the impurity, at the outset. One gentleman tells me that he has been here nine weeks, and has regularly gained a pound a week during that time. Another one who has been here four weeks has had the same result in his case. How I shall come out, remains to be seen; but if as portly as a London alderman, it will not be owing either to roast turkey or turtle soup. It will, however, be genuine flesh, accompanied by no tendency to gout or apoplexy.

After a fortnight's experiment to-night, I am prepared to pass an opinion upon this mode of cure, and to give a certificate in its favor, as against every other. We have now upwards of twenty patients, and it is both curious and surprising to see what the application of water alone has done, or is doing, for them. In almost every instance, virulent humors are driven to the surface of the body, or of the limbs, so as to present an extraordinary appearance. When these pass off, it generally indicates a renovated system, and the patient may go on his way rejoicing.

Speaking of water, I am reminded of the falls of Niagara. How very natural! Well, you have seen them, and heard them, and taken their dimensions. Pray how did you feel in their presence? A tailor, on seeing them, is reported to have exclaimed, "What a place to sponge a coat!" — and a dandy, surveying them with his eye-glass, cried out admiringly — "Upon my soul, they do infinite credit to the artist!" [3] — An hydropathist would probably call them Nature's "douche bath." Soberly, I suppose every attempt to describe their sublimity and grandeur must fail. Did you and your good company venture across on the wire bridge? Or take a trip in the "Maid of the Mist," which I see is described as peculiarly thrilling? [4] Then, as to Canada. Doubtless, you saw a mighty contrast between its condition and that of the Empire State. While the people of Canada are willing to remain in colonial vassalage, they will never rise far above their present condition. What they need is to be free and independent, and thus thrown upon their own resources, and clothed with their own responsibilities. Then they will begin to exhibit thrift, enterprise, and proofs of social, intellectual and moral improvement. As to being annexed to this Union, I trust that will never be done while a slave remains on our soil.

To-morrow is the memorable first of August. What a day for rejoicing! what an occasion on which to derive strength to continue the conflict with the Slave Power in our own land! Of course, you will be at the gathering of free hearts and grateful spirits in Lynn. I shall be there too — in spirit — and also in all the islands of the West Indies, in which slavery expired on that day. May you and I be spared to see an American jubilee — every fetter riven, every captive set free!

In consequence of not being able to find precisely the tenement I wanted before I left Boston — the difficulty of my visiting the city to superintend the removal of my furniture, while going through the "cure" — the uncertainty as to the time my case may require — and certain domestic considerations — I have concluded to remain in Pine-street until the spring. During the interim, there will be a good opportunity to examine houses, both in the city and its vicinity, and to choose with care and deliberation. Wendell [Phillips] thought this the wisest course.

I shall send this letter by my brother-in-law, Mr. Benson, one of the noblest of the human race, who is now in quest of business, having forfeited his situation as agent of the factory here, in consequence of his freedom from religious bigotry, and especially for the awful crime of being the President of the Anti-Sabbath Convention. If you can suggest to him any thing that may be useful in the way of business, I am sure you will gladly do so.

Please remember Northampton, and come with Eliza [Jackson Merriam] as soon as convenient, to whom remember me affectionately and admiringly, and also to Harriet [Mrs. Francis Jackson] and James [Jackson], and Edmund [Jackson] and his dear family.

Yours, with boundless esteem,

Wm. Lloyd Garrison.

Francis Jackson.

ALS: Garrison Papers, Boston Public Library.

1. Garrison supplies on the manuscript, apparently at a later date, the correct place "Northampton" instead of the erroneous "Boston."
2. Either I Peter 3:21 or an adaptation of II Corinthians 7:1.
3. The quotation "What a place to sponge a coat!" comes from a book of remarks written by visitors to the Table Rock House at the falls. (Letter to the

editor from Marjorie F. Williams, city historian, Niagara Falls, New York, June 3, 1971.) The comment of the dandy has not been identified but is probably from the same source.

4. The *Maid of the Mist* was a vessel which left a landing near the foot of the American Falls and went past them almost to the very foot of the Horseshoe Falls before the engine was turned off and the boat drifted downstream again in the torrent. The ride did and still does give a feeling of daring adventure, even though it is not actually dangerous. The name of the boat derives from the legend that each year the Indians sent their fairest maiden over the falls in a canoe to appease the thunder god living below. (Thomas Tugby, *Tugby's Guide to Niagara Falls*, Niagara Falls, 1890.)

---

2 4 5

TO ELIZA JACKSON MERRIAM

Northampton, Aug. 9, 1848.

My Dear Friend:

Helen desires me to enclose a few lines in her letter to you, and I would gladly send you many, if I thought they would repay a perusal.[1] In the quiet retreat in which I am now located, we have nothing occurring, from day to day, beyond the usual routine of taking one bath after another; and as we receive intelligence from abroad only occasionally, we have little to suggest topics of conversation, and still less to place on record. The number of patients at the "Cure" is twenty-three — of whom thirteen are ladies, with one exception, *young* ladies, though several of them are married, and therefore not in the market; luckily, neither am I. All, of both sexes, seem to be very amiable; and as there is not a single dogmatic, controversial spirit among us, it is not only impossible to get up a breeze, but it is difficult to raise even a zephyr, on any subject. The conversational powers of our party seem to be quite limited, either (as the school-boy whistled) for want of thought,[2] or because they are incorrigibly saturnine or diffident. But, in several points we are heartily agreed, and quite enthusiastic: to wit, that there is no medicine, whether taken internally or externally, like pure cold water; that, having appetites alarmingly good, it is a real pleasure to eat the simplest fare; that we are all making good progress in the cure; that our worthy doctor (being blind, you know) is a very *feeling* man, and has much physiological knowledge at *his fingers' ends*; and that Northampton is one of the prettiest places in the wide world, though few of us have seen very little of the world. Being Yankees, we *guess* that it is so. The weather is perfect — the scenery romantic — the retirement delightful; and now that the moon nightly grows in size and splendor, our evening rambles are perfectly pleasurable.

I am greatly delighted to learn, from Helen, that you and your father [Francis Jackson] ("may his shadow never be less") [3] intend visiting this place, ere long; and that though *he* will not be able to remain long — I am sorry for that, yet I know what are the demands of business — *you* will remain with us a few weeks, with the children. Having my family here, I now feel very much at home; and when you all come, it will be having cherished friends in addition to wife and progeny. Though I am not master of my time, and must take my baths at regular hours, yet I shall be able to find some leisure to show Helen and you the beauties of this romantic region.

Please give my thanks to your father for his very pleasant letter, relative to your excursion to Niagara, and as he is so capital a correspondent, I must send him another epistle to elicit another similar favor, which, by the way, is fairly due, as he left you and himself suspended on the ærial wire bridge over the roaring waters, without having time to relate the sequel. I take a long breath, however; for I am sure you both got safely across, and so were not carried over the falls, inasmuch as his letter was dated at Boston, and Helen saw you at No. 7, Hollis-street, with her own eyes. Your father admits that you had more courage than himself, as he had no intention to take such a wirey passage; but on you would go, heroine-like, and on he would follow, like an affectionate father whose love is superior to all apprehension of danger, whether real or imaginary. It seems your uncle Edmund [Jackson], with his estimable wife, could not be persuaded to "bridge the gulf" in that manner, preferring the "firm-set earth" [4] to any position in the air, however lofty or sublime. Blessings unnumbered on you all, and may all harm be kept from you, whether at home or abroad, on dry land or in "the blue above."

Yours, truly,

Wm. Lloyd Garrison.

Mrs. E. J. Meriam.

ALS: Garrison Papers, Boston Public Library.

1. Garrison frequently added a note of his own to a letter his wife was writing.
2. An allusion to Robert Blair, "The Grave," lines 58–59.
3. James J. Morier, *The Adventures of Hajji Babba of Ispahan* (1824); see reprint (New York, 1937), p. 137.
4. Shakespeare, *Macbeth*, II, i, 56.

246

TO EDMUND QUINCY

Northampton, Aug. 10, 1848.

My Dear Quincy:

If I do not scrawl at least a few lines for your perusal, you may come to the affecting conclusion, that the "water *cure*" has been the death of me, and so be induced to announce my exit in the Liberator — declaring,

> "He shall not float upon his watery bier,
> Without the meed of some melodious tear" — [1]

though why another drop should be given to a man who has been drowned, I cannot understand. It would certainly be "a drop too much," as well as "all in my eye." [2] However, I am no Lycidas, and I trust his fate will not be mine. [3]

Well, here I am, giving myself to the work of physical regeneration, by being packed, showered, drenched, plunged, *douched*, &c. &c., with the utmost zeal and fidelity. You may easily imagine that half a dozen different applications of the same redeeming element, with active exercise between each in the open air, leave but very little time either for reading or writing, even if these were not contraband engagements here to all the patients, especially if their mental machine is already overworked. I assure you that so many interruptions seriously interfere with one's continuity of thought, or disposition to drive the quill. Few, very few, are the letters written by those at this establishment, though we number about two dozen in all. We write all our joys and griefs, our comforts and deprivations, in water. "Water, water every where," and plenty of it to drink. [4] Ink is a liquid in which we do not deal. To think of it at once calls up the idea of the *black* vomit.

Thus do I submerge my epistolary delinquency, and deluge you with reasons for my silence.

Time does not hang heavily on my hands, as I apprehended it would, at this establishment. On the contrary, it runs as rapidly as water down hill, and does not grow weary in the race. I am now on my fourth week, borne along on "the tide of successful experiment"; [5] not long enough to instigate a "crisis," (which is Nature's signal of distress, indicating that relief is near,) but long enough to get a taste of the liquid, and to determine its quality. You know that I cherished a strong aversion to drugs and *die* stuffs, in consequence of my Thompsonian enlightenment; but that aversion has been increased since I have exchanged cold water for hot. Immortal honor, and a monument

higher than the tallest Egyptian pyramid, to the man who first exclaimed — "Give physic to the dogs! I'll none of it!" [6] Long life to
Priessnitz, and "to your honor" also! — for though you meddle with
no other doctors, excepting those who dose the people with *divinity*
pills, yet you sacredly perform your daily cold water ablutions, and
contrive to steer clear of "the ills that flesh is heir to." [7] I dare say you
are careful to treasure up the declaration of Solomon, as a good recipe
against disease — "A sound heart is the life of the flesh." [8]

As this letter is written for your eye, and not for the public's, I
shall try to send you something about the "Water Cure," for the
Liberator, and thus report progress to its subscribers; but I have
thought it best to give heed to the sage injunction — "Do not halloo
until you get out of the woods." [9] A part of the time I am in the woods,
and the rest in the water; but I know where I am, and feel that I am
warranted in shouting at the top of my lungs. Besides, exercise of
this kind is good for them.

Having my family almost within hailing distance of me, my
absence from Boston is not like absence from home; yet we are all
eager for the arrival of the day when we shall find ourselves located
at our old place in the city, No. 13, Pine-street.

The telegraphic intelligence from the Buffalo Convention, this evening, is, that Martin Van Buren will probably be the Presidential
nominee, almost without opposition! [10] "Through what new scenes
and changes must we pass?" [11] It is stated in the Tribune, moreover,
that Gerrit Smith has written a letter to the Convention, advising the
nomination of Van Buren! This I cannot credit, impulsive and unstable as I know him to be. "*Nous verrons.*" It is true, the Convention
appears to have adopted, as the basis of action, all that the Liberty
party dare claim Congress is constitutionally empowered to do, (and
thus has fairly swamped that party as such,) but Mr. Smith has been
very severe upon John P. Hale, and utterly condemnatory of the
Liberty party basis; and now, if he has eaten his own words, pray look
after him, and let the readers of the Liberator see how he *feeds.*

As for this Free Soil movement, I feel that great care is demanded
of us, Disunionists, both in the Standard and the Liberator, in giving
credit to whom credit is due, and yet in no case even seeming to be
satisfied with it. It is only placing the country precisely in the same
condition, on the subject of slavery, that it occupied a quarter of a
century since — to wit, that slavery ought not to be extended to new
territories; that it ought to be abolished (when or how is not stated
in the new creed) in all our territorial possessions — (nothing, I believe, is said about its abolition in the District of Columbia;) and
that Congress has no constitutional power to meddle with it in the

several States — (another repudiation of Spooner's, [William] Goodell's and Smith's dogma on that point.) [12]

Our Disunion ground is invulnerable, and to it all parties at the North must come, ere long. The temptation to vote, however, at the coming election, will be so great, that I fear a considerable number of Disunionists, and even of professed non-resistants, will fall into the snare, and try to persuade themselves that, for this once, they may innocently, and even laudably, "bow down in the house of Rimmon." [13] Calm yet earnest appeals must be made to our friends to preserve their integrity, and not to lose sight of the true issue. Already, in this region, I hear it said that a number of those who have hitherto acted with us, think they can now vote, even for Martin Van Buren! What infatuation!

I have not yet read Horace Mann's speech, as the Dr [David Ruggles]'s Liberator has suddenly disappeared.[14] I dare say it was excellent in its manner and matter, though by no means original, (for all that such men can now do is to steal our thunder,) but I have very little doubt that Horace Mann will go for the Louisiana bloodhound.[15] If he should —!

Your 1st of August celebration at Lynn appears to have been very successful. Our esteemed friend John B. Pierce, of Salem, wrote me an account of it immediately on his return home.[16] This I send to you for insertion, either in whole or in part, or not at all, as you may deem proper.[17] The [Joshua] Leavitt and [Elizur] Wright celebration at Baker's Grove, Dorchester, which the Emancipator and Chronotype puffed so prodigiously in advance, telling how many eminent men *had been invited* to speak on the occasion, seems to have been a very slim affair.[18]

Hoping that you and yours are well and happy, and wishing to be lovingly remembered to all the friends at 25, Cornhill, I remain, my dear Quincy,

Yours, in cold water or hot,

Wm. Lloyd Garrison.

ALS: Garrison Papers, Sophia Smith Collection, Smith College Library; extract printed in *The Liberator*, August 25, 1848, and in *Life*, III, 235.

1. A quotation from John Milton, *Lycidas*, lines 12 and 14, with the word "must" changed to "shall."
2. Garrison uses a slang expression meaning nonsense, humbug.
3. Garrison alludes to John Milton's poem and to Edward King (1612–1637), whose death by drowning supplied the occasion for writing it.
4. Garrison refers to Samuel Taylor Coleridge, *The Rime of the Ancient Mariner*, Part II, stanza 9, lines 3–4.
5. An adaptation of Thomas Jefferson, *First Inaugural Address*, delivered March 4, 1801.

6. Shakespeare, *Macbeth*, V, iii, 47. Garrison changes the word "throw" to "give."

7. Garrison slightly misquotes Shakespeare, *Hamlet*, III, i, 62–63, substituting the word "ills" for "shocks."

8. Proverbs 14:30.

9. Garrison uses a common maxim, the sense of which goes back to the ancient Greeks.

10. Martin Van Buren (1782–1862), eighth President of the United States (1836–1840), had earlier, as Vice-President, taken various stands in favor of states' rights and against the Garrisonian abolitionists. By the time of this letter, however, he had become convinced that the northern Democrats had yielded to the "slavocracy" long enough and was willing to be nominated for the Presidency by the Free-soil party, organized in Buffalo in August. He later alienated the Free-soilers by supporting the compromise measures of 1850.

11. Joseph Addison, *Cato*, V, i, 12.

12. Lysander Spooner (1808–1887) was a lawyer and political writer who in 1844 established the American Letter Mail Company, a private agency that carried letters between Boston and New York at the rate of five cents each. Government opposition soon forced him to give up the enterprise. He was a strong enemy of slavery, but unlike Garrison advocated political organization as a means toward abolition. His *Unconstitutionality of Slavery* (1845) was used by the Liberty party as campaign literature.

13. Garrison adapts II Kings 5:18.

14. Horace Mann (1796–1859) was a graduate of Brown University whose interest in educational reform lasted all his life. He helped to push through the Massachusetts education bill of 1837, a pioneer effort toward free public education. In 1853 he became president of Antioch College. The antislavery speech to which Garrison refers was delivered before the United States House of Representatives, June 30, 1848, and reprinted in *The Liberator*, August 4, 1848.

15. Garrison refers to Zachary Taylor (1784–1850), who, as an officer in the struggle between the United States and the Seminole Indians in 1839, found it necessary to recruit a pack of bloodhounds from Cuba to track down the Indians. In *The Liberator*, July 7, 1848, the Whig party is called the Bloodhound party and Taylor the Bloodhound candidate.

16. John B. Peirce (c. 1804–1889) was a businessman in Salem, San Francisco, and Boston, specializing in the wholesale grocery trade. He supported the temperance and abolition movements and was a Garrisonian until 1848, when he joined the Free-soil party.

17. Quincy appears not to have inserted Peirce's account of the Lynn celebration.

18. The Boston *Weekly Chronotype* was founded in 1846 by Elizur Wright, who used it to oppose the protective tariff, slavery, and life insurance companies. Wright was frequently hostile to Garrison. In 1850 the *Chronotype* was purchased by the *Weekly Commonwealth*, an organ of the Free-soil party, with Wright remaining as editor. For an identification of Wright, see Garrison's letter to Father Theobald Mathew, September 7, 1849, n. 7.

2 4 7

TO ROBERT F. WALLCUT

Northampton, Aug. 28, 1848.

Dear Wallcut:

The bundle of papers comes with regularity, and is gladly welcomed by all at our Water Cure, especially by me, of course. Thanks for your pleasant note, and love to you and yours. The object of this is simply to request you to have the following obituary notice published in this week's Liberator, as I have not time to write you a letter.[1] Indeed, as to letter-writing, it is very strictly prohibited in my case, by Dr. [David] Ruggles, and he is not at all pleased to have me engaged in corresponding even with my friends. The other day, he caught me writing in my chamber, and emphatically declared — "Now, this will never do — you might as well be in Boston as here, if you mean to use your pen — the water cure can do you no good, if you do not abstain from mental exertion, but will rather do you harm" — &c. &c. It is certainly a curious fact that, with all the cold water applications that are daily made to me, from my head to my heels, my brain loses none of its heat, (which is always too great,) though in other respects I am powerfully affected. So much for my hot-headedness! The Dr. is undoubtedly right in his injunction, and I mean to try to comply with it, as far as practicable, in justice to himself, as well as to expedite my cure. Hence, the fewness of my letters must not be a source of complaint on the part of my friends.

Helen unites with me in desiring to be kindly remembered to your dear wife and estimable aunts.

Faithfully yours,

Wm. Lloyd Garrison.

P.S. My wife is writing a letter to you, in which I have detected her counselling you to withhold my weekly bundle of newspapers, on the ground that it will do me more harm than good. In this, she is mistaken. My excitement without it would be greater than it is with it. It pleasantly relieves the otherwise intolerable monotony of my situation. But as to indulgence in writing, I am willing to curtail it to the lowest point practicable, because it requires far greater mental effort than miscellaneous reading. Perhaps, now and then, you may find a private opportunity to send the bundle; if not, let it come by express.

ALS: Garrison Papers, Sophia Smith Collection, Smith College Library.

1. Garrison refers to the obituary of Augusta V. Reed which later appeared in *The Liberator*, September 1, 1848. His handwritten copy is not with his letter in the Sophia Smith Collection and presumably has not survived.

---

2 4 8

TO NATHANIEL BARNEY

Northampton, Sept. 8, 1848.

Esteemed Friend:

It is a long time since I have heard directly from you, but I trust you are in the enjoyment of good health, one of the greatest of all earthly blessings. My own health having been much impaired by the severe illness with which I was prostrated a year ago, in Ohio, I have been trying the efficacy of the cold water treatment, at the Hydropathic establishment of Dr. [David] Ruggles in this place, for a few weeks past, in which I have great faith, both theoretically and experimentally. Here I expect to remain till about the 1st of November; though, to perfect the "cure," I ought to continue a much longer period, but my domestic and business affairs are such as to require my presence in Boston at that time.

My principal object in writing to you relates to my brother-in-law, George W. Benson, (with whom you are acquainted, I believe, both personally and by reputation,) rather than to myself.

Mr. Benson removed to this place some seven or eight years since from Brooklyn, Ct., and was one of the principal founders of the "Northampton Community"; but, for the last two or three years, he has been connected with the cotton factory as agent, &c., after the sale of it by the Community to the Messrs. Willistons.[1] He has discharged the duties of his station with admirable fidelity and unremitted vigilance, and expected to continue in it, and still make "Bensonville" the place of his residence. But the spirit of religious intolerance, when once aroused, burns fiercely, and is not easily allayed. In February last — as you are aware — a Call was issued by the friends of Christian reform, and of mental and spiritual freedom, for an Anti-Sabbath Convention, to be held in the Melodeon, Boston, toward the close of the ensuing month, for the cogent reasons duly set forth in the Call.[2] Among the noble spirits whose names were appended to it was George W. Benson. When the Convention assembled, it unanimously appointed him its President. Though modestly desirous of avoiding public conspicuity, it was not for him to "confer with flesh and blood"[3] on such an occasion, be the sacrifice or odium what it might; and, therefore, with his characteristic calmness of spirit, yet intrepidity of action, he did not hesitate for a moment to occupy the place assigned him. The Convention was worthy of the days of primitive Christianity. Its proceedings have been published in pamphlet form, and will bear rigid scrutiny.

Now, the proprietors of the factory here are rigid Presbyterians; and this public act of Mr. Benson, in connection with a more intimate acquaintance with his religious freedom and independence on other subjects, was manifestly so distasteful to them, as to make the retaining of his position no longer agreeable to either of the parties. Mr. Benson, therefore, sent in his resignation to them a few weeks ago, and is now endeavoring to establish himself in another kind of business.

In Providence, he was formerly engaged in the sale and manufacture of leather, and well understands the business. Joseph Southwick, (the husband of Thankful,) of Boston, owns a first rate tannery in Chelsea, near the city, but has not carried it on, for a year or two past, owing partly to some pecuniary reverses, including a heavy loss by fire in Maine, but mainly to the glutted state of the leather market. He is now very desirous that Mr. Benson should either take a lease of it, or unite with him in partnership, as the prospect is now very favorable for that business, and promises to be increasingly so.[4] To enable him to accept of either of these propositions, Mr. Benson must raise a sufficient capital to start the business, by the purchase of bark, hides, &c.; and for this, in the shape of a temporary loan, he must look to those who sympathize with him in spirit, who know how to appreciate his unsullied character, and whose object is to cheer on the good and the true, rather than to usurious money-lenders. How you are pecuniarily circumstanced at present, you best know; but I venture to make the inquiry — Is it in your power to grant him a loan, to the amount of two or three thousand dollars, on two years' time, with the usual interest? He desires me to say to you, that, in personal and real estate, he is good to the amount of at least six thousand dollars; but his property is so situated, that he cannot readily dispose of it, without a serious loss. He will either give you his note on his own personal security, or one conjointly with Mr. Southwick, as you may desire. The assistance which he is seeking, he has repeatedly given to other true spirits, laboring under somewhat similar difficulties; and, therefore, he naturally hopes to obtain it in a quarter not trodden by the hoofs of Mammon.

Of Mr. Benson, after an intimate acquaintance with him of nearly twenty years, I am free to say, that there is not on earth the man for whom I entertain more love or respect; that his word, his pledge, his bond, are sacred; that no man is more exact and punctual in all his dealings; that he is remarkable for the soundness of his judgment, and the prudence of his plans and engagements; that a character so well-balanced as his is rarely to be found among men; that his piety is of the genuine stamp, combining justice, conscientiousness, reverence, benevolence, self-sacrifice, and all good elements; that he is "the noblest work of God, an honest man"; [5] and that, in spite even of religious bigotry,

> "None know him but to love him,
> None name him but to praise." [6]

I am anxious to facilitate the effort he is now making to prosecute a business which he and Mr. Southwick, (long versed in the same,) are confident will yield a good remuneration, and therefore I have not hesitated to address this letter to you in his behalf, feeling assured that your reply will be such as a noble spirit will dictate, and your circumstances will allow.

My family are temporarily sojourning here with me. A few days since, Francis Jackson and his daughter, (Mrs. [Eliza Jackson] Meriam,) Edmund Jackson and his wife, of Boston, accompanied Helen and myself to the beautiful residence of our friend David Joy, on Round Hill, where we had a very pleasant interview with him and his wife.[7] They were to start the next day on a tour to Niagara Falls. He has lately sold his house.

Our warmest regards to your estimable wife. Accept for yourself the assurance that I am

Your faithful and admiring friend,

Wm. Lloyd Garrison.

Nathaniel Barney.

ALS: Merrill Collection of Garrison Papers, Wichita State University Library.

1. Garrison refers to Samuel Williston (1795–1874) and his brother John Payson Williston (1803–1872), prominent businessmen and philanthropists of Easthampton and Northampton. Samuel Williston, sometimes referred to as the "Father of Easthampton" because of his industrial and civic leadership, founded the Williston Seminary and was a generous patron of Mount Holyoke and Amherst. (*Hampshire Gazette*, July 21, 1874.) John Williston was interested both in temperance and antislavery. His house was a station on the Underground Railroad, and after the war he donated money for the establishment of southern schools to educate former slaves. (*Hampshire Gazette*, January 9 and 23, 1872.)

2. Built in 1836 as the Lion Theatre, since 1839 the Melodeon had been a popular concert and lecture hall. (William W. Clapp, "The Drama in Boston," in Justin Winsor, ed., *The Memorial History of Boston, 1630–1880*, Boston, 1881.)

3. An allusion to Galatians 1:16.

4. The proposed partnership of Benson and Southwick was never formed.

5. An adaptation of Alexander Pope, *An Essay on Man*, Epistle IV, line 248.

6. Garrison paraphrases Fitz-Greene Halleck, "On the Death of Joseph Rodman Drake," lines 3–4.

7. David Joy (1801–1875) was a native of Nantucket, where he engaged in

the cooperage and whale oil refining businesses with his brother Moses and was elected to the General Court of Massachusetts. During the 1840's he lived in Northampton and later in Hopedale, buying and selling many pieces of real estate. (Letter to the editor from Edouard A. Stackpole, president, Nantucket Historical Association, November 19, 1970; the Betty Allen Chapter, DAR, *Early Northampton*, Northampton, 1914, p. 226.)

2 4 9

TO ADELINE ROBERTS

Northampton, Sept. 20, 1848.

Esteemed Friend:

I feel honored by the kind invitation to me, on the part of the Salem Female Anti-Slavery Society, to give a lecture before the Society, on the 26th of November, on the great question of liberty to the captive, and the opening of the prison to those who are bound.[1] Most gladly will I accept of it, if circumstances permit; but, as there is some uncertainty on this point, I should prefer to have another name substituted for my own. I am here at a Water Cure establishment for the benefit of my health, which, I am happy to say, is improving; and it is now my hope and expectation to return to Boston about the 1st of November. It may turn out that I shall be compelled to remain here a few weeks longer, to complete what I have already so auspiciously begun; and it is for this reason, I think you would be more safe in procuring a substitute — though it is my intention to be in Boston at the time specified, if practicable. The list of speakers, which you have forwarded to me, for the course of lectures, is an excellent one; and I trust every one of them will readily embrace the opportunity thus presented, to plead the cause of the suffering and the dumb.[2] In that case, the lectures cannot fail to be highly interesting and profitable. May "faith, hope, charity," [3] abide with every member of the Society.

Yours, to redeem every bondman,

Wm. Lloyd Garrison.

Adeline Roberts, Cor. Sec.

ALS: Autograph Collection, Essex Institute.

Adeline Roberts (died 1904) was a schoolteacher who served for many years as corresponding secretary of the Salem Female Anti-Slavery Society. (Letter to the editor from Dorothy M. Potter, librarian, Essex Institute, Salem, June 8, 1970.)

1. The Salem Female Anti-Slavery Society was organized June 4, 1834. The president at the time of this letter and for some years to follow was Lucy G. Ives. (Letter to the editor from Dorothy M. Potter, June 8, 1970.) In his reference to "liberty to the captive," etc., Garrison adapts Isaiah 61:1.

2. According to the advertisement in *The Liberator*, October 6, 1848, the list of speakers included, besides Garrison, the Reverend C. S. Shackford, the Reverend Thomas Wentworth Higginson, Samuel Johnson, Edmund Quincy, Lucy Stone, Thomas T. Stone, and Wendell Phillips. The course of lectures was to begin October 8 and continue on successive Sunday evenings.

3. A reference to I Corinthians 13:13.

---

2 5 0

TO ELIZA JACKSON EDDY

Northampton, Oct. 8, 1848.

My Dear Friend:

To-morrow is to be one of the memorable days of your life. You are to bid adieu to the land of your nativity, the place of your birth, to relatives near and dear, to friends beloved and faithful; and to cross the Atlantic, that "great and wide sea, wherein are things creeping innumerable, both small and great beasts," and thus to take the indescribable position (for can language paint it?) of "a stranger in a strange land." [1] Happily, you will not go as an exile, but under propitious circumstances. You will be cherished and comforted by one with whose earthly destiny you have blended your own, to whom you have given your heart's best affections, and for whom it is lawful to leave both father and mother. The passage, too, will in all probability be a short one; for the Acadia is an admirable sea-boat and a quick steamer, as I know from experience, having twice crossed the ocean in her; so that, within a fortnight from the time of your departure, you may safely calculate on being at Liverpool, the "commercial emporium" of the fast anchored isle. [2] From thence, (if I correctly understood Mr. Eddy,) you are to proceed immediately to Paris, and subsequently go to Italy, &c. [3] During all the time of your absence, you will find any number of objects and scenes to challenge attention, excite admiration, and fill you with astonishment. Should your health be preserved, the tour will prove a delightful one; though it will be perfectly natural, should you

"Cast many a longing, lingering look behind,"
and feel that, after all, "there is no place like home." [4]

If I had any faith in prayer to create a smooth sea, give you a fair wind and clear weather, and deliver you from sea-sickness, during your voyage, most assuredly I would pray that you might thus be miraculously blessed; but as I have not a particle of such faith, and do not think that the laws of nature ought to be changed for the special accommodation of any body, but feel entirely satisfied that they are incapable of being amended, I can only hope that you will be so fortunate as to make a short and pleasant trip across "the big pond," as the Indians call the ocean.

I cannot help thinking, with something of sadness, how much your bright presence will be missed in our social circle of friendship, at our various reformatory meetings, at the anti-slavery fair, and at the domestic fireside. No one can fill that vacancy but yourself: it must remain unoccupied, therefore, until your return. My sympathies cluster tenderly and powerfully, at this trying hour, around your dear and noble father, to whom your absence must seem almost like a lasting bereavement. Dearer than his right hand, or his right eye, are you to his heart; and that deep, unfathomable love is fully reciprocated by you. I know how he will meet the trial — with Roman firmness, but not with Roman stoicism. He will be sustained by a sound and Christian philosophy, which, while it allows full scope for parental feeling, bows with resignation to whatever comes to pass. The possibility that you may never behold each other again on earth will give poignancy to the separation; yet such a parting must take place, some day or other, whether you are near or remote. Mrs. Hemans says of Death —

> "Thou art where billows foam;
> Thou art where music melts upon the air;
> Thou art around us in our peaceful home;
> And the world calls us far — and thou art there! " [5]

"Thou art around us in our peaceful home." Yes! as truly so as when we are where billows foam, or as when we are called afar; and, therefore, we do not materially lessen the peril by circumscribing our travels, or taking refuge by the domestic hearth. Go, dear friend! and when the summons shall come, in God's good time, to put on immortality, be it yours to shout, wherever you may be — "O Death! where is thy sting? O Grave! where is thy victory?" [6]

> "It is not all of life to live,
> Nor all of death to die." [7]

You know my views on this subject — that I deplore the popular, or, rather, the theological view taken of death, and see nothing in the tomb but the passage to eternal progress. A beneficent Creator never made our mortality to be a source of terror or disgust, but, rather, of consolation and gratitude.

I am glad, for your sake, that you are to have your brother James [8] with you; but it is taking another one from the family circle, and making two vacancies, instead of one. He has my best wishes for his perfect enjoyment during his European tour.

You will, very judiciously, leave your two children behind you.[9] On their account, you will not have any cause for anxiety, as they will be tenderly cared for, and duly guarded, until your return. But you are a mother, and a good mother's place is not easily supplied. You are a mother, and the separation must cause a deep struggle within your breast. But, O the joy of reunion at no distant day!

You will have pleasant travelling companions in Mr. and Mrs. [Charles F.] Hovey. With her I am not particularly acquainted. She must still be very youthful, as she looks very pretty and girl-like. The more I know of Mr. Hovey, the higher is my regard for him. So radically is he imbued with the spirit of reform, that, considering the fashionable and wealthy circle in which he has moved, he is a prodigy. He has generous and noble qualities — an honest, ingenuous mind, rare independence, true moral courage, an abhorrence of all shams, a deep sympathy for suffering humanity, and a most disinterested spirit. May he live to see the world revolutionized by the Genius of Human Brotherhood, and all forms of oppression destroyed! As I shall not have time to write to him, tell him I wish him a prosperous voyage, a safe return, and every blessing.

A thousand times do I congratulate myself on my rapid flight to Boston, to be present at your marriage. It was an occasion never to be forgotten. I only lament that I could find no utterance for the feelings of my heart. Never did I feel more embarrassed for words, words, words. You will be glad to learn that my journey has not interfered with my cure. I am now in the midst of another "crisis."

I send only two brief introductory letters — one to George Thompson, and the other to Elizabeth Pease — because I understand you are to proceed at once to the continent.[10]

Helen deeply regrets that she cannot be in Boston in season to give you a parting embrace. She expects to leave here, with the children, in a few days. Our united regards to Mr. Eddy, who has our best wishes. Farewell!

Yours, with great esteem,

Wm. Lloyd Garrison.

Mrs. Eliza F. Eddy.

ALS: Garrison Papers, Boston Public Library.

Mrs. Eddy, the daughter of Francis Jackson, was formerly married to Charles D. Merriam, who died in 1845. On September 21 she married James Eddy.

1. Psalms 104:25, Exodus 2:22.

2. William Cowper, *The Task*, Book II, line 151.

3. James Eddy (1806–1888) was a Providence, Rhode Island art dealer who in 1875 was to construct Bell Street Chapel for the use of those who wished to worship according to the dictates of conscience rather than the restrictions of doctrine. (*Biographical Sketch, Memorial Service, Selected Thoughts of James Eddy*, Providence, 1888.)

4. Garrison adapts Thomas Gray, "Elegy Written in a Country Churchyard,"

stanza 22, line 4, and John Howard Payne, "Home, Sweet Home," line 2, from the opera *Clari; or, the Maid of Milan.*

5. Garrison quotes Felicia Dorothea Hemans, "The Hour of Death," stanza 8, changing the word "forth" to "far" in line 4.

6. I Corinthians 15:55.

7. Garrison slightly misquotes James Montgomery, "The Issues of Life and Death," stanza 1, lines 7–8, altering line 7, which should read, " 'Tis not the whole of life to live."

8. Not further identified.

9. Garrison refers to Francis Jackson Merriam (1837–1865) and Eliza F. Merriam, children of Eliza Jackson Merriam Eddy. Francis was to serve in the United States Army as a captain in the Third South Carolina Colored Infantry. Wishing to devote his life to the antislavery cause, he contributed $600 to John Brown's raid on Harper's Ferry. He was assigned to guarding the arms left at Kennedy Farm and was therefore not captured but was able to escape to Canada. Early in the Civil War he married Minerva Caldwell of Illinois. (Oswald Garrison Villard, *John Brown*, New York, 1943, p. 685.) Nothing is known of the other child.

10. The letter to George Thompson has evidently not been preserved; the one to Elizabeth Pease (October 3, 1848) follows this one.

251

TO ELIZABETH PEASE

Boston, Oct. 3, 1848.

My Dear Friend:

The deep interest that you have long felt in the little band of faithful abolitionists, who have maintained their ground so unflinchingly in this oppressive land, will assuredly obtain at your hands, for one of the most deserving of that band, a cordial reception, on a personal introduction. The bearer of this is Mrs. Eliza F. Eddy, (formerly E. F. Meriam,) the eldest daughter of that sterling man, and my most faithful friend, Francis Jackson, of this city. For many years, she has devoted herself to the anti-slavery cause with an unreservedness of heart and hand, worthy of the highest commendation. As a member of the Boston Female Anti-Slavery Society, and one of the most active assistants at our National Bazaar, her absence will be greatly missed. I hope she will be so fortunate as to see you, either in Darlington or London, for she has long admired your character, and desired that privilege. She has recently been married to a most estimable gentleman [James Eddy], a true friend of the slave, and a liberal contributor to the funds of the American Anti-Slavery Society. The happy couple are to leave for Liverpool to-morrow, in the steamer Acadia, and on their arrival at that port intend, I believe, to proceed immediately to the continent; so that some time will elapse, probably, before this letter of introduction will be forwarded to you. As I expect to write to you again, ere long, in anticipation of the receipt of this, I shall not attempt now to give you any intelligence as to the state of things with us. Suffice it to say, the cause of emancipation is advancing mightily, and we are rejoicing in hope.

You will be glad to learn, I know, that, for the last twelve weeks, I have been faithfully trying the benefits of the Water Cure, under the care of Dr. [David] Ruggles, at Northampton. I have been packed, and plunged, and drenched, and douched — had two or three flattering crises — and am decidedly improved in health. Doubtless, to effect a radical change in my constitution, I ought to continue the treatment at least a year, but circumstances forbid. I shall pursue it at home, however, as far as practicable. My aversion to cold water has been fairly conquered. I am now its ardent advocate.

Our dear Henry C. Wright has spent his summer in Ohio, where he has been laboring with his accustomed assiduity and zeal in every good cause. He is still in that State, but will probably be in Boston at the time of the Bazaar.

I trust you have had the pleasure of greeting our absent friends Maria W. Chapman, and Caroline Weston, her sister, and also Mary G. Chapman, a relative of theirs. All our jewels are collecting on your side of the Atlantic.

It is a long time since I wrote to you, but you are as one ever by my side. I am hoping, on the arrival of every steamer, to get a letter from you, though I do not deserve any, as a matter of epistolary reciprocity.

My family have enjoyed excellent health all the summer, amidst an unusual amount of sickness. The loss of our dear little Elizabeth Pease makes a large void in our hearts.

Accept the warmest remembrances of my dear wife, and my own best wishes for your health and happiness.

Your devoted friend,

Wm. Lloyd Garrison.

Elizabeth Pease.

ALS: Garrison Papers, Boston Public Library.

2 5 2

TO HELEN E. GARRISON

Northampton, Oct. 10, 1848.
Tuesday Morning.

Dear Helen:

Yesterday afternoon, when the Doctor returned from town with his mail-bag, I inquired of him — "Have you a letter for me?" "None," was his reply. I was somewhat disappointed — but not a great deal; for though I was extremely anxious to know how you stood your long journey, and whether you and the children arrived home without any accident, I hardly supposed you would find time to send me a letter quite so soon. "Well," said I to the Doctor, "I expect you will bring me one to-morrow evening; and so I shall wait resignedly till that time." I went up into my chamber, and was engaged in reading my newspapers, when I heard a tap at my door; on opening which, Miss [Abby] Thayer informed me that there was a very interesting young lady in the parlor, who desired to see me; and her curiosity, she said, was excited to know who she was. So was mine; and I therefore hurried below, in order to learn the name of the stranger. Judge of my surprise and pleasure on beholding our friend Harriet Jackson! I had supposed she had postponed her contemplated visit, till another season. She not only informed me of your safe arrival, but gave me a long epistle from you, containing just such particulars as I wanted to know, respecting home and its affairs — your journey, &c. This gave great relief to my mind; and all the more, inasmuch as one item of intelligence was, that dear sister Sarah was once more under our roof, prompt to a day in being with you, and thus banishing (to some extent at least) the loneliness of your situation. For this new proof of her sisterly affection, she will accept my warmest thanks.

First, as to the driver who extorted 50 cents from you, for a ride from the depot. He was a knave in so doing, and he knew it; but he thought he could take advantage of you without any risk of his bones, and so he did. It is a trifling matter, to be sure, in amount, but not in principle, or as a precedent. I only wish, after tendering him the lawful charge, on his refusal to take it, you had coolly put your money into your pocket, telling him he might have it whenever he should feel disposed to call. Should you be able to identify him on my return?

Next, as to the appearance of home. I do not wonder that you felt a sensation of desolateness, on entering the house. Every thing to be properly arranged — the accumulated dust of three months covering the rooms — no food in readiness — no fire — no "help" — and five children to be cared for; — to say nothing of my absence, or of your peculiar situation. But a few days will alter the appearance of things, and once more you will feel yourself at home. I am afraid you will injure yourself by excessive labor. Be careful not to do so, for a thousand reasons.

Of the sisterly kindness of Mrs. [Eliza Jones] Garnaut and Miss Cannan, I cannot find terms strong enough to express my sense of it.[1] Such friends are to be prized more than any conceivable quantity of the gold of Ophir.[2] I trust we shall be able to make them some compensation in return, not in a business point of view, but to show that we also take pleasure in the performance of similar deeds.

You excite much uneasiness in my mind, in regard to our dear Wendell Phillips, by stating that he is not yet wholly cured of his disorder. This ought not so to be. I think there is yet considerable danger that he will go into a decline, unless he finds entire relief very speedily. I wish he had as much faith in the water cure as I have knowledge of it; so that he might be induced to try it for a few weeks, under the care of Dr. [David] Ruggles. You will give my brotherly remembrances to him and his beloved Ann. Much do I long to be by their side.

I am glad you have got in some coal, and hope it was of the right size; otherwise it may prove an annoyance to the cook. The way to ignite it is first to fill up the grate with the kindling wood, and let that get *well on fire*, and then to put a small quantity of coal upon it, which must be increased at discretion. Let William [L. Garrison, Jr.] go to Mr. Prescott,[3] and ask him to send me a cord of his best dry hard wood, for air-tight stoves, and let it be sawed twice; the boys can do the splitting and piling.

You write that George has been a very good boy, and of great ass[ista]nce to you. Such intelligence cheers my heart. I hope he will try to do his best, in aiding you, until my return. Most cheerfully will I reward him. No one can do better than himself, if he will try. May there be no quarrelling among any of the dear children, but may each of them strive to be kind and obedient in all things.

Since you and they have returned, I feel much more lonesome than I did before you all came. I go over to George's, and every thing is so quiet that it seems like a general bereavement. Little Sarah asks frequently after Fanny, who, she says, "has gone far away." Mary is very much missed.[4]

I return the $5 which you enclosed to me, because I do not need it, and shall be able to collect enough here, which is due on the Liberator, to enable me to get home. Tell dear Sarah, I take the will as for the deed. She is ever disposed to manifest a sister's love.

Why did you not buy four blankets, instead of two, at Mr. Ganett's? [5] You will certainly need them all. Get the other two without fail. The price is very low.

I am sorry that my credit is getting impaired, by lack of promptness, even in the slightest degree. How the grocery and the meat bills can amount to $45, for one month's supply, is to me inexplicable. They are so enormous, that they ought not to be paid without the most careful scrutiny.

Dear sister Charlotte has been very kind indeed, as well as sister Sarah, in supplying you with various articles, indispensable in a certain contingency. It was also very kind in Mrs. [Eliza Jackson] Eddy, in giving you a farewell token for such a purpose. Your appropriation of it was very proper, under the circumstances.

Bro. George expects to leave for Boston this forenoon, but is not certain. Should he be detained, he will put this letter into the mail. My "crisis" is improving. In a fortnight from to-day, I hope to be with you.

Ever yours,

W. L. G.

ALS: Garrison Papers, Boston Public Library.

1. It is thought that Miss Cannan lived in Boston, though she does not appear in the appropriate city directories. Since Garrison frequently associates her with Mrs. Eliza Jones Garnaut, who is known to have been the matron of a Boston orphanage, she may have been employed, perhaps as a nurse, at the same institution. (See Garrison's letter to Helen E. Garrison, October 20, 1847.)

2. The region renowned for its gold appears several times in the Bible, as in Job 28:16: "It cannot be valued with the gold of Ophir, with the precious onyx, or the sapphire."

3. Edward Prescott of the firm of Prescott and Chapin, wood and coal dealers, Liverpool Wharf, Boston. (Boston city directory.)

4. Mary Benson was the sister who had died in 1842.

5. Garrison refers to J. A. Ganett of the J. M. Beebe Company, 90 Hanover Street, Boston. (Boston city directory.)

253

TO HELEN E. GARRISON

Northampton, Oct. 18, 1848.
Wednesday evening.

Dear Wife:

I hardly expected to hear from you again before my return to Boston, but have just had the pleasure of receiving a letter from you, dated yesterday. I sit down to write a few lines in return, before taking my evening bath.

My calculation still is, to be in Boston on Saturday, as I intimated in my last letter. You must not be uneasy, if I should not happen to arrive at that time. Possibly, something may happen to detain me a day or two longer; but I hope not. I have been urging Catharine, to-day, to let Anne accompany me, in advance of the rest of the family. She will do so, if she can get her clothes ready; so you may expect her. As next week is to be a stirring one in Boston — a Whig torch-light procession on Tuesday evening, and the grand celebration of the introduction of the Long Pond water into the city — I thought it would be a favorable time for Anne to be there.[1]

On Sunday afternoon, I rode up to the Bridgemans, with bro. George, to see Mrs. [Nathaniel] Paul.[2] She is boarding with an old lady, and is very comfortably situated; and, on the whole, she professed to be very well satisfied. I think, however, she will not be contented, until she is an inmate of Mr. Bridgeman's family; and he is willing to take her, in case she shall strongly desire it. She inquired particularly after you and the children — spoke of Charlie as the dear boy, who was so kind and obliging to her — and was profuse, as usual, with her expressions of gratitude for what had been done for her. Yesterday, after dinner, I again visited her, carrying a large bundle of newspapers with me for her perusal, and walking the distance (four miles) on foot. I cannot tell, of course, what sort of weather you had in Boston; but, here, it was as warm as a day in July. The atmosphere was sultry — yellow butterflies started up in my pathway, as though summer had really come again — the crickets were chirrupping merrily — the birds uttered their pleasant notes, and gaily flitted from tree to tree — and the cattle were lying down in the shadow of the trees. To-day, the change in the weather is any thing but agreeable to the feelings, though certainly very much needed. It is not very cold, but the air is damp and chilly, and it has rained pretty steadily during the day; consequently, I have taken but very little exercise out of doors, as I have a great aversion to getting wet, beyond what the "water cure" absolutely requires. Mrs. Paul was very glad to get so many papers, especially as there were several from England among them; and I hope they will beguile her of many a weary hour, in her lonely situation. Her health, now, seems to be very good; but her life is one of peculiar uncertainty, no doubt. On returning home, I took tea with our venerable friends, Mr. and Mrs. Ross, and had no conscientious or hydropathic scruples in eating some of their nice pumpkin pies, dough-nuts, preserves, &c.[3] They expressed great regret at the thought of bro. George leaving the place. Whether he has really decided to do so, or not, I cannot say: there is, even now, some uncertainty about it. Catherine is quietly packing up her things, to move somewhere — when or where, she does not know. No doubt, however, I think, from all I can gather, they will ultimately decide to go to Chelsea. In that case, we must endeavor to accommodate them under our roof, until they can get their house in readiness, which will not, probably, occupy more than two or three days. How deeply are we indebted to them on the score of hospitality! I only regret that we are in a condition to make only a poor and meager return.

It is important that you should take every precaution not to overwork yourself at this period. Be careful in lifting, as a strain might prove very injurious.

I feel quite uneasy, in regard to the bills that I owe not being paid. Credit, once impaired, always excites suspicion of its unsoundness afterward. It is the more disagreeable, in this case, inasmuch as if I had only what is usually allotted to me on my salary, I could immediately settle every demand. Yet, as no man, or committee, is responsible to me, even to the amount of a farthing, in the shape of a salary, I have nothing to ask for in the shape of dues. This is a harrassing mode of getting along, every thing is so precarious — especially, with a large, growing, and unavoidably expensive family. If a few of my friends would combine to obviate it, by taking a share of pecuniary responsibility, which, individually, would not be onerous to them, it would relieve my mind of a heavy burden. However, I throw myself on the promise, which, thus far, has never failed me — "Trust in the Lord, and do good, and verily thou shalt be fed." [4] I will not borrow any trouble, for that would not be wise. Still, I do not mean to rush heedlessly into debt, but to use all proper circumspection and economy. The Liberator, at the commencement of another volume, will need a new typographical dress. Where is it to come from?

I am glad you have seen Miss A——r,[5] and ascertained where she resides.

My heart is full of gratitude to Mrs. [Eliza Jones] Garnaut, for her great kindness in being so much with you at this critical juncture. She needs no profusion of words from my pen to be assured of my appreciation of it. My best regards to her and Miss Cannan.

I am greatly rejoiced to hear that our dear friend, W. P[hillips]., is gaining in health and strength, as it relieves my mind of all anxiety on that score. How happy shall I be to see him and Ann once more!

Should you happen to see our dear friends the [Francis] Jacksons, the [Robert F.] Wallcuts, Mr. [Samuel] May, [Jr.,] &c., assure them of the lively and affectionate remembrance of

Your loving husband,

W. L. G.

ALS: Garrison Papers, Boston Public Library.

1. "Anne" is Anna Elizabeth Benson, daughter of George Benson. In the last sentence, Garrison refers to a Boston water project completed in 1848 which brought water from Long Pond, located fifteen miles southwest of the city, to replace the polluted water sources previously used. Long Pond was later renamed Lake Cochituate. (Nathaniel B. Shurtleff, *A Topographical and Historical Description of Boston*, Boston, 1871.)

2. Bridgeman was so common a name in the Northampton area that it is impossible to identify the specific family to which Garrison refers.

3. Austin Ross (1812–1901) had married Fidelia Rindge (1813–1902) in 1834. Garrison had apparently known the Rosses at the Northampton Association of Education and Industry, where, during the last year of the community's existence, Ross was in charge of agriculture. In later years Ross operated in the vicinity of Northampton an active station on the Underground Railroad. (*Biographical Review: Biographical Sketches of the Leading Citizens of Hampshire County, Mass.*, Boston, 1896, pp. 363–364.)

4. Garrison abridges Psalms 37:3.

5. Doubtless Garrison refers to Mary Margaret Alexander; see letter to George W. Benson, October 29, 1848, n. 4.

254

TO GEORGE W. BENSON

Boston, Sunday Afternoon,
Oct. 29, 1848.

Dear George:

Heigh-ho! The *boys* have it, out of all proportion — five to one! Should they all "live to grow up," the *Garrison* will at last be strongly *manned*. This morning, about 2 o'clock, Helen presented me with another son — [1] "a broth of a boy" [2] — with black hair, dark eyes, and "cheeks like thumping red potatoes" [3] — weighing plump ten pounds and a half. Our midwife, Miss Alexander, was residing in Dorchester, but we fortunately obtained her services at a seasonable hour.[4] It was also fortunate, in the absence of the nurse, that Mrs. [Eliza Jones] Garnaut and Miss Cannan were also with Helen all the way through. We tried the effect of ether, in this case, but it seemed to excite rather than to allay distress; so we soon threw it aside. Both mother and babe are very comfortable.

What an avalanche of anxiety is removed from the mind at the successful termination of a case of childbirth! Of course, I feel quite elastic in spirit at the event. Now for great care and good nursing, that a good beginning may have a good ending.

We have not yet positively determined upon the name of the new comer, but it will probably be, *Francis Jackson Garrison*. What do you say to that? If Henry C. Wright was simply Henry Wright — or Samuel J. May simply Samuel May — it would please us to take either of them, for the love that we bear them; but it would be too long to take the whole name, and to curtail it would not be adopting the name. Then — there is the name of our estimable friend Edmund Quincy. It deserves to be an honored name, and long remembered by posterity. It is also liquid and pleasant to the ear. But there is no better man, and we have not a more reliable friend, than Francis Jackson. Francis Jackson Garrison has a sonorous and victorious sound, and can we do better than to adopt the name?

Dear sister Sarah is now confined to her room, and much of the time to her bed. She is extremely weak, and suffers a good deal of pain in her breast and back. She has given up all expectation of being able to endure the fatigue of the journey to Northampton — at least for the present. Her breast is in a terrible condition, and the flesh rotting fearfully. Whether this is a good or a bad indication, I do not know. It looks bad, certainly; and I should not be greatly surprised if the dear sufferer should descend to the grave rapidly. I think she begins to abandon her confident hope of recovery. — Much is your presence desired at this critical moment, and we shall expect to see you in all this week.

I am beginning to feel a little after the old sort, on the score of health. I find it almost impracticable to take my baths regularly, except morning and evening. My piles are troubling me again, and I am losing considerable fresh and clotted blood. The humor still covers the surface of my body, and rather increases than otherwise. As soon as I begin to grind in the prison-house of editorial life, I expect to run down physically.

Enclosed, I send a note from Anne Weston to David Joy and his wife — probably about the Bazaar. It was sent to me at N[orthampton]., but I mislaid it. Please leave it at their house, or drop it in the Post Office, as most convenient. I also enclose a note for Miss [Abby] Thayer, at the Water Cure.

Harrison Gray Otis died yesterday in this city — a quick exit after his vile letter for Taylor.[5]

With best regards to all at home — to Mr. and Mrs. [Elisha] Hammond, to all and several of the other friends,

Yours, truly,

W. L. Garrison.

ALS: William Lloyd Garrison Papers, Massachusetts Historical Society.

1. Francis Jackson Garrison (1848–1916), who was to become an editor and publisher and the co-author of the four-volume *Life* of Garrison. (Obituary in New York *Times*, December 12, 1916.)

2. An Anglo-Irish expression used as early as 1822 by Lord Byron (*Don Juan*, Canto VIII, line 185).

3. Not identified.

4. Mary Margaret Alexander, the daughter of Mrs. Janet Alexander (the Garrisons' midwife before her death in 1845), was one of the last pupils in midwifery of Dr. James Hamilton of Edinburgh and had been practicing since 1834. (*The Liberator*, February 6, 1846, obituary of Mrs. Janet Alexander.)

5. Harrison Gray Otis (1765–1848), aristocratic Federalist statesman from Boston, served in Congress, in the Massachusetts legislature, in the United States Senate, and as mayor of Boston. Although he denounced the abolitionist movement as leading to a division in the Union, he also opposed all attempts to suppress free speech on the subject of slavery. The letter Garrison refers to, in which Otis declares himself in favor of Zachary Taylor for President, was printed in the Boston *Atlas*, October 2, 1848.

255

TO FRANCIS JACKSON

13, Pine Street,
Sunday, Nov. 5[, 1848].

My Dear Friend:

A week ago, this morning, as you are aware, a fifth son was added to my group of boys — and a fine, hearty little fellow he is, without blemish, and as full of promise as any child of his *days*. It is time that he should have a name; and as there is no one for whom I entertain a higher regard than yourself, to call him *Francis Jackson Garrison* is only to indicate, in a slight degree, my admiration of your character, and the strong desire that I feel that the new comer may, through life, be inspired by that rare example of moral courage and unbending regard for principle, in contending with popular injustice and oppression, which his namesake has so nobly given to the world. My dear wife is delighted at the choice of the name, equally with

Your faithful friend,

Wm. Lloyd Garrison.

Francis Jackson.

ALS: William Lloyd Garrison Papers, Massachusetts Historical Society.

256

TO ABBY G. THAYER

[November 17, 1848.]

My Dear Friend:

Though I sincerely agree with the venerable friend, who has written the introductory article to your Album, extolling the character of

JESUS, the sufferer and martyr, and holding up his example as worthy of all imitation under the severest trials, yet I must beg leave respectfully to dissent from some of the sentiments advanced by him for your consideration.[1]

It seems that, from an early period, it has not been in your power experimentally to exclaim with the glad poet —

> 'O, who can speak the vigorous joys of health,
> Unclogged the body, unobscured the mind?
> The morning rises gay with pleasing stealth,
> The temperate evening falls serene and kind.' [2]

For many years, you have been an invalid, confined to your room, and much of the time to your bed — baffling the skill of many physicians of high repute, and almost despairing of recovery. What hours of anguish, what days of sadness, seemingly interminable, have been yours! Dr. S—— truly says — 'This trial has not sprung out of the ground.' But he intimates that it came from above! — that a 'calamity,' so deplorable, is the direct infliction of 'a righteous and all-wise Providence'! — that it was sent, not to make you wretched, or destroy your peace, or drive you to despair, but to teach you humility, lead you to Christ, bring you to repentance, and excite you to pray!

From all this, I dissent. I think it is bad logic, and worse theology. Our heavenly Father cannot manifest any goodness in torturing any of his children; an impaired constitution is neither the condition nor the product of humility; bad digestion or spinal weakness is not promotive of repentance of sin; the way to Christ is not a calamitous, though it may be a thorny one.

Surely, my afflicted friend, no strange thing has happened to you, that renders it necessary to suppose a special divine visitation, either of discipline or judgment, in your case. When we are grievously ill, it is but the effect of a natural cause; and that cause is to be found either in bodily malformation, or the violation of some physiological law; either in hereditary taint, or the prevalence of contagion. It is neither a supernatural nor a superhuman occurrence; it is neither from above, nor from beneath; and, if curable, is to be cured by a natural process, without regard to any of the Christian graces. Dr. S., however, thinks that, if you are humble and patient, you may, on that account, hope to see 'a bright day of health and prosperity'! As if patience were the panacea of human prostration, or humility were efficacious in remedying a diseased spine! This is not adapting means to ends. It would be as rational to talk of effecting the conversion of the soul by a prescription of calomel, or purifying the heart by a dose of rhubarb. Patience is an excellent virtue; humility is a rare trait of character; but will either of these allay chronic inflammation, or cure the liver complaint? If not, then your 'bright day of health' must depend upon something more analogous to the wants of the body. I rejoice, therefore, that you are resolved to give the 'Water Cure' a faithful trial in your case, as it is equally good for saint or sinner. I rejoice, moreover, to know that you have already derived great benefit from it, and that the prospect of your complete recovery is very flattering. May the remainder of your days amply compensate you, in the enjoyment of sound health, for all the sufferings with which you have been afflicted!

While I have thus ventured to differ from the venerable Doctor in some particulars, I cordially unite with him in hoping that, whether sick or well, in prosperity or adversity, you may largely possess the spirit of Him who has set us an example that we should follow his steps — loving God with all our heart, and our neighbor as ourselves.[3]

Your sympathizing friend,

W. L. G.

Printed: *The Liberator*, November 17, 1848.

In a paragraph printed in *The Liberator* above his own letter Garrison explains that before he left Dr. David Ruggles' water-cure establishment a young lady, an invalid since childhood, asked him to write in her album, whereupon Garrison noticed an "introductory essay" written by a Calvinistic minister whose views on illness and religion were so different from Garrison's that he felt impelled to write this letter "on the succeeding pages" of the album.

1. The "venerable friend" has not with any certainty been identified, though one might speculate that he could be Daniel Stebbins (1766–1856), who was a physician and a resident of Northampton after 1806, except that Stebbins is not known to have been a minister. Stebbins was associated with Samuel Whitmarsh in the silk business which he sold to the Northampton Association of Education and Industry and was for thirty-five years treasurer of Hampshire County. (Solomon Clark, *Antiquities, Historicals, and Graduates of Northampton*, Northampton, 1882, p. 346.)

2. James Thomson, *The Castle of Indolence*, Canto II, stanza 58, lines 1–4.

3. Garrison telescopes Matthew 22:37 and 39.

257

TO SAMUEL MAY, JR.

Boston, Dec. 2, 1848.

My dear friend May: —

I am very sorry it so happens that I cannot be at your anti-slavery gathering to-morrow at North Brookfield, as it is a long time since I visited that town, or have met the friends of Worcester County in Convention; but, positively, I am neither mentally nor bodily fitted, at this time, to participate in any public meeting. My water "crisis," in the development of humor and boils, is very annoying, though I trust in the end it will be very serviceable to me. I must "wait a little longer," before it will be prudent for me to leave home even temporarily.[1] Besides, three of my children are on the sick list, with colds and coughs and some fever — Wendell, Charles and Fanny — and they need my care and presence, though not seriously ill.

All I can do is to hope that your meetings will be well attended, and your discussions judiciously adapted to the place in which you are to assemble. There is a great deal of prejudice against us in North Brookfield, and very little knowledge of what we desire and seek. Under such circumstances, the injunction of the Saviour, to "be wise as serpents, and harmless as doves," [2] is worthy of special observance. I would hide no part of the truth, of course; yet I think it would be wise to explain our own positions, religiously and politically, as to the good cause in which we are engaged, rather than to deal in much severity of speech towards those who are not yet with us. When we know there will be a spirit present, on the part of some hearers, that will readily pervert what may be unguardedly or hastily spoken, it is at such times, on such occasions, and in such places, we should be specially careful of the manner in which we present and advocate our views.

As for the "Free Soil" movement, I am for hailing it as a cheering sign of the times, and an unmistakable proof of the progress we have made, under God, in changing public sentiment. Those who have left the Whig and Democratic parties, for conscience sake, and joined that movement, deserve our commendation and sympathy; at the same time, it is our duty to show them and all others, that there is a higher position to be attained by them, or they will have the blood of the slave staining their garments. This can be done charitably, yet faithfully. On the two old parties, especially the Whig Taylor party, I would expend — *pro tempore* at least — our heaviest ammunition.

Hastily, but faithfully yours,

Wm. Lloyd Garrison.

Samuel May Jr.
Boston.

Handwritten transcription: Garrison Papers, Boston Public Library; printed partly in *Life*, III, 236.

1. Garrison refers to Charles Mackay, "The Good Time Coming," stanza 1, line 9. The context of the line Garrison quotes is interesting in the light of the physical agonies through which he is passing:

> "Cannon-balls may aid the truth,
> But thought's a weapon stronger;
> We'll win our battles by its aid; —
> Wait a little longer."

2. From Matthew 10:16.

258

TO JOSEPH CONGDON

Boston, Dec. 15, 1848.

Dear Friend:

You are aware that the prevalent superstition in regard to the holiness of the first day of the week has been found a mighty obstacle in the path of every reform, and that it is the stronghold of priestcraft, and of a pharisaical religion. The most vigorous and systematic measures are in operation to strengthen that superstition, and to make its yoke heavier upon the necks of the people. You are also aware, that, in order to do something towards counteracting these measures, disseminating rational views on the subject, and thus comprehensively aiding every reformatory enterprise, an Anti-Sabbath Convention was held in Boston, in March last. The speeches made on the occasion by Theodore Parker, Lucretia Mott, C. C. Burleigh, H. C. Wright, Parker Pillsbury, and others, embraced every important aspect of this great question, and were marked by great ability. These were reported expressly for publication by a skillful phonographer, and with the entire proceedings, the Call for the Convention, and a valuable Appendix, containing the views of Luther, Melancthon, Calvin, Tyndale, Paley, Fox, Barclay, Belsham, Whateley,[1] &c., were published in a handsome pamphlet, making [...] pages.[2] From the excitement produced by the Convention, among the clergy and the religious journals, and the interest that seemed to be awakening among reformers on this subject, the Committee on Publication were led to suppose that a large edition would be easily disposed of — certainly, in the course of a few months. Accordingly, they concluded to print 2000 copies; but only a small number has been sold, (surely, not because the pamphlet is not deserving of the widest circulation,) leaving the sum of *two hundred dollars* still due to the printers, Messrs. Andrews & Prentiss,[3] who have already kindly waited eight months for their pay, but who cannot do so any longer, being severely pressed for money to meet their bills. As I contracted for the printing of the work, they naturally look to me to liquidate the debt. This I would cheerfully do, out of my own pocket, if I had the means; but I am unable to meet my own liabilities, as the receipts of the Liberator have fallen off considerably the present year. What is to be done? Among the many *false* charges brought against us anti-sabbatarians, is there to be a *true* one, that we are unable or unwilling to pay for the printing we have had done on contract?

My object in writing to you is, to solicit your co-operation in cancelling the debt alluded to, getting other friends to join with you, if you can, for this purpose. — Thirty copies of the work will be given in return for $5, — and a similar proportion will be observed in regard to a larger or smaller sum. They can be distributed to good advantage, and cannot grow out of date while the Sabbath is a matter of controversy.

Aid me, if you can, in this exigency, by enclosing what money you can raise in a letter addressed either to me or to Robert F. Wallcut, the Treasurer of the Anti-Sabbath Convention, immediately. The pamphlets, to the amount of the money, at cost price, can be forwarded to you by express, or disposed of as you shall direct.

Yours, for mental and spiritual freedom,

Wm. Lloyd Garrison.

Joseph Congdon.

ALS: Mellen Chamberlain Autograph Collection, Boston Public Library.

Joseph Congdon (1799–1857) of New Bedford served as cashier of the Mechanics Bank from its inception in October 1831 until shortly before his death. Both Joseph and his younger brother James B. Congdon were active in the affairs of the New Bedford Lyceum. (Letter to the editor from Richard C. Kugler, director, Old Dartmouth Historical Society, April 21, 1971.)

1. Richard Whately (1787–1863), an English theologian, was archbishop of Dublin from 1831 until his death. Although an Anglican, he supported the right of Roman Catholics to emancipation and to state endowment of their clergy; and he advocated nonsectarian religious education for both Protestants and Catholics. He was the author of many religious works and the editor of Bacon's *Essays*.

2. The number of pages is not supplied.

3. The printing firm owned by Samuel G. Andrews and H. J. Prentiss, with offices at 11 Devonshire Street, Boston. (Boston city directory.)

259

TO JOSEPH RICKETSON

Boston, Jan. 2, 1849.

My Dear Friend:

I think I have forfeited the opportunity extended to me, in behalf of your Association by yourself, some time ago, to lecture before the Association, by my unintentional neglect to answer your kind letter.[1] But, it seems, by your letter of the 31st, you have not struck me off (as you would certainly have been justified in doing) from the list of lecturers; and you now write to know whether I can be with you on the evening of the 29th inst. As I am to go to Maine next week, and as the annual meeting of the Massachusetts A. S. Society [2] will be near the time you have specified, I should prefer the evening of Feb.

5th or 12th, though I should be sorry to incommode either Mr. [Theodore] Parker or Mr. [Ralph Waldo] Emerson. But as I suppose those gentlemen have their lectures already prepared, and as I have yet to prepare mine, I trust it will be more convenient for one of them to lecture for you on the 29th than myself. I will, however, try to complete my lecture in season for the 29th, so that, in case of a pinch, you may not be disappointed. Yet secure me the 5th or 12th of February, if you can. My subject will be — "The Rights of Woman." [3]

Yours, for a happy new year,

Wm. Lloyd Garrison.

ALS: Villard Papers, Harvard College Library; a typed transcription is preserved in the Garrison Papers, Boston Public Library.

1. Garrison probably refers to the New Bedford Lyceum as Ricketson's "Association." (See Garrison's letter to Ricketson, December 4, 1847.)

2. To be held in Boston's Faneuil Hall, January 24–26 (reported in *The Liberator*, February 2, 1849).

3. New Bedford newspapers and *The Liberator* supply no evidence that Garrison did in fact make this appearance.

260

TO JOSEPH RICKETSON

Boston, Jan. 22, 1849.

Dear Friend:

I wish it were in my power to say, I will be with you on the 29th, according to your desire; but I should certainly fail if I should attempt it, and therefore must take advantage of the latitude you kindly give me. It shall be my endeavor to be with you on the evening of Feb. 5th, at which time you may consider me positively engaged.

We hope to see some of our New Bedford friends at our State anniversary, this week, in the Old Cradle of Liberty.[1]

Hastily, but with great esteem,

Yours truly,

Wm. Lloyd Garrison.

Joseph Ricketson.

Typed transcription: Garrison Papers, Boston Public Library.

1. Faneuil Hall, Boston.

261

TO EDMUND QUINCY

Boston, March 16, 1849.

My dear Quincy:

Wendell has just communicated to me the sad and startling intelligence, that another of your dear children is dead, and to be buried this afternoon.[1] A few moments only, are left to me, before he goes to Dedham, to express to you and your wife, my heart-felt sympathy at this double bereavement, which must fall most heavily upon you. With my sympathy, dear Helen's is also strongly mingled. Last year, we were called to taste of this same cup, though only *one* of our beloved circle was taken.[2] We have yet six children left to us, but the one that was taken leaves a void in our hearts that nothing can ever fill, except a re-union with the departed. Twice have you been smitten, within a few days. I can imagine how your hearts must be torn, and how terrible the bereavement must be to you both. — Heaven strengthen and sustain you at this mournful crisis! True, no strange thing has happened to you; yet, when were parents ever ready to lose their offspring, or children their parents, (if they had any love in their hearts,) without feeling unutterable emotions of sorrow? I can add no more, now, except that I am, in joy or grief,

Faithfully yours,

Wm. Lloyd Garrison.

ALS: Garrison Papers, Sophia Smith Collection, Smith College Library.

1. Edmund Quincy's two young children, Morton (1845–1849) and Arthur Bromfield (1847–1849), had died respectively on March 10 and 15.
2. Elizabeth Pease Garrison died April 20, 1848.

262

TO HENRY CLAY

[March 16, 1849.]

SIR —

I have read your Letter to RICHARD PINDELL, Esq., on Slavery and Emancipation, and now give it a place in the columns of the Liberator, that others may have the same opportunity.[1] When the magnetic telegraph brought the intelligence, a few days since, that you had written such a Letter, I felt curious to see whether any, and, if any, what changes had taken place in your views and sentiments on this grave subject, since your detestable speech in the U. S. Senate.[2] Ten years of anti-slavery agitation have witnessed many changes, equally cheering and surprising, in the opinions of individuals and collective bodies, respecting the colored population of this country, especially that portion of it now held in the galling fetters of slavery at the South. I supposed it to be possible, therefore, — not probable, no, sir! — that, in the Letter now under consideration, there would be at least a slight indication that you were growing less selfish, less inhuman, less cowardly, on the question of negro emancipation. But I see no evidence of this in your epistle. Whoever else may have altered his position, you have not. My first criticisms upon your proslavery attitude, as a colonizationist, were written twenty years ago, in the 'Genius of Universal Emancipation.'[3] During all that time, I have watched the career of no man more narrowly than your own. Either you are very perverse, or I am; for I find we do not approximate any nearer to each other, even so much as a hair's breadth. Most happy should I be to give you the right hand of fellowship,[4] for I am not blind to your shining abilities; but either you or I must 'right about face,' before that grasp can be given.

I will not stop to surmise what may have been the motives that led to the writing of this Letter. In the crisis now existing in Kentucky, and the efforts now making on the part of a portion of her citizens to secure such an amendment to the Constitution as shall provide for the ultimate extinction of slavery on her soil, — to say nothing of the agitation on this subject now pervading every part of the country, — your Letter makes its appearance naturally, and at a timely period; but it is not what the time or the occasion demands. Nay, with a single exception, it is remorseless in purpose, cruel in spirit, delusive in expectation, sophistical in reasoning, tyrannous in principle. If you have feigned nothing — if you have uttered your real convictions, caring not whether you are found in the majority or the minority — it shows that you are removed from a true sense of justice, and a clear perception of human rights and obligations, as far as heaven is from the bottomless abyss. Truly, you are a pitiable object; the sands of your life are nearly run out; years are pressing heavily upon you; yet no sign of repentance do you give for the countless wrongs and outrages you have inflicted, or caused to be inflicted, on an unoffending, weak and helpless race. You have been an awful curse to them, to your country, to the world. You have long stood at the head of as cruel a conspiracy against God and man as was ever contrived — a conspiracy expressly designed and adapted to give vigor and safety to the soul-crushing system of slavery, and ample indulgence to slaveholders to continue in their iniquitous course. As the author of the

Missouri Compromise, you have done more than any other to lengthen the cords and strengthen the stakes of oppression.[5] If Texas has since been perfidiously wrested from Mexico, annexed to this country, and on its free soil slavery planted with safeguards for its perpetuity, to you preeminently attaches the guilt, in consequence of the impulse given to the slave system by the Compromise alluded to. If Mexico has been wantonly invaded, her towns and cities devastated, her people slain by thousands, and the immense territories of New Mexico and California coerced from her, for the purpose of extending the dominion of the Slave Power, the criminality is eminently yours, for the same reason. The self-complacency, therefore, which you exhibit, in speaking of the 'extravagant opinions' of those 'who believe that slavery is a blessing,' would excite in us ludicrous emotions, could we restrain our indignation in view of such profligate inconsistency. For one, sir, I am constrained to regard JOHN C. CALHOUN as a more honest, trust-worthy and harmless man than yourself, even on this question of slavery. It is true, he openly advocates slavery for all time — you only for a limited period; but, in practice, you are as bad as he is, for you hold a large number of your fellow-creatures as *bona fide* property; while you are more to be feared, and can do incomparably greater mischief, by your double-dealing and hypocrisy. He, by his monstrous and headlong advocacy of man-stealing, makes no proselytes, but repels rather than allures; you, by your pretended desire to see it come to an end, not now, but at a future period long protracted, and by your oily tongue and wily compromises, would deceive the very elect,[6] if it were possible.

I have found one exception in your letter, to save it from utter condemnation. It is contained in that portion of it in which you admit, that the principle on which slavery is advocated would equally require the enslavement of the white race with that of the black; and that intellectual inferiority can in no instance justify the holding of any human being in bondage. True, these propositions are self-evident; but their endorsement by you, at this time, and in this connexion, is of some value. You further add, that 'if indeed we possess this intellectual superiority, we ought to fulfill all the duties and obligations which it imposes, and these would require us *not to subjugate or deal unjustly by our fellow men* who are less blessed than we are, but TO INSTRUCT, TO IMPROVE, AND TO ENLIGHTEN THEM.' By this standard, then, do not complain, sir, if I measure you. You, Mr. Clay, are a slaveholder; in your household, and on your plantation, are more than sixty slaves, over whom you claim and exercise absolute power. They are reckoned and regarded by you as 'chattels personal, to all intents and purposes whatsoever.'[7] It is for you to sell them — the husband from the wife, the child from the mother — as you would cattle, or a crop of tobacco, according to your necessities or caprice. You basely 'subjugate and deal unjustly' by them, and do not attempt 'to instruct, to improve, or to enlighten them.' Are you not condemned out of your own mouth? I will not multiply epithets to describe such conduct, for they are needless.

You say that 'a vast majority of the people of the United States deplore the *necessity* of the continuance of slavery in any of the States.' This assertion is not true: 'a vast majority of the people' really care nothing about it: they are agreed in nothing so well as in despising and proscribing the colored race, whether bond or free. Besides, if the immediate abolition of slavery would prove disastrous, then why should its continuance be deplored? To deplore that which is essential to good order, the public safety, and the welfare of all classes, *pro tempore*, is not to talk sensibly. Sir, slavery is 'the sum of all villanies' [8] — it is pollution, concubinage, adultery — it is theft, robbery, kidnapping — it is ignorance, degradation, and woe — it is suffering, cruelty, and horrid injustice — it is the exaltation of a master above all that is called God — it smites the most fertile soil with barrenness, and depraves the manners and morals of all who are infected by it! This you know; and yet you dare to affirm that its continuance is a matter of 'necessity'! Ah! this is ever 'the tyrant's plea,' [9] and you are a tyrant.

It seems to you 'that it may have been among the dispensations of Providence (!) to permit the wrongs under which Africa has suffered to be inflicted, that her children might be returned to their original home, civilized, and imbued with the benign spirit of Christianity, and prepared ultimately to redeem that great continent from barbarism and idolatry.' Why, sir, if there be any such thing as impeaching Divine wisdom and goodness, surely this is; at least, it indicates that you place the common sense of mankind at a low estimate.

What strange necessities — according to your reasoning — have been imposed on Providence! Africa was to be redeemed from barbarism and idolatry. To effect this desirable object, it was necessary that her coasts should be invaded by civilized and Christianized kidnappers, her villages sacked, her blood poured out in torrents, millions of her people seized and carried across the Atlantic in the holds of those 'floating hells,' the slave ships, multitudes of them suffocated on the 'middle passage,' [10] and given to the sharks, the survivors huddled together in slave pens until they could be sold as slaves for life — and, finally, after two centuries occupied in this piratical manner, it is suggested by Providence (!) that the millions whom we have 'pealed, meted out, and trodden under foot,' [11] and systematically kept at the lowest point of physical, mental and moral degradation, would make excellent missionaries to 'redeem Africa from barbarism and idolatry, by a violent expulsion from the land of their birth, because their complexion renders it impossible for them ever to rise in the scale of humanity, so long as they remain among us white civilized and Christianized Americans! [12] And this, sir, you present as a consolatory view of 'the dispensations of Providence'! Mr. Clay, you are not a fool, neither are your readers idiots. But, sir, I must leave you in the hands of Providence for another week.

Yours, for immediate emancipation without expatriation,

WM. LLOYD GARRISON.

Printed: *The Liberator*, March 16, 1849. Clay's letter to Pindell appears in this same issue.

1. Richard Pindell (1812–1870), grandnephew of Mrs. Henry Clay, was an attorney and minor politician of Lexington, Kentucky. (Letter to the editor from James F. Hopkins, editor, *The Papers of Henry Clay*, University of Kentucky, April 28, 1970.) In his letter to Pindell, Clay defines his position on emancipation in Kentucky by three principles: first, that emancipation should be gradual, so as to avoid a convulsion of the society; second, that freed slaves should be returned to Africa, since the two races would never be able to live in harmony and equality in America; and third, that the expenses of colonization should be defrayed by money raised from the labor of each slave after his emancipation.

Garrison's quotations from Clay's letter are for the most part accurate. However, some misrepresentations do occur. For example, the quotation beginning "chattels, personal . . ." does not seem to be from the Clay letter. A more serious matter is Garrison's alteration of the quotation beginning "that it may have been among the dispensations. . . ." The correct citation should read ". . . that it may have been among the dispensations of Providence to prevent the wrongs under which Africa has suffered, to be designed that her children might be returned to their original home, civilized, imbued with the benign spirit of Christianity, and prepared ultimately to redeem that great continent from barbarism and idolatry." Another less serious error occurs in the quotation beginning "if indeed we possess . . . ," where Garrison has omitted "grateful and thankful to Him who has bestowed it" from its position immediately following "superiority"; the italics are also Garrison's.

2. The speech to which Garrison probably refers was given by Clay on February 7, 1839, and printed in *The Liberator*, February 15, 1839. In conjunction with presenting a petition against abolition from some citizens of Washington, D.C., Clay denounced the abolitionists' use of petitions as a means to make Congress take action on their cause.

3. Clay's address to the Colonization Society of Kentucky was printed in three parts in the *Genius of Universal Emancipation*, January 15, 22, and 29, 1830. The speech did not reflect a "pro-slavery" attitude except in the sense that Clay argued that, bad as the present system was, the hardships that would befall the slaves should there be immediate emancipation would be much worse. In a two-part editorial (February 12, 19, 1830) Garrison wrote a strong rebuttal to the speech. Although professing high esteem for Clay, he argued, "It is morally impossible . . . for a slaveholder to reason correctly on the subject of slavery."

4. Galatians 2:9.

5. By the Missouri Compromise of 1820 Missouri was admitted to the Union, its legislature being allowed to adopt a constitution which did not prohibit slavery in the state, on the condition that in all other areas of the Louisiana Purchase north of 36° 30′ (Missouri's southern boundary) slavery was to be excluded.

(*OHAP.*) Clay was not so much the author of this bill as its chief advocate; as Speaker of the House he was instrumental in its passage. The bill was repealed in 1854.

6. An adaptation of Matthew 24:24.

7. In law, the term "chattels personal" applied to all movable goods, such as money, plate, cattle, and, controversially, slaves.

8. An adaptation of John Wesley, *Journal*, February 12, 1772. (See *Journal*, New York, 1906, III. 461.)

9. John Milton, *Paradise Lost*, IV, 394.

10. That is, across the Atlantic.

11. An adaptation of Isaiah 18:7.

12. Garrison inserts a quotation mark before the word "redeem" but has no end quote. The phrase in Clay's letter that Garrison may be referring to occurs in paragraph 7: ". . . redeem that great continent from barbarism and idolatry." Possibly he wanted to quote only the word "redeem."

---

2 6 3

TO THEODORE PARKER

65, Suffolk Street,
Monday morning, April 9, 1849.

Esteemed Friend —

A year ago, this month, we lost our dear little babe, Elizabeth Pease. It was our melancholy yet valued privilege to have you with us on the occasion of the burial of her remains. — Again we have been smitten, and another of our children has left us for a higher and purer state of existence. Our beautiful, affectionate, intelligent, large-hearted and noble boy, Charles Follen, died last evening, after a severe illness of a week, in the seventh year of his age. His body we shall commit to the tomb to-morrow (Tuesday) afternoon, at 3 o'clock, and it will give us great pleasure to have you with us, if convenient, and to participate with others in the services of the occasion. We also hope that Mrs. Parker will be able to accompany you.

We have removed from 13 Pine street to 65 Suffolk street, above Dover, directly opposite Hanson street.

Wm. Lloyd Garrison,
Helen E. Garrison.

ALS: Garrison Papers, Boston Public Library.

2 6 4

TO *THE LIBERATOR*

NEW YORK, May 8, 1849.

MY DEAR FRIEND:

Our anniversary meeting at the Tabernacle has just terminated, a powerful impression having been visibly made upon those who were present — a great congregation, embodying a large amount of the intelligence, morality and religion of the community — most respectful in their behavior, and deeply interested in mind, with an occasional and feeble exception on the part of some tormented spirit in the galleries, whose hisses served only to call forth the louder bursts of approbation from the assembly.[1] Prayer was offered by SAMUEL MAY, JR., in the spirit of true devotion; after which, pertinent and impressive portions of Scripture were read, as applicable to the condition and perils of this oppressive nation. The Memorial from Aberdeenshire, Scotland, signed by upwards of one thousand persons, among them several ministers of various religious denominations, remonstrating with the American churches for the criminal support which they are giving to slavery, and urging them to exclude slaveholders from their communion, was laid before the meeting by the President, with some introductory remarks.[2] According to the Report of the Treasurer, FRANCIS JACKSON of Boston, the whole amount received into the treasury, during the last year, was $6992.57; the expenditures were $6975.13; leaving a balance of $17.44 on hand. EDMUND QUINCY then presented a series of resolutions, relating to the participation of the Church and the Government in the system of slavery, and setting forth the duty of every Christian and Patriot having for his motto, and carrying it out to the letter — '*No Union with Slaveholders, religiously or politically.*' PARKER PILLSBURY then took the platform and made an excellent speech, and was followed by WENDELL PHILLIPS, at considerable length, in a speech charged with an immense amount of moral electricity, and marked by all the characteristics of his opulent mind. It was just such a speech as the occasion and the times demand, and was responded to in a most gratifying manner. Said one of our Philadelphia friends, whose eulogy is worth a great deal, — 'I feel as if I could willingly go across the Atlantic to hear such a speech.' FREDERICK DOUGLASS then took the platform, and was warmly received; but, after proceeding a short time, gave way, in consequence of the lateness of the hour, much to the regret of many who had never heard him. I have not time to add more, except that it is strengthening to see the faces of old friends, and to feel the pressure of their warm grasp.

Yours, truly,

WM. LLOYD GARRISON.

Printed: *The Liberator,* May 11, 1849.

1. Garrison refers to the fifteenth annual meeting of the American Anti-Slavery Society which was held in New York City at the Broadway Tabernacle May 8–10, 1849. A complete account of the meeting appears in *The Liberator,* May 18, 1849.

2. In his opening remarks to the convention, Garrison said he declined to offer a formal address, preferring to yield to other speakers. He did take the time, however, to read passages of scripture about the ungodliness of slavery and concluded by reiterating the position of the American Anti-Slavery Society — that slavery was incompatible with the spirit of Christianity

265

TO HELEN E. GARRISON

New York, May 9, 1849.

Dear Helen:

I did not arrive in this city at so early an hour on Monday afternoon as I anticipated, in consequence of an accident which happened to our train about ten miles from the city. Owing to a switch not being properly adjusted, our engine, tender and baggage cars were thrown off the track; but, fortunately, on so level a piece of ground that no one was injured, and the shock was not violent. The engine made so deep and long a furrow as to be partially buried in the earth. After a detention of two hours, another train from the city came to our relief, during which time a portion of our passengers sought recreation and refreshment at a little shanty kept by a man who glories in the name of Oliver Cromwell,[1] and who was quite willing to help "keep their spirits up, by pouring spirits down," at so much a glass. This occurrence will serve to make me distinctly remember my first trip from Boston to New York by rail-way. Dear Wendell [Phillips], S. May, Jr., and Samuel Brooke, were with me. Brooke thinks he has derived considerable benefit to his health at the Water Cure, and will return to Northampton for a short time longer after our anniversary meetings are over.

I found them all well at friend [Isaac T.] Hopper's, and the venerable old gentleman was as full of his interesting narrations as ever.

Yesterday morning, and all day, was very dismal indeed; but our meetings were never before so well attended, and I think never was a deeper impression been made. Wendell has, if possible, surpassed himself — he is so ready, so eloquent, so morally true, so sublimely great, that I know not what we should do without him. He is really one of the best and noblest specimens of humanity in this world. Our choicest friends and advocates (many of them) are here, men and women, in strong array and with a serene front, Lucretia Mott, Lucy Stone, A. K. Foster, among the women.

We have had nothing but rainy weather, since we have been here. I dislike New York in the brightest weather. I cannot tell you what I think of it in this.

Friend [Francis] Jackson goes home this afternoon. You may expect me on Friday evening. In railway haste,

Lovingly yours,

W. L. Garrison.

ALS: Garrison Papers, Boston Public Library.

1. Not identified.

2 6 6

TO SYDNEY HOWARD GAY

New York, May 22, 1849.

My Dear Gay:

My old friend James Boyle will either call at the office, or send regularly, for a copy of the Liberator, which please deliver to him without charge. If my venerable friend Isaac T. Hopper does not receive the Liberator regularly, I want him to have it without fail, and without charge.

As for the proceedings of the New England Convention, I will endeavor to send you a slip containing them, in all next week.[1] Wendell [Phillips] thinks the employment of Dr. Houston's reporter [2] will not be practicable, on account of the alarming emptiness of our treasury, and the necessity of appropriating every cent we can raise at the Convention to meeting expenses which are inevitable in sustaining the Standard and the American A. S. Society. The reporter promises to work cheap, and seems anxious to make a report for us. We will do the best that we can in his case.

Yours, faithfully,

Wm. Lloyd Garrison.

ALS: Sydney Howard Gay Papers, Columbia University Libraries.

1. The annual New England Anti-Slavery Convention was held at the Melo-

deon and at Faneuil Hall, May 29–31, Wendell Phillips presiding. The proceedings and some of the speeches are printed in *The Liberator,* June 8, 1849.

2. Neither Dr. Houston nor his reporter has been identified.

2 6 7

TO SYDNEY HOWARD GAY

Boston, May 25, 1849.

Dear Gay:

At the request of Samuel Philbrick, I send you the following copy of the Articles of Agreement between the Messrs. [James B.] Yerrinton and myself, in regard to the printing of the Liberator. In haste,

Yours, with esteem,

W. L. Garrison.

ALS: Sydney Howard Gay Papers, Columbia University Libraries. Attached to this letter in Garrison's hand are two and one-half pages of detailed and legalistic descriptions of the articles of agreement, perhaps as a protection from such trouble as he had earlier experienced with Isaac Knapp.

2 6 8

TO SYDNEY HOWARD GAY

Boston, June 6, 1849.

My dear Gay:

I write in great haste, just to say that there is no doubt that the bearer of this is worthy of aid and sympathy in his undertaking, which he will explain to you more fully than it will do to put on the paper.[1] [James M.] McKim at Philadelphia is his treasurer. If you can advise him on whom to call, either in New York or Brooklyn, pray do so, as you love your wife, and would like to get her out of slavery, if she were in it.

Yours, truly,

Wm. Lloyd Garrison.

ALS: Sydney Howard Gay Papers, Columbia University Libraries.

1. Although the bearer of Garrison's letter has not been identified, it is known that he was trying to raise funds to buy his wife out of slavery.

2 6 9

TO ELIZABETH PEASE

Boston, June 20, 1849.

Beloved Friend:

In taking up my pen to write you a few hasty lines, I have never before had so strong a desire to be with you, face to face, at Darlington; for I have much that I wish to communicate, and it is far easier for me to use the tongue than to wield the pen. Is there never to be a labor-saving invention as to epistolary correspondence, by which writing can be made as easy as talking? The mechanical drudgery of putting legibly on paper the thoughts of the brain is growing more and more irksome to me: perhaps it is because those thoughts are too feeble to inspire the hand. At least, it is a great hindrance to my communicating with those I esteem, whether at home or abroad. I envy those who can write both plainly and rapidly, and who take real pleasure in driving the quill.

The first subject to which my mind naturally reverts is the sudden death of our noble little boy, Charles Follen. For your consolatory letter, touching this great bereavement, dear Helen unites with me in proffering heart-felt acknowledgments. In the hour of affliction, the sympathetic expressions and comforting suggestions of friends are of priceless value. These we have had, in great variety, and they have helped to mitigate our sorrow. That sorrow, however, was not caused so much by the mere fact of his removal, as by other considerations. Death itself to me is not terrible, is not repulsive, is not to be deplored. I see in it as clear an evidence of Divine wisdom and beneficence as I do in the birth of a child, in the works of creation, in all the arrangements and operations of nature. I neither fear nor regret its power. I neither expect nor supplicate to be exempted from its legitimate action. It is not to be chronicled among calamities; it is not to be styled "a mysterious dispensation of Divine Providence"; it is scarcely rational to talk of being resigned to it. For what is more natural — what more universal — what more impartial — what more serviceable — what more desirable, in God's own time, hastened neither by our ignorance nor folly? Discarding as I do, as equally absurd and monstrous, the theological dogma, that death settles forever the condition of those who die, whether for an eternity of bliss or misery for the deeds done here in the body — and believing as I do, without doubt or wavering, in the everlasting progression of the human race, in the ultimate triumph of infinite love over finite error and sinfulness, in the fatherly care and boundless goodness of that Creator, "whose tender mercies are over all the works of his hands" [1] — I see nothing strange, appalling, or even sad, in death. When, therefore, my dear friend, I tell you that the loss of my dear boy has overwhelmed me with sadness, has affected my peace by day and my repose by night, has been a staggering blow, from the shock of which I find it very difficult to recover, you will not understand me as referring to any thing pertaining to another state of existence, or as gloomily affected by a change inevitable to all: far from it. Where the cherished one who has been snatched from us is, what is his situation, or what his employment, I know not, of course; and it gives me no anxiety whatever. Until I join him at least, my responsibility to him as his guardian and protector has ceased, he does not need my aid, he cannot be benefitted by my counsel. That he will still be kindly cared for, by Him who numbers the very hairs of our heads, and without whose notice a sparrow cannot fall to the ground; [2] that he is still living, having thrown aside his mortal drapery, and occupying a higher sphere of existence; I do not entertain a doubt. My grief arises mainly from the conviction that his death was premature; that he was actually defrauded of his life through unskilful treatment; that he might have been saved, if we had not been most unfortunately situated at that time. This, to be sure, is not certain; and not being certain, it is the only ingredient of consolation that we find in our cup of bitterness. Perhaps none ever lose a beloved relative or friend, by death, without thinking that, if some other mode of treatment had been adopted, peradventure the result might have been very different. But my reasons for an opinion of this kind, in regard to Charles, are not based on any thing vague or fanciful. The day before he complained of feeling unwell, he looked so vigorous and blooming that his mother could not help recording the fact in a letter which she was then writing to a sister residing in a neighboring city. Of all our children, he was the most robust, the most beautifully developed, and the last we expected to be taken from us. During the week that we were removing from our residence in Pine-street to another in Suffolk-street, the weather was cold and stormy, and he was imprudent in neglecting to wear his overcoat, &c. On Saturday afternoon, he complained of feeling sick at the stomach, looked very much flushed in the face, and vomited occasionally. His limbs were also painfully affected, as if by rheumatism. For the first four days, I did not regard him as dangerously ill, and therefore did not seek for any medical advice. I thought he had taken a violent cold, which would yield to a very simple treatment in a short time; but I happened to be so situated as to be able to give him very little attention. Helen kept assuring me that she regarded him as a very sick child, but I thought she was unnecessarily alarmed.

Had I known that the whole force of his disease was upon the brain, I too should have been filled with the deepest anxiety. We gave him the wet sheet three or four times, but this was not what he needed. We also gave him the homœopathic prescriptions as accurately as we could discover his symptoms described in our books, but without much skill or knowledge. On Wednesday, I was at my office, not expecting to return home, as usual on that day when I am getting my Liberator ready for the press, until late at night; but at noon Helen sent me a note, saying that Charles was evidently growing worse, and urging me to come home with as little delay as possible. While hesitating whether to go for a physician, I was advised by a friend to try a medicated vapor bath, who spoke of its efficacy in the highest terms, and said that his wife would be happy to administer it, as she had given it with great success in a multitude of cases. Still erroneously supposing that Charles was suffering from a rheumatic fever, and thinking that a powerful perspiration was what he needed, I resolved to try the experiment. After some delay, the chair and apparatus were procured, and in the evening my friend's wife kindly came to give the bath. Up to that hour, Charles had been perfectly rational, though somewhat lethargic, except when moved, when the pain in his limbs made him scream with agony. While he was in the chair, some fifteen or twenty minutes, his sufferings appeared to be insupportable — he became perfectly frantic — his screams were appalling — and he begged most piteously to be released. No other person was in the room, except the lady and myself. She endeavored to soothe him as much as possible, and I appealed to his little manhood in the best way I could, thinking he was nervously affected, and urging him to bear it all with fortitude, as he would undoubtedly be benefitted by the operation. Such was my confidence in the judgment of the lady alluded to, I did not even suspect that she might be raising the steam to an undue height. Alas! on coming out of the bath, we found that the poor boy had been horribly scalded, especially where he had sat down, the skin being entirely destroyed on one side; and such was the action on the brain, so intense and overwhelming, that from that fatal hour he became delirious, and so remained until he was relieved from his sufferings by death on the subsequent Sunday evening. Dying in this manner, do you wonder, my dear friend, that our grief is excessive? or that

"We grieve the more because we grieve in vain"? [3]

True, it is not wise to brood over such a catastrophe, and we endeavor to keep the thought of it from our minds as much as possible; but we should be something less or something more than human not to be most deeply affected by it. Well, it was all kindly intended on our part; we meant it to save, not to destroy; and, as I have already remarked, there is no certainty that he would have been saved, even if this calamitous result had not made his recovery impossible. The fever struck upon the brain with great force from the beginning; and it therefore made his case a critical one, as he was a child full of warm blood and nervous excitability. An hour before his death, I said in his ear as distinctly as possible, "Dear Charley is dying!" He seemed to understand what I said, gave a gentle sigh, then smiled. Once more I said, "Charley will soon be with our darling Lizzie" — (he was passionately fond of her memory, and in health used frequently to express the wish that he might be with her) — again there was a smile, and an evident recognition of what I said. Just before he expired, he rallied for a moment, and seeing his mother standing by his bedside, and also two beloved friends, smiled upon each of them in the most expressive manner; and then insensibility followed to the end.

You have the daguerrian likenesses of Fanny and Lizzie — I wish it were in my power to send you one of Charley. But we never had his taken, though we thought of doing so a hundred times. Why I did not have one taken before his interment, I can hardly tell; perhaps because he was more altered in appearance than Lizzie. But I now lament that I did not get an artist to make an attempt. He was a beautiful boy, but in no frail or delicate sense. He had a fine intellectual and moral development, with great bodily energy; he seemed born to take a century upon his shoulders, without stooping; his eyes were large, lustrous, and charged with electric light; his voice was clear as a bugle, melodious, and ever ringing in our ears, from the dawn of day to the ushering in of night — so that since it has been stilled, our dwelling has seemed to be almost without an occupant. But, above all, he was remarkable for the strength and fervor of his affection. He loved with all his soul, mind, and might. In this respect, I have never seen his equal. All the friends who have visited us for the last three or four years have had the strongest proofs of his attachment. He would almost smother them beneath a tornado of kisses; his embraces were given with intense vital energy, and "with a will." He had not a vicious quality.

Dear little Fanny feels the bereavement greatly. He was her oracle and champion. His affection she as strongly reciprocated. Not a day passes, that she does not spontaneously allude to him in the most touching manner. But she has no idea of death that is gloomy or repulsive; for we have taught her to look upon it rationally, philosophically, and in the light of growth and progress. Through her tears she will often smile to think that "he is now with dear Lizzie," and the thought of one day joining them is to her full of thrilling pleasure. Indeed, she sometimes talks like one who is

"Dressed for the flight, and ready to be gone" [4] —

so that we are really apprehensive she will early be called away.

In the cycle of ages, the death of one person — of millions of persons — however beloved, or whatever their characteristics, is a very insignificant event; but, in its sphere and immediate relationships, it is weighty, trying, momentous. You will pardon me, therefore, my sympathising friend, in occupying so large a portion of this letter with the details of our recent bereavement. This is the first time I have attempted to give any one an account of it on paper; for, until now, I have shrunk from the performance of such a task. I need not add — for you can easily imagine — that the blow has been severely felt by my dear wife, and that her heart is still wrung with anguish, especially in view of the unfortunate circumstances attending C's sickness. But we both feel that "it is well with the child"; [5] and we are comforted in the assurance that we shall again embrace him in the arms of our love as really as we have done so on earth. O, how glorious is the thought of immortality! how glorious are the visions of eternity! "O Death, where is thy sting? O Grave, where is thy victory?" [6]

The magnetic telegraph brings the sad intelligence, to-day, that Cassius M. Clay has been killed in a rencounter with a Mr. Turner, at a public meeting in Kentucky.[7] No particulars are received, except that the parties first used pistols, which flashed in the pan, when they drew their bowie-knives, and closed in a death-struggle. Mr. Clay was stabbed to the heart, and immediately expired; and his antagonist was so dreadfully wounded that he survived only a few hours. This is an awful occurrence. You will recollect with what ardor and ability Mr. Clay espoused the anti-slavery cause in Kentucky three or four years since; how boldly he uttered his sentiments through the medium of his paper, the "True American"; how a mob of "gentlemen of property and standing" assailed his office, and destroyed his press and types, while he was lying dangerously ill; how, on his recovery, he again started his paper, with indomitable courage; how, on the commencement of the war with Mexico, he denounced it in unmeasured terms as waged for a diabolical purpose, and without the slightest provocation; how, almost in the twinkling of an eye, he espoused that war, and was placed at the head of a company of volunteers; how, as soon as he arrived on the Mexican soil, he and his party were taken prisoners by a superior Mexican force; how he remained in prison until the termination of that war, having won no glory, but a great deal of shame, and lost the respect and esteem of the friends of freedom on both sides of the Atlantic; and how he was welcomed on his return home by his old persecutors, seeing that he had suffered in their behalf. That he emancipated all his slaves will ever redound to his credit; that he earnestly desired to see slavery abolished in his native State, I have no doubt; that he enlisted in the Mexican war for the purpose of aiding in the extension of slavery, probably no one believes; that he was a man of generous impulses and warm sympathies is certain; that he had any fixed principles of justice and morality is not apparent. He was neither a coward nor a time-server; and yet his courage was more of the animal than of the moral kind, and he could not wholly crucify himself to the opinions of those among whom he dwelt. In plunging so abruptly into the Mexican war, his purposes appear to have been purely political, as (being a strong Whig) he did not wish all the "glory"(!!) of it to be monopolized by the Democratic administration — and he thought it might be the means of helping to subvert that administration, which was so rankly pro-slavery.

Within the last six months, the subject of abolishing slavery in Kentucky has attracted unusual attention, and been eliciting more and more discussion. The boldest emancipationist, however, has ventured to propose nothing better than a distant abolition of the system, in the most gradual manner, and accompanied with the condition of colonization in Africa. Cassius M. Clay has recently written and spoken freely in favor of bringing slavery to a termination in Kentucky; he has advocated the measure with his usual ardor at various public meetings, at the last of which he appears to have received his death-wound.* I presume it will appear that he was attacked by Turner, and that he fought in what is called "self-defence"; but, alas! that he should have equipped himself with such weapons to carry on a moral agitation! But his death has been caused by the murderous spirit of slavery, and must powerfully react on it.

Dear Henry C. Wright is now laboring in the great State of Ohio, where he will probably remain until next winter. I have had no letters from him for some time past; but I see, by the Cleveland "True Democrat," that he lately attended a Peace Convention in that country, which he addressed, and which was also addressed by the Hon. Joshua R. Giddings.[8] The latter was chosen a delegate to attend the Peace Convention in Paris, to be holden in September next; and it is said that he has accepted the nomination.[9] Possibly, before his

---

* A later report is, that Clay survives his wounds, but that Turner is dead.

return home, you may have an opportunity to see or hear him. For a politician, he is a man of rare integrity, humanity, and moral courage; and no one on the floor of Congress has ever run so much risk, or exhibited so much heroism, in bearding the lion of slavery in its den — the District of Columbia — as himself. But while he swears to support the Constitution of the United States, and to maintain inviolate the blood-stained American Union, his moral power must be greatly impaired, and the force of his testimonies against slavery very much weakened. I think, however, that, in spirit, he is not far from the kingdom of Disunion.

As for the Peace Convention at Paris, it will probably do some good; but I fear it will prove a somewhat sentimental affair, and proceed rather mincingly in its work. As for disarming the nations of the earth, by appealing to "the powers that be," [10] rather than to *the people*, individually and collectively, I believe it will prove chimerical; still, any agitation of the Peace question must do good, and serve to open the eyes of the people to the horrors and iniquities of war. But into what a baptism of blood is Europe about to be plunged!

I suppose you have read Henry's Autobiography.[11] How do you like it? Much of it will be familiar to you; to all its sentiments you may not be ready to subscribe. There is no evidence of care or labor in what he writes; his style is always negligent and too diffuse, and his repetitions are multitudinous; yet he is an independent thinker, a fearless advocate of whatever he believes to be the truth, a world-embracing philanthropist, and a most sturdy reformer. His abhorrence of injustice, oppression, blood-shedding, is admirably intense, and in entire accordance with the scriptural injunction, "Ye that love the Lord, hate evil." [12] His disgust at mere forms and ceremonies, to the disregard of every sound religious principle, is most hearty, and he pours his contempt upon them without measure. His estimate of man is exalted, as a being too sacred to be injured, and as of paramount importance to all human institutions. His ideas of what constitutes religion and the worship of God will doubtless startle many, and offend some; but they will lead to reflection and discussion, which are much needed on such stereotyped and traditional subjects. His letters to me injure the unity of such a volume, and break the charm of consecutive narration; but, as a whole, this Autobiography is a valuable contribution to the cause of spiritual and personal freedom, and will be better appreciated hereafter than at present. In copying from his diary as far back as 1825, he appears unconsciously to have mingled some of his latest thoughts and expressions on various religious and reformatory subjects; and thus subjects himself to the imputation of wearing a clerical garb long after he professes to have outgrown it. But these anachronisms subtract nothing from the value of his sentiments, though they afford ground for captious criticism.

You will learn from the Standard and Liberator how very interesting, enthusiastic and encouraging were our anti-slavery anniversaries in New York and Boston.[13] If you could have been present, I am sure you would have felt repaid for the trip across the Atlantic. [*En passant*, are we never to have the pleasure of seeing you here? Only think how quickly the voyage is now made!] Wendell [Phillips], as usual, produced a powerful impression by his eloquent appeals and bold avowals. He always speaks to the trinity in man — to the understanding, the conscience, and the heart. I love and admire him more and more. [Frederick] Douglass was in full strength and power, and acquitted himself to the astonishment of many, and the admiration of all. [Stephen S.] Foster was in the prophet-vein of Isaiah and Jeremiah, and made the ears of a hireling clergy and a corrupt church to tingle.[14] [Parker] Pillsbury was equally effective. We have never had so many runaway slaves on our platform as on these occasions. The remarkable case of the one who escaped in a box from Virginia, excited the deepest interest, and created a powerful sensation.[15] I presume it will be extensively noticed in England. What a country is this, what a people are we, that such expedients should be necessary to obtain liberty, even at the almost certain loss of life! Only look at the action of the two General Assemblies of the Presbyterian Church, recently, in regard to the enslavement of a population in their midst larger than that of all Scotland! The New School refusing to place slavery in the category of immoralities; and the Old School declaring its purpose not to have any thing to do with the question! Such is the American Church.

Wendell informs me that he has received a most generous donation from you towards a fund intended for the benefit of my family, which a few friends are kindly endeavoring to raise, and of which I have known nothing until recently.[16] Be assured, this fresh token of your friendship, which has been manifested on so many occasions and in so many ways, is more gratefully appreciated than words can express. It fills me with humiliation, however, to think that I am not more worthy to receive it. I know, to some extent at least, how many must be the calls upon you for pecuniary assistance at home, and how large (with your sympathetic and generous spirit) must be the drain upon your finances. As to the contemplated fund, the attempt to raise it has taken me entirely by surprise; and I am sure I have done nothing to deserve it, for I have only done my duty. Would that I could add, my whole duty! Whatever the sum may be, I do not mean or desire to have any thing to do with its expenditure. In the hands of the faithful friends who have kindly consented to act as trustees, it will find a safe deposit, and be appropriated in the most judicious manner. May my future course be such as to give no contributor regret that he ever assisted me in my necessities!

Our beloved friend Mrs. [Eliza Jackson] Eddy has safely returned from her foreign tour. How glad am I that she visited Darlington, and had the pleasure of seeing you under your own roof — a pleasure which she describes as very great on her part, diminished by nothing but the necessary brevity of the interview. To hear her speak of you and home was next to my being present in bodily form: the reminiscenses of my own visit came thronging up from the sanctuary of my memory. I may not indulge the hope of ever being permitted again to cross the Atlantic; and yet there are so many choice spirits abroad, whose faces I yearn to see, that at times I feel as if I *must* once more take them by the hand, and enjoy once more their delightful companionship. Some of them ought to come over here, by way of reciprocity: we owe them obligations which we are most anxious to discharge.

I shall send this letter by a young lady, warmly interested in the anti-slavery cause — Miss Emma Weston, the youngest sister of Maria W. Chapman.[17] She is to join her sisters in Paris, and will thus leave another vacancy in our little circle in Boston. I presume you will see her before her final return to this country, but not before the expiration of her sojourn on the continent. About the 1st of August, our estimable friend Mrs. E. L. Follen, (with her sister, Miss Cabot, and son, Charles Follen,) is also to go to Europe, where she expects to remain two or three years.[18] She is a charming woman, and the beloved of all who know her. I hope she will not fail of seeing you; for the interview could not fail to be mutually delightful. Another of our anti-slavery laborers is to visit England this summer — I mean William W. Brown, the fugitive slave, whose narrative you may have read, and who has so long and so acceptably pleaded the cause of his oppressed brethren in Massachusetts. He is very agreeable in his manners, neat in his personal appearance, persuasive in his eloquence and intelligent in his mind. I think he will make a very favorable impression on an English audience. He will do what he can to uphold genuine, uncompromising abolitionism.[19]

I have now written so much [on various domestic and public matters] that it must weary you to read it; and yet I have not even alluded to a subject of special interest and importance on which I should like to dwell at considerable length; but at present, time will not permit. I refer to the Bible discussion and other matters which have appeared in the columns of the Liberator, during the present volume, and which appear to have caused cruel grief and alarm to you and other cherished friends abroad, though not to any at home that I am aware of. One excellent friend has discontinued the Liberator for conscience sake, being unwilling any longer to receive or to circulate it! Another also declines taking the paper on the same ground. And you, in various letters to Henry C. Wright, Wendell Phillips, and myself, say that while the Liberator is the most interesting paper you receive, you feel it is a serious thing to circulate it, while it contains so much which appears to you dangerous and, as you believe, *"false* doctrine." Nay, you are deeply concerned when you think of leaving copies of it behind you, to fall into you know not whose hands, lest their everlasting salvation should be perilled by a perusal of such heresies!

My dear friend, I admire your frankness; I appreciate your friendly concern for my welfare and that of the Liberator, shown so often both by word and deed; I greatly respect your conscientious scruples; I praise your circumspection; which leads you to desire to avoid the very appearance of evil; I am sure you wish to do nothing, to say nothing, that looks like unjust proscription or sectarian intolerance; and yet I confess that your grief is inexplicable to me, and your alarm perfectly unaccountable. In vain I read what I have written and published — in vain I ask, of what sin or error I have been guilty — in vain I strive to ascertain precisely what it is in the Liberator that you so seriously object — I am only more and more perplexed, and "find no end in wandering mazes lost." [20] What! the Liberator so bad a publication, (in spite, too, of the confessedly good things it contains) that its suppression, not its circulation is deemed a duty by ———— and ———— and ———— and I know not how many others! What! are you alarmed at honest investigation, at free discussion, at the maintenance of a free press, at the disposition to favor all things and hold fast that which is good — and shocked to find that certain theological opinions, which are conscientiously held by her, are not universally received as too sacred to be examined, and too selfevident to admit of doubt! Well, this is strange, wonderful, almost incredible. My dear friend I should be quite as much amused as surprised if I did not believe that you have spoken from the depth of a sincere heart; and therefore I proceed to reason with you a little, with becoming gravity and earnest consideration.

Henry Vincent, too, it appears is disturbed at what has appeared in the Liberator, and intends writing faithfully to H. C. Wright on the subject.

My dear friend, you, and ———— and ———— and Henry Vincent are certainly wrong in this matter. You are troubled where you ought to be serene; you are alarmed at what ought to make your repose perfect;

you are not acting naturally; you occupy, in regard to these things, a sandy foundation; and therefore your anxiety, trepidation, grief! "Come, now, let us reason together," [21] and see if it be not so.

The Liberator, as you well know, is not the organ of any Anti Slavery society. For its views on any subject, I alone am responsible, to the extent that I utter or endorse them; hence, it is a perfectly independent journal, and the Anti Slavery cause, as such, is not responsible for it. None of the money contributed to the American Anti Slavery Society is used to sustain the Liberator: therefore it is not to be identified with that society, any further than there happens to be a coincidence of views in regard to the abolition of slavery; and to this alone there can be no objections in any candid mind. If therefore any of our English friends cannot conscientiously patronize the Liberator, they need withhold nothing from the American A. S. Society on that account.

The Liberator always allows both sides of every question that it may start to be fairly discussed in its columns; it maintains and exemplifies the right of free discussion; it holds with Thomas Jefferson, that "error of opinion may be safely tolerated where truth is left free to combat it;" [22] it believes and acts on the belief, that "truth is mighty, and must prevail;" [23] it affirms that ["]the righteous are as bold as a lion, but the wicked flee when no man pursueth;" [24] it maintains that there is nothing too holy to be interrogated, examined, and proved, though it does not undertake to interrogate, examine and prove all things questionable, as its distinctive purpose is the abolition of slavery, to which it has unswervingly adhered. Do you, does Henry Vincent, object to such views of discussions, to such a course of action? If not, why then so much regret and uneasiness at my maintaining a free press? Are such presses so numerous, that one can be advantageously spared? You do not dislike to see both sides of the slavery question presented; and you would smile at the idea of secreting the Liberator because it contains many proslavery articles which might injuriously affect some minds. You are not troubled on seeing both sides of the peace or nonresistance question argued in its columns, but rejoice in proportion to the activity of its discussion — do you not? You are not alarmed when you see articles freely admitted, *pro* and *con*, into a publication on the subject of temperance. Neither you nor Henry Vincent would think of remonstrating against the free utterance of sentiments in favor of religious intolerance, provided no gag was put into the mouth of the advocate of religious liberty. You both would exclaim

> "Thrice is he armed that hath his quarrel just,
> And he but naked though locked up in steel,["] [25]

who is the victim of bigotry or superstition, who is afraid to reason and investigate, who does not dare to burst a single traditional trammel, who cries out, "This is too sacred to be examined — too mysterious to be examined — and has been too long received to admit of scepticism!"

But why are you willing that these things should be freely discussed? Simply because you are persuaded that your views of anti slavery, peace, temperance, religious liberty, &c. are based on a solid foundation, and cannot be successfully overthrown; nay, the more they are attacked, the more truthful you think they will appear. Just so! hence you invite, solicit, demand, the most thorough inquiry into their validity. But the slaveholder, the warrior, the rum drinker, the bigot, do not like to see their views on slavery, war, temperance, and religious liberty brought into the arena of free debate; they are one sided, and dread nothing so much as "a fair field and no quarter." Why! because

"Tis conscience that makes cowards of them all." [26]

Their cause is a bad one, and they either know it, or suspect it; and to change their opinions might cost them their reputation, and peradventure the means by which they live.

Now what is true with regard to one subject or question is equally true in regard to every other. Whoever holds to an opinion or sentiment which he is not pleased to see dealt with boldly and searchingly gives evidence that he is conscious that it will not bear such treatment, or that he has taken it upon trust, usage, parental, educational, traditional authority and not upon his own clear wrought, unbiased convictions. Is it not so? Who shall presume to say to another, in regard to the examination of any creed, book, ordinance, day, or form of government — of any thing natural or reputedly miraculous — "Thus far shalt thou go, but no further." [27] Beloved friend, are you not in just this state of mind, in regard to certain subjects, the discussion of which you so much deplore? How is this to be accounted for? I will tell you.

You were born a member of the Society of Friends; your religious opinions you received upon authority, and you accepted them as a matter of course, sincerely and trustingly, as I did mine, and as nine tenths of those who are born in Christendom do. Your theological views of man's depravity, the atonement, eternal punishment, the divinity of Christ, the inspiration of the Bible, &c. you received as confidingly as you did your quaker views of peace, anti slavery, temperance, &c. only the latter you have advocated and carried out to an extent much beyond the ordinary teachings of quakerism on these points. But the latter views are true, and susceptible of the clearest demonstration; and their examination you court. The former are all wrong; (in my judgment, I mean — though I was brought up to believe them) admit of no satisfactory proof, much less of demonstration; and a free examination of them gives you positive uneasiness! Your peace and anti slavery views commend themselves to your understanding, your conscience, and your heart; perhaps you will discover that your theological views have really little to do with your understanding, your conscience, or your heart, independently & absolutely, like the others — (pardon my frankness) — for if they had, it seems to me you would no more be startled to see an impartial discussion of them in the Liberator, or any other periodical conducted on the same principle, than you now are to see proslavery & anti peace sentiments admitted into its columns, along with those of an opposite spirit. Is there any flaw in this reasoning? Is there any link in this chain of logic unsound? Is not the parallel perfect, the analogy exact, the illustration pertinent, the conclusion inevitable?

What is it that induces you to hide the Liberator from your friends? It cannot be that you have ever seen any thing in it, from my pen, detrimental to the peace, liberty, or happiness of mankind. Is not its standard of rectitude exalted, unswerving, absolute? Is it not boldly and continually rebuking sin and sinners in high places & in low places? Is it not hated, feared, and persecuted by all that is p[h]arisaical, intolerant, cowardly, time serving, brutal, and devilish? Does it not advocate in practical life, Love to God and love to man — peace on earth — the brotherhood of all mankind? Is it not straining every nerve to overthrow, by sublime moral instrumentalities, that horrible system in this country, by which millions of our brethren and sisters are reduced to the condition of things? Is such a paper to be secreted? Is its circulation to be a cause of disquietude to any pure mind, to any free spirit, to any philanthropic heart? I have never allowed a single number of it to go forth to the world, without feeling that it would do something to redeem that world from sin and error. My mistakes and infirmities have been numerous undoubtedly — for who is infallible? — but the moral tone of my paper I am confident, has been uniformly pure and elevated.

To what do you object, my dear friend? I hardly know; and this is the reason I am not more specific in my reply, for want of a specific charge. On the Sabbath question, I believe your mind is at rest; and the discussion of it in the Liberator is interesting rather than unpleasant to you. We hardly ever object to seeing our views supported on any subject; but when they are called in question, our complacency is not always as perfect, unless we have the utmost assurance in our own souls of their correctness. My worthy friend at ——— [28] comes

right to the point in her letter, of which the following is the introductory paragraph: —["]My dear sir[,] I am sorry to say that I cannot
read the Liberator any longer. You will, therefore, not send any more
papers to my address. Ever since the Sabbath and Scripture questions
were brought forward, I have read it only to *mourn over it*. I know
the Bible and the Author of it so well (?) that I have not any fears
for my own sentiments being injured. But I cannot put it into the
hands of my family, because I consider its sentiments on these points
calculated to bring forth the grapes of *Sodom* and the apples of
Gomorrah."

Is this good woman as careful to suppress in her family those political or religious periodicals which sanction war, the army and navy,
a monarchical government, conquests in India, and the like — all which
serve to degrade, oppress, or depopulate the human race? Even there
it would not be a parallel case of proscription because she does not
complain of any thing in the Liberator as injurious to the cause of
humanity. She believes in the holiness of the first day of the week;
will she not allow Calvin's Institutes to be in her family, in which the
Sabbath is declared to have been a purely Jewish institution? [29] Does
she repudiate Paleys Moral Philosophy, in which the same view of
the subject is taken — that the Sabbath was exclusively Jewish in its
origin and design, and is unknown to Christianity? [30] Does she put
under her ban Dymonds Essays, in which the holiness of any particular day is discarded? [31] Is she careful not to let any of her family
see a copy of the Augsburgh Confessions of Faith, drawn up by
Melancthon, in which the Sabbath is classed among those shadows
which vanished at the coming of Christ? [32] If so, she is at least consistent. But is it wise or rational for her attempt to hold absolute
mastery over the understandings and consciences of her family, by
preventing them from seeing what in her eyes savors of heresy? Is this
her way of teaching her children to obey the injunction, "Prove all
things"? [33] and may they give as a satisfactory reply to the injunction
of Jesus, "Why judge ye not of your own selves what is right?" [34]
"our mother thought it might endanger our salvation to do so."! God
forbid that I should ever take such a responsibility upon myself — that
I should ever bring my children up in this one sided manner! The one
distinct and emphatic lesson which I shall teach them is, to take
nothing upon mere authority — to dare to differ in opinion from their
father, and from all the world — to understand, as clearly as possible,
what can be said against or in favor of any doctrine or practice, &
then to accept or reject it according to their own convictions of duty.
Mrs. R. says her sentiments are too strongly fixed to be swept away;
but I am forced to believe that she has not absolute confidence in

them — else why should she refuse to read herself, or to allow her family to read, a paper in which the Sabbatarian is welcomed with his views as cordially as the Anti Sabbatarian is with his? To say — "I am sure I am right — I cannot be wrong — I will not read or hear what may be advanced in opposition to my views" — is, surely, not the way to "grow in grace," or "in the knowledge of the Lord." [35] We have all of us much to learn; for we are, to a lamentable extent, creatures of circumstances — mere imitations of others, simply because they did or did not this or that act, or accepted or rejected this or that religious or political opinion. How many seek for truth, or dare to follow her, independently? Alas! how few!

But, agreeing in the anti sabbatical views of the Liberator, your complaint is not, my dear friend, that the subject is allowed to be freely discussed in its columns. If I understand the cause of your disquietude, it is the Bible discussion which has been introduced by Henry C. Wright; it is the avowal of our belief, that the Bible is not an inspired book, in the popular sense — and, therefore, that God never sanctioned any of those exterminating wars and horrid cruelties recorded in the Old Testament and ascribed to him. But is this a settled question? Is it not worthy of serious thought and the most searching investigation? Do you believe that God is changeable in his moral attributes; that he rules arbitrarily and capriciously, without any fixed law; that it is his prerogative now to sanction war, and then to enjoin peace as a moral duty — now to command lying and deceiving, and then to speak the truth and deal honestly with all men — now to indulge in licentiousness and then to enforce purity? If so, then a lie may be as good as the truth, and wrong is equal to right under certain circumstances! What is your reverence for the Bible but traditional? Why should it not be examined, criticized, and decided upon like any other book — according to its own intrinsic merits? All that is really good in it we should prize, and it will assuredly remain; whatever we discover in it to be either obsolete, erroneous, visionary, or contradicted by fact and experience, let us treat it accordingly. But to take it as from God, credulously and to be in the fashion — is neither to honor God nor exalt the book.

In your last letter to Henry C. Wright you say, "I am afraid thou thought me very severe in the expression of my sentiments, but it arose from the depth of my grief that the work should be marred, and as I cannot but fear, *souls* led astray [from what, dear friend? This language is *so* technical and indefinite!] by the promulgation of opinions on subjects which *I do not think we can fully understand in our present state*"! Pray, what can we not understand that is essential to our welfare? And how can any be led astray by that which neither he nor his teacher can understand? Do you not see that your "fear" is without foundation? To say that a thing is mysterious, and too high for our finite minds, and yet must be implicitly accepted, that it contradict reason, experience, all the facts of history, is to advocate credulity, but not the use of our faculties. I will leave mysteries above human comprehension, to take care of themselves; I will not quarrel with any man concerning them; they constitute no part of my moral observations or duties; they are of no value to me or to others; they are not tangible, and therefore not practical; they may or may not exist, they may or may not be true, but as they are incomprehensible, they are not within the sphere of the finite, but of the Infinite. We may not, then, dogmatize about them, we may not promise salvation or threaten damnation as they are believed or denied; we may not be uncharitable towards each other, because our speculations about them differ; toward bad manners, bad principles, bad practices, we may be intolerant, but in regard to all mysteries we must be entirely catholic. Instead of this, however, how prone are religionists to be lenient towards evil practices, (and to sanction them if they are popular) and intolerant in their feelings towards those who reject their mysterious and worthless creeds? For mere religious speculations I care nothing; they decide no man's character; they determine no man's destiny; but I am concerned to see removed from the earth whatever tends to degrade, oppress, and curse mankind. I judge of men by their fruits, not by their professions, believing that a corrupt tree cannot bring forth good fruit.[36] I am for the extension of peace and liberty throughout the world, by grappling with the war spirit, and overturning every hold of tyranny. This I think was the mission of Jesus; this his mode of reconciling a hostile world; and this the spirit by which he was animated.

You fear that others, whose minds are less strong than H. C. Wrights and my own may be led astray by our sentiments. Not unless those sentiments are mischievous when reduced to practice. Besides — are we shut up to the necessity of keeping our mouths closed, lest some weak or youthful minds may misinterpret or pervert what we say? Then all discussion is wrong, and dissent leads to error!

Are we wrong in contending that war is sinful, *per se*? and therefore that it was never commanded by God, any book to the contrary? Is this to sap or to reorganize the foundation of moral obligation? "The head and front of our offending hath this extent — no more.["][37] Besides, you will remember that the Bible has had its able champions in the Liberator — such men as Henry Grew and William Goodell.[38] If the truth be with them, why is my friend so alarmed "lest souls should be led astray"? I beseech you to review this whole matter as sensibly as you would the Anti Slavery or Corn Law question; and I am confident we shall not differ widely in the result.

I doubt not that a sincere concern for the welfare of the Anti Slavery cause, and the usefulness of the Liberator, as its advocate, may give rise to the inquiry in your mind — ["]why discuss the merits of the Bible, or the question of the holiness of the first day of the week, in the Liberator? Is it not needlessly to deter persons from taking the paper, who otherwise would be disposed to subscribe for it, being desirous to promote the abolition of slavery?" My dear friend, it would give me great satisfaction to extend the subscription list of my paper much beyond what it is at present; and most solicitous am I to see every slave free, and to join in singing the song of jubilee. But I beg you and my other English friends to bear constantly in your minds the fact, that the discussion of these questions has been forced upon us by the enemies of the anti slavery and non resistance movements. Their constant cry has been, that we are desecrating the Sabbath in pleading the cause of the slave on that day, and mixing up secular with holy affairs. Thus criminated, we have naturally been led to see how this doctrine of the holiness of days affects every reformatory enterprise, and to inquire into its origin and nature. We are enlightened as we proceed in our investigations, and led to perceive not only that there is no scriptural authority for the observance of the first day of the week as the Sabbath, but that time is sanctified only as we use it aright, without regard to particular days or seasons. In short, that holiness pertains to the spirit & to its acts, not to any external arrangements or observances; and that whatever it is right to do on one day, it is right to do on every other day of the week. That this discussion has already proved highly serviceable to our cause, we have the clearest evidence.

Again, in advocating our non resistance doctrines, our opponents have resorted to the Bible, and thought to silence us by triumphantly referring to the exterminating wars recorded in the Old Testament, as expressly commanded by Jehovah. It was not conclusive for us to reply that what was obligatory once is not necessarily so now — that Christ has superseded Moses, and now forbids all war; for the answer was, if, as you assert, war is like slavery, idolatry, and the like, inherently wrong, a *malum in se*, how could it be enjoined by a sin hating God in the days of Moses, unless his moral character is mutable? our answer to this is, whoever or whatever asserts that the Creator has required, and may still require, one portion of his children to butcher another portion, for any purpose whatever, is libelling his goodness, and asserting what every thing in nature contradicts. This position we believe to be impregnable.

So, too, the controversies with the American church and clergy have all been forced upon us by those who love darkness rather than light,[39] because their deeds are evil. We are not the aggressors in any of these instances. Ought we to have abandoned our ground, and avoided the conflict? What would have been gained by it, either to the cause of the slave in particular, or of mankind universally?

But I must stop. I am sorry, dear friend, to have caused you any grief or uneasiness, but I must be true to my convictions of duty, and trust you will ever be true to yours. This is a hastily written letter, without revision or amendment, and you will kindly overlook any thought or expression in it that may appear improper or harsh.

Yours gratefully & affectionately

Wm. Lloyd Garrison

AL: Garrison Papers, Boston Public Library; printed partly in *Life*, III, 263–270. The first half of this long letter is written in Garrison's hand; the second half has been preserved only in a copy in the hand of Richard D. Webb, whose writing is so difficult to decipher that the editor cannot always vouch for the accuracy of his transcription. Certainly Webb's capitalization and punctuation are not always consistent with Garrison's usual practice; nor is Webb himself always consistent.

1. An adaptation of Psalms 145:9.
2. An allusion either to Matthew 10:29, 30 or to Luke 12:6, 7.
3. Garrison may be echoing the parallelism found in Abraham Cowley, *Anacreon*, XLIII, "Upon Gold," lines 3–4.
4. Not identified.
5. A reference to II Kings 4:26.
6. I Corinthians 15:55.
7. Garrison was mistaken, as he acknowledges subsequently in a footnote to this letter; not only did Clay survive the duel, he lived until 1903. The facts are these: the duel appears to have involved two members of the Turner family, Squire Turner (1793–1871) and his son Cyrus (died 1849). According to one account (J. Winston Coleman, Jr., *Slavery Times in Kentucky*, Chapel Hill, 1940, p. 315) Squire Turner, a proslavery man who had served in the Kentucky legislature, attacked Clay. Clay then attacked Turner. Finally Cyrus Turner attacked Clay physically and died as a result of wounds sustained in the ensuing fight. For a biography of Clay, together with an account of his newspaper, the *True American*, mentioned by Garrison later in this letter, see Garrison's letter to Unknown Recipient, July 25, 1845.
8. A peace convention was held in Painesville, Ohio, June 6, 1849. It was reported in the Cleveland *Daily True Democrat*, June 11, 1849.
9. The Congress of the Friends of Universal Peace, or "Peace Congress," a distinguished international convention with Victor Hugo as chairman, met August 22, 1849, at the Salle de Ste. Cécile, a Paris music hall. The delegates passed resolutions advocating disarmament, renunciation of war, and establishment of an international code of law and a supreme court to arbitrate disputes. Although avoiding controversial political questions, the congress listened to two former slaves, William Wells Brown and the Reverend J. W. C. Pennington, who discussed the relation between war and slavery. (Merle E. Curti, *The American Peace Crusade*, Durham, N.C., 1929, pp. 172–178.)
10. Romans 13:1.
11. Henry C. Wright's autobiography, *Human Life Illustrated in My Individual Experience as a Child, a Youth, and a Man*, was published in March 1849.

A volume of more than 400 pages, priced at one dollar, it was taken from Wright's journals of more than thirty years. A summary of the contents as well as a brief excerpt can be found in *The Liberator*, March 30 and May 11, 1849.

12. Psalms 97:10.

13. An account of the annual meeting of the American Anti-Slavery Society appeared in *The Liberator*, May 18, 1849, and an account of the New England Anti-Slavery Convention on June 8, 1849.

14. Garrison alludes either to II Kings 21:12 or to Jeremiah 19:3.

15. Garrison refers to the case of the famous Henry "Box" Brown. A slave in Richmond, Brown contrived to have himself shipped in a crate to Philadelphia by way of Adams' Express. The journey took twenty-six hours. Upon arrival, rising up in his box, ". . . he reached out his hand, saying, 'How do you do, gentlemen?'" (William Still, *The Underground Railroad*, Philadelphia, 1879, pp. 81–86).

16. The fund to which Garrison refers had been started in 1847 when his illness on his western tour revealed his precarious financial position. On January 1, 1849, Francis Jackson, Samuel Philbrick, and Ellis Gray Loring established a trust fund for Garrison at that time amounting to $2,289.79 (see *Life*, III, 265).

17. Nothing more than Garrison tells us is known of Emma Forbes Weston except her dates (1825–1888).

18. Susan Cabot 1794–1861) married Jesse P. Richardson in 1830 but after his death in 1840 took back her maiden name. She wrote *What Have We, as Individuals, to Do With Slavery?* (New York, 1855). (L. Vernon Briggs, *History and Genealogy of the Cabot Family, 1475–1927*, Boston, 1927.) Charles Follen, Jr. (1830–1872) was graduated from Harvard in 1849 with a degree in zoology. He served in the Civil War and for a time was held prisoner in Tennessee. After the war he was connected with the Port Royal experiment in South Carolina. (Letter to the editor from Jonathan Prude, researcher, July 10, 1970.)

19. The portion of the manuscript in Garrison's hand ends with this paragraph; hereafter we are transcribing from Richard D. Webb's copy.

20. Garrison adapts John Milton, *Paradise Lost*, II, 561.

21. Isaiah 1:18.

22. A slight misquotation from Thomas Jefferson, *First Inaugural Address*, March 4, 1801.

23. A common saying, usually phrased "will prevail," originally from the Apocrypha, I Esdras 4:41.

24. A transposition and slight misquotation of Proverbs 28:1.

25. Shakespeare, *2 Henry VI*, III, ii, 233–234.

26. Garrison slightly misquotes Shakespeare, *Hamlet*, III, i, 83.

27. Garrison adapts Job 38:11.

28. Later in the letter called "Mrs. R.," possibly Mrs. Mary A. Rawson.

29. Garrison refers to John Calvin, *Institutes of the Christian Religion* (first published in Basel in 1536).

30. Garrison refers to William Paley, *Principles of Moral and Political Philosophy* (1785), which had been used at Cambridge University and elsewhere as a textbook.

31. Garrison probably refers to Jonathan Dymond, *Essays on the Principles of Morality, and on the Private and Political Rights and Obligations of Mankind* (New York, 1834). When this book was first published Garrison praised Dymond in *The Liberator* (March 8, 1845), as "the Lord Bacon of our times."

32. The *Augsburg Confession*, or seventeen articles of the Evangelical faith, drawn up by Melancthon in 1530, emphasized the doctrine of justification by faith.

33. I Thessalonians 5:21.

34. A reference to Luke 12:57.

35. Garrison adapts II Peter 3:18.

36. Garrison refers to Matthew 7:16 and either to Matthew 7:18 or to Luke 6:43.

37. Garrison quotes Shakespeare, *Othello*, I, iii, 80–81, omitting the word "very" before "head."

38. Henry Grew (1781–1862) was a Philadelphia clergyman whose fundamentalist interpretation of the Bible made him question equality for women, although his daughter Mary served for twenty-three years as president of the Pennsylvania Woman Suffrage Association. Despite his views on woman's rights Grew was a supporter of Garrisonian abolitionism. (Obituary, *The Liberator*, August 15, 1862.)

39. A reference to John 3:19.

<hr>

2 7 0

TO ELIZABETH PEASE

Boston, July 17, 1849.

Dear Friend:

One of the pleasantest sights in the world to me is, the sight of a slave escaped from his dreary prison-house. I know you participate in that feeling; and therefore it is with great pleasure I introduce you to one, the bearer of this, whose Narrative you may have read, William W. Brown.[1] It is true, he has not recently escaped, but for several years past has been a lecturer in the anti-slavery cause, rehearsing in the public ear the story of the wrongs and sufferings of the millions who are still held in captivity; but it is also true, that, up to the hour of his departure for the fast-anchored isle,[2] he is by American law a chattel, and finds in "this great country" no spot on which he can legally stand in safety from his pursuers. For the last three years, he has been laboring in the service of the Massachusetts Anti-Slavery Society, during which period he has conducted himself in the most exemplary manner, and commended himself to the respect and esteem of a large circle of acquaintance. We part from him with regret, especially as the harvest here is so great, and the laborers are so few;[3] but we are reconciled to his absence by knowing that he is not to cease advocating the cause of his fettered countrymen by going abroad, but intends to labor for their deliverance with renewed zeal. Indeed, how can he help remembering those in bonds as bound with them,[4] seeing that he carries upon his person the marks of slave-holding cruelty, and in his mind the dreadful recollection of all that he saw and suffered while held as a chattel; and seeing, too, that he left behind him, when he made his escape, a mother and three sisters, who, if living, are yet groaning beneath a bondage that is hopeless?

Mr. Brown does not go out officially from any anti-slavery society, simply because he prefers to stand alone responsible for what he may say and do, and to present himself to the British public in his distinctive character as a fugitive slave from a land boasting of its freedom, independence, republicanism and piety, but under the flag of which he finds less protection than is given to cattle and household furniture. Nor does he go out to be a pecuniary burden or to make himself an unwelcome guest to any one; but he hopes that, by the sale of his Narrative, (the stereotype plates of which he takes with him,) he shall be able to meet such expenses as may arise beyond what the hospitality of friends may cover. His stay will be longer or shorter, as circumstances may determine.

It gratifies me to state, that he has been appointed a delegate to the Peace Congress which is to be held in Paris next month, by the Committee of the American Peace League, whose credentials he bears with him.[5] This is another proof that prejudice against color is gradually yielding here to the appeals of reason, to the claims of justice, to the dictates of piety. I should like to be at that Congress myself; for though it will doubtless come far short of the standard of Christian non-resistance, as taught and exemplified by Christ, yet its deliberations cannot fail to be interesting, and its testimonies I trust will be clear and emphatic against all wars, whether waged offensively or defensively.

It appears that there is now in England, a "Reverend" agent of the American Colonization Society, by the name of Miller, who is endeavoring to deceive the public and to get pecuniary aid for that Society, as did Elliott Cresson, many years ago; and it is one object of Mr. Brown, in going to England at this time, to meet and expose this wolf in sheep's clothing.[6]

Last evening, a large and an enthusiastic public meeting was held by the colored citizens of Boston, in conjunction with their white friends, to give him the parting hand, and to recognize and accredit him as their representative and mouthpiece abroad.[7] The proceedings of the meeting you will receive by another conveyance, and doubtless will have read them in print before this letter is put into your hands by Mr. Brown.

As Mr. Brown comes fresh from the anti-slavery field in the United States, and can tell you every thing about the state of our cause, as well as any private particulars you may desire to obtain respecting your anti-slavery friends and acquaintance, I need not extend this letter.

The cholera is visiting various parts of this country with great severity; but, as yet, Boston has had very few cases of it, and we are hoping that these will not be multiplied.[8] In every other respect, the city is unusually healthy.

We are all pretty well at home. The loss of our dear boy, Charles

Follen, still presses heavily upon us. Helen desires to be warmly remembered to you.

Accept afresh the assurances of my gratitude, esteem, and friendly attachment.

Wm. Lloyd Garrison.

Elizabeth Pease.

ALS: Garrison Papers, Boston Public Library.

1. Garrison refers to the *Narrative of William W. Brown, A Fugitive Slave*, Boston, 1847 (3,000 copies). A second enlarged edition appeared in 1848, and within two years four editions totaling 8,000 copies had been printed and sold.

2. William Cowper, *The Task*, Book II, line 151.

3. A reference to Luke 10:2.

4. An adaptation of Hebrews 13:3.

5. Garrison probably refers to the Peace Congress Committee formed by the League of Universal Brotherhood and the American Peace Society to enlist support for the movement and to recruit delegates to the Paris convention. The committee issued an appeal to the American people for delegates to go to Paris and held rallies in major cities to gain support. (Merle E. Curti, *The American Peace Crusade*, Durham, N.C., 1929, p. 172.)

6. John Miller (1819–1895), a Presbyterian clergyman, served as an agent of the American Colonization Society in England between pastorates in Maryland and Philadelphia. He withdrew from the Presbyterian church in 1877 and established an independent church in Princeton, New Jersey. During the Civil War he served in the Confederate Army.

7. The meeting to which Garrison refers took place at Washingtonian Hall. Besides bidding Brown farewell, the participants presented Garrison with a silver pitcher in gratitude for his efforts on behalf of abolition. A complete account of the proceedings appears in *The Liberator*, July 20, 1849.

8. During the nineteenth century several cholera epidemics struck the United States, among them one in 1849. For a complete account of the epidemics see Charles E. Rosenberg, *The Cholera Years* (Chicago, 1962).

271

TO RALPH WALDO EMERSON

Boston, July 20, 1849.

Dear Sir:

I am desired, by the Board of Managers of the Massachusetts Anti-Slavery Society, to invite you in their behalf to be present at the celebration of that ever memorable and most joyous event, the abolition of slavery in the British West India islands, at a grand mass meeting of the friends of freedom which is to be held at Worcester, "the heart of the Commonwealth," [1] on the day which has been designated by Pres. Taylor as a day of national fasting and prayer on account of the Cholera, namely, Friday, August 3rd.[2] In addition to your personal presence, which is much desired, I am requested to urge you to be one of the speakers on that occasion. Our friend Theodore Parker has pledged himself to be one of the number, and I earnestly hope you will be able to accede to this request. Like him, you exercise a strong influence over many minds in this country, which are not yet sufficiently committed to the side of the slave; like him, you are not afraid publicly and pointedly to testify against the enslavement of three millions of our countrymen. A renewal of that testimony, as opportunity may offer, is not only desirable, but important. I will not add, it is a duty; for you need no suggestion on that point. If any thing should happen to prevent your being with us, please furnish us with a letter to be read on the occasion, and make it as long as you choose; but we would much prefer to have you address us *viva voce*, in mass meeting.

We shall endeavor to have Ireland's benefactor, Father [Theobald] Mathew, with us on this joyous occasion, if his engagements will possibly allow him to do so.

Longing to see the day when not a slave shall clank his chains on the American soil, and the song of jubilee shall be heard on every Southern plantation, I remain, with great regard,

Yours, for universal freedom and happiness,

Wm. Lloyd Garrison.

Ralph Waldo Emerson.

ALS: R. W. Emerson Papers, Harvard College Library. This letter is published by courtesy of the Ralph Waldo Emerson Memorial Association.

1. A term derived from the location of Worcester in the center of the state of Massachusetts.

2. The cholera epidemic of 1849 was seen by many as a visitation from God in punishment for the sinfulness of the nation. Therefore, a fast day was declared, business suspended, and prayer meetings held. In addition to this national fast day, several states, including Massachusetts, issued supplementary proclamations. Some controversy arose over the efficacy of fasting and prayer as a remedy, since the poor who were most directly affected by cholera were also unlikely to attend special religious services. In many quarters the Fast Day was welcomed as a holiday; in New York the Long Island Railroad chartered four special trains to take people to the horse races in Brooklyn. (Charles E. Rosenberg, *The Cholera Years*, Chicago, 1962.)

The meeting at Worcester is given a full account in *The Liberator*, August 10, 1849. Of the possible participants mentioned in this letter only Father Mathew failed to attend. Both Parker and Emerson gave speeches which are printed in *The Liberator*, August 17, 1849.

2 7 2

TO THEOBALD MATHEW

BOSTON, July 26, 1849.

ESTEEMED FRIEND OF HUMANITY:

The anniversary of the most thrilling event of the nineteenth century, the abolition of slavery in the British West India islands, will be celebrated at Worcester, in this Commonwealth, on Friday, Aug. 3, commencing at 10 o'clock, A.M., under the auspices of the Massachusetts Anti-Slavery Society. In behalf of that Society, the undersigned are instructed to extend to you a cordial and an earnest invitation to be present, and to participate in the proceedings of the meeting, in such manner as may be most agreeable to your feelings. This they gladly now do; and, having no doubt of your heartfelt interest in this great event, and of your desire to see slavery every where abolished, on America, as well as on British soil, they trust that you will be able so to make your arrangements as vastly to enhance the pleasure of the occasion, by your quickening presence. The celebration is one in which all the friends of freedom may joyfully unite, without distinction of sect, party, or country. A grand mass meeting of the people is confidently anticipated at Worcester, and able and distinguished advocates of liberty have pledged themselves to be present.

In the year 1842, an '*Address from the people of Ireland to their countrymen and countrywomen in America,*' signed by Ireland's lamented champion, DANIEL O'CONNELL, YOURSELF, and *seventy thousand* other inhabitants of Ireland, was sent to this country, in which it was truly declared that 'Slavery is a sin against God and man — all who are not for it must be against it — none can be neutral;' and that 'it is in vain that American citizens attempt to conceal their own and their country's degradation under this withering curse.' Its final appeal was in the following emphatic language: — 'Irishmen and Irishwomen! *treat the colored people as your equals, as brethren.* By all your memories of Ireland, continue to love liberty — hate slavery — CLING BY THE ABOLITIONISTS — and in America, *you will do honor to the name of Ireland.*'

We deeply regret, that truth compels us to state, that the Address fell powerless on the ear and heart of the Irish population in this country; and while it urged them to exercise their moral and political power for the extension [1] of slavery, that power has been, and still is, wielded on the side of the oppressor, and against the oppressed. Religiously and politically, like the American people generally, they are in such relations to those who 'trade in slaves and the souls of men'[2] as to sanction that horrible traffic, and to prolong the unmitigated servitude of three millions of the native-born inhabitants of the American Union. This melancholy and undeniable fact will cause you much grief; and we doubt not, it will be a powerful incentive to you, to improve every suitable opportunity, while you remain in this country, to bear a clear and unequivocal testimony, both in public and in private, against the enslavement of any portion of the human family; and to tell your countrymen here again, in the words of the Address alluded to, 'America is cursed by Slavery! Never cease your efforts until perfect liberty be granted to every one of her inhabitants, the black man as well as the white man. Join with the Abolitionists every where: they are the only consistent advocates of liberty.'

It will be doubly gratifying to you to know that the Abolitionists in America are thoroughgoing teetotallers; and it would be not less so to learn, [(]what, alas! is not the fact,) that teetotallers are as uniformly Abolitionists.

Congratulating you on your safe arrival in this country, trusting that your mission of mercy will be crowned with unparalleled success, and assuring you of our sincere regard and heartfelt admiration, we remain, dear sir,

In behalf of three millions of Slaves,

Yours, for universal liberty and sobriety,

WM. LLOYD GARRISON,
FRANCIS JACKSON,
WENDELL PHILLIPS,
H. I. BOWDITCH,

} *Committee.*

REV. THEOBALD MATHEW.

Printed: *The Liberator*, August 10, 1849; also printed in *Life*, III, 248–250.

1. An obvious misprint for "extermination"; so corrected in the copy printed in *Life*.
2. A reference to Revelation 18:13.

273

TO CHARLES SUMNER

Boston, July 27, 1849.

Dear Sir:

You will see, by the advertisement in the accompanying Liberator,[1] that the most thrilling event of the nineteenth century, the entire abolition of British West India slavery, and the consequent liberation of eight hundred thousand bondmen, is to be celebrated at Worcester, on Friday, August 3rd, by a mass meeting of the friends of freedom. It is the day which Pres. [Zachary] Taylor has appointed for a national fast, and we intend to give it a practical turn in regard to the great sin of our land. I am desired, by the Committee of Arrangements, to invite you to be present, and to address the meeting on the great occasion alluded to.[2] Hoping it will be in your power to do, I remain,

Yours, with much respect,

Wm. Lloyd Garrison.

Charles Sumner, Esq.

ALS: Charles Sumner Papers, Harvard College Library.

1. July 27, 1849.
2. Sumner was not able to be present at the celebration. He did, however, send a letter of regret, which was published in *The Liberator*, August 10, 1849.

---

2 7 4

TO SAMUEL MAY, JR.

Boston, July 28, 1849.

My Dear Friend May:

I thank you for your kind invitation to me, (including my "better-half,") to visit Leicester after the Anti-Slavery Pic Nic at Worcester, and shall be most happy to avail myself of the opportunity thus presented to partake of your hospitality, (so long and so frequently proffered,) and to address the people of L. on the subject of slavery, on Sunday evening, August 5th, according to your desire. In compliance with your suggestion, I will advertise the lecture in the next Liberator — only I know not at what time it will be most suitable or convenient to hold the meeting, (probably before dark, commencing at half past 5,) or in what hall. Should you have occasion to write again before our paper goes to press, you will please decide these points.[1]

We will endeavor to have the next Liberator mailed for Worcester county in season on Wednesday, as you suggest.

By all means, send us one or two hundred Posters for this city, if you are to have some printed (and there ought to be) for Worcester and the neighboring towns. I am thoroughly satisfied it is good economy to advertise such a meeting in a very extensive manner. Too much publicity cannot be given to it. If we should fail of securing a large attendance, for want of due notice, it would be a serious drawback upon the usefulness of the meeting. Ought not an advertisement (as brief as practicable) to be inserted in good season in each of the Worcester papers, in addition to the Posters?

The Republican [2] of this city shall not be overlooked.

I do not think the meeting at Worcester can be organized properly before half past 10 o'clock; but there will be no absolute necessity to wait for the arrival of the Boston special train, before completing the organization, and settling all preliminary matters.[3]

Mr. [Francis] Jackson and others wish me to preside on the occasion.[4] Of course, I will do so, if no other can be found willing to fill the gap; but I prefer some one else. I shall endeavor to leave Boston in the 7 o'clock train, so as to confer with you and other friends in good season.

Stephen C. Phillips has given Wendell [Phillips] some encouragement that he will attend, but there is as yet no absolute assurance on his part. I presume you have invited, in behalf of the Committee, John G. Palfrey and Charles Allen.[5] As for Father [Theobald] Mathew, he will not attend. Yesterday morning, Dr. [Henry I.] Bowditch and myself had an interview with him,[6] and handed him a letter of invitation to be present at the Jubilee; but he at once declined, and declared his intention, while he remained in this country, not to commit himself on the subject of slavery. He had as much as he can do — he said — to save men from the slavery of intemperance, without attempting any thing for the emancipation of the slaves in this country. Besides, he thought it would not be proper for him to meddle with the subject of slavery. He was opposed to slavery, and should never think of advocating it; *but*, — &c. &c. I will give you the particulars of the interview when I see you. I was not greatly disappointed. He will follow in the wake of the other clergymen who have come over to this country from England. How pitiable!

We are all agreed in opinion here, that it will be better to take the *City Hall* for the speeches, and let it be compactly filled. The electric effect will be much greater, and the speakers will be much better heard. Still, you and the friends in Worcester must determine this matter, as, under all the circumstances, you shall think best. Every thing will depend upon the state of the weather.

Mrs. Garrison is sorry that she will not be able to accompany me, (perhaps little Wendell will do so,) and desire to be kindly remembered to Mrs. May and yourself.

Yours, with high regard,

Wm. Lloyd Garrison.

Samuel May, Jr.

ALS: Garrison Papers, Boston Public Library. The final page of this letter consists of a note from Joshua T. Everett to May, approving Garrison's arrangements for the Worcester meeting and urging May to invite other Unitarian clergymen sympathetic to the cause.

1. According to an advertisement in *The Liberator*, August 3, 1849, Garrison was scheduled to speak in the Unitarian church in Leicester at 5:30 p.m.

2. At the date of Garrison's letter there were in Boston two papers of this name, a daily, which was to cease publication in November, and a semiweekly, published for about four years, beginning in 1846. (*ULN.*)

3. According to *The Liberator*, August 3, 1849, a special train had been chartered to carry the participants to Worcester. It was scheduled to depart from the Worcester Depot in Albany Street, Boston, on the morning of the third at 8:45 and was to return at 4 p.m. Fares were $1.00 round trip, children under twelve half price.

4. Garrison did preside.

5. There is no evidence in the account of the meeting in *The Liberator*, August 10, 1849, that either Stephen C. Phillips or Charles Allen attended, and Garrison prints a letter of regret from John G. Palfrey. Palfrey (1796–1881) was a unique combination of clergyman and politician. He had been the minister of the church in Brattle Square, Boston, as well as Dexter Professor of Sacred Literature at Harvard before becoming a member of the state legislature (1842–1843), secretary of the Commonwealth (1844–1848), and member of Congress (1847–1849). He was also a prolific writer of articles for the *North American Review* and its owner and editor between 1835 and 1843. Not only was he an abolitionist, but he had the distinction of having freed slaves he inherited from his father.

6. Recorded in *The Liberator*, August 10, 1849.

---

2 7 5

TO ELIZABETH PEASE

Boston, July 31, 1849.

My Dear Friend:

I am delighted at the thought, that the bearer of this may have an opportunity to become acquainted with you, and you with her. Two such women, I sincerely think, are rarely to be met with on earth. Without ceremony, let me introduce to you one of the most devoted in our anti-slavery circle in Boston and its vicinity, Mrs. Eliza Lee Follen, the accomplished widow of the deeply lamented Professor Charles Follen, whose untimely fate on his passage from New York to Boston, a few years since, by the burning of the steamer Lexington, you cannot have forgotten, and whose nobleness of character is quite familiar to you. Allied by birth and education to the higher circles of Boston, she long ago openly espoused the odious anti-slavery cause, and has gone through every trial in the spirit of a moral heroine, unshrinkingly, uncompromisingly. She is a woman of the largest humanity, of fine literary attainments, combining great gentleness and firmness, and alive to every thing that pertains to the cause of suffering humanity. I am sure you will greatly enjoy each other's society, should you be so fortunate as to meet; and she has a strong desire to see one whom she has so long esteemed and loved for her work's sake — i. e. Elizabeth Pease, of Darlington. I wish I could see her too!

Within the past year, the health of Mrs. Follen has been so much impaired, that it was feared by her friends that she could not long survive. She is now better; and it is hoped that a voyage across the Atlantic, and a change of climate, will completely restore her.

She expects to be absent from us some two or three years — spending most of the time in Germany, among the relatives and friends of her deceased hsuband. She will reside awhile in Paris, where she will enjoy the society of her very intimate friends, Mrs. [Maria W.] Chapman and her sister Miss [Caroline] Weston. She is accompanied by her only son, Charles Follen, who has just graduated with much credit at Harvard University, and who gives promise of being a son worthy of such rare parents; — also by her own sister, Miss Susan Cabot, an excellent and talented woman, and a faithful abolitionist.

Thus our anti-slavery circle is thinning continually, by a kind of colonization process. Who will go next, I will not attempt to surmise. William W. Brown left us a fortnight ago for England, and by this time is probably standing on British soil, acknowledged as a man. Success attend his mission! I insist upon it, Elizabeth, that you and some other friends are bound to come over and see us awhile, by way of reciprocity.[1] Only think how easy it is to glide across the Atlantic! In ten or twelve days from Liverpool, you may be in Boston; and is Boston not worth seeing? — to say nothing of other portions of our "great country." *When* you come, there will be many made glad by your presence, but no one more so than

Your faithful friend,

Wm. Lloyd Garrison.

Elizabeth Pease.

ALS: Garrison Papers, Boston Public Library.

1. Elizabeth Pease never visited the United States.

---

2 7 6

TO THEOBALD MATHEW

[September 7, 1849.]

SIR —

I would gladly commence this letter with some expressions of personal esteem and veneration for your character, could I do so

conscientiously or sincerely; but the position which you occupy respecting the greatest crime of the age, on the American soil, forbids
my doing so.

Though I am no longer your admirer, I am still your friend; and
never have you stood so much in need of a real friend as now. You
have done a foolish and wicked thing, and foolish and wicked men
are filled with delight. It will serve to increase the number of your
parasites and flatterers, and, alas! to blind the vision, pervert the
judgment, and injure the moral sense of many who claim to be the
friends of suffering humanity, but who, to shield you from censure
will sacrifice their regard for principle to their personal partiality.
Hence the greater is the necessity of my being true to you, where so
many will prove false. 'Faithful are the wounds of a friend.' [1] Claiming
to be such, I have nothing but wounds to give at present. These shall
be inflicted with equal tenderness and fidelity. Regard me as you
choose, I will 'nothing extenuate, nor set down aught in malice.' [2]

A month has elapsed since, as chairman of a committee appointed
by the Board of Managers of the Massachusetts Anti-Slavery Society,
I waited upon you, in behalf of the Board, to extend to you an invitation to be present at the celebration of British West India emancipation at Worcester. The facts pertaining to that interview are already
before the public. To the official letter of the Committee, which was
then put into your hands, and to which an answer was respectfully
requested, you have made no reply. It was due, therefore, to the friends
of the anti-slavery cause, on both sides of the Atlantic, to state publicly
the substance of the conversation between us at the interview alluded
to. I did so, at the Worcester meeting, and through the medium of
the Liberator, as nearly *verbatim* as I could remember. It is a singular
fact, that nearly every journal that has come to your defence has
affected to doubt the accuracy of the report, while it has professed to
regard all that you are declared to have uttered as sagacious and
commendable! Why doubt that, which, instead of being unworthy of
you, only redounds to your credit? Does not the expression of such a
doubt fairly imply, that even your eulogists are conscious that the
report places you in an unenviable position? But I have not heard —
the public has not heard — either directly or indirectly, that you have
any complaint to make of that report, or that you are prepared to
deny its substantial accuracy. Your silence bears witness that I have
not misrepresented you; that silence you would break, if you could,
by impugning my statements. You certainly know how to write; but
you seem determined not even to make your mark on paper, lest it
should commit you 'in black and white' on this subject. Policy like this
may be crowned with temporary success, but its end is disaster and
disgrace.

The motives which actuated the long-tried friends of the slaves in extending to you such an invitation were pure and praise-worthy, and need no defence. In Ireland, you professed to sympathise with the American slave; you addressed your countrymen here in earnest and emphatic language, calling upon them by the most sacred considerations, to use their moral and political power for the abolition of slavery, and to join the abolitionists as the only true friends of freedom in the United States. What less, as a mark of their gratitude, respect and veneration, could the abolitionists do, on your arrival here, than to thank you for the noble testimony borne by you at home against American slavery, and to signify to you the importance of your renewing that testimony on this side of the Atlantic? If they had not done so, would not their conduct have excited surprise and animadversion on the part of the SEVENTY THOUSAND who signed the Irish Address? — not to mention the millions of hearts that are beating warmly for liberty in Ireland. If they had not done so, they could not easily have vindicated themselves from the charge of personal indifference or unpardonable forgetfulness. They purposely selected for you, *as the most unexceptionable occasion that could be presented during your sojourn in this country*, on which to express your feelings and sentiments on the subject of slavery, the anniversary of a world-thrilling event, the simultaneous emancipation of eight hundred thousand slaves in the British West India islands — an event in which it was believed you would take special pride and interest as a Briton, as the most glorious recorded on the page of British history.

In extending to you an invitation to attend an anti-slavery celebration, the friends of the slave evinced the same courtesy to you as they had shown to other distinguished transatlantic visitors. They acted neither invidiously nor singularly in this respect. Religious deputations have been repeatedly sent to this country from England, for various objects; and these have all been tested in a similar manner as to their anti-slavery principles, and in every instance they have exhibited a treacherous and cowardly spirit. At home, where it was reputable to be an abolitionist, they could declaim with zeal and fervor against slavery, and all its abettors. As soon as they landed on these shores, where it is highly disreputable to be an abolitionist, they united with the traducers and persecutors of the uncompromising advocates of emancipation. Thus they were proved to be men destitute of principle, guided by a selfish expediency, 'loving the praises of men more than the praise of God.'[3] For instance — in 1835, the Rev. Dr. Cox and the Rev. Dr. Hoby were deputed by the Baptist Association in England to visit this country, on a special mission to their American Baptist brethren.[4] They were conspicuous for their anti-slavery zeal at home; hence, they were cordially invited by the Executive Committee * of the American Anti-Slavery Society to attend its anniversary meeting in New York. They anticipated you in recreancy, but surpassed you in courtesy, for they sent a written reply to the letter of invitation — you did not. And how did they excuse themselves for not appearing on the anti-slavery platform, and bearing a strong Christian testimony against 'the sum of all villanies'? [5] They said they 'must be understood to assume a position of NEUTRALITY,' because of the 'political bearings' of the question! [6] 'It was impossible not to perceive,' they said, 'that three parties were equally eager on the subject, — the Anti-Slavery Society, their opponents, and the colonizationists' !!!

they were 'placed in a position of delicacy and difficulty' — if they had appeared at the anti-slavery meeting, 'would the special purpose of their mission, a high, a holy, and *a paramount one*, have been accomplished, or nullified? Would American and British Christians have been united in holy fellowship, or separated in mutual exasperation? Would it have been acting in the spirit of martyrdom, or in the spirit of madness?' This was the precise language of their defence. Here you have a mirror, in which you may see your own features clearly reflected; for do you not attempt to justify yourself in a similar way? What specimens of Christian ingenuousness and honesty!

But the baseness of these men did not begin or end with making out for themselves a non-committal course of policy, respecting a system of inconceivable impieties and horrors: they proceeded to denounce the abolitionist, and to apologize for the slaveholder. Their 'neutrality' amounted to positive hostility to the American Anti-Slavery Society. They not only refused to give the least countenance to the philanthropic mission of that gifted, eloquent and faithful champion of impartial liberty, GEORGE THOMPSON, their own countryman, (now a member of the British Parliament,) at that very time execrated, persecuted, and hunted for his life by the bloodhounds of slavery, but they accused him of 'employing the language of fierce invective — and invective against whom? not merely against slaveholders, but against men of elevated Christian character, zealous in promoting every good work, whose names will be immortalized when those of their calumniators will be extinct'!! They deepened the popular odium against that great advocate of freedom by declaring — 'An anti-slavery agent from Great Britain might have pursued a course which would have been wise, and must have been beneficial; which would have tended to unite the good of all classes and parties;

* Of whom Elizur Wright, the present editor of the Boston Chronotype, was a member. [7]

which would have been honorable to Britain, and felicitous for America. That course has unhappily not been pursued.' And these treacherous stabs were given by men who did not dare to open their lips publicly for the liberation of the slave!

Of course, they won for themselves — what you are winning — the smiles, the praises, the flatteries of all that was heartless, unprincipled, inhuman, apostate and tryannical in the land; and they roused up against the abolitionists new elements of hatred and vengeance. As in your case, the newspapers teemed with the vilest abuse of those who had had the 'insolence' to invite Messrs. Cox and Hoby to attend the anti-slavery anniversary; and from that time Mr. Thompson lectured at the imminent peril of his life, and abolitionists were mobbed from one end of the country to the other! The year 1835 was the most memorable of any that has occured for pro-slavery violence and lawlessness; and that was the year made equally memorable by the presence and recreancy of those English delegates. How much of this violence and lawlessness will be manifested during your sojourn here remains to be seen; but no small amount, if 'coming events cast their shadows before' [8] — if the furious and malevolent assaults of pro-slavery and doubly apostate journals should be as ferociously seconded by the mob now as they were in 1835.

What Messrs. Cox and Hoby gained in America by their truckling policy, they lost in England. At home, their craven conduct excited extreme disgust and intense indignation among all classes, even among their own religious denomination. To make out a case of justification — at least, to shield themselves in some measure from the storm of moral indignation that burst upon them — they obtained the certificates of such men as the Rev. Dr. Welch and the Rev. Dr. Sprague of Albany, Rev. Dr. Sharp and the Rev. Mr. Malcom of Boston, (men notorious for giving no countenance to the anti-slavery movement,) [9] testifying to the wisdom and excellence of their course in regard to the 'difficult and delicate question of slavery'! Most competent, most disinterested witnesses these! So, in like manner, and for a similar purpose, you can, on your return to Ireland, read the testimonials of the Catholic Observer, the Boston Pilot, the Boston Herald, the Chronotype, *et id genus omne!* [10]

The Rev. Dr. Welch testified as to the mission of Messrs. Cox and Hoby — 'There has been nothing, in my judgment, more salutary and important than the influence of your discreet and prudent example upon this subject of all-absorbing and exciting interest throughout the land' — 'it has secured to you the approbation, and raised you high in the esteem of the wise and good [i. e., the Southern slaveholders and their Northern abettors] of all parties. Your refusal to enter upon the arena of public debate, upon a subject in the highest degree exciting to the community, in which you appeared in the high character of teachers of righteousness, manifested a decision of character, and displayed a *consistency of conduct* (!!) worthy of your stations as *representatives of the English churches*, and highly honorable to yourselves and country, in the view of every reflecting man' — 'the American church ["the bulwark of slavery"] is deeply indebted to you; had you adopted a different course, the consequences would have been most unhappy to the church; whatever may be the results of your course upon your own interests, [in refusing to plead for the oppressed,] it has been most beneficial upon the interests of Zion, (!!) and has been eminently calculated to reflect honor upon our denomination'!! Dr. Welch accompanied this disgusting cant with an astounding falsehood. He said, 'Slavery is deprecated and lamented in every part of the Union . . . Our statesmen seek the means of wiping out this foul blot from our national escutcheon; the wisdom of our legislators, and the pens of our scribes, and the prayers of our churches, and the ministry of our divines, *have long been directed to this subject,* (!!) but it is still to us a question as difficult as it is distressing.'

The Rev. Dr. Sprague wrote to them, after their return home, as follows: — Of all the individuals I have ever heard speak of the course you took at New York, there has been but one who has not most decidedly approved it, and he one of George Thompson's most intimate friends. I hope you will be able to satisfy our English brethren, that the American Christians are not the friends of slavery'!! O, no! not the friends of slavery, though buying, selling and holding slaves *ad libitum*, and resisting every effort for their deliverance! Not the friends of slavery, though if the English delegates had lifted up their voices against it, they would have ruined their mission, if not jeoparded their lives!

The Rev. Dr. Sharp, of Boston, the inflexible enemy of the anti-slavery cause from its inception, and the defender of slaveholding upon Bible authority, testified in their behalf as follows: — 'Your prudence in not intermeddling with topics of a secular (!) and political (!) character, [meaning the immoral, brutal, and impious system of slavery,] when strongly urged to do so, has won for you the esteem of the most learned, upright, (!) philanthropic, (!!) and pious (!!!) men of every Christian denomination in the land . . . Such visits, *so conducted*, [discarding and not encouraging the abolitionists,] the American Baptist churches will ever hail with joy, and I trust will ever be ready to reciprocate'!

The testimony of the Rev. Howard Malcom was as follows: — 'Your position and movements in regard to the much vexed question of slavery, have been truly dignified and fortunate'! This trimmer was recently compelled to resign the Presidency of Georgetown College, a Baptist institution in Kentucky,[11] because he was so 'ultra' as to vote at the late election for the abolition of slavery in that State, 'half way between now and never'! Verily, he has his reward.

The Rev. S. H. Cone,[12] the President of the Baptist Triennial Convention, certified as follows: — 'The course they (Drs. Cox and Hoby) have pursued while in this country, in reference to the abolition question, was not only dictated by sound discretion, but was in perfect accordance with the views of the Baptist General Convention, [composed of Southern man-stealers and their Northern allies,] to which body they came as delegates. Any other course would have *completely defeated the object of their visit to the American churches*, and would have involved them in constant personal embarrassment. Did Englishmen know that the question, as now presented, is equivalent to the question — 'Shall the Union be dissolved?' they would see that foreigners could not safely enter upon its discussion.' A system which nullifies all the commands of the Decalogue, all the precepts of Jesus, and turns millions of the rational creatures of God into chattels personal, 'to all intents, constructions and purposes whatsoever,' must not be discussed by professed ministers of Christ from England, as it would endanger the American Union!

This is a long reference, but a most pertinent and instructive reminiscence. These, Father Mathew, were your recreant predecessors; in their footsteps you seem resolved to tread; their defence is yours, *their defenders yours*, AND THEIR REPROVERS YOURS. From Bishop Hughes [13] and the whole body of Catholic priests in this country, you can obtain as strong testimonials to the wisdom of your course, in turning your back to the friends of the down-trodden slave, as were procured by Drs. Cox and Hoby from the time-serving clergy of their particular sect. But these, instead of saving your reputation, will certainly serve to stain it with dishonor; purchased as they will be at the expense of consistency, honesty, justice, humanity!

I conclude this letter with the eloquent rebuke administered to the Rev. Dr. Cox, at the anniversary meeting of the American Anti-Slavery Society to which he had been invited, but which he refused to attend, by GEORGE THOMPSON, the consistent, dauntless and indefatigable opponent of injustice and crime on both sides of the Atlantic: —

'Sir, in this very fact, I behold a new proof of the power, of the omnipotence of slavery. By its torpedo touch, a man has been struck dumb, who was eloquent in England on the side of its opposers. What! is it come to this? Shall he or shall I advocate the cause of emancipation, of immediate emancipation, only because we are Englishmen? Perish the thought! Before I can entertain such an idea, I must be recreant to all the principles of the Bible, — to all the claims of truth, of honor, of humanity! No, sir: if man is not the same in every latitude; if he would advocate a cause with eloquence and ardor in Exeter Hall, in the midst of admiring thousands, but because he is in America, can close his lips, and desert the cause he once espoused, I denounce, I abjure him! Let him carry his philanthropy home again; there let him display it in the loftiest or the tenderest strains; but never let him step his foot abroad, until he is prepared to show to the world that he is the friend of his kind!" [14]

This rebuke is far more applicable to Theobald Mathew in 1849, than it was to Dr. F. A. Cox in 1835. He came to this country in a sectarian capacity, for a sectarian purpose, as a Baptist to Baptists; while you are here, not for the advantage of the Catholic Church, not as a sectarian, but as a philanthropist, consecrated to the sacred cause of suffering humanity, without regard to religious belief or national origin. And yet you will not utter a word in behalf of three millions of perishing slaves, lest it should give offence to the traffickers in human flesh! O, far heavier is the condemnation you deserve!

Your faithful friend,

WM. LLOYD GARRISON.

Printed: *The Liberator*, September 7, 1849; partly printed in *Life*, III, 255–256.

This is the first of a series of five letters to Father Mathew which were published in *The Liberator* in the fall of 1849. For the invitation which began the controversy see Garrison's letter to Theobald Mathew, July 26, 1849.

1. Proverbs 27:6.
2. Shakespeare, *Othello*, V, ii, 342–343.
3. Garrison refers to John 12:43.
4. Francis Augustus Cox (1783–1853) was a Baptist minister and graduate of the University of Edinburgh. Ordained in 1805, in 1809 he helped establish the *Baptist Magazine*. He is especially remembered for his active role in founding the University of London. A prolific author, he served as minister at Hackney, a district near Bethnal Green in London, for forty-two years.

James Hoby (1788–1871) had held Baptist pastorates in several British towns, including Aberdeen, Birmingham, Weymouth, and Twickenham. (Frederick B. Tolles, ed., *Slavery and "the Woman Question,"* Supplement No. 23 to the *Journal of the Friends' Historical Society*, Haverford, Pa., and London, 1952.)

Garrison mistakes the "Baptist Association in England" for the English Baptist Union, the major organization of Baptists in Great Britain and Ireland. Organized in 1813, the union was active in education and missionary work, at the same time recognizing the autonomy of individual congregations. (Thomas Armitage, *A History of the Baptists*, New York, 1892.)

5. Garrison refers to John Wesley, *Journal*, February 12, 1772, "That execrable sum of all villanies, commonly called the Slave Trade." (See *Journal*, New York, 1906, III, 461.)
6. The quotations "must be understood to assume a position of neutrality" and "political bearings" are from a letter from Francis Augustus Cox to the American Anti-Slavery Society dated May 12, 1835, and published in *The*

Liberator, May 23, 1835. The source of the other quotations attributed to Cox and Hoby has not been determined.

7. Elizur Wright (1804–1885) was one of the most prominent members of the New York group of moderate abolitionists. In 1833 he was corresponding secretary of the American Anti-Slavery Society. Between 1835 and 1837 he edited the *Quarterly Anti-Slavery Magazine* as well as some of the society's tracts. After the schism of 1839–1840, he edited the short-lived *Massachusetts Abolitionist* and between 1846 and 1850 the Boston *Weekly Chronotype*.

8. Thomas Campbell, "Lochiel's Warning," line 56.

9. Bartholomew T. Welch (1794–1870) was minister of Emmanuel Baptist Church in Albany from 1827 to 1848, at which time he assumed the pastorate of the Pierpont Street Church in Brooklyn. For seventeen years he was president of the American and Foreign Bible Society and was instrumental in founding the Albany Rural Cemetery. (The Reverend Henry M. King, "Historical Address," in *Services and Sermon Commemorating the Seventy-fifth Anniversary of Emmanuel Baptist Church . . .* , Albany, 1909, pp. 12–17.)

William Buell Sprague (1795–1876), clergyman, biographer, and collector of letters and autographs, was pastor of the Second Presbyterian Church in Albany from 1829 to 1869. Born in Connecticut, he was graduated from Yale in 1815 and from Princeton Theological Seminary in 1819. He wrote prolifically, his best-known work being *Annals of the American Pulpit* (1857–1869), and he edited the *Spectator*, a local paper, in 1845.

Daniel Sharp (1783–1853) served the Third Baptist Church (later Charles Street Church) in Boston from 1812 until his death. He was president of the American Baptist Foreign Mission Society and an overseer of Harvard.

Howard Malcom (1799–1879) was a Baptist clergyman who spent three years as a missionary in India, Burma, and China. After 1840 he became president of several educational and philanthropic institutions, among them Georgetown College in Kentucky, Lewisburg University (now Bucknell), and Hahnemann Medical College.

10. The Boston *Catholic Observer* began publication on January 16, 1847, and ceased sometime in 1849. It was owned by Denis and James Sadlier, who also published *Sadlier's Catholic Dictionary* and other religious works. (Letter to the editor from Ruth D. Bell, researcher, April 30, 1971.) Two Boston papers were named *Herald*, a daily founded in 1846 and a weekly founded in 1848. (*ULN.*) Garrison could be referring to either or both. The other newspapers he mentions have been previously identified.

11. Located in Georgetown and founded in 1829. (Georgetown College *Bulletin*, 1970–1971.)

12. Spencer Houghton Cone (1785–1855) was an eminent Baptist preacher. From 1841 until his death he was pastor of the First Baptist Church of New York City. From 1832 to 1841 he served as president of the Baptist General Convention. He was also a founder and head of the American and Foreign Bible Society. The Baptist Triennial Convention is another name for the Baptist General Convention for Foreign Missions, a representative body which shaped denominational activities at home and abroad. It was founded in 1814 and its board was located in Boston. (Armitage, *A History of the Baptists*.)

13. John Joseph Hughes (1797–1864) was a native of Ireland who in 1842 became bishop of New York. Although he hated slavery he did not support the Irish Address and was doubtful that emancipation would be an unmixed blessing for the slaves. During the Civil War, however, he supported the Union and became one of President Lincoln's personal agents, with authority to present the northern cause in foreign countries.

14. Garrison reproduces with fair accuracy part of the speech George Thompson delivered at the American Anti-Slavery Society Convention in 1835. The speech is printed in *The Liberator*, May 23, 1835.

2 7 7

TO THEOBALD MATHEW

[September 14, 1849.]

SIR —

Every thing seems to go prosperously with you. Whether in city or village, your reception is marked by a pomp and an enthusiasm that appear to indicate a millenium of virtue. Elegant carriages, drawn by spirited steeds, are prepared for your reception — processions are formed, with 'badges, batons and banners' — the air is filled with acclamations — your pathway is literally strewed with flowers. For a moral reformer, you are certainly 'in luck.' With the exception of a small and despised band of 'fanatics, madmen, and disorganizers,' who are stiff and stubborn in their advocacy of the hateful cause of negro emancipation, all classes are vociferously shouting your praises, and eagerly pressing forward to do you homage. Surely, this is a proof of a thorough reformatory spirit on your part! Surely, the declaration of Jesus, 'Wo unto you when all mean speak well of you,'[1] is not applicable in a land so 'free and glorious' as you are pleased to style this slavery-cursed republic! Be not deceived: 'all is not gold that glistens.'[2] The popular idolatry which is paid to you is not the evidence of any real reverence for your character, any solid appreciation of virtue, any vital interest in the success of the temperance enterprise: far otherwise. Like every other species of idolatry, it is blind, selfish, accommodating, criminal. It is true, there are those who sincerely appreciate your labors in Ireland, and who welcomed you to these shores as an uncompromising philanthropist; but their admiration is materially lessened, by perceiving that you have no higher law than that of public sentiment — that you are actuated by worldly policy, rather than by Christian principle.

You are here in a cause which is not only reputable, but popular. In Ireland, it never cost you any thing in character as a priest, or subjected you to any thing like general opprobrium or religious persecution; hence, even at home, your moral heroism was not severely tested. In this country, the time has been when to advocate teetotalism as a moral duty, and to pronounce the traffic in ardent spirits an immoral act, was deemed slanderous and fanatical in the extreme. That time I have some reason to remember, for it was then that my editorial espousal of the cause subjected me to the ridicule and denunication of the respectable, the influential, and the godly. It is twenty-two years since I became the public advocate of total abstinence, and maintained the proposition that 'Moderate drinking is the downhill road to intemperance and drunkenness.'[3] There was scarcely a pulpit or press in the land, at that time, that dared openly and unequivocally to endorse the sentiment. But 'the offence of the cross'[4] has ceased, and to be a temperance lecturer is no longer to incur the displeasure of the church or clergy, nor to subject one to insult and calumny from reputable sources. In the flood-tide of the popularity of this beneficent cause, you visit these shores, assured that you would have nothing more formidable to encounter than smiles and caresses, plaudits and benedictions; that you would be feasted and flattered, honored and rewarded, lauded and canonized; that 'no stone of stumbling, no rock of offence,'[5] would be encountered in your capacity as a friend of temperance. Adhering, therefore, to this one topic — refusing to commit yourself in favor of any other cause, however righteous, if unpopular — returning compliment for compliment, admiration for admiration, congratulation for congratulation — it is not possible for you to display any moral intrepidity or virtuous disinterestedness. Nay, not to speak out, even rarely or incidentally, against the sin of sins, of which this nation is guilty — to move about with a padlock on your lips, touching any and every question not reputably sustained in the community — is 'proof as strong as holy writ'[6] that your philanthropy is of a superficial and sentimental quality, that you are 'a coward on instinct,'[7] that you love the praises of men more than the praise of God,[8] that your regard for what is popular is stronger than your trust in the truth. Greeted with the cheers of the multitude, and overwhelmed with flattering encomiums, you can have no trial of your virtue until you venture to arraign and denounce some cherished sin of the nation; and that you are resolved not to do, on the miserable plea that a just regard for the cause of temperance requires you to be deaf, and dumb, and blind, to every thing which has not the sanction of public opinion.

Is there any unsoundness in this reasoning? any thing unjust in this conclusion? Honored and caressed as you are, do you not see that a powerful temptation is constantly held out to you not to disturb this 'era of good feelings' by any 'imprudent' avowal of unpopular sentiments?[9] It is quite certain that your compromise of principle and profound silence on the subject of slavery will greatly increase your popularity here, and cause alike fashionable wine-bibbers and the frequenters of the dram-shops to drink to 'the health of Father Mathew'; but will all this either nourish your virtue or strengthen your piety — either secure for you the approval of a good conscience, or the verdict of an impartial posterity?

Across the Atlantic, the existence of slavery in this boasted land of liberty calls forth universal astonishment and condemnation. He who denounces it in the strongest terms receives the loudest responses in any public meeting. There the American abolitionist is applauded an[d] honored; there the American slave is hailed as 'a man and a brother.' You find quite another state of things here. In England, Queen Victoria is an abolitionist, and Prince Albert can preside over an anti-slavery meeting in Exeter Hall, and the most distinguished statesmen and divines are marshalled on the side of immediate emancipation. In America, for the first time, you breathe in a pro-slavery atmosphere; you are surrounded by the foes of justice and humanity, though audaciously claiming to be Christians and republicans; all that is reputedly pious, honorable, and really influential, you see is arrayed against the abolitionists. You discover that those who are consecrating their time, means and talents to the overthrow of slavery, and whose principles and sentiments are those of WILBERFORCE and CLARKSON, O'CONNELL and BUXTON, — nay, your own, *in Ireland*, — are without political strength, and branded with the religious stigma of 'infidelity' — hooted at, maligned, and bitterly opposed by all classes, from the most refined to the most vulgar. The American Protestant Church and the American Catholic Church, with the great body of the Protestant and Catholic clergy, (especially of the latter,) agree most harmoniously in principle and practice as to their views of slavery, and leave no weapon of violence or falsehood untried to defend it from assault. Not a Catholic priest, not a Catholic journal, can be found in this great country, pleading for the liberation of the enslaved; on the contrary, they most heartily stigmatize the abolitionists and all their movements. Of the multitudes who are crowding around you, pretending to feel the deepest solicitude for the success of the cause in which you are engaged, nine-tenths would sooner see the slaves expatriated from this country to Africa, or kept in their chains forever, than to have them liberated and admitted to equal rights and privileges here.

It is under such circumstances that you are asked to indicate your abhorrence of slavery, to express your sympathy with the struggling friends of freedom, to renew your anti-slavery appeal to the millions of your countrymen who are here the veriest tools of the Slave Power, and among the most inimical to the colored population. You hesitate, falter, refuse! Not a word will you utter, calculated to offend American prejudice or tyranny! Your excuse — the excuse of your defenders — is, a jealous regard for the success of your temperance mission! Of this, I shall have more to say in a subsequent letter. The only remark I shall now make is, the excuse is not even plausible — it can hardly be sincere — it reduces moral accountability to a single point. A careful examination of all the facts in the case authorizes the conclusion, that if you had found the anti-slavery cause as popular as you have found the temperance, you would have attended the Worcester celebration with the utmost pleasure and alacrity, or, at least, sent a civil reply to a courteous invitation. It also justifies the conviction, that if the temperance cause were now struggling against wind and tide, instead of having them both in its favor, in this country — if the religious and respectable were now as strongly arrayed against it as they were twenty years ago — you would not be here to advocate the odious and proscribed cause.

Well, you seem to have made up your mind to remain dumb in regard to the afflictions and wrongs, the claims and supplications of three millions of manacled slaves, 'without God and without hope in the world.' [10] Slaveholders and slave-drivers at the South, and their abettors and defenders at the North, are greatly rejoiced, and find in your conduct a fresh occasion to pour their vials of fury upon the heads of the hated abolitionists. They now will delight to do you honor, and verily you have your reward! For this act of inhumanity and injustice, which you have committed by the substitution of expediency for principle, remember that retribution is certain, in despite of the buzzes of the crowd, or the blandishments of the affluent. In the language of another —

'One strong thing I find here below; the just thing, the true thing. My friend, if thou hadst all the artillery of Woolwich thundering at thy back in support of an unjust thing, and infinite bonfires invisibly waiting ahead of thee, to blaze centuries long for the victory on behalf of it, I would advise thee to call halt; to fling down thy baton, and say, 'In God's name, No!' Thy 'success'? What will thy success amount to? If the thing is unjust, thou has not succeeded; no, though bonfires blaze from North to South, and bells ring, and editors write leading articles, and the just thing lie trampled out of sight to all mortal eyes, an abolished and annihilated thing.' [11]

To shield you from censure, your defenders declare that you have a specific object in view — the promotion of temperance, especially among your own countrymen — from which it is quite outrageous to ask you to be diverted, even for a moment, to aid the noblest cause that ever enlisted the sympathies of the human soul. You are complimented, on all sides, for resolving to know nothing, say nothing, do nothing, except on the subject of temperance, which, it is declared, is enough to exhaust your strength and fully to absorb your time. The acme of impudence is reached by your eulogists in denouncing me, in the same breath, for seeing but one object, having but one idea, and making the liberation of the slave the one great object of my life! So that what in you excites their highest approval and admiration, in me fills them with extreme disgust and righteous displeasure! How just, impartial, magnanimous is such a spirit! — Says the Boston Pilot — 'Father Mathew sagaciously and properly refused, saying that his own slavery-abolitionism was enough for his powers.' Says the same journel — 'Why does Mr. Garrison suppose that the slavery of the American blacks is the only great evil, or devil, to be cast out of modern civilization? Why do his sympathies run rabid *in one direction?*' [12] Says the Catholic Observer — 'Father Mathew sees before him a good work to be done, for the individual and the race, and he will not swerve from the path thus marked out for him.' Says the same journal — 'Mr. Garrison's brain can contain but one idea; and to realize that idea, he would not hesitate to overthrow every thing that exists; for him the abolition of slavery is the only good to be done on earth.' [13] Says the Chronotype, while complimenting you for having but one idea — 'Garrison is stone blind on the inside; and he is so far-sighted on the outside, that he can hardly see any thing this side of the slave States.' [14] Said the Boston Herald — 'Father Mathew replied in the following excellent words: "I have as much as I can do to save men from the slavery of intemperance, without attempting the overthrow of any other kind of slavery." Says the same filthy sheet — 'Garrison knows nothing but abolitionism — thinks, speaks, dreams of nothing else.' [15] And so on to the end of the list. All this is highly consistent — is it not? What renders it particularly ludicrous and audacious is the fact, that you allow your mind no scope as to other reforms, while I have never hesitated to countenance and aid a great variety, comprehending the rights and interests of the whole human family. I have not hesitated to grapple with any system of iniquity, however gigantic or hoary, whether pertaining to the Church or the State. I am constantly stigmatized as an 'anti-church and ministry, anti-sabbath, woman's rights, non-resistance, no-government man,' aside from the odium that is heaped upon me as an abolitionist. This implies something of a discursive spirit of reform! Years ago, on this subject, I publicly said —

Doubtless, some even in the anti-slavery ranks will be offended, because I exercise this freedom — and because, as they may plausibly contend, I shall thereby injure the abolition cause. My first reply is, that in pleading for universal liberty, I cannot consent to be bound; and I ask, why am I obligated to suppress my views on all subjects, except the abolition of slavery, any more than a Methodist abolition brother is bound to be silent respecting Methodism, or a Baptist respecting the doctrine of baptism? I enter my solemn protest against the absurd conclusion, that, inasmuch as my attention and labors have been specially directed to the overthrow of slavery, therefore I have vacated my right to avow my sentiments on other subjects; and that, whenever these sentiments are uttered, they are only an exposition of the creed of abolitionists.

My second reply is, that my anxiety for the emancipation of my enslaved countrymen is continual, earnest, intense; but it is not, it ought not to be, so strong as to make me both blind and dumb to all other abuses and impositions. In assailing spiritual despotism, no injury to the natural rights of man must necessarily follow. Were it not that American slavery is upheld and sanctioned by the American church, that vast system of pollution and blood would cease to exist. How, then, can it be urged, that by exposing the abominations which take shelter in the very bosom of the church, I shall retard the progress of the anti-slavery cause? [16]

So much for my being swallowed up in the 'one idea' of anti-slavery!

Yours, to effect a world-wide reform,

WM. LLOYD GARRISON.

Printed: *The Liberator*, September 14, 1849; partly printed in *Life*, III, 256–257.

1. Luke 6:26, with the omission of the word "shall" before "speak."
2. Garrison reverses and slightly misquotes Shakespeare, *The Merchant of Venice*, II, vii, 65.
3. Garrison quotes the motto of the *National Philanthropist*, devised for the paper by William Collier, the founder and first editor.
4. Galatians 5:11.
5. An adaptation of Isaiah 8:14.
6. A slight misquotation of Shakespeare, *Othello*, III, iii, 323–324.
7. Shakespeare, *1 Henry IV*, II, iv, 301–302.
8. John 12:43.
9. The phrase "era of good feeling" refers to the two administrations of President Monroe (1817–1824), when there were practically no crucial political issues and but one party. In 1820 Monroe was reelected unanimously except for the vote of one elector. (*OHAP*, p. 400.)
10. Garrison reverses and slightly alters Ephesians 2:12.
11. This paragraph, which is quoted fairly accurately, appears in Thomas Carlyle, *Past and Present*, Book I, chapter II, "The Sphinx" (Boston, 1843), p. 11.
12. The quotation from the Boston *Pilot* is taken from an article reprinted in *The Liberator*, August 31, 1849. In this letter Garrison is reasonably accurate in all of his quotations from newspaper articles.
13. Garrison quotes from an article from the Boston *Catholic Observer* reprinted in *The Liberator*, August 24, 1849.
14. Garrison quotes from an article from the Boston *Chronotype* reprinted in *The Liberator*, August 24, 1849.
15. Garrison quotes from an article from the Boston *Herald* reprinted in *The Liberator*, August 24, 1849.
16. The editor regrets that extensive search through manuscript collections, through editorials in *The Liberator* and through speeches published in periodicals, in collections, and individually has not revealed the passage which Garrison quotes. It would seem likely that Garrison's complete public statement — probably a speech — was not published and has been preserved only in this letter.

2 7 8

TO THEOBALD MATHEW

[September 28, 1849.]

Sir —

The committee, by whom you were invited to join in the celebration of British West India Emancipation at Worcester, (as you were duly apprised at the time,) were appointed by the Board of Managers of the Massachusetts Anti-Slavery Society, and acted under special instructions. Of that committee, I was a member; and whatever praise or blame — blame there certainly was none — the act of extending this invitation to you merited, belonged as much to every one of my associates as to myself. It was neither a private nor a personal affair, but an official proceeding in behalf of the Pioneer Anti-Slavery Society in the United States.[1] The numerous ribald journals, North and South, that have rallied in your defence, — edited either by those who have openly apostatized from the cause of the slave, and repudiated every thing in the shape of moral principle, or by the consistent but unrelenting enemies of negro emancipation, — have artfully attempted to make the public believe that I acted on my own responsibility in this matter, and on my 'fierce hobby horse singled out and charged down upon the meek Irish missionary'! 'The whole act is Garrison's, and not that of [Francis] Jackson, Wendell Phillips, or Dr. [Henry I.] Bowditch — there was not so pointed a rebuff as such impudence demanded', says the apostate and venomous Chronotype. 'Garrison has had the audacity to visit Father Mathew, and make overtures to him,' says the polluted Herald. 'A most diabolical plot to cut short the useful mission of Father Mathew has been set on foot by Garrison, the abolitionist,' says the New York Morning Star. 'The notorious Wm. Lloyd Garrison, in his exclusive attachment to the *darker* side of philanthropy, has been doing his best to corner, if not to paralyze Father Mathew, in his benevolent purposes with regard to the Irish in America,' says the St. Louis Reveille.[2] Similar quotations might be multiplied indefinitely, but these must suffice. On my head, therefore, ten thousand vials of wrath and defamation are poured afresh from the four quarters of the land; whole dens of poisonous reptiles, of every size and hue, are stirred up, and endeavoring to sting me to death; all that is treacherous, base, brutal and murderous, is in full cry for my destruction, as in the earlier days of my anti-slavery labors. And for such an act!

My only complaint is, that this is doing me too much honor — putting to my credit much more than fairly belongs to me — exalting me to the disparagement of others, who are equally entitled to the same flattering distinction. It is an old trick of the enemy, whose folly and malignity are equally measureless. For twenty years, it has been my lot to stand as a target, at which every foul and every murderous missile has been sent, by a nation that is stained with blood, steeped in pollution, and 'laden with iniquity.' [3] In one half of the country, I am outlawed by the traffickers in human flesh, and a price is set on my head; in the other half, no man is so detested, calumniated, shunned, by those who are eager to 'strike hands with thieves and consent with adulterers.' [4] At the present time, these are your warmest admirers, your special eulogists, your stoutest defenders! Is this to your credit, and to my reproach? If you are not ashamed of your backers, I am not ashamed of my assailants. 'Instinct is a great matter' [5] — and instinctively whatever is treacherous in spirit, or apostate in conduct, or time-serving in character, or brutal in condition, or pharisaical in life, or tyrannical in power, or diabolical in purpose, rallies around you, avows its entire approval of your noncommittal policy on the subject of slavery, and ensures for you in all places a public reception all the more enthusiastic on account of the padlock you have voluntarily placed upon your lips. In view of facts like these, therefore — that you are now borne on the topmost wave of popularity, and that I am more dreaded, denounced and persecuted than any other living man in America — the following paragraph from the 'Catholic Observer' in this city is remarkably apposite! —

'☞ Some of our friends seem to be quite afflicted that the good Father Mathew should have been reviled by the Liberator, during his stay among us. We must confess that we almost rejoice at it. *Did not the Pharisees of old mock and insult the Baptist and the divine Redeemer himself!* Every work of God must meet with contradictions, and we rejoice that, in this instance, they have come from the Garrisonians. If the men of that tribe co-operated heartily, we would begin to fear that there was something wrong in the work itself.' [6]

That you have been 'reviled by the Liberator,' is a false accusation, though it be a 'catholic' one. It will be time enough to meet it seriously when you shall make it on your own responsibility.

'The Pharisees of old' — I need not inform you — were 'the wise and the prudent,' [7] the respectable and godly, the leaders of public sentiment, the enemies of reform, the guardians of old abuses, the devourers of widows' houses, the binders of heavy burdens, in their day: to them the praises of men were incomparably more valuable than the praise of God,[8] and therefore they mocked and insulted every one who sympathized with down-trodden humanity, or called for repentance and reformation. The cause which 'the divine Redeemer' espoused stood in relation to these, his crucifiers, precisely where the anti-slavery cause, in its integrity, now stands in relation to the same class, who are guilty of far greater crimes than their predecessors, and as eager to shed the blood of the true and good; whose hypocritical cry is the reiteration of the old one — 'This man is not of God; he keepeth not the Sabbath day' — 'he hath a devil' — 'release not this man, but Barabbas' — 'if we let this man alone, the people will believe on him' — 'away with him! crucify him! crucify him!' [9] There is a wonderful, not to say an exact, analogy between these two cases; and there is a legion of facts and occurrences all leading to the same end and to one conclusion, namely, that, in this country, a profession of faith in Jesus is an unmeaning act — is no proof of virtue, no exhibition of devotion, no evidence of genuine piety, no symptom of moral heroism — is a popular, fashionable, ceremonial act, and therefore is obsolete as a test of character; and that what Jesus was to the Jews, unmasking the scribes and pharisees, rebuking a corrupt church, and [re]proving an oppressive nation, the anti-slavery movement is to the people of the United States, demonstrating, with equal certainty, and even by stronger proof, that their religion is 'cruel, sensual, devilish,' [10] and their republicanism a sham. In the slaveholding States, it is a more perilous act to one's reputation, worldly interest, personal safety, and life itself, to be an outspoken abolitionist, than it was in Judea, eighteen hundred years ago, openly to espouse the cause of the despised Nazarine. In the non-slaveholding States, (falsely so called,) if the act is not as hazardous to life, it at least demands such sacrifices to be the uncompromising friend of the slave, that comparatively few are found able or willing to perform it. That the experience of the faithful abolitionists has been like that of the early disciples of Christ, in almost every particular, is certain. They have been cast out of the synagogues — accused of sedition and blasphemy — hunted for their lives — reviled, persecuted, defamed — made fools for the sake of Christ *in the person of the slave*, and a spectacle to the world, to angels, and to men; they have been in stripes, in imprisonments, in tumults, in labors, in watchings, in fastings; in journeyings often, in perils of robbers, in perils by their own countrymen, in perils in the city, in perils amongst false brethren — and made as the filth of the earth and the off-scouring of all things: in some instances, they have been called to lay down their lives as martyrs.[11] Behold the resemblance, identity, companionship!

'Once to every man and nation comes the moment to decide,
In the strife of Truth with Falsehood, for the good or evil side;

Some great cause, GOD'S NEW MESSIAH, offering each the bloom or
    blight,
Parts the goats upon the left hand, and the sheep upon the right,
And the choice goes by for ever 'twixt that darkness and that light.' [12]

Now for the 'Catholic Observer' to represent the abolitionists as
occupying the position of the Jewish Pharisees — of course, reputable,
powerful, at the head of society! — and you as another Jesus, despised,
hated, persecuted from city to city, and scarcely knowing where to
lay your head, (while the fact is, that you are engaged in a most
popular work, and are every where feasted and complimented by
'city authorities' and 'honorable men not a few,' [13] and also greeted
with loud applause by the multitude, and by an exhibition of fireworks,) — is in fact keenly satirical, and as the dullest vision may see
at a glance, diametrically at variance with all the facts in the case. As
the priestly editor of the Observer is not a teetotaller, it is possible
that an equal mixture of passion and alcohol may have caused this
singular reversal of parties and positions in his vision, and led to this
amusing optical delusion, while writing his article.[14]

What the Observer means to convey by its insinuations is, no doubt,
that the friends of the slave are hostile to the temperance movement!
Urge its Rev. editor to take the pledge, and to cease from his
calumnies. In the letter of invitation to which you have never had the
courtesy to reply, it was stated — 'It will be doubly gratifying to you
to know that *the abolitionists in America are thoroughgoing teetotallers,* and they trust that your mission of mercy will be crowned
with unparalleled success.' In my opinion, the cause in which you are
engaged is more indebted to them for its success and stability, than to
any other class of men; and, as teetotallers, they hailed your visit to
America with the utmost pleasure. You have never known any of
them, on visiting England, Scotland or Ireland, to shrink from giving
their public support to the cause of total abstinence, or to keep silent
in regard to it, lest they should diminish the warmth of their anti-
slavery reception. I think you would have estimated their sympathy
for suffering humanity at a very low rate indeed, if they had done
so. According to the Observer, however, you ought to suspect that
the cause which they sanction is an evil one; and as they are sturdy
teetotallers, you may find it necessary to abandon the temperance
enterprise for that reason, just as you have turned your back upon the
anti-slavery cause; in which case, your hollow admirer of the Observer
will, doubtless, be doubly gratified.

Among the many absurd things that have been said in the newspapers is, that the abolitionists were anxious to obtain your coun-

tenance, in order that they might gain in reputation by availing themselves of your present popularity! They are anxious, forsooth, to get along smoothly, and to conciliate the favor of a pro-slavery nation; — they who, in espousing the cause of the manacled slave, drew the sword, and threw away the scabbard [15] — who, in assailing the hosts of oppression, burnt the bridge over which they passed to meet them — who have avoided no sacrifice, shrunk from no peril, dreaded no opprobrium — who have cheerfully cut off the right hand, and plucked out the right eye,[16] rather than yield one jot or tittle [17] of principle — who have allowed neither sectarian ties nor party bonds, neither threats nor bribes, neither their regard for the State nor their reverence for the Church, to hold them back from demanding the Immediate abolition of slavery! They have never yet courted any man for the sake of his influence, nor resorted to any *ruse* to avoid popular odium; for their reliance is not on an arm of flesh,[18] and they know of no other policy except a faithful adherence to principle. Honored as you are, great as is your influence, they desired your co-operation as opportunity might offer among your pro-slavery countrymen, only as they invoke the aid of every philanthropic spirit to overthrow the most horrible system of oppression in the world.

As the case historically stands, you volunteered to assist the abolitionists, instead of their making overtures to you. In the anti-slavery address that you signed in 1842, in company with nineteen other Catholic priests and one Bishop, and sent over to this country, you solemnly invoked your countrymen in America to regard slavery as 'a sin against God — the most tremendous invasion of the natural, inalienable rights of man' — and declared that 'all who are not for it must be against it [19] — *none can be neutral*' — and called upon them to 'oppose it' by all the peaceful means in their power, and to 'join with the abolitionists every where, as the only consistent advocates of liberty.' [20] Most deeply do the friends of emancipation lament that, now you are on the American soil, you are too timid, or too unprincipled, to reiterate these sentiments in the ears of your countrymen; but it is for your sake — for the sake of those over whom you wield so potent an influence — for the sake of three millions of heart-broken slaves and their miserable posterity — and not for any selfish considerations.

The Boston 'Bee' [21] endeavors to use its sting for your benefit, and to my detriment, as follows: —

'W. L. Garrison, the notorious abolitionist, is denouncing Father Mathew, because the Rev. Father will not, during his stay in this country, enlist in the cause of abolition. If Garrison's face were as black as his heart, it would be impossible to tell him from his friends.' [22]

My 'friends,' it is conceded, are black — the chattelized, fettered, stricken slaves, and the nominally colored population, who are yet a proscribed and injured people. What higher panegyric could be desired or bestowed on any man? Yes, they *are* my friends — and proud am I to be identified with them by their enemies, and recognized as their unflinching advocate! The blackness of my heart is simply my absolute fidelity to their cause, under all circumstances. Observe — the Bee says they are *my* friends, not *yours!* We now, alas! occupy antagonistical positions. You are now virtually on the side of the slave-breeders and slave-despoilers of the South; and how great is their joy, to learn this fact, you can see by reading the panegyrics upon your course which you will find on the first page, and elsewhere, extracted from Southern journals which advocate eternal slavery!

Yours, for the oppressed and against the oppressor, whether at home or abroad,

WM. LLOYD GARRISON.

Printed: *The Liberator*, September 28, 1849.

1. Garrison refers to the New England Anti-Slavery Society founded in Boston in 1832; it was the first American organization favoring unconditional abolition. After 1835 the name was changed to the Massachusetts Anti-Slavery Society. (*Life.*)

2. The quotations from the Boston *Chronotype* and *Herald* and the New York *Morning Star* are reprinted in *The Liberator*, August 24, 1849; the quotation from the St. Louis *Reveille* is reprinted in the issue of September 21.

In the early and middle years of the nineteenth century three New York daily papers carried the name of *Morning Star.* The one most probably referred to in this letter began publication in February 1848; no closing date is known. The St. Louis *Reveille* was published between 1844 and 1850; it then merged with the *Daily People's Organ* to form the *Daily Organ and Reveille.* The two Boston newspapers have been previously identified. (*ULN.*)

3. Isaiah 1:4.

4. Garrison loosely adapts Psalms 50:18.

5. Shakespeare, *1 Henry IV*, II, iv, 301.

6. This quotation is not cited in *The Liberator* and remains unidentified.

7. Matthew 11:25.

8. An adaptation of John 12:43.

9. Garrison refers to John 9:16, 10:20, 18:40, 11:48, and 19:15.

10. A reference to James 3:15.

11. In this paragraph Garrison combines several passages, not always accurately quoted, from I Corinthians 4:10, 4:9, II Corinthians 6:5, 11:26, and I Corinthians 4:13.

12. Garrison quotes James Russell Lowell, "The Present Crisis," stanza 1. The poem, with the omission of line 4, was later set to music and sung as a hymn.

13. A possible reference either to Acts 17:6 or Luke 19:17 and an adaptation of Acts 17:12.

14. Garrison refers to Felix Francisco José María de la Concepción Varela y Morales, usually known as Felix Varela (1788–1853), a Catholic priest and native of Cuba, who came to the United States in 1823. From 1841 to 1844 he edited the *Catholic Expositor and Literary Magazine* and was vicar general of New York

from 1839 to 1853. (Letter to the editor from Ruth D. Bell, researcher, June 6, 1971.)

15. A common proverb, often expressed, "Who draweth his sword against his prince must throw away the scabbard."

16. A reference to Matthew 5:29, 30.

17. A phrase used in Matthew 5:18.

18. A reference to II Chronicles 32:8.

19. A reference either to Matthew 12:30, Luke 9:50, or Luke 11:23.

20. This passage is quoted fairly accurately from the Irish Address, printed in *The Liberator*, March 25, 1842.

21. Two papers shared the title of Boston *Bee*, a daily (1842–1858) and a weekly (1843–c. 1854). It is not certain to which Garrison refers, although one may infer the latter, since its title does not vary, as the daily paper's does. (*ULN.*)

22. This quotation is not cited in *The Liberator* and remains unidentified.

---

2 7 9

TO THE FINANCIAL COMMITTEE OF *THE LIBERATOR*

Boston, Sept. 28, 1849.

Dear Friends —

As you have had no meeting, as a Committee, respecting the financial condition of the Liberator, since the present year commenced, (none having been needed,) and may not be aware how the accounts stand at the present time, I find it necessary to state that, during the present quarter ending on Sunday next, (always the most barren of receipts of the whole four,) the whole amount received by the General Agent has only been sufficient to cover the expenses of the paper, exclusive of my own salary for three months, of which I have received but $32.00 — leaving a balance due of $268, reckoning in the usual manner, which sum I am owing for rent, fuel, groceries, medical attendance, clothing, &c. &c., and must look in the face the first of the week, with an empty purse and pocket. Beyond what the Liberator affords, I have no claim upon any human being for aid to the amount of a farthing; yet it is as difficult for me to support my family without means, as it was for the ancient Israelites to make bricks without straw.[1] My public position is such that I am specially anxious to maintain my credit for pecuniary punctuality in meeting my quarterly obligations, not having any credit with the public at large for any anti-slavery labors. The next quarter is sure to be more productive, and I trust will show the receipts of the paper, for the year, to have been equal to the expenditures; beyond that, we cannot reasonably hope. But my anxiety of mind relates to the quarter just expiring, as to how its obligations shall be met. I can make no appeal to you, dear friends, who have already done so much for me, and for the cause, through so many years; still it is due to you as a Committee to be informed of my situation, and the state of the Liberator treasury; and therefore I send you this statement, regretting its necessity. I will only add, that if in any way temporary relief can be devised, the amount raised shall be paid in full at the close of the next quarter, should the receipts warrant, (and every effort shall be made to collect what is due from delinquent subscribers,) or as much of it as possible.

Yours, while there is a shot in the locker,[2] and ever after,

Wm. Lloyd Garrison.

Francis Jackson,
Ellis Gray Loring,
Edmund Quincy,   } Financial Committee.
Samuel Philbrick,
Wendell Phillips,

ALS: Garrison Papers, Boston Public Library.

1. Garrison refers to Exodus 5:7.
2. A naval colloquial expression meaning "as long as one is not destitute."

---

2 8 0

TO THEOBALD MATHEW

[October 5, 1849.]

Sir —

In extending to you an invitation to attend an anti-slavery celebration in this Commonwealth, the Board of Managers of the Massachusetts A. S. Society anticipated the objections that might be raised, either by yourself or by others, to a compliance with it; — such as, the specific nature of your mission to this country — the arduousness of your labors in the temperance cause fully occupying your time, and greatly exhausting your physical energies — the impolicy and impropriety of identifying yourself with any particular phase of anti-slavery agitation — &c. &c. Hence the caution and considerateness evinced by them in selecting an occasion so appropriate, and so entirely unexceptionable, as the anniversary of British West India emancipation; hence the expression of their hope, simply, that you would 'embrace every *suitable* opportunity'[1] to renew those appeals to your countrymen here, on the subject of slavery, which were embodied in the Address signed by you in Ireland in 1842; hence their sincere declaration, that they had no wish to divert you from the special object of your visit to America; hence, too, their silence on all the controverted points among professed abolitionists, not expecting or desiring you to commit yourself one jot or tittle [2] further than you had already done in your own country. They prescribed no shibboleth; [3] they asked no endorsement as an association; they suggested no peculiar doctrines or measures for you to advocate; they left you wholly untrammelled as to thought, speech, and action; and they presented to you the fairest and most innocent occasion, (even to the eye of the most prejudiced,) that could possibly occur during your sojourn here, on which to express your sympathies with the millions in this and other lands, who are still held in the galling fetters of slavery, as well as to exult in the liberation of all those once held in the same degrading servitude by England. Their language was — 'We cordially invite you to participate in the proceedings of the meeting, *in such manner as may be most agreeable to your feelings.*' [4] Yet, for acting thus guardedly, no credit has been awarded to them; nay, they have been as fiercely assailed, on the right hand and on the left, as though they had coolly asked you wholly to abandon your own mission, and to sanction all their peculiar doctrines and measures! There is, therefore, no excuse for your conduct; the pillory on which you are placed is of your own erection; no plea, no trick, no subterfuge, can save you from the condemnation of all honest, candid, humane men.

Aware how much your time and strength were taxed by your temperance labors, our expectations as to your personal attendance at the Worcester celebration were not sanguine. Our ground of complaint is not that you were absent on the thrilling occasion alluded to: that absence created no surprise, and would have elicited no censure, but for the circumstances. *Why* you were not present, — as it was every where known that a kind and courteous invitation had been officially proffered to you, — the multitudinous gathering at Worcester naturally inquired, and had a right to be definitely informed. Our complaints are —

(1) The lack of civility, on your part, in not replying to the cordial and respectful letter sent to you by the committee of arrangements. That letter was carefully prepared, and was as important in its contents as it was commendable in its language and spirit. Our bitterest revilers — now your warmest eulogists — have neither denied nor controverted any of its statements. It was something more than a mere complimentary note: it related to a sublime occasion, to a glorious cause, and to the shameful recreancy to that cause of your countrymen in America. The intelligence communicated, on that last

point, should have startled and shocked you, and called forth from you expressions of heartfelt sorrow. The letter deserved at least a brief reply — as the committee expressed the hope that you would 'attentively read it, and answer it at your earliest convenience.' [5] Of that letter, you took no notice! Now it is worse than frivolous for any of your defenders to pretend to account for your silence, on the ground of the multiplicity of your engagements, and the numerous letters received by you in relation to the places desirous of your presence. You had more than a week in which to write a reply; and if there had been a will, doubtless there would have been a way. Who believes — especially in view of the fact, that, up to this hour, notwithstanding all that has appeared in the public journals on both sides of the Atlantic respecting your anomalous position, you continue to preserve a death-like silence — that, if the letter had related to a popular enterprise, and had emanated from a popular society, you would have allowed it to go unanswered? Is this an uncharitable conclusion? Do not all the facts in the case warrant it? Will any of your friends (?) plead, as a sufficient excuse, that you deemed no other reply necessary than what fell from your lips in my interview with you? If so, they will do so without your authority; for you have complained to a friend of mine, because I have made public a conversation, which you intended to be strictly *sub rosa*. So that this defence is worthless. Had you replied to the letter, as you were requested and expected to do, under your own signature, I should not have felt called upon to state at Worcester, or subsequently in the Liberator, the colloquy held by us on the presentation of that letter. If you said aught, on that occasion, which I either misunderstood or have misrepresented, or which you now sincerely regret, you can easily rectify the error through the medium of any of the public journals.

(2) We complain, in the second place, that, in the private interview held with you, you should volunteer the expression of a doubt, whether any specific injunction can be found in the Scriptures against the damning crime of slavery; when both the Old and the New Testament are crowded with prohibitory and condemnatory passages of it, as explicit and conclusive as language can make them. What can be more explicit than the 'golden rule' — or the precepts and example of Christ — or the teachings of the apostles — or the warnings, remonstrances and threatenings of the prophets — touching covetousness, theft, injustice, and oppression? The greater includes the less — and the less, even to the minutest act of wrong doing as between man and man, is in a thousand instances expressly condemned. Indeed, if there be one sin far more distinctly and powerfully denounced than another

in the Bible, it is the sin of oppressing the poor and needy, of with-holding the hire of the laborer, and of subjecting to bondage the weak and defenceless. But the rights of man are not dependant upon any parchment, ancient or modern: they are 'self-evident,' and there-fore not to be denied, argued or questioned, this slaveholding and slave-breeding nation being witness!

(3) We complain, in the third place, that you listened to the well-founded declaration, that your countrymen here not only give no countenance to the anti-slavery movement — neither Catholic Bishop, nor priest, nor journal — but are decidedly hostile to it, and exhibited no surprise, and expressed no regret: whereas, if you had been in principle opposed to slavery, (as in words you were in your Address,) and a true and consistent Irishman, you would have been deeply moved by this intelligence, as was DANIEL O'CONNELL, when he in-dignantly exclaimed to my face, on hearing a similar statement — 'Sir, they are not Irishmen! They are bastard Irishmen!'

(4) We complain, in the fourth place, that you uttered not a word of encouragement for those who are struggling to deliver the spoiled out of the hand of the oppressor,[6] nor evinced any interest in their success. Surely, if you deemed the interview a private one, a friendly token of sympathy and regard, to this extent, might reasonably have been expected of you.

(5) We complain, in the fifth place, that you manifested no pleasure on being apprised that the anniversary of the best and brightest achievement of British philanthropy — to wit, the emancipa-tion of every slave in the British West Indies — was to be celebrated by the friends of freedom and humanity in this Commonwealth, in order to show their appreciation of the deed, and also to derive from it hope and strength to sustain them in their conflict for the liberation of every bondman on the American soil. How, as a professed aboli-tionist, could you manifest such insensibility? Is it not to your shame?

(6) We complain, finally, and especially — and herein lies your criminality beyond all denial — that you signified your determination to be deaf, dumb and blind on the subject of slavery, while you remained in America — to go to the South with a padlock on your lips, and wear it in advance at the North — by no expression and in no manner to give offence to the traffickers in human flesh — lest your temperance mission should be less heartily welcomed. This was your avowal — you who had solemnly told your countrymen that on a question like this of human slavery, 'none can be neutral,' and that they were bound to use all their moral and political power for the extinction of this foul wrong!

Let me briefly portray the consequences of a step like this, taken by one so greatly distinguished, so much admired and esteemed, so widely reverenced, as yourself. But, first, let us take a glance at the bright side of the picture. Let us suppose you had attended the celebration, or courteously replied to the letter of invitation, and had improved the opportunity to reiterate the noble sentiments of the Address which bears your signature; what then? Under the circumstances, even the most strenuous defenders of slavery would have scarcely dreamed of raising a single outcry; surely none but the vilest of the vile, none but the unprincipled and inhuman, would have ventured to impeach your motives or assail your character. The act would have been regarded by all not thoroughly corrupted by slavery, as perfectly consistent and proper; in Ireland it would have been hailed with delight; it would have increased the veneration felt for your character by the wise and good throughout Christendom; it would have saved that character from a stain which has sullied its integrity and dimmed its lustre; and it would have exerted a salutary influence in behalf of the beneficent cause of universal emancipation.

Alas! in an evil hour, by the advice of bad counsellors, or unwilling to run any risk of incurring the censure even of men-stealers, you stood aloof, strangely remarking that you 'should never think of *advocating* slavery, though you knew of no special scriptural injunction against it.' [7] How different this, in spirit and language, from the following declarations in your Address: — 'Slavery is the most tremendous invasion of the natural, inalienable rights of man, and of some of the noblest gifts of God, "life, liberty, and the pursuit of happiness." What a spectacle does America present to the people of the earth! A land of professing Christian republicans, uniting their energies for the oppression and degradation of three millions of innocent human beings, the children of one common Father, who suffer the most grievous wrongs and utmost degradation for no crime of their ancestors or their own! Slavery is a sin against God and man. All who are not for it must be against it — none can be neutral.' [8]

You were assured, both in the letter of invitation and by myself, that the excellent Address which was signed by Daniel O'Connell, yourself, and seventy thousand others, 'fell powerless on the ear of the Irish population in this country.' To confirm this melancholy fact — to show you in what a skeptical, contemptuous, angry and abusive manner the Address was received at the time by the Irish journals and associations, and by the Catholic clergy, (Bishop John Hughes at their head) — and to demonstrate how absolutely important is the renewal of your anti-slavery appeals to your countrymen 'on every suitable occasion' — I have brought together, on the first page of the present number, a variety of articles, which will serve as a sample of a multitude of similar ones that might be collected by a little pains-taking, and which you are requested to 'read, mark, learn and inwardly digest,' [9] as best you may. Surely, it was not only proper, but their imperative duty, for the committee to apprise you of the temper in which your appeal had been treated by those to whom it had been so kindly addressed — or, rather, by the Irish priests and demagogues who mislead the unsuspecting and credulous multitude — in order that you might feel that an additional obligation was laid upon you to 'cry aloud, and spare not.' [10]

WM. LLOYD GARRISON.

Printed: *The Liberator*, October 5, 1849.

1. A misquotation from Garrison's letter to Father Mathew (July 26, 1849), in which he said "to improve every suitable opportunity."

2. An allusion to Matthew 5:18.

3. A reference to Judges 12:6.

4. Garrison slightly alters his original phraseology, which read, "In behalf of that Society, the undersigned are instructed to extend to you a cordial and an earnest invitation to be present, and to participate in the proceedings of the meeting, in such manner as may be most agreeable to your feelings."

5. This quotation is not in the original letter to Father Mathew, nor does it appear in the account of Garrison's interview with him in *The Liberator*, August 10, 1849.

6. A reference to Jeremiah 22:3.

7. Garrison quotes fairly accurately from his written description of the interview with Father Mathew.

8. Garrison quotes accurately from the address, printed in *The Liberator*, March 25, 1842.

9. A reference to *The Book of Common Prayer*, the Collect for the Second Sunday in Advent.

10. Garrison alludes to Isaiah 58:1.

281

TO THEOBALD MATHEW

[October 12, 1849.]

SIR —

The excellence of the cause in which you have been so long assiduously engaged, and the wonderful success which has crowned your efforts among your suffering countrymen, have made you conspicuous throughout Christendom, won for you the esteem and admiration of men of every sect and party, secured for you a potent influence over millions of minds, and attached unusual importance to your opinions and conduct as a distinguished benefactor of the human race. But such renown and such influence bring with them peculiar trials, great perils, solemn responsibilities. Whoever rises to eminence as a philanthropist or a reformer, should keep in constant remembrance, that with him is lodged a power for good or evil on a mighty scale; that he cannot lose himself in a crowd, nor sink into obscurity as only one among the many; that a misstep on his part is no longer an individual, but a collective calamity; that there is, unhappily, a strong tendency, among ardent friends and warm supporters, to man-worship — to a belief in the infallibility of the cherished object; and, therefore, that he shapes the destinies of a wide circle of followers, according to his fidelity to principle and inflexible adherence to the right, on the one hand, or his apostacy and truckling to worldly expediency, on the other.

You have voluntarily come to this land, in which the one great national sin that overtops every other is SLAVERY — the transformation of three millions of its inhabitants into personal property, chattels, merchandize, to the subversion of all the doctrines and precepts of Jesus Christ, to the annihilation of all human rights. In Ireland, you professed to be an uncompromising abolitionist; you found time to bear a strong testimony against American slavery, as a disgrace to the country, and a sin against God; you felt it to be your duty to implore your countrymen here to be true to the cause of liberty, by giving no countenance to oppression; you recognized the American abolitionists as worthy of their support, as the only consistent friends of freedom in the land. Now that you are on American soil, is there any reason why you should shun those whom you eulogized at home; or why you should not renew your anti-slavery appeal to your countrymen, as opportunity may offer? That the abolitionists remain true to their principles, I presume you will not deny; that your countrymen refuse to give even the slightest countenance to the anti-slavery movement, and that they spurned with indignation and contempt the address which bore your signature, as well as O'Connell's, you cannot be ignorant; that the Catholic priesthood, the Catholic church, the Catholic journalists, and the Catholic political leaders, are giving their sanction and support to the slave system, either by holding slaves, or by maintaining that it is not a crime to hold property in man, either by preserving that silence which gives consent, or by furious denunciation of those who demand the instant liberation of every bondman, is a fact too notorious to admit of denial; that the slave population has not diminished since you signed the address in Ireland, but that, on the contrary, it has been augmented to the frightful amount of at least HALF A MILLION of fresh victims, the census will fully demonstrate. Yet, behold the change! You have signified your determination to give the slave no token of your sympathy, and his oppressor no cause of uneasiness! As for the abolitionists, in no shape or manner are you willing to be identified with them! You volunteer the expression of a doubt whether there is any specific injunction in the Scriptures against slavery! You recollect that the signing of your name to the address to your countrymen here, brought a good deal of odium (?) upon you, and you are not disposed to encounter any more of it on that score, especially as you are every where feasted and flattered by a pro-slavery people!

All this is a melancholy exhibition of folly or criminality on your part. Its influence, alas! for 'evil, only evil, and that continually,' [1] on the ethics and actions of a vast multitude, may easily be traced, though not as easily measured.

Consider, now, what must be the effect of your example on the minds of your countrymen in the United States, whose number is at least as great as that of the slave population. Will they not feel justified in disregarding all the injunctions contained in your address? Will they not consider you as virtually condemning the abolitionists, and all agitation of the subject of slavery? Hitherto, their prejudices against our free colored population have been peculiarly bitter: will they not be rendered even more inimical to that persecuted class, by your apparent lack of sympathy? How can you ever consistently enjoin upon them, again, the duty to use all their moral and political power for the abolition of slavery, and to unite with the friends and advocates of immediate emancipation in one common effort? If you can find reasons to stand aloof from this question, will it be a difficult matter for them to do the same thing in their own case? Alas! the moral injury to them of your bad example, in this particular, is beyond calculation. You have confirmed them in their pro-slavery views and feelings, and made them at least the passive, if not the active subjects of the Slave Power. Thus your mission to them, in spite of the success that may crown your temperance labors, will prove a curse instead of a blessing. Three or four millions strong, if they were abolitionists, how long could the foul system of slavery remain unshaken on our soil? Now that they are strengthened in their pro-slavery position, what hope is left that that system will be overthrown by moral and peaceful instrumentalities?

Your anti-slavery defection will be known throughout Ireland. On the part of those who regard principles more than men, in your unfortunate country, it will excite grief and elicit condemnation; but the great mass of your countrymen, it is to be feared, will allow their reverence for you as a priest, and their regard for you as a temperance benefactor, to bias their judgment and blind their vision. In the nature of things, you cannot take a wrong step without leading them astray. In trying to defend your pro-slavery position in America, they will lessen their abhorrence of slavery, and injure their moral nature. Yours will be the guilt, theirs the degradation and suffering.

How your course is regarded by the cruel oppressors in the South is plainly indicated by the exultation of the press in that quarter. They are eager to give you the right hand of fellowship,[2] and are lavish of their praises in your behalf. Such prudence, forecast and wisdom as you are displaying, in being dumb on the slavery question, they have always admired and commended. Yet they heartily despise you, beyond all doubt; but the blow you have inflicted on the anti-slavery cause fills them with inexpressible delight.

It follows, 'as the night the day,'[3] that you have added to the anguish, horror and despair of the poor miserable slaves, made their yokes heavier, and fastened their chains more securely! For, in a struggle like this, and at such a crisis, whatever gladdens the hearts of the slave-mongers must proportionably agonize those of their victims. Oh, Father Mathew, by all that is implied or embodied in a system which reduces millions of your fellow-creatures to the condition of brutes, and dooms their posterity to the same degradation, forget not the apostolic injunction — 'Remember them that are in bonds as bound with them.'[4]

WM. LLOYD GARRISON.

Printed: *The Liberator*, October 12, 1849; partly printed in *Life*, III, 257–258.

1. An adaptation of Genesis 6:5.
2. Galatians 2:9.
3. Shakespeare, *Hamlet*, I, iii, 79.
4. Hebrews 13:3.

282

TO SYDNEY HOWARD GAY

Boston, Oct. 25, 1849.

My Dear Gay:

In reply to your note, I have but a moment to say, that I think the Convention you contemplate in Western New York, this season, is out of the question, so far at least as the attendance of Phillips and myself is concerned.[1] More time should have been taken to get it up, and to attempt it in a hurry would make it little more than a local meeting in the place in which it might be held. My anti-slavery engagements to lecture in these parts are numerous and positive, running to the middle of December. I think we must wait another year, (say next August or September,) before we can hold such a Convention in Western New York as will *tell* on the public mind.

In great haste,

Yours, with great regard,

Wm. Lloyd Garrison.

S. H. Gay.

ALS: Sydney Howard Gay Papers, Columbia University Libraries.

1. The convention was in fact held in Syracuse, January 15-17, 1850, and Samuel J. May was elected president. (See the incomplete report of the convention in *The Liberator*, February 1, 1850. Although the report was designated as "to be continued," the continuation seems to have been omitted from subsequent issues of the paper.)

---

2 8 3

TO FRANCIS JACKSON

65, Suffolk Street,
Dec. 13, 1849.

Dear Friend Jackson:

The name of the poor colored woman, who is desirous of reaching Philadelphia by the earliest conveyance, where she has a daughter who will be ready to succor her on her arrival, is Elizabeth Cunnard.[1] She belongs to Cincinnati; but when the cholera broke out so fearfully in that city, a few months since, she fled with others, and hoped to obtain employment in Boston.[2] But her health is so miserable, and her constitution so impaired, that she is unable to go out to service, though well qualified to perform any kind of house-work, if she were only in health. Mrs. [Lydia Maria] Child found her in a state of entire destitution, without means, without any clothing for this wintry season, and without friends who could give her any assistance; and having inquired into her case, and found that she is a truly deserving woman, she has done what she could to shelter and comfort her until a way can be provided to get her to her daughter in Philadelphia. Once in Philadelphia, she will find friends, she has no doubt, who will assist her in getting to Cincinnati. If any thing can be done by way of procuring for her a free pass over any portion of the route to Philadelphia, it will be a blessed deed, and will certainly go to disprove the common saying that "corporations have no souls."[3]

Yours, truly,

Wm. Lloyd Garrison.

Francis Jackson.

ALS: Garrison Papers, Boston Public Library.

1. Neither Elizabeth Cunnard nor her daughter has been identified.

2. Like many other American cities, Cincinnati was hit by cholera epidemics in 1832, 1849, and 1866. Since the disease was especially rampant among the poor, the large immigrant population caused Cincinnati to be especially vulnerable in 1849. Public health measures, moreover, were rendered ineffectual owing to a dispute between regular and homeopathic physicians, which resulted in the appointment to the board of health of a heterogeneous group of nonprofessionals. (Charles E. Rosenberg, *The Cholera Years*, Chicago, 1962.)

3. Garrison refers to a point of law established in English courts as early as the sixteenth century and perhaps specifically to a decision handed down by Sir Edward Coke in 1612 in the case of Sutton's Hospital.

APPENDIX

2 8 4

TO WILLIAM B. EARLE

Boston, March 13, 1841.

My dear Earle:

I am more sorry to disappoint you, by not attending your meeting on Tuesday next,[1] (as I had hoped to be able to do when we parted in Brooklyn,) than you will be at my not coming. I find, however, that I cannot be with you, without more inconvenience to my business concerns, in consequence of other engagements which I am bound to fulfill, than I ought to incur. My only regret is, that, as we have no agents in the field, it is desirable that our county meetings, in particular, should be attended by such individuals as can utter a word in season in behalf of our persecuted, yet glorious enterprise. But my absence will amount to very little — for "I am no orator as Brutus is, but a plain blunt man" — [2] and I trust those of you who shall assemble together will be individually animated to open your mouths for those who cannot speak for themselves. Make your meeting social, simple, free — and, looking to God for a blessing, you will not assemble together in vain.[3]

Yours, with much esteem,

Wm. Lloyd Garrison.

W. B. Earle.

ALS: William Lloyd Garrison-Personal (Miscellaneous), New York Public Library.

William Buffum Earle (1802–1891), who came from Leicester, Massachusetts, was the son of Pliny Earle, a successful manufacturer of card-clothing used in the process of cotton spinning. Himself an inventor, Earle had since 1819 been employed in his father's business. In his local area he was a leader in both the anti-slavery and the non-resistance movements. During the last thirty years of his life he was blind. He was also a brother of Thomas Earle, who was frequently critical of Garrison; see the letter to Helen E. Garrison, August 3, 1847.

1. Garrison refers to the quarterly meeting of the Worcester County South Division Anti-Slavery Society to be held on Tuesday, March 16. (*The Liberator*, March 5, 1841.)

2. Shakespeare, *Julius Caesar*, III, ii, 221.

3. A report of the meeting in *The Liberator*, March 26, 1841, indicated that nothing startling occurred, though dilatory abolitionists were urged to work harder.

2 8 5

TO ISAAC T. HOPPER

Boston, May 7, 1846.

Beloved and venerated friend Hopper:

Your kind letter, dated at Albany, inviting me to renew my annual sojourn at your hospitable home, during our anniversary meetings in New-York next week, was duly received. Most happy shall I be to accept of your offer, on this one imperative condition, that I put you to no special inconvenience. It will greatly refresh my spirit to see you again in the flesh, and to hold converse with you and your family, as of old. I hope to see Mrs. Child, also, but am apprehensive that she will not be in the city. Beseech her to remain. I want to converse with her specially in regard to David's going to Hayti.[1] My warm regards to her, and to all under your roof. I shall be in New-York Monday evening, *Deo volente*, via Long Island.

Yours, faithfully,

Wm. Lloyd Garrison.

ALS: Collection of Sarah Dunning Schear, Belmont, Massachusetts.

1. Search through *The Liberator* and appropriate biographies indicates that in all probability David Lee Child never made the projected trip to Haiti.

2 8 6

TO THE SECRETARIES OF THE GLASGOW EMANCIPATION SOCIETY

Boston, June 1, 1846.

Dear Coadjutors, — The last steamer from Liverpool brought me the proceedings of the meeting of the Glasgow Emancipation Society, held on the 21st April; and if ever my heart was filled with gladness — if ever I felt the power and efficacy of human cooperation, in the prosecution of a godlike enterprise — if ever I desired to bless God, and to embrace my brother man — it was when I read what was said and done at that meeting. You will see, by the last number of the *Liberator*, that I have published the proceedings without abridgment,[1] and printed a large number of extra copies for distribution. The effect upon the public mind, especially upon the religious sentiment, in this country, will be powerful. Rely upon it, at the present time, incomparably more can be done for the overthrow of American Slavery in Scotland, than in Carolina or Georgia. What is it that keeps that horrible system from an almost instantaneous suppression? It is the *religious sanction* which is extended to it, at home and abroad. I say abroad, for what is the position of the boasted "Free Church" of Scotland, in regard to the heinous crime of slaveholding, but one of warm "Christian" (!) fellowship. Now, how is it possible to think of extirpating a practice which is sustained and defended as perfectly compatible with a true Christian life, and the spirit of the gospel? There are no circumstances under which a man can innocently be a slaveholder, any more than he can innocently be a thief or a murderer. If we yield this point, the hope of the slave perishes — the slaveholder desires nothing more — we abandon a principle that is vital — and our labours for the overthrow of slavery will be futile. It is generally admitted, without hesitation, that slavery, as a *system*, is exceedingly iniquitous; but it is contended — and this is the absurd and guilty defence of the Free Church — that there are cases in which individuals may be slave-holders, not only innocently, but in a meritorious manner. What would be thought of the piety of those, who should denounce idolatry as a *system*, but maintain that idolatry, under certain circumstances, is not an anti-Christian act? But slavery is worse than idolatry. It is, as John Wesley rightly affirmed, "the sum of all villany" — the crime of crimes, both toward God and toward man.[2]

I feel highly honoured by the cordial invitation which has been extended to me, by the Glasgow Emancipation Society, to visit Scotland the present summer. I have no words to express the grateful feelings of my heart, in view of such a token of personal esteem and kindness — especially after the subtle and malignant efforts that have been made, (and in an anti-slavery garb, too,) both on this and the other side of the Atlantic, to cripple my influence, to destroy my reputation, and to make me an object of suspicion and dread. But my reliance has been on the many precious promises of God. I know that he will ever take the cunning in their own craftiness, and the counsels of the froward he will carry headlong.[3] Conscious that I have endeavoured faithfully to "remember them that are in bonds as bound with them,"[4] cost me what it might, there is nothing that disturbs my peace, or that is able to cast me down.

What shall I say to your invitation? At least, this — I leap in spirit, even at the thought of seeing you again in the flesh; but I cannot write decisively in regard to the proposed visit, by the present steamer. The subject was referred to the New England Anti-Slavery Convention, (which has just ended its sessions in this city, in Faneuil Hall,) and a resolution was cordially adopted, expressing the hope that I should be able to comply with the invitation. Nothing but almost insuperable difficulties will keep me from coming. More I dare not now add.[5]

This country is now successfully engaged in a war with poor, ill-fated, injured, almost helpless Mexico, for the entire conquest of that republic. The grand object of the war is the extension and perpetuation of slavery, indefinitely. We Abolitionists are testifying against the war, in the strongest manner, and our testimony is felt.

In great haste, I remain, with much love and esteem, yours faithfully,

WM. LLOYD GARRISON.

Printed form letter: Samuel J. May Anti-Slavery Collection, Cornell University Library.

In the heading to his letter, Garrison identifies the secretaries of the Glasgow Emancipation Society as William Smeal and John Murray.

1. *The Liberator*, May 29, 1846.
2. Garrison slightly misquotes John Wesley, *Journal*, February 12, 1772. (See *Journal*, New York, 1906, III, 461.)
3. Job 5:13, adapted.
4. Hebrews 13:3.
5. Written at the bottom of the printed letter is the following: "P.S. WLG is to sail on '16th July'." See also Garrison's letter to Elizabeth Pease, June 16, 1846, and his statement in *The Liberator*, June 26, 1846.

287

TO ELIZABETH BUFFUM CHACE

[Boston, June 26, 1847.]

. . . I deserve a good scolding, and you a long apology, for not having answered more promptly your kind letters, inviting me to visit Valley Falls and lecture on the subject of slavery. Your first letter got mislaid, and various hindrances have prevented my answering the second till now. Be assured, it would give me great pleasure to comply with your request, if my multitudinous engagements would permit. You may readily suppose that I am constantly applied to, [from] various quarters, to lecture on a variety of subjects, especially on that of slavery; and that I am often necessitated to answer in the negative. It is difficult for me to leave home at any time, and especially so at the present time. I am soon to go West to be gone at least eight weeks, and must therefore decline being absent in the meantime as much as possible. I am aware that the Anti-Slavery cause in Rhode Island needs to be greatly revived, and if it be in our power here to send you a good lecturer soon, we shall be very glad, and you shall be duly apprized of the fact. My cordial regards to your husband. . . .

Printed extract: Lillie Buffum Chace Wyman and Arthur Crawford Wyman, *Elizabeth Buffum Chace 1806–1899, Her Life and Its Environment* (Boston, 1914), I, 101.

Index of Recipients

(References are to letter numbers)

Allen, Richard, 23, 39
American Anti-Slavery Society, Executive Committee of, 32

Bailey, Gamaliel, Jr., 14
Bailey, John, 107, 110
Baring Brothers, 181
Barney, Nathaniel, 248
Benson, George W., 3, 18, 19, 20, 21, 28, 30, 33, 40, 42, 45, 46, 50, 55, 61, 62, 66, 67, 80, 85, 96, 99, 100, 101, 114, 187, 197, 203, 222, 228, 233, 235, 254
Benson, Sarah T. (Mrs. George), 81
Benson, Sarah T., 84
Bradburn, George, 36
Brown, Abel, 26
Buffum, James N., 58
Burritt, Elihu, 116

Chace, Elizabeth Buffum, 287
Chalmers, William, 97
Chapman, Henry G., 22
Chapman, Maria W., 22, 69, *et al.*, 229, 241
Child, David Lee, 65
Christian Witness, editor of, 186
Clarke, James Freeman, 185
Clarkson, Thomas, 153, 156
Clay, Henry, 262
Collins, John A., 9
Congdon, Joseph, 258
Corkran, Charles L., 25

Daily Mail, editor of, 109
Davis, Edward M., 225
Douglass, Sarah M., 27

Earle, William B., 284
Eddy, Eliza Jackson, 250. *See also*
Merriam, Eliza Jackson
Emerson, Ralph Waldo, 271
Endicott, William, 121
Estlin, John B., 154, 164, 201
Everett, Joshua T., 56

Foster, Stephen S., 214

Garrison, Helen E., 47, 48, 94, 140, 143, 145, 146, 147, 148, 151, 161, 165, 167, 206, 207, 208, 209, 210, 212, 213, 215, 216, 217, 240, 242, 243, 252, 253, 265
Garrison, James H., 1
Gay, Sydney Howard, 129, 130, 132, 137, 195, 231, 232, 266, 267, 268, 282
Glasgow Emancipation Society, secretaries of, 286

Hilditch, Sarah, 182
Hodgson, William Ballantyne, 238
Hopper, Isaac T., 285
Howitt, Mary, 163
Hudson, Erasmus D., 124
Humphrey, Louisa, 88
Humphrey, Heman, 196, 199

Jackson, Francis, 17, 71, 72, 75, 78, 115, 127, 139, 160, 218, 236, 244, 255, 283
Jackson, Phoebe, 63

Kelley, Abby, 77

The Liberator, 64, 70, 74, 79, 83, 93, 95, 174, 176, 194, 211, 264
The Liberator, Financial Committee of, 279
Lincoln, Sumner, 15
Loring, Ellis Gray, 218
Loring, Louisa Gilman, 57, 92, 108, 126, 189, 205

McKim, James Miller, 119, 122, 131, 136
Mathew, Theobald, 272, 276, 277, 278, 280, 281
May, Samuel J., 2, 37, 102, 117, 128, 188, 226, 227
May, Samuel, Jr., 257, 274

Merriam, Eliza Jackson, 245. *See also*
    Eddy, Eliza Jackson
Merrill, Joseph, 200
Morton, Marcus, 184
Mott, James, 224
Mott, Lucretia, 113, 224

Norton, John T., 49

O'Connell, Daniel, 87

Parker, Theodore, 223, 230, 263
Pease, Elizabeth, 6, 8, 10, 13, 34, 38,
    51, 60, 86, 106, 138, 150, 175, 178,
    183, 193, 234, 251, 269, 270, 275
Pillsbury, Parker, 7

Quincy, Edmund, 4, 16, 29, 43, 68, 91,
    105, 118, 141, 144, 149, 152, 159,
    168, 219, 221, 237, 246, 261

Rathbone, William, 239
Ricketson, Joseph, 220, 259, 260
Roberts, Adeline, 249
Robinson, Christopher, 104
Rogers, Nathaniel P., 11, 35

Sewall, Samuel E., 133
Stebbins, Laura, 82
Sumner, Charles, 123, 273

Thayer, Abby G., 256
Tredgold, John H., 5

Unknown Recipient, 12, 120, 135, 180

Vashon, John B., 204

Wallcut, Robert F., 247
Webb, Hannah, 53
Webb, Richard D., 24, 52, 111, 155,
    162, 166, 172, 173, 177, 179, 191,
    198
Weston, Anne Warren, 90, 190
Whipple, Charles King, 142
Williams, Henry W., 73, 76
Woodbury, Levi, 112
Wright, Henry C., 31, 44, 54, 59, 89,
    103, 125, 134, 157, 158, 169, 170,
    171, 192, 202

Yerrinton, James B., 98

Zion's Herald, editor of, 41

Index of Names

The following symbols and abbreviations are used: *, identified; AA-SS, American Anti-Slavery Society; MA-SS, Massachusetts Anti-Slavery Society; WLC, William Lloyd Garrison.

Abdy, Edward Strutt, 401, *402, 440; *Journal of a Residence in the United States*, 402
Aberdeen, Scotland, 446
Aberdeenshire, Scotland, Memorial from, 614
Académie Française, 315
Acadia (steamer), 103, 104, 448, 452, 589, 592
Adam, William, 25, *27, 41, 42, 45, 63, 74, 75, 94, 154, 254; defends Northampton Association, 137, 138; presides at Northampton meeting, 170, 177, 178; at West Indies emancipation celebration, 189, 192–193
Adam, Mrs. William, 215, 254
Adams, Charles Francis, *136, 280, 566; and Latimer case, 135
Adams, John Quincy, 280, 569; and *Amistad* case, 18, 20; and gag rule, 53, 274; and Latimer case, 135; on abolitionists, 196
Address of the Irish People to their Countrymen and Countrywomen in America. *See* Irish Address
Adshead, Joseph, 16, *18
Africa, 232, 293, 483, 486, 491, 611, 612, 623, 657
African Repository, 482, 486
Albany, N.Y., 61, 67, 68, 108, 114, 650, 682; The Temperance House, 108, 110
Albany *Argus*, 61, *63
Albany *Patriot*, 110, 296, *297, 560
Albany *Tocsin*, 67
Albatross, 513
Albert, Prince (of England), 82, 125, 356, 657; visits Liverpool, 358
Alcott, Bronson, 66, 215
Aldersgate Street, London, 348

Alexander, Mr., 514
Alexander I, Czar, 233
Alexander, Janet, 100, *101, 601
Alexander, Mary Margaret, 598, 599, *601
Allegheny Mountains, 508–509
Allegheny River, 510
Allen, Charles, *280, 644, 645
Allen, Richard, *31, 52, 127, 237, 268, 283, 289, 438, 442, 443, 488, 489; letters to, 49, 91; WLG's affection for, 29, 50, 104; letters and handwriting, 91–92; WLG sends thanks for shirts, 239; family, 239, 368, 423, 468
Allen, Mrs. Richard (Anne), 31, 93, 104, 127, 489; WLG's affection for, 50
Allen, William, 147, 230, *233, 492
Allen, Rev. William, 179, *182, 190
Alliance, Ohio, 514
Alum Rocks (Pittsburgh, Pa.), 511, *513
Ambleside, England, 407, 462
America, 29, 45, 56, 641, 642, 650, 653, 657, 661, 662, 664, 665, 669, 671, 672, 675; compared with England, 144; needs H. C. Wright, 148; slavery and the antislavery cause in, 380–381; "a great country," 497
American Agriculturist, 63
American and Foreign Anti-Slavery Society, 1, 35, 259, 327, 336, 378, 379, 383, 384; and Lewis Tappan, 459, 460
American and Foreign Sabbath Union, 546, 547
American Anti-Slavery Society, 12, 13, 16, 21, 25, 26, 27, 29, 31, 60, 61, 70, 76, 87, 95, 116, 117, 120, 136, 160,

168, 269, 282, 288, 323, 327, 334, 346, 400, 456, 460, 480, 525, 561, 567, 575, 592, 615, 616, 628, 652; letter to, 71; WLG's power in, 1; and *Emancipator*, 19; anniversary meetings: (1842) 61–62, 71–72, 84; (1843) 156–158, 162–163; (1844) 254–255, 255–257; (1846) 336–337; (1847) 477–479; (1848) 552, 553–554, 558; (1849) 543, 625, 636, 649; Executive Committee, 72, 74, 89, 161, 333, 649; and union and disunion, 71–72, 73, 74, 75, 256, 478; WLG attends meetings in New York state, 108–110; attacked by William Goodell, 110; resolutions against U.S. Constitution, 118–119; will not send delegates to London convention, 126, 146; policies, 162–163; motto, 289; and *Standard*, 309, 340–341; importance in antislavery cause, 310–311; abolition of slavery its only objective, 313–314, 386; will send WLG on British tour, 343–344; has English sympathy, 370; Anti-Slavery League to cooperate with, 378, 379; and Broad Street Committee, 396; WLG gives history of, at Edinburgh meeting, 428; WLG defends against charge of infidelity, 457–459; will pay George Thompson's expenses if he visits U.S., 472

American Colonization Society, 60, 147, 164, 230, 232–233, 486, 500, 638; WLG attacks, 481–485, 491–494
American Letter Mail Company, 583
American Manufacturer, 268
American Missionary Association, 460
American Peace League, 638–639
American Peace Society, 70, 351, 352, 639
American Phonographic Society, 304, 305
American Revolution, 47
American Seaman's Friend Society, 72
American Temperance Union, 374
American Unitarian Association, 464
American Woman Suffrage Association, 526
Ames, Mrs., 439, 440
Amherstburg, Ontario, 333
Amherst College, 68, 212, 486, 587
Amistad case, 18, 20
Andersen, Hans Christian, 374
Andover, Mass., 11, 495
Andover Theological Seminary, 26, 167, 168, 421, 486, 540

Andrews, Norman, 512, °514
Andrews, Samuel G., 605, 606
Andrews, Samuel Pearl, 304
Anelay, Henry, 414, 417
Angelette (Angelletta, Angenette, Angenetta, Angy; servant), 164, 166, 206, 208, 210, 254
Anthony, Henry, °107
Anthony, Mrs. Henry (Charlotte Benson), °107, 224, 259, 407
Anti-Corn-Law League, 126, 374
Antioch College, 194, 583
Anti-Sabbath Convention (1848), 577, 585–586; importance summarized, 540–541, 543; call for, 543, 544, 545, 547–548, 605, 606; aims, 545–546
Anti-Slavery Bazaars (Fairs), 41, 135, 136, 228, 239, 242, 397, 400, 401, 402, 405, 407, 452, 539, 548, 593, 600; gifts from England, 273; success, 469; in Ohio, 515, 517
Anti-Slavery Bugle, 73, 516, 517
Anti-Slavery Convention of American Women (1838), 143
Anti-Slavery League, 327, 369, 390, 406, 408, 415, 420, 421, 422, 427; WLG on first meeting, 377–378; formation, 378, 379, 382; purpose, 378; auxiliaries, 388, 396; WLG hopes American abolitionists will enroll in, 395
Anti-Slavery Missions. *See* British-American Institute of Science
Appleton, Wis., 215
Arch Street, Philadelphia, 60
Ardrossan, Scotland, 434, 442
Armistead, Wilson, 410
Armstrong, Mrs. George, 400, °401–°402
Army of the Rio Grande, 477
Arundel Street, London, 369
Ashburton, Lord. *See* Baring, Alexander
Ashley, George, 224, °225
Ashmun, Jehudi, 486
Ashurst, William Henry, 18, °19, 328; described, 391; WLG's visit, 394, 413, 568
Ashurst, Mrs. William Henry, 413
Atherton, Charles G., 53
Atlantic Monthly, 343
Atlantic Ocean, 14, 17, 20, 29, 49, 51, 103, 143, 174, 282–283, 354, 363, 611, 614, 623, 625, 626, 646, 647, 648, 652, 656, 683
Auburn Theological Seminary, 194, 333
Augusta, Ohio, 524
Austinburg, Ohio, 518, 524

Austrian Silesia, 268
Avery College, Pittsburgh, 512

Babb, Robert, 101
Backhouse, Jonathan, 125, °127
Backhouse, Mrs. Jonathan, 127
Bacon, Benjamin C., 70, °71; defends
  Northampton Association, 165
Bacon, Ezekiel, 196, °197
Bailey, Gamaliel, Jr., 31, °35; letter to,
  32
Bailey, John, °275; letter to, 274
Bailey, Mrs. John, 281
Balfour, James, 440
Balfour, Mrs. James (Clara Lucas),
  439, °440
Ball, William, 23, °26
Ballot Box, 147
Ballou, Adin, 238, °241, 454; speaks at
  AA-SS anniversary meeting, 256
Baltimore, Md., 320, 335
Bangor, Me., 94
Baptist Advocate, 134, 136
Baptist Association in England. *See*
  English Baptist Union
Baptist General Convention for Foreign
  Missions, 652, °654
Baptist Triennial Convention. *See* Bap-
  tist General Convention for Foreign
  Missions
Barclay, Robert, 17, °19, 98, 99, 546,
  605
Barclay Street, N.Y., 72, 337
Baring, Alexander, first Baron Ash-
  burton, °101, 450
Baring Brothers, 450; letter to, 449
Barker, Joseph, 123, °126, 150, 328,
  397, 400, 410; praised, 124; visited,
  405–406; described, 408–409
Barnes, Gilbert Hobbs, 1
Barney, Nathaniel, 271, °272, 548;
  letter to, 585; WLG asks loan for
  George W. Benson, 586
Barney, Mrs. Nathaniel, 587
Barnstable, Mass., 87
Bartlett, Mrs. Elkanah (Mary Morton),
  571, 572
Basel, University of, 45
Bassett, William, 25, °27; and Knapp
  controversy, 45, 78, 80
Batcheller (Bachelder), Dr. James,
  248–°249
Batcheller (Bachelder), Mrs. James
  (Persis Sweetser), 248, 249
Bates, Hamlett, 40, °42, 45
Bath, England, 303, 368, 382

Bath, Me., 261
Bath (Me.) Anti-Slavery Society, 101
Bayne, Walter McPherson, 568, °569
Beach, Thomas P., 101
Beaumont, Gustave de, °314–°315;
  Marie, ou l'Esclavage aux États-Unis,
  312
Beaver, Pa., 510
Beaver River, 513
Beecher, Henry Ward, 374
Beecher, Lyman, 352, °374, 421; at
  World's Temperance Convention,
  373; and Evangelical Alliance, 419
Belfast, Ireland, 368, 416, 418, 422,
  424, 428, 430, 441; antislavery meet-
  ing at, 434; tea party at, 438
Belfast Anti-Slavery Society, 423
Belfast Charitable Society, 423
Belfast *News-Letter*, 434, 435
Belgium, 42
Belsham, Thomas, 98, 99, 605
Beman, Amos, 200
Benson, Anna Elizabeth (George W.
  Benson's sister), 4, °5, °28, 41, 42,
  61, 63, 73, 75, 94, 107, 147, 166, 258;
  health, 44, 122, 132, 142, 146, 151–
  152, 153–154, 164, 167, 198, 201;
  death, 119, 202, 237, 267; tribute to,
  202–203; remembered, 225, 356
Benson, Anna Elizabeth (George W.
  Benson's daughter), 206, 597
Benson, Eliza Davis, 77, 100, 551;
  death, 73, 75
Benson, Frances, 356, 357
Benson, George, 202, °205, 356; family,
  511
Benson, Mrs. George (Sarah Thurber),
  5, °6, 7, 41, 42, 43, 44, 94, 95, 107,
  147, 152, 153, 164, 166, 167, 225,
  259; letter to, 209; health, 122, 132,
  137, 146, 201, 227, 234, 257–258;
  injured, 197, 199, 201, 213, 226, 237;
  WLG wishes her to consult Dr. Sweet,
  208, 223; WLG anxious to hear from,
  209; WLG wishes her to live with his
  family, 224; death, 260, 267; remembered, 356
Benson, George William, °5, 10, 27, 38,
  77, 119, 138, 189, 209, 211, 215, 223,
  224, 235, 247, 261, 407, 531, 532,
  537, 565, 566, 595; letters to, 8, 40,
  43, 45, 48, 61, 66, 73, 93, 100, 105,
  106, 121, 137, 151, 153, 164, 166,
  206, 225, 252, 257, 258, 260, 296,
  460, 487, 499, 537, 549, 554, 557,
  599; and James H. Garrison, 3, 4, 5;
  and Northampton Association, 95,

240, 564; and WLG's finances, 105–
106, 539; and Anna's illness, 153,
154; narrow escape, 226; family,
355–356, 499, 539, 564, 598; and
Anti-Sabbath Convention, 541, 548;
business worries, 571, 577; WLG tries
to help, 585–587; considers moving,
597–598
Benson, Mrs. George William (Catharine Knapp Stetson), 42, *43, 47,
63, 73, 95, 100, 138, 151, 153, 154,
165, 189, 209, 225, 254, 258, 297,
487, 539, 550, 565, 597; visits Garrisons, 257; thrown from carriage, 499
Benson, George W., Jr., 153
Benson, Henry Egbert (George W.
Benson's brother), 155, 356, *357
Benson, Henry Egbert (George W.
Benson's son), 153
Benson, Mary (George W. Benson's
sister), 2, 3, *5, 41, 42, 77, 106, 146;
illness, 43–46, 48; death, 48, 267;
remembered, 356
Benson, Mary (George W. Benson's
daughter), 225, *226, 565, 595
Benson, Sarah Davis, 564, 565, *566,
572, 595
Benson, Sarah Thurber, 4, *5, 41, 61,
73, 75, 94, 107, 147, 152, 164, 166,
208, 209, 215, 225, 257, 258, 259,
407, 499, 511; letter to, 222; concern
for sister Anna, 153; WLG invites to
live with his family, 224; WLG's
sympathy for, at mother's death, 260;
health, 44, 122, 132, 224, 234, 267,
461–462, 487, 531, 532, 542, 548,
550, 594, 595, 600
Benson, Thomas Davis, 100, 153, 225,
226, 565
Bentham, Jeremy, 147
Berge, E. B., 528
Berwick-upon-Tweed, Scotland, 418,
422, 423
Bevan-Naish Library, 398
Bible, 36, 66, 256, 485, 634
Bible Convention, 65, *66
Bimeler, Joseph Michael, 526
Birmingham, England, 393
Birney, James Gillespie, 31, 147, 163,
*164, 245, 265, 266, 269
Bishop and Simmson, 129
Bishop, Caroline Garrison, 462, 464
Bishop, Francis, *389, 396, 463; ar-
ranges public meeting at Exeter, 388;
names daughter for WLG, 462
Bishop, Mrs. Francis, 462
Bishop, Joel Prentiss, *7–*8, 40, 41, 45

Blackwell, Henry Brown, 526
Blagden, Rev. George Washington, 484,
*486
Blanchard, Joshua P., 575
Blantyre, Charles Walter Stewart,
twelfth Lord, 433, *435
Bolles, William, 305, *306
Bolles, W. and J., 306
Boston, 3, 4, 5, 6, 9, 10, 19, 21, 51, 52,
61, 66, 72, 89, 101, 111, 113, 135,
156, 209, 212, 236, 269, 283, 302,
323, 328, 349, 351, 352, 354, 355,
356, 358, 359, 361, 362, 401, 466,
471, 497, 499, 527, 532, 534, 542,
548, 558, 564, 579, 587, 588, 591,
597, 638, 645, 646, 654; WLG plans
to move to, 138, 185, 200–201;
WLG's departure from, on British
mission, 326–327; 1835 riots in, 360,
500
Boston, Adams House, 543
Boston, Amory Hall, 42, 228
Boston, Bunker Hill, 167, 168, 468
Boston, Chardon-Street Chapel, 10, 25,
26, 75
Boston, Church of the Disciples, 455
Boston, Custom House, 328, 503
Boston, Faneuil Hall, 3, 46, 47, 48, 53,
92, 156, 166, 168, 229, 242, 246, 254,
279, 328, 338, 340, 405, 452, 607,
617, 683
Boston, First Free Baptist Church. *See*
Boston, Tremont Temple
Boston, Hollis Street Church, 535
Boston, Lion Theatre, 587
Boston, Liverpool Wharf, 596
Boston, Long Pond water project, 597,
598
Boston, Marlboro Chapel, 65, 66, 92,
93, 107, 309, 454, 481
Boston, Marlboro Hotel, 66
Boston, Masonic Temple, 66
Boston, Melodeon, 42, 47, 351, 543,
585, 587, 616–617
Boston, Miller Tabernacle, 166, 254
Boston, Mount Vernon Congregational
Church, 363
Boston, New North Church, 464
Boston, North End, 461
Boston, Old South Church, 481, 485,
486
Boston, Roxbury Neck, 548
Boston, South Cove, 186, 196
Boston, South End, 142, 145, 208, 209
Boston, State House, 11, 46, 47, 246, 254
Boston, Temporary Home for Destitute
Females and Orphan Children, 533

Boston, Town Hall, 45
Boston, Tremont Temple, 14
Boston Anti-Slavery Bazaar. *See* Anti-Slavery Bazaars
Boston *Atlas*, 601
Boston *Bee*, 665, 666, °667
Boston *Catholic Diary*, 51, 92
Boston *Catholic Observer*, 650, °654, 659, 660, 662, 664
Boston *Chronotype*, 649, 650, 659, 660, 661, 666
Boston *Daily Mail*, 279; letter to, 277
Boston Female Anti-Slavery Society, 19, 186, 517, 567, 592
Boston *Herald*, 650, °651, 659, 660, 661, 666
Boston *Olive Branch*, 560, 561
Boston *Pilot*, 51, 92, 650, 659, 660
Boston *Post*, 291, 294
Boston Public Library, 147
Boston *Recorder*, 147, 560, 561
Boston *Republican*, 644, °645
Boston *Weekly Chronotype*, 582, 583
Boston *Weekly Commonwealth*, 583
Boswell, James, 369
Bowditch, Dr. Henry Ingersoll, °156, 542, 642, 644, 661; examines WLG, 155; on WLG's health, 165
Bowdoin College, 156, 179, 182
Bowling Bay, Scotland, 426, 433
Bowring, John, 18, °19, 328; WLG breakfasts with, 372
Boyer, Henry, 274, 275
Boyer, Jean Pierre, 49
Boyle, Augustus French, °304
Boyle, James, 100, °101, 154, 165, 173, 199, 214, 235, 253, 258, 616; at Northampton antislavery meeting, 170, 177–178; at Springfield, Mass., antislavery convention, 184; at West Indian emancipation celebration, 189, 193; at Northampton Community, 240; said to attack Garrisonians, 296
Boyle, Mrs. James (Laura), 154, 165, 199, 214, 240, 254, 296
Boylston Street, Boston, 147
Bradburn, George, 18, °19, 46, 48, 52, 64, 65, 92, 93, 103, 527, 574, 576; letter to, 87; reports on Concord, N.H., antislavery meeting, 86; term as lecturer extended, 87; joins Liberty party, 266, 273, 288
Bradbury, Elizabeth Ely, 575
Bradbury, Sarah Elizabeth, 575
Bradley, John N., 279
Brady, Mary, 403, 405, 406, °407, 409, 471, 472; WLG stays with, 402, 411

Brady, Rebecca, 405, °407, 409; WLG stays with, 402, 411
Braithwaite, Isaac, 26
Braithwaite, Mrs. Isaac (Anna), 23–24, °26
Brattleboro, Vt., 45, 307
Bridgeman family, 597, 599
Briggs, George W., °261, 521
Briggs, Simon B., 519, °521
Brighton, Mass., 75, 108
Brinkerhoff, Jacob, 474
Brisbane, William Henry, 256, °257
Bristol, England, 368, 382, 383, 401, 402; public meetings in, 390, 392; Fine Arts Academy, 380; Lewin's Mead, 402; Queen's Hotel, 389; Victoria Rooms, 387, 389
Bristol and Clifton Auxiliary Ladies' Anti-Slavery Society, 400, 401, 496
Bristol General Hospital, 390
Britannia (steamer), 16, 21, 104, 359, 361, 416, 418; runs aground, 347, 355; repaired, 349; arrives at Liverpool, 358
British-American Institute of Science, 331, 332, 389
British and Foreign Anti-Slavery Society, 13, 19, 127, 131, 232, 378, 389, 390, 402, 460; London (Broad Street) Committee, 19, 388, 389, 396, 403, 407, 417, 441
British Anti-State Church Association, 374
British Banner, 460
British Colonial Government, 260
British Friend, 228
British India, 391, 446
British India movement, 16
British India Society, 228, 440
British West Indies, 19, 233, 525; emancipation, 95, 409; celebrations of emancipation, 94–95, 189, 315, 316, 542, 543, 577, 639, 641, 642, 647, 648, 661, 668, 671
Broadway, New York City, 156, 160, 254, 336
Brook Farm, 198, 236, 316
Brooke, Samuel, 512, °514, 520, 529, 530, 532, 534, 615; at Oberlin graduation, 522; and *North Star*, 533
Brookfield, Mass., 524
Brookline, Mass., 503
Brooklyn, Conn., 3, 4, 5, 6, 7, 28, 46, 47, 165, 202, 205, 224, 511; WLG reminisces about, 355, 356
Brooklyn, N.Y., 333, 617, 640, 681
Brooklyn (N.Y.) *Advertiser*, 115

Brooklyn (N.Y.) *Freeman. See* Brooklyn *Advertiser*
Brown, Mr., 508
Brown, Abel, 57, °58, 67; letter to, 56
Brown, Henry ("Box"), 625, °636
Brown, John, 321, 340, 592
Brown, Roxcy. *See* Nickerson, Mrs. Lorenzo D.
Brown, William, 357, 359, 498
Brown, W. W., 443
Brown, William Wells, 552, °553, 554, 626, 635, 637, 638, 646; *Narrative of William Wells Brown, a Fugitive Slave*, 553, 639
Brown University, 268
Browne, John W., 546, °547, 548
Brussels Peace Congress, 302
Buck, William, 449
Buffalo, N.Y., 199, 583; Liberty party convention at, 530
Buffum, James Needham, °138, 270, 316, 340, 345, 348, 384, 405, 407, 433, 435, 468, 489, 498; letter to, 142; offers to rent WLG his Lynn house, 138, 142; in England, 323, 324; will send daguerreotype to Richard Webb, 469; family of, 517
Bulfinch, Charles, 47
Burgess, Rev. George, °66; to preach on slavery, 64–65
Burke, William, 281, °282
Burleigh, Charles Calistus, 25, °27, 323, 510, 545, 547, 548, 605; speaks at AA-SS anniversary meeting, 257; and Anti-Sabbath Convention, 544
Burnell, Barker, °168; death, 167
Burnet, Rev. John, 412, °416
Burnham, Denison R., 85, °87
Burritt, Elihu, °301–°302; letter to, 298; WLG attacks on disunion, 298–301
Burtis, Lewis B., 108, °110
Bury St. Edmunds, England, 449
Bustill, Cyrus, 60
Buxton, Sir Thomas Fowell, 18, °19, 230, 492, 494, 657
Byron, Augusta Ada, 461, 463
Byron, George Gordon, Lord, 461
Byron, Lady (Anna Isabella Milbanke), 494

Cabot, Susan, 626, °636, 646
Caldwell, Minerva, 592
Caledonia (steamer), 20, 21, 497
Calhoun, John C., 121, 179, °182, 290, 301, 560, 561, 610; speech in *Liberator*, 470, 473–474

Calhoun, William Brown, 280
California, 610
Calvin, John, 98, 99, 546, 605; *Institutes of the Christian Religion*, 631, 636
Cambria (steamer), 348, 405, 473; treatment of Douglass on, 479, 480
Cambridge, Mass., 45, 75
Cambridgeport, Mass., 44, 73, 94, 105, 138, 145, 369
Campbell, James, °459–°460
Camperdown, Nova Scotia, 348
Canada, 85, 86, 332, 389, 576–577
Canada Mission. *See* British-American Institute of Science
Candlish, Rev. Robert Smith, 426, °427, 428, 546
Cannan, Miss, 595, 596, 598, 599
Canton, Ohio, 68
Cape Cod, Mass., 87, 88, 275, 343
Cape Mesurado, 486
Cape Race, Newfoundland, 354, 358
Carleton, Edmund, 85, 86, °87
Carlisle, England, 396, 409
Carmichael, Daniel, °333–°334
Carmichael, Mrs. Daniel (Eliza Otis), °333–°334
Carmichael, Henry, 334
Carolina, 683
Carpenter, Mrs. Lant (Anna Penn), 401, °402
Carpenter, Mary, 495, °496
Carpenter, Philip, 402, 462, °463
Carr, Tagore, & Company, 126
Carroll County, Ohio, 526
Carter, James Gordon, °280
Carver Street, Boston, 201
Cass, Lewis, 574, °575
Cassey, Joseph, 343, °344
Catharine Linda case, 320–321
Catherine Lane, New York City, 135
Catherwood, Frederick, °171; *Panorama of Jerusalem*, 169, 171
Catholic Diary. See New England Reporter and Catholic Diary
Catholicism, and abolitionists, 230
Cavender, Thomas S., 308, °309
Centre Street, New York City, 463
Chace (Chase), Samuel Buffington, 685
Chace, Mrs. Samuel Buffington (Elizabeth Buffum), letter to, 684
Chace (Chase), William M., 8, 9, °10, 38
Chagrin Falls, Ohio, 520
Chalmers, Thomas, 255, 426, °427, 428
Chalmers, William, °255; letter to, 254
Chambersburg, Pa., 508
Channing, Dr. Walter, 94, °95

Channing, Rev. William Ellery, 95, 215, 316

Channing, Rev. William Henry, 315, °316, 333, 545, 546, 548; speaks at antislavery convention, 339; and *Standard,* 341

Chaplin, Conn., 218

Chaplin, William Lawrence, 109, °111

Chapman, Henry, 517, °563-°564

Chapman, Mrs. Henry (Sarah Greene), °517; leaves $100 to WLG, 539

Chapman, Henry Grafton, °19, 30, 70, 131, 145; letter to, 48; in Haiti, 18; to represent MA-SS in Haiti, 48–49; and *Liberator* controversy, 80; "Haitian Sketches," 312, 314

Chapman, Mrs. Henry Grafton (Maria Weston), °19, 25, 52, 53, 60, 70, 141, 145, 147, 161, 163, 228, 242, 273, 282, 296, 333, 393, 395, 405, 406, 440, 557, 593, 626, 646; letters to, 48, 171, 551, 566; edits *Standard,* 2, 266, 269; in Haiti, 18; to represent MA-SS in Haiti, 48–49; and Bible convention, 66; and *Liberator* controversy, 80; WLG grateful to, 173; "Haitian Sketches," 312, 314; helps Quincy edit *Liberator,* 327; and *Standard,* 341; daguerreotype for R. D. Webb, 469; signs call for Anti-Sabbath convention, 548; WLG introduces to English friends, 562, 563; her visit to Europe a loss to antislavery friends, 564; WLG praises her antislavery efforts, 567

Chapman, Mary Gray, 517, 569, 593

Chardon-Street Convention (Boston), 9, 10, 19, 23, 25–26, 27

Charles II, king of England, 96, 440

Charleston, S.C., 168, 182; supports Free Church of Scotland, 119

Charlestown, Mass., 167

Charlotte, queen of England, 494

Chartists, 125, 126, 369, 373, 374, 393, 394, 395, 396

Chase, Frances Elvira, 249, 250, 252

Chase, Isaac T., 572

Chase, Leonard, 244, °246, 249; death of wife and children, 249–250

Chase, Mrs. Leonard (Mary Isabelle Dickey), 249–250, °252

Chase, Salmon P., 302

Chatham Street, Boston, 241

Chauncy Place, Boston, 131, 173

Cheever, Rev. George B., °136, 151; defends capital punishment, 134, 144

Chelsea, Mass., 598

Cherokee Indians, 292

Chesson, F. W., 366

Chester County, Pa., 506, 526

Chesterfield, Mass., 215

Chicago *Tribune,* 520

Child, David Lee, 26–27, 41, °42, 43, 45, 60, 61, 63, 74, 94, 118, 165, 169, 173, 174, 185, 196, 199, 682; letter to, 161; editorship of *Standard,* 2, 161–162, 163, 175–176, 341; and *Liberator* controversy, 80; policies unacceptable to WLG, 164; at antislavery meeting, Northampton, 170; efforts at sugar-beet cultivation, 175; attacked by editor of Northampton *Democrat,* 181; regrets Mrs. Chapman's visit to Europe, 564

Child, Mrs. David Lee (Lydia Maria Francis), °26-°27, 60, 72, 176, 196, 677, 682; edits *Standard,* 2, 25; and H. C. Wright's English mission, 70; and *Liberator* controversy, 80

Choctaw Indians, 292

Cholera epidemic (1849), 638, 639, 640, 677, 678

Christian Monitor and Common People's Adviser, 357

Christian Observer, 205

Christian Penny Magazine, 460

Christian Pilot and Pioneer, 441

Christian Watchman, 351

Christian Witness, 460; letter to, 455

Christian Witness and Church Member's Magazine, 273, 274

Christian Work, 136

Christian Work and the Evangelist, 136

Church, Dr. Jefferson, °321

Church of Scotland, 435

Church, Sabbath and Ministry Convention. *See* Chardon-Street Convention

Cincinnati, Ohio, 30, 31, 32, 35, 298, 318, 677

Cincinnati *Philanthropist,* °35

Cincinnati Repeal Association, 229, 232

Civil War, 8, 19, 136, 241, 257, 269, 314, 425

"Clapham Sect," 205

Clapp, Henry, °270, 357, 363, 474; and N. P. Rogers, 288; attacks WLG, 414; opposed to Garrisonians, 473

Clare, Rev. Joseph, 450, °451

Clark, Ezra, 520, °521

Clark, Rev. Orange, 190, °193–°194

Clarke, James Freeman, °454-°455; letter to, 454

Clarke, John L., 137, 138, 166, 167

Clarke, Peleg, 137, °138, 305

Clarke, Sarah Jane, 511, *513
Clarke, Dr. Thaddeus, 511, *513
Clarke, Mrs. Thaddeus (Deborah), 511, 513
Clarkson, Thomas, *19, 204, 205, 233, 564, 657; letters to, 380, 385; WLG's visit to, 381, 385–386; and American Colonization Society, 493; "Hints for the American People in the Event of a Dissolution of the Union," 386–387; WLG refuses to return manuscript, 448–449
Clarkson, Mrs. Thomas (Catherine Buck), 386, *449
Clarkson, Thomas (son), 449
Clay, Cassius Marcellus, 311, *314; duel with Turner, 622–623, 635
Clay, Henry, 179, *182, 232, 266, 484, 610, 612; letter to, 608; D. L. Child supports for President, 164; position on slavery in Kentucky, 612
Cleveland, Mr., 167
Cleveland, Ohio, 194, 466, 517; antislavery meetings in, 526; Advent Chapel, 526, 528
Cleveland *Daily True Democrat*, 528, 623, 635
Cleveland *Leader*, 520
"Clique, The," 448
Cluer, John Campbell, 315, *316
Cluer, Mrs. John Campbell, 315
Clyde River, 433
Coates, Lindley, 157, *158
Cobden, Richard, 126
Coe, William, 224, *225
Coffin, Charlotte G., 463, *464, 509, 549
Coffin, Joshua, 145, *147
Coffin, Susan, 304, 305, 461, 548
Coit, William Henry, 235, *236
Cold Water Army, 190, *193
Collier, Mr. (Dr.), 379
Collier, William, 660
Collins, John A., 2, *12, 13, 14, 16, 24, 30, 31, 65, 95, 296, 465; letter to, 20; attacked by Torrey, 11; mission to England, 17–18, 20–21; attends meetings in Rochester, 108; at Farmington, N.Y., 109; health, 110, 112; and individual property, 145; and communal farm, 198; and Skaneateles community, 240, 267
Colman, Henry, 146, 150
Colonization Society of Kentucky, 612
Columbia College, Medical Department, 222
Columbia University, 194, 421
Colver, Rev. Nathaniel, *14, 22; attacks

Collins, 17; and Chardon-Street Convention, 23; delegate to antislavery convention, 146
Come-outerism, 235, 236, 245, 248, 523
Concord, Mass., 468
Concord, N.H., 16, 27, 31, 85, 86, 197, 258, 270, 360
Conder, Josiah, *417
Cone, Spencer H., 652, *654
Congdon, James B., *280, 606
Congdon, Joseph, *606; letter to, 605
Congregational Union of England and Wales, 274, 416
Congress of the Friends of Universal Peace. *See* Paris Peace Congress
Conley, Michael, 495
Connecticut, 101, 120, 158; legislature, 205
Connecticut River, 184
Convention of Friends of Social Reform, 236
Convention of the People of Massachusetts, 277, 278, 279
Cooley, Thomas, 129
Cork, Ireland, 368, 416, 418, 428, 430; House of Industry, 495
Corkran, Charles L., *55; letter to, 54
Cornelia (schooner), 275
Cornhill, Boston, 12, 32, 86, 261, 582
Corn Laws, 125, 126, 634
Coues, Elliott, 70
Coues, Samuel Elliott, 69, *70
Coventry, R.I., 137, 305
Cow Bay, Nova Scotia, 347, 348
Cowles family, 524
Cowles, Alfred, 520
Cowles, Betsey, 518, *520
Cowles, Cornelia, 518, *520
Cowles, Edwin Weed, 518, *520
Cowles, Giles Hooker, 520
Cox, Rev. Abraham Liddon, 134, *136
Cox, Francis Augustus, 648, 650, 652, *653, 654
Cox, Rev. Samuel Hanson, 136, 419, *421
Crain (Crane), Agnes, 506, 507
Crain, Col. Richard M., 508
Crandall, Prudence, 5
Creole case, 63, 101
Cresson, Elliott, 230, *232, 233, 638; and American Colonization Society, 491–492
Cromwell, Oliver, 615
Cropper, James, 230, *233, 492
Crowell, William, *351–*352
Cummings, Hiram, 113, *115
Cunard Line, 19, 21, 104, 237, 241, 408;

and prejudice against Negroes, 479, 480
Cunnard, Elizabeth, 677, 678
Cunningham, William, 426, °427, 428
Curtis, George Ticknor, °280
Curtis, John, Jr., 572, 573, 574
Cutts, John Smith. *See* John Cutts Smith
Cuyahoga County, Ohio, 517
Czechoslovakia, 268

Daily, J. B. (R.), 412, 413, 417
Danvers, Mass., 316, 494, 495
Darlington, England, 148, 344, 393, 397, 416, 418, 436, 452, 618, 626, 646; WLG visits E. Pease at, 439
Dartmouth College, 16, 26, 249, 294
Dauphin County, Pa., 506
Davis, Edward M., 308, 544; letter to, 545; and Anti-Sabbath Convention, 546, 547, 548
Davis, Mrs. Edward M. (Maria Mott), 546
Davis, Thomas, °51, 487; WLG introduces, 49–50, 52, 54
Davis, Mrs. Thomas (Eliza Chace), 51
Davis, Mrs. Thomas (Pauline Kellogg Wright), 51
Dawes, William, 522, °525
Declaration of Independence, 156, 256, 290, 478; quoted, 277–278
Dedham, Mass., 11, 64, 65, 102, 189, 192, 215, 315, 316, 608; compared with Northampton, 169
Deer Island, Mass., 463
Delaney, Dr. Martin R., 510, °513; speaks at New Brighton meeting, 511; and *North Star*, 533
Democratic party, 136, 266, 291, 292, 300, 516, 561, 604, 623; and annexation of Texas, 284
Democrats, 566
Denison, Rev. Charles Wheeler, 256–°257, 334
Detroit, Mich., 334
Devil's Island, Nova Scotia, 347, 348
Dewey, Rev. Orville, 462, °464
Diamond Alley, Pittsburgh, 510
Dickens, Charles, 328; and *Daily News*, 371, 373–374; *Dombey and Son*, 374
Dickinson College, 421
Dickinson, Rev. W. W., 449
Dickinson, Mrs. W. W. (Mary Clarkson), 449
Diet Kitchen Association, 274
District of Columbia, 581, 624
Doolittle, Dr. Adrastus, 461–462, °463
Doolittle, Rev. Horace D., 190, 215

Dorchester, Mass., 137, 582
Dorchester Heights, Mass., 468
Dorr, Thomas W., 96
Douglas Jerrold's Shilling Magazine, 373
Douglas Jerrold's Weekly Newspaper, 373
Douglass, Frederick, 46, °47, 48, 72, 109, 112, 157, 252, 275, 281, 316, 326, 327, 339–340, 345, 368, 371, 372, 374, 377, 386, 388, 389, 391, 397, 401, 403, 404, 405, 410, 412, 418, 424, 427, 429, 439, 463, 465, 480, 489, 526, 528, 552, 554, 571, 614, 625; conflict with Rev. Garnet, 200; in England, 323, 324; and formation of Anti-Slavery League, 378, 379, 382, 384, 385; to visit Clarkson, 381; at Bristol, England, 387, 390, 392, 393, 396; visits William Ashurst, 394; at Exeter, 396; at London, 400; at Sheffield, 409, 421; at Exeter Hall, 412; success in England, 415; and British and Foreign Anti-Slavery Society, 417; to remain in Britain, 422, 436; at Greenoch, Scotland, 426; at Edinburgh, 428, 430, 442; at Glasgow, 432–433; at Wrexham, 435; at Kirkcaldy, 442, 445; at Liverpool, 445; at Dundee, 445; accompanies WLG on western tour, 465–466, 498, 500; plans to return to U.S., 472, 473; family, 473; English wish to ransom from slavery, 476, 477; returns to U.S., 476; at AA-SS anniversary meeting, 479, 481; at Norristown, Pa., 505; attacked on train, 506; at Harrisburg, Pa., 507, 508; discriminated against on stagecoach, 508–509; at Pittsburgh, 509, 510; at New Brighton, Pa., 511; at Youngstown, O., 512; his founding of *North Star* and WLG, 513, 532–533; at meetings of Western Anti-Slavery Society, 515; and Cowles family, 518; ill health on western tour, 516, 519; at Munson and Twinsburg, O., 519–520; at Oberlin College, 522, 523; *Narrative of the Life of*, 47, 400, 402, 409, 415
Douglass, Mrs. Frederick, 415
Douglass, Grace Bustill, 58, 59
Douglass, Robert M. J., 59, °60
Douglass, Robert M. J., Jr., 59, °60
Douglass, Sarah Mapps, °60; letter to, 58
Dover Street, Boston, 613
Downes, George, 50, °51, 93
Dramatic Line, 104

Drogheda, Ireland, 438
Dublin, Ireland, 29, 31, 50, 54, 63, 93, 103, 104, 128, 230, 356, 359, 368, 382, 384, 393, 395, 416, 418, 423, 424, 425, 427, 441; WLG's 1840 visit to, 52, 129–130; WLG longs to revisit, 239; WLG's 1846 visit to, 431, 434, 438–439, 469; antislavery meeting at, 438–439; Burgh Quay, 233; Conciliation Hall, 232, 233; Cork Hill, 129; Corn Exchange, 232, 233
Dublin Committee, 488, 489–490
Dublin Royal Exchange, 129
Dublin Temperance Society, 398
Dublin *Weekly Herald*, 55
Dumond, Dwight L., 1
Dundee, Scotland, 416, 418, 424, 428, 429; antislavery meeting at, 430, 433, 445
Durham, University of, Medical School, 441
Duvall, W. O., 112, 115
Duxbury, Mass., 7, 40, 316
Dymond, John, 396, *398
Dymond, Mrs. John (Olive), 398
Dymond, John, Jr., *398
Dymond, Jonathan, 396, *398; *Essays on the Principles of Morality . . .* , 398, 631, 636

Earle, John Milton, 280, *281
Earle, Pliny, 681
Earle, Thomas, *505, 681; *The Life, Travels and Opinions of Benjamin Lundy*, 295
Earle, William Buffum, letter to, *681
East Abington, Mass., 88
East Boston, 67
East India Service, 84
East Orange, N.J., 194
Eastern New York Anti-Slavery Society, 58, 67
Eastern Pennsylvania Anti-Slavery Society, 60, 305, 306, 309, 344, 465; meeting at Norristown, Pa., 505
Eddy, James, 346, 589, *591, 592
Eddy, Mrs. James. *See* Merriam, Mrs. Charles D.
Edinburgh, Scotland, 282, 328, 397, 416, 418, 422; WLG in, 423, 424, 428–429, 430, 433, 445; gifts to WLG, 442, 445, 453, 503
Edinburgh, University of, 101, 435, 440, 464
Egypt, 462
Eliot, Charles W., 569

Eliza (servant), 41, 43, 75
Ellen (servant), 357, 368, 407, 416, 462, 573
Ellis, Rev. Rufus, 190
Ellon, Scotland, 435
Ellsworth, Rev. Elijah, 520, *521, 524
Emancipator, 2, *19, 147, 163, 334, 560, 582
Emerson, Ralph Waldo, 10, 215, 281, *282, 607, 640; letter to, 639; and Bible Convention, 66
Emory, Rev. Robert, 419, *421
Empire State Democrat and United States Review, 115
Endecott, John, 316
Endicott, William, *316; letter to, 315
England, 2, 3, 12, 14, 16, 19, 20, 21, 22, 26, 28, 54, 62, 63, 66, 69, 75, 90, 99, 126, 228, 238, 258, 259, 323, 359, 361, 625, 626, 638, 644, 646, 648, 650, 652, 657, 664, 669; repeal of union between Ireland and, 57; WLG's 1840 visit to, 76; WLG deplores conditions in, 125; WLG compares with America, 144; and H. C. Wright, 148, 237; and Texas, 284; WLG's 1846 visit to, 356–423, 435–440, 448–449; progress of reform in, 369–370; WLG's plans for mission in, 370; and WLG's health, 472. *See also* Great Britain
English Baptist Union, 648, *653
English Independent, 417
Ensign, Horace, 518, 521
Ensign, Mrs. Horace (Celestia Raymond), 521
Essex County, Mass., 16, 315
Essex County Anti-Slavery Society, 14, 16, 495
Essex County Washingtonian, 270
Essex Gazette, 269
Estlin, Dr. John Bishop, *383, 569; letters to, 382, 400, 495; WLG visits, 387–388; helps antislavery cause, 406
Estlin, Mary Anne, 401, *402, 406, 410, 496, 569
Europe, 54, 263, 626
Evangelical Alliance, 368, 389, 390, 393, 397, 398, 401, 405, 412, 421, 423, 435, 437, 439, 455; collapse of, 398; and slavery question, 418–420; and antislavery cause in England, 427; attacks and condemnation, 428, 436, 439, 440, 456; in Liverpool, 445; opposition to WLG, 445; at Glasgow, 447; and WLG's British mission, 463, 464

Evangelical Alliance Convention, 346, °348, 369
Evangelist, 134, °136, 147
Everett, Joshua Titus, °140, 644; letter to, 138; family, 517
Examiner. See *True American*
Exeter, England, 368, 382, 392–393, 398
Exeter Hall, London, 415, 420, 423, 455
Exeter, Mass., 14
Ezekiel, 291

Faculty of Physicians and Surgeons of Glasgow, 427
Fall River, Mass., 275, 316
Farmer, William, 442, °443
Farmington, Conn., 117
Farmington, N.Y., 101, 109, 111, 157
Farwell, Emily, 165, °166, 214
Farwell, William, 166
Farwell, Mrs. William (Rebecca), 166
Feethams, England, 443, 451
Ferris, Jacob, °111, 112; speaks, 109, 113, 157
Fifty-fifth Massachusetts Regiment, 8
Finney, Charles Grandison, 523, °525
First Free Congregational Church, 66
Fisher, John Adams, 506, °507
Fleetwood, England, 442
Florence, Mass., 226
Flournoy, John Jacobus, 346, °348
Folger, Robert H., 524, °526
Follen, Dr. Charles, 44, °45, 100, 128, 132, 343, 645, 646
Follen, Mrs. Charles (Eliza Lee Cabot), °343, 439, 626, 645, 646; and *National Anti-Slavery Standard*, 341
Follen, Charles, Jr., 626, °636, 646
Folsom, Abby, 541
Ford (Foord), Sophia, °215, 226
Forster, John, 371, °373
Forster, Josiah, 22, °25
Forten, James, 59, °60
Forten, Mrs. James, 60
Foster, George J., 94, °95
Foster, John, 98, 99
Foster, Sarah, 527, °528
Foster, Stephen Collins, 513
Foster, Stephen Symonds, 15, °16, 27, 86, 101, 252, 267, 275, 296, 323, 474, 527, 531, 532, 547; letter to, 528; WLG on speeches of, 113, 114, 625; in Pennsylvania and Ohio, 466, 510, 512, 515, 519, 522, 523; WLG asks for financial help, 528–529; and Anti-Sabbath Convention, 548
Foster, Mrs. Stephen Symonds (Abby Kelley), 16, 25, °27, 46, 52, 209, 252,

257, 296, 323, 332, 337, 510, 616; at abolitionist meetings, 108, 109, 110, 112, 157, 257; daguerreotype, 469; and Anti-Sabbath Convention, 548
Fourier, François Charles Marie, 138, 236
Fowler, James, °280
Fox, George, 17, °19, 98, 99, 546, 605
Fox, Rev. William Johnson, 371, °374, 391, 394
Foxborough, Mass., 332
Franklin, Conn., 202, 208, 216, 221
Franklin, Mass., 165
Franklin Institute, 194
Free Church of Scotland, 255, 348, 418, 427, 437, 447, 546; money raised in South, 119, 339; WLG and, 326, 328, 428, 445, 456; Douglass attacks, 426; "guilty position of," 433, 683; George Thompson attacks, 436
Free Congregational Society, 95
Freedmen's Bureau, 512
Free Press, The, 268
Free-soil movement, 136, 280, 517, 553, °566, 583, 604; conventions, 564, 574, 581, 583
Free Suffrage Declaimers, 125, °126
French, Mrs. (nurse), 106, 107
French, John Robert, 120–121, 267, °269, 273, 281, 282, 285, 286, 287, 288
Friends Educational Society, 25
Friends of Social Reform, 138
Fugitive Slave Act of 1850, 280
Fuller, James Cannings, 46, °47, 48, 146
Furness, William H., °553, 554

Ganett, J. A., 596
Gardner, Mass., 35, 37, 193
Garnaut (Garneaux), Eliza Jones, 532, °533, 595, 596, 598, 599
Garnet, Rev. Henry Highland, 200
Garrison children, 227, 268, 324, 356, 404, 416, 450, 452, 462, 475, 487, 528, 531, 539, 566, 593, 595, 608. *See also individual names*
Garrison, Charles Follen, 102, 104, 106, 110, 114, 128, 132, 167, 188, 206, 208, 210, 223, 227, 240, 254, 368, 572, 604; birth, 100; teething, 122; health, 154; at Lynn, 517; welcomes WLG, 564–565, 621; Mrs. Paul praises, 597; death, 542, 613, 618–621, 638–639
Garrison, Elizabeth Pease, 467, 477, 509, 517, 568, 575, 613, 621; birth, 328,

460, 461, 471, 472, 475; WLG's poem about, 475; weaned, 532; illness and death, 542, 549–550, 551, 552, 555–556, 608; missed by family, 593

Garrison, Francis Jackson, 12, *600; birth, 542, 599; named, 600, 601

Garrison, George Thompson, *8, 39, 41, 70, 110, 114, 146, 167, 211, 223; sick, 46; education, 130, 154, 268, 532; Laura Stebbins reports on, 212–213; arrangements for, 224, 225; described, 240, 595; at Northampton Association, 268, 296, 367, 574; at Princeton, Mass., 517

Garrison, Helen Frances (Fanny), 120, 368, 405, 475, 509, 517, 564, 565–566, 575, 604; birth, *274, 288–289; WLG's delight in, 276, 356, 572; health, 367, 404, 462, 487; wants WLG home soon, 532; and Charles Follen Garrison, 621–622

Garrison, James Holley, 2, *5, 42, 68, 75, 95, 106, 146; letter to, 3; and life with Bensons, 3–4; health and problems, 8–9, 44, 100, 105; death, 106, 107, 132, 167

Garrison, Wendell Phillips, *8, 41, 47, 110, 114, 146, 167, 208, 223, 308, 368, 604, 644; health, 122; described, 210, 240; in accident, 213; at Lynn, Mass., 517

Garrison, William Lloyd

personal concerns: affection and admiration for friends, 29, 50, 52, 59, 89, 93, 103, 104, 124, 127–130, 132–133, 148, 233, 239, 262, 268, 282, 302, 324, 345, 384, 530, 562, 563, 567, 568; imagines sleighride with Irish friends, 468–469; health (his own and family's), 41–42, 64, 68, 70, 73, 76–77, 88, 114, 116, 122, 123, 128, 132, 138, 146, 154–155, 156, 165, 170–171, 172, 173, 188, 197–198, 205, 226–227, 234, 240, 247, 267–268, 275, 307, 392, 394, 404, 413, 424, 432, 487, 527, 528, 529, 538, 542, 550, 556, 585, 600, takes water cure, 542, 565, 566–567, 570–571, 574, 575–576, 578, 580–581, 584, 593; financial problems, 105–106, 227, 228, 271–272, 297, 329, 330–331, 487, 528–529, 538–539, 558, 559, 598, 667–668, trust fund for, 625, 636; concern for home and family, 114, 247–248, 354, 355–356, 367, 377, 392; rearing of children, 130, 368, 631; large family a hindrance, 462; living

arrangements, 119, 142, 170, 200–201, 208, 209, 210, 577; not suited to a quiet life, 570; impossible to get good likeness of, 575

comments on: human iniquity, 6; religion, 17, 22–24, 90, 97–99, 190–191, 192, 250–251, 602–603, 605, 632–633, 649, 683 (see also Anti-Sabbath Convention); death, bereavement, mortality, 28, 43, 58–60, 73, 77–78, 267, 345, 375, 552, 555, 590, 618–619, 622; self as correspondent, 29, 50, 51–52, 121–122, 123, 128, 133, 233, 237, 262, 322, 345, 413, 418, 495–496, 618; travel by ship, 76, 346–348, 349–351, 354–355, 451, 462, 589–590, by train, 244, 411–412, 423–425; animal magnetism, 114; state of world, 124, 195; clairvoyance, 155; natural beauties, 169–170, 172, 174–175, 184, 597; doctors, 202, 207–208, 213, 217, 218; happiness, 276; riots of 1835, 359, 360, 500; need for a common language, 350; London prostitutes, 364–365; famine in Ireland, 438

on righteousness, progress, and strategy of antislavery cause: 11, 29–30, 32, 35, 36–37, 38, 51, 53, 64–65, 91, 93, 114, 116–117, 128–129, 134–135, 139, 190, 235–236, 238–239, 255–256, 266, 283–284, 306, 307, 309, 314, 339, 380–381, 466–467, 469–470, 478, 488, 498, 503–504; response to attacks, 21–24, 41, 96–99, 139, 179–182, 230–231, 277–279, 414, 445, 446, 481–485, 490–494, 659, 661, 662, 665; describes antislavery meetings, 43, 53, 109, 112–114, 156–158, 162–163, 177–179, 184, 192–193, 255–257, 338–339, 378–379, 387, 390, 393, 396–397, 409–410, 412, 426, 477–480, 505, 507, 511, 515, 518, 519–520, 614–615, 625; and disunion, 54, 89, 128, 277–279, 288, 298–301, 470, 473, 574, 581–582; his own speeches, 94, 109, 112, 132, 159, 170, 177, 235, 245, 248, 251, 255–256, 393, 396–397, 412, 428, 434; divisions among abolitionists, 116–117, 139–140, 245; defends abolitionists against charge of prejudice, 229–230

on other reforms: nonresistance movement, 30, 54–55, 133–134, 237–238, 248, 319, 352–353, 349–350, 388, 399, 634; repeal of intermarriage law, 130–131, 134; repeal of capital pun-

ishment, 134, 144–145, 149–150;
social experimentation, 119, 145, 235,
240–241; woman's rights, 148–149,
543; temperance, 190, 349, 361–362,
363, 642, 655–656; free trade, 503
writings and lecture topics: "Repeal
of the Union," 3; *Thoughts on African
Colonization*, 120, 233, 482, 486;
"Address to the Slaves of the United
States," 155, 158, 166, 167, 168; "The
Sabbath, as a Christian Institution,"
316; "The Duty of Public Worship
Examined," 316–317; "Freedom of
the Mind," 319, 320; "The Constitution and Political Action," 335–336
Garrison, Mrs. William Lloyd (Helen
Elizabeth Benson), 2, 5, *6, 7, 27, 30,
41, 42, 44, 45, 61, 73, 75, 88–89, 95,
102, 107, 122, 147, 152, 153, 167,
173, 185, 202, 205, 224, 233, 235,
243, 268, 324, 329, 332, 422, 450,
462, 467, 474, 477, 487, 499, 503,
539, 548, 568, 578, 579, 584, 587,
591, 608, 613, 618, 619, 620, 621,
639, 643, 644; letters to, 108, 111,
246, 346, 354, 360, 362, 363, 366,
377, 392, 402, 410, 504, 506, 508,
510, 514, 522, 526, 530, 531, 534,
564, 569, 573, 594, 596, 615; health,
94, 106, 123, 132, 187–188, 234, 542,
549; births, of Charles, 100, 104, of
Fanny, 274, 288, of Elizabeth Pease,
328, 460, 461, 471; trials of, 123;
injury to arm and efforts to repair,
119–120, 197, 199, 201–202, 206–207,
209, 211, 212, 213, 216–218, 226, 227,
234, 237, 240; gratitude toward E.
Pease, 228, 272; mother's death, 260;
gratitude toward Lorings, 275–277;
WLG's concern and affection for, 354,
355–356, 363, 367–368, 403–404, 405,
411, 416, 444, 452; WLG misses mailing letter to, 360–361; misses WLG,
384; WLG urges to write, 394; expects H. C. Wright, 498; and servants,
538, 573–574; Lizzy's death, 556;
daguerreotype admired, 575; depressed by arrival home, 594–595;
Charlie's death, 619–620
Garrison, William Lloyd, Jr., *8, 41, 68,
70, 110, 114, 146, 167, 209, 211, 595;
education, 130; Laura Stebbins reports on, 212–213; to be sent home,
223; WLG welcomes, 225; described,
240; at Northampton, 367, 574; at
Princeton, Mass., 517
Gay, Sydney Howard, 60, 163, *269,

305, 333, 342; letters to, 333, 334,
336, 344, 480, 552, 553, 616, 617,
676; edits *Standard*, 2, 266, 269, 341;
at AA-SS anniversary meeting, 478;
at Norristown, Pa., meeting, 505
Gay, Mrs. Sydney Howard (Elizabeth J.
Neall), 333, *334, 335, 337, 575
Gaylord, Frederick C., 198
Geist (Guise), Dr. Christian F., 356,
*357, 367, 404, 550; treats WLG, 538
General Anti-Slavery Conference
(1854), 389
General Anti-Slavery Convention
(1843), 125–126
General Church Conference (1844),
421
General Peace Convention, 149
Genius of Universal Emancipation, 295,
334, 335, 609, 612
Georgetown College, Ky., 651, *654
Georgia, 180, 232, 683
Germany, 44, 45, 99, 357, 646
Gibbons, James Sloan, *72
Gibbons, Mrs. James Sloan (Abigail
Hopper), *72
Giddings, Joshua Reed, *517, 623–624;
at Western Anti-Slavery Society meet-
ings, 515
Gilbert, Olive, *165, 211, 224, 499;
visits Garrisons, 164–165
Gillet, Isaac, 519, *521
Gillet, Mrs. Isaac, 519
Gilpin, H. D., 302
Glasgow, Scotland, 24, 147, 328, 368,
389, 401, 416, 418, 422, 424, 428,
431; H. C. Wright's meeting at, 339;
antislavery meetings at, 434, 447;
Candleriggs, 425; City Hall, 424, 425,
432, 434, 447; Eagle Hotel, 433, 434
Glasgow, University of, 464
Glasgow *Argus*, 31, 447, 448
Glasgow Emancipation Society, 29, 31,
426, 433, 474, 683; letter to, 682;
supports disunion, 118–119; invites
WLG to Britain, 326, 344; Henry
Clapp speaks at meeting of, 473
Glasgow Female Anti-Slavery Society,
425
Glasgow *Herald*, 427
Glasgow Observatory, 14
Glasgow Theological Academy, 447
Gleason, Elizabeth, 155, 156
Gloucester, Mass., 321
Godey's Lady's Book, 452
Golden Rule, 485, 490
Goodell, William, 560, *561, 582, 633;
attacks AA-SS, 110

Gore, John C., 69, *70, 187
Goss, Roswell, *72, 337
Graeffenberg, Austria, 45, 262, 322, 359;
    H. C. Wright at, 264–265; health
    resort at, 268
Graham, Rev. Sylvester, 175, *182
Grand Banks, Newfoundland, 354, 358
Grange, Ireland, 398
Gravesend, England, 359, 364, 368
Gray, John C., *280
Gray, Thomas, 171
"Great Awakening," 471
Great Britain, 13, 72, 127, 147, 232,
    649, 650; and *Creole* case, 101;
    WLG's 1846 visit to, 326–328, 356–
    450, 496; WLG describes schedule
    for, 431–435; Unitarians and WLG's
    mission, 462–463; success of mission,
    467; AA-SS thanks, 479; Douglass'
    reception in, 509. *See also* England;
    Ireland; Scotland
Great Brunswick Street, Dublin, 55, 429,
    430
Great Queen Street, London, 233
Great Western (steamer), 402, 403,
    407, 410, 413
Greeley, Horace, 134, *136
*Green Mountain Spring Monthly Jour-
    nal*, 45
Green Mountains, Vt., 175
Greene, Christopher A., *38
Greene, Dr. Henry Bowen Clarke, 155,
    *156
Greenhow, Dr. Michael Thomas, 441
Greenhow, Mrs. Michael Thomas (Eliz-
    abeth Martineau), 439, 441, 462–
    463
Greenoch, Scotland, 424, 426, 428, 433
Greenville, Conn., 206, 209, 214, 219,
    233, 235; WLG speaks at, 236
Greenville, Tenn., 334, 335
Grenadier Guards, 435
Grew, Rev. Henry, 309, 633, *637
Grew, Mary, 637
Grisi, Giulia, 409, *410
Griswold, Bishop Alexander Viets, 135,
    *137
Gurley, Rev. Ralph Randolph, 486
Gurney, Samuel, 492, *494

Haberfield, John Kerle, 387, *389
Haiti, 18, 19, 48, 53, 70, 682
Hale, David, 156, *158
Hale, John Parker, *553, 581
Hall, Dr. Chauncey Austin, *205; diag-
    noses Helen's arm, 201, 207, 208, 211,
    213, 216, 217–218

Halifax, Nova Scotia, 346, 348, 354,
    359, 361, 366, 367; ship detained at,
    352, 355, 356, 358; Citadel, 352, 353
Hallett, Benjamin Franklin, 560, *561
Hallock, Gerard, 158
Hallowell Academy, 369
Halyard, William, 549
Hamilton, Dr. James, 101, 601
Hamilton College, 333
Hammond, Elisha Livermore, *249, 546,
    600; and WLG, 247, 252–253; plan
    for Community House, 254
Hammond, Mrs. Elisha Livermore
    (Eliza Preston), *249, 600; described,
    247, 249, 253
Hampshire Gazette, 170, 171
Hangman, The, 241
Hannah (servant), 573, 574
Hansard, Luke James, 420, *421–422
Hansard and Sons, L. and G., 422
Hanson Street, Boston, 613
Harden Company, William F., 185, 186
Harding, George, 422, 423
Harper's Ferry, 592
Harris, Rev. George, 439, *441, 462
Harrisburg, Pa., 465; and slavery, 505;
    meetings at, 507, 508
Harrisburg Gas Company, 508
Hart, John, 494–495
Hartford, Conn., 66, 205
Hartford, Ohio, 514
Harvard College, 45, 194, 272, 304, 316,
    343, 454, 464
Harvard Divinity School, 194, 304, 316,
    454
Harvard Medical School, 68, 87, 95,
    156, 205, 463
Harvard University, 27, 228, 646
Hathaway, Joseph Comstock, 109, *111,
    112, 333; report at anniversary meet-
    ing, 157
Hathaway, Mrs. Joseph Comstock (Es-
    ther Aldrich), 111
Haughton, James, *31, 50, 93, 268, 283,
    286, 289, 324, 372, 397, 438, 443;
    WLG's affection for, 29, 104; family,
    239, 368, 423, 468, 489; and Anti-
    Slavery League, 377, 379, 382, 383,
    385; and John Marsh, 389
Haughton, Mrs. James, 104, 127
Haverhill, Mass., 53
Hayden, Lewis, 334, *335
Hayward, Dr. George, 202, *205
Hayward, Josiah, *215
Hayward, Mrs. Josiah (Sarah Lord),
    215
Hazen, Miss, 210, 212

Hazen, Col. Henry, 210, °212, 222
Hazen, Mrs. Henry (Sarah Gifford), 210, 212
Headlam, Thomas Emerson, °411, 439
Hedding, Rev. Elijah, 485, 486
Hemans, Felicia Dorothea, °84; quoted, 77, 203, 590
Henry, Patrick, quoted, 277
Herald and Philanthropist. See Cincinnati *Philanthropist*
Herald of Freedom, 16, 31, 196, °197, 289, 297, 305, 308, 536; on Wright's English mission, 70; controversy over, 120–121, 252, 269, 270, 273, 281, 282, 285–288
Hewitt, Capt. John, 347, 348, 349
Hibernian Anti-Slavery Society, 31
Hicks, Elias, 513
Higginson, Rev. Thomas Wentworth, 589
Higley, Homer, 518–519, °521
Hilditch, Blanche, 439, 450
Hilditch, Sarah, 439; letter to, 450
Hill, Hamilton, 523, °525
Hill, Matilda, 194
Hill, Sir Rowland, 391
Hill, Sally, 194
Hill, Samuel L., 94, °96, 194
Hill, Thomas, 193, °194, 214
Hill Institute, Northampton, Mass., 96
Hillis (Hillas), David Duncan, 113, °115
Hillis and Morgan (law firm), 115
Hincks, William, 397, °398
Hingham, Mass., 37, 38, 88
Hinton, Rev. James Howard, °379, 383–384
Hoare, Sir Richard, 422
Hoare's Bank, 421, 422
Hoby, James, 648, 650, 652, °653, 654
Hodges, Spencer, 332
Hodgson, W. B., and Catharine Linda case, 320, 321
Hodgson, Dr. William Ballantyne, 439, °440, 498; letter to, 562
Hollis Street, Boston, 196, 579
Hooton, Charles, *St. Louis' Isle, or Texiana*, 294
Hopedale Community, 241
Hopper, Isaac T., °72, 337, 554, 615, 616; letter to, 682
House of Representatives. *See* United States Congress
Houston, Dr., 616, 617
Hovey, Charles Fox, °548, 591
Hovey, Mrs. Charles Fox, 591
Howard, John, 372, °374

Howard Street, Boston, 166, 254
Howells, H. C., 383
Howitt, William, °19, 328, 374; WLG on, 371–372, 399; WLG visits, 394
Howitt, Mrs. William (Mary Botham), 328, °374; letter to, 398; WLG describes, 371, 372; WLG visits, 394; "Memoir of William Lloyd Garrison," 394, 395, 398–399, 407, 463
Hudson, Dr. Erasmus Darwin, 74, °75–°76, 94, 170, 173, 177, 207, 214; letter to, 320; at Springfield convention, 184; at West Indies emancipation celebration, 192; examines Helen's arm, 216; in prison, 320; and Catharine Linda case, 321
Hudson, Mrs. Erasmus D. (Martha Turner), 321
Hudson, James, 72
Hudson, Timothy B., 523, °525
Hudson, N.Y., 204
Hudson River, 465
Hughes, Rev. John Joseph, °58, 652, °654, 672
Hugo, Victor, 635
Hull, Isaac, 135, °137
Humphrey, Heman, °486; letters to, 481, 490; WLG attacks, 481–485, 490–494
Humphrey, Louisa, 206, °209, 214; letter to, 233
Hunt, Rev. Thomas P., 193
Hutchinson family, 157, 158, 281, 348
Hutchinson, Abigail Jemima, °158
Hutchinson, Adoniram Judson Joseph, °158
Hutchinson, Asa, °158
Hutchinson, John Wallace, °158
Hutchinson, Minn., 158

Independent, 147
Independent Order of Odd Fellows, 167, 168
India, 18, 55, 228, 230, 631
Indiana, 158, 245
Inginac, Joseph Balthazar, 49
Institute for Colored Youth, Philadelphia, 60
Ipswich, England, 381
Ireland, 2, 18, 26, 49, 51, 52, 54, 56, 62, 120, 283, 397, 640, 641, 648, 650, 655, 657, 664, 668, 674, 675; and disunion, 57; Massachusetts Fair receives gifts from, 239; WLG in, 431, 434–435, 438–439; famine in, 438, 440; American relief for, 470–471, 476–477

Irish Address, 46, 47, 48, 51, 53, 56–57, 58, 61, 542, 641, 648, 667, 668, 671, 672, 673; significance of, 2–3; and antislavery strategy, 62–63; reception of in U.S., 92
Irish-Americans, and antislavery cause, 92, 284, 641–642, 665, 668, 671, 672, 674, 675
Irish Repeal, 57, 58, 62–63, 489
Irish Repeal Association, 61, 63, 93, 231, 232, 233
Ithaca *Journal and Advertiser*, 70
Ives, Lucy G., 588

Jackson, Mr., 518, 521
Jackson, Edmund, °407–°408, 577, 587; WLG grateful to, 404; and Anti-Sabbath Convention, 548
Jackson, Mrs. Edmund, 404, 587
Jackson, Francis, 11, °12, 13, 25, 39, 100, 161, 198, 333, 346, 379, 439, 469, 470, 487, 498, 579, 587, 592, 614, 616, 642, 644, 661, 668; letters to, 38, 183, 186, 195, 200, 297, 330, 345, 391, 534, 559, 575, 601, 677; and Knapp controversy, 45, 78, 80; finances, 105; at AA-SS meetings, 157, 478; visits WLG at Northampton, 183–184, 186, 195; and South Cove Company, 186, 188; WLG asks help in finding house, 200–201; helps finance *Liberator*, 271, 272; at Convention of the People of Massachusetts, 279; and WLG's finances, 297, 330–331, 392, 394–395, 559, 636; and Catharine Linda case, 320, 321; family, 396, 516, 534, 598; WLG grateful to, 404; Webb's letter to, 488, 489; signs call for Anti-Sabbath Convention, 548; will miss daughter, 590; Garrison's son named for, 600
Jackson, Mrs. Francis (Harriet), 185, 186, 577, 594
Jackson, James, 577, 590
Jackson, James Caleb, 108, °110; and James Boyle, 296
Jackson, Phoebe (Phebe), °155, 164, 166, 224; letter to, 154
Jamaica, 233
James, William, 401, °402, 462, 463
Jay, Peter Augustus, 135, °137
Jefferson, Thomas, 628
Jefferson Medical College, 269, 507
Jerrold, Douglas, 328, °373; WLG calls on, 370–371
Jerrold's Weekly News, 373

Jesus Christ, 17, 21, 23, 24, 36, 55, 59, 90, 97, 98, 99, 124, 139, 140, 148, 150, 221, 230, 235, 256, 290, 456, 490, 602, 629, 631, 633, 663, 670
Jesus College, Cambridge, 402
Jim Crow cars, 134, 136, 411, 416
John Hand line, 75
Johnson, Abby, 143
Johnson, Daniel, 142, °143
Johnson, Mrs. Daniel (Miriam B.), 143, 332
Johnson, John, 365, 366
Johnson, Oliver, 60, °72–°73, 100, 189, 197, 240, 242, 248, 249, 258, 480; to share house with Garrisons, 200, 208, 210; moves to Pine St., 223; intends to publish WLG's writings, 253; and *Anti-Slavery Bugle*, 517
Johnson, Mrs. Oliver (Mary Anne), 100, 208, 210, 223, 234, 240, 249, 258
Johnson, Dr. Samuel (English), 369
Johnson, Samuel (American), 589
Johnson, Ziba, 208, 209, 210
Jones, Benjamin Smith, 515, °517, 524, 527
Jones, Mrs. Benjamin Smith (Jane Elizabeth), 517, 524, 527
Jones, John, 528
Jones, Thomas, 527, °528
Jones, Mrs. Thomas (Mary Ann), 528
Journal of the American Temperance Union, 374
Joy, David, °587–°588, 600
Joy, Mrs. David, 600
Joy, Moses, 588
Judd, Hall, 194, °215
Judd, Mrs. Hall (Frances P. Birge), 192, °194, 215
Judkins, Commodore Charles, 405, °408
Judson, Andrew T., 20

Kansas, 226
Karens, 459
Keep, John, 522, °525
Kelley, Abby. *See* Foster, Mrs. Stephen S.
Kendal, England, 26
Kennedy, Mr. and Mrs., 236
Kennedy Farm, 592
Kennett Square, Pa., 309
Kentucky, 335, 346, 609, 622, 623, 651
Kilmarnock, Scotland, 434
Kimball, Joseph H., 197
King, Samuel W., 96
Kingstown, Dublin, 289

Kirk, Rev. Edwin Norris, 327, °363, 373, 421; at World's Temperance Convention, 362–363; at Anti-Slavery League meeting, 378; and antislavery movement, 384; and Evangelical Alliance, 419
Kirkcaldy, Scotland, 445
Knapp, Isaac, 2, 11, °12, 70, 271, 617; controversy with WLG over *Liberator*, 40–42, 78–84; death, 203; WLG's appraisal of, 203–204
Knapp, Mrs. Isaac (Adeline B.), 70, °71
Knapp, Jacob, 235, °236
Knapp's Liberator, 41, 42, 45, 78, 83–84

Lablache, Luigi, 409, °410
Ladd, William, 352
Lake Cochituate, Mass., 599
Lake Erie, 517
Lancaster County, Pa., 158, 506
Lancaster, N.H., 86
Lane Theological Seminary, 269, 332, 374, 522, 525
Langtree, S.D., 136
Latimer, George, case of, 110, °111, 135, 156, 157, 193
Lawrence, Kans., 5
League of Universal Brotherhood, 301, 639
Leavitt, Joshua, 117, 146, °147, 266, 582
Lee, Rev. Samuel, 248, °249, 251–252
Leeds, England, 393, 397, 399, 400, 409, 410, 414
Leeds Anti-Slavery Association, 410
Leesburg (Leesville), Ohio, 480, 524, 526
Legaré, Hugh Swinton, 167, °168
Leghorn, Italy, 18
Le Havre, France, 52, 335
Leicester, Mass., 316, 643, 645
Leominster, Mass., 138, 236
Leslie, Eliza, °452
Lewis, Samuel, 298, °302
Lexington (steamer), 128, 129, 645
Lexington, Ky., 314
Lexington, Mass., 468
Liberal Republicans, 136
Liberator, The, 1, 10, 11, 12, 18, 27, 30, 31, 37, 40, 41, 46, 47, 51, 53, 57, 66, 67, 71, 72, 85, 87, 93, 96, 98, 99, 102, 110, 115, 131, 137, 156, 181, 194, 229, 288, 316, 332, 395, 422, 567, 608, 616, 617, 620, 625, 642, 643, 647, 662, 670, 682; letters to, 156, 174, 189, 201, 216, 244, 249, 431,

437, 477, 518, 614; publicizes Irish Address, 3; supports disunion, 3, 121; Gerrit Smith supports, 9; Ashurst contributes to, 19; problems of, 41, 105, 106, 227–228, 239, 243, 271–272, 305, 306, 331, 535, 538–539, 598, 605, 667–668; and Knapp controversy, 42, 45, 78–84, 203, 204; compared to *Standard*, 60; prints account of *Creole* case, 100, 101; motto of, 118, 121, 141, 268; H. C. Wright writes for, 119, 135, 264, 322–323, 324, 380; attacked by Judge Thacher, 137; publishes political letters of D. L. Child, 164; Quincy edits, 171, 417, 466; WLG looks forward to editing again, 205; will publish "fresh testimonies," 215; prints letter from Louisa Humphrey, 234–235; call for New Bedford convention not printed in, 281, 282; prints disunion and antislavery pledges, 303, 304; founding of, 334, 335; should protest Mexican war, 353; *Punch* prints excerpts from, 371; WLG too busy to send material to, 413, 431, 440; helped by E. Pease, 444–445; and *North Star*, 533; and Anti-Sabbath Convention, 541; must exercise care with regard to Free-soil movement, 581; and religious controversy, 626–635; letter to Financial Committee, 667
Liberia, 72, 484
Liberia, 486
Liberty Bell, The, 147
Liberty Club (Cleveland), 528
Liberty League, 110, 561
Liberty party, 19, 67, 68, 108, 109, 110, 111, 164, 200, 238, 269, 296, 302, 303, 315, 402, 505, 521, 523, 526, 553, 561, 581, 583; AA-SS opposed to, 163; and new organization, 245; at Ipswich, N.H., 248; and U.S. Constitution, 265, 269; and antislavery cause, 266; Bradburn joins, 273, 288; Cincinnati convention, 298, 299; in Ohio, 516
Liberty Press, 110
Limerick, Ireland, 438
Lincoln, Abraham, 314
Lincoln, Jairus, 87, °88
Lincoln, Sumner, °37, 193; letter to, 35
Lippincott, Leander K., 513
Literary and Catholic Sentinel. See Boston *Pilot*
Littleton, N.H., 85, 86, 87
Liverpool, England, 24, 28, 50, 76, 89,

360; Prince Albert visits, 356, 358; grand meeting planned in, 429; party at Dr. Hodgson's in, 439; antislavery meetings in, 440, 442, 445; Albert Dock, 358, 360; Brown's Temperance Hotel, 357, 359, 439; Clayton Square, 357, 359, 439; Mechanics Institution, 439; Sailors' Home, 358, 360

London, England, 19, 27, 28, 52, 76, 101, 120, 147, 230; WLG in, 357, 359–384, 390–395, 396; WLG's reaction to, 363–365; antislavery meetings in, 327, 393, 396, 414. *See also* London, Crown and Anchor Tavern

London, Crown and Anchor Tavern, 369, 393; Anti-Slavery League meetings at, 327, 368, 376, 378, 382, 383–384

London, Exeter Hall, 91, 230, 233, 393, 397, 401, 405, 410, 412, 653, 657; meeting on Evangelical Alliance at, 412, 414, 415, 420–421, 423

London, Freemasons Hall, 127, 230, 232

London, Literary Institute, 348

London, "National Hall," 395, 401; antislavery meeting at, 393, 396

London, Stamford Street Chapel, 398

London, Vauxhall Gardens, 412

London, Whittington Club, 369

London, Ontario, 332

London Committee. *See* British and Foreign Anti-Slavery Society

London Convention. *See* World's Anti-Slavery Convention

London *Daily News*, 328, 371, 373

London *Inquirer*, 397, 398

London League. *See* Anti-Slavery League

London *Nonconformist*, 472

London *Patriot*, 415, 417, 420, 423, 448, 449

London Peace Society, 149

London Post Office, 360

London *Times*, on Douglass, 479, 480

London *Universe*, 382, 383

Long Pond, Mass., 597

Lorain County (Ohio) Peace Society, 525

Loring, Ellis Gray, 6, °7, 21, 141, 161, 196, 208, 329, 503, 504, 668; letter to, 534; and Knapp controversy, 45, 78, 80; and WLG's finances, 105, 636; signs protest, 118; WLG may rent house from, 138, 142, 145, 200; and *Liberator* finances, 271; WLG's regard for, 243, 276, 466, 467; at Convention of the People of Massachu-

setts, 279; and Catharine Linda case, 320, 321

Loring, Mrs. Ellis Gray (Louisa Gilman): letters to, °141, 243, 275, 329, 466, 503; WLG grateful to, 141, 243, 275–276, 329, 466

Louisiana Purchase, 612

Louisville, Ky., 314, 455

Lovett, William, 328, 372, 373, °374, 394

Lovejoy, Elijah P., 369

Lovejoy, Joseph C., 367, °369

Lovejoy, Owen, 369

Lovelace, William, first Earl of, 463

Lowell, James Russell, °343, 569; quoted, 329; and *Standard*, 341, 343

Lowell, Mass., 51, 94, 189, 192, 257, 266, 315, 316

Lower Canada, 101

Low Hampton, N.Y., 136

Lundy, Benjamin, °295, 334, 505; *Autobiography*, 335

Lupton, Joseph, 409, °410

Lurgen, Ireland, 398

Lushington, Stephen, 492, °494

Luther, Martin, 98, 99, 457, 546, 605

Lynn, Mass., 101, 138, 142, 258, 270, 468; WLG speaks at, 235; West Indies emancipation celebration at, 577, 582

Lynn *Pioneer*, 19, 270, 288, 289, 414

Lynn Women's Anti-Slavery Sewing Circle, 332

Lynn Women's Anti-Slavery Society, 143

Lyon, Mary, 212

Macaulay, Zachary, 230, °233, 492

Macclesfield, England, 421

McClintock, Thomas, 108, °110

McClintock, Mrs. Thomas (Mary Ann), 108

McClintock, Mary, 108

McDuffie, George, 179, °182, 290

Mack, David, °75, 213, 215, 235, 254

Mack, Mrs. David, 215, 254

Mackay, Charles, 448, 604

McKim, Charles Follen, 308

McKim, Lucy, 308

McKim, James Miller, °308, 617; letters to, 306, 316, 335, 343; and subscriptions for WLG's trip, 343; meets WLG in Philadelphia, 504; and Anti-Sabbath Convention, 544

McKim, Mrs. James Miller (Sarah Allibone Speakman), 336

Macleod, Dr. William, 556, *557
Macon, Georgia, 219
Madison, James, 232, 301, 302
Madison, Ohio, 518
Madison, Wis., 205
Mahan, Rev. Asa, 523, *525
Maid of the Mist, The (excursion boat),
  576, 578
Maine, 66, 94, 100, 606
Malcom, Howard, 650, 651, *654
Manchester, England, 18, 28, 416, 418,
  422, 429; antislavery meeting at, 439;
  Evangelical Alliance meeting at, 463,
  464; Free Trade Hall, 435, 437
Manchester New College, 401
Mann, Anne E., 210, *212
Mann, Horace, 582, *583
Marlborough, N.H., 248, 249
Marriott, Charles, *72; death of, 204;
  WLG praises, 204–205
Marsh, Rev. John, *374; at World's
  Temperance Convention, 373; and
  antislavery movement, 384; and James
  Haughton, 389
Marshall, John, 232
Martha Washington Societies. *See*
  Washingtonian movement
Martin, Edward, *452
Martin, Mrs. Edward (Mary), *452, 477
Martin, William, 494, *495
Martineau, Harriet, 401, 407, *408, 439,
  441, 462
Martineau, James, 400, *401, 408, 462
Martineau, Mrs. Thomas (Elizabeth
  Rankin), 439, *441, 462
Massachusetts, 2, 16, 32, 66, 120, 416,
  626, 640; repeals intermarriage law,
  130–131; and Latimer case, 193; and
  Liberty party, 266, 269, and disunion,
  277–278; Superior Court, 280; Court
  of Common Pleas, 280; and Catharine
  Linda case, 320–321; and Mexican
  war, 353. *See also* Massachusetts
  legislature
Massachusetts Abolitionist, 11, 12
Massachusetts Abolition Society, 1, 12,
  13, 25, 26
Massachusetts Anti-Slavery Fairs. *See*
  Anti-Slavery Bazaars
Massachusetts Anti-Slavery Society, 1,
  3, 7–8, 9, 12, 14, 16, 18, 20, 26, 40,
  41, 46, 47, 70, 72, 83, 85, 87, 88, 95,
  120, 136, 186, 246, 269, 275, 288,
  305, 306, 323, 325, 343, 346, 480,
  540, 542, 563, 567, 606, 637, 641,
  647, 666; Board of Managers of,
  10–11, 12–13, 26, 32, 35, 48–49, 83,

88, 639, 647, 661, 668; and Knapp
  controversy, 42; resolution on disunion, 118; convention, 173; censures
  Ricketson, 275; raises funds for
  WLG's trip, 326; will pay George
  Thompson's expenses in U.S., 472
Massachusetts General Hospital, 156,
  205
Massachusetts Historical Society, 280,
  561
Massachusetts legislature, 6, 19, 111,
  131, 134, 135, 136, 140, 168, 197,
  280, 281; and capital punishment,
  144, 149; and fugitive slaves, 157;
  petitioned for secession, 470, 473
Massilon, Ohio, 526; antislavery meet-
  ings at, 542
Mathew, Father Theobald, *51, 56, 92,
  495, 640, 642, 644, 652, 653, 656,
  659, 662, 665, 673, 676; letters to,
  641, 646, 655, 661, 668, 673; and
  Irish Address, 2, 47; unable to affect
  Irish attitude toward slavery, 285;
  WLG's displeasure with, 540, 542–
  543
May, Frederick W. G., 450
May, John Joseph, 450
May, Samuel, 227, 450
May and Company, Samuel, 449, 450
May, Rev. Samuel, Jr., *480, 598, 604,
  614, 615, 644, 645; letters to, 603,
  643; at AA-SS anniversary meeting,
  478
May, Mrs. Samuel, Jr., 644
May, Samuel J., *7, 9, 25, 45, 214, 260,
  281, 352, 357, 499, 516, 528, 534,
  599; letters to, 6, 87, 261, 302, 331,
  461, 547, 549; at funeral of James
  Garrison, 132; WLG urges to attend
  Plymouth meeting, 261; at Conven-
  tion of the People of Massachusetts,
  279; WLG's affection for, 302; and
  Anti-Sabbath Convention, 541; offers
  help with *Liberator*, 574
May, Mrs. Samuel J. (Lucretia Flagge
  Coffin), *7, 88, 304, 463, 464, 548,
  549
Medina, Ohio, 524
Melancthon, 98, 99, 605; *Augsburg
  Confession*, 631, 636
Melbourne, Australia, 421
Mellen, George W. F., *241, 238
Merriam, Charles D., 185, 186, 369
Merriam, Mrs. Charles D. (Eliza Jack-
  son; later Mrs. James Eddy), 185,
  *186, 346, 516, 534, 550, 577, 587;
  letters to, 578, 589; and WLG, 404,

590, 592; raises money for tea service duty, 503; second marriage, 591

Merriam, Eliza F., 590–591

Merriam, Francis Jackson, 590–591, °592

Merrill, Joseph, letter to, 494, °495

Merrimack River, 174

Mesmer, Friedrich, 115

Methodists, 98, 659

Methodist Episcopal Church, 113, 421, 486

Methuen, Mass., 11

Mexico, 66, 314, 465, 540; and annexation of Texas, 238, 284, 291; WLG condemns war with, 326, 338, 353, 470, 473, 476, 477, 488–489, 610, 684; Cassius Clay and war with, 622–623

Mexico City, 489

Miall, Edward, 372, °374

Middlesex Standard, 266, 269

Milford, N.H., 244–245, 246, 250

Mill, John Stuart, 374

Millbury, Mass., 94, 240

Miller, John, 638, °639

Miller, Col. Jonathan Peckham, 46, °47, 48

Miller, William, 135, °136–°137, 151, 248

Millisack, Mr., 524

Milton, John, 8

Milwaukee University, 194

Missouri Compromise, 517, 610, 612–613

Mitre Tavern, 422

Mohegan (ship), 74, 75

Monongahela River, 510

Monroe, James, 660

Monterey, Mexico, battle at, 476, 477

Montgomery, James, 403, °407; WLG copies his letter, 406; at Sheffield anti-slavery meeting, 409, 411

Monthly Repository, 374

Montreal (ship), 280

Moore, Dr. Robert, °60

Moore, Mrs. Robert (Esther), °60

Moore, Robert Ross Rowan, 440

Moore, Mrs. Robert Ross Rowan (Rebecca Fisher), 439, °440

Moral Reform Society, 533

Morgan, John, 523, °525

Morgan, J. P., 535

Moriarity, Dr. Joseph, 461, °463

Morse, Rev. Sidney Edwards, 419, °421

Morton, Marcus, 134, °136; letter to, 453

Mott, James, 27, 60, °61, 308, 336, 524;

letter to, 544; WLG stays with, 504; WLG thanks for donation, 544; signs call for Anti-Sabbath Convention, 545, 548

Mott, Mrs. James (Lucretia Coffin), 25, °27, 30, 60, 61, 72, 127, 308, 316, 333, 336, 524, 526, 547, 605, 616; letters to, 295, 544; WLG stays with, 504; at Norristown meeting, 505; at Salem meeting, 525; at Anti-Sabbath Convention, 541; WLG thanks for donation, 544; signs call for Anti-Sabbath Convention, 545, 548; and AA-SS anniversary, 552, 554

Mott Memorial Library, 222

Mott, Dr. Valentine, 219, °222

Moulton, Albanus K., 560, °561

Mount Holyoke, Mass., 169, 174, 183, 187, 511

Mount Holyoke College, 212, 587

Mount Holyoke Seminary, 210, 212

Mount Pleasant, Ohio, 335

Mount Tom, Mass., 169, 174

Mount Washington, N.H., 31, 169

Mumford, Stephen, 99

Munroe, James, 157, °158, 523

Munson, Ohio, 519–520

Murray, John, 29, °31, 268, 389, 424, 684; WLG's affection for, 104; WLG visits, 426; and H. C. Wright, 427

Murray, Mrs. John, 426

Muswell Hill, England, 381, 394, 413

Nahant, Mass., 267, 468

Naish, Arthur John, 396, 397, °398

Nantucket, 19, 47, 103, 167, 194, 272, 282, 587; fire in, 470, 471; contributes to Irish relief, 470

Napoleon Bonaparte, 186

Nashua, N.H., 47, 86, 244, 257; Central House, 47

Nassau, Bahamas, 63

Natick, Mass., 309, 320

National Academy of Art, 569

National Advocate, 60, 561

National Anti-Slavery Bazaar (1846), 328–329, 562, 567, 592

National Anti-Slavery Standard, 7, 25, 42, 43, 59, 63, 70, 72, 110, 136, 165, 242, 266, 269, 288, 371, 395, 480, 481, 505, 616, 625; established, 2; and AA-SS, 19; D. L. Child and editorship, 27, 161–162, 175–176; must be nonpolitical, 162–163; publishes political letters from D. L. Child, 164; "defective" article in, 199;

finances, 305–306, 309–314; indispensable to antislavery cause, 310; read
in southern states, 313; purpose and
policies, 313–314, 340–342; an-
nounces annual meeting of AA-SS,
333, 334; and money for WLG's trip,
344; and Free-soil movement, 581
National Convention of Colored Citi-
zens, 199, 200
National Association for the Advance-
ment of Colored People, 274
*National Enquirer and Constitutional
Advocate of Universal Liberty*, 295
National Era, 35
National Liberty Party Convention, 530
National Philanthropist, 666
National Temperance Advocate, 60
National Temperance Society of En-
gland, 348
Neall, Daniel, *337
Neill, John B., 428, 429
Nelson, Isaac, *389–*390, 422
Newark, N.J., 296
New Bedford, Mass., 112, 115, 271, 272,
274, 275, 280, 282, 315, 334, 607;
and antislavery conventions, 281, 333,
334; Bedford Commercial Bank, 536;
Merchants' Bank, 280; Sears Court,
316
New Bedford Lyceum, 536, 606, 607
New Bedford Railroad, 272
New Brighton, Pa., 509, 510–511
New Brighton *Times*, 510, 513
New Broad Street, London, 389
Newburyport, Mass., 27, 172, 174, 469
Newcastle-upon Tyne, England, 397,
418, 422, 423, 432, 436, 463; anti-
slavery meeting and public breakfast
at, 439, 441; Hanover Square Chapel,
441
New Connexion of General Baptists, 421
New England, 1, 84, 86, 121; Fast Days,
66; hospitality, 111
New England Anti-Slavery Convention:
(1841), 25, 26; (1842), 74, 75, 85,
86; (1843), 154, 155, 165, 166, 167,
168, 465; (1845), 307, 309; (1846),
described, 338–339; resolves to pay
for WLG's trip to Great Britain, 339,
340; (1847), 415, 473, 480, 481;
(1848), 558, 560; (1849), 616, 625,
636, 683
New England Anti-Slavery Society, 45,
71, 147, 325, 666; fund-raising fair,
136
New England Non-Resistance Society,
30, 31, 316, 323, 325, 454; and H. C.

Wright's mission to England, 16, 68;
Executive Committee, 70, 102, 238;
anniversary meeting, 107; and anti-
slavery movement, 264; motto of, 268
New England Puritan, 144, *147, 560,
561
*New England Reporter and Catholic
Diary*, 51, 92
New England Weekly Review, 269
New Hampshire, 16, 28, 53, 86, 87, 103,
126, 169, 242, 275, 281, 294; WLG
on, 15; WLG's tour of, 244–254; and
abolitionist cause, 252
New Hampshire Anti-Slavery Society,
16, 197; and *Herald of Freedom* con-
troversy, 120–121, 252, 267, 269, 270,
273, 285, 287; meeting at Concord,
N.H., 258
New Harmony, Ind., 147
New Haven, Conn., 26
New Ipswich, N.H., 246; WLG lectures
at, 248–249, 251–252; First Congre-
gational Church, 249
New Lanark, Scotland, 147
New London, Conn., 20, 305
New Lyme, Ohio, 515–516, 518
New Marlboro, Mass., 321
New Mexico, 610
New Orleans, La., 63
Newport, R.I., 99
New Testament, 97
Newton, Ohio, 521
New York Assay Office, 63
New York Anti-Slavery Society, 2, 19,
110, 460
New York City, 18, 25, 27, 42, 52, 70,
74, 76, 84, 89, 111, 113, 115, 129,
144, 204, 274, 280, 343, 461, 616,
617, 625, 640, 645, 649, 651, 682;
AA-SS advertises anniversary meeting
in, 336–337; change in antislavery
sentiment in, 478; Allen Street Pres-
byterian Church, 136; Apollo Hall,
156, 158, 254, 255, 479, 480; Broad-
way Tabernacle, 26, 134, 135, 156,
158, 333, 334, 336, 337, 481, 553,
614, 615; Graham Boarding House,
72, 337; South Reformed Church, 193
New York *Courier and Enquirer*, 58
New York Court of Sessions, 561
New York *Evangelist*, 144, 147
New York *Evening Post*, 269
New York *Journal of Commerce*, 156,
158
New York *Morning News*, 136
New York *Morning Star*, 661, *666
New York *Observer*, 144, *147, 421

New York state, 1, 46, 58, 68, 69, 70, 164, 269, 296, 465, 576, 676; WLG's tour of, 108–115; hospitality, 111

New York *Sun*, 269

New York *Tribune*, 134, *136, 165, 269, 480, 481, 581

New York University, 421

Niagara Falls, 498, 576, 579, 587; Table Rock House, 577; American Falls and Horseshoe Falls, 578

Nichol, John, 14

Nicholas I of Russia, 470, 471

Nickerson, Lorenzo D., 215

Nickerson, Mrs. Lorenzo D., 214, *215

Niger Valley, 513

Noah, Mordecai Manuel, 560, *561

Noah's Sunday Times, 561

Noah's Times and Weekly Messenger, 561

Nonconformist, 372, 374

Nonresistance movement, 323. *See also* New England Non-Resistance Society

Non-Resistant, 102, 133, 316

Norfolk, Va., 63, 111, 275

Norfolk County, Mass., 306

Norfolk County Anti-Slavery Society, 11, 471

Norristown, Pa., 505

North, William C., *572–*573

North, 3, 5, 7, 71, 658, 671

North American Review, 343

Northampton, Mass., 5, 42, 61, 66, 67, 68, 73, 75, 94, 95, 100, 105, 120, 138, 165, 167, 212, 213, 257, 267, 321; Garrisons spend summer in, 119, 164, 166, 169–205 *passim*; WLG on, 169–170, 171–172, 174–175, 176, 578; WLG on meetings at, 170, 173, 177–179, 180; temperance celebration at, 189–191; celebration of British West Indies emancipation, 189, 192–193; WLG's water cure at, 542, 564–572, 574–591 *passim*, 593, 600, 615; American House, 187, 188; Edwards Church, 193; First Church, 194; St. John's Parish, 193

Northampton Association of Education and Industry, 5, 10, 27, 66, 75, 76, 93, *95, 96, 101, 138, 154, 165, 170, 177, 193, 198, 199, 209, 212, 214, 215, 224, 225, 235, 236, 249, 253, 254, 268, 585, 599, 603; attacked on equal rights, 137; finances, 137; struggles for success, 184–185; F. Jackson and N. P. Rogers to stay at, 187; members at West Indies emancipation celebration, 192; and Dr.

David Ruggles, 194; Hammonds to join, 247; and Mrs. Paul, 258, 259

Northampton Community. *See* Northampton Association

Northampton *Courier*, 179, 182, 190

Northampton *Democrat*, 179–183

Northampton *Gazette*, 179

North British Advertiser, 547

North Brookfield, Mass., 603, 604

North Dennis, Mass., 343

Northern Star (Leeds), 374

North Star, 513, 533

Norton, John Treadwell, 116–*117; letter to, 116

Norwich, Conn., 202, 208, 209, 212, 214, 219

Norwich, England, 494

Nott, Samuel, 221–*222

Noyes, John Humphrey, 2, 24, *26, 101, 172

Oberlin, Ohio, 520, 523

Oberlin College, 158, 512, 525, 526; Theological Department, 332

Oberlin Collegiate Institute, 522–523, 525

Oberlin *Evangelist*, 332, 333

O'Connell, Daniel, 18, *19, 51, 56, 57, 62, 63, 89, 92, 93, 286, 492, 641, 657, 671, 672, 674; letter to, 229; and Irish Address, 2, 47; quoted, 91; letter to Cincinnati Repeal Association, 229, 232; and WLG, 231–232; and Irish attitude toward slavery, 285; death, 489, 490

O'Connor, Feargus Edward, 373, *374

Ohio, 32, 158, 332, 465, 466, 474, 497, 503, 623; WLG in, 510–533

Ohio (American) Anti-Slavery Society. *See* Western Anti-Slavery Society

Ohio River, 510

Old Dartmouth Historical Society Whaling Museum, 536

Old Kennett Meeting House, Chester County, Pa., 306

Old Testament, 97, 632, 634

Oldtown, Me., 369

Olin, Rev. Stephen, 419, *421

Oneida, N.Y., 26

Oneida Institute, 332

Oneida *Whig*, 196, 197

Onondaga Solar Salt Company, 115

Onondaga *Standard*, 115

Ordnance Survey (Ireland), 51

Oregon, 561

O'Sullivan, John Louis, 134, *136, 144

Oswald, James, 448
Otis, Harrison Gray, 600, °601
Otis, James, 479, 489
Overend, Gurney and Company, 494
Owen, Robert, °147; social doctrine, 145, 240–241, 267

Page, William, 568, °569
Paine, Byron, 521
Paine, Gen. James Harvey, 519
Paine, Oliver Dwight, 214, °215
Paine, Thomas, 97, 98, 99
Paines Corners, Ohio, 514
Painesville, Ohio, 518; antislavery meeting at, 519; peace convention at, 628, 635; American House, 518, 521
Painesville and Fairport Railroad, 521
Painesville *Telegraph*, 518, 521
Paisley, Scotland, 424, 426; antislavery meeting at, 428, 433
Paley, William, 98, 99, 605; *Principles of Moral and Political Philosophy*, 631, 636
Palfrey, John G., 644, °645
Palmer, Dr. James George, 289
Paris, France, 52, 54, 626, 635, 638, 646; Salle de Ste. Cécile, 635
Paris Peace Congress, 623, 624, 635, 638, 639; Committee, 639
Park, Miss, 401, 402
Parker, Theodore, °340, 541, 546, 547, 605, 607, 640; letters to, 543, 552, 613; speaks at Boston antislavery convention, 339; and Anti-Sabbath Convention, 545, 548; and AA-SS anniversary (1848), 552; *A Discourse of Matters Pertaining to Religion*, 340; *Sermon of War*, 351
Parker, Mrs. Theodore, 613
Parker, William F., °194, 214; and West Indies emancipation celebration, 193
Parkman, Rev. Francis, 462, °464
Parliament, British, 19, 328, 366, 374, 448, 649; House of Commons, 95, 205, 440; House of Lords, 435
Parry, J. H., 374
Path-Finder, 275
Paton, Andrew, °425, 427, 434; WLG visits, 423, 432
Paton, Catherine, °425; WLG visits, 423, 432
Patton, Rev. William, °374, 421; at World's Temperance Convention, 373; and antislavery movement, 384; and Evangelical Alliance, 419
Paul, Rev. Nathaniel, 258, °260

Paul, Mrs. Nathaniel, 558, 572; and Northampton Community, 258–259; WLG visits, 597
Peace Almanac, The, 272, 274
Peace Congress. *See* Paris Peace Congress
Peace Reading-Book (Reader), The, 272–273, 274
Peacham, Vt., 209
Peacock, H. B., 439, °440
Pearl Street, New York, 72
Pease, Elizabeth, 2, °14, 26, 146, 151, 268, 339, 402, 416, 571, 591, 639, 646, 684; letters to, 13, 16, 21, 28, 76, 88, 123, 148, 226, 272, 344, 375, 435, 443, 451, 471, 555, 592, 610, 637, 645; WLG's regard for, 22, 104, 133, 147, 226, 324, 376; health, 76, 88, 123, 364, 375, 376, 393, 407; WLG urges to visit U.S., 89, 443–444, 452, 477; and H. C. Wright, 126, 227, 472; gives financial aid to WLG, 227, 228, 239, 444; death of father, 345; WLG visits, 439, 441–442; WLG's daughter named for, 461; and Anti-Sabbath Convention, 541; and M. W. Chapman, 568; and E. J. M. Eddy, 592
Pease, John Beaumont, °452, 477
Pease, Mrs. John Beaumont, 452, 477
Pease, Joseph, °14, 18, 125, 151, 364; death of, 345, 375
Pease, Mrs. Joseph, 14, 18, 125, 151
Peck, Dr. David Jones, 510, 511, °513, 518, 519, 520; at Youngstown, Ohio, antislavery meetings, 512
Peck, John, 512, °513
Peirce, Cyrus, °304–°305
Peirce, John B., 582
Pemigewasset Inn, Plymouth, N.H., 87
Penn, William, 17, °19, 98, 99, 546
Pennington, J. W. C., 635
Pennsylvania, 99, 307, 465, 466, 474, 498, 503; beauty of, 506
Pennsylvania, University of, 45; Medical School, 205
Pennsylvania Anti-Slavery Society, 543
Pennsylvania Freeman, 59, 60, 269, 295, 309, 336, 343, 395, 505; and funds for WLG's British mission, 343
Pennsylvania-Ohio Canal, 512, 514
Pennsylvania Railroad Co., 508
People's and Howitt's Journal, 374
People's Charter, 126
People's Journal, 328, 371, 374, 398, 407, 463; prints biography of WLG, 394, 395, 414
People's Press, 275

Percy, Dr. Edward, 209
Perfectionist, 24, 26, 172
Perth, Scotland, 446
Peru, Mass., 321
Phelps, Amos A., 22, °25; at Chardon-Street Convention, 23; at London antislavery convention, 246
Philadelphia, Pa., 59, 60, 61, 70, 72, 75, 110, 267, 269, 289, 307, 308, 333, 343, 360, 412, 498, 614, 617, 677; Franklin Hall, 402; Pennsylvania Hall, 337; Temperance Hall, 309, 319
Philadelphia County, 506
Philadelphia Liberty Party Bazaar, 400, 402
Philadelphia *World*, 257
Philanthropist, 30, 31, 32
Philbrick, Samuel, 45, °85, 187, 346, 617, 668; and *Liberator*, 78, 80, 271, 272; WLG in debt to, 105, 331; and WLG's trust fund, 636
Phillips, Stephen Clarendon, °280, 315, 645
Phillips, Wendell, °19–°20, 25, 30, 35, 38, 46, 48, 56, 61, 65, 92, 93, 136, 145, 161, 228, 275, 296, 307–308, 309, 316, 333, 384, 392, 393, 402, 404, 475, 487, 497, 534, 540, 543, 546, 552, 554, 560, 569, 577, 589, 608, 614, 615, 616, 617, 625, 627, 642, 644, 661, 668, 676; travels in Italy, 18; lectures at Boston Town Hall, 45; and *Herald of Freedom* controversy, 121, 285, 536; speech, 1843, 157; at Nahant, Mass., 267; and New Bedford convention, 281; and Catharine Linda case; helps Quincy edit *Liberator*, 327; health, 337, 595, 598; and *Standard*, 341; quoted, 366, 388; and Jim Crow cars, 416; and daguerreotype of Webb, 469; offers resolution at AA-SS anniversary meeting, 478–479; care of wife, 498–499; and Anti-Sabbath Convention, 541, 548; lends WLG money, 559
Phillips, Mrs. Wendell (Ann Terry Greene), 18, °20, 475, 497, 498–499, 595, 598; health, 267
Phonography, 350, 514
Phonotypy, 350
Pierce, Elizabeth A., 224, 225
Pierpont, John, °535–°536, 537
Pillsbury, Parker, °16, 27, 252, 323, 337, 389, 460, 510, 546, 547, 605, 614, 625; letter to, 14; and *Herald of Freedom*, 273; and Anti-Sabbath Convention, 548

Pindell, Richard, 608, °612
Pine Street, Boston, 208, 209, 223, 235, 240, 357, 542, 577, 581, 613, 619
Pioneer: A Literary and Critical Magazine, 343
Pioneer and Herald of Freedom, 270, 289, 417
Pitman, Isaac, °4, 303
Pittsburgh, Pa., 465, 500; antislavery meetings at Temperance Hall, 509–510
Pittsburgh *Mystery*, 510, 513
Pittsfield Medical College, 321
Plainfield, Conn., 157
Playford Hall, Ipswich, England, 385
Plymouth, Mass., 7, 261, 316, 484
Plymouth, N.H., 85, 87
Plymouth County (Mass.) Anti-Slavery Society, 27, 28, 38, 88, 261
Polk, James K., 269, 560; on the Union, 299–301; on Mexican war, 474, 477
Portadown, Ireland, 438
Porter, Fortune R., 214, 215
Portsmouth, N.H., 70
Post, Isaac, 108, °110
Post, Mrs. Isaac, 111
Powell, William P., °72
Prentiss, H. J., 605, 606
Presbyterian church, 255, 625
Prescott, Edward, 595, °596
Prescott and Chapin, 596
Preston, James A., °529–°530
Preston, John, 420, °421
Prideaux, James, °357; illness, 366; death, 404
Prideaux, Mrs. James, 357, 404, 416; devotion to husband, 366
Priessnitz, Vincenz, 45, 268, 581
Priestly, Joseph, 98, 99
Princeton, Mass., 140
Princeton Theological Seminary, 193, 363
Princeton University, 194
Prisoner's Friend, The, 241
Protestant church, 230
Providence, R.I., 6, 10, 38, 46, 49, 51, 52, 54, 73, 94, 99, 105, 107, 202, 209, 224, 226, 229, 257, 259, 260, 267, 357, 461, 487; Bell Street Chapel, 591
Pryor, George W., 112, °115
Pugh, Sarah, °333, 410
Punch, 328, 371
Purchase Street, Boston, 575
Purdy, Edward C., 277–°279
Puritan. See *New England Puritan*
Purvis, Robert, 25, °27, 60
Putney, Vt., 26

Quakerism, 231
Quincy, Arthur B., °608
Quincy, Edmund, 6, °7, 11, 25, 38, 48, 60, 65, 145, 161, 228, 281, 333, 337, 343, 360, 361, 367, 384, 393, 439, 471, 540, 542, 546, 589, 600, 614, 668; letters to, 10, 37, 64, 102, 169, 242, 271, 305, 349, 358, 369, 378, 390, 417, 535, 537, 560, 580, 608; edits *Standard*, 2, 163, 266, 269, 341; and *Knapp's Liberator*, 45; and *Herald of Freedom* controversy, 121, 285, 536; and Bible convention, 66; and *Liberator* controversy, 78, 80; and *Non-Resistant*, 102; edits *Liberator*, 171, 327, 366, 413, 414, 417, 466, 505, 537, 560; and *Liberator*, 206, 271–272; resigns presidency of New England Non-Resistance Society, 238; annual report for MA-SS (1843), 242; and Richard Webb, 283, 469; and *North Star*, 533; and Anti-Sabbath Convention, 541, 548
Quincy, Mrs. Edmund (Lucilla P. Parker), 11, 306, 608
Quincy, Josiah, 7, 569
Quincy, Morton, 306, 608

"Rally 'Round the Flag," 158
Ram's Horn, 72
Randall, David Austin, 520, °521
Randolph, John, 484, 486
Randolph, Ohio, 529
Randolph-Macon College, 421
Rathbone, Richard, 563, °564
Rathbone, Mrs. Richard (Hannah Mary Reynolds), 564
Rathbone, William, °14, 320, 404; letter to, 563
Rathbone, Mrs. William (Elizabeth Gray), 319, °320
Rawson, Mary, 403, °407, 630, 631, 636; WLG calls on, 411
Ray, Isaiah C., 281, °282
Recorder, 136
Reed, Augusta, 206, °209, 214, 233, 235, 585
Religious Union of Associationists, 316
Remond, Charles Lenox, °26, 46, 48, 56, 58, 61, 67, 68, 103, 109, 112, 200, 275, 281, 333, 552; and Irish Address, 2, 47; WLG praises, 24
Republican party, 10, 526
Reynolds, Sir Joshua, 369
Rhode Island, 66, 96, 684; constitutional crisis in, 38, 95, 96; legislature, 51

Rhode-Island Anti-Slavery Society, 37, 38, 226, 229
Rhode Island Homœopathic Society, 138
Rice, Isaac J., 332, °333
Rice, Thomas D., 416
Richards, James B., °554
Richardson, Mrs. (of Newcastle), 477
Richardson, Jesse P., 636
Richfield, Ohio, 524
Richmond, Dr. John Lambert, 520, °521
Rickaby, James, 422, 423
Ricketson, Gilbert, 274, °275; "infamous conduct," 281
Ricketson, Joseph, Jr., °536; letters to, 536, 606, 607
Ripley, George, °198
Roberts, Adeline, letter to, °588
Robertson, Rev. James, 433, °435
Robeson, Andrew, °272, 548; and new type for *Liberator*, 271
Robinson, Christopher, °270
Rochdale, England, 418, 422, 429
Rochester, England, 416
Rochester, N.Y., 108, 110, 111; abolitionist meetings at, 108–109; Second Presbyterian Church, 109
Rodman, Samuel William, 271, °272
Rogers, Mrs., 572
Rogers, Rev. Ebenezer P., 190, °193
Rogers, Nathaniel Peabody, 2, 15, °16, 25, 28, 30, 46, 52, 101, 103, 109, 244, 296, 308, 403, 411, 414, 477; letters to, 27, 85; WLG's tour with, 31, 76; on H. C. Wright's English mission, 69; and escaped slave, 85; and James Caleb Jackson, 110; friendship and controversy with WLG, 120–121, 188, 195, 305; to visit WLG at Northampton, 187, 195; and controversy over *Herald of Freedom*, 197, 252, 266–267, 269, 270, 273, 281, 282, 285–288, 536; mental deterioration, 286–288; *A Collection from the Miscellaneous Writings of* . . . , 31
Rogers, Mrs. Nathaniel Peabody, 86
Rosherville garden, 364
Ross, Austin, 597, °599
Ross, Mrs. Austin (Fidelia Rindge), 597, 599
Round Hill, Mass., 174
Round Hill Water Cure, 205
Roxbury, Mass., 247
Royal Academy, 417
Rudder (slave), 275
Ruggles, Dr. David, °194, 214; presides at West Indies emancipation celebra-

tion, 192; and WLG's water cure, 537, 538, 542, 556, 565, 566–567, 584, 585, 593, 594, 595, 603
Rush Medical College, 512, 518
Rush, Samuel, 214
Rush, Stephen, 193, °194
Russell, Wing, °115, 302; WLG stays with, 112
Russell, Mrs. Wing (Elizabeth), 112, 115, 302
Russia, 314, 486
Russian Lotion for Chilblains, 5, 6
Rutherford, Dr. William Wilson, 506, °507–°508
Rutherford, Mrs. William Wilson (Eleanor Crain), 507, 508

Sabbath Alliance. *See* Sabbath League
Sabbath Convention, western New York, 96, 98
Sabbath League, 546, 547
Sabbath question, 17, 97–99, 255, 541. *See also* Anti-Sabbath Convention
Saco, Me., 156
Sadlier, Denis, °654
Sadlier, James, °654
St. Andrews University, 427
St. Clair, Alanson, 23, 25–°26
St. Lawrence River, 280
St. Louis, Mo., 351
St. Louis *Reveille*, 661, °666
St. Paul, 23, 139, 231, 232
Salem, Mass., 215, 280, 315; First Unitarian Church, 261, 343
Salem (Mass.) Female Anti-Slavery Society, 588
Salem, Ohio, 520, 524–525
Salem Street, Boston, 463
San Antonio, Tex., 66
San Francisco, Cal., 193; U.S. Marine Hospital, 194
Sargent, Lucius Manlius, 191, °194
Satara, Pratap Singh, Rajah of, 228, 446; public meeting about, 393; and George Thompson, 395
Saunders, John, 371, °374
Savannah, Ga., 321
Savannah *Republican*, 294
Scarborough, Philip, 46, °47
Scarborough, Theodore, 9, °10, 215
Scarborough, Mrs. Theodore (Caroline Simmons), 10, 215
Schirras (Schiras), Charles Perry, 511, °513
Scituate, Mass., 461
Scoble, Rev. John, 388, °389

Scotland, 18, 27, 30, 101, 104, 120, 263, 397, 416, 438, 614, 625, 664, 683; WLG in, 422–430, 432–434, 436, 441, 442, 443, 445–447; and Sabbath question, 546. *See also* Free Church of Scotland; Great Britain
Scott, Dred, 280
Scott, Gen. Winfield, 489, 490
Scottish Emancipation Society, 434
Scottish Guardian, 560, 561
Search, Edward. *See* Ashurst, William H.
Second Advent movement, 136–137, 150, 151, 248, 254, 545
Seminole Indians, 292, 583
Seneca Falls, N.Y., 111, 540
Seventh-day Baptists, 98, 99
Seventh-day Sabbath, 544, 545
Seventh Street, Philadelphia, 60
Sewall, Samuel E.: letter to, 338; and Catharine Linda case, 320
Shackford, Rev. C. S., 589
Sharp, Daniel, 650, 651, °654
Shaw, Judge Lemuel, 111
Shaw, Col. R. G., 569
Sheffield, England, 393, 397, 399, 402–403; antislavery meeting at, 403, 409–410, 411; Leavy Greave, 402, 406, 407, 408; Winco Bank, 411
Sheffield *Iris*, 407
Sheridan (sailing ship), 103, 104
Shields, England, 409
Sierra Leone, 233
Simmons, Judge William, 167, °168
Skaneateles, N.Y., 47, 198
Skaneateles Anti-Slavery Society, 115
Skaneateles Community, 267
Skaneateles Female Seminary, 115
Smeal, William, °31, 268, 345, 368, 389, 394, 425, 427, 429, 434, 682, 684; WLG praises, 29, 104
Smith, Anna Bustill, 60
Smith, Edward, 409, °410, 411
Smith, Elias, 100, °101, 164
Smith, Gerrit, °10, 72, 117, 582; aids *Liberator*, 9; and Liberty party, 265–266, 269; and Van Buren, 581
Smith, John Cutts, 40, °42, 45
Smith, R., 421, 422
Smith, Stephen, °115, 303; WLG stays with, 112
Smith, Mrs. Stephen, 303
Smithfield Street, Pittsburgh, 510
Society of Friends, 17, 19, 27, 72, 90, 98, 100, 101, 111, 127, 202, 387, 388, 398, 410, 411, 629; English members attack WLG, 22–24, 403; and annexa-

tion of Texas, 228, 284; Hicksite branch, 511, 513
Solly, Henry, 462, °463
Somerset, N.J., 351
Somersworth, Mass., 103
Sons of Temperance, 101
Soule, William L., 226
South, 3, 53, 57, 62, 71, 609, 658, 666, 671, 676; and *Creole* case, 63
South Carolina, 119, 182, 257
Southgate, England, 25
South Hadley, Mass., 210, 212
South Scituate, Mass., 7, 88
Southwick, Joseph, 102, 105, °106, 145; Garrisons stay with, 207; and Mrs. Paul, 258; and G. W. Benson, 586, 587
Southwick, Mrs. Joseph (Thankful Hussey), °102, 106, 145, 586; Garrisons stay with, 207; cares for Garrison boys, 210; and Mrs. Paul, 258, 259
Spear, Charles, 241
Spear, John Murray, 238, °241
Spooner, Bourne, °261
Spooner, Lysander, 582, °583
Sprague, Peleg, 7
Sprague, Seth, °7, 40, 560
Sprague, William Buell, 650, 651, °654
Springfield, Mass., 167, 173, 176, 199, 270, 280, 321; antislavery convention at, 184
Stamp Act, 279
Standard. See *National Anti-Slavery Standard*
Standfield, John, 422, °423
Stanton, Henry B., 266, °269
Stanton, Mrs. Henry B. (Elizabeth Cady), 269
State House, Boston, 7
State Street, Boston, 279
Stebbins, Daniel, 601, 602, °603
Stebbins, Laura (Mrs. Armanda Wood), 211; letter to, °212; cares for Garrison boys, 212–213
Stephens, Lemuel, 571, °572, 573
Stephens, Mrs. Lemuel (Sally Morton), 572
Stetson, Mrs. Benjamin (Mary Alexander), 257, °258
Stetson, Rev. Caleb, 315, °316
Stetson, Ebenezer Witter, 225, °226
Stetson, James A., 43, °189, 225, 226
Stetson, Mrs. James A. (Dolly W.), 225, 226
Stetson, Joseph, 46, °47; WLG stays at temperance hotel of, 244
Stevens, Abel, °99

Stewart, Alvan, °100; WLG visits, 108
Stewart, A. T., 558
Stickney, Dr. Pierre Le Breton, 267, °269–°270
Stoke Newington, England, 372
Stone, Horace E., 566
Stone, Lucy, °526, 589, 616; WLG describes, 523–524
Stone, Thomas T., °343, 589; and *Standard*, 431
Stonington, Conn., 74, 129
Stott, Joseph Hood, 430
Stow, Rev. Baron, 11, °12
Stowe, Harriet Beecher, 35, 374, 447
Strand, London, 233, 369
Stuart, Capt. Charles, 78, °84
Sturge, Joseph, 18, °19, 230, 232, 388, 397, 415, 417; attacks WLG, 17, 22; in U.S., 24–25; WLG meets, 403
Sturge, Thomas, 187, °188, 205
Suffield, Edward Harbord, Baron, 492, °494
Suffolk Street, Boston, 542, 613, 619
Suffrage party, 38, 95, 96
Sulloway (Silloway), Jason H., 66, °68, 95, 96
Sulloway, Mrs. Jason H. (Mary Eliza Pierce), 95, 96
Sully, Thomas, 60
Summer Street, Boston, 173, 212
Sumner, Charles, °319, 547, 561, 569, 643; letters to, 319, 642
Sutherland, Harriet Elizabeth Georgiana Leveson-Gower, second Duchess of, 435
Sweet, Benoni, 220, °222
Sweet, John Byron, 205
Sweet, Dr. Stephen, °205, 248–249; and Helen's injured arm, 202, 206–208, 209, 211, 212, 213, 216–218, 222–223, 227, 234, 240; other cases, 218 220; WLG recommends, 223, 224; examines WLG, 224
Sweet, Mrs. Stephen, 216
Switzerland, 99, 374
Syracuse, N.Y., 110, 115, 331; antislavery meetings at, 112–114; WLG remembers, 302–303; Library Hall, 112, 115
Syracuse Convention, 676, 677
Syracuse *Democratic Freeman*, 115

Tagore, Dwarkanath, 124, °126
Tappan, Arthur, 1, 158, 460
Tappan, Lewis, 1, 117, 459, °460, 537
Tappan and Dennet, 168
Tay River, 446

Taylor, Mr., 178–179
Taylor, Mr., 573–575
Taylor, Dan, 421
Taylor, Rinaldo, 181–182, *183
Taylor, Zachary, 540, 582, 600, 601,
604, 639, 643; and war with Mexico,
476, *477, 489, 490; and Massachu-
setts, 574; and Seminole Indians, 583
"Tenting on the Old Camp Ground,"
158
Texas: invasion of, 65, 66; annexation
of, 121, 228, 238, 266, 274, 277, 279,
284, 289, 295, 300, 304, 610; WLG
attacks Woodbury's speech on, 290–
294
Thacher, Peter Oxenbridge, 135, *137
Thames River, 364
Thayer, Abby G., *572, 594, 600; letter
to, 601; takes water cure, 571
Third South Carolina Colored Infantry,
592
Thomas, George, *390
Thomas, James, 523, *525–*526
Thompson, Mrs. (mother of George
Thompson), 357
Thompson, Amelia, 364, 366
Thompson, Edith, 364, 366
Thompson, Elizabeth, 364, 366
Thompson, Garrison, 364, 366
Thompson, George, *14, 18, 25, 31,
37, 230, 261, 327, 339, 345, 366,
372, 373, 380, 386, 389, 392, 393,
396, 397, 401, 403, 411, 413, 414,
415, 416, 422, 429, 430, 431, 439,
448, 449, 463, 523, 562, 563, 591,
651, 654; WLG's regard for, 29, 89,
104, 124, 394, 435–436, 567–568;
and India, 228; invites WLG to
Britain, 326; WLG stays with, 357,
359, 361; WLG on, 359, 361–362;
mobbed in 1835, 360, family, 368,
416, 568; and Anti-Slavery League,
377, 378, 382, 427; visits Clarkson
with WLG, 381, 386; and John
Scoble, 389; unable to attend Bristol
meeting, 390; visits Ashurst with
WLG, 391, 394; and Rajah of
Satara, 395; speaks at Birmingham,
396; at Exeter Hall, 412, 420;
praises Quincy, 417; fidelity to
Garrisonian abolitionism, 435–436;
and tour of Scotland, 437–438; at
Newcastle, 439; at Liverpool,
Edinburgh, Dundee, 442, 445; and
Wardlaw, 447–448; plans to visit
America, 472; death of daughter,
473–475; elected House of Commons,

568; and Cox and Hoby, 649, 650,
652
Thompson, Mrs. George, 357, 359,
364, 368, 394, 412, 413, 416, 442,
568
Thompson, Herbert, 364, 366
Thompson, Louisa, 364, 366
Thomson, James, 123
Thomson (Thompson), Dr. Samuel,
*10, 249; death, 220, 224; WLG
praises, 220–221
Thomsonian courses, 43, 44, 46, 68,
132, 152
Thurber, Dr., 211, 214, 224
Thurber, George, 61, *63, 66–67, 196
Thurber, Mrs. George, 61
Tilden, Daniel R., 515, *517
Tocqueville, Alexis de, *314–*315;
De La Démocratie en Amerique,
312, 314–315
Tocsin of Liberty, 58, 297
Torrey, Charles T., *12; attacks
J. A. Collins, 11; and Chardon-
Street Convention, 23; death, 338
Tottenham, England, 25, 26
Toronto, Canada, 398
Toronto Clear Grit movement, 389
Townsend, Milo A., 510, 511, *513
Townsend, Dr. Samuel P., *558–*559
Tredgold, John Harfield, *13; letter to,
12
Tremont Street, Boston, 325
Trinity College, Dublin, 51
True American (Examiner), 314, 622,
635
True Democrat, 527, 528
Truth, Sojourner, 165
Tucker, J. N. T., 112, *115
Turner, Cyrus, 622, 623, *635
Turner, Squire, *635
Twinsburg, Ohio, 520
Tyler, Daniel, 511, *513
Tyler, John, 101, 168, 290, 301; at
Bunker Hill pageant, 167; and
annexation of Texas, 238, 241
Tyndale, William, 98, 99, 546, 605
*Tyranny of Penal Legislation in Favor
of the Sabbath,* 547

Ulster, Ireland, 390
Underground Railroad, 27, 72, 87,
115, 143, 158, 194, 321, 333, 513,
521, 587
Union Theological Seminary, 374, 421
United States, 14, 19, 24, 26, 45, 47,
49, 51, 63, 89, 99, 132, 136, 232,
283, 611, 638, 646, 648, 661, 663,

675; and Irish Appeal, 63; and Great Britain in *Creole* case, 101; and Mexico, 238, 326; antislavery movement in, 455; and Liberia, 486
United States Army, 490
United States Congress, 42, 49, 121, 135, 182, 205, 215, 228, 269, 280, 289, 302, 453, 486, 553, 560, 581, 624; and gag law, 42, 43, 53, 273–274; and annexation of Texas, 238; discusses slavery, 473; House of Representatives, 51, 135, 158, 168, 473, 474, 583; Senate, 290, 291, 319, 473, 474, 561, 609
United States Constitution, 10, 118, 292, 302, 303, 304, 478; "a covenant with death," 3, 449; proslavery, 68, 178–179, 245, 269, 293, 301, 303, 516, 523; and Liberty party, 265, 269; abolition possible under, 561; Kentucky tries to amend, 609; Giddings supports, 624
United States Magazine and Democratic Review, 134, 136
United States Patent Office, 70
United States Supreme Court, 20, 294, 486
United States Treasury, 197, 269
Unknown Recipients, letters to, 28, 309, 340, 448
Upper Canada, 332
Utica, N.Y., 110, 113, 114, 194, 197; Genesee Street, 108, 198
Utica *Daily Gazette*, 115
Utica *Liberty Press*, 331, 332
Utica *Whig. See* Oneida *Whig*

Valley Falls, R.I., 684
Van Buren, Martin, 566, 581, 582
Van Renselaer, Thomas, °72
Varela, Felix, 664, °666–°667
Vashon, George B., 510, °512
Vashon, John, 510, 512; letter to, °500
Vermont, 46, 101, 169, 200, 208
Vernon, N.Y., 112
Vicksburg *Daily Sentinel*, 292, 294
Victoria, queen of England, 125, 148, 358, 657
Villard, Henry, 274
Vincent, Henry, 328, 368, °369, 628; described, 372; and formation of Anti-Slavery League, 377, 379, 382; assists WLG on British mission, 394; disturbed by *Liberator*, 627
Vincent, Mrs. Henry (Lucy Chappell Cleave), 369, 372

Vineland, N.J., 165
Virginia, 625; House of Burgesses, 279
Virginia Penitentiary, 275

W., Mrs., 210, 212
Walker, Rev. Jems, 227, °228
Walker, James W., 479, °480, 524, 529; at Ohio meetings, 512, 519; at Oberlin graduation, 522
Wall, James, 409, 410
Wallcut, Robert Folger, 88, 93, 94, 95, 342, °343, 404, 534, 567, 572, 574, 607; letter to, 584; family, 516, 598; Garrison grateful to, 531–532
Wallcut, Mrs. Robert Folger, 531–532, 534
Waltham, Mass., 166, 194, 315, 316
Walton. *See* West, Richard
War of 1812, 490
Wardlaw, Rev. Ralph, °447–°448
Waring, Maria, °289, 359, 384, 489
Warren, Dr. John Collins, 94, °95, 202, 207; examines WLG, 155, 165
Washington, Bushrod, 484, 486
Washington, George, 468, 486
Washington, D.C., 70, 101, 228, 280, 284
Washington *Daily Globe*, 291, 294
Washingtonian, 521
Washingtonian Hall, 639
Washingtonian movement, 100, 101, 246; Martha Washington Society, 101, 193; in Northampton celebration, 190; and clergy, 191
Washington *Semi-Weekly Globe*, 291, 294
Washington Street, Boston, 66, 208
Watchman-Examiner, 351
Waterford, Ireland, 438, 452
Waterloo, N.Y., 110, 111, 199; antislavery meeting at, 112; Court House, 109
Waterloo Place, London, 397
Watson, Dr. George, 426, °427, 433
Waverly Place, Boston, 575
Wayland, Francis, 263, °268
Webb, James, 397, °398, 442
Webb, James Henry, 288, °289, 359, 397, 398, 438, 442
Webb, Mrs. James Henry, 359
Webb, Richard Davis, °31, 50, 93, 131, 151, 163, 230, 268, 333, 345, 423, 425, 452, 635, 636; letters to, 51, 127, 282, 383, 396, 408, 428, 429, 441, 447, 468, 488; WLG's regard for, 29, 104, 127–128, 129–130, 282–283, 324, 359, 384,

468–469; Thomas Davis introduced to, 52; donation to *Liberator*, 239; family, 239, 289, 368, 397, 423, 429, 468, 489; urged to visit America, 282–283; meets WLG at Liverpool, 356, 359; misinformed about mail, 360; writes of WLG's safe arrival, 361; will collect articles for *Daily News*, 371; cousins, 430; WLG stays with, 438; and WLG's departure, 447

Webb, Mrs. Richard Davis (Hannah), °31, 53, 93, 104, 129, 131, 268, 283, 288, 397, 410, 423, 429, 442, 447, 468, 471, 488; letter to, 129; WLG's affection for, 129–130

Webb, Thomas, 397, °398, 410, 438, 443

Webb, Mrs. Thomas, 410

Webster, Daniel, 136, 232, 560, 561; and *Creole* case, 101; speech at Bunker Hill pageant, 167, 168

Webster-Ashburton Treaty, 101

Weaver, Dr. Charles, 510, 511, 513

Weeks, Rebecca, 101, 109, °111

Welch, Bartholomew T., 650, 651, °654

Weld, Elizabeth Clarke, 513

Weld, Theodore D., 117, 465, 513, 525; WLG rejects views of, 1

Wellington, Duke of, 186

Wells, Alfred, 69, °70

Wells, Hiram, 214, °215, 225, 226

Wenham Lake, Mass., 468

Wesley, John, 503, 613, 683

Wesleyan University, 421

Wesselhoeft, Dr. Robert, 44, °45, 74, 75, 307, 309; treats Mary Benson, 46; treats Mrs. George Benson, 122; and WLG, 132, 155, 165; treats Anna Benson, 142, 151–152, 153, 154

West, Richard, 171

West, WLG's tour, 465–466, 504–534; WLG's hopes for, 501; labor and fatigue of, 509, 516

Western Anti-Slavery Society, 101, 480, 514, 517, 522, 525; anniversary meetings of, 515–516, 518

Western College of Hómœopathic Medicine, 528

Western Reserve, 516, 517, 518

Westfield, Mass., 280

West Indies. *See* British West Indies

West Indies Emancipation Bill, 205

Weston, Anne Warren, 145, °147, 161, 173, 333, 600; letters to, 241,

467; and *Herald of Freedom* controversy, 285

Weston, Caroline, 145, °147, 173, 316, 562, 563, 566, 568, 569, 593, 646

Weston, Deborah, 173, °282

Weston, Emma Forbes, 173, 626, °636

Weston, Lucia, 173

Weston, Warren, °173, 282

Weston, Mrs. Warren (Ann or Anne), 173

Weston, Mrs. Warren (Nancy Bates), 173

Weston family, 228, 281

West Roxbury, Mass., 198

Weymouth, Mass., 172, 173, 238

Whately, Richard, 605, °606

Whig party, 96, 266, 516, 566, 583, 604, 623

Whipple, Charles King, 315, °316, 367, 546; letter to, 352; helps Quincy edit *Liberator*, 327; signs call for Anti-Sabbath Convention, 548

Whitby, Daniel, 98, 99

White, Timothy, 510, °513

White, William A., 186–187, °188

White Karens, 460

White Mountains, N.H., 30, 86, 120, 175

Whitefield, George, 469, °471

Whitmarsh, Samuel, 603

Whitney, Miss (school mistress), 131

Whittier, John Greenleaf, 35, 117, 295; and Liberty party, 265, 266, 269

Wigham, Eliza, 402

Wigham, Jane, 402

Wigham, John, Jr., °443, 445

Wilberforce, William, 204, °205, 230, 233, 657; and American Colonization Society, 491–492, 493

Wilberforce Settlement, 260

Wilbraham, Mass., 166, 206

Wiley, Rev. Charles, 190, °194, 214

Wilkins, Fanny, 155, 156

Williams, Dr. Charles D., 527, °528

Williams College, 525

Williams, Henry, 534–535

Williams, Henry Willard, 80, °87, 101, 335; letters to, 188, 197; in charge of *Liberator* office, 206

Williams, John Mason, °280

Williams, Roger, 98, °99

Williams, Thomas S., 547

Willimantic, Conn., 96, 213

Williston, John Payson, 585, 586, °587; pays Hudson's bail, 321

Williston, Samuel, 585, 586, °587

Williston Seminary, 587
Wilmot, David, proviso, 473, 474
Wilson, Hiram, 331, *332
Windham County (N.Y.) Peace Society, 352
Windship, Dr. Charles William, 463, *464
Windsor, England, 24
Winslow, Hubbard, 351, *352
Winthrop, Robert Charles, *560–*561
Witness. See *Perfectionist*
Wolcott, Mr. *See* Wallcut, Robert Folger
Wolf, Mr., 507
Woman's Journal, 526
Wood, Armanda, 212
Woodbury, Levi: letter to, 290; WLG attacks speech by, 290–*294
Woolwich, England, 658
Worcester, Mass., 206, 236, 639, 640, 641, 642, 643, 644, 645, 647, 658, 661, 669, 670; Temperance Hall, 207; City Hall, 644
Worcester County, Mass., 140, 603
Worcester County (Mass.,) North Division Anti-Slavery Society, 35, 37, 138, 140
Worcester County (Mass.,) South Division Anti-Slavery Society, 681
Worcester *Spy*, 281
World's Anti-Slavery Conventions: (1840), 19, 26, 27, 47, 61, 120, 151, 230, 327, 333, 334, 373, 440, 525; (1843), 146, 147, 148–149, 150
World's Temperance Convention, 327, 346, *348, 355, 357, 360; WLG rebuffed at, 362–363; failure, 373
Worth Street, New York, 135
Wortley, England, 408
Wrentham, Mass., 38
Wrexham, Wales, 416, 418, 429, 430; antislavery meetings at, 435, 439; Baptist Chapel, 451
Wright, Elizur, 582, 649, *654; WLG rejects views of, 1
Wright, Rev. Henry Clarke, 15, *16, 25, 37, 68, 127, 151, 283, 289, 326, 327, 345, 357, 368, 372, 373, 374, 397, 404, 405, 407, 410, 436, 438, 439, 442, 447, 463, 488, 532, 546, 547, 555, 556, 599, 605, 623, 627, 632,

633; letters to, 69, 103, 131, 143, 237, 261, 322, 338, 387, 390, 422, 423, 426, 472, 496; WLG's affection and admiration for, 59, 90–91, 124, 130, 148, 227, 237, 262–263, 282–283, 376; mission to Britain, 69, 75, 103–104, 119, 143–144, 377, 415, 427, 429, 436; return to U.S., 472, 473, 497; and Elizabeth Pease, 126, 227, 376, 441; praises Irish friends, 127, 128; WLG hopes he will attend peace convention, 149; health, 227, 228, 237, 263, 471, 472, 476; urged to come home, 237, 263–264, 323, 325, 422, 424–425; contributions to *Liberator*, 022–020, 024, 380; and nonresistance, 323; meets WLG at Liverpool, 356, 359; stays with Thompsons, 359; writes of WLG's safe arrival, 361; recommends sitz bath for Fanny, 367; and formation of Anti-Slavery League, 378, 379, 382, 383, 384, 385; *Defensive War Proved to be a Denial of Christianity* . . . , 393, 395, 425; WLG suggests testimonial for, 407; family, 424, 473; brings WLG home from Cleveland, 466, 530, 534; sent to Liberty party convention, 530–531; at New Bedford antislavery meetings, 536; and Anti-Sabbath Convention, 540, 541, 548; visiting WLG at time of Lizzy's death, 551; in Ohio, 557, 593; *Human Life Illustrated in My Individual Experience as a Child, a Youth, and a Man*, 624–625, 635–636
Wright, Mrs. Henry Clarke, 267, 324
Wright, Dr. James Harvey, *68, 75

Yale College, 12, 26, 37, 75, 222, 249, 421, 486
Yale Theological Seminary, 37, 249
Yerrinton, James Brown, *158, 407, 617; letter to, 255
Youngstown, Ohio, 512, 514
Youth's Temperance Advocate, 374

Zion's Herald, *99, 486; letter to editor, 96; WLG replies to attack, 96–99
Zoar, Ohio, 524, 526